SHORTER SIXTH EDITION
WITH ESSAYS

LITERATURE

THE HUMAN EXPERIENCE

SHORTER SIXTH EDITION
WITH ESSAYS

LITERATURE
THE HUMAN EXPERIENCE

RICHARD ABCARIAN
California State University, Northridge

MARVIN KLOTZ
Emeritus, California State University, Northridge

ST. MARTIN'S PRESS
New York

Editor: Nancy Lyman
Revisions editor: Edward Hutchinson
Development editor: Clare Payton
Managing editor: Patricia Mansfield Phelan
Project editor: Nicholas Webb
Production supervisor: Dennis Para
Art director and cover design: Lucy Krikorian
Cover art: William Low

For information, write:
St. Martin's Press, Inc.
175 Fifth Avenue
New York, NY 10010

ISBN: 0-312-11520-2

ACKNOWLEDGMENTS

Samuel Allen, "A Moment Please." © 1962 Samuel Allen. Reprinted by permission.
Woody Allen, "Death Knocks." From *Getting Even* by Woody Allen. Copyright © 1968 by
Woody Allen. Reprinted by permission of Random House, Inc.
Catherine Anderson, "Womanhood." Reprinted by permission of the author.
Anonymous, "The Ruin." From *The Earliest English Poems* translated by Michael Alexander.
(Penguin Classics, Second edition, 1977). Copyright © Michael Alexander, 1966, 1977. Reprinted
by permission of Penguin Books Ltd.
W. H. Auden, "Five Songs," "Musée des Beaux Arts," "The Unknown Citizen." From *W. H.
Auden: Collected Poems* by W. H. Auden, ed. by Edward Mendelson. Copyright 1940 and renewed
1968 by W. H. Auden. Reprinted by permission of Random House, Inc., and Faber and Faber.
Donald W. Baker, "Formal Application." Reprinted by permission of the author.
James Baldwin, "Rage." From *Notes of a Native Son* by James Baldwin. Copyright © 1955,
renewed 1983, by James Baldwin. Reprinted by permission of Beacon Press.
Toni Cade Bambara, "The Lesson." From *Gorilla, My Love* by Toni Cade Bambara. Reprinted
by permission of Random House, Inc.
Elizabeth Brewster, "Disqualification." Reprinted by permission of the author.
Elizabeth Bishop, "One Art." From *The Complete Poems 1927–1979* by Elizabeth Bishop.
Copyright © 1979, 1983 by Alice Helen Methfessel. Reprinted with permission of Farrar, Straus
& Giroux, Inc.

Acknowledgments and copyrights are continued at the back of the book on pages 1031–37, which
constitute an extension of the copyright page.
It is a violation of the law to reproduce these selections by any means whatsoever without the
written permission of the copyright holder.

To Joan and Debra

Love: a word properly applied to our delight in particular kinds of food; sometimes metaphorically spoken of the favorite objects of all our appetites.

Henry Fielding

CONTENTS

Innocence and Experience   2

For Thinking and Writing   5

Conformity and Rebellion   206

POETRY   280

DRAMA   322

ESSAYS   414

Love and Hate   466

The Presence of Death   690

Appendices   884

ALTERNATE TABLE OF CONTENTS

arranged by genre*

---

*Within each genre, authors are listed chronologically by date of birth.

POETRY

DRAMA

ESSAYS

PREFACE

And wisdom is a butterfly
And not a gloomy bird of prey.

      W. B. Yeats

With this anthology, based on the sixth edition of *Literature: The Human Experience*, we continue our practice of making a shorter version available to instructors who prefer a more compact volume. In this shorter edition, we have retained 5 plays, 27 stories, and 156 poems from the longer edition. Further, we have added a play, a Flannery O'Connor story, 2 pieces of "sudden fiction," and 6 new poems. This edition also contains 22 essays, 11 of which are new to *Literature: The Human Experience*.

Our arrangement of the works into four thematic groups—Innocence and Experience, Conformity and Rebellion, Love and Hate, and The Presence of Death—provides opportunities to explore diverse attitudes toward those great themes of human experience. Each section is introduced by a short essay that embodies some general observations on the theme and by a series of questions that may stimulate thinking, discussion, and writing. Within each thematic section, the works are grouped by genre—fiction, poetry, drama, and the essay—and arranged chronologically by author's birth date. Each work is dated to indicate its first appearance in a book; dates enclosed in parentheses indicate the date of composition or earliest appearance. We have not attempted to date traditional ballads.

Study questions and writing topics follow about half the stories and poems, all of the plays and essays, and each thematic section. These study questions are designed to help students discover the central issues in the works. The writing topics, related to the study questions that precede them, focus attention on thematic similarities among various works.

The first four appendices, "Reading Fiction," "Reading Poetry," "Reading Drama," and "Reading Essays," acquaint students with some formal concepts and historical considerations basic to the study of literature. These are general introductions that instructors will no doubt want to augment as they discuss the formal sources of readers' pleasure or, for that matter, boredom.

A "Glossary of Critical Approaches" is new to the sixth edition. Since the publication of the first edition of this anthology more than twenty years ago, the so-called New Criticism, with its unyielding emphasis on formalism, has been dethroned by a wide variety of competing critical approaches. Whatever else one might say about this development, it has certainly had the important and salutary effect of broadening and deepening the range of discourse about literature. For example, feminist criticism, like Marxism before it, has insisted on the connections between literature and the larger world of power and politics. Deconstructionism, by calling our attention to the instability and contradictory nature of language, has challenged the view that great literary works embody a consciously designed seamless web of interrelated parts. Reader-response criticism celebrates the reader by arguing that, in any meaningful sense, a literary text only comes into being when a particular reader confronts a particular work. Finally, the new historical criticism contends that knowledge of historical context is as important as any other kind of knowledge in understanding a literary work. The "Glossary of Critical Approaches" attempts to explain the basic assumptions of these various schools of critical practice. We hope that from what may seem a bewildering and even confusing array of approaches, students will at least learn that there is not some "correct" way to approach a literary work and, further, that many of the approaches complement one another.

"Writing about Literature" outlines a number of writing strategies ranging from the freewriting of a student's journal through discussions of more formal explication, analysis, and comparison and contrast essay assignments. We provide several samples of student writing to guide students in the preparation of their own papers. "Suggested Topics for Writing" offers instructors over eighty focused writing assignments. The appendix concludes with a section illustrating manuscript mechanics based on the *MLA Handbook*.

The appendix "Biographical Notes on the Authors" provides students with information about some of the major events, biographical and literary, in the career of each author. We hope these notes will not only satisfy students' natural curiosity about writers' lives but will also, from time to time, stimulate them enough to want to learn more.

A "Glossary of Literary Terms," with brief excerpts to illustrate the definitions, concludes the text.

The main thing, of course, continues to be the works themselves. We have preserved plays by Sophocles and Shakespeare, restored Ibsen's *A Doll's House*, and added *No Exit*, Sartre's examination of a new kind of hell. In *M. Butterfly*, David Henry Hwang draws on an historical event to create an extraordinary drama of sexual intrigue in the context of power politics and cross-cultural confusion. As well, we introduce Art Spiegelman's illustrated story (it seems, somehow, inappropriate to call it a comic strip) based on the suicide of his mother, who killed herself more than twenty years after she was freed from a Nazi concentration camp. Among the other new selections are stories by Robert Olen Butler, Raymond Carver, Louise Erdrich, Molly Giles, Nadine Gordimer, Bessie Head, Pam Houston, Bharati Mukherjee, and Edna O'Brien; poems by Catherine Anderson, Elizabeth Brewster, Marianne Burke, Kate Daniels, James Fenton, Tess Gallagher, William Heyen, Edward Hirsch, Linda Hogan, Denise Levertov, Katherine McAlpine, Felix Mnthali, Kathleen Norris, Mary Oliver, Molly Peacock, Marge Piercy, Alberto Ríos, May Sarton, Gjertrud

Schnackenberg, and Kathleen Wiegner; and essays by Joan Didion, Lars Eighner, Willard Gaylin, Emma Goldman, Bill McKibben, St. Paul, William Saroyan, Robert C. Solomon, Gary Soto, Jill Tweedie, and Melvin I. Urofsky.

As always, this edition is accompanied by an Instructor's Manual. This resource provides thematic discussions of each selection in *Literature: The Human Experience*, shorter sixth edition, and will assist the instructor in formulating lecture, discussion, and writing topics.

ACKNOWLEDGMENTS

We are grateful to the following colleagues across the country who took time to send us their helpful suggestions for this shorter sixth edition: Kathleen L. Bell, University of Central Florida; Nancy Dandrea, Lake Michigan College; JoAnn Goslin, Northern Virginia Community College; Margaret Griswold, West Liberty State College; Stephen P. M. Howard, Essex Community College; Reid Huntley, Ohio University; Sister Jean Klene, St. Mary's College; Pamela Monaco, Northern Virginia Community College; Laura Noell, Northern Virginia Community College; Elizabeth J. Petiprin, Jamestown Community College; Tami Phenix, University of Cincinnati; Donna J. Turner, Marshall University; and Arthur Wohlgemuth, Miami-Dade Community College–Kendall.

We wish also to thank the many people at St. Martin's Press for the care they took in the preparation of this edition, and for their good humor, particularly Clare Payton, Nancy Lyman, Edward Hutchinson, Nick Webb, Dennis Para, Lucy Krikorian, and Darby Downey.

Richard Abcarian
Marvin Klotz

SHORTER SIXTH EDITION
WITH ESSAYS

LITERATURE

THE HUMAN EXPERIENCE

Innocence and Experience

The Garden of the Peaceful Arts (Allegory of the Court of Isabelle d'Este), ca. 1530 by Lorenzo Costa

Humans strive to give order and meaning to their lives, to reduce the mystery and unpredictability that constantly threaten them. Life is infinitely more complex and surprising than we imagine, and the categories we establish to give it order and meaning are, for the most part, "momentary stays against confusion." At any time, the equilibrium of our lives, the comfortable image of ourselves and the world around us, may be disrupted suddenly by something new, forcing us into painful reevaluation. These disruptions create pain, anxiety, and terror but also wisdom and awareness.

The works in this section deal generally with the movement of a central character from moral simplicities and certainties into a more complex and problematic world. Though these works frequently issue in awareness, even wisdom, their central figures rarely act decisively; the protagonist is more often a passive figure who learns the difference between the ideal world he or she imagines and the injurious real world. If the protagonist survives the ordeal (and he or she doesn't always, emotionally or physically), the protagonist will doubtless be a better human—better able to wrest some satisfaction from a bleak and threatening world. It is no accident that so many of the works here deal with the passage from childhood to adulthood, for childhood is a time of simplicities and certainties that must give way to the complexities and uncertainties of adult life.

Almost universally, innocence is associated with childhood and youth, as experience is with age. We teach the young about an ideal world, without explaining that it has not yet been and may never be achieved. As innocents, they are terribly vulnerable to falsehood, to intrusive sexuality, and to the machinations of the wicked, who, despite all the moral tales, often do triumph.

But the terms *innocence* and *experience* range widely in meaning, and that range is reflected here. Innocence may be defined almost biologically, or it may be social—the innocence of Brown in Nathaniel Hawthorne's "Young Goodman Brown," Hulga in Flannery O'Connor's "Good Country People," or the boy in William Saroyan's "Five Ripe Pears." Or innocence may be seen as the child's ignorance of his or her own mortality, as in Gerard Manley Hopkins's "Spring and Fall" and Dylan Thomas's "Fern Hill." In works such as David

Henry Hwang's *M. Butterfly* and Robert Browning's "My Last Duchess," one discovers the tragic and violent consequences of an innocence that is blind.

The contrast between what we thought in our youth and what we have come to know, painfully, as adults stands as an emblem of the passage from innocence to experience. Yet, all of us remain, to one degree or another, innocent throughout life, since we never, except with death, stop learning from experience. Looked at in this way, experience is the ceaseless assault life makes upon our innocence, moving us to a greater wisdom about ourselves and the world around us.

FOR THINKING AND WRITING

As you read the selections in this section, consider the following questions. You may want to write out your thoughts informally in a journal or notebook as a way of preparing to respond to the selections, or you may wish to make one of these questions the basis for a formal essay.

1. Innocence is often associated with childhood and responsibility with adulthood. Were you happier or more contented as a preteen than you are now? Why? Which particular aspects of your childhood do you remember with pleasure? Which with pain? Do you look forward to the future with pleasurable anticipation or with dread? Why?

2. Do you know any adults who seem to be innocents? On what do you base your judgment? Do you know any preteens who seem to be particularly "adult" in their behavior (beyond politeness and good manners—they may, for example, have to cope with severe family difficulties)? On what do you base your judgment?

3. Most of you have spent your lives under the authority of others, such as parents, teachers, and employers. How do you deal with authorities you resent? Do you look forward to exercising authority over others (your own children, your own students, employees under your supervision)? How will your experiences affect your behavior as an authority?

4. How does the growth from innocence to experience affect one's sexual behavior? Social behavior? Political behavior?

INNOCENCE
AND
EXPERIENCE

Woman and Child on a Beach, ca. 1901 by Pablo Picasso

FICTION

Young Goodman Brown

1846

NATHANIEL HAWTHORNE   [1804–1864]

Young Goodman[1] Brown came forth at sunset into the street at Salem village; but put his head back, after crossing the threshold, to exchange a parting kiss with his young wife. And Faith, as the wife was aptly named, thrust her own pretty head into the street, letting the wind play with the pink ribbons of her cap while she called to Goodman Brown.

"Dearest heart," whispered she, softly and rather sadly, when her lips were close to his ear, "prithee put off your journey until sunrise and sleep in your own bed to-night. A lone woman is troubled with such dreams and such thoughts that she's afeared of herself sometimes. Pray tarry with me this night, dear husband, of all nights in the year."

"My love and my Faith," replied young Goodman Brown, "of all nights in the year, this one night must I tarry away from thee. My journey, as thou callest it, forth and back again, must needs be done 'twixt now and sunrise. What, my sweet, pretty wife, dost thou doubt me already, and we but three months married?"

"Then God bless you!" said Faith, with the pink ribbons; "and may you find all well when you come back."

"Amen!" cried Goodman Brown. "Say thy prayers, dear Faith, and go to bed at dusk, and no harm will come to thee."

So they parted; and the young man pursued his way until, being about to turn the corner by the meeting-house, he looked back and saw the head of Faith still peeping after him with a melancholy air, in spite of her pink ribbons.

"Poor little Faith!" thought he, for his heart smote him. "What a wretch am I to leave her on such an errand! She talks of dreams, too. Methought as she spoke there was trouble in her face, as if a dream had warned her what work is to be done to-night. But no, no; 'twould kill her to think it. Well, she's a blessed angel on earth; and after this one night I'll cling to her skirts and follow her to heaven."

---

[1] Equivalent to *Mr.*, a title given to a man below the rank of gentleman.

With this excellent resolve for the future, Goodman Brown felt himself justified in making more haste on his present evil purpose. He had taken a dreary road, darkened by all the gloomiest trees of the forest, which barely stood aside to let the narrow path creep through, and closed immediately behind. It was all as lonely as could be; and there is this peculiarity in such a solitude, that the traveller knows not who may be concealed by the innumerable trunks and the thick boughs overhead; so that with lonely footsteps he may yet be passing through an unseen multitude.

"There may be a devilish Indian behind every tree," said Goodman Brown to himself; and he glanced fearfully behind him as he added, "What if the devil himself should be at my very elbow!"

His head being turned back, he passed a crook of the road, and, looking forward again, beheld the figure of a man, in grave and decent attire, seated at the foot of an old tree. He arose at Goodman Brown's approach and walked onward side by side with him.

"You are late, Goodman Brown," said he. "The clock of the Old South[2] was striking as I came through Boston, and that is full fifteen minutes agone."

"Faith kept me back a while," replied the young man, with a tremor in his voice, caused by the sudden appearance of his companion, though not wholly unexpected.

It was now deep dusk in the forest, and deepest in that part of it where these two were journeying. As nearly as could be discerned, the second traveller was about fifty years old, apparently in the same rank of life as Goodman Brown, and bearing a considerable resemblance to him, though perhaps more in expression than features. Still they might have been taken for father and son. And yet, though the elder person was as simply clad as the younger, and as simple in manner too, he had an indescribable air of one who knew the world, and who would not have felt abashed at the governor's dinner table or in King William's[3] court, were it possible that his affairs should call him thither. But the only thing about him that could be fixed upon as remarkable was his staff, which bore the likeness of a great black snake, so curiously wrought that it might almost be seen to twist and wriggle itself like a living serpent. This, of course, must have been an ocular deception, assisted by the uncertain light.

"Come, Goodman Brown," cried his fellow-traveller, "this is a dull pace for the beginning of a journey. Take my staff, if you are so soon weary."

"Friend," said the other, exchanging his slow pace for a full stop, "having kept covenant by meeting thee here, it is my purpose now to return whence I came. I have scruples touching the matter thou wot'st of."

"Sayest thou so?" replied he of the serpent, smiling apart. "Let us walk on, nevertheless, reasoning as we go; and if I convince thee not thou shalt turn back. We are but a little way in the forest yet."

---

[2] A church in Boston.
[3] Ruler of England from 1689–1702.

"Too far! too far!" exclaimed the goodman, unconsciously resuming his walk. "My father never went into the woods on such an errand, nor his father before him. We have been a race of honest men and good Christians since the days of the martyrs;[4] and shall I be the first of the name of Brown that ever took this path and kept—"

"Such company, thou wouldst say," observed the elder person, interpreting his pause. "Well said, Goodman Brown! I have been as well acquainted with your family as with ever a one among the Puritans; and that's no trifle to say. I helped your grandfather, the constable, when he lashed the Quaker woman so smartly through the streets of Salem; and it was I that brought your father a pitch-pine knot, kindled at my own hearth, to set fire to an Indian village, in King Philip's war.[5] They were my good friends, both; and many a pleasant walk have we had along this path, and returned merrily after midnight. I would fain be friends with you for their sake."

"If it be as thou sayest," replied Goodman Brown, "I marvel they never spoke of these matters; or, verily, I marvel not, seeing that the least rumor of the sort would have driven them from New England. We are a people of prayer, and good works to boot, and abide no such wickedness."

"Wickedness or not," said the traveller, with the twisted staff, "I have a very general acquaintance here in New England. The deacons of many a church have drunk the communion wine with me; the selectmen of divers towns make me their chairman; and a majority of the Great and General Court[6] are firm supporters of my interest. The governor and I, too—But these are state secrets."

"Can this be so?" cried Goodman Brown, with a stare of amazement at his undisturbed companion. "Howbeit, I have nothing to do with the governor and council; they have their own ways, and are no rule for a simple husbandman[7] like me. But, were I to go on with thee, how should I meet the eye of that good old man, our minister, at Salem village? Oh, his voice would make me tremble both Sabbath day and lecture day."

Thus far the elder traveller had listened with due gravity; but now burst into a fit of irrepressible mirth, shaking himself so violently that his snake-like staff actually seemed to wriggle in sympathy.

"Ha! ha! ha!" shouted he again and again; then composing himself, "Well, go on, Goodman Brown, go on; but, prithee, don't kill me with laughing."

"Well, then, to end the matter at once," said Goodman Brown, considerably nettled, "there is my wife, Faith. It would break her dear little heart; and I'd rather break my own."

"Nay, if that be the case," answered the other, "e'en go thy ways, Goodman

---

[4] A reference to the persecution of Protestants in England by the Catholic monarch Mary Tudor (1553–1558).

[5] War waged (1675–1676) against the colonists of New England by the Indian chief Metacomset, also known as "King Philip."

[6] The Puritan legislature.

[7] An ordinary person.

Brown. I would not for twenty old women like the one hobbling before us that Faith should come to any harm."

As he spoke he pointed his staff at a female figure on the path, in whom Goodman Brown recognized a very pious and exemplary dame, who had taught him his catechism in youth, and was still his moral and spiritual adviser, jointly with the minister and Deacon Gookin.

"A marvel, truly, that Goody[8] Cloyse should be so far in the wilderness at nightfall," said he. "But with your leave, friend, I shall take a cut through the woods until we have left this Christian woman behind. Being a stranger to you, she might ask whom I was consorting with and whither I was going."

"Be it so," said his fellow-traveller. "Betake you to the woods, and let me keep the path."

Accordingly the young man turned aside, but took care to watch his companion, who advanced softly along the road until he had come within a staff's length of the old dame. She, meanwhile, was making the best of her way, with singular speed for so aged a woman, and mumbling some indistinct words—a prayer, doubtless—as she went. The traveller put forth his staff and touched her withered neck with what seemed the serpent's tail.

"The devil!" screamed the pious old lady.

"Then Goody Cloyse knows her old friend?" observed the traveller, confronting her and leaning on his writhing stick.

"Ah, forsooth, and is it your worship indeed?" cried the good dame. "Yea, truly is it, and in the very image of my old gossip, Goodman Brown, the grandfather of the silly fellow that now is. But—would your worship believe it?—my broomstick hath strangely disappeared, stolen, as I suspect, by that unhanged witch, Goody Cory, and that, too, when I was all anointed with the juice of smallage and cinquefoil and wolf's bane"[9]—

"Mingled with fine wheat and the fat of a new-born babe," said the shape of old Goodman Brown.

"Ah, your worship knows the recipe," cried the old lady, cackling aloud. "So, as I was saying, being all ready for the meeting, and no horse to ride on, I made up my mind to foot it; for they tell me there is a nice young man to be taken into communion to-night. But now your good worship will lend me your arm, and we shall be there in a twinkling."

"That can hardly be," answered her friend. "I may not spare you my arm, Goody Cloyse; but here is my staff, if you will."

So saying, he threw it down at her feet, where, perhaps, it assumed life, being one of the rods which its owner had formerly lent to the Egyptian magi.[10] Of this fact, however, Goodman Brown could not take cognizance. He

---

[8] A polite title for a wife of humble rank.
[9] All these plants were associated with magic and witchcraft.
[10] Allusion to the biblical magicians who turned their rods into serpents (Exodus 7:11–12).

had cast up his eyes in astonishment, and, looking down again, beheld neither Goody Cloyse nor the serpentine staff, but his fellow-traveller alone, who waited for him as calmly as if nothing had happened.

"That old woman taught me my catechism," said the young man; and there was a world of meaning in this simple comment.

They continued to walk onward, while the elder traveller exhorted his companion to make good speed and persevere in the path, discoursing so aptly that his arguments seemed rather to spring up in the bosom of his auditor than to be suggested by himself. As they went, he plucked a branch of maple to serve for a walking stick, and began to strip it of the twigs and little boughs, which were wet with evening dew. The moment his fingers touched them they became strangely withered and dried up as with a week's sunshine. Thus the pair proceeded, at a good free pace, until suddenly, in a gloomy hollow of the road, Goodman Brown sat himself on the stump of a tree and refused to go any farther.

"Friend," said he, stubbornly, "my mind is made up. Not another step will I budge on this errand. What if a wretched old woman do choose to go to the devil when I thought she was going to heaven: is that any reason why I should quit my dear Faith and go after her?"

"You will think better of this by and by," said his acquaintance, composedly. "Sit here and rest yourself a while; and when you feel like moving again, there is my staff to help you along."

Without more words, he threw his companion the maple stick, and was as speedily out of sight as if he had vanished into the deepening gloom. The young man sat for a few moments by the roadside, applauding himself greatly, and thinking with how clear a conscience he should meet the minister in his morning walk, nor shrink from the eye of good old Deacon Gookin. And what calm sleep would be his that very night, which was to have been spent so wickedly, but so purely and sweetly now, in the arms of Faith! Amidst these pleasant and praiseworthy meditations, Goodman Brown heard the tramp of horses along the road, and deemed it advisable to conceal himself within the verge of the forest, conscious of the guilty purpose that had brought him thither, though now so happily turned from it.

On came the hoof tramps and the voices of the riders, two grave old voices, conversing soberly as they drew near. These mingled sounds appeared to pass along the road, within a few yards of the young man's hiding-place; but, owing doubtless to the depth of the gloom at that particular spot, neither the travellers nor their steeds were visible. Though their figures brushed the small boughs by the wayside, it could not be seen that they intercepted, even for a moment, the faint gleam from the strip of bright sky athwart which they must have passed. Goodman Brown alternately crouched and stood on tiptoe, pulling aside the branches and thrusting forth his head as far as he durst without discerning so much as a shadow. It vexed him the more, because he could have sworn, were such a thing possible, that he recognized the voices of the minister and Deacon Gookin, jogging along qui-

etly, as they were wont to do, when bound to some ordination or ecclesiastical council. While yet within hearing, one of the riders stopped to pluck
a switch.

"Of the two, reverend sir," said the voice like the deacon's, "I had rather
miss an ordination dinner than to-night's meeting. They tell me that some of
our community are to be here from Falmouth[11] and beyond, and others from
Connecticut and Rhode Island, besides several of the Indian powwows,[12] who,
after their fashion, know almost as much deviltry as the best of us. Moreover,
there is a goodly young woman to be taken into communion."

"Mighty well, Deacon Gookin!" replied the solemn old tones of the minister. "Spur up, or we shall be late. Nothing can be done, you know, until I get
on the ground."

The hoofs clattered again; and the voices, talking so strangely in the empty
air, passed on through the forest, where no church had ever been gathered, nor
solitary Christian prayed. Whither, then, could these holy men be journeying
so deep into the heathen wilderness? Young Goodman Brown caught hold of
a tree for support, being ready to sink down on the ground, faint and over-
burdened with the heavy sickness of his heart. He looked up to the sky,
doubting whether there really was a heaven above him. Yet there was the blue
arch, and the stars brightening in it.

"With heaven above and Faith below, I will yet stand firm against the
devil!" cried Goodman Brown.

While he still gazed upward into the deep arch of the firmament and had
lifted his hands to pray, a cloud, though no wind was stirring, hurried across
the zenith and hid the brightening stars. The blue sky was still visible, except
directly overhead, where this black mass of cloud was sweeping swiftly north-
ward. Aloft in the air, as if from the depths of the cloud, came a confused and
doubtful sound of voices. Once the listener fancied that he could distinguish
the accents of towns-people of his own, men and women, both pious and
ungodly, many of whom he had met at the communion table, and had seen
others rioting at the tavern. The next moment, so indistinct were the sounds,
he doubted whether he had heard aught but the murmur of the old forest,
whispering without a wind. Then came a stronger swell of those familiar tones,
heard daily in the sunshine at Salem village, but never until now from a cloud
of night. There was one voice, of a young woman, uttering lamentations, yet
with an uncertain sorrow, and entreating for some favor, which, perhaps, it
would grieve her to obtain; and all the unseen multitude, both saints and
sinners, seemed to encourage her onward.

"Faith!" shouted Goodman Brown, in a voice of agony and desperation; and
the echoes of the forest mocked him, crying, "Faith! Faith!" as if bewildered
wretches were seeking her all through the wilderness.

---

[11] A town near Salem, Massachusetts.
[12] Medicine men.

The cry of grief, rage, and terror was yet piercing the night, when the unhappy husband held his breath for a response. There was a scream, drowned immediately in a louder murmur of voices, fading into far-off laughter, as the dark cloud swept away, leaving the clear and silent sky above Goodman Brown. But something fluttered lightly down through the air and caught on the branch of a tree. The young man seized it, and beheld a pink ribbon.

"My Faith is gone!" cried he, after one stupefied moment. "There is no good on earth; and sin is but a name. Come, devil; for to thee is this world given."

And, maddened with despair, so that he laughed loud and long, did Goodman Brown grasp his staff and set forth again, at such a rate that he seemed to fly along the forest path rather than to walk or run. The road grew wilder and drearier and more faintly traced, and vanished at length, leaving him in the heart of the dark wilderness, still rushing onward with the instinct that guides mortal man to evil. The whole forest was peopled with frightful sounds—the creaking of the trees, the howling of wild beasts, and the yell of Indians; while sometimes the wind tolled like a distant church bell, and sometimes gave a broad roar around the traveller, as if all Nature were laughing him to scorn. But he was himself the chief horror of the scene, and shrank not from its other horrors.

"Ha! ha! ha!" roared Goodman Brown when the wind laughed at him. "Let us hear which will laugh loudest. Think not to frighten me with your deviltry. Come witch, come wizard, come Indian powwow, come devil himself, and here comes Goodman Brown. You may as well fear him as he fear you."

In truth, all through the haunted forest there could be nothing more frightful than the figure of Goodman Brown. On he flew among the black pines, brandishing his staff with frenzied gestures, now giving vent to an inspiration of horrid blasphemy, and now shouting forth such laughter as set all the echoes of the forest laughing like demons around him. The fiend in his own shape is less hideous than when he rages in the breast of man. Thus sped the demoniac on his course, until, quivering among the trees, he saw a red light before him, as when the felled trunks and branches of a clearing have been set on fire, and throw up their lurid blaze against the sky, at the hour of midnight. He paused, in a lull of the tempest that had driven him onward, and heard the well of what seemed a hymn, rolling solemnly from a distance with the weight of many voices. He knew the tune; it was a familiar one in the choir of the village meeting-house. The verse died heavily away, and was lengthened by a chorus, not of human voices, but of all the sounds of the benighted wilderness pealing in awful harmony together. Goodman Brown cried out, and his cry was lost to his own ear by its unison with the cry of the desert.

In the interval of silence he stole forward until the light glared full upon his eyes. At one extremity of an open space, hemmed in by the dark wall of the forest, arose a rock, bearing some rude, natural resemblance either to an altar or a pulpit, and surrounded by four blazing pines, their tops aflame, their stems untouched, like candles at an evening meeting. The mass of foliage that had overgrown the summit of the rock was all on fire, blazing high into the night and fitfully illuminating the whole field. Each pendent twig and leafy festoon was in a blaze. As the red light arose and fell, a numerous congregation alternately shone forth, then disappeared in shadow, and again grew, as it were, out of the darkness, peopling the heart of the solitary woods at once.

"A grave and dark-clad company," quoth Goodman Brown.

In truth they were such. Among them, quivering to and fro between gloom and splendor, appeared faces that would be seen next day at the council board of the province, and others which, Sabbath after Sabbath, looked devoutly heavenward, and benignantly over the crowded pews, from the holiest pulpits in the land. Some affirm that the lady of the governor was there. At least there were high dames well known to her, and wives of honored husbands, and widows, a great multitude, and ancient maidens, all of excellent repute, and fair young girls, who trembled lest their mothers should espy them. Either the sudden gleams of light flashing over the obscure field bedazzled Goodman Brown, or he recognized a score of the church members of Salem village famous for their especial sanctity. Good old Deacon Gookin had arrived, and waited at the skirts of that venerable saint, his revered pastor. But, irreverently consorting with these grave, reputable, and pious people, these elders of the church, these chaste dames and dewy virgins, there were men of dissolute lives and women of spotted fame, wretches given over to all mean and filthy vice, and suspected even of horrid crimes. It was strange to see that the good shrank not from the wicked, nor were the sinners abashed by the saints. Scattered also among their pale-faced enemies were the Indian priests, or powwows, who had often scared their native forest with more hideous incantations than any known to English witchcraft.

"But where is Faith?" thought Goodman Brown; and, as hope came into his heart, he trembled.

Another verse of the hymn arose, a slow and mournful strain, such as the pious love, but joined to words which expressed all that our nature can conceive of sin, and darkly hinted at far more. Unfathomable to mere mortals is the lore of fiends. Verse after verse was sung; and still the chorus of the desert swelled between like the deepest tone of a mighty organ; and with the final peal of that dreadful anthem there came a sound, as if the roaring wind, the rushing streams, the howling beasts, and every other voice of the unconcerted wilderness were mingling and according with the voice of guilty man in homage to the prince of all. The four blazing pines threw up a loftier flame, and obscurely discovered shapes and visages of horror on the smoke wreaths above the impious assembly. At the same moment the fire on the rock shot redly forth and formed a glowing arch above its base, where now appeared a figure. With reverence be it spoken, the figure bore no slight similitude, both in garb and manner, to some grave divine of the New England churches.

"Bring forth the converts!" cried a voice that echoed through the field and rolled into the forest.

At the word, Goodman Brown stepped forth from the shadow of the trees and approached the congregation, with whom he felt a loathful brotherhood by the sympathy of all that was wicked in his heart. He could have well-nigh sworn that the shape of his own dead father beckoned him to advance, looking downward from a smoke wreath, while a woman, with dim features of despair, threw out her hand to warn him back. Was it his mother? But he had no power to retreat one step, nor to resist, even in thought, when the minister and good old Deacon Gookin seized his arms and led him to the blazing rock. Thither came also the slender form of a veiled female, led between Goody Cloyse, that pious teacher of the catechism, and Martha Carrier,[13] who had received the devil's promise to be queen of hell. A rampant hag was she. And there stood the proselytes beneath the canopy of fire.

"Welcome, my children," said the dark figure, "to the communion of your race. Ye have found thus young your nature and your destiny. My children, look behind you!"

They turned; and flashing forth, as it were, in a sheet of flame, the fiend worshippers were seen; the smile of welcome gleamed darkly on every visage.

"There," resumed the sable form, "are all whom ye have reverenced from youth. Ye deemed them holier than yourselves, and shrank from your own sin, contrasting it with their lives of righteousness and prayerful aspirations heavenward. Yet here are they all in my worshipping assembly. This night it shall be granted you to know their secret deeds: how hoary-bearded elders of the church have whispered wanton words to the young maids of their households; how many a woman, eager for widows' weeds, has given her husband a drink at bedtime and let him sleep his last sleep in her bosom; how beardless youths have made haste to inherit their fathers' wealth; and how fair damsels—blush not, sweet ones—have dug little graves in the garden, and bidden me, the sole guest, to an infant's funeral. By the sympathy of your human hearts for sin ye shall scent out all the places—whether in church, bed-chamber, street, field, or forest—where crime has been committed, and shall exult to behold the whole earth one stain of guilt, one mighty blood spot. Far more than this. It shall be yours to penetrate, in every bosom, the deep mystery of sin, the fountain of all wicked arts, and which inexhaustibly supplies more evil impulses than human power—than my power at its utmost—can make manifest in deeds. And now, my children, look upon each other."

They did so; and, by the blaze of the hell-kindled torches, the wretched man beheld his Faith, and the wife her husband, trembling before that unhallowed altar.

"Lo, there ye stand, my children," said the figure, in a deep and solemn tone, almost sad with its despairing awfulness, as if his once angelic nature could yet mourn for our miserable race. "Depending upon one another's hearts, ye had still hoped that virtue were not all a dream. Now are ye undeceived. Evil is the nature of mankind. Evil must be your only happiness. Welcome again, my children, to the communion of your race."

---

[13] One of the women hanged in Salem in 1697 for witchcraft.

"Welcome," repeated the fiend worshippers, in one cry of despair and triumph.

And there they stood, the only pair, as it seemed, who were yet hesitating on the verge of wickedness in this dark world. A basin was hollowed, naturally, in the rock. Did it contain water, reddened by the lurid light? or was it blood? or, perchance, a liquid flame? Herein did the shape of evil dip his hand and prepare to lay the mark of baptism upon their foreheads, that they might be partakers of the mystery of sin, more conscious of the secret guilt of others, both in deed and thought, than they could now be of their own. The husband cast one look at his pale wife, and Faith at him. What polluted wretches would the next glance show them to each other, shuddering alike at what they disclosed and what they saw!

"Faith! Faith!" cried the husband, "look up to heaven, and resist the wicked one."

Whether Faith obeyed he knew not. Hardly had he spoken when he found himself amid calm night and solitude, listening to a roar of the wind which died heavily away through the forest. He staggered against the rock, and felt it chill and damp; while a hanging twig, that had been all on fire, besprinkled his cheek with the coldest dew.

The next morning Goodman Brown came slowly into the street of Salem village, staring around him like a bewildered man. The good old minister was taking a walk along the graveyard to get an appetite for breakfast and meditate his sermon, and bestowed a blessing, as he passed, on Goodman Brown. He shrank from the venerable saint as if to avoid an anathema. Old Deacon Gookin was at domestic worship, and the holy words of his prayer were heard through the open window. "What doth the wizard pray to?" quoth Goodman Brown. Goody Cloyse, that excellent old Christian, stood in the early sunshine at her own lattice, catechizing a little girl who had brought her a pint of morning's milk. Goodman Brown snatched away the child as from the grasp of the fiend himself. Turning the corner by the meeting-house, he spied the head of Faith, with the pink ribbons, gazing anxiously forth, and bursting into such joy at sight of him that she skipped along the street and almost kissed her husband before the whole village. But Goodman Brown looked sternly and sadly into her face, and passed on without a greeting.

Had Goodman Brown fallen asleep in the forest and only dreamed a wild dream of a witch-meeting?

Be it so if you will; but, alas! it was a dream of evil omen for young Goodman Brown. A stern, a sad, a darkly meditative, a distrustful, if not a desperate man did he become from the night of that fearful dream. On the Sabbath day, when the congregation were singing a holy psalm, he could not listen because an anthem of sin rushed loudly upon his ear and drowned all the blessed strain. When the minister spoke from the pulpit with power and fervid eloquence, and, with his hand on the open Bible, of the sacred truths of our religion, and of saint-like lives and triumphant deaths, and of future bliss or misery unutterable, then did Goodman Brown turn pale, dreading lest the roof should thunder down upon the gray blasphemer and his hearers. Often, awakening suddenly at midnight, he shrank from the bosom of Faith; and at morning or eventide, when the family knelt down at prayer, he scowled and muttered to himself, and gazed sternly at his wife, and turned away. And when he had lived long, and was borne to his grave a hoary corpse, followed by Faith, an aged woman, and children and grandchildren, a goodly procession, besides neighbors not a few, they carved no hopeful verse upon his tombstone, for his dying hour was gloom.

QUESTIONS
1. At the end of the story, Hawthorne asks, "Had Goodman Brown fallen asleep in the forest and only dreamed a wild dream of a witch-meeting?" Why does he not answer the question?   **2.** How would you characterize the setting of this story?   **3.** What elements of the story can be described as allegoric or symbolic? Explain.   **4.** Write out a paraphrase of Satan's sermon.

WRITING TOPIC
Does the final paragraph of the story tell us that Brown's lifelong gloom is justified? Or does it express disapproval of Brown?

The Bride Comes to Yellow Sky

1898

STEPHEN CRANE   [1871–1900]

I

The great Pullman was whirling onward with such dignity of motion that a glance from the window seemed simply to prove that the plains of Texas were pouring eastward. Vast flats of green grass, dull-hued space of mesquit and cactus, little groups of frame houses, woods of light and tender trees, all were sweeping into the east, sweeping over the horizon, a precipice.

A newly married pair had boarded this coach at San Antonio. The man's face was reddened from many days in the wind and sun, and a direct result of his new black clothes was that his brick-colored hands were constantly performing in a most conscious fashion. From time to time he looked down respectfully at his attire. He sat with a hand on each knee, like a man waiting in a barber's shop. The glances he devoted to other passengers were furtive and shy.

The bride was not pretty, nor was she very young. She wore a dress of blue cashmere, with small reservations of velvet here and there, and with steel buttons abounding. She continually twisted her head to regard her puff sleeves, very stiff, straight, and high. They embarrassed her. It was quite apparent that she had cooked, and that she expected to cook, dutifully. The blushes caused by the careless scrutiny of some passengers as she had entered the car were strange to see upon this plain, under-class countenance, which was drawn in placid, almost emotionless lines.

They were evidently very happy. "Ever been in a parlour-car before?" he asked, smiling with delight.

"No," she answered; "I never was. It's fine, ain't it?"

"Great! And then after a while we'll go forward to the diner, and get a big lay-out. Finest meal in the world. Charge a dollar."

"Oh, do they?" cried the bride. "Charge a dollar? Why, that's too much—for us—ain't it, Jack?"

"Not this trip, anyhow," he answered bravely. "We're going to go the whole thing."

Later he explained to her about the trains. "You see, it's a thousand miles from one end of Texas to the other; and this train runs right across it, and never stops but four times." He had the pride of an owner. He pointed out to her the dazzling fittings of the coach; and in truth her eyes opened wider as she contemplated the sea-green figured velvet, the shining brass, silver, and glass, the wood that gleamed as darkly brilliant as the surface of a pool of oil. At one end a bronze figure sturdily held a support for a separated chamber, and at convenient places on the ceiling were frescos in olive and silver.

To the minds of the pair, their surroundings reflected the glory of their marriage that morning in San Antonio; this was the environment of their new estate; and the man's face in particular beamed with an elation that made him appear ridiculous to the negro porter. This individual at times surveyed them from afar with an amused and superior grin. On other occasions he bullied them with skill in ways that did not make it exactly plain to them that they were being bullied. He subtly used all the manners of the most unconquerable kind of snobbery. He oppressed them; but of this oppression they had small knowledge, and they speedily forgot that infrequently a number of travellers covered them with stares of derisive enjoyment. Historically there was supposed to be something infinitely humorous in their situation.

"We are due in Yellow Sky at 3:42," he said, looking tenderly into her eyes.

"Oh, are we?" she said, as if she had not been aware of it. To evince surprise at her husband's statement was part of her wifely amiability. She took from a pocket a little silver watch; and as she held it before her, and stared at it with a frown of attention, the new husband's face shone.

"I bought it in San Anton' from a friend of mine," he told her gleefully.

"It's seventeen minutes past twelve," she said, looking up at him with a kind of shy and clumsy coquetry. A passenger, noting this play, grew excessively sardonic, and winked at himself in one of the numerous mirrors.

At last they went to the dining-car. Two rows of negro waiters, in glowing white suits, surveyed their entrance with the interest, and also the equanimity, of men who had been forewarned. The pair fell to the lot of a waiter who happened to feel pleasure in steering them through their meal. He viewed them with the manner of a fatherly pilot, his countenance radiant with benevolence. The patronage, entwined with the ordinary deference, was not plain to them. And yet, as they returned to their coach, they showed in their faces a sense of escape.

To the left, miles down a long purple slope, was a little ribbon of mist where moved the keening Rio Grande. The train was approaching it at an angle, and the apex was Yellow Sky. Presently it was apparent that, as the distance from Yellow Sky grew shorter, the husband became commensurately restless. His brick-red hands were more insistent in their prominence. Occasionally he was even rather absent-minded and far-away when the bride leaned forward and addressed him.

As a matter of truth, Jack Potter was beginning to find the shadow of a deed weigh upon him like a leaden slab. He, the town marshal of Yellow Sky, a man known, liked, and feared in his corner, a prominent person, had gone to San Antonio to meet a girl he believed he loved, and there, after the usual prayers, had actually induced her to marry him, without consulting Yellow Sky for any part of the transaction. He was now bringing his bride before an innocent and unsuspecting community.

Of course people in Yellow Sky married as it pleased them, in accordance with a general custom; but such was Potter's thought of his duty to his friends, or of their idea of his duty, or of an unspoken form which does not control men in these matters, that he felt he was heinous. He had committed an extraordinary crime. Face to face with this girl in San Antonio, and spurred by his sharp impulse, he had gone headlong over all the social hedges. At San Antonio he was like a man hidden in the dark. A knife to sever any friendly duty, any form, was easy to his hand in that remote city. But the hour of Yellow Sky—the hour of daylight—was approaching.

He knew full well that his marriage was an important thing to his town. It could only be exceeded by the burning of the new hotel. His friends could not forgive him. Frequently he had reflected on the advisability of telling them by telegraph, but a new cowardice had been upon him. He feared to do it. And now the train was hurrying him toward a scene of amazement, glee, and reproach. He glanced out of the window at the line of haze swinging slowly in toward the train.

Yellow Sky had a kind of brass band, which played painfully, to the delight of the populace. He laughed without heart as he thought of it. If the citizens could dream of his prospective arrival with his bride, they would parade the band at the station and escort them, amid cheers and laughing congratulations, to his adobe home.

He resolved that he would use all the devices of speed and plainscraft in making the journey from the station to his house. Once within that safe citadel, he could issue some sort of verbal bulletin, and then not go among the citizens until they had time to wear off a little of their enthusiasm.

The bride looked anxiously at him. "What's worrying you, Jack?"

He laughed again. "I'm not worrying, girl; I'm only thinking of Yellow Sky."

She flushed in comprehension.

A sense of mutual guilt invaded their minds and developed a finer tenderness. They looked at each other with eyes softly aglow. But Potter often laughed the same nervous laugh; the flush upon the bride's face seemed quite permanent.

The traitor to the feelings of Yellow Sky narrowly watched the speeding landscape. "We're nearly there," he said.

Presently the porter came and announced the proximity of Potter's home. He held a brush in his hand, and, with all his airy superiority gone, he brushed Potter's new clothes as the latter slowly turned this way and that way. Potter fumbled out a coin and gave it to the porter, as he had seen others do. It was a heavy and muscle-bounded business, as that of a man shoeing his first horse.

The porter took their bag, and as the train began to slow they moved forward to the hooded platform of the car. Presently the two engines and their string of coaches rushed into the station of Yellow Sky.

"They have to take water here," said Potter, from a constricted throat and in mournful cadence, as one announcing death. Before the train stopped his eye had swept the length of the platform, and he was glad and astonished to see there was none upon it but the station-agent, who, with a slightly hurried and anxious air, was walking toward the water-tanks. When the train had halted, the porter alighted first, and placed in position a little temporary step.

"Come on, girl," said Potter, hoarsely. As he helped her down they each laughed on a false note. He took the bag from the negro, and bade his wife cling to his arm. As they slunk rapidly away, his hang-dog glance perceived that they were unloading the two trunks, and also that the station-agent, far ahead near the baggage-car, had turned and was running toward him, making gestures. He laughed, and groaned as he laughed, when he noted the first effect of his marital bliss upon Yellow Sky. He gripped his wife's arm firmly to his side, and they fled. Behind them the porter stood, chuckling fatuously.

II

The California express on the Southern Railway was due at Yellow Sky in twenty-one minutes. There were six men at the bar of the Weary Gentleman saloon. One was a drummer who talked a great deal and rapidly; three were Texans who did not care to talk at that time; and two were Mexican sheep-herders, who did not talk as a general practice in the Weary Gentleman saloon. The barkeeper's dog lay on the board walk that crossed in front of the door. His head was on his paws, and he glanced drowsily here and there with the constant vigilance of a dog that is kicked on occasion. Across the sandy street were some vivid green grass-plots, so wonderful in appearance, amid the sands that burned near them in a blazing sun, that they caused a doubt in the mind. They exactly resembled the grass mats used to represent lawns on the stage. At the cooler end of the railway station, a man without a coat sat in a tilted chair and smoked his pipe. The fresh-cut bank of the Rio Grande circled near the town, and there could be seen beyond it a great plum-coloured plain of mesquit.

Save for the busy drummer and his companions in the saloon, Yellow Sky was dozing. The new-comer leaned gracefully upon the bar, and recited many tales with the confidence of a bard who had come upon a new field.

"—and at the moment that the old man fell downstairs with the bureau in his arms, the old woman was coming up with two scuttles of coal, and of course—"

The drummer's tale was interrupted by a young man who suddenly appeared in the open door. He cried: "Scratchy Wilson's drunk, and has turned loose with both hands." The two Mexicans at once set down their glasses and faded out of the rear entrance of the saloon.

The drummer, innocent and jocular, answered: "All right, old man. S'pose he has? Come in and have a drink, anyhow."

But the information had made such an obvious cleft in every skull in the room that the drummer was obliged to see its importance. All had become instantly solemn. "Say," said he, mystified, "what is this?" His three companions made the introductory gesture of eloquent speech; but the young man at the door forestalled them.

"It means, my friend," he answered, as he came into the saloon, "that for the next two hours this town won't be a health resort."

The barkeeper went to the door, and locked and barred it; reaching out of the window, he pulled in heavy wooden shutters, and barred them. Immediately a solemn, chapel-like gloom was upon the place. The drummer was looking from one to another.

"But, say," he cried, "what is this, anyhow? You don't mean there is going to be a gun-fight?"

"Don't know whether there'll be a fight or not," answered one man, grimly; "but there'll be some shootin'—some good shootin'."

The young man who had warned them waved his hand. "Oh, there'll be a fight fast enough, if any one wants it. Anybody can get a fight out there in the street. There's a fight just waiting."

The drummer seemed to be swayed between the interest of a foreigner and a perception of personal danger.

"What did you say his name was?" he asked.

"Scratchy Wilson," they answered in chorus.

"And will he kill anybody? What are you going to do? Does this happen often? Does he rampage around like this once a week or so? Can he break in that door?"

"No; he can't break down that door," replied the barkeeper. "He's tried it three times. But when he comes you'd better lay down on the floor, stranger. He'd dead sure to shoot at it, and a bullet may come through."

Thereafter the drummer kept a strict eye upon the door. The time had not yet called for him to hug the floor, but, as a minor precaution, he sidled near the wall. "Will he kill anybody?" he said again.

The men laughed low and scornfully at the question.

"He's out to shoot, and he's out for trouble. Don't see any good in experimentin' with him."

"But what do you do in a case like this? What do you do?"

A man responded: "Why, he and Jack Potter—"

"But," in chorus the other men interrupted, "Jack Potter's in San Anton'."

"Well, who is he? What's he got to do with it?"

"Oh, he's the town marshal. He goes out and fights Scratchy when he gets on one of these tears."

"Wow!" said the drummer, mopping his brow. "Nice job he's got."

The voices had toned away to mere whisperings. The drummer wished to ask further questions, which were born of an increasing anxiety and bewilderment; but when he attempted them, the men merely looked at him in irritation and motioned him to remain silent. A tense waiting hush was upon them. In the deep shadows of the room their eyes shone as they listened for sounds from the street. One man made three gestures at the barkeeper; and the latter, moving like a ghost, handed him a glass and a bottle. The man poured a full glass of whisky, and set down the bottle noiselessly. He gulped the whiskey in a swallow, and turned again toward the door in immovable silence. The drummer saw that the barkeeper, without a sound, had taken a Winchester from beneath the bar. Later he saw this individual beckoning to him, so he tiptoed across the room.

"You better come with me back of the bar."

"No thanks," said the drummer, perspiring; "I'd rather be where I can make a break for the back door."

Whereupon the man of bottles made a kindly but peremptory gesture. The drummer obeyed it, and, finding himself seated on a box with his head below the level of the bar, balm was laid upon his soul at sight of various zinc and copper fittings that bore a resemblance to armour-plate. The barkeeper took a seat comfortably upon an adjacent box.

"You see," he whispered, "this here Scratchy Wilson is a wonder with a gun—a perfect wonder; and when he goes on the war-trail, we hunt our holes—naturally. He's about the last one of the old gang that used to hang out along the river here. He's a terror when he's drunk. When he's sober he's all right—kind of simple—wouldn't hurt a fly—nicest fellow in town. But when he's drunk—whoo!"

There were periods of stillness. "I wish Jack Potter was back from San Anton'," said the barkeeper. "He shot Wilson up once—in the leg—and he would sail in and pull out the kinks in this thing."

Presently they heard from a distance the sound of a shot, followed by three wild yowls. It instantly removed a bond from the men in the darkened saloon. There was a shuffling of feet. They looked at each other. "Here he comes," they said.

III

A man in a maroon-coloured flannel shirt, which had been purchased for purposes of decoration, and made principally by some Jewish women on the East Side of New York, rounded a corner and walked into the middle of the main street of Yellow Sky. In either hand the man held a long, heavy, blue-black revolver. Often he yelled, and these cries rang through a semblance of a deserted village, shrilly flying over the roofs in a volume that seemed to have no relation to the ordinary vocal strength of a man. It was as if the surrounding stillness formed the arch of a tomb over him. These cries of ferocious challenge rang against the walls of silence. And his boots had red tops with gilded imprints, of the kind beloved in winter by little sledding boys on the hillsides of New England.

The man's face flamed in a rage begot of whisky. His eyes, rolling, and yet keen for ambush, hunted the still doorways and windows. He walked with the creeping movement of the midnight cat. As it occurred to him, he roared menacing information. The long revolvers in his hands were as easy as straws; they were moved with an electric swiftness. The little fingers of each hand played sometimes in a musician's way. Plain from the low collar of the shirt, the cords of his neck straightened and sank, straightened and sank, as passion moved him. The only sounds were his terrible invitations. The calm adobes preserved their demeanor at the passing of this small thing in the middle of the street.

There was no offer of fight—no offer of fight. The man called to the sky. There were no attractions. He bellowed and fumed and swayed his revolvers here and everywhere.

The dog of the barkeeper of the Weary Gentleman saloon had not appreciated the advance of events. He yet lay dozing in front of his master's door. At sight of the dog, the man paused and raised his revolver humorously. At sight of the man, the dog sprang up and walked diagonally away, with a sullen head, and growling. The man yelled, and the dog broke into a gallop. As it was about to enter an alley, there was a loud noise, a whistling, and something spat the ground directly before it. The dog screamed, and, wheeling in terror, galloped headlong in a new direction. Again there was a noise, a whistling, and sand was kicked viciously before it. Fear-stricken, the dog turned and flurried like an animal in a pen. The man stood laughing, his weapons at his hips.

Ultimately the man was attracted by the closed door of the Weary Gentleman saloon. He went to it and, hammering with a revolver, demanded drink.

The door remaining imperturbable, he picked a bit of paper from the walk, and nailed it to the framework with a knife. He then turned his back contemptuously upon this popular resort and, walking to the opposite side of the street and spinning there on his heel quickly and lithely, fired at the bit of paper. He missed it by a half-inch. He swore at himself, and went away. Later he comfortably fusilladed the windows of his most intimate friend. The man was playing with this town; it was a toy for him.

But still there was no offer of fight. The name of Jack Potter, his ancient antagonist, entered his mind, and he concluded that it would be a glad thing if he should go to Potter's house and by bombardment induce him to come out and fight. He moved in the direction of his desire, chanting Apache scalp-music.

When he arrived at it, Potter's house presented the same still front as had the other adobes. Taking up a strategic position, the man howled a challenge. But this house regarded him as might a great stone god. It gave no sign. After a decent wait, the man howled further challenges, mingling with them wonderful epithets.

Presently there came the spectacle of a man churning himself into deepest rage over the immobility of a house. He fumed at it as the winter wind attacks a prairie cabin in the North. To the distance there should have gone the sound of a tumult like the fighting of two hundred Mexicans. As necessity bade him, he paused for breath or to reload his revolvers.

IV

Potter and his bride walked sheepishly and with speed. Sometimes they laughed together shamefacedly and low.

"Next corner, dear," he said finally.

They put forth the efforts of a pair walking bowed against a strong wind. Potter was about to raise a finger to point the first appearance of the new home when, as they circled the corner, they came face to face with a man in a maroon-coloured shirt, who was feverishly putting cartridges into a large revolver. Upon the instant the man dropped his revolver to the ground and, like lightning, whipped another from its holster. The second weapon was aimed at the bridegroom's chest.

There was a silence. Potter's mouth seemed to be merely a grave for his tongue. He exhibited an instinct to at once loosen his arm from the woman's grip, and he dropped the bag to the sand. As for the bride, her face had gone as yellow as old cloth. She was a slave to hideous rites, gazing at the apparitional snake.

The two men faced each other at a distance of three paces. He of the revolver smiled with a new and quiet ferocity.

"Tried to sneak up on me," he said. "Tried to sneak up on me!" His eyes grew more baleful. As Potter made a slight movement, the man thrust his revolver venomously forward. "No, don't you do it, Jack Potter. Don't you move a finger toward a gun just yet. Don't you move an eyelash. The time has come for me to settle with you, and I'm goin' to do it my own way, and loaf along with no interferin'. So if you don't want a gun bent on you, just mind what I tell you."

Potter looked at his enemy. "I ain't got a gun on me, Scratchy," he said. "Honest, I ain't." He was stiffening and steadying, but yet somewhere at the back of his mind a vision of the Pullman floated: the sea-green figured velvet, the shining brass, silver, and glass, the wood that gleamed as darkly brilliant as the surface of a pool of oil—all the glory of marriage, the environment of the new estate. "You know I fight when it comes to fighting, Scratchy Wilson; but I ain't got a gun on me. You'll have to do all the shootin' yourself."

His enemy's face went livid. He stepped forward, and lashed his weapon to and fro before Potter's chest. "Don't you tell me you ain't got no gun on you, you whelp. Don't tell me no lie like that. There ain't a man in Texas ever seen you without no gun. Don't take me for no kid." His eyes blazed with light, and his throat worked like a pump.

"I ain't takin' you for no kid," answered Potter. His heels had not moved an inch backward. "I'm takin' you for a damn fool. I tell you I ain't got a gun, and I ain't. If you're goin' to shoot me up, you better begin now; you'll never get a chance like this again."

So much enforced reasoning had told on Wilson's rage; he was calmer. "If you ain't got a gun, why ain't you got a gun?" he sneered. "Been to Sunday-school?"

"I ain't got a gun because I've just come from San Anton' with my wife. I'm married," said Potter. "And if I'd thought there was going to be any galoots like you prowling around when I brought my wife home, I'd had a gun, and don't you forget it."

"Married!" said Scratchy, not at all comprehending.

"Yes, married. I'm married," said Potter, distinctly.

"Married?" said Scratchy. Seemingly for the first time, he saw the drooping, drowning woman at the other man's side. "No!" he said. He was like a creature allowed a glimpse of another world. He moved a pace backward, and his arm, with the revolver, dropped to his side. "Is this the lady?" he asked.

"Yes; this is the lady," answered Potter.

There was another period of silence.

"Well," said Wilson at last, slowly, "I s'pose it's all off now."

"It's all off if you say so, Scratchy. You know I didn't make the trouble." Potter lifted his valise.

"Well, I 'low it's off, Jack," said Wilson. He was looking at the ground. "Married!" He was not a student of chivalry; it was merely that in the presence of this foreign condition he was a simple child of the earlier plains. He picked up his starboard revolver, and, placing both weapons in their holsters, he went away. His feet made funnel-shaped tracks in the heavy sand.

QUESTIONS

1. Scratchy is described in the final paragraph as "a simple child of the earlier plains." What does this mean? Was Potter ever a simple child of the earlier plains?   **2.** Early in the story we read that ". . . Jack Potter was beginning to find the shadow of a deed weigh upon him like a leaden slab. He, the town marshal of Yellow Sky, a man known, liked, and feared in his corner, a prominent person, had gone to San Antonio to meet a girl he believed he loved, and there, after the usual prayers, had actually induced her to marry him, without consulting Yellow Sky for any part of the transaction. He was now bringing his bride before an innocent and unsuspecting community." Jack Potter, like any man, has a right to marry. How do you account for his feelings as described in this passage?   **3.** A "drummer" is a traveling salesman. What effect does his presence have on the "myth of the West"?

WRITING TOPICS

1. How would you characterize Scratchy's behavior? How does it relate to the "myth of the West" preserved in films and Western novels? How does the description of Scratchy's shirt at the beginning of Part III affect that view of the West? Why is Scratchy disconsolate at the end?   **2.** Analyze Crane's metaphors and images. What function do they serve in the story?

Araby*

1914

JAMES JOYCE   [1882–1941]

North Richmond Street, being blind, was a quiet street except at the hour when the Christian Brothers' School set the boys free. An uninhabited house of two storeys stood at the blind end, detached from its neighbours in a square ground. The other houses of the street, conscious of decent lives within them, gazed at one another with brown imperturbable faces.

The former tenant of our house, a priest, had died in the back drawing-room. Air, musty from having been long enclosed, hung in all the rooms, and the waste room behind the kitchen was littered with old useless papers. Among these I found a few paper-covered books, the pages of which were curled and damp: *The Abbot*, by Walter Scott, *The Devout Communicant* and *The Memoirs of Vidocq*. I liked the last best because its leaves were yellow. The wild garden behind the house contained a central apple-tree and a few straggling bushes under one of which I found the late tenant's rusty bicycle pump. He had been a very charitable priest; in his will he left all his money to institutions and the furniture of his house to his sister.

When the short days of winter came dusk fell before we had well eaten our dinners. When we met in the street the houses had grown sombre. The space of sky above us was the colour of ever-changing violet and towards it the lamps of the street lifted their feeble lanterns. The cold air stung us and we played till our bodies glowed. Our shouts echoed in the silent street. The career of our play brought us through the dark muddy lanes behind the houses where we ran the gauntlet of the rough tribes from the cottages, to the back doors of the dark dripping gardens where odours arose from the ashpits, to the dark odorous stables where a coachman smoothed and combed the horse or shook music from the buckled harness. When we returned to the street light from the kitchen windows had filled the areas. If my uncle was seen turning the corner we hid in the shadow until we had seen him safely housed. Or if Mangan's sister came out on the doorstep to call her brother in to his tea we watched her from our shadow peer up and down the street. We waited to see whether she would remain or go in and, if she remained, we left our shadow and walked up to Mangan's steps resignedly. She was waiting for us, her figure defined by the light from the half-opened door. Her brother always teased her before he obeyed and I stood by the railings looking at her. Her dress swung as she moved her body and the soft rope of her hair tossed from side to side.

Every morning I lay on the floor in the front parlour watching her door. The blind was pulled down to within an inch of the sash so that I could not be seen. When she came out on the doorstep my heart leaped. I ran to the hall, seized

---

* This story is considered in the essay "Reading Fiction" at the end of the book.

my books and followed her. I kept her brown figure always in my eye and, when we came near the point at which our ways diverged, I quickened my pace and passed her. This happened morning after morning. I had never spoken to her, except for a few casual words, and yet her name was like a summons to all my foolish blood.

Her image accompanied me even in places the most hostile to romance. On Saturday evenings when my aunt went marketing I had to go to carry some of the parcels. We walked through the flaring streets, jostled by drunken men and bargaining women, amid the curses of labourers, the shrill litanies of shop-boys who stood on guard by the barrels of pigs' cheeks, the nasal chanting of street-singers, who sang a *come-all-you*[1] about O'Donovan Rossa, or a ballad about the troubles in our native land. These noises converged in a single sensation of life for me: I imagined that I bore my chalice safely through a throng of foes. Her name sprang to my lips at moments in strange prayers and praises which I myself did not understand. My eyes were often full of tears (I could not tell why) and at times a flood from my heart seemed to pour itself out into my bosom. I thought little of the future. I did not know whether I would ever speak to her or not or, if I spoke to her, how I could tell her of my confused adoration. But my body was like a harp and her words and gestures were like fingers running upon the wires.

One evening I went into the back drawing-room in which the priest had died. It was a dark rainy evening and there was no sound in the house. Through one of the broken panes I heard the rain impinge upon the earth, the fine incessant needles of water playing in the sodden beds. Some distant lamp or lighted window gleamed below me. I was thankful that I could see so little. All my senses seemed to desire to veil themselves and, feeling that I was about to slip from them, I pressed the palms of my hands together until they trembled, murmuring: "O love! O love!" many times.

At last she spoke to me. When she addressed the first words to me I was so confused that I did not know what to answer. She asked me was I going to *Araby*. I forgot whether I answered yes or no. It would be a splendid bazaar, she said she would love to go.

"And why can't you?" I asked.

While she spoke she turned a silver bracelet round and round her wrist. She could not go, she said, because there would be a retreat that week in her convent. Her brother and two other boys were fighting for their caps and I was alone at the railings. She held one of the spikes, bowing her head towards me. The light from the lamp opposite our door caught the white curve of her neck, lit up her hair that rested there, and, falling, lit up the hand upon the railing. It fell over one side of her dress and caught the white border of a petticoat, just visible as she stood at ease.

"It's well for you," she said.

---

[1] A street ballad beginning with these words. This one is about Jeremiah Donovan, a nineteenth-century Irish nationalist popularly known as O'Donovan Rossa.

"If I go," I said, "I will bring you something."

What innumerable follies laid waste my waking and sleeping thoughts after that evening! I wished to annihilate the tedious intervening days. I chafed against the work of school. At night in my bedroom and by day in the classroom her image came between me and the page I strove to read. The syllables of the word *Araby* were called to me through the silence in which my soul luxuriated and cast an Eastern enchantment over me. I asked for leave to go to the bazaar on Saturday night. My aunt was surprised and hoped it was not some Freemason affair. I answered few questions in class. I watched my master's face pass from amiability to sternness; he hoped I was not beginning to idle. I could not call my wandering thoughts together. I had hardly any patience with the serious work of life which, now that it stood between me and my desire, seemed to me child's play, ugly monotonous child's play.

On Saturday morning I reminded my uncle that I wished to go to the bazaar in the evening. He was fussing at the hallstand, looking for the hat-brush, and answered me curtly:

"Yes, boy, I know."

As he was in the hall I could not go into the front parlour and lie at the window. I left the house in bad humour and walked slowly towards the school. The air was pitilessly raw and already my heart misgave me.

When I came home to dinner my uncle had not yet been home. Still it was early. I sat staring at the clock for some time and, when its ticking began to irritate me, I left the room. I mounted the staircase and gained the upper part of the house. The high cold empty gloomy rooms liberated me and I went from room to room singing. From the front window I saw my companions playing below in the street. Their cries reached me weakened and indistinct and, leaning my forehead against the cool glass, I looked over at the dark house where she lived. I may have stood there for an hour, seeing nothing but the brown-clad figure cast by my imagination, touched discreetly by the lamplight as the curved neck, at the hand upon the railings and at the border below the dress.

When I came downstairs again I found Mrs. Mercer sitting at the fire. She was an old garrulous woman, a pawnbroker's widow, who collected used stamps for some pious purpose. I had to endure the gossip of the tea-table. The meal was prolonged beyond an hour and still my uncle did not come. Mrs. Mercer stood up to go: she was sorry she couldn't wait any longer, but it was after eight o'clock and she did not like to be out late, as the night air was bad for her. When she had gone I began to walk up and down the room, clenching my fist. My aunt said:

"I'm afraid you may put off your bazaar for this night of Our Lord."

At nine o'clock I heard my uncle's latchkey in the hall door. I heard him talking to himself and heard the hallstand rocking when it had received the weight of his overcoat. I could interpret these signs. When he was midway through his dinner I asked him to give me the money to go to the bazaar. He had forgotten.

"The people are in bed and after their first sleep now," he said.

I did not smile. My aunt said to him energetically:

"Can't you give him the money and let him go? You've kept him late enough as it is."

My uncle said he was very sorry he had forgotten. He said he believed in the old saying: "All work and no play makes Jack a dull boy." He asked me where I was going and, when I had told him a second time he asked me did I know *The Arab's Farewell to His Steed.* When I left the kitchen he was about to recite the opening lines of the piece to my aunt.

I held a florin tightly in my hand as I strode down Buckingham Street towards the station. The sight of the streets thronged with buyers and glaring with gas recalled me to the purpose of my journey. I took my seat in a third-class carriage of a deserted train. After an intolerable delay the train moved out of the station slowly. It crept onward among ruinous houses and over the twinkling river. At Westland Row Station a crowd of people pressed to the carriage doors; but the porters moved them back, saying that it was a special train for the bazaar. I remained alone in the bare carriage. In a few minutes the train drew up beside an improvised wooden platform. I passed out on to the road and saw by the lighted dial of a clock that it was ten minutes to ten. In front of me was a large building which displayed the magical name.

I could not find any sixpenny entrance and, fearing that the bazaar would be closed, I passed in quickly through a turnstile, handing a shilling to a weary-looking man. I found myself in a big hall girdled at half its height by a gallery. Nearly all the stalls were closed and the greater part of the hall was in darkness. I recognised a silence like that which pervades a church after a service. I walked into the centre of the bazaar timidly. A few people were gathered about the stalls which were still open. Before a curtain, over which the words *Café Chantant* were written in coloured lamps, two men were counting money on a salver. I listened to the fall of the coins.

Remembering with difficulty why I had come I went over to one of the stalls and examined porcelain vases and flowered tea-sets. At the door of the stall a young lady was talking and laughing with two young gentlemen. I remarked their English accents and listened vaguely to their conversation.

"O, I never said such a thing!"

"O, but you did!"

"O, but I didn't!"

"Didn't she say that?"

"Yes. I heard her."

"O, there's a . . . fib!"

Observing me the young lady came over and asked me did I wish to buy anything. The tone of her voice was not encouraging; she seemed to have spoken to me out of a sense of duty. I looked humbly at the great jars that stood like Eastern guards at either side of the dark entrance to the stall and murmured:

"No, thank you."

The young lady changed the position of one of the vases and went back to the two young men. They began to talk of the same subject. Once or twice the young lady glanced at me over her shoulder.

I lingered before her stall, though I knew my stay was useless, to make my interest in her wares seem the more real. Then I turned away slowly and walked down the middle of the bazaar. I allowed the two pennies to fall against the sixpence in my pocket. I heard a voice call from one end of the gallery that the light was out. The upper part of the hall was now completely dark.

Gazing up into the darkness I saw myself as a creature driven and derided by vanity; and my eyes burned with anguish and anger.

A Clean, Well-Lighted Place 1933

ERNEST HEMINGWAY [1899–1961]

It was late and everyone had left the café except an old man who sat in the shadow the leaves of the tree made against the electric light. In the day time the street was dusty, but at night the dew settled the dust and the old man liked to sit late because he was deaf and now at night it was quiet and he felt the difference. The two waiters inside the café knew that the old man was a little drunk, and while he was a good client they knew that if he became too drunk he would leave without paying, so they kept watch on him.

"Last week he tried to commit suicide," one waiter said.

"Why?"

"He was in despair."

"What about?"

"Nothing."

"How do you know it was nothing?"

"He has plenty of money."

They sat together at a table that was close against the wall near the door of the café and looked at the terrace where the tables were all empty except where the old man sat in the shadow of the leaves of the tree that moved slightly in the wind. A girl and a soldier went by in the street. The street light shone on the brass number on his collar. The girl wore no head covering and hurried beside him.

"The guard will pick him up," one waiter said.

"What does it matter if he gets what he's after?"

"He had better get off the street now. The guard will get him. They went by five minutes ago."

The old man sitting in the shadow rapped on his saucer with his glass. The younger waiter went over to him.

"What do you want?"

The old man looked at him. "Another brandy," he said.

"You'll be drunk," the waiter said. The old man looked at him. The waiter went away.

"He'll stay all night," he said to his colleague. "I'm sleepy now. I never get into bed before three o'clock. He should have killed himself last week."

The waiter took the brandy bottle and another saucer from the counter inside the café and marched out to the old man's table. He put down the saucer and poured the glass full of brandy.

"You should have killed yourself last week," he said to the deaf man. The old man motioned with his finger. "A little more," he said. The waiter poured on into the glass so that the brandy slopped over and ran down the stem into the top saucer of the pile. "Thank you," the old man said. The waiter took the bottle back inside the café. He sat down at the table with his colleague again.

"He's drunk now," he said.

"He's drunk every night."

"What did he want to kill himself for?"

"How should I know."

"How did he do it?"

"He hung himself with a rope."

"Who cut him down?"

"His niece."

"Why did they do it?"

"Fear for his soul."

"How much money has he got?"

"He's got plenty."

"He must be eighty years old."

"Anyway I should say he was eighty."

"I wish he would go home. I never get to bed before three o'clock. What kind of hour is that to go to bed?"

"He stays up because he likes it."

"He's lonely. I'm not lonely. I have a wife waiting in bed for me."

"He had a wife once too."

"A wife would be no good to him now."

"You can't tell. He might be better with a wife."

"His niece looks after him."

"I know. You said she cut him down."

"I wouldn't want to be that old. An old man is a nasty thing."

"Not always. This old man is clean. He drinks without spilling. Even now, drunk. Look at him."

"I don't want to look at him. I wish he would go home. He has no regard for those who must work."

The old man looked from his glass across the square, then over at the waiters.

"Another brandy," he said, pointing to his glass. The waiter who was in a hurry came over.

"Finished," he said, speaking with that omission of syntax stupid people employ when talking to drunken people or foreigners. "No more tonight. Close now."

"Another," said the old man.

"No. Finished." The waiter wiped the edge of the table with a towel and shook his head.

The old man stood up, slowly counted the saucers, took a leather coin purse from his pocket and paid for the drinks, leaving half a peseta tip.

The waiter watched him go down the street, a very old man walking unsteadily but with dignity.

"Why didn't you let him stay and drink?" the unhurried waiter asked. They were putting up the shutters. "It is not half-past two."

"I want to go home to bed."

"What is an hour?"

"More to me than to him."

"An hour is the same."

"You talk like an old man yourself. He can buy a bottle and drink at home."

"It's not the same."

"No, it is not," agreed the waiter with a wife. He did not wish to be unjust. He was only in a hurry.

"And you? You have no fear of going home before your usual hour?"

"Are you trying to insult me?"

"No, hombre, only to make a joke."

"No," the waiter who was in a hurry said, rising from pulling down the metal shutters. "I have confidence. I am all confidence."

"You have youth, confidence, and a job," the older waiter said. "You have everything."

"And what do you lack?"

"Everything but work."

"You have everything I have."

"No. I have never had confidence and I am not young."

"Come on. Stop talking nonsense and lock up."

"I am of those who like to stay late at the café," the older waiter said. "With all those who do not want to go to bed. With all those who need a light for the night."

"I want to go home and into bed."

"We are of two different kinds," the older waiter said. He was now dressed to go home. "It is not only a question of youth and confidence although those things are very beautiful. Each night I am reluctant to close up because there may be some one who needs the café."

"Hombre, there are bodegas open all night long."

"You do not understand. This is a clean and pleasant café. It is well lighted. The light is very good and also, now, there are shadows of the leaves."

"Good night," said the younger waiter.

"Good night," the other said. Turning off the electric light he continued the conversation with himself. It is the light of course but it is necessary that the place be clean and pleasant. You do not want music. Certainly you do not want music. Nor can you stand before a bar with dignity although that is all that is provided for these hours. What did he fear? It was not fear or dread. It was a nothing that he knew too well. It was all a nothing and a man was nothing too. It was only that and light was all it needed and a certain cleanness and order. Some lived in it and never felt it but he knew it was nada y pues nada y pues nada.[1] Our nada who art in nada, nada be thy name thy kingdom nada thy will be nada in nada as it is in nada. Give us this nada our daily nada and nada us our nada as we nada our nadas and nada us not into nada but deliver us from

---

[1] Nothing, and then nothing, and then nothing.

nada; pues nada. Hail nothing full of nothing, nothing is with thee. He smiled and stood before a bar with a shining steam pressure coffee machine.

"What's yours?" asked the barman.

"Nada."

"Otro loco mas,"[2] said the barman and turned away.

"A little cup," said the waiter.

The barman poured it for him.

"The light is very bright and pleasant but the bar is unpolished," the waiter said.

The barman looked at him but did not answer. It was too late at night for conversation.

"You want another copita?" the barman asked.

"No, thank you," said the waiter and went out. He disliked bars and bodegas. A clean, well-lighted café was a very different thing. Now, without thinking further, he would go home to his room. He would lie in the bed and finally, with daylight, he would go to sleep. After all, he said to himself, it is probably only insomnia. Many must have it.

QUESTION

How do the two waiters differ in their attitudes toward the old man? What bearing does that difference have on the theme of the story?

---

[2] Another crazy one.

Good Country People

1955

FLANNERY O'CONNOR [1925–1964]

Besides the neutral expression that she wore when she was alone, Mrs. Freeman had two others, forward and reverse, that she used for all her human dealings. Her forward expression was steady and driving like the advance of a heavy truck. Her eyes never swerved to left or right but turned as the story turned as if they followed a yellow line down the center of it. She seldom used the other expression because it was not often necessary for her to retract a statement, but when she did, her face came to a complete stop, there was an almost imperceptible movement of her black eyes, during which they seemed to be receding, and then the observer would see that Mrs. Freeman, though she might stand there as real as several grain sacks thrown on top of each other, was no longer there in spirit. As for getting anything across to her when this was the case, Mrs. Hopewell had given it up. She might talk her head off. Mrs. Freeman could never be brought to admit herself wrong on any point. She would stand there and if she could be brought to say anything, it was something like, "Well, I wouldn't of said it was and I wouldn't of said it wasn't," or letting her gaze range over the top kitchen shelf where there was an assortment of dusty bottles, she might remark, "I see you ain't ate many of them figs you put up last summer."

They carried on their most important business in the kitchen at breakfast. Every morning Mrs. Hopewell got up at seven o'clock and lit her gas heater and Joy's. Joy was her daughter, a large blonde girl who had an artificial leg. Mrs. Hopewell thought of her as a child though she was thirty-two years old and highly educated. Joy would get up while her mother was eating and lumber into the bathroom and slam the door, and before long, Mrs. Freeman would arrive at the back door. Joy would hear her mother call, "Come on in," and then they would talk for a while in low voices that were indistinguishable in the bathroom. By the time Joy came in, they had usually finished the weather report and were on one or the other of Mrs. Freeman's daughters, Glynese or Carramae. Joy called them Glycerin and Caramel. Glynese, a redhead, was eighteen and had many admirers; Carramae, a blonde, was only fifteen but already married and pregnant. She could not keep anything on her stomach. Every morning Mrs. Freeman told Mrs. Hopewell how many times she had vomited since the last report.

Mrs. Hopewell liked to tell people that Glynese and Carramae were two of the finest girls she knew and that Mrs. Freeman was a *lady* and that she was never ashamed to take her anywhere or introduce her to anybody they might meet. Then she would tell how she had happened to hire the Freemans in the first place and how they were a godsend to her and how she had had them four years. The reason for her keeping them so long was that they were not trash.

36

They were good country people. She had telephoned the man whose name they had given as a reference and he had told her that Mr. Freeman was a good farmer but that his wife was the nosiest woman ever to walk the earth. "She's got to be into everything," the man said. "If she don't get there before the dust settles, you can bet she's dead, that's all. She'll want to know all your business. I can stand him real good," he had said, "but me nor my wife neither could have stood that woman one more minute on this place." That had put Mrs. Hopewell off for a few days.

She had hired them in the end because there were no other applicants but she had made up her mind beforehand exactly how she would handle the woman. Since she was the type who had to be into everything, then, Mrs. Hopewell had decided, she would not only let her be into everything, she would *see* to it that she was into everything— she would give her the responsibility of everything, she would put her in charge. Mrs. Hopewell had no bad qualities of her own but she was able to use other people's in such a constructive way that she never felt the lack. She had hired the Freemans and she had kept them four years.

Nothing is perfect. This was one of Mrs. Hopewell's favorite sayings. Another was: that is life! And still another, the most important, was: well, other people have their opinions too. She would make these statements, usually at the table, in a tone of gentle insistence as if no one held them but her, and the large hulking Joy, whose constant outrage had obliterated every expression from her face, would stare just a little to the side of her, her eyes icy blue, with the look of someone who has achieved blindness by an act of will and means to keep it.

When Mrs. Hopewell said to Mrs. Freeman that life was like that, Mrs. Freeman would say, "I always said so myself." Nothing had been arrived at by anyone that had not first been arrived at by her. She was quicker than Mr. Freeman. When Mrs. Hopewell said to her after they had been on the place a while, "You know, you're the wheel behind the wheel," and winked, Mrs. Freeman had said, "I know it. I've always been quick. It's some that are quicker than others."

"Everybody is different," Mrs. Hopewell said.

"Yes, most people is," Mrs. Freeman said.

"It takes all kinds to make the world."

"I always said it did myself."

The girl was used to this kind of dialogue for breakfast and more of it for dinner; sometimes they had it for supper too. When they had no guest they ate in the kitchen because that was easier. Mrs. Freeman always managed to arrive at some point during the meal and to watch them finish it. She would stand in the doorway if it were summer but in the winter she would stand with one elbow on top of the refrigerator and look down on them, or she would stand by the gas heater, lifting the back of her skirt slightly. Occasionally she would stand against the wall and roll her head from side to side. At no time was she in any hurry to leave. All this was very trying on Mrs. Hopewell but she was a woman of great patience. She realized that nothing is perfect and that in the Freemans she had good country people and that if, in this day and age, you get good country people, you had better hang onto them.

She had had plenty of experience with trash. Before the Freemans she had averaged one tenant family a year. The wives of these farmers were not the kind you would want to be around you for very long. Mrs. Hopewell, who had divorced her husband long ago, needed someone to walk over the fields with her; and when Joy had to be impressed for these services, her remarks were usually so ugly and her face so glum that Mrs. Hopewell would say, "If you can't come pleasantly, I don't want you at all," to which the girl, standing square and rigid-shouldered with her neck thrust slightly forward, would reply, "If you want me, here I am—LIKE I AM."

Mrs. Hopewell excused this attitude because of the leg (which had been shot off in a hunting accident when Joy was ten). It was hard for Mrs. Hopewell to realize that her child was thirty-two now and that for more than twenty years she had had only one leg. She thought of her still as a child because it tore her heart to think instead of the poor stout girl in her thirties who had never danced a step or had any *normal* good times. Her name was really Joy but as soon as she was twenty-one and away from home, she had had it legally changed. Mrs. Hopewell was certain that she had thought and thought until she had hit upon the ugliest name in any language. Then she had gone and had the beautiful name, Joy, changed without telling her mother until after she had done it. Her legal name was Hulga.

When Mrs. Hopewell thought the name, Hulga, she thought of the broad blank hull of a battleship. She would not use it. She continued to call her Joy to which the girl responded but in a purely mechanical way.

Hulga had learned to tolerate Mrs. Freeman, who saved her from taking walks with her mother. Even Glynese and Carramae were useful when they occupied attention that might otherwise have been directed at her. At first she had thought she could not stand Mrs. Freeman for she had found that it was not possible to be rude to her. Mrs. Freeman would take on strange resentments and for days together she would be sullen but the source of her displeasure was always obscure; a direct attack, a positive leer, blatant ugliness to her face—these never touched her. And without warning one day, she began calling her Hulga.

She did not call her that in front of Mrs. Hopewell who would have been incensed but when she and the girl happened to be out of the house together, she would say something and add the name Hulga to the end of it, and the big spectacled Joy-Hulga would scowl and redden as if her privacy had been intruded upon. She considered the name her personal affair. She had arrived at it first purely on the basis of its ugly sound and then the full genius of its fitness had struck her. She had a vision of the name working like the ugly sweating Vulcan who stayed in the furnace and to whom, presumably, the goddess had to come when called. She saw it as the name of her highest creative act. One of her major triumphs was that her mother had not been able to turn her dust into Joy, but the greater one was that she had been able to turn it herself into Hulga. However, Mrs. Freeman's relish for using the name only irritated her. It was as if Mrs. Freeman's beady steel-pointed eyes had penetrated far enough behind her face to reach some secret fact. Something about her seemed to fascinate Mrs. Freeman and then one day Hulga realized that it was the artificial leg. Mrs. Freeman had a special fondness for the details of secret infections, hidden deformities, assaults upon children. Of diseases, she preferred the lingering or incurable. Hulga had heard Mrs. Hopewell give her the details of the hunting accident, how the leg had been literally blasted off, how she had never lost consciousness. Mrs. Freeman could listen to it any time as if it had happened an hour ago.

When Hulga stumped into the kitchen in the morning (she could walk without making the awful noise but she made it—Mrs. Hopewell was certain—because it was ugly-sounding), she glanced at them and did not speak. Mrs. Hopewell would be in her red kimono with her hair tied around her head in rags. She would be sitting at the table, finishing her breakfast and Mrs. Freeman would be hanging by her elbow outward from the refrigerator, looking down at the table. Hulga always put her eggs on the stove to boil and then stood over them with her arms folded, and Mrs. Hopewell would look at her—a kind of indirect gaze divided between her and Mrs. Freeman—and would think that if she would only keep herself up a little, she wouldn't be so bad looking. There was nothing wrong with her face that a pleasant expression wouldn't help. Mrs. Hopewell said that people who looked on the bright side of things would be beautiful even if they were not.

Whenever she looked at Joy this way, she could not help but feel that it would have been better if the child had not taken the Ph.D. It had certainly not brought her out any and now that she had it, there was no more excuse for her to go to school again. Mrs. Hopewell thought it was nice for girls to go to school to have a good time but Joy had "gone through." Anyhow, she would not have been strong enough to go again. The doctors had told Mrs. Hopewell that with the best of care, Joy might see forty-five. She had a weak heart. Joy had made it plain that if it had not been for this condition, she would be far from these red hills and good country people. She would be in a university lecturing to people who knew what she was talking about. And Mrs. Hopewell could very well picture her there, looking like a scarecrow and lecturing to more of the same. Here she went about all day in a six-year-old skirt and a yellow sweat shirt with a faded cowboy on a horse embossed on it. She thought this was funny; Mrs. Hopewell thought it was idiotic and showed simply that she was still a child. She was brilliant but she didn't have a grain of sense. It seemed to Mrs. Hopewell that every year she grew less like other people and more like herself—bloated, rude, and squint-eyed. And she said such strange things! To her own mother she had said—without warning, without excuse, standing up in the middle of a meal with her face purple and her mouth half full—"Woman! do you ever look inside? Do you ever look inside and see what you are *not*? God!" she had cried sinking down again and staring at her plate,

"Malebranche was right: we are not our own light. We are not our own light!" Mrs. Hopewell had no idea to this day what brought that on. She had only made the remark, hoping Joy would take it in, that a smile never hurt anyone.

The girl had taken the Ph.D. in philosophy and this left Mrs. Hopewell at a complete loss. You could say, "My daughter is a nurse," or "My daughter is a school teacher," or even, "My daughter is a chemical engineer." You could not say, "My daughter is a philosopher." That was something that had ended with the Greeks and Romans. All day Joy sat on her deck in a deep chair, reading. Sometimes she went for walks but she didn't like dogs or cats or birds or flowers or nature or nice young men. She looked at nice young men as if she could smell their stupidity.

One day Mrs. Hopewell had picked up one of the books the girl had just put down and opening it at random, she read, "Science, on the other hand, has to assert its soberness and seriousness afresh and declare that it is concerned solely with what-is. Nothing—how can it be for science anything but a horror and a phantasm? If science is right, then one thing stands firm: science wishes to know nothing of nothing. Such is after all the strictly scientific approach to Nothing. We know it by wishing to know nothing of Nothing." These words had been underlined with a blue pencil and they worked on Mrs. Hopewell like some evil incantation in gibberish. She shut the book quickly and went out of the room as if she were having a chill.

This morning when the girl came in, Mrs. Freeman was on Carramae. "She thrown up four times after supper," she said, "and was up twict in the night after three o'clock. Yesterday she didn't do nothing but ramble in the bureau drawer. All she did. Stand up there and see what she could run up on."

"She's got to eat," Mrs. Hopewell muttered, sipping her coffee, while she watched Joy's back at the stove. She was wondering what the child had said to the Bible salesman. She could not imagine what kind of a conversation she could possibly have had with him.

He was a tall gaunt hatless youth who had called yesterday to sell them a Bible. He had appeared at the door, carrying a large black suitcase that weighted him so heavily on one side that he had to brace himself against the door facing. He seemed on the point of collapse but he said in a cheerful voice, "Good morning, Mrs. Cedars!" and set the suitcase down on the mat. He was not a bad-looking young man though he had on a bright blue suit and yellow socks that were not pulled up far enough. He had prominent face bones and a streak of sticky-looking brown hair falling across his forehead.

"I'm Mrs. Hopewell," she said.

"Oh!" he said, pretending to look puzzled but with his eyes sparkling, "I saw it said 'The Cedars,' on the mailbox so I thought you was Mrs. Cedars!" and he burst out in a pleasant laugh. He picked up the satchel and under cover of a pant, he fell forward into her hall. It was rather as if the suitcase had moved first, jerking him after it. "Mrs. Hopewell!" he said and grabbed her hand. "I hope you are well!" and he laughed again and then all at once his face sobered completely. He paused and gave her a straight earnest look and said, "Lady, I've come to speak of serious things."

"Well, come in," she muttered, none too pleased because her dinner was almost ready. He came into the parlor and sat down on the edge of a straight chair and put the suitcase between his feet and glanced around the room as if he were sizing her up by it. Her silver gleamed on the two sideboards; she decided he had never been in a room as elegant as this.

"Mrs. Hopewell," he began, using her name in a way that sounded almost intimate, "I know you believe in Chrustian service."

"Well yes," she murmured.

"I know," he said and paused, looking very wise with his head cocked on one side, "that you're a good woman. Friends have told me."

Mrs. Hopewell never liked to be taken for a fool. "What are you selling?" she asked.

"Bibles," the young man said and his eye raced around the room before he added, "I see you have no family Bible in your parlor, I see that is the one lack you got!"

Mrs. Hopewell could not say, "My daughter is an atheist and won't let me keep the Bible in the parlor." She said, stiffening slightly, "I keep my Bible by my bedside." This was not the truth. It was in the attic somewhere.

"Lady," he said, "the word of God ought to be in the parlor."

"Well, I think that's a matter of taste," she began. "I think . . ."

"Lady," he said, "for a Chrustian, the word of God ought to be in every room in the house besides in his heart. I know you're a Chrustian because I can see it in every line of your face."

She stood up and said, "Well, young man, I don't want to buy a Bible and I smell my dinner burning."

He didn't get up. He began to twist his hands and looking down at them, he said softly, "Well lady, I'll tell you the truth—not many people want to buy one nowadays and besides, I know I'm real simple. I don't know how to say a thing but to say it. I'm just a country boy." He glanced up into her unfriendly face. "People like you don't like to fool with country people like me!"

"Why!" she cried, "good country people are the salt of the earth! Besides, we all have different ways of doing, it takes all kinds to make the world go 'round. That's life!"

"You said a mouthful," he said.

"Why, I think there aren't enough good country people in the world!" she said, stirred. "I think that's what's wrong with it!"

His face had brightened. "I didn't inraduce myself," he said. "I'm Manley Pointer from out in the country around Willohobie, not even from a place, just from near a place."

"You wait a minute," she said. "I have to see about my dinner." She went out to the kitchen and found Joy standing near the door where she had been listening.

"Get rid of the salt of the earth," she said, "and let's eat."

Mrs. Hopewell gave her a pained look and turned the heat down under the vegetables. "I can't be rude to anybody," she murmured and went back into the parlor.

He had opened the suitcase and was sitting with a Bible on each knee.

"You might as well put those up," she told him. "I don't want one."

"I appreciate your honesty," he said. "You don't see any more real honest people unless you go way out in the country."

"I know," she said, "real genuine folks!" Through the crack in the door she heard a groan.

"I guess a lot of boys come telling you they're working their way through college," he said, "but I'm not going to tell you that. Somehow," he said, "I don't want to go to college. I want to devote my life to Chrustian service. See," he said, lowering his voice, "I got this heart condition. I may not live long. When you know it's something wrong with you and you may not live long, well then, lady . . ." He paused, with his mouth open, and stared at her.

He and Joy had the same condition! She knew that her eyes were filling with tears but she collected herself quickly and murmured, "Won't you stay for dinner? We'd love to have you!" and was sorry the instant she heard herself say it.

"Yes mam," he said in an abashed voice. "I would sher love to do that!"

Joy had given him one look on being introduced to him and then throughout the meal had not glanced at him again. He had addressed several remarks to her, which she pretended not to hear. Mrs. Hopewell could not understand deliberate rudeness, although she lived with it, and she felt she had always to overflow with hospitality to make up for Joy's lack of courtesy. She urged him to talk about himself and he did. He said he was the seventh child of twelve and that his father had been crushed under a tree when he himself was eight years old. He had been crushed very badly, in fact, almost cut in two and was practically not recognizable. His mother had got along the best she could by hard working and she had always seen that her children went to Sunday School and that they read the Bible every evening. He was now nineteen years old and he had been selling Bibles for four months. In that time he had sold seventy-seven Bibles and had the promise of two more sales. He wanted to become a missionary because he thought that was the way you could do most for people. "He who losest his life shall find it," he said simply and he was so sincere, so genuine and earnest that Mrs. Hopewell would not for the world have smiled. He prevented his peas from sliding onto the table by blocking them with a piece of bread which he later cleaned his plate with. She could see Joy observing sidewise how he handled his knife and fork and she saw too that every few minutes, the boy would dart a keen appraising glance at the girl as if he were trying to attract her attention.

After dinner Joy cleared the dishes off the table and disappeared and Mrs. Hopewell was left to talk with him. He told her again about his childhood and his father's accident and about various things that had happened to him. Every five minutes or so she would stifle a yawn. He sat for two hours until finally she told him she must go because she had an appointment in town. He packed his Bibles and thanked her and prepared to leave, but in the doorway he stopped and wrung her hand and said that not on any of his trips had he met a lady as nice as her and he asked if he could come again. She had said she would always be happy to see him.

Joy had been standing in the road, apparently looking at something in the distance, when he came down the steps toward her, bent to the side with his heavy valise. He stopped where she was standing and confronted her directly. Mrs. Hopewell could not hear what he said but she trembled to think what Joy would say to him. She could see that after a minute Joy said something and that then the boy began to speak again, making an excited gesture with his free hand. After a minute Joy said something else at which the boy began to speak once more. Then to her amazement, Mrs. Hopewell saw the two of them walk off together, toward the gate. Joy had walked all the way to the gate with him and Mrs. Hopewell could not imagine what they had said to each other, and she had not yet dared to ask.

Mrs. Freeman was insisting upon her attention. She had moved from the refrigerator to the heater so that Mrs. Hopewell had to turn and face her in order to seem to be listening. "Glynese gone out with Harvey Hill again last night," she said. "She had this sty."

"Hill," Mrs. Hopewell said absently, "is that the one who works in the garage?"

"Nome, he's the one that goes to chiropracter school," Mrs. Freeman said. "She had this sty. Been had it two days. So she says when he brought her in the other night he says, 'Lemme get rid of that sty for you,' and she says. 'How?' and he says. 'You just lay yourself down acrost the seat of that car and I'll show you.' So she done it and he popped her neck. Kept on a-popping it several times until she made him quit. This morning," Mrs. Freeman said, "she ain't got no sty. She ain't got no traces of a sty."

"I never heard of that before," Mrs. Hopewell said.

"He ast her to marry him before the Ordinary," Mrs. Freeman went on, "and she told him she wasn't going to be married in no *office*."

"Well, Glynese is a fine girl," Mrs. Hopewell said. "Glynese and Carramae are both fine girls."

"Carramae said when her and Lyman was married Lyman said it sure felt sacred to him. She said he said he wouldn't take five hundred dollars for being married by a preacher."

"How much would he take?" the girl asked from the stove.

"He said he wouldn't take five hundred dollars," Mrs. Freeman repeated.

"Well we all have work to do," Mrs. Hopewell said.

"Lyman said it just felt more sacred to him," Mrs. Freeman said. "The doctor wants Carramae to eat prunes. Says instead of medicine. Says them cramps is coming from pressure. You know where I think it is?"

"She'll be better in a few weeks," Mrs. Hopewell said.

"In the tube," Mrs. Freeman said. "Else she wouldn't be as sick as she is."

Hulga had cracked her two eggs into a saucer and was bringing them to the table along with a cup of coffee that she had filled too full. She sat down carefully and began to eat, meaning to keep Mrs. Freeman there by questions if for any reason she showed an inclination to leave. She could perceive her mother's eye on her. The first roundabout question would be about the Bible salesman and she did not wish to bring it on. "How did he pop her neck?" she asked.

Mrs. Freeman went into a description of how he had popped her neck. She said he owned a '55 Mercury but that Glynese said she would rather marry a man with only a '36 Plymouth who would be married by a preacher. The girl asked what if he had a '32 Plymouth and Mrs. Freeman said what Glynese had said was a '36 Plymouth.

Mrs. Hopewell said there were not many girls with Glynese's common sense. She said what she admired in those girls was their common sense. She said that reminded her that they had a nice visitor yesterday, a young man selling Bibles. "Lord," she said, "he bored me to death but he was so sincere and genuine I couldn't be rude to him. He was just good country people, you know," she said, "—just the salt of the earth."

"I seen him walk up," Mrs. Freeman said, "and then later—I seen him walk off," and Hulga could feel the slight shift in her voice, the slight insinuation, that he had not walked off alone, had he? Her face remained expressionless but the color rose into her neck and she seemed to swallow it down with the next spoonful of egg. Mrs. Freeman was looking at her as if they had a secret together.

"Well, it takes all kinds of people to make the world go 'round," Mrs. Hopewell said. "It's very good we aren't all alike."

"Some people are more alike than others," Mrs. Freeman said.

Hulga got up and stumped, with about twice the noise that was necessary, into her room and locked the door. She was to meet the Bible salesman at ten o'clock at the gate. She had thought about it half the night. She had started thinking of it as a great joke and then she had begun to see profound implications in it. She had lain in bed imagining dialogues for them that were insane on the surface but that reached below to depths that no Bible salesman would be aware of. Their conversation yesterday had been of this kind.

He had stopped in front of her and had simply stood there. His face was bony and sweaty and bright, with a little pointed nose in the center of it, and his look was different from what it had been at the dinner table. He was gazing at her with open curiosity, with fascination, like a child watching a new fantastic animal at the zoo, and he was breathing as if he had run a great distance to reach her. His gaze seemed somehow familiar but she could not think where she had been regarded with it before. For almost a minute he didn't say anything. Then on what seemed an insuck of breath, he whispered, "You ever ate a chicken that was two days old?"

The girl looked at him stonily. He might have just put this question up for consideration at the meeting of a philosophical association. "Yes," she presently replied as if she had considered it from all angles.

"It must have been mighty small!" he said triumphantly and shook all over with little nervous giggles, getting very red in the face, and subsiding finally into his gaze of complete admiration, while the girl's expression remained exactly the same.

"How old are you?" he asked softly.

She waited some time before she answered. Then in a flat voice she said, "Seventeen."

His smiles came in succession like waves breaking on the surface of a little lake. "I see you got a wooden leg," he said. "I think you're real brave. I think you're real sweet."

The girl stood blank and solid and silent.

"Walk to the gate with me," he said. "You're a brave sweet little thing and I liked you the minute I seen you walk in the door."

Hulga began to move forward.

"What's your name?" he asked, smiling down on the top of her head.

"Hulga," she said.

"Hulga," he murmured, "Hulga. Hulga. I never heard of anybody name Hulga before. You're shy, aren't you, Hulga?" he asked.

She nodded, watching his large red hand on the handle of the giant valise.

"I like girls that wear glasses," he said. "I think a lot. I'm not like these people that a serious thought don't ever enter their heads. It's because I may die."

"I may die too," she said suddenly and looked up at him. His eyes were very small and brown, glittering feverishly.

"Listen," he said, "don't you think some people was meant to meet on account of what all they got in common and all? Like they both think serious thoughts and all?" He shifted the valise to his other hand so that the hand nearest her was free. He caught hold of her elbow and shook it a little. "I don't work on Saturday," he said. "I like to walk in the woods and see what Mother Nature is wearing. O'er the hills and far away. Pic-nics and things. Couldn't we go on a pic-nic tomorrow? Say yes, Hulga," he said and gave her a dying look as if he felt his insides about to drop out of him. He had even seemed to sway slightly toward her.

During the night she had imagined that she seduced him. She imagined that the two of them walked on the place until they came to the storage barn beyond the two back fields and there, she imagined, that things came to such a pass that she very easily seduced him and that then, of course, she had to reckon with his remorse. True genius can get an idea across even to an inferior mind. She imagined that she took his remorse in hand and changed it into a deeper understanding of life. She took all his shame away and turned it into something useful.

She set off for the gate at exactly ten o'clock, escaping without drawing Mrs. Hopewell's attention. She didn't take anything to eat, forgetting that food is usually taken on a picnic. She wore a pair of slacks and a dirty white shirt, and as an afterthought, she had put some Vapex on the collar of it since she did not own any perfume. When she reached the gate no one was there.

She looked up and down the empty highway and had the furious feeling that she had been tricked, that he had only meant to make her walk to the gate after the idea of him. Then suddenly he stood up, very tall, from behind a bush on the opposite embankment. Smiling, he lifted his hat which was new and wide-brimmed. He had not worn it yesterday and she wondered if he had bought it for the occasion. It was toast-colored with a red and white band around it and was slightly too large for him. He stepped from behind the bush still carrying the black valise. He had on the same suit and the same yellow socks sucked down in his shoes from walking. He crossed the highway and said, "I knew you'd come!"

The girl wondered acidly how he had known this. She pointed to the valise and asked, "Why did you bring your Bibles?"

He took her elbow, smiling down on her as if he could not stop. "You can never tell when you'll need the word of God, Hulga," he said. She had a moment in which she doubted that this was actually happening and then they began to climb the embankment. They went down into the pasture toward the woods. The boy walked lightly by her side, bouncing on his toes. The valise did not seem to be heavy today; he even swung it. They crossed half the pasture without saying anything and then, putting his hand easily on the small of her back, he asked softly, "Where does your wooden leg join on?"

She turned an ugly red and glared at him and for an instant the boy looked abashed. "I didn't mean you no harm," he said. "I only meant you're so brave and all. I guess God takes care of you."

"No," she said, looking forward and walking fast, "I don't even believe in God."

At this he stopped and whistled. "No!" he exclaimed as if he were too astonished to say anything else.

She walked on and in a second he was bouncing at her side, fanning with his hat. "That's very unusual for a girl," he remarked, watching her out of the corner of his eye. When they reached the edge of the wood, he put his hand on her back again and drew her against him without a word and kissed her heavily.

The kiss, which had more pressure than feeling behind it, produced that extra surge of adrenalin in the girl that enables one to carry a packed trunk out of a burning house, but in her, the power went at once to the brain. Even before he released her, her mind, clear and detached and ironic anyway, was regarding him from a great distance, with amusement but with pity. She had never been kissed before and she was pleased to discover that it was an unexceptional experience and all a matter of the mind's control. Some people might enjoy drain water if they were told it was vodka. When the boy, looking expectant but uncertain, pushed her gently away, she turned and walked on, saying nothing as if such business, for her, were common enough.

He came along panting at her side, trying to help her when he saw a root that she might trip over. He caught and held back the long swaying blades of thorn vine until she had passed beyond them. She led the way and he came breathing heavily behind her. Then they came out on a sunlit hillside, sloping softly into another one a little smaller. Beyond, they could see the rusted top of the old barn where the extra hay was stored.

The hill was sprinkled with small pink weeds. "Then you ain't saved?" he asked suddenly, stopping.

The girl smiled. It was the first time she had smiled at him at all. "In my economy," she said, "I'm saved and you are damned but I told you I didn't believe in God."

Nothing seemed to destroy the boy's look of admiration. He gazed at her now as if the fantastic animal at the zoo had put its paw through the bars and given him a loving poke. She thought he looked as if he wanted to kiss her again and she walked on before he had the chance.

"Ain't there somewheres we can sit down sometime?" he murmured, his voice softening toward the end of the sentence.

"In that barn," she said.

They made for it rapidly as if it might slide away like a train. It was a large two-story barn, cool and dark inside. The boy pointed up the ladder that led into the loft and said, "It's too bad we can't go up there."

"Why can't we?" she asked.

"Yer leg," he said reverently.

The girl gave him a contemptuous look and putting both hands on the ladder, she climbed it while he stood below, apparently awestruck. She pulled herself expertly through the opening and then looked down at him and said, "Well, come on if you're coming," and he began to climb the ladder, awkwardly bringing the suitcase with him.

"We won't need the Bible," she observed.

"You never can tell," he said, panting. After he had got into the loft, he was a few seconds catching his breath. She had sat down in a pile of straw. A wide sheath of sunlight, filled with dust particles, slanted over her. She lay back against a bale, her face turned away, looking out the front opening of the barn where hay was thrown from a wagon into the loft. The two pink-speckled hillsides lay back against a dark ridge of woods. The sky was cloudless and cold blue. The boy dropped down by her side and put one arm under her and the other over her and began methodically kissing her face, making little noises like a fish. He did not remove his hat but it was pushed far enough back not to interfere. When her glasses got in his way, he took them off of her and slipped them into his pocket.

The girl at first did not return any of the kisses but presently she began to and after she had put several on his cheek, she reached his lips and remained there, kissing him again and again as if she were trying to draw all the breath out of him. His breath was clear and sweet like a child's and the kisses were sticky like a child's. He mumbled about loving her and about knowing when he first seen her that he loved her, but the mumbling was like the sleepy fretting of a child being put to sleep by his mother. Her mind, throughout this, never stopped or lost itself for a second to her feelings. "You ain't said you love me none," he whispered finally, pulling back from her. "You got to say that."

She looked away from him off into the hollow sky and then down at a black ridge and then down farther into what appeared to be two green swelling lakes. She didn't realize he had taken her glasses but this landscape could not seem exceptional to her for she seldom paid any close attention to her surroundings.

"You got to say it," he repeated. "You got to say you love me."

She was always careful how she committed herself. "In a sense," she began, "if you use the word loosely, you might say that. But it's not a word I use. I don't have illusions. I'm one of those people who see *through* to nothing."

The boy was frowning. "You got to say it. I said it and you got to say it," he said.

The girl looked at him almost tenderly. "You poor baby," she murmured. "It's just as well you don't understand," and she pulled him by the neck, face-down, against her. "We are all damned," she said, "but some of us have taken off our blindfolds and see that there's nothing to see. It's a kind of salvation."

The boy's astonished eyes looked blankly through the ends of her hair. "Okay," he almost whined, "but do you love me or don'tcher?"

"Yes," she said and added, "in a sense. But I must tell you something. There mustn't be anything dishonest between us." She lifted his head and looked him in the eye. "I am thirty years old," she said. "I have a number of degrees."

The boy's look was irritated but dogged. "I don't care," he said. "I don't care a thing about what all you done. I just want to know if you love me or don'tcher?" and he caught her to him and wildly planted her face with kisses until she said, "Yes, yes."

"Okay then," he said, letting her go. "Prove it."

She smiled, looking dreamily out on the shifty landscape. She had seduced him without even making up her mind to try. "How?" she asked, feeling that he should be delayed a little.

He leaned over and put his lips to her ear. "Show me where your wooden leg joins on," he whispered.

The girl uttered a sharp little cry and her face instantly drained of color. The obscenity of the suggestion was not what shocked her. As a child she had sometimes been subject to feelings of shame but education had removed the last traces of that as a good surgeon scrapes for cancer; she would no more have felt it over what he was asking than she would have believed in his Bible. But she was as sensitive about the artificial leg as a peacock about his tail. No one ever touched it but her. She took care of it as someone else would his soul, in private and almost with her own eyes turned away. "No," she said.

"I known it," he muttered, sitting up. "You're just playing me for a sucker."

"Oh no no!" she cried. "It joins on at the knee. Only at the knee. Why do you want to see it?"

The boy gave her a long penetrating look. "Because," he said, "it's what makes you different. You ain't like nobody else."

She sat staring at him. There was nothing about her face or her round freezing-blue eyes to indicate that this had moved her; but she felt as if her heart had stopped and left her mind to pump her blood. She decided that for the first time in her life she was face to face with real innocence. This boy, with an instinct that came from beyond wisdom, had touched the truth about her. When after a minute, she said in a low hoarse high voice, "All right," it was like surrendering to him completely. It was like losing her own life and finding it again, miraculously, in his.

Very gently he began to roll the slack leg up. The artificial limb, in a white sock and brown flat shoe, was bound in a heavy material like canvas and ended in an ugly jointure where it was attached to the stump. The boy's face and his voice were entirely reverent as he uncovered it and said, "Now show me how to take it off and on."

She took it off for him and put it back on again and then he took it off himself, handling it as tenderly as if it were a real one. "See!" he said with a delighted child's face. "Now I can do it myself!"

"Put it back on," she said. She was thinking that she would run away with him and that every night he would take the leg off and every morning put it back on again. "Put it back on," she said.

"Not yet," he murmured, setting it on its foot out of her reach. "Leave it off for a while. You got me instead."

She gave a little cry of alarm but he pushed her down and began to kiss her again. Without the leg she felt entirely dependent on him. Her brain seemed to have stopped thinking altogether and to be about some other function that it was not very good at. Different expressions raced back and forth over her face. Every now and then the boy, his eyes like two steel spikes, would glance behind him where the leg stood. Finally she pushed him off and said, "Put it back on me now."

"Wait," he said. He leaned the other way and pulled the valise toward him and opened it. It had a pale blue spotted lining and there were only two Bibles in it. He took one of these out and opened the cover of it. It was hollow and contained a pocket flask of whiskey, a pack of cards, and a small blue box with printing on it. He laid these out in front of her one at a time in an evenly spaced row, like one presenting offerings at the shrine of a goddess. He put the blue box in her. hand. THIS PRODUCT TO BE USED ONLY FOR THE PREVENTION OF DISEASE, she read, and dropped it. The boy was unscrewing the top of the flask. He stopped and pointed, with a smile, to the deck of cards. It was not an ordinary deck but one with an obscene picture on the back of each card. "Take a swig," he said, offering her the bottle first. He held it in front of her, but like one mesmerized, she did not move.

Her voice when she spoke had an almost pleading sound. "Aren't you," she murmured, "aren't you just good country people?"

The boy cocked his head. He looked as if he were just beginning to understand that she might be trying to insult him. "Yeah," he said, curling his lip slightly, "but it ain't held me back none. I'm as good as you any day in the week."

"Give me my leg," she said.

He pushed it farther away with his foot. "Come on now, let's begin to have us a good time," he said coaxingly. "We ain't got to know one another good yet."

"Give me my leg!" she screamed and tried to lunge for it but he pushed her down easily.

"What's the matter with you all of a sudden?" he asked, frowning as he screwed the top on the flask and put it quickly inside the Bible. "You just a while ago said you didn't believe in nothing. I thought you was some girl!"

Her face was almost purple. "You're a Christian!" she hissed. "You're a fine Christian! You're just like them all—say one thing and do another. You're a perfect Christian, you're . . ."

The boy's mouth was set angrily. "I hope you don't think," he said in a lofty indignant tone, "that I believe in that crap! I may sell Bibles but I know which end is up and I wasn't born yesterday and I know where I'm going!"

"Give me my leg!" she screeched. He jumped up so quickly that she barely saw him sweep the cards and the blue box back into the Bible and throw the Bible into the valise. She saw him grab the leg and then she saw it for an instant slanted forlornly across the inside of the suitcase with a Bible at either side of its opposite ends. He slammed the lid shut and snatched up the valise and swung it down the hole and then stepped through himself.

When all of him had passed but his head, he turned and regarded her with a look that no longer had any admiration in it. "I've gotten a lot of interesting things," he said. "One time I got a woman's glass eye this way. And you needn't to think you'll catch me because Pointer ain't really my name. I use a different name at every house I call at and don't stay nowhere long. And I'll tell you another thing, Hulga," he said, using the name as if he didn't think much of it, "you ain't so smart. I been believing in nothing ever since I was born!" and then the toast-colored hat disappeared down the hole and the girl was left, sitting on the straw in the dusty sunlight. When she turned her churning face toward the opening, she saw his blue figure struggling successfully over the green speckled lake.

Mrs. Hopewell and Mrs. Freeman, who were in the back pasture, digging up onions, saw him emerge a little later from the woods and head across the meadow toward the highway. "Why, that looks like that nice dull young man that tried to sell me a Bible yesterday," Mrs. Hopewell said, squinting. "He must have been selling them to the Negroes back in there. He was so simple," she said, "but I guess the world would be better off if we were all that simple."

Mrs. Freeman's gaze drove forward and just touched him before he disappeared under the hill. Then she returned her attention to the evil-smelling onion shoot she was lifting from the ground. "Some can't be that simple," she said. "I know I never could."

QUESTIONS
1. Why does Joy feel that changing her name to Hulga is "her highest creative act"?   **2.** In what ways do Mrs. Freeman's descriptions of her daughters Glynese and Carramae contribute to the theme of the story?   **3.** Is the title ironic? Explain.

WRITING TOPICS
1. Does this story have any admirable characters or heroes in the conventional sense? Explain.   **2.** Why does Hulga agree to meet with Manley Pointer? Does Hulga's experience with Manley Pointer confirm her cynical philosophy of "nothing"?

The Lesson 1972

TONI CADE BAMBARA [b. 1939]

Back in the days when everyone was old and stupid or young and foolish and me and Sugar were the only ones just right, this lady moved on our block with nappy hair and proper speech and no makeup. And quite naturally we laughed at her, laughed the way we did at the junk man who went about his business like he was some big-time president and his sorry-ass horse his secretary. And we kinda hated her too, hated the way we did the winos who cluttered up our parks and pissed on our handball walls and stank up our hallways and stairs so you couldn't halfway play hide-and-seek without a goddamn gas mask. Miss Moore was her name. The only woman on the block with no first name. And she was black as hell, cept for her feet, which were fish-white and spooky. And she was always planning these boring-ass things for us to do, us being my cousin, mostly, who lived on the block cause we all moved North the same time and to the same apartment then spread out gradual to breathe. And our parents would yank our heads into some kinda shape and crisp up our clothes so we'd be presentable for travel with Miss Moore, who always looked like she was going to church, though she never did. Which is just one of the things the grownups talked about when they talked behind her back like a dog. But when she came calling with some sachet she'd sewed up or some gingerbread she'd made or some book, why then they'd all be too embarrassed to turn her down and we'd get handed over all spruced up. She'd been to college and said it was only right that she should take responsibility for the young ones' education, and she not even related by marriage or blood. So they'd go for it. Specially Aunt Gretchen. She was the main gofer in the family. You got some old dumb shit foolishness you want somebody to go for, you send for Aunt Gretchen. She been screwed into the go-along for so long, it's a blood-deep natural thing with her. Which is how she got saddled with me and Sugar and Junior in the first place while our mothers were in a la-de-da apartment up the block having a good ole time.

So this one day Miss Moore rounds us all up at the mailbox and it's puredee hot and she's knockin herself out about arithmetic. And school suppose to let up in summer I heard, but she don't never let up. And the starch in my pinafore scratching the shit outta me and I'm really hating this nappy-head bitch and her goddamn college degree. I'd much rather go to the pool or to the show where it's cool. So me and Sugar leaning on the mailbox being surly, which is a Miss Moore word. And Flyboy checking out what everybody brought for lunch. And Fat Butt already wasting his peanut-butter-and-jelly sandwich like the pig he is. And Junebug punchin on Q.T.'s arm for potato chips. And Rosie Giraffe shifting from one hip to the other waiting for somebody to step on her foot or ask her if she from Georgia so she can kick ass, preferably

Mercedes'. And Miss Moore asking us do we know what money is, like we a bunch of retards. I mean real money, she say, like it's only poker chips or monopoly papers we lay on the grocer. So right away I'm tired of this and say so. And would much rather snatch Sugar and go to the Sunset and terrorize the West Indian kids and take their hair ribbons and their money too. And Miss Moore files that remark away for next week's lesson on brotherhood, I can tell. And finally I say we oughta get to the subway cause it's cooler and besides we might meet some cute boys. Sugar done swiped her mama's lipstick, so we ready.

So we heading down the street and she's boring us silly about what things cost and what our parents make and how much goes for rent and how money ain't divided up right in this country. And then she gets to the part about we all poor and live in the slums, which I don't feature. And I'm ready to speak on that, but she steps out in the street and hails two cabs just like that. Then she hustles half the crew in with her and hands me a five-dollar bill and tells me to calculate 10 percent tip for the driver. And we're off. Me and Sugar and Junebug and Flyboy hangin out the window and hollering to everybody, putting lipstick on each other cause Flyboy a faggot anyway, and making farts with our sweaty armpits. But I'm mostly trying to figure how to spend this money. But they all fascinated with the meter ticking and Junebug starts laying bets as to how much it'll read when Flyboy can't hold his breath no more. Then Sugar lays bets as to how much it'll be when we get there. So I'm stuck. Don't nobody want to go for my plan, which is to jump out at the next light and run off to the first bar-b-que we can find. Then the driver tells us to get the hell out cause we there already. And the meter reads eighty-five cents. And I'm stalling to figure out the tip and Sugar say give him a dime. And I decide he don't need it bad as I do, so later for him. But then he tries to take off with Junebug foot still in the door so we talk about his mama something ferocious. Then we check out that we on Fifth Avenue and everybody dressed up in stockings. One lady in a fur coat, hot as it is. White folks crazy.

"This is the place," Miss Moore say, presenting it to us in the voice she uses at the museum. "Let's look in the windows before we go in."

"Can we steal?" Sugar asks very serious like she's getting the ground rules squared away before she plays. "I beg your pardon," say Miss Moore, and we fall out. So she leads us around the windows of the toy store and me and Sugar screamin, "This is mine, that's mine, I gotta have that, that was made for me, I was born for that," till Big Butt drowns us out.

"Hey, I'm goin to buy that there."

"That there? You don't even know what it is, stupid."

"I do so," he say punchin on Rosie Giraffe. "It's a microscope."

"Whatcha gonna do with a microscope, fool?"

"Look at things."

"Like what, Ronald?" ask Miss Moore. And Big Butt ain't got the first notion. So here go Miss Moore gabbing about the thousands of bacteria in a drop of water and the somethinorother in a speck of blood and the million and one living things in the air around us is invisible to the naked eye. And what she say that for? Junebug go to town on that "naked" and we rolling. Then Miss Moore ask what it cost. So we all jam into the window smudgin it up and the price tag say $300. So then she ask how long'd take for Big Butt and Junebug to save up their allowances. "Too long," I say. "Yeh," adds Sugar, "outgrown it by that time." And Miss Moore say no, you never outgrow learning instruments. "Why, even medical students and interns and," blah, blah, blah. And we ready to choke Big Butt for bringing it up in the first damn place.

"This here costs four hundred eighty dollars," say Rosie Giraffe. So we pile up all over her to see what she pointin out. My eyes tell me it's a chunk of glass cracked with something heavy, and different-color inks dripped into the splits, then the whole thing put into a oven or something. But for $480 it don't make sense.

"That's a paperweight made of semi-precious stones fused together under tremendous pressure," she explains slowly, with her hands doing the mining and all the factory work.

"So what's a paperweight?" asks Rosie Giraffe.

"To weigh paper with, dumbbell," say Flyboy, the wise man from the East.

"Not exactly," say Miss Moore, which is what she say when you warm or way off too. "It's to weigh paper down so it won't scatter and make your desk untidy." So right away me and Sugar curtsy to each other and then to Mercedes who is more the tidy type.

"We don't keep paper on top of the desk in my class," say Junebug, figuring Miss Moore crazy or lyin one.

"At home, then," she say. "Don't you have a calendar and pencil case and a blotter and a letter-opener on your desk at home where you do your homework?" And she know damn well what our homes look like cause she nosys around in them every chance she gets.

"I don't even have a desk," say Junebug. "Do we?"

"No. And I don't get no homework neither," says Big Butt.

"And I don't even have a home," say Flyboy like he do at school to keep the white folks off his back and sorry for him. Send this poor kid to camp posters, is his specialty.

"I do," says Mercedes. "I have a box of stationery on my desk and a picture of my cat. My godmother bought the stationery and the desk. There's a big rose on each sheet and the envelopes smell like roses."

"Who wants to know about your smelly-ass stationery," say Rosie Giraffe fore I can get my two cents in.

"It's important to have a work area all your own so that . . ."

"Will you look at this sailboat, please," say Flyboy, cuttin her off and pointin to the thing like it was his. So once again we tumble all over each other to gaze at this magnificent thing in the toy store which is just big enough to maybe sail two kittens across the pond if you strap them to the posts tight. We all start reciting the price tag like we in assembly. "Handcrafted sailboat of fiberglass at one thousand one hundred ninety-five dollars."

"Unbelievable," I hear myself say and am really stunned. I read it again for myself just in case the group recitation put me in a trance. Same thing. For some reason this pisses me off. We look at Miss Moore and she lookin at us, waiting for I dunno what.

"Who'd pay all that when you can buy a sailboat set for a quarter at Pop's, a tube of glue for a dime, and a ball of string for eight cents? It must have a motor and a whole lot else besides," I say. "My sailboat cost me about fifty cents."

"But will it take water?" say Mercedes with her smart ass.

"Took mine to Alley Pond Park once," say Flyboy. "String broke. Lost it. Pity."

"Sailed mine in Central Park and it keeled over and sank. Had to ask my father for another dollar."

"And you got the strap," laugh Big Butt. "The jerk didn't even have a string on it. My old man wailed on his behind."

Little Q.T. was staring hard at the sailboat and you could see he wanted it bad. But he too little and somebody'd just take it from him. So what the hell. "This boat for kids, Miss Moore?"

"Parents silly to buy something like that just to get all broke up," say Rosie Giraffe.

"That much money it should last forever," I figure.

"My father'd buy it for me if I wanted it."

"Your father, my ass," say Rosie Giraffe getting a chance to finally push Mercedes.

"Must be rich people shop here," say Q.T.

"You are a very bright boy," say Flyboy. "What was your first clue?" And he rap him on the head with the back of his knuckles, since Q.T. the only one he could get away with. Though Q.T. liable to come up behind you years later and get his licks in when you half expect it.

"What I want to know is," I says to Miss Moore though I never talk to her, I wouldn't give the bitch that satisfaction, "is how much a real boat costs? I figure a thousand'd get you a yacht any day."

"Why don't you check that out," she says, "and report back to the group?" Which really pains my ass. If you gonna mess up a perfectly good swim day least you could do is have some answers. "Let's go in," she say like she got something up her sleeve. Only she don't lead the way. So me and Sugar turn the corner to where the entrance is, but when we get there I kinda hang back. Not that I'm scared, what's there to be afraid of, just a toy store. But I feel funny, shame. But what I got to be shamed about? Got as much right to go in as anybody. But somehow I can't seem to get hold of the door, so I step away for Sugar to lead. But she hangs back too. And I look at her and she looks at me and this is ridiculous. I mean, damn, I have never ever been shy about doing nothing or going nowhere. But then Mercedes steps up and then Rosie Giraffe and Big Butt crowd in behind and shove, and next thing we all stuffed into the doorway with only Mercedes squeezing past us, smoothing out her jumper and walking right down the aisle. Then the rest of us tumble in like a glued-together jigsaw done all wrong. And people lookin at us. And it's like the time me and Sugar crashed into the Catholic church on a dare. But once we got in there and everything so hushed and holy and the candles and the bowin and the handkerchiefs on all the drooping heads, I just couldn't go through with the plan. Which was for me to run up to the altar and do a tap dance while Sugar played the nose flute and messed around in the holy water. And Sugar kept givin me the elbow. Then later teased me so bad I tied her up in the shower and turned it on and locked her in. And she'd be there till this day if Aunt Gretchen hadn't finally figured I was lyin about the boarder takin a shower.

Same thing in the store. We all walkin on tiptoe and hardly touchin the games and puzzles and things. And I watched Miss Moore who is steady watchin us like she waitin for a sign. Like Mama Drewery watches the sky and sniffs the air and takes note of just how much slant is in the bird formation. Then me and Sugar bump smack into each other, so busy gazing at the toys, 'specially the sailboat. But we don't laugh and go into our fat-lady bump-stomach routine. We just stare at that price tag. Then Sugar run a finger over the whole boat. And I'm jealous and want to hit her. Maybe not her, but I sure want to punch somebody in the mouth.

"Watcha bring us here for, Miss Moore?"

"You sound angry, Sylvia. Are you mad about something?" Givin me one of them grins like she tellin a grown-up joke that never turns out to be funny. And she's lookin very closely at me like maybe she planning to do my portrait from memory. I'm mad, but I won't give her that satisfaction. So I slouch around the store bein very bored and say, "Let's go."

Me and Sugar at the back of the train watchin the tracks whizzin by large then small then gettin gobbled up in the dark. I'm thinkin about this tricky toy I saw in the store. A clown that somersaults on a bar then does chin-ups just cause you yank lightly at his leg. Cost $35. I could see me askin my mother for a $35 birthday clown. "You wanna who that costs what?" she'd say, cocking her head to the side to get a better view of the hole in my head. Thirty-five dollars could buy new bunk beds for Junior and Gretchen's boy. Thirty-five dollars and the whole household could go visit Granddaddy Nelson in the country. Thirty-five dollars would pay for the rent and the piano bill too. Who are these people that spend that much for performing clowns and $1000 for toy sailboats? What kinda work they do and how they live and how come we ain't in on it? Where we are is who we are, Miss Moore always pointin out. But it don't necessarily have to be that way, she always adds then waits for somebody to say that poor people have to wake up and demand their share of the pie and don't none of us know what kind of pie she talking about in the first damn place. But she ain't so smart cause I still got her four dollars from the taxi and she sure ain't gettin it. Messin up my day with this shit. Sugar nudges me in my pocket and winks.

Miss Moore lines us up in front of the mailbox where we started from, seem like years ago, and I got a headache for thinkin so hard. And we lean all over each other so we can hold up under the draggy-ass lecture she always finishes us off with at the end before we thank her for borin us to tears. But she just looks at us like she readin tea leaves. Finally she say, "Well, what did you think of F. A. O. Schwarz?"

Rosie Giraffe mumbles, "White folks crazy."

"I'd like to go there again when I get my birthday money," says Mercedes, and we shove her out the pack so she has to lean on the mailbox by herself.

"I'd like a shower. Tiring day," say Flyboy.

Then Sugar surprises me by sayin, "You know, Miss Moore, I don't think all of us here put together eat in a year what that sailboat costs." And Miss Moore lights up like somebody goosed her. "And?" she say, urging Sugar on. Only I'm standin on her foot so she don't continue.

"Imagine for a minute what kind of society it is in which some people can spend on a toy what it would cost to feed a family of six or seven. What do you think?"

"I think," say Sugar pushing me off her feet like she never done before, cause I whip her ass in a minute, "that this is not much of a democracy if you ask me. Equal chance to pursue happiness means an equal crack at the dough, don't it?" Miss Moore is besides herself and I am disgusted with Sugar's treachery. So I stand on her foot one more time to see if she'll shove me. She shuts up, and Miss Moore looks at me, sorrowfully I'm thinkin. And somethin weird is goin on, I can feel it in my chest.

"Anybody else learn anything today?" lookin dead at me. I walk away and Sugar has to run to catch up and don't even seem to notice when I shrug her arm off my shoulder.

"Well, we got four dollars anyway," she says.

"Uh hunh."

"We could go to Hascombs and get half a chocolate layer and then go to the Sunset and still have plenty money for potato chips and ice cream sodas."

"Un hunh."

"Race you to Hascombs," she say.

We start down the block and she gets ahead which is O.K. by me cause I'm going to the West End and then over to the Drive to think this day through. She can run if she want to and even run faster. But ain't nobody gonna beat me at nuthin.

QUESTIONS

1. Characterize the narrator of this story. **2.** How does the narrator describe her neighborhood? How does she feel when Miss Moore calls the neighborhood a slum? **3.** F. A. O. Schwarz is a famous toy store on Fifth Avenue in New York City, located about three miles south of Harlem where, doubtless, the children live. What lesson does Miss Moore convey by taking them there?

WRITING TOPIC

Is there any evidence at the end of the story that the narrator has been changed by the experience?

Orbiting
1988

BHARATI MUKHERJEE   [b. 1940]

On Thanksgiving morning I'm still in my nightgown thinking of Vic when Dad raps on my apartment door. Who's he rolling joints for, who's he initiating now into the wonders of his inner space? What got me on Vic is remembering last Thanksgiving and his famous cranberry sauce with Grand Marnier, which Dad had interpreted as a sign of permanence in my life. A man who cooks like Vic is ready for other commitments. Dad cannot imagine cooking as self-expression. You cook *for* someone. Vic's sauce was a sign of his permanent isolation, if you really want to know.

Dad's come to drop off the turkey. It's a seventeen-pounder. Mr. Vitelli knows to reserve a biggish one for us every Thanksgiving and Christmas. But this November what with Danny in the Marines, Uncle Carmine having to be very careful after the bypass, and Vic taking off for outer space as well, we might as well have made do with one of those turkey rolls you pick out of the freezer. And in other years, Mr. Vitelli would not have given us a frozen bird. We were proud of that, our birds were fresh killed. I don't bring this up to Dad.

"Your mama took care of the thawing," Dad says. "She said you wouldn't have room in your Frigidaire."

"You mean Mom said Rindy shouldn't be living in a dump, right?" Mom has the simple, immigrant faith that children should do better than their parents, and her definition of better is comfortingly rigid. Fair enough—I believed it, too. But the fact is all I can afford is this third-floor studio with an art deco shower. The fridge fits under the kitchenette counter. The room has potential. I'm content with that. And I *like* my job even though it's selling, not designing, jewelry made out of seashells and semiprecious stones out of a boutique in Bellevue Plaza.

Dad shrugs. "You're an adult, Renata." He doesn't try to lower himself into one of my two deck chairs. He was a minor league catcher for a while and his knees went. The fake zebra-skin cushions piled as seats on the rug are out of the question for him. My futon bed folds up into a sofa, but the satin sheets are still lasciviously tangled. My father stands in a slat of sunlight, trying not to look embarrassed.

"Dad, I'd have come to the house and picked it up. You didn't have to make the extra trip out from Verona." A sixty-five-year-old man in wingtips and a Borsalino[1] hugging a wet, heavy bird is so poignant I have to laugh.

"You wouldn't have gotten out of bed until noon, Renata." But Dad smiles. I know what he's saying. He's saying *he's* retired and *he* should be able to stay

---

[1] A stylish brim hat.

in bed till noon if he wants to, but he can't and he'd rather drive twenty miles with a soggy bird than read the *Ledger* one more time.

Grumbling and scolding are how we deMarcos express love. It's the North Italian way, Dad used to tell Cindi, Danny, and me when we were kids. Sicilians and Calabrians are emotional; we're contained. Actually, *he's* contained, the way Vic was contained for the most part. Mom's a Calabrian and she was born and raised there. Dad's very American, so Italy's a safe source of pride for him. I once figured it out: *his* father, Arturo deMarco, was a fifteen-week-old fetus when his mother planted her feet on Ellis Island. Dad, a proud son of North Italy, had one big adventure in his life, besides fighting in the Pacific, and that was marrying a Calabrian peasant. He made it sound as though Mom was a Korean or something, and their marriage was a kind of taming of the West, and that everything about her could be explained as a cultural deficiency. Actually, Vic could talk beautifully about his feelings. He'd brew espresso, pour it into tiny blue pottery cups and analyze our relationship. I should have listened. I mean really listened. I thought he was talking about us, but I know now he was only talking incessantly about himself. I put too much faith in mail-order nightgowns and bras.

"Your mama wanted me out of the house," Dad goes on. "She didn't used to be like this, Renata."

Renata and Carla are what we were christened. We changed to Rindy and Cindi in junior high. Danny didn't have to make such leaps, unless you count dropping out of Montclair State and joining the Marines. He was always Danny, or Junior.

I lug the turkey to the kitchen sink where it can drip away at a crazy angle until I have time to deal with it.

"Your mama must have told you girls I've been acting funny since I retired."

"No, Dad, she hasn't said anything about you acting funny." What she *has* said is do we think she ought to call Doc Brunetti and have a chat about Dad? Dad wouldn't have to know. He and Doc Brunetti are, or were, on the same church league bowling team. So is, or was, Vic's dad, Vinny Riccio.

"Your mama thinks a man should have an office to drive to every day. I sat at a desk for thirty-eight years and what did I get? Ask Doc, I'm too embarrassed to say." Dad told me once Doc—his real name was Frankie, though no one ever called him that—had been called Doc since he was six years old and growing up with Dad in Little Italy. There was never a time in his life when Doc wasn't Doc, which made his professional decision very easy. Dad used to say, no one ever called me Adjuster when I was a kid. Why didn't they call me something like Sarge or Teach? Then I would have known better.

I wish I had something breakfasty in my kitchen cupboard to offer him. He wants to stay and talk about Mom, which is the way old married people have. Let's talk about me means: What do you think of Mom? I'll take the turkey over means: When will Rindy settle down? I wish this morning I had bought the Goodwill sofa for ten dollars instead of letting Vic haul off the fancy deck chairs from Fortunoff's. Vic had flash. He'd left Jersey a long time before he actually took off.

"I can make you tea."

"None of that herbal stuff."

We don't talk about Mom, but I know what he's going through. She's just started to find herself. He's not burned out, he's merely stuck. I remember when Mom refused to learn to drive, wouldn't leave the house even to mail a letter. Her litany those days was: when you've spent the first fifteen years of your life in a mountain village, when you remember candles and gaslight and carrying water from a well, not to mention holding in your water at night because of wolves and the unlit outdoor privy, you *like* being housebound. She used those wolves for all they were worth, as though imaginary wolves still nipped her heels in the Clifton Mall.

Before Mom began to find herself and signed up for a class at Paterson, she used to nag Cindi and me about finding the right men. "Men," she said; she wasn't coy, never. Unembarrassed, she'd tell me about her wedding night, about her first sighting of Dad's "thing" ("Land Ho!" Cindi giggled. "Thar she blows!" I chipped in.) and she'd giggle at our word for it, the common word, and she'd use it around us, never around Dad. Mom's peasant, she's earthy but never coarse. If I could get that across to Dad, how I admire it in men or in women, I would feel somehow redeemed of all my little mistakes with them, with men, with myself. Cindi and Brent were married on a cruise ship by the ship's captain. Tony, Vic's older brother, made a play for me my senior year. Tony's solid now. He manages a funeral home but he's invested in crayfish ponds on the side.

"You don't even own a dining table." Dad sounds petulant. He uses "even" a lot around me. Not just a judgment, but a comparative judgment. Other people have dining tables. *Lots* of dining tables. He softens it a bit, not wanting to hurt me, wanting more for me to judge him a failure. "We've always had a sit-down dinner, hon."

Okay, so traditions change. This year dinner's potluck. So I don't have real furniture. I eat off stack-up plastic tables as I watch the evening news. I drink red wine and heat a pita bread on the gas burner and wrap it around alfalfa sprouts or green linguine. The Swedish knockdown dresser keeps popping its sides because Vic didn't glue it properly. Swedish engineering, he said, doesn't need glue. Think of Volvos, he said, and Ingmar Bergman. He isn't good with directions that come in four languages. At least he wasn't.

"Trust me, Dad." This isn't the time to spring new lovers on him. "A friend made me a table. It's in the basement."

"How about chairs?" Ah, my good father. He could have said, friend? What friend?

Marge, my landlady, has all kinds of junky stuff in the basement. "Jorge and I'll bring up what we need. You'd strain your back, Dad." Shot knees, bad back: daily pain but nothing fatal. Not like Carmine.

"Jorge? Is that the new boyfriend?"

Shocking him makes me feel good. It would serve him right if Jorge were my new boyfriend. But Jorge is Marge's other roomer. He gives Marge Spanish lessons, and does the heavy cleaning and the yard work. Jorge has family in El

Salvador he's hoping to bring up. I haven't met Marge's husband yet. He works on an offshore oil rig in some emirate with a funny name.

"No, Dad." I explain about Jorge.

"El Salvador!" he repeats. "That means 'the Savior.'" He passes on the information with a kind of awe. It makes Jorge's homeland, which he's shown me pretty pictures of, seem messy and exotic, at the very rim of human comprehension.

After Dad leaves, I call Cindi, who lives fifteen minutes away on Upper Mountainside Road. She's eleven months younger and almost a natural blond, but we're close. Brent wasn't easy for me to take, not at first. He owns a discount camera and electronics store on Fifty-fourth in Manhattan. Cindi met him through Club Med. They sat on a gorgeous Caribbean beach and talked of hogs. His father is an Amish farmer in Kalona, Iowa. Brent, in spite of the obvious hairpiece and the gold chain, is a rebel. He was born Schwartz-endruber, but changed his name to Schwartz. Now no one believes the Brent, either. They call him Bernie on the street and it makes everyone more comfortable. His father's never taken their buggy out of the county.

The first time Vic asked me out, he talked of feminism and holism and macrobiotics. Then he opened up on cinema and literature, and I was very impressed, as who wouldn't be? Ro, my current lover, is very different. He picked me up in an uptown singles bar that I and sometimes Cindi go to. He bought me a Cinzano and touched my breast in the dark. He was direct, and at the same time weirdly courtly. I took him home though usually I don't, at first. I learned in bed that night that the tall brown drink with the lemon twist he'd been drinking was Tab.

I went back on the singles circuit even though the break with Vic should have made me cautious. Cindi thinks Vic's a romantic. I've told her how it ended. One Sunday morning in March he kissed me awake as usual. He'd brought in the *Times* from the porch and was reading it. I made us some cinnamon rose tea. We had a ritual, starting with the real estate pages, passing remarks on the latest tacky towers. Not for us, we'd say, the view is terrible! No room for the servants, things like that. And our imaginary children's imaginary nanny. "Hi, gorgeous," I said. He is gorgeous, not strong, but showy. He said, "I'm leaving, babe. New Jersey doesn't do it for me anymore." I said, "Okay, so where're we going?" I had an awful job at the time, taking orders for MCI. Vic said, "I didn't say we, babe." So I asked, "You mean it's over? Just like that?" And he said, "Isn't that the best way? No fuss, no hang-ups." Then I got a little whiny. "*But* why?" I wanted to know. But he was macrobiotic in lots of things, including relationships. Yin and yang, hot and sour, green and yellow. "You know, Rindy, there are *places*. You don't fall off the earth when you leave Jersey, you know. Places you see pictures of and read about. Different weathers, different trees, different everything. Places that get the Cubs on cable instead of the Mets." He was into that. For all the sophisticated things he liked to talk about, he was a very local boy. "Vic," I pleaded, "you're crazy. You need help." "I need help because I want to get out of Jersey? You gotta be kidding!"

He stood up and for a moment I thought he would do something crazy, like destroy something, or hurt me. "Don't ever call me crazy, got that? And give me the keys to the van."

He took the van. Danny had sold it to me when the Marines sent him overseas. I'd have given it to him anyway, even if he hadn't asked.

"Cindi, I need a turkey roaster," I tell my sister on the phone.

"I'll be right over," she says. "The brat's driving me crazy."

"Isn't Franny's visit working out?"

"I could kill her. I think up ways. How does that sound?"

"Why not send her home?" I'm joking. Franny is Brent's twelve-year-old and he's shelled out a lot of dough to lawyers in New Jersey and Florida to work out visitation rights.

"Poor Brent. He feels so *divided*," Cindi says. "He shouldn't have to take sides."

I want her to ask who my date is for this afternoon, but she doesn't. It's important to me that she like Ro, that Mom and Dad more than tolerate him.

All over the country, I tell myself, women are towing new lovers home to meet their families. Vic is simmering cranberries in somebody's kitchen and explaining yin and yang. I check out the stuffing recipe. The gravy calls for cream and freshly grated nutmeg. Ro brought me six whole nutmegs in a Ziplock bag from his friend, a Pakistani, who runs a spice store in SoHo.[2] The nuts look hard and ugly. I take one out of the bag and sniff it. The aroma's so exotic my head swims. On an impulse I call Ro.

The phone rings and rings. He doesn't have his own place yet. He has to crash with friends. He's been in the States three months, maybe less. I let it ring fifteen, sixteen, seventeen times.

Finally someone answers. "Yes?" The voice is guarded, the accent obviously foreign even though all I'm hearing is a one-syllable word. Ro has fled here from Kabul. He wants to take classes at NJIT and become an electrical engineer. He says he's lucky his father got him out. A friend of Ro's father, a man called Mumtaz, runs a fried chicken restaurant in Brooklyn in a neighborhood Ro calls "Little Kabul," though probably no one else has ever noticed. Mr. Mumtaz puts the legal immigrants to work as waiters out front. The illegals hide in a backroom as pluckers and gutters.

"Ro? I miss you. We're eating at three, remember?"

"Who is speaking, please?"

So I fell for the accent, but it isn't a malicious error. I *can* tell one Afghan tribe from another now, even by looking at them or by their names. I can make out some Pashto words. "Tell Ro it's Rindy. Please? I'm a friend. He wanted me to call this number."

---

[2] A neighborhood south of Houston Street in Manhattan, New York City.

"Not knowing any Ro."

"Hey, wait. Tell him it's Rindy deMarco."

The guy hangs up on me.

I'm crumbling cornbread into a bowl for the stuffing when Cindi honks half of "King Cotton" from the parking apron in the back. Brent bought her the BMW on the gray market and saved a bundle—once discount, always discount—then spent three hundred dollars to put in a horn that beeps a Sousa march. I wave a potato masher at her from the back window. She doesn't get out of the car. Instead she points to the pan in the back seat. I come down, wiping my hands on a dish towel.

"I should stay and help." Cindi sounds ready to cry. But I don't want her with me when Ro calls back.

"You're doing too much already, kiddo." My voice at least sounds comforting. "You promised one veg and the salad."

"I ought to come up and help. That or get drunk." She shifts the stick. When Brent bought her the car, the dealer threw in driving gloves to match the upholstery.

"Get Franny to shred the greens," I call as Cindi backs up the car. "Get her involved."

The phone is ringing in my apartment. I can hear it ring from the second-floor landing.

"Ro?"

"You're taking a chance, my treasure. It could have been any other admirer, then where would you be?"

"I don't have any other admirers." Ro is not a conventionally jealous man, not like the types I have known. He's totally unlike any man I have ever known. He wants men to come on to me. Lately when we go to a bar he makes me sit far enough from him so some poor lonely guy thinks I'm looking for action. Ro likes to swagger out of a dark booth as soon as someone buys me a drink. I go along. He comes from a macho culture.

"How else will I know you are as beautiful as I think you are? I would not want an unprized woman," he says. He is asking me for time, I know. In a few more months he'll know I'm something of a catch in my culture, or at least I've never had trouble finding boys. Even Brent Schwartzendruber has begged me to see him alone.

"I'm going to be a little late," Ro says. "I told you about my cousin, Abdul, no?"

Ro has three or four cousins that I know of in Manhattan. They're all named Abdul something. When I think of Abdul, I think of a giant black man with goggles on, running down a court. Abdul is the teenage cousin whom immigration officials nabbed as he was gutting chickens in Mumtaz's backroom. Abdul doesn't have the right papers to live and work in this country, and now he's been locked up in a detention center on Varick Street. Ro's afraid Abdul will be deported back to Afghanistan. If that happens, he'll be tortured.

"I have to visit him before I take the DeCamp bus. He's talking nonsense. He's talking of starting a hunger fast."

"A hunger strike! God!" When I'm with Ro I feel I am looking at America through the wrong end of a telescope. He makes it sound like a police state, with sudden raids, papers, detention centers, deportations, and torture and death waiting in the wings. I'm not a political person. Last fall I wore the Ferraro button because she's a woman and Italian.

"Rindy, all night I've been up and awake. All night I think of your splendid breasts. Like clusters of grapes, I think. I am stroking and fondling your grapes this very minute. My talk gets you excited?"

I tell him to test me, please get here before three. I remind him he can't buy his ticket on the bus.

"We got here too early, didn't we?" Dad stands just outside the door to my apartment, looking embarrassed. He's in his best dark suit, the one he wears every Thanksgiving and Christmas. This year he can't do up the top button of his jacket.

"Don't be so formal, Dad." I give him a showy hug and pull him indoors so Mom can come in.

"As if your papa ever listens to me!" Mom laughs. But she sits primly on the sofa bed in her velvet cloak, with her tote bag and evening purse on her lap. Before Dad started courting her, she worked as a seamstress. Dad rescued her from a sweatshop. He married down, she married well. That's the family story.

"She told me to rush."

Mom isn't in a mood to squabble. I think she's reached the point of knowing she won't have him forever. There was Carmine, at death's door just a month ago. Anything could happen to Dad. She says, "Renata, look what I made! Crostolis." She lifts a cake tin out of her tote bag. The pan still feels warm. And for dessert, I know, there'll be a jar of super-thick, super-rich Death by Chocolate.

The story about Grandma deMarco, Dad's mama, is that every Thanksgiving she served two full dinners, one American with the roast turkey, candied yams, pumpkin pie, the works, and another with Grandpa's favorite pastas.

Dad relaxes. He appoints himself bartender. "Don't you have more ice cubes, sweetheart?"

I tell him it's good Glenlivet. He shouldn't ruin it with ice, just a touch of water if he must. Dad pours sherry in Vic's pottery espresso cups for his women. Vic made them himself, and I used to think they were perfect blue jewels. Now I see they're lumpy, uneven in color.

"Go change into something pretty before Carla and Brent come." Mom believes in dressing up. Beaded dresses lift her spirits. She's wearing a beaded green dress today.

I take the sherry and vanish behind a four-panel screen, the kind long-legged showgirls change behind in black and white movies while their moustached lovers keep talking. My head barely shows above the screen's top, since I'm no long-legged showgirl. My best points, as Ro has said, are my clusters of grapes.

Vic found the screen at a country auction in the Adirondacks. It had filled the van. Now I use the panels as a bulletin board and I'm worried Dad'll spot the notice for the next meeting of Amnesty International, which will bother him. He will think the two words stand for draft dodger and communist. I was going to drop my membership, a legacy of Vic, when Ro saw it and approved. Dad goes to the Sons of Italy Anti-Defamation dinners. He met Frank Sinatra at one. He voted for Reagan last time because the Democrats ran an Italian woman.

Instead of a thirties lover, it's my moustached papa talking to me from the other side of the screen. "So where's this dining table?"

"Ro's got the parts in the basement. He'll bring it up, Dad."

I hear them whispering. "Bo? Now she's messing with a Southerner?" and "Shh, it's her business."

I'm just smoothing on my pantyhose when Mom screams for the cops. Dad shouts too, at Mom for her to shut up. It's my fault, I should have warned Ro not to use his key this afternoon.

I peek over the screen's top and see my lover the way my parents see him. He's a slight, pretty man with hazel eyes and a tufty moustache, so whom can he intimidate? I've seen Jews and Greeks, not to mention Sons of Italy, darker-skinned than Ro. Poor Ro resorts to his Kabuli prep-school manners.

"How do you do, Madam! Sir! My name is Roashan."

Dad moves closer to Ro but doesn't hold out his hand. I can almost read his mind: *he speaks.* "Come again?" he says, baffled.

I cringe as he spells his name. My parents are so parochial. With each letter he does a graceful dip and bow. "Try it syllable by syllable, sir. Then it is not so hard."

Mom stares past him at me. The screen doesn't hide me because I've strayed too far in to watch the farce. "Renata, you're wearing only your camisole."

I pull my crew neck over my head, then kiss him. I make the kiss really sexy so they'll know I've slept with this man. Many times. And if he asks me, I will marry him. I had not known that till now. I think my mother guesses.

He's brought flowers: four long-stemmed, stylish purple blossoms in a florist's paper cone. "For you, madam." He glides over the dirty broadloom to Mom who fills up more than half the sofa bed. "This is my first Thanksgiving dinner, for which I have much to give thanks, no?"

"He was born in Afghanistan," I explain. But Dad gets continents wrong. He says, "We saw your famine camps on TV. Well, you won't starve this afternoon."

"They smell good," Mom says. "Thank you very much but you shouldn't spend a fortune."

"No, no, madam. What you smell good is my cologne. Flowers in New York have no fragrance."

"His father had a garden estate outside Kabul." I don't want Mom to think he's putting down American flowers, though in fact he is. Along with American fruits, meats, and vegetables. "The Russians bulldozed it," I add.

Dad doesn't want to talk politics. He senses, looking at Ro, this is not the face of Ethiopian starvation. "Well, what'll it be, Roy? Scotch and soda?" I wince. It's not going well.

"Thank you but no. I do not imbibe alcoholic spirits, though I have no objection for you, sir." My lover goes to the fridge and reaches down. He knows just where to find his Tab. My father is quietly livid, staring down at his drink.

In my father's world, grown men bowl in leagues and drink the best whiskey they can afford. Dad whistles "My Way." He must be under stress. That's his usual self-therapy: how would Francis Albert handle this?

"Muslims have taboos, Dad." Cindi didn't marry a Catholic, so he has no right to be upset about Ro, about us.

"Jews," Dad mutters. "So do Jews." He knows because catty-corner from Vitelli's is a kosher butcher. This isn't the time to parade new words before him, like *halal,* the Muslim kosher. An Italian-American man should be able to live sixty-five years never having heard the word, I can go along with that. Ro, fortunately, is cosmopolitan. Outside of pork and booze, he eats anything else I fix.

Brent and Cindi take forever to come. But finally we hear his MG squeal in the driveway. Ro glides to the front window; he seems to blend with the ficus tree and hanging ferns. Dad and I wait by the door.

"Party time!" Brent shouts as he maneuvers Cindi and Franny ahead of him up three flights of stairs. He looks very much the head of the family, a rich man steeply in debt to keep up appearances, to compete, to head off middle age. He's at that age—and Cindi's nowhere near that age—when people notice the difference and quietly judge it. I know these things from Cindi—I'd never guess it from looking at Brent. If he feels divided, as Cindi says he does, it doesn't show. Misery, anxiety, whatever, show on Cindi though; they bring her cheekbones out. When I'm depressed, my hair looks rough, my skin breaks out. Right now, I'm lustrous.

Brent does a lot of whooping and hugging at the door. He even hugs Dad who looks grave and funereal like an old-world Italian gentleman because of his outdated, pinched dark suit. Cindi makes straight for the fridge with her casserole of squash and browned marshmallow. Franny just stands in the middle of the room holding two biggish Baggies of salad greens and vinaigrette in an old Dijon mustard jar. Brent actually bought the mustard in Dijon, a story that Ro is bound to hear and not appreciate. Vic was mean enough last year to tell him that he could have gotten it for more or less the same price at the Italian specialty foods store down on Watchung Plaza. Franny doesn't seem to have her own winter clothes. She's wearing Cindi's car coat over a Dolphins sweatshirt. Her mother moved down to Florida the very day the divorce became final. She's got a Walkman tucked into the pocket of her cords.

"You could have trusted me to make the salad dressing at least," I scold my sister.

Franny gives up the Baggies and the jar of dressing to me. She scrutinizes us—Mom, Dad, me and Ro, especially Ro, as though she can detect something strange about him—but doesn't take off her earphones. A smirk starts twitching her tanned, feral features. I see what she is seeing. Asian men carry their bodies differently, even these famed warriors from the Khyber Pass. Ro doesn't stand like Brent or Dad. His hands hang kind of stiffly from the shoulder joints, and when he moves, his palms are tucked tight against his thighs, his stomach sticks out like a slightly pregnant woman's. Each culture establishes its own manly posture, different ways of claiming space. Ro, hiding among my plants, holds himself in a way that seems both too effeminate and too macho. I hate Franny for what she's doing to me. I am twenty-seven years old, I should be more mature. But I see now how wrong Ro's clothes are. He shows too much white collar and cuff. His shirt and his wool-blend flare-leg pants were made to measure in Kabul. The jacket comes from a discount store on Canal Street, part of a discontinued line of two-trousered suits. I ought to know, I took him there. I want to shake Franny or smash the earphones.

Cindi catches my exasperated look. "Don't pay any attention to her. She's unsociable this weekend. We can't compete with the Depeche Mode."

I intend to compete.

Franny, her eyes very green and very hostile, turns on Brent. "How come she never gets it right, Dad?"

Brent hi-fives his daughter, which embarrasses her more than anyone else in the room. "It's a Howard Jones, hon," Brent tells Cindi.

Franny, close to tears, runs to the front window where Ro's been hanging back. She has an ungainly walk for a child whose support payments specify weekly ballet lessons. She bores in on Ro's hidey hole like Russian artillery. Ro moves back to the perimeter of family intimacy. I have no way of helping yet. I have to set out the dips and Tostitos. Brent and Dad are talking sports, Mom and Cindi are watching the turkey. Dad's going on about the Knicks. He's in despair, so early in the season. He's on his second Scotch. I see Brent try. "What do you think, Roy?" He's doing his best to get my lover involved. "Maybe we'll get lucky, huh? We can always hope for a top draft pick. End up with Patrick Ewing!" Dad brightens. "That guy'll change the game. Just wait and see. He'll fill the lane better than Russell." Brent gets angry, since for some strange Amish reason he's a Celtics fan. So was Vic. "Bird'll make a monkey out of him." He looks to Ro for support.

Ro nods. Even his headshake is foreign. "You are undoubtedly correct, Brent," he says. "I am deferring to your judgment because currently I have not familiarized myself with these practices."

Ro loves squash, but none of my relatives have ever picked up a racket. I want to tell Brent that Ro's skied in St. Moritz, lost a thousand dollars in a casino in Beirut, knows where to buy Havana cigars without getting hijacked. He's sophisticated, he could make monkeys out of us all, but they think he's a retard.

Brent drinks three Scotches to Dad's two; then all three men go down to the basement. Ro and Brent do the carrying, negotiating sharp turns in the stairwell. Dad supervises. There are two trestles and a wide, splintery plywood top. "Try not to take the wall down!" Dad yells.

When they make it back in, the men take off their jackets to assemble the table. Brent's wearing a red lamb's wool turtleneck under his camel hair blazer. Ro unfastens his cuff links—they are 24-karat gold and his father's told him to sell them if funds run low—and pushes up his very white shirt sleeves. There are scars on both arms, scars that bubble against his dark skin, scars like lightning flashes under his thick black hair. Scar tissue on Ro is the color of freshwater pearls. I want to kiss it.

Cindi checks the turkey one more time. "You guys better hurry. We'll be ready to eat in fifteen minutes."

Ro, the future engineer, adjusts the trestles. He's at his best now. He's become quite chatty. From under the plywood top, he's holding forth on the Soviet menace in Kabul. Brent may actually have an idea where Afghanistan is, in a general way, but Dad is lost. He's talking of being arrested for handing out pro-American pamphlets on his campus. Dad stiffens at "arrest" and blanks out the rest. He talks of this "so-called leader," this "criminal" named Babrak Karmal and I hear other buzz-words like Kandahār and Pamir, words that might have been Polish to me a month ago, and I can see even Brent is slightly embarrassed. It's his first exposure to Third World passion. He thought only Americans had informed political opinion—other people staged coups out of spite and misery. It's an unwelcome revelation to him that a reasonably educated and rational man like Ro would die for things that he, Brent, has never heard of and would rather laugh about. Ro was tortured in jail. Franny has taken off her earphones. Electrodes, canes, freezing tanks. He leaves nothing out. Something's gotten into Ro.

Dad looks sick. The meaning of Thanksgiving should not be so explicit. But Ro's in a daze. He goes on about how—*inshallah*[3]—his father, once a rich landlord, had stashed away enough to bribe a guard, sneak him out of this cell and hide him for four months in a tunnel dug under a servant's adobe hut until a forged American visa could be bought. Franny's eyes are wide, Dad joins Mom on the sofa bed, shaking his head. Jail, bribes, forged, what is this? I can read his mind. "For six days I must orbit one international airport to another," Ro is saying. "The main trick is having a valid ticket, that way the airline has to carry you, even if the country won't take you in. Colombo, Seoul, Bombay, Geneva, Frankfurt, I know too too well the transit lounges of many airports. We travel the world with our gym bags and prayer rugs, unrolling them in the transit lounges. The better airports have special rooms."

Brent tries to ease Dad's pain. "Say, buddy," he jokes, "you wouldn't be ripping us off, would you?"

Ro snakes his slender body from under the makeshift table. He hasn't been

---

[3] "God willing." Here, it is apparently used to mean "Thank God."

watching the effect of his monologue. "I am a working man," he says stiffly. I have seen his special permit. He's one of the lucky ones, though it might not last. He's saving for NJIT. Meantime he's gutting chickens to pay for room and board in Little Kabul. He describes the gutting process. His face is transformed as he sticks his fist into imaginary roasters and grabs for gizzards, pulls out the squishy stuff. He takes an Afghan dagger out of the pocket of his pants. You'd never guess, he looks like such a victim. "This," he says, eyes glinting. "This is all I need."

"Cool," Franny says.

"Time to eat," Mom shouts. "I made the gravy with the nutmeg as you said, Renata."

I lead Dad to the head of the table. "Everyone else sit where you want to."

Franny picks out the chair next to Ro before I can put Cindi there. I want Cindi to know him, I want her as an ally.

Dad tests the blade of the carving knife. Mom put the knife where Dad always sits when she set the table. He takes his thumb off the blade and pushes the switch. "That noise makes me feel good."

But I carry in the platter with the turkey and place it in front of Ro. "I want you to carve," I say.

He brings out his dagger all over again. Franny is practically licking his fingers. "You mean this is a professional job?"

We stare fascinated as my lover slashes and slices, swiftly, confidently, at the huge, browned, juicy beast. The dagger scoops out flesh.

Now I am the one in a daze. I am seeing Ro's naked body as though for the first time, his nicked, scarred, burned body. In his body, the blemishes seem embedded, more beautiful, like wood. I am seeing character made manifest. I am seeing Brent and Dad for the first time, too. They have their little scars, things they're proud of, football injuries and bowling elbows they brag about. Our scars are so innocent; they are invisible and come to us from rough-housing gone too far. Ro hates to talk about his scars. If I trace the puckered tissue on his left thigh and ask "How, Ro?" he becomes shy, dismissive: a pack of dogs attacked him when he was a boy. The skin on his back is speckled and lumpy from burns, but when I ask he laughs. A crazy villager whacked him with a burning stick for cheekiness, he explains. He's ashamed that he comes from a culture of pain.

The turkey is reduced to a drying, whitened skeleton. On our plates, the slices are symmetrical, elegant. I realize all in a rush how much I love this man with his blemished, tortured body. I will give him citizenship if he asks. Vic was beautiful, but Vic was self-sufficient. Ro's my chance to heal the world.

I shall teach him how to walk like an American, how to dress like Brent but better, how to fill up a room as Dad does instead of melting and blending but sticking out in the Afghan way. In spite of the funny way he holds himself and the funny way he moves his head from side to side when he wants to say yes, Ro is Clint Eastwood, scarred hero and survivor. Dad and Brent are children. I realize Ro's the only circumcised man I've slept with.

Mom asks, "Why are you grinning like that, Renata?"

QUESTIONS

1. During the conversation with her father, early in the story, Renata thinks: "This isn't the time to spring new lovers on him." Why not? Characterize Renata's previous lover, Vic.   **2.** What do Brent and Renata's father talk about before dinner? What does Ro talk about? What do you make of the differences in their interests?   **3.** How do the various members of Renata's family feel about Ro? Why?   **4.** Explain the story's title.

WRITING TOPICS

1. Describe the cultural conflicts illustrated by this story. Is there any hope that those conflicts can be resolved? Explain.   **2.** Describe from your personal life or knowledge an example of the kind of cultural conflict dealt with in this story.

The Red Convertible

LYMAN LAMARTINE

LOUISE ERDRICH [b. 1954]

1984

I was the first one to drive a convertible on my reservation. And of course it was red, a red Olds. I owned that car along with my brother Henry Junior. We owned it together until his boots filled with water on a windy night and he bought out my share. Now Henry owns the whole car, and his youngest brother Lyman (that's myself), Lyman walks everywhere he goes.

How did I earn enough money to buy my share in the first place? My own talent was I could always make money. I had a touch for it, unusual in a Chippewa. From the first I was different that way, and everyone recognized it. I was the only kid they let in the American Legion Hall to shine shoes, for example, and one Christmas I sold spiritual bouquets for the mission door to door. The nuns let me keep a percentage. Once I started, it seemed the more money I made the easier the money came. Everyone encouraged it. When I was fifteen I got a job washing dishes at the Joliet Café, and that was where my first big break happened.

It wasn't long before I was promoted to bussing tables, and then the short-order cook quit and I was hired to take her place. No sooner than you know it I was managing the Joliet. The rest is history. I went on managing. I soon became part owner, and of course there was no stopping me then. It wasn't long before the whole thing was mine.

After I'd owned the Joliet for one year, it blew over in the worst tornado ever seen around here. The whole operation was smashed to bits. A total loss. The fryalator was up in a tree, the grill torn in half like it was paper. I was only sixteen. I had it all in my mother's name, and I lost it quick, but before I lost it I had every one of my relatives, and their relatives, to dinner, and I also bought that red Olds I mentioned, along with Henry.

The first time we saw it! I'll tell you when we first saw it. We had gotten a ride up to Winnipeg, and both of us had money. Don't ask me why, because we never mentioned a car or anything, we just had all our money. Mine was cash, a big bankroll from the Joliet's insurance. Henry had two checks—a week's extra pay for being laid off, and his regular check from the Jewel Bearing Plant.

We were walking down Portage anyway, seeing the sights, when we saw it. There it was, parked, large as life. Really as *if* it was alive. I thought of the word *repose*, because the car wasn't simply stopped, parked, or whatever. That car reposed, calm and gleaming, a FOR SALE sign in its left front window. Then, before we had thought it over at all, the car belonged to us and our pockets were empty. We had just enough money for gas back home.

We went places in that car, me and Henry. We took off driving all one whole summer. We started off toward the Little Knife River and Mandaree in Fort Berthold and then we found ourselves down in Wakpala somehow, and then suddenly we were over in Montana on the Rocky Boys, and yet the summer was not even half over. Some people hang on to details when they travel, but we didn't let them bother us and just lived our everyday lives here to there.

I do remember this one place with willows. I remember I laid under those trees and it was comfortable. So comfortable. The branches bent down all around me like a tent or a stable. And quiet, it was quiet, even though there was a powwow close enough so I could see it going on. The air was not too still, not too windy either. When the dust rises up and hangs in the air around the dancers like that, I feel good. Henry was asleep with his arms thrown wide. Later on, he woke up and we started driving again. We were somewhere in Montana, or maybe on the Blood Reserve—it could have been anywhere. Anyway it was where we met the girl.

All her hair was in buns around her ears, that's the first thing I noticed about her. She was posed alongside the road with her arm out, so we stopped. That girl was short, so short her lumber shirt looked comical on her, like a night-gown. She had jeans on and fancy moccasins and she carried a little suitcase.

"Hop on in," says Henry. So she climbs in between us.

"We'll take you home," I says. "Where do you live?"

"Chicken," she says.

"Where the hell's that?" I ask her.

"Alaska."

"Okay," says Henry, and we drive.

We got up there and never wanted to leave. The sun doesn't truly set there in summer, and the night is more a soft dusk. You might doze off, sometimes, but before you know it you're up again, like an animal in nature. You never feel like you have to sleep hard or put away the world. And things would grow up there. One day just dirt or moss, the next day flowers and long grass. The girl's name was Susy. Her family really took to us. They fed us and put us up. We had our own tent to live in by their house, and the kids would be in and out of there all day and night. They couldn't get over me and Henry being broth-ers, we looked so different. We told them we knew we had the same mother, anyway.

One night Susy came in to visit us. We sat around in the tent talking of this thing and that. The season was changing. It was getting darker by that time, and the cold was even getting just a little mean. I told her it was time for us to go. She stood up on a chair.

"You never seen my hair," Susy said.

That was true. She was standing on a chair, but still, when she unclipped her buns the hair reached all the way to the ground. Our eyes opened. You couldn't tell how much hair she had when it was rolled up so neatly. Then my brother Henry did something funny. He went up to the chair and said, "Jump on my shoulders." So she did that, and her hair reached down past his waist, and he started twirling, this way and that, so her hair was flung out from side to side.

"I always wondered what it was like to have long pretty hair," Henry says. Well we laughed. It was a funny sight, the way he did it. The next morning we got up and took leave of those people.

On to greener pastures, as they say. It was down through Spokane and across Idaho then Montana and very soon we were racing the weather right along under the Canadian border through Columbus, Des Lacs, and then we were in Bottineau County and soon home. We'd made most of the trip, that summer, without putting up the car hood at all. We got home just in time, it turned out, for the army to remember Henry had signed up to join it.

I don't wonder that the army was so glad to get my brother that they turned him into a Marine. He was built like a brick outhouse anyway. We liked to tease him that they really wanted him for his Indian nose. He had a nose big and sharp as a hatchet, like the nose on Red Tomahawk, the Indian who killed Sitting Bull, whose profile is on signs all along the North Dakota highways. Henry went off to training camp, came home once during Christmas, then the next thing you know we got an overseas letter from him. It was 1970, and he said he was stationed up in the northern hill country. Whereabouts I did not know. He wasn't such a hot letter writer, and only got off two before the enemy caught him. I could never keep it straight, which direction those good Vietnam soldiers were from.

I wrote him back several times, even though I didn't know if those letters would get through. I kept him informed all about the car. Most of the time I had it up on blocks in the yard or half taken apart, because that long trip did a hard job on it under the hood.

I always had good luck with numbers, and never worried about the draft myself. I never even had to think about what my number was. But Henry was never lucky in the same way as me. It was at least three years before Henry came home. By then I guess the whole war was solved in the government's mind, but for him it would keep on going. In those years I'd put his car into almost perfect shape. I always thought of it as his car while he was gone, even though when he left he said, "Now it's yours," and threw me his key.

"Thanks for the extra key," I'd say. "I'll put it up in your drawer just in case I need it." He laughed.

When he came home, though, Henry was very different, and I'll say this: the change was no good. You could hardly expect him to change for the better, I know. But he was quiet, so quiet, and never comfortable sitting still anywhere but always up and moving around. I thought back to times we'd sat still for whole afternoons, never moving a muscle, just shifting our weight along the ground, talking to whoever sat with us, watching things. He'd always had a joke, then, too, and now you couldn't get him to laugh, or when he did it was more the sound of a man choking, a sound that stopped up the throats of other people around him. They got to leaving him alone most of the time, and I didn't blame them. It was a fact: Henry was jumpy and mean.

I'd bought a color TV set for my mom and the rest of us while Henry was away. Money still came very easy. I was sorry I'd ever bought it though, because of Henry. I was also sorry I'd bought color, because with black-and-white the pictures seem older and farther away. But what are you going to do? He sat in front of it, watching it, and that was the only time he was completely still. But it was the kind of stillness that you see in a rabbit when it freezes and before it will bolt. He was not easy. He sat in his chair gripping the armrests with all his might, as if the chair itself was moving at a high speed and if he let go at all he would rocket forward and maybe crash right through the set.

Once I was in the room watching TV with Henry and I heard his teeth click at something. I looked over, and he'd bitten through his lip. Blood was going down his chin. I tell you right then I wanted to smash that tube to pieces. I went over to it but Henry must have known what I was up to. He rushed from his chair and shoved me out of the way, against the wall. I told myself he didn't know what he was doing.

My mom came in, turned the set off real quiet, and told us she had made something for supper. So we went and sat down. There was still blood going down Henry's chin, but he didn't notice it and no one said anything, even though every time he took a bit of his bread his blood fell onto it until he was eating his own blood mixed in with the food.

While Henry was not around we talked about what was going to happen to him. There were no Indian doctors on the reservation, and my mom was afraid of trusting Old Man Pillager because he courted her long ago and was jealous of her husbands. He might take revenge through her son. We were afraid that if we brought Henry to a regular hospital they would keep him.

"They don't fix them in those places," Mom said; "they just give them drugs."

"We wouldn't get him there in the first place," I agreed, "so let's just forget about it."

Then I thought about the car.

Henry had not even looked at the car since he'd gotten home, though like I said, it was in tip-top condition and ready to drive. I thought the car might bring the old Henry back somehow. So I bided my time and waited for my chance to interest him in the vehicle.

One night Henry was off somewhere. I took myself a hammer. I went out to that car and I did a number on its underside. Whacked it up. Bent the tail pipe double. Ripped the muffler loose. By the time I was done with the car it looked worse than any typical Indian car that has been driven all its life on reservation roads, which they always say are like government promises—full of holes. It just about hurt me, I'll tell you that! I threw dirt in the carburetor and I ripped all the electric tape off the seats. I made it look just as beat up as I could. Then I sat back and waited for Henry to find it.

Still, it took him over a month. That was all right, because it was just getting warm enough, not melting, but warm enough to work outside.

"Lyman," he says, walking in one day, "that red car looks like shit."

"Well it's old," I says. "You got to expect that."

"No way!" says Henry. "That car's a classic! But you went and ran the piss right out of it, Lyman, and you know it don't deserve that. I kept that car in A-one shape. You don't remember. You're too young. But when I left, that car was running like a watch. Now I don't even know if I can get it to start again, let alone get it anywhere near its old condition."

"Well you try," I said, like I was getting mad, "but I say it's a piece of junk."

Then I walked out before he could realize I knew he'd strung together more than six words at once.

After that I thought he'd freeze himself to death working on that car. He was out there all day, and at night he rigged up a little lamp, ran a cord out the window, and had himself some light to see by while he worked. He was better than he had been before, but that's still not saying much. It was easier for him to do the things the rest of us did. He ate more slowly and didn't jump up and down during the meal to get this or that or look out the window. I put my hand in the back of the TV set, I admit, and fiddled around with it good, so that it was almost impossible now to get a clear picture. He didn't look at it very often anyway. He was always out with that car or going off to get parts for it. By the time it was really melting outside, he had it fixed.

I had been feeling down in the dumps about Henry around this time. We had always been together before. Henry and Lyman. But he was such a loner now that I didn't know how to take it. So I jumped at the chance one day when Henry seemed friendly. It's not that he smiled or anything. He just said, "Let's take that old shitbox for a spin." Just the way he said it made me think he could be coming around.

We went out to the car. It was spring. The sun was shining very bright. My only sister, Bonita, who was just eleven years old, came out and made us stand together for a picture. Henry leaned his elbow on the red car's windshield, and he took his other arm and put it over my shoulder, very carefully, as though it was heavy for him to lift and he didn't want to bring the weight down all at once.

"Smile," Bonita said, and he did.

That picture, I never look at it anymore. A few months ago, I don't know why, I got his picture out and tacked it on the wall. I felt good about Henry at the time, close to him. I felt good having his picture on the wall, until one night when I was looking at television. I was a little drunk and stoned. I looked up at the wall and Henry was staring at me. I don't know what it was, but his smile had changed, or maybe it was gone. All I know is I couldn't stay in the same room with that picture. I was shaking. I got up, closed the door, and went into the kitchen. A little later my friend Ray came over and we both went back into that room. We put the picture in a brown bag, folded the bag over and over tightly, then put it way back in a closet.

I still see that picture now, as if it tugs at me, whenever I pass that closet door. The picture is very clear in my mind. It was so sunny that day Henry had to squint against the glare. Or maybe the camera Bonita held flashed like a mirror, blinding him, before she snapped the picture. My face is right out in the sun, big and round. But he might have drawn back, because the shadows on his face are deep as holes. There are two shadows curved like little hooks around the ends of his smile, as if to frame it and try to keep it there—that one, first smile that looked like it might have hurt his face. He has his field jacket on and the worn-in clothes he'd come back in and kept wearing ever since. After Bonita took the picture, she went into the house and we got into the car. There was a full cooler in the trunk. We started off, east, toward Pembina and the Red River because Henry said he wanted to see the high water.

The trip over there was beautiful. When everything starts changing, drying up, clearing off, you feel like your whole life is starting. Henry felt it, too. The top was down and the car hummed like a top. He'd really put it back in shape, even the tape on the seats was very carefully put down and glued back in layers. It's not that he smiled again or even joked, but his face looked to me as if it was clear, more peaceful. It looked as though he wasn't thinking of anything in particular except the bare fields and windbreaks and houses we were passing.

The river was high and full of winter trash when we got there. The sun was still out, but it was colder by the river. There were still little clumps of dirty snow here and there on the banks. The water hadn't gone over the banks yet, but it would, you could tell. It was just at its limit, hard swollen glossy like an old gray scar. We made ourselves a fire, and we sat down and watched the current go. As I watched it I felt something squeezing inside me and tightening and trying to let go all at the same time. I knew I was not just feeling it myself; I knew I was feeling what Henry was going through at that moment. Except that I couldn't stand it, the closing and opening. I jumped to my feet. I took Henry by the shoulders and I started shaking him. "Wake up," I says, "wake up, wake up, wake up!" I didn't know what had come over me. I sat down beside him again.

His face was totally white and hard. Then it broke, like stones break all of a sudden when water boils up inside them.

"I know it," he says. "I know it. I can't help it. It's no use."

We start talking. He said he knew what I'd done with the car. It was obvious it had been whacked out of shape and not just neglected. He said he wanted to give the car to me for good now, it was no use. He said he'd fixed it just to give it back and I should take it.

"No way," I says, "I don't want it."

"That's okay," he says, "you take it."

"I don't want it, though," I says back to him, and then to emphasize, just to emphasize, you understand, I touch his shoulder. He slaps my hand off.

"Take that car," he says.

"No," I say, "make me," I say, and then he grabs my jacket and rips the arm loose. That jacket is a class act, suede with tags and zippers. I push Henry backwards, off the log. He jumps up and bowls me over. We go down in a clinch and come up swinging hard, for all we're worth, with our fists. He socks my jaw so hard I feel like it swings loose. Then I'm at his ribcage and land a good one under his chin so his head snaps back. He's dazzled. He looks at me and I look at him and then his eyes are full of tears and blood and at first I think he's crying. But no, he's laughing. "Ha! Ha!" he says. "Ha! Ha! Take good care of it."

"Okay," I says, "okay, no problem. Ha! Ha!"

I can't help it, and I start laughing, too. My face feels fat and strange, and after a while I get a beer from the cooler in the trunk, and when I hand it to Henry he takes his shirt and wipes my germs off. "Hoof-and-mouth disease," he says. For some reason this cracks me up, and so we're really laughing for a while, and then we drink all the rest of the beers one by one and throw them in the river and see how far, how fast, the current takes them before they fill up and sink.

"You want to go on back?" I ask after a while. "Maybe we could snag a couple nice Kashpaw girls."

He says nothing. But I can tell his mood is turning again.

"They're all crazy, the girls up here, every damn one of them."

"You're crazy too," I say, to jolly him up. "Crazy Lamartine boys!"

He looks as though he will take this wrong at first. His face twists, then clears, and he jumps up on his feet. "That's right!" he says. "Crazier 'n hell. Crazy Indians!"

I think it's the old Henry again. He throws off his jacket and starts swinging his legs out from the knees like a fancy dancer. He's down doing something between a grouse dance and a bunny hop, no kind of dance I ever saw before, but neither has anyone else on all this green growing earth. He's wild. He wants to pitch whoopee! He's up and at me and all over. All this time I'm laughing so hard, so hard my belly is getting tied up in a knot.

"Got to cool me off!" he shouts all of a sudden. Then he runs over to the river and jumps in.

There's boards and other things in the current. It's so high. No sound comes from the river after the splash he makes, so I run right over. I look around. It's getting dark. I see he's halfway across the water already, and I know he didn't swim there but the current took him. It's far. I hear his voice, though, very clearly across it.

"My boots are filling," he says.

He says this in a normal voice, like he just noticed and he doesn't know what to think of it. Then he's gone. A branch comes by. Another branch. And I go in.

By the time I get out of the river, off the snag I pulled myself onto, the sun is down. I walk back to the car, turn on the high beams, and drive it up the bank. I put it in first gear and then I take my foot off the clutch. I get out, close the door, and watch it plow softly into the water. The headlights reach in as they go down, searching, still lighted even after the water swirls over the back end. I wait. The wires short out. It is all finally dark. And then there is only the water, the sound of it going and running and going and running and running.

QUESTIONS
1. Characterize Lyman, the narrator. Why does he refer to himself in the third person in the opening paragraph?   **2.** In the sixth section of the story, why does Lyman move forward in time to describe the photograph taken by his sister and his feelings about it?   **3.** Why does Lyman feel that *repose* is the precise word to describe the red convertible?   **4.** How does the episode about Susy's hair relate to the theme of the story?   **5.** Does it make a difference that it is the Vietnam War (rather than, say, the Second World War) that Henry never recovers from? Explain.

WRITING TOPICS
1. Discuss the meaning of the red convertible to Lyman and Henry and its function in the story.   **2.** In what ways is it significant that Lyman and Henry are Native Americans?

INNOCENCE
AND
EXPERIENCE

Il castello di carte (The House of Cards) by Zinaida Serebriakova

POETRY

The Chimney Sweeper

1789

WILLIAM BLAKE   [1757–1827]

When my mother died I was very young,
And my Father sold me while yet my tongue
Could scarcely cry "'weep! 'weep! 'weep! 'weep!"
So your chimneys I sweep, and in soot I sleep.   5

There's little Tom Dacre, who cried when his head,
That curled like a lamb's back, was shaved: so I said,
"Hush, Tom! never mind it, for when your head's bare
You know that the soot cannot spoil your white hair."   10

And so he was quiet and that very night
As Tom was a-sleeping, he had such a sight!
That thousands of sweepers, Dick, Joe, Ned, and Jack,
Were all of them locked up in coffins of black.

And by came an Angel who had a bright key,   15
And he opened the coffins and set them all free;
Then down a green plain leaping, laughing, they run,
And wash in a river, and shine in the Sun.

Then naked and white, all their bags left behind,
They rise upon clouds and sport in the wind;   20
And the Angel told Tom, if he'd be a good boy,
He'd have God for his father, and never want joy.

And so Tom awoke; and we rose in the dark,
And got with our bags and our brushes to work.
Though the morning was cold, Tom was happy and warm;
So if all do their duty they need not fear harm.

The Tyger

1794

WILLIAM BLAKE [1757–1827]

Tyger! Tyger! burning bright
In the forests of the night,
What immortal hand or eye
Could frame thy fearful symmetry?

In what distant deeps or skies   5
Burnt the fire of thine eyes?
On what wings dare he aspire?
What the hand dare seize the fire?

And what shoulder, & what art,
Could twist the sinews of thy heart?   10
And when thy heart began to beat,
What dread hand? & what dread feet?

What the hammer? what the chain?
In what furnace was thy brain?
What the anvil? what dread grasp   15
Dare its deadly terrors clasp?

When the stars threw down their spears,
And water'd heaven with their tears,
Did he smile his work to see?
Did he who made the Lamb make thee?   20

Tyger! Tyger! burning bright
In the forests of the night,
What immortal hand or eye
Dare frame thy fearful symmetry?

The Garden of Love

1793

WILLIAM BLAKE [1757–1827]

I went to the Garden of Love,
And saw what I never had seen:
A Chapel was built in the midst,
Where I used to play on the green.

And the gates of this Chapel were shut,   5
And "Thou shalt not" writ over the door;
So I turn'd to the Garden of Love,
That so many sweet flowers bore,

And I saw it was filled with graves,
And tomb-stones where flowers should be: 10
And Priests in black gowns were walking their rounds,
And binding with briars my joys & desires.

QUESTIONS
1. What meanings does the word *love* have in this poem?   **2.** What is Blake's
judgment on established religion?   **3.** Explain the meaning of "Chapel" (l. 3) and of
"briars" (l. 12).

WRITING TOPIC
Read the definition of irony in the glossary of literary terms. Write an essay in which
you distinguish between the types of irony used in "The Chimney Sweeper" and
"The Garden of Love."

London   1794

WILLIAM BLAKE   [1757–1827]

I wander through each chartered¹ street,
Near where the chartered Thames does flow
And mark in every face I meet
Marks of weakness, marks of woe.

In every cry of every man,   5
In every infant's cry of fear,
In every voice; in every ban,
The mind-forged manacles I hear:

How the chimney-sweeper's cry
Every blackening church appalls,   10
And the hapless soldier's sigh
Runs in blood down palace-walls.

London
¹ Preempted by the state and leased out under royal patent.

But most, through midnight streets I hear
How the youthful harlot's curse
Blasts the new-born infant's tear,   15
And blights with plagues the marriage-hearse.

To a Mouse   1786
ON TURNING HER UP IN HER NEST
WITH THE PLOUGH, NOVEMBER, 1785

ROBERT BURNS   [1759–1796]

Wee, sleekit,° cow'rin, tim'rous beastie,   *sleck*
O, what a panic's in thy breastie!
Thou need na start awa sae hasty,
   Wi' bickering° brattle!°   *hurried/scamper*
I wad be laith° to rin an' chase thee,   *reluctant* 5
   Wi' murd'ring pattle!°   *plowstaff*

I'm truly sorry man's dominion
Has broken Nature's social union,
An' justifies that ill opinion
   Which makes thee startle   10
At me, thy poor earth-born companion,
   An' fellow-mortal!

I doubt na, whiles,° but thou may thieve;   *sometimes*
What then? poor beastie, thou maun° live!   *must*
A daimen° icker° in a thrave°   *occasional/corn-ear/shock* 15
   'S a sma' request:
I'll get a blessin wi' the lave,°   *rest*
   And never miss't!

Thy wee bit housie, too, in ruin!
Its silly wa's the win's are strewin'   20
An' naething, now, to big° a new ane,   *build*
   O' foggage° green!   *mosses*
An' bleak December's winds ensuin,
   Baith snell° an' keen!   *bitter*

Thou saw the fields laid bare and waste,   25
An' weary winter comin fast,
An' cozie here, beneath the blast,
   Thou thought to dwell,

Till crash! the cruel coulter° past   plowshare
        Out thro' thy cell.   30

That wee bit heap o' leaves an' stibble
Has cost thee mony a weary nibble!
Now thou's turned out, for a' thy trouble,
        But° house or hald,   without
To thole° the winter's sleety dribble,   endure 35
        An' cranreuch° cauld!   hoarfrost

But, Mousie, thou art no thy lane°   not alone
In proving foresight may be vain:
The best laid schemes o' mice an' men
        Gang° aft a-gley.°   go/awry 40
An' lea'e us nought but grief an' pain
        For promised joy.

Still thou art blest, compared wi' me!
The present only toucheth thee:
But och! I backward cast my e'e   45
        On prospects drear!
An' forward, tho' I canna see,
        I guess an' fear!

Lines[1]   1798

COMPOSED A FEW MILES ABOVE TINTERN ABBEY ON REVISITING THE BANKS OF THE WYE DURING A TOUR. JULY 13, 1798

WILLIAM WORDSWORTH   [1770–1850]

Five years have passed;[2] five summers, with the length
Of five long winters! and again I hear
These waters, rolling from their mountain-springs
With a soft inland murmur. Once again
Do I behold these steep and lofty cliffs,   5

Lines
   [1] Wordsworth wrote this poem during a four- or five-day walking tour through the Wye valley with his sister Dorothy.
   [2] The poet had visited the region on a solitary walking tour in August 1793 when he was twenty-three years old.

That on a wild secluded scene impress
Thoughts of more deep seclusion; and connect
The landscape with the quiet of the sky.
The day is come when I again repose
Here, under this dark sycamore, and view   10
These plots of cottage ground, these orchard tufts,
Which at this season, with their unripe fruits,
Are clad in one green hue, and lose themselves
'Mid groves and copses. Once again I see
These hedgerows, hardly hedgerows, little lines   15
Of sportive wood run wild; these pastoral farms,
Green to the very door; and wreaths of smoke
Sent up, in silence, from among the trees!
With some uncertain notice, as might seem
Of vagrant dwellers in the houseless woods,   20
Or of some Hermit's cave, where by his fire
The Hermit sits alone.

                    These beauteous forms,
Through a long absence, have not been to me
As is a landscape to a blind man's eye;
But oft, in lonely rooms, and 'mid the din   25
Of towns and cities, I have owed to them
In hours of weariness, sensations sweet,
Felt in the blood, and felt along the heart;
And passing even into my purer mind,
With tranquil restoration—feelings too   30
Of unremembered pleasure; such, perhaps,
As have no slight or trivial influence
On that best portion of a good man's life,
His little, nameless, unremembered, acts
Of kindness and of love. Nor less, I trust,   35
To them I may have owed another gift,
Of aspect more sublime; that blessed mood,
In which the burthen of the mystery,
In which the heavy and the weary weight
Of all this unintelligible world,   40
Is lightened—that serene and blessed mood,
In which the affections gently lead us on—
Until, the breath of this corporeal frame
And even the motion of our human blood
Almost suspended, we are laid asleep   45
In body, and become a living soul;
While with an eye made quiet by the power
Of harmony, and the deep power of joy,
We see into the life of things.

                        If this
Be but a vain belief, yet, oh! how oft—   50
In darkness and amid the many shapes
Of joyless daylight; when the fretful stir
Unprofitable, and the fever of the world,
Have hung upon the beatings of my heart—
How oft, in spirit, have I turned to thee,   55
O sylvan Wye! thou wanderer through the woods,
How often has my spirit turned to thee!

   And now, with gleams of half-extinguished thought
With many recognitions dim and faint,
And somewhat of a sad perplexity,   60
The picture of the mind revives again;
While here I stand, not only with the sense
Of present pleasure, but with pleasing thoughts
That in this moment there is life and food
For future years. And so I dare to hope,   65
Though changed, no doubt, from what I was when first
I came among these hills; when like a roe
I bounded o'er the mountains, by the sides
Of the deep rivers, and the lonely streams,
Wherever nature led—more like a man   70
Flying from something that he dreads than one
Who sought the thing he loved. For nature then
(The coarser pleasures of my boyish days,
And their glad animal movements all gone by)
To me was all in all.—I cannot paint   75
What then I was. The sounding cataract
Haunted me like a passion; the tall rock,
The mountain, and the deep and gloomy wood,
Their colors and their forms, were then to me
An appetite; a feeling and a love,   80
That had no need of a remoter charm,
By thought supplied, nor any interest
Unborrowed from the eye.—That time is past,
And all its aching joys are now no more,
And all its dizzy raptures. Not for this   85
Faint[3] I, nor mourn nor murmur; other gifts
Have followed; for such loss, I would believe,
Abundant recompense. For I have learned
To look on nature, not as in the hour
Of thoughtless youth; but hearing oftentimes   90

---

[3]Lose heart.

The still, sad music of humanity,
Nor harsh nor grating, though of ample power
To chasten and subdue. And I have felt
A presence that disturbs me with the joy
Of elevated thoughts; a sense sublime   95
Of something far more deeply interfused,
Whose dwelling is the light of setting suns,
And the round ocean and the living air,
And the blue sky, and in the mind of man:
A motion and a spirit, that impels   100
All thinking things, all objects of all thought,
And rolls through all things. Therefore am I still
A lover of the meadows and the woods,
And mountains; and of all that we behold
From this green earth; of all the mighty world   105
Of eye, and ear—both what they half create,
And what perceive; well pleased to recognize
In nature and the language of the sense
The anchor of my purest thoughts, the nurse,
The guide, the guardian of my heart, and soul   110
Of all my moral being.

                    Nor perchance,
If I were not thus taught, should I the more
Suffer my genial spirits to decay:
For thou art with me here upon the banks   115
Of this fair river; thou my dearest Friend,[4]
My dear, dear Friend; and in thy voice I catch
The language of my former heart, and read
My former pleasures in the shooting lights
Of thy wild eyes. Oh! yet a little while   120
May I behold in thee what I was once,
My dear, dear Sister! and this prayer I make,
Knowing that Nature never did betray
The heart that loved her; 'tis her privilege,
Through all the years of this our life, to lead   125
From joy to joy: for she can so inform
The mind that is within us, so impress
With quietness and beauty, and so feed
With lofty thoughts, that neither evil tongues,
Rash judgments, nor the sneers of selfish men,   130
Nor greetings where no kindness is, nor all

---

[4] The poet addresses his sister Dorothy.

The dreary intercourse of daily life,
Shall e'er prevail against us, or disturb
Our cheerful faith, that all which we behold
Is full of blessings. Therefore let the moon   135
Shine on thee in thy solitary walk;
And let the misty mountain winds be free
To blow against thee: and, in after years,
When these wild ecstasies shall be matured
Into a sober pleasure; when thy mind   140
Shall be a mansion for all lovely forms,
Thy memory be as a dwelling place
For all sweet sounds and harmonies; oh! then,
If solitude, or fear, or pain, or grief
Should be thy portion, with what healing thoughts   145
Of tender joy wilt thou remember me,
And these my exhortations! Nor, perchance—
If I should be where I no more can hear
Thy voice, nor catch from thy wild eyes these gleams
Of past existence[5]—wilt thou then forget   150
That on the banks of this delightful stream
We stood together; and that I, so long
A worshiper of Nature, hither came
Unwearied in that service; rather say
With warmer love—oh! with far deeper zeal   155
Of holier love. Nor wilt thou then forget,
That after many wanderings, many years
Of absence, these steep woods and lofty cliffs,
And this green pastoral landscape, were to me
More dear, both for themselves and for thy sake!   160

QUESTIONS

1. In this poem the poet distinguishes between two important periods in his life: the first is described in lines 65–83, and the second is described in lines 83–111. How does he characterize these two periods?   **2.** The poem describes a visit to a familiar scene of the poet's youth and includes a meditation upon the changes that have occurred. Are the changes in the poet, the scene itself, or both?

WRITING TOPIC

Discuss the ways in which the poet contrasts the city and the countryside.

---

[5] I.e., the poet's past experience. Note lines 116–119.

On First Looking into Chapman's Homer[1]

1816

JOHN KEATS   [1795–1821]

Much have I travelled in the realms of gold,
And many goodly states and kingdoms seen:
Round many western islands have I been
Which bards in fealty to Apollo[2] hold.
Oft of one wide expanse had I been told   5
That deep-browed Homer ruled as his demesne;°   realm
Yet did I never breathe its pure serene°   clear air
Till I heard Chapman speak out loud and bold:
Then felt I like some watcher of the skies
When a new planet swims into his ken;   10
Or like stout Cortez[3] when with eagle eyes
He stared at the Pacific—and all his men
Looked at each other with a wild surmise—
    Silent, upon a peak in Darien.

My Last Duchess

1842

ROBERT BROWNING   [1812–1889]

FERRARA

That's my last Duchess painted on the wall,
Looking as if she were alive. I call
That piece a wonder, now: Frà Pandolf's[1] hands
Worked busily a day, and there she stands.
Will't please you sit and look at her? I said   5
"Frà Pandolf" by design, for never read
Strangers like you that pictured countenance,

On First Looking into Chapman's Homer
  [1] George Chapman published translations of *The Iliad* (1611) and *The Odyssey* (1616).
  [2] The Greek and Roman god of poetry.
  [3] Keats mistakenly attributes the discovery of the Pacific Ocean by Europeans to Hernando Cortez (1485–1547), the Spanish conqueror of Mexico. Vasco Nuñez de Balboa (1475–1517) first saw the Pacific from a mountain located in eastern Panama.

My Last Duchess
  [1] Frà Pandolf and Claus of Innsbruck (mentioned in the last line) are fictitious artists.

The depth and passion of its earnest glance,
But to myself they turned (since none puts by
The curtain I have drawn for you, but I)   10
And seemed as they would ask me, if they durst,
How such a glance came there; so, not the first
Are you to turn and ask thus. Sir, 'twas not
Her husband's presence only, called that spot
Of joy into the Duchess' cheek: perhaps   15
Frà Pandolf chanced to say "Her mantle laps
"Over my lady's wrist too much," or "Paint
"Must never hope to reproduce the faint
"Half-flush that dies along her throat": such stuff
Was courtesy, she thought, and cause enough   20
For calling up that spot of joy. She had
A heart—how shall I say?—too soon made glad,
Too easily impressed; she liked whate'er
She looked on, and her looks went everywhere.
Sir, 'twas all one! My favor at her breast,   25
The dropping of the daylight in the West,
The bough of cherries some officious fool
Broke in the orchard for her, the white mule
She rode with round the terrace—all and each
Would draw from her alike the approving speech,   30
Or blush, at least. She thanked men—good! but thanked
Somehow—I know not how—as if she ranked
My gift of a nine-hundred-years-old name
With anybody's gift. Who'd stoop to blame
This sort of trifling? Even had you skill   35
In speech—which I have not—to make your will
Quite clear to such an one, and say, "Just this
"Or that in you disgusts me; here you miss,
"Or there exceed the mark"—and if she let
Herself be lessoned° so, nor plainly set   taught   40
Her wits to yours, forsooth, and made excuse,
—E'en then would be some stooping; and I choose
Never to stoop. Oh sir, she smiled, no doubt,
Whene'er I passed her; but who passed without
Much the same smile? This grew; I gave commands;   45
Then all smiles stopped together. There she stands
As if alive. Will't please you rise? We'll meet
The company below, then. I repeat,
The Count your master's known munificence°   generosity
Is ample warrant that no just pretense   50
Of mine for dowry will be disallowed;
Though his fair daughter's self, as I avowed
At starting, is my object. Nay, we'll go

Together down, sir. Notice Neptune, though,
Taming a sea-horse, thought a rarity,   55
Which Claus of Innsbruck cast in bronze for me!

QUESTIONS
1. To whom is the Duke speaking, and what is the occasion? **2.** What does a comparison between the Duke's feelings about his artworks and his feelings about his last Duchess reveal about his character? **3.** What became of the Duke's last Duchess? **4.** Does this poem rely upon irony? Explain.

WRITING TOPIC
Write an essay in which you argue that the reader is or is not meant to sympathize with the Duke's characterization of his wife.

I Felt a Funeral, in My Brain   (1861)

EMILY DICKINSON   [1830–1886]

I felt a Funeral, in my Brain,
And Mourners to and fro
Kept treading—treading—till it seemed
That Sense was breaking through—

And when they all were seated,   5
A Service, like a Drum—
Kept beating—beating—till I thought
My Mind was going numb—

And then I heard them lift a Box
And creak across my Soul   10
With those same Boots of Lead, again,
Then Space—began to toll,

As all the Heavens were a Bell,
And Being, but an Ear,
And I, and Silence, some strange Race   15
Wrecked, solitary, here—

And then a Plank in Reason, broke,
And I dropped down, and down—
And hit a World, at every plunge,
And Finished knowing—then—   20

Hap   1898

THOMAS HARDY   [1840–1928]

If but some vengeful god would call to me
From up the sky, and laugh: "Thou suffering thing,
Know that thy sorrow is my ecstasy,
That thy love's loss is my hate's profiting!"

Then would I bear it, clench myself, and die,   5
Steeled by the sense of ire unmerited;
Half-eased in that a Powerfuller than I
Had willed and meted me the tears I shed.

But not so. How arrives it joy lies slain,
And why unblooms the best hope ever sown?   10
—Crass Casualty° obstructs the sun and rain,   chance
And dicing Time for gladness casts a moan. . . .
These purblind Doomsters[1] had as readily strown
Blisses about my pilgrimage as pain.

The Ruined Maid   1902

THOMAS HARDY   [1840–1928]

"O Melia, my dear, this does everything crown!
Who could have supposed I should meet you in Town?
And whence such fair garments, such prosperi-ty?"
"O didn't you know I'd been ruined?" said she.

"You left us in tatters, without shoes or socks,   5
Tired of digging potatoes, and spudding up docks;°   digging herbs
And now you've gay bracelets and bright feathers three!"
"Yes: that's how we dress when we're ruined," said she.

"At home in the barton° you said 'thee' and 'thou,'   farmyard
And 'thik onn,' and 'theäs oon,' and 't'other'; but now   10
Your talking quite fits 'ee for high compa-ny!"
"Some polish is gained with one's ruin," said she.

Hap
[1] Those who decide one's fate.

"Your hands were like paws then, your face blue and bleak
But now I'm bewitched by your delicate cheek,
And your little gloves fit as on any la-dy!"   15
"We never do work when we're ruined," said she.

"You used to call home-life a hag-ridden dream,
And you'd sigh, and you'd sock; but at present you seem
To know not of megrims° or melancho-ly!"   sick headaches
"True. One's pretty lively when ruined," said she.   20

"I wish I had feathers, a fine sweeping gown,
And a delicate face, and could strut about Town!"
"My dear—a raw country girl, such as you be,
Cannot quite expect that. You ain't ruined," said she.

Spring and Fall   1880
TO A YOUNG CHILD

GERARD MANLEY HOPKINS   [1844–1889]

Márgarét, áre you gríeving
Over Goldengrove unleaving?°   losing leaves
Leáves, líke the things of man, you
With your fresh thoughts care for, can you?
Áh! ás the heart grows older   5
It will come to such sights colder
By and by, nor spare a sigh
Though worlds of wanwood leafmeal¹ lie;
And yet you wíll weep and know why.
Now no matter, child, the name: 10
Sórrow's spríngs are the same.
Nor mouth had, no nor mind, expressed
What heart heard of, ghost° guessed: soul
It ís the blight man was born for,
It is Margaret you mourn for.   15

QUESTIONS
1. In this poem Margaret grieves over the passing of spring and the coming of fall.
What does the coming of fall symbolize?   2. Why, when Margaret grows older, will
she not sigh over the coming of fall?   3. What are "Sorrow's springs" (l. 11)?

Spring and Fall
¹ Pale woods littered with mouldering leaves.

When I Was One-and-Twenty   1896

A. E. HOUSMAN   [1859–1936]

When I was one-and-twenty
    I heard a wise man say,
"Give crowns and pounds and guineas
    But not your heart away;
Give pearls away and rubies   5
    But keep your fancy free."
But I was one-and-twenty,
    No use to talk to me.

When I was one-and-twenty
    I heard him say again,   10
"The heart out of the bosom
    Was never given in vain;
'Tis paid with sighs a plenty
    And sold for endless rue."
And I am two-and-twenty,   15
    And oh, 'tis true, 'tis true.

Terence, This Is Stupid Stuff[1]   1896

A. E. HOUSMAN   [1859–1936]

   "Terence, this is stupid stuff:
You eat your victuals fast enough;
There can't be much amiss, 'tis clear,
To see the rate you drink your beer.
But oh, good Lord, the verse you make,   5
It gives a chap the bellyache.
The cow, the old cow, she is dead;
It sleeps well, the hornéd head:
We poor lads, 'tis our turn now
To hear such tunes as killed the cow.   10
Pretty friendship 'tis to rhyme
Your friends to death before their time

Terence, This Is Stupid Stuff
  [1] Housman originally titled the volume in which this poem appeared *The Poems of Terence Hearsay.* Terence was a Roman satiric playwright.

Moping melancholy mad:
Come, pipe a tune to dance to, lad."

Why, if 'tis dancing you would be,   15
There's brisker pipes than poetry.
Say, for what were hopyards meant,
Or why was Burton built on Trent?[2]
Oh many a peer of England brews
Livelier liquor than the Muse,   20
And malt does more than Milton can
To justify God's ways to man.[3]
Ale, man, ale's the stuff to drink
For fellows whom it hurts to think:
Look into the pewter pot   25
To see the world as the world's not.
And faith, 'tis pleasant till 'tis past:
The mischief is that 'twill not last.

Oh I have been to Ludlow fair
And left my necktie God knows where,   30
And carried halfway home, or near,
Pints and quarts of Ludlow beer:
Then the world seemed none so bad,
And I myself a sterling lad;
And down in lovely muck I've lain,   35
Happy till I woke again.
Then I saw the morning sky:
Heigho, the tale was all a lie;
The world, it was the old world yet,
I was I, my things were wet,   40
And nothing now remained to do
But begin the game anew.

Therefore, since the world has still
Much good, but much less good than ill,
And while the sun and moon endure   45
Luck's a chance, but trouble's sure,
I'd face it as a wise man would,
And train for ill and not for good.
'Tis true the stuff I bring for sale
Is not so brisk a brew as ale: 50

---

[2] The river Trent provides water for the town's brewing industry.
[3] In the invocation to *Paradise Lost*, Milton declares that his epic will "justify the ways of God to men."

Out of a stem that scored the hand
I wrung it in a weary land.
But take it: if the smack is sour,
The better for the embittered hour;
It should do good to heart and head   55
When your soul is in my soul's stead;
And I will friend you, if I may,
In the dark and cloudy day.

   There was a king reigned in the East:
There, when kings will sit to feast,   60
They get their fill before they think
With poisoned meat and poisoned drink.
He gathered all that springs to birth
From the many-venomed earth;
First a little, thence to more,   65
He sampled all her killing store;
And easy, smiling, seasoned sound,
Sate the king when healths went round.
They put arsenic in his meat
And stared aghast to watch him eat;   70
They poured strychnine in his cup
And shook to see him drink it up:
They shook, they stared as white's their shirt:
Them it was their poison hurt.
—I tell the tale that I heard told.   75
Mithridates, he died old.[4]

QUESTIONS
1. What does the speaker of the first fourteen lines object to in Terence's poetry? **2.** What is Terence's response to the criticism of his verse? What function of true poetry is implied by his comparison of bad poetry with liquor?

WRITING TOPIC
How does the story of Mithridates (ll. 59–76) illustrate the theme of the poem?

---

[4] Mithridates, the King of Pontus (in Asia Minor), reputedly immunized himself against poisons by administering to himself gradually increasing doses.

Adam's Curse

1902

WILLIAM BUTLER YEATS [1865–1939]

We sat together at one summer's end,
That beautiful mild woman, your close friend,
And you and I, and talked of poetry.
I said, 'A line will take us hours maybe;
Yet if it does not seem a moment's thought,   5
Our stitching and unstitching has been naught.

Better go down upon your marrow-bones
And scrub a kitchen pavement, or break stones
Like an old pauper, in all kinds of weather;
For to articulate sweet sounds together   10
Is to work harder than all these, and yet
Be thought an idler by the noisy set
Of bankers, schoolmasters, and clergymen
The martyrs call the world.'

          And thereupon   15
That beautiful mild woman for whose sake
There's many a one shall find out all heartache
On finding that her voice is sweet and low
Replied, 'To be born woman is to know—
Although they do not talk of it at school—   20
That we must labour to be beautiful.'

I said, 'It's certain there is no fine thing
Since Adam's fall but needs much labouring.
There have been lovers who thought love should be
So much compounded of high courtesy   25
That they would sigh and quote with learned looks
Precedents out of beautiful old books;
Yet now it seems an idle trade enough.'

We sat grown quiet at the name of love;
We saw the last embers of daylight die,   30
And in the trembling blue-green of the sky
A moon, worn as if it had been a shell
Washed by time's waters as they rose and fell
About the stars and broke in days and years.

I had a thought for no one's but your ears: 35
That you were beautiful, and that I strove

To love you in the old high way of love;
That it had all seemed happy, and yet we'd grown
As weary-hearted as that hollow moon.

Leda and the Swan[1]   1928

WILLIAM BUTLER YEATS   [1865–1939]

A sudden blow: the great wings beating still
Above the staggering girl, her thighs caressed
By the dark webs, her nape caught in his bill,
He holds her helpless breast upon his breast.

How can those terrified vague fingers push   5
The feathered glory from her loosening thighs?
And how can body, laid in that white rush,
But feel the strange heart beating where it lies?

A shudder in the loins engenders there
The broken wall, the burning roof and tower   10
And Agamemnon dead.
                    Being so caught up,
So mastered by the brute blood of the air,
Did she put on his knowledge with his power
Before the indifferent beak could let her drop?   15

Birches   1916

ROBERT FROST   [1874–1963]

When I see birches bend to left and right
Across the lines of straighter darker trees,
I like to think some boy's been swinging them.
But swinging doesn't bend them down to stay.
Ice-storms do that. Often you must have seen them   5

Leda and the Swan
[1] In Greek myth, Zeus, in the form of a swan, rapes Leda. As a consequence, Helen and
Clytemnestra are born. Each sister marries the king of a city-state; Helen marries Menelaus and
Clytemnestra marries Agamemnon. Helen, the most beautiful woman on earth, elopes with Paris,
a prince of Troy, an act that precipitates the Trojan War in which Agamemnon commands the
combined Greek armies. The war ends with the destruction of Troy. Agamemnon, when he
returns to his home, is murdered by his unfaithful wife.

Loaded with ice a sunny winter morning
After a rain. They click upon themselves
As the breeze rises, and turn many-colored
As the stir cracks and crazes their enamel.
Soon the sun's warmth makes them shed crystal shells   10
Shattering and avalanching on the snow-crust—
Such heaps of broken glass to sweep away
You'd think the inner dome of heaven had fallen.
They are dragged to the withered bracken by the load,
And they seem not to break; though once they are bowed   15
So low for long, they never right themselves:
You may see their trunks arching in the woods
Years afterwards, trailing their leaves on the ground
Like girls on hands and knees that throw their hair
Before them over their heads to dry in the sun.   20
But I was going to say when Truth broke in
With all her matter-of-fact about the ice-storm
I should prefer to have some boy bend them
As he went out and in to fetch the cows—
Some boy too far from town to learn baseball,   25
Whose only play was what he found himself,
Summer or winter, and could play alone.
One by one he subdued his father's trees
By riding them down over and over again
Until he took the stiffness out of them,   30
And not one but hung limp, not one was left
For him to conquer. He learned all there was
To learn about not launching out too soon
And so not carrying the tree away
Clear to the ground. He always kept his poise   35
To the top branches, climbing carefully
With the same pains you use to fill a cup
Up to the brim, and even above the brim.
Then he flung outward, feet first, with a swish,
Kicking his way down through the air to the ground.   40
So was I once myself a swinger of birches.
And so I dream of going back to be.
It's when I'm weary of considerations,
And life is too much like a pathless wood
Where your face burns and tickles with the cobwebs   45
Broken across it, and one eye is weeping
From a twig's having lashed across it open.
I'd like to get away from earth awhile
And then come back to it and begin over.
May no fate willfully misunderstand me   50
And half grant what I wish and snatch me away

Not to return. Earth's the right place for love:
I don't know where it's likely to go better.
I'd like to go by climbing a birch tree,
And climb black branches up a snow-white trunk   55
Toward heaven, till the tree could bear no more,
But dipped its top and set me down again.
That would be good both going and coming back.
One could do worse than be a swinger of birches.

Provide, Provide   1936

ROBERT FROST   [1874–1963]

The witch that came (the withered hag)
To wash the steps with pail and rag,
Was once the beauty Abishag,[1]

The picture pride of Hollywood.
Too many fall from great and good   5
For you to doubt the likelihood.

Die early and avoid the fate.
Or if predestined to die late,
Make up your mind to die in state.

Make the whole stock exchange your own!   10
If need be occupy a throne,
Where nobody can call *you* crone.

Some have relied on what they knew;
Others on being simply true.
What worked for them might work for you.   15

No memory of having starred
Atones for later disregard,
Or keeps the end from being hard.

Provide, Provide
   [1] "Now King David was old and advanced in years; and although they covered him with clothes,
he could not get warm. Therefore his servants said to him, 'Let a young maiden be sought for my
lord the king, and let her wait upon the king, and be his nurse; let her lie in your bosom, that my
lord the king may be warm.' So they sought for a beautiful maiden throughout all the territory of
Israel, and found Abishag, the Shunammite, and brought her to the king. The maiden was very
beautiful. . . ."—I Kings 1:1–4.

Better to go down dignified
With boughten friendship at your side   20
Than none at all. Provide, provide!

To Carry the Child   1966

STEVIE SMITH   [1902–1971]

To carry the child into adult life
Is good? I say it is not,
To carry the child into adult life
Is to be handicapped.

The child in adult life is defenceless   5
And if he is grown-up, knows it,
And the grown-up looks at the childish part
And despises it.

The child, too, despises the clever grown-up,
The man-of-the-world, the frozen,   10
For the child has the tears alive on his cheek
And the man has none of them.

As the child has colours, and the man sees no
Colours or anything,
Being easy only in things of the mind,   15
The child is easy in feeling.

Easy in feeling, easily excessive
And in excess powerful,
For instance, if you do not speak to the child
He will make trouble.   20

You would say a man had the upper hand
Of the child, if a child survive,
But I say the child has fingers of strength
To strangle the man alive.

Oh! it is not happy, it is never happy,   25
To carry the child into adulthood,
Let the children lie down before full growth
And die in their infanthood
And be guilty of no man's blood.

But oh the poor child, the poor child, what can he do,   30
Trapped in a grown-up carapace,
But peer outside of his prison room
With the eye of an anarchist?

Not Waving but Drowning   1972

STEVIE SMITH   [1902–1971]

Nobody heard him, the dead man,
But still he lay moaning:
I was much further out than you thought
And not waving but drowning.

Poor chap, he always loved larking   5
And now he's dead
It must have been too cold for him his heart gave way,
They said.

Oh, no no no, it was too cold always
(Still the dead one lay moaning)   10
I was much too far out all my life
And not waving but drowning.

QUESTIONS
1. Explain the paradox in the first and last stanzas, where the speaker describes someone dead as moaning.   **2.** Who do you suppose the *you* of line 3 is? And the *they* of line 8?   **3.** Explain the meaning of line 7. Can it be interpreted in more than one way? Explain.   **4.** Explain the meanings of *drowning*.   **5.** The only thing we learn about the dead man is that "he always loved larking." Why is this detail significant? What kind of man do you think he was?   **6.** Does the speaker know more about the dead man than his friends did? Explain.

WRITING TOPICS
1. Write an essay describing how you or someone you know suffered the experience of "not waving but drowning."   **2.** Write an essay describing how you came to the realization that someone close to you was not the person you thought he or she was.

Incident

1925

COUNTEE CULLEN   [1903–1946]

Once riding in old Baltimore,
    Heart-filled, head-filled with glee,
I saw a Baltimorean
    Keep looking straight at me.

Now I was eight and very small,   5
    And he was no whit bigger,
And so I smiled, but he poked out
    His tongue and called me, "Nigger."

I saw the whole of Baltimore
    From May until December: 10
Of all the things that happened there
    That's all that I remember.

Fern Hill

1946

DYLAN THOMAS   (1914–1953)

Now as I was young and easy under the apple boughs
About the lilting house and happy as the grass was green,
    The night above the dingle° starry,   small wooded valley
        Time let me hail and climb
    Golden in the heydays of his eyes,   5
And honored among wagons I was prince of the apple towns
And once below a time I lordly had the trees and leaves
        Trail with daisies and barley
    Down the rivers of the windfall light.

And I was green and carefree, famous among the barns   10
About the happy yard and singing as the farm was home,
    In the sun that is young once only,
        Time let me play and be
    Golden in the mercy of his means,

And green and golden I was huntsman and herdsman, the calves   15
Sang to my horn, the foxes on the hills barked clear and cold,
      And the sabbath rang slowly
    In the pebbles of the holy streams.

All the sun long it was running, it was lovely, the hay
Fields high as the house, the tunes from the chimneys, it was air   20
        And playing, lovely and watery
        And fire green as grass.
        And nightly under the simple stars
As I rode to sleep the owls were bearing the farm away,
All the moon long I heard, blessed among stables, the nightjars[1]   25
    Flying with the ricks, and the horses
      Flashing into the dark.

And then to awake, and the farm, like a wanderer white
With the dew, come back, the cock on his shoulder: it was all
    Shining, it was Adam and maiden,   30
      The sky gathered again
    And the sun grew round that very day.
So it must have been after the birth of the simple light
In the first, spinning place, the spellbound horses walking warm
    Out of the whinnying green stable   35
      On to the fields of praise.

And honored among foxes and pheasants by the gay house
Under the new made clouds and happy as the heart was long,
    In the sun born over and over,
      I ran my heedless ways,   40
    My wishes raced through the house high hay
And nothing I cared, at my sky blue trades, that time allows
In all his tuneful turning so few and such morning songs
    Before the children green and golden
      Follow him out of grace.   45

Nothing I cared, in the lamb white days, that time would take me
Up to the swallow thronged loft by the shadow of my hand,
    In the moon that is always rising,
      Nor that riding to sleep
    I should hear him fly with the high fields   50
And wake to the farm forever fled from the childless land.

---

[1] Nightjars are harsh-sounding nocturnal birds.

Oh as I was young and easy in the mercy of his means,
　　　Time held me green and dying
　　Though I sang in my chains like the sea.

QUESTIONS

1. What emotional impact does the color imagery in the poem provide? **2.** Trace the behavior of "time" in the poem. **3.** Fairy tales often begin with the words *once upon a time.* Why does Thomas alter that formula in line 7? **4.** Explain the paradox in line 53.

WRITING TOPICS

1. Lines 17–18, 30, 45–46 incorporate religious language and biblical allusion. How do those allusions clarify the poet's vision of his childhood? **2.** Compare this poem with Gerard Manley Hopkins's "Spring and Fall."

A Moment Please 　　　　　　　　　　1962

SAMUEL ALLEN [b. 1917]

When I gaze at the sun
　　I walked to the subway booth
　　for change for a dime.
and know that this great earth
　　Two adolescent girls stood there　　　　　　　　　5
　　alive with eagerness to know
is but a fragment from it thrown
　　all in their new found world
　　there was for them to know
in heat and flame a billion years ago,　　　　　　　10
　　they looked at me and brightly asked
　　"Are you Arabian?"
that when this world was lifeless
　　I smiled and cautiously
　　—for one grows cautious—　　　　　　　　　　15
　　shook my head.
as, a billion hence,
　　"Egyptian?"
It shall again be,
　　Again I smiled and shook my head　　　　　　　20
　　and walked away.
what moment is it that I am betrayed,
　　I've gone but seven paces now

oppressed, cast down,
  and from behind comes swift the sneer   25
or warm with love or triumph?
  "Or Nigger?"
  A moment, please
What is it that to fury I am roused?
  for still it takes a moment   30
What meaning for me
  and now
in this homeless clan
  I'll turn
the dupe of space   35
  and smile
the toy of time?
  and nod my head.

Constantly Risking Absurdity 1958

LAWRENCE FERLINGHETTI [b. 1919]

  Constantly risking absurdity
      and death
   whenever he performs
     above the heads
       of his audience   5
  the poet like an acrobat
    climbs on rime
     to a high wire of his own making
 and balancing on eyebeams
     above a sea of faces   10
  paces his way
    to the other side of day
 performing entrechats
    and sleight-of-foot tricks
 and other high theatrics   15
    and all without mistaking
   any thing
    for what it may not be

  For he's the super realist
      who must perforce perceive 20
   taut truth
     before the taking of each stance or step

in his supposed advance
                        toward that still higher perch
where Beauty stands and waits   25
              with gravity
                      to start her death-defying leap

And he
            a little charleychaplin man
                      who may or may not catch   30
      her fair eternal form
                  spreadeagled in the empty air
      of existence

Disqualification   1973

ELIZABETH BREWSTER   [b. 1922]

I am of puritan and loyalist ancestry
and of middle class tastes.
My father never swore in front of ladies,
as he always quaintly called women.
My mother thought that a man was no gentleman   5
if he smoked a cigar without asking her permission;
and she thought all men should be gentlemen,
even though a gentleman would not call himself one,
and all women should be ladies,
even though a lady would not call herself one.   10

I have never taken any drug
stronger than aspirin.
I have never been more than slightly drunk.
I think there are worse vices
than hypocrisy or gentility,   15
or even than voting Conservative.

If I wanted to be fucked
I should probably choose a different word.
(Anyhow, I am not quite sure
whether it is a transitive or an intransitive verb,   20
because it was never given to me to parse.)
Usually I can parse words, analyze sentences,
spell, punctuate,
and recognize the more common metrical forms.

It is almost impossible   25
that I shall ever be
a truly established poet.

This Be the Verse   1974

PHILIP LARKIN   [1922–1985]

They fuck you up, your mum and dad.
   They may not mean to, but they do.
They fill you with the faults they had
   And add some extra, just for you.

But they were fucked up in their turn   5
   By fools in old-style hats and coats,
Who half the time were soppy-stern
   And half at one another's throats.

Man hands on misery to man.
   It deepens like a coastal shelf.   10
Get out as early as you can,
   And don't have any kids yourself.

"More Light! More Light!"[1]   1961
FOR HEINRICH BLÜCHER AND HANNAH ARENDT[2]

ANTHONY HECHT   [b. 1923]

Composed in the Tower[3] before his execution
These moving verses, and being brought at that time
Painfully to the stake, submitted, declaring thus:
"I implore my God to witness that I have made no crime."

"More Light! More Light!"
  [1] These were the last words of the German poet Johann Wolfgang von Goethe (1749–1832).
  [2] Husband and wife who emigrated to the United States from Germany in 1941. Hannah Arendt wrote extensively on political totalitarianism.
  [3] The Tower of London was used as a prison for eminent political prisoners. What follows is an account of a priest's execution for the crime of heresy. The punishment was death by fire, and often a sack of gunpowder was placed at the condemned's neck to shorten the agony.

Nor was he forsaken of courage, but the death was horrible,   5
The sack of gunpowder failing to ignite.
His legs were blistered sticks on which the black sap
Bubbled and burst as he howled for the Kindly Light.

And that was but one, and by no means one of the worst;
Permitted at least his pitiful dignity;   10
And such as were by made prayers in the name of Christ,
That shall judge all men, for his soul's tranquillity.

We move now to outside a German wood.
Three men are there commanded to dig a hole
In which the two Jews are ordered to lie down   15
And be buried by the third, who is a Pole.

Not light from the shrine at Weimar[4] beyond the hill
Nor light from heaven appeared. But he did refuse.
A Lüger[5] settled back deeply in its glove.
He was ordered to change places with the Jews.   20

Much casual death had drained away their souls.
The thick dirt mounted toward the quivering chin.
When only the head was exposed the order came
To dig him out again and to get back in.

No light, no light in the blue Polish eye.   25
When he finished a riding boot packed down the earth.
The Lüger hovered lightly in its glove.
He was shot in the belly and in three hours bled to death.

No prayers or incense rose up in those hours
Which grew to be years, and every day came mute   30
Ghosts from the ovens, sifting through crisp air,
And settled upon his eyes in a black soot.

QUESTIONS
1. What relationship does the event (which occurred in sixteenth-century England) recounted in the first two stanzas bear to the event recounted in the last four stanzas?   **2.** What irony do you find in the title of the poem and the use of the word *light* in lines 8, 17, 18, and 25? How would you define *light* in each case? Can you imagine yourself in the place of the three prisoners in line 14? What would you do?

---

[4] Goethe spent most of his life in Weimar, and his humanistic achievements are honored there in the Goethe National Museum. The event recounted here occurred at Buchenwald, a World War II German concentration camp north of Weimar.

[5] A German automatic pistol.

Curiosity

1959

ALASTAIR REID   [b. 1926]

may have killed the cat; more likely
the cat was just unlucky, or else curious
to see what death was like, having no cause
to go on licking paws, or fathering
litter on litter of kittens, predictably.   5

Nevertheless, to be curious
is dangerous enough. To distrust
what is always said, what seems,
to ask odd questions, interfere in dreams,
leave home, smell rats, have hunches   10
does not endear him to those doggy circles
where well-smelt baskets, suitable wives, good lunches
are the order of things and where prevails
much wagging of incurious heads and tails.

Face it. Curiosity   15
will not cause him to die—
only lack of it will.
Never to want to see
the other side of the hill,
or that improbable country   20
where living is an idyll
(although a probable hell)
would kill us all.
Only the curious
have, if they live, a tale   25
worth telling at all.

Dogs say he loves too much, is irresponsible,
is changeable, marries too many wives,
deserts his children, chills all dinner tables
with tales of his nine lives.   30
Well, he is lucky. Let him be
nine-lived and contradictory,
curious enough to change, prepared to pay
the cat price, which is to die
and die again and again,   35
each time with no less pain.
A cat minority of one

is all that can be counted on
to tell the truth. And what he has to tell
on each return from hell   40
is this: that dying is what the living do,
that dying is what the loving do,
and that dead dogs are those who do not know
that hell is where, to live, they have to go.

First Confession   1961

X. J. KENNEDY   [b. 1929]

Blood thudded in my ears. I scuffed,
    Steps stubborn, to the telltale booth
Beyond whose curtained portal coughed
    The robed repositor of truth.

The slat shot back. The universe   5
    Bowed down his cratered dome to hear
Enumerated my each curse,
    The sip snitched from my old man's beer.

My sloth pride envy lechery,
    The dime held back from Peter's Pence   10
With which I'd bribed my girl to pee
    That I might spy her instruments.

Hovering scale-pans when I'd done
    Settled their balance slow as silt
While in the restless dark I burned   15
    Bright as a brimstone in my guilt

Until as one feeds birds he doled
    Seven Our Fathers and a Hail
Which I to double-scrub my soul
    Intoned twice at the altar rail   20

Where Sunday in seraphic light
    I knelt, as full of grace as most,
And stuck my tongue out at the priest:
    A fresh roost for the Holy Ghost.

Advice to My Son   1965

PETER MEINKE   [b. 1932]

The trick is, to live your days
as if each one may be your last
(for they go fast, and young men lose their lives
in strange and unimaginable ways)
but at the same time, plan long range   5
(for they go slow: if you survive
the shattered windshield and the bursting shell
you will arrive
at our approximation here below
of heaven or hell).   10

To be specific, between the peony and the rose
plant squash and spinach, turnips and tomatoes;
beauty is nectar
and nectar, in a desert, saves—
but the stomach craves stronger sustenance   15
than the honied vine.

Therefore, marry a pretty girl
after seeing her mother;
speak truth to one man,
work with another;   20
and always serve bread with your wine.

But, son,
always serve wine.

QUESTIONS
1. Explain how the advice of lines 17–21 is logically related to the preceding two
stanzas of this poem.   **2.** What do the final two lines tell the reader about the
speaker?

WRITING TOPIC
The advice of the first stanza seems contradictory. In what ways does the second
stanza attempt to resolve the contradiction or explain "The trick" (l. 1)? What do the
various plants and the bread and wine symbolize?

My Mother

1970

ROBERT MEZEY   [b. 1935]

My mother writes from Trenton,
a comedian to the bone
but underneath, serious
and all heart. "Honey," she says,
"be a mensch[1] and Mary too,   5
it's no good to worry, you
are doing the best you can
your Dad and everyone
thinks you turned out very well
as long as you pay your bills   10
nobody can say a word
you can tell them to drop dead
so save a dollar it can't
hurt—remember Frank you went
to highschool with? he still lives   15
with his wife's mother, his wife
works while he writes his books and
did he ever sell a one
the four kids run around naked
36 and he's never had,   20
you'll forgive my expression
even a pot to piss in
or a window to throw it,
such a smart boy he couldn't
read the footprints on the wall   25
honey you think you know all
the answers you don't, please try
to put some money away
believe me it wouldn't hurt
artist shmartist life's too short   30
for that kind of, forgive me,
horseshit, I know what you want
better than you, all that counts
is to make a good living
and the best of everything,   35
as Sholem Aleichem said
he was a great writer did

---

[1] Man, in the sense of "human being."

you ever read his books dear,
you should make what he makes a year
anyway he says some place   40
Poverty is no disgrace
but it's no honor either
that's what I say,
                    love,
                            Mother"   45

The Black Walnut Tree   1992

MARY OLIVER   [b. 1935]

My mother and I debate:
we could sell
the black walnut tree
to the lumberman,
and pay off the mortgage.   5
Likely some storm anyway
will churn down its dark boughs,
smashing the house. We talk
slowly, two women trying
in a difficult time to be wise.   10
Roots in the cellar drains,
I say, and she replies
that the leaves are getting heavier
every year, and the fruit
harder to gather away.   15
But something brighter than money
moves in our blood—an edge
sharp and quick as a trowel
that wants us to dig and sow.
So we talk, but we don't do   20
anything. That night I dream
of my fathers out of Bohemia
filling the blue fields
of fresh and generous Ohio
with leaves and vines and orchards.   25
What my mother and I both know
is that we'd crawl with shame
in the emptiness we'd made
in our own and our fathers' backyard.
So the black walnut tree   30

swings through another year
of sun and leaping winds,
of leaves and bounding fruit,
and, month after month, the whip-
crack of the mortgage.   35

QUESTIONS
1. What arguments support selling the black walnut tree?   **2.** Why do the mother
and daughter not sell it?

WRITING TOPICS
1. In an essay, describe the benefits to the mother and daughter of not selling the
tree, despite all the trouble it causes. Consider what "fathers" (ll. 22 and 29) have to
do with the issue.   **2.** Write about a time when "something brighter than money"
moved in your blood (ll. 16–17).

Memo: 1980

JUNE JORDAN   [b. 1936]

When I hear some woman say she
has finally decided you can spend time with
other women, I wonder what she means: Her
mother? My mother?
I've always despised my woman friends. Even   5
if they introduced me to a man I found
attractive I have never let them become
what you could call my intimates. Why
should I? Men are the ones with the money and
the big way with waiters and the passkey   10
to excitement in strange places of real
danger and the power to make things happen
like babies or war and all these great ideas
about mass magazines for members of the weaker sex
who need permission   15
to eat potatoes or a doctor's opinion on orgasm after death
or the latest word on what the female
executive should do, after hours, wearing
what. They must be morons: women!
Don't you think?   20
I guess you could say
I'm stuck in my ways
as
That Cosmopolitan Girl.

QUESTIONS
1. Explain the title.   **2.** What do the first three lines mean? Why would a woman feel she *can't* spend time with other women?   **3.** Does this poem accurately describe the power relations in our society? Explain.   **4.** Describe the tone of this poem.

WRITING TOPIC
Examine a few issues of *Cosmopolitan* magazine to show how it inspired this poem.

First Light   1991

LINDA HOGAN   [b. 1947]

In early morning
I forget I'm in this world
with crooked chiefs
who make federal deals.

In the first light   5
I remember who rewards me for living,
not bosses
but singing birds and blue sky.

I know I can bathe and stretch,
make jewelry and love   10
the witch and wise woman
living inside, needing to be silenced
and put at rest for work's long day.

In the first light
I offer cornmeal   15
and tobacco.
I say hello to those who came before me,
and to birds
under the eaves,
and budding plants.   20

I know the old ones are here.
And every morning I remember the song
about how buffalo left through a hole in the sky
and how the grandmothers look out from those holes
watching over us   25
from there and from there.

                          For Robin

QUESTIONS
1. Explain what "this world" of line 2 is.   **2.** Who are the "crooked chiefs"? What is a "federal" deal?   **3.** Is the speaker part of the world of chiefs and federal deals? Explain.   **4.** Why does the speaker offer cornmeal and tobacco?   **5.** Explain the title.

WRITING TOPIC
Write an essay in which you speculate on who the poet is and what might have led her to write this poem.

Our Room   1984

MOLLY PEACOCK   [b. 1947]

I tell the children in school sometimes
why I hate alcoholics: my father was one.
"Alcohol" and "disease" I use, and shun
the word "drunk" or even "drinking," since one time   5
the kids burst out laughing when I told them.
I felt as though they were laughing at me.
I waited for them, wounded, remembering how I imagined they'd howl at me
when I was in grade 5. Acting drunk   10
is a guaranteed screamer, especially
for boys. I'm quiet when I sort the junk
of my childhood for them, quiet so we
will all be quiet, and they can ask what
questions they have to and tell about what   15
happened to them, too. The classroom becomes
oddly lonely when we talk about our homes.

QUESTIONS
1. The implication of line 6 is that the children were laughing not at the speaker but at something else. What might that have been?   **2.** Describe the speaker's attitude toward her classmates.   **3.** Explain the title.

WRITING TOPIC
Have you ever experienced shame about your family? Describe what it was that caused the shame, your feelings at the time, and your present feelings about it.

Father Answers His Adversaries   1980

LAWRENCE KEARNEY   [b. 1948]

It's early March, Eisenhower still
president, & Mother's heating up supper
for the third time tonight.
We're at the table doing homework,
& she tells us Father's next in line   5
for foreman, that today he'll know for sure.
He's three hours late.

Half past eight the Chevy
screeches into the carport.
For a minute, nothing.   10
Then the sudden slam, & the thump downstairs
to the basement. Beneath our feet
Father lays into the workbench
with a sledgehammer—the jam jars
of nails, of screws, of nuts & bolts   15
he'd taken years to sort out
exploding against the wall.

Later, sheepish, he comes up,
slumps in his seat & asks for supper.
And when Mother brings his plate   20
& he looks up at her
& she takes his head on her breast,
he blushes, turns away, & spits out
that final, weary-mouthed answer
to all of it—General Motors & the bosses   25
& the union pimps & the punched-out Johnnies,
every yes-man goddam ass-lick
who'd ever been jumped to foreman
over him—*aah, crap's like cream,*
it rises.   30

QUESTIONS

1. How would you characterize the family? Happy? Unhappy? Close-knit?
Explain. **2.** Why do you suppose the father did not get the job as
foreman? **3.** Why is the father described as "sheepish" (l. 18)? Why does he blush
(l. 23)? **4.** Put into your own words the father's answer to his adversaries.

WRITING TOPIC

Write an essay describing someone you know who was unfairly passed over for a promotion (or fired from a job). Did he or she feel the same bitterness and helplessness as the father in this poem? What became of the person?

Plus C'est la Même Chose[1]   1994
LINES WRITTEN UPON CHAPERONING THE SEVENTH GRADE DANCE

KATHERINE McALPINE   [b. 1948]

When did these little girls turn into women?
Lip-glossed and groomed, alarmingly possessed
of polish, poise and, in some cases, breasts,
they're clustered at one corner of the gym in
elaborate indifference to the boys,   5
who, at the other end, convene with cables,
adjusting speakers, tuners and turntables
to make the optimum amount of noise.
If nobody plans to dance, what's this dance for?
Finally the boys all gather in formation,   10
tentatively begin a group migration
across the fearsome distance of the floor—
and then retreat, noticing no one's there.
The girls have gone, en masse, to fix their hair.

QUESTIONS

1. What is the tone of this sonnet? Point to specific elements to support your response.   **2.** Explain the title.   **3.** Explain the appropriateness of "elaborate indifference" (l. 5), "gather in formation" (l. 10), and "migration" (l. 11).

WRITING TOPIC

Write an essay in which you use one of the following as a thesis statement: (1) the poem embodies a traditional, sexist view of gender differences, or (2) the poem describes, without making a judgment, the culturally determined differences between males and females. If you disagree with both of these statements, formulate your own.

---

[1] The title comes from the French expression *plus ça change, plus ç'est la même chose,* which means "the more things change, the more they remain the same."

Womanhood

1987

CATHERINE ANDERSON   [b. 1954]

She slides over
the hot upholstery
of her mother's car,
this schoolgirl of fifteen
who loves humming & swaying   5
with the radio.
Her entry into womanhood
will be like all the other girls'—
a cigarette and a joke,
as she strides up with the rest   10
to a brick factory
where she'll sew rag rugs
from textile strips of kelly green,
bright red, aqua.

When she enters,   15
and the millgate closes,
final as a slap,
there'll be silence.
She'll see fifteen high windows
cemented over to cut out light.   20
Inside, a constant, deafening noise
and warm air smelling of oil,
the shifts continuing on . . .
All day she'll guide cloth along a line
of whirring needles, her arms & shoulders   25
rocking back & forth
with the machines—
200 porch size rugs behind her
before she can stop
to reach up, like her mother,   30
and pick the lint
out of her hair.

QUESTIONS
1. Who are the "other girls" of line 8?   **2.** Explain line 9. What is the effect of the
contrast between the "silence" (l. 18) and the "deafening noise" (l. 21)?   **3.** Ex-

plain the final four lines.   **4.** Is the speaker making a judgment or merely offering a neutral description? Explain.

WRITING TOPIC
Compare and contrast this poem with Katherine McAlpine's "Plus C'est la Même Chose" as social commentary.

INNOCENCE
AND
EXPERIENCE

Belisarius and the Boy, 1802 by Benjamin West

DRAMA

M. Butterfly   1988

DAVID HENRY HWANG   [b. 1957]

CHARACTERS

Rene Gallimard	**Comrade Chin / Suzuki / Shu-Fang**
Song Liling	**Helga**
Marc / Man No. 2 / Consul Sharpless	**Toulon / Man No. 1 / Judge**
Renee / Woman at Party / Pinup Girl	**Dancers**

Playwright's Notes

This play was suggested by international newspaper accounts of a recent es-
pionage trial. For purposes of dramatization, names have been changed, characters created, and incidents devised or altered, and this play does not purport
to be a factual record of real events or real people.

A former French diplomat and a Chinese opera singer have been sentenced
to six years in jail for spying for China after a two-day trial that traced a story
of clandestine love and mistaken sexual identity. . . .
   Mr. Bouriscot was accused of passing information to China after he fell in
love with Mr. Shi, whom he believed for twenty years to be a woman.
                                        —*The New York Times*, May 11, 1986

   I could escape this feeling
   With my China girl . . .
                            —David Bowie & Iggy Pop

Time and Place

The action of the play takes place in a Paris prison in the present, and, in recall,
during the decade 1960–1970 in Beijing, and from 1966 to the present in Paris.

Act I

SCENE I.   M. Gallimard's prison cell. Paris. 1988.

Lights fade up to reveal Rene Gallimard, sixty-five, in a prison cell. He wears a comfortable bathrobe, and looks old and tired. The sparsely furnished cell contains a wooden crate, upon which sits a hot plate with a kettle, and a portable tape recorder. Gallimard sits on the crate staring at the recorder, a sad smile on his face.

Upstage Song, who appears as a beautiful woman in traditional Chinese garb, dances a traditional piece from the Peking Opera, surrounded by the percussive clatter of Chinese music.

Then, slowly, lights and sound cross-fade; the Chinese opera music dissolves into a Western opera, the "Love Duet" from Puccini's Madame Butterfly. *Song continues dancing, now to the Western accompaniment. Though her movements are the same, the difference in music now gives them a balletic quality.*

Gallimard rises, and turns upstage towards the figure of Song, who dances without acknowledging him.

Gallimard.   Butterfly, Butterfly . . .

He forces himself to turn away, as the image of Song fades out, and talks to us.

Gallimard.   The limits of my cell are as such: four-and-a-half meters by five. There's one window against the far wall; a door, very strong, to protect me from autograph hounds. I'm responsible for the tape recorder, the hot plate, and this charming coffee table.

When I want to eat, I'm marched off to the dining room—hot, steaming slop appears on my plate. When I want to sleep, the light bulb turns itself off—the work of fairies. It's an enchanted space I occupy. The French—we know how to run a prison.

But, to be honest, I'm not treated like an ordinary prisoner. Why? Because I'm a celebrity. You see, I make people laugh.

I never dreamed this day would arrive. I've never been considered witty or clever. In fact, as a young boy, in an informal poll among my grammar school classmates, I was voted "least likely to be invited to a party." It's a title I managed to hold on to for many years. Despite some stiff competition.

But now, how the tables turn! Look at me: the life of every social function in Paris. Paris? Why be modest: My fame has spread to Amsterdam, London, New York. Listen to them! In the world's smartest parlors, I'm the one who lifts their spirits!

With a flourish, Gallimard directs our attention to another part of the stage.

SCENE II.   A party. 1988.

Lights go up on a chic-looking parlor, where a well-dressed trio, two men and one woman, make conversation. Gallimard also remains lit; he observes them from his cell.

Woman.   And what of Gallimard?
Man 1.   Gallimard?
Man 2.   Gallimard!
Gallimard *(to us).*   You see? They're all determined to say my name, as if it were some new dance.
Woman.   He still claims not to believe the truth.
Man 1.   What? Still? Even since the trial?
Woman.   Yes. Isn't it mad?
Man 2 *(laughing).*   He says . . . it was dark . . . and she was very modest!

The trio break into laughter.

Man 1.   So—what? He never touched her with his hands?
Man 2.   Perhaps he did, and simply misidentified the equipment. A compelling case for sex education in the schools.
Woman.   To protect the National Security—the Church can't argue with that.
Man 1.   That's impossible! How could he not know?
Man 2.   Simple ignorance.
Man 1.   For twenty years?
Man 2.   Time flies when you're being stupid.
Woman.   Well, I thought the French were ladies' men.
Man 2.   It seems Monsieur Gallimard was overly anxious to live up to his national reputation.
Woman.   Well, he's not very good-looking.
Man 1.   No, he's not.
Man 2.   Certainly not.
Woman.   Actually, I feel sorry for him.
Man 2.   A toast! To Monsieur Gallimard!
Woman.   Yes! To Gallimard!
Man 1.   To Gallimard!
Man 2.   *Vive la différence!*

They toast, laughing. Lights down on them.

SCENE III.   M. Gallimard's cell.

Gallimard *(smiling).*   You see? They toast me. I've become a patron saint of the socially inept. Can they really be so foolish? Men like that—they should be scratching at my door, begging to learn my secrets! For I, Rene Gallimard, you see, I have known, and been loved by . . . the Perfect Woman.

Alone in this cell, I sit night after night, watching our story play through my head, always searching for a new ending, one which redeems my honor, where she returns at last to my arms. And I imagine you—my ideal audience—who come to understand and even, perhaps just a little, to envy me.

He turns on his tape recorder. Over the house speakers, we hear the opening phrases of Madame Butterfly.

Gallimard.   In order for you to understand what I did and why, I must introduce you to my favorite opera: *Madame Butterfly.* By Giacomo Puccini. First produced at La Scala, Milan, in 1904, it is now beloved throughout the Western world.

As Gallimard describes the opera, the tape segues in and out to sections he may be describing.

Gallimard.   And why not? Its heroine, Cio-Cio-San, also known as Butterfly, is a feminine ideal, beautiful and brave. And its hero, the man for whom she gives up everything, is—(*He pulls out a naval officer's cap from under his crate, pops it on his head, and struts about*)—not very good-looking, not too bright, and pretty much a wimp: Benjamin Franklin Pinkerton of the U.S. Navy. As the curtain rises, he's just closed on two great bargains: one on a house, the other on a woman—call it a package deal.

Pinkerton purchased the rights to Butterfly for one hundred yen—in modern currency, equivalent to about . . . sixty-six cents. So, he's feeling pretty pleased with himself as Sharpless, the American consul, arrives to witness the marriage.

Marc, wearing an official cap to designate Sharpless, enters and plays the character.

Sharpless/Marc.   Pinkerton!
Pinkerton/Gallimard.   Sharpless! How's it hangin'? It's a great day, just great. Between my house, my wife, and the rickshaw ride in from town, I've saved nineteen cents just this morning.
Sharpless.   Wonderful. I can see the inscription on your tombstone already: "I saved a dollar, here I lie." (*He looks around.*) Nice house.
Pinkerton.   It's artistic. Artistic, don't you think? Like the way the shoji screens slide open to reveal the wet bar and disco mirror ball? Classy, huh? Great for impressing the chicks.
Sharpless.   "Chicks"? Pinkerton, you're going to be a married man!

Pinkerton.   Well, sort of.

Sharpless.   What do you mean?

Pinkerton.   This country—Sharpless, it is okay. You got all these geisha girls running around—

Sharpless.   I know! I live here!

Pinkerton.   Then, you know the marriage laws, right? I split for one month, it's annulled!

Sharpless.   Leave it to you to read the fine print. Who's the lucky girl?

Pinkerton.   Cio-Cio-San. Her friends call her Butterfly. Sharpless, she eats out of my hand!

Sharpless.   She's probably very hungry.

Pinkerton.   Not like American girls. It's true what they say about Oriental girls. They want to be treated bad!

Sharpless.   Oh, please!

Pinkerton.   It's true!

Sharpless.   Are you serious about this girl?

Pinkerton.   I'm marrying her, aren't I?

Sharpless.   Yes—with generous trade-in terms.

Pinkerton.   When I leave, she'll know what it's like to have loved a real man. And I'll even buy her a few nylons.

Sharpless.   You aren't planning to take her with you?

Pinkerton.   Huh? Where?

Sharpless.   Home!

Pinkerton.   You mean, America? Are you crazy? Can you see her trying to buy rice in St. Louis?

Sharpless.   So, you're not serious.

Pause.

Pinkerton/Gallimard (*as Pinkerton*).   Consul, I am a sailor in port. (*As Gallimard.*) They then proceed to sing the famous duet, "The Whole World Over."

The duet plays on the speakers. Gallimard, as Pinkerton, lip-syncs his lines from the opera.

Gallimard.   To give a rough translation: "The whole world over, the Yankee travels, casting his anchor wherever he wants. Life's not worth living unless he can win the hearts of the fairest maidens, then hotfoot it off the premises ASAP." (*He turns towards Marc.*) In the preceding scene, I played Pinkerton, the womanizing cad, and my friend Marc from school . . . (*Marc bows grandly for our benefit.*) played Sharpless, the sensitive soul of reason. In life, however, our positions were usually—no, always—reversed.

SCENE IV.   École Nationale.[1] Aix-en-Provence. 1947.

Gallimard.   No, Marc, I think I'd rather stay home.

Marc.   Are you crazy?! We are going to Dad's condo in Marseilles! You know what happened last time?

Gallimard.   Of course I do.

Marc.   Of course you don't! You never know. . . . They stripped, Rene!

Gallimard.   Who stripped?

Marc.   The girls!

Gallimard.   Girls? Who said anything about girls?

Marc.   Rene, we're a buncha university guys goin' up to the woods. What are we gonna do—talk philosophy?

Gallimard.   What girls? Where do you get them?

Marc.   Who cares? The point is, they come. On trucks. Packed in like sardines. The back flips open, babes hop out, we're ready to roll.

Gallimard.   You mean, they just—?

Marc.   Before you know it, every last one of them—they're stripped and splashing around my pool. There's no moon out, they can't see what's going on, their boobs are flapping, right? You close your eyes, reach out—it's grab bag, get it? Doesn't matter whose ass is between whose legs, whose teeth are sinking into who. You're just in there, going at it, eyes closed, on and on for as long as you can stand. *(Pause.)* Some fun, huh?

Gallimard.   What happens in the morning?

Marc.   In the morning, you're ready to talk some philosophy. *(Beat.)* So how 'bout it?

Gallimard.   Marc, I can't . . . I'm afraid they'll say no—the girls. So I never ask.

Marc.   You don't have to ask! That's the beauty—don't you see? They don't have to say yes. It's perfect for a guy like you, really.

Gallimard.   You go ahead . . . I may come later.

Marc.   Hey, Rene—it doesn't matter that you're clumsy and got zits—they're not looking!

Gallimard.   Thank you very much.

Marc.   Wimp.

Marc walks over to the other side of the stage, and starts waving and smiling at women in the audience.

Gallimard *(to us).*   We now return to my version of *Madame Butterfly* and the events leading to my recent conviction for treason.

Gallimard notices Marc making lewd gestures.

---

[1] National School.

Gallimard.   Marc, what are you doing?

Marc.   Huh? *(Sotto voce.)* Rene, there're a lotta great babes out there. They're probably lookin' at me and thinking, "What a dangerous guy."

Gallimard.   Yes—how could they help but be impressed by your cool sophistication?

Gallimard pops the Sharpless cap on Marc's head, and points him offstage. Marc exits, leering.

SCENE V.   M. Gallimard's cell.

Gallimard.   Next, Butterfly makes her entrance. We learn her age—fifteen . . . but very mature for her years.

Lights come up on the area where we saw Song dancing at the top of the play. She appears there again, now dressed as Madame Butterfly, moving to the "Love Duet." Gallimard turns upstage slightly to watch, transfixed.

Gallimard.   But as she glides past him, beautiful, laughing softly behind her fan, don't we who are men sigh with hope? We, who are not handsome, nor brave, nor powerful, yet somehow believe, like Pinkerton, that we deserve a Butterfly. She arrives with all her possessions in the folds of her sleeves, lays them all out, for her man to do with as he pleases. Even her life itself—she bows her head as she whispers that she's not even worth the hundred yen he paid for her. He's already given too much, when we know he's really had to give nothing at all.

Music and lights on Song out. Gallimard sits at his crate.

Gallimard.   In real life, women who put their total worth at less than sixty-six cents are quite hard to find. The closest we come is in the pages of these magazines. *(He reaches into his crate, pulls out a stack of girlie magazines, and begins flipping through them.)* Quite a necessity in prison. For three or four dollars, you get seven or eight women.

I first discovered these magazines at my uncle's house. One day, as a boy of twelve. The first time I saw them in his closet . . . all lined up—my body shook. Not with lust—no, with power. Here were women—a shelf-full— who would do exactly as I wanted.

The "Love Duet" creeps in over the speakers. Special comes up, revealing, not Song this time, but a pinup girl in a sexy negligee, her back to us. Gallimard turns upstage and looks at her.

Girl.   I know you're watching me.

Gallimard.   My throat . . . it's dry.

Girl.   I leave my blinds open every night before I go to bed.

Gallimard.   I can't move.

Girl.   I leave my blinds open and the lights on.

Gallimard.   I'm shaking. My skin is hot, but my penis is soft. Why?

Girl.   I stand in front of the window.

Gallimard.   What is she going to do?

Girl.   I toss my hair, and I let my lips part . . . barely.

Gallimard.   I shouldn't be seeing this. It's so dirty. I'm so bad.

Girl.   Then, slowly, I lift off my nightdress.

Gallimard.   Oh, god. I can't believe it. I can't—

Girl.   I toss it to the ground.

Gallimard.   Now, she's going to walk away. She's going to—

Girl.   I stand there, in the light, displaying myself.

Gallimard.   No. She's—why is she naked?

Girl.   To you.

Gallimard.   In front of a window? This is wrong. No—

Girl.   Without shame.

Gallimard.   No, she must . . . like it.

Girl.   I like it.

Gallimard.   She . . . she wants me to see.

Girl.   I want you to see.

Gallimard.   I can't believe it! She's getting excited!

Girl.   I can't see you. You can do whatever you want.

Gallimard.   I can't do a thing. Why?

Girl.   What would you like me to do . . . next?

Lights go down on her. Music off. Silence, as Gallimard puts away his maga-
zines. Then he resumes talking to us.

Gallimard.   Act Two begins with Butterfly staring at the ocean. Pinkerton's
been called back to the U.S., and he's given his wife a detailed schedule of
his plans. In the column marked "return date," he's written "when the robins
nest." This failed to ignite her suspicions. Now, three years have passed without a peep from him. Which brings a response from her faithful servant,
Suzuki.

Comrade Chin enters, playing Suzuki.

Suzuki.   Girl, he's a loser. What'd he ever give you? Nineteen cents and those
ugly Day-Glo stockings? Look, it's finished! Kaput! Done! And you should
be glad! I mean, the guy was a woofer! He tried before, you know—before
he met you, he went down to geisha central and plunked down his spare
change in front of the usual candidates—everyone else gagged! These are

hungry prostitutes, and they were not interested, get the picture? Now, stop slathering when an American ship sails in, and let's make some bucks—I mean, yen! We are broke!

Now, what about Yamadori? Hey, hey—don't look away—the man is a prince—figuratively, and, what's even better, literally. He's rich, he's handsome, he says he'll die if you don't marry him—and he's even willing to overlook the little fact that you've been deflowered all over the place by a foreign devil. What do you mean, "But he's Japanese?" What do you think you are? You think you've been touched by the whitey god? He was a sailor with dirty hands!

Suzuki stalks offstage.

Gallimard. She's also visited by Consul Sharpless, sent by Pinkerton on a minor errand.

Marc enters, as Sharpless.

Sharpless. I hate this job.
Gallimard. This Pinkerton—he doesn't show up personally to tell his wife he's abandoning her. No, he sends a government diplomat . . . at taxpayers' expense.
Sharpless. Butterfly? Butterfly? I have some bad—I'm going to be ill. Butterfly, I came to tell you—
Gallimard. Butterfly says she knows he'll return and if he doesn't she'll kill herself rather than go back to her own people. *(Beat.)* This causes a lull in the conversation.
Sharpless. Let's put it this way . . .
Gallimard. Butterfly runs into the next room, and returns holding—

Sound cue: a baby crying. Sharpless, "seeing" this, backs away.

Sharpless. Well, good. Happy to see things going so well. I suppose I'll be going now. Ta ta. Ciao. *(He turns away. Sound cue out.)* I hate this job. *(He exits.)*
Gallimard. At that moment, Butterfly spots in the harbor an American ship—the *Abramo Lincoln!*

Music cue: "The Flower Duet." Song, still dressed as Butterfly, changes into a wedding kimono, moving to the music.

Gallimard. This is the moment that redeems her years of waiting. With Suzuki's help, they cover the room with flowers—

Chin, as Suzuki, trudges onstage and drops a lone flower without much enthu-siasm.

Gallimard.   —and she changes into her wedding dress to prepare for Pinker-ton's arrival.

Suzuki helps Butterfly change. Helga enters, and helps Gallimard change into a tuxedo.

Gallimard.   I married a woman older than myself—Helga.
Helga.   My father was ambassador to Australia. I grew up among criminals and kangaroos.
Gallimard.   Hearing that brought me to the altar—

Helga exits.

Gallimard.   —where I took a vow renouncing love. No fantasy woman would ever want me, so, yes, I would settle for a quick leap up the career ladder. Passion, I banish, and in its place—practicality!
   But my vows had long since lost their charm by the time we arrived in China. The sad truth is that all men want a beautiful woman, and the uglier the man, the greater the want.

Suzuki makes final adjustments of Butterfly's costume, as does Gallimard of his tuxedo.

Gallimard.   I married late, at age thirty-one. I was faithful to my marriage for eight years. Until the day when, as a junior-level diplomat in puritanical Peking, in a parlor at the German ambassador's house, during the "Reign of a Hundred Flowers,"[2] I first saw her ... singing the death scene from *Madame Butterfly.*

Suzuki runs offstage.

SCENE VI.   German ambassador's house. Beijing. 1960.

The upstage special area now becomes a stage. Several chairs face upstage, representing seating for some twenty guests in the parlor. A few "diplomats"—Renee, Marc, Toulon—in formal dress enter and take seats.
   Gallimard also sits down, but turns towards us and continues to talk. Orches-tral accompaniment on the tape is now replaced by a simple piano. Song picks up the death scene from the point where Butterfly uncovers the hara-kiri knife.

---

[2] The name given to a short-lived encouragement of free expression in China in 1957.

Gallimard.   The ending is pitiful. Pinkerton, in an act of great courage, stays home and sends his American wife to pick up Butterfly's child. The truth, long deferred, has come up to her door.

Song, playing Butterfly, sings the lines from the opera in her own voice—which, though not classical, should be decent.

Song.   "Con onor muore / chi non puo serbar / vita con onore."
Gallimard (*simultaneously*).   "Death with honor / Is better than life / Life with dishonor."

The stage is illuminated; we are now completely within an elegant diplomat's residence. Song proceeds to play out an abbreviated death scene. Everyone in the room applauds. Song, shyly, takes her bows. Others in the room rush to congratulate her. Gallimard remains with us.

Gallimard.   They say in opera the voice is everything. That's probably why I'd never before enjoyed opera. Here . . . here was a Butterfly with little or no voice—but she had the grace, the delicacy . . . I believed this girl. I believed her suffering. I wanted to take her in my arms—so delicate, even I could protect her, take her home, pamper her until she smiled.

Over the course of the preceding speech, Song has broken from the upstage crowd and moved directly upstage of Gallimard.

Song.   Excuse me. Monsieur . . . ?

Gallimard turns upstage, shocked.

Gallimard.   Oh! Gallimard. Mademoiselle . . . ? A beautiful . . .
Song.   Song Liling.
Gallimard.   A beautiful performance.
Song.   Oh, please.
Gallimard.   I usually—
Song.   You make me blush. I'm no opera singer at all.
Gallimard.   I usually don't like *Butterfly.*
Song.   I can't blame you in the least.
Gallimard.   I mean, the story—
Song.   Ridiculous.
Gallimard.   I like the story, but . . . what?
Song.   Oh, you like it?
Gallimard.   I . . . what I mean is, I've always seen it played by huge women in so much bad makeup.
Song.   Bad makeup is not unique to the West.
Gallimard.   But, who can believe them?

Song.   And you believe me?

Gallimard.   Absolutely. You were utterly convincing. It's the first time—

Song.   Convincing? As a Japanese woman? The Japanese used hundreds of our people for medical experiments during the war, you know. But I gather such an irony is lost on you.

Gallimard.   No! I was about to say, it's the first time I've seen the beauty of the story.

Song.   Really?

Gallimard.   Of her death. It's a . . . a pure sacrifice. He's unworthy, but what can she do? She loves him . . . so much. It's a very beautiful story.

Song.   Well, yes, to a Westerner.

Gallimard.   Excuse me?

Song.   It's one of your favorite fantasies, isn't it? The submissive Oriental woman and the cruel white man.

Gallimard.   Well, I didn't quite mean . . .

Song.   Consider it this way: what would you say if a blonde homecoming queen fell in love with a short Japanese businessman? He treats her cruelly, then goes home for three years, during which time she prays to his picture and turns down marriage from a young Kennedy. Then, when she learns he has remarried, she kills herself. Now, I believe you would consider this girl to be a deranged idiot, correct? But because it's an Oriental who kills herself for a Westerner—ah!—you find it beautiful.

Silence.

Gallimard.   Yes . . . well . . . I see your point . . .

Song.   I will never do Butterfly again, Monsieur Gallimard. If you wish to see some real theater, come to the Peking Opera sometime. Expand your mind.

Song walks offstage. Other guests exit with her.

Gallimard (*to us*).   So much for protecting her in my big Western arms.

SCENE VII.   M. Gallimard's apartment. Beijing. 1960.

Gallimard changes from his tux into a casual suit. Helga enters.

Gallimard.   The Chinese are an incredibly arrogant people.

Helga.   They warned us about that in Paris, remember?

Gallimard.   Even Parisians consider them arrogant. That's a switch.

Helga.   What is it that Madame Su says? "We are a very old civilization." I never know if she's talking about her country or herself.

Gallimard.   I walk around here, all I hear every day, everywhere is how *old* this culture is. The fact that "old" may be synonymous with "senile" doesn't occur to them.

Helga.   You're not going to change them. "East is east, west is west, and . . ."
whatever that guy said.

Gallimard.   It's just that—silly. I met . . . at Ambassador Koening's tonight—
you should've been there.

Helga.   Koening? Oh god, no. Did he enchant you all again with the history
of Bavaria?

Gallimard.   No. I met, I suppose, the Chinese equivalent of a diva. She's a
singer in the Chinese opera.

Helga.   They have an opera, too? Do they sing in Chinese? Or maybe—in
Italian?

Gallimard.   Tonight, she did sing in Italian.

Helga.   How'd she manage that?

Gallimard.   She must've been educated in the West before the Revolution.
Her French is very good also. Anyway, she sang the death scene from
Madame Butterfly.

Helga.   *Madame Butterfly!* Then I should have come. (*She begins humming,
floating around the room as if dragging long kimono sleeves.*) Did she have a
nice costume? I think it's a classic piece of music.

Gallimard.   That's what *I* thought, too. Don't let her hear you say that.

Helga.   What's wrong?

Gallimard.   Evidently the Chinese hate it.

Helga.   She hated it, but she performed it anyway? Is she perverse?

Gallimard.   They hate it because the white man gets the girl. Sour grapes if
you ask me.

Helga.   Politics again? Why can't they just hear it as a piece of beautiful
music? So, what's in their opera?

Gallimard.   I don't know. But, whatever it is, I'm sure it must be *old.*

Helga exits.

SCENE VIII.   Chinese opera house and the streets of Beijing. 1960.

The sound of gongs clanging fills the stage.

Gallimard.   My wife's innocent question kept ringing in my ears. I asked
around, but no one knew anything about the Chinese opera. It took four
weeks, but my curiosity overcame my cowardice. This Chinese diva—this
unwilling Butterfly—what did she do to make her so proud?
    The room was hot, and full of smoke. Wrinkled faces, old women, teeth
missing—a man with a growth on his neck, like a human toad. All smiling,
pipes falling from their mouths, cracking nuts between their teeth, a live
chicken pecking at my foot—all looking, screaming, gawking . . . at her.

*The upstage area is suddenly hit with a harsh white light. It has become the stage
for the Chinese opera performance. Two dancers enter, along with Song. Galli-*

*mard stands apart, watching. Song glides gracefully amidst the two dancers.
Drums suddenly slam to a halt. Song strikes a pose, looking straight at Gallimard. Dancers exit. Light change. Pause, then Song walks right off the stage and
straight up to Gallimard.*

Song.   Yes. You. White man. I'm looking straight at you.
Gallimard.   Me?
Song.   You see any other white men? It was too easy to spot you. How often
   does a man in my audience come in a tie?

*Song starts to remove her costume. Underneath, she wears simple baggy clothes.
They are now backstage. The show is over.*

Song.   So, you are an adventurous imperialist?
Gallimard.   I . . . thought it would further my education.
Song.   It took you four weeks. Why?
Gallimard.   I've been busy.
Song.   Well, education has always been undervalued in the West, hasn't it?
Gallimard *(laughing).*   I don't think that's true.
Song.   No, you wouldn't. You're a Westerner. How can you objectively judge
   your own values?
Gallimard.   I think it's possible to achieve some distance.
Song.   Do you? *(Pause.)* It stinks in here. Let's go.
Gallimard.   These are the smells of your loyal fans.
Song.   I love them for being my fans, I hate the smell they leave behind. I too
   can distance myself from my people. *(She looks around, then whispers in his
   ear.)* "Art for the masses" is a shitty excuse to keep artists poor. *(She pops
   a cigarette in her mouth.)* Be a gentleman, will you? And light my cigarette.

Gallimard fumbles for a match.

Gallimard.   I don't . . . smoke.
Song *(lighting her own).*   Your loss. Had you lit my cigarette, I might have
   blown a puff of smoke right between your eyes. Come.

*They start to walk about the stage. It is a summer night on the Beijing streets.
Sounds of the city play on the house speakers.*

Song.   How I wish there were even a tiny café to sit in. With cappuccinos,
   and men in tuxedos and bad expatriate jazz.
Gallimard.   If my history serves me correctly, you weren't even allowed into
   the clubs in Shanghai before the Revolution.
Song.   Your history serves you poorly, Monsieur Gallimard. True, there were
   signs reading "No dogs and Chinamen." But a woman, especially a delicate

Oriental woman—we always go where we please. Could you imagine it otherwise? Clubs in China filled with pasty, big-thighed white women, while thousands of slender lotus blossoms wait just outside the door? Never. The clubs would be empty. *(Beat.)* We have always held a certain fascination for you Caucasian men, have we not?

Gallimard.   But . . . that fascination is imperialist, or so you tell me.

Song.   Do you believe everything I tell you? Yes. It is always imperialist. But sometimes . . . sometimes, it is also mutual. Oh—this is my flat.

Gallimard.   I didn't even—

Song.   Thank you. Come another time and we will further expand your mind.

Song exits. Gallimard continues roaming the streets as he speaks to us.

Gallimard.   What was that? What did she mean, "Sometimes . . . it is mutual"? Women do not flirt with me. And I normally can't talk to them. But tonight, I held up my end of the conversation.

SCENE IX.   Gallimard's bedroom. Beijing. 1960.

Helga enters.

Helga.   You didn't tell me you'd be home late.

Gallimard.   I didn't intend to. Something came up.

Helga.   Oh? Like what?

Gallimard.   I went to the . . . to the Dutch ambassador's home.

Helga.   Again?

Gallimard.   There was a reception for a visiting scholar. He's writing a six-volume treatise on the Chinese revolution. We all gathered that meant he'd have to live here long enough to actually write six volumes, and we all expressed our deepest sympathies.

Helga.   Well, I had a good night too. I went with the ladies to a martial arts demonstration. Some of those men—when they break those thick boards— *(she mimes fanning herself.)* whoo-whoo!

Helga exits. Lights dim.

Gallimard.   I lied to my wife. Why? I've never had any reason to lie before. But what reason did I have tonight? I didn't do anything wrong. That night, I had a dream. Other people, I've been told, have dreams when angels appear. Or dragons, or Sophia Loren in a towel. In my dream, Marc from school appeared.

Marc enters, in a nightshirt and cap.

Marc.   Rene! You met a girl!

Gallimard and Marc stumble down the Beijing streets. Night sounds over the speakers.

Gallimard.   It's not that amazing, thank you.
Marc.   No! It's so monumental, I heard about it halfway around the world in my sleep!
Gallimard.   I've met girls before, you know.
Marc.   Name one. I've come across time and space to congratulate you. *(He hands Gallimard a bottle of wine.)*
Gallimard.   Marc, this is expensive.
Marc.   On those rare occasions when you become a formless spirit, why not steal the best?

Marc pops open the bottle, begins to share it with Gallimard.

Gallimard.   You embarrass me. She . . . there's no reason to think she likes me.
Marc.   "Sometimes, it is mutual"?
Gallimard.   Oh.
Marc.   "Mutual"? "Mutual"? What does that mean?
Gallimard.   You heard?
Marc.   It means the money is in the bank, you only have to write the check!
Gallimard.   I am a married man!
Marc.   And an excellent one too. I cheated after . . . six months. Then again and again, until now—three hundred girls in twelve years.
Gallimard.   I don't think we should hold that up as a model.
Marc.   Of course not! My life—it is disgusting! Phooey! Phooey! But, you—you are the model husband.
Gallimard.   Anyway, it's impossible. I'm a foreigner.
Marc.   Ah, yes. She cannot love you, it is taboo, but something deep inside her heart . . . she cannot help herself . . . she must surrender to you. It is her destiny.
Gallimard.   How do you imagine all this?
Marc.   The same way you do. It's an old story. It's in our blood. They fear us, Rene. Their women fear us. And their men—their men hate us. And, you know something? They are all correct.

They spot a light in a window.

Marc.   There! There, Rene!
Gallimard.   It's her window.
Marc.   Late at night—it burns. The light—it burns for you.

Gallimard.   I won't look. It's not respectful.
Marc.   We don't have to be respectful. We're foreign devils.

Enter Song, in a sheer robe, her face completely swathed in black cloth. The "One Fine Day" aria creeps in over the speakers. With her back to us, Song mimes attending to her toilette. Her robe comes loose, revealing her white shoulders.

Marc.   All your life you've waited for a beautiful girl who would lay down for you. All your life you've smiled like a saint when it's happened to every other man you know. And you see them in magazines and you see them in movies. And you wonder, what's wrong with me? Will anyone beautiful ever want me? As the years pass, your hair thins and you struggle to hold on to even your hopes. Stop struggling, Rene. The wait is over. *(He exits.)*
Gallimard.   Marc? Marc?

At that moment, Song, her back still towards us, drops her robe. A second of her naked back, then a sound cue: a phone ringing, very loud. Blackout, followed in the next beat by a special up on the bedroom area, where a phone now sits. Gallimard stumbles across the stage and picks up the phone. Sound cue out. Over the course of his conversation, area lights fill in the vicinity of his bed. It is the following morning.

Gallimard.   Yes? Hello?
Song *(offstage).*   Is it very early?
Gallimard.   Why, yes.
Song *(offstage).*   How early?
Gallimard.   It's . . . it's 5:30. Why are you—?
Song *(offstage).*   But it's light outside. Already.
Gallimard.   It is. The sun must be in confusion today.

Over the course of Song's next speech, her upstage special comes up again. She sits in a chair, legs crossed, in a robe, telephone to her ear.

Song.   I waited until I saw the sun. That was as much discipline as I could manage for one night. Do you forgive me?
Gallimard.   Of course . . . for what?
Song.   Then I'll ask you quickly. Are you really interested in the opera?
Gallimard.   Why, yes. Yes I am.
Song.   Then come again next Thursday. I am playing *The Drunken Beauty*. May I count on you?
Gallimard.   Yes. You may.
Song.   Perfect. Well, I must be getting to bed. I'm exhausted. It's been a very long night for me.

Song hangs up; special on her goes off. Gallimard begins to dress for work.

SCENE X.   Song Liling's apartment. Beijing. 1960.

Gallimard.   I returned to the opera that next week, and the week after that
. . . she keeps our meetings so short—perhaps fifteen, twenty minutes at
most. So I am left each week with a thirst which is intensified. In this way,
fifteen weeks have gone by. I am starting to doubt the words of my friend
Marc. But no, not really. In my heart, I know she has . . . an interest in me.
I suspect this is her way. She is outwardly bold and outspoken, yet her heart
is shy and afraid. It is the Oriental in her at war with her Western education.

Song *(offstage).*   I will be out in an instant. Ask the servant for anything you
want.

Gallimard.   Tonight, I have finally been invited to enter her apartment.
Though the idea is almost beyond belief, I believe she is afraid of me.

Gallimard looks around the room. He picks up a picture in a frame, studies it.
Without his noticing, Song enters, dressed elegantly in a black gown from the
twenties. She stands in the doorway looking like Anna May Wong.[3]

Song.   That is my father.

Gallimard *(surprised).*   Mademoiselle Song . . .

She glides up to him, snatches away the picture.

Song.   It is very good that he did not live to see the Revolution. They would,
no doubt, have made him kneel on broken glass. Not that he didn't deserve
such a punishment. But he is my father. I would've hated to see it happen.

Gallimard.   I'm very honored that you've allowed me to visit your home.

Song curtseys.

Song.   Thank you. Oh! Haven't you been poured any tea?

Gallimard.   I'm really not—

Song *(to her offstage servant).*   Shu-Fang! Cha! Kwai-lah! *(To Gallimard.)* I'm
sorry. You want everything to be perfect—

Gallimard.   Please.

Song.   —and before the evening even begins—

Gallimard.   I'm really not thirsty.

Song.   —it's ruined.

Gallimard *(sharply).*   Mademoiselle Song!

Song sits down.

---

[3] (1905–1961), a beautiful Chinese-American actress.

Song.   I'm sorry.
Gallimard.   What are you apologizing for now?

Pause; Song starts to giggle.

Song.   I don't know!

Gallimard laughs.

Gallimard.   Exactly my point.
Song.   Oh, I am silly. Light-headed. I promise not to apologize for anything else tonight, do you hear me?
Gallimard.   That's a good girl.

Shu-Fang, a servant girl, comes out with a tea tray and starts to pour.

Song (*to Shu-Fang*).   No! I'll pour myself for the gentleman!

Shu-Fang, staring at Gallimard, exits.

Gallimard.   You have a beautiful home.
Song.   No, I . . . I don't even know why I invited you up.
Gallimard.   Well, I'm glad you did.

Song looks around the room.

Song.   There is an element of danger to your presence.
Gallimard.   Oh?
Song.   You must know.
Gallimard.   It doesn't concern me. We both know why I'm here.
Song.   It doesn't concern me either. No . . . well perhaps . . .
Gallimard.   What?
Song.   Perhaps I am slightly afraid of scandal.
Gallimard.   What are we doing?
Song.   I'm entertaining you. In my parlor.
Gallimard.   In France, that would hardly—
Song.   France. France is a country living in the modern era. Perhaps even ahead of it. China is a nation whose soul is firmly rooted two thousand years in the past. What I do, even pouring the tea for you now . . . it has . . . implications. The walls and windows say so. Even my own heart, strapped inside this Western dress . . . even it says things—things I don't care to hear.

Song hands Gallimard a cup of tea. Gallimard puts his hand over both the teacup and Song's hand.

Gallimard.   This is a beautiful dress.

Song.   Don't.

Gallimard.   What?

Song.   I don't even know if it looks right on me.

Gallimard.   Believe me—

Song.   You are from France. You see so many beautiful women.

Gallimard.   France? Since when are the European women—?

Song.   Oh! What am I trying to do, anyway?!

Song runs to the door, composes herself, then turns towards Gallimard.

Song.   Monsieur Gallimard, perhaps you should go.

Gallimard.   But . . . why?

Song.   There's something wrong about this.

Gallimard.   I don't see what.

Song.   I feel . . . I am not myself.

Gallimard.   No. You're nervous.

Song.   Please. Hard as I try to be modern, to speak like a man, to hold a Western woman's strong face up to my own . . . in the end, I fail. A small, frightened heart beats too quickly and gives me away. Monsieur Gallimard, I'm a Chinese girl. I've never . . . never invited a man up to my flat before. The forwardness of my actions makes my skin burn.

Gallimard.   What are you afraid of? Certainly not me, I hope.

Song.   I'm a modest girl.

Gallimard.   I know. And very beautiful. *(He touches her hair.)*

Song.   Please—go now. The next time you see me, I shall again be myself.

Gallimard.   I like you the way you are right now.

Song.   You are a cad.

Gallimard.   What do you expect? I'm a foreign devil.

Gallimard walks downstage. Song exits.

Gallimard *(to us).*   Did you hear the way she talked about Western women? Much differently than the first night. She does—she feels inferior to them—and to me.

SCENE XI.   The French embassy. Beijing. 1960.

Gallimard moves towards a desk.

Gallimard.   I determined to try an experiment. In *Madame Butterfly,* Cio-Cio-San fears that the Western man who catches a butterfly will pierce its heart with a needle, then leave it to perish. I began to wonder: had I, too, caught a butterfly who would writhe on a needle?

Marc enters, dressed as a bureaucrat, holding a stack of papers. As Gallimard speaks, Marc hands papers to him. He peruses, then signs, stamps, or rejects them.

Gallimard.   Over the next five weeks, I worked like a dynamo. I stopped going to the opera, I didn't phone or write her. I knew this little flower was waiting for me to call, and, as I wickedly refused to do so, I felt for the first time that rush of power—the absolute power of a man.

Marc continues acting as the bureaucrat, but he now speaks as himself.

Marc.   Rene! It's me.

Gallimard.   Marc—I hear your voice everywhere now. Even in the midst of work.

Marc.   That's because I'm watching you—all the time.

Gallimard.   You were always the most popular guy in school.

Marc.   Well, there's no guarantee of failure in life like happiness in high school. Somehow I knew I'd end up in the suburbs working for Renault and you'd be in the Orient picking exotic women off the trees. And they say there's no justice.

Gallimard.   That's why you were my friend?

Marc.   I gave you a little of my life, so that now you can give me some of yours. *(Pause.)* Remember Isabelle?

Gallimard.   Of course I remember! She was my first experience.

Marc.   We all wanted to ball her. But she only wanted me.

Gallimard.   I had her.

Marc.   Right. You balled her.

Gallimard.   You were the only one who ever believed me.

Marc.   Well, there's a good reason for that. *(Beat.)* C'mon. You must've guessed.

Gallimard.   You told me to wait in the bushes by the cafeteria that night. The next thing I knew, she was on me. Dress up in the air.

Marc.   She never wore underwear.

Gallimard.   My arms were pinned to the dirt.

Marc.   She loved the superior position. A girl ahead of her time.

Gallimard.   I looked up, and there was this woman . . . bouncing up and down on my loins.

Marc.   Screaming, right?

Gallimard.   Screaming, and breaking off the branches all around me, and pounding my butt up and down into the dirt.

Marc.   Huffing and puffing like a locomotive.

Gallimard.   And in the middle of all this, the leaves were getting into my mouth, my legs were losing circulation, I thought, "God. So this is *it*?"

Marc.   You thought that?

Gallimard.   Well, I was worried about my legs falling off.

Marc.   You didn't have a good time?

Gallimard.   No, that's not what I—I had a great time!

Marc.   You're sure?

Gallimard.   Yeah. Really.

Marc.   'Cuz I wanted you to have a good time.

Gallimard.   I did.

Pause.

Marc.   Shit. *(Pause.)* When all is said and done, she was kind of a lousy lay, wasn't she? I mean, there was a lot of energy there, but you never knew what she was doing with it. Like when she yelled "I'm coming!"—hell, it was so loud, you wanted to go, "Look, it's not that big a deal."

Gallimard.   I got scared. I thought she meant someone was actually coming. *(Pause.)* But, Marc?

Marc.   What?

Gallimard.   Thanks.

Marc.   Oh, don't mention it.

Gallimard.   It was my first experience.

Marc.   Yeah. You got her.

Gallimard.   I got her.

Marc.   Wait! Look at that letter again!

Gallimard picks up one of the papers he's been stamping, and rereads it.

Gallimard *(to us).*   After six weeks, they began to arrive. The letters.

Upstage special on Song, as Madame Butterfly. The scene is underscored by the "Love Duet."

Song.   Did we fight? I do not know. Is the opera no longer of interest to you? Please come—my audiences miss the white devil in their midst.

Gallimard looks up from the letter, towards us.

Gallimard *(to us).*   A concession, but much too dignified. *(Beat; he discards the letter.)* I skipped the opera again that week to complete a position paper on trade.

The bureaucrat hands him another letter.

Song.   Six weeks have passed since last we met. Is this your practice—to leave friends in the lurch? Sometimes I hate you, sometimes I hate myself, but always I miss you.

Gallimard *(to us).*   Better, but I don't like the way she calls me "friend." When a woman calls a man her "friend," she's calling him a eunuch or a homosexual. *(Beat; he discards the letter.)* I was absent from the opera for the seventh week, feeling a sudden urge to clean out my files.

Bureaucrat hands him another letter.

Song.   Your rudeness is beyond belief. I don't deserve this cruelty. Don't bother to call. I'll have you turned away at the door.

Gallimard *(to us).*   I didn't. *(He discards the letter; bureaucrat hands him another.)* And then finally, the letter that concluded my experiment.

Song.   I am out of words. I can hide behind dignity no longer. What do you want? I have already given you my shame.

Gallimard gives the letter back to Marc, slowly. Special on Song fades out.

Gallimard *(to us).*   Reading it, I became suddenly ashamed. Yes, my experiment had been a success. She was turning on my needle. But the victory seemed hollow.

Marc.   Hollow?! Are you crazy?

Gallimard.   Nothing, Marc. Please go away.

Marc *(exiting, with papers).*   Haven't I taught you anything?

Gallimard.   "I have already given you my shame." I had to attend a reception that evening. On the way, I felt sick. If there is a God, surely he would punish me now. I had finally gained power over a beautiful woman, only to abuse it cruelly. There must be justice in the world. I had the strange feeling that the ax would fall this very evening.

SCENE XII.   Ambassador Toulon's residence. Beijing. 1960.

Sound cue: party noises. Light change. We are now in a spacious residence. Toulon, the French ambassador, enters and taps Gallimard on the shoulder.

Toulon.   Gallimard? Can I have a word? Over here.

Gallimard *(to us).*   Manuel Toulon. French ambassador to China. He likes to think of us all as his children. Rather like God.

Toulon.   Look, Gallimard, there's not much to say. I've liked you. From the day you walked in. You were no leader, but you were tidy and efficient.

Gallimard.   Thank you, sir.

Toulon.   Don't jump the gun. Okay, our needs in China are changing. It's embarrassing that we lost Indochina. Someone just wasn't on the ball there. I don't mean you personally, of course.

Gallimard.   Thank you, sir.

Toulon.   We're going to be doing a lot more information-gathering in the future. The nature of our work here is changing. Some people are just going to have to go. It's nothing personal.

Gallimard.   Oh.

Toulon.   Want to know a secret? Vice-Consul LeBon is being transferred.

Gallimard *(to us).*   My immediate superior!

Toulon.   And most of his department.

Gallimard *(to us).*   Just as I feared! God has seen my evil heart—

Toulon.   But not you.

Gallimard *(to us).*   —and he's taking her away just as . . . *(To Toulon.)* Excuse me, sir?

Toulon.   Scare you? I think I did. Cheer up, Gallimard. I want you to replace LeBon as vice-consul.

Gallimard.   You—? Yes, well, thank you, sir.

Toulon.   Anytime.

Gallimard.   I . . . accept with great humility.

Toulon.   Humility won't be part of the job. You're going to coordinate the revamped intelligence division. Want to know a secret? A year ago, you would've been out. But the past few months, I don't know how it happened, you've become this new aggressive confident . . . thing. And they also tell me you get along with the Chinese. So I think you're a lucky man, Gallimard. Congratulations.

They shake hands. Toulon exits. Party noises out. Gallimard stumbles across a darkened stage.

Gallimard.   Vice-consul? Impossible! As I stumbled out of the party, I saw it written across the sky: There is no God. Or, no—say that there is a God. But that God . . . understands. Of course! God who creates Eve to serve Adam, who blesses Solomon with his harem but ties Jezebel to a burning bed[4]— that God is a man. And he understands! At age thirty-nine, I was suddenly initiated into the way of the world.

SCENE XIII.   Song Liling's apartment. Beijing. 1960.

Song enters, in a sheer dressing gown.

Song.   Are you crazy?

Gallimard.   Mademoiselle Song—

Song.   To come here—at this hour? After . . . after eight weeks?

Gallimard.   It's the most amazing—

Song.   You bang on my door? Scare my servants, scandalize the neighbors?

Gallimard.   I've been promoted. To vice-consul.

Pause.

Song.   And what is that supposed to mean to me?

Gallimard.   Are you my Butterfly?

---

[4] Biblical allusions. See Genesis 2:18–25, I Kings 11:1–8, and II Kings 9:30–37.

Song.   What are you saying?

Gallimard.   I've come tonight for an answer: are you my Butterfly?

Song.   Don't you know already?

Gallimard.   I want you to say it.

Song.   I don't want to say it.

Gallimard.   So, that is your answer?

Song.   You know how I feel about—

Gallimard.   I do remember one thing.

Song.   What?

Gallimard.   In the letter I received today.

Song.   Don't.

Gallimard.   "I have already given you my shame."

Song.   It's enough that I even wrote it.

Gallimard.   Well, then—

Song.   I shouldn't have it splashed across my face.

Gallimard.   —if that's all true—

Song.   Stop!

Gallimard.   Then what is one more short answer?

Song.   I don't want to!

Gallimard.   Are you my Butterfly? *(Silence; he crosses the room and begins to touch her hair.)* I want from you honesty. There should be nothing false between us. No false pride.

Pause.

Song.   Yes, I am. I am your Butterfly.

Gallimard.   Then let me be honest with you. It is because of you that I was promoted tonight. You have changed my life forever. My little Butterfly, there should be no more secrets: I love you.

He starts to kiss her roughly. She resists slightly.

Song.   No . . . no . . . gently . . . please, I've never . . .

Gallimard.   No?

Song.   I've tried to appear experienced, but . . . the truth is . . . no.

Gallimard.   Are you cold?

Song.   Yes. Cold.

Gallimard.   Then we will go very, very slowly.

He starts to caress her; her gown begins to open.

Song.   No . . . let me . . . keep my clothes . . .

Gallimard.   But . . .

Song.   Please . . . it all frightens me. I'm a modest Chinese girl.

Gallimard.   My poor little treasure.

Song.   I am your treasure. Though inexperienced, I am not . . . ignorant. They teach us things, our mothers, about pleasing a man.

Gallimard.   Yes?
Song.   I'll do my best to make you happy. Turn off the lights.

Gallimard gets up and heads for a lamp. Song, propped up on one elbow, tosses her hair back and smiles.

Song.   Monsieur Gallimard?
Gallimard.   Yes, Butterfly?
Song.   *"Vieni, vieni!"*
Gallimard.   "Come, darling."
Song.   *"Ah! Dolce notte!"*
Gallimard.   "Beautiful night."
Song.   *"Tutto estatico d'amor ride il ciel!"*
Gallimard.   "All ecstatic with love, the heavens are filled with laughter."

He turns off the lamp. Blackout.

Act II

SCENE I.   M. Gallimard's cell. Paris. 1988.

Lights up on Gallimard. He sits in his cell, reading from a leaflet.

Gallimard.   This, from a contemporary critic's commentary on *Madame But-terfly*: "Pinkerton suffers from . . . being an obnoxious bounder whom every man in the audience itches to kick." Bully for us men in the audience! Then, in the same note: "Butterfly is the most irresistibly appealing of Puccini's 'Little Women.' Watching the succession of her humiliations is like watching a child under torture." (*He tosses the pamphlet over his shoulder.*) I suggest that, while we men may all want to kick Pinkerton, very few of us would pass up the opportunity to *be* Pinkerton.

Gallimard moves out of his cell.

SCENE II.   Gallimard and Butterfly's flat. Beijing. 1960.

We are in a simple but well-decorated parlor. Gallimard moves to sit on a sofa, while Song, dressed in a chong sam,[5] enters and curls up at his feet.

---

[5] A tight-fitting dress with side slits in the skirt.

Gallimard (*to us*).   We secured a flat on the outskirts of Peking. Butterfly, as I was calling her now, decorated our "home" with Western furniture and Chinese antiques. And there, on a few stolen afternoons or evenings each week, Butterfly commenced her education.

Song.   The Chinese men—they keep us down.

Gallimard.   Even in the "New Society"?

Song.   In the "New Society," we are all kept ignorant equally. That's one of the exciting things about loving a Western man. I know you are not threatened by a woman's education.

Gallimard.   I'm no saint, Butterfly.

Song.   But you come from a progressive society.

Gallimard.   We're not always reminding each other how "old" we are, if that's what you mean.

Song.   Exactly. We Chinese—once, I suppose, it is true, we ruled the world. But so what? How much more exciting to be part of the society ruling the world today. Tell me—what's happening in Vietnam?

Gallimard.   Oh, Butterfly—you want me to bring my work home?

Song.   I want to know what you know. To be impressed by my man. It's not the particulars so much as the fact that you're making decisions which change the shape of the world.

Gallimard.   Not the world. At best, a small corner.

Toulon enters, and sits at a desk upstage.

SCENE III.   French embassy. Beijing. 1961.

Gallimard moves downstage, to Toulon's desk. Song remains upstage, watching.

Toulon.   And a more troublesome corner is hard to imagine.

Gallimard.   So, the Americans plan to begin bombing?

Toulon.   This is very secret, Gallimard: yes. The Americans don't have an embassy here. They're asking us to be their eyes and ears. Say Jack Kennedy signed an order to bomb North Vietnam, Laos. How would the Chinese react?

Gallimard.   I think the Chinese will squawk—

Toulon.   Uh-huh.

Gallimard.   —but, in their hearts, they don't even like Ho Chi Minh.[6]

Pause.

Toulon.   What a bunch of jerks. Vietnam was *our* colony. Not only didn't the Americans help us fight to keep them, but now, seven years

---

[6] Revolutionary leader and president of North Vietnam, 1945–1969.

later, they've come back to grab the territory for themselves. It's very ir-
ritating.

Gallimard.   With all due respect, sir, why should the Americans have won
our war for us back in 'fifty-four if we didn't have the will to win it ourselves?

Toulon.   You're kidding, aren't you?

Pause.

Gallimard.   The Orientals simply want to be associated with whoever shows
the most strength and power. You live with the Chinese, sir. Do you think
they like Communism?

Toulon.   I live in China. Not with the Chinese.

Gallimard.   Well, I—

Toulon.   *You* live with the Chinese.

Gallimard.   Excuse me?

Toulon.   I can't keep a secret.

Gallimard.   What are you saying?

Toulon.   Only that I'm not immune to gossip. So, you're keeping a native
mistress? Don't answer. It's none of my business. *(Pause.)* I'm sure she must
be gorgeous.

Gallimard.   Well . . .

Toulon.   I'm impressed. You had the stamina to go out into the streets and
hunt one down. Some of us have to be content with the wives of the
expatriate community.

Gallimard.   I do feel . . . fortunate.

Toulon.   So, Gallimard, you've got the inside knowledge—what *do* the Chinese think?

Gallimard.   Deep down, they miss the old days. You know, cappuccinos, men
in tuxedos—

Toulon.   So what do we tell the Americans about Vietnam?

Gallimard.   Tell them there's a natural affinity between the West and the
Orient.

Toulon.   And that you speak from experience?

Gallimard.   The Orientals are people too. They want the good things we can
give them. If the Americans demonstrate the will to win, the Vietnamese
will welcome them into a mutually beneficial union.

Toulon.   I don't see how the Vietnamese can stand up to American firepower.

Gallimard.   Orientals will always submit to a greater force.

Toulon.   I'll note your opinions in my report. The Americans always love to
hear how "welcome" they'll be. *(He starts to exit.)*

Gallimard.   Sir?

Toulon.   Mmmm?

Gallimard.   This . . . rumor you've heard.

Toulon.   Uh-huh?

Gallimard. How . . . widespread do you think it is?

Toulon. It's only widespread within this embassy. Where nobody talks because everybody is guilty. We were worried about you, Gallimard. We thought you were the only one here without a secret. Now you go and find a lotus blossom . . . and top us all. *(He exits.)*

Gallimard *(to us).* Toulon knows! And he approves! I was learning the benefits of being a man. We form our own clubs, sit behind thick doors, smoke—and celebrate the fact that we're still boys. *(He starts to move downstage, towards Song.)* So, over the—

Suddenly Comrade Chin enters. Gallimard backs away.

Gallimard *(to Song).* No! Why does she have to come in?

Song. Rene, be sensible. How can they understand the story without her? Now, don't embarrass yourself.

Gallimard moves down center.

Gallimard *(to us).* Now, you will see why my story is so amusing to so many people. Why they snicker at parties in disbelief. Please—try to understand it from my point of view. We are all prisoners of our time and place. *(He exits.)*

SCENE IV. Gallimard and Butterfly's flat. Beijing. 1961.

Song *(to us).* 1961. The flat Monsieur Gallimard rented for us. An evening after he has gone.

Chin. Okay, see if you can find out when the Americans plan to start bombing Vietnam. If you can find out what cities, even better.

Song. I'll do my best, but I don't want to arouse his suspicions.

Chin. Yeah, sure, of course. So, what else?

Song. The Americans will increase troops in Vietnam to 170,000 soldiers with 120,000 militia and 11,000 American advisors.

Chin *(writing).* Wait, wait, 120,000 militia and—

Song. —11,000 American—

Chin. —American advisors. *(Beat.)* How do you remember so much?

Song. I'm an actor.

Chin. Yeah. *(Beat.)* Is that how come you dress like that?

Song. Like what, Miss Chin?

Chin. Like that dress! You're wearing a dress. And every time I come here, you're wearing a dress. Is that because you're an actor? Or what?

Song. It's a . . . disguise, Miss Chin.

Chin. Actors, I think they're all weirdos. My mother tells me actors are like gamblers or prostitutes or—

Song. It helps me in my assignment.

Pause.

Chin. You're not gathering information in any way that violates Communist
  Party principles, are you?
Song. Why would I do that?
Chin. Just checking. Remember: when working for the Great Proletarian
  State, you represent our Chairman Mao in every position you take.
Song. I'll try to imagine the Chairman taking my positions.
Chin. We all think of him this way. Good-bye, comrade. (*She starts to exit.*)
  Comrade?
Song. Yes?
Chin. Don't forget: there is no homosexuality in China!
Song. Yes, I've heard.
Chin. Just checking. (*She exits.*)
Song (*to us*). What passes for a woman in modern China.

Gallimard sticks his head out from the wings.

Gallimard. Is she gone?
Song. Yes, Rene. Please continue in your own fashion.

SCENE V. Beijing. 1961–1963.

*Gallimard moves to the couch where Song still sits. He lies down in her lap, and
she strokes his forehead.*

Gallimard (*to us*). And so, over the years 1961, '62, '63, we settled into our
  routine, Butterfly and I. She would always have prepared a light snack and
  then, ever so delicately, and only if I agreed, she would start to pleasure me.
  With her hands, her mouth ... too many ways to explain, and too sad,
  given my present situation. But mostly we would talk. About my life. Perhaps there is nothing more rare than to find a woman who passionately
  listens.

*Song remains upstage, listening, as Helga enters and plays a scene downstage
with Gallimard.*

Helga. Rene, I visited Dr. Bolleart this morning.
Gallimard. Why? Are you ill?
Helga. No, no. You see, I wanted to ask him ... that question we've been
  discussing.
Gallimard. And I told you, it's only a matter of time. Why did you bring a
  doctor into this? We just have to keep trying—like a crapshoot, actually.
Helga. I went, I'm sorry. But listen: he says there's nothing wrong with me.

Gallimard. You see? Now, will you stop—?

Helga. Rene, he says he'd like you to go in and take some tests.

Gallimard. Why? So he can find there's nothing wrong with both of us?

Helga. Rene, I don't ask for much. One trip! One visit! And then, whatever you want to do about it—you decide.

Gallimard. You're assuming he'll find something defective!

Helga. No! Of course not! Whatever he finds—if he finds nothing, we decide what to do about nothing! But go!

Gallimard. If he finds nothing, we keep trying. Just like we do now.

Helga. But at least we'll know! *(Pause.)* I'm sorry. *(She starts to exit.)*

Gallimard. Do you really want me to see Dr. Bolleart?

Helga. Only if you want a child, Rene. We have to face the fact that time is running out. Only if you want a child. *(She exits.)*

Gallimard *(to Song).* I'm a modern man, Butterfly. And yet, I don't want to go. It's the same old voodoo. I feel like God himself is laughing at me if I can't produce a child.

Song. You men of the West—you're obsessed by your odd desire for equality. Your wife can't give you a child, and *you're* going to the doctor?

Gallimard. Well, you see, she's already gone.

Song. And because this incompetent can't find the defect, you now have to subject yourself to him? It's unnatural.

Gallimard. Well, what is the "natural" solution?

Song. In Imperial China, when a man found that one wife was inadequate, he turned to another—to give him his son.

Gallimard. What do you—? I can't . . . marry you, yet.

Song. Please. I'm not asking you to be my husband. But I am already your wife.

Gallimard. Do you want to . . . have my child?

Song. I thought you'd never ask.

Gallimard. But, your career . . . your—

Song. Phooey on my career! That's your Western mind, twisting itself into strange shapes again. Of course I love my career. But what would I love most of all? To feel something inside me—day and night—something I know is yours. *(Pause.)* Promise me . . . you won't go to this doctor. Who is this Western quack to set himself as judge over the man I love? I know who is a man, and who is not. *(She exits.)*

Gallimard *(to us).* Dr. Bolleart? Of course I didn't go. What man would?

SCENE VI. Beijing. 1963.

Party noises over the house speakers. Renee enters, wearing a revealing gown.

Gallimard. 1963. A party at the Austrian embassy. None of us could remember the Austrian ambassador's name, which seemed somehow appropriate.

(To Renee.) So, I tell the Americans, Diem[7] must go. The U.S. wants to be respected by the Vietnamese, and yet they're propping up this nobody seminarian as her president. A man whose claim to fame is his sister-in-law imposing fanatic "moral order" campaigns? Oriental women—when they're good, they're very good, but when they're bad, they're Christians.

Renee. Yeah.

Gallimard. And what do you do?

Renee. I'm a student. My father exports a lot of useless stuff to the Third World.

Gallimard. How useless?

Renee. You know. Squirt guns, confectioner's sugar, Hula Hoops . . .

Gallimard. I'm sure they appreciate the sugar.

Renee. I'm here for two years to study Chinese.

Gallimard. Two years!

Renee. That's what everybody says.

Gallimard. When did you arrive?

Renee. Three weeks ago.

Gallimard. And?

Renee. I like it. It's primitive, but . . . well, this is the place to learn Chinese, so here I am.

Gallimard. Why Chinese?

Renee. I think it'll be important someday.

Gallimard. You do?

Renee. Don't ask me when, but . . . that's what I think.

Gallimard. Well, I agree with you. One hundred percent. That's very far-sighted.

Renee. Yeah. Well of course, my father thinks I'm a complete weirdo.

Gallimard. He'll thank you someday.

Renee. Like when the Chinese start buying Hula Hoops?

Gallimard. There're a billion bellies out there.

Renee. And if they end up taking over the world—well, then I'll be lucky to know Chinese too, right?

Pause.

Gallimard. At this point, I don't see how the Chinese can possibly take—

Renee. You know what I *don't* like about China?

Gallimard. Excuse me? No—what?

Renee. Nothing to do at night.

Gallimard. You come to parties at embassies like everyone else.

Renee. Yeah, but they get out at ten. And then what?

---

[7] Ngo Dinh Diem (1901–1963), president of South Vietnam, 1955–1963. He was assassinated in a U.S.-supported coup d'etat.

Gallimard. I'm afraid the Chinese idea of a dance hall is a dirt floor and a man with a flute.

Renee. Are you married?

Gallimard. Yes. Why?

Renee. You wanna . . . fool around?

Pause.

Gallimard. Sure.

Renee. I'll wait for you outside. What's your name?

Gallimard. Gallimard. Rene.

Renee. Weird. I'm Renee too. *(She exits.)*

Gallimard *(to us).* And so, I embarked on my first extra-extramarital affair. Renee was picture perfect. With a body like those girls in the magazines. If I put a tissue paper over my eyes, I wouldn't have been able to tell the difference. And it was exciting to be with someone who wasn't afraid to be seen completely naked. But is it possible for a woman to be *too* uninhibited, *too* willing, so as to seem almost too . . . masculine?

Chuck Berry blares from the house speakers, then comes down in volume as Renee enters, toweling her hair.

Renee. You have a nice weenie.

Gallimard. What?

Renee. Penis. You have a nice penis.

Gallimard. Oh. Well, thank you. That's very . . .

Renee. What—can't take a compliment?

Gallimard. No, it's very . . . reassuring.

Renee. But most girls don't come out and say it, huh?

Gallimard. And also . . . what did you call it?

Renee. Oh. Most girls don't call it a "weenie," huh?

Gallimard. It sounds very—

Renee. Small, I know.

Gallimard. I was going to say, "young."

Renee. Yeah. Young, small, same thing. Most guys are pretty, uh, sensitive about that. Like, you know, I had a boyfriend back home in Denmark. I got mad at him once and called him a little weeniehead. He got so mad! He said at least I should call him a great big weeniehead.

Gallimard. I suppose I just say "penis."

Renee. Yeah. That's pretty clinical. There's "cock," but that sounds like a chicken. And "prick" is painful, and "dick" is like you're talking about someone who's not in the room.

Gallimard. Yes. It's a . . . bigger problem than I imagined.

Renee. I—I think maybe it's because I really don't know what to do with them—that's why I call them "weenies."

Gallimard.   Well, you did quite well with . . . mine.

Renee.   Thanks, but I mean, really *do* with them. Like, okay, have you ever looked at one? I mean, really?

Gallimard.   No, I suppose when it's part of you, you sort of take it for granted.

Renee.   I guess. But, like, it just hangs there. This little . . . flap of flesh. And there's so much fuss that we make about it. Like, I think the reason we fight wars is because we wear clothes. Because no one knows—between the men, I mean—who has the biggest . . . weenie. So, if I'm a guy with a small one, I'm going to build a really big building or take over a really big piece of land or write a really long book so the other men don't know, right? But, see, it never really works, that's the problem. I mean, you conquer the country, or whatever, but you're still wearing clothes, so there's no way to prove absolutely whose is bigger or smaller. And that's what we call a civilized society. The whole world run by a bunch of men with pricks the size of pins. *(She exits.)*

Gallimard *(to us)*.   This was simply not acceptable.

A high-pitched chime rings through the air. Song, dressed as Butterfly, appears in the upstage special. She is obviously distressed. Her body swoons as she attempts to clip the stems of flowers she's arranging in a vase.

Gallimard.   But I kept up our affair, wildly, for several months. Why? I believe because of Butterfly. She knew the secret I was trying to hide. But, unlike a Western woman, she didn't confront me, threaten, even pout. I remembered the words of Puccini's *Butterfly:*

Song.   *"Noi siamo gente avvezza / alle piccole cose / umili e silenziose."*

Gallimard.   "I come from a people / Who are accustomed to little / Humble and silent." I saw Pinkerton and Butterfly, and what she would say if he were unfaithful . . . nothing. She would cry, alone, into those wildly soft sleeves, once full of possessions, now empty to collect her tears. It was her tears and her silence that excited me, every time I visited Renee.

Toulon *(offstage)*.   Gallimard!

Toulon enters. Gallimard turns towards him. During the next section, Song, up center, begins to dance with the flowers. It is a drunken, reckless dance, where she breaks small pieces off the stems.

Toulon.   They're killing him.

Gallimard.   Who? I'm sorry? What?

Toulon.   Bother you to come over at this late hour?

Gallimard.   No . . . of course not.

Toulon.   Not after you hear my secret. Champagne?

Gallimard.   Um . . . thank you.

Toulon.   You're surprised. There's something that you've wanted, Gallimard. No, not a promotion. Next time. Something in the world. You're not aware of this, but there's an informal gossip circle among intelligence agents. And some of ours heard from some of the Americans—

Gallimard.   Yes?

Toulon.   That the U.S. will allow the Vietnamese generals to stage a coup . . . and assassinate President Diem.

The chime rings again. Toulon freezes. Gallimard turns upstage and looks at Butterfly, who slowly and deliberately clips a flower off its stem. Gallimard turns back towards Toulon.

Gallimard.   I think . . . that's a very wise move!

Toulon unfreezes.

Toulon.   It's what you've been advocating. A toast?

Gallimard.   Sure. I consider this a vindication.

Toulon.   Not exactly. "To the test. Let's hope you pass."

They drink. The chime rings again. Toulon freezes. Gallimard turns upstage, and Song clips another flower.

Gallimard *(to Toulon).*   The test?

Toulon *(unfreezing).*   It's a test of everything you've been saying. I personally think the generals probably will stop the Communists. And you'll be a hero. But if anything goes wrong, then your opinions won't be worth a pig's ear. I'm sure that won't happen. But sometimes it's easier when they don't listen to you.

Gallimard.   They're your opinions too, aren't they?

Toulon.   Personally, yes.

Gallimard.   So we agree.

Toulon.   But my opinions aren't on that report. Yours are. Cheers.

Toulon turns away from Gallimard and raises his glass. At that instant Song picks up the vase and hurls it to the ground. It shatters. Song sinks down amidst the shards of the vase, in a calm, childlike trance. She sings softly, as if reciting a child's nursery rhyme.

Song *(repeat as necessary).*   "The whole world over, the white man travels, setting anchor, wherever he likes. Life's not worth living, unless he finds, the finest maidens, of every land . . ."

Gallimard turns downstage towards us. Song continues singing.

Gallimard.   I shook as I left his house. That coward! That worm! To put the burden for his decisions on my shoulders!

I started for Renee's. But no, that was all I needed. A schoolgirl who would question the role of the penis in modern society. What I wanted was revenge. A vessel to contain my humiliation. Though I hadn't seen her in several weeks, I headed for Butterfly's.

Gallimard enters Song's apartment.

Song.   Oh! Rene . . . I was dreaming!

Gallimard.   You've been drinking?

Song.   If I can't sleep, then yes, I drink. But then, it gives me these dreams which—Rene, it's been almost three weeks since you visited me last.

Gallimard.   I know. There's been a lot going on in the world.

Song.   Fortunately I am drunk. So I can speak freely. It's not the world, it's you and me. And an old problem. Even the softest skin becomes like leather to a man who's touched it too often. I confess I don't know how to stop it. I don't know how to become another woman.

Gallimard.   I have a request.

Song.   Is this a solution? Or are you ready to give up the flat?

Gallimard.   It may be a solution. But I'm sure you won't like it.

Song.   Oh well, that's very important. "Like it?" Do you think I "like" lying here alone, waiting, always waiting for your return? Please—don't worry about what I may not "like."

Gallimard.   I want to see you . . . naked.

Silence.

Song.   I thought you understood my modesty. So you want me to—what— strip? Like a big cowboy girl? Shiny pasties on my breasts? Shall I fling my kimono over my head and yell "ya-hoo" in the process? I thought you respected my shame!

Gallimard.   I believe you gave me your shame many years ago.

Song.   Yes—and it is just like a white devil to use it against me. I can't believe it. I thought myself so repulsed by the passive Oriental and the cruel white man. Now I see—we are always most revolted by the things hidden within us.

Gallimard.   I just mean—

Song.   Yes?

Gallimard.   —that it will remove the only barrier left between us.

Song.   No, Rene. Don't couch your request in sweet words. Be yourself—a cad—and know that my love is enough, that I submit—submit to the worst you can give me. *(Pause.)* Well, come. Strip me. Whatever happens, know that you have willed it. Our love, in your hands. I'm helpless before my man.

Gallimard starts to cross the room.

Gallimard.   Did I not undress her because I knew, somewhere deep down, what I would find? Perhaps. Happiness is so rare that our mind can turn somersaults to protect it.

At the time, I only knew that I was seeing Pinkerton stalking towards his Butterfly, ready to reward her love with his lecherous hands. The image sickened me, pulled me to my knees, so I was crawling towards her like a worm. By the time I reached her, Pinkerton . . . had vanished from my heart. To be replaced by something new, something unnatural, that flew in the face of all I'd learned in the world—something very close to love.

He grabs her around the waist; she strokes his hair.

Gallimard.   Butterfly, forgive me.
Song.   Rene . . .
Gallimard.   For everything. From the start.
Song.   I'm . . .
Gallimard.   I want to—
Song.   I'm pregnant. *(Beat.)* I'm pregnant. *(Beat.)* I'm pregnant.

Beat.

Gallimard.   I want to marry you!

SCENE VII.   Gallimard and Butterfly's flat. Beijing. 1963.

Downstage, Song paces as Comrade Chin reads from her notepad. Upstage, Gallimard is still kneeling. He remains on his knees throughout the scene, watching it.

Song.   I need a baby.
Chin *(from pad)*.   He's been spotted going to a dorm.
Song.   I need a baby.
Chin.   At the Foreign Language Institute.
Song.   I need a baby.
Chin.   The room of a Danish girl. . . . What do you mean, you need a baby?!
Song.   Tell Comrade Kang—last night, the entire mission, it could've ended.
Chin.   What do you mean?
Song.   Tell Kang—he told me to strip.
Chin.   Strip?!
Song.   Write!
Chin.   I tell you, I don't understand nothing about this case anymore. Nothing.
Song.   He told me to strip, and I took a chance. Oh, we Chinese, we know how to gamble.

Chin *(writing).*   ". . . told him to strip."
Song.   My palms were wet, I had to make a split-second decision.
Chin.   Hey! Can you slow down?!

Pause.

Song.   You write faster, I'm the artist here. Suddenly, it hit me—"All he wants is for her to submit. Once a woman submits, a man is always ready to become 'generous.' "
Chin.   You're just gonna end up with rough notes.
Song.   And it worked! He gave in! Now, if I can just present him with a baby. A Chinese baby with blond hair—he'll be mine for life!
Chin.   Kang will never agree! The trading of babies has to be a counterrevolutionary act!
Song.   Sometimes, a counterrevolutionary act is necessary to counter a counterrevolutionary act.

Pause.

Chin.   Wait.
Song.   I need one . . . in seven months. Make sure it's a boy.
Chin.   This doesn't sound like something the Chairman would do. Maybe you'd better talk to Comrade Kang yourself.
Song.   Good. I will.

Chin gets up to leave.

Song.   Miss Chin? Why, in the Peking Opera, are women's roles played by men?
Chin.   I don't know. Maybe, a reactionary remnant of male—
Song.   No. *(Beat.)* Because only a man knows how a woman is supposed to act.

Chin exits. Song turns upstage, towards Gallimard.

Gallimard *(calling after Chin).*   Good riddance! *(To Song.)* I could forget all that betrayal in an instant, you know. If you'd just come back and become Butterfly again.
Song.   Fat chance. You're here in prison, rotting in a cell. And I'm on a plane, winging my way back to China. Your President pardoned me of our treason, you know.
Gallimard.   Yes, I read about that.
Song.   Must make you feel . . . lower than shit.
Gallimard.   But don't you, even a little bit, wish you were here with me?
Song.   I'm an artist, Rene. You were my greatest . . . acting challenge. *(She laughs.)* It doesn't matter how rotten I answer, does it? You still adore me.

That's why I love you, Rene. *(She points to us.)* So—you were telling your
audience about the night I announced I was pregnant.

*Gallimard puts his arms around Song's waist. He and Song are in the positions
they were in at the end of Scene VI.*

SCENE VIII.   Same.

Gallimard.   I'll divorce my wife. We'll live together here, and then later in
France.
Song.   I feel so . . . ashamed.
Gallimard.   Why?
Song.   I had begun to lose faith. And now, you shame me with your gener-
osity.
Gallimard.   Generosity? No, I'm proposing for very selfish reasons.
Song.   Your apologies only make me feel more ashamed. My outburst a
moment ago!
Gallimard.   Your outburst? What about my request?!
Song.   You've been very patient dealing with my . . . eccentricities. A West-
ern man, used to women freer with their bodies—
Gallimard.   It was sick! Don't make excuses for me.
Song.   I have to. You don't seem willing to make them for yourself.

Pause.

Gallimard.   You're crazy.
Song.   I'm happy. Which often looks like crazy.
Gallimard.   Then make me crazy. Marry me.

Pause.

Song.   No.
Gallimard.   What?
Song.   Do I sound silly, a slave, if I say I'm not worthy?
Gallimard.   Yes. In fact you do. No one has loved me like you.
Song.   Thank you. And no one ever will. I'll see to that.
Gallimard.   So what is the problem?
Song.   Rene, we Chinese are realists. We understand rice, gold, and guns.
You are a diplomat. Your career is skyrocketing. Now, what would happen
if you divorced your wife to marry a Communist Chinese actress?
Gallimard.   That's not being realistic. That's defeating yourself before you
begin.
Song.   We conserve our strength for the battles we can win.
Gallimard.   That sounds like a fortune cookie!
Song.   Where do you think fortune cookies come from!
Gallimard.   I don't care.

Song.   You do. So do I. And we should. That is why I say I'm not worthy. I'm
worthy to love and even to be loved by you. But I am not worthy to end the
career of one of the West's most promising diplomats.

Gallimard.   It's not that great a career! I made it sound like more than it is!

Song.   Modesty will get you nowhere. Flatter yourself, and you flatter me. I'm
flattered to decline your offer. *(She exits.)*

Gallimard *(to us).*   Butterfly and I argued all night. And, in the end, I left,
knowing I would never be her husband. She went away for several
months—to the countryside, like a small animal. Until the night I received
her call.

A baby's cry from offstage. Song enters, carrying a child.

Song.   He looks like you.

Gallimard.   Oh! *(Beat; he approaches the baby.)* Well, babies are never very
attractive at birth.

Song.   Stop!

Gallimard.   I'm sure he'll grow more beautiful with age. More like his mother.

Song.   *"Chi vide mai / a bimbo del Giappon . . ."*

Gallimard.   "What baby, I wonder, was ever born in Japan"—or China, for
that matter—

Song.   *". . . occhi azzurrini?"*

Gallimard.   "With azure eyes"—they're actually sort of brown, wouldn't you
say?

Song.   *"E il labbro."*

Gallimard.   "And such lips!" *(He kisses Song.)* And such lips.

Song.   *"E i ricciolini d'oro schietto?"*

Gallimard.   "And such a head of golden"—if slightly patchy—"curls?"

Song.   I'm going to call him "Peepee."

Gallimard.   Darling, could you repeat that because I'm sure a rickshaw just
flew by overhead.

Song.   You heard me.

Gallimard.   "Song Peepee"? May I suggest Michael, or Stephan, or Adolph?

Song.   You may, but I won't listen.

Gallimard.   You can't be serious. Can you imagine the time this child will
have in school?

Song.   In the West, yes.

Gallimard.   It's worse than naming him Ping Pong or Long Dong or—

Song.   But he's never going to live in the West, is he?

Pause.

Gallimard.   That wasn't my choice.

Song.   It is mine. And this is my promise to you: I will raise him, he will be
our child, but he will never burden you outside of China.

Gallimard.   Why do you make these promises? I want to be burdened! I want a scandal to cover the papers!

Song *(to us).*   Prophetic.

Gallimard.   I'm serious.

Song.   So am I. His name is as I registered it. And he will never live in the West.

Song exits with the child.

Gallimard *(to us).*   It is possible that her stubbornness only made me want her more. That drawing back at the moment of my capitulation was the most brilliant strategy she could have chosen. It is possible. But it is also possible that by this point she could have said, could have done . . . anything, and I would have adored her still.

    SCENE IX.   Beijing. 1966.

A *driving rhythm of Chinese percussion fills the stage.*

Gallimard.   And then, China began to change. Mao became very old, and his cult became very strong. And, like many old men, he entered his second childhood. So he handed over the reins of state to those with minds like his own. And children ruled the Middle Kingdom[8] with complete caprice. The doctrine of the Cultural Revolution[9] implied continuous anarchy. Contact between Chinese and foreigners became impossible. Our flat was confiscated. Her fame and my money now counted against us.

Two dancers in Mao suits and red-starred caps enter, and begin crudely mimicking revolutionary violence, in an agitprop fashion.

Gallimard.   And somehow the American war went wrong too. Four hundred thousand dollars were being spent for every Viet Cong[10] killed; so General Westmoreland's[11] remark that the Oriental does not value life the way Americans do was oddly accurate. Why weren't the Vietnamese people giving in? Why were they content instead to die and die and die again?

Toulon enters. Percussion and dancers continue upstage.

---

[8] From early in its history, the Chinese have called their country the Middle (or Central) Kingdom.

[9] The name given to the period from 1965 to 1967 during which any opposition to the ideological ideas of Chinese leader Mao Tse-tung was fiercely suppressed.

[10] Those in the Vietnamese Communist movement rebelling against the South Vietnam government. U.S. military forces were sent to suppress the Viet Cong.

[11] William Westmoreland commanded American military forces in Vietnam from 1964 to 1968.

Toulon. Congratulations, Gallimard.

Gallimard. Excuse me, sir?

Toulon. Not a promotion. That was last time. You're going home.

Gallimard. What?

Toulon. Don't say I didn't warn you.

Gallimard. I'm being transferred . . . because I was wrong about the American war?

Toulon. Of course not. We don't care about the Americans. We care about your mind. The quality of your analysis. In general, everything you've predicted here in the Orient . . . just hasn't happened.

Gallimard. I think that's premature.

Toulon. Don't force me to be blunt. Okay, you said China was ready to open to Western trade. The only thing they're trading out there are Western heads. And, yes, you said the Americans would succeed in Indochina. You were kidding, right?

Gallimard. I think the end is in sight.

Toulon. Don't be pathetic. And don't take this personally. You were wrong. It's not your fault.

Gallimard. But I'm going home.

Toulon. Right. Could I have the number of your mistress? (*Beat.*) Joke! Joke! Eat a croissant for me.

Toulon exits. Song, wearing a Mao suit, is dragged in from the wings as part of the upstage dance. They "beat" her, then lampoon the acrobatics of the Chinese opera, as she is made to kneel onstage.

Gallimard (*simultaneously*). I don't care to recall how Butterfly and I said our hurried farewell. Perhaps it was better to end our affair before it killed her.

Gallimard exits. Percussion rises in volume. The lampooning becomes faster, more frenetic. At its height, Comrade Chin walks across the stage with a banner reading: "The Actor Renounces His Decadent Profession!" She reaches the kneeling Song. At the moment Chin touches Song's chin, percussion stops with a thud. Dancers strike poses.

Chin. Actor-oppressor, for years you have lived above the common people and looked down on their labor. While the farmer ate millet—

Song. I ate pastries from France and sweetmeats from silver trays.

Chin. And how did you come to live in such an exalted position?

Song. I was a plaything for the imperialists!

Chin. What did you do?

Song. I shamed China by allowing myself to be corrupted by a foreigner . . .

Chin. What does this mean? The People demand a full confession!

Song. I engaged in the lowest perversions with China's enemies!

Chin.   What perversions? Be more clear!
Song.   I let him put it up my ass!

Dancers look over, disgusted.

Chin.   Aaaa-ya! How can you use such sickening language?!
Song.   My language . . . is only as foul as the crimes I committed . . .
Chin.   Yeah. That's better. So—what do you want to do . . . now?
Song.   I want to serve the people

Percussion starts up, with Chinese strings.

Chin.   What?
Song.   I want to serve the people!

Dancers regain their revolutionary smiles, and begin a dance of victory.

Chin.   What?!
Song.   I want to serve the people!!

Dancers unveil a banner: "The Actor Is Re-Habilitated!" Song remains kneeling before Chin, as the dancers bounce around them, then exit. Music out.

SCENE X.   A commune. Hunan Province. 1970.

Chin.   How you planning to do that?
Song.   I've already worked four years in the fields of Hunan, Comrade Chin.
Chin.   So? Farmers work all their lives. Let me see your hands.

Song holds them out for her inspection.

Chin.   Goddamn! Still so smooth! How long does it take to turn you actors into good anythings? Hunh. You've just spent too many years in luxury to be any good to the Revolution.
Song.   I served the Revolution.
Chin.   Served the Revolution? Bullshit! You wore dresses! Don't tell me—I was there. I saw you! You and your white vice-consul! Stuck up there in your flat, living off the People's Treasury! Yeah, I knew what was going on! You two . . . homos! Homos! Homos! *(Pause; she composes herself.)* Ah! Well . . . you will serve the people, all right. But not with the Revolution's money. This time, you use your own money.
Song.   I have no money.
Chin.   Shut up! And you won't stink up China anymore with your pervert stuff. You'll pollute the place where pollution begins—the West.
Song.   What do you mean?

Chin.   Shut up! You're going to France. Without a cent in your pocket. You find your consul's house, you make him pay your expenses—

Song.   No.

Chin.   And you give us weekly reports! Useful information!

Song.   That's crazy. It's been four years.

Chin.   Either that, or back to the rehabilitation center!

Song.   Comrade Chin, he's not going to support me! Not in France! He's a white man! I was just his plaything—

Chin.   Oh yuck! Again with the sickening language? Where's my stick?

Song.   You don't understand the mind of a man.

Pause.

Chin.   Oh no? No I don't? Then how come I'm married, huh? How come I got a man? Five, six years ago, you always tell me those kind of things, I felt very bad. But not now! Because what does the Chairman say? He tells us *I'm* now the smart one, you're now the nincompoop! *You're* the blockhead, the harebrain, the nitwit! You think you're so smart? You understand "The Mind of a Man"? Good! Then *you* go to France and be a pervert for Chairman Mao!

Chin and Song exit in opposite directions.

SCENE XI.   Paris. 1968–1970.

Gallimard enters.

Gallimard.   And what was waiting for me back in Paris? Well, better Chinese food than I'd eaten in China. Friends and relatives. A little accounting, regular schedule, keeping track of traffic violations in the suburbs. . . . And the indignity of students shouting the slogans of Chairman Mao at me—in French.

Helga.   Rene? Rene? *(She enters, soaking wet.)* I've had a . . . problem. *(She sneezes.)*

Gallimard.   You're wet.

Helga.   Yes, I . . . coming back from the grocer's. A group of students, waving red flags, they—

Gallimard fetches a towel.

Helga.   —they ran by, I was caught up along with them. Before I knew what was happening—

Gallimard gives her the towel.

Helga.   Thank you. The police started firing water cannons at us. I tried to shout, to tell them I was the wife of a diplomat, but—you know how it is . . . *(Pause.)* Needless to say, I lost the groceries. Rene, what's happening to France?

Gallimard.   What's—? Well, nothing, really.

Helga.   Nothing?! The storefronts are in flames, there's glass in the streets, buildings are toppling—and I'm wet!

Gallimard.   Nothing! . . . that I care to think about.

Helga.   And is that why you stay in this room?

Gallimard.   Yes, in fact.

Helga.   With the incense burning? You know something? I hate incense. It smells so sickly sweet.

Gallimard.   Well, I hate the French. Who just smell—period!

Helga.   And the Chinese were better?

Gallimard.   Please—don't start.

Helga.   When we left, this exact same thing, the riots—

Gallimard.   No, no . . .

Helga.   Students screaming slogans, smashing down doors—

Gallimard.   Helga—

Helga.   It was all going on in China, too. Don't you remember?!

Gallimard.   Helga! Please! *(Pause.)* You have never understood China, have you? You walk in here with these ridiculous ideas, that the West is falling apart, that China was spitting in our faces. You come in, dripping of the streets, and you leave water all over my floor. *(He grabs Helga's towel, begins mopping up the floor.)*

Helga.   But it's the truth!

Gallimard.   Helga, I want a divorce.

Pause; Gallimard continues mopping the floor.

Helga.   I take it back. China is . . . beautiful. Incense, I like incense.

Gallimard.   I've had a mistress.

Helga.   So?

Gallimard.   For eight years.

Helga.   I knew you would. I knew you would the day I married you. And now what? You want to marry her?

Gallimard.   I can't. She's in China.

Helga.   I see. You know that no one else is ever going to marry me, right?

Gallimard.   I'm sorry.

Helga.   And you want to leave. For someone who's not here, is that right?

Gallimard.   That's right.

Helga.   You can't live with her, but still you don't want to live with me.

Gallimard.   That's right.

Pause.

Helga.   Shit. How terrible that I can figure that out. *(Pause.)* I never thought I'd say it. But, in China, I was happy. I knew, in my own way, I knew that you were not everything you pretended to be. But the pretense—going on your arm to the embassy ball, visiting your office and the guards saying, "Good morning, good morning, Madame Gallimard"—the pretense . . . was very good indeed. *(Pause.)* I hope everyone is mean to you for the rest of your life. *(She exits.)*

Gallimard *(to us).*   Prophetic.

Marc enters with two drinks.

Gallimard *(to Marc).*   In China, I was different from all other men.

Marc.   Sure. You were white. Here's your drink.

Gallimard.   I felt . . . touched.

Marc.   In the head? Rene, I don't want to hear about the Oriental love goddess. Okay? One night—can we just drink and throw up without a lot of conversation?

Gallimard.   You still don't believe me, do you?

Marc.   Sure I do. She was the most beautiful, et cetera, et cetera, blasé, blasé.

Pause.

Gallimard.   My life in the West has been such a disappointment.

Marc.   Life in the West is like that. You'll get used to it. Look, you're driving me away. I'm leaving. Happy, now? *(He exits, then returns.)* Look, I have a date tomorrow night. You wanna come? I can fix you up with—

Gallimard.   Of course. I would love to come.

Pause.

Marc.   Uh—on second thought, no. You'd better get ahold of yourself first.

He exits; Gallimard nurses his drink.

Gallimard *(to us).*   This is the ultimate cruelty, isn't it? That I can talk and talk and to anyone listening, it's only air—too rich a diet to be swallowed by a mundane world. Why can't anyone understand? That in China, I once loved, and was loved by, very simply, the Perfect Woman.

Song enters, dressed as Butterfly in wedding dress.

Gallimard *(to Song).*   Not again. My imagination is hell. Am I asleep this time? Or did I drink too much?

Song.   Rene!

Gallimard.   God, it's too painful! That you speak?

Song. What are you talking about? Rene—touch me.
Gallimard. Why?
Song. I'm real. Take my hand.
Gallimard. Why? So you can disappear again and leave me clutching at the air? For the entertainment of my neighbors who—?

Song touches Gallimard.

Song. Rene?

Gallimard takes Song's hand. Silence.

Gallimard. Butterfly? I never doubted you'd return.
Song. You hadn't . . . forgotten—?
Gallimard. Yes, actually, I've forgotten everything. My mind, you see—there wasn't enough room in this hard head—not for the world *and* for you. No, there was only room for one. *(Beat.)* Come, look. See? Your bed has been waiting, with the Klimt[12] poster you like, and—see? The *xiang lu*[13] you gave me?
Song. I . . . I don't know what to say.
Gallimard. There's nothing to say. Not at the end of a long trip. Can I make you some tea?
Song. But where's your wife?
Gallimard. She's by my side. She's by my side at last.

Gallimard reaches to embrace Song. Song sidesteps, dodging him.

Gallimard. Why?!
Song *(to us).* So I did return to Rene in Paris. Where I found—
Gallimard. Why do you run away? Can't we show them how we embraced that evening?
Song. Please. I'm talking.
Gallimard. You have to do what I say! I'm conjuring you up in *my* mind!
Song. Rene, I've never done what you've said. Why should it be any different in your mind? Now split—the story moves on, and I must change.
Gallimard. I welcomed you into my home! I didn't have to, you know! I could've left you penniless on the streets of Paris! But I took you in!
Song. Thank you.
Gallimard. So . . . please . . . don't change.
Song. You know I have to. You know I will. And anyway, what difference does it make? No matter what your eyes tell you, you can't ignore the truth. You already know too much.

---

[12] Gustav Klimt (1862–1918), an Austrian painter.
[13] Incense burner.

Gallimard exits. Song turns to us.

Song.   The change I'm going to make requires about five minutes. So I thought you might want to take this opportunity to stretch your legs, enjoy a drink, or listen to the musicians. I'll be here, when you return, right where you left me.

Song goes to a mirror in front of which is a washbasin of water. She starts to remove her makeup as stagelights go to half and houselights come up.

Act III

SCENE I.   A courthouse in Paris. 1986.

As he promised, Song has completed the bulk of his transformation onstage by the time the houselights go down and the stagelights come up full. As he speaks to us, he removes his wig and kimono, leaving them on the floor. Underneath, he wears a well-cut suit.

Song.   So I'd done my job better than I had a right to expect. Well, give him some credit, too. He's right—I was in a fix when I arrived in Paris. I walked from the airport into town, then I located, by blind groping, the Chinatown district. Let me make one thing clear: whatever else may be said about the Chinese, they are stingy! I slept in doorways three days until I could find a tailor who would make me this kimono on credit. As it turns out, maybe I didn't even need it. Maybe he would've been happy to see me in a simple shift and mascara. But . . . better safe than sorry.
      That was 1970, when I arrived in Paris. For the next fifteen years, yes, I lived a very comfy life. Some relief, believe me, after four years on a fucking commune in Nowheresville, China. Rene supported the boy and me, and I did some demonstrations around the country as part of my "cultural exchange" cover. And then there was the spying.

Song moves upstage, to a chair. Toulon enters as a judge, wearing the appropriate wig and robes. He sits near Song. It's 1986, and Song is testifying in a courtroom.

Song.   Not much at first. Rene had lost all his high-level contacts. Comrade Chin wasn't very interested in parking-ticket statistics. But finally, at my urging, Rene got a job as a courier, handling sensitive documents. He'd photograph them for me, and I'd pass them on to the Chinese embassy.
Judge.   Did he understand the extent of his activity?
Song.   He didn't ask. He knew that I needed those documents, and that was enough.

Judge. But he must've known he was passing classified information.
Song. I can't say.
Judge. He never asked what you were going to do with them?
Song. Nope.

Pause.

Judge. There is one thing that the court—indeed, that all of France—would like to know.
Song. Fire away.
Judge. Did Monsieur Gallimard know you were a man?
Song. Well, he never saw me completely naked. Ever.
Judge. But surely, he must've . . . how can I put this?
Song. Put it however you like. I'm not shy. He must've felt around?
Judge. Mmmmm.
Song. Not really. I did all the work. He just laid back. Of course we did enjoy more . . . complete union, and I suppose he *might* have wondered why I was always on my stomach, but. . . . But what you're thinking is, "Of course a wrist must've brushed . . . a hand hit . . . over twenty years!" Yeah. Well, Your Honor, it was my job to make him think I was a woman. And chew on this: it wasn't all that hard. See, my mother was a prostitute along the Bundt before the Revolution. And, uh, I think it's fair to say she learned a few things about Western men. So I borrowed her knowledge. In service to my country.
Judge. Would you care to enlighten the court with this secret knowledge? I'm sure we're all very curious.
Song. I'm sure you are. *(Pause.)* Okay, Rule One is: Men always believe what they want to hear. So a girl can tell the most obnoxious lies and the guys will believe them every time—"This is my first time"—"That's the biggest I've ever seen"—or *both*, which, if you really think about it, is not possible in a single lifetime. You've maybe heard those phrases a few times in your own life, yes, Your Honor?
Judge. It's not my life, Monsieur Song, which is on trial today.
Song. Okay, okay, just trying to lighten up the proceedings. Tough room.
Judge. Go on.
Song. Rule Two: As soon as a Western man comes into contact with the East—he's already confused. The West has sort of an international rape mentality towards the East. Do you know rape mentality?
Judge. Give us your definition, please.
Song. Basically, "Her mouth says no, but her eyes say yes."
  The West thinks of itself as masculine—big guns, big industry, big money—so the East is feminine—weak, delicate, poor . . . but good at art, and full of inscrutable wisdom—the feminine mystique.
  Her mouth says no, but her eyes say yes. The West believes the East, deep down, *wants* to be dominated—because a woman can't think for herself.

Judge.   What does this have to do with my question?

Song.   You expect Oriental countries to submit to your guns, and you expect Oriental women to be submissive to your men. That's why you say they make the best wives.

Judge.   But why would that make it possible for you to fool Monsieur Gallimard? Please—get to the point.

Song.   One, because when he finally met his fantasy woman, he wanted more than anything to believe that she was, in fact, a woman. And second, I am an Oriental. And being an Oriental, I could never be completely a man.

Pause.

Judge.   Your armchair political theory is tenuous, Monsieur Song.

Song.   You think so? That's why you'll lose in all your dealings with the East.

Judge.   Just answer my question: did he know you were a man?

Pause.

Song.   You know, Your Honor, I never asked.

   SCENE II.   Same.

Music from the "Death Scene" from Butterfly *blares over the house speakers. It is the loudest thing we've heard in this play.*
   Gallimard enters, crawling towards Song's wig and kimono.

Gallimard.   Butterfly? Butterfly?

Song remains a man, in the witness box, delivering a testimony we do not hear.

Gallimard *(to us).*   In my moment of greatest shame, here, in this courtroom—with that . . . person up there, telling the world. . . . What strikes me especially is how shallow he is, how glib and obsequious . . . completely . . . without substance! The type that prowls around discos with a gold medallion stinking of garlic. So little like my Butterfly.

   Yet even in this moment my mind remains agile, flip-flopping like a man on a trampoline. Even now, my picture dissolves, and I see that . . . witness . . . talking to me.

Song suddenly stands straight up in his witness box, and looks at Gallimard.

Song.   Yes. You. White man.

Song steps out of the witness box, and moves downstage towards Gallimard. Light change.

Gallimard *(to Song).*   Who? Me?

Song.   Do you see any other white men?

Gallimard.   Yes. There're white men all around. This is a French courtroom.

Song.   So you are an adventurous imperialist. Tell me, why did it take you so long? To come back to this place?

Gallimard.   What place?

Song.   This theater in China. Where we met many years ago.

Gallimard *(to us).*   And once again, against my will, I am transported.

Chinese opera music comes up on the speakers. Song begins to do opera moves, as he did the night they met.

Song.   Do you remember? The night you gave your heart?

Gallimard.   It was a long time ago.

Song.   Not long enough. A night that turned your world upside down.

Gallimard.   Perhaps.

Song.   Oh, be honest with me. What's another bit of flattery when you've already given me twenty years' worth? It's a wonder my head hasn't swollen to the size of China.

Gallimard.   Who's to say it hasn't?

Song.   Who's to say? And what's the shame? In pride? You think I could've pulled this off if I wasn't already full of pride when we met? No, not just pride. Arrogance. It takes arrogance, really—to believe you can will, with your eyes and your lips, the destiny of another. *(He dances.)* C'mon. Admit it. You still want me. Even in slacks and a button-down collar.

Gallimard.   I don't see what the point of—

Song.   You don't? Well maybe, Rene, just maybe—I want you.

Gallimard.   You do?

Song.   Then again, maybe I'm just playing with you. How can you tell? *(Reprising his feminine character, he sidles up to Gallimard.)* "How I wish there were even a small café to sit in. With men in tuxedos, and cappuccinos, and bad expatriate jazz." Now you want to kiss me, don't you?

Gallimard *(pulling away).*   What makes you—?

Song.   —so sure? See? I take the words from your mouth. Then I wait for you to come and retrieve them. *(He reclines on the floor.)*

Gallimard.   Why?! Why do you treat me so cruelly?

Song.   Perhaps I *was* treating you cruelly. But now—I'm being nice. Come here, my little one.

Gallimard.   I'm not your little one!

Song.   My mistake. It's I who am *your* little one, right?

Gallimard.   Yes, I—

Song.   So come get your little one. If you like, I may even let you strip me.

Gallimard.   I mean, you were! Before . . . but not like this!

Song.   I was? Then perhaps I still am. If you look hard enough. *(He starts to remove his clothes.)*

Gallimard. What—what are you doing?

Song. Helping you to see through my act.

Gallimard. Stop that! I don't want to! I don't—

Song. Oh, but you asked me to strip, remember?

Gallimard. What? That was years ago! And I took it back!

Song. No. You postponed it. Postponed the inevitable. Today, the inevitable has come calling.

From the speakers, cacophony: Butterfly *mixed in with Chinese gongs.*

Gallimard. No! Stop! I don't want to see!

Song. Then look away.

Gallimard. You're only in my mind! All this is in my mind! I order you! To stop!

Song. To what? To strip? That's just what I'm—

Gallimard. No! Stop! I want you—!

Song. You want me?

Gallimard. To stop!

Song. You know something, Rene? Your mouth says no, but your eyes say yes. Turn them away. I dare you.

Gallimard. I don't have to! Every night, you say you're going to strip, but then I beg you and you stop!

Song. I guess tonight is different.

Gallimard. Why? Why should that be?

Song. Maybe I've become frustrated. Maybe I'm saying "Look at me, you fool!" Or maybe I'm just feeling . . . sexy. *(He is down to his briefs.)*

Gallimard. Please. This is unnecessary. I know what you are.

Song. You do? What am I?

Gallimard. A—a man.

Song. You don't really believe that.

Gallimard. Yes I do! I knew all the time somewhere that my happiness was temporary, my love a deception. But my mind kept the knowledge at bay. To make the wait bearable.

Song. Monsieur Gallimard—the wait is over.

Song drops his briefs. He is naked. Sound cue out. Slowly, we and Song come to the realization that what we had thought to be Gallimard's sobbing is actually his laughter.

Gallimard. Oh god! What an idiot! Of course!

Song. Rene—what?

Gallimard. Look at you! You're a man! *(He bursts into laughter again.)*

Song. I fail to see what's so funny!

Gallimard. "You fail to see—!" I mean, you never did have much of a sense of humor, did you? I just think it's ridiculously funny that I've wasted so much time on just a man!

Song.   Wait. I'm not "just a man."

Gallimard.   No? Isn't that what you've been trying to convince me of?

Song.   Yes, but what I mean—

Gallimard.   And now, I finally believe you, and you tell me it's not true? I think you must have some kind of identity problem.

Song.   Will you listen to me?

Gallimard.   Why?! I've been listening to you for twenty years. Don't I deserve a vacation?

Song.   I'm not just any man!

Gallimard.   Then, what exactly are you?

Song.   Rene, how can you ask—? Okay, what about this?

He picks up Butterfly's robes, starts to dance around. No music.

Gallimard.   Yes, that's very nice. I have to admit.

Song holds out his arm to Gallimard.

Song.   It's the same skin you've worshipped for years. Touch it.

Gallimard.   Yes, it does feel the same.

Song.   Now—close your eyes.

Song covers Gallimard's eyes with one hand. With the other, Song draws Galli-mard's hand up to his face. Gallimard, like a blind man, lets his hands run over Song's face.

Gallimard.   This skin, I remember. The curve of her face, the softness of her cheek, her hair against the back of my hand . . .

Song.   I'm your Butterfly. Under the robes, beneath everything, it was always me. Now, open your eyes and admit it—you adore me. *(He removes his hand from Gallimard's eyes.)*

Gallimard.   You, who knew every inch of my desires—how could you, of all people, have made such a mistake?

Song.   What?

Gallimard.   You showed me your true self. When all I loved was the lie. A perfect lie, which you let fall to the ground—and now, it's old and soiled.

Song.   So—you never really loved me? Only when I was playing a part?

Gallimard.   I'm a man who loved a woman created by a man. Everything else—simply falls short.

Pause.

Song.   What am I supposed to do now?

Gallimard.   You were a fine spy, Monsieur Song, with an even finer accomplice. But now I believe you should go. Get out of my life!

Song.   Go where? Rene, you can't live without me. Not after twenty years.

Gallimard.   I certainly can't live with you—not after twenty years of betrayal.

Song.   Don't be stubborn! Where will you go?

Gallimard.   I have a date . . . with my Butterfly.

Song.   So, throw away your pride. And come . . .

Gallimard.   Get away from me! Tonight, I've finally learned to tell fantasy from reality. And, knowing the difference, I choose fantasy.

Song.   *I'm* your fantasy!

Gallimard.   You? You're as real as hamburger. Now get out! I have a date with my Butterfly and I don't want your body polluting the room! *(He tosses Song's suit at him.)* Look at these—you dress like a pimp.

Song.   Hey! These are Armani slacks and—! *(He puts on his briefs and slacks.)* Let's just say . . . I'm disappointed in you, Rene. In the crush of your adoration, I thought you'd become something more. More like . . . a woman.

But no. Men. You're like the rest of them. It's all in the way we dress, and make up our faces, and bat our eyelashes. You really have so little imagination!

Gallimard.   You, Monsieur Song? Accuse me of too little imagination? You, if anyone, should know—I am pure imagination. And in imagination I will remain. Now get out!

Gallimard bodily removes Song from the stage, taking his kimono.

Song.   Rene! I'll never put on those robes again! You'll be sorry!

Gallimard *(to Song).*   I'm already sorry! *(Looking at the kimono in his hands.)* Exactly as sorry . . . as a Butterfly.

    SCENE III.   M. Gallimard's prison cell. Paris. 1988.

Gallimard.   I've played out the events of my life night after night, always searching for a new ending to my story, one where I leave this cell and return forever to my Butterfly's arms.

Tonight I realize my search is over. That I've looked all along in the wrong place. And now, to you, I will prove that my love was not in vain—by returning to the world of fantasy where I first met her.

He picks up the kimono; dancers enter.

Gallimard.   There is a vision of the Orient that I have. Of slender women in chong sams and kimonos who die for the love of unworthy foreign devils. Who are born and raised to be the perfect women. Who take whatever punishment we give them, and bounce back, strengthened by love, unconditionally. It is a vision that has become my life.

Dancers bring the washbasin to him and help him make up his face.

Gallimard.   In public, I have continued to deny that Song Liling is a man. This brings me headlines, and is a source of great embarrassment to my French colleagues, who can now be sent into a coughing fit by the mere mention of Chinese food. But alone, in my cell, I have long since faced the truth.

  And the truth demands a sacrifice. For mistakes made over the course of a lifetime. My mistakes were simple and absolute—the man I loved was a cad, a bounder. He deserved nothing but a kick in the behind, and instead I gave him . . . all my love.

  Yes—love. Why not admit it all? That was my undoing, wasn't it? Love warped my judgment, blinded my eyes, rearranged the very lines on my face . . . until I could look in the mirror and see nothing but . . . a woman.

Dancers help him put on the Butterfly wig.

Gallimard.   I have a vision. Of the Orient. That, deep within its almond eyes, there are still women. Women willing to sacrifice themselves for the love of a man. Even a man whose love is completely without worth.

Dancers assist Gallimard in donning the kimono. They hand him a knife.

Gallimard.   Death with honor is better than life . . . life with dishonor. *(He sets himself center stage, in a seppuku position.)* The love of a Butterfly can withstand many things—unfaithfulness, loss, even abandonment. But how can it face the one sin that implies all others? The devastating knowledge that, underneath it all, the object of her love was nothing more, nothing less than . . . a man. *(He sets the tip of the knife against his body.)* It is 1988. And I have found her at last. In a prison on the outskirts of Paris. My name is Rene Gallimard—also known as Madame Butterfly.

Gallimard turns upstage and plunges the knife into his body, as music from the "Love Duet" blares over the speakers. He collapses into the arms of the dancers, who lay him reverently on the floor. The image holds for several beats. Then a tight special up on Song, who stands as a man, staring at the dead Gallimard. He smokes a cigarette; the smoke filters up through the lights. Two words leave his lips.

Song.   Butterfly? Butterfly?

Smoke rises as lights fade slowly to black.

QUESTIONS
1. Explain the title of the play. Who was Madame Butterfly? What happened to her? Why does Hwang use the abbreviation *M.?*   **2.** Examine the Western stereotypes of

Chinese and Japanese women that occur in the play. What are those stereotypes? How do they contribute to the play's impact? Are such stereotypes widely accepted in your community?   **3.** What function is served by minor characters such as Marc and Helga?   **4.** Is this play about international spying? Odd and obsessive sexuality? Political systems? Or something else? Explain.

WRITING TOPICS
1. How does *M. Butterfly*'s complex structure (its movements back and forth in time, in and out of the story of *Madame Butterfly* and the Chinese Opera) contribute to the play's central themes?   **2.** In an essay, describe the implications of the play's ending. Who does Gallimard emulate? How has he changed?

INNOCENCE
AND
EXPERIENCE

Child in a Straw Hat, 1886 by Mary Cassatt

ESSAYS

Shooting an Elephant   (1936)

GEORGE ORWELL   [1903–1950]

In Moulmein, in lower Burma, I was hated by large numbers of people—the
only time in my life that I have been important enough for this to happen to
me. I was sub-divisional police officer of the town, and in an aimless, petty
kind of way anti-European feeling was very bitter. No one had the guts to raise
a riot, but if a European woman went through the bazaars alone somebody
would probably spit betel juice over her dress. As a police officer I was an
obvious target and was baited whenever it seemed safe to do so. When a
nimble Burman tripped me up on the football field and the referee (another
Burman) looked the other way, the crowd yelled with hideous laughter. This
happened more than once. In the end the sneering yellow faces of young men
that met me everywhere, the insults hooted after me when I was at a safe
distance, got badly on my nerves. The young Buddhist priests were the worst
of all. There were several thousands of them in the town and none of them
seemed to have anything to do except stand on street corners and jeer at
Europeans.

All this was perplexing and upsetting. For at that time I had already made
up my mind that imperialism was an evil thing and the sooner I chucked up
my job and got out of it the better. Theoretically—and secretly, of course—I
was all for the Burmese and all against their oppressors, the British. As for the
job I was doing, I hated it more bitterly than I can perhaps make clear. In a job
like that you see the dirty work of Empire at close quarters. The wretched
prisoners huddling in the stinking cages of the lock-ups, the grey, cowed faces
of the long-term convicts, the scarred buttocks of the men who had been
flogged with bamboos—all these oppressed me with an intolerable sense of
guilt. But I could get nothing into perspective. I was young and ill-educated
and I had had to think out my problems in the utter silence that is imposed
on every Englishman in the East. I did not even know that the British Empire
is dying, still less did I know that it is a great deal better than the younger
empires that are going to supplant it. All I knew was that I was stuck between
my hatred of the empire I served and my rage against the evil-spirited little
beasts who tried to make my job impossible. With one part of my mind I

181

thought of the British[1] as an unbreakable tyranny, as something clamped down, *in saecula saeculorum,*[2] upon the will of prostrate peoples; with another part I thought that the greatest joy in the world would be to drive a bayonet into a Buddhist priest's guts. Feelings like these are the normal by-products of imperialism; ask any Anglo-Indian official, if you can catch him off duty.

One day something happened which in a roundabout way was enlightening. It was a tiny incident in itself, but it gave me a better glimpse than I had had before of the real nature of imperialism—the real motive for which despotic governments act. Early one morning the sub-inspector at a police station the other end of the town rang me up on the 'phone and said that an elephant was ravaging the bazaar. Would I please come and do something about it? I did not know what I could do, but I wanted to see what was happening and I got on to a pony and started out. I took my rifle, an old .44 Winchester and much too small to kill an elephant, but I thought the noise might be useful *in terrorem.* Various Burmans stopped me on the way and told me about the elephant's doings. It was not, of course, a wild elephant, but a tame one which had gone "must." It had been chained up, as tame elephants always are when their attack of "must" is due, but on the previous night it had broken its chain and escaped. Its mahout,[3] the only person who could manage it when it was in that state, had set out in pursuit, but had taken the wrong direction and was now twelve hours' journey away, and in the morning the elephant had suddenly reappeared in the town. The Burmese population had no weapons and were quite helpless against it. It had already destroyed somebody's bamboo hut, killed a cow and raided some fruit-stalls and devoured the stock; also it had met the municipal rubbish van and, when the driver jumped out and took to his heels, had turned the van over and inflicted violences upon it.

The Burmese sub-inspector and some Indian constables were waiting for me in the quarter where the elephant had been seen. It was a very poor quarter, a labyrinth of squalid bamboo huts, thatched with palm-leaf, winding all over a steep hillside. I remember that it was a cloudy, stuffy morning at the beginning of the rains. We began questioning the people as to where the elephant had gone and, as usual, failed to get any definite information. That is invariably the case in the East; a story always sounds clear enough at a distance, but the nearer you get to the scene of events the vaguer it becomes. Some of the people said that the elephant had gone in one direction, some said that he had gone in another, some professed not even to have heard of any elephant. I had almost made up my mind that the whole story was a pack of lies, when we heard yells a little distance away. There was a loud, scandalized cry of "Go away, child! Go away this instant!" and an old woman with a switch in her hand came round the corner of a hut, violently shooing away a crowd of naked children. Some more women followed, clicking their tongues and exclaiming; evidently there was something that the children ought not to have

---

[1] The imperial British government of India and Burma.
[2] For eternity.
[3] The keeper and driver of an elephant.

seen. I rounded the hut and saw a man's dead body sprawling in the mud. He was an Indian, a black Dravidian coolie, almost naked, and he could not have been dead many minutes. The people said that the elephant had come suddenly upon him round the corner of the hut, caught him with its trunk, put its foot on his back and ground him into the earth. This was the rainy season and the ground was soft, and his face had scored a trench a foot deep and a couple of yards long. He was lying on his belly with arms crucified and head sharply twisted to one side. His face was coated with mud, the eyes wide open, the teeth bared and grinning with an expression of unendurable agony. (Never tell me, by the way, that the dead look peaceful. Most of the corpses I have seen look devilish.) The friction of the great beast's foot had stripped the skin from his back as neatly as one skins a rabbit. As soon as I saw the dead man I sent an orderly to a friend's house nearby to borrow an elephant rifle. I had already sent back the pony, not wanting it to go mad with fright and throw me if it smelt the elephant.

The orderly came back in a few minutes with a rifle and five cartridges, and   5 meanwhile some Burmans had arrived and told us that the elephant was in the paddy fields below, only a few hundred yards away. As I started forward practically the whole population of the quarter flocked out of the houses and followed me. They had seen the rifle and were all shouting excitedly that I was going to shoot the elephant. They had not shown much interest in the elephant when he was merely ravaging their homes, but it was different now that he was going to be shot. It was a bit of fun to them, as it would be to an English crowd; besides they wanted the meat. It made me vaguely uneasy. I had no intention of shooting the elephant—I had merely sent for the rifle to defend myself if necessary—and it is always unnerving to have a crowd following you. I marched down the hill, looking and feeling a fool, with the rifle over my shoulders and an ever-growing army of people jostling at my heels. At the bottom, when you got away from the huts, there was a metalled road and beyond that a miry waste of paddy fields a thousand yards across, not yet ploughed but soggy from the first rains and dotted with coarse grass. The elephant was standing eight yards from the road, his left side towards us. He took not the slightest notice of the crowd's approach. He was tearing up branches of grass, beating them against his knees to clean them and stuffing them into his mouth.

I had halted on the road. As soon as I saw the elephant I knew with perfect   6 certainty that I ought not to shoot him. It is a serious matter to shoot a working elephant—it is comparable to destroying a huge and costly piece of machinery—and obviously one ought not to do it if it can possibly be avoided. And at that distance, peacefully eating, the elephant looked no more dangerous than a cow. I thought then and I think now that his attack of "must" was already passing off; in which case he would merely wander harmlessly about until the mahout came back and caught him. Moreover, I did not in the least want to shoot him. I decided that I would watch him for a little while to make sure that he did not turn savage again, and then go home.

But at that moment I glanced round at the crowd that had followed me. It   7 was an immense crowd, two thousand at the least and growing every minute. It blocked the road for a long distance on either side. I looked at the sea of yellow faces above the garish clothes—faces all happy and excited over this bit of fun, all certain that the elephant was going to be shot. They were watching me as they would watch a conjurer about to perform a trick. They did not like me, but with the magical rifle in my hands I was momentarily worth watching. And suddenly I realized that I should have to shoot the elephant after all. The people expected it of me and I had got to do it; I could feel their two thousand wills pressing me forward, irresistibly. And it was at this moment, as I stood there with the rifle in my hands, that I first grasped the hollowness, the futility of the white man's dominion in the East. Here was I, the white man with his gun, standing in front of the unarmed native crowd—seemingly the leading actor of the piece; but in reality I was only an absurd puppet pushed to and fro by the will of those yellow faces behind. I perceived in this moment that when the white man turns tyrant it is his own freedoms that he destroys. He becomes a sort of hollow, posing dummy, the conventionalized figure of a sahib. For it is the condition of his rule that he shall spend his life in trying to impress the "natives," and so in every crisis he has got to do what the "natives" expect of him. He wears a mask, and his face grows to fit it. I had got to shoot the elephant. I had committed myself to doing it when I sent for the rifle. A sahib has got to act like a sahib; he has got to appear resolute, to know his own mind and do definite things. To come all that way, rifle in hand, with two thousand people marching at my heels, and then to trail feebly away, having done nothing—no, that was impossible. The crowd would laugh at me. And my whole life, every white man's life in the East, was one long struggle not to be laughed at.

But I did not want to shoot the elephant. I watched him beating his bunch of grass against his knees, with that preoccupied grandmotherly air that elephants have. It seemed to me that it would be murder to shoot him. At that age I was not squeamish about killing animals, but I had never shot an elephant and never wanted to. (Somehow it always seems worse to kill a *large* animal.) Besides, there was the beast's owner to be considered. Alive, the elephant was worth at least a hundred pounds; dead, he would only be worth the value of his tusks, five pounds, possibly. But I had to act quickly. I turned to some experienced-looking Burmans who had been there when we arrived, and asked them how the elephant had been behaving. They all said the same thing: he took no notice of you if you left him alone, but he might charge if you went too close to him.   8

It was perfectly clear to me what I ought to do. I ought to walk up to within,   9 say, twenty-five yards of the elephant and test his behavior. If he charged, I could shoot; if he took no notice of me, it would be safe to leave him until the mahout came back. But also I knew that I was going to do no such thing. I was a poor shot with a rifle and the ground was soft mud into which one would sink at every step. If the elephant charged and I missed him, I should have about as much chance as a toad under a steam-roller. But even then I was not thinking particularly of my own skin, only of the watchful yellow faces behind. For at that moment, with the crowd watching me, I was not afraid in the ordinary sense, as I would have been if I had been alone. A white man mustn't be frightened in front of "natives"; and so, in general, he isn't frightened. The sole thought in my mind was that if anything went wrong those two thousand Burmans would see me pursued, caught, trampled on and reduced to a grinning corpse like that Indian up the hill. And if that happened it was quite probable that some of them would laugh. That would never do. There was only one alternative. I shoved the cartridges into the magazine and lay down on the road to get a better aim.

The crowd grew very still, and a deep, low, happy sigh, as of people who see   10
the theatre curtain go up at last, breathed from innumerable throats. They were going to have their bit of fun after all. The rifle was a beautiful German thing with cross-hair sights. I did not then know that in shooting an elephant one would shoot to cut an imaginary bar running from ear-hole to ear-hole. I ought, therefore, as the elephant was sideways on, to have aimed straight at his ear-hole; actually I aimed several inches in front of this, thinking the brain would be further forward.

When I pulled the trigger I did not hear the bang or feel the kick—one never   11
does when a shot goes home—but I heard the devilish roar of glee that went up from the crowd. In that instant, in too short a time, one would have thought, even for the bullet to get there, a mysterious, terrible change had come over the elephant. He neither stirred nor fell, but every line of his body had altered. He looked suddenly stricken, shrunken, immensely old, as though the frightful impact of the bullet had paralysed him without knocking him down. At last, after what seemed a long time—it might have been five seconds, I dare say—he sagged flabbily to his knees. His mouth slobbered. An enormous senility seemed to have settled upon him. One could have imagined him thousands of years old. I fired again into the same spot. At the second shot he did not collapse but climbed with desperate slowness to his feet and stood weakly upright, with legs sagging and head drooping. I fired a third time. That was the shot that did for him. You could see the agony of it jolt his whole body and knock the last remnant of strength from his legs. But in falling he seemed for a moment to rise, for as his hind legs collapsed beneath him he seemed to tower upward like a huge rock toppling, his trunk reaching skywards like a tree. He trumpeted, for the first and only time. And then down he came, his belly towards me, with a crash that seemed to shake the ground even where I lay.

I got up. The Burmans were already racing past me across the mud. It was   12
obvious that the elephant would never rise again, but he was not dead. He was breathing very rhythmically with long rattling gasps, his great mound of a side painfully rising and falling. His mouth was wide open—I could see far down into caverns of pale pink throat. I waited a long time for him to die, but his breathing did not weaken. Finally I fired my two remaining shots into the spot where I thought his heart must be. The thick blood welled out of him like red velvet, but still he did not die. His body did not even jerk when the shots hit

him, the tortured breathing continued without a pause. He was dying, very slowly and in great agony, but in some world remote from me where not even a bullet could damage him further. I felt that I had got to put an end to that dreadful noise. It seemed dreadful to see the great beast lying there, powerless to move and yet powerless to die, and not even to be able to finish him. I sent back for my small rifle and poured shot after shot into his heart and down his throat. They seemed to make no impression. The tortured gasps continued as steadily as the ticking of a clock.

In the end I could not stand it any longer and went away. I heard later that   13
it took him half an hour to die. Burmans were bringing dahs[4] and baskets even before I left, and I was told they had stripped his body almost to the bones by the afternoon.

Afterwards, of course, there were endless discussions about the shooting of   14
the elephant. The owner was furious, but he was only an Indian and could do nothing. Besides, legally I had done the right thing, for a mad elephant has to be killed, like a mad dog, if its owner fails to control it. Among the Europeans opinion was divided. The older men said I was right, the younger men said it was a damn shame to shoot an elephant for killing a coolie, because an elephant was worth more than any damn Coringhee coolie. And afterwards I was very glad that the coolie had been killed; it put me legally in the right and it gave me a sufficient pretext for shooting the elephant. I often wondered whether any of the others grasped that I had done it solely to avoid looking a fool.

QUESTIONS

1. Why does Orwell disclose the significance the event had for him midway through the essay (paragraph 7) rather than saving it for the conclusion?   **2.** Examine carefully paragraphs 11 and 12, in which Orwell describes the death of the elephant. Is the reader meant to take the passage literally, or can a case be made that Orwell has imbued the elephant's death with symbolic meaning?   **3.** Orwell tells us repeatedly that his sympathies are with the Burmese. Does the language Orwell uses to describe them support his claim? Explain.

WRITING TOPIC

What does Orwell conclude regarding the position of foreign authorities in a hostile country?

---

[4] Knives.

Five Ripe Pears
1936

WILLIAM SAROYAN [1908–1981]

If old man Pollard is still alive I hope he reads this because I want him to know 1
I am not a thief and never have been. Instead of making up a lie, which I could
have done, I told the truth and got a licking. I don't care about the licking
because I got a lot of them in grammar school. They were part of my education. Some of them I deserved and some I didn't. The licking Mr. Pollard gave
me I didn't deserve, and I am going to tell him why. I couldn't tell him that
day because I didn't know how to explain what I knew.

It was about spring pears. 2

The trees grew in a yard protected by a spike fence, but some of the 3
branches grew beyond the fence. I was six, but logical. A fence, I reasoned, can
protect only that which it encloses.

Therefore, I said, the pears growing on the branches beyond the fence are 4
mine—if I can reach them.

It happened during school recess. The trees were two blocks from the school. 5

I told the Jewish boy, Isaacs, that I was going to the trees, and he said it was 6
stealing. This meant nothing, or it meant that he was afraid to go with me. I
did not bother at the time to investigate what it meant, and went running out
of the school grounds, down the street.

I reached the trees breathless but alert and smiling. The pears were fat and 7
ready. The sun was warm. The moment was a moment of numerous clarities,
air, body, and mind.

Among the leaves I watched the pears, fat and yellow and red, full of the 8
stuff of life, from the sun, and I wanted. It was a thing they could not speak
about in the second grade.

The pears were mine if I could reach them, but I couldn't. It was almost 9
enough to see them, but I had been looking at them for weeks. I had seen the
trees when they had been bare of leaf. I had seen the coming of leaves and the
coming of blossoms. I had seen the blossoms fall away before the pressure of
the hard green shapes of unripe pears.

Now the pears were ripe and ready, and I was ready. 10

But it was not to eat. It was not to steal. It was to know: *the pear*. Of 11
life—the sum of it—which *could* decay.

I was determined to get them, and remain innocent. 12

Afterwards, when they made a thief of me, I weakened and almost believed 13
I *was* a thief, but it was not so.

A misfortune of youth is that it is speechless when it has most to say, and 14
a fault of maturity is that it is garrulous when it has forgotten where to begin
or what language to use. Oh, we have been well educated in error, all right. We
at least know that we have forgotten.

I couldn't reach the pears, so I tried leaping. At first I leaped with the idea 15
of reaching a branch and lowering it, but after I had leaped two or three times
I leaped because it was fun to do so.

I was leaping when I heard the school bell ring, and I remember the ringing 16
sickened me because I knew I was going to be late. A moment afterwards,
though, I thought nothing of being late, having as justification both the ripe
pears and my discovery of leaping.

I believed it was a reasonable bargain. 17

I didn't stop to think they would ask me questions, and I wouldn't have the 18
words with which to answer them accurately.

I got five pears by using a dead tree twig. There were many more to have, 19
but I chose only five, those that were most ready. One I ate. Four I took to
class, arriving ten minutes late.

A sensible man is no less naïve at six than at sixty, but few men are sensible. 20
Four pears I took to class, showing them as the reason for lateness.

This caused an instantaneous misunderstanding, and I knew I was being 21
taken for a thief. I had nothing to say because I did have the pears. They were
both the evidence of theft and the proof of innocence. I was amazed to
discover that to Miss Larkin they were only the evidence.

She was severe and said many things. I understood only that she was angry 22
and inclined toward the opinion that I should be punished. The details are
blurred, but I remember sitting in the school office, feeling somewhat a thief,
waiting for Mr. Pollard to put in an appearance.

The pears were on his table. They were cheerless and I was frightened. 23

There was nothing else to do: I ate a pear. It was sweet, sweeter than the one 24
I had eaten by the tree. The core remained in my hand, lingering there in a
foolish way.

I ate also the core, keeping in my hand only a number of seeds. These I 25
pocketed, thinking of growing pear-trees of my own.

One pear followed another because I was frightened and disliked feeling a 26
thief.

The Principal of the school came at last. His coming was like the coming of 27
doom, and when he coughed I thought the whole world shook. He coughed a
number of times, looked at me severely a number of times, and then said: I
hear you have been stealing pears. Where are they?

I imagined he wanted to eat a pear, so I felt ashamed of myself because I had 28
none to give him, but I suppose he took it the other way around and believed
I was ashamed because I was a thief who had been caught.

I could see him taking advantage of my shame, and I knew I would be 29
punished.

It was not pleasant, either, to hear him say that I had stolen the pears. I ate 30
them, I said.

You *ate* the pears? he said. It seemed to me that he was angry. 31

Nevertheless, I said: Yes, sir. 32

How many pears? he said. 33

Four, I said.   34

You *stole* four pears, he said, and then *ate* them?   35

No, sir, I said. Five. One I ate by the tree.   36

Everything was misunderstood, but all I could do was answer questions in a   37
way that would justify his punishing me, which he did.

I cried for all I was worth, because it seemed very strange to me that no one   38
could even faintly understand why I had picked the five ripe pears.

I know Miss Larkin is dead, but if old man Pollard is still alive I hope he   39
reads this because I want him to know that I did *not* steal the pears, I created
them, and took four to class because I wanted others to see them. No hard
feelings, Mr. Pollard, but I thought I ought to tell you how it really was with
me that day.

QUESTIONS
1. Why has this event lingered in the author's memory for so many years?   **2.** Why
does the author insist that taking the pears was not stealing?   **3.** Explain what the
author means when he declares that the pears "were both the evidence of theft
and the proof of innocence" (paragraph 21).   **4.** In what sense has the author
"created" the pears, as he claims in the final paragraph?

WRITING TOPIC
Describe a childhood experience where the adult world judged you harshly or
punished you for what in your mind was an innocent act.

On Morality

(1965)

JOAN DIDION   [b. 1934]

As it happens I am in Death Valley, in a room at the Enterprise Motel and   1
Trailer Park, and it is July, and it is hot. In fact it is 119°. I cannot seem to
make the air conditioner work, but there is a small refrigerator, and I can wrap
ice cubes in a towel and hold them against the small of my back. With the help
of the ice cubes I have been trying to think, because *The American Scholar*[1]
asked me to, in some abstract way about "morality," a word I distrust more
every day, but my mind veers inflexibly toward the particular.

Here are some particulars. At midnight last night, on the road in from Las   2
Vegas to Death Valley Junction, a car hit a shoulder and turned over. The
driver, very young and apparently drunk, was killed instantly. His girl was
found alive but bleeding internally, deep in shock. I talked this afternoon to
the nurse who had driven the girl to the nearest doctor, 185 miles across the
floor of the Valley and three ranges of lethal mountain road. The nurse explained that her husband, a talc miner, had stayed on the highway with the
boy's body until the coroner could get over the mountains from Bishop, at
dawn today. "You can't just leave a body on the highway," she said. "It's
immoral."

It was one instance in which I did not distrust the word, because she meant   3
something quite specific. She meant that if a body is left alone for even a few
minutes on the desert, the coyotes close in and eat the flesh. Whether or not
a corpse is torn apart by coyotes may seem only a sentimental consideration,
but of course it is more: one of the promises we make to one another is that
we will try to retrieve our casualties, try not to abandon our dead to the
coyotes. If we have been taught to keep our promises—if, in the simplest
terms, our upbringing is good enough—we stay with the body, or have bad
dreams.

I am talking, of course, about the kind of social code that is sometimes   4
called, usually pejoratively, "wagon-train morality." In fact that is precisely
what it is. For better or worse, we are what we learned as children: my own
childhood was illuminated by graphic litanies of the grief awaiting those who
failed in their loyalties to each other. The Donner-Reed Party,[2] starving in the
Sierra snows, all the ephemera of civilization gone save that one vestigial
taboo, the provision that no one should eat his own blood kin. The Jayhawkers,
who quarreled and separated not far from where I am tonight. Some of them

---

[1] A general interest journal published by the Phi Beta Kappa Society.
[2] A group of eighty-seven people who tried to cross the mountains into California during
the stormy winter of 1846. The forty-seven who survived the ordeal ate the flesh of those who
died.

died in the Funerals[3] and some of them died down near Badwater and most of the rest of them died in the Panamints. A woman who got through gave the Valley its name. Some might say that the Jayhawkers were killed by the desert summer, and the Donner Party by the mountain winter, by circumstances beyond control; we were taught instead that they had somewhere abdicated their responsibilities, somehow breached their primary loyalties, or they would not have found themselves helpless in the mountain winter or the desert summer, would not have given way to acrimony, would not have deserted one another, would not have *failed.* In brief, we heard such stories as cautionary tales, and they still suggest the only kind of "morality" that seems to me to have any but the most potentially mendacious meaning.

You are quite possibly impatient with me by now; I am talking, you want to say, about a "morality" so primitive that it scarcely deserves the name, a code that has as its point only survival, not the attainment of the ideal good. Exactly. Particularly out here tonight, in this country so ominous and terrible that to live in it is to live with antimatter, it is difficult to believe that "the good" is a knowable quantity. Let me tell you what it is like out here tonight. Stories travel at night on the desert. Someone gets in his pickup and drives a couple of hundred miles for a beer, and he carries news of what is happening, back wherever he came from. Then he drives another hundred miles for another beer, and passes along stories from the last place as well as from the one before; it is a network kept alive by people whose instincts tell them that if they do not keep moving at night on the desert they will lose all reason. Here is a story that is going around the desert tonight: over across the Nevada line, sheriff's deputies are diving in some underground pools, trying to retrieve a couple of bodies known to be in the hole. The widow of one of the drowned boys is over there; she is eighteen, and pregnant, and is said not to leave the hole. The divers go down and come up, and she just stands there and stares into the water. They have been diving for ten days but have found no bottom to the caves, no bodies and no trace of them, only the black 90° water going down and down and down, and a single translucent fish, not classified. The story tonight is that one of the divers has been hauled up incoherent, out of his head, shouting—until they got him out of there so that the widow could not hear—about water that got hotter instead of cooler as he went down, about light flickering through the water, about magma, about underground nuclear testing.

That is the tone stories take out here, and there are quite a few of them tonight. And it is more than the stories alone. Across the road at the Faith Community Church a couple of dozen old people, come here to live in trailers and die in the sun, are holding a prayer sing. I cannot hear them and do not want to. What I can hear are occasional coyotes and a constant chorus of

---

[3] The Funerals and the Panamints are mountain ranges close to Death Valley.

"Baby the Rain Must Fall" from the jukebox in the Snake Room next door, and if I were also to hear those dying voices, those Midwestern voices drawn to this lunar country for some unimaginable atavistic rites, *rock of ages cleft for me*, I think I would lose my own reason. Every now and then I imagine I hear a rattlesnake, but my husband says that it is a faucet, a paper rustling, the wind. Then he stands by a window, and plays a flashlight over the dry wash outside.

What does it mean? It means nothing manageable. There is some sinister   7
hysteria in the air out here tonight, some hint of the monstrous perversion to which any human idea can come. "I followed my own conscience." "I did what I thought was right." How many madmen have said it and meant it? How many murderers? Klaus Fuchs said it, and the men who committed the Mountain Meadows Massacre said it, and Alfred Rosenberg[4] said it. And, as we are rotely and rather presumptuously reminded by those who would say it now, Jesus said it. Maybe we have all said it, and maybe we have been wrong. Except on that most primitive level—our loyalties to those we love—what could be more arrogant than to claim the primacy of personal conscience? ("Tell me," a rabbi asked Daniel Bell when he said, as a child, that he did not believe in God. "Do you think God cares?") At least some of the time, the world appears to me as a painting by Hieronymus Bosch;[5] were I to follow my conscience then, it would lead me out onto the desert with Marion Faye, out to where he stood in *The Deer Park*[6] looking east to Los Alamos and praying, as if for rain, that it would happen: "*. . . let it come and clear the rot and the stench and the stink, let it come for all of everywhere, just so it comes and the world stands clear in the white dead dawn.*"

Of course you will say that I do not have the right, even if I had the power,   8
to inflict that unreasonable conscience upon you; nor do I want you to inflict your conscience, however reasonable, however enlightened, upon me. ("We must be aware of the dangers which lie in our most generous wishes," Lionel Trilling[7] once wrote. "Some paradox of our nature leads us, when once we have made our fellow men the objects of our enlightened interest, to go on to make them the objects of our pity, then of our wisdom, ultimately of our coercion.") That the ethic of conscience is intrinsically insidious seems scarcely

---

[4] Klaus Fuchs fled Germany to the United States, where he worked on the development of the atomic bomb during World War II. He moved to Great Britain to assume an important position at the British atomic energy center. He was convicted and imprisoned for providing atomic energy secrets to the Soviet Union. The Mountain Meadows Massacre occurred in September 1857 in Utah. A group of 130–140 emigrants heading for California were attacked by Indians incited and joined by Mormons angry at the treatment they had received during their earlier trek across the continent. All but seventeen children were massacred. Alfred Rosenberg was a Nazi leader often called "The Grand Inquisitor of the Third Reich." He was hanged for war crimes in 1946.

[5] Hieronymus Bosch (1450?–1516), a Dutch painter of fantastic and hellish images.

[6] A novel by Norman Mailer.

[7] (1905–1975), an eminent critic of literature and modern culture.

a revelatory point, but it is one raised with increasing infrequency; even those who do raise it tend to *segue* with troubling readiness into the quite contradictory position that the ethic of conscience is dangerous when it is "wrong," and admirable when it is "right."

You see I want to be quite obstinate about insisting that we have no way of knowing—beyond that fundamental loyalty to the social code—what is "right" and what is "wrong," what is "good" and what "evil." I dwell so upon this because the most disturbing aspect of "morality" seems to me to be the frequency with which the word now appears; in the press, on television, in the most perfunctory kinds of conversation. Questions of straightforward power (or survival) politics, questions of quite indifferent public policy, questions of almost anything: they are all assigned these factitious moral burdens. There is something facile going on, some self-indulgence at work. Of course we would all like to "believe" in something, like to assuage our private guilts in public causes, like to lose our tiresome selves; like, perhaps, to transform the white flag of defeat at home into the brave white banner of battle away from home. And of course it is all right to do that; that is how, immemorially, things have gotten done. But I think it is all right only so long as we do not delude ourselves about what we are doing, and why. It is all right only so long as we remember that all the *ad hoc* committees, all the picket lines, all the brave signatures in *The New York Times*, all the tools of agitprop straight across the spectrum, do not confer upon anyone any *ipso facto* virtue. It is all right only so long as we recognize that the end may or may not be expedient, may or may not be a good idea, but in any case has nothing to do with "morality." Because when we start deceiving ourselves into thinking not that we want something or need something, not that it is a pragmatic necessity for us to have it, but that it is a *moral imperative* that we have it, then is when we join the fashionable madmen, and then is when the thin whine of hysteria is heard in the land, and then is when we are in bad trouble. And I suspect we are already there.

9

QUESTIONS

1. What instances of "wagon-train" or "primitive" morality does Didion cite? How would you characterize that morality? Why is Didion comfortable with that sort of morality?   **2.** Didion is pleased that the music from a jukebox drowns out the singing of the prayer meeting near the motel (paragraph 6). Why is she pleased? How does her identification of the musical pieces contribute to the argument of this essay?   **3.** Didion asserts that "we are what we learned as children" (paragraph 4). What does she mean by this? Are your own moral values reflections of what you learned as a child, or did those values change as you grew older? Explain.   **4.** What is the point of her including the speech from *The Deer Park* (paragraph 7)?   **5.** What names, and, by implication, events does she use to illustrate some possibilities of abstract morality? How do those names and incidents define her attitude toward abstract morality?   **6.** What role does the quotation from Lionel Trilling (paragraph 8) play in this essay?

WRITING TOPIC
Using the next-to-last sentence of this piece as the focus of your argument, write an essay in which you distinguish between *needs, wants,* and *pragmatic necessities* on one hand and *moral imperatives* on the other. Give examples to illustrate each category. Conclude with your own judgment on the usefulness or necessity of *moral imperatives.*

On Dumpster Diving[1]   1993

LARS EIGHNER   [b. 1948]

Long before I began Dumpster diving I was impressed with Dumpsters, enough   1
so that I wrote the Merriam-Webster research service to discover what I could
about the word *Dumpster*. I learned from them that it is a proprietary word
belonging to the Dempster Dumpster company. Since then I have dutifully
capitalized the word, although it was lowercased in almost all the citations
Merriam-Webster photocopied for me. Dempster's word is too apt. I have
never heard these things called anything but Dumpsters. I do not know anyone
who knows the generic name for these objects. From time to time I have heard
a wino or hobo give some corrupted credit to the original and call them Dipsy
Dumpsters.

I began Dumpster diving about a year before I became homeless.   2

I prefer the word *scavenging* and use the word *scrounging* when I mean to be   3
obscure. I have heard people, evidently meaning to be polite, use the word
foraging, but I prefer to reserve that word for gathering nuts and berries and
such, which I do also according to the season and the opportunity. *Dumpster
diving* seems to me to be a little too cute and, in my case, inaccurate because
I lack the athletic ability to lower myself into the Dumpsters as the true divers
do, much to their increased profit.

I like the frankness of the word *scavenging*, which I can hardly think of   4
without picturing a big black snail on an aquarium wall. I live from the refuse
of others. I am a scavenger. I think it a sound and honorable niche, although
if I could I would naturally prefer to live the comfortable consumer life,
perhaps—and only perhaps—as a slightly less wasteful consumer, owing to
what I have learned as a scavenger.

While Lizbeth[2] and I were still living in the shack on Avenue B as my   5
savings ran out, I put almost all my sporadic income into rent. The necessities
of daily life I began to extract from Dumpsters. Yes, we ate from them. Except
for jeans, all my clothes came from Dumpsters. Boom boxes, candles, bedding,
toilet paper, a virgin male love doll, medicine, books, a typewriter, dishes,
furnishings, and change, sometimes amounting to many dollars—I acquired
many things from the Dumpsters.

I have learned much as a scavenger. I mean to put some of what I have   6
learned down here, beginning with the practical art of Dumpster diving and
proceeding to the abstract.

*   *   *

---

[1] This chapter was composed while the author was homeless. The present tense has been
preserved [Eighner's note].

[2] The author's dog, apparently a Labrador mix.

195

What is safe to eat?　　　　　　　　　　　　　　　　　　　　　7

After all, the finding of objects is becoming something of an urban art. Even　　8
respectable employed people will sometimes find something tempting sticking
out of a Dumpster or standing beside one. Quite a number of people, not all
of them of the bohemian type, are willing to brag that they found this or that
piece in the trash. But eating from Dumpsters is what separates the dilettani
from the professionals. Eating safely from the Dumpsters involves three principles: using the senses and common sense to evaluate the condition of the
found materials, knowing the Dumpsters of a given area and checking them
regularly, and seeking always to answer the question "Why was this discarded?"

Perhaps everyone who has a kitchen and a regular supply of groceries has, at　　9
one time or another, made a sandwich and eaten half of it before discovering
mold on the bread or got a mouthful of milk before realizing the milk had
turned. Nothing of the sort is likely to happen to a Dumpster diver because he
is constantly reminded that most food is discarded for a reason. Yet a lot of
perfectly good food can be found in Dumpsters.

Canned goods, for example, turn up fairly often in the Dumpsters I fre-　　10
quent. All except the most phobic people would be willing to eat from a can,
even if it came from a Dumpster. Canned goods are among the safest of foods
to be found in Dumpsters but are not utterly foolproof.

Although very rare with modern canning methods, botulism is a possibility.　　11
Most other forms of food poisoning seldom do lasting harm to a healthy
person, but botulism is almost certainly fatal and often the first symptom is
death. Except for carbonated beverages, all canned goods should contain a
slight vacuum and suck air when first punctured. Bulging, rusty, and dented
cans and cans that spew when punctured should be avoided, especially when
the contents are not very acidic or syrupy.

Heat can break down the botulin, but this requires much more cooking than　　12
most people do to canned goods. To the extent that botulism occurs at all, of
course, it can occur in cans on pantry shelves as well as in cans from Dumpsters. Need I say that home-canned goods are simply too risky to be recommended.

From time to time one of my companions, aware of the source of my　　13
provisions, will ask, "Do you think these crackers are really safe to eat?" For
some reason it is most often the crackers they ask about.

This question has always made me angry. Of course I would not offer my　　14
companion anything I had doubts about. But more than that, I wonder why he
cannot evaluate the condition of the crackers for himself. I have no special
knowledge and I have been wrong before. Since he knows where the food
comes from, it seems to me he ought to assume some of the responsibility for
deciding what he will put in his mouth. For myself I have few qualms about
dry foods such as crackers, cookies, cereal, chips, and pasta if they are free of
visible contaminates and still dry and crisp. Most often such things are found
in the original packaging, which is not so much a positive sign as it is the
absence of a negative one.

Raw fruits and vegetables with intact skins seems perfectly safe to me,   15
excluding of course the obviously rotten. Many are discarded for minor imperfections that can be pared away. Leafy vegetables, grapes, cauliflower, broccoli, and similar things may be contaminated by liquids and may be impractical
to wash.

Candy, especially hard candy, is usually safe if it has not drawn ants. Choc-   16
olate is often discarded only because it has become discolored as the cocoa
butter de-emulsified. Candying, after all, is one method of food preservation
because pathogens do not like very sugary substances.

All of these foods might be found in any Dumpster and can be evaluated   17
with some confidence largely on the basis of appearance. Beyond these are
foods that cannot be correctly evaluated without additional information.

I began scavenging by pulling pizzas out of the Dumpster behind a pizza   18
delivery shop. In general, prepared food requires caution, but in this case I
knew when the shop closed and went to the Dumpster as soon as the last of
the help left.

Such shops often get prank orders; both the orders and the products made   19
to fill them are called *bogus*. Because help seldom stays long at these places,
pizzas are often made with the wrong topping, refused on delivery for being
cold, or baked incorrectly. The products to be discarded are boxed up because
inventory is kept by counting boxes: A boxed pizza can be written off; an
unboxed pizza does not exist.

I never placed a bogus order to increase the supply of pizzas and I believe   20
no one else was scavenging in this Dumpster. But the people in the shop
became suspicious and began to retain their garbage in the shop overnight.
While it lasted I had a steady supply of fresh, sometimes warm pizza. Because
I knew the Dumpster I knew the source of the pizza, and because I visited the
Dumpster regularly I knew what was fresh and what was yesterday's.

The area I frequent is inhabited by many affluent college students. I am not   21
here by chance; the Dumpsters in this area are very rich. Students throw out
many good things, including food. In particular they tend to throw everything
out when they move at the end of a semester, before and after breaks, and
around midterm, when many of them despair of college. So I find it advantageous to keep an eye on the academic calendar.

Students throw food away around breaks because they do not know whether   22
it has spoiled or will spoil before they return. A typical discard is a half jar of
peanut butter. In fact, nonorganic peanut butter does not require refrigeration
and is unlikely to spoil in any reasonable time. The student does not know
that, and since it is Daddy's money, the student decides not to take a chance.
Opened containers require caution and some attention to the question "Why
was this discarded?" But in the case of discards from student apartments, the
answer may be that the item was thrown out through carelessness, ignorance,
or wastefulness. This can sometimes be deduced when the item is found with
many others, including some that are obviously perfectly good.

Some students, and others, approach defrosting a freezer by chucking out   23 the whole lot. Not only do the circumstances of such a find tell the story, but also the mass of frozen goods stays cold for a long time and items may be found still frozen or freshly thawed.

Yogurt, cheese, and sour cream are items that are often thrown out while they are still good. Occasionally I find a cheese with a spot of mold, which of course I pare off, and because it is obvious why such a cheese was discarded, I treat it with less suspicion than an apparently perfect cheese found in similar circumstances. Yogurt is often discarded, still sealed, only because the expiration date on the carton had passed. This is one of my favorite finds because yogurt will keep for several days, even in warm weather.

Students throw out canned goods and staples at the end of semesters and when they give up college at midterm. Drugs, pornography, spirits, and the like are often discarded when parents are expected—Dad's Day, for example. And spirits also turn up after big party weekends, presumably discarded by the newly reformed. Wine and spirits, of course, keep perfectly well even once opened, but the same cannot be said of beer.

My test for carbonated soft drinks is whether they still fizz vigorously. Many juices or other beverages are too acidic or too syrupy to cause much concern, provided they are not visibly contaminated. I have discovered nasty molds in vegetable juices, even when the product was found under its original seal; I recommend that such products be decanted slowly into a clear glass. Liquids always require some care. One hot day I found a large jug of Pat O'Brien's Hurricane mix. The jug had been opened but was still ice cold. I drank three large glasses before it became apparent to me that someone had added the rum to the mix, and not a little rum. I never tasted the rum, and by the time I began to feel the effects I had already ingested a very large quantity of the beverage. Some divers would have considered this a boon, but being suddenly intoxicated in a public place in the early afternoon is not my idea of a good time.

I have heard of people maliciously contaminating discarded food and even handouts, but mostly I have heard of this from people with vivid imaginations who have had no experience with the Dumpsters themselves. Just before the pizza shop stopped discarding its garbage at night, jalapeños began showing up on most of the thrown-out pizzas. If indeed this was meant to discourage me, it was a wasted effort because I am a native Texan.

For myself, I avoid game, poultry, pork, and egg-based foods, whether I find them raw or cooked. I seldom have the means to cook what I find, but when I do I avail myself of plentiful supplies of beef, which is often in very good condition. I suppose fish becomes disagreeable before it becomes dangerous. Lizbeth is happy to have any such thing that is past its prime and, in fact, does not recognize fish as food until it is quite strong.

Home leftovers, as opposed to surpluses from restaurants, are very often bad. Evidently, especially among students, there is a common type of personality that carefully wraps up even the smallest leftover and shoves it into the back of the refrigerator for six months or so before discarding it. Characteristic of this type are the reused jars and margarine tubs to which the remains are committed. I avoid ethnic foods I am unfamiliar with. If I do not know what it is supposed to look like when it is good, I cannot be certain I will be able to tell if it is bad.

No matter how careful I am I still get dysentery at least once a month, oftener in warm weather. I do not want to paint too romantic a picture. Dumpster diving has serious drawbacks as a way of life. 30

I learned to scavenge gradually, on my own. Since then I have initiated several companions into the trade. I have learned that there is a predictable series of stages a person goes through in learning to scavenge. 31

At first the new scavenger is filled with disgust and self-loathing. He is ashamed of being seen and may lurk around, trying to duck behind things, or he may try to dive at night. (In fact, most people instinctively look away from a scavenger. By skulking around, the novice calls attention to himself and arouses suspicion. Diving at night is ineffective and needlessly messy.) 32

Every grain of rice seems to be a maggot. Everything seems to stink. He can wipe the egg yolk off the found can, but he cannot erase from his mind the stigma of eating garbage. 33

That stage passes with experience. The scavenger finds a pair of running shoes that fit and look and smell brand-new. He finds a pocket calculator in perfect working order. He finds pristine ice cream, still frozen, more than he can eat or keep. He begins to understand: People throw away perfectly good stuff, a lot of perfectly good stuff. 34

At this stage, Dumpster shyness begins to dissipate. The diver, after all, has the last laugh. He is finding all manner of good things that are his for the taking. Those who disparage his profession are the fools, not he. 35

He may begin to hang on to some perfectly good things for which he has neither a use nor a market. Then he begins to take note of the things that are not perfectly good but are nearly so. He mates a Walkman with broken earphones and one that is missing a battery cover. He picks up things that he can repair. 36

At this stage he may become lost and never recover. Dumpsters are full of things of some potential value to someone and also of things that never have much intrinsic value but are interesting. All the Dumpster divers I have known come to the point of trying to acquire everything they touch. Why not take it, they reason, since it is all free? This is, of course, hopeless. Most divers come to realize that they must restrict themselves to items of relatively immediate utility. But in some cases the diver simply cannot control himself. I have met several of these pack-rat types. Their ideas of the values of various pieces of junk verge on the psychotic. Every bit of glass may be a diamond, they think, and all that glisters, gold. 37

I tend to gain weight when I am scavenging. Partly this is because I always find far more pizza and doughnuts than water-packed tuna, nonfat yogurt, and fresh vegetables. Also I have not developed much faith in the reliability of 38

Dumpsters as a food source, although it has been proven to me many times. I tend to eat as if I have no idea where my next meal is coming from. But mostly I just hate to see food go to waste and so I eat much more than I should. Something like this drives the obsession to collect junk.

As for collecting objects, I usually restrict myself to collecting one kind of   39 small object at a time, such as pocket calculators, sunglasses, or campaign buttons. To live on the street I must anticipate my needs to a certain extent: I must pick up and save warm bedding I find in August because it will not be found in Dumpsters in November. As I have no access to health care, I often hoard essential drugs, such as antibiotics and antihistamines. (This course can be recommended only to those with some grounding in pharmacology. Antibiotics, for example, even when indicated are worse than useless if taken in insufficient amounts.) But even if I had a home with extensive storage space, I could not save everything that might be valuable in some contingency.

I have proprietary feelings about my Dumpsters. As I have mentioned, it is   40 no accident that I scavenge from ones where good finds are common. But my limited experience with Dumpsters in other areas suggests to me that even in poorer areas, Dumpsters, if attended with sufficient diligence, can be made to yield a livelihood. The rich students discard perfectly good kiwifruit; poorer people discard perfectly good apples. Slacks and Polo shirts are found in the one place; jeans and T-shirts in the other. The population of competitors rather than the affluence of the dumpers most affects the feasibility of survival by scavenging. The large number of competitors is what puts me off the idea of trying to scavenge in places like Los Angeles.

Curiously, I do not mind my direct competition, other scavengers, so much   41 as I hate the can scroungers.

People scrounge cans because they have to have a little cash. I have tried   42 scrounging cans with an able-bodied companion. Afoot a can scrounger simply cannot make more than a few dollars a day. One can extract the necessities of life from the Dumpsters directly with far less effort than would be required to accumulate the equivalent value in cans. (These observations may not hold in places with container redemption laws.)

Can scroungers, then, are people who must have small amounts of cash.   43 These are drug addicts and winos, mostly the latter because the amounts of cash are so small. Spirits and drugs do, like all other commodities, turn up in Dumpsters and the scavenger will from time to time have a half bottle of a rather good wine with his dinner. But the wino cannot survive on these occasional finds; he must have his daily dose to stave off the DTs. All the cans he can carry will buy about three bottles of Wild Irish Rose.

I do not begrudge them the cans, but can scroungers tend to tear up the   44 Dumpsters, mixing the contents and littering the area. They become so specialized that they can see only cans. They earn my contempt by passing up change, canned goods, and readily hockable items.

There are precious few courtesies among scavengers. But it is common   45 practice to set aside surplus items: pairs of shoes, clothing, canned goods, and such. A true scavenger hates to see good stuff go to waste, and what he cannot use he leaves in good condition in plain sight.

Can scroungers lay waste to everything in their path and will stir one of a pair of good shoes to the bottom of a Dumpster, to be lost or ruined in the muck. Can scroungers will even go through individual garbage cans, something I have never seen a scavenger do.

Individual garbage cans are set out on the public easement only on garbage days. On other days going through them requires trespassing close to a dwelling. Going through individual garbage cans without scattering litter is almost impossible. Litter is likely to reduce the public's tolerance of scavenging. Individual cans are simply not as productive as Dumpsters; people in houses and duplexes do not move so often and for some reason do not tend to discard as much useful material. Moreover, the time required to go through one garbage can that serves one household is not much less than the time required to go through a Dumpster that contains the refuse of twenty apartments.

But my strongest reservation about going through individual garbage cans is that this seems to me a very personal kind of invasion to which I would object if I were a householder. Although many things in Dumpsters are obviously meant never to come to light, a Dumpster is somehow less personal.

I avoid trying to draw conclusions about the people who dump in the Dumpsters I frequent. I think it would be unethical to do so, although I know many people will find the idea of scavenger ethics too funny for words.

Dumpsters contain bank statements, correspondence, and other documents, just as anyone might expect. But there are also less obvious sources of information. Pill bottles, for example. The labels bear the name of the patient, the name of the doctor, and the name of the drug. AIDS drugs and antipsychotic medicines, to name but two groups, are specific and are seldom prescribed for any other disorders. The plastic compacts for birth-control pills usually have complete label information.

Despite all this sensitive information, I have had only one apartment resident object to my going through the Dumpster. In that case it turned out the resident was a university athlete who was taking bets and who was afraid I would turn up his wager slips.

Occasionally a find tells a story. I once found a small paper bag containing some unused condoms, several partial tubes of flavored sexual lubricants, a partially used compact of birth-control pills, and the torn pieces of a picture of a young man. Clearly she was through with him and planning to give up sex altogether.

Dumpster things are often sad—abandoned teddy bears, shredded wedding books, despaired-of sales kits. I find many pets lying in state in Dumpsters. Although I hope to get off the streets so Lizbeth can have a long and comfortable old age, I know this hope is not very realistic. So I suppose when her time comes she too will go into a Dumpster. I will have no better place for her. And after all, it is fitting, since for most of her life her livelihood has come from the Dumpster. When she finds something I think is safe that has been spilled from a Dumpster, I let her have it. She already knows the route around the best ones. I like to think that if she survives me she will have a chance of evading the dog catcher and of finding her sustenance on the route.

Silly vanities also come to rest in the Dumpsters. I am a rather accomplished needleworker. I get a lot of material from the Dumpsters. Evidently sorority girls, hoping to impress someone, perhaps themselves, with their mastery of a womanly art, buy a lot of embroider-by-number kits, work a few stitches horribly, and eventually discard the whole mess. I pull out their stitches, turn the canvas over, and work an original design. Do not think I refrain from chuckling as I make gifts from these kits.

I find diaries and journals. I have often thought of compiling a book of literary found objects. And perhaps I will one day. But what I find is hopelessly commonplace and bad without being, even unconsciously, camp. College students also discard their papers. I am horrified to discover the kind of paper that now merits an A in an undergraduate course. I am grateful, however, for the number of good books and magazines the students throw out.

In the area I know best I have never discovered vermin in the Dumpsters, but there are two kinds of kitty surprise. One is alley cats whom I meet as they leap, claws first, out of Dumpsters. This is especially thrilling when I have Lizbeth in tow. The other kind of kitty surprise is a plastic garbage bag filled with some ponderous, amorphous mass. This always proves to be used cat litter.

City bees harvest doughnut glaze and this makes the Dumpster at the doughnut shop more interesting. My faith in the instinctive wisdom of animals is always shaken whenever I see Lizbeth attempt to catch a bee in her mouth, which she does whenever bees are present. Evidently some birds find Dumpsters profitable, for birdie surprise is almost as common as kitty surprise of the first kind. In hunting season all kinds of small game turn up in Dumpsters, some of it, sadly, not entirely dead. Curiously, summer and winter, maggots are uncommon.

The worst of the living and near-living hazards of the Dumpsters are the fire ants. The food they claim is not much of a loss, but they are vicious and aggressive. It is very easy to brush against some surface of the Dumpster and pick up half a dozen or more fire ants, usually in some sensitive area such as the underarm. One advantage of bringing Lizbeth along as I make Dumpster rounds is that, for obvious reasons, she is very alert to ground-based fire ants. When Lizbeth recognizes a fire-ant infestation around our feet, she does the Dance of the Zillion Fire Ants. I have learned not to ignore this warning from Lizbeth, whether I perceive the tiny ants or not, but to remove ourselves at Lizbeth's first pas de bourée.[3] All the more so because the ants are the worst in the summer months when I wear flip-flops if I have them. (Perhaps someone will misunderstand this. Lizbeth does the Dance of the Zillion Fire Ants

---

[3] A ballet dance step.

when she recognizes more fire ants than she cares to eat, not when she is being bitten. Since I have learned to react promptly, she does not get bitten at all. It is the isolated patrol of fire ants that falls in Lizbeth's range that deserves pity. She finds them quite tasty.)

By far the best way to go through a Dumpster is to lower yourself into it. Most of the good stuff tends to settle at the bottom because it is usually weightier than the rubbish. My more athletic companions have often demonstrated to me that they can extract much good material from a Dumpster I have already been over.

To those psychologically or physically unprepared to enter a Dumpster, I recommend a stout stick, preferably with some barb or hook at one end. The hook can be used to grab plastic garbage bags. When I find canned goods or other objects loose at the bottom of a Dumpster, I lower a bag into it, roll the desired object into the bag, and then hoist the bag out—a procedure more easily described than executed. Much Dumpster diving is a matter of experience for which nothing will do except practice.

Dumpster diving is outdoor work, often surprisingly pleasant. It is not entirely predictable; things of interest turn up every day and some days there are finds of great value. I am always very pleased when I can turn up exactly the thing I most wanted to find. Yet in spite of the element of chance, scavenging more than most other pursuits tends to yield returns in some proportion to the effort and intelligence brought to bear. It is very sweet to turn up a few dollars in change from a Dumpster that has just been gone over by a wino.

The land is now covered with cities. The cities are full of Dumpsters. If a member of the canine race is ever able to know what it is doing, then Lizbeth knows that when we go around to the Dumpsters, we are hunting. I think of scavenging as a modern form of self-reliance. In any event, after having survived nearly ten years of government service, where everything is geared to the lowest common denominator, I find it refreshing to have work that rewards initiative and effort. Certainly I would be happy to have a sinecure again, but I am no longer heartbroken that I left one.

I find from the experience of scavenging two rather deep lessons. The first is to take what you can use and let the rest go by. I have come to think that there is no value in the abstract. A thing I cannot use or make useful, perhaps by trading, has no value however rare or fine it may be. I mean useful in a broad sense—some art I would find useful and some otherwise.

I was shocked to realize that some things are not worth acquiring, but now I think it is so. Some material things are white elephants that eat up the possessor's substance. The second lesson is the transience of material being. This has not quite converted me to a dualist, but it has made some headway in that direction. I do not suppose that ideas are immortal, but certainly mental things are longer lived than other material things.

Once I was the sort of person who invests objects with sentimental value. Now I no longer have those objects, but I have the sentiments yet.

Many times in our travels I have lost everything but the clothes I was wearing and Lizbeth. The things I find in Dumpsters, the love letters and rag dolls of so many lives, remind me of this lesson. Now I hardly pick up a thing without envisioning the time I will cast it aside. This I think is a healthy state of mind. Almost everything I have now has already been cast out at least once, proving that what I own is valueless to someone.

Anyway, I find my desire to grab for the gaudy bauble has been largely sated. 67 I think this is an attitude I share with the very wealthy—we both know there is plenty more where what we have came from. Between us are the rat-race millions who nightly scavenge the cable channels looking for they know not what.

I am sorry for them. 68

QUESTIONS

1. What purpose does the opening paragraph serve?   **2.** What kind of reader is the author writing for?   **3.** Do Eighner's comments about students ring true? **4.** Eighner asserts that he has "come to think that there is no value in the abstract. A thing I cannot use or make useful, perhaps by trading, has no value however rare or fine it may be" (paragraph 63). Do you agree? What things had value for you as a child? Does the movement from "innocence" to "experience" alter the value of things? Explain.   **5.** What, in your opinion, are the writer's outstanding personality traits?   **6.** How would you characterize the tone and style of this essay?   **7.** What is your reaction to the conclusion of the essay, particularly the final sentence?

WRITING TOPICS

1. Describe how Eighner's essay altered your views about homelessness and Dumpster diving.   **2.** Use the following comment by the reviewer for the *New Yorker* magazine as the basis for an analysis of the tone and style of Eighner's essay: "Part of the fascination of reading Eighner comes from the cleavage between his stately, slightly fussbudget diction and the indignity of his circumstances."

Innocence and Experience

QUESTIONS AND WRITING TOPICS

1. What support do the works in this section provide for Thomas Gray's well-known observation that "where ignorance is bliss, / 'Tis folly to be wise"? **Writing Topic:** Use Gray's observation as the basis for an analysis of Flannery O'Connor's "Good Country People" or Toni Cade Bambara's "The Lesson."

2. In such poems as William Blake's "The Garden of Love," William Wordsworth's "Lines Composed a Few Miles above Tintern Abbey," Robert Frost's "Birches," and Stevie Smith's "To Carry the Child," growing up is seen as a growing away from a kind of truth and reality; in other poems, such as Gerard Manley Hopkins's "Spring and Fall," and Dylan Thomas's "Fern Hill," growing up is seen as growing into truth and reality. Do these two groups of poems embody contradictory and mutually exclusive conceptions of childhood? Explain. **Writing Topic:** Select one poem from each of these two groups, and contrast the conception of childhood embodied in each.

3. An eighteenth-century novelist wrote: "Oh Innocence, how glorious and happy a portion art thou to the breast that possesses thee! Thou fearest neither the eyes nor the tongues of men. Truth, the most powerful of all things, is thy strongest friend; and the brighter the light is in which thou art displayed, the more it discovers thy transcendent beauties." Which works in this section support this assessment of innocence? Which works contradict it? How would you characterize the relationship between "truth" and "innocence" in the fiction and the drama presented here? **Writing Topic:** Use this observation as the basis for an analysis of *M. Butterfly*.

4. James Joyce's "Araby" and Flannery O'Connor's "Good Country People" deal with some aspect of sexuality as a force that moves the protagonist from innocence toward experience. How does the recognition of sexuality function in each of the stories? **Writing Topic:** Discuss the relationship between sexuality and innocence in these stories.

5. Which poems in this section depend largely on irony for their force? Can you suggest why irony is a useful device in literature that portrays innocence and experience? **Writing Topic:** Write an analysis of the function of irony in Blake's "The Garden of Love" and Hardy's "The Ruined Maid."

6. Some authors treat the passage from innocence to experience as comedy, while others treat it more seriously, even as tragedy. Do you find one or the other treatment more satisfying? Explain. **Writing Topic:** Select one short story and show how the author achieves either a comic or serious tone.

Conformity
and
Rebellion

Chez Aubert, galerie vero dodat.

Le Ventre Législatif, 1834 by Honoré Daumier

$\mathbf{A}$lthough the works in this section, like those in "Innocence and Experience," may also feature a violation of innocence, the events are usually based on the clash between the two well-articulated positions; the rebel, on principle, confronts and struggles with established authority. Central in these works is the sense of tremendous external forces—the state, the church, tradition—which can be obeyed only at the expense of conscience and humanity. At the most general level, these works confront a dilemma older than Antigonê's Thebes: the very organizations men and women establish to protect and nurture the individual demand—on pain of economic ruin, social ostracism, even spiritual or physical death—that they violate their most deeply cherished beliefs. When individuals refuse such a demand, they translate their awareness of a hostile social order into action against it and precipitate a crisis. In *Antigonê*, the issue is drawn with utter clarity: Antigonê must obey either the state (Creon) or the gods. In Henrik Ibsen's *A Doll's House*, Nora finally realizes that dehumanization is too high a price to pay for security. On a different note, in "Bartleby the Scrivener," Bartleby's "preference" not to conform to the established structures of Wall Street results in a crisis of passive resistance.

Many of the works in this section, particularly the poems, do not treat the theme of conformity and rebellion quite so explicitly and dramatically. Some, like "Eleanor Rigby," describe a world devoid of human communion and community without directly accounting for it; others, like W. H. Auden's "The Unknown Citizen," tell us that the price exacted for total conformity to the industrial superstate is spiritual death. In "Easter 1916," William Butler Yeats meditates upon the awesome meaning of the lives and deaths of political revolutionaries, and in "Harlem," Langston Hughes warns that an inflexible and constricting social order will generate explosion.

Two basic modes, then, inform the literary treatment of conformity and rebellion. While in many of the works, the individual is caught up in a crisis that forces him or her into rebellion, in other works, especially the poems, the focus may be on the individual's failure to move from awareness into action, as in Amy Lowell's "Patterns." Indeed, the portraits of Auden's unknown citizen and of E. E. Cummings's "Cambridge ladies" affirm the necessity for rebellion by rendering so effectively the hollow life of mindless conformity.

However diverse in treatment and technique, all the works in this section are about individuals trapped by complex sets of external forces that regulate and define their lives. Social beings—men and women—sometimes submit to these forces, but it is always an uneasy submission, for the purpose of these forces is to curb and control people. Individuals may recognize that they must be controlled for some larger good; yet they are aware that established social power is often abusive. The tendency of power, at its best, is to act as a conserving force that brakes the disruptive impulse to abandon and destroy, without cause, old ways and ideas. At its worst, power is self-serving. The individual must constantly judge which tendency power is enhancing. And because the power of the individual is most often negligible beside that of frequently abusive social forces, it is not surprising that many artists since the advent of the great nation-states have found a fundamental human dignity in the resistance of the individual to organized society. One of humanity's ancient and profound recognitions, after all, is that the impulse of a Creon is always to make unknown citizens of us all.

FOR THINKING AND WRITING

As you read the selections in this section, consider the following questions. You may want to write out your thoughts informally in a journal or notebook as a way of preparing to respond to the selections, or you may wish to make one of these questions the basis for a formal essay.

1. How would you define *conformity?* What forms of rebellion are possible for a person in your situation? Do you perceive yourself as a conformist? A rebel? Some combination of the two? Explain.

2. How would you define *sanity?* Based on your own definition, do you know an insane person? What form does that insanity take? Do you agree or disagree with Emily Dickinson's assertion that "Much Madness Is Divinest Sense"? Explain.

3. Discuss this proposition: Governments routinely engage in behavior that would cause an individual to be imprisoned or institutionalized.

4. Give an extended response to each of the following questions. Is war sane? Should one obey an "unjust" law? Should one be guided absolutely by religious principles?

CONFORMITY
AND
REBELLION

The Trial, 1950 by Keith Vaughan

FICTION

Bartleby the Scrivener
A STORY OF WALL STREET

1853

HERMAN MELVILLE [1819–1891]

I am a rather elderly man. The nature of my avocations, for the last thirty years, has brought me into more than ordinary contact with what would seem an interesting and somewhat singular set of men, of whom, as yet, nothing, that I know of, has ever been written—I mean, the law-copyists, or scriveners. I have known very many of them, professionally and privately, and, if I pleased, could relate divers histories, at which good-natured gentlemen might smile, and sentimental souls might weep. But I waive the biographies of all other scriveners, for a few passages in the life of Bartleby, who was a scrivener, the strangest I ever saw, or heard of. While, of other law-copyists, I might write the complete life, of Bartleby nothing of that sort can be done. I believe that no materials exist for a full and satisfactory biography of this man. It is an irreparable loss to literature. Bartleby was one of those beings of whom nothing is ascertainable, except from the original sources, and, in his case, those are very small. What my own astonished eyes saw of Bartleby, *that* is all I know of him, except, indeed, one vague report, which will appear in the sequel.

Ere introducing the scrivener, as he first appeared to me, it is fit I make some mention of myself, my employees, my business, my chambers, and general surroundings; because some such description is indispensable to an adequate understanding of the chief character about to be presented. Imprimis: I am a man who, from his youth upwards, has been filled with a profound conviction that the easiest way of life is the best. Hence, though I belong to a profession proverbially energetic and nervous, even to turbulence, at times, yet nothing of that sort have I ever suffered to invade my peace. I am one of those unambitious lawyers who never addresses a jury, or in any way draws down public applause; but, in the cool tranquillity of a snug retreat, do a snug business among rich men's bonds, and mortgages, and title-deeds. All who know me, consider me an eminently *safe* man. The late John Jacob Astor,[1] a

---

[1]A poor immigrant who rose to become one of the great business tycoons of the nineteenth century.

personage little given to poetic enthusiasm, had no hesitation in pronouncing my first grand point to be prudence; my next, method. I do not speak it in vanity, but simply record the fact, that I was not unemployed in my profession by the late John Jacob Astor; a name which, I admit, I love to repeat; for it hath a rounded and orbicular sound to it, and rings like unto bullion. I will freely add, that I was not insensible to the late John Jacob Astor's good opinion.

Some time prior to the period at which this little history begins, my avocations had been largely increased. The good old office, now extinct in the State of New York, of a Master in Chancery,[2] had been conferred upon me. It was not a very arduous office, but very pleasantly remunerative. I seldom lose my temper; much more seldom indulge in dangerous indignation at wrongs and outrages; but, I must be permitted to be rash here, and declare that I consider the sudden and violent abrogation of the office of Master in Chancery, by the new Constitution, as a—premature act; inasmuch as I had counted upon a life-lease of the profits, whereas I only received those of a few short years. But this is by the way.

My chambers were up stairs, at No. ——— Wall Street. At one end, they looked upon the white wall of the interior of a spacious sky-light shaft, penetrating the building from top to bottom.

This view might have been considered rather tame than otherwise, deficient in what landscape painters call "life." But, if so, the view from the other end of my chambers offered, at least, a contrast, if nothing more. In that direction, my windows commanded an unobstructed view of a lofty brick wall, black by age and everlasting shade; which wall required no spyglass to bring out its lurking beauties, but, for the benefit of all near-sighted spectators, was pushed up to within ten feet of my window panes. Owing to the great height of the surrounding buildings, and my chambers being on the second floor, the interval between this wall and mine not a little resembled a huge square cistern.

At the period just preceding the advent of Bartleby, I had two persons as copyists in my employment, and a promising lad as an office-boy. First, Turkey; second, Nippers; third, Ginger Nut. These may seem names, the like of which are not usually found in the Directory. In truth, they were nicknames, mutually conferred upon each other by my three clerks, and were deemed expressive of their respective persons or characters. Turkey was a short, pursy Englishman, of about my own age—that is, somewhere not far from sixty. In the morning, one might say, his face was of a fine florid hue, but after twelve o'clock, meridian—his dinner hour—it blazed like a grate full of Christmas coals; and continued blazing—but, as it were, with a gradual wane—till six o'clock P.M., or thereabouts; after which, I saw no more of the proprietor of the face, which, gaining its meridian with the sun, seemed to set with it, to rise, culminate, and decline the following day, with the like regularity and undiminished glory. There are many singular coincidences I have known in the

---

[2] Courts of Chancery often adjudicated business disputes.

course of my life, not the least among which was the fact, that, exactly when Turkey displayed his fullest beams from his red and radiant countenance, just then, too, at that critical moment, began the daily period when I considered his business capacities as seriously disturbed for the remainder of the twenty-four hours. Not that he was absolutely idle, or averse to business, then; far from it. The difficulty was, he was apt to be altogether too energetic. There was a strange, inflamed, flurried, flighty recklessness of activity about him. He would be incautious in dipping his pen into his inkstand. All his blots upon my documents were dropped there after twelve o'clock meridian. Indeed, not only would he be reckless, and sadly given to making blots in the afternoon, but, some days, he went further, and was rather noisy. At such times, too, his face flamed with augmented blazonry, as if cannel coal had been heaped on anthracite. He made an unpleasant racket with his chair; spilled his sand-box; in mending his pens, impatiently split them all to pieces, and threw them on the floor in a sudden passion; stood up, and leaned over his table, boxing his papers about in a most indecorous manner, very sad to behold in an elderly man like him. Nevertheless, as he was in many ways a most valuable person to me, and all the time before twelve o'clock meridian, was the quickest, steadiest creature, too, accomplishing a great deal of work in a style not easily to be matched—for these reasons, I was willing to overlook his eccentricities, though, indeed, occasionally, I remonstrated with him. I did this very gently, however, because, though the civilest, nay, the blandest and most reverential of men in the morning, yet, in the afternoon, he was disposed, upon provocation, to be slightly rash with his tongue—in fact, insolent. Now, valuing his morning services as I did, and resolved not to lose them—yet, at the same time, made uncomfortable by his inflamed ways after twelve o'clock—and being a man of peace, unwilling by my admonitions to call forth unseemly retorts from him, I took upon me, one Saturday noon (he was always worse on Saturdays) to hint to him, very kindly, that, perhaps, now that he was growing old, it might be well to abridge his labors; in short, he need not come to my chambers after twelve o'clock, but, dinner over, had best go home to his lodgings, and rest himself till tea-time. But no; he insisted upon his afternoon devotions. His countenance became intolerably fervid, as he oratorically assured me—gesticulating with a long ruler at the other end of the room—that if his services in the morning were useful, how indispensable, then, in the afternoon?

"With submission, sir," said Turkey, on this occasion, "I consider myself your right-hand man. In the morning I but marshal and deploy my columns; but in the afternoon I put myself at their head, and gallantly charge the foe, thus"—and he made a violent thrust with the ruler.

"But the blots, Turkey," intimated I.

"True; but, with submission, sir, behold these hairs! I am getting old. Surely, sir, a blot or two of a warm afternoon is not to be severely urged against gray hairs. Old age—even if it blot the page—is honorable. With submission, sir, we *both* are getting old."

This appeal to my fellow-feeling was hardly to be resisted. At all events, I saw that go he would not. So, I made up my mind to let him stay, resolving, nevertheless, to see to it that, during the afternoon, he had to do with my less important papers.

Nippers, the second on my list, was a whiskered, sallow, and, upon the whole, rather piratical-looking young man, of about five and twenty. I always deemed him the victim of two evil powers—ambition and indigestion. The ambition was evinced by a certain impatience of the duties of a mere copyist, an unwarrantable usurpation of strictly professional affairs, such as the original drawing up of legal documents. The indigestion seemed betokened in an occasional nervous testiness and grinning irritability, causing the teeth to audibly grind together over mistakes committed in copying; unnecessary male-dictions, hissed, rather than spoken, in the heat of business; and especially by a continual discontent with the height of the table where he worked. Though of a very ingenious, mechanical turn, Nippers could never get this table to suit him. He put chips under it, blocks of various sorts, bits of pasteboard, and at last went so far as to attempt an exquisite adjustment, by final pieces of folded blotting paper. But no invention would answer. If, for the sake of easing his back, he brought the table-lid at a sharp angle well up towards his chin, and wrote there like a man using the steep roof of a Dutch house for his desk, then he declared that it stopped the circulation in his arms. If now he lowered the table to his waistbands, and stooped over it in writing, then there was a sore aching in his back. In short, the truth of the matter was, Nippers knew not what he wanted. Or, if he wanted anything, it was to be rid of a scrivener's table altogether. Among the manifestations of his diseased ambition was a fondness he had for receiving visits from certain ambiguous-looking fellows in seedy coats, whom he called his clients. Indeed, I was aware that not only was he, at times, considerable of a ward-politician, but he occasionally did a little business at the Justices' courts, and was not unknown on the steps of the Tombs.[3] I have good reason to believe, however, that one individual who called upon him at my chambers, and who, with a grand air, he insisted was his client, was no other than a dun, and the alleged title-deed, a bill. But, with all his failings, and the annoyances he caused me, Nippers, like his compatriot Tur-key, was a very useful man to me; wrote a neat, swift hand; and, when he chose, was not deficient in a gentlemanly sort of deportment. Added to this, he always dressed in a gentlemanly sort of way; and so, incidentally, reflected credit upon my chambers. Whereas, with respect to Turkey, I had much ado to keep him from being a reproach to me. His clothes were apt to look oily, and smell of eating houses. He wore his pantaloons very loose and baggy in summer. His coats were execrable, his hat not to be handled. But while the hat was a thing of indifference to me, inasmuch as his natural civility and deference, as a dependent Englishman, always led him to doff it the moment he entered the room, yet his coat was another matter. Concerning his coats, I reasoned with

---

[3]A prison in New York City.

him; but with no effect. The truth was, I suppose, that a man with so small an income could not afford to sport such a lustrous face and a lustrous coat at one and the same time. As Nippers once observed, Turkey's money went chiefly for red ink. One winter day, I presented Turkey with a highly respectable-looking coat of my own—a padded gray coat, of a most comfortable warmth, and which buttoned straight up from the knee to the neck. I thought Turkey would appreciate the favor, and abate his rashness and obstreperousness of after-noons. But no; I verily believe that buttoning himself up in so downy and blanket-like a coat had a pernicious effect upon him—upon the same principle that too much oats are bad for horses. In fact, precisely as a rash, restive horse is said to feel his oats, so Turkey felt his coat. It made him insolent. He was a man whom prosperity harmed.

Though, concerning the self-indulgent habits of Turkey, I had my own private surmises, yet, touching Nippers, I was well persuaded that, whatever might be his faults in other respects, he was, at least, a temperate young man. But, indeed, nature herself seemed to have been his vintner, and, at his birth, charged him so thoroughly with an irritable, brandy-like disposition, that all subsequent potations were needless. When I consider how, amid the stillness of my chambers, Nippers would sometimes impatiently rise from his seat, and stooping over his table, spread his arms wide apart, seize the whole desk, and move it, and jerk it, with a grim, grinding motion on the floor, as if the table were a perverse voluntary agent and vexing him, I plainly perceive that, for Nippers, brandy-and-water were altogether superfluous.

It was fortunate for me that, owing to its peculiar cause—indigestion—the irritability and consequent nervousness of Nippers were mainly observable in the morning, while in the afternoon he was comparatively mild. So that, Turkey's paroxysms only coming on about twelve o'clock, I never had to do with their eccentricities at one time. Their fits relieved each other, like guards. When Nippers's was on, Turkey's was off; and *vice versa*. This was a good natural arrangement, under the circumstances.

Ginger Nut, the third on my list, was a lad, some twelve years old. His father was a car-man, ambitious of seeing his son on the bench instead of a cart, before he died. So he sent him to my office, as student at law, errandboy, cleaner and sweeper, at the rate of one dollar a week. He had a little desk to himself; but he did not use it much. Upon inspection, the drawer exhibited a great array of shells of various sorts of nuts. Indeed, to this quick-witted youth, the whole noble science of the law was contained in a nutshell. Not the least among the employments of Ginger Nut, as well as one which he discharged with the most alacrity, was his duty as cake and apple purveyor for Turkey and Nippers. Copying law-papers being proverbially a dry, husky sort of business, my two scriveners were fain to moisten their mouths very often with Spitzen-bergs,[4] to be had at the numerous stalls nigh the Custom House and Post Office. Also, they sent Ginger Nut very frequently for that peculiar cake—

---

[4] A variety of apple.

small, flat, round, and very spicy—after which he had been named by them. Of a cold morning, when business was but dull, Turkey would gobble up scores of these cakes, as if they were mere wafers—indeed, they sell them at the rate of six or eight for a penny—the scrape of his pen blending with the crunching of the crisp particles in his mouth. Rashest of all the fiery afternoon blunders and flurried rashnesses of Turkey, was his once moistening a ginger-cake between his lips, and clapping it on to a mortgage, for a seal. I came within an ace of dismissing him then. But he mollified me by making an oriental bow, and saying—

"With submission, sir, it was generous of me to find you in stationery on my own account."

Now my original business—that of a conveyancer and title hunter, and drawer-up of recondite documents of all sorts—was considerably increased by receiving the master's office. There was now great work for scriveners. Not only must I push the clerks already with me, but I must have additional help.

In answer to my advertisement, a motionless young man one morning stood upon my office threshold, the door being open, for it was summer. I can see that figure now—pallidly neat, pitiably respectable, incurably forlorn! It was Bartleby.

After a few words touching his qualifications, I engaged him, glad to have among my corps of copyists a man of so singularly sedate an aspect, which I thought might operate beneficially upon the flighty temper of Turkey, and the fiery one of Nippers.

I should have stated before that ground-glass folding-doors divided my premises into two parts, one of which was occupied by my scriveners, the other by myself. According to my humor, I threw open these doors, or closed them. I resolved to assign Bartleby a corner by the folding-doors, but on my side of them, so as to have this quiet man within easy call, in case any trifling thing was to be done. I placed his desk close up to a small side-window in that part of the room, a window which originally had afforded a lateral view of certain grimy backyards and bricks, but which, owing to subsequent erections, commanded at present no view at all, though it gave some light. Within three feet of the panes was a wall, and the light came down from far above, between two lofty buildings, as from a very small opening in a dome. Still further to a satisfactory arrangement, I procured a high green folding screen, which might entirely isolate Bartleby from my sight, though not remove him from my voice. And thus, in a manner, privacy and society were conjoined.

At first, Bartleby did an extraordinary quantity of writing. As if long famishing for something to copy, he seemed to gorge himself on my documents. There was no pause for digestion. He ran a day and night line, copying by sun-light and by candle-light. I should have been quite delighted with his application, had he been cheerfully industrious. But he wrote on silently, palely, mechanically.

It is, of course, an indispensable part of a scrivener's business to verify the accuracy of his copy, word by word. Where there are two or more scriveners in an office, they assist each other in this examination, one reading from the copy, the other holding the original. It is a very dull, wearisome, and lethargic affair. I can readily imagine that, to some sanguine temperaments, it would be altogether intolerable. For example, I cannot credit that the mettlesome poet, Byron, would have contentedly sat down with Bartleby to examine a law document of, say five hundred pages, closely written in a crimpy hand.

Now and then, in the haste of business, it had been my habit to assist in comparing some brief document myself, calling Turkey or Nippers for this purpose. One object I had, in placing Bartleby so handy to me behind the screen, was to avail myself of his services on such trivial occasions. It was on the third day, I think, of his being with me, and before any necessity had arisen for having his own writing examined, that, being much hurried to complete a small affair I had in hand, I abruptly called to Bartleby. In my haste and natural expectancy of instant compliance, I sat with my head bent over the original on my desk, and my right hand sideways, and somewhat nervously extended with the copy, so that, immediately upon emerging from his retreat, Bartleby might snatch it and proceed to business without the least delay.

In this very attitude did I sit when I called to him, rapidly stating what it was I wanted him to do—namely, to examine a small paper with me. Imagine my surprise, nay, my consternation, when, without moving from his privacy, Bartleby, in a singularly mild, firm voice, replied, "I would prefer not to."

I sat awhile in perfect silence, rallying my stunned faculties. Immediately it occurred to me that my ears had deceived me, or Bartleby had entirely misunderstood my meaning. I repeated my request in the clearest tone I could assume; but in quite as clear a one came the previous reply, "I would prefer not to."

"Prefer not to," echoed I, rising in high excitement, and crossing the room with a stride. "What do you mean? Are you moon-struck? I want you to help me compare this sheet here—take it," and I thrust it towards him.

"I would prefer not to," said he.

I looked at him steadfastly. His face was leanly composed; his gray eye dimly calm. Not a wrinkle of agitation rippled him. Had there been the least uneasiness, anger, impatience, or impertinence in his manner; in other words, had there been any thing ordinarily human about him, doubtless I should have violently dismissed him from the premises. But as it was, I should have as soon thought of turning my pale plaster-of-paris bust of Cicero out of doors. I stood gazing at him awhile, as he went on with his own writing, and then reseated myself at my desk. This is very strange, thought I. What had one best do? But my business hurried me. I concluded to forget the matter for the present, reserving it for my future leisure. So calling Nippers from the other room, the paper was speedily examined.

A few days after this, Bartleby concluded four lengthy documents, being quadruplicates of a week's testimony taken before me in my High Court of Chancery. It became necessary to examine them. It was an important suit, and great accuracy was imperative. Having all things arranged, I called Turkey,

Nippers, and Ginger Nut from the next room, meaning to place the four copies in the hands of my four clerks, while I should read from the original. Accordingly, Turkey, Nippers, and Ginger Nut had taken their seats in a row, each with his document in his hand, when I called to Bartleby to join this interesting group.

"Bartleby! quick, I am waiting."

I heard a slow scrape of his chair legs on the uncarpeted floor, and soon he appeared standing at the entrance of his hermitage.

"What is wanted?" said he, mildly.

"The copies, the copies," said I, hurriedly. "We are going to examine them. There—" and I held towards him the fourth quadruplicate.

"I would prefer not to," he said, and gently disappeared behind the screen.

For a few moments I was turned into a pillar of salt, standing at the head of my seated column of clerks. Recovering myself, I advanced towards the screen, and demanded the reason for such extraordinary conduct.

"*Why* do you refuse?"

"I would prefer not to."

With any other man I should have flown outright into a dreadful passion, scorned all further words, and thrust him ignominiously from my presence. But there was something about Bartleby that not only strangely disarmed me, but in a wonderful manner, touched and disconcerted me. I began to reason with him.

"These are your own copies we are about to examine. It is labor saving to you, because one examination will answer for your four papers. It is common usage. Every copyist is bound to help examine his copy. Is it not so? Will you not speak? Answer!"

"I prefer not to," he replied in a flutelike tone. It seemed to me that, while I had been addressing him, he carefully revolved every statement that I made; fully comprehended the meaning; could not gainsay the irresistible conclusion; but, at the same time, some paramount consideration prevailed with him to reply as he did.

"You are decided, then, not to comply with my request—a request made according to common usage and common sense?"

He briefly gave me to understand, that on that point my judgment was sound. Yes: his decision was irreversible.

It is not seldom the case that, when a man is browbeaten in some unprecedented and violently unreasonable way, he begins to stagger in his own plainest faith. He begins, as it were, vaguely to surmise that, wonderful as it may be, all the justice and all the reason is on the other side. Accordingly, if any disinterested persons are present, he turns to them for some reinforcement of his own faltering mind.

"Turkey," said I, "what do you think of this? Am I not right?"

"With submission, sir," said Turkey, in his blandest tone, "I think that you are."

"Nippers," said I, "what do *you* think of it?"

"I think I should kick him out of the office."

(The reader, of nice perceptions, will here perceive that, it being morning, Turkey's answer is couched in polite and tranquil terms, but Nippers replies in ill-tempered ones. Or, to repeat a previous sentence, Nippers's ugly mood was on duty, and Turkey's off.)

"Ginger Nut," said I, willing to enlist the smallest suffrage in my behalf, "what do *you* think of it?"

"I think, sir, he's a little *luny*," replied Ginger Nut, with a grin.

"You hear what they say," said I, turning towards the screen, "come forth and do your duty."

But he vouchsafed no reply. I pondered a moment in sore perplexity. But once more business hurried me. I determined again to postpone the consideration of this dilemma to my future leisure. With a little trouble we made out to examine the papers without Bartleby, though at every page or two Turkey deferentially dropped his opinion, that this proceeding was quite out of the common; while Nippers, twitching in his chair with a dyspeptic nervousness, ground out, between his set teeth, occasional hissing maledictions against the stubborn oaf behind the screen. And for his (Nippers's) part, this was the first and the last time he would do another man's business without pay.

Meanwhile Bartleby sat in his hermitage, oblivious to everything but his own peculiar business there.

Some days passed, the scrivener being employed upon another lengthy work. His late remarkable conduct led me to regard his ways narrowly. I observed that he never went to dinner; indeed, that he never went anywhere. As yet I had never, of my personal knowledge, known him to be outside of my office. He was a perpetual sentry in the corner. At about eleven o'clock though, in the morning, I noticed that Ginger Nut would advance toward the opening in Bartleby's screen, as if silently beckoned thither by a gesture invisible to me where I sat. The boy would then leave the office, jingling a few pence, and reappear with a handful of ginger-nuts, which he delivered in the hermitage, receiving two of the cakes for his trouble.

He lives, then, on ginger-nuts, thought I; never eats a dinner, properly speaking; he must be a vegetarian, then; but no; he never eats even vegetables; he eats nothing but ginger-nuts. My mind then ran on in reveries concerning the probable effects upon the human constitution of living entirely on ginger-nuts. Ginger-nuts are so called, because they contain ginger as one of their peculiar constituents, and the final flavoring one. Now, what was ginger? A hot, spicy thing. Was Bartleby hot and spicy? Not at all. Ginger, then, had no effect upon Bartleby. Probably he preferred it should have none.

Nothing so aggravates an earnest person as a passive resistance. If the individual so resisted be of a not inhumane temper, and the resisting one perfectly harmless in his passivity, then, in the better moods of the former, he will endeavor charitably to construe to his imagination what proves impossible to be solved by his judgement. Even so, for the most part, I regarded Bartleby and his ways. Poor fellow! thought I, he means no mischief; it is plain he intends no insolence; his aspect sufficiently evinces that his eccentricities are involuntary. He is useful to me. I can get along with him. If I turn him away, the chances are he will fall in with some less-indulgent employer, and then he will be rudely treated, and perhaps driven forth miserably to starve. Yes. Here I can cheaply purchase a delicious self-approval. To befriend Bartleby; to humor him in his strange willfulness, will cost me little or nothing, while I lay up in my soul what will eventually prove a sweet morsel for my conscience. But this mood was not invariable with me. The passiveness of Bartleby sometimes irritated me. I felt strangely goaded on to encounter him in new opposition—to elicit some angry spark from him answerable to my own. But, indeed, I might as well have essayed to strike fire with my knuckles against a bit of Windsor soap. But one afternoon the evil impulse in me mastered me, and the following little scene ensued:

"Bartleby," said I, "when those papers are all copied, I will compare them with you."

"I would prefer not to."

"How? Surely you do not mean to persist in that mulish vagary?"

No answer.

I threw open the folding-doors near by, and, turning upon Turkey and Nippers, exclaimed:

"Bartleby a second time says, he won't examine his papers. What do you think of it, Turkey?"

It was afternoon, be it remembered. Turkey sat glowing like a brass boiler; his bald head steaming; his hands reeling among his blotted papers.

"Think of it?" roared Turkey; "I think I'll just step behind his screen, and black his eyes for him!"

So saying, Turkey rose to his feet and threw his arms into a pugilistic position. He was hurrying away to make good his promise, when I detained him, alarmed at the effect of incautiously rousing Turkey's combativeness after dinner.

"Sit down, Turkey," said I, "and hear what Nippers has to say. What do you think of it, Nippers? Would I not be justified in immediately dismissing Bartleby?"

"Excuse me, that is for you to decide, sir. I think his conduct quite unusual, and, indeed, unjust, as regards Turkey and myself. But it may only be a passing whim."

"Ah," exclaimed I, "you have strangely changed your mind, then—you speak very gently of him now."

"All beer," cried Turkey; "gentleness is effects of beer—Nippers and I dined together to-day. You see how gentle I am, sir. Shall I go and black his eyes?"

"You refer to Bartleby, I suppose. No, not to-day, Turkey," I replied; "pray, put up your fists."

I closed the doors, and again advanced towards Bartleby. I felt additional incentives tempting me to my fate. I burned to be rebelled against again. I remembered that Bartleby never left the office.

"Bartleby," said I, "Ginger Nut is away; just step around to the post office, won't you? (it was but a three minutes' walk), and see if there is anything for me."

"I would prefer not to."

"You *will* not?"

"I *prefer* not."

I staggered to my desk, and sat there in a deep study. My blind inveteracy returned. Was there any other thing in which I could procure myself to be ignominiously repulsed by this lean, penniless wight?—my hired clerk? What added thing is there, perfectly reasonable, that he will be sure to refuse to do? "Bartleby!"

No answer.

"Bartleby," in a louder tone.

No answer.

"Bartleby," I roared.

Like a very ghost, agreeably to the laws of magical invocation, at the third summons, he appeared at the entrance of his hermitage.

"Go to the next room, and tell Nippers to come to me."

"I prefer not to," he respectfully and slowly said and mildly disappeared.

"Very good, Bartleby," said I, in a quiet sort of serenely-severe, self-possessed tone, intimating the unalterable purpose of some terrible retribution very close at hand. At the moment I half intended something of the kind. But upon the whole, as it was drawing towards my dinner-hour, I thought it best to put on my hat and walk home for the day, suffering much from perplexity and distress of mind.

Shall I acknowledge it? The conclusion of this whole business was, that it soon became a fixed fact of my chambers, that a pale young scrivener, by the name of Bartleby, had a desk there; that he copied for me at the usual rate of four cents a folio (one hundred words); but he was permanently exempt from examining the work done by him, that duty being transferred to Turkey and Nippers, out of compliment, doubtless, to their superior acuteness; moreover, said Bartleby was never, on any account, to be dispatched on the most trivial errand of any sort; and that even if entreated to take upon him such a matter, it was generally understood that he would "prefer not to"—in other words, he would refuse point blank.

As days passed on, I became considerably reconciled to Bartleby. His steadiness, his freedom from all dissipation, his incessant industry (except when he chose to throw himself into a standing revery behind his screen), his great stillness, his unalterableness of demeanor under all circumstances, made him a valuable acquisition. One prime thing was this—*he was always there*—first in the morning, continually through the day, and the last at night. I had a singular confidence in his honesty. I felt my most precious papers perfectly safe in his hands. Sometimes, to be sure, I could not, for the very soul of me, avoid falling into sudden spasmodic passions with him. For it was exceeding difficult to bear in mind all the time those strange peculiarities, privileges, and unheard of exemptions, forming the tacit stipulations on Bartleby's part under which he remained in my office. Now and then, in the eagerness of dispatching pressing business, I would inadvertently summon Bartleby, in a short, rapid tone, to put his finger, say, on the incipient tie of a bit of red tape with which I was about compressing some papers. Of course, from behind the screen the usual answer, "I prefer not to," was sure to come; and then, how could a human creature, with the common infirmities of our nature, refrain from bitterly exclaiming upon such perverseness—such unreasonableness? However, every added repulse of this sort which I received only tended to lessen the probability of my repeating the inadvertence.

Here it must be said, that according to the custom of most legal gentlemen occupying chambers in densely-populated law buildings, there were several keys to my door. One was kept by a woman residing in the attic, which person weekly scrubbed and daily swept and dusted my apartments. Another was kept by Turkey for convenience sake. The third I sometimes carried in my own pocket. The fourth I knew not who had.

Now, one Sunday morning I happened to go to Trinity Church, to hear a celebrated preacher, and finding myself rather early on the ground I thought I would walk round to my chambers for a while. Luckily I had my key with me; but upon applying it to the lock, I found it resisted by something inserted from the inside. Quite surprised, I called out; when to my consternation a key was turned from within; and thrusting his lean visage at me, and holding the door ajar, the apparition of Bartleby appeared, in his shirt sleeves, and otherwise in a strangely tattered *déshabillé*, saying quietly that he was sorry, but he was deeply engaged just then, and—preferred not admitting me at present. In a brief word or two, he moreover added, that perhaps I had better walk around the block two or three times, and by that time he would probably have concluded his affairs.

Now, the utterly unsurmised appearance of Bartleby, tenanting my law-chambers of a Sunday morning, with his cadaverously gentlemanly *nonchalance*, yet withal firm and self-possessed, had such a strange effect upon me, that incontinently I slunk away from my own door, and did as desired. But not without sundry twinges of impotent rebellion against the mild effrontery of this unaccountable scrivener. Indeed, it was his wonderful mildness chiefly, which not only disarmed me, but unmanned me as it were. For I consider that one, for the time, is somehow unmanned when he tranquilly permits his hired clerk to dictate to him, and order him away from his own premises. Furthermore, I was full of uneasiness as to what Bartleby could possibly be doing in my office in his shirt sleeves, and in an otherwise dismantled condition of a Sunday morning. Was anything amiss going on? Nay, that was out of the question. It was not to be thought of for a moment that Bartleby was an immoral person. But what could he be doing there?—copying? Nay again, whatever might be his eccentricities, Bartleby was an eminently decorous person. He would be the last man to sit down to his desk in any state approaching to nudity. Besides, it was Sunday; and there was something about

Bartleby that forbade the supposition that he would by any secular occupation violate the proprieties of the day.

Nevertheless, my mind was not pacified; and full of a restless curiosity, at last I returned to the door. Without hindrance I inserted my key, opened it, and entered. Bartleby was not to be seen. I looked round anxiously, peeped behind his screen; but it was very plain that he was gone. Upon more closely examining the place, I surmised that for an indefinite period Bartleby must have eaten, dressed, and slept in my office, and that, too, without plate, mirror, or bed. The cushioned seat of a rickety old sofa in one corner bore the faint impress of a lean, reclining form. Rolled away under his desk, I found a blanket; under the empty grate, a blacking box and brush; on a chair, a tin basin, with soap and a ragged towel; in a newspaper a few crumbs of ginger-nuts and a morsel of cheese. Yes, thought I, it is evident enough that Bartleby has been making his home here, keeping bachelor's hall all by himself. Immediately then the thought came sweeping across me, what miserable friendlessness and loneliness are here revealed! His poverty is great; but his solitude, how horrible! Think of it. Of a Sunday, Wall Street is deserted as Petra;[5] and every night of every day it is an emptiness. This building, too, which of week-days hums with industry and life, at nightfall echoes with sheer vacancy, and all through Sunday is forlorn. And here Bartleby makes his home; sole spectator of a solitude which he has seen all populous—a sort of innocent and transformed Marius brooding among the ruins of Carthage![6]

For the first time in my life a feeling of over-powering stinging melancholy seized me. Before, I had never experienced aught but a not unpleasing sadness. The bond of a common humanity now drew me irresistibly to gloom. A fraternal melancholy! For both I and Bartleby were sons of Adam. I remembered the bright silks and sparkling faces I had seen that day, in gala trim, swan-like sailing down the Mississippi of Broadway; and I contrasted them with the pallid copyist, and thought to myself, Ah, happiness courts the light, so we deem the world is gay; but misery hides aloof, so we deem that misery there is none. These sad fancyings—chimeras, doubtless, of a sick and silly brain—led on to other and more special thoughts, concerning the eccentricities of Bartleby. Presentiments of strange discoveries hovered round me. The scrivener's pale form appeared to me laid out, among uncaring strangers, in its shivering winding sheet.

Suddenly I was attracted by Bartleby's closed desk, the key in open sight left in the lock.

I mean no mischief, seek the gratification of no heartless curiosity, thought I; besides, the desk is mine, and its contents, too, so I will make bold to look within. Everything was methodically arranged, the papers smoothly placed.

---

[5]A city in Jordan found by explorers in 1812. It had been deserted and lost for centuries.
[6]Gaius Marius (155–86 B.C.), a plebeian general who was forced to flee from Rome. Nineteenth-century democratic literature sometimes pictured him old and alone among the ruins of Carthage.

The pigeon holes were deep, and removing the files of documents, I groped into their recesses. Presently I felt something there, and dragged it out. It was an old bandanna handkerchief, heavy and knotted. I opened it, and saw it was a saving's bank.

I now recalled all the quiet mysteries which I had noted in the man. I remembered that he never spoke but to answer; that, though at intervals he had considerable time to himself, yet I had never seen him reading—no, not even a newspaper; that for long periods he would stand looking out, at his pale window behind the screen, upon the dead brick wall; I was quite sure he never visited any refectory or eating house; while his pale face clearly indicated that he never drank beer like Turkey; or tea and coffee even, like other men; that he never went anywhere in particular that I could learn; never went out for a walk, unless, indeed, that was the case at present; that he had declined telling who he was, or whence he came, or whether he had any relatives in the world; that though so thin and pale, he never complained of ill health. And more than all, I remembered a certain unconscious air of pallid—how shall I call it?—of pallid haughtiness, say, or rather an austere reserve about him, which had positively awed me into my tame compliance with his eccentricities, when I had feared to ask him to do the slightest incidental thing for me, even though I might know, from his long-continued motionlessness, that behind his screen he must be standing in one of those dead-wall reveries of his.

Revolving all these things, and coupling them with the recently discovered fact, that he made my office his constant abiding place and home, and not forgetful of his morbid moodiness; revolving all these things, a prudential feeling began to steal over me. My first emotions had been those of pure melancholy and sincerest pity; but just in proportion as the forlornness of Bartleby grew and grew to my imagination, did that same melancholy merge into fear, that pity into repulsion. So true it is, and so terrible, too, that up to a certain point the thought or sight of misery enlists our best affections; but, in certain special cases, beyond that point it does not. They err who would assert that invariably this is owing to the inherent selfishness of the human heart. It rather proceeds from a certain hopelessness of remedying excessive and organic ill. To a sensitive being, pity is not seldom pain. And when at last it is perceived that such pity cannot lead to effectual succor, common sense bids the soul be rid of it. What I saw that morning persuaded me that the scrivener was the victim of innate and incurable disorder. I might give alms to his body; but his body did not pain him; it was his soul that suffered, and his soul I could not reach.

I did not accomplish the purpose of going to Trinity Church that morning. Somehow, the things I had seen disqualified me for the time from churchgoing. I walked homeward, thinking what I would do with Bartleby. Finally, I resolved upon this—I would put certain calm questions to him the next morning, touching his history, etc., and if he declined to answer them openly and unreservedly (and I supposed he would prefer not), then to give him a twenty dollar bill over and above whatever I might owe him, and tell him his services were no longer required; but that if in any other way I could assist him, I would be happy to do so, especially if he desired to return to his native place, wherever that might be, I would willingly help to defray the expenses. Moreover, if, after reaching home, he found himself at any time in want of aid, a letter from him would be sure of a reply.

The next morning came.

"Bartleby," said I, gently calling to him behind his screen.

No reply.

"Bartleby," said I, in a still gentler tone, "come here; I am not going to ask you to do anything you would prefer not to do—I simply wish to speak to you."

Upon this he noiselessly slid into view.

"Will you tell me, Bartleby, where you were born?"

"I would prefer not to."

"Will you tell me *anything* about yourself?"

"I would prefer not to."

"But what reasonable objection can you have to speak to me? I feel friendly towards you."

He did not look at me while I spoke, but kept his glance fixed upon my bust of Cicero, which, as I then sat, was directly behind me, some six inches above my head.

"What is your answer, Bartleby," said I, after waiting a considerable time for a reply, during which his countenance remained immovable, only there was the faintest conceivable tremor of the white attenuated mouth.

"At present I prefer to give no answer," he said, and retired into his hermitage.

It was rather weak in me I confess, but his manner, on this occasion, nettled me. Not only did there seem to lurk in it a certain calm disdain, but his perverseness seemed ungrateful, considering the undeniable good usage and indulgence he had received from me.

Again I sat ruminating what I should do. Mortified as I was at his behavior, and resolved as I had been to dismiss him when I entered my office, nevertheless I strangely felt something superstitious knocking at my heart, and forbidding me to carry out my purpose, and denouncing me for a villain if I dared to breathe one bitter word against this forlornest of mankind. At last, familiarly drawing my chair behind his screen, I sat down and said: "Bartleby, never mind, then, about revealing your history; but let me entreat you, as a friend, to comply as far as may be with the usages of this office. Say now, you will help to examine papers to-morrow or next day: in short, say now, that in a day or two you will begin to be a little reasonable:—say so, Bartleby."

"At present I would prefer not to be a little reasonable," was his mildly cadaverous reply.

Just then the folding-doors opened, and Nippers approached. He seemed suffering from an unusually bad night's rest, induced by severer indigestion than common. He overheard those final words of Bartleby.

"*Prefer not*, eh?" gritted Nippers—"I'd *prefer* him, if I were you, sir," addressing me—"I'd *prefer* him; I'd give him preferences, the stubborn mule! What is it, sir, pray, that he *prefers* not to do now?"

Bartleby moved not a limb.

"Mr. Nippers," said I, "I'd prefer that you would withdraw for the present."

Somehow, of late, I had got into the way of involuntarily using this word "prefer" upon all sorts of not exactly suitable occasions. And I trembled to think that my contact with the scrivener had already and seriously affected me in a mental way. And what further and deeper aberration might it not yet produce? This apprehension had not been without efficacy in determining me to summary measures.

As Nippers, looking very sour and sulky, was departing, Turkey blandly and deferentially approached.

"With submission, sir," said he, "yesterday I was thinking about Bartleby here, and I think that if he would but prefer to take a quart of good ale every day, it would do much towards mending him, and enabling him to assist in examining his papers."

"So you have got the word, too," said I, slightly excited.

"With submission, what word, sir," asked Turkey, respectfully crowding himself into the contracted space behind the screen, and by so doing, making me jostle the scrivener. "What word, sir?"

"I would prefer to be left alone here," said Bartleby, as if offended at being mobbed in his privacy.

"*That's* the word, Turkey," said I—"*that's* it."

"Oh, *prefer?* oh yes—queer word. I never use it myself. But, sir, as I was saying, if he would but prefer—"

"Turkey," interrupted I, "you will please withdraw."

"Oh certainly, sir, if you prefer that I should."

As he opened the folding-door to retire, Nippers at his desk caught a glimpse of me, and asked whether I would prefer to have a certain paper copied on blue paper or white. He did not in the least roguishly accent the word prefer. It was plain that it involuntarily rolled from his tongue. I thought to myself, surely I must get rid of a demented man, who already has in some degree turned the tongues, if not the heads of myself and clerks. But I thought it prudent not to break the dismission at once.

The next day I noticed that Bartleby did nothing but stand at his window in his dead-wall revery. Upon asking him why he did not write, he said that he had decided upon doing no more writing.

"Why, how now? What next?" exclaimed I, "do no more writing?"

"No more."

"And what is the reason?"

"Do you not see the reason for yourself?" he indifferently replied.

I looked steadfastly at him, and perceived that his eyes looked dull and glazed. Instantly it occurred to me, that his unexampled diligence in copying by his dim window for the first few weeks of his stay with me might have temporarily impaired his vision.

I was touched. I said something in condolence with him. I hinted that of course he did wisely in abstaining from writing for a while; and urged him to embrace that opportunity of taking wholesome exercise in the open air. This, however, he did not do. A few days after this, my other clerks being absent, and being in a great hurry to dispatch certain letters by the mail, I thought that, having nothing else earthly to do, Bartleby would surely be less inflexible than usual, and carry these letters to the post office. But he blankly declined. So, much to my inconvenience, I went myself.

Still added days went by. Whether Bartleby's eyes improved or not, I could not say. To all appearance, I thought they did. But when I asked him if they did, he vouchsafed no answer. At all events, he would do no copying. At last, in reply to my urgings, he informed me that he had permanently given up copying.

"What!" exclaimed I; "suppose your eyes should get entirely well—better than ever before—would you not copy then?"

"I have given up copying," he answered, and slid aside.

He remained as ever, a fixture in my chamber. Nay—if that were possible— he became still more of a fixture than before. What was to be done? He would do nothing in the office; why should he stay there? In plain fact, he had now become a millstone to me, not only useless as a necklace, but afflictive to bear. Yet I was sorry for him. I speak less than truth when I say that, on his own account, he occasioned me uneasiness. If he would but have named a single relative or friend, I would instantly have written, and urged their taking the poor fellow away to some convenient retreat. But he seemed alone, absolutely alone in the universe. A bit of wreck in the mid-Atlantic. At length, necessities connected with my business tyrannized over all other considerations. Decently as I could, I told Bartleby that in six days time he must unconditionally leave the office. I warned him to take measures, in the interval, for procuring some other abode. I offered to assist him in this endeavor, if he himself would but take the first step towards a removal. "And when you finally quit me, Bartleby," added I, "I shall see that you go not away entirely unprovided. Six days from this hour, remember."

At the expiration of that period, I peeped behind the screen, and lo! Bartleby was there.

I buttoned up my coat, balanced myself; advanced slowly towards him, touched his shoulder, and said, "The time has come; you must quit this place; I am sorry for you; here is money; but you must go."

"I would prefer not," he replied, with his back still towards me.

"You *must.*"

He remained silent.

Now I had an unbounded confidence in this man's common honesty. He had frequently restored to me sixpences and shillings carelessly dropped upon the floor, for I am apt to be very reckless in such shirt-button affairs. The proceeding, then, which followed will not be deemed extraordinary.

"Bartleby," said I, "I owe you twelve dollars on account; here are thirty-two, the odd twenty are yours—Will you take it?" and I handed the bills towards him.

But he made no motion.

"I will leave them here, then," putting them under a weight on the table. Then taking my hat and cane and going to the door, I tranquilly turned and added—"After you have removed your things from these offices, Bartleby, you will of course lock the door—since every one is now gone for the day but you—and if you please, slip your key underneath the mat, so that I may have it in the morning. I shall not see you again; so good-by to you. If, hereafter, in your new place of abode, I can be of any service to you, do not fail to advise me by letter. Good-by, Bartleby, and fare you well."

But he answered not a word; like the last column of some ruined temple, he remained standing mute and solitary in the middle of the otherwise deserted room.

As I walked home in a pensive mood, my vanity got the better of my pity. I could not but highly plume myself on my masterly management in getting rid of Bartleby. Masterly I call it, and such it must appear to any dispassionate thinker. The beauty of my procedure seemed to consist in its perfect quietness. There was no vulgar bullying, no bravado of any sort, no choleric hectoring, and striding to and fro across the apartment, jerking out vehement commands for Bartleby to bundle himself off with his beggarly traps. Nothing of the kind. Without loudly bidding Bartleby depart—as an inferior genius might have done—I *assumed* the ground that depart he must; and upon that assumption built all I had to say. The more I thought over my procedure, the more I was charmed with it. Nevertheless, next morning, upon awakening, I had my doubts—I had somehow slept off the fumes of vanity. One of the coolest and wisest hours a man has, is just after he awakes in the morning. My procedure seemed as sagacious as ever—but only in theory. How it would prove in practice—there was the rub. It was truly a beautiful thought to have assumed Bartleby's departure; but, after all, that assumption was simply my own, and none of Bartleby's. The great point was, not whether I had assumed that he would quit me, but whether he would prefer to do so. He was more a man of preferences than assumptions.

After breakfast, I walked down town, arguing the probabilities *pro* and *con*. One moment I thought it would prove a miserable failure, and Bartleby would be found all alive at my office as usual; the next moment it seemed certain that I should find his chair empty. And so I kept veering about. At the corner of Broadway and Canal Street, I saw quite an excited group of people standing in earnest conversation.

"I'll take odds he doesn't," said a voice as I passed.

"Doesn't go?—done!" said I; "put up your money."

I was instinctively putting my hand in my pocket to produce my own, when I remembered that this was an election day. The words I had overheard bore no reference to Bartleby, but to the success or non-success of some candidate for the mayoralty. In my intent frame of mind, I had, as it were, imagined that all Broadway shared in my excitement, and were debating the same question with me. I passed on, very thankful that the uproar of the street screened my momentary absent-mindedness.

As I had intended, I was earlier than usual at my office door. I stood listening for a moment. All was still. He must be gone. I tried the knob. The door was locked. Yes, my procedure had worked to a charm; he indeed must be vanished. Yet a certain melancholy mixed with this: I was almost sorry for my brilliant success. I was fumbling under the door mat for the key, which Bartleby was to have left there for me, when accidentally my knee knocked against a panel, producing a summoning sound, and in response a voice came to me from within—"Not yet; I am occupied."

It was Bartleby.

I was thunderstruck. For an instant I stood like the man who, pipe in mouth, was killed one cloudless afternoon long ago in Virginia, by summer lightning; at his own warm open window he was killed, and remained leaning out there upon the dreamy afternoon, till some one touched him, when he fell.

"Not gone!" I murmured at last. But again obeying that wondrous ascendancy which the inscrutable scrivener had over me, and from which ascendancy, for all my chafing, I could not completely escape, I slowly went down stairs and out into the street, and while walking round the block, considered what I should next do in this unheard-of perplexity. Turn the man out by an actual thrusting I could not; to drive him away by calling him hard names would not do; calling in the police was an unpleasant idea; and yet, permit him to enjoy his cadaverous triumph over me—this, too, I could not think of. What was to be done? or, if nothing could be done, was there anything further that I could *assume* in the matter? Yes, as before I had prospectively assumed that Bartleby would depart, so now I might retrospectively assume that departed he was. In the legitimate carrying out of this assumption, I might enter my office in a great hurry, and pretending not to see Bartleby at all, walk straight against him as if he were air. Such a proceeding would in a singular degree have the appearance of a home-thrust. It was hardly possible that Bartleby could withstand such an application of the doctrine of assumption. But upon second thoughts the success of the plan seemed rather dubious. I resolved to argue the matter over with him again.

"Bartleby," said I, entering the office, with a quietly severe expression, "I am seriously displeased. I am pained, Bartleby. I had thought better of you. I had imagined you of such a gentlemanly organization, that in any delicate dilemma a slight hint would suffice—in short, an assumption. But it appears I am deceived. Why," I added, unaffectedly starting, "you have not even touched that money yet," pointing to it, just where I had left it the evening previous.

He answered nothing.

"Will you, or will you not, quit me?" I now demanded in a sudden passion, advancing close to him.

"I would prefer *not* to quit you," he replied, gently emphasizing the *not*.

"What earthly right have you to stay here? Do you pay any rent? Do you pay my taxes? Or is this property yours?"

He answered nothing.

"Are you ready to go on and write now? Are your eyes recovered? Could you copy a small paper for me this morning? or help examine a few lines? or step round to the post office? In a word, will you do anything at all, to give a coloring to your refusal to depart the premises?"

He silently retired into his hermitage.

I was now in such a state of nervous resentment that I thought it but prudent to check myself at present from further demonstrations. Bartleby and I were alone. I remembered the tragedy of the unfortunate Adams and the still more unfortunate Colt in the solitary office of the latter; and how poor Colt, being dreadfully incensed by Adams, and imprudently permitting himself to get wildly excited, was at unawares hurried into his fatal act—an act which certainly no man could possibly deplore more than the actor himself.[7] Often it had occurred to me in my ponderings upon the subject that had that altercation taken place in the public street, or at a private residence, it would not have terminated as it did. It was the circumstance of being alone in a solitary office, up stairs, of a building entirely unhallowed by humanizing domestic associations—an uncarpeted office, doubtless, of a dusty, haggard sort of appearance—this it must have been, which greatly helped to enhance the irritable desperation of the hapless Colt.

But when this old Adam of resentment rose in me and tempted me concerning Bartleby, I grappled him and threw him. How? Why, simply by recalling the divine injunction: "A new commandment give I unto you, that ye love one another." Yes, this it was that saved me. Aside from higher considerations, charity often operates as a vastly wise and prudent principle—a great safeguard to its possessor. Men have committed murder for jealousy's sake, and anger's sake, and hatred's sake, and selfishness' sake, and spiritual pride's sake; but no man, that ever I heard of, ever committed a diabolical murder for sweet charity's sake. Mere self-interest, then, if no better motive can be enlisted, should, especially with high-tempered men, prompt all beings to charity and philanthropy. At any rate, upon the occasion in question, I strove to drown my exasperated feelings towards the scrivener by benevolently construing his conduct. Poor fellow, poor fellow! thought I, he don't mean anything; and besides, he has seen hard times, and ought to be indulged.

I endeavored, also, immediately to occupy myself, and at the same time to comfort my despondency. I tried to fancy, that in the course of the morning, at such time as might prove agreeable to him, Bartleby, of his own free accord, would emerge from his hermitage and take up some decided line of march in the direction of the door. But no. Half-past twelve o'clock came; Turkey began to glow in the face, overturn his inkstand, and become generally obstreperous; Nippers abated down into quietude and courtesy; Ginger Nut munched his noon apple; and Bartleby remained standing at his window in one of his profoundest dead-wall reveries. Will it be credited? Ought I to acknowledge it? That afternoon I left the office without saying one further word to him.

---

[7]A sensational homicide case in which Colt murdered Adams in a fit of passion.

Some days now passed, during which, at leisure intervals I looked a little into "Edwards on the Will," and "Priestley on Necessity."[8] Under the circumstances, those books induced a salutary feeling. Gradually I slid into the persuasion that these troubles of mine, touching the scrivener, had been all predestinated from eternity, and Bartleby was billeted upon me for some mysterious purpose of an all-wise Providence, which it was not for a mere mortal like me to fathom. Yes, Bartleby, stay there behind your screen, thought I; I shall persecute you no more; you are harmless and noiseless as any of these old chairs; in short, I never feel so private as when I know you are here. At last I see it, I feel it; I penetrate to the predestinated purpose of my life. I am content. Others may have loftier parts to enact; but my mission in this world, Bartleby, is to furnish you with office-room for such period as you may see fit to remain.

I believe that this wise and blessed frame of mind would have continued with me, had it not been for the unsolicited and uncharitable remarks obtruded upon me by my professional friends who visited the rooms. But thus it often is, that the constant friction of illiberal minds wears out at last the best resolves of the more generous. Though to be sure, when I reflected upon it, it was not strange that people entering my office should be struck by the peculiar aspect of the unaccountable Bartleby, and so be tempted to throw out some sinister observations concerning him. Sometimes an attorney, having business with me, and calling at my office, and finding no one but the scrivener there, would undertake to obtain some sort of precise information from him touching my whereabouts; but without heeding his idle talk, Bartleby would remain standing immovable in the middle of the room. So after contemplating him in that position for a time, the attorney would depart, no wiser than he came.

Also, when a reference was going on, and the room full of lawyers and witnesses, and business driving fast, some deeply-occupied legal gentleman present, seeing Bartleby wholly unemployed, would request him to run round to his (the legal gentleman's) office and fetch some papers for him. Thereupon, Bartleby would tranquilly decline, and yet remain idle as before. Then the lawyer would give a great stare, and turn to me. And what could I say? At last I was made aware that all through the circle of my professional acquaintance, a whisper of wonder was running round, having reference to the strange creature I kept at my office. This worried me very much. And as the idea came upon me of his possibly turning out a long-lived man, and keep occupying my chambers, and denying my authority; and perplexing my visitors; and scandalizing my professional reputation; and casting a general gloom over the premises; keeping soul and body together to the last upon his savings (for doubtless he spent but half a dime a day), and in the end perhaps outlive me, and claim possession of my office by right of his perpetual occupancy: as all these dark anticipations crowded upon me more and more, and my friends continually intruded their relentless remarks upon the apparition in my room;

---

[8]Jonathan Edwards (1703–1758), American theologian, and Joseph Priestley (1733–1804), English clergyman and chemist, both held that man's life was predetermined.

a great change was wrought in me. I resolved to gather all my faculties together, and forever rid me of this intolerable incubus.

Ere revolving any complicated project, however, adapted to this end, I first simply suggested to Bartleby the propriety of his permanent departure. In a calm and serious tone, I commended the idea to his careful and mature consideration. But, having taken three days to meditate upon it, he apprised me, that his original determination remained the same; in short, that he still preferred to abide with me.

What shall I do? I now said to myself, buttoning up my coat to the last button. What shall I do? what ought I to do? what does conscience say I *should* do with this man, or, rather, ghost. Rid myself of him, I must; go, he shall. But how? You will not thrust him, the poor, pale, passive mortal—you will not thrust such a helpless creature out of your door? you will not dishonor yourself by such cruelty? No, I will not, I cannot do that. Rather would I let him live and die here, and then mason up his remains in the wall. What, then, will you do? For all your coaxing, he will not budge. Bribes he leaves under your own paper-weight on your table; in short, it is quite plain that he prefers to cling to you.

Then something severe, something unusual must be done. What! surely you will not have him collared by a constable, and commit his innocent pallor to the common jail? And upon what ground could you procure such a thing to be done?—a vagrant, is he? What! he a vagrant, a wanderer, who refuses to budge? It is because he will *not* be a vagrant, then, that you seek to count him *as* a vagrant. That is too absurd. No visible means of support: there I have him. Wrong again: for indubitably he *does* support himself, and that is the only unanswerable proof that any man can show of his possessing the means so to do. No more, then. Since he will not quit me, I must quit him. I will change my offices; I will move elsewhere, and give him fair notice, that if I find him on my new premises I will then proceed against him as a common trespasser.

Acting accordingly, next day I thus addressed him: "I find these chambers too far from the City Hall; the air is unwholesome. In a word, I propose to remove my offices next week, and shall no longer require your services. I tell you this now, in order that you may seek another place."

He made no reply, and nothing more was said.

On the appointed day I engaged carts and men, proceeded to my chambers, and, having but little furniture, everything was removed in a few hours. Throughout, the scrivener remained standing behind the screen, which I directed to be removed the last thing. It was withdrawn; and, being folded up like a huge folio, left him the motionless occupant of a naked room. I stood in the entry watching him a moment, while something from within me upbraided me.

I re-entered, with my hand in my pocket—and—and my heart in my mouth.

"Good-by, Bartleby; I am going—good-by, and God some way bless you; and take that," slipping something in his hand. But it dropped upon the floor, and then—strange to say—I tore myself from him whom I had so longed to be rid of.

Established in my new quarters, for a day or two I kept the door locked, and started at every footfall in the passages. When I returned to my rooms, after any little absence, I would pause at the threshold for an instant, and attentively listen, ere applying my key. But these fears were needless. Bartleby never came nigh me.

I thought all was going well, when a perturbed-looking stranger visited me, inquiring whether I was the person who had recently occupied rooms at No. —— Wall Street.

Full of forebodings, I replied that I was.

"Then, sir," said the stranger, who proved a lawyer, "you are responsible for the man you left there. He refuses to do any copying; he refuses to do anything; he says he prefers not to; and he refuses to quit the premises."

"I am very sorry, sir," said I, with assumed tranquillity, but an inward tremor, "but, really, the man you allude to is nothing to me—he is no relation or apprentice of mine, that you should hold me responsible for him."

"In mercy's name, who is he?"

"I certainly cannot inform you. I know nothing about him. Formerly I employed him as a copyist; but he has done nothing for me now for some time past."

"I shall settle him, then—good morning, sir."

Several days passed, and I heard nothing more; and, though I often felt a charitable prompting to call at the place and see poor Bartleby, yet a certain squeamishness, of I know not what, withheld me.

All is over with him, by this time, thought I, at last, when, through another week, no further intelligence reached me. But, coming to my room the day after, I found several persons waiting at my door in a high state of nervous excitement.

"That's the man—here he comes," cried the foremost one, whom I recognized as the lawyer who had previously called upon me alone.

"You must take him away, sir, at once," cried a portly person among them, advancing upon me, and whom I knew to be the landlord of No. —— Wall Street. "These gentlemen, my tenants, cannot stand it any longer; Mr. B——," pointing to the lawyer, "has turned him out of his room, and he now persists in haunting the building generally, sitting upon the banisters of the stairs by day, and sleeping in the entry by night. Everybody is concerned; clients are leaving the offices; some fears are entertained of a mob; something you must do, and that without delay."

Aghast at this torrent, I fell back before it, and would fain have locked myself in my new quarters. In vain I persisted that Bartleby was nothing to me—no more than to any one else. In vain—I was the last person known to have anything to do with him, and they held me to the terrible account. Fearful, then, of being exposed in the papers (as one person present obscurely threatened), I considered the matter, and, at length, said, that if the lawyer would give me a confidential interview with the scrivener, in his (the lawyer's) own room, I would, that afternoon, strive my best to rid them of the nuisance they complained of.

Going up stairs to my old haunt, there was Bartleby silently sitting upon the banister at the landing.

"What are you doing here, Bartleby?" said I.

"Sitting upon the banister," he mildly replied.

I motioned him into the lawyer's room, who then left us.

"Bartleby," said I, "are you aware that you are the cause of great tribulation to me, by persisting in occupying the entry after being dismissed from the office?"

No answer.

"Now one of two things must take place. Either you must do something, or something must be done to you. Now what sort of business would you like to engage in? Would you like to re-engage in copying for some one?"

"No; I would prefer not to make any change."

"Would you like a clerkship in a dry-goods store?"

"There is too much confinement about that. No, I would not like a clerkship; but I am not particular."

"Too much confinement," I cried, "why, you keep yourself confined all the time!"

"I would prefer not to take a clerkship," he rejoined, as if to settle that little item at once.

"How would a bar-tender's business suit you? There is no trying of the eyesight in that."

"I would not like it at all; though, as I said before, I am not particular."

His unwonted wordiness inspirited me. I returned to the charge.

"Well, then, would you like to travel through the country collecting bills for the merchants? That would improve your health."

"No, I would prefer to be doing something else."

"How, then, would going as a companion to Europe, to entertain some young gentleman with your conversation—how would that suit you?"

"Not at all. It does not strike me that there is anything definite about that. I like to be stationary. But I am not particular."

"Stationary you shall be, then," I cried, now losing all patience, and, for the first time in all my exasperating connection with him, fairly flying into a passion. "If you do not go away from these premises before night, I shall feel bound—indeed, I *am* bound—to—to—to quit the premises myself!" I rather absurdly concluded, knowing not with what possible threat to try to frighten his immobility into compliance. Despairing of all further efforts, I was precipitately leaving him, when a final thought occurred to me—one which had not been wholly unindulged before.

"Bartleby," said I, in the kindest tone I could assume under such exciting circumstances, "will you go home with me now—not to my office, but my dwelling—and remain there till we can conclude upon some convenient arrangement for you at our leisure? Come, let us start now, right away."

"No: at present I would prefer not to make any change at all."

I answered nothing; but, effectually dodging every one by the suddenness and rapidity of my flight, rushed from the building, ran up Wall Street towards Broadway, and, jumping into the first omnibus, was soon removed from pursuit. As soon as tranquillity returned, I distinctly perceived that I had now done all that I possibly could, both in respect to the demands of the landlord and his tenants, and with regard to my own desire and sense of duty, to benefit Bartleby, and shield him from rude persecution. I now strove to be entirely care-free and quiescent; and my conscience justified me in the attempt; though, indeed, it was not so successful as I could have wished. So fearful was I of being again hunted out by the incensed landlord and his exasperated tenants, that, surrendering my business to Nippers, for a few days, I drove about the upper part of the town and through the suburbs, in my rockaway; crossed over to Jersey City and Hoboken, and paid fugitive visits to Manhattanville and Astoria. In fact, I almost lived in my rockaway for the time.

When again I entered my office, lo, a note from the landlord lay upon the desk. I opened it with trembling hands. It informed me that the writer had sent to the police, and had Bartleby removed to the Tombs as a vagrant. Moreover, since I knew more about him than any one else, he wished me to appear at that place, and make a suitable statement of the facts. These tidings had a conflicting effect upon me. At first I was indignant; but, at last, almost approved. The landlord's energetic, summary disposition, had led him to adopt a procedure which I do not think I would have decided upon myself; and yet, as a last resort, under such peculiar circumstances, it seemed the only plan.

As I afterwards learned, the poor scrivener, when told that he must be conducted to the Tombs, offered not the slightest obstacle, but, in his pale, unmoving way, silently acquiesced.

Some of the compassionate and curious by-standers joined the party; and headed by one of the constables arm in arm with Bartleby, the silent procession filed its way through all the noise, and heat, and joy of the roaring thoroughfares at noon.

The same day I received the note, I went to the Tombs, or, to speak more properly, the Halls of Justice. Seeking the right officer, I stated the purpose of my call, and was informed that the individual I described was, indeed, within. I then assured the functionary that Bartleby was a perfectly honest man, and greatly to be compassionated, however unaccountably eccentric. I narrated all I knew, and closed by suggesting the idea of letting him remain in as indulgent confinement as possible, till something less harsh might be done—though, indeed, I hardly knew what. At all events, if nothing else could be decided upon, the alms-house must receive him. I then begged to have an interview.

Being under no disgraceful charge, and quite serene and harmless in all his ways, they had permitted him freely to wander about the prison, and, especially, in the inclosed grass-platted yards thereof. And so I found him there, standing all alone in the quietest of the yards, his face towards a high wall, while all around, from the narrow slits of the jail windows, I thought I saw peering out upon him the eyes of murderers and thieves.

"Bartleby!"

"I know you," he said, without looking round—"and I want nothing to say to you."

"It was not I that brought you here, Bartleby," said I, keenly pained at his implied suspicion. "And to you, this should not be so vile a place. Nothing reproachful attaches to you by being here. And see, it is not so sad a place as one might think. Look, there is the sky, and here is the grass."

"I know where I am," he replied, but would say nothing more, and so I left him.

As I entered the corridor again, a broad meat-like man, in an apron, accosted me, and, jerking his thumb over his shoulder, said—"Is that your friend?"

"Yes."

"Does he want to starve? If he does, let him live on the prison fare, that's all."

"Who are you?" asked I, not knowing what to make of such an unofficially speaking person in such a place.

"I am the grub-man. Such gentlemen as have friends here, hire me to provide them with something good to eat."

"Is this so?" said I, turning the turnkey.

He said it was.

"Well, then," said I, slipping some silver into the grub-man's hands (for so they called him), "I want you to give particular attention to my friend there; let him have the best dinner you can get. And you must be as polite to him as possible."

"Introduce me, will you?" said the grub-man, looking at me with an expression which seemed to say he was all impatience for an opportunity to give a specimen of his breeding.

Thinking it would prove of benefit to the scrivener, I acquiesced; and, asking the grub-man his name, went up with him to Bartleby.

"Bartleby, this is a friend; you will find him very useful to you."

"Your sarvant, sir, your sarvant," said the grub-man, making a low salutation behind his apron. "Hope you find it pleasant here, sir; nice grounds—cool apartments—hope you'll stay with us some time—try to make it agreeable. What will you have for dinner to-day?"

"I prefer not to dine to-day," said Bartleby, turning away. "It would disagree with me; I am unused to dinners." So saying, he slowly moved to the other side of the inclosure, and took up a position fronting the deadwall.

"How's this?" said the grub-man, addressing me with a stare of astonishment. "He's odd, ain't he?"

"I think he is a little deranged," said I, sadly.

"Deranged? deranged is it? Well, now, upon my word, I thought that friend of yourn was a gentleman forger; they are always pale and genteel-like, them forgers. I can't help pity 'em—can't help it, sir. Did you know Monroe Edwards?" he added, touchingly, and paused. Then, laying his hand piteously on my shoulder, sighed, "he died of consumption at Sing-Sing.[9] So you weren't acquainted with Monroe?"

"No, I was never socially acquainted with any forgers. But I cannot stop longer. Look to my friend yonder. You will not lose by it. I will see you again."

Some few days after this, I again obtained admission to the Tombs, and went through the corridors in quest of Bartleby; but without finding him.

"I saw him coming from his cell not long ago," said a turnkey, "may be he's gone to loiter in the yards."

So I went in that direction.

"Are you looking for the silent man?" said another turnkey, passing me. "Yonder he lies—sleeping in the yard there. 'Tis not twenty minutes since I saw him lie down."

The yard was entirely quiet. It was not accessible to the common prisoners. The surrounding walls of amazing thickness, kept off all sounds behind them. The Egyptian character of the masonry weighed upon me with its gloom. But a soft imprisoned turf grew under foot. The heart of the eternal pyramids, it seemed, wherein, by some strange magic, through the clefts, grass-seed, dropped by birds, had sprung.

Strangely huddled at the base of the wall, his knees drawn up, and lying on his side, his head touching the cold stones, I saw the wasted Bartleby. But nothing stirred. I paused; then went close up to him; stooped over, and saw that his dim eyes were open; otherwise he seemed profoundly sleeping. Something prompted me to touch him. I felt his hand, when a tingling shiver ran up my arm and down my spine to my feet.

The round face of the grub-man peered upon me now. "His dinner is ready. Won't he dine to-day, either? Or does he live without dining?"

"Lives without dining," said I, and closed the eyes.

"Eh!—He's asleep, ain't he?"

"With kings and counselors," murmured I.

There would seem little need for proceeding further in this history. Imagination will readily supply the meagre recital of poor Bartleby's interment. But, ere parting with the reader, let me say, that if this little narrative has sufficiently interested him, to awaken curiosity as to who Bartleby was, and what manner of life he led prior to the present narrator's making his acquaintance, I can only reply, that in such curiosity I fully share, but am wholly unable to gratify it. Yet here I hardly know whether I should divulge one little item of rumor, which came to my ear a few months after the scrivener's decease. Upon what basis it rested, I could never ascertain; and hence, how true it is I cannot now tell. But, inasmuch as this vague report has not been without a certain suggestive interest to me, however said, it may prove the same with some

---

[9]The state prison near Ossining, New York.

others; and so I will briefly mention it. The report was this: that Bartleby had been a subordinate clerk in the Dead Letter[10] Office at Washington, from which he had been suddenly removed by a change in the administration. When I think over this rumor, hardly can I express the emotions which seize me. Dead letters! does it not sound like dead men? Conceive a man by nature and misfortune prone to a pallid hopelessness, can any business seem more fitted to heighten it than that of continually handling these dead letters, and assorting them for the flames? For by the cart-load they are annually burned. Some times from out the folded paper the pale clerk takes a ring—the finger it was meant for, perhaps, moulders in the grave; a bank-note sent in swiftest charity—he whom it would relieve, nor eats nor hungers any more; pardon for those who died despairing; hope for those who died unhoping; good tidings for those who died stifled by unrelieved calamities. On errands of life, these letters speed to death.

Ah, Bartleby! Ah, humanity!

QUESTIONS

1. What is it about Bartleby that so intrigues and fascinates the narrator? Why does the narrator continue to feel a moral obligation to an employee who refuses to work and curtly rejects kindly offers of help?   **2.** With his final utterance, "Ah, Bartleby! Ah, humanity!" the narrator apparently penetrates the mystery of Bartleby. The comments seem to suggest that for the narrator Bartleby is a representative of humanity. In what sense might the narrator come to see Bartleby in this light?   **3.** What functions do Turkey and Nippers serve?   **4.** Would it be fair to describe Bartleby as a rebel without a cause, as a young man who refuses to participate in a comfortable and well-ordered business world but fails to offer any alternative way of life? Justify your answer.

WRITING TOPICS

1. Readers differ as to whether this is the story of Bartleby or the story of the lawyer-narrator. What is your view?   **2.** Why does Melville allow the narrator (and the reader) to discover so little about Bartleby and the causes of his behavior? All we learn of Bartleby's past is contained in the next-to-last paragraph. What, if anything, in this paragraph establishes a link between Bartleby and the narrator?

---

[10]A letter that, for some reason, is undeliverable.

The Greatest Man in the World 1935

JAMES THURBER [1894–1961]

Looking back on it now, from the vantage point of 1950, one can only marvel that it hadn't happened long before it did. The United States of America had been, ever since Kitty Hawk, blindly constructing the elaborate petard by which, sooner or later, it must be hoist. It was inevitable that some day there would come roaring out of the skies a national hero of insufficient intelligence, background, and character successfully to endure the mounting orgies of glory prepared for aviators who stayed up a long time or flew a great distance. Both Lindbergh and Byrd, fortunately for national decorum and international amity, had been gentlemen; so had our other famous aviators. They wore their laurels gracefully, withstood the awful weather of publicity, married excellent women, usually of fine family, and quietly retired to private life and the enjoyment of their varying fortunes. No untoward incidents, on a worldwide scale, marred the perfection of their conduct on the perilous heights of fame. The exception to the rule was, however, bound to occur and it did, in July, 1937, when Jack ("Pal") Smurch, erstwhile mechanics' helper in a small garage in Westfield, Iowa, flew a second-hand, single-motored Bresthaven Dragon-Fly III monoplane all the way around the world, without stopping.

Never before in the history of aviation had such a flight as Smurch's ever been dreamed of. No one had even taken seriously the weird floating auxiliary gas tanks, invention of the mad New Hampshire professor of astronomy, Dr. Charles Lewis Gresham, upon which Smurch placed full reliance. When the garage worker, a slightly built, surly, unprepossessing young man of twenty-two, appeared at Roosevelt Field in early July, 1937, slowly chewing a great quid of scrap tobacco, and announced "Nobody ain't seen no flyin' yet," the newspapers touched briefly and satirically upon his projected twenty-five-thousand-mile flight. Aeronautical and automotive experts dismissed the idea curtly, implying that it was a hoax, a publicity stunt. The rusty, battered, second-hand plane wouldn't go. The Gresham auxiliary tanks wouldn't work. It was simply a cheap joke.

Smurch, however, after calling on a girl in Brooklyn who worked in the flap-folding department of a large paper-box factory, a girl whom he later described as his "sweet patootie," climbed nonchalantly into his ridiculous plane at dawn of the memorable seventh of July, 1937, spat a curve of tobacco juice into the still air, and took off, carrying with him only a gallon of bootleg gin and six pounds of salami.

When the garage boy thundered out over the ocean the papers were forced to record, in all seriousness, that a mad, unknown young man—his name was variously misspelled—had actually set out upon a preposterous attempt to span the world in a rickety, one-engined contraption, trusting to the long-distance refueling device of a crazy schoolmaster. When, nine days later, without having stopped once, the tiny plane appeared above San Francisco Bay, headed for New York, spluttering and choking, to be sure, but still magnificently and miraculously aloft, the headlines, which long since had crowded everything else off the front page—even the shooting of the Governor of Illinois by the Vileti gang—swelled to unprecedented size, and the news stories began to run to twenty-five and thirty columns. It was noticeable, however, that the accounts of the epoch-making flight touched rather lightly upon the aviator himself. This was not because facts about the hero as a man were too meagre, but because they were too complete.

Reporters, who had been rushed out to Iowa when Smurch's plane was first sighted over the little French coast town of Serly-le-Mar, to dig up the story of the great man's life, had promptly discovered that the story of his life could not be printed. His mother, a sullen short-order cook in a shack restaurant on the edge of a tourists' camping ground near Westfield, met all enquiries as to her son with an angry, "Ah, the hell with him; I hope he drowns." His father appeared to be in jail somewhere for stealing spotlights and laprobes from tourists' automobiles; his younger brother, a weak-minded lad, had but recently escaped from the Preston, Iowa, Reformatory and was already wanted in several Western towns for the theft of money-order blanks from post offices. These alarming discoveries were still piling up at the very time that Pal Smurch, the greatest hero of the twentieth century, blear-eyed, dead for sleep, half-starved, was piloting his crazy junk-heap high above the region in which the lamentable story of his private life was being unearthed, headed for New York under greater glory than any man of his time had ever known.

The necessity for printing some account in the papers of the young man's career and personality had led to a remarkable predicament. It was of course impossible to reveal the facts, for a tremendous popular feeling in favor of the young hero had sprung up, like a grass fire, when he was halfway across Europe on his flight around the globe. He was, therefore, described as a modest chap, taciturn, blond, popular with his friends, popular with girls. The only available snapshot of Smurch, taken at the wheel of a phony automobile in a cheap photo studio at an amusement park, was touched up so that the little vulgarian looked quite handsome. His twisted leer was smoothed into a pleasant smile. The truth was, in this way, kept from the youth's ecstatic compatriots; they did not dream that the Smurch family was despised and feared by its neighbors in the obscure Iowa town, nor that the hero himself, because of numerous unsavory exploits, had come to be regarded in Westfield as a nuisance and a menace. He had, the reporters discovered, once knifed the principal of his high school—not mortally, to be sure, but he had knifed him; and on another occasion, surprised in the act of stealing an altar-cloth from a church, he had bashed the sacristan over the head with a pot of Easter lilies; for each of these offences he had served a sentence in the reformatory.

Inwardly, the authorities, both in New York and in Washington, prayed that an understanding Providence might, however awful such a thing seemed, bring disaster to the rusty, battered plane and its illustrious pilot, whose unheard-of flight had aroused the civilized world to hosannas of hysterical praise. The authorities were convinced that the character of the renowned aviator was such that the limelight of adulation was bound to reveal him to all the world, as a congenital hooligan mentally and morally unequipped to cope with his own prodigious fame. "I trust," said the Secretary of State, at one of many secret Cabinet meetings called to consider the national dilemma, "I trust that his mother's prayer will be answered," by which he referred to Mrs. Emma Smurch's wish that her son might be drowned. It was, however, too late for that—Smurch had leaped the Atlantic and then the Pacific as if they were millponds. At three minutes after two o'clock in the afternoon of 17 July, 1937, the garage boy brought his idiotic plane into Roosevelt Field for a perfect three-point landing.

It had, of course, been out of the question to arrange a modest little reception for the greatest flier in the history of the world. He was received at Roosevelt Field with such elaborate and pretentious ceremonies as rocked the world. Fortunately, however, the worn and spent hero promptly swooned, had to be removed bodily from his plane, and was spirited from the field without having opened his mouth once. Thus he did not jeopardize the dignity of this first reception, a reception illumined by the presence of the Secretaries of War and the Navy, Mayor Michael J. Moriarity of New York, the Premier of Canada, Governors Fanniman, Groves, McFeely, and Critchfield, and a brilliant array of European diplomats. Smurch did not, in fact, come to in time to take part in the gigantic hullabaloo arranged at City Hall for the next day. He was rushed to a secluded nursing home and confined to bed. It was nine days before he was able to get up, or to be more exact, before he was permitted to get up. Meanwhile the greatest minds in the country, in solemn assembly, had arranged a secret conference of city, state and government officials, which Smurch was to attend for the purpose of being instructed in the ethics and behavior of heroism.

On the day that the little mechanic was finally allowed to get up and dress and, for the first time in two weeks, took a great chew of tobacco, he was permitted to receive the newspapermen—this by way of testing him out. Smurch did not wait for questions. "Youse guys," he said—and the *Times* man winced—"youse guys can tell the cock-eyed world dat I put it over on Lindbergh, see? Yes—an' made an ass o' them two frogs." The "two frogs" was a reference to a pair of gallant French fliers who, in attempting a flight only halfway round the world, had, two weeks before, unhappily been lost at sea. The *Times* man was bold enough, at this point, to sketch out for Smurch the accepted formula for interviews in cases of this kind; he explained that there should be no arrogant statements belittling the achievements of other heroes, particularly heroes of foreign nations. "Ah, the hell with that," said Smurch. "I did it, see? I did it, an' I'm talkin' about it." And he did talk about it.

None of this extraordinary interview was, of course, printed. On the contrary, the newspapers, already under the disciplined direction of a secret directorate created for the occasion and composed of statesmen and editors, gave out to a panting and restless world that "Jacky," as he had been arbitrarily nicknamed, would consent to say only that he was very happy and that anyone could have done what he did. "My achievement has been, I fear, slightly exaggerated," the *Times* man's article had him protest, with a modest smile. These newspaper stories were kept from the hero, a restriction which did not serve to abate the rising malevolence of his temper. The situation was, indeed, extremely grave, for Pal Smurch was, as he kept insisting, "rarin' to go." He could not much longer be kept from a nation clamorous to lionize him. It was the most desperate crisis the United States of America had faced since the sinking of the *Lusitania*.

On the afternoon of the twenty-seventh of July, Smurch was spirited away to a conference-room in which were gathered mayors, governors, government officials, behaviorist psychologists, and editors. He gave them each a limp, moist paw and a brief unlovely grin. "Hah ya?" he said. When Smurch was seated, the Mayor of New York arose and, with obvious pessimism, attempted to explain what he must say and how he must act when presented to the world, ending his talk with a high tribute to the hero's courage and integrity. The Mayor was followed by Governor Fanniman of New York, who, after a touching declaration of faith, introduced Cameron Spottiswood, Second Secretary of the American Embassy in Paris, the gentleman selected to coach Smurch in the amenities of public ceremonies. Sitting in a chair, with a soiled yellow tie in his hand and his shirt open at the throat, unshaved, smoking a rolled cigarette, Jack Smurch listened with a leer on his lips. "I get ya, I get ya," he cut in nastily. "Ya want me to ack like a softy, huh? Ya want me to ack like that—baby-faced Lindbergh, huh? Well, nuts to that, see?" Everyone took in his breath sharply; it was a sigh and a hiss. "Mr. Lindbergh," began a United States Senator, purple with rage, "and Mr. Byrd—" Smurch, who was paring his nails with a jackknife, cut in again. "Byrd!" he exclaimed. "Aw fa God's sake, dat big—" Somebody shut off his blasphemies with a sharp word. A newcomer had entered the room. Everyone stood up, except Smurch, who, still busy with his nails, did not even glance up. "Mr. Smurch," said someone sternly, "the President of the United States!" It had been thought that the presence of the Chief Executive might have a chastening effect upon the young hero, and the former had been, thanks to the remarkable co-operation of the press, secretly brought to the obscure conference-room.

A great, painful silence fell. Smurch looked up, waved a hand at the President. "How ya comin'?" he asked, and began rolling a fresh cigarette. The silence deepened. Someone coughed in a strained way. "Geez, it's hot, ain't it?" said Smurch. He loosened two more shirt buttons, revealing a hairy chest and the tattooed word "Sadie" enclosed in a stenciled heart. The great and important men in the room, faced by the most serious crisis in recent American history, exchanged worried frowns. Nobody seemed to know how to proceed. "Come awn, come awn," said Smurch. "Let's get the hell out of here! When do I start cuttin' in on de parties, huh? And what's they goin' to be *in* it?" He rubbed a thumb and a forefinger together meaningly. "Money!" exclaimed a state senator, shocked, pale. "Yeh, money," said Pal, flipping his cigarette out of a window, "an' big money." He began rolling a fresh cigarette. "Big money," he repeated, frowning over the rice paper. He tilted back in his chair, and leered at each gentleman, separately, the leer of an animal that knows its power, the leer of a leopard loose in a bird-and-dog shop. "Aw, fa God's sake, let's get some place where it's cooler," he said. "I been cooped up plenty for three weeks!"

Smurch stood up and walked over to an open window, where he stood staring down into the street, nine floors below. The faint shouting of newsboys floated up to him. He made out his name. "Hot dog!" he cried, grinning, ecstatic. He leaned out over the sill. "You tell 'em, babies!" he shouted down. "Hot diggity dog!" In the tense little knot of men standing behind him, a quick, mad impulse flared up. An unspoken word of appeal, of command, seemed to ring through the room. Yet it was deadly silent. Charles K. L. Brand, secretary to the Mayor of New York City, happened to be standing nearest Smurch; he looked inquiringly at the President of the United States. The President, pale, grim, nodded shortly. Brand, a tall, powerfully built man, once a tackle at Rutgers, stepped forward, seized the greatest man in the world by his left shoulder and the seat of his pants, and pushed him out of the window.

"My God, he's fallen out the window!" cried a quick-witted editor.

"Get me out of here!" cried the President. Several men sprang to his side and he was hurriedly escorted out of a door toward a side-entrance to the building. The editor of the Associated Press took charge, being used to such things. Crisply he ordered certain men to leave, others to stay; quickly he outlined a story which all the papers were to agree on, sent two men to the street to handle that end of the tragedy, commanded a Senator to sob and two Congressmen to go to pieces nervously. In a word, he skillfully set the stage for the gigantic task that was to follow, the task of breaking to a grief-stricken world the sad story of the untimely, accidental death of its most illustrious and spectacular figure.

The funeral was, as you know, the most elaborate, the finest, the solemnest, and the saddest ever held in the United States of America. The monument in Arlington Cemetery, with its clean white shaft of marble and the simple device of a tiny plane carved on its base, is a place for pilgrims, in deep reverence, to visit. The nations of the world paid lofty tributes to little Jacky Smurch, America's greatest hero. At a given hour there were two minutes of silence throughout the nation. Even the inhabitants of the small, bewildered town of Westfield, Iowa, observed this touching ceremony; agents of the Department of Justice saw to that. One of them was especially assigned to stand grimly in the doorway of a little shack restaurant on the edge of the tourists' camping ground just outside the town. There, under his stern scrutiny, Mrs. Emma Smurch bowed her head above two hamburger steaks sizzling on her grill— bowed her head and turned away, so that the Secret Service man could not see the twisted, strangely familiar, leer on her lips.

Something for the Time Being   1965

NADINE GORDIMER   [b. 1923]

He thought of it as discussing things with her, but the truth was that she did not help him out at all. She said nothing, while she ran her hand up the ridge of bone behind the rim of her child-sized yellow-brown ear, and raked her fingers tenderly into her hairline along the back of her neck as if feeling out some symptom in herself. Yet her listening was very demanding; when he stopped at the end of a supposition or a suggestion, her silence made the stop inconclusive. He had to take up again what he had said, carry it—where?

"Ve vant to give you a tsance, but you von't let us," he mimicked; and made a loud glottal click, half angry, resentfully amused. He knew it wasn't because Kalzin Brothers were Jews that he had lost his job at last, but just because he had lost it, Mr. Solly's accent suddenly presented to him the irresistibly vulnerable. He had come out of prison nine days before after spending three months as an awaiting-trial prisoner in a political case that had just been quashed—he was one of those who would not accept bail. He had been in prison three or four times since 1952; his wife Ella and the Kalzin Brothers were used to it. Until now, his employers had always given him his job back when he came out. They were importers of china and glass and he was head packer in a team of black men who ran the dispatch department. "Well, what the hell, I'll get something else," he said. "Hey?"

She stopped the self-absorbed examination of the surface of her skin for a slow moment and shrugged, looking at him.

He smiled.

Her gaze loosened hold like hands falling away from a grasp. The ends of her nails pressed at small imperfections in the skin of her neck. He drank his tea and tore off pieces of bread to dip in it; then he noticed the tin of sardines she had opened, and sopped up the pale matrix of oil in which ragged flecks of silver were suspended. She offered him more tea, without speaking.

They lived in one room of a three-roomed house belonging to someone else; it was better for her that way, since he was often likely to have to be away for long stretches. She worked in a textile factory that made knitted socks; there was no one at home to look after their one child, a girl, and the child lived with a grandmother in a dusty peaceful village a day's train journey from the city.

He said, dismissing it as of no importance, "I wonder what chance they meant? You can imagine. I don't suppose they were going to give me an office with my name on it." He spoke as if she would appreciate the joke. She had known when she married him that he was a political man; she had been proud of him because he didn't merely want something for himself, like the other young men she knew, but everything, and for *the people*. It had excited her, under his influence, to change her awareness of herself as a young black girl to

244

awareness of herself as belonging to the people. She knew that everything wasn't like something—a hand-out, a wangled privilege, a trinket you could hold. She would never get something from him.

Her hand went on searching over her skin as if it must come soon, come anxiously, to the flaw, the sickness, the evidence of what was wrong with her; for on this Saturday afternoon, all these things that she knew had deserted her. She had lost her wits. All that she could understand was the one room, the child growing up far away in the mud house, and the fact that you couldn't keep a job if you kept being away from work for weeks at a time.

"I think I'd better look up Flora Donaldson," he said. Flora Donaldson was a white woman who had set up an office to help political prisoners. "Sooner the better. Perhaps she'll dig up something for me by Monday. It's the beginning of the month."

He got on all right with those people. Ella had met Flora Donaldson once; she was a pretty white woman who looked just like any white woman who would automatically send a black face round to the back door, but she didn't seem to know that she was white and you were black.

He pulled the curtain that hung across one corner of the room and took out his suit. It was a thin suit, of the kind associated with holiday-makers in American clothing advertisements, and when he was dressed in it, with a sharpbrimmed grey hat tilted back on his small head, he looked a wiry, boyish figure, rather like one of those boy-men who sing and shake before a microphone, and whose clothes admirers try to touch as a talisman.

He kissed her good-bye, obliging her to put down, the lowering of a defence, the piece of sewing she held. She had cleared away the dishes from the table and set up the sewing machine, and he saw that the shapes of cut material that lay on the table were the parts of a small girl's dress.

She spoke suddenly. "And when the next lot gets tired of you?"

"When that lot gets tired of me, I'll get another job again, that's all."

She nodded, very slowly, and her hand crept back to her neck.

"Who was that?" Madge Chadders asked.

Her husband had been out into the hall to answer the telephone.

"Flora Donaldson. I wish you'd explain to these people exactly what sort of factory I've got. It's so embarrassing. She's trying to find a job for some chap, he's a skilled packer. There's no skilled packing done in my workshop, no skilled jobs at all done by black men. What on earth can I offer the fellow? She says he's desperate and anything will do."

Madge had the broken pieces of a bowl on a newspaper spread on the Persian carpet. "Mind the glue, darling! There, just next to your foot. Well, anything is better than nothing. I suppose it's someone who was in the Soganiland sedition case. Three months awaiting trial taken out of their lives, and now they're chucked back to fend for themselves."

William Chadders had not had any black friends or mixed with coloured people in any but master-servant terms until he married Madge, but his views on the immorality and absurdity of the colour bar were sound; sounder, she often felt, than her own, for they were backed by the impersonal authority of a familiarity with the views of great thinkers, saints, and philosophers, with history, political economy, sociology, and anthropology. She knew only what she felt. And she always did something, at once, to express what she felt. She never measured the smallness of her personal protest against the establishment she opposed; she marched with Flora and five hundred black women in a demonstration against African women's being forced to carry passes; outside the university where she had once been a student, she stood between sandwichboards bearing messages of mourning because a bill had been passed closing the university, for the future, to all but white students; she had living in her house for three months a young African who wanted to write and hadn't the peace or space to get on with it in a Location.[1] She did not stop to consider the varying degrees of usefulness of the things she did, and if others pointed this out to her and suggested that she might make up her mind to throw her weight on the side of either politics or philanthropy, she was not resentful but answered candidly that there was so little it was possible to do that she simply took any and every chance to get off her chest her disgust at the colour bar. When she had married William Chadders, her friends had thought that her protestant activities would stop; they underestimated not only Madge, but also William, who, although he was a wealthy businessman, subscribed to the necessity of personal freedom as strictly as any bohemian. Besides he was not fool enough to want to change in any way the person who had enchanted him just as she was.

She reacted upon him, rather than he upon her; she, of course, would not hesitate to go ahead and change anybody. (But why not? she would have said, astonished. If it's to the good?) The attitude she sought to change would occur to her as something of independent existence, she would not see it as a cell in the organism of personality, whose whole structure would have to regroup itself round the change. She had the boldness of being unaware of these consequences.

William did not carry a banner in the streets, of course; he worked up there, among his first principles and historical precedents and economic necessities, but now they were translated from theory to practice of an anonymous, large-scale, and behind-the-scenes sort—he was the brains and some of the money in a scheme to get Africans some economic power besides their labour, through the setting up of an all-African trust company and investment corporation. A number of Madge's political friends, both white and black, thought this was putting the middle-class cart before the proletarian horse, but most of the African leaders welcomed the attempt as an essential backing to popular movements on other levels—something to count on outside the unpredictability of

---

[1]A township where Africans, who make up a majority of South Africa's population, were forced to live under *apartheid*, the white South African system of racial separation.

mobs. Sometimes it amused Madge to think that William, making a point at a meeting in a boardroom, fifteen floors above life in the streets, might achieve in five minutes something of more value than she did in all her days of turning her hand to anything—from sorting old clothes to duplicating a manifesto or driving people during a bus boycott. Yet this did not knock the meaning out of her own life, for her; she knew that she had to see, touch, and talk to people in order to care about them, that was all there was to it.

Before she and her husband dressed to go out that evening, she finished sticking together the broken Chinese bowl, and showed it to him with satisfaction. To her, it was whole again. But it was one of a set, that had belonged together, and whose unity had illustrated certain philosophical concepts. William had bought them long ago, in London; for him, the whole set was damaged forever.

He said nothing to her, but he was thinking of the bowls when she said to him as they drove off, "Will you see that chap, on Monday, yourself?"

He changed gear deliberately, attempting to follow her out of his preoccupation. But she said, "The man Flora's sending. What was his name?"

He opened his hand on the steering wheel, indicating that the name escaped him.

"See him yourself?"

"I'll have to leave it to the works manager to find something for him to do," he said.

"Yes, I know. But see him yourself, too?"

Her anxious voice made him feel very fond of her. He turned and smiled at her suspiciously. "Why?"

She was embarrassed at his indulgent manner. She said, frank and wheedling, "Just to show him. You know. That you know about him and it's not much of a job."

"All right," he said, "I'll see him myself."

He met her in town straight from the office on Monday and they went to the opening of an exhibition of paintings and on to dinner and to see a play, with friends. He had not been home at all, until they returned after midnight. It was a summer night and they sat for a few minutes on their terrace, where it was still mild with the warmth of the day's sun coming from the walls in the darkness, and drank lime juice and water to quench the thirst that wine and the stuffy theatre had given them. Madge made gasps and groans of pleasure at the release from the pressures of company and noise. Then she lay quiet for a while, her voice lifting now and then in fragments of unrelated comment on the evening—the occasional chirp of a bird that has already put its head under its wing for the night.

By the time they went in, they were free of the evening. Her black dress, her earrings, and her bracelets felt like fancy dress; she shed the character and sat on the bedroom carpet, and, passing her, he said, "Oh—that chap of Flora's came today, but I don't think he'll last. I explained to him that I didn't have the sort of job he was looking for."

"Well, that's all right, then," she said, inquiringly. "What more could you do?"

"Yes," he said, deprecating. "But I could see he didn't like the idea much. It's a cleaner's job; nothing for him. He's an intelligent chap. I didn't like having to offer it to him."

She was moving about her dressing table, piling out upon it the contents of her handbag. "Then I'm sure he'll understand. It'll give him something for the time being, anyway, darling. You can't help it if you don't need the sort of work he does."

"Huh, he won't last. I could see that. He accepted it, but only with his head. He'll get fed up. Probably won't turn up tomorrow. I had to speak to him about his Congress[2] button, too. The works manager came to me."

"What about his Congress button?" she said.

He was unfastening his shirt and his eyes were on the evening paper that lay folded on the bed. "He was wearing one," he said inattentively.

"I know, but what did you have to speak to him about it for?"

"He was wearing it in the workshop all day."

"Well, what about it?" She was sitting at her dressing table, legs spread, as if she had sat heavily and suddenly. She was not looking at him, but at her own face.

He gave the paper a push and drew his pyjamas from under the pillow. Vulnerable and naked, he said authoritatively, "You can't wear a button like that among the men in the workshop."

"Good heavens," she said, almost in relief, laughing, backing away from the edge of tension, chivvying him out of a piece of stuffiness. "And why can't you?"

"You can't have someone clearly representing a political organization like Congress."

"But he's not there *representing* anything, he's there as a workman!" Her mouth was still twitching with something between amusement and nerves.

"Exactly."

"Then why can't he wear a button that signifies his allegiance to an organization in his private life outside the workshop? There's no rule about not wearing tie-pins or club buttons or anything, in the workshop, is there?"

"No, there isn't, but that's not quite the same thing."

"My dear William," she said, "it is exactly the same. It's nothing to do with the works manager whether the man wears a Rotary button, or an Elvis Presley button, or an African National Congress button. It's damn all his business."

"No, Madge, I'm sorry," William said, patient, "but it's not the same. I can give the man a job because I feel sympathetic toward the struggle he's in, but I can't put him in the workshop as a Congress man. I mean that wouldn't be

---

[2]The African National Congress, a predominantly black political party, struggled, sometimes violently, to successfully replace *apartheid* with majority rule.

fair to Fowler. That I can't do to Fowler." He was smiling as he went towards the bathroom but his profile, as he turned into the doorway, was incisive.

She sat on at her dressing table, pulling a comb through her hair, dragging it down through knots. Then she rested her face on her palms, caught sight of herself, and became aware, against her fingers, of the curving shelf of bone, like the lip of a strong shell, under each eye. Everyone has his own intimations of mortality. For her, the feel of the bone beneath the face, in any living creature, brought her the message of the skull. Once hollowed out of this, outside the world, too. For what it's worth. It's worth a lot, the world, she affirmed, as she always did, life rising at once in her as a fish opens its jaws to a fly. It's worth a lot; and she sighed and got up with the sigh.

She went into the bathroom and sat down on the edge of the bath. He was lying there in the water, his chin relaxed on his chest, and he smiled at her. She said, "You mean you don't want Fowler to know."

"Oh," he said, seeing where they were, again. "What is it I don't want Fowler to know?"

"You don't want your partner to know that you slip black men with political ideas into your workshop. Cheeky kaffir agitators. Specially a man who's just been in jail for getting people to defy the government!—What was his name; you never said?"

"Daniel something. I don't know. Mongoma or Ngoma. Something like that."

A line like a cut appeared between her eyebrows. "Why can't you remember his name?" Then she went on at once, "You don't want Fowler to know what you think, do you? That's it? You want to pretend you're like him, you don't mind the native in his place. You want to pretend that to please Fowler. You don't want Fowler to think you're cracked, or Communist, or whatever it is that good-natured, kind, jolly rich people like old Fowler think about people like us."

"I couldn't have less interest in what Fowler thinks outside our boardroom. And inside it, he never thinks about anything but how to sell more earthmoving gear."

"I don't mind the native in his place. You want him to think you go along with all that." She spoke aloud, but she seemed to be telling herself rather than him.

"Fowler and I run a factory. Our only common interest is the efficient running of that factory. Our *only* one. The factory depends on a stable, satisfied black labour force, and that we've got. Right, you and I know that the whole black wage standard is too low, right, we know that they haven't a legal union to speak for them, *right*, we know that the conditions they live under make it impossible for them really to be stable. All that. But the fact is, so far as accepted standards go in this crazy country, they're a stable, satisfied labour force with better working conditions than most. So long as I'm a partner in a business that lives by them, I can't officially admit an element that represents dissatisfaction with their lot."

"A green badge with a map of Africa on it," she said.

"If you make up your mind not to understand, you don't, and there it is," he said indulgently.

"You give him a job but you make him hide his Congress button."

He began to soap himself. She wanted everything to stop while she inquired into things, she could not go on while a remark was unexplained or a problem unsettled, but he represented a principle she subscribed to but found so hard to follow, that life must go on, trivially, commonplace, the trailing hem of the only power worth clinging to. She smoothed the film of her thin nightgown over the shape of her knees, again and again, and presently she said, in exactly the flat tone of statement that she had used before, the flat tone that was the height of belligerence in her, "He can say and do what he likes, he can call for strikes and boycotts and anything he likes, outside the factory, but he mustn't wear his Congress button at work."

He was standing up, washing his body that was full of scars; she knew them all, from the place on his left breast where a piece of shrapnel had gone in, all the way back to the place under his arm where he had torn himself on barbed wire as a child. "Yes, of course, anything he likes."

Anything except his self-respect. Pretend, pretend. Pretend he doesn't belong to a political organization. Pretend he doesn't want to be a man. Pretend he hasn't been to prison for what he believes. Suddenly she spoke to her husband. "You'll let him have anything except the one thing worth giving."

They stood in uncomfortable proximity to each other, in the smallness of the bathroom. They were at once aware of each other as people who live in intimacy are only when hostility returns each to the confines of himself. He felt himself naked before her, where he had stepped out onto the towelling mat, and he took a towel and slowly covered himself, pushing the free end in round his waist. She felt herself an intrusion and, in silence, went out.

Her hands were tingling. She walked up and down the bedroom floor like someone waiting to be summoned, called to account. I'll forget about it, she kept thinking, very fast, I'll forget about it again. Take a sip of water. Read another chapter. Let things flow, cover up, go on.

But when he came into the room with his wet hair combed and his stranger's face, and he said, "You're angry," it came from her lips, a black bird in the room, before she could understand what she had released—"I'm not angry. I'm beginning to get to know you."

Ella Mgoma knew he was going to a meeting that evening and didn't expect him home early. She put the paraffin lamp on the table so that she could see to finish the child's dress. It was done, buttons and all, by the time he came in at half past ten.

"Well, now we'll see what happens. I've got them to accept, *in principle*, that in future we won't take bail. You should have seen Ben Tsolo's face when I said that we lent the government our money interest-free when we paid bail. That really hit him. That was language he understood." He laughed, and did not seem to want to sit down, the heat of the meeting still upon him. "*In principle*. Yes, it's easy to accept in principle. We'll see."

She pumped the primus and set a pot of stew to warm up for him. "Ah, that's nice"—he saw the dress. "Finished already?" And she nodded vociferously in pleasure; but at once she noticed his forefinger run lightly along the line of braid round the neck, and the traces of failure that were always at the bottom of her cup tasted on her tongue again. Probably he was not even aware of it, or perhaps his instinct for what was true—the plumb line, the coin with the right ring—led him absently to it, but the fact was that she had botched the neck.

She had an almost Oriental delicacy about not badgering him, and she waited until he had washed and sat down to eat before she asked, "How did the job go?"

"Oh that," he said. "It went." He was eating quickly, moving his tongue strongly round his mouth to marshal the bits of meat that escaped his teeth. She was sitting with him, feeling, in spite of herself, the rest of satisfaction in her evening's work. "Didn't you get it?"

"It got *me*. But I got loose again, all right."

She watched his face to see what he meant. "They don't want you to come back tomorrow?"

He shook his head, no, no, no, to stem the irritation of her suppositions. He finished his mouthful and said, "Everything very nice. Boss takes me into his office, apologizes for the pay, he knows it's not the sort of job I should have and so forth. So I go off and clean up in the assembly shop. Then at lunch time he calls me into the office again: they don't want me to wear my ANC badge at work. Flora Donaldson's sympathetic white man, who's going to do me the great favour of paying me three pounds a week." He laughed. "Well, there you are."

She kept on looking at him. Her eyes widened and her mouth tightened; she was trying to prime herself to speak, or was trying not to cry. The idea of tears exasperated him and he held her with a firm, almost belligerently inquiring gaze. Her hand went up round the back of her neck under her collar, anxiously exploratory. "Don't do that!" he said. "You're like a monkey catching lice."

She took her hand down swiftly and broke into trembling, like a sweat. She began to breathe hysterically. "You couldn't put it in your pocket, for the day," she said wildly, grimacing at the bitterness of malice towards him.

He jumped up from the table. "Christ! I knew you'd say it! I've been waiting for you to say it. You've been wanting to say it for five years. Well, now it's out. Out with it. Spit it out!" She began to scream softly as if he were hitting her. The impulse to cruelty left him and he sat down before his dirty plate, where the battered spoon lay among bits of gristle and potato eyes. Presently he spoke. "You come out and you think there's everybody waiting for you. The truth is, there isn't anybody. You think straight in prison because you've got nothing to lose. Nobody thinks straight, outside. They don't want to hear you. What are you all going to do with me, Ella? Send me back to prison as quickly as possible? Perhaps I'll get a banishment order next time. That'd do. That's what you've got for me. I must keep myself busy with that kind of thing."

He went over to her and said, in a kindly voice, kneading her shoulder with spread fingers, "Don't cry. Don't cry. You're just like any other woman."

QUESTIONS

1. What do the contrasting reactions of Ella Mgoma and Madge Chadders to Daniel's wearing of the badge tell us about the theme of the story?   **2.** What do Daniel's final words mean?   **3.** What does the author mean when she says that Madge "would not hesitate to go ahead and change anybody. . . . The attitude she sought to change would occur to her as something of independent existence, she would not see it as a cell in the organism of personality, whose whole structure would have to regroup itself round the change. She had the boldness of being unaware of these consequences"?   **4.** How do the contrasting reactions of Madge and William reflect their attitudes toward Daniel?   **5.** Does the portrayal of the two wives and the two husbands reflect gender differences?

WRITING TOPIC

Daniel's political activities are the focus of the story. How would you characterize his politics? Compare and contrast the reaction to his political activities of his wife, Ella; William Chadders; and Madge Chadders. Which of the four characters do you find most sympathetic? Which the least? Explain.

The Ones Who Walk Away from Omelas

1974

URSULA K. LE GUIN [b. 1929]

With a clamor of bells that set the swallows soaring, the Festival of Summer came to the city Omelas, bright-towered by the sea. The rigging of the boats in harbor sparkled with flags. In the streets between houses with red roofs and painted walls, between old moss-grown gardens and under avenues of trees, past great parks and public buildings, processions moved. Some were decorous: old people in long stiff robes of mauve and grey, grave master workmen, quiet, merry women carrying their babies and chatting as they walked. In other streets the music beat faster, a shimmering of gong and tambourine, and the people went dancing, the procession was a dance. Children dodged in and out, their high calls rising like the swallows' crossing flights over the music and the singing. All the processions wound towards the north side of the city, where on the great water-meadow called the Green Fields boys and girls, naked in the bright air, with mud-stained feet and ankles and long, lithe arms, exercised their restive horses before the race. The horses wore no gear at all but a halter without bit. Their manes were braided with streamers of silver, gold, and green. They flared their nostrils and pranced and boasted to one another; they were vastly excited, the horse being the only animal who has adopted our ceremonies as his own. Far off to the north and west the mountains stood up half encircling Omelas on her bay. The air of morning was so clear that the snow still crowning the Eighteen Peaks burned with white-gold fire across the miles of sunlit air, under the dark blue of the sky. There was just enough wind to make the banners that marked the racecourse snap and flutter now and then. In the silence of the broad green meadows one could hear the music winding through the city streets, farther and nearer and ever approaching, a cheerful faint sweetness of the air that from time to time trembled and gathered together and broke out into the great joyous clanging of the bells.

Joyous! How is one to tell about joy? How describe the citizens of Omelas?

They were not simple folk, you see, though they were happy. But we do not say the words of cheer much any more. All smiles have become archaic. Given a description such as this one tends to make certain assumptions. Given a description such as this one tends to look next for the King, mounted on a splendid stallion and surrounded by his noble knights, or perhaps in a golden litter borne by great-muscled slaves. But there was no king. They did not use swords, or keep slaves. They were not barbarians. I do not know the rules and laws of their society, but I suspect that they were singularly few. As they did without monarchy and slavery, so they also got on without the stock exchange, the advertisement, the secret police, and the bomb. Yet I repeat that these were not simple folk, not dulcet shepherds, noble savages, bland utopians. They were not less complex than us. The trouble is that we have a bad habit, encouraged by pedants and sophisticates, of considering happiness as something rather stupid. Only pain is intellectual, only evil interesting. This is the treason of the artist: a refusal to admit the banality of evil and the terrible boredom of pain. If you can't lick 'em, join 'em. If it hurts, repeat it. But to praise despair is to condemn delight, to embrace violence is to lose hold of everything else. We have almost lost hold; we can no longer describe a happy man, nor make any celebration of joy. How can I tell you about the people of Omelas? They were not naïve and happy children—though their children were, in fact, happy. They were mature, intelligent, passionate adults whose lives were not wretched. O miracle! but I wish I could describe it better. I wish I could convince you. Omelas sounds in my words like a city in a fairy tale, long ago and far away, once upon a time. Perhaps it would be best if you imagined it as your own fancy bids, assuming it will rise to the occasion, for certainly I cannot suit you all. For instance, how about technology? I think that there would be no cars or helicopters in and above the streets; this follows from the fact that the people of Omelas are happy people. Happiness is based on a just discrimination of what is necessary, what is neither necessary nor destructive, and what is destructive. In the middle category, however—that of the unnecessary but undestructive, that of comfort, luxury, exuberance, etc.—they could perfectly well have central heating, subway trains, washing machines, and all kinds of marvelous devices not yet invented here, floating light-sources, fuelless power, a cure for the common cold. Or they could have none of that: it doesn't matter. As you like it. I incline to think that people from towns up and down the coast have been coming in to Omelas during the last days before the Festival on very fast little trains and double-decker trams, and that the train station of Omelas is actually the handsomest building in town, though plainer than the magnificent Farmers' Market. But even granted trains, I fear that Omelas so far strikes some of you as goody-goody. Smiles, bells, parades, horses, bleh. If so, please add an orgy. If an orgy would help, don't hesitate. Let us not, however, have temples from which issue beautiful nude priests and priestesses already half in ecstasy and ready to copulate with any man or woman, lover or stranger, who desires union with the deep godhead of the blood, although that was my first idea. But really it would be better not to have any temples in Omelas—at least, not manned temples. Religion yes, clergy no. Surely the beautiful nudes can just wander about, offering themselves like divine soufflés to the hunger of the needy and the rapture of the flesh. Let them join the processions. Let tambourines be struck above the copulations, and the glory of desire be proclaimed upon the gongs, and (a not unimportant point) let the offspring of these delightful rituals be beloved and looked after by all. One thing I know there is none of in Omelas is guilt. But what else should there be? I thought at first there were no drugs, but that is puritanical. For those who like it, the faint insistent sweetness of *drooz* may perfume the ways of the city, *drooz* which first brings a great lightness and brilliance to the mind and limbs, and then after some hours a dreamy languor, and wonderful visions at last of the very arcana and inmost secrets of the Universe, as well as exciting the pleasure of sex beyond all belief; and it is not habit-forming. For more modest tastes I think there ought to be beer. What else, what else belongs in the joyous city? The sense of victory, surely, the celebration of courage. But as we did without clergy, let us do without soldiers. The joy built upon successful slaughter is not the right kind of joy; it will not do; it is fearful and it is trivial. A boundless and generous contentment, a magnanimous triumph felt not against some outer enemy but in communion with the finest and fairest in the souls of all men everywhere and the splendor of the world's summer: this is what swells the hearts of the people of Omelas, and the victory they celebrate is that of life. I really don't think many of them need to take *drooz*.

Most of the processions have reached the Green Fields by now. A marvelous smell of cooking goes forth from the red and blue tents of the provisioners. The faces of small children are amiably sticky; in the benign grey beard of a man a couple of crumbs of rich pastry are entangled. The youths and girls have mounted their horses and are beginning to group around the starting line of the course. An old woman, small, fat, and laughing, is passing out flowers from a basket, and tall young men wear her flowers in their shining hair. A child of nine or ten sits at the edge of the crowd, alone, playing on a wooden flute. People pause to listen, and they smile, but they do not speak to him, for he never ceases playing and never sees them, his dark eyes wholly rapt in the sweet, thin magic of the tune.

He finishes, and slowly lowers his hands holding the wooden flute.

As if that little private silence were the signal, all at once a trumpet sounds from the pavilion near the starting line: imperious, melancholy, piercing. The horses rear on their slender legs, and some of them neigh in answer. Sober-faced, the young riders stroke the horses' necks and soothe them, whispering, "Quiet, quiet, there my beauty, my hope. . . . " They begin to form in rank along the starting line. The crowds along the racecourse are like a field of grass and flowers in the wind. The Festival of Summer has begun.

Do you believe? Do you accept the festival, the city, the joy? No? Then let me describe one more thing.

In a basement under one of the beautiful public buildings of Omelas, or perhaps in the cellar of one of its spacious private homes, there is a room. It has one locked door, and no window. A little light seeps in dustily between cracks in the boards, secondhand from a cobwebbed window somewhere across the cellar. In one corner of the little room a couple of mops, with stiff, clotted, foul-smelling heads, stand near a rusty bucket. The floor is dirt, a little damp to the touch, as cellar dirt usually is. The room is about three paces long and two wide: a mere broom closet or disused tool room. In the room a child is sitting. It could be a boy or a girl. It looks about six, but actually is nearly ten. It is feeble-minded. Perhaps it was born defective, or perhaps it has become imbecile through fear, malnutrition, and neglect. It picks its nose and occasionally fumbles vaguely with its toes or genitals, as it sits hunched in the corner farthest from the bucket and the two mops. It is afraid of the mops. It finds them horrible. It shuts its eyes, but it knows the mops are still standing there; and the door is locked; and nobody will come. The door is always locked; and nobody ever comes, except that sometimes—the child has no understanding of time or interval—sometimes the door rattles terribly and opens, and a person, or several people, are there. One of them may come in and kick the child to make it stand up. The others never come close, but peer in at it with frightened, disgusted eyes. The food bowl and the water jug are hastily filled, the door is locked, the eyes disappear. The people at the door never say anything, but the child, who has not always lived in the tool room, and can remember sunlight and its mother's voice, sometimes speaks. "I will be good," it says. "Please let me out. I will be good!" They never answer. The child used to scream for help at night, and cry a good deal, but now it only makes a kind of whining, "eh-haa, eh-haa," and it speaks less and less often. It is so thin there are no calves to its legs; its belly protrudes; it lives on a half-bowl of corn meal and grease a day. It is naked. Its buttocks and thighs are a mass of festered sores, as it sits in its own excrement continually.

They all know it is there, all the people of Omelas. Some of them have come to see it, others are content merely to know it is there. They all know that it has to be there. Some of them understand why, and some do not, but all understand that their happiness, the beauty of their city, the tenderness of their friendships, the health of their children, the wisdom of their scholars, the skill of their makers, even the abundance of their harvest and the kindly weathers of their skies, depend wholly on this child's abominable misery.

This is usually explained to children when they are between eight and twelve, whenever they seem capable of understanding; and most of those who come to see the child are young people, though often enough an adult comes, or comes back, to see the child. No matter how well the matter has been explained to them, these young spectators are always shocked and sickened at the sight. They feel disgust, which they had thought themselves superior to. They feel anger, outrage, impotence, despite all the explanations. They would like to do something for the child. But there is nothing they can do. If the child were brought up into the sunlight out of that vile place, if it were cleaned and fed and comforted, that would be a good thing, indeed; but if it were done, in that day and hour all the prosperity and beauty and delight of Omelas would wither and be destroyed. Those are the terms. To exchange all the goodness and grace of every life in Omelas for that single, small improvement: to throw away the happiness of thousands for the chance of the happiness of one: that would be to let guilt within the walls indeed.

The terms are strict and absolute; there may not even be a kind word spoken to the child.

Often the young people go home in tears, or in a tearless rage, when they have seen the child and faced this terrible paradox. They may brood over it for weeks or years. But as time goes on they begin to realize that even if the child could be released, it would not get much good of its freedom: a little vague pleasure of warmth and food, no doubt, but little more. It is too degraded and imbecile to know any real joy. It has been afraid too long ever to be free of fear. Its habits are too uncouth for it to respond to humane treatment. Indeed, after so long it would probably be wretched without walls about it to protect it, and darkness for its eyes, and its own excrement to sit in. Their tears at the bitter injustice dry when they begin to perceive the terrible justice of reality, and to accept it. Yet it is their tears and anger, the trying of their generosity and the acceptance of their helplessness, which are perhaps the true source of the splendor of their lives. Theirs is no vapid, irresponsible happiness. They know that they, like the child, are not free. They know compassion. It is the existence of the child, and their knowledge of its existence, that makes possible the nobility of their architecture, the poignancy of their music, the profundity of their science. It is because of the child that they are so gentle with children. They know that if the wretched one were not there snivelling in the dark, the other one, the flute-player, could make no joyful music as the young riders line up in their beauty for the race in the sunlight of the first morning of summer.

Now do you believe in them? Are they not more credible? But there is one more thing to tell, and this is quite incredible.

At times one of the adolescent girls or boys who go to see the child does not go home to weep or rage, does not, in fact, go home at all. Sometimes also a man or woman much older falls silent for a day or two, and then leaves home. These people go out into the street, and walk down the street alone. They keep walking, and walk straight out of the city of Omelas, through the beautiful gates. They keep walking across the farmlands of Omelas. Each one goes alone, youth or girl, man or woman. Night falls; the traveler must pass down village streets, between the houses with yellow-lit windows, and on out into the darkness of the fields. Each alone, they go west or north, towards the mountains. They go on. They leave Omelas, they walk ahead into the darkness, and they do not come back. The place they go towards is a place even less imaginable to most of us than the city of happiness. I cannot describe it at all. It is possible that it does not exist. But they seem to know where they are going, the ones who walk away from Omelas.

"Repent, Harlequin!" Said the Ticktockman

1965

HARLAN ELLISON   [b. 1934]

There are always those who ask, what is it all about? For those who need to ask, for those who need points sharply made, who need to know "where it's at," this:

> The mass of men serve the state thus, not as men mainly, but as machines, with their bodies. They are the standing army, and the militia, jailors, constables, posse comitatus, etc. In most cases there is no free exercise whatever of the judgment or of the moral sense; but they put themselves on a level with wood and earth and stones; and wooden men can perhaps be manufactured that will serve the purpose as well. Such command no more respect than men of straw or a lump of dirt. They have the same sort of worth only as horses and dogs. Yet such as these even are commonly esteemed good citizens. Others—as most legislators, politicians, lawyers, ministers, and officeholders—serve the state chiefly with their heads; and, as they rarely make any moral distinctions, they are as likely to serve the Devil, without intending it, as God. A very few, as heroes, patriots, martyrs, reformers in the great sense, and men, serve the state with their consciences also, and so necessarily resist it for the most part; and they are commonly treated as enemies by it.
>
> Henry David Thoreau
CIVIL DISOBEDIENCE

That is the heart of it. Now begin in the middle, and later learn the beginning; the end will take care of itself.

But because it was the very world it was, the very world they had allowed it to *become*, for months his activities did not come to the alarmed attention of The Ones Who Kept The Machine Functioning Smoothly, the ones who poured the very best butter over the cams and mainsprings of the culture. Not until it had become obvious that somehow, someway, he had become a notoriety, a celebrity, perhaps even a hero for (what Officialdom inescapably tagged) "an emotionally disturbed segment of the populace," did they turn it over to the Ticktockman and his legal machinery. But by then, because it was the very world it was, and they had no way to predict he would happen—possibly a strain of disease long-defunct, now, suddenly, reborn in a system where immunity had been forgotten, had lapsed—he had been allowed to become too real. Now he had form and substance.

He had become a *personality*, something they had filtered out of the system many decades before. But there it was, and there *he* was, a very definitely imposing personality. In certain circles—middle-class circles—it was thought disgusting. Vulgar ostentation. Anarchistic. Shameful. In others, there was only sniggering: those strata where thought is subjugated to form and ritual, niceties, proprieties. But down below, ah, down below, where the people always needed their saints and sinners, their bread and circuses, their heroes and villains, he was considered a Bolivar; a Napoleon; a Robin Hood; a Dick Bong (Ace of Aces); a Jesus; a Jomo Kenyatta.

And at the top—where, like socially-attuned Shipwreck Kellys, every tremor and vibration threatening to dislodge the wealthy, powerful and titled from their flagpoles—he was considered a menace; a heretic; a rebel; a disgrace; a peril. He was known down the line, to the very heart-meat core, but the important reactions were high above and far below. At the very top, at the very bottom.

So his file was turned over, along with his time-card and his cardioplate, to the office of the Ticktockman.

The Ticktockman: very much over six feet tall, often silent, a soft purring man when things went timewise. The Ticktockman.

Even in the cubicles of the hierarchy, where fear was generated, seldom suffered, he was called the Ticktockman. But no one called him that to his mask.

You don't call a man a hated name, not when that man, behind his mask, is capable of revoking the minutes, the hours, the days and nights, the years of your life. He was called the Master Timekeeper to his mask. It was safer that way.

"That is *what* he is," said the Ticktockman with genuine softness, "but not *who* he is. This time-card I'm holding in my left hand has a name on it, but it is the name of *what* he is, not *who* he is. The cardioplate here in my right hand is also named, but not *whom* named, merely *what* named. Before I can exercise proper revocation, I have to know *who* this *what* is."

To his staff, all the ferrets, all the loggers, all the finks, all the commex, even the mineez, he said, "Who is this Harlequin?"

He was not purring smoothly. Timewise, it was jangle.

However, it *was* the longest speech they had ever heard him utter at one time, the staff, the ferrets, the loggers, the finks, the commex, but not the mineez, who usually weren't around to know, in any case. But even they scurried to find out.

Who is the Harlequin?

High above the third level of the city, he crouched on the humming aluminum-frame platform of the air-boat (foof! air-boat, indeed! swizzleskid is what it was, with a tow-rack jerry-rigged) and he stared down at the neat Mondrian arrangement of the buildings.

Somewhere nearby, he could hear the metronomic left-right-left of the 2:47 PM shift, entering the Timkin roller-bearing plant in their sneakers. A minute later, precisely, he heard the softer right-left-right of the 5:00 AM formation, going home.

An elfin grin spread across his tanned features, and his dimples appeared for a moment. Then, scratching at his thatch of auburn hair, he shrugged within his motley, as though girding himself for what came next, and threw the joystick forward, and bent into the wind as the air-boat dropped. He skimmed over a slidewalk, purposely dropping a few feet to crease the tassels of the ladies of fashion, and—inserting thumbs in large ears—he stuck out his tongue, rolled his eyes and went wugga-wugga-wugga. It was a minor diversion. One pedestrian skittered and tumbled, sending parcels everywhichway, another wet herself, a third keeled slantwise and the walk was stopped automatically by the servitors till she could be resuscitated. It was a minor diversion.

Then he swirled away on a vagrant breeze, and was gone. Hi-ho.

As he rounded the cornice of the Time-Motion Study Building, he saw the shift, just boarding the slidewalk. With practiced motion and an absolute conservation of movement, they sidestepped up onto the slow-strip and (in a chorus line reminiscent of a Busby Berkeley film of the antediluvian 1930s) advanced across the strips ostrich-walking till they were lined up on the expresstrip.

Once more, in anticipation, the elfin grin spread, and there was a tooth missing back there on the left side. He dipped, skimmed, and swooped over them; and then, scrunching about on the air-boat, he released the holding pins that fastened shut the ends of the home-made pouring troughs that kept his cargo from dumping prematurely. And as he pulled the trough-pins, the air-boat slid over the factory workers and one hundred and fifty thousand dollars' worth of jelly beans cascaded down on the expresstrip.

Jelly beans! Millions and billions of purples and yellows and greens and licorice and grape and raspberry and mint and round and smooth and crunchy outside and soft-mealy inside and sugary and bouncing jouncing tumbling clittering clattering skittering fell on the heads and shoulders and hardhats and carapaces of the Timkin workers, tinkling on the slidewalk and bouncing away and rolling about underfoot and filling the sky on their way down with all the colors of joy and childhood and holidays, coming down in a steady rain, a solid wash, a torrent of color and sweetness out of the sky from above, and entering a universe of sanity and metronomic order with quite-mad coocoo newness. Jelly beans!

The shift workers howled and laughed and were pelted, and broke ranks, and the jelly beans managed to work their way into the mechanism of the slidewalks after which there was a hideous scraping as the sound of a million fingernails rasped down a quarter of a million blackboards, followed by a coughing and a sputtering, and then the slidewalks all stopped and everyone was dumped thisawayandthataway in a jackstraw tumble, still laughing and popping little jelly bean eggs of childish color into their mouths. It was a holiday, and a jollity, an absolute insanity, a giggle. But . . .

The shift was delayed seven minutes.

They did not get home for seven minutes.

The master schedule was thrown off by seven minutes.

Quotas were delayed by inoperative slidewalks for seven minutes.

He had tapped the first domino in the line, and one after another, like chik chik chik, the others had fallen.

The System had been seven minutes' worth of disrupted. It was a tiny matter, one hardly worthy of note, but in a society where the single driving force was order and unity and equality and promptness and clocklike precision and attention to the clock, reverence of the gods of the passage of time, it was a disaster of major importance.

So he was ordered to appear before the Ticktockman. It was broadcast across every channel of the communications web. He was ordered to be *there* at 7:00 dammit on time. And they waited, and they waited, but he didn't show up till almost ten-thirty, at which time he merely sang a little song about moonlight in a place no one had ever heard of, called Vermont, and vanished again. But they had all been waiting since seven, and it wrecked *hell* with their schedules. So the question remained: Who is the Harlequin?

But the *unasked* question (more important of the two) was: how did we get *into* this position, where a laughing, irresponsible japer of jabberwocky and jive could disrupt our entire economic and cultural life with a hundred and fifty thousand dollars' worth of jelly beans . . .

Jelly for God's sake *beans!* This is madness! Where did he get the money to buy a hundred and fifty thousand dollars' worth of jelly beans? (They knew it would have cost that much, because they had a team of Situation Analysts pulled off another assignment, and rushed to the slidewalk scene to sweep up and count the candies, and produce findings, which disrupted *their* schedules and threw their entire branch at least a day behind.) Jelly beans! Jelly . . . *beans?* Now wait a second—a second accounted for—no one has manufactured jelly beans for over a hundred years. Where did he get jelly beans?

That's another good question. More than likely it will never be answered to your complete satisfaction. But then, how many questions ever are?

The middle you know. Here is the beginning. How it starts:

A desk pad. Day for day, and turn each day. 9:00—open the mail. 9:45—appointment with planning commission board. 10:30—discuss installation progress charts with J.L. 11:45—pray for rain. 12:00—lunch. *And so it goes.*

"I'm sorry, Miss Grant, but the time for interviews was set at 2:30, and it's almost five now. I'm sorry you're late, but those are the rules. You'll have to wait till next year to submit application for this college again." *And so it goes.*

The 10:10 local stops at Cresthaven, Galesville, Tonawanda Junction, Selby and Farnhurst, but not at Indiana City, Lucasville and Colton, except on Sunday. The 10:35 express stops at Galesville, Selby and Indiana City, except on Sundays & Holidays, at which time it stops at . . . *and so it goes.*

"I couldn't wait, Fred. I had to be at Pierre Cartain's by 3:00, and you said you'd meet me under the clock in the terminal at 2:45, and you weren't there, so I had to go on. You're always late, Fred. If you'd been there, we could have sewed it up together, but as it was, well, I took the order alone . . ." *And so it goes.*

Dear Mr. and Mrs. Atterley: In reference to your son Gerold's constant tardiness, I am afraid we will have to suspend him from school unless some more reliable method can be instituted guaranteeing he will arrive at his classes on time. Granted he is an exemplary student, and his marks are high, his constant flouting of the schedules of this school makes it impractical to maintain him in a system where the other children seem capable of getting where they are supposed to be on time *and so it goes.*

YOU CANNOT VOTE UNLESS YOU APPEAR AT 8:45 AM.

"I don't care if the script is *good,* I need it Thursday!"

CHECK-OUT TIME IS 2:00 PM.

"You got here late. The job's taken. Sorry."

YOUR SALARY HAS BEEN DOCKED FOR TWENTY MINUTES TIME LOST.

"God, what time is it, I've gotta run!"

And so it goes. And so it goes. And so it goes. And so it goes goes goes goes goes tick tock tick tock tick tock and one day we no longer let time serve us, we serve time and we are slaves of the schedule, worshippers of the sun's passing, bound into a life predicated on restrictions because the system will not function if we don't keep the schedule tight.

Until it becomes more than a minor inconvenience to be late. It becomes a sin. Then a crime. Then a crime punishable by this:

EFFECTIVE 15 JULY 2389 12:00:00 midnight, the office of the Master Timekeeper will require all citizens to submit their time-cards and cardioplates for processing. In accordance with Statute 555-7-SGH-999 governing the revocation of time per capita, all cardioplates will be keyed to the individual holder and—

What they had done, was devise a method of curtailing the amount of life a person could have. If he was ten minutes late, he lost ten minutes of his life. An hour was proportionately worth more revocation. If someone was consistently tardy, he might find himself, on a Sunday night, receiving a communiqué from the Master Timekeeper that his time had run out, and he would be "turned off" at high noon on Monday, please straighten your affairs, sir, madame or bisex.

And so, by this simple scientific expedient (utilizing a scientific process held dearly secret by the Ticktockman's office) the System was maintained. It was the only expedient thing to do. It was, after all, patriotic. The schedules had to be met. After all, there *was* a war on!

But, wasn't there always?

"Now that is really disgusting," the Harlequin said, when Pretty Alice showed him the wanted poster. "Disgusting and *highly* improbable. After all, this isn't the Day of the Desperado. A *wanted* poster!"

"You know," Pretty Alice noted, "you speak with a great deal of inflection."

"I'm sorry," said the Harlequin, humbly.

"No need to be sorry. You're always saying 'I'm sorry.' You have such massive guilt, Everett, it's really very sad."

"I'm sorry," he said again, then pursed his lips so the dimples appeared momentarily. He hadn't wanted to say that at all. "I have to go out again. I have to *do* something."

Pretty Alice slammed her coffee-bulb down on the counter. "Oh for God's *sake*, Everett, can't you stay home just *one* night! Must you always be out in that ghastly clown suit, running around annoying people?"

"I'm—" He stopped, and clapped the jester's hat onto his auburn thatch with a tiny tingling of bells. He rose, rinsed out his coffee-bulb at the spray, and put it into the dryer for a moment. "I have to go."

She didn't answer. The faxbox was purring, and she pulled a sheet out, read it, threw it toward him on the counter. "It's about you. Of course. You're ridiculous."

He read it quickly. It said the Ticktockman was trying to locate him. He didn't care, he was going out to be late again. At the door, dredging for an exit line, he hurled back petulantly, "Well, *you* speak with inflection, *too!*"

Pretty Alice rolled her pretty eyes heavenward. "You're ridiculous." The Harlequin stalked out, slamming the door, which sighed shut softly, and locked itself.

There was a gentle knock, and Pretty Alice got up with an exhalation of exasperated breath, and opened the door. He stood there. "I'll be back about ten-thirty, okay?"

She pulled a rueful face. "Why do you tell me that? Why? You *know* you'll be late! You *know* it! You're *always* late, so why do you tell me these dumb things?" She closed the door.

On the other side, the Harlequin nodded to himself. *She's right. She's always right. I'll be late. I'm always late. Why do I tell her these dumb things?*

He shrugged again, and went off to be late once more.

He had fired off the firecracker rockets that said: I will attend the 115th annual International Medical Association Invocation at 8:00 PM precisely. I do hope you will all be able to join me.

The words had burned in the sky, and of course the authorities were there, lying in wait for him. They assumed, naturally, that he would be late. He arrived twenty minutes early, while they were setting up the spiderwebs to trap and hold him. Blowing a large bullhorn, he frightened and unnerved them so, their own moisturized encirclement webs sucked closed, and they were hauled up, kicking and shrieking, high above the amphitheater's floor. The Harlequin laughed and laughed, and apologized profusely. The physicians, gathered in solemn conclave, roared with laughter, and accepted the Harlequin's apologies with exaggerated bowing and posturing, and a merry time was had by all, who thought the Harlequin was a regular foofaraw in fancy pants; all, that is, but the authorities, who had been sent out by the office of the Ticktockman; they hung there like so much dockside cargo, hauled up above the floor of the amphitheater in a most unseemly fashion.

(In another part of the same city where the Harlequin carried on his "activities," totally unrelated in every way to what concerns us here, save that it illustrates the Ticktockman's power and import, a man named Marshall Delahanty received his turn-off notice from the Ticktockman's office. His wife received the notification from the gray-suited minee who delivered it, with the traditional "look of sorrow" plastered hideously across his face. She knew what it was, even without unsealing it. It was a billet-doux of immediate recognition to everyone these days. She gasped, and held it as though it were a glass slide tinged with botulism, and prayed it was not for her. Let it be for Marsh, she thought, brutally, realistically, or one of the kids, but not for me, please dear God, not for me. And then she opened it, and it *was* for Marsh, and she was at one and the same time horrified and relieved. The next trooper in the line had caught the bullet. "Marshall," she screamed, "Marshall! Termination, Marshall! OhmiGod, Marshall, whattl we do, whattl we do, Marshall omigod-marshall . . ." and in their home that night was the sound of tearing paper and fear, and the stink of madness went up the flue and there was nothing, absolutely nothing they could do about it.

(But Marshall Delahanty tried to run. And early the next day, when turnoff time came, he was deep in the Canadian forest two hundred miles away, and the office of the Ticktockman blanked his cardioplate, and Marshall Delahanty keeled over, running, and his heart stopped, and the blood dried up on its way to his brain, and he was dead that's all. One light went out on the sector map in the office of the Master Timekeeper, while notification was entered for fax reproduction, and Georgette Delahanty's name was entered on the dole roles till she could remarry. Which is the end of the footnote, and all the point that need be made, except don't laugh, because that is what would happen to the Harlequin if ever the Ticktockman found out his real name. It isn't funny.)

The shopping level of the city was thronged with the Thursday-colors of the buyers. Women in canary yellow chitons and men in pseudo-Tyrolean outfits that were jade and leather and fit very tightly, save for the balloon pants.

When the Harlequin appeared on the still-being-constructed shell of the new Efficiency Shopping Center, his bullhorn to his elfishly-laughing lips, everyone pointed and stared, and he berated them:

"Why let them order you about? Why let them tell you to hurry and scurry like ants or maggots? Take your time! Saunter a while! Enjoy the sunshine, enjoy the breeze, let life carry you at your own pace! Don't be slaves of time, it's a helluva way to die, slowly, by degrees . . . down with the Ticktockman!"

Who's the nut? most of the shoppers wanted to know. Who's the nut oh wow I'm gonna be late I gotta run . . .

And the construction gang on the Shopping Center received an urgent order from the office of the Master Timekeeper that the dangerous criminal known as the Harlequin was atop their spire, and their aid was urgently needed in apprehending him. The work crew said no, they would lose time on their construction schedule, but the Ticktockman managed to pull the proper threads of governmental webbing, and they were told to cease work and catch that nitwit up there on the spire; up there with the bullhorn. So a dozen and more burly workers began climbing into their construction platforms, releasing the a-grav plates, and rising toward the Harlequin.

After the debacle (in which, through the Harlequin's attention to personal safety, no one was seriously injured), the workers tried to reassemble, and assault him again, but it was too late. He had vanished. It had attracted quite a crowd, however, and the shopping cycle was thrown off by hours, simply hours. The purchasing needs of the system were therefore falling behind, and so measures were taken to accelerate the cycle for the rest of the day, but it got bogged down and speeded up and they sold too many float-valves and not nearly enough wegglers, which meant that the popli ratio was off, which made it necessary to rush cases and cases of spoiling Smash-O to stores that usually needed a case only every three or four hours. The shipments were bollixed, the transshipments were misrouted, and in the end, even the swizzleskid industries felt it.

"Don't come back till you have him!" the Ticktockman said, very quietly, very sincerely, extremely dangerously.

They used dogs. They used probes. They used cardioplate crossoffs. They used teepers. They used bribery. They used stiktytes. They used intimidation. They used torment. They used torture. They used finks. They used cops. They used search&seizure. They used fallaron. They used betterment incentive. They used fingerprints. They used the Bertillon system. They used cunning. They used guile. They used treachery. They used Raoul Mitgong, but he didn't help much. They used applied physics. They used techniques of criminology.

And what the hell: they caught him.

After all, his name was Everett C. Marm, and he wasn't much to begin with, except a man who had no sense of time.

"Repent, Harlequin!" said the Ticktockman.

"Get stuffed!" the Harlequin replied, sneering.

"You've been late a total of sixty-three years, five months, three weeks, two days, twelve hours, forty-one minutes, fifty-nine seconds, point oh three six one one one microseconds. You've used up everything you can, and more. I'm going to turn you off."

"Scare someone else. I'd rather be dead than live in a dumb world with a bogeyman like you."

"It's my job."

"You're full of it. You're a tyrant. You have no right to order people around and kill them if they show up late."

"You can't adjust. You can't fit in."

"Unstrap me, and I'll fit my fist into your mouth."

"You're a nonconformist."

"That didn't used to be a felony."

"It is now. Live in the world around you."

"I hate it. It's a terrible world."

"Not everyone thinks so. Most people enjoy order."

"I don't, and most of the people I know don't."

"That's not true. How do you think we caught you?"

"I'm not interested."

"A girl named Pretty Alice told us who you were."

"That's a lie."

"It's true. You unnerve her. She wants to belong; she wants to conform; I'm going to turn you off."

"Then do it already, and stop arguing with me."

"I'm not going to turn you off."

"You're an idiot!"

"Repent, Harlequin!" said the Ticktockman.

"Get stuffed."

So they sent him to Coventry. And in Coventry they worked him over. It was just like what they did to Winston Smith in NINETEEN EIGHTY-FOUR, which was a book none of them knew about, but the techniques are really quite ancient, and so they did it to Everett C. Marm; and one day, quite a long time later, the Harlequin appeared on the communications web, appearing elfin and dimpled and bright-eyed, and not at all brainwashed, and he said he had been wrong, that it was a good, a very good thing indeed, to belong, to be right on time hip-ho and away we go, and everyone stared up at him on the public screens that covered an entire city block, and they said to themselves, well, you see, he was just a nut after all, and if that's the way the system is run, then let's do it that way, because it doesn't pay to fight city hall, or in this case, the Ticktockman. So Everett C. Marm was destroyed, which was a loss, because of what Thoreau said earlier, but you can't make an omelet without breaking a few eggs, and in every revolution a few die who shouldn't, but they have to, because that's the way it happens, and if you make only a little change, then it seems to be worthwhile. Or, to make the point lucidly:

"Uh, excuse me, sir, I, uh, don't know how to uh, to uh, tell you this, but you were three minutes late. The schedule is a little, uh, bit off."

He grinned sheepishly.

"That's ridiculous!" murmured the Ticktockman behind his mask. "Check your watch." And then he went into his office, going *mrmee, mrmee, mrmee, mrmee.*

Everyday Use 1973

FOR YOUR GRANDMAMA

ALICE WALKER [b. 1944]

I will wait for her in the yard that Maggie and I made so clean and wavy yesterday afternoon. A yard like this is more comfortable than most people know. It is not just a yard. It is like an extended living room. When the hard clay is swept clean as a floor and the fine sand around the edges lined with tiny, irregular grooves anyone can come and sit and look up into the elm tree and wait for the breezes that never come inside the house.

Maggie will be nervous until after her sister goes: she will stand hopelessly in corners homely and ashamed of the burn scars down her arms and legs, eyeing her sister with a mixture of envy and awe. She thinks her sister has held life always in the palm of one hand, that "no" is a word the world never learned to say to her.

You've no doubt seen those TV shows where the child who has "made it" is confronted, as a surprise, by her own mother and father, tottering in weakly from backstage. (A pleasant surprise, of course: What would they do if parent and child came on the show only to curse out and insult each other?) On TV mother and child embrace and smile into each other's faces. Sometimes the mother and father weep, the child wraps them in her arms and leans across the table to tell how she would not have made it without their help. I have seen these programs.

Sometimes I dream a dream in which Dee and I are suddenly brought together on a TV program of this sort. Out of a dark and soft-seated limousine I am ushered into a bright room filled with many people. There I meet a smiling, gray, sporty man like Johnny Carson who shakes my hand and tells me what a fine girl I have. Then we are on the stage and Dee is embracing me with tears in her eyes. She pins on my dress a large orchid, even though she has told me once that she thinks orchids are tacky flowers.

In real life I am a large, big-boned woman with rough, man-working hands. In the winter I wear flannel nightgowns to bed and overalls during the day. I can kill and clean a hog as mercilessly as a man. My fat keeps me hot in zero weather. I can work outside all day, breaking ice to get water for washing. I can eat pork liver cooked over the open fire minutes after it comes steaming from the hog. One winter I knocked a bull calf straight in the brain between the eyes with a sledge hammer and had the meat hung up to chill before nightfall. But of course all this does not show on television. I am the way my daughter would want me to be: a hundred pounds lighter, my skin like an uncooked barley pancake. My hair glistens in the hot bright lights. Johnny Carson has much to do to keep up with my quick and witty tongue.

But that is a mistake. I know even before I wake up. Who ever knew a Johnson with a quick tongue? Who can even imagine me looking a strange white man in the eye? It seems to me I have talked to them always with one foot raised in flight, with my head turned in whichever way is farthest from them. Dee, though. She would always look anyone in the eye. Hesitation was no part of her nature.

"How do I look, Mama?" Maggie says, showing just enough of her thin body enveloped in pink skirt and red blouse for me to know she's there, almost hidden by the door.

"Come out into the yard," I say.

Have you ever seen a lame animal, perhaps a dog run over by some careless person rich enough to own a car, sidle up to someone who is ignorant enough to be kind to him? That is the way my Maggie walks. She has been like this, chin on chest, eyes on ground, feet in shuffle, ever since the fire that burned the other house to the ground.

Dee is lighter than Maggie, with nicer hair and a fuller figure. She's a woman now, though sometimes I forget. How long ago was it that the other house burned? Ten, twelve years? Sometimes I can still hear the flames and feel Maggie's arms sticking to me, her hair smoking and her dress falling off her in little black papery flakes. Her eyes seemed stretched open, blazed open by the flames reflected in them. And Dee. I see her standing off under the sweet gum tree she used to dig gum out of; a look of concentration on her face as she watched the last dingy gray board of the house fall in toward the red-hot brick chimney. Why don't you do a dance around the ashes? I'd wanted to ask her. She had hated the house that much.

I used to think she hated Maggie, too. But that was before we raised the money, the church and me, to send her to Augusta to school. She used to read to us without pity; forcing words, lies, other folks' habits, whole lives upon us two, sitting trapped and ignorant underneath her voice. She washed us in a river of make-believe, burned us with a lot of knowledge we didn't necessarily need to know. Pressed us to her with the serious way she read, to shove us away at just the moment, like dimwits, we seemed about to understand.

Dee wanted nice things. A yellow organdy dress to wear to her graduation from high school; black pumps to match a green suit she'd made from an old suit somebody gave me. She was determined to stare down any disaster in her efforts. Her eyelids would not flicker for minutes at a time. Often I fought off the temptation to shake her. At sixteen she had a style of her own: and knew what style was.

I never had an education myself. After second grade the school was closed down. Don't ask me why: in 1927 colored asked fewer questions than they do now. Sometimes Maggie reads to me. She stumbles along good-naturedly but can't see well. She knows she is not bright. Like good looks and money, quickness passed her by. She will marry John Thomas (who has mossy teeth in an earnest face) and then I'll be free to sit here and I guess just sing church songs to myself. Although I never was a good singer. Never could carry a tune. I was always better at a man's job. I used to love to milk till I was hoofed in the side in '49. Cows are soothing and slow and don't bother you, unless you try to milk them the wrong way.

I have deliberately turned my back on the house. It is three rooms, just like the one that burned, except the roof is tin; they don't make shingle roofs any more. There are no real windows, just some holes cut in the sides, like the portholes in a ship, but not round and not square, with rawhide holding the shutters up on the outside. This house is in a pasture, too, like the other one. No doubt when Dee sees it she will want to tear it down. She wrote me once that no matter where we "choose" to live, she will manage to come see us. But she will never bring her friends. Maggie and I thought about this and Maggie asked me, "Mama, when did Dee ever *have* any friends?"

She had a few. Furtive boys in pink shirts hanging about on washday after school. Nervous girls who never laughed. Impressed with her they worshiped the well-turned phrase, the cute shape, the scalding humor that erupted like bubbles in lye. She read to them.

When she was courting Jimmy T she didn't have much time to pay to us, but turned all her faultfinding power on him. He *flew* to marry a cheap gal from a family of ignorant flashy people. She hardly had time to recompose herself.

When she comes I will meet—but there they are!

Maggie attempts to make a dash for the house, in her shuffling way, but I stay her with my hand. "Come back here," I say. And she stops and tries to dig a well in the sand with her toe.

It is hard to see them clearly through the strong sun. But even the first glimpse of leg out of the car tells me it is Dee. Her feet were always neatlooking, as if God himself had shaped them with a certain style. From the other side of the car comes a short, stocky man. Hair is all over his head a foot long and hanging from his chin like a kinky mule tail. I hear Maggie suck in her breath. "Uhnnnh," is what it sounds like. Like when you see the wriggling end of a snake just in front of your foot on the road. "Uhnnnh."

Dee next. A dress down to the ground, in this hot weather. A dress so loud it hurts my eyes. There are yellows and oranges enough to throw back the light of the sun. I feel my whole face warming from the heat waves it throws out. Earrings, too, gold and hanging down to her shoulders. Bracelets dangling and making noises when she moves her arm up to shake the folds of the dress out of her armpits. The dress is loose and flows, and as she walks closer, I like it. I hear Maggie go "Uhnnnh" again. It is her sister's hair. It stands straight up like the wool on a sheep. It is black as night and around the edges are two long pigtails that rope about like small lizards disappearing behind her ears.

"Wa-su-zo-Tean-o!" she says, coming on in that gliding way the dress makes her move. The short stocky fellow with the hair to his navel is all grinning and he follows up with "Asalamalakim, my mother and sister!" He moves to hug

Maggie but she falls back, right up against the back of my chair. I feel her trembling there and when I look up I see the perspiration falling off her chin.

"Don't get up," says Dee. Since I am stout it takes something of a push. You can see me trying to move a second or two before I make it. She turns, showing white heels through her sandals, and goes back to the car. Out she peeks next with a Polaroid. She stoops down quickly and lines up picture after picture of me sitting there in front of the house with Maggie cowering behind me. She never takes a shot without making sure the house is included. When a cow comes nibbling around the edge of the yard she snaps it and me and Maggie *and* the house. Then she puts the Polaroid in the back seat of the car, and comes up and kisses me on the forehead.

Meanwhile Asalamalakim is going through motions with Maggie's hand. Maggie's hand is as limp as a fish, and probably as cold, despite the sweat, and she keeps trying to pull it back. It looks like Asalamalakim wants to shake hands but wants to do it fancy. Or maybe he don't know how people shake hands. Anyhow, he soon gives up on Maggie.

"Well," I say. "Dee."

"No, Mama," she says. "Not 'Dee,' Wangero Leewanika Kemanjo!"

"What happened to 'Dee'?" I wanted to know.

"She's dead," Wangero said. "I couldn't bear it any longer being named after the people who oppress me."

"You know as well as me you was named after your aunt Dicie," I said. Dicie is my sister. She named Dee. We called her "Big Dee" after Dee was born.

"But who was *she* named after?" asked Wangero.

"I guess after Grandma Dee," I said.

"And who was she named after?" asked Wangero.

"Her mother," I said, and saw Wangero was getting tired. "That's about as far back as I can trace it," I said. Though, in fact, I probably could have carried it back beyond the Civil War through the branches.

"Well," said Asalamalakim, "there you are."

"Uhnnnh," I heard Maggie say.

"There I was not," I said, "before 'Dicie' cropped up in our family, so why should I try to trace it that far back?"

He just stood there grinning, looking down on me like somebody inspecting a Model A car. Every once in a while he and Wangero sent eye signals over my head.

"How do you pronounce this name?" I asked.

"You don't have to call me by it if you don't want to," said Wangero.

"Why shouldn't I?" I asked. "If that's what you want us to call you, we'll call you."

"I know it might sound awkward at first," said Wangero.

"I'll get used to it," I said. "Ream it out again."

Well, soon we got the name out of the way. Asalamalakim had a name twice as long and three times as hard. After I tripped over it two or three times he told me to just call him Hakim-a-barber. I wanted to ask him was he a barber, but I didn't really think he was, so I didn't ask.

"You must belong to those beef-cattle peoples down the road," I said. They said "Asalamalakim" when they met you, too, but they didn't shake hands. Always too busy: feeding the cattle, fixing the fences, putting up salt-lick shelters, throwing down hay. When the white folks poisoned some of the herd the men stayed up all night with rifles in their hands. I walked a mile and a half just to see the sight.

Hakim-a-barber said, "I accept some of their doctrines, but farming and raising cattle is not my style." (They didn't tell me, and I didn't ask, whether Wangero [Dee] had really gone and married him.)

We sat down to eat and right away he said he didn't eat collards and pork was unclean. Wangero, though, went on through the chitlins and corn bread, the greens and everything else. She talked a blue streak over the sweet potatoes. Everything delighted her. Even the fact that we still used the benches her daddy made for the table when we couldn't afford to buy chairs.

"Oh, Mama!" she cried. Then turned to Hakim-a-barber. "I never knew how lovely these benches are. You can feel the rump prints," she said, running her hands underneath her and along the bench. Then she gave a sigh and her hand closed over Grandma Dee's butter dish. "That's it!" she said. "I knew there was something I wanted to ask you if I could have." She jumped up from the table and went over in the corner where the churn stood, the milk in its clabber by now. She looked at the churn and looked at it.

"This churn top is what I need," she said. "Didn't Uncle Buddy whittle it out of a tree you all used to have?"

"Yes," I said.

"Uh huh," she said happily. "And I want the dasher, too."

"Uncle Buddy whittle that, too?" asked the barber.

Dee (Wangero) looked up at me.

"Aunt Dee's first husband whittled the dash," said Maggie so low you almost couldn't hear her. "His name was Henry, but they called him Stash."

"Maggie's brain is like an elephant's," Wangero said, laughing. "I can use the churn top as a centerpiece for the alcove table," she said, sliding a plate over the churn, "and I'll think of something artistic to do with the dasher."

When she finished wrapping the dasher the handle stuck out. I took it for a moment in my hands. You didn't even have to look close to see where hands pushing the dasher up and down to make butter had left a kind of sink in the wood. In fact, there were a lot of small sinks; you could see where thumbs and fingers had sunk into the wood. It was beautiful light yellow wood, from a tree that grew in the yard where Big Dee and Stash had lived.

After dinner Dee (Wangero) went to the trunk at the foot of my bed and started rifling through it. Maggie hung back in the kitchen over the dishpan. Out came Wangero with two quilts. They had been pieced by Grandma Dee and then Big Dee and me had hung them on the quilt frames on the front porch and quilted them. One was in the Lone Star pattern. The other was Walk Around the Mountain. In both of them were scraps of dresses Grandma Dee had worn fifty and more years ago. Bits and pieces of Grandpa Jarrell's Paisley shirts. And one teeny faded blue piece, about the size of a penny matchbox, that was from Great Grandpa Ezra's uniform that he wore in the Civil War.

"Mama," Wangero said sweet as a bird. "Can I have these old quilts?"

I heard something fall in the kitchen, and a minute later the kitchen door slammed.

"Why don't you take one or two of the others?" I asked. "These old things was just done by me and Big Dee from some tops your grandma pieced before she died."

"No," said Wangero. "I don't want those. They are stitched around the borders by machine."

"That'll make them last better," I said.

"That's not the point," said Wangero. "These are all pieces of dresses Grandma used to wear. She did all this stitching by hand. Imagine!" She held the quilts securely in her arms, stroking them.

"Some of the pieces, like those lavender ones, come from old clothes her mother handed down to her," I said, moving up to touch the quilts. Dee (Wangero) moved back just enough so that I couldn't reach the quilts. They already belonged to her.

"Imagine!" she breathed again, clutching them closely to her bosom.

"The truth is," I said, "I promised to give them quilts to Maggie, for when she marries John Thomas."

She gasped like a bee had stung her.

"Maggie can't appreciate these quilts!" she said. "She'd probably be backward enough to put them to everyday use."

"I reckon she would," I said. "God knows I been saving 'em for long enough with nobody using 'em. I hope she will!" I didn't want to bring up how I had offered Dee (Wangero) a quilt when she went away to college. Then she had told me they were old-fashioned, out of style.

"But they're *priceless!*" she was saying now, furiously; for she has a temper. "Maggie would put them on the bed and in five years they'd be in rags. Less than that!"

"She can always make some more," I said. "Maggie knows how to quilt."

Dee (Wangero) looked at me with hatred. "You just will not understand. The point is these quilts, *these* quilts!"

"Well," I said, stumped. "What would *you* do with them?"

"Hang them," she said. As if that was the only thing you *could* do with quilts.

Maggie by now was standing in the door. I could almost hear the sound her feet made as they scraped over each other.

"She can have them, Mama," she said, like somebody used to never winning anything, or having anything reserved for her. "I can 'member Grandma Dee without the quilts."

I looked at her hard. She had filled her bottom lip with checkerberry snuff and it gave her face a kind of dopey, hangdog look. It was Grandma Dee and Big Dee who taught her how to quilt herself. She stood there with her scarred hands hidden in the folds of her skirt. She looked at her sister with something like fear but she wasn't mad at her. This was Maggie's portion. This was the way she knew God to work.

When I looked at her like that something hit me in the top of my head and ran down to the soles of my feet. Just like when I'm in church and the spirit of God touches me and I get happy and shout. I did something I never had done before: hugged Maggie to me, then dragged her on into the room, snatched the quilts out of Miss Wangero's hands and dumped them into Maggie's lap. Maggie just sat there on my bed with her mouth open.

"Take one or two of the others," I said to Dee.

But she turned without a word and went out to Hakim-a-barber.

"You just don't understand," she said, as Maggie and I came out to the car.

"What don't I understand?" I wanted to know.

"Your heritage," she said. And then she turned to Maggie, kissed her, and said, "You ought to try to make something of yourself, too, Maggie. It's really a new day for us. But from the way you and Mama still live you'd never know it."

She put on some sunglasses that hid everything above the tip of her nose and her chin.

Maggie smiled; maybe at the sunglasses. But a real smile, not scared. After we watched the car dust settle I asked Maggie to bring me a dip of snuff. And then the two of us sat there just enjoying, until it was time to go in the house and go to bed.

Winter Count 1973: Geese, They Flew Over in a Storm 1981

BARRY HOLSTUN LOPEZ [b. 1945]

He followed the bellboy off the elevator, through a foyer with forlorn leather couches, noting how low the ceiling was, with its white plaster flowers in bas-relief—and that there were no windows. He followed him down a long corridor dank with an air of fugitives, past dark, impenetrable doors. At the distant end of the next corridor he saw gray thunderheads and the black ironwork of a fire escape. The boy slowed down and reached out to slide a thick key into the lock and he heard the sudden alignment of steel tumblers and their ratchet click. The door swung open and the boy entered, with the suitcase bouncing against the crook at the back of his knee.

He tipped the boy, having no idea what amount was now thought proper. The boy departed, leaving the room sealed off as if in a vacuum. The key with the ornate brass fob lay on a glass table. The man stood by the bed with his hands folded at his lips as though in prayer. Slowly he cleared away the drapes, the curtains and the blinds and stared out at the bare sky. Wind whipped rain in streaks across the glass. He had never been to New Orleans. It was a vague streamer blowing in his memory, like a boyhood acquaintance with Lafcadio Hearn. Natchez Trace. Did Choctaw live here? he wondered. Or Chitamacha? Before them, worshippers of the sun.

He knew the plains better. Best. The high plains north of the Platte River.

He took off his shoes and lay on the bed. He was glad for the feel of the candlewick bedspread. Or was it chenille? He had had this kind of spread on his bed when he was a child. He removed his glasses and pinched the bridge of his nose. In all these years he had delivered so few papers, had come to enjoy much more listening to them, to the stories unfolding in them. It did not matter to him that the arguments were so abstruse they were all but impregnable, that the thought in them would turn to vapor, an arrested breath. He came to hear a story unfold, to regard its shape and effect. He thought one unpacked history, that it came like pemmican in a parfleche and was to be consumed in a hard winter.

The wind sucked at the windows and released them suddenly to rattle in their metal frames. It made him think of home, of the Sand Hills. He lay motionless on the bed and thought of the wind. Crow men racing naked in an April rain, with their hair, five-foot-long black banners, spiraling behind, splashing on the muscled rumps of white horses with brown ears.

>   1847 One man alone defended the Hat in a fight with the Crow
>
>   1847 White buffalo, Dusk killed it
>
>   1847 Daughter of Turtle Head, her clothes caught fire and she was burned up
>
>   1847 Three men who were women came

He got up and went to his bag. He took out three stout willow sticks and bound them as a tripod. From its apex he hung a beaded bag of white elk hide with long fringe. The fringe was wrinkled from having been folded against itself in his suit pocket.

1891 Medicine bundles, police tore them open

What did they want from him? A teacher. He taught, he did not write papers. He told the story of people coming up from the Tigris-Euphrates, starting there. Other years he would start in a different place—Olduvai, Afar Valley. Or in Tierra del Fuego with the Onas. He could as easily start in the First World of the Navajo. The point, he told his students, was not this. There was no point. It was a slab of meat. It was a rhythm to dance to. It was a cloak that cut the wind when it blew hard enough to crack your soul.

1859 Ravens froze, fell over
1804 Heavy spring snow. Even the dogs went snow-blind

He slept. In his rumpled suit. In the flat, reflected storm light his face appeared ironed smooth. The wind fell away from the building and he dreamed.

For a moment he was lost. Starlight Room. Tarpon Room. Oak Room. He was due—he thought suddenly of aging, of illness: *when our children, they had strangulations of the throat,* of the cure for *any* illness as he scanned the long program—in the Creole Room. He was due in the Creole Room. Roger Callahan, Nebraska State College: "Winter Counts from the Dakota, the Crow and the Blackfeet: Personal Histories." Jesus, he thought, why had he come? He had been asked. They had asked.
    "Aha, Roger."
    "I'm on time? I got—"
    "You come right this way. I want you in front here. Everyone is very excited, very excited, you know. We're very glad you came. And how is Margaret?"
    "Yes—. Margaret died. She died two years ago."

1837 Straight Calf took six horses from the Crow and gave them to Blue Cloud
      Woman's father and took her
1875 White Hair, he was killed in a river by an Omaha man
1943 John Badger Heart killed in an automobile crash

He did not hear the man. He sat. The histories began to cover him over like willows, thick as creek willows, and he reached out to steady himself in the pool of time.
    He listened patiently to the other papers. Edward Rice Phillips, Purdue: "The Okipa Ceremony and Mandan Sexual Habits." The Mandan, he thought, they were all dead. Who would defend them? Renata Morrison, University of Texas: "The Role of Women in Northern Plains Religious Ceremonials."

1818 Sparrow Woman promised the Sun Dance in winter if the Cree didn't find us

1872 Comes Out of the Water, she ran off the Assiniboine horses

1904 Moving Gently, his sister hung herself

He tried to listen, but the words fell away like tumbled leaves. Cottonwoods. Winters so bad they would have to cut down cottonwood trees for the horses to eat. *So cold we got water from beaver holes only.* And years when they had to eat the horses. *We killed our ponies and ate them. No buffalo.*

Inside the windowless room (he could not remember which floor the elevator had opened on) everyone was seated in long rows. From the first row he could not see anyone. He shifted in his seat and his leather bag fell with a slap against the linoleum floor. How long had he been carrying papers from one place to another like this? He remembered a friend's poem about a snowy owl dead behind glass in a museum, no more to soar, to hunch and spread his wings and tail and fall silent as moonlight.

1809 Blue feathers found on the ground from unknown birds

1811 Weasel Sits Down came into camp with blue feathers tied in his hair

There was distant applause, like dry brush rattling in the wind.

Years before, defense of theory had concerned him. Not now. "I've thrown away everything that is no good," he told a colleague one summer afternoon on his porch, as though shouting over the roar of a storm. "I can no longer think of anything worse than proving you are right." He took what was left and he went on from there.

1851 No meat in camp. A man went to look for buffalo and was killed by two Arapaho

1854 The year they dragged the Arapaho's head through camp

". . . and my purpose in aligning these four examples is to clearly demonstrate an irrefutable, or what I consider an irrefutable, relationship: the Arikara never . . ."

When he was a boy his father had taken him one April morning to watch whooping cranes on estuaries of the Platte, headed for Alberta. The morning was crucial in the unfolding of his own life.

1916 My father drives east for hours in silence. We walk out into a field covered all over with river fog. The cranes, just their legs are visible

His own count would be personal, more personal, as though he were the only one.

1918 Father, shot dead. Argonne forest

The other years came around him now like soft velvet noses of horses touching his arms in the dark.

". . . while the Cheyenne, contrary to what Greenwold has had to say on this point but reinforcing what has been stated previously by Gregg and Houston, were more inclined . . ."

He wished for something to hold, something to touch, to strip leaves barehanded from a chokecherry branch or to hear rain falling on the surface of a lake. In this windowless room he ached.

> 1833 Stars blowing around like snow. Some fall to the earth
>
> 1856 Reaches into the Enemy's Tipi has a dream and can't speak
>
> 1869 Fire Wagon, it comes

Applause.

He stood up and walked in quiet shoes to the stage. (Once in the middle of class he had stopped to explain his feeling about walking everywhere in silence.) He set his notes on the podium and covered them with his hands. In a clear voice, without apology for his informality or a look at his papers, he unfolded the winter counts of the Sioux warrior Blue Thunder, of the Blackfeet Bad Head, and of the Crow Extends His Paw. He stated that these were personal views of history, sometimes metaphorical, bearing on a larger, tribal history. He spoke of the confusion caused by translators who had tried to force agreement among several winter counts or who mistook mythic time for some other kind of real time. He concluded by urging less contention. "As professional historians, we have too often subordinated one system to another and forgotten all together the individual view, the poetic view, which is as close to the truth as the consensus. Or it can be as distant."

He felt the necklace of hawk talons pressing against his clavicles under the weight of his shirt.

The applause was respectful, thin, distracted. As he stepped away from the podium he realized it was perhaps foolish to have accepted the invitation. He could no longer make a final point. He had long ago lost touch with the definitive, the awful distance of reason. He wanted to go back to the podium. You can only tell the story as it was given to you, he wanted to say. Do not lie. Do not make it up.

He hesitated for a moment at the edge of the stage. He wished he were back in Nebraska with his students, to warn them: it is too dangerous for everyone to have the same story. The same things do not happen to everyone.

He passed through the murmuring crowd, through a steel fire door, down a hallway, up a flight of stairs, another, and emerged into palms in the lobby.

> 1823 A man, he was called Fifteen Horses, who was heyoka, a contrary, sacred clown, ran at the Crow backwards, shooting arrows at his own people. The Crow shot him in midair like a quail. He couldn't fool them

He felt the edge of self-pity, standing before a plate-glass window as wide as the spread of his arms and as tall as his house. He watched the storm that still raged, which he could not hear, which he had not been able to hear, bend trees to breaking, slash the surface of Lake Pontchartrain and raise air boiling over the gulf beyond. "Everything is held together with stories," he thought. "That is all that is holding us together, stories and compassion."

He turned quickly from the cold glass and went up in the silent elevator and ordered dinner. When it came, he threw back the drapes and curtains and opened the windows. The storm howled through his room and roared through his head. He breathed the wet air deep into his lungs. In the deepest distance, once, he heard the barking-dog sounds of geese, running like horses before a prairie thunderstorm.

QUESTIONS

1. Why do you suppose Roger Callahan carries a "medicine bag" and wears a hawk talon necklace?   **2.** What did tribal historians record in their "winter counts"? How do such records differ from the events recorded by academic historians?   **3.** Locate Callahan's own winter count observation. How does it differ from typical historical treatments of World War I?   **4.** Is there any relationship between the last winter count anecdote about the "contrary" who ran backwards and Callahan? Explain.

WRITING TOPICS

1. In an essay, expand on Callahan's statement to his colleague: "I can no longer think of anything worse than proving you are right."   **2.** Mindful of the contrast between Indian historical observations and the learned papers being read at the academic meeting, discuss Callahan's concluding remark: "As professional historians we have too often subordinated one system to another and forgotten all together the individual view, the poetic view, which is as close to the truth as the consensus. Or it can be as distant."

CONFORMITY
AND
REBELLION

Adam and Eve, Sistine Chapel (restored figures) 1509–10 by Michelangelo

POETRY

from

Paradise Lost[1]

JOHN MILTON   [1608–1674]

"Is this the region, this the soil, the clime,"
Said then the lost archangel, "this the seat
That we must change for Heaven? this mournful gloom
For that celestial light? Be it so, since he
Who now is sovereign can dispose and bid   5
What shall be right: farthest from him is best,
Whom reason hath equaled, force hath made supreme
Above his equals. Farewell, happy fields,
Where joy forever dwells! Hail, horrors! hail,
Infernal world! and thou, profoundest Hell,   10
Receive thy new possessor, one who brings
A mind not to be changed by place or time.
The mind is its own place, and in itself
Can make a Heaven of Hell, a Hell of Heaven.
What matter where, if I be still the same,   15
And what I should be, all but° less than he   only
Whom thunder hath made greater? Here at least
We shall be free; th' Almighty hath not built
Here for his envy, will not drive us hence:
Here we may reign secure; and, in my choice,   20
To reign is worth ambition, though in Hell:
Better to reign in Hell than serve in Heaven.
But wherefore let we then our faithful friends,
Th' associates and copartners of our loss,
Lie thus astonished on th' oblivious pool,   25
And call them not to share with us their part
In this unhappy mansion, or once more
With rallied arms to try what may be yet
Regained in Heaven, or what more lost in Hell?"

Paradise Lost
   [1]The first part of *Paradise Lost*, a poem on the expulsion of Adam and Eve from the Garden of Eden, tells the story of Satan's rebellion against God, his defeat and expulsion from heaven. In this passage, Satan surveys the infernal region to which God has banished him.

281

QUESTIONS
1. Is the statement in line 22 a logical extension of the statement in lines 13–14? Explain.   **2.** Is the rebellious Satan heroic or ignoble? Defend your answer.   **3.** What are the political implications of Satan's analysis of power (ll. 4–8)?

The World Is
Too Much with Us   1807

WILLIAM WORDSWORTH   [1770–1850]

The world is too much with us; late and soon,
Getting and spending, we lay waste our powers;
Little we see in Nature that is ours;
We have given our hearts away, a sordid boon!
This Sea that bares her bosom to the moon,   5
The winds that will be howling at all hours,
And are up-gathered now like sleeping flowers,
For this, for everything, we are out of tune;
It moves us not.—Great God! I'd rather be
A Pagan suckled in a creed outworn;   10
So might I, standing on this pleasant lea,
Have glimpses that would make me less forlorn;
Have sight of Proteus rising from the sea;
Or hear old Triton blow his wreathèd horn.[1]

QUESTIONS
1. What does "world" mean in line 1?   **2.** What does Wordsworth complain of in the first four lines?   **3.** In lines 4–8 Wordsworth tells us what we have lost; in the concluding lines he suggests a remedy. What is that remedy? What do Proteus and Triton symbolize?

WRITING TOPIC
In what ways does Wordsworth's use of images both define what we have lost and suggest a remedy for this loss?

---

[1]Proteus and Triton are both figures from Greek mythology. Proteus had the power to assume different forms; Triton was often represented as blowing on a conch shell.

Ulysses[1]   (1833)

ALFRED, LORD TENNYSON   [1809–1892]

It little profits that an idle king,
By this still hearth, among these barren crags,
Matched with an aged wife, I mete and dole
Unequal laws unto a savage race,
That hoard, and sleep, and feed, and know not me.   5

  I cannot rest from travel; I will drink
Life to the lees. All times I have enjoyed
Greatly, have suffered greatly, both with those
That loved me, and alone; on shore, and when
Through scudding drifts the rainy Hyades[2]   10
Vexed the dim sea. I am become a name;
For always roaming with a hungry heart
Much have I seen and known—cities of men
And manners, climates, councils, governments,
Myself not least, but honored of them all—   15
And drunk delight of battle with my peers,
Far on the ringing plains of windy Troy.
I am a part of all that I have met;
Yet all experience is an arch wherethrough
Gleams that untraveled world whose margin fades   20
Forever and forever when I move.
How dull it is to pause, to make an end,
To rust unburnished, not to shine in use!
As though to breathe were life. Life piled on life
Were all too little, and of one to me   25
Little remains; but every hour is saved
From that eternal silence, something more,
A bringer of new things; and vile it were
For some three suns to store and hoard myself,
And this gray spirit yearning in desire   30
To follow knowledge like a sinking star,
Beyond the utmost bound of human thought.

  This is my son, mine own Telemachus,
To whom I leave the scepter and the isle—

---

[1]Ulysses, according to Greek legend, was the king of Ithaca and a hero of the Trojan War. Tennyson represents him as eager to resume the life of travel and adventure.
[2]A group of stars in the constellation Taurus. According to Greek mythology, the rising of these stars with the sun foretold rain.

Well-loved of me, discerning to fulfill   35
This labor, by slow prudence to make mild
A rugged people, and through soft degrees
Subdue them to the useful and the good.
Most blameless is he, centered in the sphere
Of common duties, decent not to fail   40
In offices of tenderness, and pay
Meet° adoration to my household gods,   proper
When I am gone. He works his work, I mine.

   There lies the port; the vessel puffs her sail;
There gloom the dark, broad seas. My mariners,   45
Souls that have toiled, and wrought, and thought with me—
That ever with a frolic welcome took
The thunder and the sunshine, and opposed
Free hearts, free foreheads—you and I are old;
Old age hath yet his honor and his toil.   50
Death closes all; but something ere the end,
Some work of noble note, may yet be done,
Not unbecoming men that strove with Gods.
The lights begin to twinkle from the rocks;
The long day wanes; the slow moon climbs; the deep   55
Moans round with many voices. Come, my friends,
'Tis not too late to seek a newer world.
Push off, and sitting well in order smite
The sounding furrows; for my purpose holds
To sail beyond the sunset, and the baths   60
Of all the western stars, until I die.
It may be that the gulfs will wash us down;
It may be we shall touch the Happy Isles,[3]
And see the great Achilles, whom we knew.
Though much is taken, much abides; and though   65
We are not now that strength which in old days
Moved earth and heaven, that which we are, we are—
One equal temper of heroic hearts,
Made weak by time and fate, but strong in will
To strive, to seek, to find, and not to yield.   70

QUESTIONS

1. Is Ulysses' desire to abdicate his duties as king irresponsible? Defend your answer.   **2.** Contrast Ulysses with his son, Telemachus, as the latter is described in lines 33–43. Is Telemachus admirable? Explain.

---

[3]The Islands of the Blessed (also Elysium), thought to be in the far western oceans, where those favored by the gods, such as Achilles, enjoyed life after death.

WRITING TOPIC
At the conclusion of the poem, Ulysses is determined not to yield. Yield to what?

Much Madness
Is Divinest Sense   (1862)

EMILY DICKINSON   [1830–1886]

Much Madness is divinest Sense—
To a discerning Eye—
Much Sense—the starkest Madness—
'Tis the Majority
In this, as All, prevail—
Assent—and you are sane—
Demur—you're straightway dangerous—   5
And handled with a Chain—

What Soft—
Cherubic Creatures   (ca. 1862)

EMILY DICKINSON   [1830–1886]

What Soft—Cherubic Creatures—
These Gentlewomen are—
One would as soon assault a Plush—
Or violate a Star—

Such Dimity Convictions—   5
A Horror so refined
Of freckled Human Nature—
Of Deity—ashamed—

It's such a common-Glory—
A Fisherman's—Degree—
Redemption—Brittle Lady—   10
Be so—ashamed of Thee—

She Rose to His Requirement   (ca. 1863)

EMILY DICKINSON   [1830–1886]

She rose to His Requirement—dropt
The Playthings of Her Life
To take the honorable Work
Of Woman, and of Wife—

If ought° She missed in Her new Day,   anything 5
Of Amplitude, or Awe—
Or first Prospective—Or the Gold
In using, wear away,

It lay unmentioned—as the Sea
Develope Pearl, and Weed,   10
But only to Himself—be known
The Fathoms they abide—

QUESTIONS

1. What are the "Playthings" referred to in line 2? Could the word be construed as ironic? Explain.   **2.** Why does the poet refer to both "Woman" and "Wife" in line 4, since a wife is also a woman?   **3.** The second stanza alludes to some losses the woman might have suffered in "Her new Day" (i.e., her marriage). Look up in your dictionary *amplitude, awe,* and *prospective,* and consider how these words help you to understand what those losses are.   **4.** What does "It" in the third stanza refer to?   **5.** Why is the sea image at the end of the poem appropriate? What does the contrast between "Pearl" and "Weed" suggest?   **6.** The last word of the poem, *abide,* has several meanings. Which of them are relevant to the meaning of the poem?

WRITING TOPICS

1. Write an essay describing a woman you know who gave up an important part of herself to be a wife.   **2.** Write an essay comparing and contrasting the attitudes toward marriage in this poem and in Helen Sorrells's "From a Correct Address in a Suburb of a Major City."

Easter 1916[1]   (1916)

WILLIAM BUTLER YEATS   [1865–1939]

I have met them at close of day
Coming with vivid faces
From counter or desk among grey
Eighteenth-century houses.
I have passed with a nod of the head   5
Or polite meaningless words,
Or have lingered awhile and said
Polite meaningless words,
And thought before I had done
Of a mocking tale or a gibe   10
To please a companion
Around the fire at the club,
Being certain that they and I
But lived where motley is worn:
All changed, changed utterly: 15
A terrible beauty is born.

That woman's days were spent
In ignorant good-will,
Her nights in argument
Until her voice grew shrill.   20
What voice more sweet than hers
When, young and beautiful,
She rode to harriers?
This man had kept a school
And rode our wingéd horse;[2]   25
This other his helper and friend
Was coming into his force;
He might have won fame in the end,
So sensitive his nature seemed,
So daring and sweet his thought.   30
This other man I had dreamed

---

[1]On Easter Sunday of 1916, a group of Irish nationalists seized key points in Ireland, including the Dublin Post Office, from which they proclaimed an independent Irish Republic. At first, most Irishmen were indifferent to the nationalists' futile and heroic gesture, but as the rebellion was crushed and the leaders executed, they became heroes in their countrymen's eyes. Some of those leaders are alluded to in the second stanza and are named in lines 75 and 76.

[2]In Greek mythology, a winged horse is associated with poetic inspiration.

A drunken, vainglorious lout.
He had done most bitter wrong
To some who are near my heart,
Yet I number him in the song;   35
He, too, has resigned his part
In the casual comedy;
He, too, has been changed in his turn,
Transformed utterly:
A terrible beauty is born.   40

Hearts with one purpose alone
Through summer and winter seem
Enchanted to a stone
To trouble the living stream.
The horse that comes from the road,   45
The rider, the birds that range
From cloud to tumbling cloud,
Minute by minute they change;
A shadow of cloud on the stream
Changes minute by minute;   50
A horse-hoof slides on the brim,
And a horse plashes within it;
The long-legged moor-hens dive,
And hens to moor-cocks call;
Minute by minute they live: 55
The stone's in the midst of all.

Too long a sacrifice
Can make a stone of the heart.
O when may it suffice?
That is Heaven's part, our part   60
To murmur name upon name,
As a mother names her child
When sleep at last has come
On limbs that had run wild.
What is it but nightfall?   65
No, no, not night but death;
Was it needless death after all?
For England may keep faith
For all that is done and said.
We know their dream; enough   70
To know they dreamed and are dead;
And what if excess of love
Bewildered them till they died?
I write it out in a verse—
MacDonagh and MacBride   75

And Connolly and Pearse
Now and in time to be,
Wherever green is worn,
Are changed, changed utterly:
A terrible beauty is born.   80

QUESTIONS

1. What is "changed utterly," and in what sense can beauty be "terrible"?   **2.** What does "they" in line 55 refer to? What does the "stone" in lines 43 and 56 symbolize? What is Yeats contrasting?   **3.** How does the poet answer the question he asks in line 67?

WRITING TOPIC

In the first stanza the attitude of the poet toward the people he is describing is indifferent, even contemptuous. How is that attitude modified in the rest of the poem?

Miniver Cheevy   1910

EDWIN ARLINGTON ROBINSON   [1869–1935]

Miniver Cheevy, child of scorn,
    Grew lean while he assailed the seasons;
He wept that he was ever born,
    And he had reasons.

                                                  5

Miniver loved the days of old
    When swords were bright and steeds were prancing;
The vision of a warrior bold
    Would set him dancing.

Miniver sighed for what was not,   10
    And dreamed, and rested from his labors;
He dreamed of Thebes and Camelot,
    And Priam's neighbors.[1]

Miniver mourned the ripe renown
    That made so many a name so fragrant,

Miniver Cheevy
  [1]Thebes was an ancient Greek city, famous in history and legend; Camelot was the site of the legendary King Arthur's court; Priam was king of Troy during the Trojan War.

He mourned Romance, now on the town,   15
    And Art, a vagrant.

Miniver loved the Medici,[2]
    Albeit he had never seen one;
He would have sinned incessantly
    Could he have been one.   20

Miniver cursed the commonplace
    And eyed a khaki suit with loathing;
He missed the medieval grace
    Of iron clothing.

Miniver scorned the gold he sought,   25
    But sore annoyed was he without it;
Miniver thought, and thought, and thought,
    And thought about it.

Miniver Cheevy, born too late,
    Scratched his head and kept on thinking;   30
Miniver coughed, and called it fate,
    And kept on drinking.

We Wear the Mask   1896

PAUL LAURENCE DUNBAR   [1872–1906]

We wear the mask that grins and lies,
It hides our cheeks and shades our eyes—
This debt we pay to human guile;
With torn and bleeding hearts we smile,
And mouth with myriad subtleties.   5

Why should the world be over-wise,
In counting all our tears and sighs?
Nay, let them only see us, while
    We wear the mask.

We smile, but, O great Christ, our cries   10
To thee from tortured souls arise.

Miniver Cheevy
    [2]A family of bankers and statesmen, notorious for their cruelty, who ruled Florence for nearly two centuries during the Italian Renaissance.

We sing, but oh the clay is vile
Beneath our feet, and long the mile;
But let the world dream otherwise,
    We wear the mask!   15

Patterns   1916

AMY LOWELL   [1874–1925]

I walk down the garden-paths,
And all the daffodils
Are blowing, and the bright blue squills.
I walk down the patterned garden-paths
In my stiff, brocaded gown.   5
With my powdered hair and jeweled fan,
I too am a rare
Pattern. As I wander down
The garden-paths.
My dress is richly figured,   10
And the train
Makes a pink and silver stain
On the gravel, and the thrift
Of the borders.
Just a plate of current fashion,   15
Tripping by in high-heeled, ribboned shoes.
Not a softness anywhere about me,
Only whalebone and brocade.
And I sink on a seat in the shade
Of a lime tree. For my passion   20
Wars against the stiff brocade.
The daffodils and squills
Flutter in the breeze
As they please.
And I weep;   25
For the lime-tree is in blossom
And one small flower has dropped upon my bosom.

And the plashing of waterdrops
In the marble fountain
Comes down the garden-paths.   30
The dripping never stops.
Underneath my stiffened gown
Is the softness of a woman bathing in a marble basin,
A basin in the midst of hedges grown

So thick, she cannot see her lover hiding,   35
But she guesses he is near,
And the sliding of the water
Seems the stroking of a dear
Hand upon her.
What is Summer in a fine brocaded gown!   40
I should like to see it lying in a heap upon the ground.
All the pink and silver crumpled up on the ground.

I would be the pink and silver as I ran along the paths,
And he would stumble after,
Bewildered by my laughter.   45
I should see the sun flashing from his sword-hilt and the buckles on his
    shoes.
I would choose
To lead him in a maze along the patterned paths,
A bright and laughing maze for my heavy-booted lover.
Till he caught me in the shade,   50
And the buttons of his waistcoat bruised my body as he clasped me,
Aching, melting, unafraid.
With the shadows of the leaves and the sundrops,
And the plopping of the waterdrops,
All about us in the open afternoon—   55
I am very like to swoon
With the weight of this brocade,
For the sun sifts through the shade.

Underneath the fallen blossom
In my bosom   60
Is a letter I have hid.
It was brought to me this morning by a rider from the Duke.
"Madam, we regret to inform you that Lord Hartwell
Died in action Thursday se'nnight."[1]
As I read it in the white, morning sunlight,   65
The letters squirmed like snakes.
"Any answer, Madam," said my footman.
"No," I told him.
"See that the messenger takes some refreshment.
No, no answer."   70
And I walked into the garden,
Up and down the patterned paths,
In my stiff, correct brocade.

---

[1]Seven nights (i.e., a week) ago.

The blue and yellow flowers stood up proudly in the sun,
Each one.   75
I stood upright too,
Held rigid to the pattern
By the stiffness of my gown;
Up and down I walked,
Up and down.   80

In a month he would have been my husband.
In a month, here, underneath this lime,
We would have broke the pattern;
He for me, and I for him,
He as Colonel, I as Lady,   85
On this shady seat.
He had a whim
That sunlight carried blessing.
And I answered, "It shall be as you have said."
Now he is dead.   90

In Summer and in Winter I shall walk
Up and down
The patterned garden-paths
In my stiff, brocaded gown.
The squills and daffodils   95
Will give place to pillared roses, and to asters, and to snow.
I shall go
Up and down
In my gown.
Gorgeously arrayed,   100
Boned and stayed.
And the softness of my body will be guarded from embrace
By each button, hook, and lace.
For the man who should loose me is dead,
Fighting with the Duke in Flanders,[2]   105
In a pattern called a war.
Christ! What are patterns for?

QUESTIONS
1. What period of time does the poem seem to be set in? Explain.   **2.** Identify the
various kinds of patterns in the poem.   **3.** In line 83, the speaker refers to the pattern

---

[2]A region of Belgium where battles were fought during wars in the eighteenth, nineteenth,
and twentieth centuries.

"We would have broke." What is that pattern? How might it have been broken?   **4.** Does the poem provide an answer to the question the speaker asks in the final line? Explain.

WRITING TOPICS

1. Describe a pattern in your family that has limited your life.   **2.** Describe a societal pattern that has limited your life.   **3.** Write an essay in which you argue that patterns, while perhaps limiting, are necessary.

Sunday Morning   1923

WALLACE STEVENS   [1879–1955]

beauty of nature
in cyclical beauty

I

Complacencies of the peignoir, and late
Coffee and oranges in a sunny chair,
And the green freedom of a cockatoo
Upon a rug mingle to dissipate
The holy hush of ancient sacrifice.   5
She dreams a little, and she feels the dark
Encroachment of that old catastrophe,
As a calm darkens among water-lights.
The pungent oranges and bright, green wings
Seem things in some procession of the dead,   10
Winding across wide water, without sound.
The day is like wide water, without sound,
Stilled for the passing of her dreaming feet
Over the seas, to silent Palestine,
Dominion of the blood and sepulchre.   15

II

Why should she give her bounty to the dead?
What is divinity if it can come
Only in silent shadows and in dreams?
Shall she not find in comforts of the sun,
In pungent fruit and bright, green wings, or else   20
In any balm or beauty of the earth,
Things to be cherished like the thought of heaven?
Divinity must live within herself:
Passions of rain, or moods in falling snow;

Grievings in loneliness, or unsubdued   25
Elations when the forest blooms; gusty
Emotions on wet roads on autumn nights;
All pleasures and all pains, remembering
The bough of summer and the winter branch.
These are the measures destined for her soul.   30

III

Jove in the clouds had his inhuman birth.[1]
No mother suckled him, no sweet land gave
Large-mannered motions to his mythy mind.
He moved among us, as a muttering king,
Magnificent, would move among his hinds,°   farm servants 35
Until our blood, commingling, virginal,
With heaven, brought such requital to desire
The very hinds discerned it, in a star.
Shall our blood fail? Or shall it come to be
The blood of paradise? And shall the earth   40
Seem all of paradise that we shall know?
The sky will be much friendlier then than now,
A part of labor and a part of pain,
And next in glory to enduring love,
Not this dividing and indifferent blue.   45

IV

She says, "I am content when wakened birds,
Before they fly, test the reality
Of misty fields, by their sweet questionings;
But when the birds are gone, and their warm fields
Return no more, where, then, is paradise?"   50
There is not any haunt of prophecy,
Nor any old chimera[2] of the grave,
Neither the golden underground, nor isle
Melodious, where spirits gat them home,
Nor visionary south, nor cloudy palm   55
Remote on heaven's hill, that has endured
As April's green endures; or will endure
Like her remembrance of awakened birds,

---

[1]Jove is Jupiter, the principal god of the Romans, who, unlike Jesus, had an "inhuman birth."
[2]A monster with a lion's head, a goat's body, and a serpent's tail. Here an emblem for the belief in other worlds described in the following lines.

Or her desire for June and evening, tipped
By the consummation of the swallow's wings.   60

V

She says, "But in contentment I still feel
The need of some imperishable bliss."
Death is the mother of beauty; hence from her,
Alone, shall come fulfilment to our dreams
And our desires. Although she strews the leaves   65
Of sure obliteration on our paths,
The path sick sorrow took, the many paths
Where triumph rang its brassy phrase, or love
Whispered a little out of tenderness,
She makes the willow shiver in the sun   70
For maidens who were wont to sit and gaze
Upon the grass, relinquished to their feet.
She causes boys to pile new plums and pears
On disregarded plate. The maidens taste
And stray impassioned in the littering leaves.   75

VI

Is there no change of death in paradise?
Does ripe fruit never fall? Or do the boughs
Hang always heavy in that perfect sky,
Unchanging, yet so like our perishing earth,
With rivers like our own that seek for seas   80
They never find, the same receding shores
That never touch with inarticulate pang?
Why set the pear upon those river-banks
Or spice the shores with odors of the plum?
Alas, that they should wear our colors there,   85
The silken weavings of our afternoons,
And pick the strings of our insipid lutes!
Death is the mother of beauty, mystical,
Within whose burning bosom we devise
Our earthly mothers waiting, sleeplessly.   90

VII

Supple and turbulent, a ring of men
Shall chant in orgy on a summer morn
Their boisterous devotion to the sun,
Not as a god, but as a god might be,

(handwritten margin note: w/o death, you can not appreciate beauty)

Naked among them, like a savage source.   95
Their chant shall be a chant of paradise,
Out of their blood, returning to the sky;
And in their chant shall enter, voice by voice,
The windy lake wherein their lord delights,
The trees, like serafin, and echoing hills,   100
That choir among themselves long afterward.
They shall know well the heavenly fellowship
Of men that perish and of summer morn.
And whence they came and whither they shall go
The dew upon their feet shall manifest.   105

VIII

She hears, upon that water without sound,
A voice that cries, "The tomb in Palestine
Is not the porch of spirits lingering.
It is the grave of Jesus, where he lay."
We live in an old chaos of the sun,   110
Or old dependency of day and night,
Or island solitude, unsponsored, free,
Of that wide water, inescapable.
Deer walk upon our mountains, and the quail
Whistle about us their spontaneous cries;   115
Sweet berries ripen in the wilderness;
And, in the isolation of the sky,
At evening, casual flocks of pigeons make
Ambiguous undulations as they sink,
Downward to darkness, on extended wings.   120

QUESTIONS

1. In the opening stanza, the woman's enjoyment of a late Sunday morning breakfast in a relaxed and sensuous atmosphere is troubled by thoughts of what Sunday morning should mean to her. What are the thoughts that disturb her complacency?   **2.** What does the speaker mean when he says, "Death is the mother of beauty" (ll. 63 and 88)?   **3.** In stanza VI, what is the speaker's attitude toward the conventional Christian conception of paradise?   **4.** Stanza VII presents the speaker's vision of an alternative religion. How does it differ from the paradise of stanza VI?   **5.** In what ways does the cry of the voice in the final stanza (ll. 107–109) state the woman's dilemma? How do the lines about the pigeons at the end of the poem sum up the speaker's belief?

WRITING TOPIC

This poem is, in a sense, a commentary by the speaker on the woman's desire for truth and certainty more enduring than the physical world can provide. Is the speaker sympathetic to her quest? Explain.

If We Must Die

1922

CLAUDE McCKAY [1890–1948]

If we must die, let it not be like hogs
Hunted and penned in an inglorious spot,
While round us bark the mad and hungry dogs,
Making their mock at our accursèd lot.
If we must die, O let us nobly die,   5
So that our precious blood may not be shed
In vain; then even the monsters we defy
Shall be constrained to honor us though dead!
O kinsmen! we must meet the common foe!
Though far outnumbered let us show us brave,   10
And for their thousand blows deal one deathblow!
What though before us lies the open grave?
Like men we'll face the murderous, cowardly pack,
Pressed to the wall, dying, but fighting back!

the Cambridge ladies
who live in furnished souls

1923

E. E. CUMMINGS [1894–1962]

the Cambridge ladies who live in furnished souls
are unbeautiful and have comfortable minds
(also, with the church's protestant blessings
daughters, unscented shapeless spirited)
they believe in Christ and Longfellow, both dead,   5
are invariably interested in so many things—
at the present writing one still finds
delighted fingers knitting for the is it Poles?
perhaps. While permanent faces coyly bandy
scandal of Mrs. N. and Professor D   10
.... the Cambridge ladies do not care, above
Cambridge if sometimes in its box of
sky lavender and cornerless, the
moon rattles like a fragment of angry candy

QUESTIONS

1. What images does the poet use to describe "the Cambridge ladies"? What do the
images suggest?   **2.** What is the effect of the interruption "is it" in line 8?   **3.** In the

final lines, the moon seems to protest against the superficiality of these women. What is the effect of comparing the moon to a fragment of candy?

WRITING TOPIC
Compare this poem with Emily Dickinson's "What Soft—Cherubic Creatures."

Harlem   1951

LANGSTON HUGHES   [1902–1967]

What happens to a dream deferred?

>   Does it dry up
>   like a raisin in the sun?
>   Or fester like a sore—
>   And then run?   5
>   Does it stink like rotten meat?
>   Or crust and sugar over—
>   like a syrupy sweet?
>
>   Maybe it just sags
>   like a heavy load.   10
>
>   *Or does it explode?*

Same in Blues   1951

LANGSTON HUGHES   [1902–1967]

I said to my baby,
Baby take it slow.
I can't, she said, I can't!
I got to go!

>   *There's a certain*   5
>   *amount of traveling*
>   *in a dream deferred.*

Lulu said to Leonard,
I want a diamond ring.
Leonard said to Lulu,   10
You won't get a goddam thing!

> *A certain*
> *amount of nothing*
> *in a dream deferred.*

Daddy, daddy, daddy,   15
All I want is you.
You can have me, baby—
but my lovin' days is through.

> *A certain*
> *amount of impotence*   20
> *in a dream deferred.*

Three parties
On my party line—
But that third party,
Lord, ain't mine!   25

> *There's liable*
> *to be confusion*
> *in a dream deferred.*

From river to river
Uptown and down,   30
There's liable to be confusion
when a dream gets kicked around.

The Unknown Citizen   1940
(TO JS/07/M/378
THIS MARBLE MONUMENT
IS ERECTED BY THE STATE)

W. H. AUDEN   [1907–1973]

He was found by the Bureau of Statistics to be
One against whom there was no official complaint,
And all the reports on his conduct agree
That, in the modern sense of an old-fashioned word, he was a saint,
For in everything he did he served the Greater Community.   5
Except for the War till the day he retired
He worked in a factory and never got fired,
But satisfied his employers, Fudge Motors Inc.

Yet he wasn't a scab or odd in his views,
For his Union reports that he paid his dues,   10
(Our report on his Union shows it was sound)
And our Social Psychology workers found
That he was popular with his mates and liked a drink.
The Press are convinced that he bought a paper every day
And that his reactions to advertisements were normal in every way.   15
Policies taken out in his name prove that he was fully insured,
And his Health-card shows he was once in hospital but left it cured.
Both Producers Research and High-Grade Living declare
He was fully sensible to the advantages of the Installment Plan
And had everything necessary to the Modern Man,   20
A phonograph, radio, a car and a frigidaire.
Our researchers into Public Opinion are content
That he held the proper opinions for the time of year;
When there was peace, he was for peace; when there was war, he went.
He was married and added five children to the population,   25
Which our Eugenist says was the right number for a parent of his generation,
And our teachers report that he never interfered with their education.
Was he free? Was he happy? The question is absurd:
Had anything been wrong, we should certainly have heard.

From a Correct Address in a Suburb of a Major City   1971

HELEN SORRELLS   [b. 1908]

She wears her middle age like a cowled
gown, sleeved in it, folded high
at the breast,

charming, proper at cocktails
but the inner one raging   5
and how to hide her,

how to keep her leashed, contain
the heat of her, the soaring cry
never yet loosed,

demanding a chance before the years devour her,   10
before the marrow of her fine long legs
congeals and she

settles forever for this street, this house,
her face set to the world
sweet, sweet   15

above the shocked, astonished
hunger.

Myth   1973

MURIEL RUKEYSER [1913–1980]

Long afterward, Oedipus, old and blinded, walked the
roads.[1]   He smelled a familiar smell.   It was
the Sphinx.   Oedipus said, "I want to ask one question.
Why didn't I recognize my mother?"   "You gave the   5
wrong answer," said the Sphinx.   "But that was what
made everything possible," said Oedipus.   "No," she said.
"When I asked, What walks on four legs in the morning,
two at noon, and three in the evening, you answered,
Man.   You didn't say anything about woman."   10
"When you say Man," said Oedipus, "you include women
too. Everyone knows that."   She said, "That's what
you think."

Ballad of Birmingham   1969

(ON THE BOMBING OF A CHURCH IN
BIRMINGHAM, ALABAMA, 1963)

DUDLEY RANDALL [b. 1914]

"Mother dear, may I go downtown
Instead of out to play,
And march the streets of Birmingham
In a Freedom March today?"

Myth

[1]Oedipus became King of Thebes when he solved the riddle of the Sphinx quoted in the poem. He blinded himself when he discovered that he had married his own mother.

"No, baby, no, you may not go,   5
For the dogs are fierce and wild,
And clubs and hoses, guns and jails
Aren't good for a little child."

"But, mother, I won't be alone.
Other children will go with me,   10
And march the streets of Birmingham
To make our country free."

"No, baby, no, you may not go,
For I fear those guns will fire.
But you may go to church instead   15
And sing in the children's choir."

She has combed and brushed her night-dark hair,
And bathed rose petal sweet.
And drawn white gloves on her small brown hands,
And white shoes on her feet.   20

The mother smiled to know her child
Was in the sacred place,
But that smile was the last smile
To come upon her face.

For when she heard the explosion,   25
Her eyes grew wet and wild.
She raced through the streets of Birmingham
Calling for her child.

She clawed through bits of glass and brick,
Then lifted out a shoe.   30
"Oh, here's the shoe my baby wore,
But, baby, where are you?"

Naming of Parts   1946

HENRY REED   [b. 1914]

Today we have naming of parts. Yesterday,
We had daily cleaning. And tomorrow morning
We shall have what to do after firing. But today,
Today we have naming of parts. Japonica
Glistens like coral in all of the neighboring gardens,   5
    And today we have naming of parts.

This is the lower sling swivel. And this
Is the upper sling swivel, whose use you will see,
When you are given your slings. And this is the piling swivel,
Which in your case you have not got. The branches   10
Hold in the gardens their silent, eloquent gestures,
   Which in our case we have not got.

This is the safety-catch, which is always released
With an easy flick of the thumb. And please do not let me
See anyone using his finger. You can do it quite easy   15
If you have any strength in your thumb. The blossoms
Are fragile and motionless, never letting anyone see
   Any of them using their finger.

And this you can see is the bolt. The purpose of this
Is to open the breech, as you see. We can slide it   20
Rapidly backwards and forwards: we call this
Easing the spring. And rapidly backwards and forwards
The early bees are assaulting and fumbling the flowers:
   They call it easing the Spring.

They call it easing the Spring: it is perfectly easy   25
If you have any strength in your thumb: like the bolt,
And the breech, and the cocking-piece, and the point of balance,
Which in our case we have not got; and the almond-blossom
Silent in all of the gardens and the bees going backwards and forwards,
   For today we have naming of parts.   30

QUESTIONS
1. The poem has two speakers. Identify their voices, and characterize the speakers.   **2.** The last line of each stanza repeats a phrase from within the stanza. What
is the effect of the repetition?

WRITING TOPIC
This poem incorporates a subtle underlying sexuality. Trace the language that generates it. What function does that sexuality serve in the poem?

from
The Children of the Poor   (1949)

GWENDOLYN BROOKS   [b. 1917]

4

First fight. Then fiddle. Ply the slipping string
With feathery sorcery; muzzle the note
With hurting love, the music that they wrote
Bewitch, bewilder. Qualify to sing
Threadwise. Devise no salt, no hempen thing   5
For the dear instrument to bear. Devote
The bow to silks and honey. Be remote
A while from malice and from murdering.
But first to arms, to armor. Carry hate
In front of you and harmony behind.   10
Be deaf to music and to beauty blind.
Win war. Rise bloody, maybe not too late
For having first to civilize a space
Wherein to play your violin with grace.

11

Life for my child is simple, and is good.
He knows his wish. Yes, but that is not all.
Because I know mine too.
And we both want joy of undeep and unabiding things,
Like kicking over a chair or throwing blocks out of a window   5
Or tipping over an icebox pan
Or snatching down curtains or fingering an electric outlet
Or a journey or a friend or an illegal kiss.
No. There is more to it than that.
It is that he has never been afraid.   10
Rather, he reaches out and lo the chair falls with a beautiful crash,
And the blocks fall, down on the people's heads,
And the water comes slooshing sloppily out across the floor.
And so forth.
Not that success, for him, is sure, infallible.   15
But never has he been afraid to reach.
His lesions are legion.
But reaching is his rule.

QUESTIONS
1. In sonnet 4, the poet advises the children: "First fight. Then fiddle." The meaning of "fight" is clear. What does "fiddle" symbolize?   **2.** Why does the poet advocate violence?   **3.** Is the child described in poem 11 different from the children addressed in sonnet 4?   **4.** Explain the meaning of line 4 in poem 11.   **5.** What does "reaching" in the last line mean?

In Goya's Greatest Scenes   1958

LAWRENCE FERLINGHETTI   [b. 1919]

In Goya's greatest scenes[1] we seem to see
                            the people of the world
        exactly at the moment when
                they first attained the title of
                                'suffering humanity'
            They writhe upon the page
                        in a veritable rage
                            of adversity
        Heaped up
                groaning with babies and bayonets
                            under cement skies
            in an abstract landscape of blasted trees
                bent statues bats wings and beaks
                    slippery gibbets
                cadavers and carnivorous cocks   15
        and all the final hollering monsters
                of the
                    'imagination of disaster'
            they are so bloody real
                        it is as if they really still existed

    And they do
            Only the landscape is changed

    They still are ranged along the roads
            plagued by legionaires
                        false windmills and demented roosters   25

    They are the same people
                        only further from home

---

[1] Francisco José de Goya (1746–1828), famous Spanish artist, celebrated for his representations of "suffering humanity."

on freeways fifty lanes wide
        on a concrete continent
                spaced with bland billboards   30
        illustrating imbecile illusions of happiness

The scene shows fewer tumbrils[2]
        but more maimed citizens
                in painted cars
and they have strange license plates   35
and engines
        that devour America

QUESTIONS
1. To whom does the word "they" refer in line 26?   **2.** What is responsible for the "suffering" of modern American "humanity"?

Formal Application   (1963)

DONALD W. BAKER   [b. 1923]

"The poets apparently want to rejoin the human race."   TIME

I shall begin by learning to throw
the knife, first at trees, until it sticks
in the trunk and quivers every time;

next from a chair, using only wrist
and fingers, at a thing on the ground,   5
a fresh ant hill or a fallen leaf;

then at a moving object, perhaps
a pine cone swinging on twine, until
I pot it at least twice in three tries.

Meanwhile, I shall be teaching the birds   10
that the skinny fellow in sneakers
is a source of suet and bread crumbs,

first putting them on a shingle nailed
to a pine tree, next scattering them
on the needles, closer and closer   15

In Goya's Greatest Scenes
[2] Carts in which prisoners were conducted to the place of execution.

to my seat, until the proper bird,
a towhee, I think, in black and rust
and gray, takes tossed crumbs six feet away.

Finally, I shall coordinate
conditioned reflex and functional   20
form and qualify as Modern Man.

You see the splash of blood and feathers
and the blade pinning it to the tree?
It's called an "Audubon Crucifix."

The phrase has pleasing (even pious)   25
connotations, like *Arbeit Macht Frei,*
"Molotov Cocktail," and *Enola Gay.*[1]

QUESTIONS

1. What did *Time* mean by the line Baker uses as an epigraph to this poem? How, for example, are poets not members of the human race? What does the title of the poem mean?   **2.** In what sense does "Audubon Crucifix" have "pleasing (even pious) connotations"? What are the pleasing connotations of the expressions in the last two lines? According to this poem, what are the attributes necessary to join the human race?

Hard Rock Returns to Prison from the Hospital for the Criminal Insane   1968

ETHERIDGE KNIGHT   [1933–1991]

Hard Rock was "known not to take no shit
From nobody," and he had the scars to prove it:
Split purple lips, lumped ears, welts above
His yellow eyes, and one long scar that cut

Formal Application
[1] *Arbeit Macht Frei,* the motto of the German Nazi party, means "labor liberates." A Molotov cocktail is a homemade hand grenade named after Vyacheslav M. Molotov, the foreign minister of the Soviet Union during the reign of Joseph Stalin. *Enola Gay* was the name of the United States plane that dropped the atomic bomb on Hiroshima in 1945.

Across his temple and plowed through a thick   5
Canopy of kinky hair.

The WORD was that Hard Rock wasn't a mean nigger
Anymore, that the doctors had bored a hole in his head,
Cut out part of his brain, and shot electricity
Through the rest. When they brought Hard Rock back,   10
Handcuffed and chained, he was turned loose,
Like a freshly gelded stallion, to try his new status.
And we all waited and watched, like Indians at a corral,
To see if the WORD was true.

As we waited we wrapped ourselves in the cloak   15
Of his exploits: "Man, the last time, it took eight
Screws to put him in the Hole." "Yeah, remember when he
Smacked the captain with his dinner tray?" "He set
The record for time in the Hole—67 straight days!"
"Ol Hard Rock! man, that's one crazy nigger."   20
And then the jewel of a myth that Hard Rock had once bit
A screw on the thumb and poisoned him with syphilitic spit.

The testing came, to see if Hard Rock was really tame.
A hillbilly called him a black son of a bitch
And didn't lose his teeth, a screw who knew Hard Rock   25
From before shook him down and barked in his face.
And Hard Rock did *nothing*. Just grinned and looked silly,
His eyes empty like knot holes in a fence.

And even after we discovered that it took Hard Rock
Exactly 3 minutes to tell you his first name,   30
We told ourselves that he had just wised up,
Was being cool; but we could not fool ourselves for long,
And we turned away, our eyes on the ground. Crushed.

He had been our Destroyer, the doer of things
We dreamed of doing but could not bring ourselves to do,   35
The fears of years, like a biting whip,
Had cut grooves too deeply across our backs.

The Stranglehold of English Lit.   1961
(FOR MOLARA OGUNDIPE-LESLIE)

FELIX MNTHALI [b. 1933]

Those questions, sister,
those questions
        stand
        stab
        jab   5
    and gore
too close to the centre!

For if we had asked
why Jane Austen's people[1]
carouse all day   10
and do no work

would Europe in Africa
have stood
the test of time?
and would she still maul   15
the flower of our youth
in the south?
Would she?

Your elegance of deceit,
Jane Austen,   20
lulled the sons and daughters
of the dispossessed
into a calf-love
with irony and satire
around imaginary people.   25

While history went on mocking
the victims of branding irons
and sugar-plantations
that made Jane Austen's people
wealthy beyond compare!   30

---

[1]Characters in the novels of Jane Austen (1775–1817), a standard author in English literature courses. Her ironic domestic comedies are peopled with English country gentlefolk who,
apparently, do not have to work for a living.

Eng. Lit., my sister,
was more than a cruel joke—
it was the heart
of alien conquest.

How could questions be asked   35
at Makerere and Ibadan,
Dakar and Ford Hare[2]—
with Jane Austen
at the centre?
How could they be answered?   40

QUESTIONS
1. Malawi, the poet's birthplace, was a part of British South Africa, a colonial possession, before it achieved independence. How would the school curriculum reflect this fact?   **2.** Some would argue that studying Jane Austen is appropriate because her work embodies "universal" values. Does the poet agree? Explain.   **3.** In the fifth stanza, the poet moves from derision to an attack; discuss the issues he raises.   **4.** Do you agree with the assertion of the sixth stanza? Explain.

WRITING TOPIC
Discuss the political and cultural implications of the poem's title.

I Would Like   (trans. 1987)

YEVGENY YEVTUSHENKO   [b. 1933]

I would like
            to be born
                        in every country,
have a passport
            for them all,
to throw
            all foreign offices
                        into panic,
be every fish
            in every ocean
and every dog
            along the path.

The Stranglehold of English Lit.
    [2]The sites of major African universities whose students, among others, participated in Africa's struggle to free itself from European domination.

I don't want to bow down
                         before any idols
or play at being   15
                 an Orthodox church hippy,
but I would like to plunge
                     deep into Lake Baikal[1]
and surface snorting
                 somewhere,
                             why not in the Mississippi?
In my beloved universe
                 I would like
to be a lonely weed,
                 but not a delicate Narcissus[2]
kissing his own mug
                 in the mirror.
I would like to be
                 any of God's creatures
right down to the last mangy hyena—   30
but never a tyrant
                 or even the cat of a tyrant.
I would like to be
                 reincarnated as a man
                             in any circumstance:
a victim of Paraguayan prison tortures,
a homeless child in the slums of Hong Kong,
a living skeleton in Bangladesh,
a holy beggar in Tibet,
a black in Cape Town,   40
but never
         in the image of Rambo
The only people whom I hate
                 are the hypocrites—
pickled hyenas   45
             in heavy syrup.
I would like to lie
             under the knives of all the surgeons in the world,
be hunchbacked, blind,
                 suffer all kinds of diseases,
                             wounds and scars,

---

[1]A large lake in Siberia, just north of Mongolia.
[2]In Greek myth, a beautiful youth who pined away for love of his own reflection and was changed into a flower.

be a victim of war,
                or a sweeper of cigarette butts,
just so a filthy microbe of superiority
                                doesn't creep inside.   55
I would not like to be in the elite,
nor of course,
                in the cowardly herd,
nor be a guard-dog of that herd,
nor a shepherd,   60
                sheltered by that herd.
And I would like happiness,
                        but not at the expense of the unhappy,
and I would like freedom,
                        but not at the expense of the unfree. 65
I would like to love
                all the women in the world,
and I would like to be a woman, too—
                                just once. . . .
Men have been diminished   70
                by Mother Nature.
Suppose she'd given motherhood
                        to men?
If an innocent child
                stirred   75
                        below his heart,
man would probably
                not be so cruel.
I would like to be man's daily bread—
say,   80
        a cup of rice
                for a Vietnamese woman in mourning,
cheap wine
        in a Neapolitan workers' trattoria,[3]
or a tiny tube of cheese   85
                        in orbit round the moon:
let them eat me,
                let them drink me,
only let my death
                be of some use.   90
I would like to belong to all times,
                        shock all history so much

---

[3]A small inexpensive restaurant in Italy.

that it would be amazed
                                    what a smart aleck I was.
I would like to bring Nefertiti   95
                                    to Pushkin in a troika.[4]
I would like to increase
                            the space of a moment
                                            a hundredfold,
so that in the same moment   100
                            I could drink vodka with fishermen in Siberia
and sit together with Homer,
                                    Dante,
                                            Shakespeare,
                                                    and Tolstoy,   105
drinking anything,
                            except of course,
                                            Coca-Cola,
—dance to the tom-toms in the Congo,
—strike at Renault,   110
—chase a ball with Brazilian boys
                            at Copacabana Beach.
I would like
                    to know every language,
                                    the secret waters under the earth,   115
and do all kinds of work at once.
                            I would make sure
that one Yevtushenko was merely a poet,
                            the second—an underground fighter,
                                                    somewhere,   120
I couldn't say where
                            for security reasons,
the third—a student at Berkeley,
                            the fourth—a jolly Georgian[5] drinker,
and the fifth—   125
                    maybe a teacher of Eskimo children in Alaska,
the sixth—
                    a young president,
                            somewhere, say even in Sierra Leone,
the seventh—   130
                    would still be shaking a rattle in his stroller,

---

[4]Nefertiti was a famously beautiful fourteenth-century B.C. queen of Egypt. Aleksandr Sergeyevich Pushkin (1799–1837) was, perhaps, the greatest Russian writer and poet of his time. A troika is a Russian vehicle drawn by a team of three horses.
[5]Georgia is one of the republics that made up the former Soviet Union. It lies along the east coast of the Black Sea.

and the tenth . . .
                    the hundredth . . .
                              the millionth . . .
For me it's not enough to be myself,   135
                    let me be everyone!
Every creature
          usually has a double,
but God was stingy
                    with the carbon paper,   140
and in his Paradise Publishing Company
                              made a unique copy of me.
But I shall muddle up
          all God's cards—
                              I shall confound God!   145
I shall be in a thousand copies
                    to the end of my days,
so that the earth buzzes with me,
                    and computers go berserk
in the world census of me.   150
I would like to fight on all your barricades,
                              humanity,
dying each night
          an exhausted moon,
and being resurrected each morning   155
                    like a newborn sun,
with an immortal soft spot
          on my skull.
And when I die,
          a smart-aleck Siberian François Villon,[6]   160
do not lay me in the earth
                    of France
                              or Italy,
but in our Russian, Siberian earth,
                    on a still green hill,   165
where I first felt
          that I was
                    everyone.

QUESTIONS

1. The poet declares that he would like to be a certain kind of person. What kind of person? What concrete images lead you to your judgment?   **2.** What kind of person does he *not* wish to be? What images support your conclusion?   **3.** Discuss the

---

[6]A French balladeer, born in 1431, who was often in trouble with the law.

images that address chronological time. Discuss those that address geographical distance. Discuss those that address a sort of chain of being among creatures, moving from "low" to "high." How does Yevtushenko use these images to define his social and political views?

WRITING TOPIC

In an essay, characterize the poet's notion of an ideal person, and speculate on how that person would get along in the real world. Do you accept, or would you modify, Yevtushenko's ideal? Explain.

Eleanor Rigby   1966

JOHN LENNON [1940–1980] **and PAUL McCARTNEY** [b. 1942]

Ah, look at all the lonely people!
Ah, look at all the lonely people!
Eleanor Rigby picks up the rice
    in the church
Where a wedding has been.   5
Lives in a dream.
Waits at the window, wearing the face
    that she keeps in a jar by the door.
Who is it for?

All the lonely people,   10
    where do they all come from?
All the lonely people,
    where do they all belong?

Father McKenzie writing the words
    of a sermon that no one will hear—   15
No one comes near. Look at him
    working, darning his socks in the night
    when there's nobody there.
What does he care?

All the lonely people,   20
    where do they all come from?
All the lonely people,
    where do they all belong?

Ah, look at all the lonely people!
Ah, look at all the lonely people!   25

Eleanor Rigby died in the church and
    was buried along with her name.
Nobody came.
Father McKenzie wiping the dirt from
    his hands as he walks from the grave.   30
No one was saved.

All the lonely people,
    where do they all come from?
All the lonely people,
    where do they all belong?   35

QUESTIONS
1. How does the first stanza establish Eleanor Rigby's character? What is the meaning of lines 7–8?   **2.** What does the portrait of Father McKenzie contribute to our understanding of the theme of the lyric?   **3.** What significance has the juxtaposition of Father McKenzie's writing "a sermon that no one will hear" and "darning his socks in the night" (stanza 3)?   **4.** What is the significance of Eleanor Rigby's dying in the church? Why was "No one saved" (l. 31)?   **5.** What answers, if any, does the poem suggest to the questions in the last stanza?

Conversation with a Fireman from Brooklyn   1984

TESS GALLAGHER   [b. 1943]

He offers, between planes,
to buy me a drink. I've never talked
to a fireman before, not one from Brooklyn
anyway. Okay. Fine, I say. Somehow
the subject is bound to come up, women   5
firefighters, and since I'm
a woman and he's a fireman, between
the two of us, we know something
about this subject. Already
he's telling me he doesn't mind   10
women firefighters, but what
they look like
after fighting a fire, well
they lose all respect. He's sorry, but
he looks at them   15
covered with the cinders of someone's

lost hope, and he feels disgust, he just
wants to turn the hose on them, they
are that sweaty and stinking, just like
him, of course, but not the woman he   20
wants, you get me? and to come to that—
isn't it too bad, to be despised
for what you do to prove yourself
among men
who want to love you, to love you,   25
love you.

QUESTIONS

1. Do you think the speaker agrees to have a drink with the fireman because she is
sexually attracted to him? Explain.   **2.** Why does the speaker describe a woman
firefighter as "covered with the cinders of someone's / lost hope" (ll. 16–
17)?   **3.** How does the phrase "you get me?" (l. 21) help establish the tone of the
poem?   **4.** Why does the speaker repeat "to love you" at the end of the
poem?   **5.** In a few sentences, summarize the speaker's response to the fireman.

WRITING TOPIC

Write an essay in which you argue that women should or should not be excluded
from such traditional male occupations as firefighting.

Dreams   1968

NIKKI GIOVANNI   [b. 1943]

i used to dream militant
dreams of taking
over america to show
these white folks how it should be
done   5
i used to dream radical dreams
of blowing everyone away with my perceptive powers
of correct analysis
i even used to think i'd be the one
to stop the riot and negotiate the peace   10
then i awoke and dug
that if i dreamed natural
dreams of being a natural
woman doing what a woman
does when she's natural   15
i would have a revolution

For Saundra

1968

NIKKI GIOVANNI   [b. 1943]

i wanted to write
a poem
that rhymes
but revolution doesn't lend
itself to be-bopping   5

then my neighbor
who thinks i hate
asked—do you ever write
tree poems—i like trees
so i thought   10

i'll write a beautiful green tree poem
peeked from my window
to check the image
noticed the school yard was covered
with asphalt   15
no green—no trees grow
in manhattan

then, well, i thought the sky
i'll do a big blue sky poem

but all the clouds have winged   20
low since no-Dick[1] was elected

so i thought again
and it occurred to me
maybe i shouldn't write
at all   25
but clean my gun
and check my kerosene supply

perhaps these are not poetic
times
at all   30

---

[1]A derogatory reference to Richard Nixon.

Today Is a Day of Great Joy   1968

VICTOR HERNÁNDEZ CRUZ   [b. 1949]

when they stop poems
in the mail & clap
their hands & dance to
them
when women become pregnant   5
by the side of poems
the strongest sounds making
the river go along

it is a great day

as poems fall down to   10

movie crowds in restaurants
in bars

when poems start to
knock down walls to
choke politicians   15
when poems scream &
begin to break the air

that is the time of
true poets that is
the time of greatness   20

a true poet aiming
poems & watching things
fall to the ground

it is a great day.

The Colonel

1981

CAROLYN FORCHÉ   [b. 1950]

What you have heard is true. I was in his house. His wife carried a tray of coffee and sugar. His daughter filed her nails, his son went out for the night. There were daily papers, pet dogs, a pistol on the cushion beside him. The moon swung bare on its black cord over the house. On the television was a cop show. It was in English. Broken bottles were embedded in the walls round the house to scoop the kneecaps from a man's legs or cut his hands to lace. On the windows there were gratings like those in liquor stores. We had dinner, rack of lamb, good wine, a gold bell was on the table for calling the maid. The maid brought green mangoes, salt, a type of bread. I was asked how I enjoyed the country. There was a brief commercial in Spanish. His wife took everything away. There was some talk then of how difficult it had become to govern. The parrot said hello on the terrace. The colonel told it to shut up, and pushed himself from the table. My friend said to me with his eyes: say nothing. The colonel returned with a sack used to bring groceries home. He spilled many human ears on the table. They were like dried peach halves. There is no other way to say this. He took one of them in his hands, shook it in our faces, dropped it into a water glass. It came alive there. I am tired of fooling around he said. As for the rights of anyone, tell your people they can go fuck themselves. He swept the ears to the floor with his arm and held the last of his wine in the air. Something for your poetry, no? he said. Some of the ears on the floor caught this scrap of his voice. Some of the ears on the floor were pressed to the ground.

QUESTIONS

1. What is the occasion of this poem? Where is it set? How would you characterize the colonel's family?   **2.** "There was some talk then of how difficult it had become to govern." Can you suggest why it had become difficult to govern? How does the colonel respond to these difficulties?   **3.** What does the last sentence suggest?

WRITING TOPIC

This piece is printed as if it were prose. Does it have any of the formal characteristics of a poem?

CONFORMITY
AND
REBELLION

Self-Portrait, c. 1900 by Gwen John

DRAMA

Antigonê*

(ca. 441 B.C.)

SOPHOCLES [496?–406 B.C.]

CHARACTERS

Antigonê
Ismenê
Eurydicê
Creon
Haimon

Teiresias
A Sentry
A Messenger
Chorus

SCENE

Before the Palace of Creon, King of Thebes. A central double door, and two lateral doors. A platform extends the length of the façade, and from this platform three steps lead down into the "orchestra," or chorus-ground.

TIME

Dawn of the day after the repulse of the Argive army from the assault on Thebes.

Prologue

[*Antigonê and Ismenê enter from the central door of the Palace.*]

Antigonê.   Ismenê, dear sister,
   You would think that we had already suffered enough
   For the curse on Oedipus:[1]

---

   * An English version by Dudley Fitts and Robert Fitzgerald.
   [1] Oedipus, a former king of Thebes, unwittingly killed his father and married his own mother, Iocastê. By her he had four children, the sisters Antigonê and Ismenê and the brothers Polyneicês and Eteoclês. When Oedipus realized what he had done, he blinded himself and left Thebes. Eteoclês drove Polyneicês out of Thebes after a quarrel, but Polyneicês returned with an army and laid siege to Thebes. In the ensuing struggle, the brothers killed each other. Creon became king and, as a punishment, decreed that Polyneicês be denied the rites of burial.

I cannot imagine any grief
That you and I have not gone through. And now—   5
Have they told you of the new decree of our King Creon?
Ismenê.   I have heard nothing: I know
That two sisters lost two brothers, a double death
In a single hour; and I know that the Argive army
Fled in the night; but beyond this, nothing.   10
Antigonê.   I thought so. And that is why I wanted you
To come out here with me. There is something we must do.
Ismenê.   Why do you speak so strangely?
Antigonê.   Listen, Ismenê:
Creon buried our brother Eteoclês   15
With military honors, gave him a soldier's funeral,
And it was right that he should; but Polyneicês,
Who fought as bravely and died as miserably,—
They say that Creon has sworn
No one shall bury him, no one mourn for him,   20
But his body must lie in the fields, a sweet treasure
For carrion birds to find as they search for food.
That is what they say, and our good Creon is coming here
To announce it publicly; and the penalty—
Stoning to death in the public square!   25
                                    There it is,
And now you can prove what you are:
A true sister, or a traitor to your family.
Ismenê.   Antigonê, you are mad! What could I possibly do?
Antigonê.   You must decide whether you will help me or not.   30
Ismenê.   I do not understand you. Help you in what?
Antigonê.   Ismenê, I am going to bury him. Will you come?
Ismenê.   Bury him! You have just said the new law forbids it.
Antigonê.   He is my brother. And he is your brother, too.
Ismenê.   But think of the danger! Think what Creon will do!   35
Antigonê.   Creon is not strong enough to stand in my way.
Ismenê.   Ah sister!
Oedipus died, everyone hating him
For what his own search brought to light, his eyes
Ripped out by his own hand; and Iocastê died,   40
His mother and wife at once: she twisted the cords
That strangled her life; and our two brothers died,
Each killed by the other's sword. And we are left:
But oh, Antigonê,
Think how much more terrible than these   45
Our own death would be if we should go against Creon
And do what he has forbidden! We are only women,
We cannot fight with men, Antigonê!

The law is strong, we must give in to the law
In this thing, and in worse. I beg the Dead   50
To forgive me, but I am helpless: I must yield
To those in authority. And I think it is dangerous business
To be always meddling.
Antigonê.   If that is what you think,
I should not want you, even if you asked to come.   55
You have made your choice, you can be what you want to be.
But I will bury him; and if I must die,
I say that this crime is holy: I shall lie down
With him in death, and I shall be as dear
To him as he to me.   60
                    It is the dead,
Not the living, who make the longest demands:
We die for ever . . .
                    You may do as you like,
Since apparently the laws of the gods mean nothing to you.   65
Ismenê.   They mean a great deal to me; but I have no strength
To break laws that were made for the public good.
Antigonê.   That must be your excuse, I suppose. But as for me,
I will bury the brother I love.
Ismenê.   Antigonê,
I am so afraid for you!
Antigonê.   You need not be:
You have yourself to consider, after all.
Ismenê.   But no one must hear of this, you must tell no one!
I will keep it a secret, I promise!   75
Antigonê.   Oh tell it! Tell everyone!
Think how they'll hate you when it all comes out
If they learn that you knew about it all the time!
Ismenê.   So fiery! You should be cold with fear.
Antigonê.   Perhaps. But I am doing only what I must.   80
Ismenê.   But can you do it? I say that you cannot.
Antigonê.   Very well: when my strength gives out, I shall do no more.
Ismenê.   Impossible things should not be tried at all.
Antigonê.   Go away, Ismenê:
I shall be hating you soon, and the dead will too,   85
For your words are hateful. Leave me my foolish plan:
I am not afraid of the danger; if it means death,
It will not be the worst of deaths—death without honor.
Ismenê.   Go then, if you feel you must.
You are unwise,   90
But a loyal friend indeed to those who love you.

[*Exit into the Palace. Antigonê goes off, L. Enter the Chorus.*]

Párodos[2]

Chorus.   Now the long blade of the sun, lying   [*Strophe 1*]
    Level east to west, touches with glory
    Thebes of the Seven Gates. Open, unlidded
    Eye of golden day! O marching light
    Across the eddy and rush of Dircê's stream,[3]   5
    Striking the white shields of the enemy
    Thrown headlong backward from the blaze of morning!
Choragos.[4]   Polyneicês their commander
    Roused them with windy phrases,
    He the wild eagle screaming   10
    Insults above our land,
    His wings their shields of snow,
    His crest their marshalled helms.

Chorus.   Against our seven gates in a yawning ring   [*Antistrophe 1*]
    The famished spears came onward in the night;   15
    But before his jaws were sated with our blood,
    Or pinefire took the garland of our towers,
    He was thrown back; and as he turned, great Thebes—
    No tender victim for his noisy power—
    Rose like a dragon behind him, shouting war.   20
Choragos.   For God hates utterly
    The bray of bragging tongues;
    And when he beheld their smiling,
    Their swagger of golden helms,
    The frown of his thunder blasted   25
    Their first man from our walls.

Chorus.   We heard his shout of triumph high in the air   [*Strophe 2*]
    Turn to a scream; far out in a flaming arc
    He fell with his windy torch, and the earth struck him.
    And others storming in fury no less than his   30
    Found shock of death in the dusty joy of battle.
Choragos.   Seven captains at seven gates
    Yielded their clanging arms to the god
    That bends the battle-line and breaks it.
    These two only, brothers in blood,   35

---

[2] The *Párodos* is the ode sung by the Chorus as it entered the theater and moved down the aisles to the playing area. The *strophe*, in Greek tragedy, is the unit of verse the Chorus chanted as it moved to the left in a dance rhythm. The Chorus sang the *antistrophe* as it moved to the right, and the *epode* while standing still.
[3] A stream near Thebes.
[4] Choragos is the leader of the Chorus.

Face to face in matchless rage,
Mirroring each the other's death,
Clashed in long combat.

Chorus.   But now in the beautiful morning of victory   [*Antistrophe* 2]
Let Thebes of the many chariots sing for joy!   40
With hearts for dancing we'll take leave of war:
Our temples shall be sweet with hymns of praise,
And the long night shall echo with our chorus.

Scene I

Choragos.   But now at last our new King is coming:
Creon of Thebes, Menoikeus' son.
In this auspicious dawn of his reign
What are the new complexities
That shifting Fate has woven for him?
What is his counsel? Why has he summoned
The old men to hear him?

[*Enter Creon from the Palace, C. He addresses the Chorus from the top step.*]

Creon.   Gentlemen: I have the honor to inform you that our Ship of State,
which recent storms have threatened to destroy, has come safely to harbor
at last, guided by the merciful wisdom of Heaven. I have summoned you
here this morning because I know that I can depend upon you: your devotion to King Laïos was absolute; you never hesitated in your duty to our late
ruler Oedipus; and when Oedipus died, your loyalty was transferred to his
children. Unfortunately, as you know, his two sons, the princes Eteoclês and
Polyneicês, have killed each other in battle; and I, as the next in blood, have
succeeded to the full power of the throne.
   I am aware, of course, that no Ruler can expect complete loyalty from his
subjects until he has been tested in office. Nevertheless, I say to you at the
very outset that I have nothing but contempt for the kind of Governor who
is afraid, for whatever reason, to follow the course that he knows is best for
the State; and as for the man who sets private friendship above the public
welfare,—I have no use for him, either. I call God to witness that if I saw
my country headed for ruin, I should not be afraid to speak out plainly; and
I need hardly remind you that I would never have any dealings with an
enemy of the people. No one values friendship more highly than I; but we
must remember that friends made at the risk of wrecking our Ship are not
real friends at all.
   These are my principles, at any rate, and that is why I have made the
following decision concerning the sons of Oedipus: Eteoclês, who died as
a man should die, fighting for his country, is to be buried with full mil-

itary honors, with all the ceremony that is usual when the greatest heroes die; but his brother Polyneicês, who broke his exile to come back with fire and sword against his native city and the shrines of his fathers' gods, whose one idea was to spill the blood of his blood and sell his own people into slavery—Polyneicês, I say, is to have no burial: no man is to touch him or say the least prayer for him; he shall lie on the plain, unburied; and the birds and the scavenging dogs can do with him whatever they like.

   This is my command, and you can see the wisdom behind it. As long as I am King, no traitor is going to be honored with the loyal man. But whoever shows by word and deed that he is on the side of the State,—he shall have my respect while he is living and my reverence when he is dead.

Choragos.   If that is your will, Creon, son of Menoikeus,
   You have the right to enforce it: we are yours.
Creon.   That is my will. Take care that you do your part.
Choragos.   We are old men: let the younger ones carry it out.
Creon.   I do not mean that: the sentries have been appointed.
Choragos.   Then what is it that you would have us do?
Creon.   You will give no support to whoever breaks this law.
Choragos.   Only a crazy man is in love with death!
Creon.   And death it is; yet money talks, and the wisest
   Have sometimes been known to count a few coins too many.

[Enter Sentry from L.]

Sentry.   I'll not say that I'm out of breath from running, King, because every time I stopped to think about what I have to tell you, I felt like going back. And all the time a voice kept saying, "You fool, don't you know you're walking straight into trouble?"; and then another voice: "Yes, but if you let somebody else get the news to Creon first, it will be even worse than that for you!" But good sense won out, at least I hope it was good sense, and here I am with a story that makes no sense at all; but I'll tell it anyhow, because, as they say, what's going to happen's going to happen, and—
Creon.   Come to the point. What have you to say?
Sentry.   I did not do it. I did not see who did it. You must not punish me for what someone else has done.
Creon.   A comprehensive defense! More effective, perhaps,
   If I knew its purpose. Come: what is it?
Sentry.   A dreadful thing . . . I don't know how to put it—
Creon.   Out with it!
Sentry.   Well, then;
   The dead man—
                  Polyneicês—

[Pause. The Sentry is overcome, fumbles for words. Creon waits impassively.]

out there—

someone,—

New dust on the slimy flesh!

[*Pause. No sign from Creon.*]

Someone has given it burial that way, and
Gone . . .

[*Long pause. Creon finally speaks with deadly control.*]

Creon.   And the man who dared do this?
Sentry.   I swear I
Do not know! You must believe me!

Listen:

The ground was dry, not a sign of digging, no,
Not a wheeltrack in the dust, no trace of anyone.
It was when they relieved us this morning: and one of them,
The corporal, pointed to it.

There it was,

The strangest—

Look:

The body, just mounded over with light dust: you see?
Not buried really, but as if they'd covered it
Just enough for the ghost's peace. And no sign
Of dogs or any wild animal that had been there.

And then what a scene there was! Every man of us
Accusing the other: we all proved the other man did it,
We all had proof that we could not have done it.
We were ready to take hot iron in our hands,
Walk through fire, swear by all the gods,
It was not I!
I do not know who it was, but it was not I!

[*Creon's rage has been mounting steadily, but the Sentry is too intent upon his
story to notice it.*]

And then, when this came to nothing, someone said
A thing that silenced us and made us stare
Down at the ground: you had to be told the news,
And one of us had to do it! We threw the dice,
And the bad luck fell to me. So here I am,
No happier to be here than you are to have me:
Nobody likes the man who brings bad news.

Choragos.   I have been wondering, King: can it be that the gods have done
  this?
Creon [*furiously*].   Stop!
  Must you doddering wrecks
  Go out of your heads entirely? "The gods!"
  Intolerable!
  The gods favor this corpse? Why? How had he served them?
  Tried to loot their temples, burn their images,
  Yes, and the whole State, and its laws with it!
  Is it your senile opinion that the gods love to honor bad men?
  A pious thought!—
                            No, from the very beginning
  There have been those who have whispered together,
  Stiff-necked anarchists, putting their heads together,
  Scheming against me in alleys. These are the men,
  And they have bribed my own guard to do this thing.
  [*Sententiously.*] Money!
  There's nothing in the world so demoralizing as money.
  Down go your cities,
  Homes gone, men gone, honest hearts corrupted,
  Crookedness of all kinds, and all for money!
  [*To Sentry.*]   But you—!
  I swear by God and by the throne of God,
  The man who has done this thing shall pay for it!
  Find that man, bring him here to me, or your death
  Will be the least of your problems: I'll string you up
  Alive, and there will be certain ways to make you
  Discover your employer before you die;
  And the process may teach you a lesson you seem to have missed:
  The dearest profit is sometimes all too dear:
  That depends on the source. Do you understand me?
  A fortune won is often misfortune.
Sentry.   King, may I speak?
Creon.   Your very voice distresses me.
Sentry.   Are you sure that it is my voice, and not your conscience?
Creon.   By God, he wants to analyze me now!
Sentry.   It is not what I say, but what has been done, that hurts you.
Creon.   You talk too much.
Sentry.   Maybe; but I've done nothing.
Creon.   Sold your soul for some silver: that's all you've done.
Sentry.   How dreadful it is when the right judge judges wrong!
Creon.   Your figures of speech
  May entertain you now; but unless you bring me the man,
  You will get little profit from them in the end.

[*Exit Creon into the Palace.*]

Sentry.   "Bring me the man"—!
  I'd like nothing better than bringing him the man!
  But bring him or not, you have seen the last of me here.
  At any rate, I am safe!

[*Exit Sentry.*]

Ode I

Chorus.   Numberless are the world's wonders, but none   [*Strophe 1*]
  More wonderful than man; the stormgray sea
  Yields to his prows, the huge crests bear him high;
  Earth, holy and inexhaustible, is graven
  With shining furrows where his plows have gone   5
  Year after year, the timeless labor of stallions.

  The lightboned birds and beasts that cling to cover,   [*Antistrophe 1*]
  The lithe fish lighting their reaches of dim water,
  All are taken, tamed in the net of his mind;
  The lion on the hill, the wild horse windy-maned,   10
  Resign to him; and his blunt yoke has broken
  The sultry shoulders of the mountain bull.

  Words also, and thought as rapid as air,   [*Strophe 2*]
  He fashions to his good use; statecraft is his,
  And his the skill that deflects the arrows of snow,   15
  The spears of winter rain: from every wind
  He has made himself secure—from all but one:
  In the late wind of death he cannot stand.

  O clear intelligence, force beyond all measure!   [*Antistrophe 2*]
  When the laws are kept, how proudly his city stands!   20
  When the laws are broken, what of his city then?
  Never may the anarchic man find rest at my hearth,
  Never be it said that my thoughts are his thoughts.

praising the glory of man conquering nature · life in order except for death god vs. state (who is higher)

Scene II

[*Re-enter Sentry leading Antigonê.*]

Choragos.   What does this mean? Surely this captive woman
  Is the Princess, Antigonê. Why should she be taken?

Sentry.   Here is the one who did it! We caught her
In the very act of burying him.—Where is Creon?
Choragos.   Just coming from the house.   5

[*Enter Creon, C.*]

Creon.   What has happened?
Why have you come back so soon?
Sentry [*expansively*].   O King,
A man should never be too sure of anything:
I would have sworn   10
That you'd not see me here again: your anger
Frightened me so, and the things you threatened me with;
But how could I tell then
That I'd be able to solve the case so soon?
No dice-throwing this time: I was only too glad to come!   15

Here is this woman. She is the guilty one:
We found her trying to bury him.
Take her, then; question her; judge her as you will.
I am through with the whole thing now, and glad of it.
Creon.   But this is Antigonê! Why have you brought her here?   20
Sentry.   She was burying him, I tell you!
Creon [*severely*].   Is this the truth?
Sentry.   I saw her with my own eyes. Can I say more?
Creon.   The details: come, tell me quickly!
Sentry.   It was like this: 25
After those terrible threats of yours, King,
We went back and brushed the dust away from the body.
The flesh was soft by now, and stinking,
So we sat on a hill to windward and kept guard.
No napping this time! We kept each other awake.   30
But nothing happened until the white round sun
Whirled in the center of the round sky over us:
Then, suddenly,
A storm of dust roared up from the earth, and the sky
Went out, the plain vanished with all its trees   35
In the stinging dark. We closed our eyes and endured it.
The whirlwind lasted a long time, but it passed;
And then we looked, and there was Antigonê!
I have seen
A mother bird come back to a stripped nest, heard   40
Her crying bitterly a broken note or two
For the young ones stolen. Just so, when this girl

Found the bare corpse, and all her love's work wasted,
She wept, and cried on heaven to damn the hands
That had done this thing.   45
                    And then she brought more dust
And sprinkled wine three times for her brother's ghost.
We ran and took her at once. She was not afraid,
Not even when we charged her with what she had done.
She denied nothing.   50
                    And this was a comfort to me,
And some uneasiness: for it is a good thing
To escape from death, but it is no great pleasure
To bring death to a friend.
                    Yet I always say   55
There is nothing so comfortable as your own safe skin!
Creon [*slowly, dangerously*].   And you, Antigonê,
    You with your head hanging,—do you confess this thing?
Antigonê.   I do. I deny nothing.
Creon [*to Sentry*].   You may go.   60

[*Exit Sentry.*]

[*To Antigonê.*] Tell me, tell me briefly:
    Had you heard my proclamation touching this matter?

Antigonê.   It was public. Could I help hearing it?
Creon.   And yet you dared defy the law.
Antigonê.   I dared.   65
    It was not God's proclamation. That final Justice
    That rules the world below makes no such laws.

    Your edict, King, was strong,
    But all your strength is weakness itself against
    The immortal unrecorded laws of God.   70
    They are not merely now: they were, and shall be,
    Operative for ever, beyond man utterly.

    I knew I must die, even without your decree:
    I am only mortal. And if I must die
    Now, before it is my time to die,   75
    Surely this is no hardship: can anyone
    Living, as I live, with evil all about me,
    Think Death less than a friend? This death of mine
    Is of no importance; but if I had left my brother
    Lying in death unburied, I should have suffered.   80

Now I do not.
                    You smile at me. Ah Creon,
Think me a fool, if you like; but it may well be
That a fool convicts me of folly.
Choragos.   Like father, like daughter: both headstrong, deaf to reason!   85
She has never learned to yield.
Creon.   She has much to learn.
The inflexible heart breaks first, the toughest iron
Cracks first, and the wildest horses bend their necks
At the pull of the smallest curb.   90
                              Pride? In a slave?
This girl is guilty of a double insolence,
Breaking the given laws and boasting of it.
Who is the man here,
She or I, if this crime goes unpunished?   95
Sister's child, or more than sister's child,
Or closer yet in blood—she and her sister
Win bitter death for this!
[*To servants.*]   Go, some of you,
Arrest Ismenê. I accuse her equally.   100
Bring her: you will find her sniffling in the house there.

Her mind's a traitor: crimes kept in the dark
Cry for light, and the guardian brain shudders;
But how much worse than this
Is brazen boasting of barefaced anarchy!   105
Antigonê.   Creon, what more do you want than my death?
Creon.   Nothing.
That gives me everything.
Antigonê.   Then I beg you: kill me.
This talking is a great weariness: your words   110
Are distasteful to me, and I am sure that mine
Seem so to you. And yet they should not seem so:
I should have praise and honor for what I have done.
All these men here would praise me
Were their lips not frozen shut with fear of you.   115
[*Bitterly.*] Ah the good fortune of kings,
Licensed to say and do whatever they please!
Creon.   You are alone here in that opinion.
Antigonê.   No, they are with me. But they keep their tongues in leash.
Creon.   Maybe. But you are guilty, and they are not.   120
Antigonê.   There is no guilt in reverence for the dead.
Creon.   But Eteoclês—was he not your brother too?
Antigonê.   My brother too.
Creon.   And you insult his memory?
Antigonê [*softly*].   The dead man would not say that I insult it.   125

Creon.   He would: for you honor a traitor as much as him.
Antigonê.   His own brother, traitor or not, and equal in blood.
Creon.   He made war on his country. Eteoclês defended it.
Antigonê.   Nevertheless, there are honors due all the dead.
Creon.   But not the same for the wicked as for the just.   130
Antigonê.   Ah Creon, Creon,
  Which of us can say what the gods hold wicked?
Creon.   An enemy is an enemy, even dead.
Antigonê.   It is my nature to join in love, not hate.
Creon [*finally losing patience*].   Go join them, then; if you must have   135
  your love,
    Find it in hell!
Choragos.   But see, Ismenê comes:

[*Enter Ismenê, guarded.*]

  Those tears are sisterly, the cloud
  That shadows her eyes rains down gentle sorrow.   140

Creon.   You too, Ismenê,
  Snake in my ordered house, sucking my blood
  Stealthily—and all the time I never knew
  That these two sisters were aiming at my throne!
                                                       Ismenê,   145
  Do you confess your share in this crime, or deny it?
  Answer me.
Ismenê.   Yes, if she will let me say so. I am guilty.
Antigonê [*coldly*].   No, Ismenê. You have no right to say so.
  You would not help me, and I will not have you help me.   150
Ismenê.   But now I know what you meant; and I am here
  To join you, to take my share of punishment.
Antigonê.   The dead man and the gods who rule the dead
  Know whose act this was. Words are not friends.
Ismenê.   Do you refuse me, Antigonê? I want to die with you: 155
  I too have a duty that I must discharge to the dead.
Antigonê.   You shall not lessen my death by sharing it.
Ismenê.   What do I care for life when you are dead?
Antigonê.   Ask Creon. You're always hanging on his opinions.
Ismenê.   You are laughing at me. Why, Antigonê?   160
Antigonê.   It's a joyless laughter, Ismenê.
Ismenê.   But can I do nothing?
Antigonê.   Yes. Save yourself. I shall not envy you.
  There are those who will praise you; I shall have honor, too.
Ismenê.   But we are equally guilty!   165
Antigonê.   No more, Ismenê.
  You are alive, but I belong to Death.

Creon [*to the Chorus*].   Gentlemen, I beg you to observe these girls:
     One has just now lost her mind; the other,
     It seems, has never had a mind at all.   170
Ismenê.   Grief teaches the steadiest minds to waver, King.
Creon.   Yours certainly did, when you assumed guilt with the guilty!
Ismenê.   But how could I go on living without her?
Creon.   You are.
     She is already dead.   175
Ismenê.   But your own son's bride!
Creon.   There are places enough for him to push his plow.
     I want no wicked women for my sons!
Ismenê.   O dearest Haimon, how your father wrongs you!
Creon.   I've had enough of your childish talk of marriage!   180
Choragos.   Do you really intend to steal this girl from your son?
Creon.   No; Death will do that for me.
Choragos.   Then she must die?
Creon [*ironically*].   You dazzle me.
                              —But enough of this talk!   185
     [*To Guards.*] You there, take them away and guard them well:
     For they are but women, and even brave men run
     When they see Death coming.

[*Exeunt Ismenê, Antigonê, and Guards.*]

Ode II

Chorus.   Fortunate is the man who has never tasted   [*Strophe 1*]
          God's vengeance!
     Where once the anger of heaven has struck, that house is shaken
     For ever: damnation rises behind each child
     Like a wave cresting out of the black northeast,   5
     When the long darkness under sea roars up
     And bursts drumming death upon the windwhipped sand.

     I have seen this gathering sorrow from time long past   [*Antistrophe 1*]
     Loom upon Oedipus' children: generation from generation
     Takes the compulsive rage of the enemy god.   10
     So lately this last flower of Oedipus' line
     Drank the sunlight! but now a passionate word
     And a handful of dust have closed up all its beauty.

          What mortal arrogance   [*Strophe 2*]
          Transcends the wrath of Zeus?   15

Sleep cannot lull him, nor the effortless long months
Of the timeless gods: but he is young for ever,
And his house is the shining day of high Olympos.
    And that is and shall be,
    And all the past, is his.   20
No pride on earth is free of the curse of heaven.

    The straying dreams of men   [*Antistrophe 2*]
    May bring them ghosts of joy:
But as they drowse, the waking embers burn them;
Or they walk with fixed eyes, as blind men walk.   25
But the ancient wisdom speaks for our own time:
    Fate works most for woe
    With Folly's fairest show.
Man's little pleasure is the spring of sorrow.

Scene III

Choragos.   But here is Haimon, King, the last of all your sons.
Is it grief for Antigonê that brings him here,
And bitterness at being robbed of his bride?

[*Enter Haimon.*]

Creon.   We shall soon see, and no need of diviners.
                                   —Son,   5
You have heard my final judgment on that girl:
Have you come here hating me, or have you come
With deference and with love, whatever I do?
Haimon.   I am your son, father. You are my guide.
You make things clear for me, and I obey you.   10
No marriage means more to me than your continuing wisdom.
Creon.   Good. That is the way to behave: subordinate
Everything else, my son, to your father's will.
This is what a man prays for, that he may get
Sons attentive and dutiful in his house,   15
Each one hating his father's enemies,
Honoring his father's friends. But if his sons
Fail him, if they turn out unprofitably,
What has he fathered but trouble for himself
And amusement for the malicious?   20
                         So you are right
Not to lose your head over this woman.

Your pleasure with her would soon grow cold, Haimon,
And then you'd have a hellcat in bed and elsewhere.
Let her find her husband in Hell!   25
Of all the people in this city, only she
Has had contempt for my law and broken it.

Do you want me to show myself weak before the people?
Or to break my sworn word? No, and I will not.
The woman dies.   30
I suppose she'll plead "family ties." Well, let her.
If I permit my own family to rebel,
How shall I earn the world's obedience?
Show me the man who keeps his house in hand,
He's fit for public authority.   35
                              I'll have no dealings
With law-breakers, critics of the government:
Whoever is chosen to govern should be obeyed—
Must be obeyed, in all things, great and small,
Just and unjust! O Haimon,   40
The man who knows how to obey, and that man only,
Knows how to give commands when the time comes.
You can depend on him, no matter how fast
The spears come: he's a good soldier, he'll stick it out.
Anarchy, anarchy! Show me a greater evil!   45
This is why cities tumble and the great houses rain down,
This is what scatters armies!

No, no: good lives are made so by discipline.
We keep the laws then, and the lawmakers,
And no woman shall seduce us. If we must lose,   50
Let's lose to a man, at least! Is a woman stronger than we?
Choragos.   Unless time has rusted my wits,
What you say, King, is said with point and dignity.
Haimon [*boyishly earnest*].   Father:
Reason is God's crowning gift to man, and you are right   55
To warn me against losing mine. I cannot say—
I hope that I shall never want to say!—that you
Have reasoned badly. Yet there are other men
Who can reason, too; and their opinions might be helpful.
You are not in a position to know everything   60
That people say or do, or what they feel:
Your temper terrifies them—everyone
Will tell you only what you like to hear.
But I, at any rate, can listen; and I have heard them

Muttering and whispering in the dark about this girl.   65
They say no woman has ever, so unreasonably,
Died so shameful a death for a generous act:
"She covered her brother's body. Is this indecent?
She kept him from dogs and vultures. Is this a crime?
Death?—She should have all the honor that we can give her!"   70

This is the way they talk out there in the city.

You must believe me:
Nothing is closer to me than your happiness.
What could be closer? Must not any son
Value his father's fortune as his father does his?   75
I beg you, do not be unchangeable:
Do not believe that you alone can be right.
The man who thinks that,
The man who maintains that only he has the power
To reason correctly, the gift to speak, the soul—   80
A man like that, when you know him, turns out empty.
It is not reason never to yield to reason!

In flood time you can see how some trees bend
And because they bend, even their twigs are safe,
While stubborn trees are torn up, roots and all.   85
And the same thing happens in sailing:
Make your sheet fast, never slacken—and over you go,
Head over heels and under: and there's your voyage.
Forget you are angry! Let yourself be moved!
I know I am young; but please let me say this: 90
The ideal condition
Would be, I admit, that men should be right by instinct;
But since we are all too likely to go astray,
The reasonable thing is to learn from those who can teach.
Choragos.   You will do well to listen to him, King,   95
   If what he says is sensible. And you, Haimon,
   Must listen to your father.—Both speak well.
Creon.   You consider it right for a man of my years and experience
   To go to school to a boy?
Haimon.   It is not right   100
   If I am wrong. But if I am young, and right,
   What does my age matter?
Creon.   You think it right to stand up for an anarchist?
Haimon.   Not at all. I pay no respect to criminals.
Creon.   Then she is not a criminal?   105

Haimon.   The City would deny it, to a man.
Creon.   And the City proposes to teach me how to rule?
Haimon.   Ah. Who is it that's talking like a boy now?
Creon.   My voice is the one voice giving orders in this City!
Haimon.   It is no City if it takes orders from one voice.   110
Creon.   The State is the King!
Haimon.   Yes, if the State is a desert.

[*Pause.*]

Creon.   This boy, it seems, has sold out to a woman.
Haimon.   If you are a woman: my concern is only for you.
Creon.   So? Your "concern"! In a public brawl with your father!   115
Haimon.   How about you, in a public brawl with justice?
Creon.   With justice, when all that I do is within my rights?
Haimon.   You have no right to trample on God's right.
Creon [*completely out of control*].   Fool, adolescent fool! Taken in by a woman!
Haimon.   You'll never see me taken in by anything vile.   120
Creon.   Every word you say is for her!
Haimon [*quietly, darkly*].   And for you.
     And for me. And for the gods under the earth.
Creon.   You'll never marry her while she lives.
Haimon.   Then she must die.—But her death will cause another.   125
Creon.   Another?
     Have you lost your senses? Is this an open threat?
Haimon.   There is no threat in speaking to emptiness.
Creon.   I swear you'll regret this superior tone of yours!
     You are the empty one!   130
Haimon.   If you were not my father,
     I'd say you were perverse.
Creon.   You girlstruck fool, don't play at words with me!
Haimon.   I am sorry. You prefer silence.
Creon.   Now, by God—!   135
     I swear, by all the gods in heaven above us,
     You'll watch it, I swear you shall!
     [*To the servants.*]   Bring her out!
     Bring the woman out! Let her die before his eyes!
     Here, this instant, with her bridegroom beside her!   140
Haimon.   Not here, no; she will not die here, King.
     And you will never see my face again.
     Go on raving as long as you've a friend to endure you.

[*Exit Haimon.*]

Choragos.   Gone, gone.
     Creon, a young man in a rage is dangerous!   145

Creon.   Let him do, or dream to do, more than a man can.
　　He shall not save these girls from death.
Choragos.　　　　　　　　　　These girls?
　　You have sentenced them both?
Creon.　　　　　　　　No, you are right.　　　　　　　150
　　I will not kill the one whose hands are clean.
Choragos.   But Antigonê?
Creon [*somberly*].   I will carry her far away
　　Out there in the wilderness, and lock her
　　Living in a vault of stone. She shall have food,　　　155
　　As the custom is, to absolve the State of her death.
　　And there let her pray to the gods of hell:
　　They are her only gods:
　　Perhaps they will show her an escape from death,
　　Or she may learn,　　　　　　　　　　　　160
　　　　　　　though late,
　　That piety shown the dead is pity in vain.

[*Exit Creon.*]

Ode III

Chorus.   Love, unconquerable　　　　　　　[*Strophe*]
　　Waster of rich men, keeper
　　Of warm lights and all-night vigil
　　In the soft face of a girl:
　　Sea-wanderer, forest-visitor!　　　　　　　　5
　　Even the pure Immortals cannot escape you,
　　And mortal man, in his one day's dusk,
　　Trembles before your glory.

　　Surely you swerve upon ruin　　　　　　　[*Antistrophe*]
　　The just man's consenting heart,　　　　　　　10
　　As here you have made bright anger
　　Strike between father and son—
　　And none had conquered but Love!
　　A girl's glance working the will of heaven:
　　Pleasure to her alone who mocks us,　　　　　　15
　　Merciless Aphroditê.⁵

---

⁵ Aphroditê is the goddess of love.

Scene IV

Choragos [*as Antigonê enters guarded*].   But I can no longer stand in awe of
     this,
  Nor, seeing what I see, keep back my tears.
  Here is Antigonê, passing to that chamber
  Where all find sleep at last.   5

Antigonê.   Look upon me, friends, and pity me   [*Strophe 1*]
  Turning back at the night's edge to say
  Good-by to the sun that shines for me no longer;
  Now sleepy Death
  Summons me down to Acheron,[6] that cold shore: 10
  There is no bridesong there, nor any music.
Chorus.   Yet not unpraised, not without a kind of honor,
  You walk at last into the underworld;
  Untouched by sickness, broken by no sword.
  What woman has ever found your way to death?   15

Antigonê.   How often I have heard the story of Niobê,[7]   [*Antistrophe 1*]
  Tantalos' wretched daughter, how the stone
  Clung fast about her, ivy-close: and they say
  The rain falls endlessly   20
  And sifting soft snow; her tears are never done.
  I feel the loneliness of her death in mine.
Chorus.   But she was born of heaven, and you
  Are woman, woman-born. If her death is yours,
  A mortal woman's, is this not for you   25
  Glory in our world and in the world beyond?

Antigonê.   You laugh at me. Ah, friends, friends,   [*Strophe 2*]
  Can you not wait until I am dead? O Thebes,
  O men many-charioted, in love with Fortune,
  Dear springs of Dircê, sacred Theban grove,   30
  Be witnesses for me, denied all pity,
  Unjustly judged! and think a word of love
  For her whose path turns
  Under dark earth, where there are no more tears.
Chorus.   You have passed beyond human daring and come at last   35
  Into a place of stone where Justice sits.

---

[6] A river of Hades.
  [7] Niobê married an ancestor of Oedipus named Amphion. Her fourteen children were killed
by Apollo and Artemis after Niobê boasted to their mother, Leto, that her children were superior to them. She wept incessantly and was finally transformed into a rock on Mt. Sipylos,
whose streams are her tears.

I cannot tell
What shape of your father's guilt appears in this.

Antigonê.   You have touched it at last: that bridal bed   [*Antistrophe 2*]
    Unspeakable, horror of son and mother mingling:
    Their crime, infection of all our family!   40
    O Oedipus, father and brother!
    Your marriage strikes from the grave to murder mine.
    I have been a stranger here in my own land:
    All my life
    The blasphemy of my birth has followed me.   45

Chorus.   Reverence is a virtue, but strength
    Lives in established law: that must prevail.
    You have made your choice,
    Your death is the doing of your conscious hand.

Antigonê.   Then let me go, since all your words are bitter,   [*Epode*]   50
    And the very light of the sun is cold to me.
    Lead me to my vigil, where I must have
    Neither love nor lamentation; no song, but silence.

[*Creon interrupts impatiently.*]

Creon.   If dirges and planned lamentations could put off death,   55
    Men would be singing for ever.
    [*To the servants.*]   Take her, go!
    You know your orders: take her to the vault
    And leave her alone there. And if she lives or dies,
    That's her affair, not ours: our hands are clean.   60

Antigonê.   O tomb, vaulted bride-bed in eternal rock,
    Soon I shall be with my own again
    Where Persephonê[8] welcomes the thin ghosts underground:
    And I shall see my father again, and you, mother,
    And dearest Polyneicês—   65
                dearest indeed
    To me, since it was my hand
    That washed him clean and poured the ritual wine:
    And my reward is death before my time!

    And yet, as men's hearts know, I have done no wrong,   70
    I have not sinned before God. Or if I have,
    I shall know the truth in death. But if the guilt

---

[8] Queen of Hades.

Lies upon Creon who judged me, then, I pray,
May his punishment equal my own.
Choragos.   O passionate heart,   75
Unyielding, tormented still by the same winds!
Creon.   Her guards shall have good cause to regret their delaying.
Antigonê.   Ah! That voice is like the voice of death!
Creon.   I can give you no reason to think you are mistaken.
Antigonê.   Thebes, and you my fathers' gods,   80
And rulers of Thebes, you see me now, the last
Unhappy daughter of a line of kings,
Your kings, led away to death. You will remember
What things I suffer, and at what men's hands,
Because I would not transgress the laws of heaven.   85
[*To the guards, simply.*] Come: let us wait no longer.

[*Exit Antigonê, L., guarded.*]

Ode IV

Chorus.   All Danaê's[9] beauty was locked away   [*Strophe 1*]
In a brazen cell where the sunlight could not come:
A small room, still as any grave, enclosed her.
Yet she was a princess too,
And Zeus in a rain of gold poured love upon her.   5
O child, child,
No power in wealth or war
Or tough sea-blackened ships
Can prevail against untiring Destiny!

And Dryas' son[10] also, that furious king,   [*Antistrophe 1*] 10
Bore the god's prisoning anger for his pride:
Sealed up by Dionysos in deaf stone,
His madness died among echoes.
So at the last he learned what dreadful power
His tongue had mocked: 15
For he had profaned the revels,
And fired the wrath of the nine
Implacable Sisters[11] that love the sound of the flute.

---

[9] Though Danaê, a beautiful princess of Aìgos, was confined by her father, Zeus visited her in the form of a shower of gold, and she gave birth to Perseus as a result.
[10] Lycurgus, King of Thrace, who was driven mad by Dionysos, the god of wine.
[11] The Muses.

And old men tell a half-remembered tale   [*Strophe* 2]
Of horror where a dark ledge splits the sea   20
And a double surf beats on the gray shores:
How a king's new woman,[12] sick
With hatred for the queen he had imprisoned,
Ripped out his two sons' eyes with her bloody hands
While grinning Arês[13] watched the shuttle plunge   25
Four times: four blind wounds crying for revenge,

Crying, tears and blood mingled.—Piteously born,   [*Antistrophe* 2]
Those sons whose mother was of heavenly birth!
Her father was the god of the North Wind
And she was cradled by gales,   30
She raced with young colts on the glittering hills
And walked untrammeled in the open light:
But in her marriage deathless Fate found means
To build a tomb like yours for all her joy.

Scene V

[*Enter blind Teiresias, led by a boy. The opening speeches of Teiresias should be in singsong contrast to the realistic lines of Creon.*]

Teiresias.   This is the way the blind man comes, Princes, Princes,
    Lock-step, two heads lit by the eyes of one.
Creon.   What new thing have you to tell us, old Teiresias?
Teiresias.   I have much to tell you: listen to the prophet, Creon.
Creon.   I am not aware that I have ever failed to listen.   5
Teiresias.   Then you have done wisely, King, and ruled well.
Creon.   I admit my debt to you. But what have you to say?
Teiresias.   This, Creon: you stand once more on the edge of fate.
Creon.   What do you mean? Your words are a kind of dread.
Teiresias.   Listen, Creon: 10
    I was sitting in my chair of augury, at the place
    Where the birds gather about me. They were all a-chatter,
    As is their habit, when suddenly I heard
    A strange note in their jangling, a scream, a

---

[12] The ode alludes to a story indicating the uselessness of high birth against implacable fate. The king's new woman is Eidothea, the second wife of King Phineus. Though Cleopatra, his first wife, was the daughter of Boreas, the north wind, and Phineus was descended from kings, yet Eidothea, out of hatred for Cleopatra, blinded her two sons.

[13] The god of war.

Whirring fury; I knew that they were fighting,   15
Tearing each other, dying
In a whirlwind of wings clashing. And I was afraid.
I began the rites of burnt-offering at the altar,
But Hephaistos[14] failed me: instead of bright flame,
There was only the sputtering slime of the fat thigh-flesh   20
Melting: the entrails dissolved in gray smoke;
The bare bone burst from the welter. And no blaze!

This was a sign from heaven. My boy described it,
Seeing for me as I see for others.

I tell you, Creon, you yourself have brought   25
This new calamity upon us. Our hearths and altars
Are stained with the corruption of dogs and carrion birds
That glut themselves on the corpse of Oedipus' son.
The gods are deaf when we pray to them, their fire
Recoils from our offering, their birds of omen   30
Have no cry of comfort, for they are gorged
With the thick blood of the dead.
                                          O my son,
These are no trifles! Think: all men make mistakes,
But a good man yields when he knows his course is wrong,   35
And repairs the evil. The only crime is pride.

Give in to the dead man, then: do not fight with a corpse—
What glory is it to kill a man who is dead?
Think, I beg you:
It is for your own good that I speak as I do.   40
You should be able to yield for your own good.
Creon.   It seems that prophets have made me their especial province.
All my life long
I have been a kind of butt for the dull arrows
Of doddering fortune-tellers!   45
                              No, Teiresias:
If your birds—if the great eagles of God himself
Should carry him stinking bit by bit to heaven,
I would not yield. I am not afraid of pollution:
No man can defile the gods.   50
                              Do what you will,
Go into business, make money, speculate
In India gold or that synthetic gold from Sardis,

---

[14] The god of fire.

Get rich otherwise than by my consent to bury him.
Teiresias, it is a sorry thing when a wise man   55
Sells his wisdom, lets out his words for hire!
Teiresias.   Ah Creon! Is there no man left in the world—
Creon.   To do what?—Come, let's have the aphorism!
Teiresias.   No man who knows that wisdom outweighs any wealth?
Creon.   As surely as bribes are baser than any baseness.   60
Teiresias.   You are sick, Creon! You are deathly sick!
Creon.   As you say: it is not my place to challenge a prophet.
Teiresias.   Yet you have said my prophecy is for sale.
Creon.   The generation of prophets has always loved gold.
Teiresias.   The generation of kings has always loved brass.   65
Creon.   You forget yourself! You are speaking to your King.
Teiresias.   I know it. You are a king because of me.
Creon.   You have a certain skill; but you have sold out.
Teiresias.   King, you will drive me to words that—
Creon.   Say them, say them!   70
Only remember: I will not pay you for them.
Teiresias.   No, you will find them too costly.
Creon.   No doubt. Speak:
Whatever you say, you will not change my will.
Teiresias.   Then take this, and take it to heart!   75
The time is not far off when you shall pay back
Corpse for corpse, flesh of your own flesh.
You have thrust the child of this world into living night,
You have kept from the gods below the child that is theirs:
The one in a grave before her death, the other,   80
Dead, denied the grave. This is your crime:
And the Furies and the dark gods of Hell
Are swift with terrible punishment for you.

Do you want to buy me now, Creon?
                                  Not many days,   85
And your house will be full of men and women weeping,
And curses will be hurled at you from far
Cities grieving for sons unburied, left to rot
Before the walls of Thebes.
These are my arrows, Creon: they are all for you.   90

[*To boy.*] But come, child: lead me home.
Let him waste his fine anger upon younger men.
Maybe he will learn at last
To control a wiser tongue in a better head.   95

[*Exit Teiresias.*]

Choragos.   The old man has gone, King, but his words
   Remain to plague us. I am old, too,
   But I cannot remember that he was ever false.
Creon.   That is true. . . . It troubles me.   100
   Oh it is hard to give in! but it is worse
   To risk everything for stubborn pride.
Choragos.   Creon: take my advice.
Creon.   What shall I do?
Choragos.   Go quickly: free Antigonê from her vault   105
   And build a tomb for the body of Polyneicês.
Creon.   You would have me do this?
Choragos.   Creon, yes!
   And it must be done at once: God moves
   Swiftly to cancel the folly of stubborn men.   110
Creon.   It is hard to deny the heart! But I
   Will do it: I will not fight with destiny.
Choragos.   You must go yourself, you cannot leave it to others.
Creon.   I will go.
                —Bring axes, servants:
   Come with me to the tomb. I buried her, I   115
   Will set her free.
                Oh quickly!
   My mind misgives—
   The laws of the gods are mighty, and a man must serve them
   To the last days of his life!   120

[*Exit Creon.*]

Paean[15]

Choragos.   God of many names   [*Strophe 1*]
Chorus.   O Iacchos[16]
                          son
   of Kadmeian Sémelê
                     O born of the Thunder!   5
   Guardian of the West
                     Regent
   of Eleusis's plain

---

[15] A hymn.
[16] Iacchos is a name for Dionysos. His mother was Sémelê, daughter of Kadmos, the founder of Thebes. His father was Zeus. The Maenads were priestesses of Dionysos who cry "evohé evohé."

O Prince of maenad Thebes
and the Dragon Field by rippling Ismenos:[17]   10

Choragos.   God of many names   [*Antistrophe 1*]
Chorus.   the flame of torches
flares on our hills
                    the nymphs of Iacchos
dance at the spring of Castalia:[18]   15
from the vine-close mountain
                                  come ah come in ivy:
Evohé evohé! sings through the streets of Thebes

Choragos.   God of many names   [*Strophe 2*]
Chorus.   Iacchos of Thebes   20
heavenly Child
                    of Sémelê bride of the Thunderer!
The shadow of plague is upon us:
                                  come
with clement feet   25
                    oh come from Parnasos
down the long slopes
                    across the lamenting water

Choragos.   Iô Fire! Chorister of the throbbing stars!   [*Antistrophe 2*]
O purest among the voices of the night!   30
Thou son of God, blaze for us!
Chorus.   Come with choric rapture of circling Maenads
Who cry *Iô Iacche!*
                    God of many names!

Exodos

[*Enter Messenger, L.*]

Messenger.   Men of the line of Kadmos, you who live
Near Amphion's[19] citadel:
                    I cannot say

---

[17] A river of Thebes, sacred to Apollo. Dragon Field refers to the legend that the ancestors of Thebes sprang from the dragon's teeth sown by Kadmos.

[18] A spring on Mt. Parnasos.

[19] A child of Zeus and Antiope. He is noted for building the walls of Thebes by charming the stones into place with a lyre.

Of any condition of human life "This is fixed,
This is clearly good, or bad." Fate raises up,   5
And Fate casts down the happy and unhappy alike:
No man can foretell his Fate.
                                    Take the case of Creon:
Creon was happy once, as I count happiness:
Victorious in battle, sole governor of the land,   10
Fortunate father of children nobly born.
And now it has all gone from him! Who can say
That a man is still alive when his life's joy fails?
He is a walking dead man. Grant him rich,
Let him live like a king in his great house: 15
If his pleasure is gone, I would not give
So much as the shadow of smoke for all he owns.
Choragos.   Your words hint at sorrow: what is your news for us?
Messenger.   They are dead. The living are guilty of their death.
Choragos.   Who is guilty? Who is dead? Speak!   20
Messenger.   Haimon.
Haimon is dead; and the hand that killed him
Is his own hand.
Choragos.   His father's? or his own?
Messenger.   His own, driven mad by the murder his father had done.   25
Choragos.   Teiresias, Teiresias, how clearly you saw it all!
Messenger.   This is my news: you must draw what conclusions you can from
it.
Choragos.   But look: Eurydicê, our Queen:
Has she overheard us?   30

[*Enter Eurydicê from the Palace, C.*]

Eurydicê.   I have heard something, friends:
As I was unlocking the gate of Pallas'[20] shrine,
For I needed her help today, I heard a voice
Telling of some new sorrow. And I fainted
There at the temple with all my maidens about me.   35
But speak again: whatever it is, I can bear it:
Grief and I are no strangers.
Messenger.   Dearest lady,
I will tell you plainly all that I have seen.
I shall not try to comfort you: what is the use,   40
Since comfort could lie only in what is not true?

---

[20] Pallas Athene, goddess of wisdom.

The truth is always best.
                    I went with Creon
To the outer plain where Polyneicês was lying,
No friend to pity him, his body shredded by dogs.   45
We made our prayers in that place to Hecatê[21]
And Pluto,[22] that they would be merciful. And we bathed
The corpse with holy water, and we brought
Fresh-broken branches to burn what was left of it,
And upon the urn we heaped up a towering barrow   50
Of the earth of his own land.
                     When we were done, we ran
To the vault where Antigonê lay on her couch of stone.
One of the servants had gone ahead,
And while he was yet far off he heard a voice   55
Grieving within the chamber, and he came back
And told Creon. And as the King went closer,
The air was full of wailing, the words lost,
And he begged us to make all haste. "Am I a prophet?"
He said, weeping, "And must I walk this road,   60
The saddest of all that I have gone before?
My son's voice calls me on. Oh quickly, quickly!
Look through the crevice there, and tell me
If it is Haimon, or some deception of the gods!"

We obeyed; and in the cavern's farthest corner   65
We saw her lying:
She had made a noose of her fine linen veil
And hanged herself. Haimon lay beside her,
His arms about her waist, lamenting her,
His love lost under ground, crying out   70
That his father had stolen her away from him.

When Creon saw him the tears rushed to his eyes
And he called to him: "What have you done, child? Speak to me.
What are you thinking that makes your eyes so strange?
O my son, my son, I come to you on my knees!"   75
But Haimon spat in his face. He said not a word,
Staring—
          And suddenly drew his sword

---

[21] Hecatê is often identified with Persephone, a goddess of Hades; generally Hecatê is a goddess of sorcery and witchcraft.
[22] King of Hades and brother of Zeus and Poseidon.

And lunged. Creon shrank back, the blade missed; and the boy,
Desperate against himself, drove it half its length   80
Into his own side, and fell. And as he died
He gathered Antigonê close in his arms again,
Choking, his blood bright red on her white cheek.
And now he lies dead with the dead, and she is his
At last, his bride in the houses of the dead.   85

[*Exit Eurydicê into the Palace.*]

Choragos.   She has left us without a word. What can this mean?
Messenger.   It troubles me, too; yet she knows what is best,
    Her grief is too great for public lamentation,
    And doubtless she has gone to her chamber to weep
    For her dead son, leading her maidens in his dirge.   90
Choragos.   It may be so: but I fear this deep silence.

[*Pause.*]

Messenger.   I will see what she is doing. I will go in.

[*Exit Messenger into the Palace.*]
[*Enter Creon with attendants, bearing Haimon's body.*]

Choragos.   But here is the King himself: oh look at him,
    Bearing his own damnation in his arms.
Creon.   Nothing you say can touch me any more.   95
    My own blind heart has brought me
    From darkness to final darkness. Here you see
    The father murdering, the murdered son—
    And all my civic wisdom!
    Haimon my son, so young to die,   100
    I was the fool, not you; and you died for me.
Choragos.   That is the truth; but you were late in learning it.
Creon.   This truth is hard to bear. Surely a god
    Has crushed me beneath the hugest weight of heaven,
    And driven me headlong a barbaric way   105
    To trample out the thing I held most dear.

    The pains that men will take to come to pain!

[*Enter Messenger from the Palace.*]

Messenger.   The burden you carry in your hands is heavy,
   But it is not all: you will find more in your house.
Creon.   What burden worse than this shall I find there?   110
Messenger.   The Queen is dead.
Creon.   O port of death, deaf world,
   Is there no pity for me? And you, Angel of evil,
   I was dead, and your words are death again.
   Is it true, boy? Can it be true?   115
   Is my wife dead? Has death bred death?
Messenger.   You can see for yourself.

[*The doors are opened, and the body of Eurydicê is disclosed within.*]

Creon.   Oh pity!
   All true, all true, and more than I can bear!
   O my wife, my son!   120
Messenger.   She stood before the altar, and her heart
   Welcomed the knife her own hand guided,
   And a great cry burst from her lips for Megareus[23] dead,
   And for Haimon dead, her sons; and her last breath
   Was a curse for their father, the murderer of her sons,   125
   And she fell, and the dark flowed in through her closing eyes.
Creon.   O God, I am sick with fear.
   Are there no swords here? Has no one a blow for me?
Messenger.   Her curse is upon you for the deaths of both.
Creon.   It is right that it should be. I alone am guilty.   130
   I know it, and I say it. Lead me in,
   Quickly, friends.
   I have neither life nor substance. Lead me in.
Choragos.   You are right, if there can be right in so much wrong.
   The briefest way is best in a world of sorrow.   135
Creon.   Let it come,
   Let death come quickly, and be kind to me.
   I would not ever see the sun again.
Choragos.   All that will come when it will; but we, meanwhile,
   Have much to do. Leave the future to itself.   140
Creon.   All my heart was in that prayer!
Choragos.   Then do not pray any more: the sky is deaf.
Creon.   Lead me away. I have been rash and foolish.
   I have killed my son and my wife.
   I look for comfort; my comfort lies here dead.   145

---

[23] Son of Creon who was killed in the attack on Thebes.

Whatever my hands have touched has come to nothing.
Fate has brought all my pride to a thought of dust.

[*As Creon is being led into the house, the Choragos advances and speaks directly
to the audience.*]

Choragos.   There is no happiness where there is no wisdom;
No wisdom but in submission to the gods.
Big words are always punished,   150
And proud men in old age learn to be wise.

QUESTIONS
1. Critics have traditionally divided over the question of whether Antigonê or Creon
is the protagonist in the play. How does the answer to this question affect one's
interpretation of the play?   **2.** How does the Prologue establish the mood and theme
of the play?   **3.** Does the character of Antigonê change during the course of the
play?   **4.** Does the action of the play prepare us for the change in Creon—that is, for
his realization that he has been wrong?   **5.** Is there any justification for Antigonê's
cold refusal to allow Ismenê to share her martyrdom? Explain.

WRITING TOPICS
1. Can *Antigonê* be read as a justification for civil disobedience? Explain.   **2.** To
what extent and in what ways does the Chorus contribute to the dramatic development and tension of the play?

A Doll's House*   (1879)

HENRIK IBSEN   [1828–1906]

CHARACTERS

Torvald Helmer, a lawyer
Nora, his wife
Dr. Rank
Mrs. Linde
Krogstad

The Helmers' three small children
Anne, the children's nurse
A Maid
A Porter

Act I

SCENE.   *A room furnished comfortably and tastefully, but not extravagantly. At the back, a door to the right leads to the entrance hall, another to the left leads to Helmer's study. Between the doors stands a piano. In the middle of the left-hand wall is a door, and beyond it a window. Near the window are a round table, armchairs and a small sofa. In the right-hand wall, at the farther end, another door; and on the same side, nearer the footlights, a stove, two easy chairs and a rocking-chair; between the stove and the door, a small table. Engravings on the walls; a cabinet with china and other small objects; a small book-case with well-bound books. The floors are carpeted, and a fire burns in the stove. It is winter.*

A bell rings in the hall; shortly afterwards the door is heard to open. Enter Nora, *humming a tune and in high spirits. She is in out-door dress and carries a number of parcels; these she lays on the table to the right. She leaves the outer door open after her, and through it is seen a* Porter *who is carrying a Christmas tree and a basket, which he gives to the* Maid *who has opened the door.*

Nora.   Hide the Christmas tree carefully, Helen. Be sure the children do not see it till this evening, when it is dressed. (*To the Porter, taking out her purse.*) How much?

---

* Translated by R. Farquharson Sharp.

Porter.   Sixpence.

Nora.   There is a shilling. No, keep the change. (*The Porter thanks her, and goes out. Nora shuts the door. She is laughing to herself, as she takes off her hat and coat. She takes a packet of macaroons from her pocket and eats one or two; then goes cautiously to her husband's door and listens.*) Yes, he is in.

[*Still humming, she goes to the table on the right.*]

Helmer (*calls out from his room*).   Is that my little lark twittering out there?

Nora (*busy opening some of the parcels*).   Yes, it is!

Helmer.   Is it my little squirrel bustling about?

Nora.   Yes!

Helmer.   When did my squirrel come home?

Nora.   Just now. (*Puts the bag of macaroons into her pocket and wipes her mouth.*) Come in here, Torvald, and see what I have bought.

Helmer.   Don't disturb me. (*A little later, he opens the door and looks into the room, pen in hand.*) Bought, did you say? All these things? Has my little spendthrift been wasting money again?

Nora.   Yes, but, Torvald, this year we really can let ourselves go a little. This is the first Christmas that we have not needed to economise.

Helmer.   Still, you know, we can't spend money recklessly.

Nora.   Yes, Torvald, we may be a wee bit more reckless now, mayn't we? Just a tiny wee bit! You are going to have a big salary and earn lots and lots of money.

Helmer.   Yes, after the New Year; but then it will be a whole quarter before the salary is due.

Nora.   Pooh! we can borrow till then.

Helmer.   Nora! (*Goes up to her and takes her playfully by the ear.*) The same little featherhead! Suppose, now, that I borrowed fifty pounds to-day, and you spent it all in the Christmas week, and then on New Year's Eve a slate fell on my head and killed me, and——

Nora (*putting her hands over his mouth*).   Oh! don't say such horrid things.

Helmer.   Still, suppose that happened,—what then?

Nora.   If that were to happen, I don't suppose I should care whether I owed money or not.

Helmer.   Yes, but what about the people who had lent it?

Nora.   They? Who would bother about them? I should not know who they were.

Helmer.   That is like a woman! But seriously, Nora, you know what I think about that. No debt, no borrowing. There can be no freedom or beauty about a home life that depends on borrowing and debt. We two have kept bravely on the straight road so far, and we will go on the same way for the short time longer that there need be any struggle.

Nora (*moving towards the stove*).   As you please, Torvald.

Helmer (*following her*).   Come, come, my little skylark must not droop her wings. What is this! Is my little squirrel out of temper? (*Taking out his purse.*) Nora, what do you think I have got here?

Nora (*turning round quickly*).   Money!

Helmer.   There you are. (*Gives her some money.*) Do you think I don't know what a lot is wanted for house-keeping at Christmas-time?

Nora (*counting*).   Ten shillings—a pound—two pounds! Thank you, thank you, Torvald; that will keep me going for a long time.

Helmer.   Indeed it must.

Nora.   Yes, yes, it will. But come here and let me show you what I have bought. And all so cheap! Look, here is a new suit for Ivar, and a sword; and a horse and a trumpet for Bob; and a doll and dolly's bedstead for Emmy,— they are very plain, but anyway she will soon break them in pieces. And here are dress-lengths and handkerchiefs for the maids; old Anne ought really to have something better.

Helmer.   And what is in this parcel?

Nora (*crying out*).   No, no! you mustn't see that till this evening.

Helmer.   Very well. But now tell me something reasonable that you would particularly like to have.

Nora.   No, I really can't think of anything—unless, Torvald——

Helmer.   Well?

Nora (*playing with his coat buttons, and without raising her eyes to his*).   If you really want to give me something, you might—you might——

Helmer.   Well, out with it!

Nora (*speaking quickly*).   You might give me money, Torvald. Only just as much as you can afford; and then one of these days I will buy something with it.

Helmer.   But, Nora——

Nora.   Oh, do! dear Torvald; please, please do! Then I will wrap it up in beautiful gilt paper and hang it on the Christmas tree. Wouldn't that be fun?

Helmer.   What are little people called that are always wasting money?

Nora.   Spendthrifts—I know. Let us do as you suggest, Torvald, and then I shall have time to think what I am most in want of. That is a very sensible plan, isn't it?

Helmer (*smiling*).   Indeed it is—that is to say, if you were really to save out of the money I give you, and then really buy something for yourself. But if you spend it all on the housekeeping and any number of unnecessary things, then I merely have to pay up again.

Nora.   Oh but, Torvald——

Helmer.   You can't deny it, my dear little Nora. (*Puts his arm round her waist.*) It's a sweet little spendthrift, but she uses up a deal of money. One would hardly believe how expensive such little persons are!

Nora.   It's a shame to say that. I do really save all I can.

Helmer (*laughing*).   That's very true,—all you can. But you can't save any-thing!

Nora (*smiling quietly and happily*).   You haven't any idea how many expenses we skylarks and squirrels have, Torvald.

Helmer.   You are an odd little soul. Very like your father. You always find some new way of wheedling money out of me, and, as soon as you have got it, it seems to melt in your hands. You never know where it has gone. Still, one must take you as you are. It is in the blood; for indeed it is true that you can inherit these things, Nora.

Nora.   Ah, I wish I had inherited many of papa's qualities.

Helmer.   And I would not wish you to be anything but just what you are, my sweet little skylark. But, do you know, it strikes me that you are looking rather—what shall I say—rather uneasy to-day?

Nora.   Do I?

Helmer.   You do, really. Look straight at me.

Nora (*looks at him*).   Well?

Helmer (*wagging his finger at her*).   Hasn't Miss Sweet-Tooth been breaking rules in town to-day?

Nora.   No; what makes you think that?

Helmer.   Hasn't she paid a visit to the confectioner's?

Nora.   No, I assure you, Torvald——

Helmer.   Not been nibbling sweets?

Nora.   No, certainly not.

Helmer.   Not even taken a bite at a macaroon or two?

Nora.   No, Torvald, I assure you really——

Helmer.   There, there, of course I was only joking.

Nora (*going to the table on the right*).   I should not think of going against your wishes.

Helmer.   No, I am sure of that! Besides, you gave me your word—— (*Going up to her.*) Keep your little Christmas secrets to yourself, my darling. They will all be revealed to-night when the Christmas tree is lit, no doubt.

Nora.   Did you remember to invite Doctor Rank?

Helmer.   No. But there is no need; as a matter of course he will come to dinner with us. However, I will ask him, when he comes in this morning. I have ordered some good wine. Nora, you can't think how I am looking forward to this evening.

Nora.   So am I! And how the children will enjoy themselves, Torvald!

Helmer.   It is splendid to feel that one has a perfectly safe appointment, and a big enough income. It's delightful to think of, isn't it?

Nora.   It's wonderful!

Helmer.   Do you remember last Christmas? For a full three weeks before-hand you shut yourself up every evening till long after midnight, making ornaments for the Christmas tree and all the other fine things that were to be a surprise to us. It was the dullest three weeks I ever spent!

Nora.   I didn't find it dull.

Helmer (*smiling*).   But there was precious little result, Nora.

Nora.   Oh, you shouldn't tease me about that again. How could I help the cat's going in and tearing everything to pieces?

Helmer.   Of course you couldn't, poor little girl. You had the best of intentions to please us all, and that's the main thing. But it is a good thing that our hard times are over.

Nora.   Yes, it is really wonderful.

Helmer.   This time I needn't sit here and be dull all alone, and you needn't ruin your dear eyes and your pretty little hands——

Nora *(clapping her hands).*   No, Torvald, I needn't any longer, need I! It's wonderfully lovely to hear you say so! *(Taking his arm.)* Now I will tell you how I have been thinking we ought to arrange things, Torvald. As soon as Christmas is over—— *(A bell rings in the hall.)* There's the bell. *(She tidies the room a little.)* There's someone at the door. What a nuisance!

Helmer.   If it is a caller, remember I am not at home.

Maid *(in the doorway).*   A lady to see you, ma'am,—a stranger.

Nora.   Ask her to come in.

Maid *(to Helmer).*   The doctor came at the same time, sir.

Helmer.   Did he go straight into my room?

Maid.   Yes, sir.

[Helmer goes into his room. The Maid ushers in Mrs. Linde, who is in traveling dress, and shuts the door.]

Mrs. Linde   *(in a dejected and timid voice).* How do you do, Nora?

Nora *(doubtfully).*   How do you do——

Mrs. Linde.   You don't recognise me, I suppose.

Nora.   No, I don't know—yes, to be sure, I seem to—— *(Suddenly.)* Yes! Christine! Is it really you?

Mrs. Linde.   Yes, it is I.

Nora.   Christine! To think of my not recognising you! And yet how could I—— *(In a gentle voice.)* How you have altered, Christine!

Mrs. Linde.   Yes, I have indeed. In nine, ten long years——

Nora.   Is it so long since we met? I suppose it is. The last eight years have been a happy time for me, I can tell you. And so now you have come into the town, and have taken this long journey in winter—that was plucky of you.

Mrs. Linde.   I arrived by steamer this morning.

Nora.   To have some fun at Christmas-time, of course. How delightful! We will have such fun together! But take off your things. You are not cold, I hope. *(Helps her.)* Now we will sit down by the stove, and be cosy. No, take this arm-chair; I will sit here in the rocking-chair. *(Takes her hands.)* Now you look like your old self again; it was only the first moment—— You are a little paler, Christine, and perhaps a little thinner.

Mrs. Linde.   And much, much older, Nora.

Nora.   Perhaps a little older; very, very little; certainly not much. *(Stops suddenly and speaks seriously.)* What a thoughtless creature I am, chattering away like this. My poor, dear Christine, do forgive me.

Mrs. Linde.   What do you mean, Nora?

Nora *(gently)*.   Poor Christine, you are a widow.

Mrs. Linde.   Yes; it is three years ago now.

Nora.   Yes, I knew; I saw it in the papers. I assure you, Christine, I meant ever so often to write to you at the time, but I always put it off and something always prevented me.

Mrs. Linde.   I quite understand, dear.

Nora.   It was very bad of me, Christine. Poor thing, how you must have suffered. And he left you nothing?

Mrs. Linde.   No.

Nora.   And no children?

Mrs. Linde.   No.

Nora.   Nothing at all, then?

Mrs. Linde.   Not even any sorrow or grief to live upon.

Nora *(looking incredulously at her)*.   But, Christine, is that possible?

Mrs. Linde *(smiles sadly and strokes her hair)*.   It sometimes happens, Nora.

Nora.   So you are quite alone. How dreadfully sad that must be. I have three lovely children. You can't see them just now, for they are out with their nurse. But now you must tell me all about it.

Mrs. Linde.   No, no; I want to hear you.

Nora.   No, you must begin. I mustn't be selfish to-day, to-day I must only think of your affairs. But there is one thing I must tell you. Do you know we have just had a great piece of good luck?

Mrs. Linde.   No, what is it?

Nora.   Just fancy, my husband has been made manager of the Bank!

Mrs. Linde.   Your husband? What good luck!

Nora.   Yes, tremendous! A barrister's profession is such an uncertain thing, especially if he won't undertake unsavoury cases; and naturally Torvald has never been willing to do that, and I quite agree with him. You may imagine how pleased we are! He is to take up his work in the Bank at the New Year, and then he will have a big salary and lots of commissions. For the future we can live quite differently—we can do just as we like. I feel so relieved and so happy, Christine! It will be splendid to have heaps of money and not need to have any anxiety, won't it?

Mrs. Linde.   Yes, anyhow I think it would be delightful to have what one needs.

Nora.   No, not only what one needs, but heaps and heaps of money.

Mrs. Linde *(smiling)*.   Nora, Nora, haven't you learnt sense yet? In our school-days you were a great spendthrift.

Nora *(laughing)*.   Yes, that is what Torvald says now *(Wags her finger at her.)* But "Nora, Nora" is not so silly as you think. We have not been in a position for me to waste money. We have both had to work.

Mrs. Linde.   You too?

Nora.   Yes; odds and ends, needlework, crochet-work, embroidery, and that kind of thing. *(Dropping her voice.)* And other things as well. You know Torvald left his office when we were married? There was no prospect of promotion there, and he had to try and earn more than before. But during the first year he overworked himself dreadfully. You see, he had to make money every way he could, and he worked early and late; but he couldn't stand it, and fell dreadfully ill, and the doctors said it was necessary for him to go south.

Mrs. Linde. You spent a whole year in Italy, didn't you?

Nora. Yes. It was no easy matter to get away, I can tell you. It was just after Ivar was born; but naturally we had to go. It was a wonderfully beautiful journey, and it saved Torvald's life. But it cost a tremendous lot of money, Christine.

Mrs. Linde. So I should think.

Nora. It cost about two hundred and fifty pounds. That's a lot, isn't it?

Mrs. Linde. Yes, and in emergencies like that it is lucky to have the money.

Nora. I ought to tell you that we had it from papa.

Mrs. Linde. Oh, I see. It was just about that time that he died, wasn't it?

Nora. Yes; and, just think of it, I couldn't go and nurse him. I was expecting little Ivar's birth every day and I had my poor sick Torvald to look after. My dear, kind father—I never saw him again, Christine. That was the saddest time I have known since our marriage.

Mrs. Linde. And your husband came back quite well?

Nora. As sound as a bell!

Mrs. Linde. But—the doctor?

Nora. What doctor?

Mrs. Linde. I thought your maid said the gentleman who arrived here just as I did was the doctor?

Nora. Yes, that was Doctor Rank, but he doesn't come here professionally. He is our greatest friend, and comes in at least once every day. No, Torvald has not had an hour's illness since then, and our children are strong and healthy and so am I. *(Jumps up and claps her hands.)* Christine! Christine! it's good to be alive and happy!—— But how horrid of me; I am talking of nothing but my own affairs. *(Sits on a stool near her, and rests her arms on her knees.)* You mustn't be angry with me. Tell me, is it really true that you did not love your husband? Why did you marry him?

Mrs. Linde. My mother was alive then, and was bedridden and helpless, and I had to provide for my two younger brothers; so I did not think I was justified in refusing his offer.

Nora. No, perhaps you were quite right. He was rich at that time, then?

Mrs. Linde. I believe he was quite well off. But his business was a precarious one; and, when he died, it all went to pieces and there was nothing left.

Nora. And then?——

Mrs. Linde. Well, I had to turn my hand to anything I could find—first a small shop, then a small school, and so on. The last three years have seemed like one long working-day, with no rest. Now it is at an end, Nora. My poor mother needs me no more, for she is gone; and the boys do not need me either; they have got situations and can shift for themselves.

Nora.   What a relief you must feel it——

Mrs. Linde.   No, indeed; I only feel my life unspeakably empty. No one to live for any more. (*Gets up restlessly.*) That was why I could not stand the life in my little backwater any longer. I hope it may be easier here to find something which will busy me and occupy my thoughts. If only I could have the good luck to get some regular work—office work of some kind——

Nora.   But, Christine, that is so frightfully tiring, and you look tired out now. You had far better go away to some watering-place.

Mrs. Linde (*walking to the window*).   I have no father to give me money for a journey, Nora.

Nora (*rising*).   Oh, don't be angry with me.

Mrs. Linde (*going up to her*).   It is you that must not be angry with me, dear. The worst of a position like mine is that it makes one so bitter. No one to work for, and yet obliged to be always on the look-out for chances. One must live, and so one becomes selfish. When you told me of the happy turn your fortunes have taken—you will hardly believe it—I was delighted not so much on your account as on my own.

Nora.   How do you mean?—Oh, I understand. You mean that perhaps Torvald could get you something to do.

Mrs. Linde.   Yes, that was what I was thinking of.

Nora.   He must, Christine. Just leave it to me; I will broach the subject very ، cleverly—I will think of something that will please him very much. It will make me so happy to be of some use to you.

Mrs. Linde.   How kind you are, Nora, to be so anxious to help me! It is doubly kind in you, for you know so little of the burdens and troubles of life.

Nora.   I——? I know so little of them?

Mrs. Linde (*smiling*).   My dear! Small household cares and that sort of thing!—You are a child, Nora.

Nora (*tosses her head and crosses the stage.*)   You ought not to be so superior.

Mrs. Linde.   No?

Nora.   You are just like the others. They all think that I am incapable of anything really serious——

Mrs. Linde.   Come, come——

Nora.   —that I have gone through nothing in this world of cares.

Mrs. Linde.   But, my dear Nora, you have just told me all your troubles.

Nora.   Pooh!—those were trifles. (*Lowering her voice.*) I have not told you the important thing.

Mrs. Linde.   The important thing? What do you mean?

Nora.   You look down upon me altogether, Christine—but you ought not to. You are proud, aren't you, of having worked so hard and so long for your mother?

Mrs. Linde.   Indeed, I don't look down on any one. But it is true that I am both proud and glad to think that I was privileged to make the end of my mother's life almost free from care.

Nora.   And you are proud to think of what you have done for your brothers.

Mrs. Linde. I think I have the right to be.

Nora. I think so, too. But now, listen to this; I too have something to be proud and glad of.

Mrs. Linde. I have no doubt you have. But what do you refer to?

Nora. Speak low. Suppose Torvald were to hear! He mustn't on any account—no one in the world must know, Christine, except you.

Mrs. Linde. But what is it?

Nora. Come here. *(Pulls her down on the sofa beside her.)* Now I will show you that I too have something to be proud and glad of. It was I who saved Torvald's life.

Mrs. Linde. "Saved"? How?

Nora. I told you about our trip to Italy. Torvald would never have recovered if he had not gone there——

Mrs. Linde. Yes, but your father gave you the necessary funds.

Nora *(smiling).* Yes, that is what Torvald and all the others think, but——

Mrs. Linde. But——

Nora. Papa didn't give us a shilling. It was I who procured the money.

Mrs. Linde. You? All that large sum?

Nora. Two hundred and fifty pounds. What do you think of that?

Mrs. Linde. But, Nora, how could you possibly do it? Did you win a prize in the Lottery?

Nora *(contemptuously).* In the Lottery? There would have been no credit in that.

Mrs. Linde. But where did you get it from, then?

Nora. *(humming and smiling with an air of mystery).* Hm, hm! Aha!

Mrs. Linde. Because you couldn't have borrowed it.

Nora. Couldn't I? Why not?

Mrs. Linde. No, a wife cannot borrow without her husband's consent.

Nora *(tossing her head).* Oh, if it is a wife who has any head for business—a wife who has the wit to be a little bit clever——

Mrs. Linde. I don't understand it at all, Nora.

Nora. There is no need you should. I never said I had borrowed the money. I may have got it some other way. *(Lies back on the sofa.)* Perhaps I got it from some other admirer. When anyone is as attractive as I am——

Mrs. Linde. You are a mad creature.

Nora. Now, you know you're full of curiosity, Christine.

Mrs. Linde. Listen to me, Nora dear. Haven't you been a little bit imprudent?

Nora *(sits up straight).* Is it imprudent to save your husband's life?

Mrs. Linde. It seems to me imprudent, without his knowledge, to——

Nora. But it was absolutely necessary that he should not know! My goodness, can't you understand that? It was necessary he should have no idea what a dangerous condition he was in. It was to me that the doctors came and said that his life was in danger, and that the only thing to save him was to live in the south. Do you suppose I didn't try, first of all, to get what I wanted as if it were for myself? I told him how much I should love to travel abroad like other young wives; I tried tears and entreaties with him; I told him that he ought to remember the condition I was in, and that he ought to be kind and indulgent to me; I even hinted that he might raise a loan. That nearly made him angry, Christine. He said I was thoughtless, and that it was his duty as my husband not to indulge me in my whims and caprices—as I believe he called them. Very well I thought, you must be saved—and that was how I came to devise a way out of the difficulty——

Mrs. Linde. And did your husband never get to know from your father that the money had not come from him?

Nora. No, never. Papa died just at that time. I had meant to let him into the secret and beg him never to reveal it. But he was so ill then—alas, there never was any need to tell him.

Mrs. Linde. And since then have you never told your secret to your husband?

Nora. Good Heavens, no! How could you think so? A man who has such strong opinions about these things! And besides, how painful and humiliating it would be for Torvald, with his manly independence, to know that he owed me anything! It would upset our mutual relations altogether; our beautiful happy home would no longer be what it is now.

Mrs. Linde. Do you mean never to tell him about it?

Nora (*meditatively, and with a half smile*). Yes—some day, perhaps, after many years, when I am no longer as nice-looking as I am now. Don't laugh at me! I mean, of course, when Torvald is no longer as devoted to me as he is now; when my dancing and dressing-up and reciting have palled on him; then it may be a good thing to have something in reserve—— (*Breaking off.*) What nonsense! That time will never come. Now, what do you think of my great secret, Christine? Do you still think I am of no use? I can tell you, too, that this affair has caused me a lot of worry. It has been by no means easy for me to meet my engagements punctually. I may tell you that there is something that is called, in business, quarterly interest, and another thing called payment in instalments, and it is always so dreadfully difficult to manage them. I have had to save a little here and there, where I could, you understand. I have not been able to put aside much from my house-keeping money, for Torvald must have a good table. I couldn't let my children be shabbily dressed; I have felt obliged to use up all he gave me for them, the sweet little darlings!

Mrs. Linde. So it has all had to come out of your own necessaries of life, poor Nora?

Nora. Of course. Besides, I was the one responsible for it. Whenever Torvald has given me money for new dresses and such things, I have never spent more than half of it; I have always bought the simplest and cheapest things. Thank Heaven, any clothes look well on me, and so Torvald has never noticed it. But it was often very hard on me, Christine—because it is delightful to be really well dressed, isn't it?

Mrs. Linde. Quite so.

Nora. Well, then I have found other ways of earning money. Last winter I was lucky enough to get a lot of copying to do; so I locked myself up and sat writing every evening until quite late at night. Many a time I was desperately tired; but all the same it was a tremendous pleasure to sit there working and earning money. It was like being a man.

Mrs. Linde. How much have you been able to pay off in that way?

Nora. I can't tell you exactly. You see, it is very difficult to keep an account of a business matter of that kind. I only know that I have paid every penny that I could scrape together. Many a time I was at my wits' end. (*Smiles.*) Then I used to sit here and imagine that a rich old gentleman had fallen in love with me——

Mrs. Linde. What! Who was it?

Nora. Be quiet!—that he had died; and that when his will was opened it contained, written in big letters, the instruction: "The lovely Mrs. Nora Helmer is to have all I possess paid over to her at once in cash."

Mrs. Linde. But, my dear Nora—who could the man be?

Nora. Good gracious, can't you understand? There was no old gentleman at all; it was only something that I used to sit here and imagine, when I couldn't think of any way of procuring money. But it's all the same now; the tiresome old person can stay where he is, as far as I am concerned; I don't care about him or his will either, for I am free from care now. (*Jumps up.*) My goodness, it's delightful to think of, Christine! Free from care! To be able to be free from care, quite free from care; to be able to play and romp with the children; to be able to keep the house beautifully and have everything just as Torvald likes it! And, think of it, soon the spring will come and the big blue sky! Perhaps we shall be able to take a little trip—perhaps I shall see the sea again! Oh, it's a wonderful thing to be alive and be happy. (*A bell is heard in the hall.*)

Mrs. Linde (*rising*). There is the bell; perhaps I had better go.

Nora. No, don't go; no one will come in here; it is sure to be for Torvald.

Servant (*at the hall door*). Excuse me, ma'am—there is a gentleman to see the master, and as the doctor is with him——

Nora. Who is it?

Krogstad (*at the door*). It is I, Mrs. Helmer. (*Mrs. Linde starts, trembles, and turns to the window.*)

Nora (*takes a step towards him, and speaks in a strained, low voice*). You? What is it? What do you want to see my husband about?

Krogstad. Bank business—in a way. I have a small post in the Bank, and I hear your husband is to be our chief now——

Nora. Then it is——

Krogstad. Nothing but dry business matters, Mrs. Helmer; absolutely nothing else.

Nora. Be so good as to go into the study, then. (*She bows indifferently to him and shuts the door into the hall; then comes back and makes up the fire in the stove.*)

Mrs. Linde.   Nora—who was that man?

Nora.   A lawyer, of the name of Krogstad.

Mrs. Linde.   Then it really was he.

Nora.   Do you know the man?

Mrs. Linde.   I used to—many years ago. At one time he was a solicitor's clerk in our town.

Nora.   Yes, he was.

Mrs. Linde.   He is greatly altered.

Nora.   He made a very unhappy marriage.

Mrs. Linde.   He is a widower now, isn't he?

Nora.   With several children. There now, it is burning up.

[Shuts the door of the stove and moves the rocking-chair aside.]

Mrs. Linde.   They say he carries on various kinds of business.

Nora.   Really! Perhaps he does; I don't know anything about it. But don't let us think of business; it is so tiresome.

Doctor Rank (*comes out of Helmer's study. Before he shuts the door he calls to him*).   No, my dear fellow, I won't disturb you; I would rather go into your wife for a little while. (*Shuts the door and sees Mrs. Linde.*) I beg your pardon; I am afraid I am disturbing you too.

Nora.   No, not at all. (*Introducing him.*) Doctor Rank, Mrs. Linde.

Rank.   I have often heard Mrs. Linde's name mentioned here. I think I passed you on the stairs when I arrived, Mrs. Linde?

Mrs. Linde.   Yes, I go up very slowly; I can't manage stairs well.

Rank.   Ah! some slight internal weakness?

Mrs. Linde.   No, the fact is I have been overworking myself.

Rank.   Nothing more than that? Then I suppose you have come to town to amuse yourself with our entertainments?

Mrs. Linde.   I have come to look for work.

Rank.   Is that a good cure for overwork?

Mrs. Linde.   One must live, Doctor Rank.

Rank.   Yes, the general opinion seems to be that it is necessary.

Nora.   Look here, Doctor Rank—you know you want to live.

Rank.   Certainly. However wretched I may feel, I want to prolong the agony as long as possible. All my patients are like that. And so are those who are morally diseased; one of them, and a bad case too, is at this very moment with Helmer——

Mrs. Linde (*sadly*).   Ah!

Nora.   Whom do you mean?

Rank.   A lawyer of the name of Krogstad, a fellow you don't know at all. He suffers from a diseased moral character, Mrs. Helmer; but even he began talking of its being highly important that he should live.

Nora.   Did he? What did he want to speak to Torvald about?

Rank.   I have no idea; I only heard that is was something about the Bank.

Nora. I didn't know this—what's his name—Krogstad had anything to do with the Bank.

Rank. Yes, he has some sort of appointment there. *(To Mrs. Linde.)* I don't know whether you find also in your part of the world that there are certain people who go zealously snuffing about to smell out moral corruption, and, as soon as they have found some, put the person concerned into some lucrative position where they can keep their eye on him. Healthy natures are left out in the cold.

Mrs. Linde. Still I think the sick are those who most need taking care of.

Rank *(shrugging his shoulders)*. Yes, there you are. That is the sentiment that is turning Society into a sickhouse.

[Nora, who has been absorbed in her thoughts, breaks out into smothered laughter and claps her hands.]

Rank. Why do you laugh at that? Have you any notion what Society really is?

Nora. What do I care about tiresome Society? I am laughing at something quite different, something extremely amusing. Tell me, Doctor Rank, are all the people who are employed in the Bank dependent on Torvald now?

Rank. Is that what you find so extremely amusing?

Nora *(smiling and humming)*. That's my affair! *(Walking about the room.)* It's perfectly glorious to think that we have—that Torvald has so much power over so many people. *(Takes the packet from her pocket.)* Doctor Rank, what do you say to a macaroon?

Rank. What, macaroons? I thought they were forbidden here.

Nora. Yes, but these are some Christine gave me.

Mrs. Linde. What! I?—

Nora. Oh, well, don't be alarmed! You couldn't know that Torvald had forbidden them. I must tell you that he is afraid they will spoil my teeth. But, bah!—once in a way—— That's so, isn't it, Doctor Rank? By your leave? *(Puts a macaroon into his mouth.)* You must have one too, Christine. And I shall have one, just a little one—or at most two. *(Walking about.)* I am tremendously happy. There is just one thing in the world now that I should dearly love to do.

Rank. Well, what is that?

Nora. It's something I should dearly love to say, if Torvald could hear me.

Rank. Well, why can't you say it?

Nora. No, I daren't; it's so shocking.

Mrs. Linde. Shocking?

Rank. Well, I should not advise you to say it. Still, with us you might. What is it you would so much like to say if Torvald could hear you?

Nora. I should just love to say—Well, I'm damned!

Rank. Are you mad?

Mrs. Linde. Nora, dear——!

Rank.   Say it, here he is!
Nora (*hiding the packet*).   Hush! Hush! Hush!

[*Helmer comes out of his room, with his coat over his arm and his hat in his hand.*]

Nora.   Well, Torvald dear, have you got rid of him?
Helmer.   Yes, he has just gone.
Nora.   Let me introduce you—this is Christine, who has come to town.
Helmer.   Christine——? Excuse me, but I don't know——
Nora.   Mrs. Linde, dear; Christine Linde.
Helmer.   Of course. A school friend of my wife's, I presume?
Mrs. Linde.   Yes, we have known each other since then.
Nora.   And just think, she has taken a long journey in order to see you.
Helmer.   What do you mean?
Mrs. Linde.   No, really, I——
Nora.   Christine is tremendously clever at book-keeping, and she is frightfully anxious to work under some clever man, so as to perfect herself——
Helmer.   Very sensible, Mrs. Linde.
Nora.   And when she heard you had been appointed manager of the Bank— the news was telegraphed, you know—she travelled here as quick as she could, Torvald, I am sure you will be able to do something for Christine, for my sake, won't you?
Helmer.   Well, it is not altogether impossible. I presume you are a widow, Mrs. Linde?
Mrs. Linde.   Yes.
Helmer.   And have had some experience of book-keeping?
Mrs. Linde.   Yes, a fair amount.
Helmer.   Ah! well, it's very likely I may be able to find something for you——
Nora (*clapping her hands*).   What did I tell you? What did I tell you?
Helmer.   You have just come at a fortunate moment, Mrs. Linde.
Mrs. Linde.   How am I to thank you?
Helmer.   There is no need. (*Puts on his coat.*) But to-day you must excuse me——
Rank.   Wait a minute; I will come with you.

[*Brings his fur coat from the hall and warms it at the fire.*]

Nora.   Don't be long away, Torvald dear.
Helmer.   About an hour, not more.
Nora.   Are you going too, Christine?
Mrs. Linde (*putting on her cloak*).   Yes, I must go and look for a room.
Helmer.   Oh, well then, we can walk down the street together.
Nora (*helping her*).   What a pity it is we are so short of space here; I am afraid it is impossible for us——

Mrs. Linde.   Please don't think of it! Good-bye, Nora dear, and many thanks.

Nora.   Good-bye for the present. Of course you will come back this evening. And you too, Dr. Rank. What do you say? If you are well enough? Oh, you must be! Wrap yourself up well.

[*They go to the door all talking together. Children's voices are heard on the staircase.*]

Nora.   There they are. There they are! (*She runs to open the door. The Nurse comes in with the children.*) Come in! Come in! (*Stoops and kisses them.*) Oh, you sweet blessings! Look at them, Christine! Aren't they darlings.?

Rank.   Don't let us stand here in the draught.

Helmer.   Come along, Mrs. Linde; the place will only be bearable for a mother now!

[*Rank, Helmer and Mrs. Linde go downstairs. The Nurse comes forward with the children; Nora shuts the hall door.*]

Nora.   How fresh and well you look! Such red cheeks!—like apples and roses. (*The children all talk at once while she speaks to them.*) Have you had great fun? That's splendid! What, you pulled both Emmy and Bob along on the sledge?—both at once?—that *was* good. You are a clever boy, Ivar. Let me take her for a little, Anne. My sweet little baby doll! (*Takes the baby from the Maid and dances it up and down.*) Yes, yes, mother will dance with Bob too. What! Have you been snowballing? I wish I had been there too! No, no, I will take their things off, Anne; please let me do it, it is such fun. Go in now, you look half frozen. There is some hot coffee for you on the stove.

[*The Nurse goes into the room on the left. Nora takes off the children's things and throws them about, while they all talk to her at once.*]

Nora.   Really! Did a big dog run after you? But it didn't bite you? No, dogs don't bite nice little dolly children. You mustn't look at the parcels, Ivar. What are they? Ah, I daresay you would like to know. No, no—it's something nasty! Come, let us have a game! What shall we play at? Hide and Seek? Yes, we'll play Hide and Seek. Bob shall hide first. Must I hide? Very well, I'll hide first.

[*She and the children laugh and shout, and romp in and out of the room; at last Nora hides under the table, the children rush in and look for her, but do not see her; they hear her smothered laughter, run to the table, lift up the cloth and find her. Shouts of laughter. She crawls forward and pretends to frighten them. Fresh laughter. Meanwhile there has been a knock at the hall door, but none of them has noticed it. The door is half opened, and Krogstad appears. He waits a little; the game goes on.*]

Krogstad. Excuse me, Mrs. Helmer.

Nora *(with a stifled cry, turns round and gets up on to her knees).*   Ah! what do you want?

Krogstad. Excuse me, the outer door was ajar; I suppose someone forgot to shut it.

Nora *(rising).*   My husband is out, Mr. Krogstad.

Krogstad. I know that.

Nora. What do you want here, then?

Krogstad. A word with you.

Nora. With me?— *(to the children, gently.)* Go in to nurse. What? No, the strange man won't do mother any harm. When he has gone we will have another game. *(She takes the children into the room on the left, and shuts the door after them.)* You want to speak to me?

Krogstad. Yes, I do.

Nora. To-day? It is not the first of the month yet.

Krogstad. No, it is Christmas Eve, and it will depend on yourself what sort of a Christmas you will spend.

Nora. What do you want? To-day it is absolutely impossible for me——

Krogstad. We won't talk about that till later on. This is something different. I presume you can give me a moment?

Nora. Yes—yes, I can—although——

Krogstad. Good. I was in Olsen's Restaurant and saw your husband going down the street——

Nora. Yes?

Krogstad. With a lady.

Nora. What then?

Krogstad. May I make so bold as to ask if it was a Mrs. Linde?

Nora. It was.

Krogstad. Just arrived in town?

Nora. Yes, to-day.

Krogstad. She is a great friend of yours, isn't she?

Nora. She is. But I don't see——

Krogstad. I knew her too, once upon a time.

Nora. I am aware of that.

Krogstad. Are you? So you know all about it; I thought as much. Then I can ask you, without beating about the bush—is Mrs. Linde to have an appointment in the Bank?

Nora. What right have you to question me, Mr. Krogstad?—You, one of my husband's subordinates! But since you ask, you shall know. Yes, Mrs. Linde *is* to have an appointment. And it was I who pleaded her cause, Mr. Krogstad, let me tell you that.

Krogstad. I was right in what I thought, then.

Nora *(walking up and down the stage).*   Sometimes one has a tiny little bit of influence, I should hope. Because one is a woman, it does not necessarily follow that——. When anyone is in a subordinate position, Mr. Krog-

stad, they should really be careful to avoid offending anyone who—
who——

Krogstad. Who has influence?

Nora. Exactly.

Krogstad (*changing his tone*). Mrs. Helmer, you will be so good as to use your
influence on my behalf.

Nora. What? What do you mean?

Krogstad. You will be so kind as to see that I am allowed to keep my subordinate position in the Bank.

Nora. What do you mean by that? Who proposes to take your post away
from you?

Krogstad. Oh, there is no necessity to keep up the pretence of ignorance. I
can quite understand that your friend is not very anxious to expose herself
to the chance of rubbing shoulders with me; and I quite understand, too,
whom I have to thank for being turned off.

Nora. But I assure you——

Krogstad. Very likely; but, to come to the point, the time has come when I
should advise you to use your influence to prevent that.

Nora. But, Mr. Krogstad, I *have* no influence.

Krogstad. Haven't you? I thought you said yourself just now——

Nora. Naturally I did not mean you to put that construction on it. I! What
should make you think I have any influence of that kind with my husband?

Krogstad. Oh, I have known your husband from our student days. I don't
suppose he is any more unassailable than other husbands.

Nora. If you speak slightingly of my husband, I shall turn you out of the
house.

Krogstad. You are bold, Mrs. Helmer.

Nora. I am not afraid of you any longer. As soon as the New Year comes, I
shall in a very short time be free of the whole thing.

Krogstad (*controlling himself*). Listen to me, Mrs. Helmer. If necessary, I am
prepared to fight for my small post in the Bank as if I were fighting for my
life.

Nora. So it seems.

Krogstad. It is not only for the sake of the money; indeed, that weighs least
with me in the matter. There is another reason—well, I may as well tell you.
My position is this. I daresay you know, like everybody else, that once, many
years ago, I was guilty of an indiscretion.

Nora. I think I have heard something of the kind.

Krogstad. The matter never came into court; but every way seemed to be
closed to me after that. So I took to the business that you know of. I had
to do something; and, honestly, I don't think I've been one of the worst. But
now I must cut myself free from all that. My sons are growing up; for their
sake I must try and win back as much respect as I can in the town. This post
in the Bank was like the first step up for me—and now your husband is
going to kick me downstairs again into the mud.

Nora.   But you must believe me, Mr. Krogstad; it is not in my power to help you at all.

Krogstad.   Then it is because you haven't the will; but I have means to compel you.

Nora.   You don't mean that you will tell my husband that I owe you money?

Krogstad.   Hm!—suppose I were to tell him?

Nora.   It would be perfectly infamous of you. *(Sobbing.)* To think of his learning my secret, which has been my joy and pride, in such an ugly, clumsy way—that he should learn it from you! And it would put me in a horribly disagreeable position——

Krogstad.   Only disagreeable?

Nora *(impetuously)*.   Well, do it, then!—and it will be the worse for you. My husband will see for himself what a blackguard you are, and you certainly won't keep your post then.

Krogstad.   I asked you if it was only a disagreeable scene at home that you were afraid of?

Nora.   If my husband does get to know of it, of course he will at once pay you what is still owing, and we shall have nothing more to do with you.

Krogstad *(coming a step nearer)*.   Listen to me, Mrs. Helmer. Either you have a very bad memory or you know very little of business. I shall be obliged to remind you of a few details.

Nora.   What do you mean?

Krogstad.   When your husband was ill, you came to me to borrow two hundred and fifty pounds.

Nora.   I didn't know anyone else to go to.

Krogstad.   I promised to get you that amount——

Nora.   Yes, and you did so.

Krogstad.   I promised to get you that amount, on certain conditions. Your mind was so taken up with your husband's illness, and you were so anxious to get the money for your journey, that you seem to have paid no attention to the conditions of our bargain. Therefore it will not be amiss if I remind you of them. Now, I promised to get the money on the security of a bond which I signed.

Nora.   Yes, and which I signed.

Krogstad.   Good. But below your signature there were a few lines constituting your father a surety for the money; those lines your father should have signed.

Nora.   Should? He did sign them.

Krogstad.   I had left the date blank; that is to say your father should himself have inserted the date on which he signed the paper. Do you remember that?

Nora.   Yes, I think I remember——

Krogstad.   Then I gave you the bond to send by post to your father. Is that not so?

Nora.   Yes.

Krogstad. And you naturally did so at once, because five or six days afterwards you brought me the bond with your father's signature. And then I gave you the money.

Nora. Well, haven't I been paying it off regularly?

Krogstad. Fairly so, yes. But—to come back to the matter in hand—that must have been a very trying time for you, Mrs. Helmer?

Nora. It was, indeed.

Krogstad. Your father was very ill, wasn't he?

Nora. He was very near his end.

Krogstad. And died soon afterwards?

Nora. Yes.

Krogstad. Tell me, Mrs. Helmer, can you by any chance remember what day your father died?—on what day of the month, I mean.

Nora. Papa died on the 29th of September.

Krogstad. That is correct; I have ascertained it for myself. And, as that is so, there is a discrepancy *(taking a paper from his pocket)* which I cannot account for.

Nora. What discrepancy? I don't know——

Krogstad. The discrepancy consists, Mrs. Helmer, in the fact that your father signed this bond three days after his death.

Nora. What do you mean? I don't understand——

Krogstad. Your father died on the 29th of September. But, look here; your father has dated his signature the 2nd of October. It is a discrepancy, isn't it? *(Nora is silent.)* Can you explain it to me? *(Nora is still silent.)* It is a remarkable thing, too, that the words "2nd of October," as well as the year, are not written in your father's handwriting but in one that I think I know. Well, of course it can be explained; your father may have forgotten to date his signature, and someone else may have dated it haphazard before they knew of his death. There is no harm in that. It all depends on the signature of the name; and *that* is genuine, I suppose, Mrs. Helmer? It was your father himself who signed his name here?

Nora *(after a short pause, throws her head up and looks defiantly at him).* No, it was not. It was I that wrote papa's name.

Krogstad. Are you aware that is a dangerous confession?

Nora. In what way? You shall have your money soon.

Krogstad. Let me ask you a question; why did you not send the paper to your father?

Nora. It was impossible; papa was so ill. If I had asked him for his signature, I should have had to tell him what the money was to be used for; and when he was so ill himself I couldn't tell him that my husband's life was in danger—it was impossible.

Krogstad. It would have been better for you if you had given up your trip abroad.

Nora. No, that was impossible. That trip was to save my husband's life; I couldn't give that up.

Krogstad.   But did it never occur to you that you were committing a fraud on me?

Nora.   I couldn't take that into account; I didn't trouble myself about you at all. I couldn't bear you, because you put so many heartless difficulties in my way, although you knew what a dangerous condition my husband was in.

Krogstad.   Mrs. Helmer, you evidently do not realise clearly what it is that you have been guilty of. But I can assure you that my one false step, which lost me all my reputation, was nothing more or nothing worse than what you have done.

Nora.   You? Do you ask me to believe that you were brave enough to run a risk to save your wife's life?

Krogstad.   The law cares nothing about motives.

Nora.   Then it must be a very foolish law.

Krogstad.   Foolish or not, it is the law by which you will be judged, if I produce this paper in court.

Nora.   I don't believe it. Is a daughter not to be allowed to spare her dying father anxiety and care? Is a wife not to be allowed to save her husband's life? I don't know much about law; but I am certain that there must be laws permitting such things as that. Have you no knowledge of such laws—you who are a lawyer? You must be a very poor lawyer, Mr. Krogstad.

Krogstad.   Maybe. But matters of business—such business as you and I have had together—do you think I don't understand that? Very well. Do as you please. But let me tell you this—if I lose my position a second time, you shall lose yours with me.

[He bows, and goes out through the hall.]

Nora *(appears buried in thought for a short time, then tosses her head).*   Nonsense! Trying to frighten me like that—I am not so silly as he thinks. *(Begins to busy herself putting the children's things in order.)* And yet——? No, it's impossible! I did it for love's sake.

The Children *(in the doorway on the left).*   Mother, the stranger man has gone out through the gate.

Nora.   Yes, dears, I know. But don't tell anyone about the stranger man. Do you hear? Not even papa.

Children.   No, mother; but will you come and play again?

Nora.   No, no,—not now.

Children.   But, mother, you promised us.

Nora.   Yes, but I can't now. Run away in; I have such a lot to do. Run away in, my sweet little darlings. *(She gets them into the room by degrees and shuts the door on them; then sits down on the sofa, takes up a piece of needlework and sews a few stitches, but soon stops.)* No! *(Throws down the work, gets up, goes to the hall door and calls out.)* Helen! bring the tree in. *(Goes to the table on the left, opens a drawer, and stops again.)* No, no! it is quite impossible!

Maid *(coming in with the tree).*   Where shall I put it, ma'am?

Nora.   Here, in the middle of the floor.

Maid.   Shall I get you anything else?

Nora.   No, thank you. I have all I want.

[Exit Maid.]

Nora *(begins dressing the tree).*   A candle here—and flowers here——. The horrible man! It's all nonsense—there's nothing wrong. The tree shall be splendid! I will do everything I can think of to please you, Torvald!—I will sing for you, dance for you—*(Helmer comes in with some papers under his arm.)* Oh! are you back already?

Helmer.   Yes. Has anyone been here?

Nora.   Here? No.

Helmer.   That is strange. I saw Krogstad going out of the gate.

Nora.   Did you? Oh yes, I forgot, Krogstad was here for a moment.

Helmer.   Nora, I can see from your manner that he has been here begging you to say a good word for him.

Nora.   Yes.

Helmer.   And you were to appear to do it of your own accord; you were to conceal from me the fact of his having been here; didn't he beg that of you too?

Nora.   Yes, Torvald, but——

Helmer.   Nora, Nora, and you would be a party to that sort of thing? To have any talk with a man like that, and give him any sort of promise? And to tell me a lie into the bargain?

Nora.   A lie——?

Helmer.   Didn't you tell me no one had been here? *(Shakes his finger at her.)* My little song-bird must never do that again. A song-bird must have a clean beak to chirp with—no false notes! *(Puts his arm round her waist.)* That is so, isn't it? Yes, I am sure it is. *(Lets her go.)* We will say no more about it. *(Sits down by the stove.)* How warm and snug it is here!

[Turns over his papers.]

Nora   *(after a short pause, during which she busies herself with the Christmas tree).* Torvald!

Helmer.   Yes.

Nora.   I am looking forward tremendously to the fancy dress ball at the Stenborgs' the day after to-morrow.

Helmer.   And I am tremendously curious to see what you are going to surprise me with.

Nora.   It was very silly of me to want to do that.

Helmer.   What do you mean?

Nora.   I can't hit upon anything that will do; everything I think of seems so silly and insignificant.

Helmer.   Does my little Nora acknowledge that at last?

Nora   (*standing behind his chair with her arms on the back of it*). Are you very busy, Torvald?

Helmer.   Well——

Nora.   What are all those papers?

Helmer.   Bank business.

Nora.   Already?

Helmer.   I have got authority from the retiring manager to undertake the necessary changes in the staff and in the rearrangement of the work; and I must make use of the Christmas week for that, so as to have everything in order for the new year.

Nora.   Then that was why this poor Krogstad——

Helmer.   Hm!

Nora (*leans against the back of his chair and strokes his hair*).   If you hadn't been so busy I should have asked you a tremendously big favour, Torvald.

Helmer.   What is that? Tell me.

Nora.   There is no one has such good taste as you. And I do so want to look nice at the fancy-dress ball. Torvald, couldn't you take me in hand and decide what I shall go as, and what sort of a dress I shall wear?

Helmer.   Aha! so my obstinate little woman is obliged to get someone to come to her rescue?

Nora.   Yes, Torvald, I can't get along a bit without your help.

Helmer.   Very well, I will think it over, we shall manage to hit upon something.

Nora.   That *is* nice of you. (*Goes to the Christmas tree. A short pause.*) How pretty the red flowers look——. But, tell me, was it really something very bad that this Krogstad was guilty of?

Helmer.   He forged someone's name. Have you any idea what that means?

Nora.   Isn't it possible that he was driven to do it by necessity?

Helmer.   Yes; or, as in so many cases, by imprudence. I am not so heartless as to condemn a man altogether because of a single false step of that kind.

Nora.   No you wouldn't, would you, Torvald?

Helmer.   Many a man has been able to retrieve his character, if he has openly confessed his fault and taken his punishment.

Nora.   Punishment——?

Helmer.   But Krogstad did nothing of that sort; he got himself out of it by a cunning trick, and that is why he has gone under altogether.

Nora.   But do you think it would——?

Helmer.   Just think how a guilty man like that has to lie and play the hypocrite with everyone, how he has to wear a mask in the presence of those near and dear to him, even before his own wife and children. And about the children—that is the most terrible part of it all, Nora.

Nora.   How?

Helmer.   Because such an atmosphere of lies infects and poisons the whole life of a home. Each breath the children take in such a house is full of the germs of evil.

Nora (*coming nearer him*).   Are you sure of that?

Helmer.   My dear, I have often seen it in the course of my life as a lawyer. Almost everyone who has gone to the bad early in life has had a deceitful mother.

Nora.   Why do you only say—mother?

Helmer.   It seems most commonly to be the mother's influence, though naturally a bad father's would have the same result. Every lawyer is familiar with the fact. This Krogstad, now, has been persistently poisoning his own children with lies and dissimulation; that is why I say he has lost all moral character. *(Holds out his hands to her.)* That is why my sweet little Nora must promise me not to plead his cause. Give me your hand on it. Come, come, what is this? Give me your hand. There now, that's settled. I assure you it would be quite impossible for me to work with him; I literally feel physically ill when I am in the company of such people.

Nora *(takes her hand out of his and goes to the opposite side of the Christmas tree).*   How hot it is in here; and I have such a lot to do.

Helmer *(getting up and putting his papers in order).*   Yes, and I must try and read through some of these before dinner; and I must think about your costume, too. And it is just possible I may have something ready in gold paper to hang up on the tree. *(Puts his hand on her head.)* My precious little singing-bird!

[He goes into his room and shuts the door after him.]

Nora   *(after a pause, whispers).* No, no—it isn't true. It's impossible; it must be impossible.

[The Nurse opens the door on the left.]

Nurse.   The little ones are begging so hard to be allowed to come in to mamma.

Nora.   No, no, no! Don't let them come in to me! You stay with them, Anne.

Nurse.   Very well, ma'am.

[Shuts the door.]

Nora *(pale with terror).*   Deprave my little children? Poison my home? *(A short pause. Then she tosses her head.)* It's not true. It can't possibly be true.

Act II

THE SAME SCENE.   *The Christmas tree is in the corner by the piano, stripped of its ornaments and with burnt-down candle-ends on its dishevelled branches. Nora's cloak and hat are lying on the sofa. She is alone in the room, walking about uneasily. She stops by the sofa and takes up her cloak.*

Nora *(drops the cloak).*   Someone is coming now! *(Goes to the door and listens.)* No—it is no one. Of course, no one will come to-day, Christmas

Day—nor tomorrow either. But, perhaps—(*Opens the door and looks out*). No, nothing in the letter-box; it is quite empty. (*Comes forward.*) What rubbish! of course he can't be in earnest about it. Such a thing couldn't happen; it is impossible—I have three little children.

[*Enter the Nurse from the room on the left, carrying a big cardboard box.*]

Nurse. At last I have found the box with the fancy dress.

Nora. Thanks; put it on the table.

Nurse (*doing so*). But it is very much in want of mending.

Nora. I should like to tear it into a hundred thousand pieces.

Nurse. What an idea! It can easily be put in order—just a little patience.

Nora. Yes, I will go and get Mrs. Linde to come and help me with it.

Nurse. What, out again? In this horrible weather? You will catch cold, ma'am, and make yourself ill.

Nora. Well, worse than that might happen. How are the children?

Nurse. The poor little souls are playing with their Christmas presents, but——

Nora. Do they ask much for me?

Nurse. You see, they are so accustomed to have their mamma with them.

Nora. Yes, but, nurse, I shall not be able to be so much with them now as I was before.

Nurse. Oh well, young children easily get accustomed to anything.

Nora. Do you think so? Do you think they would forget their mother if she went away altogether?

Nurse. Good heavens!—went away altogether?

Nora. Nurse, I want you to tell me something I have often wondered about— how could you have the heart to put your own child out among strangers?

Nurse. I was obliged to, if I wanted to be little Nora's nurse.

Nora. Yes, but how could you be willing to do it?

Nurse. What, when I was going to get such a good place by it? A poor girl who has got into trouble should be glad to. Besides, that wicked man didn't do a single thing for me.

Nora. But I suppose your daughter has quite forgotten you.

Nurse. No, indeed she hasn't. She wrote to me when she was confirmed, and when she was married.

Nora (*putting her arms round her neck*). Dear old Anne, you were a good mother to me when I was little.

Nurse. Little Nora, poor dear, had no other mother but me.

Nora. And if my little ones had no other mother, I am sure you would—— What nonsense I am talking! (*Opens the box.*) Go in to them. Now I must——. You will see to-morrow how charming I shall look.

Nurse. I am sure there will be no one at the ball so charming as you, ma'am.

[*Goes into the room on the left.*]

Nora (*begins to unpack the box, but soon pushes it away from her*).   If only I dared go out. If only no one would come. If only I could be sure nothing would happen here in the meantime. Stuff and nonsense! No one will come. Only I mustn't think about it. I will brush my muff. What lovely, lovely gloves! Out of my thoughts, out of my thoughts! One, two, three, four, five, six—— (*Screams.*) Ah! there is someone coming——

[*Makes a movement towards the door, but stands irresolute. Enter Mrs. Linde from the hall, where she has taken off her cloak and hat.*]

Nora.   Oh, it's you, Christine. There is no one else out there, is there? How good of you to come!

Mrs. Linde.   I heard you were up asking for me.

Nora.   Yes, I was passing by. As a matter of fact, it is something you could help me with. Let us sit down here on the sofa. Look here. To-morrow evening there is to be a fancy-dress ball at the Stenborgs', who live above us; and Torvald wants me to go as a Neapolitan fisher-girl, and dance the Tarantella that I learnt at Capri.

Mrs. Linde.   I see; you are going to keep up the character.

Nora.   Yes, Torvald wants me to. Look, here is the dress; Torvald had it made for me there, but now it is all so torn, and I haven't any idea——

Mrs. Linde.   We will easily put that right. It is only some of the trimming come unsewn here and there. Needle and thread? Now then, that's all we want.

Nora.   It *is* nice of you.

Mrs. Linde (*sewing*).   So you are going to be dressed up to-morrow, Nora. I will tell you what—I shall come in for a moment and see you in your fine feathers. But I have completely forgotten to thank you for a delightful evening yesterday.

Nora (*gets up, and crosses the stage*).   Well I don't think yesterday was as pleasant as usual. You ought to have come to town a little earlier, Christine. Certainly Torvald does understand how to make a house dainty and attractive.

Mrs. Linde.   And so do you, it seems to me; you are not your father's daughter for nothing. But tell me, is Doctor Rank always as depressed as he was yesterday?

Nora.   No; yesterday it was very noticeable. I must tell you that he suffers from a very dangerous disease. He has consumption of the spine, poor creature. His father was a horrible man who committed all sorts of excesses; and that is why his son was sickly from childhood, do you understand?

Mrs. Linde (*dropping her sewing*).   But, my dearest Nora, how do you know anything about such things?

Nora (*walking about*).   Pooh! When you have three children, you get visits now and then from—from married women, who know something of medical matters, and they talk about one thing and another.

Mrs. Linde (*goes on sewing. A short silence*).   Does Doctor Rank come here every day?

Nora.   Every day regularly. He is Torvald's most intimate friend, and a great friend of mine too. He is just like one of the family.

Mrs. Linde.   But tell me this—is he perfectly sincere? I mean, isn't he the kind of man that is very anxious to make himself agreeable?

Nora.   Not in the least. What makes you think that?

Mrs. Linde.   When you introduced him to me yesterday, he declared he had often heard my name mentioned in this house; but afterwards I noticed that your husband hadn't the slightest idea who I was. So how could Doctor Rank——?

Nora.   That is quite right, Christine. Torvald is so absurdly fond of me that he wants me absolutely to himself, as he says. At first he used to seem almost jealous if I mentioned any of the dear folk at home, so naturally I gave up doing so. But I often talk about such things with Doctor Rank, because he likes hearing about them.

Mrs. Linde.   Listen to me, Nora. You are still very like a child in many things, and I am older than you in many ways and have a little more experience. Let me tell you this—you ought to make an end of it with Doctor Rank.

Nora.   What ought I to make an end of?

Mrs. Linde.   Of two things, I think. Yesterday you talked some nonsense about a rich admirer who was to leave you money——

Nora.   An admirer who doesn't exist, unfortunately! But what then?

Mrs. Linde.   Is Doctor Rank a man of means?

Nora.   Yes, he is.

Mrs. Linde.   And has no one to provide for?

Nora.   No, no one; but——

Mrs. Linde.   And comes here every day?

Nora.   Yes, I told you so.

Mrs. Linde.   But how can this well-bred man be so tactless?

Nora.   I don't understand you at all.

Mrs. Linde.   Don't prevaricate, Nora. Do you suppose I don't guess who lent you the two hundred and fifty pounds?

Nora.   Are you out of your senses? How can you think of such a thing! A friend of ours, who comes here every day! Do you realise what a horribly painful position that would be?

Mrs. Linde.   Then it really isn't he?

Nora.   No, certainly not. It would never have entered into my head for a moment. Besides, he had no money to lend then; he came into his money afterwards.

Mrs. Linde.   Well, I think that was lucky for you, my dear Nora.

Nora.   No, it would never have come into my head to ask Doctor Rank. Although I am quite sure that if I had asked him——

Mrs. Linde.   But of course you won't.

Nora.   Of course not. I have no reason to think it could possibly be necessary. But I am quite sure that if I told Doctor Rank——

Mrs. Linde.   Behind your husband's back?

Nora.   I must make an end of it with the other one, and that will be behind his back too. I *must* make an end of it with him.

Mrs. Linde.   Yes, that is what I told you yesterday, but——

Nora (*walking up and down*).   A man can put a thing like that straight much easier than a woman——

Mrs. Linde.   One's husband, yes.

Nora.   Nonsense! (*Standing still.*) When you pay off a debt you get your bond back, don't you?

Mrs. Linde.   Yes, as a matter of course.

Nora.   And can tear it into a hundred thousand pieces, and burn it up—the nasty dirty paper!

Mrs. Linde (*looks hard at her, lays down her sewing and gets up slowly*).   Nora, you are concealing something from me.

Nora.   Do I look as if I were?

Mrs. Linde.   Something has happened to you since yesterday morning. Nora, what is it?

Nora (*going nearer to her*).   Christine! (*Listens.*) Hush! there's Torvald come home. Do you mind going in to the children for the present? Torvald can't bear to see dressmaking going on. Let Anne help you.

Mrs. Linde (*gathering some of the things together*).   Certainly—but I am not going away from here till we have had it out with one another.

[*She goes into the room on the left, as Helmer comes in from the hall.*]

Nora (*going up to Helmer*).   I have wanted you so much, Torvald dear.

Helmer.   Was that the dressmaker?

Nora.   No, it was Christine; she is helping me to put my dress in order. You will see I shall look quite smart.

Helmer.   Wasn't that a happy thought of mine, now?

Nora.   Splendid! But don't you think it is nice of me, too, to do as you wish?

Helmer.   Nice?—because you do as your husband wishes? Well, well, you little rogue, I am sure you did not mean it in that way. But I am not going to disturb you; you will want to be trying on your dress, I expect.

Nora.   I suppose you are going to work.

Helmer.   Yes. (*Shows her a bundle of papers.*) Look at that. I have just been into the bank.

[*Turns to go into his room.*]

Nora.   Torvald.

Helmer.   Yes.

Nora. If your little squirrel were to ask you for something very, very prettily——?

Helmer. What then?

Nora. Would you do it?

Helmer. I should like to hear what it is, first.

Nora. Your squirrel would run about and do all her tricks if you would be
nice, and do what she wants.

Helmer. Speak plainly.

Nora. Your skylark would chirp about in every room, with her song rising and
falling——

Helmer. Well, my skylark does that anyhow.

Nora. I would play the fairy and dance for you in the moonlight, Torvald.

Helmer. Nora—you surely don't mean that request you made of me this
morning?

Nora (*going near him*). Yes, Torvald, I beg you so earnestly——

Helmer. Have you really the courage to open up that question again?

Nora. Yes, dear, you *must* do as I ask; you *must* let Krogstad keep his post in
the Bank.

Helmer. My dear Nora, it is his post that I have arranged Mrs. Linde shall
have.

Nora. Yes, you have been awfully kind about that; but you could just as well
dismiss some other clerk instead of Krogstad.

Helmer. This simply incredible obstinacy! Because you chose to give him a
thoughtless promise that you would speak for him, I am expected to——

Nora. That isn't the reason, Torvald. It is for your own sake. This fellow
writes in the most scurrilous newspapers; you have told me so yourself. He
can do you an unspeakable amount of harm. I am frightened to death of
him——

Helmer. Ah, I understand; it is recollections of the past that scare you.

Nora. What do you mean?

Helmer. Naturally you are thinking of your father.

Nora. Yes—yes, of course. Just recall to your mind what these malicious
creatures wrote in the papers about papa, and how horribly they slandered
him. I believe they would have procured his dismissal if the Department
had not sent you over to inquire into it, and if you had not been so kindly
disposed and helpful to him.

Helmer. My little Nora, there is an important difference between your father
and me. Your father's reputation as a public official was not above suspicion. Mine is, and I hope it will continue to be so, as long as I hold my
office.

Nora. You never can tell what mischief these men may contrive. We ought
to be so well off, so snug and happy here in our peaceful home, and have
no cares—you and I and the children, Torvald! That is why I beg of you so
earnestly——

Helmer. And it is just by interceding for him that you make it impossible for me to keep him. It is already known at the Bank that I mean to dismiss Krogstad. Is it to get about now that the new manager has changed his mind at his wife's bidding——

Nora.   And what if it did?

Helmer.   Of course!—if only this obstinate little person can get her way! Do you suppose I am going to make myself ridiculous before my whole staff, to let people think that I am a man to be swayed by all sorts of outside influence? I should very soon feel the consequences of it, I can tell you! And besides, there is one thing that makes it quite impossible for me to have Krogstad in the Bank as long as I am manager.

Nora.   Whatever is that?

Helmer.   His moral failings I might perhaps have overlooked, if necessary——

Nora.   Yes, you could—couldn't you?

Helmer.   And I hear he is a good worker, too. But I knew him when we were boys. It was one of those rash friendships that so often prove an incubus in after life. I may as well tell you plainly, we were once on very intimate terms with one another. But this tactless fellow lays no restraint on himself when other people are present. On the contrary, he thinks it gives him the right to adopt a familiar tone with me, and every minute it is "I say, Helmer, old fellow!" and that sort of thing. I assure you it is extremely painful for me. He would make my position in the Bank intolerable.

Nora.   Torvald, I don't believe you mean that.

Helmer.   Don't you? Why not?

Nora.   Because it is such a narrow-minded way of looking at things.

Helmer.   What are you saying? Narrow-minded? Do you think I am narrow-minded?

Nora.   No, just the opposite, dear—and it is exactly for that reason.

Helmer.   It's the same thing. You say my point of view is narrow-minded, so I must be so too. Narrow-minded! Very well—I must put an end to this. *(Goes to the hall-door and calls.)* Helen!

Nora.   What are you going to do?

Helmer *(looking among his papers).*   Settle it. *(Enter Maid.)* Look here; take this letter and go downstairs with it at once. Find a messenger and tell him to deliver it, and be quick. The address is on it, and here is the money.

Maid.   Very well, sir.

[Exit with the letter.]

Helmer   *(putting his papers together).* Now then, little Miss Obstinate.

Nora *(breathlessly).*   Torvald—what was that letter?

Helmer.   Krogstad's dismissal.

Nora.   Call her back, Torvald! There is still time. Oh Torvald, call her back! Do it for my sake—for your own sake—for the children's sake! Do you hear me, Torvald? Call her back! You don't know what that letter can bring upon us.

Helmer.   It's too late.

Nora.   Yes, it's too late.

Helmer. My dear Nora, I can forgive the anxiety you are in, although really it is an insult to me. It is, indeed. Isn't it an insult to think that I should be afraid of a starving quill-driver's vengeance? But I forgive you nevertheless, because it is such eloquent witness to your great love for me. *(Takes her in his arms.)* And that is as it should be, my darling Nora. Come what will, you may be sure I shall have both courage and strength if they be needed. You will see I am man enough to take everything upon myself.

Nora *(in a horror-stricken voice).* What do you mean by that?

Helmer. Everything, I say——

Nora *(recovering herself).* You will never have to do that.

Helmer. That's right. Well, we will share it, Nora, as man and wife should. That is how it shall be. *(Caressing her.)* Are you content now? There! there!—not these frightened dove's eyes! The whole thing is only the wildest fancy!—Now, you must go and play through the Tarantella and practise with your tambourine. I shall go into the inner office and shut the door, and I shall hear nothing; you can make as much noise as you please. *(Turns back at the door.)* And when Rank comes, tell him where he will find me.

[Nods to her, takes his papers and goes into his room, and shuts the door after him.]

Nora *(bewildered with anxiety, stands as if rooted to the spot, and whispers).* He was capable of doing it. He will do it. He will do it in spite of everything.—No, not that! Never, never! Anything rather than that! Oh, for some help, some way out of it! *(The door-bell rings.)* Doctor Rank! Anything rather than that—anything, whatever it is!

[She puts her hands over her face, pulls herself together, goes to the door and opens it. Rank is standing without, hanging up his coat. During the following dialogue it begins to grow dark.]

Nora. Good-day, Doctor Rank. I knew your ring. But you mustn't go into Torvald now; I think he is busy with something.

Rank. And you?

Nora *(brings him in and shuts the door after him).* Oh, you know very well I always have time for you.

Rank. Thank you. I shall make use of as much of it as I can.

Nora. What do you mean by that? As much of it as you can?

Rank. Well, does that alarm you?

Nora. It was such a strange way of putting it. Is anything likely to happen?

Rank. Nothing but what I have long been prepared for. But certainly didn't expect it to happen so soon.

Nora *(gripping him by the arm).* What have you found out? Doctor Rank, you must tell me.

Rank *(sitting down by the stove).* It is all up with me. And it can't be helped.

Nora (*with a sigh of relief*).   Is it about yourself?

Rank.   Who else? It is no use lying to one's self. I am the most wretched of all my patients, Mrs. Helmer. Lately I have been taking stock of my internal economy. Bankrupt! Probably within a month I shall lie rotting in the churchyard.

Nora.   What an ugly thing to say!

Rank.   The thing itself is cursedly ugly, and the worst of it is that I shall have to face so much more that is ugly before that. I shall only make one more examination of myself; when I have done that, I shall know pretty certainly when it will be that the horrors of dissolution will begin. There is something I want to tell you. Helmer's refined nature gives him an unconquerable disgust at everything that is ugly; I won't have him in my sick-room.

Nora.   Oh, but, Doctor Rank——

Rank.   I won't have him there. Not on any account. I bar my door to him. As soon as I am quite certain that the worst has come, I shall send you my card with a black cross on it, and then you will know that the loathsome end has begun.

Nora.   You are quite absurd to-day. And I wanted you so much to be in a really good humour.

Rank.   With death stalking beside me?—To have to pay this penalty for another man's sin! Is there any justice in that? And in every single family, in one way or another, some such inexorable retribution is being exacted——

Nora (*putting her hands over her ears*).   Rubbish! Do talk of something cheerful.

Rank.   Oh, it's a mere laughing matter, the whole thing. My poor innocent spine has to suffer for my father's youthful amusements.

Nora (*sitting at the table on the left*).   I suppose you mean that he was too partial to asparagus and pâté de foie gras, don't you.

Rank.   Yes, and to truffles.

Nora.   Truffles, yes. And oysters too, I suppose?

Rank.   Oysters, of course, that goes without saying.

Nora.   And heaps of port and champagne. It is sad that all these nice things should take their revenge on our bones.

Rank.   Especially that they should revenge themselves on the unlucky bones of those who have not had the satisfaction of enjoying them.

Nora.   Yes, that's the saddest part of it all.

Rank (*with a searching look at her*).   Hm!——

Nora (*after a short pause*).   Why did you smile?

Rank.   No, it was you that laughed.

Nora.   No, it was you that smiled, Doctor Rank!

Rank (*rising*).   You are a greater rascal than I thought.

Nora.   I am in a silly mood to-day.

Rank.   So it seems.

Nora *(putting her hands on his shoulders).*   Dear, dear Doctor Rank, death mustn't take you away from Torvald and me.

Rank.   It is a loss you would easily recover from. Those who are gone are soon forgotten.

Nora *(looking at him anxiously).*   Do you believe that?

Rank.   People form new ties, and then——

Nora.   Who will form new ties?

Rank.   Both you and Helmer, when I am gone. You yourself are already on the high road to it, I think. What did that Mrs. Linde want here last night?

Nora.   Oho!—you don't mean to say you are jealous of poor Christine?

Rank.   Yes, I am. She will be my successor in this house. When I am done for, this woman will—

Nora.   Hush! don't speak so loud. She is in that room.

Rank.   To-day again. There, you see.

Nora.   She has only come to sew my dress for me. Bless my soul, how unreasonable you are! *(Sits down on the sofa.)* Be nice now, Doctor Rank, and to-morrow you will see how beautifully I shall dance, and you can imagine I am doing it all for you—and for Torvald too, of course. *(Takes various things out of the box.)* Doctor Rank, come and sit down here, and I will show you something.

Rank *(sitting down).*   What is it?

Nora.   Just look at those!

Rank.   Silk stockings.

Nora.   Flesh-coloured. Aren't they lovely? It is so dark here now, but to-morrow—. No, no, no! you must only look at the feet. Oh well, you may have leave to look at the legs too.

Rank.   Hm!—

Nora.   Why are you looking so critical? Don't you think they will fit me?

Rank.   I have no means of forming an opinion about that.

Nora *(looks at him for a moment).*   For shame! *(Hits him lightly on the ear with the stockings.)* That's to punish you. *(Folds them up again.)*

Rank.   And what other nice things am I to be allowed to see?

Nora.   Not a single thing more, for being so naughty. *(She looks among the things, humming to herself.)*

Rank *(after a short silence).*   When I am sitting here, talking to you as intimately as this, I cannot imagine for a moment what would have become of me if I had never come into this house.

Nora *(smiling).*   I believe you do feel thoroughly at home with us.

Rank *(in a lower voice, looking straight in front of him).*   And to be obliged to leave it all——

Nora.   Nonsense, you are not going to leave it.

Rank *(as before).*   And not be able to leave behind one the slightest token of one's gratitude, scarcely even a fleeting regret—nothing but an empty place which the first comer can fill as well as any other.

Nora.   And if I asked you now for a—? No!

Rank.   For what?

Nora.   For a big proof of your friendship——

Rank.   Yes, yes!

Nora.   I mean a tremendously big favour——

Rank.   Would you really make me so happy for once?

Nora.   Ah, but you don't know what it is yet.

Rank.   No—but tell me.

Nora.   I really can't, Doctor Rank. It is something out of all reason; it means advice, and help, and a favour——

Rank.   The bigger a thing it is the better. I can't conceive what it is you mean. Do tell me. Haven't I your confidence?

Nora.   More than anyone else. I know you are my truest and best friend, and so I will tell you what it is. Well, Doctor Rank, it is something you must help me to prevent. You know how devotedly, how inexpressibly deeply Torvald loves me; he would never for moment hesitate to give his life for me.

Rank (*leaning towards her*).   Nora—do you think he is the only one——?

Nora (*with a slight start*).   The only one—?

Rank.   The only one who would gladly give his life for your sake.

Nora (*sadly*).   Is that it?

Rank.   I was determined you should know it before I went away, and there will never be a better opportunity than this. Now you know it, Nora. And now you know, too, that you can trust me as you would trust no one else.

Nora (*rises, deliberately and quietly*).   Let me pass.

Rank (*makes room for her to pass him, but sits still*).   Nora!

Nora (*at the hall door*).   Helen, bring in the lamp. (*Goes over to the stove.*) Dear Doctor Rank, that was really horrid of you.

Rank.   To have loved you as much as anyone else does? Was that horrid?

Nora.   No, but to go and tell me so. There was really no need——

Rank.   What do you mean? Did you know—? (*Maid enters with lamp, puts it down on the table, and goes out.*) Nora—Mrs. Helmer—tell me, had you any idea of this?

Nora.   Oh, how do I know whether I had or whether I hadn't? I really can't tell you— To think you could be so clumsy, Doctor Rank! We were getting on so nicely.

Rank.   Well, at all events you know now that you can command me, body and soul. So won't you speak out?

Nora (*looking at him*).   After what happened?

Rank.   I beg you to let me know what it is.

Nora.   I can't tell you anything now.

Rank.   Yes, yes. You mustn't punish me in that way. Let me have permission to do for you whatever a man may do.

Nora.   You can do nothing for me now. Besides, I really don't need any help at all. You will find that the whole thing is merely fancy on my part. It really is so—of course it is! (*Sits down in the rocking-chair, and looks at him with* *a smile.*) You are a nice sort of man, Doctor Rank!—don't you feel ashamed of yourself, now the lamp has come?

Rank. Not a bit. But perhaps I had better go—forever?

Nora. No, indeed, you shall not. Of course you must come here just as before. You know very well Torvald can't do without you.

Rank. Yes, but you?

Nora. Oh, I am always tremendously pleased when you come.

Rank. It is just that, that put me on the wrong track. You are a riddle to me. I have often thought that you would almost as soon be in my company as in Helmer's.

Nora. Yes—you see there are some people one loves best, and others whom one would almost always rather have as companions.

Rank. Yes, there is something in that.

Nora. When I was at home, of course I loved papa best. But I always thought it tremendous fun if I could steal down into the maids' room, because they never moralised at all, and talked to each other about such entertaining things.

Rank. I see—it is *their* place I have taken.

Nora (*jumping up and going to him*). Oh, dear, nice Doctor Rank, I never meant that at all. But surely you can understand that being with Torvald is a little like being with papa——

[*Enter Maid from the hall.*]

Maid. If you please, ma'am. (*Whispers and hands her a card.*)

Nora (*glancing at the card*). Oh! (*Puts it in her pocket.*)

Rank. Is there anything wrong?

Nora. No, no, not in the least. It is only something—it is my new dress——

Rank. What? Your dress is lying there.

Nora. Oh, yes, that one; but this is another. I ordered it. Torvald mustn't know about it——

Rank. Oho! Then that was the great secret.

Nora. Of course. Just go in to him; he is sitting in the inner room. Keep him as long as——

Rank. Make your mind easy; I won't let him escape. (*Goes into Helmer's room.*)

Nora (*to the Maid*). And he is standing waiting in the kitchen?

Maid. Yes; he came up the back stairs.

Nora. But didn't you tell him no one was in?

Maid. Yes, but it was no good.

Nora. He won't go away?

Maid. No; he says he won't until he has seen you, ma'am.

Nora. Well, let him come in—but quietly. Helen, you mustn't say anything about it to anyone. It is a surprise for my husband.

Maid. Yes ma'am, I quite understand.   [*Exit.*]

Nora.   This dreadful thing is going to happen! It will happen in spite of me! No, no, no, it can't happen—it shan't happen!

[*She bolts the door of Helmer's room. The Maid opens the hall door for Krogstad and shuts it after him. He is wearing a fur coat, high boots and a fur cap.*]

Nora (*advancing towards him.*)   Speak low—my husband is at home.

Krogstad.   No matter about that.

Nora.   What do you want of me?

Krogstad.   An explanation of something.

Nora.   Make haste then. What is it?

Krogstad.   You know, I suppose, that I have got my dismissal.

Nora.   I couldn't prevent it, Mr. Krogstad. I fought as hard as I could on your side, but it was no good.

Krogstad.   Does your husband love you so little, then? He knows what I can expose you to, and yet he ventures——

Nora.   How can you suppose that he has any knowledge of the sort?

Krogstad.   I didn't suppose so at all. It would not be the least like our dear Torvald Helmer to show so much courage—

Nora.   Mr. Krogstad, a little respect for my husband, please.

Krogstad.   Certainly—all the respect he deserves. But since you have kept the matter so carefully to yourself, I make bold to suppose that you have a little clearer idea, than you had yesterday, of what it actually is that you have done?

Nora.   More than you could ever teach me.

Krogstad.   Yes, such a bad lawyer as I am.

Nora.   What is it you want of me?

Krogstad.   Only to see how you were, Mrs. Helmer. I have been thinking about you all day long. A mere cashier, a quill-driver, a—well, a man like me—even he has a little of what is called feeling, you know.

Nora.   Show it, then; think of my little children.

Krogstad.   Have you and your husband thought of mine? But never mind about that. I only wanted to tell you that you need not take this matter too seriously. In the first place there will be no accusation made on my part.

Nora.   No, of course not; I was sure of that.

Krogstad.   The whole thing can be arranged amicably; there is no reason why anyone should know anything about it. It will remain a secret between us three.

Nora.   My husband must never get to know anything about it.

Krogstad.   How will you be able to prevent it? Am I to understand that you can pay the balance that is owing?

Nora.   No, not just at present.

Krogstad.   Or perhaps that you have some expedient for raising the money soon?

Nora.   No expedient that I mean to make use of.

Krogstad.   Well, in any case, it would have been of no use to you now. If you stood there with ever so much money in your hand, I would never part with your bond.

Nora.   Tell me what purpose you mean to put it to.

Krogstad.   I shall only preserve it—keep it in my possession. No one who is not concerned in the matter shall have the slightest hint of it. So that if the thought of it has driven you to any desperate resolution——

Nora.   It has.

Krogstad.   If you had it in your mind to run away from your home——

Nora.   I had.

Krogstad.   Or even something worse——

Nora.   How could you know that?

Krogstad.   Give up the idea.

Nora.   How did you know I had thought of *that?*

Krogstad.   Most of us think of that at first. I did, too—but I hadn't the courage.

Nora (*faintly*).   No more had I.

Krogstad (*in a tone of relief*).   No, that's it, isn't it—you hadn't the courage either?

Nora.   No, I haven't—I haven't.

Krogstad.   Besides, it would have been a great piece of folly. Once the first storm at home is over—. I have a letter for your husband in my pocket.

Nora.   Telling him everything?

Krogstad.   In as lenient a manner as I possibly could.

Nora (*quickly*).   He mustn't get the letter. Tear it up. I will find some means of getting money.

Krogstad.   Excuse me, Mrs. Helmer, but I think I told you just now——

Nora.   I am not speaking of what I owe you. Tell me what sum you are asking my husband for, and I will get the money.

Krogstad.   I am not asking your husband for a penny.

Nora.   What do you want, then?

Krogstad.   I will tell you. I want to rehabilitate myself, Mrs. Helmer; I want to get on; and in that your husband must help me. For the last year and a half I have not had a hand in anything dishonourable, and all that time I have been struggling in most restricted circumstances. I was content to work my way up step by step. Now I am turned out, and I am not going to be satisfied with merely being taken into favour again. I want to get on, I tell you. I want to get into the Bank again, in a higher position. Your husband must make a place for me——

Nora.   That he will never do!

Krogstad.   He will; I know him; he dare not protest. And as soon as I am in there again with him, then you will see! Within a year I shall be the manager's right hand. It will be Nils Krogstad and not Torvald Helmer who manages the Bank.

Nora.   That's a thing you will never see!

Krogstad.   Do you mean that you will——?

Nora.   I have courage enough for it now.

Krogstad.   Oh, you can't frighten me. A fine, spoilt lady like you——

Nora.   You will see, you will see.

Krogstad.   Under the ice, perhaps? Down into the cold, coal-black water? And then, in the spring, to float up to the surface, all horrible and unrecognisable, with your hair fallen out——

Nora.   You can't frighten me.

Krogstad.   Nor you me. People don't do such things, Mrs. Helmer. Besides, what use would it be? I should have him completely in my power all the same.

Nora.   Afterwards? When I am no longer——

Krogstad.   Have you forgotten that it is I who have the keeping of your reputation? (*Nora stands speechlessly looking at him.*) Well, now, I have warned you. Do not do anything foolish. When Helmer has had my letter, I shall expect a message from him. And be sure you remember that it is your husband himself who has forced me into such ways as this again. I will never forgive him for that. Good-bye, Mrs. Helmer.

[Exit through the hall.]

Nora (*goes to the hall door, opens it slightly and listens*).   He is going. He is not putting the letter in the box. Oh no, no! that's impossible! (*Opens the door by degrees.*) He is going. He is standing outside. He is not going downstairs. Is he hesitating? Can he——

[A letter drops into the box; then Krogstad's footsteps are heard, till they die away as he goes downstairs. Nora utters a stifled cry and runs across the room to the table by the sofa. A short pause.]

Nora.   In the letter-box. (*Steals across to the hall door.*) There it lies—Torvald, Torvald, there is no hope for us now!

[Mrs. Linde comes in from the room on the left carrying the dress.]

Mrs. Linde.   There, I can't see anything more to mend now. Would you like to try it on——?

Nora (*in a hoarse whisper*).   Christine, come here.

Mrs. Linde   (*throwing the dress down on the sofa*). What is the matter with you? You look so agitated!

Nora.   Come here. Do you see that letter? There look—you can see it through the glass in the letter-box.

Mrs. Linde.   Yes, I see it.

Nora.   That letter is from Krogstad.

Mrs. Linde.   Nora—it was Krogstad who lent you the money!

Nora.   Yes, and now Torvald will know all about it.

Mrs. Linde.   Believe me, Nora, that's the best thing for both of you.

Nora.   You don't know all. I forged a name.

Mrs. Linde.   Good heavens——!

Nora.   I only want to say this to you, Christine—you must be my witness.

Mrs. Linde.   Your witness? What do you mean? What am I to—?

Nora.   If I should go out of my mind—and it might easily happen——

Mrs. Linde.   Nora!

Nora.   Or if anything else should happen to me—anything, for instance, that might prevent my being here—

Mrs. Linde.   Nora! Nora! you are quite out of your mind.

Nora.   And if it should happen that there were someone who wanted to take all the responsibility, all the blame, you understand——

Mrs. Linde.   Yes, yes—but how can you suppose—?

Nora.   Then you must be my witness, that it is not true, Christine. I am not out of my mind at all; I am in my right senses now, and I tell you no one else has known anything about it; I, and I alone, did the whole thing. Remember that.

Mrs. Linde.   I will, indeed. But I don't understand all this.

Nora.   How should you understand it? A wonderful thing is going to happen.

Mrs. Linde.   A wonderful thing?

Nora.   Yes, a wonderful thing!—But it is so terrible, Christine; it *mustn't* happen, not for all the world.

Mrs. Linde.   I will go at once and see Krogstad.

Nora.   Don't go to him; he will do you some harm.

Mrs. Linde.   There was a time when he would gladly do anything for my sake.

Nora.   He?

Mrs. Linde.   Where does he live?

Nora.   How should I know—? Yes (*feeling in her pocket*) here is his card. But the letter, the letter——!

Helmer   (*calls from his room, knocking at the door*). Nora!

Nora (*cries out anxiously*).   Oh, what's that? What do you want?

Helmer.   Don't be so frightened. We are not coming in; you have locked the door. Are you trying on your dress?

Nora.   Yes, that's it. I look so nice, Torvald.

Mrs. Linde (*who has read the card*).   I see he lives at the corner here.

Nora.   Yes, but it's no use. It is hopeless. The letter is lying there in the box.

Mrs. Linde.   And your husband keeps the key?

Nora.   Yes, always.

Mrs. Linde.   Krogstad must ask for his letter back unread, he must find some pretence——

Nora.   But it is just at this time that Torvald generally——

Mrs. Linde.   You must delay him. Go in to him in the meantime. I will come back as soon as I can.

[*She goes out hurriedly through the hall door.*]

Nora (*goes to Helmer's door, opens it and peeps in*).   Torvald!

Helmer (*from the inner room*).   Well? May I venture at last to come into my own room again? Come along, Rank, now you will see— (*Halting in the doorway.*) But what is this?

Nora.   What is what, dear?

Helmer.   Rank led me to expect a splendid transformation.

Rank (*in the doorway*).   I understood so, but evidently I was mistaken.

Nora.   Yes, nobody is to have the chance of admiring me in my dress until to-morrow.

Helmer.   But, my dear Nora, you look so worn out. Have you been practising too much?

Nora.   No, I have not practised at all.

Helmer.   But you will need to—

Nora.   Yes, indeed I shall, Torvald. But I can't get on a bit without you to help me; I have absolutely forgotten the whole thing.

Helmer.   Oh, we will soon work it up again.

Nora.   Yes, help me, Torvald. Promise that you will! I am so nervous about it—all the people—. You must give yourself up to me entirely this evening. Not the tiniest bit of business—you mustn't even take a pen in your hand. Will you promise, Torvald dear?

Helmer.   I promise. This evening I will be wholly and absolutely at your service, you helpless little mortal. Ah, by the way, first of all I will just——

[*Goes towards the hall door.*]

Nora.   What are you going to do there?

Helmer.   Only see if any letters have come.

Nora.   No, no! don't do that, Torvald!

Helmer.   Why not?

Nora.   Torvald, please don't. There is nothing there.

Helmer.   Well, let me look. (*Turns to go to the letter-box. Nora at the piano, plays the first bars of the Tarantella. Helmer stops in the doorway.*) Aha!

Nora.   I can't dance to-morrow if I don't practise with you.

Helmer (*going up to her*).   Are you really so afraid of it, dear?

Nora.   Yes, so dreadfully afraid of it. Let me practise at once; there is time now, before we go to dinner. Sit down and play for me, Torvald dear; criticise me, and correct me as you play.

Helmer.   With great pleasure, if you wish me to.

[*Sits down at the piano.*]

Nora (*takes out of the box a tambourine and a long variegated shawl. She hastily drapes the shawl round her. Then she springs to the front of the stage and calls out*).   Now play for me! I am going to dance!

[*Helmer plays and Nora dances. Rank stands by the piano behind Helmer and looks on.*]

Helmer (*as he plays*).   Slower, slower!
Nora.   I can't do it any other way.
Helmer.   Not so violently, Nora!
Nora.   This is the way.
Helmer (*stops playing*).   No, no—that is not a bit right.
Nora (*laughing and swinging the tambourine*).   Didn't I tell you so?
Rank.   Let me play for her.
Helmer (*getting up*).   Yes, do. I can correct her better then.

[*Rank sits down at the piano and plays. Nora dances more and more wildly. Helmer has taken up a position beside the stove, and during her dance gives her frequent instructions. She does not seem to hear him; her hair comes down and falls over her shoulders; she pays no attention to it, but goes on dancing. Enter Mrs. Linde.*]

Mrs. Linde (*standing as if spell-bound in the doorway*).   Oh!——
Nora (*as she dances*).   Such fun, Christine!
Helmer.   My dear darling Nora, you are dancing as if your life depended on it.
Nora.   So it does.
Helmer.   Stop, Rank; this is sheer madness. Stop, I tell you! (*Rank stops playing, and Nora suddenly stands still. Helmer goes up to her.*) I could never have believed it. You have forgotten everything I taught you.
Nora (*throwing away the tambourine*).   There, you see.
Helmer.   You will want a lot of coaching.
Nora.   Yes, you see how much I need it. You must coach me up to the last minute. Promise me that, Torvald!
Helmer.   You can depend on me.
Nora.   You must not think of anything but me, either to-day or to-morrow; you mustn't open a single letter—not even open the letter-box——
Helmer.   Ah, you are still afraid of that fellow——
Nora.   Yes, indeed I am.
Helmer.   Nora, I can tell from your looks that there is a letter from him lying there.
Nora.   I don't know; I think there is; but you must not read anything of that kind now. Nothing horrid must come between us till this is all over.
Rank (*whispers to Helmer*).   You mustn't contradict her.
Helmer (*taking her in his arms*).   The child shall have her way. But to-morrow night, after you have danced——
Nora.   Then you will be free.

[*The Maid appears in the doorway to the right.*]

Maid.   Dinner is served, ma'am.
Nora.   We will have champagne, Helen.

Maid. Very good, ma'am.

[Exit.]

Helmer. Hullo!—are we going to have a banquet?

Nora. Yes, a champagne banquet till the small hours. *(Calls out.)* And a few macaroons, Helen—lots, just for once!

Helmer. Come, come, don't be so wild and nervous. Be my own little skylark, as you used.

Nora. Yes, dear, I will. But go in now and you too, Doctor Rank. Christine, you must help me to do up my hair.

Rank *(whispers to Helmer as they go out).* I suppose there is nothing—she is not expecting anything?

Helmer. Far from it, my dear fellow; it is simply nothing more than this childish nervousness I was telling you of.

[They go into the right-hand room.]

Nora. Well!

Mrs. Linde. Gone out of town.

Nora. I could tell from your face.

Mrs. Linde. He is coming home to-morrow evening. I wrote a note for him.

Nora. You should have let it alone; you must prevent nothing. After all, it is splendid to be waiting for a wonderful thing to happen.

Mrs. Linde. What is it that you are waiting for?

Nora. Oh, you wouldn't understand. Go in to them, I will come in a moment. *(Mrs. Linde goes into the dining-room. Nora stands still for a little while, as if to compose herself. Then she looks at her watch.)* Five o'clock. Seven hours till midnight. Then the Tarantella will be over. Twenty-four and seven? Thirty-one hours to live.

Helmer *(from the doorway on the right).* Where's my little skylark?

Nora *(going to him with her arms outstretched).* Here she is!

Act III

THE SAME SCENE.   *The table has been placed in the middle of the stage, with chairs round it. A lamp is burning on the table. The door into the hall stands open. Dance music is heard in the room above. Mrs. Linde is sitting at the table idly turning over the leaves of a book; she tries to read, but does not seem able to collect her thoughts. Every now and then she listens intently for a sound at the outer door.*

Mrs. Linde *(looking at her watch).*   Not yet—and the time is nearly up. If only he does not—. *(Listens again.)* Ah, there he is. *(Goes into the hall and opens the outer door carefully. Light footsteps are heard on the stairs. She whispers.)* Come in. There is no one here.

Krogstad (*in the doorway*).   I found a note from you at home. What does this mean?

Mrs. Linde.   It is absolutely necessary that I should have a talk with you.

Krogstad.   Really? And is it absolutely necessary that it should be here?

Mrs. Linde.   It is impossible where I live; there is no private entrance to my rooms. Come in; we are quite alone. The maid is asleep, and the Helmers are at the dance upstairs.

Krogstad (*coming into the room*).   Are the Helmers really at a dance to-night?

Mrs. Linde.   Yes, why not?

Krogstad.   Certainly—why not?

Mrs. Linde.   Now, Nils, let us have a talk.

Krogstad.   Can we two have anything to talk about?

Mrs. Linde.   We have a great deal to talk about.

Krogstad.   I shouldn't have thought so.

Mrs. Linde.   No, you have never properly understood me.

Krogstad.   Was there anything else to understand except what was obvious to all the world—a heartless woman jilts a man when a more lucrative chance turns up?

Mrs. Linde.   Do you believe I am as absolutely heartless as all that? And do you believe that I did it with a light heart?

Krogstad.   Didn't you?

Mrs. Linde.   Nils, did you really think that?

Krogstad.   If it were as you say, why did you write to me as you did at the time?

Mrs. Linde.   I could do nothing else. As I had to break with you, it was my duty also to put an end to all that you felt for me.

Krogstad (*wringing his hands*).   So that was it. And all this—only for the sake of money!

Mrs. Linde.   You must not forget that I had a helpless mother and two little brothers. We couldn't wait for you, Nils; your prospects seemed hopeless then.

Krogstad.   That may be so, but you had no right to throw me over for anyone else's sake.

Mrs. Linde.   Indeed I don't know. Many a time did I ask myself if I had the right to do it.

Krogstad (*more gently*).   When I lost you, it was as if all the solid ground went from under my feet. Look at me now—I am a shipwrecked man clinging to a bit of wreckage.

Mrs. Linde.   But help may be near.

Krogstad.   It *was* near; but then you came and stood in my way.

Mrs. Linde.   Unintentionally, Nils. It was only to-day that I learnt it was your place I was going to take in the Bank.

Krogstad.   I believe you, if you say so. But now that you know it, are you not going to give it up to me?

Mrs. Linde.   No, because that would not benefit you in the least.

Krogstad.   Oh, benefit, benefit—I would have done it whether or no.

Mrs. Linde.   I have learnt to act prudently. Life, and hard, bitter necessity have taught me that.

Krogstad.   And life has taught me not to believe in fine speeches.

Mrs. Linde.   Then life has taught you something very reasonable. But deeds you must believe in?

Krogstad.   What do you mean by that?

Mrs. Linde.   You said you were like a shipwrecked man clinging to some wreckage.

Krogstad.   I had good reason to say so.

Mrs. Linde.   Well, I am like a shipwrecked woman clinging to some wreckage—no one to mourn for, no one to care for.

Krogstad.   It was your own choice.

Mrs. Linde.   There was no other choice—then.

Krogstad.   Well, what now?

Mrs. Linde.   Nils, how would it be if we two shipwrecked people could join forces?

Krogstad.   What are you saying?

Mrs. Linde.   Two on the same piece of wreckage would stand a better chance than each on their own.

Krogstad.   Christine!

Mrs. Linde.   What do you suppose brought me to town?

Krogstad.   Do you mean that you gave me a thought?

Mrs. Linde.   I could not endure life without work. All my life, as long as I can remember, I have worked, and it has been my greatest and only pleasure. But now I am quite alone in the world—my life is so dreadfully empty and I feel so forsaken. There is not the least pleasure in working for one's self. Nils, give me someone and something to work for.

Krogstad.   I don't trust that. It is nothing but a woman's overstrained sense of generosity that prompts you to make such an offer of yourself.

Mrs. Linde.   Have you ever noticed anything of the sort in me?

Krogstad.   Could you really do it? Tell me—do you know all about my past life?

Mrs. Linde.   Yes.

Krogstad.   And do you know the what they think of me here?

Mrs. Linde.   You seemed to me to imply that with me you might have been quite another man.

Krogstad.   I am certain of it.

Mrs. Linde.   Is it too late now?

Krogstad.   Christine, are you saying this deliberately? Yes, I am sure you are. I see it in your face. Have you really the courage then—?

Mrs. Linde.   I want to be a mother to someone, and your children need a mother. We two need each other. Nils, I have faith in your real character—I can dare anything together with you.

Krogstad (*grasps her hands*).   Thanks, thanks, Christine! Now I shall find a way to clear myself in the eyes of the world. Ah, but I forgot——

Mrs. Linde (*listening*).   Hush! The Tarantella! Go, go!

Krogstad. Why? What is it?

Mrs. Linde. Do you hear them up there? When that is over, we may expect them back.

Krogstad. Yes, yes—I will go. But it is all no use. Of course you are not aware what steps I have taken in the matter of the Helmers.

Mrs. Linde. Yes, I know all about that.

Krogstad. And in spite of that have you the courage to—?

Mrs. Linde. I understand very well to what lengths a man like you might be driven by despair.

Krogstad. If I could only undo what I have done!

Mrs. Linde. You cannot. Your letter is lying in the letter-box now.

Krogstad. Are you sure of that?

Mrs. Linde. Quite sure, but——

Krogstad (*with a searching look at her*). Is that what it all means?—that you want to save your friend at my cost? Tell me frankly. Is that it?

Mrs. Linde. Nils, a woman who has once sold herself for another's sake, doesn't do it a second time.

Krogstad. I will ask for my letter back.

Mrs. Linde. No, no.

Krogstad. Yes, of course I will. I will wait here till Helmer comes; I will tell him he must give me my letter back—that it only concerns my dismissal— that he is not to read it——

Mrs. Linde. No, Nils, you must not recall your letter.

Krogstad. But, tell me, wasn't it for that very purpose that you asked me to meet you here?

Mrs. Linde. In my first moment of fright, it was. But twenty-four hours have elapsed since then, and in that time I have witnessed incredible things in this house. Helmer must know all about it. This unhappy secret must be disclosed; they must have a complete understanding between them, which is impossible with all this concealment and falsehood going on.

Krogstad. Very well, if you will take the responsibility. But there is one thing I can do in any case, and I shall do it at once.

Mrs. Linde (*listening*). You must be quick and go! The dance is over; we are not safe a moment longer.

Krogstad. I will wait for you below.

Mrs. Linde. Yes, do. You must see me back to my door.

Krogstad. I have never had such an amazing piece of good fortune in my life.

[*Goes out through the outer door. The door between the room and the hall remains open.*]

Mrs. Linde (*tidying up the room and laying her hat and cloak ready*). What a difference! what a difference! Someone to work for and live for—a home to bring comfort into. That I will do, indeed. I wish they would be quick and come— (*Listens.*) Ah, there they are now. I must put on my things.

[Takes up her hat and cloak. Helmer's and Nora's voices are heard outside; a key is turned, and Helmer brings Nora almost by force into the hall. She is in an Italian costume with a large black shawl round her; he is in evening dress and a black domino[1] which is flying open.]

Nora *(hanging back in the doorway, and struggling with him.)*   No, no, no!— don't take me in. I want to go upstairs again; I don't want to leave so early.

Helmer.   But, my dearest Nora——

Nora.   Please, Torvald dear—please, *please*—only an hour more.

Helmer.   Not a single minute, my sweet Nora. You know that was our agreement. Come along into the room; you are catching cold standing there.

[He brings her gently into the room, in spite of her resistance.]

Mrs. Linde.   Good evening.

Nora.   Christine!

Helmer.   You here, so late, Mrs. Linde?

Mrs. Linde.   Yes, you must excuse me; I was so anxious to see Nora in her dress.

Nora.   Have you been sitting here waiting for me?

Mrs. Linde.   Yes, unfortunately I came too late, you had already gone upstairs; and I thought I couldn't go away again without having seen you.

Helmer *(taking off Nora's shawl).*   Yes, take a good look at her. I think she is worth looking at. Isn't she charming, Mrs. Linde?

Mrs. Linde.   Yes, indeed she is.

Helmer.   Doesn't she look remarkably pretty? Everyone thought so at the dance. But she is terribly self-willed, this sweet little person. What are we to do with her? You will hardly believe that I had almost to bring her away by force.

Nora.   Torvald, you will repent not having let me stay, even if it were only for half an hour.

Helmer.   Listen to her, Mrs. Linde! She had danced her Tarantella, and it had been a tremendous success, as it deserved—although possibly the performance was a trifle too realistic—a little more so, I mean, than was strictly compatible with the limitations of art. But never mind about that! The chief thing is, she had made a success—she had made a tremendous success. Do you think I was going to let her remain there after that, and spoil the effect? No indeed! I took my charming little Capri maiden—my capricious little Capri maiden, I should say—on my arm; took one quick turn round the room; a curtsey on either side, and, as they say in novels, the beautiful apparition disappeared. An exit ought always to be effective, Mrs. Linde; but that is what I cannot make Nora understand. Pooh! this room is

---

[1] A long loose hooded cloak.

hot. (*Throws his domino on a chair and opens the door of his room.*) Hullo! it's dark in here. Oh, of course—excuse me——.

[*He goes in and lights some candles.*]

Nora (*in a hurried and breathless whisper*).   Well?

Mrs. Linde (*in a low voice*).   I have had a talk with him.

Nora.   Yes, and——

Mrs. Linde.   Nora, you must tell your husband all about it.

Nora (*in an expressionless voice*).   I knew it.

Mrs. Linde.   You have nothing to be afraid of as far as Krogstad is concerned; but you must tell him.

Nora.   I won't tell him.

Mrs. Linde.   Then the letter will.

Nora.   Thank you, Christine. Now I know what I must do. Hush——!

Helmer (*coming in again*).   Well, Mrs. Linde, have you admired her?

Mrs. Linde.   Yes, and now I will say good-night.

Helmer.   What, already? Is this yours, this knitting?

Mrs. Linde (*taking it*).   Yes, thank you, I have very nearly forgotten it.

Helmer.   So you knit?

Mrs. Linde.   Of course.

Helmer.   Do you know, you ought to embroider.

Mrs. Linde.   Really? Why?

Helmer.   Yes, it's far more becoming. Let me show you. You hold the embroidery thus in your left hand, and use the needle with the right—like this—with a long, easy sweep. Do you see?

Mrs. Linde.   Yes, perhaps——

Helmer.   But in the case of knitting—that can never be anything but ungraceful; look here—the arms close together, the knitting-needles going up and down—it has a sort of Chinese effect—. That was really excellent champagne they gave us.

Mrs. Linde.   Well,—good-night, Nora, and don't be self-willed any more.

Helmer.   That's right, Mrs. Linde.

Mrs. Linde.   Good-night, Mr. Helmer.

Helmer (*accompanying her to the door*).   Good-night, good-night. I hope you will get home all right. I should be very happy to—but you haven't any great distance to go. Good-night, good-night. (*She goes out; he shuts the door after her, and comes in again.*) Ah!—at last we have got rid of her. She is a frightful bore, that woman.

Nora.   Aren't you very tired, Torvald?

Helmer.   No, not in the least.

Nora.   Nor sleepy?

Helmer.   Not a bit. On the contrary, I feel extraordinarily lively. And you?— you really look both tired and sleepy.

Nora.   Yes, I am very tired. I want to go to sleep at once.

Helmer.   There, you see it was quite right of me not to let you stay there any longer.

Nora.   Everything you do is quite right, Torvald.

Helmer (*kissing her on the forehead*).   Now my little skylark is speaking reasonably. Did you notice what good spirits Rank was in this evening?

Nora.   Really? Was he? I didn't speak to him at all.

Helmer.   And I very little, but I have not for a long time seen him in such good form. (*Looks for a while at her and then goes nearer to her.*) It is delightful to be at home by ourselves again, to be all alone with you—you fascinating, charming little darling!

Nora.   Don't look at me like that, Torvald.

Helmer.   Why shouldn't I look at my dearest treasure?—at all the beauty that is mine, all my very own?

Nora (*going to the other side of the table*).   You mustn't say things like that to me to-night.

Helmer (*following her*).   You have still got the Tarantella in your blood, I see. And it makes you more captivating than ever. Listen—the guests are beginning to go now. (*In a lower voice.*) Nora—soon the whole house will be quiet.

Nora.   Yes, I hope so.

Helmer.   Yes, my own darling Nora. Do you know, when I am out at a party with you like this, why I speak so little to you, keep away from you, and only send a stolen glance in your direction now and then?—do you know why I do that? It is because I make believe to myself that we are secretly in love, and you are my secretly promised bride, and that no one suspects there is anything between us.

Nora.   Yes, yes—I know very well your thoughts are with me all the time.

Helmer.   And when we are leaving, and I am putting the shawl over your beautiful young shoulders—on your lovely neck—then I imagine that you are my young bride and that we have just come from the wedding, and I am bringing you for the first time into our home—to be alone with you for the first time—quite alone with my shy little darling! All this evening I have longed for nothing but you. When I watched the seductive figures of the Tarantella, my blood was on fire; I could endure it no longer, and that was why I brought you down so early——

Nora.   Go away, Torvald! You must let me go. I won't——

Helmer.   What's that? You're joking, my little Nora! You won't—you won't? Am I not your husband—?

[*A knock is heard at the outer door.*]

Nora (*starting*).   Did you hear——?

Helmer (*going into the hall*).   Who is it?

Rank (*outside*).   It is I. May I come in for a moment?

Helmer (*in a fretful whisper*).   Oh, what does he want now? (*Aloud.*) Wait a minute? (*Unlocks the door.*) Come, that's kind of you not to pass by our door.

Rank.   I thought I heard your voice, and felt as if I should like to look in. (*With a swift glance round.*) Ah, yes!—these dear familiar rooms. You are very happy and cosy in here, you two.

Helmer.   It seems to me that you looked after yourself pretty well upstairs too.

Rank.   Excellently. Why shouldn't I? Why shouldn't one enjoy everything in this world?—at any rate as much as one can, and as long as one can. The wine was capital——

Helmer.   Especially the champagne.

Rank.   So you noticed that too? It is almost incredible how much I managed to put away!

Nora.   Torvald drank a great deal of champagne tonight, too.

Rank.   Did he?

Nora.   Yes, and he is always in such good spirits afterwards.

Rank.   Well, why should one not enjoy a merry evening after a well-spent day?

Helmer.   Well spent? I am afraid I can't take credit for that.

Rank (*clapping him on the back*).   But I can, you know!

Nora.   Doctor Rank, you must have been occupied with some scientific investigation to-day.

Rank.   Exactly.

Helmer.   Just listen—little Nora talking about scientific investigations!

Nora.   And may I congratulate you on the result?

Rank.   Indeed you may.

Nora.   Was it favourable, then?

Rank.   The best possible, for both doctor and patient—certainty.

Nora (*quickly and searchingly*).   Certainty?

Rank.   Absolute certainty. So wasn't I entitled to make a merry evening of it after that?

Nora.   Yes, you certainly were, Doctor Rank.

Helmer.   I think so too, so long as you don't have to pay for it in the morning.

Rank.   Oh well, one can't have anything in this life without paying for it.

Nora.   Doctor Rank—are you fond of fancy-dress balls?

Rank.   Yes, if there is a fine lot of pretty costumes.

Nora.   Tell me—what shall we two wear at the next?

Helmer.   Little featherbrain!—are you thinking of the next already?

Rank.   We two? Yes, I can tell you. You shall go as a good fairy——

Helmer.   Yes, but what do you suggest as an appropriate costume for that?

Rank.   Let your wife go dressed just as she is in everyday life.

Helmer.   That was really very prettily turned. But can't you tell us what you will be?

Rank.   Yes, my dear friend, I have quite made up my mind about that.

Helmer.   Well?

Rank.   At the next fancy dress ball I shall be invisible.

Helmer.   That's a good joke!

Rank.   There is a big black hat—have you never heard of hats that make you invisible? If you put one on, no one can see you.

Helmer *(suppressing a smile)*.   Yes, you are quite right.

Rank.   But I am clean forgetting what I came for. Helmer, give me a cigar— one of the dark Havanas.

Helmer.   With the greatest pleasure.

[Offers him his case.]

Rank *(takes a cigar and cuts off the end)*.   Thanks.

Nora *(striking a match)*.   Let me give you a light.

Rank.   Thank you. *(She holds the match for him to light his cigar.)* And now good-bye!

Helmer.   Good-bye, good-bye, dear old man!

Nora.   Sleep well, Doctor Rank.

Rank.   Thank you for that wish.

Nora.   Wish me the same.

Rank.   You? Well, if you want me to—sleep well! And thanks for the light.

[He nods to them both and goes out.]

Helmer *(in a subdued voice)*.   He has drunk more than he ought.

Nora *(absently)*.   Maybe. *(Helmer takes a bunch of keys out of his pocket and goes into the hall.)* Torvald! what are you going to do there?

Helmer.   Empty the letter-box; it is quite full; there will be no room to put the newspaper in to-morrow morning.

Nora.   Are you going to work to-night?

Helmer.   You know quite well I'm not. What is this? Some one has been at the lock.

Nora.   At the lock—?

Helmer.   Yes, someone has. What can it mean? I should never have thought the maid—. Here is a broken hairpin. Nora, it is one of yours.

Nora *(quickly)*.   Then it must have been the children—

Helmer.   Then you must get them out of those ways. There, at last I have got it open. *(Takes out the contents of the letter-box, and calls to the kitchen.)* Helen!—Helen, put out the light over the front door. *(Goes back into the room and shuts the door into the hall. He holds out his hand full of letters.)* Look at that—look what a heap of them there are. *(Turning them over.)* What on earth is that?

Nora *(at the window)*.   The letter—No! Torvald, no!

Helmer.   Two cards—of Rank's.

Nora.   Of Doctor Rank's?

Helmer *(looking at them)*.   Doctor Rank. They were on the top. He must have put them in when he went out.

Nora.   Is there anything written on them?

Helmer.   There is a black cross over the name. Look there—what an uncomfortable idea! It looks as if he were announcing his own death.

Nora.   It is just what he is doing.

Helmer.   What? Do you know anything about it? Has he said anything to you?

Nora.   Yes. He told me that when the cards came it would be his leave-taking from us. He means to shut himself up and die.

Helmer.   My poor old friend. Certainly I knew we should not have him very long with us. But so soon! And so he hides himself away like a wounded animal.

Nora.   If it has to happen, it is best it should be without a word—don't you think so, Torvald?

Helmer (*walking up and down*).   He had so grown into our lives. I can't think of him as having gone out of them. He, with his sufferings and his loneliness, was like a cloudy background to our sunlit happiness. Well, perhaps it is best so. For him, anyway. (*Standing still.*) And perhaps for us too, Nora. We two are thrown quite upon each other now. (*Puts his arms round her.*) My darling wife, I don't feel as if I could hold you tight enough. Do you know, Nora, I have often wished that you might be threatened by some great danger, so that I might risk my life's blood, and everything, for your sake.

Nora (*disengages herself, and says firmly and decidedly*).   Now you must read your letters, Torvald.

Helmer.   No, no; not to-night. I want to be with you, my darling wife.

Nora.   With the thought of your friend's death——

Helmer.   You are right, it has affected us both. Something ugly has come between us—the thought of the horrors of death. We must try and rid our minds of that. Until then—we will each go to our own room.

Nora (*hanging on his neck*).   Good-night, Torvald—Good-night!

Helmer (*kissing her on the forehead*).   Good-night, my little singing-bird. Sleep sound, Nora. Now I will read my letters through.

[*He takes his letters and goes into his room, shutting the door after him.*]

Nora (*gropes distractedly about, seizes Helmer's domino, throws it round her, while she says in quick, hoarse, spasmodic whispers*). Never to see him again. Never! Never! (*Puts her shawl over her head.*) Never to see my children again either—never again. Never! Never!—Ah! the icy, black water—the unfathomable depths—If only it were over! He has got it now—now he is reading it. Good-bye, Torvald and my children!

[*She is about to rush out through the hall, when Helmer opens his door hurriedly and stands with an open letter in his hand.*]

Helmer. Nora!

Nora. Ah!——

Helmer. What is this? Do you know what is in this letter?

Nora. Yes, I know. Let me go! Let me get out!

Helmer *(holding her back)*. Where are you going?

Nora *(trying to get free)*. You shan't save me, Torvald!

Helmer *(reeling)*. True? Is this true, what I read here? Horrible! No, no—it is impossible that it can be true.

Nora. It is true. I have loved you above everything else in the world.

Helmer. Oh, don't let us have any silly excuses.

Nora *(taking a step towards him)*. Torvald——!

Helmer. Miserable creature—what have you done?

Nora. Let me go. You shall not suffer for my sake. You shall not take it upon yourself.

Helmer. No tragedy airs, please. *(Locks the hall door.)* Here you shall stay and give me an explanation. Do you understand what you have done? Answer me? Do you understand what you have done?

Nora *(looks steadily at him and says with a growing look of coldness in her face)*. Yes, now I am beginning to understand thoroughly.

Helmer *(walking about the room)*. What a horrible awakening! All these eight years—she who was my joy and pride—a hypocrite, a liar—worse, worse—a criminal! The unutterable ugliness of it all! For shame! For shame! *(Nora is silent and looks steadily at him. He stops in front of her.)* I ought to have suspected that something of the sort would happen. I ought to have foreseen it. All your father's want of principle—be silent!—all your father's want of principle has come out in you. No religion, no morality, no sense of duty—. How I am punished for having winked at what he did! I did it for your sake, and this is how you repay me.

Nora. Yes, that's just it.

Helmer. Now you have destroyed all my happiness. You have ruined all my future. It is horrible to think of! I am in the power of an unscrupulous man; he can do what he likes with me, ask anything he likes of me, give me any orders he pleases—I dare not refuse. And I must sink to such miserable depths because of a thoughtless woman!

Nora. When I am out of the way, you will be free.

Helmer. No fine speeches, please. Your father had always plenty of those ready, too. What good would it be to me if you were out of the way, as you say? Not the slightest. He can make the affair known everywhere; and if he does, I may be falsely suspected of having been a party to your criminal action. Very likely people will think I was behind it all—that it was I who prompted you! And I have to thank you for all this—you whom I have cherished during the whole of our married life. Do you understand now what it is you have done for me?

Nora *(coldly and quietly)*. Yes.

Helmer. It is so incredible that I can't take it in. But we must come to some understanding. Take off that shawl. Take it off, I tell you. I must try and appease him some way or another. The matter must be hushed up at any cost. And as for you and me, it must appear as if everything between us were just as before—but naturally only in the eyes of the world. You will still remain in my house, that is a matter of course. But I shall not allow you to bring up the children; I dare not trust them to you. To think that I should be obliged to say so to one whom I have loved so dearly, and whom I still——. No, that is all over. From this moment happiness is not the question; all that concerns us is to save the remains, the fragments, the appearance——

[*A ring is heard at the front-door bell.*]

Helmer (*with a start*). What is that? So late! Can the worst——? Can he——? Hide yourself, Nora. Say you are ill.

[*Nora stands motionless. Helmer goes and unlocks the hall door.*]

Maid (*half-dressed, comes to the door*). A letter for the mistress.

Helmer. Give it to me. (*Takes the letter, and shuts the door.*) Yes, it is from him. You shall not have it; I will read it myself.

Nora. Yes, read it.

Helmer (*standing by the lamp*). I scarcely have the courage to do it. It may mean ruin for both of us. No, I must know. (*Tears open the letter, runs his eye over a few lines, looks at a paper enclosed and gives a shout of joy.*) Nora! (*She looks at him questioningly.*) Nora!—No, I must read it once again——. Yes, it is true! I am saved! Nora, I am saved!

Nora. And I?

Helmer. You too, of course; we are both saved, both you and I. Look, he sends you your bond back. He says he regrets and repents—that a happy change in his life—never mind what he says! We are saved, Nora! No one can do anything to you. Oh, Nora, Nora!—no, first I must destroy these hateful things. Let me see——. (*Takes a look at the bond.*) No, no, I won't look at it. The whole thing shall be nothing but a bad dream to me. (*Tears up the bond and both letters, throws them all into the stove, and watches them burn.*) There—now it doesn't exist any longer. He says that since Christmas Eve you——. These must have been three dreadful days for you, Nora.

Nora. I have fought a hard fight these three days.

Helmer. And suffered agonies, and seen no way out but——. No, we won't call any of the horrors to mind. We will only shout with joy, and keep saying, "It's all over! It's all over!" Listen to me, Nora. You don't seem to realise that it is all over. What is this?—such a cold, set face! My poor little Nora, I quite understand; you don't feel as if you could believe that I have forgiven you. But it is true, Nora, I swear it; I have forgiven you everything. I know that what you did, you did out of love for me.

Nora.   That is true.

Helmer.   You have loved me as a wife ought to love her husband. Only you had not sufficient knowledge to judge of the means you used. But do you suppose you are any the less dear to me, because you don't understand how to act on your own responsibility? No, no; only lean on me; I will advise you and direct you. I should not be a man if this womanly helplessness did not just give you a double attractiveness in my eyes. You must not think any more about the hard things I said in my first moment of consternation, when I thought everything was going to overwhelm me. I have forgiven you, Nora; I swear to you I have forgiven you.

[She goes out through the door to the right.]

Helmer.   No, don't go———. *(Looks in.)* What are you doing in there?

Nora *(from within).*   Taking off my fancy dress.

Helmer *(standing at the open door).*   Yes, do. Try and calm yourself, and make your mind easy again, my frightened little singing-bird. Be at rest, and feel secure; I have broad wings to shelter you under. *(Walks up and down by the door.)* How warm and cosy our home is, Nora. Here is shelter for you; here I will protect you like a hunted dove that I have saved from a hawk's claws. I will bring peace to your poor beating heart. It will come, little by little, Nora, believe me. Tomorrow morning you will look upon it all quite differently; soon everything will be just as it was before. Very soon you won't need me to assure you that I have forgiven you; you will yourself feel the certainty that I have done so. Can you suppose I should ever think of such a thing as repudiating you, or even reproaching you? You have no idea what a true man's heart is like, Nora. There is something so indescribably sweet and satisfying, to a man, in the knowledge that he has forgiven his wife— forgiven her freely, and with all his heart. It seems as if that had made her, as it were, doubly his own; he has given her a new life, so to speak; and she has in a way become both wife and child to him. So you shall be for me after this, my little scared, helpless darling. Have no anxiety about anything, Nora; only be frank and open with me, and I will serve as will and con- science both to you———. What is this? Not gone to bed? Have you changed your things?

Nora   *(in everyday dress).* Yes, Torvald, I have changed my things now.

Helmer.   But what for?—so late as this.

Nora.   I shall not sleep to-night.

Helmer.   But, my dear Nora——

Nora *(looking at her watch).*   It is not so very late. Sit down here, Torvald. You and I have much to say to one another.

[She sits down at one side of the table.]

Helmer.   Nora—what is this?—this cold, set face?

Nora.   Sit down. It will take some time; I have a lot to talk over with you.

Helmer (*sits down at the opposite side of the table*). You alarm me, Nora!—and I don't understand you.

Nora. No, that is just it. You don't understand me, and I have never understood you either—before to-night. No, you mustn't interrupt me. You must simply listen to what I say. Torvald, this is a settling of accounts.

Helmer. What do you mean by that?

Nora (*after a short silence*). Isn't there one thing that strikes you as strange in our sitting here like this?

Helmer. What is that?

Nora. We have been married now eight years. Does it not occur to you that this is the first time we two, you and I, husband and wife, have had a serious conversation?

Helmer. What do you mean by serious?

Nora. In all these eight years—longer than that—from the very beginning of our acquaintance, we have never exchanged a word on any serious subject.

Helmer. Was it likely that I would be continually and for ever telling you about worries that you could not help me to bear?

Nora. I am not speaking about business matters. I say that we have never sat down in earnest together to try and get at the bottom of anything.

Helmer. But, dearest Nora, would it have been any good to you?

Nora. That is just it; you have never understood me. I have been greatly wronged, Torvald—first by papa and then by you.

Helmer. What! By us two—by us two, who have loved you better than anyone else in the world?

Nora (*shaking her head*). You have never loved me. You have only thought it pleasant to be in love with me.

Helmer. Nora, what do I hear you saying?

Nora. It is perfectly true, Torvald. When I was at home with papa, he told me his opinion about everything, and so I had the same opinions; and if I differed from him I concealed the fact, because he would not have liked it. He called me his doll-child, and he played with me just as I used to play with my dolls. And when I came to live with you——

Helmer. What sort of an expression is that to use about our marriage?

Nora (*undisturbed*). I mean that I was simply transferred from papa's hands into yours. You arranged everything according to your own taste, and so I got the same tastes as you—or else I pretended to, I am really not quite sure which—I think sometimes the one and sometimes the other. When I look back on it, it seems to me as if I had been living here like a poor woman—just from hand to mouth. I have existed merely to perform tricks for you, Torvald. But you would have it so. You and papa have committed a great sin against me. It is your fault that I have made nothing of my life.

Helmer. How unreasonable and how ungrateful you are, Nora! Have you not been happy here?

Nora. No, I have never been happy. I thought I was, but it has never really been so.

Helmer. Not—not happy!

Nora. No, only merry. And you have always been so kind to me. But our home has been nothing but a playroom. I have been your doll-wife, just as at home I was papa's doll-child; and here the children have been my dolls. I thought it great fun when you played with me, just as they thought it great fun when I played with them. That is what our marriage has been, Torvald.

Helmer. There is some truth in what you say—exaggerated and strained as your view of it is. But for the future it shall be different. Playtime shall be over, and lesson-time shall begin.

Nora. Whose lessons? Mine, or the children's?

Helmer. Both your and the children's, my darling Nora.

Nora. Alas, Torvald, you are not the man to educate me into being a proper wife for you.

Helmer. And you can say that!

Nora. And I—how am I fitted to bring up the children?

Helmer. Nora!

Nora. Didn't you say so yourself a little while ago—that you dare not trust me to bring them up?

Helmer. In a moment of anger! Why do you pay any heed to that?

Nora. Indeed, you were perfectly right. I am not fit for the task. There is another task I must undertake first. I must try and educate myself—you are not the man to help me in that. I must do that for myself. And that is why I am going to leave you now.

Helmer (*springing up*). What do you say?

Nora. I must stand quite alone, if I am to understand myself and everything about me. It is for that reason that I cannot remain with you any longer.

Helmer. Nora! Nora!

Nora. I am going away from here now, at once. I am sure Christine will take me in for the night——

Helmer. You are out of your mind! I won't allow it! I forbid you!

Nora. It is no use forbidding me anything any longer. I will take with me what belongs to myself. I will take nothing from you, either now or later.

Helmer. What sort of madness is this!

Nora. To-morrow I shall go home—I mean, to my old home. It will be easiest for me to find something to do there.

Helmer. You blind, foolish woman!

Nora. I must try and get some sense, Torvald.

Helmer. To desert your home, your husband and your children! And you don't consider what people will say!

Nora. I cannot consider that at all. I only know that it is necessary for me.

Helmer. It's shocking. This is how you would neglect your most sacred duties.

Nora. What do you consider my most sacred duties?

Helmer. Do I need to tell you that? Are they not your duties to your husband and your children?

Nora. I have other duties just as sacred.

Helmer. That you have not. What duties could those be?

Nora. Duties to myself.

Helmer. Before all else, you are a wife and a mother.

Nora. I don't believe that any longer. I believe that before all else I am a reasonable human being, just as you are—or, at all events, that I must try and become one. I know quite well, Torvald, that most people would think you right, and that views of that kind are to be found in books; but I can no longer content myself with what most people say, or with what is found in books. I must think over things for myself and get to understand them.

Helmer. Can you not understand your place in your own home? Have you not a reliable guide in such matters as that?—have you no religion?

Nora. I am afraid, Torvald, I do not exactly know what religion is.

Helmer. What are you saying?

Nora. I know nothing but what the clergyman said, when I went to be confirmed. He told us that religion was this, and that, and the other. When I am away from all this, and am alone, I will look into that matter too. I will see if what the clergyman said is true, or at all events if it is true for me.

Helmer. This is unheard of in a girl of your age! But if religion cannot lead you aright, let me try and awaken your conscience. I suppose you have some moral sense? Or—answer me—am I to think you have none?

Nora. I assure you, Torvald, that is not an easy question to answer. I really don't know. The thing perplexes me altogether. I only know that you and I look at it in quite another light. I am learning, too, that the law is quite another thing from what I supposed; but I find it impossible to convince myself that the law is right. According to it a woman has no right to spare her old dying father, or to save her husband's life. I can't believe that.

Helmer. You talk like a child. You don't understand the conditions of the world in which you live.

Nora. No, I don't. But now I am going to try. I am going to see if I can make out who is right, the world or I.

Helmer. You are ill, Nora; you are delirious; I almost think you are out of your mind.

Nora. I have never felt my mind so clear and certain as to-night.

Helmer. And is it with a clear and certain mind that you forsake your husband and your children?

Nora. Yes, it is.

Helmer. Then there is only one possible explanation.

Nora. What is that?

Helmer. You do not love me any more.

Nora. No, that is just it.

Helmer. Nora!—and you can say that?

Nora. It gives me great pain, Torvald, for you have always been so kind to me, but I cannot help it. I do not love you any more.

Helmer (*regaining his composure*). Is that a clear and certain conviction too?

Nora. Yes, absolutely clear and certain. That is the reason why I will not stay here any longer.

Helmer. And can you tell me what I have done to forfeit your love?

Nora. Yes, indeed I can. It was to-night, when the wonderful thing did not happen; then I saw you were not the man I had thought you.

Helmer. Explain yourself better—I don't understand you.

Nora. I have waited so patiently for eight years; for, goodness knows, I knew very well that wonderful things don't happen every day. Then this horrible misfortune came upon me; and then I felt quite certain that the wonderful thing was going to happen at last. When Krogstad's letter was lying out there, never for a moment did I imagine that you would consent to accept this man's conditions. I was so absolutely certain that you would say to him: Publish the thing to the whole world. And when that was done——

Helmer. Yes, what then?—when I had exposed my wife to shame and disgrace?

Nora. When that was done, I was so absolutely certain, you would come forward and take everything upon yourself, and say: I am the guilty one.

Helmer. Nora——!

Nora. You mean that I would never have accepted such a sacrifice on your part? No, of course not. But what would my assurances have been worth against yours? That was the wonderful thing which I hoped for and feared; and it was to prevent that, that I wanted to kill myself.

Helmer. I would gladly work night and day for you, Nora—bear sorrow and want for your sake. But no man would sacrifice his honour for the one he loves.

Nora. It is a thing hundreds of thousands of women have done.

Helmer. Oh, you think and talk like a heedless child.

Nora. Maybe. But you neither think nor talk like the man I could bind myself to. As soon as your fear was over—and it was not fear for what threatened me, but for what might happen to you—when the whole thing was past, as far as you were concerned it was exactly as if nothing at all had happened. Exactly as before, I was your little skylark, your doll, which you would in future treat with doubly gentle care, because it was so brittle and fragile. (*Getting up.*) Torvald—it was then it dawned upon me that for eight years I had been living here with a strange man, and had borne him three children——. Oh, I can't bear to think of it! I could tear myself into little bits!

Helmer (*sadly*). I see, I see. An abyss has opened between us—there is no denying it. But, Nora, would it not be possible to fill it up?

Nora. As I am now, I am no wife for you.

Helmer. I have it in me to become a different man.

Nora. Perhaps—if your doll is taken away from you.

Helmer. But to part!—to part from you! No, no, Nora, I can't understand that idea.

Nora *(going out to the right).*   That makes it all the more certain that it must be done.

[She comes back with her cloak and hat and a small bag which she puts on a chair by the table.]

Helmer.   Nora, Nora, not now! Wait till to-morrow.

Nora *(putting on her cloak).*   I cannot spend the night in a strange man's room.

Helmer.   But can't we live here like brother and sister——?

Nora *(putting on her hat).*   You know very well that would not last long. *(Puts the shawl round her.)* Good-bye, Torvald. I won't see the little ones. I know they are in better hands than mine. As I am now, I can be of no use to them.

Helmer.   But some day, Nora—some day?

Nora.   How can I tell? I have no idea what is going to become of me.

Helmer.   But you are my wife, whatever becomes of you.

Nora.   Listen, Torvald. I have heard that when a wife deserts her husband's house, as I am doing now, he is legally freed from all obligations towards her. In any case I set you free from all your obligations. You are not to feel yourself bound in the slightest way, any more than I shall. There must be perfect freedom on both sides. See here is your ring back. Give me mine.

Helmer.   That too?

Nora.   That too.

Helmer.   Here it is.

Nora.   That's right. Now it is all over. I have put the keys here. The maids know all about everything in the house—better than I do. To-morrow, after I have left her, Christine will come here and pack up my own things that I brought with me from home. I will have them sent after me.

Helmer.   All over! All over!—Nora, shall you never think of me again?

Nora.   I know I shall often think of you and the children and this house.

Helmer.   May I write to you, Nora?

Nora.   No—never. You must not do that.

Helmer.   But at least let me send you——

Nora.   Nothing—nothing——

Helmer.   Let me help you if you are in want.

Nora.   No. I can receive nothing from a stranger.

Helmer.   Nora—can I never be anything more than a stranger to you?

Nora *(taking her bag).* Ah, Torvald, the most wonderful thing of all would have to happen.

Helmer.   Tell me what that would be!

Nora.   Both you and I would have to be so changed that——. Oh, Torvald, I don't believe any longer in wonderful things happening.

Helmer.   But I will believe in it. Tell me? So changed that——?

Nora.   That our life together would be a real wedlock. Good-bye.

[She goes out through the hall.]

Helmer *(sinks down on a chair at the door and buries his face in his hands).* Nora! Nora! *(Looks round, and rises.)* Empty. She is gone. *(A hope flashes across his mind.)* The most wonderful thing of all——?

[The sound of a door shutting is heard from below.]

QUESTIONS
1. What evidence does the play provide that *A Doll's House* is about not only Nora's marriage but the institution of marriage itself?   **2.** On a number of occasions Nora recalls her father. What relevance do these recollections have to the development of the theme?   **3.** Is Krogstad presented as a stock villain, or are we meant to sympathize with him?   **4.** What function does Dr. Rank serve in the play?

WRITING TOPICS
1. Does the fact that Nora abandons her children undermine her otherwise heroic decision to walk out on a hollow marriage? For an 1880 German production of the play, Ibsen—in response to public demand—provided an alternate ending in which Nora, after struggling with her conscience, decides that she cannot abandon her children. Is this ending better than the original ending? Explain.   **2.** How does the subplot involving the relationship between Mrs. Linde and Krogstad add force to the main plot of *A Doll's House?*

CONFORMITY
AND
REBELLION

The Accused, 1886 by Odilon Redon

ESSAYS

A Modest Proposal   1729

JONATHAN SWIFT   [1667–1745]

It is a melancholy object to those who walk through this great town[1] or travel   1
in the country, when they see the streets, the roads, and cabin doors, crowded
with beggars of the female sex, followed by three, four, or six children, all in
rags and importuning every passenger for an alms. These mothers, instead of
being able to work for their honest livelihood, are forced to employ all their
time in strolling to beg sustenance for their helpless infants, who, as they grow
up, either turn thieves for want of work, or leave their dear native country to
fight for the Pretender in Spain, or sell themselves to the Barbados.[2]

I think it is agreed by all parties that this prodigious number of children in   2
the arms, or on the backs, or at the heels of their mothers, and frequently of
their fathers, is in the present deplorable state of the kingdom a very great
additional grievance; and therefore whoever could find out a fair, cheap, and
easy method of making these children sound, useful members of the commonwealth would deserve so well of the public as to have his statue set up for
a preserver of the nation.

But my intention is very far from being confined to provide only for the   3
children of professed beggars; it is of a much greater extent, and shall take
in the whole number of infants at a certain age who are born of parents in
effect as little able to support them as those who demand our charity in the
streets.

As to my own part, having turned my thoughts for many years upon this   4
important subject, and maturely weighed the several schemes of other projec-
tors,[3] I have always found them grossly mistaken in their computation. It is
true, a child just dropped from its dam may be supported by her milk for a
solar year, with little other nourishment; at most not above the value of two

---

[1] Dublin.
[2] Many Irish men joined the army of the exiled James Stuart (1688–1766), who laid claim
to the British throne. Others exchanged their labor for passage to the British colony of Barbados, in the Caribbean.
[3] People with projects.

shillings,[4] which the mother may certainly get, or the value in scraps, by her lawful occupation of begging; and it is exactly at one year that I propose to provide for them in such a manner as instead of being a charge upon their parents or the parish, or wanting food and raiment for the rest of their lives, they shall on the contrary contribute to the feeding, and partly to the clothing, of many thousands.

There is likewise another great advantage in my scheme, that it will prevent those voluntary abortions, and that horrid practice of women murdering their bastard children, alas, too frequent among us, sacrificing the poor innocent babes, I doubt, more to avoid the expense than the shame, which would move tears and pity in the most savage and inhuman breast.   5

The number of souls in this kingdom being usually reckoned one million and a half, of these I calculate there may be about two hundred thousand couples whose wives are breeders; from which number I subtract thirty thousand couples who are able to maintain their own children, although I apprehend there cannot be so many under the present distress of the kingdom; but this being granted, there will remain an hundred and seventy thousand breeders. I again subtract fifty thousand for those women who miscarry, or whose children die by accident or disease within the year. There only remain an hundred and twenty thousand children of poor parents annually born. The question therefore is, how this number shall be reared and provided for, which, as I have already said, under the present situation of affairs, is utterly impossible by all the methods hitherto proposed. For we can neither employ them in handicraft or agriculture; we neither build houses (I mean in the country) nor cultivate land. They can very seldom pick up a livelihood by stealing till they arrive at six years old except where they are of towardly parts;[5] although I confess they learn the rudiments much earlier, during which time they can however be looked upon only as probationers, as I have been informed by a principal gentleman in the country of Cavan, who protested to me that he never knew above one or two instances under the age of six, even in a part of the kingdom so renowned for the quickest proficiency in that art.   6

I am assured by our merchants that a boy or a girl before twelve years old is no salable commodity; and even when they come to this age they will not yield above three pounds, or three pounds and half a crown at most on the Exchange;[6] which cannot turn to account either to the parents or the kingdom, the charge of nutriment and rags having been at least four times that value.   7

I shall now therefore humbly propose my own thoughts, which I hope will not be liable to the least objection.   8

I have been assured by a very knowing American of my acquaintance in London, that a young healthy child well nursed is at a year old a most delicious, nourishing, and wholesome food, whether stewed, roasted, baked, or   9

---

[4] A shilling was worth about twenty-five cents.
[5] Able and eager to learn.
[6] A pound was twenty shillings; a crown, five shillings.

boiled; and I make no doubt that it will equally serve in a fricassee or a ragout.

I do therefore humbly offer it to public consideration that of the hundred and twenty thousand children, already computed, twenty thousand may be reserved for breed, whereof only one fourth part to be males, which is more than we allow to sheep, black cattle, or swine; and my reason is that these children are seldom the fruits of marriage, a circumstance not much regarded by our savages, therefore one male will be sufficient to serve four females. That the remaining hundred thousand may at a year old be offered in sale to the persons of quality and fortune through the kingdom, always advising the mother to let them suck plentifully in the last month, so as to render them plump and fat for a good table. A child will make two dishes at an entertainment for friends; and when the family dines alone, the fore or hind quarter will make a reasonable dish, and seasoned with a little pepper or salt will be very good boiled on the fourth day, especially in winter.   10

I have reckoned upon a medium that a child just born will weigh twelve pounds, and in a solar year if tolerably nursed increaseth to twenty-eight pounds.   11

I grant this food will be somewhat dear, and therefore very proper for landlords, who, as they have already devoured most of the parents, seem to have the best title to the children.   12

Infant's flesh will be in season throughout the year, but more plentiful in March, and a little before and after. For we are told by a grave author, an eminent French physician,[7] that fish being a prolific diet, there are more children born in Roman Catholic countries about nine months after Lent than at any other season; therefore, reckoning a year after Lent, the markets will be more glutted than usual, because the number of popish infants is at least three to one in this kingdom; and therefore it will have one other collateral advantage, by lessening the number of Papists among us.   13

I have already computed the charge of nursing a beggar's child (in which list I reckon all cottagers, laborers, and four-fifths of the farmers) to be about two shillings per annum, rags included; and I believe no gentleman would repine to give ten shillings for the carcass of a good fat child, which, as I have said, will make four dishes of excellent nutritive meat, when he hath only some particular friend or his own family to dine with him. Thus the squire will learn to be a good landlord, and grow popular among the tenants; the mother will have eight shillings net profit, and be fit for work till she produces another child.   14

Those who are more thrifty (as I must confess the times require) may flay the carcass; the skin of which artificially[8] dressed will make admirable gloves for ladies, and summer boots for fine gentlemen.   15

As to our city of Dublin, shambles[9] may be appointed for this purpose in the   16

---

[7] François Rabelais, sixteenth-century French comic writer.
[8] Skillfully.
[9] Slaughterhouses.

most convenient parts of it, and butchers we may be assured will not be wanting; although I rather recommend buying the children alive, and dressing them hot from the knife as we do roasting pigs.

A very worthy person, a true lover of his country, and whose virtues I highly esteem, was lately pleased in discoursing on this matter to offer a refinement upon my scheme. He said that many gentlemen of his kingdom, having of late destroyed their deer, he conceived that the want of venison might be well supplied by the bodies of young lads and maidens, not exceeding fourteen years of age nor under twelve, so great a number of both sexes in every country being now ready to starve for want of work or service; and these to be disposed of by their parents, if alive, or otherwise by their nearest relations. But with due deference to so excellent a friend and so deserving a patriot, I cannot be altogether in his sentiments; for as to the males, my American acquaintance assured me from frequent experience that their flesh was generally tough and lean, like that of our schoolboys, by continual exercise, and their taste disagreeable; and to fatten them would not answer the charge. Then as to the females; it would, I think with humble submission, be a loss to the public, because they soon would become breeders themselves; and besides, it is not improbable that some scrupulous people might be apt to censure such a practice (although indeed very unjustly) as a little bordering upon cruelty; which, I confess, hath always been with me the strongest objection against any project, how well soever intended.

But in order to justify my friend, he confessed that this expedient was put into his head by the famous Psalmanazar,[10] a native of the island Formosa, who came from thence to London above twenty years ago, and in conversation told my friend that in his country when any young person happened to be put to death, the executioner sold the carcass to persons of quality as a prime dainty; and that in his time the body of a plump girl of fifteen, who was crucified for an attempt to poison the emperor, was sold to his Imperial Majesty's prime minister of state, and other great mandarins of the court, in joints from the gibbet, at four hundred crowns. Neither indeed can I deny that if the same use were made of several plump young girls in this town, who without one single groat[11] to their fortunes cannot stir abroad without a chair,[12] and appear at the playhouse and assemblies in foreign fineries which they never will pay for, the kingdom would not be the worse.

Some persons of a desponding spirit are in great concern about the vast number of poor people who are aged, diseased, or maimed, and I have been desired to employ my thoughts what course may be taken to ease the nation of so grievous an encumbrance. But I am not in the least pain upon the matter, because it is very well known that they are every day dying and rotting by cold and famine, and filth and vermin, as fast as can be reasonably ex-

17

18

19

---

[10] George Psalmanazar was a Frenchman who passed himself off as a native of Formosa.
[11] A coin worth about four cents.
[12] A sedan chair, an enclosed chair carried by poles on the front and back.

pected. And as to the younger laborers, they are now in almost as hopeful a condition. They cannot get work, and consequently pine away for want of nourishment to a degree that if any time they are accidently hired to common labor, they have not the strength to perform it; and thus the country and themselves are happily delivered from the evils to come.

I have too long digressed, and therefore I shall return to my subject. I think   20
the advantages by the proposal which I have made are obvious and many, as well as of the highest importance.

For first, I have already observed, it would greatly lessen the number of   21
Papists, with whom we are yearly overrun, being the principal breeders of the nation as well as our most dangerous enemies; and who stay at home on purpose to deliver the kingdom to the Pretender, hoping to take their advantage by the absence of so many good Protestants, who have chose rather to leave their country than to stay at home and pay tithes against their conscience to an Episcopal curate.

Secondly, the poorer tenants will have something valuable of their own,   22
which by law may be made liable to distress,[13] and help to pay their landlord's rent, their corn and cattle being already seized and money a thing unknown.

Thirdly, whereas the maintenance of a hundred thousand children, from   23
two years old and upwards, cannot be computed at less than ten shillings a piece per annum, the nation's stock will be thereby increased fifty thousand pounds per annum, besides the profit of a new dish introduced to the tables of all gentlemen of fortune in the kingdom who have any refinement in taste. And all the money will circulate among ourselves, the goods being entirely of our own growth and manufacture.

Fourthly, the constant breeders, besides the gain of eight shillings sterling   24
per annum by the sale of their children, will be rid of the charge of maintaining them after the first year.

Fifthly, this food would likewise bring great custom to taverns, where the   25
vintners will certainly be so prudent as to procure the best receipts[14] for dressing it to perfection, and consequently have their houses frequented by all the fine gentlemen, who justly value themselves upon their knowledge in good eating; and a skillful cook, who understands how to oblige his guests, will contrive to make it as expensive as they please.

Sixthly, this would be a great inducement to marriage, which all wise na-   26
tions have either encouraged by rewards or enforced by laws and penalties. It would increase the care and tenderness of mothers towards their children, when they were sure of a settlement for life to the poor babes, provided in some sort by the public, to their annual profit instead of expense. We should see an honest emulation among the married women, which of them could bring the fattest child to the market. Men would become as fond of their wives

---

[13] Seizure for payment of debts.
[14] Recipes.

during the time of their pregnancy as they are now of their mares in foal, their cows in calf, or sows when they are ready to farrow; nor offer to beat or kick them (as is too frequent a practice) for fear of a miscarriage.

Many other advantages might be enumerated. For instance, the addition of some thousand carcasses in our exportation of barreled beef, the propagation of swine's flesh, and improvements in the art of making good bacon, so much wanted among us by the great destruction of pigs, too frequent at our tables, which are no way comparable in taste or magnificence to a well-grown, fat, yearling child, which roasted whole will make a considerable figure at a lord mayor's feast or any other public entertainment. But this and many others I omit, being studious of brevity.   27

Supposing that one thousand families in this city would be constant customers for infants' flesh, besides others who might have it at merry meetings, particularly weddings and christenings, I compute that Dublin would take off annually about twenty thousand carcasses, and the rest of the kingdom (where probably they will be sold somewhat cheaper) the remaining eighty thousand.   28

I can think of no one objection that will possibly be raised against this proposal unless it should be urged that the number of people will be thereby much lessened in the kingdom. This I freely own, and it was indeed one principal design in offering it to the world. I desire the reader will observe, that I calculate my remedy for this one individual kingdom of Ireland and for no other that ever was, is, or I think ever can be upon earth. Therefore let no man talk to me of other expedients: of taxing our absentees at five shillings a pound: of using neither clothes nor household furniture except what is of our own growth and manufacture: of utterly rejecting the materials and instruments that promote foreign luxury: of curing the expensiveness of pride, vanity, idleness, and gaming in our women: of introducing a vein of parsimony, prudence, and temperance: of learning to love our country, in the want of which we differ even from Laplanders and the inhabitants of Topinamboo:[15] of quitting our animosities and factions, nor acting any longer like the Jews, who were murdering one another at the very moment their city was taken:[16] of being a little cautious not to sell our country and conscience for nothing: of teaching landlords to have at least one degree of mercy toward their tenants: lastly, of putting a spirit of honesty, industry, and skill into our shopkeepers; who, if a resolution could now be taken to buy only our native goods, would immediately unite to cheat and exact upon us in the price, the measure, and the goodness, nor could ever yet be brought to make one fair proposal of just dealing, though often and earnestly invited to it.   29

Therefore, I repeat, let no man talk to me of these and the like expedients,   30

---

[15] A district in Brazil, inhabited in Swift's day by primitive tribes.
[16] While the Roman emperor Titus laid siege to Jerusalem in 70 A.D., bloody fighting erupted among factions within the city.

till he hath at least some glimpse of hope that there will be some hearty and sincere attempt to put them in practice.

But as to myself, having been wearied out for many years of offering vain, idle, visionary thoughts, and at length utterly despairing of success, I fortunately fell upon this proposal, which, as it is wholly new, so it hath something solid and real, of no expense and little trouble, full in our own power, and whereby we can incur no danger in disobliging England. For this kind of commodity will not bear exportation, the flesh being of too tender a consistence to admit a long continuance in salt, although perhaps I could name a country[17] which would be glad to eat up our whole nation without it.

After all, I am not so violently bent upon my own opinion as to reject any offer proposed by wise men, which shall be found equally innocent, cheap, easy, and effectual. But before something of that kind shall be advanced in contradiction to my scheme, and offering a better, I desire the author or authors will be pleased maturely to consider two points. First, as things now stand, how they will be able to find food and raiment for an hundred thousand useless mouths and backs. And secondly, there being a round million of creatures in human figure throughout this kingdom, whose sole subsistence put into a common stock would leave them in debt two millions of pounds sterling, adding those who are beggars by profession to the bulk of farmers, cottagers, and laborers, with their wives and children who are beggars in effect; I desire those politicians who dislike my overture, and may perhaps be so bold to attempt to answer, that they will first ask the parents of these mortals whether they would not at this day think it a great happiness to have been sold for food at a year old in this manner I prescribe, and thereby have avoided such a perpetual scene of misfortunes as they have since gone through by the oppression of landlords, the impossibility of paying rent without money or trade, the want of common sustenance, with neither house nor clothes to cover them from the inclemencies of the weather, and the most inevitable prospect of entailing the like or greater miseries upon their breed forever.

I profess, in the sincerity of my heart, that I have not the least personal interest in endeavoring to promote this necessary work, having no other motive than the public good of my country, by advancing our trade, providing for infants, relieving the poor, and giving some pleasure to the rich. I have no children by which I can propose to get a single penny; the youngest being nine years old, and my wife past childbearing.

QUESTIONS
1. In what sense is Swift's proposal "modest"?   **2.** What are the major divisions of the essay? What function does each serve?   **3.** What function does paragraph 29

---

[17] England.

serve?   **4.** Explain what Swift means when he says in paragraph 20 that "I have too long digressed. . . . "   **5.** Characterize the tone of the essay, paying particular attention to the speaker's use of diction.

WRITING TOPIC
Some knowledge of Swift's life and other works would make it clear that in this essay he is being satiric. Without that knowledge, that is, on the basis of the essay alone, how would you demonstrate that Swift is writing satire?

Defense[1]   1916

EMMA GOLDMAN   [1869–1940]

Your Honor: My presence before you this afternoon proves conclusively that there is no free speech in the city or county of New York. I hope that there is free speech in your court.

I have delivered the lecture which caused my arrest in at least fifty cities throughout the country, always in the presence of detectives. I have never been arrested. I delivered the same address in New York City seven times, prior to my arrest, always in the presence of detectives, because in my case, your honor, "the police never cease out of the land." Yet for some reason unknown to me I have never been molested until February 11th, nor would I have been then, if free speech were a living factor, and not a dead letter to be celebrated only on the 4th of July.

Your Honor, I am charged with the crime of having given information to men and women as to how to prevent conception. For the last three weeks, every night before packed houses, a stirring social indictment is being played at the Candler Theatre. I refer to "Justice" by John Galsworthy.[2] The council for the Defense in summing up the charge against the defendant says among other things: "Your Honor: back of the commission of every crime, is life, palpitating life."

Now what is the palpitating life back of my crime? I will tell you, Your Honor. According to the bulletin of the Department of Health, 30,000,000 people in America are underfed. They are always in a state of semi-starvation. Not only because their average income is too small to sustain them properly— the bulletin states that eight hundred dollars a year is the minimum income necessary for every family—but because there are too many members in each family to be sustained on a meagre income. Hence 30,000,000 people in this land go through life underfed and overworked.

Your Honor: what kind of children do you suppose these parents can bring into the world? I will tell you: children so poor and anemic that they take their leave from this, our kind world, before their first year of life. In that way, 300,000 babies, according to the baby welfare association, are sacrificed in the United States each year. This, Your Honor, is the palpitating life which has

---

[1] Emma Goldman was arrested while lecturing in New York on February 11, 1916. She was charged with violating Section 1142 of the New York Penal Code, which made it a misdemeanor to "sell, lend, or give away" or to advertise, loan, or distribute "any recipe, drug, or medicine for the prevention of conception." Tried and convicted on April 20, she was offered the choice between a hundred-dollar fine or fifteen days in jail. As a matter of principle, she chose jail.

[2] John Galsworthy (1867–1933), English novelist and playwright, whose play *Justice* (1909) deals with crime and disproportionate punishment.

confronted me for many years, and which is back of the commission of my crime. I have been part of the great social struggle of this country for twenty-six years, as nurse, as lecturer, as publisher. During this time I have gone up and down the land in the large industrial centres, in the mining region, in the slums of our large cities. I have seen conditions appalling and heart-rending, which no creative genius could adequately describe. I do not intend to take up the time of the court to go into many of these cases, but I must mention a few.

A woman, married to a consumptive husband has eight children, six are in the tuberculosis hospital. She is on the way with the ninth child.   6

A woman whose husband earns $12 per week has six children, on the way with the seventh child.   7

A woman with twelve children living in three squalid rooms, dies in con-finement with the 13th child, the oldest, now the mainstay of the 12 orphans, is 14 years of age.   8

These are but very few of the victims of our economic grinding mill, which sets a premium upon poverty, and our puritanic law which maintains a con-spiracy of silence.   9

Your Honor: if giving one's life for the purpose of awakening race conscious-ness in the masses, a consciousness which will impel them to bring quality and not quantity into society, if that be a crime, I am glad to be such a criminal. But I assure you I am in good company. I have as my illustrious colleagues the greatest men and women of our time; scientists, political economists, artists, men of letters in Europe and America. And what is even more important, I have the working class, and women in every walk of life, to back me. No isolated individuals here and there, but thousands of them.   10

After all, the question of birth control is largely a workingman's question, above all a workingwoman's question. She it is who risks her health, her youth, her very life in giving out of herself the units of the race. She it is who ought to have the means and the knowledge to say how many children she shall give, and to what purpose she shall give them, and under what conditions she shall bring forth life.   11

Statesmen, politicians, men of the cloth, men, who own the wealth of the world, need a large race, no matter how poor in quality. Who else would do their work, and fight their wars? But the people who toil and drudge and create, and receive a mere pittance in return, what reason have they to bring hapless children into the world? They are beginning to realize their debt to the children already in existence, and in order to make good their obligations, they absolutely refuse to go on like cattle breeding more and more.   12

That which constitutes my crime, Your Honor, is therefore, enabling the mass of humanity to give to the world fewer and better children—birth con-trol, which in the last two years has grown to such gigantic dimensions that no amount of laws can possibly stop the ever-increasing tide.   13

And this is true, not only because of what I may or may not say, or of how many propagandists may or may not be sent to jail; there is a much profounder reason for the tremendous growth and importance of birth control. That   14 reason is conditioned in the great modern social conflict, or rather social war, I should say. A war not for military conquest or material supremacy, a war of the oppressed and disinherited of the earth against their enemies, capitalism and the state, a war for a seat at the table of life, a war for well-being, for beauty, for liberty. Above all, this war is for a free motherhood and a joyous playful, glorious childhood.

Birth control, Your Honor, is only one of the ways which leads to the victory   15
in that war, and I am glad and proud to be able to indicate that way.

QUESTIONS
1. Regardless of your own personal feelings on the issue, how would you evaluate the strengths and weaknesses of Goldman's rhetoric?   **2.** Is Goldman right to characterize birth control as "largely a workingman's question, above all a working-woman's question" (paragraph 11)? Explain.   **3.** Are Goldman's arguments equally relevant to the issue of abortion? Explain.

WRITING TOPIC
Write an essay in which you compare and contrast Goldman's methods of persuasion and substantive arguments with those used by Margaret Sanger in her essay "The Turbid Ebb and Flow of Misery."

What if Shakespeare Had Had a Sister? [1]

1928

VIRGINIA WOOLF [1882–1941]

It was disappointing not to have brought back in the evening some important   1
statement, some authentic fact. Women are poorer than men because—this
or that. Perhaps now it would be better to give up seeking for the truth, and
receiving on one's head an avalanche of opinion hot as lava, discoloured as
dish-water. It would be better to draw the curtains; to shut out distractions; to
light the lamp; to narrow the enquiry and to ask the historian, who records not
opinions but facts, to describe under what conditions women lived, not
throughout the ages, but in England, say in the time of Elizabeth.

For it is a perennial puzzle why no woman wrote a word of that extraordi-   2
nary literature when every other man, it seemed, was capable of song or sonnet.
What were the conditions in which women lived, I asked myself; for fiction,
imaginative work that is, is not dropped like a pebble upon the ground, as
science may be; fiction is like a spider's web, attached ever so lightly perhaps,
but still attached to life at all four corners. Often the attachment is scarcely
perceptible; Shakespeare's plays, for instance, seem to hang there complete by
themselves. But when the web is pulled askew, hooked up at the edge, torn in
the middle, one remembers that these webs are not spun in midair by incor-
poreal creatures, but are the work of suffering human beings, and are attached
to grossly material things, like health and money and the houses we live in.

I went, therefore, to the shelf where the histories stand and took down one   3
of the latest, Professor Trevelyan's *History of England*. Once more I looked up
Women, found "position of," and turned to the pages indicated. "Wife-
beating," I read, "was a recognized right of man, and was practiced without
shame by high as well as low. . . . Similarly," the historian goes on, "the daughter who refused to marry the gentleman of her parents' choice was liable to be
locked up, beaten and flung about the room, without any shock being inflicted
on public opinion. Marriage was not an affair of personal affection, but of
family avarice, particularly in the 'chivalrous' upper classes. . . . Betrothal often
took place while one or both of the parties was in the cradle, and marriage
when they were scarcely out of the nurses' charge." That was about 1470, soon
after Chaucer's time. The next reference to the position of women is some two

---

[1] *A Room of One's Own*, from which this essay is taken, is based on two lectures Woolf delivered on women and literature at Newnham College and Girton College, Cambridge University. In the opening chapter, Woolf declares that without "money and a room of her own" a
woman cannot write fiction. In the following chapter, she recounts her unsuccessful attempt to
turn up information at the British Library on the lives of women. This essay is from Chapter
3, from which a few passages are omitted. It ends with the concluding paragraph of the book.

hundred years later, in the time of the Stuarts. "It was still the exception for women of the upper and middle class to choose their own husbands, and when the husband had been assigned, he was lord and master, so far at least as law and custom could make him. Yet even so," Professor Trevelyan concludes, "neither Shakespeare's women nor those of authentic seventeenth-century memoirs, like the Verneys and the Hutchinsons, seem wanting in personality and character." Certainly, if we consider it, Cleopatra must have had a way with her; Lady Macbeth, one would suppose, had a will of her own; Rosalind, one might conclude, was an attractive girl. Professor Trevelyan is speaking no more than the truth when he remarks that Shakespeare's women do not seem wanting in personality and character. Not being a historian, one might go even further and say that women have burnt like beacons in all the works of all the poets from the beginning of time—Clytemnestra, Antigone, Cleopatra, Lady Macbeth, Phèdre, Cressida, Rosalind, Desdemona, the Duchess of Malfi, among the dramatists; then among the prose writers: Millamant, Clarissa, Becky Sharp, Anna Karenina, Emma Bovary, Madame de Guermantes[2]—the names flock to mind, nor do they recall women "lacking in personality and character." Indeed, if woman had no existence save in the fiction written by men, one would imagine her a person of the utmost importance; very various; heroic and mean; splendid and sordid; infinitely beautiful and hideous in the extreme; as great as a man, some think even greater. But this is woman in fiction. In fact, as Professor Trevelyan points out, she was locked up, beaten and flung about the room.

A very queer, composite being thus emerges. Imaginatively she is of the highest importance; practically she is completely insignificant. She pervades poetry from cover to cover; she is all but absent from history. She dominates the lives of kings and conquerors in fiction; in fact she was the slave of any boy whose parents forced a ring upon her finger. Some of the most inspired words, some of the most profound thoughts in literature fell from her lips; in real life she could hardly read, could scarcely spell, and was the property of her husband.   4

It was certainly an odd monster that one made up by reading the historians first and the poets afterwards—a worm winged like an eagle; the spirit of life and beauty in a kitchen chopping up suet. But these monsters, however amusing to the imagination, have no existence in fact. What one must do to bring her to life was to think poetically and prosaically at one and the same moment, thus keeping in touch with fact—that she is Mrs. Martin, aged thirty-six, dressed in blue, wearing a black hat and brown shoes; but not losing sight of fiction either—that she is a vessel in which all sorts of spirits and forces are coursing and flashing perpetually. The moment, however, that one tries this method with the Elizabethan woman, one branch of illumination fails; one is held up by the scarcity of facts. One knows nothing detailed, nothing perfectly   5

---

[2] Female characters from great works of literature.

true and substantial about her. History scarcely mentions her. And I turned to Professor Trevelyan again to see what history meant to him. I found by looking at his chapter headings that it meant—

"The Manor Court and the Methods of Open-field Agriculture . . . The   6
Cistercians and Sheep-farming . . . The Crusades . . . The University . . . The House of Commons . . . The Hundred Years' War . . . The Wars of the Roses . . . The Renaissance Scholars . . . The Dissolution of the Monasteries . . . Agrarian and Religious Strife . . . The Origin of English Seapower . . . The Armada . . . " and so on. Occasionally an individual woman is mentioned, an Elizabeth, or a Mary; a queen or a great lady. But by no possible means could middle-class women with nothing but brains and character at their command have taken part in any one of the great movements which, brought together, constitute the historian's view of the past. Nor shall we find her in any collection of anecdotes. Aubrey hardly mentions her.[3] She never writes her own life and scarcely keeps a diary; there are only a handful of her letters in existence. She left no plays or poems by which we can judge her. . . . Here am I asking why women did not write poetry in the Elizabethan age, and I am not sure how they were educated; whether they were taught to write; whether they had sitting-rooms to themselves; how many women had children before they were twenty-one; what, in short, they did from eight in the morning till eight at night. They had no money evidently; according to Professor Trevelyan they were married whether they liked it or not before they were out of the nursery, at fifteen or sixteen very likely. It would have been extremely odd, even upon this showing, had one of them suddenly written the plays of Shakespeare, I concluded, and I thought of that old gentleman, who is dead now, but was a bishop, I think, who declared that it was impossible for any woman, past, present, or to come, to have the genius of Shakespeare. He wrote to the papers about it. He also told a lady who applied to him for information that cats do not as a matter of fact go to heaven, though they have, he added, souls of a sort. How much thinking those old gentlemen used to save one! How the borders of ignorance shrank back at their approach! Cats do not go to heaven. Women cannot write the plays of Shakespeare.

Be that as it may, I could not help thinking, as I looked at the works of   7
Shakespeare on the shelf, that the bishop was right at least in this; it would have been impossible, completely and entirely, for any woman to have written the plays of Shakespeare in the age of Shakespeare. Let me imagine, since facts are so hard to come by, what would have happened had Shakespeare had a wonderfully gifted sister, called Judith, let us say. Shakespeare himself went, very probably—his mother was an heiress—to the grammar school, where he may have learnt Latin—Ovid, Virgil and Horace—and the elements of grammar and logic. He was, it is well known, a wild boy who poached rabbits, perhaps shot a deer, and had, rather sooner than he should have done, to marry

---

[3] John Aubrey (1626–1697), author of *Brief Lives*, a biographical work.

a woman in the neighbourhood, who bore him a child rather quicker than was right. That escapade sent him to seek his fortune in London. He had, it seemed, a taste for the theatre; he began by holding horses at the stage door. Very soon he got work in the theatre, became a successful actor, and lived in the hub of the universe, meeting everybody, knowing everybody, practising his art on the boards, exercising his wits in the streets, and even getting access to the palace of the queen. Meanwhile his extraordinarily gifted sister, let us suppose, remained at home. She was as adventurous, as imaginative, as agog to see the world as he was. But she was not sent to school. She had no chance of learning grammar and logic, let alone of reading Horace and Virgil. She picked up a book now and then, one of her brother's perhaps, and read a few pages. But then her parents came in and told her to mend the stockings or mind the stew and not moon about with books and papers. They would have spoken sharply but kindly, for they were substantial people who knew the conditions of life for a woman and loved their daughter—indeed, more likely than not she was the apple of her father's eye. Perhaps she scribbled some pages up in an apple loft on the sly, but was careful to hide them or set fire to them. Soon, however, before she was out of her teens, she was to be betrothed to the son of a neighbouring wool-stapler. She cried out that marriage was hateful to her, and for that she was severely beaten by her father. Then he ceased to scold her. He begged her instead not to hurt him, not to shame him in this matter of her marriage. He would give her a chain of beads or a fine petticoat, he said; and there were tears in his eyes. How could she disobey him? How could she break his heart? The force of her own gift alone drove her to it. She made up a small parcel of her belongings, let herself down by a rope one summer's night and took the road to London. She was not seventeen. The birds that sang in the hedge were not more musical than she was. She had the quickest fancy, a gift like her brother's, for the tune of words. Like him, she had a taste for the theatre. She stood at the stage door; she wanted to act, she said. Men laughed in her face. The manager—a fat, loose-lipped man—guffawed. He bellowed something about poodles dancing and women acting—no woman, he said, could possibly be an actress.[4] He hinted—you can imagine what. She could get no training in her craft. Could she even seek her dinner in a tavern or roam the streets at midnight? Yet her genius was for fiction and lusted to feed abundantly upon the lives of men and women and the study of their ways. At last—for she was very young, oddly like Shakespeare the poet in her face, with the same grey eyes and rounded brows—at last Nick Greene the actor-manager took pity on her; she found herself with child by that gentleman and so—who shall measure the heat and violence of the poet's heart when caught and tangled in a woman's body?—killed herself one winter's night and lies buried at some cross-roads where the omnibuses now stop outside the Elephant and Castle.[5]

---

[4] In Shakespeare's day, women's roles were played by boys.
[5] A London neighborhood.

That, more or less, is how the story would run, I think, if a woman in   8
Shakespeare's day had had Shakespeare's genius. But for my part, I agree with
the deceased bishop, if such he was—it is unthinkable that any woman in
Shakespeare's day should have had Shakespeare's genius. For genius like
Shakespeare's is not born among labouring, uneducated, servile people. It was
not born in England among the Saxons and the Britons. It is not born today
among the working classes. How, then, could it have been born among women
whose work began, according to Professor Trevelyan, almost before they were
out of the nursery, who were forced to it by their parents and held to it by all
the power of law and custom? Yet genius of a sort must have existed among
women as it must have existed among the working classes. Now and again an
Emily Brontë or a Robert Burns blazes out and proves its presence.[6] But
certainly it never got itself on to paper. When, however, one reads of a witch
being ducked, of a woman possessed by devils, of a wise woman selling herbs,
or even of a very remarkable man who had a mother, then I think we are on
the track of a lost novelist, a suppressed poet, of some mute and inglorious[7]
Jane Austen, some Emily Brontë who dashed her brains out on the moor or
mopped and mowed about the highways crazed with the torture that her gift
had put her to. Indeed, I would venture to guess that Anon, who wrote so
many poems without signing them, was often a woman. It was a woman
Edward Fitzgerald,[8] I think, suggested who made the ballads and the folk-
songs, crooning them to her children, beguiling her spinning with them, or the
length of the winter's night.

This may be true or it may be false—who can say?—but what is true in it,   9
so it seemed to me, reviewing the story of Shakespeare's sister as I had made
it, is that any woman born with a great gift in the sixteenth century would
certainly have gone crazed, shot herself, or ended her days in some lonely
cottage outside the village, half witch, half wizard, feared and mocked at. For
it needs little skill in psychology to be sure that a highly gifted girl who had
tried to use her gift for poetry would have been so thwarted and hindered by
other people, so tortured and pulled asunder by her own contrary instincts,
that she must have lost her health and sanity to a certainty. No girl could have
walked to London and stood at a stage door and forced her way into the
presence of actor-managers without doing herself a violence and suffering an
anguish which may have been irrational—for chastity may be a fetish invented
by certain societies for unknown reasons—but were none the less inevitable.
Chastity had then, it has even now, a religious importance in a woman's life,
and has so wrapped itself round with nerves and instincts that to cut it free and
bring it to the light of day demands courage of the rarest. To have lived a free

---

[6] Emily Brontë (1818–1848), English novelist, and Robert Burns (1759–1796), Scottish
poet.
[7] Thomas Gray's description in "Elegy Written in a Country Churchyard" of a peasant
whose underdeveloped poetic genius might be as powerful as the great John Milton's.
[8] Edward Fitzgerald (1809–1883), translator and poet.

life in London in the sixteenth century would have meant for a woman who was poet and playwright a nervous stress and dilemma which might well have killed her. Had she survived, whatever she had written would have been twisted and deformed, issuing from a strained and morbid imagination. And undoubtedly, I thought, looking at the shelf where there are no plays by women, her work would have gone unsigned. That refuge she would have sought certainly. It was the relic of the sense of chastity that dictated anonymity to women even so late as the nineteenth century. Currer Bell, George Eliot, George Sand,[9] all the victims of inner strife as their writings prove, sought ineffectively to veil themselves by using the name of a man. Thus they did homage to the convention, which if not implanted by the other sex was liberally encouraged by them (the chief glory of a woman is not to be talked of, said Pericles,[10] himself a much-talked-of man), that publicity in women is detestable. . . .

That woman, then, who was born with a gift of poetry in the sixteenth   10 century, was an unhappy woman, a woman at strife against herself. All the conditions of her life, all her own instincts, were hostile to the state of mind which is needed to set free whatever is in the brain. But what is the state of mind that is most propitious to the act of creation, I asked? Can one come by any notion of the state that furthers and makes possible that strange activity? Here I opened the volume containing the Tragedies of Shakespeare. What was Shakespeare's state of mind, for instance, when he wrote *Lear* and *Antony and Cleopatra?* It was certainly the state of mind most favourable to poetry that there has ever existed. But Shakespeare himself said nothing about it. We only know casually and by chance that he "never blotted a line."[11] Nothing indeed was ever said by the artist himself about his state of mind until the eighteenth century perhaps. Rousseau[12] perhaps began it. At any rate, by the nineteenth century self-consciousness had developed so far that it was the habit for men of letters to describe their minds in confessions and autobiographies. Their lives also were written, and their letters were printed after their deaths. Thus, though we do not know what Shakespeare went through when he wrote *Lear,* we do know what Carlyle went through when he wrote the *French Revolution;* what Flaubert went through when he wrote *Madame Bovary;* what Keats was going through when he tried to write poetry against the coming of death and the indifference of the world.

And one gathers from this enormous modern literature of confession and   11 self-analysis that to write a work of genius is almost always a feat of prodigious difficulty. Everything is against the likelihood that it will come form the writer's mind whole and entire. Generally material circumstances are against

---

[9] The pseudonyms of Charlotte Brontë (1816–1855) and Mary Ann Evans (1819–1880), English novelists, and Amandine Aurore Lucie Dupin (1804–1876), French novelist.

[10] Pericles (d. 429 B.C.), Athenian statesman and general.

[11] According to Ben Jonson, Shakespeare's contemporary.

[12] Jean-Jacques Rousseau (1712–1778), French philosopher, author of *The Confessions of Jean-Jacques Rousseau.*

it. Dogs will bark; people will interrupt; money must be made; health will break down. Further, accentuating all these difficulties and making them harder to bear is the world's notorious indifference. It does not ask people to write poems and novels and histories; it does not need them. It does not care whether Flaubert finds the right word or whether Carlyle scrupulously verifies this or that fact. Naturally, it will not pay for what it does not want. And so the writer, Keats, Flaubert, Carlyle, suffers, especially in the creative years of youth, every form of distraction and discouragement. A curse, a cry of agony, rises from those books of analysis and confession. "Mighty poets in their misery dead"[13]—that is the burden of their song. If anything comes through in spite of this, it is a miracle, and probably no book is born entire and uncrippled as it was conceived.

But for women, I thought, looking at the empty shelves, these difficulties were infinitely more formidable. In the first place, to have a room of her own, let alone a quiet room or a sound-proof room, was out of the question, unless her parents were exceptionally rich or very noble, even up to the beginning of the nineteenth century. Since her pin money, which depended on the good will of her father, was only enough to keep her clothed, she was debarred from such alleviations as came even to Keats or Tennyson or Carlyle, all poor men, from a walking tour, a little journey to France, from the separate lodging which, even if it were miserable enough, sheltered them from the claims and tyrannies of their families. Such material difficulties were formidable; but much worse were the immaterial. The indifference of the world which Keats and Flaubert and other men of genius have found so hard to bear was in her case not indifference but hostility. The world did not say to her as it said to them, Write if you choose; it makes no difference to me. The world said with a guffaw, Write? What's the good of your writing? . . .

I told you in the course of this paper that Shakespeare had a sister; but do not look for her in Sir Sidney Lee's life of the poet. She died young—alas, she never wrote a word. She lies buried where the omnibuses now stop, opposite the Elephant and Castle. Now my belief is that this poet who never wrote a word and was buried at the cross-roads still lives. She lives in you and me, and in many other women who are not here tonight, for they are washing up the dishes and putting the children to bed. But she lives; for great poets do not die; they are continuing presences; they need only the opportunity to walk among us in the flesh. This opportunity, as I think, it is now coming within your power to give her. For my belief is that if we live another century or so—I am talking of the common life which is the real life and not of the little separate lives which we live as individuals—and have five hundred a year each of us and rooms of our own; if we have the habit of freedom and the courage to write exactly what we think; if we escape a little from the common sitting-room and

---

[13] From William Wordsworth's poem "Resolution and Independence."

see human beings not always in their relation to each other but in relation to reality; and the sky, too, and the trees or whatever it may be in themselves; if we look past Milton's bogey, for no human being should shut out the view; if we face the fact, for it is a fact, that there is no arm to cling to, but that we go alone and that our relation is to the world of reality and not only to the world of men and women, then the opportunity will come and the dead poet who was Shakespeare's sister will put on the body which she has so often laid down. Drawing her life from the lives of the unknown who were her forerunners, as her brother did before her, she will be born. As for her coming without that preparation, without that effort on our part, without that determination that when she is born again she shall find it possible to live and write her poetry, that we cannot expect, for that would be impossible. But I maintain that she would come if we worked for her, and that so to work, even in poverty and obscurity, is worth while.

QUESTIONS

1. How does Woolf explain the contrast between the women of fact and the women of fiction? **2.** Analyze the effect of Woolf's concluding remarks about the bishop (paragraph 6): "Cats do not go to heaven. Women cannot write the plays of Shakespeare." In this connection, consider her later comment (paragraph 8) that "I agree with the deceased bishop, if such he was—it is unthinkable that any woman in Shakespeare's day should have had Shakespeare's genius." Does this contradict what she has been saying? **3.** Explain the link Woolf makes (paragraph 9) between chastity and the problem of the gifted woman writer.

WRITING TOPIC

Speculate on why it was the case that, while women were little more than men's servants throughout history, they were portrayed in fiction "as great as a man, some think even greater" (paragraph 3)?

The Turbid Ebb and Flow of Misery[1]

1938

MARGARET SANGER   [1883–1966]

Every night and every morn
Some to misery are born,
Every morn and every night
Some are born to sweet delight.
Some are born to sweet delight,
Some are born to endless night.
William Blake

During these years [about 1912] in New York trained nurses were in great demand. Few people wanted to enter hospitals; they were afraid they might be "practiced" upon, and consented to go only in desperate emergencies. Sentiment was especially vehement in the matter of having babies. A woman's own bedroom, no matter how inconveniently arranged, was the usual place for her lying-in. I was not sufficiently free from domestic duties to be a general nurse, but I could ordinarily manage obstetrical cases because I was notified far enough ahead to plan my schedule. And after serving my two weeks I could get home again.

Sometimes I was summoned to small apartments occupied by young clerks, insurance salesmen, or lawyers, just starting out, most of them under thirty and whose wives were having their first or second baby. They were always eager to know the best and latest method in infant care and feeding. In particular, Jewish patients, whose lives centered around the family, welcomed advice and followed it implicitly.

But more and more my calls began to come from the Lower East Side, as though I were being magnetically drawn there by some force outside my control. I hated the wretchedness and hopelessness of the poor, and never experienced that satisfaction in working among them that so many noble women have found. My concern for my patients was now quite different from my earlier hospital attitude. I could see that much was wrong with them which did not appear in the physiological or medical diagnosis. A woman in childbirth was not merely a woman in childbirth. My expanded outlook included a

---

[1] The title of this chapter from Sanger's *Autobiography* is taken from Matthew Arnold's pessimistic poem "Dover Beach" (p. 535). In this essay, Sanger describes a time when using or advocating the use of contraceptives was illegal in the United States. As late as 1957 Connecticut and Massachusetts continued to enforce laws that prevented physicians from offering information about contraception—even to married women for whom pregnancy might be fatal.

view of her background, her potentialities as a human being, the kind of children she was bearing, and what was going to happen to them.

The wives of small shopkeepers were my most frequent cases, but I had   4
carpenters, truck drivers, dishwashers, and pushcart vendors. I admired intensely the consideration most of these people had for their own. Money to pay doctor and nurse had been carefully saved months in advance—parents-in-law, grandfathers, grandmothers, all contributing.

As soon as the neighbors learned that a nurse was in the building they came   5
in a friendly way to visit, often carrying fruit, jellies, or gefüllter fish made after a cherished recipe. It was infinitely pathetic to me that they, so poor themselves, should bring me food. Later they drifted in again with the excuse of getting the plate, and sat down for a nice talk; there was no hurry. Always back of the little gift was the question, "I am pregnant (or my daughter, or my sister is). Tell me something to keep from having another baby. We cannot afford another yet."

I tried to explain the only two methods I had ever heard of among the middle   6
classes, both of which were invariably brushed aside as unacceptable. They were of no certain avail to the wife because they placed the burden of responsibility solely upon the husband—a burden which he seldom assumed. What she was seeking was self-protection she could herself use, and there was none.

Below this stratum of society was one in truly desperate circumstances. The   7
men were sullen and unskilled, picking up odd jobs now and then, but more often unemployed, lounging in and out of the house at all hours of the day and night. The women seemed to slink on their way to market and were without neighborliness.

These submerged, untouched classes were beyond the scope of organized   8
charity and religion. No labor union, no church, not even the Salvation Army reached them. They were apprehensive of everyone and rejected help of any kind, ordering all intruders to keep out; both birth and death they considered their own business. Social agents, who were just beginning to appear, were profoundly mistrusted because they pried into homes and lives, asking questions about wages, how many were in the family, had any of them ever been in jail. Often two or three had been there or were now under suspicion of prostitution, shoplifting, purse snatching, petty thievery, and, in consequence, passed furtively by the big blue uniform on the corner.

The utmost depression came over me as I approached this surreptitious   9
region. Below Fourteenth Street I seemed to be breathing a different air, to be in another world and country where the people had habits and customs alien to anything I had ever heard about.

There were then approximately ten thousand apartments in New York into   10
which no sun ray penetrated directly; such windows as they had opened only on a narrow court from which rose fetid odors. It was seldom cleaned, though garbage and refuse often went down into it. All these dwellings were pervaded by the foul breath of poverty, that moldy, indefinable, indescribable smell which cannot be fumigated out, sickening to me but apparently unnoticed by

those who lived there. When I set to work with antiseptics, their pungent sting, at least temporarily, obscured the stench.

I remember one confinement case to which I was called by the doctor of an insurance company. I climbed up the five flights and entered the airless rooms, but the baby had come with too great speed. A boy of ten had been the only assistant. Five flights was a long way; he had wrapped the placenta in a piece of newspaper and dropped it out the window into the court.

Many families took in "boarders," as they were termed, whose small contributions paid the rent. These derelicts, wanderers, alternately working and drinking, were crowded in with the children; a single room sometimes held as many as six sleepers. Little girls were accustomed to dressing and undressing in front of the men, and were often violated, occasionally by their own fathers or brothers, before they reached the age of puberty.

Pregnancy was a chronic condition among the women of this class. Suggestions as to what to do for a girl who was "in trouble" or a married woman who was "caught" passed from mouth to mouth—herb teas, turpentine, steaming, rolling downstairs, inserting slippery elm, knitting needles, shoe-hooks. When they had word of a new remedy they hurried to the drugstore, and if the clerk were inclined to be friendly he might say, "Oh, that won't help you, but here's something that may." The younger druggists usually refused to give advice, because, if it were to be known, they would come under the law; midwives were even more fearful. The doomed women implored me to reveal the "secret" rich people had, offering to pay me extra to tell them; many really believed I was holding back information for money. They asked everybody and tried anything, but nothing did them any good. On Saturday nights I have seen groups of from fifty to one hundred with their shawls over their heads waiting outside the office of a five-dollar abortionist.

Each time I returned to this district, which was becoming a recurrent nightmare, I used to hear that Mrs. Cohen "had been carried to a hospital, but had never come back," or that Mrs. Kelly "had sent the children to a neighbor and had put her head into the gas oven." Day after day such tales were poured into my ears—a baby born dead, great relief—the death of an older child, sorrow but again relief of a sort—the story told a thousand times of death from abortion and children going into institutions. I shuddered with horror as I listened to the details and studied the reasons back of them—destitution linked with excessive childbearing. The waste of life seemed utterly senseless. One by one worried, sad, pensive, and aging faces marshaled themselves before me in my dreams, sometimes appealingly, sometimes accusingly.

These were not merely "unfortunate conditions among the poor" such as we read about. I knew the women personally. They were living, breathing, human beings, with hopes, fears, and aspirations like my own, yet their weary, misshapen bodies, "always ailing, never failing," were destined to be thrown on the scrap heap before they were thirty-five. I could not escape from the facts of their wretchedness; neither was I able to see any way out. My own cozy and comfortable family existence was becoming a reproach to me.

Then one stifling mid-July day of 1912 I was summoned to a Grand Street   16
tenement. My patient was a small, slight Russian Jewess, about twenty-eight
years old, of the special cast of feature to which suffering lends a madonna-like
expression. The cramped three-room apartment was in a sorry state of turmoil.
Jake Sachs, a truck driver scarcely older than his wife, had come home to find
the three children crying and her unconscious from the effects of a self-
induced abortion. He had called the nearest doctor, who in turn had sent for
me. Jake's earnings were trifling, and most of them had gone to keep the
none-too-strong children clean and properly fed. But his wife's ingenuity had
helped them to save a little, and this he was glad to spend on a nurse rather
than have her go to a hospital.

The doctor and I settled ourselves to the task of fighting the septicemia.   17
Never had I worked so fast, never so concentratedly. The sultry days and nights
were melted into a torpid inferno. It did not seem possible there could be such
heat, and every bit of food, ice, and drugs had to be carried up three flights of
stairs.

Jake was more kind and thoughtful than many of the husbands I had   18
encountered. He loved his children, and had always helped his wife wash and
dress them. He had brought water up and carried garbage down before he left
in the morning, and did as much as he could for me while he anxiously
watched her progress.

After a fortnight Mrs. Sachs' recovery was in sight. Neighbors, ordinarily   19
fatalistic as to the results of abortion, were genuinely pleased that she had
survived. She smiled wanly at all who came to see her and thanked them
gently, but she could not respond to their hearty congratulations. She appeared to be more despondent and anxious than she should have been, and
spent too much time in meditation.

At the end of three weeks, as I was preparing to leave the fragile patient to   20
take up her difficult life once more, she finally voiced her fears. "Another baby
will finish me, I suppose?"

"It's too early to talk about that," I temporized.   21

But when the doctor came to make his last call, I drew him aside. "Mrs.   22
Sachs is terribly worried about having another baby."

"She well may be," replied the doctor, and then he stood before her and   23
said, "Any more such capers, young woman, and there'll be no need to send for
me."

"I know, doctor," she replied timidly, "but," and she hesitated as though it   24
took all her courage to say it, "what can I do to prevent it?"

The doctor was a kindly man, and he had worked hard to save her, but such   25
incidents had become so familiar to him that he·had long since lost whatever
delicacy he might once have had. He laughed good-naturedly. "You want to
have your cake and eat it too, do you? Well, it can't be done."

Then picking up his hat and bag to depart he said, "Tell Jake to sleep on the   26
roof."

I glanced quickly at Mrs. Sachs. Even through my sudden tears I could see   27 stamped on her face an expression of absolute despair. We simply looked at each other, saying no word until the door had closed behind the doctor. Then she lifted her thin, blue-veined hands and clasped them beseechingly. "He can't understand. He's only a man. But you do, don't you? Please tell me the secret, and I'll never breathe it to a soul. *Please!*

What was I to do? I could not speak the conventionally comforting phrases   28
which would be of no comfort. Instead, I made her as physically easy as I could and promised to come back in a few days to talk with her again. A little later, when she slept, I tiptoed away.

Night after night the wistful image of Mrs. Sachs appeared before me. I   29
made all sorts of excuses to myself for not going back. I was busy on other cases; I really did not know what to say to her or how to convince her of my own ignorance; I was helpless to avert such monstrous atrocities. Time rolled by and I did nothing.

The telephone rang one evening three months later, and Jake Sachs' agi-   30
tated voiced begged me to come at once; his wife was sick again and from the same cause. For a wild moment I thought of sending someone else, but actually, of course, I hurried into my uniform, caught up my bag, and started out. All the way I longed for a subway wreck, an explosion, anything to keep me from having to enter that home again. But nothing happened, even to delay me. I turned into the dingy doorway and climbed the familiar stairs once more. The children were there, young little things.

Mrs. Sachs was in a coma and died within ten minutes. I folded her still   31
hands across her breast, remembering how they had pleaded with me, begging so humbly for the knowledge which was her right. I drew a sheet over her pallid face. Jake was sobbing, running his hands through his hair and pulling it out like an insane person. Over and over again he wailed, "My God! My God!"

I left him pacing desperately back and forth, and for hours I myself walked   32
and walked and walked through the hushed streets. When I finally arrived home and let myself quietly in, all the household was sleeping. I looked out my window and down upon the dimly lighted city. Its pains and griefs crowded in upon me, a moving picture rolled before my eyes with photographic clearness: women writhing in travail to bring forth little babies; the babies themselves naked and hungry, wrapped in newspapers to keep them from the cold; six-year-old children with pinched, pale, wrinkled faces, old in concentrated wretchedness, pushed into gray and fetid cellars, crouching on stone floors, their small scrawny hands scuttling through rags, making lamp shades, artifi-cial flowers; white coffins, black coffins, coffins, coffins interminably passing in never-ending succession. The scenes piled one upon another on another. I could bear it no longer.

As I stood there the darkness faded. The sun came up and threw its reflec-   33
tion over the house tops. It was the dawn of a new day in my life also. The doubt and questioning, the experimenting and trying, were now to be put behind me. I knew I could not go back merely to keeping people alive.

I went to bed, knowing that no matter what it might cost, I was finished   34 with palliatives and superficial cures; I was resolved to seek out the root of evil, to do something to change the destiny of mothers whose miseries were vast as the sky.

QUESTIONS

1. What arguments and assumptions would justify a law prohibiting discussion of contraception and the use of contraceptives? What arguments and assumptions would justify contraception?   **2.** What assumptions would justify the prohibition of abortion? What assumptions would justify abortion?   **3.** Characterize the source of Sanger's determination to change the conditions that contributed to Mrs. Sachs's death. Was her decision emotional? Explain.

WRITING TOPIC

Write an argumentative essay addressed to a board of education in which you either support or oppose high school classes in sex education that discuss contraception and abortion. At the outset, state the principle you support; then marshal the arguments that support it.

What's So Special about Being Human?   1990

WILLARD GAYLIN   [b. 1925]

We are in urgent need of reacquainting ourselves with our nature. Our self-
respect as a species is alarmingly low. The late twentieth century has seen a
confluence of events destined to diminish self-confidence and self-esteem.
Along with the great wars, the Depression, the Holocaust, and the ecological
disasters—enough to drive any introspective creature to self-doubts—have
come a series of seemingly unrelated intellectual movements that have independently and unwittingly diminished our stature in our own eyes.

The "dignity of man" is attacked indirectly by those who, drawing from
modern biology and using the principles of sociobiology, have consciously
attempted to lessen the distinction between us and our fellow creatures. Anthropologists in particular—Lorenz, Tiger, Fox, Morris, and others—have
tended to emphasize the hostile, aggressive, and territorial aspects of human
nature while ignoring the caring and nurturing aspects. They have envisioned
man at best as a naked ape, and at worst as a marauding beast.

Fortunately, some of our most literate, respected, and brilliant biologists,
while marveling at, and honoring the lower animals, have had no doubts about
the special quality of being human. Such great humanistic twentieth-century
biologists as Dobzhansky, Tax, and Portmann have been elegant spokesmen
within their disciplines for the special nature of human beings. They have not,
however, gone beyond their disciplines to indicate the moral implications of
our biological uniqueness.

The reputation of our species is also under attack, in a way that is half direct
and half indirect, through what has come to be known as the animal-rights
movement. The purpose of the people in this movement is not to diminish
Homo sapiens but to protect the beast. They do so by elevating animals, often
endowing them anthropomorphically with features the animals do not possess.
Their purpose is noble—to protect helpless creatures from unnecessary suffering—but one untoward consequence of this decent enterprise is a reduction
of the distance between the nature of people and that of animals. Animal
rights advocates constantly emphasize the similarity between the human and
the subhuman in a worthy attempt to mitigate our abuses of the subhuman.
But in so doing they seriously undermine the special nature of being human.

Peter Singer,[1] perhaps the most eloquent spokesman for animal rights,
acknowledges a quantitative difference between the worth of lower animals

---

[1] Peter Singer (b. 1946), author of *Animal Liberation* (1975) and *In Defense of Animals*
(1985).

440

and human beings. (Some of his colleagues do not.) He rejects, however, any suggestion that there is a qualitative difference, which would preclude *any* measurement of the worth of a human life against that of an animal life, seeing such a construction as immoral in itself. On the contrary, he insists, the failure to consider such a calculus constitutes a breach of ethics.

This leads him into the dangerous readiness to measure humans and animals on the same scale. Although he certainly would not equate the life of a rat with the life of a human being, he has inevitably been forced to take a position whereby thousands of rats would be judged more worthy of life than one child, since he is prepared to see differences only in degree.   6

I am not clear where on his social scale the cockroach would need to be in relation to the rat, so that we might extrapolate the number of cockroaches necessary to balance the life of a child.   7

I see a danger in the animal-rights movement that is more than theoretical. It is beginning to impinge on the lifesaving research necessary to solve such human miseries as AIDS, cancer, and degenerative diseases of the nervous system. I acknowledge my bias. In my world, trees may have standing but animals have no "rights." In the world of morality—as in the world of politics—the animate (and inanimate) exist—valued, considered, dealt with, or destroyed, all in the service of the purposes and interests of humankind.   8

This position has been attacked in the past as being unfairly anthropocentric. Anthropocentric it certainly is. But what else can a human being be? Beyond man are only the claims of nature or the hand of God. Though not a religious person myself, I have profound respect for religion, and I would point out to critics that the position I hold was most firmly established, not out of the anthropocentricism of science and psychology, but in the religious tradition of the Old Testament and as confirmed, in that same tradition, by such modern philosophers as Kant.[2]   9

Kant was capable of a great tenderness toward animals, as Mary Midgeley observed in her excellent book *Beast and Man*, citing the following statement by Kant: "Liebnitz used a tiny worm for purposes of observation and then carefully replaced it with its leaf on the tree so that it should not come to harm through any act of his. He would have been sorry—a natural feeling for a humane man—to destroy such a creature for no reason."   10

Yet the very same Kant, with the inherent self-confidence of his Lutheran morality, said: "The first time he [man] ever said to the sheep, 'Nature has given you the skin you wear for my use, not for yours' . . . he became aware of the way in which his nature privileged and raised him above all animals."   11

I oppose the attribution of rights to animals not out of any religious conviction or invocation of divine authority, and not because I have no affection for animals, but because I fear animal-rights arguments diminish the special status of *Homo sapiens*. Respect for human beings requires that dignity be   12

[2] Immanuel Kant (1724–1804), German philosopher.

granted our species beyond any qualitative comparison with others. In insisting on that dignity, I do not shirk our responsibility toward other creatures. A position of such privilege and power imposes a special moral obligation on our species. That is why only we human beings are capable of, willing to, and even obliged to agonize about other species.

It is directly within the purposes of humankind to treat animals with compassion, even empathy; to have reverence for those common qualities we share with the higher primates; and to be aware that, given the mutability of our nature, the way we honor and revere other creatures and other things will define the degree to which we have been true to our humanity. If human nature is so perverted as to be indifferent to suffering and blind to beauty, what is left is no longer "human" and therefore not worthy of its special role in the moral universe.   13

All animals are not created equal, however. Some animals have less value even than inanimate structures; some have negative value. I do not grieve for the destruction of *Treponema pallidum*, that beautiful and delicate spiral organism that is the cause of human syphilis. To destroy this entire species would be a blessing; whereas blowing up the Grand Tetons or willfully destroying Michelangelo's *David* would constitute a greater moral crime, these are inanimate "things."   14

Recently I was confronted with a difficult case of the ethical permissibility of using chimpanzee hearts in experimentation to facilitate human organ transplants. Chimpanzees have enormous charm, sensitivity, great intelligence, and a strong kinship to humanity. Should they be sacrificed for human ends? If so, what are the limits?   15

It seems to me that the implicit issue evolved into the following dilemmas. Assuming a promising and prudent research procedure, would you sacrifice a chimpanzee for a trivial human need? I suspect most of us would not. Would you sacrifice a chimpanzee for a child's life? I know most of us would. Would you sacrifice the entire species of chimpanzees for the entire species of *Homo sapiens?* I hope most of us would. Finally, the hard question: would you risk sacrificing the entire species of chimpanzees, a real and not just a theoretical possibility, to relieve the pain and suffering and premature death of many children? I emphatically would. Others would not. It is here that my bias for the specialness, for the extraordinary specialness, of the human being emerges.   16

Our current understanding of anthropology is replete with the suggestion of humanoid species—*higher* than the chimpanzee—that have become extinct for unknown reasons of climate or competition. Such is the moral indifference of nature. It is only with the introduction of human sensibility, human empathy, and human capacity for identification that we—alone among creatures—even consider the "rights" of other species.   17

The nobility of the human being is expressed in this readiness of some of our misguided members to sacrifice human children for the preservation of a kindred living creature. To these spokesmen the overvaluation of the human child is a form of "anthropocentrism," a prejudice like racism or sexism. I am   18 pleased about the presence of such advocates—their unselfishness does honor to our species—even while I reject their sentimentalities. But with my coarser sensibilities, my willingness to sacrifice the chimpanzee, I am still within the limits of decency that define that glorious creature whom I defend, *Homo sapiens.*

QUESTIONS

1. Some proponents of animal rights make an important distinction between animals that experience pain and those that (apparently) don't. These proponents argue that humans have a moral obligation not to inflict pain on any creature for whatever reason. How do you think Gaylin would respond to such a distinction?   **2.** Do you agree with Gaylin's assertion that emphasizing the similarity between humans and animals and attributing rights to animals "seriously undermine[s] the special nature of being human" (paragraph 4)? Explain.   **3.** Gaylin's arguments are philosophical and theoretical. Do you see any practical problems if his view were accepted? For example, how would Gaylin deal with the dissection of animals in biology classes or experiments on animals to develop new cosmetics?

WRITING TOPICS

1. Describe the reactions of an animal-rights advocate to Gaylin's arguments. You might get these reactions either by reading or by personally interviewing someone. **2.** Compare the ways in which Gaylin and Bill McKibben in "A Path of More Resistance" appeal to religion or religious sentiment to support their arguments.

Letter from Birmingham Jail[1]   1963

MARTIN LUTHER KING, JR.   [1929–1968]

MY DEAR FELLOW CLERGYMEN:

While confined here in the Birmingham city jail, I came across your recent statement calling my present activities "unwise and untimely." Seldom do I pause to answer criticism of my work and ideas. If I sought to answer all the criticisms that cross my desk, my secretaries would have little time for anything other than such correspondence in the course of the day, and I would have no time for constructive work. But since I feel that you are men of genuine good will and that your criticisms are sincerely set forth, I want to try to answer your statement in what I hope will be patient and reasonable terms.

I think I should indicate why I am here in Birmingham, since you have been influenced by the view which argues against "outsiders coming in." I have the honor of serving as president of the Southern Christian Leadership Conference, an organization operating in every southern state, with headquarters in Atlanta, Georgia. We have some eighty-five affiliated organizations across the South, and one of them is the Alabama Christian Movement for Human Rights. Frequently we share staff, educational, and financial resources with our affiliates. Several months ago the affiliate here in Birmingham asked us to be on call to engage in a nonviolent direct-action program if such were deemed necessary. We readily consented, and when the hour came we lived up to our promise. So I, along with several members of my staff, am here because I was invited here. I am here because I have organizational ties here.

But more basically, I am in Birmingham because injustice is here. Just as the prophets of the eighth century B.C. left their villages and carried their "thus saith the Lord" far beyond the boundaries of their home towns, and just as the Apostle Paul left his village of Tarsus[2] and carried the gospel of Jesus Christ to the far corners of the Greco-Roman world, so am I compelled to carry the gospel of freedom beyond my own home town. Like Paul, I must constantly respond to the Macedonian call for aid.[3]

Moreover, I am cognizant of the interrelatedness of all communities and

---

[1] This response to a published statement by eight fellow clergymen from Alabama (Bishop C. C. J. Carpenter, Bishop Joseph A. Durick, Rabbi Hilton L. Grafman, Bishop Paul Hardin, Bishop Holan B. Harmon, the Reverend George M. Murray, the Reverend Edward V. Ramage and the Reverend Earl Stallings) was composed under somewhat constricting circumstances. Begun on the margins of the newspaper in which the statement appeared while I was in jail, the letter was continued on scraps of writing paper supplied by a friendly Negro trusty, and concluded on a pad my attorneys were eventually permitted to leave me. Although the text remains in substance unaltered, I have indulged in the author's prerogative of polishing it for publication [King's note].
[2] Birthplace of St. Paul, in present-day Turkey.
[3] St. Paul was frequently called upon to aid the Christian community in Macedonia.

states. I cannot sit idly by in Atlanta and not be concerned about what happens in Birmingham. Injustice anywhere is a threat to justice everywhere. We are caught in an inescapable network of mutuality, tied in a single garment of destiny. Whatever affects one directly, affects all indirectly. Never again can we afford to live with the narrow, provincial "outside agitator" idea. Anyone who lives inside the United States can never be considered an outsider anywhere within its bounds.

You deplore the demonstrations taking place in Birmingham. But your statement, I am sorry to say, fails to express a similar concern for the conditions that brought about the demonstrations. I am sure that none of you would want to rest content with the superficial kind of social analysis that deals merely with effects and does not grapple with the underlying causes. It is unfortunate that demonstrations are taking place in Birmingham, but it is even more unfortunate that the city's white power structure left the Negro community with no alternative.

In any nonviolent campaign there are four basic steps: collection of the facts to determine whether injustices exist; negotiation; self-purification; and direct action. We have gone through all these steps in Birmingham. There can be no gainsaying the fact that racial injustice engulfs this community. Birmingham is probably the most thoroughly segregated city in the United States. Its ugly record of brutality is widely known. Negroes have experienced grossly unjust treatment in the courts. There have been more unsolved bombings of Negro homes and churches in Birmingham than in any other city in the nation. These are the hard, brutal facts of the case. On the basis of these conditions, Negro leaders sought to negotiate with the city fathers. But the latter consistently refused to engage in good-faith negotiation.

Then, last September, came the opportunity to talk with leaders of Birmingham's economic community. In the course of the negotiations, certain promises were made by the merchants—for example, to remove the stores' humiliating racial signs. On the basis of these promises, the Reverend Fred Shuttlesworth and the leaders of the Alabama Christian Movement for Human Rights agreed to a moratorium on all demonstrations. As the weeks and months went by, we realized that we were the victims of a broken promise. A few signs, briefly removed, returned; the others remained.

As in so many past experiences, our hopes had been blasted, and the shadow of deep disappointment settled upon us. We had no alternative except to prepare for direct action, whereby we would present our very bodies as a means of laying our case before the conscience of the local and the national community. Mindful of the difficulties involved, we decided to undertake a process of self-purification. We began a series of workshops on nonviolence, and we repeatedly asked ourselves: "Are you able to accept blows without retaliating?" "Are you able to endure the ordeal of jail?" We decided to schedule our direct-action program for the Easter season, realizing that except for Christmas, this is the main shopping period of the year. Knowing that a strong economic-withdrawal program would be the by-product of direct action, we felt that this would be the best time to bring pressure to bear on the merchants for the needed change.

Then it occurred to us that Birmingham's mayoral election was coming up in March, and we speedily decided to postpone action until after election-day. When we discovered that the Commissioner of Public Safety, Eugene "Bull" Connor, had piled up enough votes to be in the run-off, we decided again to postpone action until the day after the run-off so that the demonstrations could not be used to cloud the issues. Like many others, we waited to see Mr. Connor defeated, and to this end we endured postponement after postponement. Having aided in this community need, we felt that our direct-action program could be delayed no longer. 9

You may well ask, "Why direct action? Why sit-ins, marches, and so forth? Isn't negotiation a better path?" You are quite right in calling for negotiation. Indeed, this is the very purpose of direct action. Nonviolent direct action seeks to create such a crisis and foster such a tension that a community which has constantly refused to negotiate is forced to confront the issue. It seeks so to dramatize the issue that it can no longer be ignored. My citing the creation of tension as part of the work of the nonviolent-resister may sound rather shocking. But I must confess that I am not afraid of the word "tension." I have earnestly opposed violent tension, but there is a type of constructive, nonviolent tension which is necessary for growth. Just as Socrates[4] felt that it was necessary to create a tension in the mind so that individuals could rise from the bondage of myths and half-truths to the unfettered realm of creative analysis and objective appraisal, so must we see the need for nonviolent gadflies to create the kind of tension in society that will help men rise from the dark depths of prejudice and racism to the majestic heights of understanding and brotherhood. 10

The purpose of our direct-action program is to create a situation so crisis-packed that it will inevitably open the door to negotiation. I therefore concur with you in your call for negotiation. Too long has our beloved Southland been bogged down in a tragic effort to live in monologue rather than dialogue. 11

One of the basic points in your statement is that the action that I and my associates have taken in Birmingham is untimely. Some have asked: "Why didn't you give the new city administration time to act?" The only answer that I can give to this query is that the new Birmingham administration must be prodded about as much as the outgoing one, before it will act. We are sadly mistaken if we feel that the election of Albert Boutwell as mayor will bring the millennium to Birmingham. While Mr. Boutwell is a much more gentle person than Mr. Connor, they are both segregationists, dedicated to maintenance of the status quo. I have hoped that Mr. Boutwell will be reasonable enough to see the futility of massive resistance to desegregation. But he will not see this 12

---

[4] Socrates (469–399 B.C.), a Greek philosopher who often pretended ignorance in arguments in order to expose the errors in his opponent's reasoning.

without pressure from devotees of civil rights. My friends, I must say to you that we have not made a single gain in civil rights without determined legal and nonviolent pressure. Lamentably, it is an historical fact that privileged groups seldom give up their privileges voluntarily. Individuals may see the moral light and voluntarily give up their unjust posture; but, as Reinhold Niebuhr[5] has reminded us, groups tend to be more immoral than individuals.

We know through painful experience that freedom is never voluntarily given   13 by the oppressor; it must be demanded by the oppressed. Frankly, I have yet to engage in a direct-action campaign that was "well timed" in the view of those who have not suffered unduly from the disease of segregation. For years now I have heard the word "Wait!" It rings in the ear of every Negro with piercing familiarity. This "Wait" has almost always meant "Never." We must come to see, with one of our distinguished jurists, that "justice too long delayed is justice denied."

We have waited for more than 340 years for our constitutional and God-   14 given rights. The nations of Asia and Africa are moving with jetlike speed toward gaining political independence, but we still creep at horse-and-buggy pace toward gaining a cup of coffee at a lunch counter. Perhaps it is easy for those who have never felt the stinging darts of segregation to say, "Wait." But when you have seen vicious mobs lynch your mothers and fathers at will and drown your sisters and brothers at whim; when you have seen hate-filled policemen curse, kick, and even kill your black brothers and sisters; when you see the vast majority of your twenty million Negro brothers smothering in an airtight cage of poverty in the midst of an affluent society; when you suddenly find your tongue twisted and your speech stammering as you seek to explain to your six-year-old daughter why she can't go to the public amusement park that has just been advertised on television, and see tears welling up in her eyes when she is told that Funtown is closed to colored children, and see ominous clouds of inferiority beginning to form in her little mental sky, and see her beginning to distort her personality by developing an unconscious bitterness toward white people; when you have to concoct an answer for a five-year-old son who is asking, "Daddy, why do white people treat colored people so mean?"; when you take a cross-country drive and find it necessary to sleep night after night in the uncomfortable corners of your automobile because no motel will accept you; when you are humiliated day in and day out by nagging signs reading "white" and "colored"; when your first name becomes "nigger," your middle name becomes "boy" (however old you are) and your last name becomes "John," and your wife and mother are never given the respected title "Mrs."; when you are harried by day and haunted by night by the fact that you are a Negro, living constantly at tiptoe stance, never quite knowing what to expect next, and are plagued with inner fears and outer resentments; when you are forever fighting a degenerating sense of "nobodiness"—then you will un-

---

[5] Reinhold Niebuhr (1892–1971), American philosopher and theologian.

derstand why we find it difficult to wait. There comes a time when the cup of endurance runs over, and men are no longer willing to be plunged into the abyss of despair. I hope, sirs, you can understand our legitimate and unavoidable impatience.

You express a great deal of anxiety over our willingness to break laws. This is certainly a legitimate concern. Since we so diligently urge people to obey the Supreme Court's decision of 1954 outlawing segregation in the public schools, at first glance it may seem rather paradoxical for us consciously to break laws. One may well ask: "How can you advocate breaking some laws and obeying others?" The answer lies in the fact that there are two types of laws: just and unjust. I would be the first to advocate obeying just laws. One has not only a legal but a moral responsibility to obey just laws. Conversely, one has a moral responsibility to disobey unjust laws. I would agree with St. Augustine that "an unjust law is no law at all." 15

Now, what is the difference between the two? How does one determine whether a law is just or unjust? A just law is a man-made code that squares with the moral law or the law of God. An unjust law is a code that is out of harmony with the moral law. To put it in the terms of St. Thomas Aquinas: An unjust law is a human law that is not rooted in eternal law and natural law. Any law that uplifts human personality is just. Any law that degrades human personality is unjust. All segregation statutes are unjust because segregation distorts the soul and damages the personality. It gives the segregator a false sense of superiority and the segregated a false sense of inferiority. Segregation, to use the terminology of the Jewish philosopher Martin Buber, substitutes an "I-it" relationship for an "I-thou" relationship and ends up relegating persons to the status of things. Hence segregation is not only politically, economically, and sociologically unsound, it is morally wrong and sinful. Paul Tillich has said that sin is separation. Is not segregation an existential expression of man's tragic separation, his awful estrangement, his terrible sinfulness? Thus it is that I can urge men to obey the 1954 decision of the Supreme Court, for it is morally right; and I can urge them to disobey segregation ordinances, for they are morally wrong. 16

Let us consider a more concrete example of just and unjust laws. An unjust law is a code that a numerical or power majority group compels a minority group to obey but does not make binding on itself. This is *difference* made legal. By the same token, a just law is a code that a majority compels a minority to follow and that it is willing to follow itself. This is *sameness* made legal. 17

Let me give another explanation. A law is unjust if it is inflicted on a minority that, as a result of being denied the right to vote, had no part in enacting or devising the law. Who can say that the legislature of Alabama which set up that state's segregation laws was democratically elected? Throughout Alabama all sorts of devious methods are used to prevent Negroes from becoming registered voters, and there are some counties in which, even though Negroes constitute a majority of the population, not a single Negro is regis- 18 tered. Can any law enacted under such circumstances be considered democratically structured?

Sometimes a law is just on its face and unjust in its application. For instance, I have been arrested on a charge of parading without a permit. Now, there is nothing wrong in having an ordinance which requires a permit for a parade. But such an ordinance becomes unjust when it is used to maintain segregation and to deny citizens the First-Amendment privilege of peaceful assembly and protest.

I hope you are able to see the distinction I am trying to point out. In no sense do I advocate evading or defying the law, as would the rabid segregationist. That would lead to anarchy. One who breaks an unjust law must do so openly, lovingly, and with a willingness to accept the penalty. I submit that an individual who breaks a law that conscience tells him is unjust, and who willingly accepts the penalty of imprisonment in order to arouse the conscience of the community over its injustice, is in reality expressing the highest respect for law.

Of course, there is nothing new about this kind of civil disobedience. It was evidenced sublimely in the refusal of Shadrach, Meshach, and Abednego to obey the laws of Nebuchadnezzar, on the ground that a higher moral law was at stake.[6] It was practiced superbly by the early Christians, who were willing to face hungry lions and the excruciating pain of chopping blocks rather than submit to certain unjust laws of the Roman Empire. To a degree, academic freedom is a reality today because Socrates practiced civil disobedience. In our own nation, the Boston Tea Party represented a massive act of civil disobedience.

We should never forget that everything Adolf Hitler did in Germany was "legal" and everything the Hungarian freedom fighters did in Hungary was "illegal." It was "illegal" to aid and comfort a Jew in Hitler's Germany. Even so, I am sure that, had I lived in Germany at the time, I would have aided and comforted my Jewish brothers. If today I lived in a Communist country where certain principles dear to the Christian faith are suppressed, I would openly advocate disobeying that country's anti-religious laws.

I must make two honest confessions to you, my Christian and Jewish brothers. First, I must confess that over the past few years I have been gravely disappointed with the white moderate. I have almost reached the regrettable conclusion that the Negro's great stumbling block in his stride toward freedom is not the white Citizen's Counciler[7] or the Ku Klux Klanner, but the white moderate, who is more devoted to "order" than to justice; who prefers a negative peace which is the absence of tension to a positive peace which is the presence of justice; who constantly says, "I agree with you in the goal you seek, but I cannot agree with your methods of direct action"; who paternalistically

19

20

21

22

23

---

[6] See Daniel 1:7–3:30.
[7] White Citizen's Councils sprang up in the South after 1954 (the year the Supreme Court declared segregated education unconstitutional) to fight against desegregation.

believes he can set the timetable for another man's freedom; who lives by a mythical concept of time and who constantly advises the Negro to wait for a "more convenient season." Shallow understanding from people of good will is more frustrating than absolute misunderstanding from people of ill will. Lukewarm acceptance is much more bewildering than outright rejection.

I had hoped that the white moderate would understand that law and order   24
exist for the purpose of establishing justice and that when they fail in this purpose they become the dangerously structured dams that block the flow of social progress. I had hoped that the white moderate would understand that the present tension in the South is a necessary phase of the transition from an obnoxious negative peace, in which the Negro passively accepted his unjust plight, to a substantive and positive peace, in which all men will respect the dignity and worth of human personality. Actually, we who engage in nonviolent direct action are not the creators of tension. We merely bring to the surface the hidden tension that is already alive. We bring it out in the open, where it can be seen and dealt with. Like a boil that can never be cured so long as it is covered up but must be opened with all its ugliness to the natural medicines of air and light, injustice must be exposed, with all the tension its exposure creates, to the light of human conscience and the air of national opinion, before it can be cured.

In your statement you assert that our actions, even though peaceful, must be   25
condemned because they precipitate violence. But is this a logical assertion? Isn't this like condemning a robbed man because his possession of money precipitated the evil act of robbery? Isn't this like condemning Socrates because his unswerving commitment to truth and his philosophical inquiries precipitated the act by the misguided populace in which they made him drink hemlock? Isn't this like condemning Jesus because his unique God-consciousness and neverceasing devotion to God's will precipitated the evil act of crucifixion? We must come to see that, as the federal courts have consistently affirmed, it is wrong to urge an individual to cease his efforts to gain his basic constitutional rights because the quest may precipitate violence. Society must protect the robbed and punish the robber.

I had also hoped that the white moderate would reject the myth concerning   26
time in relation to the struggle for freedom. I have just received a letter from a white brother in Texas. He writes: "All Christians know that the colored people will receive greater equal rights eventually, but it is possible that you are in too great a religious hurry. It has taken Christianity almost two thousand years to accomplish what it has. The teachings of Christ take time to come to earth." Such an attitude stems from a tragic misconception of time, from the strangely irrational notion that there is something in the very flow of time that will inevitably cure all ills. Actually, time itself is neutral; it can be used either destructively or constructively. More and more I feel that the people of ill will have used time much more effectively than have the people of good will. We will have to repent in this generation not merely for the hateful words and actions of the bad people, but for the appalling silence of the good people.

Human progress never rolls in on wheels of inevitability; it comes through the tireless efforts of men willing to be co-workers with God, and without this hard work, time itself becomes an ally of the forces of social stagnation. We must use time creatively, in the knowledge that the time is always ripe to do right. Now is the time to make real the promise of democracy and transform our pending national elegy into a creative psalm of brotherhood. Now is the time to lift our national policy from the quicksand of racial injustice to the solid rock of human dignity.

You speak of our activity in Birmingham as extreme. At first I was rather   27
disappointed that fellow clergymen would see my nonviolent efforts as those of an extremist. I began thinking about the fact that I stand in the middle of two opposing forces in the Negro community. One is a force of complacency, made up in part of Negroes, who, as a result of long years of oppression, are so drained of self-respect and a sense of "somebodiness" that they have adjusted to segregation; and in part of a few middle-class Negroes who, because of a degree of academic and economic security and because in some ways they profit by segregation, have become insensitive to the problems of the masses. The other force is one of bitterness and hatred, and it comes perilously close to advocating violence. It is expressed in the various black nationalist groups that are springing up across the nation, the largest and best-known being Elijah Muhammad's Muslim movement.[8] Nourished by the Negro's frustration over the continued existence of racial discrimination, this movement is made up of people who have lost faith in America, who have absolutely repudiated Christianity, and who have concluded that the white man is an incorrigible "devil."

I have tried to stand between these two forces, saying that we need emulate   28
neither the "do-nothingism" of the complacent nor the hatred and despair of the black nationalist. For there is the more excellent way of love and nonviolent protest. I am grateful to God that, through the influence of the Negro church, the way of nonviolence became an integral part of our struggle.

If this philosophy had not emerged, by now many streets of the South   29
would, I am convinced, be flowing with blood. And I am further convinced that if our white brothers dismiss as "rabble-rousers" and "outside agitators" those of us who employ nonviolent direct action, and if they refuse to support our nonviolent efforts, millions of Negroes will, out of frustration and despair, seek solace and security in black-nationalist ideologies—a development that would inevitably lead to a frightening racial nightmare.

Oppressed people cannot remain oppressed forever. The yearning for free-   30
dom eventually manifests itself, and that is what has happened to the American Negro. Something within has reminded him of his birthright of freedom, and something without has reminded him that it can be gained. Consciously

---

[8] Elijah Muhammad (1897–1975), leader of the Nation of Islam, a black Muslim religious group that rejected integration and called upon blacks to fight to establish their own nation.

or unconsciously, he has been caught up by the *Zeitgeist*,[9] and with his black brothers of Africa and his brown and yellow brothers of Asia, South America, and the Caribbean, the United States Negro is moving with a sense of great urgency toward the promised land of racial justice. If one recognizes this vital urge that has engulfed the Negro community, one should readily understand why public demonstrations are taking place. The Negro has many pent-up resentments and latent frustrations, and he must release them. So let him march; let him make prayer pilgrimages to the city hall; let him go on freedom rides[10]—and try to understand why he must do so. If his repressed emotions are not released in nonviolent ways, they will seek expression through violence; this is not a threat but a fact of history. So I have not said to my people, "Get rid of your discontent." Rather, I have tried to say that this normal and healthy discontent can be channeled into the creative outlet of nonviolent direct action. And now this approach is being termed extremist.

But though I was initially disappointed at being categorized as an extremist, as I continued to think about the matter I gradually gained a measure of satisfaction from the label. Was not Jesus an extremist for love: "Love your enemies, bless them that curse you, do good to them that hate you, and pray for them that despitefully use you, and persecute you." Was not Amos an extremist for justice: "Let justice roll down like waters and righteousness like an ever-flowing stream." Was not Paul an extremist for the Christian gospel: "I bear in my body the marks of the Lord Jesus." Was not Martin Luther an extremist: "Here I stand; I cannot do otherwise, so help me God." And John Bunyan: "I will stay in jail to the end of my days before I make a butchery of my conscience." And Abraham Lincoln: "This nation cannot survive half slave and half free." And Thomas Jefferson: "We hold these truths to be self-evident, that all men are created equal. . . . " So the question is not whether we will be extremists, but what kind of extremists we will be. Will we be extremists for the preservation of injustice or for the extension of justice? In that dramatic scene on Calvary's hill three men were crucified. We must never forget that all three were crucified for the same crime—the crime of extremism. Two were extremists for immorality, and thus fell below their environment. The other, Jesus Christ, was an extremist for love, truth, and goodness, and thereby rose above his environment. Perhaps the South, the nation, and the world are in dire need of creative extremists.

I had hoped that the white moderate would see this need. Perhaps I was too optimistic; perhaps I expected too much. I suppose I should have realized that few members of the oppressor race can understand the deep groans and passionate yearnings of the oppressed race, and still fewer have the vision to see that injustice must be rooted out by strong, persistent, and determined action.

31

32

---

[9] The spirit of the time.

[10] In 1961, hundreds of blacks and whites, under the direction of the Congress of Racial Equality (CORE), deliberately violated laws in southern states that required segregation in buses and bus terminals.

I am thankful, however, that some of our white brothers in the South have grasped the meaning of this social revolution and committed themselves to it. They are still all too few in quantity, but they are big in quality. Some—such as Ralph McGill, Lillian Smith, Harry Golden, James McBride Dabbs, Ann Braden, and Sarah Patton Boyle—have written about our struggle in eloquent and prophetic terms. Others have marched with us down nameless streets of the South. They have languished in filthy, roach-infested jails, suffering the abuse and brutality of policemen who view them as "dirty nigger-lovers." Unlike so many of their moderate brothers and sisters, they have recognized the urgency of the moment and sensed the need for powerful "action" antidotes to combat the disease of segregation.

Let me take note of my other major disappointment. I have been so greatly   33 disappointed with the white church and its leadership. Of course, there are some notable exceptions. I am not unmindful of the fact that each of you has taken some significant stands on this issue. I commend you, Reverend Stallings, for your Christian stand on this past Sunday, in welcoming Negroes to your worship service on a nonsegregated basis. I commend the Catholic leaders of this state for integrating Spring Hill College several years ago.

But despite these notable exceptions, I must honestly reiterate that I have   34 been disappointed with the church. I do not say this as one of those negative critics who can always find something wrong with the church. I say this as a minister of the gospel, who loves the church; who was nurtured in its bosom; who has been sustained by its spiritual blessings and who will remain true to it as long as the cord of life shall lengthen.

When I was suddenly catapulted into the leadership of the bus protest in   35 Montgomery, Alabama, a few years ago, I felt we would be supported by the white church. I felt that the white ministers, priests, and rabbis of the South would be among our strongest allies. Instead, some have been outright opponents, refusing to understand the freedom movement and misrepresenting its leaders; all too many others have been more cautious than courageous and have remained silent behind the anesthetizing security of stained-glass windows.

In spite of my shattered dreams, I came to Birmingham with the hope that   36 the white religious leadership of this community would see the justice of our cause and, with deep moral concern, would serve as the channel through which our just grievances could reach the power structure. I had hoped that each of you would understand. But again I have been disappointed.

I have heard numerous southern religious leaders admonish their worshipers   37 to comply with a desegregation decision because it is the law, but I have longed to hear white ministers declare: "Follow this decree because integration is morally right and because the Negro is your brother." In the midst of blatant injustices inflicted upon the Negro, I have watched white churchmen stand on the sideline and mouth pious irrelevancies and sanctimonious trivialities. In the midst of a mighty struggle to rid our nation of racial and economic injustice, I have heard many ministers say: "Those are social issues, with which the gospel has no real concern." And I have watched many churches commit themselves to a completely otherworldly religion which makes a strange, unBiblical distinction between body and soul, between the sacred and the secular.

I have traveled the length and breadth of Alabama, Mississippi, and all the other southern states. On sweltering summer days and crisp autumn mornings I have looked at the South's beautiful churches with their lofty spires pointing heavenward. I have beheld the impressive outlines of her massive religious-education buildings. Over and over I have found myself asking: "What kind of people worship here? Who is their God? Where were their voices when the lips of Governor Barnett dripped with words of interposition and nullification? Where were they when Governor Wallace gave a clarion call for defiance and hatred? Where were their voices of support when bruised and weary Negro men and women decided to rise from the dark dungeons of complacency to the bright hills of creative protest?"

Yes, these questions are still in mind. In deep disappointment I have wept over the laxity of the church. But be assured that my tears have been tears of love. There can be no deep disappointment where there is not deep love. Yes, I love the church. How could I do otherwise? I am in the rather unique position of being the son, the grandson, and the great-grandson of preachers. Yes, I see the church as the body of Christ. But, oh! How we have blemished and scarred the body through social neglect and through fear of being non-conformists.

There was a time when the church was very powerful—in the time when the early Christians rejoiced at being deemed worthy to suffer for what they believed. In those days the church was not merely a thermometer that transformed the mores of society. Whenever the early Christians entered a town, the people in power became disturbed and immediately sought to convict the Christians for being "disturbers of the peace" and "outside agitators." But the Christians pressed on, in the conviction that they were "a colony of heaven," called to obey God rather than man. Small in number, they were big in commitment. They were too God-intoxicated to be "astronomically intimidated." By their effort and example they brought an end to such ancient evils as infanticide and gladiatorial contests.

Things are different now. So often the contemporary church is a weak, ineffectual voice with an uncertain sound. So often it is an archdefender of the status quo. Far from being disturbed by the presence of the church, the power structure of the average community is consoled by the church's silent—and often even vocal—sanction of things as they are.

But the judgment of God is upon the church as never before. If today's church does not recapture the sacrificial spirit of the early church, it will lose its authenticity, forfeit the loyalty of millions, and be dismissed as an irrelevant social club with no meaning for the twentieth century. Every day I meet young people whose disappointment with the church has turned into outright disgust.

Perhaps I have once again been too optimistic. Is organized religion too   43
inextricably bound to the status quo to save our nation and the world? Perhaps
I must turn my faith to the inner spiritual church, the church within the
church, as the true *ekklesia*[11] and the hope of the world. But again I am
thankful to God that some noble souls from the ranks of organized religion
have broken loose from the paralyzing chains of conformity and joined us as
active partners in the struggle for freedom. They have left their secure congregations and walked the streets of Albany, Georgia, with us. They have gone
down the highways of the South on tortuous rides for freedom. Yes, they have
gone to jail with us. Some have been dismissed from their churches, have lost
the support of their bishops and fellow ministers. But they have acted in the
faith that right defeated is stronger than evil triumphant. Their witness has
been the spiritual salt that has preserved the true meaning of the gospel in
these troubled times. They have carved a tunnel of hope through the dark
mountain of disappointment.

I hope that the church as a whole will meet the challenge of this decisive   44
hour. But even if the church does not come to the aid of justice, I have no
despair about the future. I have no fear about the outcome of our struggle in
Birmingham, even if our motives are at present misunderstood. We will reach
the goal of freedom in Birmingham and all over the nation, because the goal
of America is freedom. Abused and scorned though we may be, our destiny is
tied up with America's destiny. Before the pilgrims landed at Plymouth, we
were here. Before the pen of Jefferson etched the majestic words of the Declaration of Independence across the pages of history, we were here. For more
than two centuries our forebears labored in this country without wages; they
made cotton king; they built the homes of their masters while suffering gross
injustice and shameful humiliation—and yet out of a bottomless vitality they
continued to thrive and develop. If the inexpressible cruelties of slavery could
not stop us, the opposition we now face will surely fail. We will win our
freedom because the sacred heritage of our nation and the eternal will of God
are embodied in our echoing demands.

Before closing I feel impelled to mention one other point in your statement   45
that has troubled me profoundly. You warmly commended the Birmingham
police force for keeping "order" and "preventing violence." I doubt that you
would have so warmly commended the police force if you had seen its dogs
sinking their teeth into unarmed, nonviolent Negroes. I doubt that you would
so quickly commend the policemen if you were to observe their ugly and
inhumane treatment of Negroes here in the city jail; if you were to watch them
push and curse old Negro women and young Negro girls; if you were to see
them slap and kick old Negro men and young boys; if you were to observe
them, as they did on two occasions, refuse to give us food because we wanted

---

[11] The Greek *New Testament* word for the early Christian church.

to sing our grace together. I cannot join you in your praise of the Birmingham police department.

It is true that the police have exercised a degree of discipline in handling the demonstrators. In this sense they have conducted themselves rather "nonviolently" in public. But for what purpose? To preserve the evil system of segregation. Over the past few years I have consistently preached that nonviolence demands that the means we use must be as pure as the ends we seek. I have tried to make clear that it is wrong to use immoral means to attain moral ends. But now I must affirm that it is just as wrong, or perhaps even more so, to use moral means to preserve immoral ends. Perhaps Mr. Connor and his policemen have been rather nonviolent in public, as was Chief Pritchett in Albany, Georgia, but they have used the moral means of nonviolence to maintain the immoral end of racial injustice. As T. S. Eliot[12] has said, "The last temptation is the greatest treason: To do the right deed for the wrong reason."

I wish you had commended the Negro sit-inners and demonstrators of Birmingham for their sublime courage, their willingness to suffer, and their amazing discipline in the midst of great provocation. One day the South will recognize its real heroes. They will be the James Merediths,[13] with the noble sense of purpose that enables them to face jeering and hostile mobs, and with the agonizing loneliness that characterizes the life of the pioneer. They will be old, oppressed, battered Negro women, symbolized in a seventy-two-year-old woman in Montgomery, Alabama, who rose up with a sense of dignity and with her people decided not to ride segregated buses, and who responded with ungrammatical profundity to one who inquired about her weariness: "My feets is tired, but my soul is at rest." They will be the young high school and college students, the young ministers of the gospel and a host of their elders, courageously and nonviolently sitting in at lunch counters and willingly going to jail for conscience' sake. One day the South will know that when these disinherited children of God sat down at lunch counters, they were in reality standing up for what is best in the American dream and for the most sacred values in our Judaeo-Christian heritage, thereby bringing our nation back to those great wells of democracy which were dug deep by the founding fathers in their formulation of the Constitution and the Declaration of Independence.

Never before have I written so long a letter. I'm afraid it is much too long to take your precious time. I can assure you that it would have been much shorter if I had been writing from a comfortable desk, but what else can one do when he is alone in a narrow jail cell, other than write long letters, think long thoughts, and pray long prayers?

If I have said anything in this letter that overstates the truth and indicates an unreasonable impatience, I beg you to forgive me. If I have said anything

---

[12] Thomas Stearns Eliot (1888–1965), American-born poet.
[13] James Meredith was the first black to be admitted as a student at the University of Mississippi.

that understates the truth and indicates my having a patience that allows me to settle for anything less than brotherhood, I beg God to forgive me.

I hope this letter finds you strong in the faith. I hope that circumstances will soon make it possible for me to meet each of you, not as an intregationist or a civil-rights leader but as a fellow clergyman and a Christian brother. Let us all hope that the dark clouds of a racial prejudice will soon pass away and the deep fog of misunderstanding will be lifted from our fear-drenched communities, and in some not too distant tomorrow the radiant stars of love and brotherhood will shine over our great nation with all their scintillating beauty. 50

> Yours for the cause of Peace and Brotherhood,
> MARTIN LUTHER KING, JR.

QUESTIONS

1. What is King's definition of civil disobedience?   **2.** Does your own experience bear out King's distinction (paragraph 10) between "violent" and "nonviolent" tension?   **3.** Summarize and explain the argument King makes in paragraph 46 about "means" and "ends."   **4.** Those opposed to civil disobedience frequently argue that in a democratic society such as ours, change should be pursued through legislation and the courts because if people are allowed to disobey laws with which they disagree, we will have chaos and violence. How does King seek to allay these fears?   **5.** Readers have often found King's tone and style strongly influenced by pulpit oratory in its eloquence, elevated diction, biblical allusions, and didacticism. Select a passage (one or two paragraphs) from the essay and show how it reflects these qualities.

WRITING TOPIC

King offers a philosophical justification for civil disobedience (paragraphs 15–22), at the heart of which is his distinction between a just and an unjust law. Defend or take issue with that distinction.

A Path of More Resistance   1989

BILL McKIBBEN   [b. 1960]

Several years ago, Jim Stolz shouldered a pack at the Mexican border and hiked   1
eight or nine hundred miles north to the Idaho mountains for a meeting of a
small environmental group.

This, he told me as we sat by a stream three months later, was not all that   2
unusual for him. Some years earlier, he had walked the Appalachian Trail,
Georgia to Maine. "I spent the next two years going coast to coast. I took the
northern route—I spent a couple of months on snowshoes through Wisconsin
and Minnesota." He'd never seen the Pacific till he got there on his own two
feet. After that, he walked the Continental Divide trail. And then he began to
lay out a new trek—the Grand West Trail, he calls it. It runs north and south
between the Pacific Crest and the Continental Divide trails, traversing the
Grand Canyon and the lava plains, climbing over the Sawtooths. All it lacks is
people. "I spent one nine-and-a-half-day stretch this trip when I didn't see
anyone," Stolz said. "I see someone else maybe every fourth day."

In the course of his long walks he had twelve times come across grizzly bears,   3
the continent's grandest mammals, now nearly gone from the lower forty-
eight. "The last one, he stood on his hind legs, clicked his jaws, woofed three
times. I was too close to him, and he was just letting me know. Another one
circled me about forty feet away and wouldn't look me in the eye. When you
get that close, you realize you're part of the food chain. When we go into
grizzly country, we're going into *their* home. We're the intruders. We're used
to being top dog. But in griz country we're part of the food chain."

That seemed a quietly radical idea to me—the idea that we don't necessarily   4
belong at the top in every way. It seemed to me, thinking about it later, that
it might be a good way to describe a philosophy that is the opposite of the
defiant, consumptive course we've traditionally followed. What would it mean
to our ways of life, our demographics, our economics, our output of carbon
dioxide and methane if we began to truly and viscerally think of ourselves as
just one species among many?

The logic of our present thinking—that we should increase in numbers and,   5
especially, in material wealth and ease—leads inexorably in the direction of the
managed world. It is, as a few rebels have maintained, a rut, a system of beliefs
in which we are trapped. When Thoreau declared that the masses of men lead
lives of quiet desperation,[1] it was to this rut that he referred. He went to live
at Walden Pond to prove how little man needed to survive—$61.99¾ for eight
months, including the cost of his house.

---

[1] Henry David Thoreau (1817–1862) made this declaration in *Walden, or Life in the Woods*
(1854).

But most of us have lived in that rut without rebelling. A few, often under   6
Thoreau's influence, may have chucked their sophomore year to live in a tent
by some wild lake, but even most of them returned to normal society. Thoreau's explanation—that we think there's no choice—may help explain this
fact. But the terrible truth is that most of us rather like the rut. We like
acquiring more things; the aphorists notwithstanding, they make us happy.
We like the easy life. I was skimming through an old copy of the *New Yorker*
not long ago and came across an advertisement, from what in 1949 was still the
Esso Company, that summed up our century to this point. "The better you
live," it shouted, "the more oil you use." And we live well. The world, as most
of us in the West experience it in the late twentieth century, is a reasonably
sweet place. That is why there aren't more hippies camped by the lake. We like
to camp, but for the weekend.

The only trouble is that this system of beliefs, this pleasant rut, seems not   7
to be making *the planet* happy. The atmosphere and the forests are less satisfied than we are. In fact, they are changing, dying. And those changes affect
us, body and soul. The end of nature sours all my material pleasures. The
prospect of living in a genetically engineered world sickens me. And yet it is
toward such a world that our belief in endless material advancement hurries
us.

As long as that desire drives us, there is no way to set limits. We won't   8
develop genetic engineering to eradicate disease and not use it to manufacture
perfectly efficient chickens; there is nothing in the logic of our ingrained
beliefs that would lead us to draw those lines. Direct our beliefs into a new
stream, and that stream would soon be a torrent just like the present one: if we
use fusion energy instead of coal, we will still plow ahead at our basic business,
accumulation, with all its implications for the natural world. If there is one
notion that virtually every successful politician on earth—socialist or fascist or
capitalist—agrees on, it is that "economic growth" is good, necessary, the
proper end of organized human activity. But where does economic growth
end? It ends—or, at least, it runs straight through—the genetically engineered
dead world that the optimists envision. That is, provided we can surmount our
present environmental troubles.

Those troubles, though, just might give us the chance to change the way we   9
think. What if they gave us a practical—as opposed to a moral or an aesthetic—reason to climb out of our rut and find a new one that leads in some
different direction? A reason based on atmospheric chemistry, not Eastern
spirituality. That is why Stolz's phrase caught my ear, his notion that we might
be no more important than anything else. If a new idea—a *humble* idea, in
contrast to the conventional defiant attitude—is going to rise out of the
wreckage we have made of the world, this is the gut feeling, the impulse, it will
come from.

The idea that the rest of creation might count for as much as we do is   10
spectacularly foreign, even to most environmentalists. The ecological move-

ment has always had its greatest success in convincing people that we are threatened by some looming problem—or, if we are not threatened directly, then some creature that we find appealing, such as the seal or the whale or the songbird. The tropical rain forests must be saved because they contain millions of species of plants that may have medical uses—that was the single most common argument against tropical deforestation until it was replaced by the greenhouse effect. Even the American wilderness movement, in some ways a radical crusade, has argued for wilderness largely as places for man—places big enough for backpackers to lose themselves in and for stressed city dwellers to find themselves.

But what if we began to believe in the rain forest *for its own sake?* This attitude has very slowly begun to spread in recent years, both in America and abroad, as the effects of man's domination have become clearer. Some few people have begun to talk of two views of the world—the traditional, man-centered—anthropocentric—view and the biocentric vision of people as a part of the world, just like bears. 11

Many of those who take the biocentric view are, of course, oddballs, the sort who would walk two thousand miles instead of flying. (Prophets, false or true, are inevitably oddballs. There's not much need for prophets who are in synch with their society.) And theirs is, admittedly, a radical idea, almost an unrealistic idea. It strikes at the root of our identities. But we live at a radical, unrealistic moment. We live at the end of nature, the moment when the essential character of the world we've known since we stopped swinging from our tails is suddenly changing. I'm not intrinsically attracted to radical ideas anymore. I have a house, and a bank account, and I'd like my life, all other things being equal, to continue in its current course. But all other things are not equal—we live at an odd moment in human history when the most basic elements of our lives are changing. I love the trees outside my window; they are a part of my life. I don't want to see them shrivel in the heat, nor sprout in perfect cloned rows. The damage we have done to the planet, and the damage we seem set to do in a genetically engineered business-as-usual future, make me wonder if there isn't some other way. If there isn't a humbler alternative— one that would let us hew closer to what remains of nature, and give it room to recover, if it can. An alternative that would involve changing not only the way we act but also the way we think. 12

Such ideas are not brand-new. Almost as far back as people have gathered in societies, there are records of ascetics and hermits. Thoreau diluted the religion in this strain of thinking and injected it into the modern bloodstream, but, as we have seen, he went to the woods to redeem man, not nature. (It is curious, in fact, just how little description of nature *Walden* contains.) His is an intensely anthropocentric account—man's desecration of nature worried him less than man's desecration of himself. Nature mattered, but as a wonderful text. "Let us spend one day as deliberately as Nature," he pleads, "and 13

not be thrown off the track by every nutshell and mosquito wing that falls on
the rails. Let us rise early and fast, or break fast, gently and without pertur-
bation." Nature was a lesson.

The crucial next step in the development of this humble philosophy—the   14
idea that the rest of creation mattered for its own sake, and that man didn't
matter all that much—awaited other writers. It is implicit throughout the
works of John Muir,[2] and sometimes it is explicit. In the journal of his
thousand-mile hike to the Gulf of Mexico, for instance, there is a passage
that stands in perfect contrast to Professor Baxter's argument that men matter entirely and penguins not at all.[3] Muir is writing about alligators, animals
as revolting by our standards as any on the continent. He acknowledges that
alligators "cannot be called the friends of man" (though he had heard of
"one big fellow that was caught young and partially civilized and made to
work in harness"). But that, he declares, is not the point. "Many good people believe the alligators were created by the Devil, thus accounting for their
all-consuming appetite and ugliness. But doubtless these creatures are happy
and fill the place assigned for them by the great Creator of us all. Fierce and
cruel they appear to us, but beautiful in the eyes of God." This is more than
an ecological, Darwinian vision; it is a moral one: "How narrow we selfish,
conceited creatures are in our sympathies! How blind to the rights of all the
rest of creation! . . . Though alligators, snakes etc. naturally repel us, they are
not mysterious evils. They dwell happily in these flowery wilds, are part of
God's family, unfallen, undepraved, and cared for with the same species of
tenderness as is bestowed on angels in heaven or saints on earth." Muir ends
his swampy sermonette with a benediction that stands as a good epigram for
this humbler approach: "Honorable representatives of the great saurians of
older creation, may you long enjoy your lilies and rushes, and be blessed now
and then with a mouthful of terror-stricken man by way of dainty!"

Of the many heirs to this philosophical tradition, the most striking was   15
Edward Abbey. A funny, moving novelist and an able critic, Abbey was, more
than anything else, an apostle of a place—the desert Southwest, where he lived
for many years. Abbey, who died in the spring of 1989, spent long stretches
working for the government in various fire towers and ranger shacks—long
stretches utterly alone. And alone in the part of nature—the desert—that
seems least hospitable, most alienating. Though he loved the desert's beauty,
he also recognized its overwhelming alienness. In one of the essays in his first
collection he wrote: "The desert says nothing. Completely passive, acted upon
but never acting, the desert lies there like the bare skeleton of Being, spare,
sparse, austere, utterly worthless, inviting not love but contemplation. In its
simplicity and order it suggests the classical, except that *the desert is a realm*

---

[2] John Muir (1838–1914), American naturalist and writer.
[3] William F. Baxter, *People or Penguins: The Case for Optimal Pollution* (1974).

beyond the human and in the classicist view only the human is regarded as significant or even recognized as real."

The idea of "a realm beyond the human" but still on this earth is at odds with our deepest notions, our sense of all creation as our private domain. It is no accident that Abbey wrote from the desert. If you lived in the Garden of Eden, or even in, say, Fort Lauderdale, it might be possible to think that the earth had been made for you and your pleasure. But not if you lived in the desert of the Southwest. If the desert was made for you, why is there so little water? It's infinitely more plausible that the desert was made for buzzards. 16

No wonder, then, that in all the world the desert of the Southwest was one of the last places left more or less untouched. Prospectors had come and gone, and their traces could still be seen in the preserving sand, but when Abbey arrived most of the area lay in its natural state. As a result, he got to watch the developers, miners, and promoters lay their defiant siege to the land. Abbey wrote a novel, *The Monkey Wrench Gang*, out of his anger at the uranium mines and the copper smelters fouling the clean air, and at the endless road building and river damming. Though it is an "action novel," a wild account of a campaign of sabotage against bulldozers and dams, it crystallizes in a single scene the difference between our conventional, defiant view of the world and the biocentric vision. 17

Early in the book, Hayduke, the hero, decides to disrupt the construction of a road that is being laid out through the Arizona desert. As he follows the planned route, pulling up the surveyor's orange flags, he comes to the stony rim of a small canyon. On the opposite wall, four hundred feet away, he could see the line of stakes, with their Day-Glo ribbons, marching on. "This canyon, then, was going to be bridged. It was only a small and little known canyon, to be sure, with a tiny stream coursing down its bed, meandering in lazy bights over the sand, lolling in pools under the acid-green leafery of the cottonwoods, falling over lip of stone into basin below, barely enough water even in spring to sustain a resident population of spotted toads, red-winged dragonflies, a snake or two, a few canyon wrens, nothing special. And yet Hayduke demurred; he didn't want a bridge here, ever; he liked this little canyon, which he had never seen before, the name of which he didn't even know, quite well enough as it was. Hayduke knelt and wrote a message in the sand to all highway construction contractors: 'Go home.' " This canyon is not Yosemite, or even Hetch Hetchy—there is no way to rally a crowd to its defense by virtue of its splendor or its opportunities for recreation. It has no human use. If the road isn't built, no one will ever come here. This canyon can only be paved over or be left alone to no constructive end. Abbey's radicalism was that he chose the latter. 18

QUESTIONS

1. Are you persuaded by McKibben's arguments? Explain. **2.** What does McKibben mean by "a path of more resistance"? **3.** What does McKibben mean when he asserts that the destructive changes inflicted on the planet "affect us, body and soul?" (paragraph 7)?   **4.** What does it mean "to believe in the rain forest *for its own sake*" (paragraph 11)?

WRITING TOPIC
Write a paper in the form of a debate with three characters: a moderator (who introduces the subject), Willard Gaylin, and Bill McKibben.

Conformity and Rebellion

QUESTIONS AND WRITING TOPICS

1. What support do the works in this section offer for Emily Dickinson's assertion that "Much Madness is Divinest Sense"? **Writing Topic:** The central characters in Melville's "Bartleby the Scrivener" and Ellison's " 'Repent, Harlequin!' Said the Ticktockman" are viewed by society as mad. How might it be argued that they exhibit "divinest sense"?

2. Which works in this section can be criticized on the grounds that while they attack the established order, they fail to provide any alternatives? **Writing Topic:** Discuss the validity of this objection for two of the following poems: Wordsworth's "The World is Too Much with Us," Lowell's "Patterns," Reed's "Naming of Parts," Baker's "Formal Application."

3. In a number of these works, a single individual rebels against society and suffers defeat or death. Are these works therefore pessimistic and despairing? If not, then what is the purpose of the rebellions, and why do the authors choose to bring their characters to such ends? **Writing Topic:** Compare two works from this section that offer support for the idea that a single individual can have a decisive effect on society.

4. Examine some of the representatives of established order—the lawyer in "Bartleby the Scrivener," William Chadders in "Something for the Time Being," Creon in *Antigonê*, the Ticktockman—and discuss what attitudes they share and how effectively they function as spokespeople for law and order. **Writing Topic:** Compare and evaluate the kinds of order that each represents.

5. Amy Lowell's "Patterns," Lawrence Ferlinghetti's "In Goya's Greatest Scenes," and Henry Reed's "Naming of Parts" are, in different ways, antiwar poems. In which of these poems do you find the most articulate and convincing antiwar statement? **Writing Topic:** Discuss the argument that, while condemning war, none of these poems examines the specific reasons that a nation may be obliged to fight—self-defense and national self-interest, for example—and that consequently they are irresponsible.

6. Most of us live out our lives in the ordinary and humdrum world that is rejected in such poems as Wordsworth's "The World is Too Much with Us," Auden's "The Unknown Citizen," and Lennon and McCartney's "Eleanor Rigby." Can it be said that these poems are counsels to social irresponsibility? **Writing Topic:** Consider whether "we" in Wordsworth's poem, the unknown citizen, Father McKenzie, and Eleanor Rigby are simply objects of scorn or whether they deserve sympathy and perhaps even respect.

7. Characters in several pieces included here—the Harlequin, Bartleby, Daniel Mgoma, Jack Smurch, and Antigonê—are rebels. Are they comparable? **Writing Topic:** Explain how the attitudes and actions of these characters constitute an attack on the status quo.

8. Many works in this section deal explicitly with the relationship between the individual and the state. What similarities of outlook do you find among them? **Writing Topic:** Compare and contrast the way that relationship is perceived in Ellison's " 'Repent, Harlequin!' Said the Ticktockman" and King's "Letter from Birmingham Jail."

9. Essays by Willard Gaylin and Bill McKibben take differing views on the relationship between humans and their environment. Which view do you find most convincing? Why? **Writing Topic:** Compare and contrast the views put forward in these two essays, and argue for the position you favor.

Love and Hate

Mr. and Mrs. Clark and Percy, 1970–1971 by David Hockney.

Love and death, it is often noted, are the two great themes of literature. Many of the literary works we have placed in the sections "Innocence and Experience" and "Conformity and Rebellion" speak of love and death as well. But in those works, other thematic interests dominate. In this section, we gather a number of works in which love and hate are thematically central.

The rosy conception of love presented in many popular and sentimental stories ill prepares us for the complicated reality we face. We know that the course of true love never runs smooth, but in those popular stories the obstacles that hinder the lovers are simple and external. If the young lover can land the high-paying job or convince the beloved's parents that he or she is worthy despite social differences, all will be well. But love in life is rarely that simple. The external obstacles may be insuperable, or the obstacles may lie deep within the personality. The major obstacle may well be an individual's difficult and painful effort to understand that he or she has been deceived by an immature and sentimental conception of love.

In this age of psychoanalytic awareness, the claims of the flesh are well recognized. But psychoanalytic theory teaches us, as well, to recognize the aggressive aspect of the human condition. The omnipresent selfishness that civilization attempts to check may be aggressively violent as well as lustful. Thus, on one hand, we have the simple eroticism of Kate Chopin's "The Storm," and on the other, the macabre behavior of Faulkner's Emily Grierson in "A Rose for Emily." And Matthew Arnold in "Dover Beach" finds love the only refuge from a chaotic world in which "ignorant armies clash by night."

The cliché has it that love and hate are closely related, and much evidence supports this proposition. But why should love and hate, seeming opposites, lie so close together in the emotional lives of men and women? We are all egos, separate from each other. And as separate individuals, we develop elaborate behavior mechanisms that defend us from each other. But the erotic love relationship differs from other relationships in that it may be defined as a rejection of separateness. The common metaphor speaks of two lovers as joining, as merging into one. That surrender of the "me" to join in an "us" leaves lovers uniquely vulnerable to psychic injury. In short, the defenses are down, and the self-esteem of each of the lovers depends importantly on the behavior of the other. If the lover is betrayed by the beloved, the emotional consequences are uniquely disastrous—hence the peculiarly close relationship of passionate hatred with erotic love.

Words like *love* and *hate* are so general that poets rarely use them except as one term in a metaphor designed to project sharply some aspect of emotional life. The simple sexuality in such poems as Marvell's "To His Coy Mistress," Marlowe's "The Passionate Shepherd to His Love," and Campion's "I Care Not for These Ladies" may be juxtaposed with the hatred and violence generated in Othello by sexual jealousy or with the quick reprisal of the slighted Barbara Allan. And Shakespeare's description of lust in "Th' expense of spirit in a waste of shame" notes an aspect of love quite overlooked by Edmund Waller in his song, "Go, Lovely Rose!"

Perhaps more than anything, the works in this section celebrate the elemental impulses of men and women that run counter to those rational formulations by which we govern our lives. We pursue Othello's love for Desdemona and Iago's hate for Othello and arrive at an irreducible mystery, for neither Othello's love nor Iago's hate yields satisfactorily to rational explanation. Reason does not tell us why Othello and Desdemona love one another or why Iago hates rather than honors Othello.

Love is an act of faith springing from our deep-seated need to join with another human being not only in physical nakedness but in emotional and spiritual nakedness as well. While hate is a denial of that faith and, therefore, a retreat into spiritual isolation, love is an attempt to break out of the isolation.

FOR THINKING AND WRITING

As you read the selections in this section, consider the following questions. You may want to write out your thoughts informally in a journal or notebook as a way of preparing to respond to the selections, or you may wish to make one of these questions the basis for a formal essay.

1. What is love? What is the source of your definition (literature, personal observation, discussions with those you trust)? Have you ever been in love? How did you know? Do you know someone who is in love? How do you know?

2. Have you ever truly hated someone or something? Describe the circumstances, and characterize your hatred.

3. Do you believe that love and hate are closely related? Have you experienced a change from love to hatred, or do you know someone who has? Explain.

4. There are different kinds of love—love of family, of humankind, of God. There are, of course, sexual love and the love of a cause. Characterize several different kinds of love, and examine your own motives and behavior in different love relationships. In what ways do certain kinds of love necessarily generate certain hatreds?

469

LOVE
AND
HATE

A Husband Parting from His Wife and Child, 1799 by William Blake

FICTION

The Storm   (1898)

KATE CHOPIN   [1851–1904]

I

The leaves were so still that even Bibi thought it was going to rain. Bobinôt, who was accustomed to converse on terms of perfect equality with his little son, called the child's attention to certain sombre clouds that were rolling with sinister intention from the west, accompanied by a sullen, threatening roar. They were at Friedheimer's store and decided to remain there till the storm had passed. They sat within the door on two empty kegs. Bibi was four years old and looked very wise.

"Mama'll be 'fraid, yes," he suggested with blinking eyes.

"She'll shut the house. Maybe she got Sylvie helpin' her this evenin'," Bobinôt responded reassuringly.

"No; she ent got Sylvie. Sylvie was helpin' her yistiday," piped Bibi.

Bobinôt arose and going across to the counter purchased a can of shrimps, of which Calixta was very fond. Then he returned to his perch on the keg and sat stolidly holding the can of shrimps while the storm burst. It shook the wooden store and seemed to be ripping great furrows in the distant field. Bibi laid his little hand on his father's knee and was not afraid.

II

Calixta, at home, felt no uneasiness for their safety. She sat at a side window sewing furiously on a sewing machine. She was greatly occupied and did not notice the approaching storm. But she felt very warm and often stopped to mop her face on which the perspiration gathered in beads. She unfastened her white sacque at the throat. It began to grow dark, and suddenly realizing the situation she got up hurriedly and went about closing windows and doors.

Out on the small front gallery she had hung Bobinôt's Sunday clothes to air and she hastened out to gather them before the rain fell. As she stepped outside, Alcée Laballière rode in at the gate. She had not seen him very often since her marriage, and never alone. She stood there with Bobinôt's coat in her hands, and the big rain drops began to fall. Alcée rode his horse under the shelter of a side projection where the chickens had huddled and there were plows and a harrow piled up in the corner.

"May I come and wait on your gallery till the storm is over, Calixta?" he asked.

"Come 'long in, M'sieur Alcée."

His voice and her own startled her as if from a trance, and she seized Bobinôt's vest. Alcée, mounting to the porch, grabbed the trousers and snatched Bibi's braided jacket that was about to be carried away by a sudden gust of wind. He expressed an intention to remain outside, but it was soon apparent that he might as well have been out in the open: the water beat in upon the boards in driving sheets, and he went inside, closing the door after him. It was even necessary to put something beneath the door to keep the water out.

"My! what a rain! It's good two years sence it rain' like that," exclaimed Calixta as she rolled up a piece of bagging and Alcée helped her to thrust it beneath the crack.

She was a little fuller of figure than five years before when she married; but she had lost nothing of her vivacity. Her blue eyes still retained their melting quality; and her yellow hair, dishevelled by the wind and rain, kinked more stubbornly than ever about her ears and temples.

The rain beat upon the low, shingled roof with a force and clatter that threatened to break an entrance and deluge them there. They were in the dining room—the sitting room—the general utility room. Adjoining was her bed room, with Bibi's couch along side her own. The door stood open, and the room with its white, monumental bed, its closed shutters, looked dim and mysterious.

Alcée flung himself into a rocker and Calixta nervously began to gather up from the floor the lengths of a cotton sheet which she had been sewing.

"If this keeps up, *Dieu sait*[1] if the levees goin' to stan' it!" she exclaimed.

"What have you got to do with the levees?"

"I got enough to do! An' there's Bobinôt with Bibi out in that storm—if he only didn' left Friedheimer's!"

"Let us hope, Calixta, that Bobinôt's got sense enough to come in out of a cyclone."

She went and stood at the window with a greatly disturbed look on her face. She wiped the frame that was clouded with moisture. It was stiflingly hot. Alcée got up and joined her at the window, looking over her shoulder. The rain was coming down in sheets obscuring the view of far-off cabins and enveloping the distant wood in a gray mist. The playing of the lightning was incessant. A bolt struck a tall chinaberry tree at the edge of the field. It filled all visible space with a blinding glare and the crash seemed to invade the very boards they stood upon.

Calixta put her hands to her eyes, and with a cry, staggered backward.

---

[1] God knows.

Alcée's arm encircled her, and for an instant he drew her close and spasmodically to him.

"*Bonté!*"[2] she cried, releasing herself from his encircling arm and retreating from the window, "the house'll go next! If I only knew w'ere Bibi was!" She would not compose herself; she would not be seated. Alcée clasped her shoulders and looked into her face. The contact of her warm, palpitating body when he had unthinkingly drawn her into his arms, had aroused all the old-time infatuation and desire for her flesh.

"Calixta," he said, "don't be frightened. Nothing can happen. The house is too low to be struck, with so many tall trees standing about. There! aren't you going to be quiet? say, aren't you?" He pushed her hair back from her face that was warm and steaming. Her lips were as red and moist as pomegranate seed. Her white neck and a glimpse of her full, firm bosom disturbed him powerfully. As she glanced up at him the fear in her liquid blue eyes had given place to a drowsy gleam that unconsciously betrayed a sensuous desire. He looked down into her eyes and there was nothing for him to do but to gather her lips in a kiss. It reminded him of Assumption.[3]

"Do you remember—in Assumption, Calixta?" he asked in a low voice broken by passion. Oh! she remembered; for in Assumption he had kissed her and kissed and kissed her; until his senses would well nigh fail, and to save her he would resort to a desperate flight. If she was not an immaculate dove in those days, she was still inviolate; a passionate creature whose very defenselessness had made her defense, against which his honor forbade him to prevail. Now—well, now—her lips seemed in a manner free to be tasted, as well as her round, white throat and her whiter breasts.

They did not heed the crashing torrents, and the roar of the elements made her laugh as she lay in his arms. She was a revelation in that dim, mysterious chamber; as white as the couch she lay upon. Her firm, elastic flesh that was knowing for the first time its birthright, was like a creamy lily that the sun invites to contribute its breath and perfume to the undying life of the world.

The generous abundance of her passion, without guile or trickery, was like a white flame which penetrated and found response in depths of his own sensuous nature that had never yet been reached.

When he touched her breasts they gave themselves up in quivering ecstasy, inviting his lips. Her mouth was a fountain of delight. And when he possessed her, they seemed to swoon together at the very borderland of life's mystery.

He stayed cushioned upon her, breathless, dazed, enervated, with his heart beating like a hammer upon her. With one hand she clasped his head, her lips lightly touching his forehead. The other hand stroked with a soothing rhythm his muscular shoulders.

The growl of the thunder was distant and passing away. The rain beat softly

---

[2] An exclamation: Goodness!
[3] A holiday commemorating the ascent of the Virgin Mary to heaven. Assumption is also the name of a Louisiana parish (county) where Calixta and Alcée had had a rendezvous in an earlier story.

upon the shingles, inviting them to drowsiness and sleep. But they dared not yield.

The rain was over; and the sun was turning the glistening green world into a palace of gems. Calixta, on the gallery, watched Alcée ride away. He turned and smiled at her with a beaming face; and she lifted her pretty chin in the air and laughed aloud.

III

Bobinôt and Bibi, trudging home, stopped without at the cistern to make themselves presentable.

"My! Bibi, w'at will yo' mama say! You ought to be ashame'. You oughtn' put on those good pants. Look at 'em! An' that mud on yo' collar! How you got that mud on yo' collar, Bibi? I never saw such a boy!" Bibi was the picture of pathetic resignation. Bobinôt was the embodiment of serious solicitude as he strove to remove from his own person and his son's the signs of their tramp over heavy roads and through wet fields. He scraped the mud off Bibi's bare legs and feet with a stick and carefully removed all traces from his heavy brogans. Then, prepared for the worst—the meeting with an over-scrupulous housewife, they entered cautiously at the back door.

Calixta was preparing supper. She had set the table and was dripping coffee at the hearth. She sprang up as they came in.

"Oh, Bobinôt! You back! My! but I was uneasy. W'ere you been during the rain? An' Bibi? he ain't wet? he ain't hurt?" She had clasped Bibi and was kissing him effusively. Bobinôt's explanations and apologies which he had been composing all along the way, died on his lips as Calixta felt him to see if he were dry, and seemed to express nothing but satisfaction at their safe return.

"I brought you some shrimps, Calixta," offered Bobinôt, hauling the can from his ample side pocket and laying it on the table.

"Shrimps! Oh, Bobinôt! you too good fo' anything!" and she gave him a smacking kiss on the cheek that resounded. "*J'vous réponds,*[4] we'll have a feas' to night! umph-umph!"

Bobinôt and Bibi began to relax and enjoy themselves, and when the three seated themselves at table they laughed much and so loud that anyone might have heard them as far away as Laballière's.

IV

Alcée Laballière wrote to his wife, Clarisse, that night. It was a loving letter, full of tender solicitude. He told her not to hurry back, but if she and the babies liked it at Biloxi, to stay a month longer. He was getting on nicely; and

---

[4] I'm telling you.

though he missed them, he was willing to bear the separation a while longer—
realizing that their health and pleasure were the first things to be considered.

V

As for Clarisse, she was charmed upon receiving her husband's letter. She and
the babies were doing well. The society was agreeable; many of her old friends
and acquaintances were at the bay. And the first free breath since her marriage
seemed to restore the pleasant liberty of her maiden days. Devoted as she was
to her husband, their intimate conjugal life was something which she was more
than willing to forego for a while.

So the storm passed and everyone was happy.

Theater

1923

JEAN TOOMER   [1894–1967]

Life of nigger alleys, of pool rooms and restaurants and near-beer saloons soaks into the walls of Howard Theater and sets them throbbing jazz songs. Black-skinned, they dance and shout above the tick and trill of white-walled build-ings. At night, they open doors to people who come in to stamp their feet and shout. At night, road-shows volley songs into the mass-heart of black people. Songs soak the walls and seep out to the nigger life of alleys and near-beer saloons, of the Poodle Dog and Black Bear cabarets. Afternoons, the house is dark, and the walls are sleeping singers until rehearsal begins. Or until John comes within them. Then they start throbbing to a subtle syncopation. And the space-dark air grows softly luminous.

John is the manager's brother. He is seated at the center of the theater, just before rehearsal. Light streaks down upon him from a window high above. One half his face is orange in it. One half his face is in shadow. The soft glow of the house rushes to, and compacts about, the shaft of light. John's mind coincides with the shaft of light. Thoughts rush to, and compact about it. Life of the house and of the slowly awakening stage swirls to the body of John, and thrills it. John's body is separate from the thoughts that pack his mind.

Stage-lights, soft, as if they shine through clear pink fingers. Beneath them, hid by the shadow of a set, Dorris. Other chorus girls drift in. John feels them in the mass. And as if his own body were the mass-heart of a black audience listening to them singing, he wants to stamp his feet and shout. His mind, contained above desires of his body, singles the girls out, and tries to trace origins and plot destinies.

A pianist slips into the pit and improvises jazz. The walls awake. Arms of the girls, and their limbs, which . . . jazz, jazz . . . by lifting up their tight street skirts they set free, jab the air and clog the floor in rhythm to the music. (Lift your skirts, Baby, and talk to papa!) Crude, individualized, and yet . . . mo-notonous. . . .

John: Soon the director will herd you, my full-lipped, distant beauties, and tame you, and blunt your sharp thrusts in loosely suggestive movements, ap-propriate to Broadway. (O dance!) Soon the audience will paint your dusk faces white, and call you beautiful. (O dance!) Soon I . . . (O dance!) I'd like . . .

Girls laugh and shout. Sing discordant snatches of other jazz songs. Whirl with loose passion into the arms of passing show-men.

John: Too thick. Too easy. Too monotonous. Her whom I'd love I'd leave before she knew that I was with her. Her? Which? (O dance!) I'd like to . . .

Girls dance and sing. Men clap. The walls sing and press inward. They press the men and girls, they press John towards a center of physical ecstasy. Go to it, Baby! Fan yourself, and feed your papa! Put . . . nobody lied . . . and take . . .

when they said I cried over you. No lie! The glitter and color of stacked scenes, the gilt and brass and crimson of the house, converge towards a center of physical ecstasy. John's feet and torso and his blood press in. He wills thought to rid his mind of passion.

"All right, girls. Alaska. Miss Reynolds, please."

The director wants to get the rehearsal through with.

The girls line up. John sees the front row: dancing ponies. The rest are in shadow. The leading lady fits loosely in the front. Lack-life, monotonous. "One, two, three—" Music starts. The song is somewhere where it will not strain the leading lady's throat. The dance is somewhere where it will not strain the girls. Above the staleness, one dancer throws herself into it. Dorris. John sees her. Her hair, crisp-curled, is bobbed. Bushy, black hair bobbing about her lemon-colored face. Her lips are curiously full, and very red. Her limbs in silk purple stockings are lovely. John feels them. Desires her. Holds off.

John: Stage-door johnny; chorus-girl. No, that would be all right. Dictie,[1] educated, stuck-up; show-girl. Yep. Her suspicion would be stronger than her passion. It wouldn't work. Keep her loveliness. Let her go.

Dorris sees John and knows that he is looking at her. Her own glowing is too rich a thing to let her feel the slimness of his diluted passion.

"Who's that?" she asks her dancing partner.

"Th manager's brother. Dictie. Nothin doin, hon."

Dorris tosses her head and dances for him until she feels she has him. Then, withdrawing disdainfully, she flirts with the director.

Dorris: Nothin doin? How come? Aint I as good as him? Couldnt I have got an education if I'd wanted one? Dont I know respectable folks, lots of em, in Philadelphia and New York and Chicago? Aint I had men as good as him? Better. Doctors an lawyers. Whats a manager's brother, anyhow?

Two steps back, and two steps front.

"Say, Mame, where do you get that stuff?"

"Whatshmean, Dorris?"

"If you two girls cant listen to what I'm telling you, I know where I can get some who can. Now listen."

Mame: Go to hell, you black bastard.

Dorris: Whats eatin at him, anyway?

"Now follow me in this, you girls. Its three counts to the right, three counts to the left, and then you shimmy—"

John:—and then you shimmy. I'll bet she can. Some good cabaret, with rooms upstairs. And what in hell do you think you'd get from it? Youre going wrong. Here's right: get her to herself—(Christ, but how she'd bore you after the first five minutes)—not if you get her right she wouldnt. Touch her, I mean. To herself—in some room perhaps. Some cheap, dingy bedroom. Hell no. Cant be done. But the point is, brother John, it can be done. Get her to

---

[1] A snob.

herself somewhere, anywhere. Go down in yourself—and she'd be calling you all sorts of asses while you were in the process of going down. Hold em, bud. Cant be done. Let her go. (Dance and I'll love you!) And keep her loveliness.

"All right now, Chicken Chaser. Dorris and girls. Where's Dorris? I told you to stay on the stage, didnt I? Well? Now thats enough. All right. All right there, Professor?[2] All right. One, two, three—"

Dorris swings to the front. The line of girls, four deep, blurs within the shadow of suspended scenes. Dorris wants to dance. The director feels that and steps to one side. He smiles, and picks her for a leading lady, one of these days. Odd ends of stage-men emerge from the wings, and stare and clap. A crap game in the alley suddenly ends. Black faces crowd the rear stage doors. The girls, catching joy from Dorris, whip up within the footlights' glow. They forget set steps; they find their own. The director forgets to bawl them out. Dorris dances.

John: Her head bobs to Broadway. Dance from yourself. Dance! O just a little more.

Dorris' eyes burn across the space of seats to him.

Dorris: I bet he can love. Hell, he cant love. He's too skinny. His lips are too skinny. He wouldn't love me anyway, only for that. But I'd get a pair of silk stockings out of it. Red silk. I got purple. Cut it, kid. You cant win him to respect you that away. He wouldnt anyway. Maybe he would. Maybe he'd love. I've heard em say that men who look like him (what does he look like?) will marry if they love. O will you love me? And give me kids, and a home, and everything? (I'd like to make your nest, and honest, hon, I wouldnt run out on you.) You will if I make you. Just watch me.

Dorris dances. She forgets her tricks. She dances.

Glorious songs are the muscles of her limbs.

And her singing is of canebrake loves and mangrove feastings.

The walls press in, singing. Flesh of a throbbing body, they press close to John and Dorris. They close them in. John's heart beats tensely against her dancing body. Walls press his mind within his heart. And then, the shaft of light goes out the window high above him. John's mind sweeps up to follow it. Mind pulls him upward into dream. Dorris dances . . . John dreams:

> Dorris is dressed in a loose black gown, splashed with lemon ribbons. Her feet taper long and slim from trim ankles. She waits for him just inside the stage door. John, collar and tie colorful and flaring, walks towards the stage door. There are no trees in the alley. But his feet feel as though they step on autumn leaves whose rustle has been pressed out of them by the passing of a million satin slippers. The air is sweet with roasting chestnuts, sweet with bonfires of old leaves. John's melancholy is a deep thing that seals all senses but his eyes, and makes him whole.
>
> Dorris knows that he is coming. Just at the right moment she steps from the door, as if there were no door. Her face is tinted like the autumn alley.

---

[2] A piano player.

Of old flowers, or of a southern canefield, her perfume. "Glorious Dorris." So his eyes speak. And their sadness is too deep for sweet untruth. She barely touches his arm. They glide off with footfalls softened on the leaves, the old leaves powdered by a million satin slippers.

They are in a room. John knows nothing of it. Only, that the flesh and blood of Dorris are its walls. Singing walls. Lights, soft, as if they shine through clear pink fingers. Soft lights, and warm.

John reaches for a manuscript of his, and reads. Dorris, who has no eyes, has eyes to understand him. He comes to a dancing scene. The scene is Dorris. She dances. Dorris dances. Glorious Dorris. Dorris whirls, whirls, dances. . . .

Dorris dances. The pianist crashes a bumper chord. The whole stage claps. Dorris, flushed, looks quick at John. His whole face is in shadow. She seeks for her dance in it. She finds it a dead thing in the shadow which is his dream. She rushes from the stage. Falls down the steps into her dressing-room. Pulls her hair. Her eyes, over a flood of tears, stare at the whitewashed ceiling. (Smell of dry paste, and paint, and soiled clothing.) Her pal comes in. Dorris flings herself into the old safe arms, and cries bitterly.

"I told you nothin doing," is what Mame says to comfort her.

QUESTIONS

1. State the nature of the conflict in John.   **2.** How does Toomer achieve dramatic conflict between John and Dorris even though they do not speak to each other?   **3.** How does the opening paragraph establish the mood and the values of the story?

A Rose for Emily   1931

WILLIAM FAULKNER   [1897–1962]

I

When Miss Emily Grierson died, our whole town went to her funeral: the men through a sort of respectful affection for a fallen monument, the women mostly out of curiosity to see the inside of her house, which no one save an old manservant—a combined gardener and cook—had seen in at least ten years.

It was a big, squarish frame house that had once been white, decorated with cupolas and spires and scrolled balconies in the heavily lightsome style of the seventies, set on what had once been our most select street. But garages and cotton gins had encroached and obliterated even the august names of that neighborhood; only Miss Emily's house was left, lifting its stubborn and coquettish decay above the cotton wagons and the gasoline pumps—an eyesore among eyesores. And now Miss Emily had gone to join the representatives of those august names where they lay in the cedar-bemused cemetery among the ranked and anonymous graves of Union and Confederate soldiers who fell at the battle of Jefferson.

Alive, Miss Emily had been a tradition, a duty, and a care; a sort of hereditary obligation upon the town, dating from that day in 1894 when Colonel Sartoris, the mayor—he who fathered the edict that no Negro woman should appear on the streets without an apron—remitted her taxes, the dispensation dating from the death of her father on into perpetuity. Not that Miss Emily would have accepted charity. Colonel Sartoris invented an involved tale to the effect that Miss Emily's father had loaned money to the town, which the town, as a matter of business, preferred this way of repaying. Only a man of Colonel Sartoris' generation and thought could have invented it, and only a woman could have believed it.

When the next generation, with its more modern ideas, became mayors and aldermen, this arrangement created some little dissatisfaction. On the first of the year they mailed her a tax notice. February came, and there was no reply. They wrote her a formal letter, asking her to call at the sheriff's office at her convenience. A week later the mayor wrote her himself, offering to call or to send his car for her, and received in reply a note on paper of an archaic shape, in a thin, flowing calligraphy in faded ink, to the effect that she no longer went out at all. The tax notice was also enclosed, without comment.

They called a special meeting of the Board of Aldermen. A deputation waited upon her, knocked at the door through which no visitor had passed since she ceased giving china-painting lessons eight or ten years earlier. They were admitted by the old Negro into a dim hall from which a stairway mounted into still more shadow. It smelled of dust and disuse—a close, dank smell. The

Negro led them into the parlor. It was furnished in heavy, leather-covered furniture. When the Negro opened the blinds of one window, they could see that the leather was cracked; and when they sat down, a faint dust rose sluggishly about their thighs, spinning with slow motions in the single sun-ray. On a tarnished gilt easel before the fireplace stood a crayon portrait of Miss Emily's father.

They rose when she entered—a small, fat woman in black, with a thin gold chain descending to her waist and vanishing into her belt, leaning on an ebony cane with a tarnished gold head. Her skeleton was small and spare; perhaps that was why what would have been merely plumpness in another was obesity in her. She looked bloated, like a body long submerged in motionless water, and of that pallid hue. Her eyes, lost in the fatty ridges of her face, looked like two small pieces of coal pressed into a lump of dough as they moved from one face to another while the visitors stated their errand.

She did not ask them to sit. She just stood in the door and listened quietly until the spokesman came to a stumbling halt. Then they could hear the invisible watch ticking at the end of the gold chain.

Her voice was dry and cold. "I have no taxes in Jefferson. Colonel Sartoris explained it to me. Perhaps one of you can gain access to the city records and satisfy yourselves."

"But we have. We are the city authorities, Miss Emily. Didn't you get a notice from the sheriff, signed by him?"

"I received a paper, yes," Miss Emily said. "Perhaps he considers himself the sheriff . . . I have no taxes in Jefferson."

"But there is nothing on the books to show that, you see. We must go by the—"

"See Colonel Sartoris." (Colonel Sartoris had been dead almost ten years.) "I have no taxes in Jefferson. Tobe!" The Negro appeared. "Show these gentlemen out."

II

So she vanquished them, horse and foot, just as she had vanquished their fathers thirty years before about the smell. That was two years after her father's death and a short time after her sweetheart—the one we believed would marry her—had deserted her. After her father's death she went out very little; after her sweetheart went away, people hardly saw her at all. A few of the ladies had the temerity to call, but were not received, and the only sign of life about the place was the Negro man—a young man then—going in and out with a market basket.

"Just as if a man—any man—could keep a kitchen properly," the ladies said; so they were not surprised when the smell developed. It was another link between the gross, teeming world and the high and mighty Griersons.

A neighbor, a woman, complained to the mayor, Judge Stevens, eighty years old.

"But what will you have me do about it, madam?" he said.

"Why, send her word to stop it," the woman said. "Isn't there a law?"

"I'm sure that won't be necessary," Judge Stevens said. "It's probably just a snake or a rat that nigger of hers killed in the yard. I'll speak to him about it."

The next day he received two more complaints, one from a man who came in diffident deprecation. "We really must do something about it, Judge. I'd be the last one in the world to bother Miss Emily, but we've got to do something." That night the Board of Aldermen met—three graybeards and one younger man, a member of the rising generation.

"It's simple enough," he said. "Send her word to have her place cleaned up. Give her a certain time to do it in, and if she don't . . ."

"Dammit, sir," Judge Stevens said, "will you accuse a lady to her face of smelling bad?"

So the next night, after midnight, four men crossed Miss Emily's lawn and slunk about the house like burglars, sniffing along the base of the brickwork and at the cellar openings while one of them performed a regular sowing motion with his hand out of a sack slung from his shoulder. They broke open the cellar door and sprinkled lime there, and in all the outbuildings. As they recrossed the lawn, a window that had been dark was lighted and Miss Emily sat in it, the light behind her, and her upright torso motionless as that of an idol. They crept quietly across the lawn and into the shadow of the locusts that lined the street. After a week or two the smell went away.

That was when people had begun to feel really sorry for her. People in our town, remembering how old lady Wyatt, her great-aunt, had gone completely crazy at last, believed that the Griersons held themselves a little too high for what they really were. None of the young men were quite good enough for Miss Emily and such. We had long thought of them as a tableau, Miss Emily a slender figure in white in the background, her father a spraddled silhouette in the foreground, his back to her and clutching a horsewhip, the two of them framed by the back-flung front door. So when she got to be thirty and was still single, we were not pleased exactly, but vindicated; even with insanity in the family she wouldn't have turned down all of her chances if they had really materialized.

When her father died, it got about that the house was all that was left to her; and in a way, people were glad. At last they could pity Miss Emily. Being left alone, and a pauper, she had become humanized. Now she too would know the old thrill and the old despair of a penny more or less.

The day after his death all the ladies prepared to call at the house and offer condolence and aid, as is our custom. Miss Emily met them at the door, dressed as usual and with no trace of grief on her face. She told them that her father was not dead. She did that for three days, with the ministers calling on her, and the doctors, trying to persuade her to let them dispose of the body. Just as they were about to resort to law and force, she broke down, and they buried her father quickly.

We did not say she was crazy then. We believed she had to do that. We remembered all the young men her father had driven away, and we knew that with nothing left, she would have to cling to that which had robbed her, as people will.

III

She was sick for a long time. When we saw her again, her hair was cut short, making her look like a girl, with a vague resemblance to those angels in colored church windows—sort of tragic and serene.

The town had just let the contracts for paving the sidewalks, and in the summer after her father's death they began the work. The construction company came with niggers and mules and machinery, and a foreman named Homer Barron, a Yankee—a big, dark, ready man, with a big voice and eyes lighter than his face. The little boys would follow in groups to hear him cuss the niggers, and the niggers singing in time to the rise and fall of picks. Pretty soon he knew everybody in town. Whenever you heard a lot of laughing anywhere about the square, Homer Barron would be in the center of the group. Presently we began to see him and Miss Emily on Sunday afternoons driving in the yellow-wheeled buggy and the matched team of bays from the livery stable.

At first we were glad that Miss Emily would have an interest, because the ladies all said, "Of course a Grierson would not think seriously of a Northerner, a day laborer." But there were still others, older people, who said that even grief could not cause a real lady to forget *noblesse oblige*—without calling it *noblesse oblige*. They just said, "Poor Emily. Her kinsfolk should come to her." She had some kin in Alabama; but years ago her father had fallen out with them over the estate of old lady Wyatt, the crazy woman, and there was no communication between the two families. They had not even been represented at the funeral.

And as soon as the old people said, "Poor Emily," the whispering began. "Do you suppose it's really so?" they said to one another. "Of course it is. What else could . . ." This behind their hands; rustling of craned silk and satin behind jalousies closed upon the sun of Sunday afternoon as the thin, swift clop-clop-clop of the matched team passed: "Poor Emily."

She carried her head high enough—even when we believed that she was fallen. It was as if she demanded more than ever the recognition of her dignity as the last Grierson; as if it had wanted that touch of earthiness to reaffirm her imperviousness. Like when she bought the rat poison, the arsenic. That was over a year after they had begun to say "Poor Emily," and while the two female cousins were visiting her.

"I want some poison," she said to the druggist. She was over thirty then, still a slight woman, though thinner than usual, with cold, haughty black eyes in a face the flesh of which was strained across the temples and about the eye-sockets as you imagine a lighthouse-keeper's face ought to look. "I want some poison," she said.

"Yes, Miss Emily. What kind? For rats and such? I'd recom—"

"I want the best you have. I don't care what kind."

The druggist named several. "They'll kill anything up to an elephant. But what you want is—"

"Arsenic," Miss Emily said. "Is that a good one?"

"Is . . . arsenic? Yes, ma'am. But what you want—"

"I want arsenic."

The druggist looked down at her. She looked back at him, erect, her face like a strained flag. "Why, of course," the druggist said. "If that's what you want. But the law requires you to tell what you are going to use it for."

Miss Emily just stared at him, her head tilted back in order to look him eye for eye, until he looked away and went and got the arsenic and wrapped it up. The Negro delivery boy brought her package; the druggist didn't come back. When she opened the package at home there was written on the box, under the skull and bones: "For rats."

IV

So the next day we all said, "She will kill herself"; and we said it would be the best thing. When she had first begun to be seen with Homer Barron, we had said, "She will marry him." Then we said, "She will persuade him yet," because Homer himself had remarked—he liked men, and it was known that he drank with the younger men in the Elks' Club—that he was not a marrying man. Later we said, "Poor Emily" behind the jalousies as they passed on Sunday afternoon in the glittering buggy, Miss Emily with her head high and Homer Barron with his hat cocked and a cigar in his teeth, reins and whip in a yellow glove.

Then some of the ladies began to say that it was a disgrace to the town and a bad example to the young people. The men did not want to interfere, but at last the ladies forced the Baptist minister—Miss Emily's people were Episcopal—to call upon her. He would never divulge what happened during that interview, but he refused to go back again. The next Sunday they again drove about the streets, and the following day the minister's wife wrote to Miss Emily's relations in Alabama.

So she had blood-kin under her roof again and we sat back to watch developments. At first nothing happened. Then we were sure that they were to be married. We learned that Miss Emily had been to the jeweler's and ordered a man's toilet set in silver, with the letters H.B. on each piece. Two days later we learned that she had bought a complete outfit of men's clothing, including a nightshirt, and we said, "They are married." We were really glad. We were glad because the two female cousins were even more Grierson than Miss Emily had ever been.

So we were not surprised when Homer Barron—the streets had been finished some time since—was gone. We were a little disappointed that there was not a public blowing-off, but we believed that he had gone on to prepare for Miss Emily's coming, or to give her a chance to get rid of the cousins. (By that time it was a cabal, and we were all Miss Emily's allies to help circumvent the cousins.) Sure enough, after another week they departed. And, as we had expected all along, within three days Homer Barron was back in town. A neighbor saw the Negro man admit him at the kitchen door at dusk one evening.

And that was the last we saw of Homer Barron. And of Miss Emily for some time. The Negro man went in and out with the market basket, but the front door remained closed. Now and then we would see her at the window for a moment, as the men did that night when they sprinkled the lime, but for almost six months she did not appear on the streets. Then we knew that this was to be expected too; as if that quality of her father which had thwarted her woman's life so many times had been too virulent and too furious to die.

When we next saw Miss Emily, she had grown fat and her hair was turning gray. During the next few years it grew grayer and grayer until it attained an even pepper-and-salt iron-gray, when it ceased turning. Up to the day of her death at seventy-four it was still that vigorous iron-gray, like the hair of an active man.

From that time on her front door remained closed, save during a period of six or seven years, when she was about forty, during which she gave lessons in china-painting. She fitted up a studio in one of the downstairs rooms, where the daughters and granddaughters of Colonel Sartoris' contemporaries were sent to her with the same regularity and in the same spirit that they were sent to church on Sundays with a twenty-five-cent piece for the collection plate. Meanwhile her taxes had been remitted.

Then the newer generation became the backbone and the spirit of the town, and the painting pupils grew up and fell away and did not send their children to her with boxes of color and tedious brushes and pictures cut from the ladies' magazines. The front door closed upon the last one and remained closed for good. When the town got free postal delivery, Miss Emily alone refused to let them fasten the metal numbers above her door and attach a mailbox to it. She would not listen to them.

Daily, monthly, yearly we watched the Negro grow grayer and more stooped, going in and out with the market basket. Each December we sent her a tax notice, which would be returned by the post office a week later, unclaimed. Now and then we would see her in one of the downstairs windows—she had evidently shut up the top floor of the house—like the carven torso of an idol in a niche, looking or not looking at us, we could never tell which. Thus she passed from generation to generation—dear, inescapable, impervious, tranquil, and perverse.

And so she died. Fell ill in the house filled with dust and shadows, with only a doddering Negro man to wait on her. We did not even know she was sick; we had long since given up trying to get any information from the Negro. He talked to no one, probably not even to her, for his voice had grown harsh and rusty, as if from disuse.

She died in one of the downstairs rooms, in a heavy walnut bed with a curtain, her gray head propped on a pillow yellow and moldy with age and lack of sunlight.

V

The Negro met the first of the ladies at the front door and let them in, with their hushed, sibilant voices and their quick, curious glances, and then he disappeared. He walked right through the house and out the back and was not seen again.

The two female cousins came at once. They held the funeral on the second day, with the town coming to look at Miss Emily beneath a mass of bought flowers, with the crayon face of her father musing profoundly above the bier and the ladies sibilant and macabre; and the very old men—some in their brushed Confederate uniforms—on the porch and the lawn, talking of Miss Emily as if she had been a contemporary of theirs, believing they had danced with her and courted her perhaps, confusing time with its mathematical progression, as the old do, to whom all the past is not a diminishing road but, instead, a huge meadow which no winter ever quite touches, divided from them now by the narrow bottle-neck of the most recent decade of years.

Already we knew that there was one room in that region above stairs which no one had seen in forty years, and which would have to be forced. They waited until Miss Emily was decently in the ground before they opened it.

The violence of breaking down the door seemed to fill this room with pervading dust. A thin, acrid pall as of the tomb seemed to lie everywhere upon this room decked and furnished as for a bridal: upon the valance curtains of faded rose color, upon the rose-shaded lights, upon the dressing table, upon the delicate array of crystal and the man's toilet things backed with tarnished silver, silver so tarnished that the monogram was obscured. Among them lay a collar and tie, as if they had just been removed, which, lifted, left upon the surface a pale crescent in the dust. Upon a chair hung the suit, carefully folded; beneath it the two mute shoes and the discarded socks.

The man himself lay in the bed.

For a long while we just stood there, looking down at the profound and fleshless grin. The body had apparently once lain in the attitude of an embrace, but now the long sleep that outlasts love, that conquers even the grimace of love, had cuckolded him. What was left of him, rotted beneath what was left of the nightshirt, had become inextricable from the bed in which he lay; and upon him and upon the pillow beside him lay that even coating of the patient and biding dust.

Then we noticed that in the second pillow was the indentation of a head. One of us lifted something from it, and leaning forward, that faint and invisible dust dry and acrid in the nostrils, we saw a long strand of iron-gray hair.

QUESTIONS
1. Describe the narrator. Is he sympathetic to Emily? Explain. Why does Faulkner title the narrative "A Rose for Emily"? **2.** Why does Faulkner devote the second paragraph to a description of Emily's house? **3.** Why doesn't Faulkner present the story in chronological order? **4.** What is the effect of the final paragraph?

WRITING TOPIC
In the second paragraph of part V, the narrator refers to some old men "talking of Miss Emily as if she had been a contemporary of theirs, believing they had danced with her and courted her perhaps, confusing time with its mathematical progression, as the old do, to whom all the past is not a diminishing road but, instead, a huge meadow which no winter ever quite touches, divided from them now by the narrow bottle-neck of the most recent decade of years." Use this passage as the basis for a comparison of the narrator's and Emily's view of time.

The Intruder* 1966

JORGE LUIS BORGES [1899–1986]

2 Samuel 1:26[1]

They claim (improbably) that the story was told by Eduardo, the younger of the Nilsen brothers, at the wake for Cristian, the elder, who died of natural causes at some point in the 1890s, in the district of Morón. Someone must certainly have heard it from someone else, in the course of that long, idle night, between servings of maté, and passed it on to Santiago Dabove, from whom I learned it. Years later, they told it to me again in Turdera, where it had all happened. The second version, considerably more detailed, substantiated Santiago's, with the usual small variations and departures. I write it down now because, if I am not wrong, it reflects briefly and tragically the whole temper of life in those days along the banks of the River Plate. I shall put it down scrupulously; but already I see myself yielding to the writer's temptation to heighten or amplify some detail or other.

In Turdera, they were referred to as the Nilsens. The parish priest told me that his predecessor remembered with some astonishment seeing in that house a worn Bible, bound in black, with Gothic characters; in the end pages, he glimpsed handwritten names and dates. It was the only book in the house. The recorded misfortunes of the Nilsens, lost as all will be lost. The old house, now no longer in existence, was built of unstuccoed brick; beyond the hallway, one could make out a patio of colored tile, and another with an earth floor. In any case, very few ever went there; the Nilsens were jealous of their privacy. In the dilapidated rooms, they slept on camp beds; their indulgences were horses, riding gear, short-bladed daggers, a substantial fling on Saturdays, and belligerent drinking. I know that they were tall, with red hair which they wore long. Denmark, Ireland, places they would never hear tell of, stirred in the blood of those two *criollos*.[2] The neighborhood feared them, as they did all red-haired people; nor is it impossible that they might have been responsible for someone's death. Once, shoulder to shoulder, they tangled with the police. The younger one was said to have had an altercation with Juan Iberra in which he did not come off worst; which, according to what we hear, is indeed something. They were cowboys, team drivers, rustlers, and, at times, cheats. They

---

* Translated by Alastair Reid.

[1] A verse from David's lament upon the death of his brother-in-law and friend Jonathan: "I am distressed for you, my brother Jonathan; / very pleasant have you been to me, / your love to me was wonderful, passing the love of woman."

[2] Creole, a person of European parentage born in South America, Central America, or the West Indies.

had a reputation for meanness, except when drinking and gambling made them expansive. Of their ancestry or where they came from, nothing was known. They owned a wagon and a yoke of oxen.

Physically, they were quite distinct from the roughneck crowd of settlers who lent the Costa Brava their own bad name. This, and other things we do not know, helps to explain how close they were; to cross one of them meant having two enemies.

The Nilsens were roisterers, but their amorous escapades had until then been confined to hallways and houses of ill fame. Hence, there was no lack of local comment when Cristian brought Juliana Burgos to live with him. True enough, in that way he got himself a servant; but it is also true that he showered her with gaudy trinkets, and showed her off at fiestas—the poor tenement fiestas, where the more intimate figures of the tango were forbidden and where the dancers still kept a respectable space between them. Juliana was dark-complexioned, with large wide eyes; one had only to look at her to make her smile. In a poor neighborhood, where work and neglect wear out the women, she was not at all bad looking.

At first, Eduardo went about with them. Later, he took a journey to Arrecifes on some business or other; he brought back home with him a girl he had picked up along the way. After a few days, he threw her out. He grew more sullen; he would get drunk alone at the local bar, and would have nothing to do with anyone. He was in love with Cristian's woman. The neighborhood, aware of it possibly before he was, looked forward with malicious glee to the subterranean rivalry between the brothers.

One night, when he came back late from the bar at the corner, Eduardo saw Cristian's black horse tethered to the fence. In the patio, the elder brother was waiting for him, all dressed up. The woman came and went, carrying maté. Cristian said to Eduardo:

"I'm off to a brawl at the Farías'. There's Juliana for you. If you want her, make use of her."

His tone was half-commanding, half-cordial. Eduardo kept still, gazing at him; he did not know what to do. Cristian rose, said goodbye to Eduardo but not to Juliana, who was an object to him, mounted, and trotted off, casually.

From that night on, they shared her. No one knew the details of that sordid conjunction, which outraged the proprieties of the poor locality. The arrangement worked well for some weeks, but it could not last. Between them, the brothers never uttered the name of Juliana, not even to summon her, but they sought out and found reasons for disagreeing. They argued over the sale of some skins, but they were really arguing about something else. Cristian would habitually raise his voice, while Eduardo kept quiet. Without realizing it, they were growing jealous. In that rough settlement, no man ever let on to others, or to himself, that a woman would matter, except as something desired or possessed, but the two of them were in love. For them, that in its way was a humiliation.

One afternoon, in the Plaza de Lomos, Eduardo ran into Juan Iberra, who congratulated him on the beautiful "dish" he had fixed up for himself. It was then, I think, that Eduardo roughed him up. No one, in his presence, was going to make fun of Cristian.

The woman waited on the two of them with animal submissiveness; but she could not conceal her preference, unquestionably for the younger one, who, although he had not rejected the arrangement, had not sought it out.

One day, they told Juliana to get two chairs from the first patio, and to keep out of the way, for they had to talk. Expecting a long discussion, she lay down for her siesta, but soon they summoned her. They had her pack a bag with all she possessed, not forgetting the glass rosary and the little crucifix her mother had left her. Without any explanation, they put her on the wagon, and set out on a wordless and wearisome journey. It had rained; the roads were heavy going and it was eleven in the evening when they arrived at Morón. There they passed her over to the *patrona* of the house of prostitution. The deal had already been made; Cristian picked up the money, and later on he divided it with Eduardo.

In Turdera, the Nilsens, floundering in the meshes of that outrageous love (which was also something of a routine), sought to recover their old ways, of men among men. They went back to their poker games, to fighting, to occasional binges. At times, perhaps, they felt themselves liberated, but one or other of them would quite often be away, perhaps genuinely, perhaps not. A little before the end of the year, the younger one announced that he had business in Buenos Aires. Cristian went to Morón; in the yard of the house we already know, he recognized Eduardo's piebald. He entered; the other was inside, waiting his turn. It seems that Cristian said to him, "If we go on like this, we'll wear out the horses. It's better that we do something about her."

He spoke with the *patrona*, took some coins from his money belt, and they went off with her. Juliana went with Cristian; Eduardo spurred his horse so as not to see them.

They returned to what has already been told. The cruel solution had failed; both had given in to the temptation to dissimulate. Cain's mark was there, but the bond between the Nilsens was strong—who knows what trials and dangers they had shared—and they preferred to vent their furies on others. On a stranger, on the dogs, on Juliana, who had brought discord into their lives.

March was almost over and the heat did not break. One Sunday (on Sundays it is the custom to retire early), Eduardo, coming back from the corner bar, saw Cristian yoking up the oxen. Cristian said to him, "Come on. We have to leave some hides off at the Pardos'. I've already loaded them. Let us take advantage of the cool."

The Pardo place lay, I think, to the south of them; they took the Camino de las Tropas, and then a detour. The landscape was spreading out slowly under the night.

They skirted a clump of dry reeds. Cristian threw away the cigarette he had lit and said casually, "Now, brother, to work. Later on, the buzzards will give us a hand. Today I killed her. Let her stay here with all her finery, and not do us any more harm."

They embraced, almost in tears. Now they shared an extra bond; the woman sorrowfully sacrificed and the obligation to forget her.

The Chase*   1967

ALBERTO MORAVIA   [1907–1990]

I have never been a sportsman—or, rather, I have been a sportsman only once, and that was the first and last time. I was a child, and one day, for some reason or other, I found myself together with my father, who was holding a gun in his hand, behind a bush, watching a bird that had perched on a branch not very far away. It was a large, gray bird—or perhaps it was brown—with a long—or perhaps a short—beak; I don't remember. I only remember what I felt at that moment as I looked at it. It was like watching an animal whose vitality was rendered more intense by the very fact of my watching it and of the animal's not knowing that I was watching it.

At that moment, I say, the notion of wildness entered my mind, never again to leave it; everything is wild which is autonomous and unpredictable and does not depend upon us. Then all of a sudden there was an explosion; I could no longer see the bird and I thought it had flown away. But my father was leading the way, walking in front of me through the undergrowth. Finally he stooped down, picked up something and put it in my hand. I was aware of something warm and soft and I lowered my eyes: there was a bird in the palm of my hand, its dangling, shattered head crowned with a plume of already-thickening blood. I burst into tears and dropped the corpse on the ground, and that was the end of my shooting experience.

I thought again of this remote episode in my life this very day after watching my wife, for the first and also the last time, as she was walking through the streets of the city. But let us take things in order.

What had my wife been like; what was she like now? She once had been, to put it briefly, "wild"—that is, entirely autonomous and unpredictable; latterly she had become "tame"—that is, predictable and dependent. For a long time she had been like the bird that, on that far-off morning in my childhood, I had seen perching on the bough; latterly, I am sorry to say, she had become like a hen about which one knows everything in advance—how it moves, how it eats, how it lays eggs, how it sleeps, and so on.

Nevertheless I would not wish anyone to think that my wife's wildness consisted of an uncouth, rough, rebellious character. Apart from being extremely beautiful, she is the gentlest, politest, most discreet person in the world. Rather her wildness consisted of the air of charming unpredictability, of independence in her way of living, with which during the first years of our marriage she acted in my presence, both at home and abroad. Wildness signified intimacy, privacy, secrecy. Yes, my wife as she sat in front of her dressing table, her eyes fixed on the looking glass, passing the hairbrush with a repeated

---

* Translated by Angus Davidson.

motion over her long, loose hair, was just as wild as the solitary quail hopping forward along a sun-filled furrow or the furtive fox coming out into a clearing and stopping to look around before running on. She was wild because I, as I looked at her, could never manage to foresee when she would give a last stroke with the hairbrush and rise and come toward me; wild to such a degree that sometimes when I went into our bedroom the smell of her, floating in the air, would have something of the acrid quality of a wild beast's lair.

Gradually she became less wild, tamer. I had had a fox, a quail, in the house, as I have said; then one day I realized that I had a hen. What effect does a hen have on someone who watches it? It has the effect of being, so to speak, an automaton in the form of a bird; automatic are the brief, rapid steps with which it moves about; automatic its hard, terse pecking; automatic the glance of the round eyes in its head that nods and turns; automatic its ready crouching down under the cock; automatic the dropping of the egg wherever it may be and the cry with which it announces that the egg has been laid. Goodby to the fox; good-by to the quail. And her smell—this no longer brought to my mind, in any way, the innocent odor of a wild animal; rather I 'detected in it the chemical suavity of some ordinary French perfume.

Our flat is on the first floor of a big building in a modern quarter of the town; our windows look out on a square in which there is a small public garden, the haunt of nurses and children and dogs. One day I was standing at the window, looking in a melancholy way at the garden. My wife, shortly before, had dressed to go out; and once again, watching her, I had noticed the irrevocable and, so to speak, invisible character of her gestures and personality: something which gave one the feeling of a thing already seen and already done and which therefore evaded even the most determined observation. And now, as I stood looking at the garden and at the same time wondering why the adorable wildness of former times had so completely disappeared, suddenly my wife came into my range of vision as she walked quickly across the garden in the direction of the bus stop. I watched her and then I almost jumped for joy; in a movement she was making to pull down a fold of her narrow skirt and smooth it over her thigh with the tips of her long, sharp nails, in this movement I recognized the wildness that in the past had made me love her. It was only an instant, but in that instant I said to myself: She's become wild again because she's convinced that I am not there and am not watching her. Then I left the window and rushed out.

But I did not join her at the bus stop; I felt that I must not allow myself to be seen. Instead I hurried to my car, which was standing nearby, got in and waited. A bus came and she got in together with some other people; the bus started off again and I began following it. Then there came back to me the memory of that one shooting expedition in which I had taken part as a child, and I saw that the bus was the undergrowth with its bushes and trees, my wife the bird perching on the bough while I, unseen, watched it living before my eyes. And the whole town, during this pursuit, became, as though by magic, a fact of nature like the countryside: the houses were hills, the streets valleys, the vehicles hedges and woods, and even the passers-by on the pavements had something unpredictable and autonomous—that is, wild—about them. And in my mouth, behind my clenched teeth, there was the acrid, metallic taste of gunfire; and my eyes, usually listless and wandering, had become sharp, watchful, attentive.

These eyes were fixed intently upon the exit door when the bus came to the end of its run. A number of people got out, and then I saw my wife getting out. Once again I recognized, in the manner in which she broke free of the crowd and started off toward a neighboring street, the wildness that pleased me so much. I jumped out of the car and started following her.

She was walking in front of me, ignorant of my presence, a tall woman with an elegant figure, long-legged, narrow-hipped, broad-backed, her brown hair falling on her shoulders.

Men turned around as she went past; perhaps they were aware of what I myself was now sensing with an intensity that quickened the beating of my heart and took my breath away: the unrestricted, steadily increasing, irresistible character of her mysterious wildness.

She walked hurriedly, having evidently some purpose in view, and even the fact that she had a purpose of which I was ignorant added to her wildness; I did not know where she was going, just as on that far-off morning I had not known what the bird perching on the bough was about to do. Moreover I thought the gradual, steady increase in this quality of wildness came partly from the fact that as she drew nearer to the object of this mysterious walk there was an increase in her—how shall I express it?—of biological tension, of existential excitement, of vital effervescence. Then, unexpectedly, with the suddenness of a film, her purpose was revealed.

A fair-haired young man in a leather jacket and a pair of corduroy trousers was leaning against the wall of a house in that ancient, narrow street. He was idly smoking as he looked in front of him. But as my wife passed close to him, he threw away his cigarette with a decisive gesture, took a step forward and seized her arm. I was expecting her to rebuff him, to move away from him, but nothing happened: evidently obeying the rules of some kind of erotic ritual, she went on walking beside the young man. Then after a few steps, with a movement that confirmed her own complicity, she put her arm around her companion's waist and he put his around her.

I understood then that this unknown man who took such liberties with my wife was also attracted by wildness. And so, instead of making a conventional appointment with her, instead of meeting in a café with a handshake, a falsely friendly and respectful welcome, he had preferred, by agreement with her, to take her by surprise—or, rather, to pretend to do so—while she was apparently taking a walk on her own account. All this I perceived by intuition, noticing that at the very moment when he stepped forward and took her arm her wildness had, so to speak, given an upward bound. It was years since I had seen my wife so alive, but alas, the source of this life could not be traced to me.

They walked on thus entwined and then, without any preliminaries, just like two wild animals, they did an unexpected thing: they went into one of the dark doorways in order to kiss. I stopped and watched them from a distance, peering into the darkness of the entrance. My wife was turned away from me and was bending back with the pressure of his body, her hair hanging free. I looked at that long, thick mane of brown hair, which as she leaned back fell free of her shoulders, and I felt at that moment her vitality reached its diapason, just as happens with wild animals when they couple and their customary wildness is redoubled by the violence of love. I watched for a long time and then, since this kiss went on and on and in fact seemed to be prolonged beyond the limits of my power of endurance, I saw that I would have to intervene.

I would have to go forward, seize my wife by the arm—or actually by that hair, which hung down and conveyed so well the feeling of feminine passivity—then hurl myself with clenched fists upon the blond young man. After this encounter I would carry off my wife, weeping, mortified, ashamed, while I was raging and broken-hearted, upbraiding her and pouring scorn upon her.

But what else would this intervention amount to but the shot my father fired at that free, unknowing bird as it perched on the bough? The disorder and confusion, the mortification, the shame, that would follow would irreparably destroy the rare and precious moment of wildness that I was witnessing inside the dark doorway. It was true that this wildness was directed against me; but I had to remember that wildness, always and everywhere, is directed against everything and everybody. After the scene of my intervention it might be possible for me to regain control of my wife, but I should find her shattered and lifeless in my arms like the bird that my father placed in my hand so that I might throw it into the shooting bag.

The kiss went on and on: well, it was a kiss of passion—that could not be denied. I waited until they finished, until they came out of the doorway, until they walked on again still linked together. Then I turned back.

The Girls in Their Summer Dresses

1939

IRWIN SHAW [1913–1984]

Fifth Avenue was shining in the sun when they left the Brevoort.[1] The sun was warm, even though it was February, and everything looked like Sunday morning—the buses and the well-dressed people walking slowly in couples and the quiet buildings with the windows closed.

Michael held Frances' arm tightly as they walked toward Washington Square[2] in the sunlight. They walked lightly, almost smiling, because they had slept late and had a good breakfast and it was Sunday. Michael unbuttoned his coat and let it flap around him in the mild wind.

"Look out," Frances said as they crossed Eighth Street. "You'll break your neck." Michael laughed and Frances laughed with him.

"She's not so pretty," Frances said. "Anyway, not pretty enough to take a chance of breaking your neck."

Michael laughed again. "How did you know I was looking at her?"

Frances cocked her head to one side and smiled at her husband under the brim of her hat. "Mike, darling," she said.

"O.K.," he said. "Excuse me."

Frances patted his arm lightly and pulled him along a little faster toward Washington Square. "Let's not see anybody all day," she said. "Let's just hang around with each other. You and me. We're always up to our neck in people, drinking their Scotch or drinking our Scotch; we only see each other in bed. I want to go out with my husband all day long. I want him to talk only to me and listen only to me."

"What's to stop us?" Michael asked.

"The Stevensons. They want us to drop by around one o'clock and they'll drive us into the country."

"The cunning Stevensons," Mike said. "Transparent. They can whistle. They can go driving in the country by themselves."

"Is it a date?"

"It's a date."

Frances leaned over and kissed him on the tip of the ear.

"Darling," Michael said, "this is Fifth Avenue."

"Let me arrange a program," Frances said. "A planned Sunday in New York for a young couple with money to throw away."

---

[1] The Brevoort was a New York hotel on lower Fifth Avenue. At the time that this story was written, the Brevoort's bar was famous as a gathering place for literary people.

[2] A park at the south end of Fifth Avenue.

"Go easy."

"First let's go to the Metropolitan Museum of Art," Frances suggested, because Michael had said during the week he wanted to go. "I haven't been there in three years and there're at least ten pictures I want to see again. Then we can take the bus down to Radio City and watch them skate. And later we'll go down to Cavanagh's and get a steak as big as a blacksmith's apron, with a bottle of wine, and after that there's a French picture at the Filmarte that everybody says—say, are you listening to me?"

"Sure," he said. He took his eyes off the hatless girl with the dark hair, cut dancer-style like a helmet, who was walking past him.

"That's the program for the day," Frances said flatly. "Or maybe you'd just rather walk up and down Fifth Avenue."

"No," Michael said. "Not at all."

"You always look at other women," Frances said. "Everywhere. Every damned place we go."

"No, darling," Michael said, "I look at everything. God gave me eyes and I look at women and men in subway excavations and moving pictures and the little flowers of the field. I casually inspect the universe."

"You ought to see the look in your eye," Frances said, "as you casually inspect the universe on Fifth Avenue."

"I'm a happily married man." Michael pressed her elbow tenderly. "Example for the whole twentieth century—Mr. and Mrs. Mike Loomis. Hey, let's have a drink," he said, stopping.

"We just had breakfast."

"Now listen, darling," Mike said, choosing his words with care, "it's a nice day and we both felt good and there's no reason why we have to break it up. Let's have a nice Sunday."

"All right. I don't know why I started this. Let's drop it. Let's have a good time."

They joined hands consciously and walked without talking among the baby carriages and the old Italian men in their Sunday clothes and the young women with Scotties in Washington Square Park.

"At least once a year everyone should go to the Metropolitan Museum of Art," Frances said after a while, her tone a good imitation of the tone she had used at breakfast and at the beginning of their walk. "And it's nice on Sunday. There're a lot of people looking at the pictures and you get the feeling maybe Art isn't on the decline in New York City, after all—"

"I want to tell you something," Michael said very seriously. "I have not touched another woman. Not once. In all the five years."

"All right," Frances said.

"You believe that, don't you?"

"All right."

They walked between the crowded benches, under the scrubby city-park trees.

"I try not to notice it," Frances said, "but I feel rotten inside, in my stomach, when we pass a woman and you look at her and I see that look in your eye and that's the way you looked at me the first time. In Alice Maxwell's house. Standing there in the living room, next to the radio, with a green hat on and all those people."

"I remember the hat," Michael said.

"The same look," Frances said. "And it makes me feel bad. It makes me feel terrible."

"Sh-h-h, please, darling, sh-h-h."

"I think I would like a drink now," Frances said.

They walked over to a bar on Eighth Street, not saying anything, Michael automatically helping her over curbstones and guiding her past automobiles. They sat near a window in the bar and the sun streamed in and there was a small, cheerful fire in the fireplace. A little Japanese waiter came over and put down some pretzels and smiled happily at them.

"What do you order after breakfast?" Michael asked.

"Brandy, I suppose," Frances said.

"Courvoisier," Michael told the waiter. "Two Courvoisiers."

The waiter came with the glasses and they sat drinking the brandy in the sunlight. Michael finished half his and drank a little water.

"I look at women," he said. "Correct. I don't say it's wrong or right. I look at them. If I pass them on the street and I don't look at them, I'm fooling you, I'm fooling myself."

"You look at them as though you want them," Frances said, playing with her brandy glass. "Every one of them."

"In a way," Michael said, speaking softly and not to his wife, "in a way that's true. I don't do anything about it, but it's true."

"I know it. That's why I feel bad."

"Another brandy," Michael called. "Waiter, two more brandies."

He sighed and closed his eyes and rubbed them gently with his fingers. "I love the way women look. One of the things I like best about New York is the battalions of women. When I first came to New York from Ohio that was the first thing I noticed, the million wonderful women, all over the city. I walked around with my heart in my throat."

"A kid," Frances said. "That's a kid's feeling."

"Guess again," Michael said. "Guess again. I'm older now. I'm a man getting near middle age, putting on a little fat, and I still love to walk along Fifth Avenue at three o'clock on the east side of the street between Fiftieth and Fifty-seventh Streets. They're all out then, shopping, in their furs and their crazy hats, everything all concentrated from all over the world into seven blocks—the best furs, the best clothes, the handsomest women, out to spend money and feeling good about it."

The Japanese waiter put the two drinks down, smiling with great happiness.

"Everything is all right?" he asked.

"Everything is wonderful," Michael said.

"If it's just a couple of fur coats," Frances said, "and forty-five dollar hats—"

"It's not the fur coats. Or the hats. That's just the scenery for that particular kind of woman. Understand," he said, "you don't have to listen to this."

"I want to listen."

"I like the girls in the offices. Neat with their eyeglasses, smart, chipper, knowing what everything is about. I like the girls on Forty-fourth Street at lunchtime, the actresses, all dressed up on nothing a week. I like the salesgirls in the stores, paying attention to you first because you're a man, leaving the lady customers waiting. I got all this stuff accumulated in me because I've been thinking about it for ten years and now you've asked for it and here it is."

"Go ahead," Frances said.

"When I think of New York City, I think of all the girls on parade in the city. I don't know whether it's something special with me or whether every man in the city walks around with the same feeling inside him, but I feel as though I'm at a picnic in this city. I like to sit near the women in the theatres, the famous beauties who've taken six hours to get ready and look it. And the young girls at the football games, with the red cheeks, and when the warm weather comes, the girls in their summer dresses." He finished his drink. "That's the story."

Frances finished her drink and swallowed two or three times extra. "You say you love me?"

"I love you."

"I'm pretty, too," Frances said. "As pretty as any of them."

"You're beautiful," Michael said.

"I'm good for you," Frances said, pleading. "I've made a good wife, a good housekeeper, a good friend. I'd do any damn thing for you."

"I know," Michael said. He put his hand out and grasped hers.

"You'd like to be free to—" Frances said.

"Sh-h-h."

"Tell the truth." She took her hand away from under his.

Michael flicked the edge of his glass with his finger. "O.K.," he said gently. "Sometimes I feel I would like to be free."

"Well," Frances said, "any time you say."

"Don't be foolish." Michael swung his chair around to her side of the table and patted her thigh.

She began to cry silently into her handkerchief, bent over just enough so that nobody else in the bar would notice. "Someday," she said, crying, "you're going to make a move."

Michael didn't say anything. He sat watching the bartender slowly peel a lemon.

"Aren't you?" Frances asked harshly. "Come on, tell me. Talk. Aren't you?"

"Maybe," Michael said. He moved his chair back again. "How the hell do I know?"

"You know," Frances persisted. "Don't you know?"

"Yes," Michael said after a while, "I know."·

Frances stopped crying then. Two or three snuffles into the handkerchief and she put it away and her face didn't tell anything to anybody. "At least do me one favor," she said.

"Sure."

"Stop talking about how pretty this woman is or that one. Nice eyes, nice breasts, a pretty figure, good voice." She mimicked his voice. "Keep it to yourself. I'm not interested."

Michael waved to the waiter. "I'll keep it to myself," he said.

Frances flicked the corners of her eyes. "Another brandy," she told the waiter.

"Two," Michael said.

"Yes, ma'am, yes, sir," said the waiter, backing away.

Frances regarded Michael coolly across the table. "Do you want me to call the Stevensons?" she asked. "It'll be nice in the country."

"Sure," Michael said. "Call them."

She got up from the table and walked across the room toward the telephone. Michael watched her walk, thinking what a pretty girl, what nice legs.

QUESTIONS

1. Is Frances's anger justified? Explain.   **2.** What is the effect of the final sentence of the story?

Sin

(1994)

EDNA O'BRIEN [b. 1936]

They were in. In. Mother, father, and daughter. She waited to hear them come in, stayed awake. She would be awake anyhow, because sleep was paying her less and less court as the years went on. Occasionally, she took a tablet, but dreaded being at the mercy of any drug and had a secondary dread of one day not being able to get it, or not being able to afford it. In those wide-awake vigils she prayed or tried to, but prayer, like sleep, was on the wane now, at the very time when she should be pressing her maker for favors. The prayers came only from her lips, not from deep within—she had lost that heartfelt rapport she once had with God. When the prayers became meaningless, she went around her house in her mind and thought of improvements she would make this year or next—new wallpaper in the big room, where the pink was soiled around the window frames, brown smears from all the damp. And then in the vacant room, where apples were stored, the wallpaper had been hung upside-down and had survived the years without anyone knowing that the acorns and the branches were the wrong way around. She might have that replaced, too, just to get the better of those fools who hung it incorrectly. She was a woman who liked to be always in the right. Funny that on the day the paper was hung she had consulted some seer in the city about a certain matter and had been told that she would go home and find these fruits and bobbins the wrong way up, and she did. In other quarters of her house, she was more spartan with her improvements; she thought of maybe a new strip of linoleum inside the hall door, to save the tiles from trampling boots. Scrubbing was hard for her now, hard on her lower back. Then there were little things, like new towels and tea towels and dishcloths—dishcloths smelled of milk no matter how she soaked or boiled them. They had that sour, gone-off smell. Smell was her strongest sense, and when these paying guests arrived that morning she smelled the woman's perfume and the daughter's—identical, and yet nothing else about them seemed alike. The daughter, Samantha, blond and cocksure, screwed up her eyes as if she were thinking something mathematical, when all she was thinking was Look at me, admire me. She touted for their attention. Her hair was her chief weapon—long hair, which she swept along the table as she looked carefully at the wallpaper or at her parents or at a picture over the whatnot, of pussycats who were trying to move the hands of a clock on to feeding time. She kept insisting that her parents have a bite of her toast, or a taste of her porridge, because it was yummy. Her skirt was nothing short of nude—a bib, really, to draw attention to her thighs, like pillars of solid nougat inside her cream lace stockings. The mother was dark and plump and made a habit of touching the daughter whenever she jumped up in one of her fits of simulated exuberance. The father smoked a pipe. He was a handsome man, tall and distant.

They ate breakfast, then had to have a basket packed with hard-boiled eggs and sandwiches for their boating expedition. She explained that they must make their own arrangements for dinner. When they came back, she heard them say "Sh-h-h-, sh-h-h" repeatedly as they climbed the stairs. They used the bathroom in turn. She could tell by their footsteps, and had to concede that they were doing their best to be quiet—that is, until something went crash-crash and the mother went to the rescue of the daughter. She reckoned it was the china tooth mug. She loved that tooth mug, cream with green fluting and little garlands of shamrock, and she wanted to get up and tackle them, but something stopped her. Also, she did not have a dressing gown. Would they be in their dressing gowns? The woman possibly yes, and the man in his shirtsleeves. She would miss the tooth mug, she would mourn it. Her things had become her beloveds, all else gone, or scattered in distant places. She knew—oh yes, she knew—that the love of children gets fainter and fainter, like a garment that's washed and rewashed until it is only a shadow of its original color, its crimson or royal blue. Their daughter, like Samantha, would be like that soon, would skedaddle once she had other interests, men and so forth.

The parents had the blue room, which had been her and her husband's bridal room, the one where her children were born and where as the years went on she slept as little as possible and went only when she was compelled to, when he roared for her. She went to keep him quiet, to keep him off the batter—went in disgust and stayed in disgust and afterward rinsed and washed herself of it all. Five children were enough for any woman. Four scattered children and one dead, and a daughter-in-law who had made her son, her only son, the essence of graspingness. Still, she must not be too hard on them. The girls remembered when they remembered, they sent gifts, especially the one overseas, and next time when asked what she wanted she would say a dressing gown, and then she could confront her lodgers.

She only kept people in summer, partly because they only came then but also because to heat the house in winter would be impossible, as it swallowed up tankers of oil. Moreover, she never kept people for more than two nights, believing they might get forward and start to think the house was theirs, opening wardrobes and doors, making free. Her other reason was more of a secret. She was afraid that she might grow attached to them and ask them to stay. With the takings, she made improvements to the house but never indulged in a luxury herself except for the jams and tins of biscuits for her sweet tooth.

Yes, they were in her marriage bed, a wide bed with an oak headboard that rattled and a rose quilt that she had made during her betrothal, stitching all her dreamings into it. She imagined them, man and wife, lying side by side, the square pouches of the quilt rising and sinking with their breath, and she remembered the clutching of it and the plucking of some of the feathers as her husband made wrathful and unloving love to her. How might it have been with another man, a gentler, more considerate man? The girl was probably not asleep, but shaping her eyebrows or brushing the long spill of hair, brushing it slowly and maybe even examining herself in the mirror, admiring her plump, firm little figure inside her short nightgown. After they went out to dinner, she had peered into their rooms. She did not open their suitcases, as a point of honor, but she studied some of their possessions, the woman's string of pearls, her cosmetics, and her dark-brown hair net, which lay stealthily next to his pipes, pipes of different-colored wood, and a folded swag of mulchy tobacco. Their money, English money, was piled into two little banks—his money and her money, she felt. On the girl's dressing table there was only the hairbrush, cotton buds, and baby oil. The diaphanous nightie was laid out on the pillow and looked lifelike, as if there were a doll inside it.

Sleep would not come. She got up, intending to go look at the broken tooth mug, but as soon as she reached the door something prevented her. She was ashamed of being heard by them. It was as if the house had become theirs and she, the lodger, beholden to them. Something about their being a family and all over each other, and blowing about what a brilliant time they were having galled her. She paced. Pacing was one of the things she did at night, but now she felt that it, too, was wrong—revealing—and so she crept back into her bed and waited for the blessing of sleep. Sleep often came unbeknownst to her. It was not preceded by yawning or drowsiness. There she would be, totting up what guests owed her, taking it and putting it in the big orange bowl where the spoils of the summer were kept, and all of a sudden it would be morning, the sun giving a rich, red-wine glow to the velvet curtains, or the rain pouring down and her little dog, Gigi, on his hind legs, looking up at her window, waiting for her to get up and come down and open the back door and serve him a saucer of tea with milk. Over the years, he had grown more like a human and was undoubtedly her most faithful friend.

With some visitors she found it more difficult to get to sleep. They unnerved her or she began thinking about them, speculating about their lives, their earnings, their happiness, and so forth, and so it was with these three. It was as if she had to be awake, to keep a watch.

Exactly half an hour after they had retired, it happened. She heard a creak, the girl's door opening slowly, and she thought it was bathroom need, but, no, she heard her go toward their room on tiptoe and then she heard a tap, a series of taps, light and playful—not the tapping of a sick or overwrought child, not the tapping of someone disturbed by a mouse or a bumblebee—and in that second she knew it. Her whole body went into spasm. She heard the girl go into their room, and then everything became so silent, the atmosphere so tense, that her hand, jerking her own doorknob, made her jump. She opened her door very softly and moved in their direction, not certain what exactly she would do. The whole house seemed to wait. They were not talking, yet what reached her ears could not be called silence. Something terrible was being enacted in there, a rite of whispering and tittering and lewd laughter. She could not see, yet her eyes seemed to penetrate through the panelled door as if it were sheer glass and she could picture them—hands, mouths, limbs, all searching for one another. They had not dared to put on a light. The girl was probably naked, or else wore her scarf like a sarong, moving with them in their macabre dance, yielding, allowing them to fondle her, the man fondling her in one place, the woman fondling her elsewhere—an orgy of caresses and whispers and sighs that rent the air. Those sighs and whispers magnified.

She would break the door down. It was not enough simply to open it. She would catch them out, the man, lord of his harem, straddled over a girl who was in no way his daughter, and the woman ministering, because that was the only way she could hold on to him. Vile. Vile. There was a poker in there, in the coal scuttle, left since her last confinement, thirty years ago, and she was already picking it up. She would break it on their bare romping bodies. What detained her she could not say. Everything determined that she go in, and yet she waited in some wanton hesitation, as if she were waiting for their smell.

Their exclamations were what sent her scurrying back to her own room, the three pitches of sound so different—the woman's loud and gusty, the girl's helpless, almost as if she were crying, and, sometime later, his, like a jackass down in the woods with his lady love. She sat on the edge of her bed in a simmer. They would have to go in the morning. She would let them know why. She would convey it to them, insinuate that the girl was not their daughter, but she would never know for sure, and that, plus the vile pageant in the dark, would torment her and be a plague on her house until the day she died.

QUESTIONS

1. Is the woman who owns the house presented sympathetically? Explain.   **2.** What is the connection between the woman's loss of religious faith noted in the opening paragraph and her surmises about the guests?   **3.** In what ways does the woman's past help to explain her reaction to the guests?   **4.** Explain the meaning of the final sentence of the story.   **5.** How do you interpret the title of the story?

WRITING TOPICS

1. Write an essay in which you argue for or against the proposition that the woman who owns the house is justified in her surmises about who the guests are and what they are doing in their room.   **2.** Write an essay on your personal response to the story, focussing on your feelings about the woman.

What We Talk About
When We Talk About Love
1981

RAYMOND CARVER [1938–1989]

My friend Mel McGinnis was talking. Mel McGinnis is a cardiologist, and sometimes that gives him the right.

The four of us were sitting around his kitchen table drinking gin. Sunlight filled the kitchen from the big window behind the sink. There were Mel and me and his second wife, Teresa—Terri, we called her—and my wife, Laura. We lived in Albuquerque then. But we were all from somewhere else.

There was an ice bucket on the table. The gin and the tonic water kept going around, and we somehow got on the subject of love. Mel thought real love was nothing less than spiritual love. He said he'd spent five years in a seminary before quitting to go to medical school. He said he still looked back on those years in the seminary as the most important years in his life.

Terri said the man she lived with before she lived with Mel loved her so much he tried to kill her. Then Terri said, "He beat me up one night. He dragged me around the living room by my ankles. He kept saying, 'I love you, I love you, you bitch.' He went on dragging me around the living room. My head kept knocking on things." Terri looked around the table. "What do you do with love like that?"

She was a bone-thin woman with a pretty face, dark eyes, and brown hair that hung down her back. She liked necklaces made of turquoise, and long pendant earrings.

"My God, don't be silly. That's not love, and you know it," Mel said. "I don't know what you'd call it, but I sure know you wouldn't call it love."

"Say what you want to, but I know it was," Terri said. "It may sound crazy to you, but it's true just the same. People are different, Mel. Sure, sometimes he may have acted crazy. Okay. But he loved me. In his own way maybe, but he loved me. There was love there, Mel. Don't say there wasn't."

Mel let out his breath. He held his glass and turned to Laura and me. "The man threatened to kill me," Mel said. He finished his drink and reached for the gin bottle. "Terri's a romantic. Terri's of the kick-me-so-I'll-know-you-love-me school. Terri, hon, don't look that way." Mel reached across the table and touched Terri's cheek with his fingers. He grinned at her.

"Now he wants to make up," Terri said.

"Make up what?" Mel said. "What is there to make up? I know what I know. That's all."

"How'd we get started on this subject, anyway?" Terri said. She raised her glass and drank from it. "Mel always has love on his mind," she said. "Don't you, honey?" She smiled, and I thought that was the last of it.

"I just wouldn't call Ed's behavior love. That's all I'm saying, honey," Mel said. "What about you guys?" Mel said to Laura and me. "Does that sound like love to you?"

"I'm the wrong person to ask," I said. "I didn't even know the man. I've only heard his name mentioned in passing. I wouldn't know. You'd have to know the particulars. But I think what you're saying is that love is an absolute."

Mel said, "The kind of love I'm talking about is. The kind of love I'm talking about, you don't try to kill people."

Laura said, "I don't know anything about Ed, or anything about the situation. But who can judge anyone else's situation?"

I touched the back of Laura's hand. She gave me a quick smile. I picked up Laura's hand. It was warm, the nails polished, perfectly manicured. I encircled the broad wrist with my fingers, and I held her.

"When I left, he drank rat poison," Terri said. She clasped her arms with her hands. "They took him to the hospital in Santa Fe. That's where we lived then, about ten miles out. They saved his life. But his gums went crazy from it. I mean they pulled away from his teeth. After that, his teeth stood out like fangs. My God," Terri said. She waited a minute, then let go of her arms and picked up her glass.

"What people won't do!" Laura said.

"He's out of the action now," Mel said. "He's dead."

Mel handed me the saucer of limes. I took a section, squeezed it over my drink, and stirred the ice cubes with my finger.

"It gets worse," Terri said. "He shot himself in the mouth. But he bungled that too. Poor Ed," she said. Terri shook her head.

"Poor Ed nothing," Mel said. "He was dangerous."

Mel was forty-five years old. He was tall and rangy with curly soft hair. His face and arms were brown from the tennis he played. When he was sober, his gestures, all his movements, were precise, very careful.

"He did love me though, Mel. Grant me that," Terri said. "That's all I'm asking. He didn't love me the way you love me. I'm not saying that. But he loved me. You can grant me that, can't you?"

"What do you mean, he bungled it?" I said.

Laura leaned forward with her glass. She put her elbows on the table and held her glass in both hands. She glanced from Mel to Terri and waited with a look of bewilderment on her open face, as if amazed that such things happened to people you were friendly with.

"How'd he bungle it when he killed himself?" I said.

"I'll tell you what happened," Mel said. "He took this twenty-two pistol he'd bought to threaten Terri and me with. Oh, I'm serious, the man was always threatening. You should have seen the way we lived in those days. Like fugitives. I even bought a gun myself. Can you believe it? A guy like me? But I did. I bought one for self-defense and carried it in the glove compartment. Sometimes I'd have to leave the apartment in the middle of the night. To go to the hospital, you know? Terri and I weren't married then, and my first wife had the house and kids, the dog, everything, and Terri and I were living in this apartment here. Sometimes, as I say, I'd get a call in the middle of the night and have to go in to the hospital at two or three in the morning. It'd be dark out there in the parking lot, and I'd break into a sweat before I could even get to my car. I never knew if he was going to come up out of the shrubbery or from behind a car and start shooting. I mean, the man was crazy. He was capable of wiring a bomb, anything. He used to call my service at all hours and say he needed to talk to the doctor, and when I'd return the call, he'd say, 'Son of a bitch, your days are numbered.' Little things like that. It was scary, I'm telling you."

"I still feel sorry for him," Terri said.

"It sounds like a nightmare," Laura said. "But what exactly happened after he shot himself?"

Laura is a legal secretary. We'd met in a professional capacity. Before we knew it, it was a courtship. She's thirty-five, three years younger than I am. In addition to being in love, we like each other and enjoy one another's company. She's easy to be with.

"What happened?" Laura said.

Mel said, "He shot himself in the mouth in his room. Someone heard the shot and told the manager. They came in with a passkey, saw what had happened, and called an ambulance. I happened to be there when they brought him in, alive but past recall. The man lived for three days. His head swelled up to twice the size of a normal head. I'd never seen anything like it, and I hope I never do again. Terri wanted to go in and sit with him when she found out about it. We had a fight over it. I didn't think she should see him like that. I didn't think she should see him, and I still don't."

"Who won the fight?" Laura said.

"I was in the room with him when he died," Terri said. "He never came up out of it. But I sat with him. He didn't have anyone else."

"He was dangerous," Mel said. "If you call that love, you can have it."

"It was love," Terri said. "Sure, it's abnormal in most people's eyes. But he was willing to die for it. He did die for it."

"I sure as hell wouldn't call it love," Mel said. "I mean, no one knows what he did it for. I've seen a lot of suicides, and I couldn't say anyone ever knew what they did it for."

Mel put his hands behind his neck and tilted his chair back. "I'm not interested in that kind of love," he said. "If that's love, you can have it."

Terri said, "We were afraid. Mel even made a will out and wrote to his brother in California who used to be a Green Beret. Mel told him who to look for if something happened to him."

Terri drank from her glass. She said, "But Mel's right—we lived like fugitives. We were afraid. Mel was, weren't you, honey? I even called the police at one point, but they were no help. They said they couldn't do anything until Ed actually did something. Isn't that a laugh?" Terry said.

She poured the last of the gin into her glass and waggled the bottle. Mel got up from the table and went to the cupboard. He took down another bottle.

"Well, Nick and I know what love is," Laura said. "For us, I mean," Laura said. She bumped my knee with her knee. "You're supposed to say something now," Laura said, and turned her smile on me.

For an answer, I took Laura's hand and raised it to my lips. I made a big production out of kissing her hand. Everyone was amused.

"We're lucky," I said.

"You guys," Terri said. "Stop that now. You're making me sick. You're still on the honeymoon, for God's sake. You're still gaga, for crying out loud. Just wait. How long have you been together now? How long has it been? A year? Longer than a year?"

"Going on a year and a half," Laura said, flushed and smiling.

"Oh, now," Terri said. "Wait a while."

She held her drink and gazed at Laura.

"I'm only kidding," Terri said.

Mel opened the gin and went around the table with the bottle.

"Here, you guys," he said. "Let's have a toast. I want to propose a toast. A toast to love. To true love," Mel said.

We touched glasses.

"To love," we said.

Outside in the backyard, one of the dogs began to bark. The leaves of the aspen that leaned past the window ticked against the glass. The afternoon sun was like a presence in this room, the spacious light of ease and generosity. We could have been anywhere, somewhere enchanted. We raised our glasses again and grinned at each other like children who had agreed on something forbidden.

"I'll tell you what real love is," Mel said. "I mean, I'll give you a good example. And then you can draw your own conclusions." He poured more gin into his glass. He added an ice cube and a sliver of lime. We waited and sipped our drinks. Laura and I touched knees again. I put a hand on her warm thigh and left it there.

"What do any of us really know about love?" Mel said. "It seems to me we're just beginners at love. We say we love each other and we do, I don't doubt it. I love Terri and Terri loves me, and you guys love each other too. You know the kind of love I'm talking about now. Physical love, that impulse that drives you to someone special, as well as love of the other person's being, his or her essence, as it were. Carnal love and, well, call it sentimental love, the day-to-day caring about the other person. But sometimes I have a hard time accounting for the fact that I must have loved my first wife too. But I did, I know I did. So I suppose I am like Terri in that regard. Terri and Ed." He thought about it and then he went on. "There was a time when I thought I loved my first wife more than life itself. But now I hate her guts. I do. How do you explain that?

What happened to that love? What happened to it, is what I'd like to know. I wish someone could tell me. Then there's Ed. Okay, we're back to Ed. He loves Terri so much he tries to kill her and he winds up killing himself." Mel stopped talking and swallowed from his glass. "You guys have been together eighteen months and you love each other. It shows all over you. You glow with it. But you both loved other people before you met each other. You've both been married before, just like us. And you probably loved other people before that too, even. Terri and I have been together five years, been married for four. And the terrible thing, the terrible thing is, but the good thing too, the saving grace, you might say, is that if something happened to one of us—excuse me for saying this—but if something happened to one of us tomorrow I think the other one, the other person, would grieve for a while, you know, but then the surviving party would go out and love again, have someone else soon enough. All this, all of this love we're talking about, it would just be a memory. Maybe not even a memory. Am I wrong? Am I way off base? Because I want you to set me straight if you think I'm wrong. I want to know. I mean, I don't know anything, and I'm the first one to admit it."

"Mel, for God's sake," Terri said. She reached out and took hold of his wrist. "Are you getting drunk? Honey? Are you drunk?"

"Honey, I'm just talking," Mel said. "All right? I don't have to be drunk to say what I think. I mean, we're all just talking, right?" Mel said. He fixed his eyes on her.

"Sweetie, I'm not criticizing," Terri said.

She picked up her glass.

"I'm not on call today," Mel said. "Let me remind you of that. I am not on call," he said.

"Mel, we love you," Laura said.

Mel looked at Laura. He looked at her as if he could not place her, as if she was not the woman she was.

"Love you too, Laura," Mel said. "And you, Nick, love you too. You know something?" Mel said. "You guys are our pals," Mel said.

He picked up his glass.

Mel said, "I was going to tell you about something. I mean, I was going to prove a point. You see, this happened a few months ago, but it's still going on right now, and it ought to make us feel ashamed when we talk like we know what we're talking about when we talk above love."

"Come on now," Terri said. "Don't talk like you're drunk if you're not drunk."

"Just shut up for once in your life," Mel said very quietly. "Will you do me a favor and do that for a minute? So as I was saying, there's this old couple who had this car wreck out on the interstate. A kid hit them and they were all torn to shit and nobody was giving them much chance to pull through."

Terri looked at us and then back at Mel. She seemed anxious, or maybe that's too strong a word.

Mel was handing the bottle around the table.

"I was on call that night," Mel said. "It was May or maybe it was June. Terri and I had just sat down to dinner when the hospital called. There'd been this thing out on the interstate. Drunk kid, teenager, plowed his dad's pickup into this camper with this old couple in it. They were up in their mid-seventies, that couple. The kid—eighteen, nineteen, something—he was DOA. Taken the steering wheel through his sternum. The old couple, they were alive, you understand. I mean, just barely. But they had everything. Multiple fractures, internal injuries, hemorrhaging, contusions, lacerations, the works, and they each of them had themselves concussions. They were in a bad way, believe me. And, of course, their age was two strikes against them. I'd say she was worse off than he was. Ruptured spleen along with everything else. Both kneecaps broken. But they'd been wearing their seatbelts and, God knows, that's what saved them for the time being."

"Folks, this is an advertisement for the National Safety Council," Terri said. "This is your spokesman, Dr. Melvin R. McGinnis, talking." Terri laughed. "Mel," she said, "sometimes you're just too much. But I love you, hon," she said.

"Honey, I love you," Mel said.

He leaned across the table. Terri met him halfway. They kissed.

"Terri's right," Mel said as he settled himself again. "Get those seatbelts on. But seriously, they were in some shape, those oldsters. By the time I got down there, the kid was dead, as I said. He was off in a corner, laid out on a gurney. I took one look at the old couple and told the ER nurse to get me a neurologist and an orthopedic man and a couple of surgeons down there right away."

He drank from his glass. "I'll try to keep this short," he said. "So we took the two of them up to the OR and worked like fuck on them most of the night. They had these incredible reserves, those two. You see that once in a while. So we did everything that could be done, and toward morning we're giving them a fifty-fifty chance, maybe less than that for her. So here they are, still alive the next morning. So, okay, we move them into the ICU, which is where they both kept plugging away at it for two weeks, hitting it better and better on all the scopes. So we transfer them out to their own room."

Mel stopped talking. "Here," he said, "let's drink this cheapo gin the hell up. Then we're going to dinner, right? Terri and I know a new place. That's where we'll go, to this new place we know about. But we're not going until we finish up this cut-rate, lousy gin."

Terri said, "We haven't actually eaten there yet. But it looks good. From the outside, you know."

"I like food," Mel said. "If I had it to do all over again, I'd be a chef, you know? Right, Terri?" Mel said.

He laughed. He fingered the ice in his glass.

"Terri knows," he said. "Terri can tell you. But let me say this. If I could come back again in a different life, a different time and all, you know what? I'd like to come back as a knight. You were pretty safe wearing all that armor. It was all right being a knight until gunpowder and muskets and pistols came along."

"Mel would like to ride a horse and carry a lance," Terri said.

"Carry a woman's scarf with you everywhere," Laura said.

"Or just a woman," Mel said.

"Shame on you," Laura said.

Terri said, "Suppose you came back as a serf. The serfs didn't have it so good in those days," Terri said.

"The serfs never had it good," Mel said. "But I guess even the knights were vessels to someone. Isn't that the way it worked? But then everyone is always a vessel to someone. Isn't that right? Terri? But what I liked about knights, besides their ladies, was that they had that suit of armor, you know, and they couldn't get hurt very easy. No cars in those days, you know? No drunk teenagers to tear into your ass."

"Vassals," Terri said.

"What?" Mel said.

"Vassals," Terri said. "They were called vassals, not vessels."

"Vassals, vessels," Mel said, "what the fuck's the difference? You knew what I meant anyway. All right," Mel said. "So I'm not educated. I learned my stuff. I'm a heart surgeon, sure, but I'm just a mechanic. I go in and I fuck around and I fix things. Shit," Mel said.

"Modesty doesn't become you," Terri said.

"He's just a humble sawbones," I said. "But sometimes they suffocated in all that armor, Mel. They'd even have heart attacks if it got too hot and they were too tired and worn out. I read somewhere that they'd fall off their horses and not be able to get up because they were too tired to stand with all that armor on them. They got trampled by their own horses sometimes."

"That's terrible," Mel said. "That's a terrible thing, Nicky. I guess they'd just lay there and wait until somebody came along and made a shish kebab out of them."

"Some other vessel," Terri said.

"That's right," Mel said. "Some vassal would come along and spear the bastard in the name of love. Or whatever the fuck it was they fought over in those days."

"Same things we fight over these days," Terri said.

Laura said, "Nothing's changed."

The color was still high in Laura's cheeks. Her eyes were bright. She brought her glass to her lips.

Mel poured himself another drink. He looked at the label closely as if studying a long row of numbers. Then he slowly put the bottle down on the table and slowly reached for the tonic water.

"What about the old couple?" Laura said. "You didn't finish that story you started."

Laura was having a hard time lighting her cigarette. Her matches kept going out.

The sunshine inside the room was different now, changing, getting thinner. But the leaves outside the window were still shimmering, and I stared at the pattern they made on the panes and on the Formica counter. They weren't the same patterns, of course.

"What about the old couple?" I said.

"Older but wiser," Terri said.

Mel stared at her.

Terri said, "Go on with your story, hon. I was only kidding. Then what happened?"

"Terri, sometimes," Mel said.

"Please, Mel," Terri said. "Don't always be so serious, sweetie. Can't you take a joke?"

"Where's the joke?" Mel said.

He held his glass and gazed steadily at his wife.

"What happened?" Laura said.

Mel fastened his eyes on Laura. He said, "Laura, if I didn't have Terri and if I didn't love her so much, and if Nick wasn't my best friend, I'd fall in love with you, I'd carry you off, honey," he said.

"Tell your story," Terri said. "Then we'll go to that new place, okay?"

"Okay," Mel said. "Where was I?" he said. He stared at the table and then he began again.

"I dropped in to see each of them every day, sometimes twice a day if I was up doing other calls anyway. Casts and bandages, head to foot, the both of them. You know, you've seen it in the movies. That's just the way they looked, just like in the movies. Little eye-holes and nose-holes and mouth-holes. And she had to have her legs slung up on top of it. Well, the husband was very depressed for the longest while. Even after he found out that his wife was going to pull through, he was still very depressed. Not about the accident, though. I mean, the accident was one thing, but it wasn't everything. I'd get up to his mouth-hole, you know, and he'd say no, it wasn't the accident exactly but it was because he couldn't see her through his eye-holes. He said that was what was making him feel so bad. Can you imagine? I'm telling you, the man's heart was breaking because he couldn't turn his goddamn head and *see* his goddamn wife."

Mel looked around the table and shook his head at what he was going to say.

"I mean, it was killing the old fart just because he couldn't *look* at the fucking woman."

We all looked at Mel.

"Do you see what I'm saying?" he said.

Maybe we were a little drunk by then. I know it was hard keeping things in focus. The light was draining out of the room, going back through the window where it had come from. Yet nobody made a move to get up from the table to turn on the overhead light.

"Listen," Mel said. "Let's finish this fucking gin. There's about enough left here for one shooter all around. Then let's go eat. Let's go to the new place."

"He's depressed," Terri said. "Mel, why don't you take a pill?"

Mel shook his head. "I've taken everything there is."

"We all need a pill now and then," I said.

"Some people are born needing them," Terri said.

She was using her finger to rub at something on the table. Then she stopped rubbing.

"I think I want to call my kids," Mel said. "Is that all right with everybody? I'll call my kids," he said.

Terri said, "What if Marjorie answers the phone? You guys, you've heard us on the subject of Marjorie? Honey, you know you don't want to talk to Marjorie. It'll make you feel even worse."

"I don't want to talk to Marjorie," Mel said. "But I want to talk to my kids."

"There isn't a day goes by that Mel doesn't say he wishes she'd get married again. Or else die," Terri said. "For one thing," Terri said, "she's bankrupting us. Mel says it's just to spite him that she won't get married again. She has a boyfriend who lives with her and the kids, so Mel is supporting the boyfriend too."

"She's allergic to bees," Mel said. "If I'm not praying she'll get married again, I'm praying she'll get herself stung to death by a swarm of fucking bees."

"Shame on you," Laura said.

"Bzzzzzzz," Mel said, turning his fingers into bees and buzzing them at Terri's throat. Then he let his hands drop all the way to his sides.

"She's vicious," Mel said. "Sometimes I think I'll go up there dressed like a beekeeper. You know, that hat that's like a helmet with the plate that comes down over your face, the big gloves, and the padded coat? I'll knock on the door and let loose a hive of bees in the house. But first I'd make sure the kids were out, of course."

He crossed one leg over the other. It seemed to take him a lot of time to do it. Then he put both feet on the floor and leaned forward, elbows on the table, his chin cupped in his hands.

"Maybe I won't call the kids, after all. Maybe it isn't such a hot idea. Maybe we'll just go eat. How does that sound?"

"Sounds fine to me," I said. "Eat or not eat. Or keep drinking. I could head right on out into the sunset."

"What does that mean, honey?" Laura said.

"It just means what I said," I said. "It means I could just keep going. That's all it means."

"I could eat something myself," Laura said. "I don't think I've ever been so hungry in my life. Is there something to nibble on?"

"I'll put out some cheese and crackers," Terri said.

But Terri just sat there. She did not get up to get anything.

Mel turned his glass over. He spilled it out on the table.

"Gin's gone," Mel said.

Terri said, "Now what?"

I could hear my heart beating. I could hear everyone's heart. I could hear the human noise we sat there making, not one of us moving, not even when the room went dark.

QUESTIONS

1. How would you characterize the relationship between Mel and Terri? Between Nick and Laura?   **2.** What is your reaction to Mel? Is he likable? Why does Carver make him a scientist and a cardiologist?   **3.** The story begins in the sunlight of midday and ends in darkness. Does this transition help us understand what the author is saying about love and marriage? Explain.   **4.** Do you agree with Mel or with Terri about Ed? Explain.

WRITING TOPIC

Examine the various marriages (including the relationship between Terri and Ed) and discuss how they provide an explanation for the title of the story.

How to Talk to a Hunter   1990

PAM HOUSTON   [b. 1962]

When he says "Skins or blankets?" it will take you a moment to realize that he's asking which you want to sleep under. And in your hesitation he'll decide that he wants to see your skin wrapped in the big black moosehide. He carried it, he'll say, soaking wet and heavier than a dead man, across the tundra for two—was it hours or days or weeks? But the payoff, now, will be to see it fall across one of your white breasts. It's December, and your skin is never really warm, so you will pull the bulk of it around you and pose for him, pose for his camera, without having to narrate this moose's death.

You will spend every night in this man's bed without asking yourself why he listens to top-forty country. Why he donated money to the Republican party. Why he won't play back his messages while you are in the room. You are there so often the messages pile up. Once, you noticed the bright green counter reading as high as fifteen.

He will have lured you here out of a careful independence that you spent months cultivating; though it will finally be winter, the dwindling daylight and the threat of Christmas, that makes you give in. Spending nights with this man means suffering the long face of your sheep dog, who likes to sleep on your bed, who worries when you don't come home. But the hunter's house is so much warmer than yours, and he'll give you a key, and just like a woman, you'll think that means something. It will snow hard for thirteen straight days. Then it will really get cold. When it is sixty below there will be no wind and no clouds, just still air and cold sunshine. The sun on the windows will lure you out of bed, but he'll pull you back under. The next two hours he'll devote to your body. With his hands, with his tongue, he'll express what will seem to you like the most eternal of loves. Like the house key, this is just another kind of lie. Even in bed; especially in bed, you and he cannot speak the same language. The machine will answer the incoming calls. From under an ocean of passion and hide and hair you'll hear a woman's muffled voice between the beeps.

Your best female friend will say, "So what did you think? That a man who sleeps under a dead moose is capable of commitment?"

This is what you learned in college: A man desires the satisfaction of his desire; a woman desires the condition of desiring.

The hunter will talk about spring in Hawaii, summer in Alaska. The man who says he was always better at math will form the sentences so carefully it will be impossible to tell if you are included in these plans. When he asks you if you would like to open a small guest ranch way out in the country, understand that

515

this is a rhetorical question. Label these conversations future perfect, but don't expect the present to catch up with them. Spring is an inconceivable distance from the December days that just keep getting shorter and gray.

He'll ask you if you've ever shot anything, if you'd like to, if you ever thought about teaching your dog to retrieve. Your dog will like him too much, will drop the stick at his feet every time, will roll over and let the hunter scratch his belly.

One day he'll leave you sleeping to go split wood or get the mail and his phone will ring again. You'll sit very still while a woman who calls herself something like Patty Coyote leaves a message on his machine: she's leaving work, she'll say, and the last thing she wanted to hear was the sound of his beautiful voice. Maybe she'll talk only in rhyme. Maybe the counter will change to sixteen. You'll look a question at the mule deer on the wall, and the dark spots on either side of his mouth will tell you he shares more with this hunter than you ever will. One night, drunk, the hunter told you he was sorry for taking that deer, that every now and then there's an animal that isn't meant to be taken, and he should have known that deer was one.

Your best male friend will say, "No one who needs to call herself Patty Coyote can hold a candle to you, but why not let him sleep alone a few nights, just to make sure?"

The hunter will fill your freezer with elk burger, venison sausage, organic potatoes, fresh pecans. He'll tell you to wear your seat belt, to dress warmly, to drive safely. He'll say you are always on his mind, that you're the best thing that's ever happened to him, that you make him glad that he's a man.

Tell him it don't come easy, tell him freedom's just another word for nothing left to lose.

These are the things you'll know without asking: The coyote woman wears her hair in braids. She uses words like "howdy." She's man enough to shoot a deer.

A week before Christmas you'll rent *It's a Wonderful Life* and watch it together, curled on your couch, faces touching. Then you'll bring up the word "monogamy." He'll tell you how badly he was hurt by your predecessor. He'll tell you he couldn't be happier spending every night with you. He'll say there's just a few questions he doesn't have the answers for. He'll say he's just scared and confused. Of course this isn't exactly what he means. Tell him you understand. Tell him you are scared too. Tell him to take all the time he needs. Know that you could never shoot an animal, and be glad of it.

Your best female friend will say, "You didn't tell him you loved him, did you?" Don't even tell her the truth. If you do, you'll have to tell her that he said this: "I feel exactly the same way."

Your best male friend will say, "Didn't you know what would happen when you said the word 'commitment'?"

But that isn't the word that you said.

He'll say, "Commitment, monogamy, it all means just one thing."

The coyote woman will come from Montana with the heavier snows. The hunter will call you on the day of the solstice to say he has a friend in town and can't see you. He'll leave you hanging your Christmas lights; he'll give new meaning to the phrase "longest night of the year." The man who has said he's not so good with words will manage to say eight things about his friend without using a gender-determining pronoun. Get out of the house quickly. Call the most understanding person you know that will let you sleep in his bed.

Your best female friend will say, "So what did you think? That he was capable of living outside his gender?"

When you get home in the morning there's a candy tin on your pillow. Santa, obese and grotesque, fondles two small children on the lid. The card will say something like, From your not-so-secret admirer. Open it. Examine each carefully made truffle. Feed them, one at a time, to the dog. Call the hunter's machine. Tell him you don't speak chocolate.

Your best female friend will say, "At this point, what is it about him that you could possibly find appealing?"

Your best male friend will say, "Can't you understand that this is a good sign? Can't you understand that this proves how deep he's in with you?" Hug your best male friend. Give him the truffles the dog wouldn't eat.

Of course the weather will cooperate with the coyote woman. The highways will close, she will stay another night. He'll tell her he's going to work so he can come and see you. He'll even leave her your number and write "Me at Work" on the yellow pad of paper by his phone. Although you shouldn't, you'll have to be there. It will be you and your nauseous dog and your half-trimmed tree all waiting for him like a series of questions.

This is what you learned in graduate school: in every assumption is contained the possibility of its opposite.

In your kitchen he'll hug you like you might both die there. Sniff him for coyote. Don't hug him back.

He will say whatever he needs to win. He'll say it's just an old friend. He'll say the visit was all the friend's idea. He'll say the night away from you has given him time to think about how much you mean to him. Realize that nothing short of sleeping alone will ever make him realize how much you mean to him. He'll say that if you can just be a little patient, some good will come out of this for the two of you after all. He still won't use a gender-specific pronoun.

Put your head in your hands. Think about what it means to be patient. Think about the beautiful, smart, strong, clever woman you thought he saw when he looked at you. Pull on your hair. Rock your body back and forth. Don't cry.

He'll say that after holding you it doesn't feel right holding anyone else. For "holding," substitute "fucking." Then take it as a compliment.

He will get frustrated and rise to leave. He may or may not be bluffing. Stall for time. Ask a question he can't immediately answer. Tell him you want to make love on the floor. When he tells you your body is beautiful, say, "I feel exactly the same way." Don't, under any circumstances, stand in front of the door.

Your best female friend will say, "They lie to us, they cheat on us, and we love them more for it." She'll say, "It's our fault. We raise them to be like that."

Tell her it can't be your fault. You've never raised anything but dogs.

The hunter will say it's late and he has to go home to sleep. He'll emphasize the last word in the sentence. Give him one kiss that he'll remember while he's fucking the coyote woman. Give him one kiss that ought to make him cry if he's capable of it, but don't notice when he does. Tell him to have a good night.

Your best male friend will say, "We all do it. We can't help it. We're self-destructive. It's the old bad-boy routine. You have a male dog, don't you?"

The next day the sun will be out and the coyote woman will leave. Think about how easy it must be for the coyote woman and a man who listens to top-forty country. The coyote woman would never use a word like "monogamy"; the coyote woman will stay gentle on his mind.

If you can, let him sleep alone for at least one night. If you can't, invite him over to finish trimming your Christmas tree. When he asks how you are, tell him you think it's a good idea to keep your sense of humor during the holidays.

Plan to be breezy and aloof and full of interesting anecdotes about all the other men you've ever known. Plan to be hotter than ever before in bed, and a little cold out of it. Remember that necessity is the mother of invention. Be flexible.

First, he will find the faulty bulb that's been keeping all the others from lighting. He will explain in great detail the most elementary electrical principles. You will take turns placing the ornaments you and other men, he and other women, have spent years carefully choosing. Under the circumstances, try to let this be a comforting thought.

He will thin the clusters of tinsel you put on the tree. He'll say something ambiguous like, Next year you should string popcorn and cranberries. Finally, his arm will stretch just high enough to place the angel on the top of the tree.

Your best female friend will say, "Why can't you ever fall in love with a man who will be your friend?"

Your best male friend will say, "You ought to know this by now: Men always cheat on the best women."

This is what you learned in the pop psychology book: Love means letting go of fear.

Play Willie Nelson's "Pretty Paper." He'll ask you to dance, and before you can answer he'll be spinning you around your wood stove, he'll be humming in your ear. Before the song ends he'll be taking off your clothes, setting you lightly under the tree, hovering above you with tinsel in his hair. Through the spread of the branches the all-white lights you insisted on will shudder and blur, outlining the ornaments he brought: a pheasant, a snow goose, a deer.

The record will end. Above the crackle of the wood stove and the rasp of the hunter's breathing you'll hear one long low howl break the quiet of the frozen night: your dog, chained and lonely and cold. You'll wonder if he knows enough to stay in his dog house. You'll wonder if he knows that the nights are getting shorter now.

QUESTIONS
1. What is the difference between the advice offered by the male and the female friend? Which is more accurate and useful? Explain.   **2.** Describe the difference between the narrator and the "coyote woman." What does the narrator think of the "coyote woman"?   **3.** What specific advice does the narrator give about talking to a hunter?   **4.** Why does the story end with the narrator's thoughts about the dog?

WRITING TOPIC
What common relationship between men and women does this story reflect? Does the relationship in this story parallel your own courtship experiences?

LOVE
AND
HATE

La Fontana della Giovinezza, Eroe e Eroina, 15th century by Giacomo Jaquerio

POETRY

With His Venom*

SAPPHO   [ca. 610–ca. 580 B.C.]

With his venom

Irresistible
and bittersweet

that loosener
of limbs, Love   5

reptile-like
strikes me down

Bonny Barbara Allan

ANONYMOUS

It was in and about the Martinmas[1] time,
   When the green leaves were a falling,
That Sir John Graeme, in the West Country,
   Fell in love with Barbara Allan.

He sent his man down through the town,   5
   To the place where she was dwelling:
"O haste and come to my master dear,
   Gin° ye be Barbara Allan."   if

O hooly,° hooly rose she up,   slowly
   To the place where he was lying,   10
And when she drew the curtain by:
   "Young man, I think you're dying."

With His Venom
  * Translated by Mary Barnard.
Bonny Barbara Allan
  [1] November 11.

521

"O it's I'm sick, and very, very sick,
   And 'tis a' for Barbara Allan."
"O the better for me ye s'° never be,   ye shall 15
   Tho your heart's blood were a-spilling.

"O dinna° ye mind,° young man," said she,   don't/remember
   "When ye was in the tavern a drinking,
That ye made the healths gae° round and round,   go
   And slighted Barbara Allan?"   20

He turned his face unto the wall,
   And death was with him dealing:
"Adieu, adieu, my dear friends all,
   And be kind to Barbara Allan."

And slowly, slowly raise she up,   25
   And slowly, slowly left him,
And sighing said she could not stay,
   Since death of life had reft him.

She had not gane a mile but twa,
   When she heard the dead-bell ringing,   30
And every jow° that the dead-bell geid,°   stroke/gave
   It cried, "Woe to Barbara Allan!"

"O mother, mother, make my bed!
   O make it saft and narrow!
Since my love died for me to-day,   35
   I'll die for him to-morrow."

The Passionate Shepherd
to His Love[1]   1600

CHRISTOPHER MARLOWE [1564–1593]

Come live with me and be my love,
And we will all the pleasures prove
That valleys, groves, hills, and fields,
Woods, or steepy mountain yields.

The Passionate Shepherd . . .
  [1] This poem has elicited many responses over the centuries. Sir Walter Ralegh's early answer follows. C. Day Lewis's twentieth-century response appears on p. 543.

And we will sit upon the rocks,   5
Seeing the shepherds feed their flocks,
By shallow rivers to whose falls
Melodious birds sing madrigals.

And I will make thee beds of roses
And a thousand fragrant posies,   10
A cap of flowers, and a kirtle°   skirt
Embroidered all with leaves of myrtle;

A gown made of the finest wool
Which from our pretty lambs we pull;
Fair lined slippers for the cold,   15
With buckles of the purest gold;

A belt of straw and ivy buds,
With coral clasps and amber studs:
And if these pleasures may thee move,
Come live with me, and be my love.   20

The shepherds' swains shall dance and sing
For thy delight each May morning:
If these delights thy mind may move,
Then live with me and be my love.

The Nymph's Reply
to the Shepherd   1600

SIR WALTER RALEGH   [1554–1618]¹

If all the world and love were young,
And truth in every shepherd's tongue,
These pretty pleasures might me move
To live with thee and be thy love.

Time drives the flocks from field to fold,   5
When rivers rage and rocks grow cold,
And Philomel° becometh dumb;   the nightingale
The rest complains of cares to come.

The Nymph's Reply . . .
   ¹ Chronology has been dispensed with here to facilitate comparison with Marlowe's "Passionate Shepherd."

The flowers do fade, and wanton fields
To wayward winter reckoning yields;   10
A honey tongue, a heart of gall,
Is fancy's spring, but sorrow's fall.

Thy gowns, thy shoes, thy beds of roses,
Thy cap, thy kirtle, and thy posies
Soon break, soon wither, soon forgotten—   15
In folly ripe, in reason rotten.

Thy belt of straw and ivy buds,
Thy coral clasps and amber studs,
All these in me no means can move
To come to thee and be thy love.   20

But could youth last and love still breed,
Had joys no date° nor age no need,   end
Then these delights my mind might move
To live with thee and be thy love.

Sonnets   1609

WILLIAM SHAKESPEARE   [1564–1616]

18

Shall I compare thee to a summer's day?
Thou art more lovely and more temperate:
Rough winds do shake the darling buds of May,
And summer's lease hath all too short a date:
Sometime too hot the eye of heaven shines,   5
And often is his gold complexion dimmed;
And every fair from fair sometimes declines,
By chance or nature's changing course untrimmed;
But thy eternal summer shall not fade,
Nor lose possession of that fair thou ow'st,°   owns   10
Nor shall death brag thou wander'st in his shade,
When in eternal lines to time thou grow'st:
     So long as men can breathe, or eyes can see,
     So long lives this, and this gives life to thee.

QUESTIONS
1. Why does the poet argue that "a summer's day" is an inappropriate metaphor for his beloved?   **2.** What is "this" in line 14?

29

When, in disgrace with fortune and men's eyes,
I all alone beweep my outcast state
And trouble deaf heaven with my bootless cries
And look upon myself and curse my fate,
Wishing me like to one more rich in hope,   5
Featured like him, like him with friends possessed,
Desiring this man's art and that man's scope,
With what I most enjoy contented least;
Yet in these thoughts myself almost despising,
Haply I think on thee, and then my state,   10
Like to the lark at break of day arising
From sullen earth, sings hymns at heaven's gate;
     For thy sweet love remembered such wealth brings
     That then I scorn to change my state with kings.

129

Th' expense of spirit in a waste of shame
Is lust in action; and till action, lust
Is perjured, murderous, bloody, full of blame,
Savage, extreme, rude, cruel, not to trust;
Enjoyed no sooner but despiséd straight;   5
Past reason hunted; and no sooner had,
Past reason hated, as a swallowed bait,
On purpose laid to make the taker mad:
Mad in pursuit, and in possession so;
Had, having, and in quest to have, extreme;   10
A bliss in proof,° and proved, a very woe;   experience
Before, a joy proposed; behind, a dream.
     All this the world well knows; yet none knows well
     To shun the heaven that leads men to this hell.

QUESTIONS
1. Paraphrase "Th' expense of spirit in a waste of shame / Is lust in action."
2. Describe the sound patterns and metrical variations in lines 3 and 4. What do they contribute to the "sense" of the lines?

WRITING TOPIC
How do the sound patterns, the metrical variations, and the paradox in the final couplet contribute to the sense of this sonnet?

130

My mistress' eyes are nothing like the sun;
Coral is far more red than her lips' red;
If snow be white, why then her breasts are dun;
If hairs be wires, black wires grow on her head.
I have seen roses damasked,° red and white,   variegated   5
But no such roses see I in her cheeks;
And in some perfumes is there more delight
Than in the breath that from my mistress reeks.
I love to hear her speak, yet well I know
That music hath a far more pleasing sound;   10
I grant I never saw a goddess go;
My mistress, when she walks, treads on the ground.
    And yet, by heaven, I think my love as rare
    As any she belied with false compare.[1]

I Care Not for These Ladies   1601

THOMAS CAMPION   [1567–1620]

I care not for these ladies,
That must be wooed and prayed:
Give me kind Amaryllis,[1]
The wanton country maid.
Nature art disdaineth,   5
Her beauty is her own.
    Who, when we court and kiss,
    She cries, "Forsooth, let go!"
    But when we come where comfort is,
    She never will say no.   10

If I love Amaryllis,
She gives me fruit and flowers:
But if we love these ladies,
We must give golden showers.
Give them gold, that sell love,   15
Give me the nut-brown lass,
    Who, when we court and kiss,
    She cries, "Forsooth, let go!"
    But when we come where comfort is,
    She never will say no.   20

Sonnet 130
    [1] I.e., as any woman misrepresented with false comparisons.
I Care Not for These Ladies
    [1] A conventional name for a country girl in pastoral poetry.

These ladies must have pillows,
And beds by strangers wrought;
Give me a bower of willows,
Of moss and leaves unbought,
And fresh Amaryllis,   25
With milk and honey fed;
 Who, when we court and kiss,
 She cries, "Forsooth, let go!"
 But when we come where comfort is,
 She never will say no.   30

A Valediction: Forbidding Mourning

1633

JOHN DONNE [1572–1631]

As virtuous men pass mildly away,
 And whisper to their souls to go,
Whilst some of their sad friends do say
 The breath goes now, and some say, No;

So let us melt, and make no noise,   5
 No tear-floods, nor sigh-tempests move,
'Twere profanation of our joys
 To tell the laity our love.

Moving of th' earth° brings harms and fears,   earthquake
 Men reckon what it did and meant;   10
But trepidation of the spheres,
 Though greater far, is innocent.[1]

Dull sublunary° lovers' love   under the moon
 (Whose soul is sense) cannot admit
Absence, because it doth remove   15
 Those things which elemented it.

But we by a love so much refined
 That our selves know not what it is,
Inter-assuréd of the mind,
 Care less, eyes, lips, and hands to miss.   20

A Valediction: Forbidding Mourning
 [1] The movement of the heavenly spheres is harmless.

Our two souls therefore, which are one,
   Though I must go, endure not yet
A breach, but an expansion,
   Like gold to airy thinness beat.

If they be two, they are two so   25
   As stiff twin compasses are two;
Thy soul, the fixed foot, makes no show
   To move, but doth, if th' other do.

And though it in the center sit,
   Yet when the other far doth roam,   30
It leans and harkens after it,
   And grows erect, as that comes home.

Such wilt thou be to me, who must
   Like th' other foot, obliquely run;
Thy firmness makes my circle just,   35
   And makes me end where I begun.

QUESTIONS
1. Two kinds of love are described in this poem—spiritual and physical. How does the simile drawn in the first two stanzas help define the differences between them? **2.** How does the contrast between earthquakes and the movement of the spheres in stanza 3 further develop the contrast between the two types of lovers? **3.** Explain the comparison between a drawing compass and the lovers in the last three stanzas.

Go, Lovely Rose!   1645

EDMUND WALLER [1606–1687]

   Go, lovely rose!
Tell her that wastes her time and me
   That now she knows,
When I resemble° her to thee,   compare
How sweet and fair she seems to be.   5

   Tell her that's young,
And shuns to have her graces spied,
   That hadst thou sprung
In deserts, where no men abide,
Thou must have uncommended died.   10

    Small is the worth
Of beauty from the light retired;
    Bid her come forth,
Suffer herself to be desired,
And not blush so to be admired.   15

    Then die! that she
The common fate of all things rare
    May read in thee;
How small a part of time they share
That are so wondrous sweet and fair!   20

To His Coy Mistress   1681

ANDREW MARVELL   [1621–1678]

    Had we but world enough, and time,
This coyness, lady, were no crime.
We would sit down, and think which way
To walk, and pass our long love's day.
Thou by the Indian Ganges' side   5
Shouldst rubies find; I by the tide
Of Humber would complain. I would
Love you ten years before the flood,
And you should, if you please, refuse
Til the conversion of the Jews.   10
My vegetable love should grow
Vaster than empires and more slow;
An hundred years should go to praise
Thine eyes, and on thy forehead gaze;
Two hundred to adore each breast,   15
But thirty thousand to the rest;
An age at least to every part,
And the last age should show your heart.
For, lady, you deserve this state,
Nor would I love at lower rate.   20
    But at my back I always hear
Time's wingéd chariot hurrying near;
And yonder all before us lie
Deserts of vast eternity.
Thy beauty shall no more be found,   25
Nor, in thy marble vault, shall sound
My echoing song; then worms shall try
That long-preserved virginity,

And your quaint honor turn to dust,
And into ashes all my lust: 30
The grave's a fine and private place,
But none, I think, do there embrace.
   Now therefore, while the youthful hue
Sits on thy skin like morning dew,
And while thy willing soul transpires   35
At every pore with instant fires,
Now let us sport us while we may,
And now, like amorous birds of prey,
Rather at once our time devour
Than languish in his slow-chapped° power.   slow-jawed   40
Let us roll our strength and all
Our sweetness up into one ball,
And tear our pleasures with rough strife
Thorough° the iron gates of life: through
Thus, though we cannot make our sun   45
Stand still, yet we will make him run.

QUESTIONS

1. State the argument of the poem (see ll. 1–2, 21–22, 33–34).   **2.** Compare the figures of speech in the first verse paragraph with those in the last. How do they differ?   **3.** Characterize the attitude toward life recommended by the poet.

WRITING TOPIC

In what ways does the conception of love in this poem differ from that in Donne's "A Valediction: Forbidding Mourning"? In your discussion consider the imagery in both poems.

A Poison Tree   1794

WILLIAM BLAKE   [1757–1827]

I was angry with my friend:
I told my wrath, my wrath did end.
I was angry with my foe:
I told it not, my wrath did grow.

And I watered it in fears,   5
Night & morning with my tears;

And I sunnéd it with smiles,
And with soft deceitful wiles.

And it grew both day and night,
Till it bore an apple bright.   10
And my foe beheld it shine,
And he knew that it was mine,

And into my garden stole,
When the night had veil'd the pole;
In the morning glad I see   15
My foe outstretched beneath the tree.

QUESTIONS
1. Is anything gained from the parallel readers might draw between this tree and the
tree in the Garden of Eden? Explain.   **2.** Can you articulate what the "poison"
is?   **3.** Does your own experience verify the first stanza of the poem?

A Red, Red Rose   1796

ROBERT BURNS   [1759–1796]

O My Luve's like a red, red rose,
    That's newly sprung in June;
O My Luve's like a melodie
    That's sweetly played in tune.

As fair art thou, my bonnie lass,   5
    So deep in luve am I;
And I will luve thee still, my dear,
    Til a' the seas gang dry.

Till a' the seas gang dry, my dear,
    And the rocks melt wi' the sun: 10
O I will love thee still, my dear,
    While the sands o' life shall run.

And fare thee weel, my only luve,
    And fare thee weel awhile!
And I will come again, my luve,   15
    Though it were ten thousand mile.

Porphyria's Lover[1]   1842

ROBERT BROWNING   [1812–1889]

The rain set early in tonight,
    The sullen wind was soon awake,
It tore the elm-tops down for spite,
    And did its worst to vex the lake:
    I listened with heart fit to break.   5
When glided in Porphyria; straight
    She shut the cold out and the storm,
And kneeled and made the cheerless grate
    Blaze up, and all the cottage warm;
    Which done, she rose, and from her form   10
Withdrew the dripping cloak and shawl,
    And laid her soiled gloves by, untied
Her hat and let the damp hair fall,
    And, last, she sat down by my side
    And called me. When no voice replied,   15
She put my arm about her waist,
    And made her smooth white shoulder bare,
And all her yellow hair displaced,
    And, stooping, made my cheek lie there,
    And spread, o'er all, her yellow hair,   20
Murmuring how she loved me—she
    Too weak, for all her heart's endeavor,
To set its struggling passion free
    From pride, and vainer ties dissever,
    And give herself to me forever.   25
But passion sometimes would prevail,
    Nor could tonight's gay feast restrain
A sudden thought of one so pale
    For love of her, and all in vain:
    So, she was come through wind and rain.   30
Be sure I looked up at her eyes
    Happy and proud; at last I knew
Porphyria worshiped me: surprise
    Made my heart swell, and still it grew
    While I debated what to do.   35
That moment she was mine, mine, fair,
    Perfectly pure and good: I found

---

[1] First published with a complementary poem, whose speaker is also a psychopath, under the cover title *Madhouse Cells*.

A thing to do, and all her hair
   In one long yellow string I wound
   Three times her little throat around,   40
And strangled her. No pain felt she;
   I am quite sure she felt no pain.
As a shut bud that holds a bee,
   I warily oped her lids: again
   Laughed the blue eyes without a stain.   45
And I untightened next the tress
   About her neck; her cheek once more
Blushed bright beneath my burning kiss:
   I propped her head up as before,
   Only, this time my shoulder bore   50
Her head, which droops upon it still:
   The smiling rosy little head,
So glad it has its utmost will,
   That all it scorned at once is fled,
   And I, its love, am gained instead!   55
Porphyria's love: she guessed not how
   Her darling one wish would be heard.
And thus we sit together now,
   And all night long we have not stirred,
   And yet God has not said a word!   60

QUESTIONS

1. How do the first five lines set the scene and suggest that there may be something strange about the speaker? **2.** What kind of person is Porphyria? **3.** Some critics find the poem weak because it relies on horror rather than character. Do you agree? Explain. **4.** Why does the speaker's realization that "at last I knew / Porphyria worshiped me" lead him to murder her? **5.** The speaker declares his intent to kill Porphyria with the words, "I found / A thing to do. . . ." How does this phrasing help establish the tone of the poem? What would be the difference if he had said instead, "I had / To kill her now"? **6.** How do the meter and rhythm help create the tone?

WRITING TOPIC

Write a character sketch of Porphyria's lover. Use your imagination in speculating on his past.

from
Song of Myself   1855
WALT WHITMAN   [1819–1892]

11

Twenty-eight young men bathe by the shore,
Twenty-eight young men and all so friendly;
Twenty-eight years of womanly life and all so lonesome.

She owns the fine house by the rise of the bank,
She hides handsome and richly drest aft the blinds of the window.   5

Which of the young men does she like the best?
Ah the homeliest of them is beautiful to her.

Where are you off to, lady? for I see you,
You splash in the water there, yet stay stock still in your room.

Dancing and laughing along the beach came the twenty-ninth bather,   10
The rest did not see her, but she saw them and loved them.

The beards of the young men glisten'd with wet, it ran from their long
    hair,
Little streams pass'd all over their bodies.

An unseen hand also pass'd over their bodies,
It descended tremblingly from their temples and ribs.   15

The young men float on their backs, their white bellies bulge to the sun,
    they do not ask who seizes fast to them,
They do not know who puffs and declines with pendant and bending
    arch,
They do not think whom they souse with spray.

Dover Beach   1867

MATTHEW ARNOLD   [1822–1888]

The sea is calm tonight.
The tide is full, the moon lies fair
Upon the straits; on the French coast the light
Gleams and is gone; the cliffs of England stand,
Glimmering and vast, out in the tranquil bay.   5
Come to the window, sweet is the night-air!
Only, from the long line of spray
Where the sea meets the moon-blanched land,
Listen! you hear the grating roar
Of pebbles which the waves draw back, and fling,   10
At their return, up the high strand,
Begin, and cease, and then again begin,
With tremulous cadence slow, and bring
The eternal note of sadness in.

Sophocles long ago   15
Heard it on the Aegean, and it brought
Into his mind the turbid ebb and flow
Of human misery; we
Find also in the sound a thought,
Hearing it by this distant northern sea.   20

The Sea of Faith
Was once, too, at the full, and round earth's shore
Lay like the folds of a bright girdle furled.
But now I only hear
Its melancholy, long, withdrawing roar,   25
Retreating, to the breath
Of the night-wind, down the vast edges drear
And naked shingles° of the world.   pebble beaches

Ah, love, let us be true
To one another! for the world, which seems   30
To lie before us like a land of dreams,
So various, so beautiful, so new,
Hath really neither joy, nor love, nor light,
Nor certitude, nor peace, nor help for pain;
And we are here as on a darkling plain   35
Swept with confused alarms of struggle and flight,
Where ignorant armies clash by night.

Handwritten annotations:
- wrote about tragedy on human life
- Social
- turbid - sediment stirred up; disorder
- flow - incoming or rise of the tide
- ebb - period of fading away; declining, diminishing. To waste or fall away
- hear misery in the sea
- God →
- sea of faith / world used to have faith
- religion leaving
- land / love →
- be true because world is cruel
- our really
- light of God
- ?

Pied Beauty   1877

GERARD MANLEY HOPKINS   [1844–1889]

Glory be to God for dappled things—
   For skies of couple-colour as a brinded° cow;   brindled
     For rose-moles all in stipple upon trout that swim;
Fresh-firecoal chestnut-falls;[1] finches' wings;
   Landscape plotted and pierced[2]—fold, fallow, and plough;   5
     And all trades, their gear and tackle, and trim.°   equipment
All things counter,° original, spare, strange;   contrasted
   Whatever is fickle, freckled (who knows how?)
     With swift, slow; sweet, sour; adazzle, dim;
He fathers-forth whose beauty is past change: 10
        Praise him.

Fire and Ice   1923

ROBERT FROST   [1874–1963]

Some say the world will end in fire,
Some say in ice,
From what I've tasted of desire
I hold with those who favor fire.
But if it had to perish twice,   5
I think I know enough of hate
To say that for destruction ice
Is also great
And would suffice.

Pied Beauty
  [1] Fallen chestnuts, with the outer husks removed, colored like fresh fire coal.
  [2] Reference to the variegated pattern of land put to different uses.

The Love Song
of J. Alfred Prufrock

1917

T. S. ELIOT   [1888–1965]

S'io credessi che mia risposta fosse
a persona che mai tornasse al mondo,
questa fiamma staria senza più scosse.
Ma per ciò che giammai di questo fondo
non tornò vivo alcun, s'i'odo il vero,
senza tema d'infamia ti rispondo.[1]

Let us go then, you and I,
When the evening is spread out against the sky
Like a patient etherized upon a table;
Let us go, through certain half-deserted streets,
The muttering retreats   5
Of restless nights in one-night cheap hotels
And sawdust restaurants with oyster shells:
Streets that follow like a tedious argument
Of insidious intent
To lead you to an overwhelming question . . .   10
Oh, do not ask, "What is it?"
Let us go and make our visit.

In the room the women come and go
Talking of Michelangelo.

The yellow fog that rubs its back upon the windowpanes,
The yellow smoke that rubs its muzzle on the windowpanes   15
Licked its tongue into the corners of the evening,
Lingered upon the pools that stand in drains,
Let fall upon its back the soot that falls from chimneys,
Slipped by the terrace, made a sudden leap,
And seeing that it was a soft October night,   20
Curled once about the house, and fell asleep.

And indeed there will be time
For the yellow smoke that slides along the street,

---

[1] From Dante, *Inferno*, XXVII, 61–66. The speaker is Guido da Montefeltro, who is imprisoned in a flame in the level of Hell reserved for false counselors. He tells Dante and Virgil, "If I thought my answer were given to one who might return to the world, this flame would stay without further movement. But since from this depth none has ever returned alive, if what I hear is true, I answer you without fear of infamy."

Rubbing its back upon the windowpanes; 25
There will be time, there will be time
To prepare a face to meet the faces that you meet;
There will be time to murder and create,
And time for all the works and days of hands
That lift and drop a question on your plate; 30
Time for you and time for me,
And time yet for a hundred indecisions,
And for a hundred visions and revisions,
Before the taking of a toast and tea.

In the room the women come and go 35
Talking of Michelangelo.

And indeed there will be time
To wonder, "Do I dare?" and, "Do I dare?"
Time to turn back and descend the stair,
With a bald spot in the middle of my hair— 40
(They will say: "How his hair is growing thin!")
My morning coat, my collar mounting firmly to the chin,
My necktie rich and modest, but asserted by a simple pin—
(They will say: "But how his arms and legs are thin!")
Do I dare 45
Disturb the universe?
In a minute there is time
For decisions and revisions which a minute will reverse.

For I have known them all already, known them all—
Have known the evenings, mornings, afternoons,
I have measured out my life with coffee spoons;
I know the voices dying with a dying fall
Beneath the music from a farther room. 50
    So how should I presume?

And I have known the eyes already, known them all— 55
The eyes that fix you in a formulated phrase,
And when I am formulated, sprawling on a pin,
When I am pinned and wriggling on the wall,
Then how should I begin
To spit out all the butt-ends of my days and ways? 60
    And how should I presume?

And I have known the arms already, known them all—
Arms that are braceleted and white and bare
(But in the lamplight, downed with light brown hair!)

Is it perfume from a dress   65
That makes me so digress?
Arms that lie along a table, or wrap about a shawl.
　　And should I then presume?
　　And how should I begin?

　　　　　　　.　.　.　.

Shall I say, I have gone at dusk through narrow streets   70
And watched the smoke that rises from the pipes
Of lonely men in shirt-sleeves, leaning out of windows? . . .

traveling
through   I should have been a pair of ragged claws
hell?   Scuttling across the floors of silent seas.

　　　　　　　.　.　.　.

And the afternoon, the evening, sleeps so peacefully!   75
Smoothed by long fingers,
Asleep . . . tired . . . or it malingers,
Stretched on the floor, here beside you and me.
Should I, after tea and cakes and ices,
Have the strength to force the moment to its crisis?   80
But though I have wept and fasted, wept and prayed,
Though I have seen my head (grown slightly bald) brought in upon a platter,[2]
I am no prophet—and here's no great matter;
I have seen the moment of my greatness flicker,
And I have seen the eternal Footman hold my coat, and snicker,   85
And in short, I was afraid.

And would it have been worth it, after all,
After the cups, the marmalade, the tea,
Among the porcelain, among some talk of you and me,
Would it have been worth while,   90
To have bitten off the matter with a smile,
To have squeezed the universe into a ball
To roll it toward some overwhelming question,
To say: "I am Lazarus,[3] come from the dead,
Come back to tell you all, I shall tell you all"—   95
If one, settling a pillow by her head,
　　Should say: "That is not what I meant at all.
　　That is not it, at all."

And would it have been worth it, after all,
Would it have been worth while,   100
After the sunsets and the dooryards and the sprinkled streets,

---

[2] Like the head of John the Baptist. See Matthew 14:3–12.
[3] See John 11:1–14 and Luke 16:19–26.

After the novels, after the teacups, after the skirts that trail along the floor—
And this, and so much more?—
It is impossible to say just what I mean!
But as if a magic lantern threw the nerves in patterns on a screen: 105
Would it have been worth while
If one, settling a pillow or throwing off a shawl,
And turning toward the window, should say:
    "That is not it at all,
    That is not what I meant, at all."   110

          .   .   .   .

No! I am not Prince Hamlet, nor was meant to be;
Am an attendant lord, one that will do
To swell a progress,° start a scene or two,   state journey
Advise the prince; no doubt, an easy tool,
Deferential, glad to be of use,   115
Politic, cautious, and meticulous;
Full of high sentence,° but a bit obtuse;   sententiousness
At times, indeed, almost ridiculous—
Almost, at times, the Fool.

I grow old . . . I grow old . . .   120
I shall wear the bottoms of my trousers rolled.°   cuffed

Shall I part my hair behind? Do I dare to eat a peach?
I shall wear white flannel trousers, and walk upon the beach.
neaven I have heard the mermaids singing, each to each.

I do not think that they will sing to me.   125

I have seen them riding seaward on the waves
Combing the white hair of the waves blown back
When the wind blows the water white and black.

We have lingered in the chambers of the sea
By sea-girls wreathed with seaweed red and brown   130
Till human voices wake us, and we drown.

QUESTIONS
1. This poem may be understood as a stream of consciousness passing through the mind of Prufrock. The "you and I" of line 1 may be different aspects of his personality. Or perhaps the "you and I" is parallel to Guido who speaks the epigraph and Dante to whom he tells the story that resulted in his damnation—hence, "you" is the reader and "I" is Prufrock. Apparently, Prufrock is on his way to a tea and is pondering his relationship with a certain woman. The poem is disjointed because it

proceeds by psychological rather than logical stages. To what social class does Prufrock belong? How does Prufrock respond to the attitudes and values of his class? Does he change in the course of the poem?   **2.** Line 92 provides a good example of literary allusion (see the last stanza of Marvell, "To His Coy Mistress," especially ll. 41–42). How does an awareness of the allusion contribute to the reader's response to the stanza here?   **3.** What might the song of the mermaids (l. 124) signify, and why does Prufrock think they will not sing to him (l. 125)?   **4.** T. S. Eliot once said that some poetry "can communicate without being understood." Is this such a poem?

WRITING TOPIC
What sort of man is J. Alfred Prufrock? How does the poet establish his characteristics?

if everything happens that can't be done   1944

E. E. CUMMINGS   [1894–1962]

if everything happens that can't be done
(and anything's righter
than books
could plan)
the stupidest teacher will almost guess   5
(with a run
skip
around we go yes)
there's nothing as something as one

one hasn't a why or because or although   10
(and buds know better
than books
don't grow)
one's anything old being everything new
(with a what   15
which
around we come who)
one's everyanything so

so world is a leaf so tree is a bough
(and birds sing sweeter   20
than books

tell how)
so here is away and so your is a my
(with a down
up   25
around again fly)
forever was never till now

now i love you and you love me
(and books are shuter
than books   30
can be)
and deep in the high that does nothing but fall
(with a shout
each
around we go all)   35
there's somebody calling who's we

we're anything brighter than even the sun
(we're everything greater
than books
might mean)   40
we're everyanything more than believe
(with a spin
leap
alive we're alive)
we're wonderful one times one   45

QUESTIONS

1. What fundamental contrast is stated by the poem?   **2.** Lines 2–4 and 6–8 of each stanza could be printed as single lines. Why do you think Cummings decided to print them as he does?   **3.** What common attitude toward lovers is expressed by the last lines of the stanzas?   **4.** Is the poem free verse or formal verse?

WRITING TOPIC

What relation do the parenthetical lines in each stanza bear to the poem as a whole?

Song[1]   1935

C. DAY LEWIS   [1904–1972]

Come, live with me and be my love,
And we will all the pleasures prove
Of peace and plenty, bed and board,
That chance employment may afford.

I'll handle dainties on the docks   5
And thou shalt read of summer frocks:
At evening by the sour canals
We'll hope to hear some madrigals.

Care on thy maiden brow shall put
A wreath of wrinkles, and thy foot
Be shod with pain: not silken dress   10
But toil shall tire thy loveliness.

Hunger shall make thy modest zone
And cheat fond death of all but bone—
If these delights thy mind may move,
Then live with me and be my love.   15

from
Five Songs   (1937)

W. H. AUDEN   [1907–1973]

That night when joy began
Our narrowest veins to flush,
We waited for the flash
Of morning's levelled gun.

But morning let us pass,
And day by day relief
Outgrew his nervous laugh,   5
Grows credulous of peace.

Song
[1] See Christopher Marlowe's "The Passionate Shepherd to His Love," p. 522.

As mile by mile is seen
No trespasser's reproach,   10
And love's best glasses reach
No fields but are his own.

QUESTIONS
1. Describe the sound relationships among the last words in the lines of each stanza.   **2.** What is the controlling metaphor in the poem? Is it appropriate for a love poem?   **3.** If it were suggested that the poem describes a homosexual relationship, would your response to the poem's figurative language change?

My Papa's Waltz   1948

THEODORE ROETHKE   [1908–1963]

The whiskey on your breath
Could make a small boy dizzy;
But I hung on like death:
Such waltzing was not easy.

We romped until the pans   5
Slid from the kitchen shelf;
My mother's countenance
Could not unfrown itself.

The hand that held my wrist
Was battered on one knuckle;   10
At every step you missed
My right ear scraped a buckle.

You beat time on my head
With a palm caked hard by dirt,
Then waltzed me off to bed   15
Still clinging to your shirt.

QUESTIONS
1. Why is iambic trimeter an appropriate meter for this poem?   **2.** Identify the details that reveal the kind of person the father is.   **3.** How would you characterize the boy's feelings about his father? The father's about the boy?

WRITING TOPIC
Robert Hayden's "Those Winter Sundays," Ted Hughes's "Crow's First Lesson," and

Sylvia Plath's "Daddy" also deal with a child's feelings about a parent. Compare one of them with this poem.

One Art†   1976

ELIZABETH BISHOP [1911–1979]

The art of losing isn't hard to master;
so many things seem filled with the intent
to be lost that their loss is no disaster.

Lose something every day. Accept the fluster
of lost door keys, the hour badly spent.   5
The art of losing isn't hard to master.

Then practice losing farther, losing faster:
places, and names, and where it was you meant
to travel. None of these will bring disaster.

I lost my mother's watch. And look! my last, or   10
next-to-last, of three loved houses went.
The art of losing isn't hard to master.

I lost two cities, lovely ones. And, vaster,
some realms I owned, two rivers, a continent.
I miss them, but it wasn't a disaster.   15

—Even losing you (the joking voice, a gesture
I love) I shan't have lied. It's evident
the art of losing's not too hard to master
though it may look like (*Write* it!) like disaster.

AIDS   1988

MAY SARTON   [b. 1912]

We are stretched to meet a new dimension
Of love, a more demanding range
Where despair and hope must intertwine.
How grow to meet it? Intention
Here can neither move nor change   5

The raw truth. Death is on the line.
It comes to separate and estrange
Lover from lover in some reckless design.
Where do we go from here?

Fear.   Fear.   Fear.   Fear.   10

Our world has never been more stark
Or more in peril.
It is very lonely now in the dark.
Lonely and sterile.

And yet in the simple turn of a head   15
Mercy lives. I heard it when someone said
"I must go now to a dying friend.
Every night at nine I tuck him into bed,
And give him a shot of morphine,"
And added, "I go where I have never been."   20
I saw he meant into a new discipline
He had not imagined before, and a new grace.

Every day now we meet it face to face.
Every day now devotion is the test.
Through the long hours, the hard, caring nights   25
We are forging a new union. We are blest.

As closed hands open to each other
Closed lives open to strange tenderness.
We are learning the hard way how to mother.
Who says it is easy? But we have the power.   30
I watch the faces deepen all around me.
It is the time of change, the saving hour.
The word is not fear, the word we live,
But an old word suddenly made new,
As we learn it again, as we bring it alive: 35

Love.   Love.   Love.   Love.

QUESTIONS
1. Paraphrase the first three lines.   **2.** Explain the difference between "separate"
and "estrange" (l. 7).   **3.** What is the meaning of "reckless design" (l. 8)?   **4.** What
does the speaker mean by "new discipline" (l. 21) and "new grace" (l. 22)?
5. Who are the "We" of line 26, and why are they "blest"?

WRITING TOPIC
Argue either for or against the assertion that the specter of AIDS has brought about a "time of change" and that fear is giving way to love.

Those Winter Sundays   1975

ROBERT HAYDEN   [1913–1980]

Sundays too my father got up early
and put his clothes on in the blueblack cold,
then with cracked hands that ached
from labor in the weekday weather made
banked fires blaze. No one ever thanked him.   5

I'd wake and hear the cold splintering, breaking.
When the rooms were warm, he'd call,
and slowly I would rise and dress,
fearing the chronic angers of that house,

Speaking indifferently to him,   10
who had driven out the cold
and polished my good shoes as well.
What did I know, what did I know
of love's austere and lonely offices?

A Late Aubade   1968

RICHARD WILBUR   [b. 1921]

You could be sitting now in a carrel
Turning some liver-spotted page,
Or rising in an elevator-cage
Toward Ladies' Apparel.

You could be planting a raucous bed   5
Of salvia, in rubber gloves,
Or lunching through a screed of someone's loves
With pitying head,

Or making some unhappy setter
Heel, or listening to a bleak   10

Lecture on Schoenberg's serial technique.[1]
Isn't this better?

Think of all the time you are not
Wasting, and would not care to waste,
Such things, thank God, not being to your taste.   15
Think what a lot

Of time, by woman's reckoning,
You've saved, and so may spend on this,
You who had rather lie in bed and kiss
Than anything.   20

It's almost noon, you say? If so,
Time flies, and I need not rehearse
The rosebuds-theme of centuries of verse.[2]
If you *must* go,

Wait for a while, then slip downstairs   25
And bring us up some chilled white wine,
And some blue cheese, and crackers, and some fine
Ruddy-skinned pears.

QUESTIONS
1. Explain the title.   **2.** Is the speaker a sexist? Explain.   **3.** Explain lines 16–18.

The Dover Bitch   1968
A CRITICISM OF LIFE

ANTHONY HECHT   [b. 1923]

So there stood Matthew Arnold and this girl
With the cliffs of England crumbling away behind them,
And he said to her, "Try to be true to me,
And I'll do the same for you, for things are bad
All over, etc., etc."   5
Well now, I knew this girl. It's true she had read
Sophocles in a fairly good translation

A *Late Aubade*
   [1]Arnold Schoenberg (1874–1951), Austrian-born composer.
   [2]The *Carpe Diem* theme (see Glossary of Literary Terms).

And caught that bitter allusion to the sea,
But all the time he was talking she had in mind
The notion of what his whiskers would feel like   10
On the back of her neck. She told me later on
That after a while she got to looking out
At the lights across the channel, and really felt sad,
Thinking of all the wine and enormous beds
And blandishments in French and the perfumes.   15
And then she got really angry. To have been brought
All the way down from London, and then be addressed
As a sort of mournful cosmic last resort
Is really tough on a girl, and she was pretty.
Anyway, she watched him pace the room   20
And finger his watch-chain and seem to sweat a bit,
And then she said one or two unprintable things.
But you mustn't judge her by that. What I mean to say is,
She's really all right. I still see her once in a while
And she always treats me right. We have a drink
And I give her a good time, and perhaps it's a year
Before I see her again, but there she is,
Running to fat, but dependable as they come,
And sometimes I bring her a bottle of *Nuit d'Amour*.

[handwritten annotations: "Flattering comments"; "night of love"; "(cheap perfume)"; and diagonal note: "She read Sophocles but doesn't see his allusion, but rather literal sadness across the channel / the things great all she can't have / sadness doesn't have for her"]

QUESTIONS

1. This poem is a response to Matthew Arnold's "Dover Beach," which appears earlier in this section. Arnold's poem is often read as a pained response to the breakdown of religious tradition and social and political order in the mid-nineteenth century. Is this poem, in contrast, optimistic? Is the relationship between the speaker and the girl at the end of the poem admirable? Explain.   **2.** Do you suppose Hecht was moved to write this poem out of admiration for "Dover Beach"? Explain.

WRITING TOPIC

What is the fundamental difference between the speaker's conception of love in Arnold's poem and the "girl's" conception of love as reported in this poem?

The Mutes   1967

DENISE LEVERTOV [b. 1923]

Those groans men use
passing a woman on the street
or on the steps of the subway

to tell her she is a female
and their flesh knows it,   5

are they a sort of tune,
an ugly enough song, sung
by a bird with a slit tongue

but meant for music?

Or are they the muffled roaring   10
of deafmutes trapped in a building that is
slowly filling with smoke?

Perhaps both.

Such men most often
look as if groan were all they could do,   15
yet a woman, in spite of herself,

knows it's a tribute:
if she were lacking all grace
they'd pass her in silence:

so it's not only to say she's   20
a warm hole. It's a word

in grief-language, nothing to do with
primitive, not an ur-language;[1]
language stricken, sickened, cast down

in decrepitude. She wants to   25
throw the tribute away, dis-
gusted, and can't,

it goes on buzzing in her ear,
it changes the pace of her walk,
the torn posters in echoing corridors   30

spell it out, it
quakes and gnashes as the train comes in.
Her pulse sullenly

---

[1] Primordial language.

had picked up speed,
but the cars slow down and   35
jar to a stop while her understanding

keeps on translating:
'Life after life after life goes by

without poetry,
without seemliness,   40
without love.'

QUESTIONS
1. Explain the title.   **2.** Why does the tribute go on "buzzing in her ear" (l. 28)?
3. Is this poem an attack on men? Explain.

Bitch   1984

CAROLYN KIZER   [b. 1925]

Now, when he and I meet, after all these years,
I say to the bitch inside me, don't start growling.
He isn't a trespasser anymore,
Just an old acquaintance tipping his hat.
My voice says, "Nice to see you,"   5
As the bitch starts to bark hysterically.
He isn't an enemy now,
Where are your manners, I say, as I say,
"How are the children? They must be growing up."
At a kind word from him, a look like the old days,   10
The bitch changes her tone: she begins to whimper.
She wants to snuggle up to him, to cringe.
Down, girl! Keep your distance
Or I'll give you a taste of the choke-chain.
"Fine, I'm just fine," I tell him.   15
She slobbers and grovels.
After all, I am her mistress. She is basically loyal.
It's just that she remembers how she came running
Each evening, when she heard his step;
How she lay at his feet and looked up adoringly   20
Though he was absorbed in his paper;
Or, bored with her devotion, ordered her to the kitchen
Until he was ready to play.
But the small careless kindnesses

When he'd had a good day, or a couple of drinks,   25
Come back to her now, seem more important
Than the casual cruelties, the ultimate dismissal.
"It's nice to know you are doing so well," I say.
He couldn't have taken you with him;
You were too demonstrative, too clumsy,   30
Not like the well-groomed pets of his new friends.
"Give my regards to your wife," I say. You gag
As I drag you off by the scruff,
Saying, "Goodbye! Goodbye! Nice to have seen you again."

QUESTIONS
1. Who is being addressed in lines 13 and 14?   **2.** In what ways does the title suit
the poem? Consider the tone of "Bitch," as well as the many connotations of the
word, in answering this question.   **3.** What is "the ultimate dismissal" referred to in
line 27?   **4.** How would you describe the speaker's present feelings about her
former relationship?

The Farmer's Wife   1960

ANNE SEXTON   [1928–1974]

From the hodge porridge
of their country lust,
their local life in Illinois,
where all their acres look
like a sprouting broom factory,   5
they name just ten years now
that she has been his habit;
as again tonight he'll say
honey bunch let's go
and she will not say how there   10
must be more to living
than this brief bright bridge
of the raucous bed or even
the slow braille touch of him
like a heavy god grown light,   15
that old pantomime of love
that she wants although
it leaves her still alone,
built back again at last,
minds apart from him, living   20
her own self in her own words

and hating the sweat of the house
they keep when they finally lie
each in separate dreams
and then how she watches him,   25
still strong in the blowzy bag
of his usual sleep while
her young years bungle past
their same marriage bed
and she wishes him cripple, or poet,   30
or even lonely, or sometimes,
better, my lover, dead.

Living in Sin   1955

ADRIENNE RICH [b. 1929]

She had thought the studio would keep itself;
no dust upon the furniture of love.
Half heresy, to wish the taps less vocal,
the panes relieved of grime. A plate of pears,
a piano with a Persian shawl, a cat   5
stalking the picturesque amusing mouse
had risen at his urging.
Not that at five each separate stair would writhe
under the milkman's tramp; that morning light
so coldly would delineate the scraps   10
of last night's cheese and three sepulchral bottles;
that on the kitchen shelf among the saucers
a pair of beetle-eyes would fix her own—
Envoy from some village in the moldings . . .
Meanwhile, he, with a yawn,   15
sounded a dozen notes upon the keyboard,
declared it out of tune, shrugged at the mirror,
rubbed at his beard, went out for cigarettes;
while she, jeered by the minor demons,
pulled back the sheets and made the bed and found   20
a towel to dust the table-top,
and let the coffee-pot boil over on the stove.
By evening she was back in love again,
though not so wholly but throughout the night
she woke sometimes to feel the daylight coming   25
like a relentless milkman up the stairs.

Crow's First Lesson[1]

1970

TED HUGHES [b. 1930]

God tried to teach Crow how to talk.
"Love," said God. "Say, Love."
Crow gaped, and the white shark crashed into the sea *predator*
And went rolling downwards, discovering its own depth.

"No, no," said God, "Say Love, Now try it. LOVE." *gape—1) to open* 5
Crow gaped, and a bluefly, a tsetse, a mosquito *mouth wide,*
Zoomed out and down *represent disease* *2) 2 stare, as with*
To their sundry flesh-pots. *the mouth open*

retched - vomit

"A final try," said God. "Now, LOVE."
Crow convulsed, gaped, retched and 10
Man's bodiless prodigious head *prodigious - enormous,*
Bulbed out onto the earth, with swivelling eyes, *extraordinary*
Jabbering protest—

And Crow retched again, before God could stop him.
And woman's vulva dropped over man's neck and tightened. 15
The two struggled together on the grass.
God struggled to part them, cursed, wept—

Crow flew guiltily off.

Daddy

1965

SYLVIA PLATH [1932–1963]

You do not do, you do not do
Any more, black shoe
In which I have lived like a foot
For thirty years, poor and white,
Barely daring to breathe or Achoo. 5

Daddy, I have had to kill you,
You died before I had time—

Crow's First Lesson
[1] In Hughes's collection of poems about him, Crow seems to be a demigod, combining human and animal traits. His exploits form a kind of creation myth.

Marble-heavy, a bag full of God, *father dies*
Ghastly statue with one gray toe
Big as a Frisco seal   10

And a head in the freakish Atlantic
Where it pours bean green over blue
In the waters off beautiful Nauset.
I used to pray to recover you.
Ach, du.[1]   15

In the German tongue, in the Polish town
Scraped flat by the roller
Of wars, wars, wars.
But the name of the town is common.
My Polack friend   20   *use german/jewish imagery*

Says there are a dozen or two.
So I never could tell where you
Put your foot, your root,
I never could talk to you.
The tongue stuck in my jaw.   25

It stuck in a barb wire snare.
Ich, ich, ich, ich,[2]
I could hardly speak.
I thought every German was you.
And the language obscene   30

An engine, an engine
Chuffing me off like a Jew.
A Jew to Dachau, Auschwitz, Belsen.
I began to talk like a Jew.
I think I may well be a Jew.   35

The snows of the Tyrol, the clear beer of Vienna   *Tyrol – a region & former*
Are not very pure or true.   *Austrian crown territory in*
With my gypsy ancestress and my weird luck   *W. Austria & N. Italy*
And my Taroc pack and my Taroc pack   *Taroc – card game*
I may be a bit of a Jew.   40

I have always been scared of *you*,
With your Luftwaffe,[3] your gobbledygoo.

---

[1] German for "Ah, you."
[2] German for "I, I, I, I."
[3] Name of the German air force during World War II.

And your neat mustache
And your Aryan eye, bright blue.   *Aryan- Nazi ideology,*
Panzer-man,[4] panzer-man, O You—   *a Caucasian gentile, esp.*   45
    of Nordic type

Not God but a swastika
So black no sky could squeak through.
Every woman adores a Fascist,
The boot in the face, the brute
Brute heart of a brute like you.   50

You stand at the blackboard, daddy,
In the picture I have of you,
A cleft in your chin instead of your foot   *cleft - divide, split*
But no less a devil for that, no not
Any less the black man who   55

Bit my pretty red heart in two.
I was ten when they buried you.
At twenty I tried to die
And get back, back, back to you.
I thought even the bones would do   60

But they pulled me out of the sack,
And they stuck me together with glue.
And then I knew what to do.
I made a model of you,
A man in black with a Meinkampf[5] look   65

who she { And a love of the rack and the screw.
marries { And I said I do, I do.
So daddy, I'm finally through.
The black telephone's off at the root,
The voices just can't worm through.   70

If I've killed one man, I've killed two—
The vampire who said he was you
And drank my blood for a year,
Seven years, if you want to know.
Daddy, you can lie back now.   75

---

[4] Panzer refers to German armored divisions during World War II.
[5] *My Battle,* the title of Adolf Hitler's political autobiography.

There's a stake in your fat black heart
And the villagers never liked you.
They are dancing and stamping on you.
They always *knew* it was you.
Daddy, daddy, you bastard, I'm through.   80

QUESTIONS

1. How do the allusions to Nazism function in the poem?   **2.** Does the poem exhibit the speaker's love for her father or her hatred for him? Explain.   **3.** What sort of man does the speaker marry (see stanzas 13 and 14)?   **4.** How does the speaker characterize her husband and her father in the last two stanzas? Might the "Daddy" of the last line of the poem refer to something more than the speaker's father? Explain.

WRITING TOPIC

What is the effect of the peculiar structure, idiosyncratic rhyme, unusual words (such as *achoo, gobbledygoo*), and repetitions in the poem? What emotional associations does the title "Daddy" possess? Are those associations reinforced or contradicted by the poem?

Power¹   1978

AUDRE LORDE   [1934–1992]

The difference between poetry and rhetoric
is being
ready to kill
yourself
instead of your children.   5

I am trapped on a desert of raw gunshot wounds
and a dead child dragging his shattered black
face off the edge of my sleep
blood from his punctured cheeks and shoulders

Power
    ¹ " 'Power' . . . is a poem written about Clifford Glover, the ten-year-old Black child shot by a cop who was acquitted by a jury on which a Black woman sat. In fact, the day I heard on the radio that O'Shea had been acquitted, I was going across town on Eighty-eighth Street and I had to pull over. A kind of fury rose up in me; the sky turned red. I felt so sick. I felt as if I would drive this car into a wall, into the next person I saw. So I pulled over. I took out my journal just to air some of my fury, to get it out of my fingertips. Those expressed feelings are that poem" (Audre Lorde, "My Words Will Be There," in *Black Women Writers (1950–1980)*, ed. Mari Evans, New York, 1983, p. 266).

is the only liquid for miles and my stomach   10
churns at the imagined taste while
my mouth splits into dry lips
without loyalty or reason
thirsting for the wetness of his blood
as it sinks into the whiteness   15
of the desert where I am lost
without imagery or magic
trying to make power out of hatred and destruction
trying to heal my dying son with kisses
only the sun will bleach his bones quicker.   20

The policeman who shot down a 10-year-old in Queens[2]
stood over the boy with his cop shoes in childish blood
and a voice said "Die you little motherfucker" and
there are tapes to prove that. At his trial
this policeman said in his own defense   25
"I didn't notice the size or nothing else
only the color." and
there are tapes to prove that, too.

Today that 37-year-old white man with 13 years of police forcing
has been set free   30
by 11 white men who said they were satisfied
justice had been done
and one black woman who said
"They convinced me" meaning
they had dragged her 4' 10" black woman's frame   35
over the hot coals of four centuries of white male approval
until she let go the first real power she ever had
and lined her own womb with cement
to make a graveyard for our children.

I have not been able to touch the destruction within me.   40
But unless I learn to use
the difference between poetry and rhetoric
my power too will run corrupt as poisonous mold
or lie limp and useless as an unconnected wire
and one day I will take my teenaged plug   45
and connect it to the nearest socket
raping an 85-year-old white woman
who is somebody's mother

---

[2] Queens is a borough in New York City.

and as I beat her senseless and set a torch to her bed
a greek chorus will be singing in ¾ time[3]   50
"Poor thing. She never hurt a soul. What beasts they are."

There Is a Girl Inside   1977

LUCILLE CLIFTON   [b. 1936]

there is a girl inside.
she is randy as a wolf.
she will not walk away
and leave these bones
to an old woman.   5

she is a green tree
in a forest of kindling.
she is a green girl
in a used poet.

she has waited   10
patient as a nun
for the second coming,
when she can break through gray hairs
into blossom

and her lovers will harvest   15
honey and thyme
and the woods will be wild
with the damn wonder of it.

QUESTIONS

1. Who is the "girl" of this poem? What is she "inside" of?   **2.** What are the "bones" of the first stanza? What does the speaker's statement that she will not defer to old women tell us about her?   **3.** Describe the prevailing metaphor of the poem.

WRITING TOPIC

Compare this poem with Helen Sorrells's "From a Correct Address in a Suburb of a Major City." What do the two speakers share? In what ways are they different?

Power
   [3] In classical Greek tragedy, a chorus chanted in response to the action in the play. Three-quarter time is waltz rhythm.

Hard Mornings (1)   1973

KATHLEEN WIEGNER   [b. 1938]

You would take
everything
I had

and say
you'd earned it   5

with your
young body
and occasional
concern

as if it were hard.   10

At times
you stand
at the bedroom
window excited
by the girls' legs   15
flashing in the street

as if I had not
been with you
all night
long.   20

One time
you got excited
just talking
about them,

God, you said,   25
those short skirts
and I was lying
beside you
with nothing on.

The Trains   1984

WILLIAM HEYEN   [b. 1940]

Signed by Franz Paul Stangl, Commandant,
there is in Berlin a document,
an order of transmittal from Treblinka:[1]

248 freight cars of clothing,
400,000 gold watches,   5
25 freight cars of women's hair.

Some clothing was kept, some pulped for paper.
The finest watches were never melted down.
All the women's hair was used for mattresses, or dolls.

Would these words like to use some of that same paper?   10
One of those watches may pulse in your own wrist.
Does someone you know collect dolls, or sleep on human hair?

He is dead at last, Commandant Stangl of Treblinka,
but the camp's three syllables still sound like freight cars
straining around a curve, Treblinka,   15

Treblinka. Clothing, time in gold watches,
women's hair for mattresses and dolls' heads.
Treblinka. The trains from Treblinka.

QUESTIONS
1. Show how the language of this poem (diction, imagery, sound pattern) evokes an emotional response.   **2.** How can such language, quietly celebrating the thrift and productivity of the Treblinka staff, generate such a response?   **3.** Discuss the poet's use of *Treblinka* as a pattern of sound.

WRITING TOPIC
Compare this poem with Anthony Hecht's "'More Light! More Light!'" and analyze the techniques each poet uses to move his readers.

---

[1] A notorious Nazi concentration camp and extermination center located in Poland, northeast of Warsaw.

Sex without Love   1984

SHARON OLDS   [b. 1942]

How do they do it, the ones who make love
without love? Beautiful as dancers,
gliding over each other like ice skaters
over the ice, fingers hooked
inside each other's bodies, faces   5
red as steak, wine, wet as the
children at birth whose mothers are going to
give them away. How do they come to the
come to the   come to the   God   come to the
still waters, and not love   10
the one who came there with them, light
rising slowly as steam off their joined
skin? These are the true religious,
the purists, the pros, the ones who will not
accept a false Messiah, love the   15
priest instead of the God. They do not
mistake the lover for their own pleasure,
they are like great runners: they know they are alone
with the road surface, the cold, the wind,
the fit of their shoes, their over-all cardio-   20
vascular health—just factors, like the partner
in the bed, and not the truth, which is the
single body alone in the universe
against its own best time.

QUESTIONS
1. Characterize the speaker's attitude toward "the ones who make love without
love."   **2.** Who are the "These" of line 13?   **3.** What is the effect of the repetitions
in lines 8 and 9?   **4.** What does "factors" of line 21 refer to?   **5.** Put into your own
words the "truth" referred to in the final three lines. Is the speaker using the word
straightforwardly or ironically? Explain.

Say You Love Me   1989

MOLLY PEACOCK   [b. 1947]

What happened earlier I'm not sure of.
Of course he was drunk, but often he was.
His face looked like a ham on a hook above

me—I was pinned to the chair because
he'd hunkered over me with arms like jaws   5
pried open by the chair arms. "Do you love

me?" he began to sob. "Say you love me!"
I held out. I was probably fifteen.
What had happened? Had my mother—had she

said or done something? Or had he just been   10
drinking too long after work? "He'll get *mean*,"
my sister hissed, "just *tell* him." I brought my knee

up to kick him, but was too scared. Nothing
could have got the words out of me then. Rage
shut me up, yet "DO YOU?" was beginning   15

to peel, as of live layers of skin, age
from age from age from him until he gazed
through hysteria as a wet baby thing

repeating, "Do you love me? Say you do,"
in baby chokes, only loud, for they came   20
from a man. There wouldn't be a rescue

from my mother, still at work. The same
choking sobs said, "Love me, love me," and my game
was breaking down because I couldn't do

anything, not escape into my own   25
refusal, *I won't, I won't*, not fantasize
a kind, rich father, not fill the narrowed zone,

empty except for confusion until the size
of my fear ballooned as I saw his eyes,
blurred, taurean—my sister screamed—unknown,   30

unknown to me, a voice rose and leveled
off, "I love you," I said. *"Say 'I love you,
Dad!' "* "I love you, Dad," I whispered, leveled

by defeat into a cardboard image, untrue,
unbending. I was surprised I could move   35
as I did to get up, but he stayed, burled

onto the chair—my monstrous fear—she screamed,
my sister, "Dad, the phone! Go answer it!"
The phone wasn't ringing, yet he seemed

to move toward it, and I ran. He had a fit—   40
"It's not ringing!"—but I was at the edge of it
as he collapsed into the chair and blamed

both of us at a distance. No, the phone
was not ringing. There was no world out there,
so there we remained, completely alone.   45

QUESTIONS

1. Is the speaker a child or an adult? Explain.   **2.** How do the images of the sixth
stanza capture the speaker's feelings?   **3.** When the speaker finally capitulates to
her father's demand, she describes herself as "leveled / by defeat into a cardboard
image, untrue, / unbending." What does she mean?   **4.** Explain what the speaker
means by "my game" (l. 23).

WRITING TOPIC

What would motivate a parent, even a drunken one, to make the kind of demand the
father makes on his daughter?

The Sunday News   1986

DANA GIOIA   [b. 1950]

Looking for something in the Sunday paper,
I flipped by accident through *Local Weddings*,
Yet missed the photograph until I saw
Your name among the headings.

And there you were, looking almost unchanged,   5
Your hair still long, though now long out of style,

And you still wore that stiff and serious look
You called a smile.

I felt as though we sat there face to face.
My stomach tightened. I read the item through.   10
It said too much about both families,
Too little about you.

Finished at last, I threw the paper down,
Stung by jealousy, my mind aflame,
Hating this man, this stranger whom you loved,   15
This printed name.

And yet I clipped it out to put away
Inside a book like something I might use,
A scrap I knew I wouldn't read again
But couldn't bear to lose.   20

WRITING TOPIC

Write an essay in which you analyze the feelings that might cause a rejected suitor
to do what the speaker describes doing in the final stanza.

Teodoro Luna's Two Kisses   1990

ALBERTO RÍOS   [b. 1952]

Mr. Teodoro Luna in his later years had taken to kissing
His wife
Not so much with his lips as with his brows.
This is not to say he put his forehead
Against her mouth—   5
Rather, he would lift his eyebrows, once, quickly:
Not so vigorously he might be confused with the villain
Famous in the theaters, but not so little as to be thought
A slight movement, one of accident. This way
He kissed her   10
Often and quietly, across tables and through doorways,
Sometimes in photographs, and so through the years themselves.
This was his passion, that only she might see. The chance
He might feel some movement on her lips
Toward laughter.   15

QUESTIONS
1. Characterize the tone of this poem.   **2.** What kind of person is Teodoro Luna?
What kind of person is his wife?   **3.** What is the purpose of Teodoro Luna's second
kind of kiss? Do we know whether he achieves his purpose? Explain.

WRITING TOPIC
Use your imagination to speculate on the nature of Teodoro Luna's marriage and
how it might have led him to devise his unusual way of kissing his wife.

Self-Portrait with Politics   1984

KATE DANIELS   [b. 1953]

At the dinner table, my brother says something
Republican he knows I will hate.
He has said it only for me, hoping
I will rise to the argument as I usually do
so he can call me "communist"   5
and accuse me of terrible things—not loving
the family, hating the country, unsatisfied
with my life. I feel my fingers tighten
on my fork and ask for more creamed potatoes
to give me time to think.   10

He's right: It's true I am not satisfied
with life. Each time I come home
my brother hates me more for the life
of the mind I have chosen to live.
He works in a factory and can never understand   15
why I am paid a salary for teaching poetry
just as I can never understand his factory job
where everyone loves or hates the boss like god.
He was so intelligent as a child
his teachers were scared of him.   20
He did everything well and fast
and then shot rubberbands at the girls' legs
and metal lunchboxes lined up neatly beneath the desks.
Since then, something happened I don't know about.
Now he drives a forklift every day.   25
He moves things in boxes from one place
to another place. I have never worked

in a factory and can only imagine
the tedium, the thousand escapes
the bright mind must make.   30

But tonight I will not fight again.
I just nod and swallow and in spite
of everything remember my brother as a child.
When I was six and he was five, I taught him everything
I learned in school each day while we waited for dinner.   35
I remember his face—smiling always,
the round, brown eyes, and how his lower lip
seemed always wet and ready to kiss.
I remember for a long time his goal in life
was to be a dog, how we were forced   40
to scratch his head, the pathetic sound
of his human bark. Now he glowers
and acts like a tyrant and cannot eat
and thinks I think
I am superior to him.   45

The others ignore him as they usually do:
My mother with her bristly hair.
My father just wanting to get back to the TV.
My husband rolling his eyes in a warning at me.

It has taken a long time to get a politics   50
I can live with in a world that gave me
poetry and my brother an assembly line.
I accept my brother for what he is
and believe in the beauty of work
but also know the reality of waste,   55
the good minds ground down through circumstance
and loss. I mourn the loss of all I think
he could have been, and this is what he feels,
I guess, and cannot face and hates me
for reminding him of what is gone and wasted   60
and won't come back.

For once, it's too sad to know all this.
So I give my brother back his responsibility
or blandly blame it all on sociology,
and imagine sadly how it could have been different,   65
how it will be different for the son I'll bear.
And how I hope in thirty years he'll touch

his sister as they touched as children
and let nothing come between the blood they share.

QUESTIONS
1. Characterize the speaker's feelings toward her brother. Does her brother have
reason to think she feels superior to him? Explain.   **2.** The speaker says that her
brother is right that she is not satisfied with her life. Is her brother satisfied with his
life? Explain.   **3.** Explain the effect of the simile in line 18.   **4.** What do lines
39–42 add to the speaker's self-portrait?   **5.** Paraphrase lines 62–64.

WRITING TOPICS
1. Write an essay or a letter as if you were the speaker's brother responding to the
poem.   **2.** If you have had an experience similar to the one described in this poem
of becoming alienated from a brother or sister because your lives have taken different
directions, describe how and when the estrangement occurred and how you have
dealt with it.

Complaint   1985

GJERTRUD SCHNACKENBERG   [b. 1953]

I lean over the rail toward the dark town,
The rail a streak of cloud in piled snow,
The stairs cloud-piled around the balcony.
His house is lit below,

One light among the branches at my feet.   5
I look, and press my hands into the snow.
I think that I am inconsolable.
No path to him, I know

Of none but that I follow into sleep
To where he waits, I hurry through the snow   10
To where the man stands waiting in the dream.
He loves, he tells me so,

He kisses me until the ceiling dome
Parts overhead and snow is coming through,
Until heaven itself, empty of snow,   15
Opens above us too,

His hands melting the snow into my hair
Until I wake. Since he'll not have me, no,

I come out to the balcony and press
My hands into the snow,   20

And close my eyes, since he is blind to me.
Since he'll not hear me, then I'll be deaf too,
And draw my hair into a set of strings
I'll take a scissors to.

QUESTIONS
1. Characterize the speaker.   **2.** What is her problem?   **3.** What is her only path to
the man she loves? Characterize her "meeting" with him.   **4.** How does she propose to deal with her inability to attract the man?

WRITING TOPIC
Describe the unusual metrical pattern and rhyme scheme in this poem. Defend the
proposition that the formal structure of the poem reinforces its sense.

LOVE
AND
HATE

Judith and Her Maidservant with the Head of Holofernes, ca. 1625 by Artemisia Gentileschi

DRAMA

Othello

ca. 1604

WILLIAM SHAKESPEARE [1564–1616]

CHARACTERS

Duke of Venice
Brabantio, a Senator
Senators
Gratiano, Brother to Brabantio
Lodovico, Kinsman to Brabantio
Othello, a noble Moor; in the service of the Venetian State
Cassio, his Lieutenant
Iago, his Ancient
Roderigo, a Venetian Gentleman

Montano, Othello's predecessor in the Government of Cyprus
Clown, Servant to Othello
Desdemona, Daughter to Brabantio, and Wife to Othello
Emilia, Wife to Iago
Bianca, Mistress to Cassio
Sailor, Officers, Gentlemen, Messengers, Musicians, Heralds, Attendants

SCENE

For the first Act, in Venice; during the rest of the Play, at a Sea-port in Cyprus

Act I

SCENE 1. *Venice. A Street.*

(*Enter Roderigo and Iago.*)

Roderigo.   Tush! Never tell me; I take it much unkindly
  That thou, Iago, who has had my purse
  As if the strings were thine, shouldst know of this.[1]
Iago.   'Sblood,[2] but you will not hear me:

---

[1] I.e., Othello's successful courtship of Desdemona.   [2] By God's blood.

If ever I did dream of such a matter,   5
   Abhor me.
Roderigo.   Thou told'st me thou didst hold him[3] in thy hate.
Iago.   Despise me if I do not. Three great ones of the city,
   In personal suit to make me his lieutenant,
   Off-capp'd[4] to him; and, by the faith of man,   10
   I know my price, I am worth no worse a place;
   But he, as loving his own pride and purposes,
   Evades them, with a bombast circumstance[5]
   Horribly stuff'd with epithets of war;
   And, in conclusion,   15
   Nonsuits[6] my mediators;[7] for, 'Certes,'[8] says he,
   'I have already chosen my officer.'
   And what was he?
   Forsooth, a great arithmetician,
   One Michael Cassio, a Florentine,   20
   A fellow almost damn'd in a fair wife;[9]
   That never set a squadron in the field,
   Nor the division of a battle knows
   More than a spinster; unless[10] the bookish theoric,[11]
   Wherein the toged consuls can propose   25
   As masterly as he: mere prattle, without practice,
   Is all his soldiership. But he, sir, had the election;
   And I—of whom his eyes had seen the proof
   At Rhodes, at Cyprus, and on other grounds
   Christian and heathen—must be be-lee'd[12] and calm'd   30
   By debitor and creditor; this counter-caster,[13]
   He, in good time, must his lieutenant be,
   And I—God bless the mark!—his Moorship's ancient.[14]
Roderigo.   By heaven, I rather would have been his hangman.
Iago.   Why, there's no remedy: 'tis the curse of service,   35
   Preferment goes by letter and affection,
   Not by the old gradation,[15] where each second
   Stood heir to the first. Now, sir, be judge yourself,
   Whe'r[16] I in any just term am affin'd[17]
   To love the Moor.
Roderigo.   I would not follow him then.   40

---

[3] I.e., Othello.   [4] Took off their caps.   [5] Pompous wordiness, circumlocution.
[6] Turns down.   [7] Spokesmen.   [8] In truth.   [9] A much debated phrase. In the
Italian source the Captain (i.e., Cassio) was married, and it may be that Shakespeare originally
intended Bianca to be Cassio's wife but later changed his mind and failed to alter the phrase
here accordingly. Or perhaps Iago simply sneers at Cassio as a notorious ladies' man.
[10] Except.   [11] Theory.   [12] Left without wind for my sails.   [13] Bookkeeper (cf.
"arithmetician" above).   [14] Ensign (but Iago's position in the play seems to be that of
Othello's aide-de-camp).   [15] Seniority.   [16] Whether.   [17] Obliged.

Iago. O! sir, content you;
  I follow him to serve my turn upon him;
  We cannot all be masters, nor all masters
  Cannot be truly follow'd. You shall mark
  Many a duteous and knee-crooking knave,   45
  That, doting on his own obsequious bondage,
  Wears out his time, much like his master's ass,
  For nought but provender, and when he's old, cashier'd;
  Whip me such honest knaves. Others there are
  Who, trimm'd in forms and visages of duty,   50
  Keep yet their hearts attending on themselves,
  And, throwing but shows of service on their lords,
  Do well thrive by them, and when they have lin'd their coats
  Do themselves homage: these fellows have some soul;
  And such a one do I profess myself. For, sir,   55
  It is as sure as you are Roderigo,
  Were I the Moor, I would not be Iago:
  In following him, I follow but myself;
  Heaven is my judge, not I for love and duty,
  But seeming so, for my peculiar end: 60
  For when my outward action doth demonstrate
  The native act and figure of my heart
  In compliment extern,[18] 'tis not long after
  But I will wear my heart upon my sleeve
  For daws to peck at: I am not what I am.   65
Roderigo. What a full fortune does the thick-lips owe,[19]
  If he can carry 't thus!
Iago.   Call up her father;
  Rouse him, make after him, poison his delight,
  Proclaim him in the streets, incense her kinsmen,
  And, though he in a fertile climate dwell,[20]   70
  Plague him with flies; though that his joy be joy,
  Yet throw such changes of vexation on 't
  As it may lose some colour.
Roderigo. Here is her father's house; I'll call aloud.
Iago. Do; with like timorous[21] accent and dire yell   75
  As when, by night and negligence, the fire
  Is spied in populous cities.
Roderigo. What, ho! Brabantio: Signior Brabantio, ho!
Iago. Awake! what, ho! Brabantio! thieves! thieves! thieves!
  Look to your house, your daughter, and your bags!   80
  Thieves! thieves!

---

[18] External show.   [19] Own.   [20] I.e., is fortunate.   [21] Frightening.

(*Enter Brabantio, above, at a window.*)

Brabantio.   What is the reason of this terrible summons?
  What is the matter there?
Roderigo.   Signior, is all your family within?
Iago.   Are your doors lock'd?   85
Brabantio.   Why? wherefore ask you this?
Iago.   'Zounds![22] sir, you're robb'd; for shame, put on your gown;
  Your heart is burst, you have lost half your soul;
  Even now, now, very now, an old black ram
  Is tupping[23] your white ewe. Arise, arise!
  Awake the snorting[24] citizens with the bell,   90
  Or else the devil will make a grandsire of you.
  Arise, I say.
Brabantio.   What! have you lost your wits?
Roderigo.   Most reverend signior, do you know my voice?
Brabantio.   Not I, what are you?   95
Roderigo.   My name is Roderigo.
Brabantio.   The worser welcome:
  I have charg'd thee not to haunt about my doors:
  In honest plainness thou hast heard me say
  My daughter is not for thee; and now, in madness,
  Being full of supper and distempering draughts,
  Upon malicious knavery dost thou come   100
  To start my quiet.
Roderigo.   Sir, sir, sir!
Brabantio.   But thou must needs be sure
  My spirit and my place[25] have in them power
  To make this bitter to thee.
Roderigo.   Patience, good sir.
Brabantio.   What tell'st thou me of robbing? this is Venice;   105
  My house is not a grange.[26]
Roderigo.   Most grave Brabantio,
  In simple and pure soul I come to you.
Iago.   'Zounds! sir, you are one of those that will not serve God if the devil
  bid you. Because we come to do you service and you think we are ruffians,
  you'll have your daughter covered with a Barbary horse; you'll have your
  nephews neigh to you; you'll have coursers for cousins and gennets[27] for
  germans.[28]
Brabantio.   What profane wretch art thou?

---

[22] By God's wounds.   [23] Copulating.   [24] Snoring.   [25] Position.   [26] Isolated
farm house.   [27] Spanish horses.   [28] Blood relations.

Iago.   I am one, sir, that comes to tell you, your daughter and the Moor are
  now making the beast with two backs.

Brabantio.   Thou art a villain.

Iago.   You are—a senator.

Brabantio.   This thou shalt answer; I know thee, Roderigo.

Roderigo.   Sir, I will answer any thing. But, I beseech you,   120
  If 't be your pleasure and most wise consent,—
  As partly, I find, it is,—that your fair daughter,
  At this odd-even[29] and dull watch o' the night,
  Transported with no worse nor better guard
  But with a knave of common hire, a gondolier,   125
  To the gross clasps of a lascivious Moor,—
  If this be known to you, and your allowance,[30]
  We then have done you bold and saucy wrongs;
  But if you know not this, my manners tell me
  We have your wrong rebuke. Do not believe   130
  That, from[31] the sense of all civility,
  I thus would play and trifle with your reverence:
  Your daughter, if you have not given her leave,
  I say again, hath made a gross revolt;
  Tying her duty, beauty, wit and fortunes   135
  In[32] an extravagant[33] and wheeling stranger
  Of here and every where. Straight satisfy yourself:
  If she be in her chamber or your house,
  Let loose on me the justice of the state
  For thus deluding you.

Brabantio.   Strike on the tinder, ho!   140
  Give me a taper! call up all my people!
  This accident[34] is not unlike my dream;
  Belief of it oppresses me already.
  Light, I say! light!   (*Exit, from above.*)

Iago.   Farewell, for I must leave you:
  It seems not meet nor wholesome to my place   145
  To be produc'd,[35] as, if I stay, I shall,
  Against the Moor; for I do know the state,
  However this may gall him with some check,[36]
  Cannot with safety cast him; for he's embark'd
  With such loud reason to the Cyprus wars,—   150
  Which even now stand in act,—that, for their souls,

---

[29] Between night and morning.   [30] By your approval.   [31] Away from.   [32] To.
[33] Expatriate.   [34] Happening.   [35] I.e., as a witness.   [36] Restraining adversity.

Another of his fathom[37] they have none,
To lead their business; in which regard,
Though I do hate him as I do hell-pains,
Yet, for necessity of present life,   155
I must show out a flag and sign of love,
Which is indeed but sign. That you shall surely find him,
Lead to the Sagittary[38] the raised search;
And there will I be with him. So, farewell.   (*Exit.*)

(*Enter below, Brabantio, and servants with torches.*)

Brabantio.   It is too true an evil: gone she is,   160
   And what's to come of my despised time
   Is nought but bitterness. Now, Roderigo,
   Where didst thou see her? O, unhappy girl!
   With the Moor, sayst thou? Who would be a father!
   How didst thou know 'twas she? O, she deceives me   165
   Past thought. What said she to you? Get more tapers!
   Raise all my kindred! Are they married, think you?
Roderigo.   Truly, I think they are.
Brabantio.   O heaven! How got she out? O treason of the blood:
   Fathers, from hence trust not your daughters' minds   170
   By what you see them act. Are there not charms
   By which the property of youth and maidhood
   May be abus'd? Have you not read, Roderigo,
   Of some such thing?
Roderigo.   Yes, sir, I have indeed.
Brabantio.   Call up my brother. O! that you had had her.   175
   Some one way, some another! Do you know
   Where we may apprehend her and the Moor?
Roderigo.   I think I can discover him, if you please
   To get good guard and go along with me.
Brabantio.   Pray you, lead on. At every house I'll call;   180
   I may command at most. Get weapons, ho!
   And raise some special officers of night.
   On, good Roderigo; I'll deserve[39] your pains.   (*Exeunt.*)

SCENE 2.   *Another Street.*

(*Enter Othello, Iago, and Attendants, with torches.*)

Iago.   Though in the trade of war I have slain men,

---

[37] Caliber, ability.   [38] The name of an inn (?).   [39] I.e., reward.

Yet do I hold it very stuff o' the conscience
To do no contriv'd murder: I lack iniquity
Sometimes to do me service. Nine or ten times
I had thought to have yerk'd[40] him here under the ribs.   5
Othello.   'Tis better as it is.
Iago.   Nay, but he prated,
And spoke such scurvy and provoking terms
Against your honour
That, with the little godliness I have,
I did full hard forbear him. But, I pray, sir,   10
Are you fast married? Be assur'd of this,
That the magnifico[41] is much belov'd,
And hath in his effect a voice potential
As double[42] as the duke's; he will divorce you,
Or put upon you what restraint and grievance   15
The law—with all his might to enforce it on—
Will give him cable.[43]
Othello.   Let him do his spite:
My services which I have done the signiory[44]
Shall out-tongue his complaints. 'Tis yet to know,[45]
Which when I know that boasting is an honour   20
I shall promulgate, I fetch my life and being
From men of royal siege, and my demerits[46]
May speak unbonneted[47] to as proud a fortune
As this[48] that I have reach'd; for know, Iago,
But that I love the gentle Desdemona,   25
I would not my unhoused[49] free condition
Put into circumscription and confine
For the sea's worth. But, look! what lights come yond?
Iago.   Those are the raised[50] father and his friends:
You were best[51] go in.
Othello.   Not I; I must be found: 30
My parts, my title, and my perfect[52] soul
Shall manifest me rightly. Is it they?
Iago.   By Janus,[53] I think no.

(*Enter Cassio and certain Officers, with torches.*)

Othello.   The servants of the duke, and my lieutenant.

---

[40] Stabbed.   [41] One of the grandees, or rulers, of Venice; here, Brabantio.   [42] Iago
means that Brabantio's influence equals that of the Doge's with his double vote.   [43] I.e.,
scope.   [44] The Venetian government.   [45] I.e., the signiory does not as yet know.
[46] Merits.   [47] I.e., as equals.   [48] I.e., that of Desdemona's family.   [49] Unconfined.
[50] Aroused.   [51] Had better.   [52] Untroubled by a bad conscience.   [53] The two-
faced Roman god of portals and doors and (hence) of beginnings and ends.

The goodness of the night upon you, friends!⁣   35
What is the news?
Cassio.   The duke does greet you, general,
And he requires your haste-post-haste appearance,
Even on the instant.
Othello.   What is the matter, think you?
Cassio. Something from Cyprus, as I may divine.
It is a business of some heat;⁵⁴ the galleys   40
Have sent a dozen sequent⁵⁵ messengers
This very night at one another's heels,
And many of the consuls,⁵⁶ rais'd and met,
Are at the duke's already. You have been hotly call'd for;
When, being not at your lodging to be found,   45
The senate hath sent about three several⁵⁷ quests
To search you out.
Othello.   'Tis well I am found by you.
I will but spend a word here in the house,
And go with you.   (*Exit.*)
Cassio.   Ancient, what makes he here?
Iago. Faith, he to-night hath boarded a land carrack;⁵⁸   50
If it prove lawful prize, he's made for ever.
Cassio. I do not understand.
Iago.   He's married.
Cassio.   To who?

(*Re-enter Othello.*)

Iago. Marry,⁵⁹ to—Come, captain, will you go?
Othello.   Have with you.
Cassio. Here comes another troop to seek for you.
Iago. It is Brabantio. General, be advis'd;   55
He comes to bad intent.

(*Enter Brabantio, Roderigo, and Officers, with torches and weapons.*)

Othello.   Holla! stand there!
Roderigo. Signior, it is the Moor.
Brabantio.   Down with him, thief!

(*They draw on both sides.*)

---

⁵⁴ Urgency.   ⁵⁵ Following one another.   ⁵⁶ I.e., senators.   ⁵⁷ Separate.
⁵⁸ Treasure ship.   ⁵⁹ By the Virgin Mary.

Iago.   You, Roderigo! Come, sir, I am for you.[60]

Othello.   Keep up your bright swords, for the dew will rust them.

    Good signior, you shall more command with years   60

    Than with your weapons.

Brabantio.   O thou foul thief! where hast thou stow'd my daughter?

    Damn'd as thou art, thou hast enchanted her;

    For I'll refer me to all things of sense,

    If she in chains of magic were not bound,   65

    Whether a maid so tender, fair, and happy,

    So opposite to marriage that she shunn'd

    The wealthy curled darlings of our nation,

    Would ever have, to incur a general mock,

    Run from her guardage to the sooty bosom   70

    Of such a thing as thou; to fear, not to delight.

    Judge me the world, if 'tis not gross in sense[61]

    That thou hast practis'd on her with foul charms,

    Abus'd her delicate youth with drugs or minerals

    That weaken motion:[62] I'll have 't disputed on;   75

    'Tis probable, and palpable to thinking.

    I therefore apprehend and do attach[63] thee

    For an abuser of the world, a practiser

    Of arts inhibited and out of warrant.[64]

    Lay hold upon him: if he do resist,   80

    Subdue him at his peril.

Othello.   Hold your hands,

    Both you of my inclining,[65] and the rest:

    Were it my cue to fight, I should have known it

    Without a prompter. Where will you that I go

    To answer this your charge?

Brabantio.   To prison; till fit time   85

    Of law and course of direct session[66]

    Call thee to answer.

Othello.   What if I do obey?

    How may the duke be therewith satisfied,

    Whose messengers are here about my side,

    Upon some present[67] business of the state   90

    To bring me to him?

Officer.   'Tis true, most worthy signior;

    The duke's in council, and your noble self,

    I am sure, is sent for.

---

[60] Let you and me fight.   [61] Obvious.   [62] Normal reactions.   [63] Arrest.
[64] Prohibited and illegal.   [65] Party.   [66] Normal process of law.   [67] Immediate,
pressing.

Brabantio.   How! the duke in council!
  In this time of the night! Bring him away.   95
  Mine's not an idle cause: the duke himself,
  Or any of my brothers of the state,[68]
  Cannot but feel this wrong as 'twere their own;
  For if such actions may have passage free,
  Bond-slaves and pagans shall our statesmen be.   (*Exeunt.*)   100

SCENE 3.   *A Council Chamber.*

(*The Duke and Senators sitting at a table. Officers attending.*)

Duke.   There is no composition[69] in these news
  That gives them credit.
First Senator.   Indeed, they are disproportion'd;
  My letters say a hundred and seven galleys.
Duke.   And mine, a hundred and forty.
Second Senator.   And mine, two hundred:
  But though they jump[70] not on a just[71] account,—   5
  As in these cases, where the aim[72] reports,
  'Tis oft with difference,—yet do they all confirm
  A Turkish fleet, and bearing up to Cyprus.
Duke.   Nay, it is possible enough to judgment:
  I do not so secure me in[73] the error,   10
  But the main article[74] I do approve[75]
  In fearful sense.
Sailor (*within*).   What, ho! what, ho! what, ho!
Officer.   A messenger from the galleys.

(*Enter a Sailor.*)

Duke.   Now, what's the business?
Sailor.   The Turkish preparation makes for Rhodes;
  So was I bid report here to the state   15
  By Signior Angelo.
Duke.   How say you by this change?
First Senator.   This cannot be
  By no[76] assay[77] of reason; 'tis a pageant[78]
  To keep us in false gaze.[79] When we consider
  The importancy of Cyprus to the Turk,   20

---

[68] Fellow senators.   [69] Consistency, agreement.   [70] Coincide.   [71] Exact.
[72] Conjecture.   [73] Draw comfort from.   [74] Substance.   [75] Believe.
[76] Any.   [77] Test.   [78] (Deceptive) show.   [79] Looking in the wrong direction.

And let ourselves again but understand,
That as it more concerns the Turk than Rhodes,
So may he with more facile question bear[80] it,
For that it stands not in such warlike brace,[81]
But altogether lacks the abilities   25
That Rhodes is dress'd in: if we make thought of this,
We must not think the Turk is so unskilful
To leave that latest which concerns him first,
Neglecting an attempt of ease and gain,
To wake and wage a danger profitless.   30
Duke.   Nay, in all confidence, he's not for Rhodes.
Officer.   Here is more news.

(*Enter a Messenger.*)

Messenger.   The Ottomites,[82] reverend and gracious,
  Steering with due course toward the isle of Rhodes,
  Have there injointed[83] them with an after fleet.[84]   35
First Senator.   Ay, so I thought. How many, as you guess?
Messenger.   Of thirty sail; and now they do re-stem[85]
  Their backward course, bearing with frank appearance
  Their purposes toward Cyprus. Signior Montano,
  Your trusty and most valiant servitor,   40
  With his free duty[86] recommends[87] you thus,
  And prays you to believe him.
Duke.   'Tis certain then, for Cyprus.
  Marcus Luccicos, is not he in town?
First Senator.   He's now in Florence.   45
Duke.   Write from us to him; post-post-haste dispatch.
First Senator.   Here comes Brabantio and the valiant Moor.

(*Enter Brabantio, Othello, Iago, Roderigo, and Officers.*)

Duke.   Valiant Othello, we must straight employ you
  Against the general enemy Ottoman.
  (*To Brabantio.*) I did not see you; welcome, gentle signior;   50
  We lack'd your counsel and your help to-night.
Brabantio.   So did I yours. Good your Grace, pardon me;
  Neither my place nor aught I heard of business
  Hath rais'd me from my bed, nor doth the general care
  Take hold of me, for my particular grief   55

---

[80] More easily capture.   [81] State of defense.   [82] Turks.   [83] Joined.   [84] Fleet
that followed after.   [85] Steer again.   [86] Unqualified expressions of respect.
[87] Informs.

Is of so flood-gate[88] and o'erbearing nature
That it engluts and swallows other sorrows
And it is still itself.

Duke.   Why, what's the matter?

Brabantio.   My daughter! O! my daughter.

Duke. }
Senators. }   Dead?

Brabantio.   Ay, to me;
 She is abus'd, stol'n from me, and corrupted   60
 By spells and medicines bought of mountebanks;
 For nature so preposterously to err,
 Being not deficient, blind, or lame of sense,
 Sans[89] witchcraft could not.

Duke.   Whoe'er he be that in this foul proceeding   65
 Hath thus beguil'd your daughter of herself
 And you of her, the bloody book of law
 You shall yourself read in the bitter letter
 After your own sense; yea, though our proper[90] son
 Stood[91] in your action.[92]

Brabantio.   Humbly I thank your Grace.   70
 Here is the man, this Moor; whom now, it seems,
 Your special mandate for the state affairs
 Hath hither brought.

Duke. }
Senators. }   We are very sorry for it.

Duke (*to Othello*).   What, in your own part, can you say to this?

Brabantio.   Nothing, but this is so.   75

Othello.   Most potent, grave, and reverend signiors,
 My very noble and approv'd[93] good masters,
 That I have ta'en away this old man's daughter,
 It is most true; true, I have married her:
 The very head and front of my offending   80
 Hath this extent, no more. Rude am I in my speech,
 And little bless'd with the soft phrase of peace;
 For since these arms of mine had seven years' pith,[94]
 Till now some nine moons wasted,[95] they have us'd
 Their dearest action in the tented field;   85
 And little of this great world can I speak,
 More than pertains to feats of broil and battle;
 And therefore little shall I grace my cause
 In speaking for myself. Yet, by your gracious patience,

---

[88] Torrential.   [89] Without.   [90] Own.   [91] Were accused.   [92] Suit.
[93] Tested (by past experience).   [94] Strength.   [95] Past.

I will a round[96] unvarnish'd tale deliver   90
Of my whole course of love; what drugs, what charms,
What conjuration, and what mighty magic,
For such proceeding I am charg'd withal,
I won his daughter.
Brabantio.   A maiden never bold;
Of spirit so still and quiet, that her motion   95
Blush'd at herself;[97] and she, in spite of nature,
Of years, of country, credit, every thing,
To fall in love with what she fear'd to look on!
It is a judgment maim'd and most imperfect
That will confess[98] perfection so could err   100
Against all rules of nature, and must be driven
To find out practices of cunning hell,
Why this should be. I therefore vouch again
That with some mixtures powerful o'er the blood,
Or with some dram conjur'd to this effect,   105
He wrought upon her.
Duke.   To vouch this, is no proof,
Without more certain and more overt test
Than these thin habits[99] and poor likelihoods
Of modern[100] seeming do prefer against him.
First Senator.   But, Othello, speak: 110
Did you by indirect and forced courses
Subdue and poison this young maid's affections;
Or came it by request and such fair question[101]
As soul to soul affordeth?
Othello.   I do beseech you;
Send for the lady to the Sagittary,   115
And let her speak of me before her father:
If you do find me foul in her report,
The trust, the office I do hold of you,
Not only take away, but let your sentence
Even fall upon my life.
Duke.   Fetch Desdemona hither.   120
Othello.   Ancient, conduct them; you best know the place.

(*Exeunt Iago and Attendants.*)

And, till she come, as truly as to heaven
I do confess the vices of my blood,

---

[96] Blunt.   [97] I.e., (her modesty was such that) she blushed at her own emotions; or: could not move without blushing.   [98] Assert.   [99] Weak appearances.   [100] Commonplace.   [101] Conversation.

So justly to your grave ears I'll present
How I did thrive in this fair lady's love,   125
And she in mine.
Duke. Say it, Othello.
Othello. Her father lov'd me; oft invited me;
Still[102] question'd me the story of my life
From year to year, the battles, sieges, fortunes   130
That I have pass'd.
I ran it through, even from my boyish days
To the very moment that he bade me tell it;
Wherein I spake of most disastrous chances,
Of moving accidents by flood and field,   135
Of hair-breadth 'scapes i' the imminent deadly breach,
Of being taken by the insolent foe
And sold to slavery, of my redemption thence
And portance[103] in my travel's history;
Wherein of antres[104] vast and deserts idle,[105]   140
Rough quarries, rocks, and hills whose heads touch heaven,
It was my hint[106] to speak, such was the process;
And of the Cannibals that each other eat,
The Anthropophagi,[107] and men whose heads
Do grow beneath their shoulders. This to hear   145
Would Desdemona seriously incline;
But still the house-affairs would draw her thence;
Which ever as she could with haste dispatch,
She'd come again, and with a greedy ear
Devour up my discourse. Which I observing,   150
Took once a pliant[108] hour, and found good means
To draw from her a prayer of earnest heart
That I would all my pilgrimage dilate,[109]
Whereof by parcels[110] she had something heard,
But not intentively:[111] I did consent;   155
And often did beguile her of her tears,
When I did speak of some distressful stroke
That my youth suffer'd. My story being done,
She gave me for my pains a world of sighs:
She swore, in faith, 'twas strange, 'twas passing[112] strange;   160
'Twas pitiful, 'twas wondrous pitiful:
She wish'd she had not heard it, yet she wish'd

---

[102] Always, regularly.   [103] Behavior.   [104] Caves.   [105] Empty, sterile.
[106] Opportunity.   [107] Man-eaters.   [108] Suitable.   [109] Relate in full.
[110] Piecemeal.   [111] In sequence.   [112] Surpassing.

That heaven had made her[113] such a man; she thank'd me,
And bade me, if I had a friend that lov'd her,
I should but teach him how to tell my story,   165
And that would woo her. Upon this hint I spake.
She lov'd me for the dangers I had pass'd,
And I lov'd her that she did pity them.
This only is the witchcraft I have us'd:
Here comes the lady; let her witness it.   170

(*Enter Desdemona, Iago, and Attendants.*)

Duke.   I think this tale would win my daughter too.
   Good Brabantio,
   Take up this mangled matter at the best;
   Men do their broken weapons rather use
   Than their bare hands.
Brabantio.   I pray you, hear her speak: 175
   If she confess that she was half the wooer,
   Destruction on my head, if my bad blame
   Light on the man! Come hither, gentle mistress:
   Do you perceive in all this noble company
   Where most you owe obedience?
Desdemona.   My noble father,   180
   I do perceive here a divided duty:
   To you I am bound for life and education;
   My life and education both do learn[114] me
   How to respect you; you are the lord of duty,
   I am hitherto your daughter: but here's my husband;   185
   And so much duty as my mother show'd
   To you, preferring you before her father,
   So much I challenge[115] that I may profess
   Due to the Moor my lord.
Brabantio.   God be with you! I have done.
   Please it your Grace, on to the state affairs;   190
   I had rather to adopt a child than get it.
   Come hither, Moor:
   I here do give thee that with all my heart
   Which, but thou hast[116] already, with all my heart
   I would keep from thee. For your sake,[117] jewel,   195
   I am glad at soul I have no other child;
   For thy escape would teach me tyranny,
   To hang clogs on them. I have done, my lord.

---

[113] Direct object; not "for her."   [114] Teach.   [115] Claim as right.   [116] Didn't you
have it.   [117] Because of you.

Duke.   Let me speak like yourself and lay a sentence,[118]
Which as a grize[119] or step, may help these lovers   200
Into your favour.
When remedies are past, the griefs are ended
By seeing the worst, which[120] late on hopes depended.
To mourn a mischief that is past and gone
Is the next way to draw new mischief on.   205
What cannot be preserv'd when Fortune takes,
Patience her injury a mockery makes.[121]
The robb'd that smiles steals something from the thief;
He robs himself that spends a bootless grief.

Brabantio.   So let the Turk of Cyprus us beguile;   210
We lose it not so long as we can smile.
He bears the sentence[122] well that nothing bears
But the free comfort which from thence he hears;
But he bears both the sentence and the sorrow
That, to pay grief, must of poor patience borrow.   215
These sentences, to sugar, or to gall,
Being strong on both sides, are equivocal:[123]
But words are words: I never yet did hear
That the bruis'd heart was pierced[124] through the ear.
I humbly beseech you, proceed to the affairs of state.   220

Duke.   The Turk with a most mighty preparation makes for Cyprus. Othello,
the fortitude[125] of the place is best known to you; and though we have there
a substitute of most allowed sufficiency,[126] yet opinion, a sovereign mistress
of effects, throws a more safer voice on you:[127] you must therefore be content
to slubber[128] the gloss of your new fortunes with this more stubborn[129] and
boisterous expedition.

Othello.   The tyrant custom, most grave senators,
Hath made the flinty and steel couch of war
My thrice-driven[130] bed of down: I do agnize[131]
A natural and prompt alacrity   230
I find in hardness, and do undertake
These present wars against the Ottomites.
Most humbly therefore bending to your state,[132]
I crave fit disposition[133] for my wife,
Due reference of place and exhibition,[134]   235

---

[118] Provide a maxim.   [119] Step.   [120] The antecedent is "griefs."   [121] To   suffer
an irreparable loss patiently is to make light of injury (i.e., to triumph over adversity).
[122] (1) Verdict, (2) Maxim.   [123] Sententious comfort (like the Duke's trite maxims) can
hurt as well as soothe.   [124] (1) Lanced (i.e., cured), (2) Wounded.   [125] Strength.
[126] Admitted competence.   [127] General opinion, which mainly determines action, thinks
Cyprus safer with you in command.   [128] Besmear.   [129] Rough.   [130] Made as soft
as possible.   [131] Recognize.   [132] Submitting to your authority.   [133] Disposal.
[134] Provision.

With such accommodation and besort[135]
As levels with[136] her breeding.
Duke.   If you please,
Be 't at her father's.
Brabantio.   I'll not have it so.
Othello.   Nor I.
Desdemona.   Nor I; I would not there reside,
To put my father in impatient thoughts   240
By being in his eye. Most gracious duke,
To my unfolding[137] lend your gracious ear;
And let me find a charter[138] in your voice
To assist my simpleness.
Duke.   What would you, Desdemona?   245
Desdemona.   That I did love the Moor to live with him,
My downright violence and storm of fortunes
May trumpet to the world; my heart's subdu'd
Even to the very quality of my lord;[139]
I saw Othello's visage in his mind,   250
And to his honours and his valiant parts
Did I my soul and fortunes consecrate.
So that, dear lords, if I be left behind,
A moth of peace, and he go to the war,
The rites[140] for which I love him are bereft me,   255
And I a heavy interim shall support[141]
By his dear[142] absence. Let me go with him.
Othello.   Let her have your voices.
Vouch with me, heaven, I therefore beg it not
To please the palate of my appetite,   260
Nor to comply with heat,—the young affects[143]
In me defunct,—and proper satisfaction,
But to be free and bounteous to her mind;
And heaven defend[144] your good souls that you think
I will your serious and great business scant   265
For[145] she is with me. No, when light-wing'd toys
Of feather'd Cupid seel[146] with wanton dullness
My speculative and offic'd instruments,[147]
That[148] my disports corrupt and taint my business,
Let housewives make a skillet of my helm,   270

---

[135] Fitness.   [136] Is proper to.   [137] Explanation.   [138] Permission.   [139] I.e.,
I have become a soldier, like Othello.   [140] I.e., of marriage, or of war, or of both.
[141] Endure.   [142] Closely concerning (i.e., Desdemona).   [143] The passions of youth
(hence, here, *immoderate* sexual passion).   [144] Forbid.   [145] Because.   [146] Blind
(v.) by sewing up the eyelids (a term from falconry).   [147] Reflective and executive faculties and organs.   [148] So that.

And all indign[149] and base adversities
Make head against my estimation![150]
Duke. Be it as you shall privately determine,
   Either for her stay or going. The affair cries haste,
   And speed must answer it.   275
First Senator. You must away to-night.
Othello.   With all my heart.
Duke. At nine i' the morning here we'll meet again.
   Othello, leave some officer behind,
   And he shall our commission bring to you;
   With such things else of quality and respect   280
   As doth import you.[151]
Othello.   So please your Grace, my ancient;
   A man he is of honesty and trust:
   To his conveyance I assign my wife,
   With what else needful your good grace shall think
   To be sent after me.
Duke.   Let it be so.   285
   Good-night to every one. (*To Brabantio.*) And, noble signior,
   If virtue no delighted[152] beauty lack,
   Your son-in-law is far more fair than black.
First Senator. Adieu, brave Moor! use Desdemona well.
Brabantio. Look to her, Moor, if thou hast eyes to see: 290
   She has deceiv'd her father, and may thee.

                              (*Exeunt Duke, Senators, Officers, &c.*)

Othello. My life upon her faith! Honest Iago,
   My Desdemona must I leave to thee:
   I prithee, let thy wife attend on her;
   And bring them after in the best advantage.[153]   295
   Come, Desdemona; I have but an hour
   Of love, of worldly matters and direction,
   To spend with thee: we must obey the time.

                              (*Exeunt Othello and Desdemona.*)

Roderigo. Iago!
Iago. What sayst thou, noble heart?   300
Roderigo. What will I do, think'st thou?
Iago. Why, go to bed, and sleep.

---

[149] Shameful.   [150] Reputation.   [151] Concern.   [152] Delightful.   [153] Opportunity.

Roderigo.   I will incontinently[154] drown myself.

Iago.   Well, if thou dost, I shall never love thee after.
Why, thou silly gentleman!   305

Roderigo.   It is silliness to live when to live is torment; and then have we a prescription to die when death is our physician.

Iago.   O! villainous; I have looked upon the world for four times seven years, and since I could distinguish betwixt a benefit and an injury, I never found man that knew how to love himself. Ere I would say, I would drown myself for the love of a guinea-hen, I would change my humanity with a baboon.

Roderigo.   What should I do? I confess it is my shame to be so fond;[155] but it is not in my virtue[156] to amend it.

Iago.   Virtue! a fig! 'tis in ourselves that we are thus, or thus. Our bodies are our gardens, to the which our wills are gardeners; so that if we will plant nettles or sow lettuce, set hyssop and weed up thyme, supply it with one gender[157] of herbs or distract it with many, either to have it sterile with idleness or manured with industry, why, the power and corrigible[158] authority of this lies in our wills. If the balance of our lives had not one scale of reason to poise another of sensuality, the blood and baseness of our natures would conduct us to most preposterous conclusions; but we have reason to cool our raging motions, our carnal stings, our unbitted[159] lusts, whereof I take this that you call love to be a sect or scion.[160]

Roderigo.   It cannot be.

Iago.   It is merely a lust of the blood and a permission of the will. Come, be a man. Drown thyself! drown cats and blind puppies. I have professed me thy friend, and I confess me knit to thy deserving with cables of perdurable toughness; I could never better stead thee than now. Put money in thy purse; follow these wars; defeat thy favour[161] with a usurped[162] beard; I say, put money in thy purse. It cannot be that Desdemona should long continue her love to the Moor,—put money in thy purse,—nor he his to her. It was a violent commencement in her, and thou shalt see an answerable sequestration;[163] put but money in thy purse. These Moors are changeable in their wills;—fill thy purse with money:—the food that to him now is as luscious as locusts,[164] shall be to him shortly as bitter as coloquintida.[165] She must change for youth: when she is sated with his body, she will find the error of her choice. She must have change, she must: therefore put money in thy purse. If thou wilt needs damn thyself, do it a more delicate way than drowning. Make all the money thou canst. If sanctimony and a frail vow betwixt an erring[166] barbarian and a supersubtle[167] Venetian be not too hard for my wits and all the tribe of hell, thou shalt enjoy her;

---

[154] Forthwith.   [155] Infatuated.   [156] Strength.   [157] Kind.   [158] Corrective.
[159] I.e., uncontrolled.   [160] Offshoot.   [161] Change thy appearance (for the worse?).
[162] Assumed.   [163] Estrangement.   [164] Sweet-tasting fruits (perhaps the carob, the edible seed-pod of an evergreen tree in the Mediterranean area).   [165] Purgative derived from a bitter apple.   [166] Vagabond.   [167] Exceedingly refined.

therefore make money. A pox of drowning thyself! it is clean out of the way: seek thou rather to be hanged in compassing thy joy than to be drowned and go without her.

Roderigo.   Wilt thou be fast to my hopes, if I depend on the issue?[168]

Iago.   Thou art sure of me: go, make money. I have told thee often, and I retell thee again and again, I hate the Moor; my cause is hearted; thine hath no less reason. Let us be conjunctive[169] in our revenge against him; if thou canst cuckold him, thou dost thyself a pleasure, me a sport. There are many events in the womb of time which will be delivered. Traverse;[170] go: provide thy money. We will have more of this to-morrow. Adieu.

Roderigo.   Where shall we meet i' the morning?

Iago.   At my lodging.

Roderigo.   I'll be with thee betimes.

Iago.   Go to: farewell. Do you hear, Roderigo?   355

Roderigo.   What say you?

Iago.   No more of drowning, do you hear?

Roderigo.   I am changed. I'll sell all my land.

Iago.   Go to; farewell! put money enough in your purse.   (*Exit Roderigo.*)
  Thus do I ever make my fool my purse;   360
  For I mine own gain'd knowledge should profane,
  If I would time expend with such a snipe[171]
  But for my sport and profit. I hate the Moor,
  And it is thought abroad[172] that 'twixt my sheets
  He has done my office: I know not if 't be true,   365
  But I, for mere suspicion in that kind,
  Will do as if for surety.[173] He holds me well;[174]
  The better shall my purpose work on him.
  Cassio's a proper[175] man; let me see now:
  To get his place; and to plume up[176] my will   370
  In double knavery; how, how? Let's see:
  After some time to abuse Othello's ear
  That he[177] is too familiar with his wife:
  He hath a person and a smooth dispose[178]
  To be suspected; framed[179] to make women false,   375
  The Moor is of a free and open nature,
  That thinks men honest that but seem to be so,
  And will as tenderly be led by the nose
  As asses are.
  I have 't; it is engender'd: hell and night   380
  Must bring this monstrous birth to the world's light.   (*Exit.*)

---

[168] Rely on the outcome.   [169] Allied.   [170] March.   [171] Dupe.   [172] People think.   [173] As if it were certain.   [174] In high regard.   [175] Handsome. [176] Make ready.   [177] I.e., Cassio.   [178] Bearing.   [179] Designed, apt.

Act II

SCENE 1.   *A Sea-port Town in Cyprus. An open place near the Quay.*

(Enter Montano and two Gentlemen.)

Montano.   What from the cape can you discern at sea?
First Gentleman.   Nothing at all: it is a high-wrought flood;
  I cannot 'twixt the heaven and the main[180]
  Descry a sail.
Montano.   Methinks the wind hath spoke aloud at land;   5
  A fuller blast ne'er shook our battlements;
  If it hath ruffian'd so upon the sea,
  What ribs of oak, when mountains melt on them,
  Can hold the mortise?[181] What shall we hear of this?
Second Gentleman.   A segregation[182] of the Turkish fleet;   10
  For do but stand upon the foaming shore,
  The chidden billow seems to pelt the clouds;
  The wind-shak'd surge, with high and monstrous mane,
  Seems to cast water on the burning bear[183]
  And quench the guards of the ever-fixed pole:[184]   15
  I never did like[185] molestation view
  On the enchafed[186] flood.
Montano.   If that[187] the Turkish fleet
  Be not enshelter'd and embay'd, they are drown'd;
  It is impossible they bear it out.

(Enter a Third Gentleman.)

Third Gentleman.   News, lad! our wars are done.   20
  The desperate tempest hath so bang'd the Turks
  That their designment halts;[188] a noble ship of Venice
  Hath seen a grievous wrack and suffrance[189]
  On most part of their fleet.
Montano.   How! is this true?
Third Gentleman.   The ship is here put in,   25
  A Veronesa;[190] Michael Cassio,

---

[180] Ocean.   [181] Hold the joints together.   [182] Scattering.   [183] Ursa Minor (the Little Dipper).   [184] Polaris, the North Star, almost directly above the Earth's axis, is part of the constellation of the Little Bear, or Dipper.   [185] Similar.   [186] Agitated. [187] If.   [188] Plan is stopped.   [189] Damage.   [190] Probably a *type* of ship, rather than a ship from Verona—not only because Verona is an inland city but also because of "a noble ship of Venice" above.

Lieutenant to the warlike Moor Othello,
Is come on shore: the Moor himself's at sea,
And is in full commission here for Cyprus.
Montano.   I am glad on 't; 'tis a worthy governor.   30
Third Gentleman.   But this same Cassio, though he speak of comfort
Touching the Turkish loss, yet he looks sadly
And prays the Moor be safe; for they were parted
With foul and violent tempest.
Montano.   Pray heaven he be;
For I have serv'd him, and the man commands   35
Like a full soldier. Let's to the sea-side, ho!
As well to see the vessel that's come in
As to throw out our eyes for brave Othello,
Even till we make the main and the aerial blue
An indistinct regard.[191]
Third Gentleman.   Come, let's do so;   40
For every minute is expectancy
Of more arrivance.

(*Enter Cassio.*)

Cassio.   Thanks, you the valiant of this warlike isle,
That so approve the Moor. O! let the heavens
Give him defence against the elements,   45
For I have lost him on a dangerous sea.
Montano.   Is he well shipp'd?
Cassio.   His bark is stoutly timber'd, and his pilot
Of very expert and approv'd allowance;[192]
Therefore my hopes, not surfeited to death,[193]   50
Stand in bold cure.[194]

(*Within, 'A sail!—a sail!—a sail!' Enter a Messenger.*)

Cassio.   What noise?
Messenger.   The town is empty; on the brow o' the sea
Stand ranks of people, and they cry 'A sail!'
Cassio.   My hopes do shape him for the governor.   55

(*Guns heard.*)

Second Gentleman.   They do discharge their shot of courtesy;
Our friends at least.

---

[191] Till our (straining) eyes can no longer distinguish sea and sky.   [192] Admitted and
proven to be expert.   [193] Overindulged.   [194] With good chance of being fulfilled.

Cassio.   I pray you, sir, go forth.
And give us truth who 'tis that is arriv'd.   60
Second Gentleman.   I shall.   (*Exit.*)
Montano.   But, good lieutenant, is your general wiv'd?   60
Cassio.   Most fortunately: he hath achiev'd a maid
    That paragons[195] description and wild fame;
    One that excels the quirks[196] of blazoning pens,
    And in th' essential vesture of creation[197]
    Does tire the ingener.[198]

(*Re-enter Second Gentleman.*)

                      How now! who has put in?   65
Second Gentleman.   'Tis one Iago, ancient to the general.
Cassio.   He has had most favourable and happy speed:
    Tempests themselves, high seas, and howling winds,
    The gutter'd[199] rocks, and congregated sands,
    Traitors ensteep'd[200] to clog the guiltless keel,   70
    As having sense of beauty, do omit
    Their mortal[201] natures, letting go safely by
    The divine Desdemona.
Montano.   What is she?
Cassio.   She that I spake of, our great captain's captain,
    Left in the conduct of the bold Iago,   75
    Whose footing[202] here anticipates our thoughts
    A se'nnight's[203] speed. Great Jove, Othello guard,
    And swell his sail with thine own powerful breath,
    That he may bless this bay with his tall[204] ship,
    Make love's quick pants in Desdemona's arms,   80
    Give renew'd fire to our extinced spirits,
    And bring all Cyprus comfort!

(*Enter Desdemona, Emilia, Iago, Roderigo, and Attendants.*)

                      O! behold,
    The riches of the ship is come on shore.
    Ye men of Cyprus, let her have your knees.
    Hail to thee, lady! and the grace of heaven,   85
    Before, behind thee, and on every hand,
    Enwheel thee round!

---

[195] Exceeds, surpasses.   [196] Ingenuities.   [197] I.e., just as God made her; or: (even in) the (mere) essence of human nature.   [198] Inventor (i.e., of her praises?).   [199] Jagged; or: submerged.   [200] Submerged.   [201] Deadly.   [202] Landing.   [203] Week's.
[204] Brave.

Desdemona.   I thank you, valiant Cassio.
　What tidings can you tell me of my lord?
Cassio.　He is not yet arriv'd; nor know I aught
　But that he's well, and will be shortly here.　　　　　　　　90
Desdemona.　O! but I fear—How lost you company?
Cassio.　The great contention of the sea and skies
　Parted our fellowship. But hark! a sail.

(*Cry within, 'A sail—a sail!' Guns heard.*)

Second Gentleman.　They give their greeting to the citadel:
　This likewise is a friend.
Cassio.　　　　　　　　See for the news!　　　(*Exit Gentleman.*)　95
　Good ancient, you are welcome:—(*To Emilia*) welcome, mistress.
　Let it not gall your patience, good Iago,
　That I extend my manners; 'tis my breeding
　That gives me this bold show of courtesy.　　　　　　(*Kissing her.*)
Iago.　Sir, would she give you so much of her lips　　　　100
　As of her tongue she oft bestows on me,
　You'd have enough.
Desdemona.　　　　　Alas! she has no speech.
Iago.　In faith, too much;
　I find it still when I have list[205] to sleep:
　Marry, before your ladyship, I grant,　　　　　　　　　105
　She puts her tongue a little in her heart,
　And chides with thinking.[206]
Emilia.　You have little cause to say so.
Iago.　Come on, come on; you are pictures[207] out of doors,
　Bells[208] in your parlours, wild cats in your kitchens,　　　110
　Saints in your injuries, devils being offended,
　Players[209] in your housewifery,[210] and housewives[211] in your beds.
Desdemona.　O! fie upon thee, slanderer.
Iago.　Nay, it is true, or else I am a Turk:
　You rise to play and go to bed to work.　　　　　　　115
Emilia.　You shall not write my praise.
Iago.　　　　　　　　　　No, let me not.
Desdemona.　What wouldst thou write of me, if thou shouldst praise me?
Iago.　O gentle lady, do not put me to 't,
　For I am nothing if not critical.
Desdemona.　Come on; assay. There's one gone to the harbour?　　120
Iago.　Ay, madam.

---

[205] Wish.　　[206] I.e., without words.　　[207] I.e., made up, "painted."　　[208] I.e., jangly.
[209] Triflers, wastrels.　　[210] Housekeeping.　　[211] (1) Hussies, (2) (unduly) frugal with
their sexual favors, (3) businesslike, serious.

Desdemona (*aside*).   I am not merry, but I do beguile
   The thing I am by seeming otherwise.
   (*To Iago.*) Come, how wouldst thou praise me?
Iago.   I am about it; but indeed my invention   125
   Comes from my pate[212] as birdlime does from frize;[213]
   It plucks out brains and all: but my muse labours
   And thus she is deliver'd.
   If she be fair and wise, fairness and wit,
   The one's for use, the other useth it.   130
Desdemona.   Well prais'd! How if she be black and witty?
Iago.   If she be black,[214] and thereto have a wit,
   She'll find a white that shall her blackness fit.
Desdemona.   Worse and worse.
Emilia.   How if fair and foolish?   135
Iago.   She never yet was foolish that was fair,
   For even her folly[215] help'd to an heir.
Desdemona.   These are old fond[216] paradoxes to make fools laugh i' the
   alehouse. What miserable praise has thou for her that's foul and foolish?
Iago.   There's none so foul and foolish thereunto,   140
   But does foul pranks which fair and wise ones do.
Desdemona.   O heavy ignorance! thou praisest the worst best. But what
   praise couldst thou bestow on a deserving woman indeed, one that, in the
   authority of her merit, did justly put on the vouch[217] of very malice itself?
Iago.   She that was ever fair and never proud,   145
   Had tongue at will and yet was never loud,
   Never lack'd gold and yet went never gay,
   Fled from her wish and yet said 'Now I may,'
   She that being anger'd, her revenge being nigh,
   Bade her wrong stay and her displeasure fly,   150
   She that in wisdom never was so frail
   To change the cod's head for the salmon's tail,[218]
   She that could think and ne'er disclose her mind,
   See suitors following and not look behind,
   She was a wight, if ever such wight were,—   155
Desdemona.   To do what?
Iago.   To suckle fools and chronicle small beer.[219]
Desdemona.   O most lame and impotent conclusion! Do not learn of him,
   Emilia, though he be thy husband. How say you, Cassio? Is he not a most
   profane and liberal[220] counsellor?   160

---

[212] Head.   [213] Coarse cloth.   [214] Brunette, dark haired.   [215] Here also, wanton-
ness.   [216] Foolish.   [217] Compel the approval.   [218] To make a foolish exchange
(a bawdy secondary meaning is probable).   [219] I.e., keep petty household accounts.
[220] Free-spoken, licentious.

Cassio.   He speaks home,[221] madam; you may relish him more in the soldier than in[222] the scholar.

Iago (*aside*).   He takes her by the palm: ay, well said, whisper; with as little a web as this will I ensnare as great a fly as Cassio. Ay, smile upon her, do; I will gyve[223] thee in thine own courtship. You say true, 'tis so, indeed. If such tricks as these strip you out of your lieutenantry, it had been better you had not kissed your three fingers so oft, which now again you are most apt to play the sir[224] in. Very good; well kissed! an excellent courtesy! 'tis so, indeed. Yet again your fingers to your lips? would they were clyster-pipes[225] for your sake! (*A trumpet heard.*) The Moor! I know his trumpet.[226]   170

Cassio.   'Tis truly so.

Desdemona.   Let's meet him and receive him.

Cassio.   Lo! where he comes.

(*Enter Othello and Attendants.*)

Othello.   O my fair warrior!

Desdemona.   My dear Othello!

Othello.   It gives me wonder great as my content   175
To see you here before me. O my soul's joy!
If after every tempest come such calms,
May the winds blow till they have waken'd death!
And let the labouring bark climb hills of seas
Olympus-high, and duck again as low   180
As hell's from heaven! If it were now to die,
'Twere now to be most happy, for I fear
My soul hath her content so absolute
That not another comfort like to this
Succeeds in unknown fate.   185

Desdemona.   The heavens forbid
But that our loves and comforts should increase
Even as our days do grow!

Othello.   Amen to that, sweet powers!
I cannot speak enough of this content;   190
It stops me here; it is too much of joy:
And this, and this, the greatest discords be   (*Kissing her.*)
That e'er our hearts shall make!

Iago (*aside*).   O! you are well tun'd now,
But I'll set down[227] the pegs that make this music,
As honest as I am.

Othello.   Come, let us to the castle.   195
News, friends; our wars are done, the Turks are drown'd.

---

[221] To the mark, aptly.   [222] As . . . as.   [223] Entangle.   [224] Gentleman.
[225] Syringes, enema pipes.   [226] I.e., Othello's distinctive trumpet call.   [227] Loosen.

How does my old acquaintance of this isle?
Honey, you shall be well desir'd[228] in Cyprus;
I have found great love amongst them. O my sweet,
I prattle out of fashion, and I dote   200
In mine own comforts. I prithee, good Iago,
Go to the bay and disembark my coffers.
Bring thou the master to the citadel;
He is a good one, and his worthiness
Does challenge much respect. Come, Desdemona,   205
Once more well met at Cyprus.

(Exeunt all except Iago and Roderigo.)

Iago.   Do thou meet me presently at the harbour. Come hither. If thou be'st valiant, as they say base men being in love have then a nobility in their natures more than is native to them, list[229] me. The lieutenant to-night watches on the court of guard:[230] first, I must tell thee this, Desdemona is directly in love with him.

Roderigo.   With him! Why, 'tis not possible.

Iago.   Lay thy finger thus, and let thy soul be instructed. Mark me with what violence she first loved the Moor but for bragging and telling her fantastical lies; and will she love him still for prating? let not thy discreet heart think it. Her eye must be fed; and what delight shall she have to look on the devil? When the blood is made dull with the act of sport, there should be, again to inflame it, and to give satiety a fresh appetite, loveliness in favour, sympathy in years, manners, and beauties; all which the Moor is defective in. Now, for want of these required conveniences, her delicate tenderness will find itself abused, begin to heave the gorge,[231] disrelish and abhor the Moor; very nature will instruct her in it, and compel her to some second choice. Now, sir, this granted, as it is a most pregnant[232] and unforced position, who stands so eminently in the degree of this fortune as Cassio does? a knave very voluble, no further conscionable[233] than in putting on the mere form of civil and humane seeming, for the better compassing of his salt[234] and most hidden loose affection? why, none; why, none: a slip-per[235] and subtle knave, a finder-out of occasions, that has an eye can stamp and counterfeit advantages, though true advantage never present itself; a devilish knave! Besides, the knave is handsome, young, and hath all those requisites in him that folly and green minds look after; a pestilent complete knave! and the woman hath found him already.

Roderigo.   I cannot believe that in her; she is full of most blessed condition.

Iago.   Blessed fig's end! the wine she drinks is made of grapes;[236] if she had

---

[228] Welcomed.   [229] Listen to.   [230] Guardhouse.   [231] Vomit.   [232] Obvious.
[233] Conscientious.   [234] Lecherous.   [235] Slippery   [236] I.e., she is only flesh and blood.

been blessed she would never have loved the Moor; blessed pudding! Didst
thou not see her paddle with the palm of his hand? didst not mark that?

Roderigo.   Yes, that I did; but that was but courtesy.

Iago.   Lechery, by this hand! an index[237] and obscure prologue to the history
of lust and foul thoughts. They met so near with their lips, that their
breaths embraced together. Villanous thoughts, Roderigo! when these mu-
tualities so marshal the way, hard at hand comes the master and main
exercise, the incorporate[238] conclusion. Pish![239] But, sir, be you ruled by
me: I have brought you from Venice. Watch you to-night; for the command, I'll lay 't upon you: Cassio knows you not. I'll not be far from you:
do you find some occasion to anger Cassio, either by speaking too loud, or
tainting[240] his discipline; or from what other course you please, which the
time shall more favourably minister.

Roderigo.   Well.

Iago.   Sir, he is rash and very sudden in choler, and haply may strike at you:
provoke him, that he may; for even out of that will I cause these of Cyprus
to mutiny, whose qualification[241] shall come into no true taste again but by
the displanting of Cassio. So shall you have a shorter journey to your desires
by the means I shall then have to prefer[242] them; and the impediment most
profitably removed, without the which there were no expectation of our
prosperity.

Roderigo.   I will do this, if I can bring it to any opportunity.

Iago.   I warrant thee. Meet me by and by at the citadel: I must fetch his
necessaries ashore. Farewell.

Roderigo.   Adieu.   (*Exit.*)

Iago.   That Cassio loves her, I do well believe it;   260
That she loves him, 'tis apt,[243] and of great credit:[244]
The Moor, howbeit that I endure him not,
Is of a constant, loving, noble nature;
And I dare think he'll prove to Desdemona
A most dear[245] husband. Now, I do love her too;   265
Not out of absolute lust,—though peradventure[246]
I stand accountant[247] for as great a sin,—
But partly led to diet my revenge,
For that I do suspect the lusty Moor
Hath leap'd into my seat; the thought whereof   270
Doth like a poisonous mineral gnaw my inwards;
And nothing can or shall content my soul
Till I am even'd with him, wife for wife;
Or failing so, yet that I put the Moor

---

[237] Pointer.   [238] Carnal.   [239] Exclamation of disgust.   [240] Disparaging.
[241] Appeasement.   [242] Advance.   [243] Natural, probable.   [244] Easily, believable.
[245] A pun on the word in the sense of expensive.   [246] Perchance, perhaps.   [247] Ac-
countable.

At least into a jealousy so strong   275
That judgment cannot cure. Which thing to do,
If this poor trash[248] of Venice, whom I trash[249]
For his quick hunting, stand the putting-on,[250]
I'll have our Michael Cassio on the hip;
Abuse him to the Moor in the rank garb,[251]   280
For I fear Cassio with my night-cap too,
Make the Moor thank me, love me, and reward me
For making him egregiously an ass
And practising upon his peace and quiet
Even to madness. 'Tis here, but yet confus'd: 285
Knavery's plain face is never seen till us'd.   (*Exit.*)

SCENE 2.   *A Street.*

(*Enter a Herald with a proclamation; people following.*)

Herald.   It is Othello's pleasure, our noble and valiant general, that, upon
certain tidings now arrived, importing the mere[252] perdition of the Turkish
fleet, every man put himself into triumph; some to dance, some to make
bonfires, each man to what sport and revels his addiction leads him; for,
besides these beneficial news, it is the celebration of his nuptial. So much
was his pleasure should be proclaimed. All offices[253] are open, and there is
full liberty of feasting from this present hour of five till the bell have told
eleven. Heaven bless the isle of Cyprus and our noble general Othello!
                                                                (*Exeunt.*)

SCENE 3.   *A Hall in the Castle.*

(*Enter Othello, Desdemona, Cassio, and Attendants.*)

Othello.   Good Michael, look you to the guard to-night:
Let's teach ourselves that honourable stop,[254]
Not to outsport discretion.
Cassio.   Iago hath direction what to do:
But, notwithstanding, with my personal[255] eye   5
Will I look to 't.
Othello.   Iago is most honest.
Michael, good-night; to-morrow with your earliest
Let me have speech with you. (*To Desdemona.*) Come, my dear love,

---

[248] I.e., Roderigo.   [249] Check, control.   [250] Inciting.   [251] Gross manner.
[252] Utter.   [253] Kitchens and storehouses.   [254] Discipline.   [255] Own.

The purchase made, the fruits are to ensue;
That profit's yet to come 'twixt me and you.   10
Good-night.

(*Exeunt Othello, Desdemona, and Attendants.*)

(*Enter Iago.*)

Cassio. Welcome, Iago; we must to the watch.

Iago. Not this hour, lieutenant; 'tis not yet ten o' the clock. Our general casts us thus early for the love of his Desdemona, who let us not therefore blame; he hath not yet made wanton the night with her, and she is sport for Jove.

Cassio. She's a most exquisite lady.

Iago. And, I'll warrant her, full of game.

Cassio. Indeed, she is a most fresh and delicate creature.

Iago. What an eye she has! methinks it sounds a parley[256] of provocation.

Cassio. An inviting eye: and yet methinks right modest.   20

Iago. And when she speaks, is it not an alarum[257] to love?

Cassio. She is indeed perfection.

Iago. Well, happiness to their sheets! Come, lieutenant, I have a stoup of wine, and here without are a brace[258] of Cyprus gallants that would fain have a measure to the health of black Othello.   25

Cassio. Not to-night, good Iago: I have very poor and unhappy brains for drinking: I could well wish courtesy would invent some other custom of entertainment.

Iago. O! they are our friends; but one cup: I'll drink for you.

Cassio. I have drunk but one cup to-night, and that was craftily qualified[259] too, and, behold, what innovation[260] it makes here: I am unfortunate in the infirmity, and dare not task my weakness with any more.

Iago. What, man! 'tis a night of revels; the gallants desire it.

Cassio. Where are they?

Iago. Here at the door; I pray you, call them in.   35

Cassio. I'll do 't; but it dislikes me.   (*Exit.*)

Iago. If I can fasten but one cup upon him,
With that which he hath drunk to-night already,
He'll be as full of quarrel and offence
As my young mistress' dog. Now, my sick fool Roderigo,   40
Whom love has turn'd almost the wrong side out,
To Desdemona hath to-night carous'd
Potations pottle-deep;[261] and he's to watch.
Three lads of Cyprus, noble swelling spirits,
That hold their honours in a wary distance,[262]   45

---

[256] Conference.   [257] Call-to-arms.   [258] Pair.   [259] Diluted.   [260] Change, revolution.   [261] Bottoms-up.   [262] Take offense easily.

The very elements[263] of this warlike isle,
Have I to-night fluster'd with flowing cups,
And they watch too. Now, 'mongst this flock of drunkards,
Am I to put our Cassio in some action
That may offend the isle. But here they come.   50
If consequence[264] do but approve my dream,
My boat sails freely, both with wind and stream.

(Re-enter Cassio, with him Montano, and Gentlemen. Servant following with wine.)

Cassio.   'Fore God, they have given me a rouse[265] already.
Montano.   Good faith, a little one; not past a pint, as I am a soldier.
Iago.   Some wine, ho!   55
   (Sings.)   And let me the canakin[266] clink, clink;
           And let me the canakin clink:
           A soldier's a man;
           A life's but a span;
           Why then let a soldier drink.   60
   Some wine, boys!
Cassio.   'Fore God, an excellent song.
Iago.   I learned it in England, where indeed they are most potent in potting;
   your Dane, your German, and your swag-bellied[267] Hollander,—drink ho!—
   are nothing to your English.   65
Cassio.   Is your Englishman so expert in his drinking?
Iago.   Why, he drinks you[268] with facility your Dane dead drunk; he sweats
   not to overthrow your Almain;[269] he gives your Hollander a vomit ere the
   next pottle can be filled.
Cassio.   To the health of our general!   70
Montano.   I am for it, lieutenant; and I'll do you justice.
Iago.   O sweet England!
   (Sings.)   King Stephen was a worthy peer,
               His breeches cost him but a crown;
           He held them sixpence all too dear,   75
               With that he call'd the tailor lown.[270]
           He was a wight of high renown,
               And thou art but of low degree:
           'Tis pride that pulls the country down,
               Then take thine auld cloak about thee.   80
   Some wine, ho!
Cassio.   Why, this is a more exquisite song than the other.

---

[263] Types.   [264] Succeeding events.   [265] Drink.   [266] Small cup.   [267] With a pendulous belly.   [268] The "ethical" dative, i.e., you'll see that he drinks.   [269] German.   [270] Lout, rascal.

Iago.   Will you hear 't again?

Cassio.   No; for I hold him to be unworthy of his place that does those things. Well, God's above all; and there be souls must be saved, and there be souls must not be saved.

Iago.   It's true, good lieutenant.

Cassio.   For mine own part,—no offence to the general, nor any man of quality,—I hope to be saved.

Iago.   And so do I too, lieutenant.   90

Cassio.   Ay; but, by your leave, not before me; the lieutenant is to be saved before the ancient. Let's have no more of this; let's to our affairs. God forgive us our sins! Gentlemen, let's look to our business. Do not think, gentlemen, I am drunk: this is my ancient; this is my right hand, and this is my left hand. I am not drunk now; I can stand well enough, and speak well enough.

All.   Excellent well.

Cassio.   Why, very well, then; you must not think then that I am drunk.

(Exit.)

Montano.   To the platform, masters; come, let's set the watch.

Iago.   You see this fellow that is gone before;   100
    He is a soldier fit to stand by Caesar
    And give direction; and do but see his vice;
    'Tis to his virtue a just equinox,[271]
    The one as long as the other; 'tis pity of him.
    I fear the trust Othello puts him in,   105
    On some odd time of his infirmity,
    Will shake this island.

Montano.   But is he often thus?

Iago.   'Tis evermore the prologue to his sleep;
    He'll watch the horologe a double set,[272]
    If drink rock not his cradle.

Montano.   It were well   110
    The general were put in mind of it.
    Perhaps he sees it not; or his good nature
    Prizes the virtue that appears in Cassio,
    And looks not on his evils. Is not this true?

(Enter Roderigo.)

Iago *(aside to him).*   How now, Roderigo!   115
    I pray you, after the lieutenant; go.   *(Exit Roderigo.)*

Montano.   And 'tis great pity that the noble Moor
    Should hazard such a place as his own second
    With one of an ingraft[273] infirmity;

---

[271] Equivalent.   [272] Stand watch twice twelve hours.   [273] Ingrained.

It were an honest action to say   120
  So to the Moor.
Iago.   Not I, for this fair island:
  I do love Cassio well, and would do much
  To cure him of this evil. But hark! what noise?

(*Cry within*, 'Help! Help!' *Re-enter Cassio, driving in Roderigo.*)

Cassio.   You rogue! you rascal!
Montano.   What's the matter, lieutenant?
Cassio.   A knave teach me my duty!   125
  I'll beat the knave into a twiggen[274] bottle.
Roderigo.   Beat me!
Cassio.   Dost thou prate, rogue?

(*Striking Roderigo.*)

Montano (*staying him*).   Nay, good lieutenant;
  I pray you, sir, hold your hand.
Cassio.   Let me go, sir,
  Or I'll knock you o'er the mazzard.[275]
Montano.   Come, come; you're drunk.   130
Cassio.   Drunk!

(*They fight.*)

Iago (*aside to Roderigo*).   Away, I say! go out, and cry a mutiny.
                        (*Exit Roderigo.*)
  Nay, good lieutenant! God's will, gentlemen!
  Help, ho! Lieutenant! sir! Montano! sir!
  Help, masters! Here's a goodly watch indeed!

(*Bell rings.*)

  Who's that that rings the bell? Diablo, ho!   135
  The town will rise: God's will! lieutenant, hold!
  You will be sham'd for ever.

(*Re-enter Othello and Attendants.*)

Othello.   What is the matter here?
Montano.   'Zounds! I bleed still; I am hurt to the death.

(*He faints.*)

---

[274] Wicker.   [275] Head.

Othello.   Hold, for your lives!
Iago.   Hold, ho, lieutenant! Sir! Montano! gentlemen!   140
  Have you forgot all sense of place and duty?
  Hold! the general speaks to you; hold for shame!
Othello.   Why, how now, ho! from whence ariseth this?
  Are we turn'd Turks, and to ourselves do that
  Which heaven hath forbid the Ottomites?   145
  For Christian shame put by this barbarous brawl;
  He that stirs next to carve for his own rage
  Holds his soul light; he dies upon his motion.
  Silence that dreadful bell! it frights the isle
  From her propriety. What is the matter, masters?   150
  Honest Iago, that look'st dead with grieving,
  Speak, who began this? On thy love, I charge thee.
Iago.   I do not know; friends all but now, even now,
  In quarter[276] and in terms like bride and groom
  Devesting[277] them for bed; and then, but now,—   155
  As if some planet had unwitted men,—
  Swords out, and tilting one at other's breast,
  In opposition bloody. I cannot speak
  Any beginning to this peevish odds,[278]
  And would in action glorious I had lost   160
  Those legs that brought me to a part of it!
Othello.   How comes it, Michael, you are thus forgot?
Cassio.   I pray you, pardon me; I cannot speak.
Othello.   Worthy Montano, you were wont be civil;
  The gravity and stillness of your youth   165
  The world hath noted, and your name is great
  In mouths of wisest censure:[279] what's the matter,
  That you unlace[280] your reputation thus
  And spend your rich opinion[281] for the name
  Of a night-brawler? give me answer to it.   170
Montano.   Worthy Othello, I am hurt to danger;
  Your officer, Iago, can inform you,
  While I spare speech, which something now offends[282] me,
  Of all that I do know; nor know I aught
  By me that 's said or done amiss this night,   175
  Unless self-charity be sometimes a vice,
  And to defend ourselves it be a sin
  When violence assails us.
Othello.   Now, by heaven,

---

[276] On duty.   [277] Undressing.   [278] Silly quarrel.   [279] Judgment.   [280] Undo.
[281] High reputation.   [282] Pains, harms.

My blood begins my safer guides to rule,
And passion, having my best judgment collied,[283]   180
Assays to lead the way. If I once stir,
Or do but lift this arm, the best of you
Shall sink in my rebuke. Give me to know
How this foul rout began, who set it on;
And he that is approv'd[284] in this offence,   185
Though he had twinn'd with me—both at a birth—
Shall lose me. What! in a town of war,
Yet wild, the people's hearts brimful of fear,
To manage private and domestic quarrel,
In night, and on the court and guard of safety!   190
'Tis monstrous. Iago, who began 't?
Montano.   If partially affin'd,[285] or leagu'd in office,
Thou dost deliver more or less than truth,
Thou art not soldier.
Iago.   Touch me not so near;
I had rather[286] have this tongue cut from my mouth   195
Than it should do offence to Michael Cassio;
Yet, I persuade myself, to speak the truth
Shall nothing wrong him. Thus it is, general.
Montano and myself being in speech,
There comes a fellow crying out for help,   200
And Cassio following with determin'd sword
To execute upon him. Sir, this gentleman
Steps in to Cassio, and entreats his pause;
Myself the crying fellow did pursue,
Lest by his clamour, as it so fell out,   205
The town might fall in fright; he, swift of foot,
Outran my purpose, and I return'd the rather
For that I heard the clink and fall of swords,
And Cassio high in oath, which till to-night
I ne'er might say before. When I came back,—   210
For this was brief,—I found them close together,
At blow and thrust, even as again they were
When you yourself did part them.
More of this matter can I not report:
But men are men; the best sometimes forget: 215
Though Cassio did some little wrong to him,
As men in rage strike those that wish them best,
Yet, surely Cassio, I believe, receiv'd

---

[283] Clouded.   [284] Proved (i.e., guilty).   [285] Favorably biased (by ties of friendship, or
as Cassio's fellow officer).   [286] More quickly.

From him that fled some strange indignity,
Which patience could not pass.
Othello.   I know, Iago.   220
Thy honesty and love doth mince[287] this matter,
Making it light to Cassio. Cassio, I love thee;
But never more be officer of mine.

(*Enter Desdemona, attended.*)

Look! if my gentle love be not rais'd up;
(*To Cassio.*) I'll make thee an example.
Desdemona.   What's the matter?   225
Othello.   All's well now, sweeting; come away to bed.
Sir, for your hurts, myself will be your surgeon.
Lead him off.   (*Montano is led off.*)
Iago, look with care about the town,
And silence those whom this vile brawl distracted.   230
Come, Desdemona; 'tis the soldier's life,
To have their balmy slumbers wak'd with strife.

(*Exeunt all but Iago and Cassio.*)

Iago.   What! are you hurt, lieutenant?
Cassio.   Ay; past all surgery.
Iago.   Marry, heaven forbid!   235
Cassio.   Reputation, reputation, reputation! O! I have lost my reputation. I
have lost the immortal part of myself, and what remains is bestial. My
reputation, Iago, my reputation!
Iago.   As I am an honest man, I thought you had received some bodily
wound; there is more offence in that than in reputation. Reputation is an
idle and most false imposition;[288] oft got without merit, and lost without
deserving: you have lost no reputation at all, unless you repute yourself such
a loser. What! man; there are ways to recover the general again; you are but
now cast in his mood,[289] a punishment more in policy[290] than in malice;
even so as one would beat his offenceless dog to affright an imperious lion.
Sue to him again, and he is yours.
Cassio.   I will rather sue to be despised than to deceive so good a commander
with so slight, so drunken and so indiscreet an officer. Drunk! and speak
parrot![291] and squabble, swagger, swear, and discourse fustian[292] with one's

---

[287] Tone down.   [288] Something external.   [289] Dismissed because he is angry.
[290] I.e., more for the sake of the example, or to show his fairness.   [291] I.e., without thinking.   [292] I.e., nonsense.

own shadow! O thou invisible spirit of wine! if thou hast no name to be known by, let us call thee devil!

Iago. What was he that you followed with your sword? What hath he done to you?

Cassio. I know not.

Iago. Is 't possible?

Cassio. I remember a mass of things, but nothing distinctly; a quarrel, but nothing wherefore. O God! that men should put an enemy in their mouths to steal away their brains; that we should, with joy, pleasance,[293] revel, and applause, transform ourselves into beasts.

Iago. Why, but you are now well enough; how came you thus recovered?

Cassio. It hath pleased the devil drunkenness to give place to the devil wrath; one unperfectness shows me another, to make me frankly despise myself.

Iago. Come, you are too severe a moraler. As the time, the place, and the condition of this country stands, I could heartily wish this had not befallen, but since it is as it is, mend it for your own good.

Cassio. I will ask him for my place again; he shall tell me I am a drunkard! Had I as many mouths as Hydra,[294] such an answer would stop them all. To be now a sensible man, by and by a fool, and presently a beast! O strange! Every inordinate cup is unblessed and the ingredient[295] is a devil.

Iago. Come, come; good wine is a good familiar creature if it be well used; exclaim no more against it. And, good lieutenant, I think you think I love you.

Cassio. I have well approved it, sir. I drunk!

Iago. You or any man living may be drunk at some time, man. I'll tell you what you shall do. Our general's wife is now the general; I may say so in this respect, for that he hath devoted and given up himself to the contemplation, mark, and denotement of her parts and graces: confess yourself freely to her; importune her; she'll help to put you in your place again. She is of so free, so kind, so apt, so blessed a disposition, that she holds it a vice in her goodness not to do more than she is requested. This broken joint between you and her husband entreat her to splinter;[296] and, my fortunes against any lay[297] worth naming, this crack of your love shall grow stronger than it was before.

Cassio. You advise me well.

Iago. I protest, in the sincerity of love and honest kindness.

Cassio. I think it freely; and betimes in the morning I will beseech the virtuous Desdemona to undertake for me. I am desperate of my fortunes if they check me here.

Iago. You are in the right. Good-night, lieutenant; I must to the watch.

---

[293] Pleasure.   [294] Many-headed snake in Greek mythology.   [295] Contents.
[296] Bind up with splints.   [297] Wager.

Cassio.   Good-night, honest Iago!   (*Exit.*)
Iago.   And what's he then that says I play the villain?
   When this advice is free I give and honest,
   Probal[298] to thinking and indeed the course
   To win the Moor again? For 'tis most easy   295
   The inclining Desdemona to subdue
   In any honest suit; she's fram'd as fruitful[299]
   As the free elements. And then for her
   To win the Moor, were 't to renounce his baptism,
   All seals and symbols of redeemed sin,   300
   His soul is so enfetter'd to her love,
   That she may make, unmake, do what she list,
   Even as her appetite shall play the god
   With his weak function.[300] How am I then a villain
   To counsel Cassio to this parallel[301] course,   305
   Directly to his good? Divinity of hell!
   When devils will the blackest sins put on,
   They do suggest at first with heavenly shows,
   As I do now; for while this honest fool
   Plies Desdemona to repair his fortunes,   310
   And she for him pleads strongly to the Moor,
   I'll pour this pestilence into his ear
   That she repeals[302] him for her body's lust;
   And, by how much she strives to do him good,
   She shall undo her credit with the Moor.   315
   So will I turn her virtue into pitch,
   And out of her own goodness make the net
   That shall enmesh them all.

(*Re-enter Roderigo.*)

                How now, Roderigo!
Roderigo.   I do follow here in the chase, not like a hound that hunts, but one
   that fills up the cry.[303] My money is almost spent; I have been to-night
   exceedingly well cudgelled; and I think the issue will be, I shall have so
   much experience for my pains; and so, with no money at all and a little
   more wit, return again to Venice.
Iago.   How poor are they that have not patience!
   What wound did ever heal but by degrees?   325
   Thou know'st we work by wit and not by witchcraft,
   And wit depends on dilatory time.

---

[298] Provable.   [299] Generous.   [300] Faculties.   [301] Purposeful.   [302] I.e., seeks
to recall.   [303] Pack (hunting term).

Does 't not go well? Cassio hath beaten thee,
And thou by that small hurt hast cashiered Cassio.
Though other things grow fair against the sun,   330
Yet fruits that blossom first will first be ripe:
Content thyself awhile. By the mass, 'tis morning;
Pleasure and action make the hours seem short.
Retire thee; go where thou art billeted:
Away, I say; thou shalt know more hereafter: 335
Nay, get thee gone. (*Exit Roderigo.*) Two things are to be done,
My wife must move for Cassio to her mistress;
I'll set her on;
Myself the while to draw the Moor apart,
And bring him jump[304] when he may Cassio find   340
Soliciting his wife: ay, that's the way:
Dull not device by coldness and delay.   (*Exit.*)

Act III

SCENE 1.   *Cyprus. Before the Castle.*

(*Enter Cassio, and some Musicians.*)

Cassio.   Masters, play here, I will content your pains;[305]
    Something that's brief; and bid 'Good-morrow, general.'   (*Music.*)

(*Enter Clown.*)

Clown.   Why, masters, have your instruments been in Naples, that they
    speak i' the nose[306] thus?
First Musician.   How, sir, how?   5
Clown.   Are these, I pray you, wind-instruments?
First Musician.   Ay, marry, are they, sir.
Clown.   O! thereby hangs a tale.
First Musician.   Whereby hangs a tale, sir?
Clown.   Marry, sir, by many a wind-instrument that I know. But, masters,
    here's money for you; and the general so likes your music, that he desires
    you, for love's sake, to make no more noise with it.
First Musician.   Well, sir, we will not.

---

[304] At the exact moment.   [305] Reward your efforts.   [306] Naples was notorious for venereal disease, and syphilis was believed to affect the nose.

Clown.   If you have any music that may not be heard, to 't again; but, as they
say, to hear music the general does not greatly care.   15

First Musician.   We have none such, sir.

Clown.   Then put up your pipes in your bag, for I'll away.
Go; vanish into air; away!   (*Exeunt Musicians.*)

Cassio.   Dost thou hear, mine honest friend?

Clown.   No, I hear not your honest friend; I hear you.   20

Cassio.   Prithee, keep up thy quillets.[307] There's a poor piece of gold for thee.
If the gentlewoman that attends the general's wife be stirring, tell her
there's one Cassio entreats her a little favour of speech: wilt thou do this?

Clown.   She is stirring, sir: if she will stir hither, I shall seem to notify unto
her.   25

Cassio.   Do, good my friend.   (*Exit Clown.*)

(*Enter Iago.*)

In happy time, Iago.

Iago.   You have not been a-bed, then?

Cassio.   Why, no; the day had broke
Before we parted. I have made bold, Iago,
To send in to your wife; my suit to her   30
Is, that she will to virtuous Desdemona
Procure me some access.

Iago.   I'll send her to you presently;
And I'll devise a mean to draw the Moor
Out of the way, that your converse and business
May be more free.

Cassio.   I humbly thank you for 't.   (*Exit Iago.*)
I never knew   35
A Florentine more kind and honest.[308]

(*Enter Emilia.*)

Emilia.   Good-morrow, good lieutenant: I am sorry
For your displeasure,[309] but all will soon be well.
The general and his wife are talking of it,
And she speaks for you stoutly: the Moor replies   40
That he you hurt is of great fame in Cyprus
And great affinity,[310] and that in wholesome wisdom
He might not but refuse you; but he protests he loves you,

---

[307] Quibbles.   [308] Cassio means that not even a fellow Florentine could behave to him in
a friendlier fashion than does Iago.   [309] Disgrace.   [310] Family connection.

And needs no other suitor but his likings
To take the safest occasion by the front[311]   45
To bring you in again.[312]
Cassio.   Yet, I beseech you,
If you think fit, or that it may be done,
Give me advantage of some brief discourse
With Desdemona alone.
Emilia.   Pray you, come in:
I will bestow you where you shall have time   50
To speak your bosom[313] freely.
Cassio.   I am much bound to you.   (*Exeunt.*)

SCENE 2.   *A Room in the Castle.*

(*Enter Othello, Iago, and Gentlemen.*)

Othello.   These letters give, Iago, to the pilot,
And by him do my duties to the senate;
That done, I will be walking on the works;
Repair there to me.
Iago.   Well, my good lord, I'll do 't.
Othello.   This fortification, gentlemen, shall we see 't?   5
Gentlemen.   We'll wait upon your lordship.   (*Exeunt.*)

SCENE 3.   *Before the Castle.*

(*Enter Desdemona, Cassio, and Emilia.*)

Desdemona.   Be thou assur'd, good Cassio, I will do
All my abilities in thy behalf.
Emilia.   Good madam, do: I warrant it grieves my husband,
As if the case were his.   5
Desdemona.   O! that's an honest fellow. Do not doubt, Cassio,
But I will have my lord and you again
As friendly as you were.
Cassio.   Bounteous madam,
Whatever shall become of Michael Cassio,
He's never any thing but your true servant.
Desdemona.   I know 't; I thank you. You do love my lord;   10
You have known him long; and be you well assur'd

---

[311] Forelock.   [312] Restore you (to Othello's favor).   [313] Heart, inmost thoughts.

He shall in strangeness[314] stand no further off
Than in a politic[315] distance.
Cassio.   Ay, but, lady,
That policy may either last so long,
Or feed upon such nice[316] and waterish diet,   15
Or breed itself so out of circumstance,
That, I being absent and my place supplied,
My general will forget my love and service.
Desdemona.   Do not doubt[317] that; before Emilia here
I give thee warrant of thy place. Assure thee,   20
If I do vow a friendship, I'll perform it
To the last article; my lord shall never rest;
I'll watch him tame,[318] and talk him out of patience;
His bed shall seem a school, his board a shrift;[319]
I'll intermingle every thing he does   25
With Cassio's suit. Therefore be merry, Cassio;
For thy solicitor shall rather die
Than give thy cause away.[320]

(*Enter Othello, and Iago at a distance.*)

Emilia.   Madam, here comes my lord.
Cassio.   Madam, I'll take my leave.   30
Desdemona.   Why, stay, and hear me speak.
Cassio.   Madam, not now; I am very ill at ease,
Unfit for mine own purposes.
Desdemona.   Well, do your discretion.   (*Exit Cassio.*)
Iago.   Ha! I like not that.
Othello.   What dost thou say?   35
Iago.   Nothing, my lord: or if—I know not what.
Othello.   Was not that Cassio parted from my wife?
Iago.   Cassio, my lord? No, sure, I cannot think it,
That he would steal away so guilty-like,
Seeing you coming.
Othello.   I do believe 'twas he.   40
Desdemona.   How now, my lord!
I have been talking with a suitor here,
A man that languishes in your displeasure.
Othello.   Who is 't you mean?
Desdemona.   Why, your lieutenant, Cassio. Good my lord,   45
If I have any grace or power to move you,

---

[314] Aloofness.   [315] I.e., dictated by policy.   [316] Slight, trivial.   [317] Fear.
[318] Outwatch him (i.e., keep him awake) till he submits.   [319] Confessional.
[320] Abandon your cause.

His present[321] reconciliation take;
For if he be not one that truly loves you,
That errs in ignorance and not in cunning,
I have no judgment in an honest face.   50
I prithee[322] call him back.
Othello.   Went he hence now?
Desdemona.   Ay, sooth; so humbled,
   That he hath left part of his grief with me,
   To suffer with him. Good love, call him back.
Othello.   Not now, sweet Desdemona; some other time.   55
Desdemona.   But shall 't be shortly?
Othello.   The sooner, sweet, for you.
Desdemona.   Shall 't be to-night at supper?
Othello.   No, not to-night.
Desdemona.   To-morrow dinner, then?
Othello.   I shall not dine at home;
   I meet the captains at the citadel.
Desdemona.   Why, then, to-morrow night; or Tuesday morn;   60
   Or Tuesday noon, or night; or Wednesday morn:
   I prithee name the time, but let it not
   Exceed three days: in faith, he's penitent;
   And yet his trespass, in our common reason,—
   Save that they say, the wars must make examples   65
   Out of their best,—is not almost[323] a fault
   To incur a private check.[324] When shall he come?
   Tell me, Othello: I wonder in my soul,
   What you could ask me, that I should deny,
   Or stand so mammering[325] on. What! Michael Cassio,   70
   That came a wooing with you, and so many a time,
   When I have spoke of you dispraisingly,
   Hath ta'en your part; to have so much to do
   To bring him in! Trust me, I could do much,—
Othello.   Prithee, no more; let him come when he will;   75
   I deny thee nothing.
Desdemona.   Why, this is not a boon;
   'Tis as I should entreat you wear your gloves,
   Or feed on nourishing dishes, or keep you warm,
   Or sue to you to do a peculiar profit
   To your own person: nay, when I have a suit   80
   Wherein I mean to touch your love indeed,
   It shall be full of poise[326] and difficult weight,

---

[321] Immediate.   [322] Pray thee.   [323] Hardly.   [324] (Even) a private reprimand.
[325] Shilly-shallying.   [326] Weight.

And fearful to be granted.

Othello.   I will deny thee nothing:
Whereon, I do beseech thee, grant me this,
To leave me but a little to myself.   85

Desdemona.   Shall I deny you? no: farewell, my lord.

Othello.   Farewell, my Desdemona: I'll come to thee straight.

Desdemona.   Emilia, come. Be as your fancies teach you;
Whate'er you be, I am obedient.   (*Exit, with Emilia.*)

Othello.   Excellent wretch![327] Perdition catch my soul,   90
But I do love thee! and when I love thee not,
Chaos is[328] come again.

Iago.   My noble lord,—

Othello.   What dost thou say, Iago?

Iago.   Did Michael Cassio, when you woo'd my lady,
Know of your love?   95

Othello.   He did, from first to last: why dost thou ask?

Iago.   But for a satisfaction of my thought;
No further harm.

Othello.   Why of thy thought, Iago?

Iago.   I did not think he had been acquainted with her.

Othello.   O! yes; and went between us very oft.   100

Iago.   Indeed!

Othello.   Indeed! ay, indeed; discern'st thou aught in that?
Is he not honest?

Iago.   Honest, my lord?

Othello.   Honest! ay, honest.

Iago.   My lord, for aught I know.

Othello.   What dost thou think?

Iago.   Think, my lord!

Othello.   Think, my lord!   105
By heaven, he echoes me,
As if there were some monster in his thought
Too hideous to be shown. Thou dost mean something:
I heard thee say but now, thou lik'dst not that,
When Cassio left my wife; what didst not like?   110
And when I told thee he was of my counsel
In my whole course of wooing, thou criedst, 'Indeed!'
And didst contract and purse thy brow together,
As if thou then hadst shut up in thy brain
Some horrible conceit.[329] If thou dost love me,   115
Show me thy thought.

Iago.   My lord, you know I love you.

---

[327] Here, a term of endearment.   [328] Will have.   [329] Fancy.

Othello.   I think thou dost;
  And, for[330] I know thou art full of love and honesty,
  And weigh'st thy words before thou givest them breath,
  Therefore these stops[331] of thine fright me the more;   120
  For such things in a false disloyal knave
  Are tricks of custom, but in a man that's just
  They are close dilations,[332] working from the heart
  That passion cannot rule.
Iago.   For Michael Cassio,
  I dare be sworn I think that he is honest.   125
Othello.   I think so too.
Iago.   Men should be what they seem;
  Or those that be not, would they might seem none!
Othello.   Certain men should be what they seem.
Iago.   Why then, I think Cassio's an honest man.
Othello.   Nay, yet there's more in this.   130
  I pray thee, speak to me as to thy thinkings,
  As thou dost ruminate, and give thy worst of thoughts
  The worst of words.
Iago.   Good my lord, pardon me;
  Though I am bound to every act of duty,
  I am not bound to[333] that all slaves are free to.   135
  Utter my thoughts? Why, say they are vile and false;
  As where's that palace whereinto foul things
  Sometimes intrude not? who has a breast so pure
  But some uncleanly apprehensions[334]
  Keep leets and law-days,[335] and in session sit   140
  With meditations lawful?
Othello.   Thou dost conspire against thy friend, Iago,
  If thou but think'st him wrong'd, and mak'st his ear
  A stranger to thy thoughts.
Iago.   I do beseech you,
  Though I perchance am vicious in my guess,—   145
  As, I confess, it is my nature's plague
  To spy into abuses, and oft my jealousy[336]
  Shapes faults that are not,—that your wisdom yet,
  From one that so imperfectly conceits,
  Would take no notice, nor build yourself a trouble   150
  Out of his scattering and unsure observance.
  It were not for your quiet nor your good,

---

[330] Because.   [331] Interruptions, hesitations.   [332] Secret (i.e., involuntary, unconscious) revelations.   [333] Bound with regard to.   [334] Conceptions.   [335] Sittings of the lo-cal courts.   [336] Suspicion.

Nor for my manhood, honesty, or wisdom,
  To let you know my thoughts.
Othello.   What dost thou mean?
Iago.   Good name in man and woman, dear my lord,   155
  Is the immediate jewel of[337] their souls:
  Who steals my purse steals trash; 'tis something, nothing;
  'Twas mine, 'tis his, and has been slave to thousands;
  But he that filches from me my good name
  Robs me of that which not enriches him,   160
  And makes me poor indeed.
Othello.   By heaven, I'll know thy thoughts.
Iago.   You cannot, if my heart were in your hand;
  Nor shall not, whilst 'tis in my custody.
Othello.   Ha!
Iago.   O! beware, my lord, of jealousy;   165
  It is the green-ey'd monster which doth mock
  The meat it feeds on: that cuckold[338] lives in bliss
  Who, certain of his fate, loves not his wronger;
  But, O! what damned minutes tells[339] he o'er
  Who dotes, yet doubts; suspects, yet soundly loves!   170
Othello.   O misery!
Iago.   Poor and content is rich, and rich enough,
  But riches fineless[340] is as poor as winter
  To him that ever fears he shall be poor.
  Good heaven, the souls of all my tribe defend   175
  From jealousy!
Othello.   Why, why is this?
  Think'st thou I'd make a life of jealousy,
  To follow still the changes of the moon
  With fresh suspicions? No; to be once in doubt
  Is once to be resolved. Exchange me for a goat   180
  When I shall turn the business of my soul
  To such exsufflicate[341] and blown[342] surmises,
  Matching thy inference. 'Tis not to make me jealous
  To say my wife is fair, feeds well, loves company,
  Is free of speech, sings, plays, and dances well;   185
  Where virtue is, these are more virtuous:
  Nor from mine own weak merits will I draw
  The smallest fear, or doubt of her revolt;
  For she had eyes, and chose me. No, Iago;
  I'll see before I doubt; when I doubt, prove;   190

---

[337] Jewel closest to.   [338] Husband of an adulterous woman.   [339] Counts.
[340] Boundless.   [341] Spat out (?).   [342] Fly-blown.

And, on the proof, there is no more but this,
Away at once with love or jealousy!
Iago.   I am glad of it; for now I shall have reason
  To show the love and duty that I bear you
  With franker spirit; therefore, as I am bound,   195
  Receive it from me; I speak not yet of proof.
  Look to your wife; observe her well with Cassio; ←
  Wear your eye thus, not jealous nor secure:
  I would not have your free and noble nature
  Out of self-bounty[343] be abus'd; look to 't: 200
  I know our country disposition[344] well;
  In Venice they do let heaven see the pranks
  They dare not show their husbands; their best conscience
  Is not to leave 't undone, but keep 't unknown.
Othello.   Dost thou say so?   205
Iago.   She did deceive her father, marrying you;
  And when she seem'd to shake and fear your looks,
  She lov'd them most.
Othello.   And so she did.
Iago.   Why, go to,[345] then;
  She that so young could give out such a seeming,
  To seel her father's eyes up close as oak,   210
  He thought 'twas witchcraft; but I am much to blame;
  I humbly do beseech you of your pardon
  For too much loving you.
Othello.   I am bound to thee for ever.
Iago.   I see, this hath a little dash'd your spirits.
Othello.   Not a jot, not a jot.
Iago.   I' faith, I fear it has.   215
  I hope you will consider what is spoke
  Comes from my love. But I do see you're mov'd;
  I am to pray you not to strain my speech
  To grosser issues nor to larger reach
  Than to suspicion.   220
Othello.   I will not.
Iago.   Should you do so, my lord,
  My speech should fall into such vile success
  As my thoughts aim not at. Cassio's my worthy friend—
  My lord, I see you're mov'd.
Othello.   No, not much mov'd:
  I do not think but Desdemona's honest.[346]   225

---

[343] Innate generosity.   [344] I.e., that of Venice.   [345] Colloquialism;   here,   something
like "all right."   [346] Chaste.

Iago.   Long live she so! and long live you to think so!
Othello.   And yet, how nature erring from itself,—
Iago.   Ay, there's the point: as, to be bold with you,
    Not to affect many proposed matches
    Of her own clime,[347] complexion, and degree,[348]   230
    Whereto, we see, in all things nature tends;
    Foh! one may smell in such, a will most rank,
    Foul disproportion, thoughts unnatural.
    But pardon me; I do not in position[349]
    Distinctly[350] speak of her, though I may fear   235
    Her will, recoiling[351] to her better judgment,
    May fall to match you with her country forms
    And happily[352] repent.
Othello.   Farewell, farewell:
    If more thou dost perceive, let me know more;
    Set on thy wife to observe. Leave me, Iago.   240
Iago.   My lord, I take my leave.   *(Going.)*
Othello.   Why did I marry? This honest creature, doubtless,
    Sees and knows more, much more, than he unfolds.
Iago *(returning).*   My lord, I would I might entreat your honour
    To scan this thing no further; leave it to time.
    Although 'tis fit that Cassio have his place,   245
    For, sure he fills it up with great ability,
    Yet, if you please to hold him off awhile,
    You shall by that perceive him and his means:
    Note if your lady strain his entertainment[353]   250
    With any strong or vehement importunity;
    Much will be seen in that. In the mean time,
    Let me be thought too busy[354] in my fears,
    As worthy cause I have to fear I am,
    And hold her free, I do beseech your honour.   255
Othello.   Fear not my government.
Iago.   I once more take my leave.   *(Exit.)*
Othello.   This fellow's of exceeding honesty,
    And knows all qualities, with a learned spirit,
    Of human dealings; if I do prove her haggard,[355]   260
    Though that her jesses[356] were my dear heart-strings,
    I'd whistle her off and let her down the wind,[357]
    To prey at fortune. Haply, for I am black,
    And have not those soft parts of conversation

---

[347] Country.   [348] Social rank.   [349] In definite assertion.   [350] Specifically.
[351] Reverting.   [352] Perhaps.   [353] Urge his re-welcome (i.e., to Othello's trust and favor).   [354] Meddlesome.   [355] Wild hawk.   [356] Leather thongs by which the hawk's legs were strapped to the trainer's wrist.   [357] I'd let her go and take care of herself.

That chamberers[358] have, or, for I am declin'd   265
Into the vale of years—yet that's not much—
She's gone, I am abus'd;[359] and my relief
➤ Must be to loathe her. O curse of marriage!
That we can call these delicate creatures ours,
And not their appetites. I had rather be a toad,   270
And live upon the vapour of a dungeon,
Than keep a corner in the thing I love
For others' uses. Yet, 'tis the plague of great ones;
Prerogativ'd[360] are they less than the base;
'Tis destiny unshunnable, like death: 275
Even then this forked plague[361] is fated to us
When we do quicken.[362]
      Look! where she comes.
If she be false, O! then heaven mocks itself.
I'll not believe it.

(*Re-enter Desdemona and Emilia.*)

Desdemona.   How now, my dear Othello!
 Your dinner and the generous[363] islanders   280
 By you invited, do attend your presence.
Othello. I am to blame.
Desdemona.   Why do you speak so faintly?
 Are you not well?
Othello. I have a pain upon my forehead here.[364]
Desdemona. Faith, that's with watching; 'twill away again: 285
 Let me but bind it hard, within this hour
 It will be well.
Othello.   Your napkin[365] is too little:

(*She drops her handkerchief.*)

 Let it alone. Come, I'll go in with you.
Desdemona. I am very sorry that you are not well.

       (*Exeunt Othello and Desdemona.*)

Emilia. I am glad I have found this napkin;   290
 This was her first remembrance from the Moor;

---

[358] Courtiers; or (more specifically): gallants, frequenters of bed chambers. [359] Deceived.
[360] Privileged. [361] I.e., the cuckold's proverbial horns. [362] Are conceived, come alive.
[363] Noble. [364] Othello again refers to his cuckoldom. [365] Handkerchief.

My wayward husband hath a hundred times
Woo'd me to steal it, but she so loves the token,
For he conjur'd her she should ever keep it,
That she reserves it evermore about her   295
To kiss and talk to. I'll have the work ta'en out,[366]
And giv 't Iago:
What he will do with it heaven knows, not I;
I nothing but[367] to please his fantasy.[368]

(*Enter Iago.*)

Iago.   How now! what do you here alone?   300
Emilia.   Do not you chide; I have a thing for you.
Iago.   A thing for me? It is a common thing—
Emilia.   Ha!
Iago.   To have a foolish wife.
Emilia.   O! is that all? What will you give me now   305
   For that same handkerchief?
Iago.   What handkerchief?
Emilia.   What handkerchief!
   Why, that the Moor first gave to Desdemona:
   That which so often you did bid me steal.
Iago.   Hath stol'n it from her?   310
Emilia.   No, faith; she let it drop by negligence,
   And, to the advantage, I, being there, took 't up.
   Look, here it is.
Iago.   A good wench; give it me.
Emilia.   What will you do with 't, that you have been so earnest
   To have me filch it?
Iago.   Why, what's that to you?   (*Snatches it.*)   315
Emilia.   If it be not for some purpose of import
   Give 't me again; poor lady! she'll run mad
   When she shall lack it.
Iago.   Be not acknown on 't;[369] I have use for it.
   Go, leave me.   (*Exit Emilia.*)   320
   I will in Cassio's lodging lose this napkin,
   And let him find it; trifles light as air
   Are to the jealous confirmations strong
   As proofs of holy writ; this may do something.
   The Moor already changes with my poison: 325
   Dangerous conceits are in their natures poisons,

---

[366] Pattern copied.   [367] I.e., only want.   [368] Whim.   [369] You   know   nothing
about it.

Which at the first are scarce found to distaste,[370]
But with a little act upon the blood,
Burn like the mines of sulphur. I did say so:
Look! where he comes!

(*Enter Othello.*)

Not poppy,[371] nor mandragora,[372]   330
Nor all the drowsy syrups[373] of the world,
Shall ever medicine thee to that sweet sleep
Which thou ow'dst yesterday.

Othello.   Ha! ha! false to me?
Iago.   Why, how now, general! no more of that.
Othello.   Avaunt! be gone! thou hast set me on the rack;   335
  I swear 'tis better to be much abus'd
  Than but to know 't a little.
Iago.   How now, my lord!
Othello.   What sense had I of her stol'n hours of lust?
  I saw 't not, thought it not, it harm'd not me;
  I slept the next night well, was free and merry;   340
  I found not Cassio's kisses on her lips;
  He that is robb'd, not wanting what is stol'n,
  Let him not know 't, and he's not robb'd at all.
Iago.   I am sorry to hear this.
Othello.   I had been happy, if the general camp,[374]   345
  Pioners[375] and all, had tasted her sweet body,
  So[376] I had nothing known. O! now, for ever
  Farewell the tranquil mind; farewell content!
  Farewell the plumed troop and the big wars
  That make ambition virtue! O, farewell!   350
  Farewell the neighing steed, and the shrill trump,
  The spirit-stirring drum, the ear-piercing fife,
  The royal banner, and all quality,
  Pride, pomp, and circumstance[377] of glorious war!
  And, O you mortal engines,[378] whose rude throats   355
  The immortal Jove's dread clamours counterfeit,
  Farewell! Othello's occupation's gone!
Iago.   Is it possible, my lord?
Othello.   Villain, be sure thou prove my love a whore,
  Be sure of it; give me the ocular proof;   360

---

[370] Scarce can be tasted.   [371] Opium.   [372] A soporific.   [373] I.e., soporifics.
[374] Whole army.   [375] Lowest rank of manual laborers in the army.   [376] As long as.
[377] Pageantry.   [378] Deadly artillery.

Or, by the worth of mine eternal soul,
Thou hadst been better have been born a dog
Than answer my wak'd wrath.

Iago.   Is 't come to this?

Othello.   Make me to see 't; or, at the least, so prove it,
That the probation[379] bear no hinge nor loop   365
To hang a doubt on; or woe upon thy life!

Iago.   My noble lord—

Othello.   If thou dost slander her and torture me,
Never pray more; abandon all remorse;
On horror's head horrors accumulate;   370
Do deeds to make heaven weep, all earth amaz'd;
For nothing canst thou to damnation add
Greater than that.

Iago.   O grace! O heaven forgive me!
Are you a man! have you a soul or sense?
God be wi' you; take mine office. O wretched fool!   375
That liv'st to make thine honesty a vice.
O monstrous world! Take note, take note, O world!
To be direct and honest is not safe.
I thank you for this profit,[380] and, from hence
I'll love no friend, sith[381] love breeds such offence.   380

Othello.   Nay, stay; thou shouldst be honest.

Iago.   I should be wise; for honesty's a fool,
And loses that it works for.

Othello.   By the world,
I think my wife be honest and think she is not;
I think that thou art just and think thou art not.   385
I'll have some proof. Her name, that was as fresh
As Dian's[382] visage, is now begrim'd and black
As mine own face. If there be cords or knives,
Poison or fire or suffocating streams,
I'll not endure it. Would I were satisfied!   390

Iago.   I see, sir, you are eaten up with passion.
I do repent me that I put it to you.
You would be satisfied?

Othello.   Would! nay, I will.

Iago.   And may; but how? how satisfied, my lord?
Would you, the supervisor,[383] grossly gape on;   395
Behold her tupp'd?

Othello.   Death and damnation! O!

---

[379] Proof.   [380] Lesson.   [381] Since.   [382] Diana's, the goddess of the moon.
[383] Observer.

Iago.   It were a tedious[384] difficulty, I think,
    To bring them to that prospect; damn them then,
    If ever mortal eyes do see them bolster[385]
    More[386] than their own! What then? how then?   400
    What shall I say? Where's satisfaction?
    It is impossible you should see this,
    Were they as prime[387] as goats, as hot as monkeys,
    As salt as wolves in pride,[388] and fools as gross
    As ignorance made drunk; but yet, I say,   405
    If imputation, and strong circumstances,
    Which lead directly to the door of truth,
    Will give you satisfaction, you may have it.
Othello.   Give me a living reason she's disloyal.
Iago.   I do not like the office;   410
    But, sith I am enter'd in this cause so far,
    Prick'd to 't by foolish honesty and love,
    I will go on. I lay with Cassio lately;
    And, being troubled with a raging tooth,
    I could not sleep.   415
    There are a kind of men so loose of soul
    That in their sleeps will mutter their affairs;
    One of this kind is Cassio.
    In sleep I heard him say, 'Sweet Desdemona,
    Let us be wary, let us hide our loves!'   420
    And then, sir, would he gripe[389] and wring my hand,
    Cry, 'O, sweet creature!' and then kiss me hard,
    As if he pluck'd up kisses by the roots,
    That grew upon my lips; then laid his leg
    Over my thigh, and sigh'd, and kiss'd; and then   425
    Cried, 'Cursed fate, that gave thee to the Moor!'
Othello.   O monstrous! monstrous!
Iago.   Nay, this was but his dream.
Othello.   But this denoted a foregone conclusion:[390]
    'Tis a shrewd doubt,[391] though it be but a dream.
Iago.   And this may help to thicken other proofs   430
    That do demonstrate thinly.
Othello.   I'll tear her all to pieces.
Iago.   Nay, but be wise; yet we see nothing done;
    She may be honest yet. Tell me but this:
    Have you not sometimes seen a handkerchief
    Spotted with strawberries in your wife's hand?   435

---

[384] Laborious.   [385] Lie together.   [386] Other.   [387] Lustful.   [388] Heat.
[389] Seize.   [390] Previous consummation.   [391] (1) Cursed, (2) Acute suspicion.

Othello. I gave her such a one; 'twas my first gift.

➤**Iago.** I know not that; but such a handkerchief—
  I am sure it was your wife's—did I to-day
  See Cassio wipe his beard with.

Othello.   If it be that,—

Iago. If it be that, or any that was hers,   440
  It speaks against her with the other proofs.

Othello. O! that the slave had forty thousand lives;
  One is too poor, too weak for my revenge.
  Now do I see 'tis true. Look here, Iago;

➤All my fond love thus do I blow to heaven: 445
  'Tis gone.
  Arise, black vengeance, from the hollow hell!
  Yield up, O love! thy crown and hearted throne
  To tyrannous hate. Swell, bosom, with thy fraught,[392]
  For 'tis of aspics'[393] tongues!

Iago.   Yet be content.[394]   450

Othello. O! blood, blood, blood!

Iago. Patience, I say; your mind, perhaps, may change.

Othello. Never, Iago. Like to the Pontic sea,[395]
  Whose icy current and compulsive course
  Ne'er feels retiring ebb, but keeps due on   455
  To the Propontic and the Hellespont,[396]
  Even so my bloody thoughts, with violent pace,
  Shall ne'er look back, ne'er ebb to humble love,
  Till that a capable[397] and wide revenge
  Swallow them up.   (*Kneels.*)
                      Now, by yond marble heaven,   460
  In the due reverence of a sacred vow
  I here engage my words.

Iago.   Do not rise yet.   (*Kneels.*)
  Witness, you ever-burning lights above!
  You elements that clip[398] us round about!
  Witness, that here Iago doth give up   465
  The execution of his wit, hands, heart,
  To wrong'd Othello's service! Let him command,
  And to obey shall be in me remorse,[399]
  What bloody business ever.[400]   (*They rise.*)

Othello.   I greet thy love,
  Not with vain thanks, but with acceptance bounteous,   470

---

[392] Burden.   [393] Poisonous snake.   [394] Patient.   [395] The Black Sea.   [396] The Sea of Marmara, the Dardanelles.   [397] Comprehensive.   [398] Encompass.
[399] Probably a corrupt line; the meaning appears to be: "to obey shall be my solemn obligation."   [400] Soever.

And will upon the instant put thee to 't:
Within these three days let me hear thee say
That Cassio 's not alive.

Iago.   My friend is dead; 'tis done at your request:
But let her live.

Othello.   Damn her, lewd minx! O, damn her!   475
Come, go with me apart; I will withdraw
To furnish me with some swift means of death
For the fair devil. Now art thou my lieutenant.

Iago.   I am your own for ever.   (*Exeunt.*)

SCENE 4.   *Before the Castle.*

(*Enter Desdemona, Emilia, and Clown.*)

Desdemona.   Do you know, sirrah,[401] where Lieutenant Cassio lies?[402]

Clown.   I dare not say he lies any where.

Desdemona.   Why, man?

Clown.   He is a soldier; and for one to say a soldier lies, is stabbing.[403]

Desdemona.   Go to;[404] where lodges he?   5

Clown.   To tell you where he lodges is to tell you where I lie.

Desdemona.   Can anything be made of this?

Clown.   I know not where he lodges, and for me to devise[405] a lodging, and
say he lies here or he lies there, were to lie in mine own throat.

Desdemona.   Can you inquire him out, and be edified by report?   10

Clown.   I will catechize the world for him; that is, make questions, and by
them answer.

Desdemona.   Seek him, bid him come hither; tell him I have moved my lord
in his behalf, and hope all will be well.

Clown.   To do this is within the compass of man's wit, and therefore I will
attempt the doing it.   (*Exit.*)

Desdemona.   Where should I lose that handkerchief, Emilia?

Emilia.   I know not, madam.

Desdemona.   Believe me, I had rather have lost my purse
Full of cruzadoes;[406] and, but my noble Moor   20
Is true of mind, and made of no such baseness
As jealous creatures are, it were enough
To put him to ill thinking.

Emilia.   Is he not jealous?

Desdemona.   Who! he? I think the sun where he was born
Drew all such humours from him.

---

[401] Common form of address to inferiors.   [402] Lives.   [403] I.e., is cause for stabbing.
[404] Here apparently: "Come on!"   [405] Invent.   [406] Portuguese gold coins.

Emilia.   Look! where he comes.   25
Desdemona.   I will not leave him now till Cassio
  Be call'd to him.

(*Enter Othello.*)

               How is 't with you, my lord?
Othello.   Well, my good lady. (*Aside.*) O! hardness to dissemble.
  How do you, Desdemona?
Desdemona.   Well, my good lord.
Othello.   Give me your hand. This hand is moist,[407] my lady.   30
Desdemona.   It yet has felt no age nor known no sorrow.
Othello.   This argues fruitfulness and liberal[408] heart;
  Hot, hot, and moist; this hand of yours requires
  A sequester[409] from liberty, fasting and prayer,
  Much castigation, exercise devout;   35
  For here 's a young and sweating devil here,
  That commonly rebels. 'Tis a good hand,
  A frank one.
Desdemona.   You may, indeed, say so;
  For 'twas that hand that gave away my heart.
Othello.   A liberal hand; the hearts of old gave hands,   40
  But our new heraldry[410] is hands not hearts.
Desdemona.   I cannot speak of this. Come now, your promise.
Othello.   What promise, chuck?[411]
Desdemona.   I have sent to bid Cassio come speak with you.
Othello.   I have a salt and sorry rheum offends me.   45
  Lend me thy handkerchief.
Desdemona.   Here, my lord.
Othello.   That which I gave you.
Desdemona.   I have it not about me.
Othello.   Not?
Desdemona.   No, indeed, my lord.
Othello.   That is a fault.
  That handkerchief
  Did an Egyptian[412] to my mother give;   50
  She was a charmer,[413] and could almost read
  The thoughts of people; she told her, while she kept it,
  'Twould make her amiable[414] and subdue my father
  Entirely to her love, but if she lost it

---

[407] A supposed symptom of a lustful nature.   [408] With overtones of: too free, loose.
[409] Separation.   [410] I.e., new heraldic symbolism (Othello means that the new way is not
to give the heart together with the hand).   [411] Common term of endearment.
[412] Gypsy.   [413] Sorceress.   [414] Lovable, desirable.

Or made a gift of it, my father's eye   55
Should hold her loathed, and his spirits should hunt
After new fancies.[415] She dying gave it me;
And bid me, when my fate would have me wive,
To give it her. I did so; and take heed on 't;
Make it a darling like your precious eye;   60
To lose 't or give 't away, were such perdition
As nothing else could match.
Desdemona.   Is 't possible?
Othello.   'Tis true; there 's magic in the web of it;
A sibyl,[416] that had number'd in the world
The sun to course two hundred compasses,   65
In her prophetic fury sew'd the work;
The worms were hallow'd that did breed the silk,
And it was dy'd in mummy[417] which the skilful
Conserv'd of maidens' hearts.
Desdemona.   Indeed! is 't true?
Othello.   Most veritable; therefore look to 't well.   70
Desdemona.   Then would to heaven that I had never seen it!
Othello.   Ha! wherefore?
Desdemona.   Why do you speak so startingly and rash?
Othello.   Is 't lost? is 't gone? speak, is it out o' the way?
Desdemona.   Heaven bless us!   75
Othello.   Say you?
Desdemona.   It is not lost; but what an if[418] it were?
Othello.   How!
Desdemona.   I say, it is not lost.
Othello.   Fetch 't, let me see 't!
Desdemona.   Why, so I can, sir, but I will not now.
This is a trick to put me from my suit: 80
Pray you let Cassio be receiv'd again.
Othello.   Fetch me the handkerchief; my mind misgives.
Desdemona.   Come, come;
You'll never meet a more sufficient[419] man.
Othello.   The handkerchief!
Desdemona.   I pray, talk[420] me of Cassio.   85
Othello.   The handkerchief!
Desdemona.   A man that all his time
Hath founded his good fortunes on your love,
Shar'd dangers with you,—
Othello.   The handkerchief!

---

[415] Loves.   [416] Prophetess.   [417] Drug (medicinal or magic) derived from embalmed
bodies.   [418] If.   [419] Adequate.   [420] Talk to.

Desdemona. In sooth, you are to blame.   90
Othello. Away!   *(Exit.)*
Emilia. Is not this man jealous?
Desdemona. I ne'er saw this before.
    Sure, there's some wonder in this handkerchief;
    I am most unhappy in the loss of it.   95
Emilia. 'Tis not a year or two shows us a man;
    They are all but[421] stomachs, and we all but[421] food;
    They eat us hungerly, and when they are full
    They belch us. Look you! Cassio and my husband.

(Enter Iago and Cassio.)

Iago. There is no other way; 'tis she must do 't: 100
    And, lo! the happiness;[422] go and importune her.
Desdemona. How now, good Cassio! what 's the news with you?
Cassio. Madam, my former suit: I do beseech you
    That by your virtuous means I may again
    Exist, and be a member of his love   105
    Whom I with all the office[423] of my heart
    Entirely honour; I would not be delay'd.
    If my offence be of such mortal kind
    That nor my service past, nor present sorrows,
    Nor purpos'd merit in futurity,   110
    Can ransom me into his love again,
    But to know so must be my benefit;
    So shall I clothe me in a forc'd content,
    And shut myself up in some other course
    To fortune's alms.
Desdemona.   Alas! thrice-gentle Cassio!   115
    My advocation is not now in tune;
    My lord is not my lord, nor should I know him,
    Were he in favour[424] as in humour alter'd.
    So help me every spirit sanctified,
    As I have spoken for you all my best   120
    And stood within the blank of[425] his displeasure
    For my free speech. You must awhile be patient;
    What I can do I will, and more I will
    Than for myself I dare: let that suffice you.
Iago. Is my lord angry?
Emilia.   He went hence but now,   125
    And certainly in strange unquietness.

---

[421] Only . . . only.   [422] "What luck!"   [423] Duty.   [424] Appearance.
[425] As the target for.

Iago.   Can he be angry? I have seen the cannon,
  When it hath blown his ranks[426] into the air,
  And, like the devil, from his very arm
  Puff'd his own brother; and can he be angry?   130
  Something of moment[427] then; I will go meet him;
  There's matter in 't indeed, if he be angry.
Desdemona.   I prithee, do so. (*Exit Iago.*) Something, sure, of state,[428]
  Either from Venice, or some unhatch'd[429] practice
  Made demonstrable here in Cyprus to him,   135
  Hath puddled[430] his clear spirit; and, in such cases
  Men's natures wrangle with inferior things,
  Though great ones are their object. 'Tis even so;
  For let our finger ache, and it indues[431]
  Our other healthful members even to that sense   140
  Of pain. Nay, we must think men are not gods,
  Nor of them look for such observancy[432]
  As fits the bridal.[433] Beshrew me much, Emilia,
  I was—unhandsome warrior as I am—
  Arraigning his unkindness with[434] my soul;   145
  But now I find I had suborn'd the witness,[435]
  And he 's indicted falsely.
Emilia.   Pray heaven it be state matters, as you think,
  And no conception,[436] nor no jealous toy[437]
  Concerning you.   150
Desdemona.   Alas the day! I never gave him cause.
Emilia.   But jealous souls will not be answer'd so;
  They are not ever jealous for the cause,
  But jealous for they are jealous; 'tis a monster
  Begot upon itself, born on itself.   155
Desdemona.   Heaven keep that monster from Othello's mind!
Emilia.   Lady, amen.
Desdemona.   I will go seek him. Cassio, walk hereabout;
  If I do find him fit, I'll move your suit
  And seek to effect it to my uttermost.   160
Cassio.   I humbly thank your ladyship.

                              (*Exeunt Desdemona and Emilia.*)
(*Enter Bianca.*)

Bianca.   Save you, friend Cassio!
Cassio.   What make you from home?

---

[426] I.e., his soldiers.   [427] Important.   [428] Public affairs.   [429] Abortive or budding plot.   [430] Muddied.   [431] Brings, leads.   [432] Attention.   [433] Wedding.   [434] To.   [435] I.e., caused my soul to bring in wrong charges.   [436] Fancy,
supposition.   [437] Fancy.

How is it with you, my most fair Bianca?
I' faith, sweet love, I was coming to your house.

Bianca.   And I was going to your lodging, Cassio.   165
What! keep a week away? seven days and nights?
Eight score eight hours? and lovers' absent hours,
More tedious than the dial eight score times?
O weary reckoning!

Cassio.   Pardon me, Bianca,
I have this while with leaden thoughts been press'd;   170
But I shall, in a more continuate[438] time,
Strike off[439] this score of absence. Sweet Bianca,

(*Giving her Desdemona's handkerchief.*)

Take me this work out.

Bianca.   O Cassio! whence came this?
This is some token from a newer friend;
To the felt absence now I feel a cause;   175
Is 't come to this? Well, well.

Cassio.   Go to, woman!
Throw your vile guesses in the devil's teeth,
From whence you have them. You are jealous now
That this is from some mistress, some remembrance:
No, in good troth, Bianca.

Bianca.   Why, whose is it?   180

Cassio.   I know not, sweet; I found it in my chamber.
I like the work well; ere it be demanded,—[440]
As like enough it will,—I'd have it copied;
Take it and do 't; and leave me for this time.

Bianca.   Leave you! wherefore?   185

Cassio.   I do attend here on[441] the general,
And think it no addition,[442] nor my wish,
To have him see me woman'd.

Bianca.   Why, I pray you?

Cassio.   Not that I love you not.

Bianca.   But that you do not love me.
I pray you, bring me on the way a little   190
And say if I shall see you soon at night.

Cassio.   'Tis but a little way that I can bring you,
For I attend here; but I'll see you soon.

Bianca.   'Tis very good; I must be circumstanc'd.[443]   (*Exeunt.*)

---

[438] Uninterrupted.   [439] Cancel (i.e., make up for).   [440] Asked for.   [441] Wait
for.   [442] Advantage, credit.   [443] Governed by circumstances.

Act IV

SCENE 1.   *Cyprus. Before the Castle.*

(Enter Othello and Iago.)

Iago.   Will you think so?
Othello.   Think so, Iago!
Iago.   What!
   To kiss in private?
Othello.   An unauthoriz'd kiss.
Iago.   Or to be naked with her friend a-bed
   An hour or more, not meaning any harm?
Othello.   Naked a-bed, Iago, and not mean harm?   5
   It is hypocrisy against the devil:[444]
   They that mean virtuously, and yet do so,
   The devil their virtue tempts, and they tempt heaven.
Iago.   If they do nothing, 'tis a venial slip;
   But if I give my wife a handkerchief,—   10
Othello.   What then?
Iago.   Why, then, 'tis hers, my lord; and, being hers,
   She may, I think, bestow 't on any man.
Othello.   She is protectress of her honour too;
   May she give that?   15
Iago.   Her honour is an essence that 's not seen;
   They have it very oft that have it not:[445]
   But for the handkerchief,—
Othello.   By heaven, I would most gladly have forgot it:—
   Thou said'st,—O! it comes o'er my memory,   20
   As doth the raven[446] o'er the infected house,
   Boding to all,—he had my handkerchief.
Iago.   Ay, what of that?
Othello.   That's not so good now.
Iago.   What,
   If I had said I had seen him do you wrong?
   Or heard him say, as knaves be such abroad,[447]   25
   Who having, by their own importunate suit,
   Or voluntary dotage[448] of some mistress,
   Convinced or supplied them,[449] cannot choose

---

[444] I.e., by not committing the sin which the situation invites.   [445] I.e., some unchaste
women are thought chaste.   [446] (1) A bad omen, (2) A carrier of the plague.
[447] As there are some such in the world.   [448] Foolish affection.   [449] Overcome
(their reluctance) or satisfied (their desires).

But they must blab.

Othello.   Hath he said any thing?

Iago.   He hath, my lord; but be you well assur'd,   30
No more than he'll unswear.

Othello.   What hath he said?

Iago.   Faith, that he did—I know not what he did.

Othello.   What? what?

Iago.   Lie—

Othello.   With her?

Iago.   With her, on her; what you will.

Othello.   Lie with her; lie on her! We say, lie on her, when they belie her. Lie
with her! that's fulsome. Handkerchief,—confessions,—handkerchief! To
confess, and be hanged for his labour. First, to be hanged, and then to
confess: I tremble at it. Nature would not invest herself in such shadowing
passion without some instruction.[450] It is not words that shake me thus.
Pish! Noses, ears, and lips. It is possible?—Confess!—Handkerchief!—O
devil!

(*Falls in a trance.*)

Iago.   Work on,
My medicine, work! Thus credulous fools are caught;
And many worthy and chaste dames even thus,
All guiltless, meet reproach. What, ho! my lord!   45
My lord, I say! Othello!

(*Enter Cassio.*)

How now, Cassio!

Cassio.   What's the matter?

Iago.   My lord is fallen into an epilepsy;[451]
This is his second fit; he had one yesterday.

Cassio.   Rub him about the temples.

Iago.   No, forbear;   50
The lethargy[452] must have his quiet course,
If not, he foams at mouth, and by and by
Breaks out to savage madness. Look! he stirs;
Do you withdraw yourself a little while,
He will recover straight; when he is gone,   55
I would on great occasion[453] speak with you.   (*Exit Cassio.*)
How is it, general? have you not hurt your head?

---

[450] I would not fall into such passion unless there were some real grounds for it.   [451] Seizure, fit.   [452] Coma.   [453] Important matter.

Othello.   Dost thou mock me?[454]
Iago.   I mock you! no, by heaven.
  Would you would bear your fortune like a man!
Othello.   A horned man's a monster and a beast.   60
Iago.   There's many a beast then, in a populous city,
  And many a civil[455] monster.
Othello.   Did he confess it?
Iago.   Good sir, be a man;
  Think every bearded fellow that's but yok'd
  May draw[456] with you; there's millions now alive   65
  That nightly lie in those unproper[457] beds
  Which they dare swear peculiar;[458] your case is better.
  O! 'tis the spite of hell, the fiend's arch-mock,
  To lip[459] a wanton in a secure[460] couch,
  And to suppose her chaste. No, let me know;   70
  And knowing what I am, I know what she shall be.
Othello.   O! thou art wise; 'tis certain.
Iago.   Stand you awhile apart;
  Confine yourself but in a patient list.[461]
  Whilst you were here o'erwhelmed with your grief,—
  A passion most unsuiting such a man,—   75
  Cassio came hither; I shifted him away,
  And laid good 'scuse upon your ecstasy;[462]
  Bade him anon return and here speak with me;
  The which he promis'd. Do but encave yourself,
  And mark the fleers, the gibes, and notable scorns,   80
  That dwell in every region of his face;
  For I will make him tell the tale anew,
  Where, how, how oft, how long ago, and when
  He hath, and is again to cope[463] your wife:
  I say, but mark his gesture. Marry, patience;   85
  Or I shall say you are all in all in spleen,[464]
  And nothing of a man.
Othello.   Dost thou hear, Iago?
  I will be found most cunning in my patience;
  But—dost thou hear?—most bloody.
Iago.   That's not amiss:
  But yet keep time[465] in all. Will you withdraw? (*Othello goes apart.*)   90
  Now will I question Cassio of Bianca,

---

[454] Another allusion to the cuckold's horns.   [455] Citizen.   [456] I.e., pull the burden
of cuckoldom.   [457] Not exclusively their own.   [458] Exclusively their own.
[459] Kiss.   [460] I.e., without suspicion of having a rival.   [461] Bounds of patience.
[462] Derangement, trance.   [463] Close with.   [464] Completely overcome by passion.
[465] Maintain control.

A housewife[466] that by selling her desires
Buys herself bread and clothes; it is a creature
That dotes on Cassio; as 'tis the strumpet's plague
To beguile many and be beguil'd by one.   95
He, when he hears of her, cannot refrain
From the excess of laughter. Here he comes:

(*Re-enter Cassio.*)

As he shall smile, Othello shall go mad;
And his unbookish[467] jealousy must construe
Poor Cassio's smiles, gestures, and light behaviour   100
Quite in the wrong. How do you now, lieutenant?
Cassio.   The worser that you give me the addition[468]
Whose want[469] even kills me.
Iago.   Ply Desdemona well, and you are sure on 't.
(*Speaking lower.*) Now, if this suit lay in Bianca's power,   105
How quickly should you speed!
Cassio.   Alas! poor caitiff![470]
Othello.   Look! how he laughs already!
Iago.   I never knew woman love man so.
Cassio.   Alas! poor rogue, I think i' faith, she loves me.
Othello.   Now he denies it faintly, and laughs it out.   110
Iago.   Do you hear, Cassio?
Othello.   Now he importunes him
To tell it o'er: go to; well said, well said.
Iago.   She gives it out that you shall marry her;
Do you intend it?
Cassio.   Ha, ha, ha!   115
Othello.   Do you triumph, Roman?[471] do you triumph?
Cassio.   I marry her! what? a customer?[472] I prithee, bear some charity to my
wit;[473] do not think it so unwholesome. Ha, ha, ha!
Othello.   So, so, so, so. They laugh that win.[474]
Iago.   Faith, the cry goes that you shall marry her.   120
Cassio.   Prithee, say true.
Iago.   I am a very villain else.
Othello.   Have you scored me?[475] Well.
Cassio.   This is the monkey's own giving out: she is persuaded I will marry
her, out of her own love and flattery, not out of my promise.   125

---

[466] Hussy.   [467] Unpracticed, naive.   [468] Title.   [469] The want of which.
[470] Wretch.   [471] I.e., one who triumphs.   [472] Courtesan, prostitute.   [473] Give
me credit for some sense.   [474] "He who laughs last laughs longest" (?).   [475] Wounded,
defaced (?); or: settled my account (?).

Othello. Iago beckons me;[476] now he begins the story.

Cassio. She was here even now; she haunts me in every place. I was the other day talking on the sea-bank with certain Venetians, and thither comes this bauble,[477] and, by this hand, she falls me thus about my neck;—

Othello. Crying, 'O dear Cassio!' as it were; his gesture imports it.   130

Cassio. So hangs and lolls and weeps upon me; so hales[478] and pulls me; ha, ha, ha!

Othello. Now he tells how she plucked him to my chamber. O! I see that nose of yours, but not the dog I shall throw it to.

Cassio. Well, I must leave her company.   135

Iago. Before me![479] look, where she comes.

Cassio. 'Tis such another fitchew![480] marry, a perfumed one.

(*Enter Bianca.*)

What do you mean by this haunting of me?

Bianca. Let the devil and his dam haunt you! What did you mean by that same handkerchief you gave me even now? I was a fine fool to take it. I must take out the work! A likely piece of work, that you should find it in your chamber, and not know who left it there! This is some minx's token, and I must take out the work! There, give it your hobby-horse;[481] wheresoever you had it I'll take out no work on 't.

Cassio. How now, my sweet Bianca! how now, how now!   145

Othello. By heaven, that should be[482] my handkerchief!

Bianca. An you'll come to supper to-night, you may; an you will not, come when you are next prepared[483] for.   (*Exit.*)

Iago. After her, after her.

Cassio. Faith, I must; she'll rail in the street else.   150

Iago. Will you sup there?

Cassio. Faith, I intend so.

Iago. Well, I may chance to see you, for I would very fain[484] speak with you.

Cassio. Prithee come; will you?

Iago. Go to; say no more.   (*Exit Cassio.*)   155

Othello (*advancing*). How shall I murder him, Iago?

Iago. Did you perceive how he laughed at his vice?

Othello. O! Iago!

Iago. And did you see the handkerchief?

Othello. Was that mine?   160

Iago. Yours, by this hand; and to see how he prizes the foolish woman your wife! she gave it him, and he hath given it his whore.

---

[476] Signals.   [477] Plaything.   [478] Hauls.   [479] An exclamation of surprise.
[480] Polecat, noted both for its strong smell and for its lechery.   [481] Harlot.   [482] I.e., I think that is.   [483] Expected (Bianca means that if he does not come that night, she will never want to see him again).   [484] Gladly.

Othello.   I would have him nine years a-killing. A fine woman! a fair woman! a sweet woman!

Iago.   Nay, you must forget that.   165

Othello.   Ay, let her rot, and perish, and be damned to-night; for she shall not live. No, my heart is turned to stone; I strike it, and it hurts my hand. O! the world hath not a sweeter creature; she might lie by an emperor's side and command him tasks.

Iago.   Nay, that's not your way.[485]   170

Othello.   Hang her! I do but say what she is. So delicate with her needle! An admirable musician! O, she will sing the savageness out of a bear. Of so high and plenteous wit and invention!

Iago.   She's the worse for all this.

Othello.   O! a thousand, a thousand times. And then, of so gentle a condition![486]

Iago.   Ay, too gentle.[487]

Othello.   Nay, that's certain;—but yet the pity of it, Iago!
   O! Iago, the pity of it, Iago!

Iago.   If you are so fond over her iniquity, give her patent to offend; for, if it touch not you, it comes near nobody.

Othello.   I will chop her into messes.[488] Cuckold me!

Iago.   O! 'tis foul in her.

Othello.   With mine officer!

Iago.   That's fouler.   185

Othello.   Get me some poison, Iago; this night: I'll not expostulate with her, lest her body and beauty unprovide my mind again.[489] This night, Iago.

Iago.   Do it not with poison, strangle her in her bed, even the bed she hath contaminated.

Othello.   Good, good; the justice of it pleases; very good.   190

Iago.   And for Cassio, let me be his undertaker;[490] you shall hear more by midnight.

Othello.   Excellent good. (*A trumpet within.*) What trumpet is that same?

Iago.   Something from Venice, sure. 'Tis Lodovico,
   Come from the duke; and see, your wife is with him.   195

(*Enter Lodovico, Desdemona, and Attendants.*)

Lodovico.   God save you, worthy general!

Othello.   With all my heart, sir.

Lodovico.   The duke and senators of Venice greet you.

---

[485] Proper course.   [486] So much the high-born lady.   [487] I.e., yielding.   [488] Bits.
[489] Unsettle my intention.   [490] Dispatcher.

(*Gives him a packet.*)

Othello.   I kiss the instrument of their pleasures.

(*Opens the packet, and reads.*)

Desdemona.   And what's the news, good cousin Lodovico?
Iago.   I am very glad to see you, signior;   200
   Welcome to Cyprus.
Lodovico.   I thank you. How does Lieutenant Cassio?
Iago.   Lives, sir.
Desdemona.   Cousin, there's fall'n between him and my lord
   An unkind[491] breach; but you shall make all well.   205
Othello.   Are you sure of that?
Desdemona.   My lord?
Othello (*reads*).   'This fail you not to do, as you will'—
Lodovico.   He did not call; he's busy in the paper.
   Is there division[492] twixt my lord and Cassio?   210
Desdemona.   A most unhappy one; I would do much
   To atone[493] them, for the love I bear to Cassio.
Othello.   Fire and brimstone!
Desdemona.   My lord?
Othello.   Are you wise?
Desdemona.   What! is he angry?
Lodovico.   May be the letter mov'd him;
   For, as I think, they do command him home,   215
   Deputing Cassio in his government.
Desdemona.   Trust me, I am glad on 't.
Othello.   Indeed!
Desdemona.   My lord?
Othello.   I am glad to see you mad.
Desdemona.   Why, sweet Othello?
Othello.   Devil!   (*Strikes her.*)   220
Desdemona.   I have not deserved this.
Lodovico.   My lord, this would not be believ'd in Venice,
   Though I should swear I saw 't; 'tis very much;
   Make her amends, she weeps.
Othello.   O devil, devil!
   If that the earth could teem with woman's tears,   225
   Each drop she falls[494] would prove a crocodile.[495]

---

[491] Unnatural.   [492] Estrangement.   [493] Reconcile.   [494] Lets fall.   [495] The crocodile's tears were supposed to be hypocritical.

Out of my sight!
Desdemona.   I will not stay to offend you.   (*Going.*)
Lodovico.   Truly, an obedient lady;
    I do beseech your lordship, call her back.
Othello.   Mistress!
Desdemona.   My lord?
Othello.   What would you with her, sir?   230
Lodovico.   Why, I, my lord?
Othello.   Ay; you did wish that I would make her turn:
    Sir, she can turn, and turn, and yet go on,
    And turn again; and she can weep, sir, weep;
    And she's obedient, as you say, obedient,   235
    Very obedient. Proceed you in your tears.
    Concerning this, sir—O well-painted passion!—
    I am commanded home. Get you away;
    I'll send for you anon. Sir, I obey the mandate,
    And will return to Venice. Hence! avaunt![496]   (*Exit Desdemona.*)   240
    Cassio shall have my place. And, sir, to-night,
    I do entreat that we may sup together;
    You are welcome, sir, to Cyprus. Goats and monkeys!   (*Exit.*)
Lodovico.   Is this the noble Moor whom our full senate
    Call all-in-all sufficient? is this the noble nature   245
    Whom passion could not shake? whose solid virtue
    The shot of accident nor dart of chance
    Could neither graze nor pierce?
Iago.   He is much chang'd.
Lodovico.   Are his wits safe? is he not light of brain?
Iago.   He's that he is; I may not breathe my censure.   250
    What he might be, if, what he might, he is not,
    I would to heaven he were![497]
Lodovico.   What! strike his wife!
Iago.   Faith, that was not so well; yet would I knew
    That stroke would prove the worst!
Lodovico.   Is it his use?
    Or did the letters work upon his blood,   255
    And new-create this fault?
Iago.   Alas, alas!
    It is not honesty in me to speak
    What I have seen and known. You shall observe him,
    And his own courses[498] will denote him so

---

[496] Begone!   [497] Another of Iago's gnomic speeches; perhaps approximately: "If now he is not himself, I wish he would be what he could be!"   [498] Actions.

That I may save my speech. Do but go after   260
    And mark how he continues.
Lodovico.   I am sorry that I am deceiv'd in him.   (*Exeunt.*)

SCENE 2.   *A Room in the Castle.*

(*Enter Othello and Emilia.*)

Othello.   You have seen nothing, then?
Emilia.   Nor ever heard, nor ever did suspect.
Othello.   Yes, you have seen Cassio and her together.
Emilia.   But then I saw no harm, and then I heard
    Each syllable that breath made up between them.   5
Othello.   What! did they never whisper?
Emilia.   Never, my lord.
Othello.   Nor send you out o' the way?
Emilia.   Never.
Othello.   To fetch her fan, her gloves, her mask, nor nothing?[499]
Emilia.   Never, my lord.   10
Othello.   That's strange.
Emilia.   I durst, my lord, to wager she is honest,
    Lay down my soul at stake: if you think other,
    Remove your thought; it doth abuse your bosom.
    If any wretch have put this in your head,   15
    Let heaven requite it with the serpent's curse!
    For, if she be not honest, chaste, and true,
    There's no man happy; the purest of their wives
    Is foul as slander.
Othello.   Bid her come hither; go.   (*Exit Emilia.*)
    She says enough; yet she 's a simple[500] bawd   20
    That cannot say as much. This is a subtle whore,
    A closet lock and key of villanous secrets;
    And yet she 'll kneel and pray; I have seen her do 't.

(*Re-enter Emilia with Desdemona.*)

Desdemona.   My lord, what is your will?
Othello.   Pray, chuck, come hither.
Desdemona.   What is your pleasure?
Othello.   Let me see your eyes;   25
    Look in my face.
Desdemona.   What horrible fancy 's this?

---

[499] Anything.   [500] Simpleminded.

Othello (*to Emilia*).   Some of your function,[501] mistress;
 Leave procreants alone and shut the door;
 Cough or cry 'hem' if any body come;
 Your mystery,[502] your mystery; nay, dispatch. (*Exit Emilia.*) 30
Desdemona.   Upon my knees, what doth your speech import?
 I understand a fury in your words,
 But not the words.
Othello.   Why, what art thou?
Desdemona.   Your wife, my lord; your true
 And loyal wife.
Othello.   Come, swear it, damn thyself;   35
 Lest, being like one of heaven, the devils themselves
 Should fear to seize thee; therefore be double-damn'd;
 Swear thou art honest.
Desdemona.   Heaven doth truly know it.
Othello.   Heaven truly knows that thou art false as hell.
Desdemona.   To whom, my lord? with whom? how am I false? 40
Othello.   Ah! Desdemona; away, away, away!
Desdemona.   Alas, the heavy day!—Why do you weep?
 Am I the motive of these tears, my lord?
 If haply you my father do suspect
 An instrument of this your calling back,   45
 Lay not your blame on me; if you have lost him,
 Why, I have lost him too.
Othello.   Had it pleas'd heaven
 To try me with affliction, had he rain'd
 All kinds of sores and shames on my bare head,
 Steep'd me in poverty to the very lips,   50
 Given to captivity me and my utmost hopes,
 I should have found in some part of my soul
 A drop of patience; but, alas! to make me
 The fixed figure for the time of scorn[503]
 To point his slow and moving finger at;   55
 Yet could I bear that too; well, very well:
 But there, where I have garner'd[504] up my heart,
 Where either I must live or bear no life,
 The fountain from the which my current runs
 Or else dries up; to be discarded thence!   60
 Or keep it as a cistern for foul toads
 To knot and gender in![505] Turn thy complexion there,[506]

---

[501] To your duty, business. [502]Trade. [503] I.e., the scornful world. [504] Stored.
[505] Bunch up and procreate. [506] I.e., change your color to suit the "cistern for foul toads."

Patience, thou young and rose-lipp'd cherubin;
Ay, there, look grim as hell!
Desdemona. I hope my noble lord esteems me honest. 65
Othello. O! ay; as summer flies are in the shambles,[507]
That quicken even with blowing. O thou weed!
Who art so lovely fair and smell'st so sweet
That the sense aches at thee, would thou hadst ne'er been born.
Desdemona. Alas! what ignorant sin have I committed? 70
Othello. Was this fair paper, this most goodly book,
Made to write 'whore' upon? What committed!
Committed! O thou public commoner![508]
I should make very forges of my cheeks,
That would to cinders burn up modesty, 75
Did I but speak thy deeds. What committed!
Heaven stops the nose at it and the moon winks,[509]
The bawdy wind that kisses all it meets
Is hush'd within the hollow mine of earth,
And will not hear it. What committed! 80
Impudent strumpet!
Desdemona.   By heaven, you do me wrong.
Othello. Are not you a strumpet?
Desdemona.   No, as I am a Christian.
If to preserve this vessel for my lord
From any other foul unlawful touch
Be not to be a strumpet, I am none. 85
Othello. What! not a whore?
Desdemona.   No, as I shall be sav'd.
Othello. Is it possible?
Desdemona. O! heaven forgive us.
Othello.   I cry you mercy,[510] then;
I took you for that cunning whore of Venice
That married with Othello. You, mistress, 90
That have the office opposite to Saint Peter,
And keep the gate of hell!

(*Re-enter Emilia.*)

                    You, you, ay, you!
We have done our course; there's money for your pains.
I pray you, turn the key and keep our counsel.   (*Exit.*)
Emilia. Alas! what does this gentleman conceive?[511] 95

---

[507] Slaughterhouse.   [508] Harlot.   [509] Closes her eyes.   [510] Beg your pardon.
[511] Imagine.

How do you, madam? how do you, my good lady?
Desdemona.   Faith, half asleep.
Emilia.   Good madam, what 's the matter with my lord?
Desdemona.   With who?
Emilia.   Why, with my lord, madam.   100
Desdemona.   Who is thy lord?
Emilia.   He that is yours, sweet lady.
Desdemona.   I have none; do not talk to me, Emilia;
    I cannot weep, nor answer have I none,
    But what should go by water.[512] Prithee, to-night
    Lay on my bed my wedding sheets—remember;   105
    And call thy husband hither.
Emilia.   Here is a change indeed!   (*Exit.*)
Desdemona.   'Tis meet I should be us'd so, very meet.
    How have I been behav'd, that he might stick
    The small'st opinion on my least misuse?[513]

(*Re-enter Emilia, with Iago.*)

Iago.   What is your pleasure, madam? How is it with you?   110
Desdemona.   I cannot tell. Those that do teach young babes
    Do it with gentle means and easy tasks;
    He might have chid me so; for, in good faith,
    I am a child to chiding.
Iago.   What 's the matter, lady?
Emilia.   Alas, Iago, my lord hath so bewhor'd her,   115
    Thrown such despite[514] and heavy terms upon her,
    As true hearts cannot bear.
Desdemona.   Am I that name, Iago?
Iago.   What name, fair lady?
Desdemona.   Such as she says my lord did say I was.
Emilia.   He call'd her whore; a beggar in his drink   120
    Could not have laid such terms upon his callat.[515]
Iago.   Why did he so?
Desdemona.   I do not know; I am sure I am none such.
Iago.   Do not weep, do not weep. Alas the day!
Emilia.   Has she forsook so many noble matches,   125
    Her father and her country and her friends,
    To be call'd whore? would it not make one weep?
Desdemona.   It is my wretched fortune.
Iago.   Beshrew[516] him for it!

---

[512] Be conveyed by means of tears.   [513] The least suspicion on my slightest misconduct.
[514] Abuse.   [515] Slut.   [516] Curse.

How comes this trick upon him?
Desdemona.   Nay, heaven doth know.
Emilia.   I will be hang'd, if some eternal villain,   130
    Some busy and insinuating rogue,
    Some cogging[517] cozening slave, to get some office,
    Have not devis'd this slander; I'll be hang'd else.
Iago.   Fie! there is no such man; it is impossible.
Desdemona.   If any such there be, heaven pardon him!   135
Emilia.   A halter pardon him, and hell gnaw his bones!
    Why should he call her whore? who keeps her company?
    What place? what time? what form? what likelihood?
    The Moor 's abus'd by some most villanous knave,
    Some base notorious knave, some scurvy fellow.   140
    O heaven! that such companions[518] thou'dst unfold,
    And put in every honest hand a whip
    To lash the rascals naked through the world,
    Even from the east to west!
Iago.   Speak within door.
Emilia.   O! fie upon them. Some such squire he was   145
    That turn'd your wit the seamy side without,[519]
    And made you to suspect me with the Moor.
Iago.   You are a fool; go to.
Desdemona.   O good Iago,
    What shall I do to win my lord again?
    Good friend, go to him; for, by this light of heaven,   150
    I know not how I lost him. Here I kneel:
    If e'er my will did trespass 'gainst his love,
    Either in discourse of thought or actual deed,
    Or that mine eyes, mine ears, or any sense,
    Delighted them[520] in any other form;   155
    Or that I do not yet,[521] and ever did,
    And ever will, though he do shake me off
    To beggarly divorcement, love him dearly,
    Comfort forswear me! Unkindness may do much;
    And his unkindness may defeat[522] my life,   160
    But never taint my love. I cannot say 'whore':
    It does abhor me now I speak the word;
    To do the act that might the addition earn
    Not the world's mass of vanity could make me.
Iago.   I pray you be content, 'tis but his humour;   165

---

[517] Cheating.   [518] Fellows (derogatory).   [519] Outward.   [520] Found delight.
[521] Still.   [522] Destroy.

The business of the state does him offence,
And he does chide with you.
Desdemona.   If 'twere no other,—
Iago.   'Tis but so, I warrant.   (*Trumpets.*)
   Hark! how these instruments summon to supper;
   The messengers of Venice stay the meat: 170
   Go in, and weep not; all things shall be well.

                                 (*Exeunt Desdemona and Emilia.*)

(*Enter Roderigo.*)

   How now, Roderigo!
Roderigo.   I do not find that thou dealest justly with me.
Iago.   What in the contrary?[523]
Roderigo.   Every day thou daffest me[524] with some device, Iago; and rather,
   as it seems to me now, keepest from me all conveniency,[525] than suppliest
   me with the least advantage of hope. I will indeed no longer endure it, nor
   am I yet persuaded to put up[526] in peace what already I have foolishly
   suffered.
Iago.   Will you hear me, Roderigo?
Roderigo.   Faith, I have heard too much, for your words and performances
   are no kin together.
Iago.   You charge me most unjustly.
Roderigo.   With nought but truth. I have wasted myself out of my means.
   The jewels you have had from me to deliver to Desdemona would half have
   corrupted a votarist;[527] you have told me she has received them, and re-
   turned me expectations and comforts of sudden respect[528] and acquain-
   tance, but I find none.
Iago.   Well; go to; very well.
Roderigo.   Very well! go to! I cannot go to, man; nor 'tis not very well: by this
   hand, I say, it is very scurvy, and begin to find myself fobbed[529] in it.
Iago.   Very well.
Roderigo.   I tell you 'tis not very well. I will make myself known to Desdemona; if she will return me my jewels, I will give over my suit and repent
   my unlawful solicitation; if not, assure yourself I will seek satisfaction of
   you.
Iago.   You have said now.[530]
Roderigo.   Ay, and said nothing, but what I protest intendment of doing.
Iago.   Why, now I see there's mettle in thee, and even from this instant do
   build on thee a better opinion than ever before. Give me thy hand, Rod-

---

[523] I.e., what reason do you have for saying that.   [524] You put me off.   [525] Favor-
able circumstances.   [526] Put up with.   [527] Nun.   [528] Immediate consideration.
[529] Cheated.   [530] I.e., "I suppose you're through?" (?); or: "Now you're talking" (?).

erigo; thou hast taken against me a most just exception; but yet, I protest, I have dealt most directly in thy affair.

Roderigo.   It hath not appeared.

Iago.   I grant indeed it hath not appeared, and your suspicion is not without wit and judgment. But, Roderigo, if thou hast that in thee indeed, which I have greater reason to believe now than ever, I mean purpose, courage, and valour, this night show it: if thou the next night following enjoy not Desdemona, take me from this world with treachery and devise engines for[531] my life.

Roderigo.   Well, what is it? is it within reason and compass?

Iago.   Sir, there is especial commission come from Venice to depute Cassio in Othello's place.

Roderigo.   Is that true? why, then Othello and Desdemona return again to Venice.

Iago.   O, no! he goes into Mauritania, and takes away with him the fair Desdemona, unless his abode be lingered here by some accident; wherein none can be so determinate[532] as the removing of Cassio.

Roderigo.   How do you mean, removing of him?

Iago.   Why, by making him uncapable of Othello's place; knocking out his brains.

Roderigo.   And that you would have me do?

Iago.   Ay; if you dare do yourself a profit and a right. He sups to-night with a harlotry,[533] and thither will I go to him; he knows not yet of his honourable fortune. If you will watch his going thence,—which I will fashion to fall out between twelve and one,—you may take him at your pleasure; I will be near to second your attempt, and he shall fall between us. Come, stand not amazed at it, but go along with me; I will show you such a necessity in his death that you shall think yourself bound to put it on him. It is now high supper-time, and the night grows to waste; about it.

Roderigo.   I will hear further reason for this.

Iago.   And you shall be satisfied.   (*Exeunt.*)

SCENE 3.   *Another Room in the Castle.*

(*Enter Othello, Lodovico, Desdemona, Emilia, and Attendants.*)

Lodovico.   I do beseech you, sir, trouble yourself no further.

Othello.   O! pardon me; 'twill do me good to walk.

Lodovico.   Madam, good-night; I humbly thank your ladyship.

Desdemona.   Your honour is most welcome.

Othello.   Will you walk, sir?

O! Desdemona,—   5

---

[531] Devices against.   [532] Effective.   [533] Harlot.

Desdemona. My lord?

Othello. Get you to bed on the instant; I will be returned forthwith; dismiss
your attendant there; look it be done.

Desdemona. I will, my lord. (*Exeunt Othello, Lodovico, and Attendants.*)

Emilia. How goes it now? He looks gentler than he did. 10

Desdemona. He says he will return incontinent;[534]
He hath commanded me to go to bed,
And bade me to dismiss you.

Emilia.   Dismiss me!

Desdemona. It was his bidding; therefore, good Emilia,
Give me my nightly wearing, and adieu: 15
We must not now displease him.

Emilia. I would you had never seen him.

Desdemona. So would not I; my love doth so approve him,
That even his stubbornness,[535] his checks[536] and frowns,—
Prithee, unpin me,—have grace and favour in them. 20

Emilia. I have laid those sheets you bade me on the bed.

Desdemona. All's one.[537] Good faith! how foolish are our minds!
If I do die before thee, prithee, shroud me
In one of those same sheets.

Emilia.   Come, come, you talk.

Desdemona. My mother had a maid call'd Barbara; 25
She was in love, and he she lov'd prov'd mad[538]
And did forsake her; she had a song of 'willow';
An old thing 'twas, but it express'd her fortune,
And she died singing it; that song to-night
Will not go from my mind; I have much to do 30
But to go hang my head all at one side,
And sing it like poor Barbara. Prithee, dispatch.

Emilia. Shall I go fetch your night-gown?

Desdemona.   No, unpin me here.
This Lodovico is a proper man.

Emilia. A very handsome man. 35

Desdemona. He speaks well.

Emilia. I know a lady in Venice would have walked barefoot to Palestine for
a touch of his nether lip.

Desdemona (*sings*).
The poor soul sat sighing by a sycamore tree,
Sing all a green willow; 40
Her hand on her bosom, her head on her knee,
Sing willow, willow, willow:
The fresh streams ran by her, and murmur'd her moans;

---

[534] At once.   [535] Roughness.   [536] Rebukes.   [537] I.e., it doesn't matter.
[538] Wild.

> Sing willow, willow, willow:
>> Her salt tears fell from her and soften'd the stones;—   45

> Lay by these:—
>> Sing willow, willow, willow:

> Prithee, hie thee;[539] he 'll come anon.—

>> Sing all a green willow must be my garland.
> Let nobody blame him, his scorn I approve,—   50
> Nay, that's not next. Hark! who is it that knocks?

Emilia.   It is the wind.

Desdemona.
> I call'd my love false love; but what said he then?
>> Sing willow, willow, willow:
> If I court moe[540] women, you 'll couch with moe men.   55

> So, get thee gone; good-night. Mine eyes do itch;
> Doth that bode weeping?

Emilia.   'Tis neither here nor there.

Desdemona.   I have heard it said so. O! these men, these men!
> Dost thou in conscience think, tell me, Emilia,
> That there be women do abuse their husbands   60
> In such gross kind?

Emilia.   There be some such, no question.

Desdemona.   Wouldst thou do such a deed for all the world?

Emilia.   Why, would not you?

Desdemona.   No, by this heavenly light!

Emilia.   Nor I neither by this heavenly light;
> I might do 't as well i' the dark.   65

Desdemona.   Wouldst thou do such a deed for all the world?

Emilia.   The world is a huge thing; 'tis a great price
> For a small vice.

Desdemona.   In troth, I think thou wouldst not.

Emilia.   In troth, I think I should, and undo 't when I had done. Marry, I
> would not do such a thing for a joint-ring,[541] nor measures of lawn,[542] nor
> for gowns, petticoats, nor caps, nor any petty exhibition;[543] but for the
> whole world, who would not make her husband a cuckold to make him a
> monarch? I should venture purgatory for 't.

Desdemona.   Beshrew me, if I would do such a wrong   75
> For the whole world.

Emilia.   Why, the wrong is but a wrong i' the world; and having the world for

---

[539] Hurry.   [540] More.   [541] Ring made in separable halves.   [542] Fine linen.
[543] Offer, gift.

your labour, 'tis a wrong in your own world, and you might quickly make it
right.
Desdemona.   I do not think there is any such woman.
Emilia.   Yes, a dozen; and as many to the vantage,[544] as   80
Would store[545] the world they played for.
But I do think it is their husbands' faults
If wives do fall. Say that they slack their duties,
And pour our treasures into foreign laps,
Or else break out in peevish jealousies,   85
Throwing restraint upon us; or say they strike us,
Or scant[546] our former having[547] in despite;
Why, we have galls;[548] and though we have some grace,
Yet have we some revenge. Let husbands know
Their wives have sense like them; they see and smell,   90
And have their palates both for sweet and sour,
As husbands have. What is it that they do
When they change us for others? Is it sport?[549]
I think it is; and doth affection breed it?
I think it doth; is 't frailty that thus errs?   95
It is so too; and have not we affections,
Desires for sport, and frailty, as men have?
Then, let them use us well; else let them know,
The ills we do, their ills instruct us so.
Desdemona.   Good-night, good night; heaven me such usage[550] send,   100
Not to pick bad from bad, but by bad mend!   (*Exeunt.*)

Act V

SCENE 1.   *Cyprus. A Street.*

(*Enter Iago and Roderigo.*)

Iago.   Here, stand behind this bulk,[551] straight will he come:
Wear thy good rapier bare, and put it home.
Quick, quick; fear nothing; I 'll be at thy elbow.
It makes us, or it mars us; think on that,
And fix most firm thy resolution.   5
Roderigo.   Be near at hand; I may miscarry in 't.

---

[544] Over and above.   [545] Populate.   [546] Reduce.   [547] Allowance.
[548] Spirits, temper.   [549] Lust, sexual enjoyment.   [550] Habits (?), treatment (?).
[551] Jutting part of a wall.

Iago. Here, at thy hand: be bold, and take thy stand. (*Retires.*)
Roderigo. I have no great devotion to the deed;
    And yet he has given me satisfying reasons:
    'Tis but a man gone: forth, my sword; he dies. 10
Iago. I have rubb'd this young quat[552] almost to the sense,[553]
    And he grows angry. Now, whether he kill Cassio,
    Or Cassio him, or each do kill the other,
    Every way makes my gain: live Roderigo,
    He calls me to a restitution large 15
    Of gold and jewels that I bobb'd[554] from him,
    As gifts to Desdemona;
    It must not be: if Cassio do remain,
    He hath a daily beauty in his life
    That makes me ugly: and, besides, the Moor 20
    May unfold me to him; there stand I in much peril.
    No, he must die. But so;[555] I hear him coming.

(*Enter Cassio.*)

Roderigo. I know his gait; 'tis he. Villain, thou diest!

(*Makes a pass at Cassio.*)

Cassio. That thrust had been mine enemy indeed
    But that my coat is better than thou know'st; 25
    I will make proof of thine.

(*Draws, and wounds Roderigo.*)

Roderigo.   O! I am slain.

(*Iago from behind wounds Cassio in the leg, and exit.*)

Cassio. I am maim'd for ever. Help, ho! murder! murder! (*Falls.*)

(*Enter Othello, at a distance.*)

Othello. The voice of Cassio: Iago keeps his word.
Roderigo. O! villain that I am!
Othello.   It is e'en so.
Cassio. O, help, ho! light! a surgeon! 30
Othello. 'Tis he: O brave Iago, honest and just!

---

[552] Pimple.   [553] To the quick.   [554] Swindled.   [555] I.e., that's the only way.

That hast such noble sense of thy friend's wrong;
Thou teachest me. Minion,[556] your dear lies dead,
And your unblest fate hies; strumpet, I come!
Forth of my heart those charms, thine eyes, are blotted;   35
Thy bed lust-stain'd shall with lust's blood be spotted.   (*Exit.*)

(*Enter Lodovico and Gratiano, at a distance.*)

Cassio.   What ho! no watch? no passage?[557] murder! murder!
Gratiano.   'Tis some mischance; the cry is very direful.
Cassio.   O, help!
Lodovico.   Hark!   40
Roderigo.   O wretched villain!
Lodovico.   Two or three groans: it is a heavy[558] night;
   These may be counterfeits; let 's think 't unsafe
   To come in to the cry[559] without more help.
Roderigo.   Nobody come? then shall I bleed to death.   45
Lodovico.   Hark!

(*Re-enter Iago, with a light.*)

Gratiano.   Here 's one comes in his shirt, with light and weapons.
Iago.   Who 's there? whose noise is this that cries on murder?
Lodovico.   We do not know.
Iago.   Did not you hear a cry?
Cassio.   Here, here! for heaven's sake, help me.
Iago.   What's the matter?   50
Gratiano.   This is Othello's ancient, as I take it.
Lodovico.   The same indeed; a very valiant fellow.
Iago.   What are you here that cry so grievously?
Cassio.   Iago? O! I am spoil'd, undone by villains!
   Give me some help.   55
Iago.   O me, lieutenant! what villains have done this?
Cassio.   I think that one of them is hereabout,
   And cannot make away.
Iago.   O treacherous villains!
   (*To Lodovico and Gratiano.*) What are you there? come in, and
   give some help.
Roderigo.   O! help me here.   60
Cassio.   That's one of them.
Iago.   O murderous slave! O villain!

---

[556] (Cassio's) darling, i.e., Desdemona.   [557] Passer-by.   [558] Dark.   [559] Where
the cry comes from.

(Stabs Roderigo.)

Roderigo.   O damn'd Iago! O inhuman dog!
Iago.   Kill men i' the dark! Where be these bloody thieves?
  How silent is this town! Ho! murder! murder!
  What may you be? are you of good or evil?   65
Lodovico.   As you shall prove us, praise us.
Iago.   Signior Lodovico?
Lodovico.   He, sir.
Iago.   I cry you mercy. Here 's Cassio hurt by villains.
Gratiano.   Cassio!   70
Iago.   How is it, brother?
Cassio.   My leg is cut in two.
Iago.   Marry, heaven forbid.
  Light, gentlemen; I 'll bind it with my shirt.

(Enter Bianca.)

Bianca.   What is the matter, ho? who is 't that cried?
Iago.   Who is 't that cried!   75
Bianca.   O my dear Cassio! my sweet Cassio!
  O Cassio, Cassio, Cassio!
Iago.   O notable strumpet! Cassio, may you suspect
  Who they should be that have thus mangled you?
Cassio.   No.   80
Gratiano.   I am sorry to find you thus; I have been to seek you.
Iago.   Lend me a garter. So. O! for a chair,
  To bear him easily hence!
Bianca.   Alas; he faints! O Cassio, Cassio, Cassio!
Iago.   Gentlemen all, I do suspect this trash[560]   85
  To be a party in this injury.
  Patience awhile, good Cassio. Come, come.
  Lend me a light. Know we this face, or no?
  Alas! my friend and my dear countryman,
  Roderigo? no: yes, sure, O heaven! Roderigo.   90
Gratiano.   What! of Venice?
Iago.   Even he, sir, did you know him?
Gratiano.   Know him! ay.
Iago.   Signior Gratiano? I cry you gentle pardon;
  These bloody accidents must excuse my manners,
  That so neglected you.
Gratiano.   I am glad to see you.   95

---

[560] I.e., Bianca.

Iago.   How do you, Cassio? O! a chair, a chair!
Gratiano.   Roderigo!

(*A chair brought in.*)

Iago.   He, he, 'tis he,—O! that 's well said; the chair:
  Some good men bear him carefully from hence;
  I 'll fetch the general's surgeon. (*To Bianca.*) For you, mistress,   100
  Save you your labour. He that lies slain here, Cassio,
  Was my dear friend. What malice was between you?
Cassio.   None in the world; nor do I know that man.
Iago (*to Bianca*).   What! look you pale? O! bear him out o' the air—

(*Cassio and Roderigo are borne off.*)

  Stay you, good gentlemen. Look you pale, mistress?—   105
  Do you perceive the gastness[561] of her eye?
  Nay, if you stare, we shall hear more anon.
  Behold her well; I pray you, look upon her.
  Do you see, gentlemen? nay, guiltiness will speak
  Though tongues were out of use.   110

(*Enter Emilia.*)

Emilia.   'Las! what 's the matter? what 's the matter, husband?
Iago.   Cassio hath here been set on in the dark
  By Roderigo and fellows that are 'scaped:
  He 's almost slain, and Roderigo dead.
Emilia.   Alas! good gentleman; alas! good Cassio!   115
Iago.   This is the fruit of whoring. Prithee, Emilia,
  Go know of Cassio where he supp'd to-night.
  (*To Bianca.*) What! do you shake at that?
Bianca.   He supp'd at my house; but I therefore shake not.
Iago.   O! did he so? I charge you, go with me.   120
Emilia.   Fie, fie, upon thee, strumpet!
Bianca.   I am no strumpet, but of life as honest
  As you that thus abuse me.
Emilia.   As I! foh! fie upon thee!
Iago.   Kind gentlemen, let 's go see poor Cassio dress'd.[562]
  Come, mistress, you must tell 's another tale.   125
  Emilia, run you to the citadel,
  And tell my lord and lady what hath happ'd.

---

[561] Terror.   [562] Bandaged.

Will you go on afore? (*Aside.*) This is the night
That either makes me or fordoes[563] me quite.   (*Exeunt.*)

SCENE 2.   *A Bedchamber in the Castle. Desdemona in bed asleep. A light burning.*

(*Enter Othello.*)

Othello.   It is the cause,[564] it is the cause, my soul;
   Let me not name it to you, you chaste stars!
   It is the cause. Yet I 'll not shed her blood,
   Nor scar that whiter skin of hers than snow,
   And smooth as monumental alabaster.   5
   Yet she must die, else she 'll betray more men.
   Put out the light, and then put out the light:
   If I quench thee, thou flaming minister,[565]
   I can again thy former light restore,
   Should I repent me; but once put out thy light,   10
   Thou cunning'st[566] pattern of excelling nature,
   I know not where is that Promethean[567] heat
   That can thy light relume.[568] When I have pluck'd the rose,
   I cannot give it vital growth again,
   It needs must wither: I 'll smell it on the tree. (*Kisses her.*) 15
   O balmy breath, that dost almost persuade
   Justice to break her sword! One more, one more.
   Be thus when thou art dead, and I will kill thee,
   And love thee after. One more, and this the last:
   So sweet was ne'er so fatal. I must weep,   20
   But they are cruel tears; this sorrow 's heavenly,
   It strikes where it doth love. She wakes.
Desdemona.   Who 's there? Othello?
Othello.   Ay, Desdemona.
Desdemona.   Will you come to bed, my lord?
Othello.   Have you pray'd to-night, Desdemona?
Desdemona.   Ay, my lord.   25
Othello.   If you bethink yourself of any crime
   Unreconcil'd as yet to heaven and grace,
   Solicit for it straight.
Desdemona.   Alas! my lord, what may you mean by that?

---

[563] Ruins.   [564] I.e., Desdemona's unchastity (Othello means that the severity of the punishment is required by the nature of her sin).   [565] I.e., the candle.   [566] Most intricately wrought.   [567] In Greek mythology the demi-god Prometheus stole fire from the gods and gave it to man.   [568] Relight.

Othello.   Well, do it, and be brief; I will walk by:[569]   30
   I would not kill thy unprepared spirit;
   No; heaven forfend![570] I would not kill thy soul.
Desdemona.   Talk you of killing?
Othello.   Ay, I do.
Desdemona.   Then heaven
   Have mercy on me!
Othello.   Amen! with all my heart.
Desdemona.   If you say so, I hope you will not kill me.   35
Othello.   Hum!
Desdemona.   And yet I fear you; for you are fatal then
   When your eyes roll so. Why I should fear I know not,
   Since guiltiness I know not; but yet I feel I fear.
Othello.   Think on thy sins.
Desdemona.   They are loves I bear to you.   40
Othello.   Ay, and for that thou diest.
Desdemona.   That death's unnatural that kills for loving.
   Alas! why gnaw you so your nether lip?
   Some bloody passion shakes your very frame;
   These are portents,[571] but yet, I hope, I hope   45
   They do not point on me.
Othello.   Peace, and be still!
Desdemona.   I will so. What 's the matter?
Othello.   That handkerchief which I so lov'd and gave thee
   Thou gav'st to Cassio.
Desdemona.   No, by my life and soul!
   Send for the man and ask him.
Othello.   Sweet soul, take heed,   50
   Take heed of perjury; thou 'rt on thy death-bed.
Desdemona.   Ay, but not yet to die.
Othello.   Yes, presently;[572]
   Therefore confess thee freely of thy sin;
   For to deny each article with oath
   Cannot remove nor choke the strong conception[573]   55
   That I do groan withal. Thou art to die.
Desdemona.   Then Lord have mercy on me!
Othello.   I say, amen.
Desdemona.   And have you mercy too! I never did
   Offend you in my life; never lov'd Cassio
   But with such general warranty[574] of heaven   60
   As I might love; I never gave him token.

---

[569] Nearby.   [570] Forbid.   [571] Omens.   [572] At once.   [573] Belief.
[574] Permission.

Othello.   By heaven, I saw my handkerchief in 's hand.
  O perjur'd woman! thou dost stone[575] my heart,
  And mak'st me call what I intend to do
  A murder, which I thought a sacrifice: 65
  I saw the handkerchief.
Desdemona.   He found it then;
  I never gave it him. Send for him hither;
  Let him confess a truth.
Othello.   He had confessed.
Desdemona.   What, my lord?
Othello.   That he hath us'd thee.
Desdemona.   How? Unlawfully?
Othello.   Ay.   70
Desdemona.   He will not say so.
Othello.   No; his mouth is stopp'd:
  Honest Iago hath ta'en order for 't.[576]
Desdemona.   O! my fear interprets. What! is he dead?
Othello.   Had all his hairs been lives, my great revenge
  Had stomach[577] for them all.   75
Desdemona.   Alas! he is betray'd and I undone.
Othello.   Out, strumpet! Weep'st thou for him to my face?
Desdemona.   O! banish me, my lord, but kill me not!
Othello.   Down, strumpet!
Desdemona.   Kill me to-morrow; let me live to-night!   80
Othello.   Nay, if you strive,—
Desdemona.   But half an hour!
Othello.   Being done, there is no pause.
Desdemona.   But while I say one prayer!
Othello.   It is too late.   (*He smothers her.*)
Emilia (*within*).   My lord, my lord! what, ho! my lord, my lord!
Othello.   What noise is this? Not dead? Not yet quite dead? 85
  I that am cruel am yet merciful;
  I would not have thee linger in thy pain.
  So, so.
Emilia (*within*).   What, ho! my lord, my lord!
Othello.   Who's there?
Emilia (*within*).   O! good my lord, I would speak a word with you!   90
Othello.   Yes; 'tis Emilia: by and by.[578] She's dead.
  'Tis like[579] she comes to speak of Cassio's death;
  The noise was high. Ha! no more moving?
  Still as the grave. Shall she come in? were 't good?[580]

---

[575] Turn to stone.   [576] Taken steps.   [577] Appetite.   [578] I.e., "just a moment."
[579] Likely.   [580] Would that be wise.

I think she stirs again: no. What 's best to do?   95
If she come in she'll sure speak to my wife:
My wife! my wife! what wife? I have no wife;
O, insupportable! O heavy hour!
Methinks it should be now a huge eclipse
Of sun and moon, and that the affrighted globe   100
Should yawn[581] at alteration.
Emilia (*within*).   I do beseech you
That I may speak with you, O! good my lord.
Othello.   I had forgot thee: O! come in, Emilia:
Soft, by and by: let me the curtains draw.
Where art thou?   (*Unlocks the door.*)

(*Enter Emilia.*)

                  What 's the matter with thee now?   105
Emilia.   O! my good lord, yonder 's foul murder done.
Othello.   What! now?
Emilia.   But now, my lord.
Othello.   It is the very error[582] of the moon;
She comes more near the earth than she was wont,   110
And makes men mad.
Emilia.   Cassio, my lord, has kill'd a young Venetian
Call'd Roderigo.
Othello.   Roderigo kill'd!
And Cassio kill'd?
Emilia.   No, Cassio is not kill'd.
Othello.   Not Cassio kill'd! then murder 's out of tune,   115
And sweet revenge grows harsh.
Desdemona.   O! falsely, falsely murder'd.
Emilia.   Alas! what cry is that?
Othello.   That! what?
Emilia.   Out, and alas! that was my lady's voice:
Help! Help, ho! help! O lady, speak again!   120
Sweet Desdemona! O! sweet mistress, speak.
Desdemona.   A guiltless death I die.
Emilia.   O! who hath done this deed?
Desdemona.   Nobody; I myself; farewell:
Commend me to my kind lord. O! farewell!   (*Dies.*)   125
Othello.   Why, how should she be murder'd?
Emilia.   Alas! who knows?

---

[581] Open up (as in an earthquake).   [582] Straying.

Othello.   You heard her say herself it was not I.

Emilia.   She said so; I must needs report the truth.

Othello.   She 's like a liar gone to burning hell;   130
'Twas I that kill'd her.

Emilia.   O! the more angel she,
And you the blacker devil.

Othello.   She turn'd to folly, and she was a whore.

Emilia.   Thou dost belie her, and thou art a devil.

Othello.   She was false as water.

Emilia.   Thou art rash as fire to say
That she was false! O! she was heavenly true.   135

Othello.   Cassio did tup her; ask thy husband else.
O! I were damn'd beneath all depth in hell
But that I did proceed[583] upon just grounds
To this extremity. Thy husband knew it all.

Emilia.   My husband!   140

Othello.   Thy husband.

Emilia.   That she was false to wedlock?

Othello.   Ay, with Cassio. Nay, had she been true,
If heaven would make me such another world
Of one entire and perfect chrysolite,[584]   145
I'd not have sold her for it.

Emilia.   My husband!

Othello.   Ay, 'twas he that told me first:
An honest man he is, and hates the slime
That sticks on filthy deeds.

Emilia.   My husband!

Othello.   What needs this iterance,[585] woman? I say thy husband.   150

Emilia.   O mistress! villany hath made mocks with love.
My husband say that she was false!

Othello.   He, woman;
I say, thy husband: dost understand the word?
My friend, thy husband, honest, honest Iago.

Emilia.   If he say so, may his pernicious soul   155
Rot half a grain a day! he lies to the heart:
She was too fond of her most filthy bargain.[586]

Othello.   Ha!

Emilia.   Do thy worst:
This deed of thine is no more worthy heaven   160
Than thou wast worthy her.

Othello.   Peace! you were best.[587]

---

[583] Had I not proceeded.   [584] Topaz.   [585] Repetition.   [586] I.e., Othello.
[587] You'd better be quiet.

Emilia.   Thou hast not half the power to do me harm
As I have to be hurt. O gull! O dolt!
As ignorant as dirt! thou hast done a deed,—
I care not for thy sword; I'll make thee known,   165
Though I lost twenty lives. Help! help, ho! help!
The Moor has kill'd my mistress! murder! murder!

(*Enter Montano, Gratiano, Iago, and others.*)

Montano.   What is the matter? How now, general!
Emilia.   O! are you come, Iago? you have done well,
That men must lay their murders on your neck.   170
Gratiano.   What is the matter?
Emilia.   Disprove this villain if thou be'st a man:
He says thou told'st him that his wife was false.
I know thou didst not, thou 'rt not such a villain.
Speak, for my heart is full.   175
Iago.   I told him what I thought, and told no more
Than what he found himself was apt and true.
Emilia.   But did you ever tell him she was false?
Iago.   I did.
Emilia.   You told a lie, an odious damned lie;   180
Upon my soul, a lie, a wicked lie;
She false with Cassio! Did you say with Cassio?
Iago.   With Cassio, mistress. Go to, charm[588] your tongue.
Emilia.   I will not charm my tongue; I am bound to speak.
My mistress here lies murder'd in her bed.   185
All.   O heavens forfend!
Emilia.   And your reports have set the murder on.
Othello.   Nay, stare not, masters; it is true, indeed.
Gratiano.   'Tis a strange truth.
Montano.   O monstrous act!
Emilia.   Villany! villany! villany!   190
I think upon 't, I think, I smell 't; O villany!
I thought so then;[589] I'll kill myself for grief.
O! villany, villany!
Iago.   What! are you mad? I charge you, get you home.
Emilia.   Good gentlemen, let me have leave to speak: 195
'Tis proper I obey him, but not now.
Perchance, Iago, I will ne'er go home.

---

[588] I.e., into silence.   [589] *Cf.* "I will be hang'd, if some eternal villain, / Some busy and insinuating rogue, / Some cogging cozening slave, to get some office, / Have not devis'd this slander; ... " (IV, ii, 130 ff.). Emilia means, not that she guessed Iago's guilt, but that she rightly guessed the slanderer's motive.

Othello.   O! O! O!   (*Falls on the bed.*)
Emilia.   Nay, lay thee down and roar,
   For thou hast kill'd the sweetest innocent
   That e'er did lift up eye.
Othello.   O! she was foul.   (*Rises.*) 200
   I scarce did know you, uncle. There lies your niece,
   Whose breath, indeed, these hands have newly stopp'd:
   I know this act shows terrible and grim.
Gratiano.   Poor Desdemona! I am glad thy father 's dead.
   Thy match was mortal to him, and pure grief   205
   Shore[590] his old thread in twain: did he live now,
   This sight would make him do a desperate turn,
   Yea, curse his better angel from his side,
   And fall to reprobation.[591]
Othello.   'Tis pitiful; but yet Iago knows   210
   That she with Cassio hath the act of shame
   A thousand times committed; Cassio confess'd it:
   And she did gratify[592] his amorous works
   With that recognizance and pledge of love
   Which I first gave her. I saw it in his hand: 215
   It was a handkerchief, an antique token
   My father gave my mother.
Emilia.   O heaven! O heavenly powers!
Iago.   Come, hold your peace.
Emilia.   'Twill out, 'twill out; I hold my peace, sir? no;
   No, I will speak as liberal as the north;[593]   220
   Let heaven and men and devils, let them all,
   All, all, cry shame against me, yet I'll speak.
Iago.   Be wise, and get you home.
Emilia.   I will not.

(*Iago threatens to stab Emilia.*)

Gratiano.   Fie!
   Your sword upon a woman!
Emilia.   O thou dull Moor! that handkerchief thou speak'st of   225
   I found by fortune and did give my husband;
   For often, with a solemn earnestness,
   More than, indeed, belong'd to such a trifle,
   He begg'd of me to steal it.
Iago.   Villainous whore!

---

[590] Cut.   [591] Damnation.   [592] Reward.   [593] I.e., the north wind (?), the supposedly free-spoken people of north England (?).

Emilia.   She give it Cassio! no, alas! I found it,   230
    And I did give 't my husband.
Iago.   Filth, thou liest!
Emilia.   By heaven, I do not, I do not, gentlemen.
    O murderous coxcomb![594] what should such a fool
    Do with so good a wife?
Othello.   Are there no stones[595] in heaven
    But what serve for the thunder? Precious villain!   235

(*He runs at Iago. Iago stabs Emilia.*)

Gratiano.   The woman falls; sure, he has kill'd his wife.   (*Exit Iago.*)
Emilia.   Ay, ay; O! lay me by my mistress' side.
Gratiano.   He 's gone; but his wife 's kill'd.
Montano.   'Tis a notorious[596] villain. Take you this weapon,
    Which I have here recover'd from the Moor.   240
    Come, guard the door without; let him not pass,
    But kill him rather. I'll after that same villain,
    For 'tis a damned slave.   (*Exeunt Montano and Gratiano.*)
Othello.   I am not valiant neither,
    But every puny whipster[597] gets my sword.
    But why should honour outlive honesty?   245
    Let it go all.
Emilia.   What did thy song bode, lady?
    Hark, canst thou hear me? I will play the swan,
    And die in music:—
    (*Sings.*)   Willow, willow, willow.
    Moor, she was chaste; she lov'd thee, cruel Moor;
    So come my soul to bliss as I speak true;   250
    So speaking as I think, I die, I die.   (*Dies.*)
Othello.   I have another weapon in this chamber;
    It is a sword of Spain, the ice-brook's temper.[598]
    O! here it is. Uncle, I must come forth.
Gratiano (*within*).   If thou attempt it, it will cost thee dear: 255
    Thou hast no weapon, and perforce must suffer.
Othello.   Look in upon me then, and speak with me,
    Or, naked[599] as I am, I will assault thee.

(*Re-enter Gratiano.*)

Gratiano.   What is the matter?

---

[594] Idiot.   [595] I.e., thunderbolts (to strike Iago down).   [596] Notable.   [597] I.e.,
a small boy whipping a top.   [598] Tempered in icy water (or the reference may be to Innsbruck, famed for the quality of its steel, but this hardly fits "a sword of Spain").   [599] Unarmed.

Othello.   Behold! I have a weapon;
  A better never did itself sustain   260
  Upon a soldier's thigh: I have seen the day,
  That with this little arm, and this good sword,
  I have made my way through more impediments
  Than twenty times your stop: but, O vain boast!
  Who can control his fate? 'tis not so now.   265
  Be not afraid, though you do see me weapon'd;
  Here is my journey's end, here is my butt,[600]
  And very sea-mark of my utmost sail.[601]
  Do you go back dismay'd? 'tis a lost fear;
  Man but a rush[602] against Othello's breast,   270
  And he retires. Where should Othello go?
  Now how dost thou look now? O ill-starr'd wench!
  Pale as thy smock! when we shall meet at compt,[603]
  This look of thine will hurl my soul from heaven,
  And fiends will snatch at it. Cold, cold, my girl!   275
  Even like thy chastity.
  O! cursed, cursed slave. Whip me, ye devils,
  From the possession of this heavenly sight!
  Blow me about in winds! roast me in sulphur!
  Wash me in steep-down gulfs of liquid fire!   280
  O Desdemona! Desdemona! dead!
  Oh! Oh! Oh!

(*Enter Lodovico, Montano, Cassio carried in a chair, and Officers with Iago, prisoner.*)

Lodovico.   Where is this rash and most unfortunate man?
Othello.   That's he that was Othello; here I am.
Lodovico.   Where is that viper? bring the villain forth.   285
Othello.   I look down towards his feet;[604] but that 's a fable.
  If that thou be'st a devil, I cannot kill thee.   (*Wounds Iago.*)
Lodovico.   Wrench his sword from him.   (*Othello is disarmed.*)
Iago.   I bleed, sir; but not kill'd.
Othello.   I am not sorry neither; I'd have thee live;
  For, in my sense,[605] 'tis happiness to die.   290
Lodovico.   O thou Othello! that wert once so good,
  Fall'n in the practice[606] of a damned slave,[607]
  What shall be said to thee?
Othello.   Why, any thing:

---

[600] Goal, end, limit.   [601] Destination of my farthest journey.   [602] Wield but a reed.
[603] On the day of judgment.   [604] I.e., for the Devil's cloven hoof.   [605] The way I
feel.   [606] Plot, machination.   [607] I.e., Iago.

An honourable murderer, if you will;
For nought did I in hate, but all in honour.   295
Lodovico.   This wretch hath part confess'd his villany:
Did you and he consent in Cassio's death?
Othello.   Ay.
Cassio.   Dear general, I never gave you cause.
Othello.   I do believe it, and I ask your pardon.   300
Will you, I pray, demand that demi-devil
Why he hath thus ensnar'd my soul and body?
Iago.   Demand me nothing: what you know, you know:
From this time forth I never will speak word.
Lodovico.   What! not to pray?
Gratiano.   Torments will ope[608] your lips.   305
Othello.   Well, thou dost best.
Lodovico.   Sir, you shall understand what hath befall'n,
Which, as I think, you know not. Here is a letter
Found in the pocket of the slain Roderigo,
And here another; the one of them imports   310
The death of Cassio to be undertook
By Roderigo.
Othello.   O villain!
Cassio.   Most heathenish and most gross!
Lodovico.   Now here's another discontented paper,
Found in his pocket too; and this, it seems,   315
Roderigo meant to have sent this damned villain,
But that, belike,[609] Iago in the interim[610]
Came in and satisfied him.
Othello.   O the pernicious caitiff!
How came you, Cassio, by that handkerchief
That was my wife's?
Cassio.   I found it in my chamber;   320
And he himself confess'd but even now
That there he dropp'd it for a special purpose
Which wrought to his desire.
Othello.   O fool! fool! fool!
Cassio.   There is besides in Roderigo's letter
How he upbraids Iago that he made him   325
Brave me upon the watch; whereon it came
That I was cast:[611] and even but now he spake,
After long seeming dead, Iago hurt him,
Iago set him on.
Lodovico.   You must forsake this room and go with us;   330

---

[608] Open.   [609] Most likely.   [610] In the meantime.   [611] Dismissed.

Your power and your command is taken off,
And Cassio rules in Cyprus. For this slave,
If there be any cunning cruelty
That can torment him much and hold him long,
It shall be his. You shall close prisoner rest,   335
Till that the nature of your fault be known
To the Venetian state. Come, bring him away.
Othello.   Soft you; a word or two before you go.
    I have done the state some service, and they know 't;
    No more of that. I pray you, in your letters,   340
    When you shall these unlucky deeds relate,
    Speak of me as I am; nothing extenuate,
    Nor set down aught[612] in malice: then, must you speak
    Of one that lov'd not wisely but too well;
    Of one not easily jealous, but, being wrought,   345
    Perplex'd[613] in the extreme; of one whose hand
    Like the base Indian,[614] threw a pearl away
    Richer than all his tribe; of one whose subdu'd[615] eyes
    Albeit unused to the melting mood,
    Drop tears as fast as the Arabian trees   350
    Their med'cinable gum. Set you down this;
    And say besides, that in Aleppo once,
    Where a malignant and a turban'd Turk
    Beat a Venetian and traduc'd the state,
    I took by the throat the circumcised dog,   355
    And smote him, thus.   (*Stabs himself.*)
Lodovico.   O bloody period![616]
Gratiano.   All that's spoke is marr'd.
Othello.   I kiss'd thee ere I killed thee; no way but this.
                                            (*Falling upon Desdemona.*)
    Killing myself to die upon a kiss.   (*Dies.*)
Cassio.   This did I fear, but thought he had no weapon;   360
    For he was great of heart.
Lodovico   (*to Iago*).   O Spartan dog!
    More fell[617] than anguish, hunger, or the sea.
    Look on the tragic loading of this bed;
    This is thy work; the object poisons sight;
    Let it be hid. Gratiano, keep the house,   365
    And seize upon the fortunes of the Moor,
    For they succeed on you. To you, lord governor,

---

[612] Anything.   [613] Distracted.   [614] The Folio reads "Iudean." Both readings denote the foolish infidel who fails to appreciate the treasure he possesses.   [615] Overcome   (by grief).   [616] Ending.   [617] Grim, cruel.

Remains the censure of this hellish villain,
The time, the place, the torture; O! enforce it.
Myself will straight aboard, and to the state   370
This heavy act with heavy heart relate.   (*Exeunt.*)

QUESTIONS

1. In what sense might it be said that Othello is responsible for his own down-fall?   **2.** Compare the speeches of Cassio and Iago in Act II, Scene 1. What does the difference in language and style reveal about their characters?   **3.** Carefully deter-mine how much time elapses between the arrival at Cyprus and the end of the action. Can you find narrated events that could not possibly have occurred within that time? Do the chronological inconsistencies disturb you? Explain.   **4.** The first part of Act IV, Scene 2 (until Othello exits), is sometimes called the "brothel" scene. What features of Othello's language and behavior justify that designation?   **5.** Discuss the relationship between love and hate in this play.

WRITING TOPICS

1. Examine the reasons Iago gives for his actions. Do you find them consistent and convincing? Explain.   **2.** Discuss the functions of the minor characters, such as Roderigo, Bianca, and Emilia, in the play.   **3.** Othello crumbles in Act III, Scene 3, as Iago creates the jealousy that destroys Othello's self-confidence and peace of mind. Is the rapidity of Othello's emotional collapse justified? Does his being black have anything to do with his emotional turmoil?

LOVE
AND
HATE

Grosse Heidelberger Liederhandschrift "Codex Manesse" fol. 249

ESSAYS

from

1 Corinthians 13 (ca. 56)

PAUL [d. ca. A.D. 64]

If I speak in the tongues of men* and of angels, but have not love, I am a noisy 1
gong or a clanging cymbal. ² And if I have prophetic powers, and understand
all mysteries and all knowledge, and if I have all faith, so as to remove mountains, but have not love, I am nothing. ³ If I give away all I have, and if I deliver
my body to be burned, but have not love, I gain nothing.

⁴ Love is patient and kind; love is not jealous or boastful; ⁵ it is not arrogant 2
or rude. Love does not insist on its own way; it is not irritable or resentful; ⁶ it
does not rejoice at wrong, but rejoices in the right. ⁷ Love bears all things,
believes all things, hopes all things, endures all things.

⁸ Love never ends; as for prophesies, they will pass away; as for tongues, they 3
will cease; as for knowledge, it will pass away. ⁹ For our knowledge is imperfect
and our prophecy is imperfect; ¹⁰ but when the perfect comes, the imperfect
will pass away. ¹¹ When I was a child, I spoke like a child, I thought like a child,
I reasoned like a child; when I became a man, I gave up childish ways. ¹² For
now we see in a mirror dimly, but then face to face. Now I know in part; then
I shall understand fully, even as I have been fully understood. ¹³ So faith, hope,
love abide, these three; but the greatest of these is love.

QUESTIONS
1. How does Paul emphasize the significance of love in verses 1–3? **2.** Analyze
Paul's technique for defining love in verses 4–8. **3.** What does Paul mean by
"now" and "then" in verse 12?

WRITING TOPICS
1. Read Paul's First Epistle to the Corinthians (preferably in a well-annotated study
Bible) and, in an essay, analyze the relationship of Chapter 13 to the rest of the
epistle. **2.** In an essay, describe how "love" or the absence of "love" (as Paul
defines it), influences your own behavior.

---

* Glossolalia, the ecstatic uttering of unintelligible sounds that some interpret as a deeply
religious experience.

The Iks
1974

LEWIS THOMAS [1913–1993]

The small tribe of Iks, formerly nomadic hunters and gatherers in the mountain valley of northern Uganda, have become celebrities, literary symbols of the ultimate fate of disheartened, heartless mankind at large. Two disastrously conclusive things happened to them: the government decided to have a national park, so they were compelled by law to give up hunting in the valleys and become farmers on poor hillside soil, and then they were visited for two years by an anthropologist who detested them and wrote a book about them.

The message of the book is that the Iks have transformed themselves into an irreversibly disagreeable collection of unattached, brutish creatures, totally selfish and loveless, in response to the dismantling of their traditional culture. Moreover, this is what the rest of us are like in our inner selves, and we will all turn into Iks when the structure of our society comes all unhinged.

The argument rests, of course, on certain assumptions about the core of human beings, and is necessarily speculative. You have to agree in advance that man is fundamentally a bad lot, out for himself alone, displaying such graces as affection and compassion only as learned habits. If you take this view, the story of the Iks can be used to confirm it. These people seem to be living together, clustered in small, dense villages, but they are really solitary, unrelated individuals with no evident use for each other. They talk, but only to make ill-tempered demands and cold refusals. They share nothing. They never sing. They turn the children out to forage as soon as they can walk, and desert the elders to starve whenever they can, and the foraging children snatch food from the mouths of the helpless elders. It is a mean society.

They breed without love or even casual regard. They defecate on each other's doorsteps. They watch their neighbors for signs of misfortune, and only then do they laugh. In the book they do a lot of laughing, having so much bad luck. Several times they even laughed at the anthropologist, who found this especially repellent (one senses, between the lines, that the scholar is not himself the world's luckiest man). Worse, they took him into the family, snatched his food, defecated on his doorstep, and hooted dislike at him. They gave him two bad years.

It is a depressing book. If, as he suggests, there is only Ikness at the center of each of us, our sole hope for hanging onto the name of humanity will be in endlessly mending the structure of our society, and it is changing so quickly and completely that we may never find the threads in time. Meanwhile, left to ourselves alone, solitary, we will become the same joyless, zestless, untouching lone animals.

But this may be too narrow a view. For one thing, the Iks are extraordinary.   6
They are absolutely astonishing, in fact. The anthropologist has never seen
people like them anywhere, nor have I. You'd think, if they were simply
examples of the common essence of mankind, they'd seem more recognizable.
Instead, they are bizarre, anomalous. I have known my share of peculiar,
difficult, nervous, grabby people, but I've never encountered any genuinely,
consistently detestable human beings in all my life. The Iks sound more like
abnormalities, maladies.

I cannot accept it. I do not believe that the Iks are representative of isolated,   7
revealed man, unobscured by social habits. I believe their behavior is something extra, something laid on. This unremitting, compulsive repellence is a
kind of complicated ritual. They must have learned to act this way; they copied
it, somehow.

I have a theory, then. The Iks have gone crazy.   8

The solitary Ik, isolated in the ruins of an exploded culture, has built a new   9
defense for himself. If you live in an unworkable society you can make up one
of your own, and this is what the Iks have done. Each Ik has become a group,
a one-man tribe on its own, a constituency.

Now everything falls into place. This is why they do seem, after all, vaguely   10
familiar to all of us. We've seen them before. This is precisely the way groups
of one size or another, ranging from communities to nations, behave. It is, of
course, this aspect of humanity that has lagged behind the rest of evolution,
and this is why the Ik seems so primitive. In his absolute selfishness, his
incapacity to give anything away, no matter what, he is a successful committee. When he stands at the door of his hut, shouting insults at his neighbors
in a loud harangue, he is a city addressing another city.

Cities have all the Ik characteristics. They defecate on doorsteps, in rivers   11
and lakes, their own or anyone else's. They leave rubbish. They detest all
neighboring cities, give nothing away. They even build institutions for desert-
ing elders out of sight.

Nations are the most Iklike of all. No wonder the Iks seem familiar. For   12
total greed, rapacity, heartlessness, and irresponsibility there is nothing to
match a nation. Nations, by law, are solitary, self-centered, withdrawn into
themselves. There is no such thing as affection between nations, and certainly no nation ever loved another. They bawl insults from their doorsteps,
defecate into whole oceans, snatch all the food, survive by detestation, take
joy in the bad luck of others, celebrate the death of others, live for the death
of others.

That's it, and I shall stop worrying about the book. It does not signify that   13
man is a sparse, inhuman thing at his center. He's all right. It only says what
we've always known and never had enough time to worry about, that we
haven't yet learned how to stay human when assembled in masses. The Ik, in
his despair, is acting out this failure, and perhaps we should pay closer attention. Nations have themselves become too frightening to think about, but we
might learn some things by watching these people.

QUESTIONS

1. To what, in the "civilized" world, do the Iks correspond? Is this essay about the Iks or about us? Explain.   **2.** What is Thomas's view of human nature in this essay? How does it differ from the anthropologist's?

WRITING TOPIC

Analyze the sentence structure of the next to last paragraph. The paragraph defines *nation* with sentences of disparate length and forcefulness. Describe the relationship between the paragraph's rhetorical structure (i.e., sentence length, rhythm, balance, sequence of assertions) and the message it conveys.

Rage   (1955)

JAMES BALDWIN   [1924–1987]

... The year which preceded my father's death had made a great change in   1
my life. I had been living in New Jersey, working in defense plants, working
and living among southerners, white and black. I knew about the south, of
course, and about how southerners treated Negroes and how they expected
them to behave, but it had never entered my mind that anyone would look
at me and expect *me* to behave that way. I learned in New Jersey that to be
a Negro meant, precisely, that one was never looked at but was simply at the
mercy of the reflexes the color of one's skin caused in other people. I acted
in New Jersey as I had always acted, that is as though I thought a great deal
of myself—I had to *act* that way—with results that were, simply, unbelievable. I had scarcely arrived before I had earned the enmity, which was extraordinarily ingenious, of all my superiors and nearly all my co-workers. In
the beginning, to make matters worse, I simply did not know what was happening. I did not know what I had done, and I shortly began to wonder what
anyone could possibly do, to bring about such unanimous, active, and unbearably vocal hostility. I knew about jim-crow but I had never experienced
it. I went to the same self-service restaurant three times and stood with all
the Princeton boys before the counter, waiting for a hamburger and coffee;
it was always an extraordinarily long time before anything was set before me,
but it was not until the fourth visit that I learned that, in fact, nothing had
ever been set before me: I had simply picked something up. Negroes were
not served there, I was told, and they had been waiting for me to realize that
I was always the only Negro present. Once I was told this, I determined to
go there all the time. But now they were ready for me and, though some
dreadful scenes were subsequently enacted in that restaurant, I never ate
there again.

It was the same story all over New Jersey, in bars, bowling alleys, diners,   2
places to live. I was always being forced to leave, silently, or with mutual
imprecations. I very shortly became notorious and children giggled behind
me when I passed and their elders whispered or shouted—they really believed that I was mad. And it did begin to work on my mind, of course; I
began to be afraid to go anywhere and to compensate for this I went places
to which I really should not have gone and where, God knows, I had no
desire to be. My reputation in town naturally enhanced my reputation at
work and my working day became one long series of acrobatics designed to
keep me out of trouble. I cannot say that these acrobatics succeeded. It
began to seem that the machinery of the organization I worked for was turning over, day and night, with but one aim: to eject me. I was fired once, and
contrived, with the aid of a friend from New York, to get back on the pay-

roll; was fired again, and bounced back again. It took a while to fire me for a third time, but the third time took. There were no loopholes anywhere. There was not even any way of getting back inside the gates.

That year in New Jersey lives in my mind as though it were the year during   3
which, having unsuspected predilection for it, I first contracted some dread, chronic disease, the unfailing symptom of which is a kind of blind fever, a pounding in the skull and fire in the bowels. Once this disease is contracted, one can never be really carefree again, for the fever, without an instant's warning, can recur at any moment. It can wreck more important things than race relations. There is not a Negro alive who does not have this rage in his blood—one has the choice, merely, of living with it consciously or surrendering to it. As for me, this fever has recurred in me, and does, and will until the day I die.

My last night in New Jersey, a white friend from New York took me to the   4
nearest big town, Trenton, to go to the movies and have a few drinks. As it turned out, he also saved me from, at the very least, a violent whipping. Almost every detail of that night stands out very clearly in my memory. I even remember the name of the movie we saw because its title impressed me as being so patly ironical. It was a movie about the German occupation of France, starring Maureen O'Hara and Charles Laughton and called *This Land is Mine*. I remember the name of the diner we walked into when the movie ended: it was the "American Diner." When we walked in the counterman asked what we wanted and I remember answering with the casual sharpness which had become my habit: "We want a hamburger and a cup of coffee, what do you think we want?" I do not know why, after a year of such rebuffs, I so completely failed to anticipate his answer, which was, of course, "We don't serve Negroes here." This reply failed to discompose me, at least for the moment. I made some sardonic comment about the name of the diner and we walked out into the streets.

This was the time of what was called the "brown-out," when the lights in   5
all American cities were very dim. When we re-entered the streets something happened to me which had the force of an optical illusion, or a nightmare. The streets were very crowded and I was facing north. People were moving in every direction but it seemed to me, in that instant, that all of the people I could see, and many more than that, were moving toward me, against me, and that everyone was white. I remember how their faces gleamed. And I felt, like a physical sensation, a *click* at the nape of my neck as though some interior string connecting my head to my body had been cut. I began to walk. I heard my friend call after me, but I ignored him. Heaven only knows what was going on in his mind, but he had the good sense not to touch me—I don't know what would have happened if he had—and to keep me in sight. I don't know what was going on in my mind, either; I certainly had no conscious plan. I wanted to do something to crush these white faces, which were crushing me. I walked for perhaps a block or

two until I came to an enormous, glittering, and fashionable restaurant in which I knew not even the intercession of the Virgin would cause me to be served. I pushed through the doors and took the first vacant seat I saw, at a table for two, and waited.

I do not know how long I waited and I rather wonder, until today, what I could possibly have looked like. Whatever I looked like, I frightened the waitress who shortly appeared, and the moment she appeared all of my fury flowed towards her. I hated her for her white face, and for her great, astounded, frightened eyes. I felt that if she found a black man so frightening I would make her fright worthwhile. 6

She did not ask me what I wanted, but repeated, as though she had learned it somewhere, "We don't serve Negroes here." She did not say it with the blunt, derisive hostility to which I had grown so accustomed, but, rather, with a note of apology in her voice, and fear. This made me colder and more murderous than ever. I felt I had to do something with my hands. I wanted her to come close enough for me to get her neck between my hands. 7

So I pretended not to have understood her, hoping to draw her closer. And she did step a very short step closer, with her pencil poised incongruously over her pad, and repeated the formula: " . . . don't serve Negroes here." 8

Somehow, with the repetition of that phrase, which was already ringing in my head like a thousand bells of a nightmare, I realized that she would never come any closer and that I would have to strike from a distance. There was nothing on the table but an ordinary watermug half full of water, and I picked this up and hurled it with all my strength at her. She ducked and it missed her and shattered against the mirror behind the bar. And, with that sound, my frozen blood abruptly thawed, I returned from wherever I had been, I *saw*, for the first time, the restaurant, the people with their mouths open, already, as it seemed to me, rising as one man, and I realized what I had done, and where I was, and I was frightened. I rose and began running for the door. A round, potbellied man grabbed me by the nape of the neck just as I reached the doors and began to beat me about the face. I kicked him and got loose and ran into the streets. My friend whispered, *"Run!"* and I ran. 9

My friend stayed outside the restaurant long enough to misdirect my pursuers and the police, who arrived, he told me, at once. I do not know what I said to him when he came to my room that night. I could not have said much. I felt, in the oddest, most awful way, that I had somehow betrayed him. I lived it over and over and over again, the way one relives an automobile accident after it has happened and one finds oneself alone and safe. I could not get over two facts, both equally difficult for the imagination to grasp, and one was that I could have been murdered. But the other was that I had been ready to commit murder. I saw nothing very clearly but I did see this: that my life, my *real* life, was in danger, and not from anything other people might do but from the hatred I carried in my own heart. 10

QUESTIONS

1. What does Baldwin mean in the opening paragraph when he says, "I acted . . . as though I thought a great deal of myself—I had to *act* that way"? **2.** What are the various stages Baldwin passes through in his response to racism? **3.** Does Baldwin's powerful description of the rage he felt support his generalization at the end of paragraph 3: "There is not a Negro alive who does not have this rage in his blood . . . "? **4.** What does Baldwin mean by the final sentence of the essay?

WRITING TOPIC

Describe how hatred in you or someone you know became self-destructive.

The Experience   1979

JILL TWEEDIE   [1936–1993]

> *"Some day my prince will come . . . "*

I have no particular qualifications to write about love but then, who has? There   1
are no courses of higher learning offered in the subject except at the University
of Life, as they say, and there I have put in a fair amount of work. So I offer
my own thoughts, experiences and researches into love in the only spirit
possible to such an enterprise—a combination of absolute humility and utter
arrogance that will cause the reader either to deride my wrongheadedness or,
with luck, to recognize some of the same lessons.

I am a white, Anglo-Saxon, heterosexual, happily married, middle-income   2
female whose experience of what is called love spans forty years of the mid-
twentieth century in one of the most fortunate parts of the globe. I mention
this because I am profoundly aware of the limits these facts give to my vision;
also because, in spite of such advantages, my experience of love has hardly
been uplifting and yet, because of them too, I have at least been vouchsafed
a glimpse of what love might be, some day.

I took my first steps in what I was told was love when the idea of high   3
romance and living happily ever after still held sway. They said that whatever
poisoned apple I might bite would surely be dislodged by a Prince's kiss and I
would then rise from all the murderous banalities of living and, enfolded in a
strong man's arms, gallop away on a white charger to the better land called
love. The way it turned out, this dream of love did not do much to irradiate
my life. The ride was nice enough but 'twas better to travel than to arrive
and—oh, shame—there was more than one Prince. Of two previous marriages
and a variety of other lovings, very little remains and that mostly ugly. However
sweet love's initial presence, when it goes it leaves horrid scars. Unlike friendship and other forms of love, the tide of male/female sex love does not ebb
imperceptibly, leaving the stones it reveals gleaming and covetable. No. It only
shows that what was taken to be precious is simply a bare, dull pebble like any
other.

Loving, lovers fill each other's lives, Siamese twins joined at the heart, bees   4
that suck honey from each other's blossoms. When love ebbs, nothing remains. Ex-lovers rarely meet again or write or offer each other even those small
kindnesses and comforts that strangers would not withhold. Birthdays, high
days and holidays pass unmarked where once they were entered in New Year
diaries and planned for months ahead. Photographs of the beloved are discarded or curl up, yellowing, in some dusty drawer. What was once the world
becomes a no-man's land, fenced with barbed wire, where trespassers are
prosecuted and even the civilities given a passing acquaintance are forbidden.
What was the most intimate—private thoughts, dreams, nightmares and child-

hood panics soothed in warm arms—are now merely coinage for a pub joke, a hostess flippancy, worth a line or two in the local paper or the old school magazine. Divorced. Separated. Split.

For the first man I thought I loved, and therefore married, I bear, at most, 5 a distant anger for injuries received. For the second I carefully suppress the good times, burying them with the bad. All those hours, weeks, months, years passed in the same bed have vanished, leaving only the traces of an old wound, an ache where a growth was removed.

Was either a part of love, ever? Of a kind. The best we could manage at the 6 time, a deformed seedling planted in fertile ground. The three of us, each of them and me, carried loads on our backs when we met, all the clobber of past generations. This I must do, that you must be, this is good, that is bad, you must, I must, we must. By the time we met, we were already proficient puppeteers, hands stuck up our stage dolls, our real selves well concealed behind the striped canvas. You Punch, me Judy. Me Jane, you Tarzan.

I had a conventional 1940s and 1950s childhood, cut to the pattern of time. 7 I adored and admired my father and my father did not adore or admire me. My mother was there like the curtains and the carpets were there, taken for loving granted in early childhood and then ruthlessly discarded, the living symbol of everything my world did not regard and that I, therefore, did not wish to become. Rejecting her caused a very slight wreckage inside, nothing you'd notice, though transfusions would later be necessary. Powerful unloving father, powerless loving mother. Cliché.

So I did what I could to make my way and married an older man. Love and 8 marriage go together like a horse and carriage. This act imposed certain conditions. First of all, you cannot grow up if you marry a father figure because this is no part of the contract, and besides, growing up is a disagreeable occupation. Then, of course, a continuing virginity of mind, if not of body, is essential because Daddy's girl has never known other men and any evidence of sexual curiosity or, worse, a touch of ribaldry might cause him to withdraw his protection. Indeed, a daughter must not know much of anything at all because Daddy must teach and daughter learn, for ever. Competence, independence, self-sufficiency, talent in anything but the most girlish endeavours, toughness of any kind, is against the rules. Light-heartedness, giggling, little tantrums and a soupçon of mischief are permitted because Daddy is a Daddy, after all, and likes to be amused after a long day or even smack a naughty bum, in his wisdom. My first marriage was a romper room and each day I laid plans to negotiate the next, with my thumb stuck endearingly in my mouth.

To begin with, we both enjoyed the game we didn't know we were playing. 9 He was a proper husband in the eyes of the outside world, protective and admonitory, and I was a proper wife, that is to say, a child; charming and irresponsible. But quite soon these playful rituals began to harden into concrete, so that we could no longer move, even if we wished, as long as we were together. For a few years I was satisfied enough, the drama of my life absorbed me, it was a stage and I was the star. First a house to play with and later, in case the audience began to cough and fidget, a pregnancy to hold them riveted. Later, like Alice in Wonderland, I came across the cake labelled 'eat me' and whenever my husband was away at work, I ate and I grew. My legs stuck out of the windows, my arms snaked round the doors, my head above an endless neck loomed through the chimney and my heartbeat rocked the room. Each day, just before 5 P.M., I nibbled the other side of Alice's cake and, in the nick of time, shrank to being a little woman again. Hullo, darling, how was your day? Me? Oh, nothing happened. Terrified, I knew that one day I wouldn't make it down again and my husband, returning from work, would fall back in horror at the monster who had taken over his home and push me out into the big wide world.[1]

Writing this now perhaps suggests that I was aware of a pretence and set up   10
my false self knowingly, for reward. Not so. The boundaries given me in girlhood were strictly defined, allowing only minimum growth and that mainly physical. To sprout the titivating secondary sexual characteristics was expected, but woe betide the *enfant terrible* who tried to burst that tight cocoon and emerge as a full-grown adult in mind as well as body. The penalty was ill-defined but all-pervasive, like those sci-fi novels of a postnuclear generation bred to fear the radioactive world above their subterranean tunnels that threatens isolation, mutilation and death. The reward for my self-restraint (in the most literal sense) was a negative one—be good and tractable and you will be looked after—but it was none the less powerful for that. So my real self, or hints of it, was as frightening to me as I feared it would be to my husband, a dark shadow given to emerging at less and less acceptable times. I was Mr. Rochester[2] secure in his mansion but I was also his mad wife in the attic. I had to conceal her existence to preserve my way of life but all the time she was setting matches to the bedding, starting a flame at the hem of the curtains, hoping to burn the mansion down.

Things became more and more schizoid. The demure façade of a prim girl   11
hid a raucous fishwife who folded her massive arms against her chest and cursed. She horrified me, so much so—threatening, as she did, my exile from society—that in spite of increasing marital quarrels and even spurts of pure hatred, never once did I let that fishwife out to hurl the oaths she could have hurled or yelled the truths she knew. How could I, without revealing what I really was, to him and to myself?

The inner split opened wider. When my husband said he loved me, I knew   12
he meant he loved the doll I had created and I accepted his love smugly enough, on her behalf. She was worth it. She wore the right clothes, she said the right things, the span of her waist would bring tears to your eyes and the tiny staccato of her heels across a floor would melt the sternest heart. She turned her head upon its graceful stem just so and her camellia hands, laced

---

[1] The allusion to *Alice in Wonderland* refers to a number of affairs Tweedie had during her first marriage.
[2] The hero of Charlotte Brontë's novel *Jane Eyre* (1847), who keeps his insane wife secluded.

on her lap, could make a stone bleed. She smiled just enough to give a man the wildest expectations and frowned just enough to make him feel safe. This doll is a good doll. This doll is a marriagable doll. This doll is a real doll.

I knew, of course, that my doll self was only a front but it was the one I had 13 deliberately created in response to popular demand. My real self knew all the things the doll did not wish to know. She was human and therefore hopelessly unfeminine, she had no pretty ways. Her voice was harsh, pumped from the guts instead of issuing sweetly from the throat, and every now and then she howled and the doll was forced to look at her face, bare as a picked bone. No wonder the poor dolly gathered up her ruffled skirts and ran shrieking down corridors to find reassurance in a man's eyes. See my soft red lips, my white skin, feel how smooth the shaven legs, smell the scented underarms, tell me you love me, dolly me.

There were, of course, other ways to accommodate the spectre within and 14 other ways became more necessary as the spectre grew stronger and rattled the bars of the cage. My husband was a man of uncertain temper. I was quite aware of this before we married. He came from a country ravaged by war, his home had been destroyed, his brother killed, his family made refugees and he, corralled off the streets of his town, had spent two years starving in the polar wastes of a Russian prison camp. Understandably, he was outside the conventional pale. I was afraid of him.

The fear was seductive. The dolly shook with it at times, was martyred by it. 15 Hit, punched, she fell to the floor and lay, a poor pale victim, her lashes fanned against an appealingly white cheek stained, briefly, dull red. Later, kindly, she accepted the remorse of her attacker, grovelling before her. Yes, I forgive you, she said. And well she might forgive, because down in the dungeon beneath, her other self was quiet for the time being, gorged to quiescence on the thick hot adrenaline provided by the man. A small price to pay.

I do not know how many people stand at the altar repeating the marriage 16 vows and knowing, however unclearly, that what they say is false and what they do calamitous. My doll stood stiffly in her stiff dress, the groom beside her, and there was not a hope for them. Upbringing had set us against each other from the start and each was busily preparing to hammer the other into an appropriate frame. After the service well-wishers launched our raft with champagne; lashed together, not far out, we sank.

Next time, I chose more carefully. The doll, anyway, was aware that her days 17 were numbered. Winning ways must be adjusted if they are to go on being useful and a good actress acknowledges that she has aged out of *ingénue* roles before the casting director says don't call us. Besides, I was no longer enamoured of my puppet and did not want to extend her life much further. She had become more obstacle than defence, the way a wall, originally built to keep enemies out, can come to be a prison keeping you in.

So I let my real self out on probation, to be called in only now and then for 18 discipline. And now I needed a male with all the right worldly appurtenances, whom I could use as a hermit crab uses a shell, to reach full growth without exposing vulnerable flesh. Using him, I could flex my own muscles in safety until they were strong enough to risk exposure.

So I fell in love with my second husband. This time, the emotion was much   19
more powerful because I knew he had seen something of my real self before he took me on. I thought him beautiful, a golden man, flamboyant and seductively hollow, like a rocket into which I could squeeze myself and guide the flight, using his engines. He was so large he filled a room, his laugh set it shaking, his shining head topped everyone, he drew all eyes. In the turmoil of his wake I found breathing space, I could advance or retreat as I chose. He had another desirable asset and that was his lack of self-restraint. He never talked if he could shout, he never saved if he could spend, he was full of tall stories and the drinks were always on him. All of which combined to make him a natural force and natural forces can be harnessed for other ends. By his noisy, infuriating, unpredictable, ebullient and blustering existence he made me look, in comparison, a good, calm, reasonable and deeply feminine woman and thus I was able, over the years with him, to allow my real self out for airings in the sure knowledge that though I might not be as adorable as the doll, I was bound to appear more acceptable than I actually was.

There were drawbacks, of course. Originally, the space within our relation-   20
ship was almost entirely taken up with the volume of his ego and I made do in a little left-over corner. He breathed deeply, his lungs fully expanded, and I breathed lightly, in short thin gasps, and there was air enough for both of us. But then things changed. I learned a trade, began to work, worked hard and earned money. Hey, he said, getting a little stuffy in here, isn't it? Sorry, darling, I said. I breathed more deeply and new ideas rushed in. The voices of American women reached me, ideas on women's rights that linked me to the clamour of the outside world. For the first time I saw myself face to face, recognized myself, realised that I was not my own creation, uniquely formed in special circumstances, but much of a muchness with other women, a fairly standard female product made by a conveyor-belt society. Inner battles, to be fought for myself alone, became outer battles, to be fought alongside the whole female sex. Release, euphoria. Look, said my husband, I haven't enough room. Neither have I, I said. I would not placate, I would not apologise, I would not give ground any more because I was connected now to a larger army that waged a bigger war, and rescue was at hand. The slaves had revolted and even the most abject gained strength for their individual skirmishes from the growing awareness that they were not personally slavish but merely enslaved. My poor man had his problems, too, but I felt no pity, then. The walls of our relationship were closing in, we fought each other as the oxygen gave out and finally I made it into the cold, invigorating fresh air. The dolly died of double pneumonia but I was still alive.

That is a brief sketch of two marriages, founded on something we all called   21
love because we lived in the romantic West and what other reason is allowed

for marriage, if not love? On the surface, of course, the upheavals were not so apparent, being thought of as private quarrels, and I have anyway condensed them greatly—they were actually spread over seven years each, the seven years they say it takes a human to replace every cell of body skin. In the lulls between there were good times, when we laughed together and shared quite a deal of tenderness and celebrated the birth of children, and just ordinary times when we went about the business of marriage, the paying of bills, the buying of goods, the cooking and the cleaning and the entertainment of friends, as every couple does. I make very little of them because the world made so much, crowding around the happy wife, the successful husband, and abruptly turning away, turning a blind and embarrassed eye to the sobbing wife and the angry, frustrated husband. Besides, the violence was endemic and perhaps because of that, ignored as much as possible. Each of us thought we were building new houses, especially designed for us, but we didn't know about the quicksand beneath or the death-watch beetles munching the timbers. An all-pervading dishonesty hung over our enterprise. I was not what I pretended and neither were they. I sold my soul for a mess of sacrificial femininity, sugar and spice and all things nice. They built a prison with their own masculinity, so con-stricting it made them red in the face, choleric. And the impulsion to act on our roles, the sheer effort it took, left little time or energy to investigate small sounds of protest within. What reward, anyway, would there be for such investigation? In fact, only penalties would be paid. Loss of social approval, isolation from friends and family, accusations of bizarre behaviour and, for the woman, selfishness, that sin forbidden to any female unless she be extraordi-narily rich, beautiful or old. To let the human being show behind the mask of gender was to risk even madness. They might come and take us away to the funny farm, make arrangements for derangement.

Much safer to be what they wanted, what was considered respectable. Much   22
better to lean heavily upon each other for support and set up a quarrel, some drama, whenever the inner voices grew querulous and needed to be drowned. *Men*, said my mother, wiping my tears away. *Women*, said my father, soothing a husband. They sounded calm and quite pleased. Well, it was all very natural, wasn't it?

Long before all this, in my very first close encounter with the opposite sex,   23
the pattern was laid down. I was ten at the time and jaunted daily back and forth to school on a bus. Every morning a boy was also waiting at the stop, he with his mates and I with mine. I liked the way he looked, I laughed a little louder when he was about. One afternoon, on the way home, it happened. I was sitting right at the front of the bus and he was two rows behind. There came a rustle, sounds of suppressed mirth, a hand stuck itself over my shoulder and thrust a small piece of paper at me. I unfolded it. There upon the graph-lined page were fat letters in pencil. "Dear Girl," said the letters, "I love you."

I read the message and stared out of the window and watched the grass that   24
lined the road grow as green as emeralds, as if a light had been lit under every

leaf. An ache started at my chest and spread through every vein until I was heavy, drugged with glucose, banjaxed by that most potent of love-surrogates—thick undiluted narcissism. A boy, a stranger, a member of the male sex, encased in his own unknown life, lying on his unknown bed, had thought of me and, by doing so, given me surreality. Until that moment "I" was who I thought I was. From then on for a very long time, "I" was whoever a man thought I was. That pencilled note signalled the end of an autonomy I was not to experience again for many years. As I turned towards that boy, tilting my chin, narrowing my eyes, pulling down my underlip to show my pearly teeth, giving him my first consciously manufactured, all synthetic skin-deep smile, I entered into my flawed inheritance.

Looking back on all this and other episodes of lust and affection, encounters that lasted a week or a year, the picture seems at first glance chaotic and a gloomy sort of chaos at that. Love and failure. By the standards of my time, success in love is measured in bronze and gold and diamonds, anniversaries of the day when love was firstly publicly seen to be there, at the altar. Thus I am found wanting, like any other whose marriage and relationships have ended in separation, and to be found wanting is meant to induce a sense of failure because those who do not conform must be rendered impotent.   25

In fact, people of my generation, like all the generations before, have had little chance of success in love of any kind. Many of those who offer the longevity of their marriage as proof of enduring love are often only revealing their own endurance in the face of ravaging compromises and a resulting anaesthesia that has left them half-way dead. In the name of that love they have jettisoned every grace considered admirable in any other part or act of life: honesty, dignity, self-respect, courtesy, kindness, integrity, steadfastness of principle. They have said those things to each other that are unsayable and done those things that are undoable and there is no health in them. They have not been true to themselves and therefore they are false to everyone else, including their children. The man has become and been allowed to become an autocrat, a tin-pot dictator in love's police state. The woman has lowered herself upon the floor to lick his jackboots. Or, sometimes, vice versa. What would never have been permitted strangers is given a free licence under love—abuse, insults, petty denigration, physical attack, intrusions on personal privacy, destruction of personal beliefs, destruction of any other friendships, destruction of sex itself. In order to enter the kingdom of love they have shrunk themselves to the space of less than one and, atrophied in every part, they claim love's crown. Two individuals who could have reached some stature have settled for being pygmies whose life's work, now, is the similar distortion of their offspring.   26

If love takes any other form than this tight, monogamous, heterosexual, lifelong reproductive unit, blessed by the law, the State, the priests and sanctified by gods, it is dismissed as an aberration, hounded as a perversion, insulted as a failure and refused the label "love." The incredible shrinking   27 couple is presented to the world as the central aim and reward of life, a holy grail for which it is never too early to begin searching. Worst of all, we are given to believe that these dwarfish twosomes form the rock upon which all the rest of life is built, from the mental health of children to whole political systems and to remain outside it is to opt out of a cosmic responsibility and threaten the very roots of the human community. Love is all, they say. Love makes the world go round, they say. And you know it's true love, they say, when two people remain together from youth to death.

But you don't and it doesn't and you can't. The truth is that we have not yet created upon this earth the conditions in which true love can exist. Most of us are quite aware that most of mankind's other developments, emotional or technological, have been dependent upon certain prerequisites. Fire had to be discovered before we could develop a taste for cooked food and a pot to cook it in. Mass literacy was only possible after the invention of printing and printing itself depended on the much earlier Chinese discovery of paper-making. The geodesic dome was an absolute impossibility before the computer age. The emotions are based on something of the same rules. Men's lives were not overshadowed by the certainty of death (and this is still so in some primitive tribes) until life itself was safer and death could be seen inevitably to arrive without sudden injury or accident. Unlike his fellow Greeks, Xenophanes[3] was a monotheist, largely because he guessed that the physical characteristics of the earth changed with time and belief in one universal god is dependent upon belief in universal rules. And man can only be said to have become truly self-conscious after Freud's delineation of the unconscious. Just so has love its necessary prerequisites, its birth-time in history, its most favourable climatic conditions. 28

So for all that we lay claim to an eternal heritage of love, man's bosom companion since the dawn of time, we have got it wrong. We have called other emotions love and they do not smell as sweet. Love itself has been very nearly impossible for most of us most of our history and is only just becoming possible today. I failed in love, like many others, because given the tools I had to hand the work could not be done. More hopelessly still, the very blueprint was flawed, rough sketch of the eventual edifice without a single practical instruction, without a brick or a nail, without a vital part or principle. Dreams are not enough. 29

QUESTIONS
1. What function does the epigraph to this essay serve? If it were a symbol, what would it symbolize?   **2.** How do Tweedie's first and second husbands differ? Suggest a "cause" for the divorce in each case.   **3.** In paragraph 27, Tweedie rather bitterly describes the prevailing social attitudes (those taught to the young) toward love and marriage. How do you feel about her description? Explain.   **4.** In para-

---

[3] Greek philosopher (b. ca. 570 B.C.).

graph 28, the author asserts that "we have not yet created upon this earth the conditions in which true love can exist." What do you suppose she means by "true love"? Do you agree or disagree? Explain.

WRITING TOPICS

1. In an essay, describe the circumstances of a divorce you know about. Was one of the parties clearly at fault? Could (or should) the divorce have been prevented?   **2.** Write about a successful marriage you know of; what makes it successful?   **3.** Write an essay in which you define your own understanding of "true love"; describe what you expect to contribute and what you expect your partner to contribute to the love relationship.

Love Stories

1988

ROBERT C. SOLOMON   [b. 1942]

> Tell me *who*—
> Who wrote the book of love?
>
> —THE MONOTOMES, 1957

At the root of "romantic" love is the romance—a story. Love is not just a [1] momentary passion but an emotional development, a structured *narrative* that is so familiar and seemingly "natural" to us that we rarely think of it as a story, a scenario that we are taught to follow, with all of its predictable progressions and conflicts and resolutions. When we hear the folk tales of other cultures, it is often easy to find them quaint or peculiar, but it is essential that we recognize our own romantic heritage as itself an anthropological oddity, a conflict-ridden and sometimes destructive set of scenarios. For example, our romantic love stories often center on the very young, though the fact is that love is just as inspiring and important to those of us who have made it past the watershed age of thirty. Our romantic protagonists are often rich, spoiled and exotic, though love since the last century or so has become thoroughly domesticated, middle-class and democratic. Indeed, our favorite protagonists are typically ill suited for long-term love, and it is not unusual for them to be killed off while still in their prime. The paradigm of romance is often forbidden or impossible love, from Lancelot's illicit love for Guinevere to the consumptive love of *La Bohème*.[1] Or else the story is cut off with a happy ending, with an embrace and a suspicious "happily ever after." But whether the story is a tragedy or a "happily ever after," it excludes the rich development of love over time.

I once asked a group of graduate literature students what made *Romeo and* [2] *Juliet*—supposedly our paradigmatic love story—romantic. They listed, in order of elicitation, the fact that the two lovers:

> die
> don't get to know each other
> face serious opposition to their love
> face danger
> live in an exotic setting
> have to meet secretly
> confide in each other
> are young and beautiful

---

[1] Lancelot, a knight at King Arthur's Court, has an adulterous relationship with Arthur's Queen Guinevere. Puccini's opera *La Bohème* ends with the tragic death of the consumptive Mimi.

make speeches proclaiming their love
are impatient, full of longing and passion
have confidence in themselves
are obstinate
have no concern for pragmatics or practicability
can't think of anyone else
have a strong sexual urge for each other

One doesn't have to be a romantic scholar to be struck by this list, which 3 quite innocently dismisses couples over twenty, not beautiful, living in Lake Wobegon, Minnesota,[2] who enjoy the approval of parents and friends, date in the open and don't have to die at the end of the fifth act. The fact is that our favorite love story gives a very misleading impression of the nature of love and its narrative, and yet it and stories like it have defined the genre of romance since at least the twelfth century, with the first popular stories of Lancelot and Guinevere, whose love was adulterous and destroyed a kingdom.

But even without the illicitness, secrecy and fatality, it is not hard to pin- 4 point our paradigm love story: "Boy meets girl. Boy loses girl. Boy gets girl." (Why not vice versa?) They live "happily ever after." Our first question should be why we use "girl" and "boy" when love is or ought to be the main concern of adulthood, not just adolescence. It is also worth noting how unthinkingly we assume that two lovers have to *meet* one another. That is, they didn't grow up together. They encounter each other essentially *as* lovers, and all other attributes are pretty much beside the point. Presumably they are strangers, meeting most likely by chance. And what is worse is the ending. We cut off the real story line before it even begins with the disingenuous phrase "happily ever after." Marriage signifies the culmination of love rather than its vehicle. (Of course, weddings aren't often included. They're not usually dramatic events.)

Of course the heart of the love story, what makes it romantic, is the "prob- 5 lem," the conflict, the suspense. This is where romance writers get to ply their skill, rend our hearts, purple our language. Love is a challenge, an enormous and often pathologically stubborn effort to overcome misunderstandings, tragedies and apparent betrayals. "Why doesn't she just get herself another fellow?" is not one of the options. Love is perseverance and agony, even to the point of personal destruction. Of necessity the love story ends when the "problem" is solved and done away with. "Boy gets girl"—or vice versa. That is when we get the quasi-literary cop-out ("and they lived happily ever after") or the death of one or preferably both of the lovers (*Love Story, Romeo and Juliet, Tristan and Isolde, Sophie's Choice*). Occasionally the love abruptly ends (*Gone with the Wind*) or suffers a heroic parting (*Casablanca*), but all of these options are, on reflection, utterly remarkable: our paradigm story of love leaves out the heart of love. It includes the initial melodrama but excludes the countless continuing details of real-life love. The story of love, in other words,

---

[2] A fictional town, created and populated by humor writer Garrison Keillor, used here to represent the antithesis of exoticism.

leaves out love. It does not deny that love demands a protracted and possibly lifelong time together ("happily ever after" and premature death both point to that), but it totally ignores this. How, then, are we supposed to live our lives according to it? Surely we should not emulate those brief periods in history, for example the time of the publication of Goethe's unhappy romantic novel *The Sorrows of Young Werther* in 1774, when literary fashion dictated a rash of suicides among the young and lovelorn.

But here is another love story, one that, you can be sure, would not make   6
it into a Harlequin romance.[3] That elderly couple walk into breakfast at a Wisconsin Holiday Inn. They are sharing the morning paper and he offers dutifully to see to the acquisition of coffee and Danish. Their story is one of lifelong companionship. One can dimly imagine a brief but clumsy court-ship, but this possibly forgettable or even (in their own minds) laughable experience is of little importance to this love story. They may remember some little misunderstanding, some early rival for affection, but probably not. They may remember the wedding, but most likely they were both too dazed and confused at the time. There may have been passion. There may have been some doubts at the beginning, but those were on page twenty of a 1,600-page novel. It is not hard to imagine that there have been days, weeks or even years of anger, resentment, contempt, even violence, but these passions, too, disperse into the mist of the years together. One can be sure that they rarely talk of love, perhaps an occasional "I love you" (on anni-versaries), but certainly no philosophical discussions of love, no metaphysical skepticism about whether or not it's "the real thing," no agonizing personal reflections about "Is this what I really want?" and whether love is actually narcissism or an unjustifiable need for dependency. No question about its going on (the word "forever" would be superfluous). Their love just *is*. It is as real and as solid a foundation as the Midwestern granite they walk on. It does not even need a name.

It is tragic and absurd that our idealized storybook romance should be so   7
different and so detached from the real story of love and our conception of love should, consequently, be so divided into two wholly separate parts, one ro-mantic and exciting but unrealistic and the other a dull tale of domesticity and endurance, devoid of the excitement that many of us now insist upon to make life worthwhile. The two parts of this unfortunate conception of love comple-ment each other in a thoroughly disappointing way. The romantic story is all about the thrill of newfound love, but it is so filled with suspense and excite-ment or pathos that it cannot bear the weight of the future. "Forever" is thus an evasion of time rather than a celebration of it. The infinitely less romantic part of the story is about the formation and working out of a partnership, legally defined as such by marriage. It is a topic fit for accountants, advisers and counselors, in which the market virtues of honesty and fair exchange and

---

[3] A publisher's imprint noted for overheated love stories.

the business skills of negotiation and compromise are of great value. Or, for the less affluent, there is a lifetime of "seeing it through," raising children, waiting for grandchildren, earning the mortgage, coping with life. In other words, first there is the thrill, then there is the coping. In the beginning there are two independent people engaged in a melodrama; then they have to "work it out." One reason why love fades, it is not unreasonable to hypothesize, is because we define it in such a hopelessly schizoid and ultimately dreary way. By definition the suspense and excitement of romance cannot continue, the partners become compatible and confident in their love for each other, and, besides, there are simply too many other things to do.

The flaws in the two-part story of love are as conducive to unhappiness as they are unliterary. A good novel doesn't climax in the second chapter, five hundred pages from the end. Romantic love is not just the story of the initial melodrama, nor is what follows anything so dreary as a mere partnership. Love is not initial conquest followed by a relationship, much less by "happily ever after." It is the continuing story of self-definition, in which plots, themes, characters, beginnings, middles and ends are very much up to the authorship of the indeterminate selves engaged in love. Indeed, another problem with our love stories is that they sound as if they give us a complete outline and a detailed recipe for love, when in fact every romance just gives us one possible version of it. Even at the beginning, every story is different, and once one gets to the reality hidden beneath the "happily ever after" cop-out, it is every couple for themselves. We get disappointed when we don't have a storybook romance, but the truth is that all of us have to create our own story, our own romance.

Not all love stories get told; some of them we are forced to live, and at least some of the love stories with which we are most familiar are not all romantic. Emotions are learned in standard behavioral situations, in what philosopher Ronald De Sousa calls paradigm scenarios. Anger, for example, is learned in a situation where one is frustrated and learns to blame other people. And so we should ask "What is the paradigm scenario of love?" It is embarrassing to say that, for most of us, it was the *dating* situation. How should we describe this? It is an extremely artificially contrived circumstance in which two people are wrenched away from familiar contexts and the support of friends and forced to seek a complete stranger's approval, admiration and more. In other words, the story of love begins for most of us, not with a blank page, but with a character who has been imposed upon us, no background or history to appeal to and no real sense of who or what we are supposed to be or do. No wonder we need the comfort of the more sentimental love stories to soothe us through such an ordeal. And no wonder our current conception of love is so much at odds with our more general notions of comfort and sociability, so private and exclusive and so walled off from all other sources of support and appeal. We learn love in these conditions of total isolation, and we learn it as a cruel game of acceptance and rejection. And so of course finding love strikes us as both a necessity and a great relief. As one recent book puts it, an overwhelming reason for falling in love and living with someone is that one doesn't have to date anymore.

Life is notoriously sloppy, from a literary point of view. It begins before we know how to narrate and we never know how it will end. Philosophers such as Nietzsche[4] may insist that we should "live life as a work of art," but the truth is that no work of art could be so complex, could fill up such a vast amount of time or deal with such a bewildering array of details. But in love, more than anywhere else, we recognize our urge for living life as a simple story, following a narrative with a beginning, a plot, a development and a climax. Of course it is not always clear where the climax is to be found (first kiss, making love, saying "I love you," marriage, first child, death?), but *closure* is what every story must have. It is its resolution. A novel might end just after the climax, but our story must go on. We try to live our lives as narrative, but we always find ourselves in the middle. And so when we try to find closure in any particular culmination of love—whether first kiss or marriage—we are haunted by the literary phrase "happily ever after." For us there is no phrase, just more life to live, more to work out. And so we try to start the story again, keeping conflict and frustrating plot twists to a minimum, or we invent sequels, which, as in the movies, too often seem imitative and inferior to the originals. We want to close it off and seal it with a definitive word or phrase—like all of those familiar romances. But we go on. And, paradoxically though not surprisingly, we periodically try to create closure, by provoking a crisis, by walking out, for "no" creates a closure where "yes" only means that the story must go on. And there is nothing worse than a boring story, even if—especially if—it is one's own.

10

QUESTIONS
1. Solomon argues that young people's idea of love is created by stories. Do you agree or disagree? Defend your position.   **2.** What dangers await lovers whose notions of love and marriage are formed by stories? Is there a solution to this problem? How, in a reasonable society, should young people learn what "love" is? **3.** In some detail, explain the meaning of "happily ever after." In what sense does this typical conclusion begin rather than end an interesting story?

WRITING TOPICS
1. Write an essay in which you, first, analyze Solomon's warnings about the pernicious effects of both tragic and happy love stories on the young, and second, suggest some solutions to this problem.   **2.** Write a definition of love.   **3.** Write an account of an experience you had that either validates or contradicts Solomon's argument.

---

[4] Friedrich Wilhelm Nietzsche (1844–1900), a German philosopher.

Love and Hate

QUESTIONS AND WRITING TOPICS

1. Almost every story in this section incorporates some sexual element. Distinguish among the functions served by the sexual aspects of the stories. **Writing Topic:** Contrast the function of sexuality in Moravia's "The Chase" and Faulkner's "A Rose for Emily."

2. Examine the works in this section in terms of the support they provide for the contention that love and hate are closely related emotions. **Writing Topic:** Discuss the relationship between love and hate in Faulkner's "A Rose for Emily" and Shakespeare's *Othello.*

3. What images are characteristically associated with love in the prose and poetry of this section? What images are associated with hate? **Writing Topic:** Compare the image patterns in Shakespeare's sonnets 18 and 130 or the image patterns in Donne's "A Valediction: Forbidding Mourning" and Christopher Marlowe's "The Passionate Shepherd to His Love."

4. The Greeks have three words that can be translated by the English word *love: eros, agape,* and *philia.* Describe the difference among these three types of love. **Writing Topic:** Find a story or poem that you think is representative of each type of love. In analyzing each work, discuss the extent to which the primary notion of love being addressed or celebrated is tempered by the other two types.

5. Blake's "A Poison Tree," Plath's "Daddy," and Thomas's "The Iks" all seem to describe aspects of hate. How can one distinguish the different varieties of hatred being expressed? **Writing Topic:** Compare and contrast the source of the hatred in two of these selections.

6. Chopin's "The Storm" and Moravia's "The Chase" deal with infidelity. Distinguish between the attitudes toward infidelity developed in these stories. **Writing Topic:** Describe the effects of marital infidelity on the lives of the major characters in each story.

7. What are the sources of the hatred described in Thomas's "The Iks" and Baldwin's "Rage"? **Writing Topic:** Defend or refute the assertion that Baldwin's confrontation with an Ik-like society is responsible for his rage.

8. Moravia's "The Chase," Borges's "The Intruder," and Shaw's "The Girls in Their Summer Dresses" deal with jealousy. Contrast both the sources of the jealousy and the resolution of the problems caused by jealousy in the stories. **Writing Topic:** Who in your opinion has the better reason for being jealous, the husband in "The Chase," the brothers in "The Intruder," or the wife in "The Girls in Their Summer Dresses"? Explain.

9. Which works in this section treat love or hate in a way that corresponds with your own experience or conception of those emotional states? Which contradict your experience? **Writing Topic:** Isolate, in each case, the elements in the work that provoke your response and discuss them in terms of their "truth" or "falsity."

The Presence of Death

Dream of a Sunday Afternoon in the Alameda, 1947–1948 by Diego Rivera

The inevitability of death is not implied in the Biblical story of creation; it required an act of disobedience before an angry God passed sentence of hard labor and mortality on humankind: "In the sweat of your face you shall eat bread till you return to the ground, for out of it you were taken; you are dust and to dust you shall return." These words, written down some 2,800 years ago, preserve an ancient explanation for a condition of life that yet remains persistently enigmatic—the dissolution of the flesh and the personality as accident or age culminates in death, the "undiscovered country, from whose bourn / No traveller returns." Though we cannot know what death is like, from earliest times men and women have attempted to characterize death, to cultivate beliefs about it. The mystery of it and the certainty of it make death, in every age, an important theme for literary art.

Beliefs about the nature of death vary widely. The ancient Jews of the Pentateuch reveal no conception of immortality. Ancient Buddhist writings describe death as a mere translation from one painful life to another in an ongoing expiation that only the purest can avoid. The Christians came to conceive of a soul, separate from the body, which at the body's death is freed for a better (or worse) disembodied eternal life. More recently in the Western world, the history of the attitudes about death reflects the great intellectual revolutions that affected all thought—the Copernican revolution, which displaced the earth from the center of the solar system; the Darwinian revolution, which replaced humans, the greatest glory of God's creation, with upright primates with opposable thumbs whose days, like the dinosaur's, are likely to be numbered by the flux between the fire and ice of geological history; and the Freudian revolution, which robbed men and women of their proudest certainty, the conviction that they possessed a dependable and controlling rational mind. All these ideological changes serve to diminish us, to mock our self-importance, and, inevitably, to alter our conception of death.

But despite the impact of intellectual history, death remains invested with a special awe—perhaps because it infallibly mediates between all human differences. For the churchly, death, like birth and marriage, is the occasion for solemn ritual that reaffirms for the congregation its own communal life and the promise of a better life hereafter—though the belief in immortality does not eliminate sadness and regret. For those for whom there is no immortality, death is nonetheless a ceremonial affair, full of awe, for nothing human is so purely defined, so utterly important, as a life ended. Furthermore, both the religious and the secular see death in moral terms. For both, the killer is hateful. For both, there are some deaths that are deserved, some deaths that human weakness makes inevitable, some deaths that are outrageously unfair. For both, there are courageous deaths, which exalt the community, and cowardly deaths too embarrassing to recognize.

The speaker in Robert Frost's "Stopping by Woods on a Snowy Evening" gazes into the dark woods filling up with snow, momentarily drawn toward the peace it represents. But Frost's is a secular poem and the speaker turns back to life. In much religious poetry—John Donne's sonnet "Death, Be Not Proud" is an outstanding example—death is celebrated as a release from a burdensome existence into the eternal happiness of the afterlife. Another view that establishes death as the great leveler, bringing citizens and emperors to that selfsame dust, reassures the impoverished when they contrast their misery with the wealth of the mighty.

That leveling aspect of death, apparent in Shelley's "Ozymandias," leads easily and logically to the tradition wherein life itself is made absurd by the fact of death. You may remember that Macbeth finally declares that life is "a tale / Told by an idiot, full of sound and fury, / Signifying nothing." And the contemplation of suicide, which the pain and absurdity of life would seem to commend, provokes such diverse responses as Spiegelman's macabre story "Prisoner on the Hell Planet" and Edwin Arlington Robinson's ironic "Richard Cory." Some rage against death—Dylan Thomas in "Do Not Go Gentle into That Good Night"; others caution a quiet resignation—Frost in "After Apple-Picking" and Catherine Davis in her answer to Thomas, "After a Time." Much fine poetry on death is elegiac; it speaks the melancholy response of the living to the fact of death in such poems as Housman's "To an Athlete Dying Young," and Roethke's "Elegy for Jane."

In short, literary treatments of death display immense diversity. Selzer's "The Discus Thrower" reveals the rage of a dying patient, while in Tolstoy's *The Death of Iván Ilých*, dying leads to a redemptive awareness. In Malamud's tragicomic "Idiots First," the protagonist insists upon and wins fair treatment from death, and in Cummings's "nobody loses all the time" and in Woody Allen's "Death Knocks," the comic lightens the weight of death. The inevitability of death and the way one confronts it paradoxically lend to life its meaning and its value.

FOR THINKING AND WRITING

As you read the selections in this section, consider the following questions. You may want to write out your thoughts informally in a journal or notebook as a way of preparing to respond to the selections, or you may wish to make one of these questions the basis for a formal essay.

1. Have you had a close relative or friend who died? Was the person young or old, vigorous or feeble? How did you feel? How might the circumstances of death alter one's feelings toward death, or toward the person who died?

2. Do you believe that some essential part of you will survive the death of your body? On what do you base the belief? How does it alter your feelings about the death of people close to you? How does it alter your own behavior?

3. Are there any circumstances that justify suicide? Explain. If you feel that some suicides are justifiable, would it also be justifiable to help someone end his or her life? Explain.

4. Are there any circumstances that justify killing someone? Explain.

5. Imagine as best you can and describe the circumstances of your own death.

THE
PRESENCE
OF DEATH

The Dead Mother, 1897 by Edvard Munch

FICTION

The Death of Iván Ilých*   1886

LEO TOLSTOY   [1828–1910]

CHAPTER I

During an interval in the Melvínski trial in the large building of the Law Courts the members and public prosecutor met in Iván Egórovich Shébek's private room, where the conversation turned on the celebrated Krasóvski case. Fëdor Vasílievich warmly maintained that it was not subject to their jurisdiction, Iván Egórovich maintained the contrary, while Peter Ivánovich, not having entered into the discussion at the start, took no part in it but looked through the *Gazette* which had just been handed in.

"Gentlemen," he said, "Iván Ilých has died!"

"You don't say so!"

"Here, read it yourself," replied Peter Ivánovich, handing Fëdor Vasílievich the paper still damp from the press. Surrounded by a black border were the words: "Praskóvya Fëdorovna Goloviná, with profound sorrow, informs relatives and friends of the demise of her beloved husband Iván Ilých Golovín, Member of the Court of Justice, which occurred on February the 4th of this year 1882. The funeral will take place on Friday at one o'clock in the afternoon."

Iván Ilých had been a colleague of the gentlemen present and was liked by them all. He had been ill for some weeks with an illness said to be incurable. His post had been kept open for him, but there had been conjectures that in case of his death Alexéev might receive his appointment, and that either Vínnikov or Shtábel would succeed Alexéev. So on receiving the news of Iván Ilých's death the first thought of each of the gentlemen in that private room was of the changes and promotions it might occasion among themselves or their acquaintances.

"I shall be sure to get Shtábel's place or Vínnikov's," thought Fëdor Vasílievich. "I was promised that long ago, and the promotion means an extra eight hundred rubles a year for me besides the allowance."

---

* Translated by Aylmer Maude.

"Now I must apply for my brother-in-law's transfer from Kalúga," thought Peter Ivánovich. "My wife will be very glad, and then she won't be able to say that I never do anything for her relations."

"I thought he would never leave his bed again," said Peter Ivánovich aloud. "It's very sad."

"But what really was the matter with him?"

"The doctors couldn't say—at least they could, but each of them said something different. When last I saw him I thought he was getting better."

"And I haven't been to see him since the holidays. I always meant to go."

"Had he any property?"

"I think his wife had a little—but something quite trifling."

"We shall have to go to see her, but they live so terribly far away."

"Far away from you, you mean. Everything's far away from your place."

"You see, he never can forgive my living on the other side of the river," said Peter Ivánovich, smiling at Shébek. Then, still talking of the distances between different parts of the city, they returned to the Court.

Besides considerations as to the possible transfers and promotions likely to result from Iván Ilých's death, the mere fact of the death of a near acquaintance aroused, as usual, in all who heard of it the complacent feeling that, "it is he who is dead and not I."

Each one thought or felt, "Well, he's dead but I'm alive!" But the more intimate of Iván Ilých's acquaintances, his so-called friends, could not help thinking also that they would now have to fulfill the very tiresome demands of propriety by attending the funeral service and paying a visit of condolence to the widow.

Fëdor Vasílievich and Peter Ivánovich had been his nearest acquaintances. Peter Ivánovich had studied law with Iván Ilých and had considered himself to be under obligations to him.

Having told his wife at dinner-time of Iván Ilých's death, and of his conjecture that it might be possible to get her brother transferred to their circuit, Peter Ivánovich sacrificed his usual nap, put on his evening clothes, and drove to Iván Ilých's house.

At the entrance stood a carriage and two cabs. Leaning against the wall in the hall downstairs near the cloak-stand was a coffin-lid covered with cloth of gold, ornamented with gold cord and tassels, that had been polished up with metal powder. Two ladies in black were taking off their fur cloaks. Peter Ivánovich recognized one of them as Iván Ilých's sister, but the other was a stranger to him. His colleague Schwartz was just coming downstairs, but on seeing Peter Ivánovich enter he stopped and winked at him, as if to say: "Iván Ilých has made a mess of things—not like you and me."

Schwartz's face with his Piccadilly whiskers, and his slim figure in evening dress, had as usual an air of elegant solemnity which contrasted with the playfulness of his character and had a special piquancy here, or so it seemed to Peter Ivánovich.

Peter Ivánovich allowed the ladies to precede him and slowly followed them upstairs. Schwartz did not come down but remained where he was, and Peter Ivánovich understood that he wanted to arrange where they should play bridge that evening. The ladies went upstairs to the widow's room, and Schwartz with seriously compressed lips but a playful look in his eyes, indicated by a twist of his eyebrows the room to the right where the body lay.

Peter Ivánovich, like everyone else on such occasions, entered feeling uncertain what he would have to do. All he knew was that at such times it is always safe to cross oneself. But he was not quite sure whether one should make obeisances while doing so. He therefore adopted a middle course. On entering the room he began crossing himself and made a slight movement resembling a bow. At the same time, as far as the motion of his head and arm allowed, he surveyed the room. Two young men—apparently nephews, one of whom was a high-school pupil—were leaving the room, crossing themselves as they did so. An old woman was standing motionless, and a lady with strangely arched eyebrows was saying something to her in a whisper. A vigorous, resolute Church Reader, in a frock-coat, was reading something in a loud voice with an expression that precluded any contradiction. The butler's assistant, Gerásim, stepping lightly in front of Peter Ivánovich, was strewing something on the floor. Noticing this, Peter Ivánovich was immediately aware of a faint odour of a decomposing body.

The last time he had called on Iván Ilých, Peter Ivánovich had seen Gerásim in the study. Iván Ilých had been particularly fond of him and he was performing the duty of a sick nurse.

Peter Ivánovich continued to make the sign of the cross slightly inclining his head in an intermediate direction between the coffin, the Reader, and the icons on the table in a corner of the room. Afterwards, when it seemed to him that this movement of his arm in crossing himself had gone on too long, he stopped and began to look at the corpse.

The dead man lay, as dead men always lie, in a specially heavy way, his rigid limbs sunk in the soft cushions of the coffin, with the head forever bowed on the pillow. His yellow waxen brow with bald patches over his sunken temples was thrust up in the way peculiar to the dead, the protruding nose seeming to press on the upper lip. He was much changed and had grown even thinner since Peter Ivánovich had last seen him, but, as is always the case with the dead, his face was handsomer and above all more dignified than when he was alive. The expression on the face said that what was necessary had been accomplished, and accomplished rightly. Besides this there was in that expression a reproach and a warning to the living. This warning seemed to Peter Ivánovich out of place, or at least not applicable to him. He felt a certain discomfort and so he hurriedly crossed himself once more and turned and went out of the door—too hurriedly and too regardless of propriety, as he himself was aware.

Schwartz was waiting for him in the adjoining room with legs spread wide apart and both hands toying with his top-hat behind his back. The mere sight of that playful, well-groomed, and elegant figure refreshed Peter Ivánovich. He felt that Schwartz was above all these happenings and would not surrender to any depressing influences. His very look said that this incident of a church service for Iván Ilých could not be a sufficient reason for infringing the order of the session—in other words, that it would certainly not prevent his unwrapping a new pack of cards and shuffling them that evening while a footman placed four fresh candles on the table: in fact, there was no reason for supposing that this incident would hinder their spending the evening agreeably. Indeed he said this in a whisper as Peter Ivánovich passed him, proposing that they should meet for a game at Fëdor Vasílievich's. But apparently Peter Ivánovich was not destined to play bridge that evening. Praskóvya Fëdorovna (a short, fat woman who despite all efforts to the contrary had continued to broaden steadily from her shoulders downwards and who had the same extraordinarily arched eyebrows as the lady who had been standing by the coffin), dressed all in black, her head covered with lace, came out of her own room with some other ladies, conducted them to the room where the dead body lay, and said: "The service will begin immediately. Please go in."

Schwartz, making an indefinite bow, stood still, evidently neither accepting nor declining this invitation. Praskóvya Fëdorovna recognizing Peter Ivánovich, sighed, went close up to him, took his hand, and said: "I know you were a true friend to Iván Ilých . . ." and looked at him awaiting some suitable response. And Peter Ivánovich knew that, just as it had been the right thing to cross himself in that room, so what he had to do here was to press her hand, sigh, and say, "Believe me . . ." So he did all this and as he did it felt that the desired result had been achieved: that both he and she were touched.

"Come with me. I want to speak to you before it begins," said the widow. "Give me your arm."

Peter Ivánovich gave her his arm and they went to the inner rooms, passing Schwartz who winked at Peter Ivánovich compassionately.

"That does for our bridge! Don't object if we find another player. Perhaps you can cut in when you do escape," said his playful look.

Peter Ivánovich sighed still more deeply and despondently, and Praskóvya Fëdorovna pressed his arm gratefully. When they reached the drawing-room, upholstered in pink cretonne and lighted by a dim lamp, they sat down at the table—she on a sofa and Peter Ivánovich on a low pouffe, the springs of which yielded spasmodically under his weight. Praskóvya Fëdorovna had been on the point of warning him to take another seat, but felt that such a warning was out of keeping with her present condition and so changed her mind. As he sat down on the pouffe Peter Ivánovich recalled how Iván Ilých had arranged this room and had consulted him regarding this pink cretonne with green leaves. The whole room was full of furniture and knick-knacks, and on her way to the sofa the lace of the widow's black shawl caught on the carved edge of the table. Peter Ivánovich rose to detach it, and the springs of the pouffe, relieved of his weight, rose also and gave him a push. The widow began detaching her shawl herself, and Peter Ivánovich again sat down, suppressing the rebellious springs of the pouffe under him. But the widow had not quite freed herself and Peter

Ivánovich got up again, and again the pouffe rebelled and even creaked. When this was all over she took out a clean cambric handkerchief and began to weep. The episode with the shawl and the struggle with the pouffe had cooled Peter Ivánovich's emotions and he sat there with a sullen look on his face. This awkward situation was interrupted by Sokolóv, Iván Ilých's butler, who came to report that the plot in the cemetery that Praskóvya Fëdorovna had chosen would cost two hundred rubles. She stopped weeping and, looking at Peter Ivánovich with the air of a victim, remarked in French that it was very hard for her. Peter Ivánovich made a silent gesture signifying his full conviction that it must indeed be so.

"Please smoke," she said in a magnanimous yet crushed voice, and turned to discuss with Sokolóv the price of the plot for the grave.

Peter Ivánovich while lighting his cigarette heard her inquiring very circumstantially into the price of different plots in the cemetery and finally decide which she would take. When that was done she gave instructions about engaging the choir. Sokolóv then left the room.

"I look after everything myself," she told Peter Ivánovich, shifting the albums that lay on the table; and noticing that the table was endangered by his cigarette-ash, she immediately passed him an ashtray, saying as she did so: "I consider it an affectation to say that my grief prevents my attending to practical affairs. On the contrary, if anything can—I won't say console me, but—distract me, it is seeing to everything concerning him." She again took out her handkerchief as if preparing to cry, but suddenly, as if mastering her feeling, she shook herself and began to speak calmly. "But there is something I want to talk to you about."

Peter Ivánovich bowed, keeping control of the springs of the pouffe, which immediately began quivering under him.

"He suffered terribly the last few days."

"Did he?" said Peter Ivánovich.

"Oh, terribly! He screamed unceasingly, not for minutes but for hours. For the last three days he screamed incessantly. It was unendurable. I cannot understand how I bore it; you could hear him three rooms off. Oh, what I have suffered!"

"Is it possible that he was conscious all that time?" asked Peter Ivánovich.

"Yes," she whispered. "To the last moment. He took leave of us a quarter of an hour before he died, and asked us to take Volódya away."

The thought of the sufferings of this man he had known so intimately, first as a merry little boy, then as a school-mate, and later as a grown-up colleague, suddenly struck Peter Ivánovich with horror, despite an unpleasant consciousness of his own and this woman's dissimulation. He again saw that brow, and that nose pressing down on the lip, and felt afraid for himself.

"Three days of frightful suffering and then death! Why, that might suddenly, at any time, happen to me," he thought, and for a moment felt terrified. But—he did not himself know how—the customary reflection at once occurred to him that this had happened to Ivan Ilých and not to him, and that it should not and could not happen to him, and that to think that it could would be yielding to depression which he ought not to do, as Schwartz's expression plainly showed. After which reflection Peter Ivánovich felt reassured, and began to ask with interest about the details of Iván Ilých's death, as though death was an accident natural to Iván Ilých but certainly not to himself.

After many details of the really dreadful physical sufferings Iván Ilých had endured (which details he learnt only from the effect those sufferings had produced on Praskóvya Fëdorovna's nerves) the widow apparently found it necessary to get to business.

"Oh, Peter Ivánovich, how hard it is! How terribly, terribly hard!" and she again began to weep.

Peter Ivánovich sighed and waited for her to finish blowing her nose. When she had done so he said, "Believe me . . ." and she again began talking and brought out what was evidently her chief concern with him—namely, to question him as to how she could obtain a grant of money from the government on the occasion of her husband's death. She made it appear that she was asking Peter Ivánovich's advice about her pension, but he soon saw that she already knew about that to the minutest detail, more even than he did himself. She knew how much could be got out of the government in consequence of her husband's death, but wanted to find out whether she could not possibly extract something more. Peter Ivánovich tried to think of some means of doing so, but after reflecting for a while and, out of propriety, condemning the government for its niggardliness, he said he thought that nothing more could be got. Then she sighed and evidently began to devise means of getting rid of her visitor. Noticing this, he put out his cigarette, rose, pressed her hand, and went out into the anteroom.

In the dining-room where the clock stood that Iván Ilých had liked so much and had bought at an antique shop, Peter Ivánovich met a priest and a few acquaintances who had come to attend the service, and he recognized Iván Ilých's daughter, a handsome young woman. She was in black and her slim figure appeared slimmer than ever. She had a gloomy, determined, almost angry expression, and bowed to Peter Ivánovich as though he were in some way to blame. Behind her, with the same offended look, stood a wealthy young man, an examining magistrate, whom Peter Ivánovich also knew and who was her fiancé, as he had heard. He bowed mournfully to them and was about to pass into the death-chamber, when from under the stairs appeared the figure of Iván Ilých's schoolboy son, who was extremely like his father. He seemed a little Iván Ilých, such as Peter Ivánovich remembered when they studied law together. His tear-stained eyes had in them the look that is seen in the eyes of boys of thirteen or fourteen who are not pure-minded. When he saw Peter Ivánovich he scowled morosely and shamefacedly. Peter Ivánovich nodded to him and entered the death-chamber. The service began: candles, groans, incense, tears, and sobs. Peter Ivánovich stood looking gloomily down at his feet. He did not look once at the dead man, did not yield to any depressing influence, and was one of the first to leave the room. There was no one in the anteroom, but Gerásim darted out of the dead man's room, rummaged with his strong hands among the fur coats to find Peter Ivánovich's and helped him on with it.

"Well, friend Gerásim," said Peter Ivánovich, so as to say something. "It's a sad affair, isn't it?"

"It's God's will. We shall all come to it some day," said Gerásim, displaying his teeth—the even, white teeth of a healthy peasant—and, like a man in the thick of urgent work, he briskly opened the front door, called the coachman, helped Peter Ivánovich into the sledge, and sprang back to the porch as if in readiness for what he had to do next.

Peter Ivánovich found the fresh air particularly pleasant after the smell of incense, the dead body, and carbolic acid.

"Where to, sir?" asked the coachman.

"It's not too late even now. . . . I'll call round on Fëdor Vasílievich."

He accordingly drove there and found them just finishing the first rubber, so that it was quite convenient for him to cut in.

CHAPTER II

Iván Ilých's life had been most simple and most ordinary and therefore most terrible.

He had been a member of the Court of Justice, and died at the age of forty-five. His father had been an official who after serving in various ministries and departments in Petersburg had made the sort of career which brings men to positions from which by reason of their long service they cannot be dismissed, though they are obviously unfit to hold any responsible position, and for whom therefore posts are specially created, which though fictitious carry salaries of from six to ten thousand rubles that are not fictitious, and in receipt of which they live on to a great age.

Such was the Privy Councillor and superfluous member of various superfluous institutions, Ilyá Epímovich Golovín.

He had three sons, of whom Iván Ilých was the second. The eldest son was following in his father's footsteps only in another department, and was already approaching that stage in the service at which a similar sinecure would be reached. The third son was a failure. He had ruined his prospects in a number of positions and was now serving in the railway department. His father and brothers, and still more their wives, not merely disliked meeting him, but avoided remembering his existence unless compelled to do so. His sister had married Baron Greff, a Petersburg official of her father's type. Iván Ilých was *le phénix de la famille*[1] as people said. He was neither as cold and formal as his elder brother nor as wild as the younger, but was a happy mean between them—an intelligent, polished, lively and agreeable man. He had studied with

---

[1] The phoenix of the family, here meaning "rare bird" or "prodigy."

his younger brother at the School of Law, but the latter had failed to complete the course and was expelled when he was in the fifth class. Iván Ilých finished the course well. Even when he was at the School of Law he was just what he remained for the rest of his life: a capable, cheerful, good-natured, and sociable man, though strict in the fulfilment of what he considered to be his duty: and he considered his duty to be what was so considered by those in authority. Neither as a boy nor as a man was he a toady, but from early youth was by nature attracted to people of high station as a fly is drawn to the light, assimilating their ways and views of life and establishing friendly relations with them. All the enthusiasms of childhood and youth passed without leaving much trace on him; he succumbed to sensuality, to vanity, and latterly among the highest classes to liberalism, but always within limits which his instinct unfailingly indicated to him as correct.

At school he had done things which had formerly seemed to him very horrid and made him feel disgusted with himself when he did them; but when later on he saw that such actions were done by people of good position and that they did not regard them as wrong, he was able not exactly to regard them as right, but to forget about them entirely or not be at all troubled at remembering them.

Having graduated from the School of Law and qualified for the tenth rank of the civil service, and having received money from his father for his equipment, Iván Ilých ordered himself clothes at Scharmer's, the fashionable tailor, hung a medallion inscribed *respice finem*[2] on his watch-chain, took leave of his professor and the prince who was patron of the school, had a farewell dinner with his comrades at Donon's first-class restaurant, and with his new and fashionable portmanteau, linen, clothes, shaving and other toilet appliances, and a travelling rug, all purchased at the best shops, he set off for one of the provinces where, through his father's influence, he had been attached to the Governor as an official for special service.

In the province Iván Ilých soon arranged as easy and agreeable a position for himself as he had had at the School of Law. He performed his official tasks, made his career, and at the same time amused himself pleasantly and decorously. Occasionally he paid official visits to country districts, where he behaved with dignity both to his superiors and inferiors, and performed the duties entrusted to him, which related chiefly to the sectarians,[3] with an exactness and incorruptible honesty of which he could not but feel proud.

In official matters, despite his youth and taste for frivolous gaiety, he was exceedingly reserved, punctilious, and even severe; but in society he was often amusing and witty, and always good-natured, correct in his manner, and *bon enfant*, as the governor and his wife—with whom he was like one of the family—used to say of him.

---

[2] Regard the end.
[3] A large sect, whose members were placed under many legal restrictions, which broke away from the Orthodox Church in the seventeenth century.

In the provinces he had an affair with a lady who made advances to the elegant young lawyer, and there was also a milliner; and there were carousals with aides-de-camp who visited the district, and after-supper visits to a certain outlying street of doubtful reputation; and there was too some obsequiousness to his chief and even to his chief's wife, but all this was done with such a tone of good breeding that no hard names could be applied to it. It all came under the heading of the French saying: "Il faut que jeunesse se passe."[4] It was all done with clean hands, in clean linen, with French phrases, and above all among people of the best society and consequently with the approval of people of rank.

So Iván Ilých served for five years and then came a change in his official life. The new and reformed judicial institutions were introduced, and new men were needed. Iván Ilých became such a new man. He was offered the post of Examining Magistrate, and he accepted it though the post was in another province and obliged him to give up the connections he had formed and to make new ones. His friends met to give him a send-off; they had a group-photograph taken and presented him with a silver cigarette-case, and he set off to his new post.

As examining magistrate Iván Ilých was just as *comme il faut*[5] and decorous a man, inspiring general respect and capable of separating his official duties from his private life, as he had been when acting as an official on special service. His duties now as examining magistrate were far more interesting and attractive than before. In his former position it had been pleasant to wear an undress uniform made by Scharmer, and to pass through the crowd of petitioners and officials who were timorously awaiting an audience with the governor, and who envied him as with free and easy gait he went straight into his chief's private room to have a cup of tea and a cigarette with him. But not many people had then been directly dependent on him—only police officials and the sectarians when he went on special missions—and he liked to treat them politely, almost as comrades, as if he were letting them feel that he who had the power to crush them was treating them in this simple, friendly way. There were then but few such people. But now, as an examining magistrate, Iván Ilých felt that everyone without exception, even the most important and self-satisfied, was in his power, and that he need only write a few words on a sheet of paper with a certain heading, and this or that important, self-satisfied person would be brought before him in the role of an accused person or a witness, and if he did not choose to allow him to sit down, would have to stand before him and answer his questions. Iván Ilých never abused his power; he tried on the contrary to soften its expression, but the consciousness of it and of the possibility of softening its effect, supplied the chief interest and attraction of his office. In his work itself, especially in his examinations, he very soon

---

[4] Youth must have its fling.
[5] Proper.

acquired a method of eliminating all considerations irrelevant to the legal aspect of the case, and reducing even the most complicated case to a form in which it would be presented on paper only in its externals, completely excluding his personal opinion of the matter, while above all observing every prescribed formality. The work was new and Iván Ilých was one of the first men to apply the new Code of 1864.[6]

On taking up the post of examining magistrate in a new town, he made new acquaintances and connections, placed himself on a new footing, and assumed a somewhat different tone. He took up an attitude of rather dignified aloofness towards the provincial authorities, but picked out the best circle of legal gentlemen and wealthy gentry living in the town and assumed a tone of slight dissatisfaction with the government, of moderate liberalism, and of enlightened citizenship. At the same time, without at all altering the elegance of his toilet, he ceased shaving his chin and allowed his beard to grow as it pleased.

Iván Ilých settled down very pleasantly in this new town. The society there, which inclined towards opposition to the Governor, was friendly, his salary was larger, and he began to play *vint*,[7] which he found added not a little to the pleasure of life, for he had a capacity for cards, played good-humouredly, and calculated rapidly and astutely, so that he usually won.

After living there for two years he met his future wife, Praskóvya Fëdorovna Míkhel, who was the most attractive, clever, and brilliant girl of the set in which he moved, and among other amusements and relaxations from his labours as examining magistrate, Iván Ilých established light and playful relations with her.

While he had been an official on special service he had been accustomed to dance, but now as an examining magistrate it was exceptional for him to do so. If he danced now, he did it as if to show that though he served under the reformed order of things, and had reached the fifth official rank, yet when it came to dancing he could do it better than most people. So at the end of an evening he sometimes danced with Praskóvya Fëdorovna, and it was chiefly during these dances that he captivated her. She fell in love with him. Iván Ilých had at first no definite intention of marrying, but when the girl fell in love with him he said to himself: "Really, why shouldn't I marry?"

Praskóvya Fëdorovna came of a good family, was not bad looking and had some little property. Iván Ilých might have aspired to a more brilliant match, but even this was good. He had his salary, and she, he hoped, would have an equal income. She was well connected, and was a sweet, pretty, and thoroughly correct young woman. To say that Iván Ilých married because he fell in love with Praskóvya Fëdorovna and found that she sympathized with his views of life would be as incorrect as to say that he married because his social circle approved of the match. He was swayed by both these considerations: the

---

[6] Judicial procedures were thoroughly reformed after the emancipation of the serfs in 1861.
[7] A card game similar to bridge.

marriage gave him personal satisfaction, and at the same time it was considered the right thing by the most highly placed of his associates.

So Iván Ilých got married.

The preparations for marriage and the beginning of married life, with its conjugal caresses, the new furniture, new crockery, and new linen, were very pleasant until his wife became pregnant—so that Iván Ilých had begun to think that marriage would not impair the easy, agreeable, gay and always decorous character of his life, approved of by society and regarded by himself as natural, but would even improve it. But from the first months of his wife's pregnancy, something new, unpleasant, depressing, and unseemly, and from which there was no way of escape, unexpectedly showed itself.

His wife, without any reason—*de gaieté de coeur*[8] as Iván Ilých expressed it to himself—began to disturb the pleasure and propriety of their life. She began to be jealous without any cause, expected him to devote his whole attention to her, found fault with everything, and made coarse and ill-mannered scenes.

At first Iván Ilých hoped to escape from the unpleasantness of this state of affairs by the same easy and decorous relation to life that had served him heretofore: he tried to ignore his wife's disagreeable moods, continued to live in his usual easy and pleasant way, invited friends to his house for a game of cards, and also tried going out to his club or spending his evenings with friends. But one day his wife began upbraiding him so vigorously, using such coarse words, and continued to abuse him every time he did not fulfil her demands, so resolutely and with such evident determination not to give way till he submitted—that is, till he stayed at home and was bored just as she was—that he became alarmed. He now realized that matrimony—at any rate with Praskóvya Fëdorovna—was not always conducive to the pleasures and amenities of life but on the contrary often infringed both comfort and propriety, and that he must therefore entrench himself against such infringement. And Iván Ilých began to seek for means of doing so. His official duties were the one thing that imposed upon Praskóvya Fëdorovna, and by means of his official work and the duties attached to it he began struggling with his wife to secure his own independence.

With the birth of their child, the attempts to feed it and the various failures in doing so, and with the real and imaginary illnesses of mother and child, in which Iván Ilých's sympathy was demanded but about which he understood nothing, the need of securing for himself an existence outside his family life became still more imperative.

As his wife grew more irritable and exacting and Iván Ilých transferred the centre of gravity of his life more and more to his official work, so did he grow to like his work better and became more ambitious than before.

Very soon, within a year of his wedding, Iván Ilých had realized that marriage, though it may add some comforts to life, is in fact a very intricate

---

[8] From sheer exuberance.

and difficult affair towards which in order to perform one's duty, that is, to lead a decorous life approved of by society, one must adopt a definite attitude just as towards one's official duties.

And Iván Ilých evolved such an attitude towards married life. He only required of it those conveniences—dinner at home, housewife, and bed—which it could give him, and above all that propriety of external forms required by public opinion. For the rest he looked for light-hearted pleasure and propriety, and was very thankful when he found them, but if he met with antagonism and querulousness he at once retired into his separate fenced-off world of official duties, where he found satisfaction.

Iván Ilých was esteemed a good official, and after three years was made Assistant Public Prosecutor. His new duties, their importance, the possibility of indicting and imprisoning anyone he chose, the publicity his speeches received, and the success he had in all these things, made his work still more attractive.

More children came. His wife became more and more querulous and ill-tempered, but the attitude Iván Ilých had adopted towards his home life rendered him almost impervious to her grumbling.

After seven years' service in that town he was transferred to another province as Public Prosecutor. They moved, but were short of money and his wife did not like the place they moved to. Though the salary was higher the cost of living was greater, besides which two of their children died and family life became still more unpleasant for him.

Praskóvya Fëdorovna blamed her husband for every inconvenience they encountered in their new home. Most of the conversations between husband and wife, especially as to the children's education, led to topics which recalled former disputes, and those disputes were apt to flare up again at any moment. There remained only those rare periods of amorousness which still came to them at times but did not last long. These were islets at which they anchored for a while and then again set out upon that ocean of veiled hostility which showed itself in their aloofness from one another. This aloofness might have grieved Iván Ilých had he considered that it ought not to exist, but he now regarded the position as normal, and even made it the goal at which he aimed in family life. His aim was to free himself more and more from those unpleasantnesses and to give them a semblance of harmlessness and propriety. He attained this by spending less and less time with his family, and when obliged to be at home he tried to safeguard his position by the presence of outsiders. The chief thing however was that he had his official duties. The whole interest of his life now centered in the official world and that interest absorbed him. The consciousness of his power, being able to ruin anybody he wished to ruin, the importance, even the external dignity of his entry into court, or meetings with his subordinates, his success with superiors and inferiors, and above all his masterly handling of cases, of which he was conscious—all this gave him pleasure and filled his life, together with chats with his colleagues, dinners, and bridge. So that on the whole Iván Ilých's life continued to flow as he considered it should do—pleasantly and properly.

So things continued for another seven years. His eldest daughter was already sixteen, another child had died, and only one son was left, a schoolboy and a subject of dissension. Iván Ilých wanted to put him in the School of Law, but to spite him Praskóvya Fëdorovna entered him at the High School. The daughter had been educated at home and had turned out well: the boy did not learn badly either.

CHAPTER III

So Iván Ilých lived for seventeen years after his marriage. He was already a Public Prosecutor of long standing, and had declined several proposed transfers while awaiting a more desirable post, when an unanticipated and unpleasant occurrence quite upset the peaceful course of his life. He was expecting to be offered the post of presiding judge in a University town, but Happe somehow came to the front and obtained the appointment instead. Iván Ilých became irritable, reproached Happe, and quarreled both with him and with his immediate superiors—who became colder to him and again passed him over when other appointments were made.

This was in 1880, the hardest year of Iván Ilých's life. It was then that it became evident on the one hand that his salary was insufficient for them to live on, and on the other that he had been forgotten, and not only this, but that what was for him the greatest and most cruel injustice appeared to others a quite ordinary occurrence. Even his father did not consider it his duty to help him. Iván Ilých felt himself abandoned by everyone, and that they regarded his position with a salary of 3,500 rubles as quite normal and even fortunate. He alone knew that with the consciousness of the injustices done him, with his wife's incessant nagging, and with the debts he had contracted by living beyond his means, his position was far from normal.

In order to save money that summer he obtained leave of absence and went with his wife to live in the country at her brother's place.

In the country, without his work, he experienced *ennui* for the first time in his life, and not only *ennui* but intolerable depression, and he decided that it was impossible to go on living like that, and that it was necessary to take energetic measures.

Having passed a sleepless night pacing up and down the veranda, he decided to go to Petersburg and bestir himself, in order to punish those who had failed to appreciate him and to get transferred to another ministry.

Next day, despite many protests from his wife and her brother, he started for Petersburg with the sole object of obtaining a post with a salary of five thousand rubles a year. He was no longer bent on any particular department, or tendency, or kind of activity. All he now wanted was an appointment to another post with a salary of five thousand rubles, either in the administration, in the banks, with the railways, in one of the Empress Márya's Institutions,[9] or even in the customs—but it had to carry with it a salary of five thousand rubles and be in a ministry other than that in which they had failed to appreciate him.

And this quest of Iván Ilých's was crowned with remarkable and unexpected success. At Kursk an acquaintance of his, F. I. Ilyín, got into the first-class carriage, sat down beside Iván Ilých, and told him of a telegram just received by the Governor of Kursk announcing that a change was about to take place in the ministry: Peter Ivánovich was to be superseded by Iván Semënovich.

The proposed change, apart from its significance for Russia, had a special significance for Iván Ilých, because by bringing forward a new man, Peter Petróvich, and consequently his friend Zachár Ivánovich, it was highly favourable for Iván Ilých, since Zachár Ivánovich was a friend and colleague of his.

In Moscow this news was confirmed, and on reaching Petersburg Iván Ilých found Zachár Ivánovich and received a definite promise of an appointment in his former Department of Justice.

A week later he telegraphed to his wife: "Zachár in Miller's place. I shall receive appointment on presentation of report."

Thanks to this change of personnel, Iván Ilých had unexpectedly obtained an appointment in his former ministry which placed him two stages above his former colleagues besides giving him five thousand rubles salary and three thousand five hundred rubles for expenses connected with his removal. All his ill humour towards his former enemies and the whole department vanished, and Iván Ilých was completely happy.

He returned to the country more cheerful and contented than he had been for a long time. Praskóvya Fëdorovna also cheered up and a truce was arranged between them. Iván Ilých told of how he had been fêted by everybody in Petersburg, how all those who had been his enemies were put to shame and now fawned on him, how envious they were of his appointment, and how much everybody in Petersburg had liked him.

Praskóvya Fëdorovna listened to all this and appeared to believe it. She did not contradict anything, but only made plans for their life in the town to which they were going. Iván Ilých saw with delight that these plans were his plans, that he and his wife agreed, and that, after a stumble, his life was regaining its due and natural character of pleasant lightheartedness and decorum.

Iván Ilých had come back for a short time only, for he had to take up his new duties on the 10th of September. Moreover, he needed time to settle into the new place, to move all his belongings from the province, and to buy and order many additional things: in a word, to make such arrangements as he had

---

[9] A charitable organization founded in the late eighteenth century.

resolved on, which were almost exactly what Praskóvya Fëdorovna too had decided on.

Now that everything had happened so fortunately, and that he and his wife were at one in their aims and moreover saw so little of one another, they got on together better than they had done since the first years of marriage. Iván Ilých had thought of taking his family away with him at once, but the insistence of his wife's brother and her sister-in-law, who had suddenly become particularly amiable and friendly to him and his family, induced him to depart alone.

So he departed, and the cheerful state of mind induced by his success and by the harmony between his wife and himself, the one intensifying the other, did not leave him. He found a delightful house, just the thing both he and his wife had dreamt of. Spacious, lofty reception rooms in the old style, a convenient and dignified study, rooms for his wife and daughter, a study for his son—it might have been specially built for them. Iván Ilých himself superintended the arrangements, chose the wallpapers, supplemented the furniture (preferably with antiques which he considered particularly *comme il faut*), and supervised the upholstering. Everything progressed and progressed and approached the ideal he had set himself: even when things were only half completed they exceeded his expectations. He saw what a refined and elegant character, free from vulgarity, it would all have when it was ready. On falling asleep he pictured to himself how the reception-room would look. Looking at the yet unfinished drawing-room he could see the fireplace, the screen, the what-not, the little chairs dotted here and there, the dishes and plates on the walls, and the bronzes, as they would be when everything was in place. He was pleased by the thought of how his wife and daughter, who shared his taste in this matter, would be impressed by it. They were certainly not expecting as much. He had been particularly successful in finding, and buying cheaply, antiques which gave a particularly aristocratic character to the whole place. But in his letters he intentionally understated everything in order to be able to surprise them. All this so absorbed him that his new duties—though he liked his official work—interested him less than he had expected. Sometimes he even had moments of absent-mindedness during the Court Sessions, and would consider whether he should have straight or curved cornices for his curtains. He was so interested in it all that he often did things himself, rearranging the furniture, or rehanging the curtains. Once when mounting a step-ladder to show the upholsterer, who did not understand, how he wanted the hangings draped, he made a false step and slipped, but being a strong and agile man he clung on and only knocked his side against the knob of the window frame. The bruised place was painful but the pain soon passed, and he felt particularly bright and well just then. He wrote: "I feel fifteen years younger." He thought he would have everything ready by September, but it dragged on till mid-October. But the result was charming not only in his eyes but to everyone who saw it.

In reality it was just what is usually seen in the houses of people of moderate means who want to appear rich, and therefore succeed only in resembling others like themselves: there were damasks, dark wood, plants, rugs, and dull and polished bronzes—all the things people of a certain class have in order to resemble other people of that class. His house was so like the others that it would never have been noticed, but to him it all seemed to be quite exceptional. He was very happy when he met his family at the station and brought them to the newly furnished house all lit up, where a footman in a white tie opened the door into the hall decorated with plants, and when they went on into the drawing room and the study uttering exclamations of delight. He conducted them everywhere, drank in their praises eagerly, and beamed with pleasure. At tea that evening, when Praskóvya Fëdorovna among other things asked him about his fall, he laughed and showed them how he had gone flying and had frightened the upholsterer.

"It's a good thing I'm a bit of an athlete. Another man might have been killed, but I merely knocked myself, just here; it hurts when it's touched, but it's passing off already—it's only a bruise."

So they began living in their new home—in which, as always happens, when they got thoroughly settled in they found they were just one room short—and with the increased income, which as always was just a little (some five hundred rubles) too little, but it was all very nice.

Things went particularly well at first, before everything was finally arranged and while something had still to be done: this thing bought, that thing ordered, another thing moved, and something else adjusted. Though there were some disputes between husband and wife, they were both so well satisfied and had so much to do that it all passed off without any serious quarrels. When nothing was left to arrange it became rather dull and something seemed to be lacking, but they were then making acquaintances, forming habits, and life was growing fuller.

Iván Ilých spent his mornings at the law court and came home to dinner, and at first he was generally in a good humour, though he occasionally became irritable just on account of his house. (Every spot on the tablecloth or the upholstery, and every broken window-blind string, irritated him. He had devoted so much trouble to arranging it all that every disturbance of it distressed him.) But on the whole his life ran its course as he believed life should do: easily, pleasantly, and decorously.

He got up at nine, drank his coffee, read the paper, and then put on his undress uniform and went to the law courts. There the harness in which he worked had already been stretched to fit him and he donned it without a hitch: petitioners, inquiries at the chancery, the chancery itself, and the sittings public and administrative. In all this the thing was to exclude everything fresh and vital, which always disturbs the regular course of official business, and to admit only official relations with people, and then only on official grounds. A man would come, for instance, wanting some information. Iván Ilých, as one in whose sphere the matter did not lie, would have nothing to do with him: but if the man had some business with him in his official capacity, something that could be expressed on officially stamped paper, he would do everything, positively everything he could within the limits of such relations, and in doing so would maintain the semblance of friendly human relations, that is, would observe the courtesies of life. As soon as the official relations ended, so did everything else. Iván Ilých possessed this capacity to separate his real life from the official side of affairs and not mix the two, in the highest degree, and by long practice and natural aptitude had brought it to such a pitch that sometimes, in the manner of a virtuoso, he would even allow himself to let the human and official relations mingle. He let himself do this just because he felt that he could at any time he chose resume the strictly official attitude again and drop the human relation. And he did it all easily, pleasantly, correctly, and even artistically. In the intervals between the sessions he smoked, drank tea, chatted a little about politics, a little about general topics, a little about cards, but most of all about official appointments. Tired, but with the feelings of a virtuoso—one of the first violins who has played his part in an orchestra with precision—he would return home to find that his wife and daughter had been out paying calls, or had a visitor, and that his son had been to school, had done his homework with his tutor, and was duly learning what is taught at High Schools. Everything was as it should be. After dinner, if they had no visitors, Iván Ilých sometimes read a book that was being much discussed at the time, and in the evening settled down to work, that is, read official papers, compared the depositions of witnesses, and noted paragraphs of the Code applying to them. This was neither dull nor amusing. It was dull when he might have been playing bridge, but if no bridge was available it was at any rate better than doing nothing or sitting with his wife. Iván Ilých's chief pleasure was giving little dinners to which he invited men and women of good social position, and just as his drawing-room resembled all other drawing-rooms so did his enjoyable little parties resemble all other such parties.

Once they even gave a dance. Iván Ilých enjoyed it and everything went off well, except that it led to a violent quarrel with his wife about the cakes and sweets. Praskóvya Fëdorovna had made her own plans, but Iván Ilých insisted on getting everything from an expensive confectioner and ordered too many cakes, and the quarrel occurred because some of those cakes were left over and the confectioner's bill came to forty-five rubles. It was a great and disagreeable quarrel. Praskóvya Fëdorovna called him "a fool and an imbecile," and he clutched at his head and made angry allusions to divorce.

But the dance itself had been enjoyable. The best people were there, and Iván Ilých had danced with Princess Trúfonova, a sister of the distinguished founder of the Society "Bear My Burden."

The pleasures connected with his work were pleasures of ambition; his social pleasures were those of vanity; but Iván Ilých's greatest pleasure was playing bridge. He acknowledged that whatever disagreeable incident happened in his life, the pleasure that beamed like a ray of light above everything else was to sit down to bridge with good players, not noisy partners, and of course to fourhanded bridge (with five players it was annoying to have to stand out, though one pretended not to mind), to play a clever and serious game (when the cards allowed it) and then to have supper and drink a glass of wine. After a game of bridge, especially if he had won a little (to win a large sum was unpleasant), Iván Ilých went to bed in specially good humour.

So they lived. They formed a circle of acquaintances among the best people and were visited by people of importance and by young folk. In their views as to their acquaintances, husband, wife, and daughter were entirely agreed, and tacitly and unanimously kept at arm's length and shook off the various shabby friends and relations who, with much show of affection, gushed into the drawing-room with its Japanese plates on the walls. Soon these shabby friends ceased to obtrude themselves and only the best people remained in the Golovíns' set.

Young men made up to Lisa, and Petríshchev, an examining magistrate and Dmítri Ivanovich Petríshchev's son and sole heir, began to be so attentive to her that Iván Ilých had already spoken to Praskóvya Fëdorovna about it, and considered whether they should not arrange a party for them or get up some private theatricals.

So they lived, and all went well, without change, and life flowed pleasantly.

CHAPTER IV

They were all in good health. It could not be called ill health if Iván Ilých sometimes said that he had a queer taste in his mouth and felt some discomfort in his left side.

But this discomfort increased and, though not exactly painful, grew into a sense of pressure in his side accompanied by ill humour. And his irritability became worse and worse and began to mar the agreeable, easy, and correct life that had established itself in the Golovín family. Quarrels between husband and wife became more and more frequent, and soon the ease and amenity disappeared and even the decorum was barely maintained. Scenes again became frequent, and very few of those islets remained on which husband and wife could meet without explosion. Praskóvya Fëdorovna now had good reason to say that her husband's temper was trying. With characteristic exaggeration she said he had always had a dreadful temper, and that it had needed all her good nature to put up with it for twenty years. It was true that now the quarrels were started by him. His bursts of temper always came just before dinner, often just as he began to eat his soup. Sometimes he noticed that a plate or dish was chipped, or the food was not right, or his son put his elbow on the table, or his daughter's hair was not done as he liked it, and for all this he blamed Praskóvya Fëdorovna. At first she retorted and said disagreeable things to him, but once or twice he fell into such a rage at the beginning of dinner that she realized it was due to some physical derangement brought on by taking food, and so she restrained herself and did not answer, but only hurried to get the dinner over. She regarded this self-restraint as highly praiseworthy. Having come to the conclusion that her husband had a dreadful temper and made her life miserable, she began to feel sorry for herself, and the more she pitied herself the more she hated her husband. She began to wish he would die; yet she did not want him to die because then his salary would cease. And this irritated her against him still more. She considered herself dreadfully unhappy just because not even his death could save her, and though she concealed her exasperation, that hidden exasperation of hers increased his irritation also.

After one scene in which Iván Ilých had been particularly unfair and after which he had said in explanation that he certainly was irritable but that it was due to his not being well, she said that if he was ill it should be attended to, and insisted on his going to see a celebrated doctor.

He went. Everything took place as he had expected and as it always does. There was the usual waiting and the important air assumed by the doctor, with which he was so familiar (resembling that which he himself assumed in court), and the sounding and listening, and the questions which called for answers that were foregone conclusions and were evidently unnecessary, and the look of importance which implied that "if only you put yourself in our hands we will arrange everything—we know indubitably how it has to be done, always in the same way for everybody alike." It was all just as it was in the law courts. The doctor put on just the same air towards him as he himself put on towards an accused person.

The doctor said that so-and-so indicated that there was so-and-so inside the patient, but if the investigation of so-and-so did not confirm this, then he must assume that and that. If he assumed that and that, then . . . and so on. To Iván Ilých only one question was important: was his case serious or not? But the doctor ignored that inappropriate question. From his point of view it was not the one under consideration, the real question was to decide between a floating kidney, chronic catarrh, or appendicitis. It was not a question of Iván Ilých's life or death, but one between a floating kidney and appendicitis. And that question the doctor solved brilliantly, as it seemed to Iván Ilých, in favour of the appendix, with the reservation that should an examination of the urine give fresh indications the matter would be reconsidered. All this was just what Iván Ilých had himself brilliantly accomplished a thousand times in dealing with men on trial. The doctor summed up just as brilliantly, looking over his spectacles triumphantly and even gaily at the accused. From the doctor's summing up Iván Ilých concluded that things were bad, but that for the doctor, and perhaps for everybody else, it was a matter of indifference, though for him it was bad. And this conclusion struck him painfully, arousing in him a great feeling of pity for himself and of bitterness towards the doctor's indifference to a matter of such importance.

He said nothing of this, but rose, placed the doctor's fee on the table, and remarked with a sigh: "We sick people probably often put inappropriate questions. But tell me, in general, is this complaint dangerous, or not? . . ."

The doctor looked at him sternly over his spectacles with one eye, as if to say: "Prisoner, if you will not keep to the questions put to you, I shall be obliged to have you removed from the court."

"I have already told you what I consider necessary and proper. The analysis may show something more." And the doctor bowed.

Iván Ilých went out slowly, seated himself disconsolately in his sledge, and drove home. All the way home he was going over what the doctor had said, trying to translate those complicated, obscure, scientific phrases into plain language and find in them an answer to the question: "Is my condition bad? Is it very bad? Or is there as yet nothing much wrong?" And it seemed to him that the meaning of what the doctor had said was that it was very bad. Everything in the streets seemed depressing. The cabmen, the houses, the passers-by, and the shops, were dismal. His ache, this dull gnawing ache that never ceased for a moment, seemed to have acquired a new and more serious significance from the doctor's dubious remarks. Iván Ilých now watched it with a new and oppressive feeling.

He reached home and began to tell his wife about it. She listened, but in the middle of his account his daughter came in with her hat on, ready to go out with her mother. She sat down reluctantly to listen to this tedious story, but could not stand it long, and her mother too did not hear him to the end.

"Well, I am very glad," she said. "Mind now to take your medicine regularly. Give me the prescription and I'll send Gerásim to the chemist's." And she went to get ready to go out.

While she was in the room Iván Ilých had hardly taken time to breathe, but he sighed deeply when she left it.

"Well," he thought, "perhaps it isn't so bad after all."

He began taking his medicine and following the doctor's directions, which had been altered after the examination of the urine. But then it happened that there was a contradiction between the indications drawn from the examination of the urine and the symptoms that showed themselves. It turned out that what was happening differed from what the doctor had told him, and that he had either forgotten, or blundered, or hidden something from him. He could not, however, be blamed for that, and Iván Ilých still obeyed his orders implicitly and at first derived some comfort from doing so.

From the time of his visit to the doctor, Iván Ilých's chief occupation was the exact fulfilment of the doctor's instructions regarding hygiene and the taking of medicine, and the observation of his pain and his excretions. His chief interests came to be people's ailments and people's health. When sickness, deaths, or recoveries were mentioned in his presence, especially when the illness resembled his own, he listened with agitation which he tried to hide, asked questions, and applied what he heard to his own case.

The pain did not grow less, but Iván Ilých made efforts to force himself to think that he was better. And he could do this so long as nothing agitated him. But as soon as he had any unpleasantness with his wife, any lack of success in his official work, or held bad cards at bridge, he was at once acutely sensible of his disease. He had formerly borne such mischances, hoping soon to adjust what was wrong, to master it and attain success, or make a grand slam. But now every mischance upset him and plunged him into despair. He would say to himself: "There now, just as I was beginning to get better and the medicine had begun to take effect, comes this accursed misfortune, or unpleasantness. . . ." And he was furious with the mishap, or with the people who were causing the unpleasantness and killing him, for he felt that this fury was killing him but could not restrain it. One would have thought that it should have been clear to him that this exasperation with circumstances and people aggravated his illness, and that he ought therefore to ignore unpleasant occurrences. But he drew the very opposite conclusion: he said that he needed peace, and he watched for everything that might disturb it and became irritable at the slightest infringement of it. His condition was rendered worse by the fact that he read medical books and consulted doctors. The progress of his disease was so gradual that he could deceive himself when comparing one day with another—the difference was so slight. But when he consulted the doctors it seemed to him that he was getting worse, and even very rapidly. Yet despite this he was continually consulting them.

That month he went to see another celebrity, who told him almost the same as the first had done but put his questions rather differently, and the interview with this celebrity only increased Iván Ilých's doubts and fears. A friend of a friend of his, a very good doctor, diagnosed his illness again quite differently from the others, and though he predicted recovery, his questions and suppositions bewildered Iván Ilých still more and increased his doubts. A homeopathist diagnosed the disease in yet another way, and prescribed medicine which Iván Ilých took secretly for a week. But after a week, not feeling any improvement and having lost confidence both in the former doctor's treatment and in this one's, he became still more despondent. One day a lady acquaintance mentioned a cure effected by a wonder-working icon. Iván Ilých caught himself listening attentively and beginning to believe that it had occurred. This incident alarmed him. "Has my mind really weakened to such an extent?" he asked himself. "Nonsense! It's all rubbish. I mustn't give way to nervous fears but having chosen a doctor must keep strictly to his treatment. That is what I will do. Now it's all settled. I won't think about it, but will follow the treatment seriously till summer, and then we shall see. From now there must be no more of this wavering!" This was easy to say but impossible to carry out. The pain in his side oppressed him and seemed to grow worse and more incessant, while the taste in his mouth grew stranger and stranger. It seemed to him that his breath had a disgusting smell, and he was conscious of a loss of appetite and strength. There was no deceiving himself: something terrible, new, and more important than anything before in his life, was taking place within him of which he alone was aware. Those about him did not understand or would not understand it, but thought everything in the world was going on as usual. That tormented Iván Ilých more than anything. He saw that his household, especially his wife and daughter who were in a perfect whirl of visiting, did not understand anything of it and were annoyed that he was so depressed and so exacting, as if he were to blame for it. Though they tried to disguise it he saw that he was an obstacle in their path, and that his wife had adopted a definite line in regard to his illness and kept to it regardless of anything he said or did. Her attitude was this: "You know," she would say to her friends, "Iván Ilých can't do as other people do, and keep to the treatment prescribed for him. One day he'll take his drops and keep strictly to his diet and go to bed in good time, but the next day unless I watch him he'll suddenly forget his medicine, eat sturgeon—which is forbidden—and sit up playing cards till one o'clock in the morning."

"Oh, come, when was that?" Iván Ilých would ask in vexation. "Only once at Peter Ivánovich's."

"And yesterday with Shébek."

"Well, even if I hadn't stayed up, this pain would have kept me awake."

"Be that as it may you'll never get well like that, but will always make us wretched."

Praskóvya Fëdorovna's attitude to Iván Ilých's illness, as she expressed it both to others and to him, was that it was his own fault and was another of the annoyances he caused her. Iván Ilých felt that this opinion escaped her involuntarily—but that did not make it easier for him.

At the law courts too, Iván Ilých noticed, or thought he noticed, a strange attitude towards himself. It sometimes seemed to him that people were watching him inquisitively as a man whose place might soon be vacant. Then again, his friends would suddenly begin to chaff him in a friendly way about his low spirits, as if the awful, horrible, and unheard-of thing that was going on within him, incessantly gnawing at him and irresistibly drawing him away, was a very agreeable subject for jests. Schwartz in particular irritated him by his jocularity, vivacity, and *savoir-faire*, which reminded him of what he himself had been ten years ago.

Friends came to make up a set and they sat down to cards. They dealt, bending the new cards to soften them, and he sorted the diamonds in his hand and found he had seven. His partner said "No trumps" and supported him with two diamonds. What more could be wished for? It ought to be jolly and lively. They would make a grand slam. But suddenly Iván Ilých was conscious of that gnawing pain, that taste in his mouth, and it seemed ridiculous that in such circumstances he should be pleased to make a grand slam.

He looked at his partner Mikháil Mikháylovich, who rapped the table with his strong hand and instead of snatching up the tricks pushed the cards courteously and indulgently towards Iván Ilých that he might have the pleasure of gathering them up without the trouble of stretching out his hand for them. "Does he think I am too weak to stretch out my arm?" thought Iván Ilých, and forgetting what he was doing he over-trumped his partner, missing the grand slam by three tricks. And what was most awful of all was that he saw how upset Mikháil Mikháylovich was about it but did not himself care. And it was dreadful to realize why he did not care.

They all saw that he was suffering and said: "We can stop if you are tired. Take a rest." Lie down? No, he was not at all tired, and he finished the rubber. All were gloomy and silent. Iván Ilých felt that he had diffused this gloom over them and could not dispel it. They had supper and went away, and Iván Ilých was left alone with the consciousness that his life was poisoned and was poisoning the lives of others, and that this poison did not weaken but penetrated more and more deeply into his whole being.

With this consciousness, and with physical pain besides the terror, he must go to bed, often to lie awake the greater part of the night. Next morning he had to get up again, dress, go to the law courts, speak, and write; or if he did not go out, spend at home those twenty-four hours a day each of which was a torture. And he had to live thus all alone on the brink of an abyss, with no one who understood or pitied him.

CHAPTER V

So one month passed and then another. Just before the New Year his brother-in-law came to town and stayed at their house. Iván Ilých was at the law courts and Praskóvya Fëdorovna had gone shopping. When Iván Ilých came home and entered his study he found his brother-in-law there—a healthy, florid man—unpacking his portmanteau himself. He raised his head on hearing Iván Ilých's footsteps and looked up at him for a moment without a word. That stare told Iván Ilých everything. His brother-in-law opened his mouth to utter an exclamation of surprise but checked himself, and that action confirmed it all.

"I have changed, eh?"

"Yes, there is a change."

And after that, try as he would to get his brother-in-law to return to the subject of his looks, the latter would say nothing about it. Praskóvya Fëdorovna came home and her brother went out to her. Iván Ilých locked the door and began to examine himself in the glass, first full face, then in profile. He took up a portrait of himself taken with his wife, and compared it with what he saw in the glass. The change in him was immense. Then he bared his arms to the elbow, looked at them, drew the sleeves down again, sat down on an ottoman, and grew blacker than night.

"No, no, this won't do!" he said to himself, and jumped up, went to the table, took up some law papers and began to read them, but could not continue. He unlocked the door and went into the reception-room. The door leading to the drawing room was shut. He approached it on tiptoe and listened.

"No, you are exaggerating!" Praskóvya Fëdorovna was saying.

"Exaggerating! Don't you see it? Why, he's a dead man! Look at his eyes—there's no light in them. But what is it that is wrong with him?"

"No one knows. Nikoláevich (that was another doctor) said something, but I don't know what. And Leshchetítsky (this was the celebrated specialist) said quite the contrary . . ."

Iván Ilých walked away, went to his own room, lay down, and began musing: "The kidney, a floating kidney." He recalled all the doctors had told him of how it detached itself and swayed about. And by an effort of imagination he tried to catch that kidney and arrest it and support it. So little was needed for this, it seemed to him. "No, I'll go to see Peter Ivánovich again." (That was the friend whose friend was a doctor.) He rang, ordered the carriage, and got ready to go.

"Where are you going, Jean?" asked his wife, with a specially sad and exceptionally kind look.

This exceptionally kind look irritated him. He looked morosely at her. "I must go to see Peter Ivánovich."

He went to see Peter Ivánovich, and together they went to see his friend, the doctor. He was in, and Iván Ilých had a long talk with him.

Reviewing the anatomical and physiological details of what in the doctor's opinion was going on inside him, he understood it all.

There was something, a small thing, in the vermiform appendix. It might all come right. Only stimulate the energy of one organ and check the activity of another, then absorption would take place and everything would come right. He got home rather late for dinner, ate his dinner, and conversed cheerfully, but could not for a long time bring himself to go back to work in his room. At last, however, he went to his study and did what was necessary, but the consciousness that he had put something aside—an important, intimate matter which he would revert to when his work was done—never left him. When he had finished his work he remembered that this intimate matter was the thought of his vermiform appendix. But he did not give himself up to it, and went to the drawing-room for tea. There were callers there, including the examining magistrate who was a desirable match for his daughter, and they were conversing, playing the piano and singing. Iván Ilých, as Praskóvya Fëdorovna remarked, spent that evening more cheerfully than usual, but he never for a moment forgot that he had postponed the important matter of the appendix. At eleven o'clock he said good-night and went to his bedroom. Since his illness he had slept alone in a small room next to his study. He undressed and took up a novel by Zola, but instead of reading it he fell into thought, and in his imagination that desired improvement in the vermiform appendix occurred. There was the absorption and evacuation and the reestablishment of normal activity. "Yes, that's it!" he said to himself. "One need only assist nature, that's all." He remembered his medicine, rose, took it, and lay down on his back watching for the beneficent action of the medicine and for it to lessen the pain. "I need only take it regularly and avoid all injurious influences. I am already feeling better, much better." He began touching his side: it was not painful to the touch. "There, I really don't feel it. It's much better already." He put out the light and turned on his side . . . "The appendix is getting better, absorption is occurring." Suddenly he felt the old, familiar, dull, gnawing pain, stubborn and serious. There was the same familiar loathsome taste in his mouth. His heart sank and he felt dazed. "My God! My God!" he muttered. "Again, again! and it will never cease." And suddenly the matter presented itself in a quite different aspect. "Vermiform appendix! Kidney!" he said to himself. "It's not a question of appendix or kidney, but of life and . . . death. Yes, life was there and now it is going, going and I cannot stop it. Yes. Why deceive myself? Isn't it obvious to everyone but me that I'm dying, and that it's only a question of weeks, days . . . it may happen this moment. There was light and now there is darkness. I was here and now I'm going there! Where?" A chill came over him, his breathing ceased, and he felt only the throbbing of his heart.

"When I am not, what will there be? There will be nothing. Then where shall I be when I am no more? Can this be dying? No, I don't want to!" He jumped up and tried to light the candle, felt for it with trembling hands, dropped candle and candlestick on the floor, and fell back on his pillow.

"What's the use? It makes no difference," he said to himself, staring with wide-open eyes into the darkness. "Death. Yes, death. And none of them know or wish to know it, and they have no pity for me. Now they are playing." (He heard through the door the distant sound of a song and its accompaniment.) "It's all the same to them, but they will die too! Fools! I first, and they later, but it will be the same for them. And now they are merry . . . the beasts!"

Anger choked him and he was agonizingly, unbearably miserable. "It is impossible that all men have been doomed to suffer this awful horror!" He raised himself.

"Something must be wrong. I must calm myself—must think it all over from the beginning." And he again began thinking. "Yes, the beginning of my illness: I knocked my side, but I was still quite well that day and the next. It hurt a little, then rather more. I saw the doctors, then followed despondency and anguish, more doctors, and I drew nearer to the abyss. My strength grew less and I kept coming nearer and nearer, and now I have wasted away and there is no light in my eyes. I think of the appendix—but this is death! I think of mending the appendix, and all the while here is death! Can it really be death?" Again terror seized him and he gasped for breath. He leant down and began feeling for the matches, pressing with his elbow on the stand beside the bed. It was in his way and hurt him, he grew furious with it, pressed on it still harder, and upset it. Breathless and in despair he fell on his back, expecting death to come immediately.

Meanwhile the visitors were leaving. Praskóvya Fëdorovna was seeing them off. She heard something fall and came in.

"What has happened?"

"Nothing. I knocked it over accidentally."

She went out and returned with a candle. He lay there panting heavily, like a man who has run a thousand yards, and stared upwards at her with a fixed look.

"What is it, Jean?"

"No . . . o . . . thing. I upset it." ("Why speak of it? She won't understand," he thought.)

And in truth she did not understand. She picked up the stand, lit his candle, and hurried away to see another visitor off. When she came back he still lay on his back, looking upwards.

"What is it? Do you feel worse?"

"Yes."

She shook her head and sat down.

"Do you know, Jean, I think we must ask Leshchetítsky to come and see you here."

This meant calling in the famous specialist, regardless of expense. He smiled malignantly and said "No." She remained a little longer and then went up to him and kissed his forehead.

While she was kissing him he hated her from the bottom of his soul and with difficulty refrained from pushing her away.

"Good-night. Please God you'll sleep."

"Yes."

CHAPTER VI

Iván Ilých saw that he was dying, and he was in continual despair.

In the depth of his heart he knew he was dying, but not only was he not accustomed to the thought, he simply did not and could not grasp it.

The syllogism he had learnt from Kiezewetter's Logic:[10] "Caius is a man, men are mortal, therefore Caius is mortal," had always seemed to him correct as applied to Caius, but certainly not as applied to himself. That Caius—man in the abstract—was mortal, was perfectly correct, but he was not Caius, not an abstract man, but a creature quite, quite separate from all others. He had been little Ványa, with a mamma and a papa; with Mitya and Volódya, and the toys, a coachman and a nurse, afterwards with Kátenka and with all the joys, griefs, and delights of childhood, boyhood, and youth. What did Caius know of the smell of that striped leather ball Ványa had been so fond of? Had Caius kissed his mother's hand like that, and did the silk of her dress rustle so for Caius? Had he rioted like that at school when the pastry was bad? Had Caius been in love like that? Could Caius preside at a session as he did? "Caius really was mortal, and it was right for him to die; but for me, little Ványa, Iván Ilých, with all my thoughts and emotions, it's altogether a different matter. It cannot be that I ought to die. That would be too terrible."

Such was his feeling.

"If I had to die like Caius I should have known it was so. An inner voice would have told me so, but there was nothing of the sort in me and I and all my friends felt that our case was quite different from that of Caius. And now here it is!" he said to himself. "It can't be. It's impossible! But here it is. How is this? How is one to understand it?"

---

[10] Karl Kiezewetter (1766–1819), author of an outline of logic widely used in Russian schools at the time.

He could not understand it, and tried to drive this false, incorrect, morbid thought away and to replace it by other proper and healthy thoughts. But that thought, and not the thought only but the reality itself, seemed to come and confront him.

And to replace that thought he called up a succession of others, hoping to find in them some support. He tried to get back into the former current of thoughts that had once screened the thought of death from him. But strange to say, all that had formerly shut off, hidden, and destroyed his consciousness of death, no longer had that effect. Iván Ilých now spent most of his time in attempting to re-establish that old current. He would say to himself: "I will take up my duties again—after all I used to live by them." And banishing all doubts he would go to the law courts, enter into conversation with his colleagues, and sit carelessly as was his wont, scanning the crowd with a thoughtful look and leaning both his emaciated arms on the arms of his oak chair; bending over as usual to a colleague and drawing his papers nearer he would interchange whispers with him, and then suddenly raising his eyes and sitting erect would pronounce certain words and open the proceedings. But suddenly in the midst of those proceedings the pain in his side, regardless of the stage the proceedings had reached, would begin its own gnawing work. Iván Ilých would turn his attention to it and try to drive the thought of it away, but without success. *It* would come and stand before him and look at him, and he would be petrified and the light would die out of his eyes, and he would again begin asking himself whether *It* alone was true. And his colleagues and subordinates would see with surprise and distress that he, the brilliant and subtle judge, was becoming confused and making mistakes. He would shake himself, try to pull himself together, manage somehow to bring the sitting to a close, and return home with the sorrowful consciousness that his judicial labours could not as formerly hide from him what he wanted them to hide, and could not deliver him from *It*. And what was worst of all was that *It* drew his attention to itself not in order to make him take some action but only that he should look at *It*, look it straight in the face: look at it and without doing anything, suffer inexpressibly.

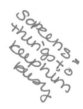

And to save himself from this condition Iván Ilých looked for consolations—new screens—and new screens were found and for a while seemed to save him, but then they immediately fell to pieces or rather became transparent, as if *It* penetrated them and nothing could veil *It*.

In these latter days he would go into the drawing-room he had arranged—that drawing-room where he had fallen and for the sake of which (how bitterly ridiculous it seemed) he had sacrificed his life—for he knew that his illness originated with that knock. He would enter and see that something had scratched the polished table. He would look for the cause of this and find that it was the bronze ornamentation of an album, that had got bent. He would take up the expensive album which he had lovingly arranged, and feel vexed with his daughter and her friends for their untidiness—for the album was torn here and there and some of the photographs turned upside down. He would put it carefully in order and bend the ornamentation back into position. Then it would occur to him to place all those things in another corner of the room, near the plants. He could call the footman, but his daughter or wife would come to help him. They would not agree, and his wife would contradict him, and he would dispute and grow angry. But that was all right, for then he did not think about *It*. *It* was invisible.

But then, when he was moving something himself, his wife would say: "Let the servants do it. You will hurt yourself again." And suddenly *It* would flash through the screen and he would see it. It was just a flash, and he hoped it would disappear, but he would involuntarily pay attention to his side. "It sits there as before, gnawing just the same!" And he could no longer forget *It*, but could distinctly see it looking at him from behind the flowers. "What is it all for?"

"It really is so! I lost my life over that curtain as I might have done when storming a fort. Is that possible? How terrible and how stupid. It can't be true! It can't, but it is."

He would go to his study, lie down, and again be alone with *It*: face to face with *It*. And nothing could be done with *It* except to look at it and shudder.

CHAPTER VII

How it happened it is impossible to say because it came about step by step, unnoticed, but in the third month of Iván Ilých's illness, his wife, his daughter, his son, his acquaintances, the doctors, the servants, and above all he himself, were aware that the whole interest he had for other people was whether he would soon vacate his place, and at last release the living from the discomfort caused by his presence and be himself released from his sufferings.

He slept less and less. He was given opium and hypodermic injections of morphine, but this did not relieve him. The dull depression he experienced in a somnolent condition at first gave him a little relief, but only as something new, afterwards it became as distressing as the pain itself or even more so.

Special foods were prepared for him by the doctors' orders, but all those foods became increasingly distasteful and disgusting to him.

For his excretions also special arrangements had to be made, and this was a torment to him every time—a torment from the uncleanliness, the unseemliness, and the smell, and from knowing that another person had to take part in it.

But just through this most unpleasant matter Iván Ilých obtained comfort. Gerásim, the butler's young assistant, always came in to carry the things out. Gerásim was a clean, fresh peasant lad, grown stout on town food and always cheerful and bright. At first the sight of him, in his clean Russian peasant costume, engaged on that disgusting task embarrassed Iván Ilých.

Once when he got up from the commode too weak to draw up his trousers, he dropped into a soft armchair and looked with horror at his bare, enfeebled thighs with the muscles so sharply marked on them.

Gerásim with a firm light tread, his heavy boots emitting a pleasant smell of tar and fresh winter air, came in wearing a clean Hessian apron, the sleeves of his print shirt tucked up over his strong bare young arms; and refraining from looking at his sick master out of consideration for his feelings, and restraining the joy of life that beamed from his face, he went up to the commode.

"Gerásim!" said Iván Ilých in a weak voice.

Gerásim started, evidently afraid he might have committed some blunder, and with a rapid movement turned his fresh, kind, simple young face which just showed the first downy signs of a beard.

"Yes, sir?"

"That must be very unpleasant for you. You must forgive me. I am helpless."

"Oh, why, sir," and Gerásim's eyes beamed and he showed his glistening white teeth, "what's a little trouble? It's a case of illness with you, sir."

And his deft strong hands did their accustomed task, and he went out of the room stepping lightly. Five minutes later he as lightly returned.

Iván Ilých was still sitting in the same position in the armchair.

"Gerásim," he said when the latter had replaced the freshly-washed utensil. "Please come here and help me." Gerásim went up to him. "Lift me up. It is hard for me to get up, and I have sent Dmítri away."

Gerásim went up to him, grasped his master with his strong arms deftly but gently, in the same way that he stepped—lifted him, supported him with one hand, and with the other drew up his trousers and would have set him down again, but Iván Ilých asked to be led to the sofa. Gerásim, without an effort and without apparent pressure, led him, almost lifting him, to the sofa and placed him on it.

"Thank you. How easily and well you do it all!"

Gerásim smiled again and turned to leave the room. But Iván Ilých felt his presence such a comfort that he did not want to let him go.

"One thing more, please move up that chair. No, the other one—under my feet. It is easier for me when my feet are raised."

Gerásim brought the chair, set it down gently in place, and raised Iván Ilých's legs on to it. It seemed to Iván Ilých that he felt better while Gerásim was holding up his legs.

"It's better when my legs are higher," he said. "Place that cushion under them."

Gerásim did so. He again lifted the legs and placed them, and again Iván Ilých felt better while Gerásim held his legs. When he set them down Iván Ilých fancied he felt worse.

"Gerásim," he said. "Are you busy now?"

"Not at all, sir," said Gerásim, who had learnt from the townsfolk how to speak to gentlefolk.

"What have you still to do?"

"What have I to do? I've done everything except chopping the logs for tomorrow."

"Then hold my legs up a bit higher, can you?"

"Of course I can. Why not?" And Gerásim raised his master's legs higher and Iván Ilých thought that in that position he did not feel any pain at all.

"And how about the logs?"

"Don't trouble about that, sir. There's plenty of time."

Iván Ilých told Gerásim to sit down and hold his legs, and began to talk to him. And strange to say it seemed to him that he felt better while Gerásim held his legs up.

After that Iván Ilých would sometimes call Gerásim and get him to hold his legs on his shoulders, and he liked talking to him. Gerásim did it all easily, willingly, simply, and with a good nature that touched Iván Ilých. Health, strength, and vitality in other people were offensive to him, but Gerásim's strength and vitality did not mortify but soothed him.

What tormented Iván Ilých most was the deception, the lie, which for some reason they all accepted, that he was not dying but was simply ill, and that he only need keep quiet and undergo a treatment and then something very good would result. He however knew that do what they would nothing would come of it, only still more agonizing suffering and death. This deception tortured him—their not wishing to admit what they all knew and what he knew, but wanting to lie to him concerning his terrible condition, and wishing and forcing him to participate in that lie. Those lies—lies enacted over him on the eve of his death and destined to degrade this awful, solemn act to the level of their visitings, their curtains, their sturgeon for dinner—were a terrible agony for Iván Ilých. And strangely enough, many times when they were going through their antics over him he had been within a hairbreadth of calling out to them: "Stop lying! You know and I know that I am dying. Then at least stop lying about it!" But he had never had the spirit to do it. The awful, terrible act of his dying was, he could see, reduced by those about him to the level of a casual, unpleasant, and almost indecorous incident (as if someone entered a drawing-room diffusing an unpleasant odour) and this was done by that very decorum which he had served all his life long. He saw that no one felt for him, because no one even wished to grasp his position. Only Gerásim recognized it and pitied him. And so Iván Ilých felt at ease only with him. He felt comforted when Gerásim supported his legs (sometimes all night long) and refused to go to bed, saying, "Don't you worry, Iván Ilých. I'll get sleep enough later on," or when he suddenly became familiar and exclaimed: "If you weren't sick it would be another matter, but as it is, why should I grudge a little trouble?" Gerásim alone did not lie; everything showed that he alone understood the facts of the case and did not consider it necessary to disguise them, but simply felt sorry for his emaciated and enfeebled master. Once when Iván Ilých was sending him away he even said straight out: "We shall all of us die, so why should I grudge a little trouble?"—expressing the fact that he did not think his work burdensome, because he was doing it for a dying man and hoped someone would do the same for him when his time came.

Apart from this lying, or because of it, what most tormented Iván Ilých was that no one pitied him as he wished to be pitied. At certain moments after prolonged suffering he wished most of all (though he would have been ashamed to confess it) for someone to pity him as a sick child is pitied. He longed to be petted and comforted. He knew he was an important functionary, that he had a beard turning grey, and that therefore what he longed for was impossible, but still he longed for it. And in Gerásim's attitude towards him there was something akin to what he wished for, and so that attitude comforted him. Iván Ilých wanted to weep, wanted to be petted and cried over, and then his colleague Shébek would come, and instead of weeping and being petted, Iván Ilých would assume a serious, severe, and profound air, and by force of habit would express his opinion on a decision of the Court of Cassation and would stubbornly insist on that view. This falsity around him and within him did more than anything else to poison his last days.

CHAPTER VIII

It was morning. He knew it was morning because Gerásim had gone, and Peter the footman had come and put out the candles, drawn back one of the curtains, and begun quietly to tidy up. Whether it was morning or evening, Friday or Sunday, made no difference, it was all just the same: the gnawing, unmitigated, agonizing pain, never ceasing for an instant, the consciousness of life inexorably waning but not yet extinguished, that approach of that ever dreaded and hateful Death which was the only reality, and always the same falsity. What were days, weeks, hours, in such a case?

"Will you have some tea, sir?"

"He wants things to be regular, and wishes the gentlefolk to drink tea in the morning," thought Iván Ilých, and only said "No."

"Wouldn't you like to move onto the sofa, sir?"

"He wants to tidy up the room, and I'm in the way. I am uncleanliness and disorder," he thought, and said only:

"No, leave me alone."

The man went on bustling about. Iván Ilých stretched out his hand. Peter came up, ready to help.

"What is it, sir?"

"My watch."

Peter took the watch which was close at hand and gave it to his master.

"Half-past eight. Are they up?"

"No, sir, except Vladímir Ivánich" (the son) "who has gone to school. Praskóvya Fëdorovna ordered me to wake her if you asked for her. Shall I do so?"

"No, there's no need to." "Perhaps I'd better have some tea," he thought, and added aloud: "Yes, bring me some tea."

Peter went to the door but Iván Ilých dreaded being left alone. "How can I keep him here? Oh yes, my medicine." "Peter, give me my medicine." "Why not? Perhaps it may still do me some good." He took a spoonful and swallowed it. "No, it won't help. It's all tomfoolery, all deception," he decided as soon as he became aware of the familiar, sickly, hopeless taste. "No, I can't believe in it any longer. But the pain, why this pain? If it would only cease just for a moment!" And he moaned. Peter turned towards him. "It's all right. Go and fetch me some tea."

Peter went out. Left alone Iván Ilých groaned not so much with pain, terrible though that was, as from mental anguish. Always and for ever the same, always these endless days and nights. If only it would come quicker! If only *what* would come quicker? Death, darkness? . . . No, no! Anything rather than death!

When Peter returned with the tea on a tray, Iván Ilých stared at him for a time in perplexity, not realizing who and what he was. Peter was disconcerted by that look and his embarrassment brought Iván Ilých to himself.

"Oh, tea! All right, put it down. Only help me to wash and put on a clean shirt."

And Iván Ilých began to wash. With pauses for rest, he washed his hands and then his face, cleaned his teeth, brushed his hair, and looked in the glass. He was terrified by what he saw, especially by the limp way in which his hair clung to his pallid forehead.

While his shirt was being changed he knew that he would be still more frightened at the sight of his body, so he avoided looking at it. Finally he was ready. He drew on a dressing-gown, wrapped himself in a plaid, and sat down in the armchair to take his tea. For a moment he felt refreshed, but as soon as he began to drink the tea he was again aware of the same taste, and the pain also returned. He finished it with an effort, and then lay down stretching out his legs, and dismissed Peter.

Always the same. Now a spark of hope flashes up, then a sea of despair rages, and always pain; always pain, always despair, and always the same. When alone he had a dreadful and distressing desire to call someone, but he knew beforehand that with others present it would be still worse. "Another dose of morphine—to lose consciousness. I will tell him, the doctor, that he must think of something else. It's impossible, impossible, to go on like this."

An hour and another pass like that. But now there is a ring at the door bell. Perhaps it's the doctor? It is. He comes in fresh, hearty, plump, and cheerful, with that look on his face that seems to say: "There now, you're in a panic about something, but we'll arrange it all for you directly!" The doctor knows this expression is out of place here, but he has put it on once for all and can't take it off—like a man who has put on a frock-coat in the morning to pay a round of calls.

The doctor rubs his hands vigorously and reassuringly.

"Brr! How cold it is! There's such a sharp frost; just let me warm myself!" he says, as if it were only a matter of waiting till he was warm, and then he would put everything right.

"Well now, how are you?"

Iván Ilých feels that the doctor would like to say: "Well, how are our affairs?" but that even he feels that this would not do, and says instead: "What sort of a night have you had?"

Iván Ilých looks at him as much as to say: "Are you really never ashamed of lying?" But the doctor does not wish to understand this question, and Iván Ilých says: "Just as terrible as ever. The pain never leaves me and never subsides. If only something . . ."

"Yes, you sick people are always like that. . . . There, now I think I am warm enough. Even Praskóvya Fëdorovna, who is so particular, could find no fault with my temperature. Well, now I can say good-morning," and the doctor presses his patient's hand.

Then, dropping his former playfulness, he begins with a most serious face to examine the patient, feeling his pulse and taking his temperature, and then begins the sounding and auscultation.

Iván Ilých knows quite well and definitely that all this is nonsense and pure deception, but when the doctor, getting down on his knee, leans over him, putting his ear first higher then lower, and performs various gymnastic movements over him with a significant expression on his face, Iván Ilých submits to it all as he used to submit to the speeches of the lawyers, though he knew very well that they were all lying and why they were lying.

The doctor, kneeling on the sofa, is still sounding him when Praskóvya Fëdorovna's silk dress rustles at the door and she is heard scolding Peter for not having let her know of the doctor's arrival.

She comes in, kisses her husband, and at once proceeds to prove that she has been up a long time already, and only owing to a misunderstanding failed to be there when the doctor arrived.

Iván Ilých looks at her, scans her all over, sets against her the whiteness and plumpness and cleanness of her hands and neck, the gloss of her hair, and the sparkle of her vivacious eyes. He hates her with his whole soul. And the thrill of hatred he feels for her makes him suffer from her touch.

Her attitude towards him and his disease is still the same. Just as the doctor had adopted a certain relation to his patient which he could not abandon, so had she formed one towards him—that he was not doing something he ought to do and was himself to blame, and that she reproached him lovingly for this—and she could not now change that attitude.

"You see he doesn't listen to me and doesn't take his medicine at the proper time. And above all he lies in a position that is no doubt bad for him—with his legs up."

She described how he made Gerásim hold his legs up.

The doctor smiled with a contemptuous affability that said: "What's to be done? These sick people do have foolish fancies of that kind, but we must forgive them."

When the examination was over the doctor looked at his watch, and then Praskóvya Fëdorovna announced to Iván Ilých that it was of course as he pleased, but she had sent to-day for a celebrated specialist who would examine him and have a consultation with Michael Danílovich (their regular doctor).

"Please don't raise any objections. I am doing this for my own sake," she said ironically, letting it be felt that she was doing it all for his sake and only said this to leave him no right to refuse. He remained silent, knitting his brows. He felt that he was so surrounded and involved in a mesh of falsity that it was hard to unravel anything.

Everything she did for him was entirely for her own sake, and she told him she was doing for herself what she actually was doing for herself, as if that was so incredible that he must understand the opposite.

At half-past eleven the celebrated specialist arrived. Again the sounding began and the significant conversations in his presence and in another room, about the kidneys and the appendix, and the questions and answers, with such an air of importance that again, instead of the real question of life and death which now alone confronted him, the question arose of the kidney and appendix which were not behaving as they ought to and would now be attacked by Michael Danílovich and the specialist and forced to amend their ways.

The celebrated specialist took leave of him with a serious though not hopeless look, and in reply to the timid question Iván Ilých, with eyes glistening with fear and hope, put to him as to whether there was a chance of recovery, said that he could not vouch for it but there was a possibility. The look of hope with which Iván Ilých watched the doctor out was so pathetic that Praskóvya Fëdorovna, seeing it, even wept as she left the room to hand the doctor his fee.

The gleam of hope kindled by the doctor's encouragement did not last long. The same room, the same pictures, curtains, wall-paper, medicine bottles, were all there, and the same aching suffering body, and Iván Ilých began to moan. They gave him a subcutaneous injection and he sank into oblivion.

It was twilight when he came to. They brought him his dinner and he swallowed some beef tea with difficulty, and then everything was the same again and night was coming on.

After dinner, at seven o'clock, Praskóvya Fëdorovna came into the room in evening dress, her full bosom pushed up by her corset, and with traces of powder on her face. She had reminded him in the morning that they were going to the theater. Sarah Bernhardt was visiting the town and they had a box, which he had insisted on their taking. Now he had forgotten about it and her toilet offended him, but he concealed his vexation when he remembered that he had himself insisted on their securing a box and going because it would be an instructive and aesthetic pleasure for the children.

Praskóvya Fëdorovna came in, self-satisfied but yet with a rather guilty air. She sat down and asked how he was, but, as he saw, only for the sake of asking and not in order to learn about it, knowing that there was nothing to learn—and then went on to what she really wanted to say: that she would not on any account have gone but that the box had been taken and Helen and their daughter were going, as well as Petríshchev (the examining magistrate, their daughter's fiancé) and that it was out of the question to let them go alone; but that she would have much preferred to sit with him for a while; and he must be sure to follow the doctor's orders while she was away.

"Oh, and Fëdor Petróvich" (the fiancé) "would like to come in. May he? And Lisa?"

"All right."

Their daughter came in in full evening dress, her fresh young flesh exposed (making a show of that very flesh which in his own case caused so much suffering), strong, healthy, evidently in love, and impatient with illness, suffering, and death, because they interfered with her happiness.

Fëdor Petróvich came in too, in evening dress, his hair curled *á la Capoul*, a tight stiff collar round his long sinewy neck, an enormous white shirt-front and narrow black trousers tightly stretched over his strong thighs. He had one white glove tightly drawn on, and was holding his opera hat in his hand.

Following him the schoolboy crept in unnoticed, in a new uniform, poor little fellow, and wearing gloves. Terribly dark shadows showed under his eyes, the meaning of which Iván Ilých knew well.

His son had always seemed pathetic to him, and now it was dreadful to see the boy's frightened look of pity. It seemed to Iván Ilých that Vásya was the only one besides Gerásim who understood and pitied him.

They all sat down and again asked how he was. A silence followed. Lisa asked her mother about the opera-glasses, and there was an altercation between mother and daughter as to who had taken them and where they had been put. This occasioned some unpleasantness.

Fëdor Petróvich inquired of Iván Ilých whether he had ever seen Sarah Bernhardt. Iván Ilých did not at first catch the question, but then replied: "No, have you seen her before?"

"Yes, in *Adrienne Lecouvreur*."[11]

Praskóvya Fëdorovna mentioned some roles in which Sarah Bernhardt was particularly good. Her daughter disagreed. Conversation sprang up as to the elegance and realism of her acting—the sort of conversation that is always repeated and is always the same.

In the midst of the conversation Fëdor Petróvich glanced at Iván Ilých and became silent. The others also looked at him and grew silent. Iván Ilých was staring with glittering eyes straight before him, evidently indignant with them. This had to be rectified, but it was impossible to do so. The silence had to be broken, but for a time no one dared to break it and they all became afraid that the conventional deception would suddenly become obvious and the truth become plain to all. Lisa was the first to pluck up courage and break that silence, but by trying to hide what everybody was feeling, she betrayed it.

"Well, if we are going it's time to start," she said, looking at her watch, a present from her father, and with a faint and significant smile at Fëdor Petróvich

---

[11] A play by the French dramatist Eugène Scribe (1791–1861).

relating to something known only to them. She got up with a rustle of her dress.

They all rose, said good-night, and went away.

When they had gone it seemed to Iván Ilých that he felt better; the falsity had gone with them. But the pain remained—that same pain and that same fear that made everything monotonously alike, nothing harder and nothing easier. Everything was worse.

Again minute followed minute and hour followed hour. Everything remained the same and there was no cessation. And the inevitable end of it all became more and more terrible.

"Yes, send Gerásim here," he replied to a question Peter asked.

CHAPTER IX

His wife returned late at night. She came in on tiptoe, but he heard her, opened his eyes, and made haste to close them again. She wished to send Gerásim away and to sit with him herself, but he opened his eyes and said: "No, go away."

"Are you in great pain?"

"Always the same."

"Take some opium."

He agreed and took some. She went away.

Till about three in the morning he was in a state of stupefied misery. It seemed to him that he and his pain were being thrust into a narrow, deep black sack, but though they were pushed further and further in they could not be pushed to the bottom. And this, terrible enough in itself, was accompanied by suffering. He was frightened yet wanted to fall through the sack, he struggled but yet co-operated. And suddenly he broke through, fell, and regained consciousness. Gerásim was sitting at the foot of the bed dozing quietly and patiently, while he himself lay with his emaciated stockinged legs resting on Gerásim's shoulders; the same shaded candle was there and the same unceasing pain.

"Go away, Gerásim," he whispered.

"It's all right, sir. I'll stay a while."

"No. Go away."

He removed his legs from Gerásim's shoulders, turned sideways onto his arm, and felt sorry for himself. He only waited till Gerásim had gone into the next room and then restrained himself no longer but wept like a child. He wept on account of his helplessness, his terrible loneliness, the cruelty of man, the cruelty of God, and the absence of God.

"Why hast Thou done all this? Why hast Thou brought me here? Why, why dost Thou torment me so terribly?"

He did not expect an answer and yet wept because there was no answer and could be none. The pain again grew more acute, but he did not stir and did not call. He said to himself: "Go on! Strike me! But what is it for? What have I done to Thee? What is it for?"

Then he grew quiet and not only ceased weeping but even held his breath and became all attention. It was as though he were listening not to an audible voice but to the voice of his soul, to the current of thoughts arising within him.

"What is it you want?" was the first clear conception capable of expression in words, that he heard.

"What do you want? What do you want?" he repeated to himself.

"What do I want? To live and not to suffer," he answered.

And again he listened with such concentrated attention that even his pain did not distract him.

"To live? How?" asked his inner voice.

"Why, to live as I used to—well and pleasantly."

"As you lived before, well and pleasantly?" the voice repeated.

And in imagination he began to recall the best moments of his pleasant life. But strange to say none of those best moments of his pleasant life now seemed at all what they had then seemed—none of them except the first recollections of childhood. There, in childhood, there had been something really pleasant with which it would be possible to live if it could return. But the child who had experienced that happiness existed no longer, it was like a reminiscence of somebody else.

As soon as the period began which had produced the present Iván Ilých, all that had then seemed joys now melted before his sight and turned into something trivial and often nasty.

And the further he departed from childhood and the nearer he came to the present the more worthless and doubtful were the joys. This began with the School of Law. A little that was really good was still found there—there was light-heartedness, friendship, and hope. But in the upper classes there had already been fewer of such good moments. Then during the first years of his official career, when he was in the service of the Governor, some pleasant moments again occurred: they were the memories of love for a woman. Then all became confused and there was still less of what was good; later on again there was still less that was good, and the further he went the less there was. His marriage, a mere accident, then the disenchantment that followed it, his wife's bad breath and the sensuality and hypocrisy: then that deadly official life and those preoccupations about money, a year of it, and two, and ten, and twenty, and always the same thing. And the longer it lasted the more deadly it became.

→ "It is as if I had been going downhill while I imagined I was going up. And that is really what it was. I was going up in public opinion, but to the same extent life was ebbing away from me. And now it is all done and there is only death."

"Then what does it mean? Why? It can't be that life is so senseless and horrible. But if it really has been so horrible and senseless, why must I die and die in agony? There is something wrong!"

"Maybe I did not live as I ought to have done," it suddenly occurred to him. "But how could that be, when I did everything properly?" he replied, and immediately dismissed from his mind this, the sole solution of all the riddles of life and death, as something quite impossible.

"Then what do you want now? To live? Live how? Live as you lived in the law courts when the usher proclaimed 'The judge is coming!' " "The judge is coming, the judge!" he repeated to himself. "Here he is, the judge. But I am not guilty!" he exclaimed angrily. "What is it for?" And he ceased crying, but turning his face to the wall continued to ponder on the same question: Why, and for what purpose, is there all this horror? But however much he pondered he found no answer. And whenever the thought occurred to him, as it often did, that it all resulted from his not having lived as he ought to have done, he at once recalled the correctness of his whole life and dismissed so strange an idea.

CHAPTER X

Another fortnight passed. Iván Ilých now no longer left his sofa. He would not lie in bed but lay on the sofa, facing the wall nearly all the time. He suffered ever the same unceasing agonies and in his loneliness pondered always on the same insoluble question: "What is this? Can it be that it is Death?" And the inner voice answered: "Yes, it is Death."

"Why these sufferings?" And the voice answered, "For no reason—they just are so." Beyond and besides this there was nothing.

From the very beginning of his illness, ever since he had first been to see the doctor, Iván Ilých's life had been divided between two contrary and alternating moods: now it was despair and the expectation of this uncomprehended and terrible death, and now hope and an intently interested observation of the functioning of his organs. Now before his eyes there was only a kidney or an intestine that temporarily evaded its duty, and now only that incomprehensible and dreadful death from which it was impossible to escape.

These two states of mind had alternated from the very beginning of his illness, but the further it progressed the more doubtful and fantastic became the conception of the kidney, and the more real the sense of impending death.

He had but to call to mind what he had been three months before and what he was now, to call to mind with what regularity he had been going downhill, for every possibility of hope to be shattered.

Latterly during that loneliness in which he found himself as he lay facing the back of the sofa, a loneliness in the midst of a populous town and surrounded by numerous acquaintances and relations but that yet could not have been more complete anywhere—either at the bottom of the sea or under the earth—during that terrible loneliness Iván Ilých had lived only in memories of the past. Pictures of his past rose before him one after another. They always began with what was nearest in time and then went back to what was most remote—to his childhood—and rested there. If he thought of the stewed prunes that had been offered him that day, his mind went back to the raw shrivelled French plums of his childhood, their peculiar flavor and the flow of saliva when he sucked their stones, and along with the memory of that taste came a whole series of memories of those days: his nurse, his brother, and their toys. "No, I mustn't think of that. . . . It is too painful," Iván Ilých said to himself, and brought himself back to the present—to the button on the back of the sofa and the creases in its morocco. "Morocco is expensive, but it does not wear well: There had been a quarrel about it. It was a different kind of quarrel and a different kind of morocco that time when we tore father's portfolio and were punished, and mamma brought us some tarts. . . ." And again his thoughts dwelt on his childhood, and again it was painful and he tried to banish them and fix his mind on something else.

Then again together with that chain of memories another series passed through his mind—of how his illness had progressed and grown worse. There also the further back he looked the more life there had been. There had been more of what was good in life and more of life itself. The two merged together. "Just as the pain went on getting worse and worse so my life grew worse and worse," he thought. "There is one bright spot there at the back, at the beginning of life, and afterwards all becomes blacker and blacker and proceeds more and more rapidly—in inverse ratio to the square of the distance from death," thought Iván Ilých. And the example of a stone falling downwards with increasing velocity entered his mind. Life, a series of increasing sufferings, flies, further and further towards its end—the most terrible suffering. "I am flying. . . ." He shuddered, shifted himself, and tried to resist, but was already aware that resistance was impossible, and again with eyes weary of gazing but unable to cease seeing what was before them, he stared at the back of the sofa and waited—awaiting that dreadful fall and shock and destruction.

"Resistance is impossible!" he said to himself. "If I could only understand what it is all for! But that too is impossible. An explanation would be possible if it could be said that I have not lived as I ought to. But it is impossible to say that," and he remembered all the legality, correctitude, and propriety of his life. "That at any rate can certainly not be admitted," he thought, and his lips smiled ironically as if someone could see that smile and be taken in by it. "There is no explanation! Agony, death. . . . What for?"

CHAPTER XI

Another two weeks went by in this way and during that fortnight an event occurred that Iván Ilých and his wife had desired. Petríshchev formally proposed. It happened in the evening. The next day Praskóvya Fëdorovna came into her husband's room considering how best to inform him of it, but that very night there had been a fresh change for the worse in his condition. She found him still lying on the sofa but in a different position. He lay on his back, groaning and staring fixedly straight in front of him.

She began to remind him of his medicines, but he turned his eyes towards her with such a look that she did not finish what she was saying; so great an animosity, to her in particular, did that look express.

"For Christ's sake, let me die in peace!" he said.

She would have gone away, but just then their daughter came in and went up to say good morning. He looked at her as he had done at his wife, and in reply to her inquiry about his health said dryly that he would soon free them all of himself. They were both silent and after sitting with him for a while went away.

"Is it our fault?" Lisa said to her mother. "It's as if we were to blame! I am sorry for papa, but why should we be tortured?"

The doctor came at his usual time. Iván Ilých answered "Yes" and "No," never taking his angry eyes from him, and at last said: "You know you can do nothing for me, so leave me alone."

"We can ease your sufferings."

"You can't even do that. Let me be."

The doctor went into the drawing-room and told Praskóvya Fëdorovna that the case was very serious and that the only resource left was opium to allay her husband's sufferings, which must be terrible.

It was true, as the doctor said, that Iván Ilých's physical sufferings were terrible, but worse than the physical sufferings were his mental sufferings which were his chief torture.

His mental sufferings were due to the fact that that night, as he looked at Gerásim's sleepy, good-natured face with its prominent cheek-bones, the question suddenly occurred to him: "What if my whole life has really been wrong?"

It occurred to him that what had appeared perfectly impossible before, namely that he had not spent his life as he should have done, might after all be true. It occurred to him that his scarcely perceptible attempts to struggle against what was considered good by the most highly placed people, those scarcely noticeable impulses which he had immediately suppressed, might have been the real thing, and all the rest false. And his professional duties and the whole arrangement of his life and of his family, and all his social and official interests, might all have been false. He tried to defend all those things to himself and suddenly felt the weakness of what he was defending. There was nothing to defend.

"But if that is so," he said to himself, "and I am leaving this life with the consciousness that I have lost all that was given me and it is impossible to rectify it—what then?"

He lay on his back and began to pass his life in review in quite a new way. In the morning when he saw first his footman, then his wife, then his daughter, and then the doctor, their every word and movement confirmed to him the awful truth that had been revealed to him during the night. In them he saw himself—all that for which he had lived—and saw clearly that it was not real at all, but a terrible and huge deception which had hidden both life and death. This consciousness intensified his physical suffering tenfold. He groaned and tossed about, and pulled at his clothing which choked and stifled him. And he hated them on that account.

He was given a large dose of opium and became unconscious, but at noon his sufferings began again. He drove everybody away and tossed from side to side.

His wife came to him and said:

"Jean, my dear, do this for me. It can't do any harm and often helps. Healthy people often do it."

He opened his eyes wide.

"What? Take communion? Why? It's unnecessary! However. . . ."

She began to cry.

"Yes, do, my dear. I'll send for our priest. He is such a nice man."

"All right. Very well," he muttered.

When the priest came and heard his confession, Iván Ilých was softened and seemed to feel a relief from his doubts and consequently from his sufferings, and for a moment there came a ray of hope. He again began to think of the vermiform appendix and the possibility of correcting it. He received the sacrament with tears in his eyes.

When they laid him down again afterwards he felt a moment's ease, and the hope that he might live awoke in him again. He began to think of the operation that had been suggested to him. "To live! I want to live!" he said to himself.

His wife came in to congratulate him after his communion, and when uttering the usual conventional words she added:

"You feel better, don't you?"

Without looking at her he said "Yes."

Her dress, her figure, the expression of her face, the tone of her voice, all revealed the same thing. "This is wrong, it is not as it should be. All you have lived for and still live for is falsehood and deception, hiding life and death from you." And as soon as he admitted that thought, his hatred and his agonizing physical suffering again sprang up, and with that suffering a consciousness of the unavoidable, approaching end. And to this was added a new sensation of grinding shooting pain and a feeling of suffocation.

The expression of his face when he uttered that "yes" was dreadful. Having uttered it, he looked her straight in the eyes, turned on his face with a rapidity extraordinary in his weak state and shouted:

"Go away! Go away and leave me alone!"

CHAPTER XII

From that moment the screaming began that continued for three days, and was so terrible that one could not hear it through two closed doors without horror. At the moment he answered his wife he realized that he was lost, that there was no return, that the end had come, the very end, and his doubts were still unsolved and remained doubts.

"Oh! Oh! Oh!" he cried in various intonations. He had begun by screaming "I won't!" and continued screaming on the letter "o."

For three whole days, during which time did not exist for him, he struggled in that black sack into which he was being thrust by an invisible, resistless force. He struggled as a man condemned to death struggles in the hands of the executioner, knowing that he cannot save himself. And every moment he felt that despite all his efforts he was drawing nearer and nearer to what terrified him. He felt that his agony was due to his being thrust into that black hole and still more to his not being able to get right into it. He was hindered from getting into it by his conviction that his life had been a good one. That very justification of his life held him fast and prevented his moving forward, and it caused him most torment of all.

Suddenly some force struck him in the chest and side, making it still harder to breathe, and he fell through the hole and there at the bottom was a light. What had happened to him was like the sensation one sometimes experiences in a railway carriage when one thinks one is going backwards while one is really going forwards and suddenly becomes aware of the real direction.

"Yes, it was all not the right thing," he said to himself, "but that's no matter. It can be done. But what *is* the right thing?" he asked himself, and suddenly grew quiet.

This occurred at the end of the third day, two hours before his death. Just then his schoolboy son had crept softly in and gone up to the bedside. The dying man was still screaming desperately and waving his arms. His hand fell on the boy's head, and the boy caught it, pressed it to his lips, and began to cry.

At that very moment Iván Ilých fell through and caught sight of the light, and it was revealed to him that though his life had not been what it should have been, this could still be rectified. He asked himself, "What *is* the right thing?" and grew still, listening. Then he felt that someone was kissing his hand. He opened his eyes, looked at his son, and felt sorry for him. His wife came up to him and he glanced at her. She was gazing at him open-mouthed, with undried tears on her nose and cheek and a despairing look on her face. He felt sorry for her too.

"Yes, I am making them wretched," he thought. "They are sorry, but it will be better for them when I die." He wished to say this but had not the strength to utter it. "Besides, why speak? I must act," he thought. With a look at his wife he indicated his son and said: "Take him away . . . sorry for him . . . sorry for you too. . . ." He tried to add, "forgive me," but said "forego" and waved his hand, knowing that He whose understanding mattered would understand.

And suddenly it grew clear to him that what had been oppressing him and would not leave him was all dropping away at once from two sides, from ten sides, and from all sides. He was sorry for them, he must act so as not to hurt them: release them and free himself from these sufferings. "How good and how simple!" he thought. "And the pain?" he asked himself. "What has become of it? Where are you, pain?"

He turned his attention to it.

"Yes, here it is. Well, what of it? Let the pain be."

"And death . . . where is it?"

He sought his former accustomed fear of death and did not find it.

"Where is it? What death?" There was no fear because there was no death. In place of death there was light.

"So that's what it is!" he suddenly exclaimed aloud. "What joy!"

To him all this happened in a single instant, and the meaning of that instant did not change. For those present his agony continued for another two hours. Something rattled in his throat, his emaciated body twitched, then the gasping and rattle became less and less frequent.

"It is finished!" said someone near him.

He heard these words and repeated them in his soul.

"Death is finished," he said to himself. "It is no more!"

He drew in a breath, stopped in the midst of a sigh, stretched out, and died.

QUESTIONS

1. Why does Tolstoy begin the story immediately after Ilých's death and then move back to recount his life? **2.** Is there any evidence that Ilých's death is a moral judgment—that is, a punishment for his life? Explain. **3.** Why is Gerásim, Ilých's peasant servant, most sympathetic to his plight?

WRITING TOPIC

At the very end, Ilých achieves peace and understanding, and the questions that have been torturing him are resolved. He realizes that "though his life had not been what it should have been, this could still be rectified." What does this mean?

Idiots First

1963

BERNARD MALAMUD   [1914–1986]

The thick ticking of the tin clock stopped. Mendel, dozing in the dark, awoke in fright. The pain returned as he listened. He drew on his cold embittered clothing, and wasted minutes sitting at the edge of the bed.

"Isaac," he ultimately sighed.

In the kitchen, Isaac, his astonished mouth open, held six peanuts in his palm. He placed each on the table. "One . . . two . . . nine."

He gathered each peanut and appeared in the doorway. Mendel, in loose hat and long overcoat, still sat on the bed. Isaac watched with small eyes and ears, thick hair graying the sides of his head.

"Schlaf," he nasally said.

"No," muttered Mendel. As if stifling he rose. "Come, Isaac."

He wound his old watch though the sight of the stopped clock nauseated him.

Isaac wanted to hold it to his ear.

"No, it's late." Mendel put the watch carefully away. In the drawer he found the little paper bag of crumpled ones and fives and slipped it into his overcoat pocket. He helped Isaac on with his coat.

Isaac looked at one dark window, then at the other. Mendel stared at both blank windows.

They went slowly down the darkly lit stairs, Mendel first, Isaac watching the moving shadows on the wall. To one long shadow he offered a peanut.

"Hungrig."

In the vestibule the old man gazed through the thin glass. The November night was cold and bleak. Opening the door he cautiously thrust his head out. Though he saw nothing he quickly shut the door.

"Ginzburg, that he came to see me yesterday," he whispered in Isaac's ear.

Isaac sucked air.

"You know who I mean?"

Isaac combed his chin with his fingers.

"That's the one, with the black whiskers. Don't talk to him or go with him if he asks you."

Isaac moaned.

"Young people he don't bother so much," Mendel said in afterthought.

It was suppertime and the street was empty but the store windows dimly lit their way to the corner. They crossed the deserted street and went on. Isaac, with a happy cry, pointed to the three golden balls. Mendel smiled but was exhausted when they got to the pawnshop.

738

The pawnbroker, a red-bearded man with black horn-rimmed glasses, was eating a whitefish at the rear of the store. He craned his head, saw them, and settled back to sip his tea.

In five minutes he came forward, patting his shapeless lips with a large white handkerchief.

Mendel, breathing heavily, handed him the worn gold watch. The pawnbroker, raising his glasses, screwed in his eyepiece. He turned the watch over once. "Eight dollars."

The dying man wet his cracked lips. "I must have thirty-five."

"So go to Rothschild."

"Cost me myself sixty."

"In 1905." The pawnbroker handed back the watch. It had stopped ticking. Mendel wound it slowly. It ticked hollowly.

"Isaac must go to my uncle that he lives in California."

"It's a free country," said the pawnbroker.

Isaac, watching a banjo, snickered.

"What's the matter with him?" the pawnbroker asked.

"So let be eight dollars," muttered Mendel, "but where will I get the rest till tonight?"

"How much for my hat and coat?" he asked.

"No sale." The pawnbroker went behind the cage and wrote out a ticket. He locked the watch in a small drawer but Mendel still heard it ticking.

In the street he slipped the eight dollars into the paper bag, then searched in his pockets for a scrap of writing. Finding it, he strained to read the address by the light of the street lamp.

As they trudged to the subway, Mendel pointed to the sprinkled sky.

"Isaac, look how many stars are tonight."

"Eggs," said Isaac.

"First we will go to Mr. Fishbein, after we will eat."

They got off the train in upper Manhattan and had to walk several blocks before they located Fishbein's house.

"A regular palace," Mendel murmured, looking forward to a moment's warmth.

Isaac stared uneasily at the heavy door of the house.

Mendel rang. The servant, a man with long sideburns, came to the door and said Mr. and Mrs. Fishbein were dining and could see no one.

"He should eat in peace but we will wait till he finishes."

"Come back tomorrow morning. Tomorrow morning Mr. Fishbein will talk to you. He don't do business or charity at this time of the night."

"Charity I am not interested—"

"Come back tomorrow."

"Tell him it's life or death—"

"Whose life or death?"

"So if not his, then mine."

"Don't be such a big smart aleck."

"Look me in my face," said Mendel, "and tell me if I got time till tomorrow morning?"

The servant stared at him, then at Isaac, and reluctantly let them in.

The foyer was a vast high-ceilinged room with many oil paintings on the walls, voluminous silken draperies, a thick flowered rug at foot, and a marbled staircase.

Mr. Fishbein, a paunchy bald-headed man with hairy nostrils and small patent leather feet, ran lightly down the stairs, a large napkin tucked under a tuxedo coat button. He stopped on the fifth step from the bottom and examined his visitors.

"Who comes on Friday night to a man that he has guests, to spoil him his supper?"

"Excuse me that I bother you, Mr. Fishbein," Mendel said. "If I didn't come now I couldn't come tomorrow."

"Without more preliminaries, please state your business. I'm a hungry man."

"Hungrig," wailed Isaac.

Fishbein adjusted his pince-nez. "What's the matter with him?"

"This is my son Isaac. He is like this all his life."

Isaac mewled.

"I am sending him to California."

"Mr. Fishbein don't contribute to personal pleasure trips."

"I am a sick man and he must go tonight on the train to my Uncle Leo."

"I never give to unorganized charity," Fishbein said, "but if you are hungry I will invite you downstairs in my kitchen. We having tonight chicken with stuffed derma."

"All I ask is thirty-five dollars for the train ticket to my uncle in California. I have already the rest."

"Who is your uncle? How old a man?"

"Eighty-one years, a long life to him."

Fishbein burst into laughter. "Eighty-one years and you are sending him this halfwit."

Mendel, flailing both arms, cried, "Please, without names."

Fishbein politely conceded.

"Where is open the door there we go in the house," the sick man said. "If you will kindly give me thirty-five dollars, God will bless you. What is thirty-five dollars to Mr. Fishbein? Nothing. To me, for my boy, is everything."

Fishbein drew himself up to his tallest height.

"Private contributions I don't make—only to institutions. This is my fixed policy."

Mendel sank to his creaking knees on the rug.

"Please, Mr. Fishbein, if not thirty-five, give maybe twenty."

"Levinson!" Fishbein angrily called.

The servant with the long sideburns appeared at the top of the stairs.

"Show this party where is the door—unless he wishes to partake food before leaving the premises."

"For what I got chicken won't cure it," Mendel said.

"This way if you please," said Levinson, descending.

Isaac assisted his father up.

"Take him to an institution," Fishbein advised over the marble balustrade. He ran quickly up the stairs and they were at once outside, buffeted by winds.

The walk to the subway was tedious. The wind blew mournfully. Mendel, breathless, glanced furtively at shadows. Isaac, clutching his peanuts in his frozen fist, clung to his father's side. They entered a small park to rest for a minute on a stone bench under a leafless two-branched tree. The thick right branch was raised, the thin left one hung down. A very pale moon rose slowly. So did a stranger as they approached the bench.

"Gut yuntif" [Happy holiday], he said hoarsely.

Mendel, drained of blood, waved his wasted arms. Isaac yowled sickly. Then a bell chimed and it was only ten. Mendel let out a piercing anguished cry as the bearded stranger disappeared into the bushes. A policeman came running, and though he beat the bushes with his nightstick, could turn up nothing. Mendel and Isaac hurried out of the little park. When Mendel glanced back the dead tree had its thin arm raised, the thick one down. He moaned.

They boarded a trolley, stopping at the home of a former friend, but he had died years ago. On the same block they went into a cafeteria and ordered two fried eggs for Isaac. The tables were crowded except where a heavy-set man sat eating soup with kasha. After one look at him they left in haste, although Isaac wept.

Mendel had another address on a slip of paper but the house was too far away, in Queens, so they stood in a doorway shivering.

What can I do, he frantically thought, in one short hour?

He remembered the furniture in the house. It was junk but might bring a few dollars. "Come, Isaac." They went once more to the pawnbroker's to talk to him, but the shop was dark and an iron gate—rings and gold watches glinting through it—was drawn tight across his place of business.

They huddled behind a telephone pole, both freezing. Isaac whimpered.

"See the big moon, Isaac. The whole sky is white."

He pointed but Isaac wouldn't look.

Mendel dreamed for a minute of the sky lit up, long sheets of light in all directions. Under the sky, in California, sat Uncle Leo drinking tea with lemon. Mendel felt warm but woke up cold.

Across the street stood an ancient brick synagogue.

He pounded on the huge door but no one appeared. He waited till he had breath and desperately knocked again. At last there were footsteps within, and the synagogue door creaked open on its massive brass hinges.

A darkly dressed sexton, holding a dripping candle, glared at them.

"Who knocks this time of night with so much noise on the synagogue door?"

Mendel told the sexton his troubles. "Please, I would like to speak to the rabbi."

"The rabbi is an old man. He sleeps now. His wife won't let you see him. Go home and come back tomorrow."

"To tomorrow I said goodbye already. I am a dying man."

Though the sexton seemed doubtful he pointed to an old wooden house next door. "In there he lives." He disappeared into the synagogue with his lit candle casting shadows around him.

Mendel, with Isaac clutching his sleeve, went up the wooden steps and rang the bell. After five minutes a big-faced, gray-haired bulky woman came out on the porch with a torn robe thrown over her nightdress. She emphatically said the rabbi was sleeping and could not be waked.

But as she was insisting, the rabbi himself tottered to the door. He listened a minute and said, "Who wants to see me let them come in."

They entered a cluttered room. The rabbi was an old skinny man with bent shoulders and a wisp of white beard. He wore a flannel nightgown and black skullcap; his feet were bare.

"Vey is mir" [Woe is me], his wife muttered. "Put on shoes or tomorrow comes sure pneumonia." She was a woman with a big belly, years younger than her husband. Staring at Isaac, she turned away.

Mendel apologetically related his errand. "All I need more is thirty-five dollars."

"Thirty-five?" said the rabbi's wife. "Why not thirty-five thousand? Who has so much money? My husband is a poor rabbi. The doctors take away every penny."

"Dear friend," said the rabbi, "if I had I would give you."

"I got already seventy," Mendel said, heavy-hearted. "All I need more is thirty-five."

"God will give you," said the rabbi.

"In the grave," said Mendel. "I need tonight. Come, Isaac."

"Wait," called the rabbi.

He hurried inside, came out with a fur-lined caftan, and handed it to Mendel.

"Yascha," shrieked his wife, "not your new coat!"

"I got my old one. Who needs two coats for one body?"

"Yascha, I am screaming—"

"Who can go among poor people, tell me, in a new coat?"

"Yascha," she cried, "what can this man do with your coat? He needs tonight the money. The pawnbrokers are asleep."

"So let him wake them up."

"No." She grabbed the coat from Mendel.

He held on to a sleeve, wrestling her for the coat. Her I know, Mendel thought. "Shylock," he muttered. Her eyes glittered.

The rabbi groaned and tottered dizzily. His wife cried out as Mendel yanked the coat from her hands.

"Run," cried the rabbi.

"Run, Isaac."

They ran out of the house and down the steps.

"Stop, you thief," called the rabbi's wife.

The rabbi pressed both hands to his temples and fell to the floor.

"Help!" his wife wept. "Heart attack! Help!"

But Mendel and Isaac ran through the streets with the rabbi's new fur-lined caftan. After them noiselessly ran Ginzburg.

It was very late when Mendel bought the train ticket in the only booth open.

There was no time to stop for a sandwich so Isaac ate his peanuts and they hurried to the train in the vast deserted station.

"So in the morning," Mendel gasped as they ran, "there comes a man that he sells sandwiches and coffee. Eat but get change. When reaches California the train, will be waiting for you on the station Uncle Leo. If you don't recognize him he will recognize you. Tell him I send best regards."

But when they arrived at the gate to the platform it was shut, the light out.

Mendel, groaning, beat on the gate with his fists.

"Too late," said the uniformed ticket collector, a bulky, bearded man with hairy nostrils and a fishy smell.

He pointed to the station clock. "Already past twelve."

"But I see standing there still the train," Mendel said, hopping in his grief.

"It just left—in one more minute."

"A minute is enough. Just open the gate."

"Too late I told you."

Mendel socked his bony chest with both hands. "With my whole heart I beg you this little favor."

"Favors you had enough already. For you the train is gone. You shoulda been dead already at midnight. I told you that yesterday. This is the best I can do."

"Ginzburg!" Mendel shrank from him.

"Who else?" The voice was metallic, eyes glittered, the expression amused.

"For myself," the old man begged, "I don't ask a thing. But what will happen to my boy?"

Ginzburg shrugged slightly. "What will happen happens. This isn't my responsibility. I got enough to think about without worrying about somebody on one cylinder."

"What then is your responsibility?"

"To create conditions. To make happen what happens. I ain't in the anthropomorphic business."

"Whatever business you in, where is your pity?"

"This ain't my commodity. The law is the law."

"Which law is this?"

"The cosmic universal law, goddamit, the one I got to follow myself."

"What kind of a law is it?" cried Mendel. "For God's sake, don't you understand what I went through in my life with this poor boy? Look at him. For thirty-nine years, since the day he was born, I wait for him to grow up, but he don't. Do you understand what this means in a father's heart? Why don't you let him go to his uncle?" His voice had risen and he was shouting.

Isaac mewled loudly.

"Better calm down or you'll hurt somebody's feelings," Ginzburg said with a wink toward Isaac.

"All my life," Mendel cried, his body trembling, "what did I have? I was poor. I suffered from my health. When I worked I worked too hard. When I didn't work was worse. My wife died a young woman. But I didn't ask from anybody nothing. Now I ask a small favor. Be so kind, Mr. Ginzburg."

The ticket collector was picking his teeth with a match stick.

"You ain't the only one, my friend, some got it worse than you. That's how it goes in this country."

"You dog you." Mendel lunged at Ginzburg's throat and began to choke. "You bastard, don't you understand what it means human?"

They struggled nose to nose, Ginzburg, though his astonished eyes bulged, began to laugh. "You pipsqueak nothing. I'll freeze you to pieces."

His eyes lit in rage and Mendel felt an unbearable cold like an icy dagger invading his body, all of his parts shriveling.

Now I die without helping Isaac.

A crowd gathered. Isaac yelped in fright.

Clinging to Ginzburg in his last agony, Mendel saw reflected in the ticket collector's eyes the depth of his terror. But he saw that Ginzburg, staring at himself in Mendel's eyes, saw mirrored in them the extent of his own awful wrath. He beheld a shimmering, starry, blinding light that produced darkness.

Ginzburg looked astounded. "Who me?"

His grip on the squirming old man slowly loosened, and Mendel, his heart barely beating, slumped to the ground.

"Go." Ginzburg muttered, "take him to the train."

"Let pass," he commanded a guard.

The crowd parted. Isaac helped his father up and they tottered down the steps to the platform where the train waited, lit and ready to go.

Mendel found Isaac a coach seat and hastily embraced him. "Help Uncle Leo, Isaakil. Also remember your father and mother."

"Be nice to him," he said to the conductor. "Show him where everything is."

He waited on the platform until the train began slowly to move. Isaac sat at the edge of his seat, his face strained in the direction of his journey. When the train was gone, Mendel ascended the stairs to see what had become of Ginzburg.

QUESTIONS

1. Can this story be read as a religious drama? In this connection, consider the rabbi, the only person who helps Mendel. His compassion and his indifference to material things reveal him as a man of God. What does the supernatural Ginzburg represent?   **2.** What is the significance of the fact that Isaac, for whom Mendel is determined to provide before death claims him, is an idiot?   **3.** Mendel wins his battle with Ginzburg. What does that victory signify?

WRITING TOPIC

How do the various episodes in this story establish Mendel's character and prepare the reader for the final, climactic confrontation between Mendel and Ginzburg?

Looking for a Rain God

1977

BESSIE HEAD [1937–1986]

It is lonely at the lands where the people go to plough. These lands are vast clearings in the bush, and the wild bush is lonely too. Nearly all the lands are within walking distance from the village. In some parts of the bush where the underground water is very near the surface, people made little rest camps for themselves and dug shallow wells to quench their thirst while on their journey to their own lands. They experienced all kinds of things once they left the village. They could rest at shady watering places full of lush, tangled trees with delicate pale-gold and purple wildflowers springing up between soft green moss and the children could hunt around for wild figs and any berries that might be in season. But from 1958, a seven-year drought fell upon the land and even the watering places began to look as dismal as the dry open thornbush country; the leaves of the trees curled up and withered; the moss became dry and hard and, under the shade of the tangled trees, the ground turned a powdery black and white, because there was no rain. People said rather humorously that if you tried to catch the rain in a cup it would only fill a teaspoon. Toward the beginning of the seventh year of drought, the summer had become an anguish to live through. The air was so dry and moisture-free that it burned the skin. No one knew what to do to escape the heat and tragedy was in the air. At the beginning of that summer, a number of men just went out of their homes and hung themselves to death from trees. The majority of the people had lived off crops, but for two years past they had all returned from the lands with only their rolled-up skin blankets and cooking utensils. Only the charlatans, incanters, and witch doctors made a pile of money during this time because people were always turning to them in desperation for little talismans and herbs to rub on the plough for the crops to grow and the rain to fall.

The rains were late that year. They came in early November, with a promise of good rain. It wasn't the full, steady downpour of the years of good rain but thin, scanty, misty rain. It softened the earth and a rich growth of green things sprang up everywhere for the animals to eat. People were called to the center of the village to hear the proclamation of the beginning of the ploughing season; they stirred themselves and whole families began to move off to the lands to plough.

The family of the old man, Mokgobja, were among those who left early for the lands. They had a donkey cart and piled everything onto it, Mokgobja—who was over seventy years old; two girls, Neo and Boseyong; their mother Tiro and an unmarried sister, Nesta; and the father and supporter of the family, Ramadi, who drove the donkey cart. In the rush of the first hope of rain, the man, Ramadi, and the two women, cleared the land of thornbush and then hedged their vast ploughing area with this same thornbush to protect the future crop from the goats they had brought along for milk. They cleared out and deepened the old well with its pool of muddy water and still in this light, misty rain, Ramadi inspanned two oxen and turned the earth over with a hand plough.

The land was ready and ploughed, waiting for the crops. At night, the earth was alive with insects singing and rustling about in search of food. But suddenly, by mid-November, the rain flew away; the rain clouds fled away and left the sky bare. The sun danced dizzily in the sky, with a strange cruelty. Each day the land was covered in a haze of mist as the sun sucked up the last drop of moisture out of the earth. The family sat down in despair, waiting and waiting. Their hopes had run so high; the goats had started producing milk, which they had eagerly poured on their porridge, now they ate plain porridge with no milk. It was impossible to plant the corn, maize, pumpkin, and watermelon seeds in the dry earth. They sat the whole day in the shadow of the huts and even stopped thinking, for the rain had fled away. Only the children, Neo and Boseyong, were quite happy in their little-girl world. They carried on their game of making house like their mother and chattered to each other in light, soft tones. They made children from sticks around which they tied rags, and scolded them severely in an exact imitation of their own mother. Their voices could be heard scolding the day long: "You stupid thing, when I send you to draw water, why do you spill half of it out of the bucket!" "You stupid thing! Can't you mind the porridge pot without letting the porridge burn!" And then they would beat the rag dolls on their bottoms with severe expressions.

The adults paid no attention to this; they did not even hear the funny chatter; they sat waiting for rain; their nerves were stretched to the breaking-point willing the rain to fall out of the sky. Nothing was important, beyond that. All their animals had been sold during the bad years to purchase food, and of all their herd only two goats were left. It was the women of the family who finally broke down under the strain of waiting for rain. It was really the two women who caused the death of the little girls. Each night they started a weird, high-pitched wailing that began on a low, mournful note and whipped up to a frenzy. Then they would stamp their feet and shout as though they had lost their heads. The men sat quiet and self-controlled; it was important for men to maintain their self control at all times but their nerve was breaking too. They knew the women were haunted by the starvation of the coming year.

Finally, an ancient memory stirred in the old man, Mokgobja. When he was very young and the customs of the ancestors still ruled the land, he had been witness to a rain-making ceremony. And he came alive a little, struggling to recall the details which had been buried by years and years of prayer in a Christian church. As soon as the mists cleared a little, he began consulting in whispers with his youngest son, Ramadi. There was, he said, a certain rain god who accepted only the sacrifice of the bodies of children. Then the rain would fall; then the crops would grow, he said. He explained the ritual and as he talked, his memory became a conviction and he began to talk with unshakable authority. Ramadi's nerves were smashed by the nightly wailing of the women and soon the two men began whispering with the two women. The children continued their game: "You stupid thing! How could you have lost the money on the way to the shop! You must have been playing again!"

After it was all over and the bodies of the two little girls had been spread across the land, the rain did not fall. Instead, there was a deathly silence at night and the devouring heat of the sun by day. A terror, extreme and deep, overwhelmed the whole family. They packed, rolling up their skin blankets and pots, and fled back to the village.

People in the village soon noted the absence of the two little girls. They had died at the lands and were buried there, the family said. But people noted their ashen, terror-stricken faces and a murmur arose. What had killed the children, they wanted to know? And the family replied they had just died. And people said amongst themselves that it was strange that the two deaths had occurred at the same time. And there was a feeling of great unease at the unnatural looks of the family. Soon the police came around. The family told them the same story of death and burial at the lands. They did not know what the children had died of. So the police asked to see the graves. At this, the mother of the children broke down and told everything.

Throughout that terrible summer the story of the children hung like a dark cloud of sorrow over the village, and the sorrow was not assuaged when the old man and Ramadi were sentenced to death for ritual murder. All they had on the statute books was that ritual murder was against the law and must be stamped out with the death penalty. The subtle story of strain and starvation and breakdown was inadmissible evidence at court; but all the people who lived off the crops knew in their hearts that only a hair's breadth had saved them from sharing a fate similar to that of the Mokgobja family. They could have killed something to make the rain fall.

QUESTIONS

1 Characterize the lives of the people in the story. What do they live on? What are the consequences of the long drought?   **2.** How do the two little girls' games affect you as a reader?   **3.** Consider the story's final paragraph. Do you feel the men should be executed? Explain.

WRITING TOPICS

1. Look up the references to animal and human sacrifices in the Hebrew Bible. As well, consider Christianity's view of the crucifixion of Jesus. In an essay, discuss the history of blood sacrifices in the Judeo-Christian tradition. Who performed them? Why?   **2.** Write a reminiscence about a crisis in your own life and discuss the "sacrifices" you offered in exchange for a resolution of your problem.

Rough Translations   1985

MOLLY GILES   [b. 1942]

There was so much to do that Ramona felt dizzy, and when Ramona felt dizzy, Ramona lay down; once down she stayed for the count and then some. Shadow and sun took their turns on her ceiling, the phone rang unanswered, a Mozart sonata spun silently on the turntable by the window. Ramona dozed, and dreamed she was dancing. When she awoke she found her own hands clinging to her own ribs as if for dear life. It's the funeral, she decided. It's the funeral that's killing me.

She must have spoken out loud because her son Potter stared from the doorway. He was balancing a bag of groceries in one arm and his pet cat and violin case in the other. In his slipped-down glasses and long brown ponytail he looked as careworn as any young housewife, and Ramona felt the familiar urge to apologize, an urge she stifled with a shamed little laugh and a wave from the pillows. If my timing had been better, she thought, Potter could be touring Europe right now, playing music with his friends, having some fun . . . can Potter have fun? Potter frowned and said, "What is it? You okay?"

"Alive," Ramona cried gaily, "and kicking." She lifted one moccasined foot to demonstrate and knocked the phone book off the bedspread. Potter's frown deepened. He had never smiled at Ramona's jokes, nor had his sister Nora; finding their mother unamusing was the one trait they shared. Sometimes Ramona thought: It's because they can't forgive me. Other times she thought: It's because they have no sense of humor. She watched as Potter, frowning, put down his burdens and moved into her room. He snapped the record player off, drew the curtains closed, turned the lamp on, plumped her pillows, and pressed his lips gingerly to her forehead to feel her temperature. Ramona, tucked under his chin like a violin being tuned, tried to sound the right note. "I had the funniest dream," she said, but even as she began to tell the dream she saw Potter didn't think it was funny; his face was so pained she started to lie. One lie, as always, led to another, and down she went, deeper and deeper. "So there I was," she finished, breathless, "tap-dancing among the gravestones like Ginger Rogers in a horror film. Isn't that a scream?"

"It might make a good drawing for *The Beacon*," Potter said. Ramona bowed her head, contrite. She knew what Potter thought of her drawings. She had heard him describe the cartoons she did for the village weekly as "illustrated idioms, the kind you find on cocktail napkins," which she supposed was a fair description—not kind, but fair. A few days before, propped up in bed, she had finished her last assignment: a pen and ink sketch of a little ark floating on a sea of question marks with a caption that read "Flooded by Doubts." Her very favorite submission, "Tour de Force," had showed a docent dragging a group of tourists through the Louvre at gunpoint, and it was true she had seen a cartoon much like it etched onto a highball glass at the church rummage sale; she had bought the glass, of course, and pitched it into a garbage bin at once. She tried now to imagine how she would draw her dancing dream. She'd sketch herself as she was: a small, wide-eyed old woman with bad posture and a frizz of gray bangs. She'd dress herself in a straw hat and tux and set herself among the headstones at Valley View . . . Valley View? Was that right? Was that the cemetery she had finally decided on? Or was that the one where Hale had been buried? Should she be buried by Hale after all? Would he want her there? Would he let her stay? Her fingers started to clutch at her ribs again, and again she sighed and said, "So much to do. So many decisions. I hope you never have to go through this, Potter."

"Right," said Potter. He replaced the phone book on the bed, gave Ramona another of his shy hard stares, and left with the cat meowing at his heels to start cooking their dinner.

Ramona reached for her glasses, picked up the phone book, and turned again to the back. She had memorized the five listings for Funerals, but she had not yet found the nerve to dial. She stared at the ads again, narrowing in on the Manis Funeral Home, which said, "Call at Any Time," and The Evergreens, which advertised air-conditioned chapels. The air-conditioning tempted her, for the summer afternoons had been growing warm, but when she finally started to dial and her finger slipped, she took it as an omen. She did not think the Manis Home, despite its insistence, should receive calls at dinner time; she'd call them tomorrow too.

She fell into her old habit of reading the phone book, leafing through the classifieds for Mourners, then for Paid Professional Mourners, then finally for Mummers. She still wondered where Hale had found that little blonde who wept so competently at his graveside—a waitress Ramona had not been told about? an extra secretary? How delicious it would be, she thought, if I could hire the equivalent of that little blonde—some good-looking young boy, an acting student down on his luck . . . someone who would be willing to fling himself down on the coffin . . . She shivered happily, thinking how that would shock Nora, and then, penitent, she reached for the phone again and dialed Nora's number, the words "I hate to bother you" already forming on her lips. She knew Nora would be busy. Nora was always busy. Right now, Ramona feared, Nora would be kneading a loaf of whole wheat bran bread, knitting a sweater, cutting the baby's hair, balancing her husband's business accounts, checking the twins' homework, and drafting a proposal for a new gymnasium while her old mother, with nothing better to do, lay slumped in a filthy bathrobe on an unmade bed covered with overdue library books, wanting a chat. Oh Lord, Ramona thought, gazing around her cluttered room, but Potter and I live like two French whores, underwear everywhere, and jars full of dead roses. I can never have the funeral here. The best thing to do is go to Nora's at once and get buried in Nora's backyard like a pet hamster in a shoe box.

"I can't decide between the Manis or The Evergreens," she said, when Nora picked up the phone. "How can I find out which one is the best?"

"I'll find out for you," Nora said. "Next?"

Nora's knitting needles clicked like static on the other end of the line while Ramona tried to think of something else to ask for. "Medication?" Nora suggested. "Has Potter been giving you the right medication?"

"I think so." Ramona glanced at the bottle by the bed, rechecked it to be sure it was labeled for her and not the cat, and leaned back. "It's just planning this funeral."

"Do you know what I'd do about that funeral if I were you?" Nora said. Ramona waited, grateful.

"I'd forget it," Nora said. "I'd file it away in my Not-to-Worry drawer."

"Not-to-Worry drawer?"

"That's right. I'd file it away and swallow the key. Do you understand?"

"I'm not a child," Ramona began, but Nora, her voice flat, sweet, and dangerous, said, "Have Potter cook you some real food for once. I'll come by and see you in the morning. I don't like the idea of you thinking about your funeral all day. It's not healthy."

Not healthy? thought Ramona. That's a good one. She said good-bye to Nora and lay back. Her heart began to race and her fingers raced too, drumming and tapping on top of the phone book. What should she do, what should she do? Perhaps there was still enough time to go crazy? She had always meant to spend her last days tiptoeing around in a flowered hat with a fingertip pressed to her lips, but no luck. These were her last days and she felt no crazier than usual. She felt as she always had when there were decisions to be made: harassed and dreamy, wildly anxious and unable to move. She reached up to twist one earring off, realizing, with dismay, that one was all she was wearing; in her haste to prove she could still dress herself she had forgotten to put on the other. Her bathrobe buttons—were they closed? They were. She wished she could push a button and make herself disappear, right now, before her body became a burden to them all, before they learned how complicated, dull, and expensive it was to dispose of even a small person's final remains.

"You know who I admire?" she said to Potter as she joined him in the kitchen for dinner. "Junie Poole. Junie sat down in the hall outside the coroner's office one night and tried to kill herself by drinking a thermos of gin mixed with pills. When they arrested her she was too drunk to talk, but they found this note pinned to her mink coat saying she hoped her children would appreciate the fact that she had at least taken herself to the morgue. Of course, no one's appreciated anything Junie's ever done, before or since, but that's not the point. The point is that she did try to make things easy for her family. I want to make things easy too." She picked up her fork and looked down at her plate. "Liver? Won't Nora be impressed." She tried to eat a little. But when she saw the cat, in the corner, licking from an identical plate, she put the fork down and regarded Potter, who had done this to her before, once with canned salmon and once with pickled herring. He was either trying to be very economical or his values were more confused than she suspected. "Potter," she said, watching the old gray cat huddled murmurously over its plate, "do you think I should just crawl off to the woods?"

"There aren't any woods within crawling distance," said Potter. Ramona smiled; Potter did not. "I think . . ." Potter began. He stopped. Ramona folded her hands and waited. Potter, born when she was over forty, had been a talkative child, full of ideas and advice and so original that even Hale had paid attention, but Potter had stopped talking years ago, at least to her. "I think," Potter repeated, one thin hand fluttering before his downcast face, "that you are using this funeral to mask your real feelings."

Ramona waited, her own head bent. "And what are my real feelings?" she asked at last.

"Rage," Potter said, his shy eyes severe behind his smudged glasses. "Terror. Awe. Grief. Self-pity."

"Heavens," said Ramona. She was impressed. Once again she wished she were the mother her children deserved, and once again she found herself having to tell them she was not. "I'm afraid, Potter," she said, "you give me credit. I don't feel any more of those 'real' feelings now than I ever have. What I feel now is a sort of social panic, the same old panic I used to feel when Hale wanted me to give a dinner party for his clients and the guests would arrive and I'd still be in my slip clutching a bucket of live lobsters. I'm sorry, dear, I can't eat this. I'm too nervous. I'm going to have to make a list."

She sat at her drawing desk, staring at a piece of paper, wondering where to start after printing "To File in the Worry Drawer" across the top of the page. In the next room Potter talked to Nora on the telephone, his voice reluctant and slow. If only my children liked each other, Ramona thought. She sighed and pressed her palm to a few of the places that hurt. Sometimes the pains were gone for hours altogether and sometimes they felt like ripping cloth; sometimes they widened and sometimes they narrowed and sometimes they overwhelmed her completely. Right now she was being treated to a new pain, a persistent jabbing in her chest that tapped back and forth like an admonishing finger. It feels like I'm being lectured by a bully, she thought. Lectured on my failures. If I had been lovable, Hale would have loved me, and if Hale had loved me, I would have loved myself, and if I'd loved myself, Nora would have loved me, and if Nora had loved me, Potter would have loved her, and then Potter wouldn't have had to grow up loving nothing but his music and his wretched cat. Hale and I, she thought, set a bad example for the children as far as loving went . . . the children! she thought. She pushed her chair back and stood up. "Tell Nora," she called out to Potter, "tell Nora I'm sorry but this is going to be an adults-only funeral, X-rated, no grandchildren allowed. Maybe the boys, but by no means the twins. By no means the baby. I've seen little children at funerals before," she added, when Potter finally returned from the phone, "and it's no picnic, believe me."

"Nora said to give you this." He handed Ramona a mug of warm milk and his eyes were so sad that she drank it all down even though there was a cat whisker floating on top.

That night Ramona dreamed her funeral was held outdoors on the slope of a mountain; it was a bright summer afternoon and everyone she'd ever cared about was there: her parents, her grandparents, Hale, all her friends from childhood on. She was there herself, hovering in the sky like a Chagall[1] bride, her pretty shroud rippling around her crossed ankles. She had never felt so happy. Tables set up under flowering trees were laden with cakes and roasts and sparkling wines; music came from somewhere; there were rainbows, fountains. The conversations she overheard made her laugh with pleasure; people were saying kind, affectionate, funny things to each other, some of them so wonderful, so insightful, that Ramona could scarcely wait to wake up and write them down.

Half-asleep, she groped for pencil and pad and quickly, in the dark, jotted down every scrap of conversation she could remember. In the morning, unsurprised, she studied her notes. They were illegible, as frail and choppy as an EKG. Lost, she thought. Like everything else. Lost like all the words I've tried to string together throughout my life. For a brief, bitter second she thought of all the poems, stories, prayers, and revelations that had evaporated like breath in cold air when she tried to express them. I have never said anything right, she decided. Even my jokes, even the drawings I do for *The Beacon* are wrong—rough translations of a foreign language I hear but cannot master.

She took her pen and quickly tied all the choppy lines on the paper together, making a scrawl across the top, and then she drew herself at the bottom of the page, an anxious old lady staring straight up, and then she wrote "Over My Dead Body" and tore the paper up.

She took the day's second dose of Percodan into her palm and thought again of Junie Poole passed out in front of the coroner's office. It was then she saw how her own funeral truly would be: a small gathering of silent relatives sitting in uncomfortable pews in a little Consolation Chapel somewhere. Pink and yellow light would fall through the stained-glass window over the casket where she lay. The air would smell unwholesomely floral. Muzak would be piped in. She would be wearing an evening gown that Nora, at the last minute, would have had to alter to fit, a terrible dress, mauve, with long sleeves and net at the neck. Her nails would be painted mauve to match, and her lips. Her five grandchildren would be wild with horror and boredom. The boys would be thinking about basketball and sex, basketball and sex. The twins would be cracking their knuckles, glancing cross-eyed at each other, giggling. The baby, whose damp quick hands were never still, would be digging a design into the plush seat with a thumbnail, a design no one but the baby would know was a skull and red flames. Nora would be shushing and clucking the children as she counted the heads in the chapel, trying to decide if she had made enough potato salad. A minister chosen by Nora's husband would give a speech. The

---

[1] Marc Chagall (1889–1985) was a Russian-born French painter who often depicted people floating in the sky.

minister would say that Ramona was in a far better place than she had been before. Potter, picking cat hair off his pressed blue jeans, would think about this. He would regret he had not gone to Europe with his friends when he had the chance; he could be in a better place, too, he would think, if it weren't for his mother. After the ceremony the mourners would bunch on the sidewalk in the sun, ill-at-ease and restless . . . and I'll still be lying beneath the pink and yellow lights, Ramona thought, reeking of hairspray and formaldehyde—and the garnet necklace I want Nora to save for the baby will still be around my neck, forgotten in that damn mauve net.

She eased herself out of bed, walked unsteadily toward her closet, opened the door, and peered in. The darkness surprised her. At first she could not see the mauve dress and she even had a wild hope she had thrown it out, years ago, but then she saw it, hanging in its plastic bag like a hideous orchid. As she reached up to strike it off the clothes rod, she lost her balance and fainted forward. It was so strange to fall face forward into soft dark clothes that when she came to she was not even frightened. She tried to tell Potter how strange it had been, how comfortable, how sexy really, like falling into outheld arms, like dancing. Oh but that time Hale twirled her at the Christmas party and she was feeling almost beautiful that night and so deeply in love and as she came out of the twirl Hale turned to another woman, neglecting to catch her, and she lost her balance and spun across the dance floor, all the colored lights a blur, and she was completely alone and she was laughing, even before she fell and cracked her coccyx she was laughing, prepared for the laughter of others, prepared to say, "It's all right, I'm not hurt a bit," even though it wasn't all right, even though she *was* hurt a bit. Quite a bit. Always after that she saw herself as Hale saw her: a clumsy woman with breasts that were too big and lips that were too wide and little awkward hands that couldn't hold a man. She saw herself as someone who could be dropped. "Oh Ramona bounces back," Hale drawled and didn't she though, bouncing back like any old kickball. Well, the secret was not to take yourself too seriously. No matter where they kicked you it couldn't hurt if you didn't let it, if you got right down there with the dancing shoes and laughed—if you could do that, you could rise like a rose in the air when they toed you.

"I have something to say," she said to Potter. "I have a statement to make. Are you ready? You should write this down. It's very important. Listen, Potter. Words of wisdom: Lie low. Move fast. Bounce."

"Don't try to talk," Potter said. He knelt beside her, stroking her forehead with the same light scratchy touch he used on the cat. "Don't keep making jokes. You don't have to be funny any more. Just breathe slow. Relax."

Ramona flushed with temper and turned her head away. She could not relax. She was angry at Potter and at Hale and at Nora and at herself too, angry at everything that wasn't funny any more, angry at everyone who had let her down, down, so far down that when young Dr. Seton stood up from the chair by her bed it was as if he were stretching up toward the ceiling and she was sinking down through the floor, sinking faster and faster, and only the thought of her funeral made her stop: the last straw, she thought, and wouldn't you know it's the one straw I reach for. "Good girl," Dr. Seton said. "You're coming back to us."

Coming back? Of course she was coming back. How could she leave? There was so much to do. There was her life to understand and Hale to forgive and Nora to charm and Potter to cheer up. There was the novel. Where was the novel? Lying in a cardboard box somewhere, half-alive, unfinished, unformed. There were all the paintings, the little canvasses of pastel flower arrangements that Hale had called "stillborns" instead of "still lifes"—where were those? Facing the walls of the garage? She didn't want anyone seeing those paintings; she didn't want anyone reading the journal she had kept in the first years after Hale's death, or playing the tapes she had made of her own voice, singing her own songs to her own accompaniment on an old guitar. She was not ready to be judged; her work wasn't done yet; it wasn't begun; she didn't even know what her work was, for God's sake. "You seem to have developed a faintly comedic point of view," her last art teacher had told her. "Have you thought of doing cartoons?" And he had dismissed her, turning his head, stifling his yawn; he had dropped her, not bothering to watch the direction of his kick, nor the way it hooked, nor the way she bounced, landing on both flat, splayed, calloused feet before the editor of *The Beacon* with a sheaf of drawings in one shaking hand. She had an occupation now. But was that her work?

"Those cartoons," she said, looking up into Nora's puzzled face, "those cartoons were the hardest things I ever did and they were never what I meant to do. I meant to do something quite important and beautiful with my life, you see—something that would astonish and delight and make you all proud."

"Still trying to talk," Nora said. "Half-alive and she's still trying to talk. She's probably worried we're going to take her to the hospital. Well, don't worry, Mother. Dr. Seton said you might as well stay here—although why you'd want to, I'm sure I don't know. The house is a mess. It's filthy dirty and there's nothing in the cupboards but cat food. I've sent the boys out to rake the yard and the twins are making cocoa, and the baby, here's the baby, the baby will keep you company while I discuss a few things with Potter. And his cat."

After Nora left the room, the baby—a lanky, curt, fast-moving four-year-old whose given name, Hope, was so unsuitable that Ramona had never been able to use it—sidled close and peered down into Ramona's face. "Ba?" said Ramona. It was all she could say. "Ba? Ah wa pa."

"You. Want. Paper," the child repeated.

Ramona pointed toward her desk and Hope tugged at the drawers until she found the drawing supplies. She gave Ramona one pad and one pencil and then, engrossed, she chose a thicker pad, a sharper pencil, for herself. Ramona struggled upright in her bed. For a long time she and Hope sat quietly, thinking. Then Hope ducked over her pad and started to draw a city. Ramona sat immobile. Even if I try, she thought, I won't succeed. I've never been able to organize my life; how dare I attempt to order my death? My funeral will be as disastrous a failure as my childhood, my marriage, my motherhood, my dotage. There will be the same dry coughs, the same scraping of chairs, the same artificial smiles I've seen all my life. I'll be put to rest like all the rest, and no one will ever know how much I had to give the world, or how I longed to give it. She glanced at her granddaughter's page. Hope had finished the city and was peopling it quickly with vampires and werewolves. It's enough to make the old blood stagger, Ramona thought. In the next room Potter and Nora were arguing. The smell of burnt cocoa drifted in from the kitchen. Ramona dozed. She dreamt Hale was in bed with her, asleep, his back turned to her, his weight warm, familiar, a great comfort, and she snuggled close, glad to have him there but afraid to wake him, afraid he might awaken saying some other woman's name.

When she opened her eyes it was dark in the house. She turned on her light, picked up the pad and pencil, and began to write. She had just had the one idea that would make her funeral the successful occasion she knew it could be. She knew the music, the foods, the psalm, the location. She wrote quickly, covering the page. She wrote until she had said everything she had to say, and then, content, she slipped the paper into the top drawer of her nightstand, lay back, and slept.

It was a restless, busy, broken sleep and it seemed to go on for a long long time. Dreams came and went, some of them nightmares, some so full of light she fought to stay in them. Nora nursed her with unsmiling vigilance, bathing and dressing her with swift cool hands. Nora's children took over the house, the boys mowing and trimming the lawn, the twins scrubbing the kitchen and bathrooms. Only the baby refused to pitch in. She sat at the desk beside Ramona's bed, covering page after page with intricate, disordered drawings. Potter too ignored Nora's orders; he locked himself in his room with the cat and tuned and retuned his violin. Ramona, listening to him play over the sound of the vacuum and the dishwasher, felt a robot was playing to her from the moon, so strange and cold and simple the music. Sometimes one of the children would drag a chair to the bureau and bring her the photos she asked for—portraits of Hale, his smile lean, gleaming, and enticing as ever, group pictures of old school friends standing arm in arm in sunny gardens, photos of her own children as children and herself as child, girl, and mother. When Ramona looked from these pictures to the face in the mirror Nora held up, she was pleased. She finally had a face she liked, sharp-boned, flushed, with enormous eyes—a stylish face, at last. She still could not speak clearly enough to be understood and when visitors told her she looked beautiful she could only tip her head, a queen accepting homage. There's a price tag to all this glamour, she wanted to tell them. Nothing big. A pay-later plan.

One afternoon Nora said, "Come on, Potter, help me for once. I want to carry Mother outside." The two of them linked hands and carried Ramona out into the garden, pausing to point out the bright banks of amaryllis and filling her bathrobe skirts with Japanese plums from the unpruned trees against the fence. Ramona looked into their pale distracted faces and said, "If you two would just like each other a little, I think I could go to heaven this second," and Nora said, "Still trying to talk? I wish she'd give up," and Potter said, "She can't give up; she's tough; she's not like us," and Nora said, "Speak for yourself; I don't slop around feeling sorry for myself all day," and Potter said, "That's because you don't know how to feel anything, period," and they carried Ramona into the house and dropped her on the bed a little too roughly. That night Potter announced that since Nora had taken over so well, he was leaving. He was moving in with another unemployed musician who had a house by the sea. "I'd like to move to a house by the sea," Ramona said suddenly, and this first clear sentence after weeks of gibberish made Potter turn and Nora stop in mid-sentence. "I'd like to go there right now," Ramona said, "and never come back."

"Don't make me cry," Nora said sharply.

"She means she wants to die," Potter said.

"I know what she means," Nora said.

Potter picked up the cat and held it close to his heart, then laid it by Ramona's side like a bouquet of gray flowers. Nora came and stood beside them. "She's asleep again," Nora said. "No I'm not," Ramona said. "There's so much I've wanted to tell her," Nora said. "But I don't have her gift. I've never known how to put things."

"Well," Ramona answered, pleased, "I thank you and I think I finally have put things in place myself. I've taken care of everything at last." But nobody heard her. It was dark in her room and she was alone. Why look at me, she thought. I've gone and died with my big mouth wide open. She started to laugh and in that same second she started to spin, which made her laugh harder, for she knew that with this last breath she would fall, fall and break herself and bounce, bounce far beyond laughter forever.

The cat leapt off the bed and meowed for Potter, but Potter and Nora were sitting in the kitchen drinking coffee together and talking about a time when they had both thought their mother the gayest and most beautiful woman in the world, their father the richest and kindest man. The only one who heard the cat cry was the baby. The baby had slipped from her sleeping bag and was prowling through the house, searching for paper. She let herself into Ramona's room and went to the desk, but the drawers were depleted, all paper gone. In the top drawer of the nightstand by the bed she found some paper, one side ruined by her grandmother's writing, but the other side fresh and clean. She turned to the clean side and went to the window. Squatting in the moonlight with the cat winding around her, the baby drew the dream that had awakened her: a woman shooting off the edge of the planet, her lips like two red wings, flapping up toward the stars. She studied the drawing, shook her head, and tore it up.

Nora made the arrangements for the funeral. It didn't take long. She was pretty sure she knew what her mother wanted. She found a long purplish evening dress in the closet that looked brand new, and she gave it with instructions for matching nail polish to the cosmetician at The Evergreens. Her husband knew a minister who agreed to say a few words. After the service, which was mercifully short for such a warm afternoon, the mourners were asked to return to the house for refreshments. Most of the mourners seemed to be truly mourning; some of them were weeping. Ramona had been so brave, they said, so uncomplaining. She had kept her sense of humor to the end, they said, and they paused to study the display of drawings from *The Beacon*, their faces long and somber. The cat wandered companionably through the crowd. Potter sat in the garden with his violin, playing a song that everyone knew but no one could place. The notes seemed to come together in little rushes, rise, fade off, rush in again. "My Mother's Voice," Potter said, when the minister asked the name of the piece. The baby, swaying to the music, pushed open the door of Ramona's room, climbed the chair by the bureau, brought down all the photographs, and dropped them out the window, chanting "Bury Bury" as they fluttered down. She was about to throw a garnet necklace out too when her father caught her and gave her a spanking. Nora, handsome in black, was too busy to pay attention to her daughter's screams; she was telling everyone how childlike Ramona had seemed toward the end, how dependent and docile. "It was as if I were the mother . . ." Nora began, but she was interrupted by a large lady named Junie Poole who hugged her impulsively, spilling gin down her dress. "This is the best funeral I've ever been to," Junie declared, and although the others turned away to hide their smiles, they all said later they agreed. It was a good funeral. The weather was fine and sunny, the house was welcoming. The only thing missing was Ramona herself.

QUESTIONS

1. Do Potter's and Nora's attitudes toward their mother's dying differ? Explain.   **2.** What do Ramona's dreams tell us about her state of mind?   **3.** What does Ramona mean when she characterizes her work as a "rough translation of a foreign language I hear but cannot master"?   **4.** What role does Junie Poole play in the story?

WRITING TOPIC

Is the reader meant to accept as accurate Ramona's evaluation of her life as a failure?

Preparation

1992

ROBERT OLEN BUTLER [b. 1945]

Though Thūy's dead body was naked under the sheet, I had not seen it since we were girls together and our families took us to the beaches of Nha Trang. This was so even though she and I were best friends for all our lives and she became the wife of Lê Văn Lý, the man I once loved. Thūy had a beautiful figure and breasts that were so tempting in the tight bodice of our aó dàis[1] that Lý could not resist her. But the last time I saw Thūy's naked body, she had no breasts yet at all, just the little brown nubs that I also had at seven years old, and we ran in the white foam of the breakers and we watched the sampans out beyond the coral reefs.

We were not common girls, the ones who worked the fields and seemed so casual about their bodies. And more than that, we were Catholics, and Mother Mary was very modest, covered from her throat to her ankles, and we made up our toes beautifully, like the statue of Mary in the church, and we were very modest about all the rest. Except Thūy could seem naked when she was clothed. We both ran in the same surf, but somehow her flesh learned something there that mine did not. She could move like the sea, her body filled her clothes like the living sea, fluid and beckoning. Her mother was always worried about her because the boys grew quiet at her approach and noisy at her departure, and no one was worried about me. I was an expert pair of hands, to bring together the herbs for the lemon grass chicken or to serve the tea with the delicacy of a wind chime or to scratch the eucalyptus oil into the back of a sick child.

And this won for me a good husband, though he was not Lê Văn Lý, nor could ever have been. But he was a good man and a surprised man to learn that my hands could also make him very happy even if my breasts did not seem so delightful in the tight bodice of my aó dài. That man died in the war which came to our country, a war we were about to lose, and I took my sons to America and I settled in this place in New Orleans called Versailles that has only Vietnamese. Soon my best friend Thūy also came to this place, with her husband Lê Văn Lý and her children. They left shortly for California, but after three years they returned, and we all lived another decade together and we expected much longer than that, for Thūy and I would have become fifty years old within a week of each other next month.

Except that Thūy was dead now and lying before me in this place that Mr. Hoa, the mortician for our community, called the "preparation room," and she

---

[1] The national dress of Vietnamese women. It consists of an ankle length dress with a tight bodice, slit to the hip on both sides. It is worn over loose black slacks.

was waiting for me to put the makeup on her face and comb her hair for the last time. She died very quickly, but she knew enough to ask for the work of my hands to make her beautiful in the casket. She let on to no one—probably not even herself—when the signs of the cancer growing in her ovaries caused no pain. She was a fearful person over foolish little things, and such a one as that will sometimes ignore the big things until it is too late. But thank God that when the pain did come and the truth was known, the end came quickly afterward.

She clutched my hand in the hospital room, the curtain drawn around us, and my own grip is very strong, but on that morning she hurt me with the power of her hand. This was a great surprise to me. I looked at our locked hands, and her lovely, slender fingers were white with the strength in them and yet the nails were still perfect, each one a meticulously curved echo of the others, each one carefully stroked with the red paint the color of her favorite Winesap apples. This was a very sad moment for me. It made me sadder even than the sounds of her pain, this hand with its sudden fearful strength and yet the signs of her lovely vanity still there.

But I could not see her hands as I stood beside her in the preparation room. They were somewhere under the sheet and I had work to do, so I looked at her face. Her closed eyes showed the mostly Western lids, passed down by more than one Frenchman among her ancestors. This was a very attractive thing about her, I always knew, though Lý never mentioned her eyes, even though they were something he might well have complimented in public. He could have said to people, "My wife has such beautiful eyes," but he did not. And his certain regard for her breasts, of course, was kept very private. Except with his glance.

We three were young, only sixteen, and Thūy and I were at the Cirque Sportif in Saigon. This was where we met Lý for the first time. We were told that if Mother Mary had known the game of tennis, she would have allowed her spiritual children to wear the costume for the game, even if our legs did show. We loved showing our legs. I have very nice legs, really. Not as nice as Thūy's but I was happy to have my legs bare when I met Lê Văn Lý for the first time. He was a ball boy at the tennis court, and when Thūy and I played, he would run before us and pick up the balls and return them to us. I was a more skillful player than Thūy and it wasn't until too late that I realized how much better it was to hit the ball into the net and have Lý dart before me on this side and then pick up my tennis ball and return it to me. Thūy, of course, knew this right away and her game was never worse than when we played with Lê Văn Lý poised at the end of the net waiting for us to make a mistake.

And it was even on that first meeting that I saw his eyes move to Thūy's breasts. It was the slightest of glances but full of meaning. I knew this because I was very attuned to his eyes from the start. They were more like mine, with nothing of the West but everything of our ancestors back to the Kindly Dragon, whose hundred children began Vietnam. But I had let myself forget that the Kindly Dragon married a fairy princess, not a solid homemaker, so my hopes were still real at age sixteen. He glanced at Thūy's breasts, but he smiled at me when I did miss a shot and he said, very low so only I could hear it, "You're a very good player." It sounded to me at sixteen that this was something he would begin to build his love on. I was a foolish girl.

But now she lay before me on a stainless-steel table, her head cranked up on a chrome support, her hair scattered behind her and her face almost plain. The room had a faint smell, a little itch in the nose of something strong, like the smell when my sons killed insects for their science classes in school. But over this was a faint aroma of flowers, though not real flowers, I knew. I did not like this place and I tried to think about what I'd come for. I was standing before Thūy and I had not moved since Mr. Hoa left me. He tied the smock I was wearing at the back and he told me how he had washed Thūy's hair already. He turned up the air conditioner in the window, which had its glass panes painted a chalky white, and he bowed himself out of the room and closed the door tight.

I opened the bag I'd placed on the high metal chair and I took out Thūy's pearl-handled brush and I bent near her. We had combed each other's hair all our lives. She had always worn her hair down, even as she got older. Even to the day of her death, with her hair laid carefully out on her pillow, something she must have done herself, very near the end, for when Lý and their oldest son and I came into the room that evening and found her, she was dead and her hair was beautiful.

So now I reached out to Thūy and I stroked her hair for the first time since her death and her hair resisted the brush and the resistance sent a chill through me. Her hair was still alive. The body was fixed and cold and absolutely passive, but the hair defied the brush, and though Thūy did not cry out at this first brush stroke as she always did, the hair insisted that she was still alive and I felt something very surprising at that. From the quick fisting of my mind at the image of Thūy, I knew I was angry. From the image of her hair worn long even after she was middle aged instead of worn in a bun at the nape of the neck like all the Vietnamese women our age. I was angry and then I realized that I was angry because she was not completely dead, and this immediately filled me with a shame so hot that it seemed as if I would break into a sweat.

The shame did not last very long. I straightened and turned my face to the flow of cool air from the air conditioner and I looked at all the instruments hanging behind the glass doors of the cabinet in the far wall, all the glinting clamps and tubes and scissors and knives. This was not the place of the living. I looked at Thūy's face and her pale lips were tugged down into a faint frown and I lifted the brush and stroked her hair again and once again, and though it felt just the way it always had felt when I combed it, I continued to brush.

And I spoke a few words to Thūy. Perhaps her spirit was in the room and could hear me. "It's all right, Thūy. The things I never blamed you for in life I won't blame you for now." She had been a good friend. She had always appreciated me. When we brushed each other's hair, she would always say how beautiful mine was and she would invite me also to leave it long, even though I am nearly fifty and I am no beauty at all. And she would tell me how wonderful my talents were. She would urge me to date some man or other in Versailles. I would make such and such a man a wonderful wife, she said. These men were successful men that she recommended, very well off. But they were always older men, in their sixties or seventies. One man was eighty-one, and this one she did not suggest to me directly but by saying casually how she had seen him last week and he was such a vigorous man, such a fine and vigorous man.

And her own husband, Lê Văn Lý, was of course more successful than any of them. And he is still the finest-looking man in Versailles. How fine he is. The face of a warrior. I have seen the high cheeks and full lips of Lê Văn Lý in the statues of warriors in the Saigon Museum, the men who threw the Chinese out of our country many centuries ago. And I lifted Thūy's hair and brushed it out in narrow columns and laid the hair carefully on the bright silver surface behind the support, letting the ends dangle off the table. The hair was very soft and it was yielding to my hands now and I could see this hair hanging perfectly against the back of her pale blue aó dài as she and Lý strolled away across the square near the Continental Palace Hotel.

I wish there had been some clear moment, a little scene; I would even have been prepared not to seem so solid and level-headed; I would have been prepared to weep and even to speak in a loud voice. But they were very disarming in the way they let me know how things were. We had lemonades on the veranda of the Continental Palace Hotel, and I thought it would be like all the other times, the three of us together in the city, strolling along the river or through the flower markets at Nguyễn Huệ or the bookstalls on Lê Lọ'i. We had been three friends together for nearly two years, ever since we'd met at the club. There had been no clear choosing, in my mind. Lý was a very traditional boy, a courteous boy, and he never forced the issue of romance, and so I still had some hopes.

Except that I had unconsciously noticed things, so when Thūy spoke to me and then, soon after, the two of them walked away from the hotel together on the eve of Lý's induction into the Army, I realized something with a shock that I actually had come to understand slowly all along. Like suddenly noticing that you are old. The little things gather for a long time, but one morning you look in the mirror and you understand them in a flash. At the flower market on Nguyễn Huệ I would talk with great spirit of how to arrange the flowers, which ones to put together, how a home would be filled with this or that sort of flower on this or that occasion. But Thūy would be bending into the flowers, her hair falling through the petals, and she would breathe very deeply and rise up and she would be inflated with the smell of flowers and of course her breasts would seem to have grown even larger and more beautiful and Lý would look at them and then he would close his eyes softly in appreciation. And at the bookstalls—I would be the one who asked for the bookstalls—I would be lost in what I thought was the miracle of all these little worlds inviting me in, and I was unaware of the little world near my elbow, Thủy looking at the postcards and talking to Lý about trips to faraway places.

I suppose my two friends were as nice to me as possible at the Continental Palace Hotel, considering what they had to do. Thủy asked me to go to the rest room with her and we were laughing together at something Lý had said. We went to the big double mirror and our two faces were side by side, two girls eighteen years old, and yet beside her I looked much older. Already old. I could see that. And she said, "I am so happy."

We were certainly having fun on this day, but I couldn't quite understand her attitude. After all, Lý was going off to fight our long war. But I replied, "I am, too."

Then she leaned near me and put her hand on my shoulder and she said, "I have a wonderful secret for you. I couldn't wait to tell it to my dear friend."

She meant these words without sarcasm. I'm sure of it. And I still did not understand what was coming.

She said, "I am in love."

I almost asked who it was that she loved. But this was only the briefest final pulse of naïveté. I knew who she loved. And after laying her head on the point of my shoulder and smiling at me in the mirror with such tenderness for her dear friend, she said, "And Lý loves me, too."

How had this subject not come up before? The answer is that the two of us had always spoken together of what a wonderful boy Lý was. But my own declarations were as vivid and enthusiastic as Thủy's—rather more vivid, in fact. So if I was to assume that she loved Lý from all that she'd said, then my own declaration of love should have been just as clear. But obviously it wasn't, and that was just as I should have expected it. Thủy never for a moment had considered me a rival for Lý. In fact, it was unthinkable to her that I should even love him in vain.

She lifted her head from my shoulder and smiled at me as if she expected me to be happy. When I kept silent, she prompted me. "Isn't it wonderful?"

I had never spoken of my love for Lý and I knew that this was the last chance I would have. But what was there to say? I could look back at all the little signs now and read them clearly. And Thủy was who she was and I was different from that and the feeling between Lý and her was already decided upon. So I said the only reasonable thing that I could. "It is very wonderful."

This made Thủy even happier. She hugged me. And then she asked me to comb her hair. We had been outside for an hour before coming to the hotel and her long, straight hair was slightly ruffled and she handed me the pearl-handled brush that her mother had given her and she turned her back to me. And I began to brush. The first stroke caught a tangle and Thủy cried out in a pretty, piping voice. I paused briefly and almost threw the brush against the wall and walked out of this place. But then I brushed once again and again, and she was turned away from the mirror so she could not see the terrible pinch of my face when I suggested that she and Lý spend their last hours now alone together. She nearly wept in joy and appreciation at this gesture from her dear friend, and I kept on brushing until her hair was perfect.

And her hair was perfect now beneath my hands in the preparation room. And I had a strange thought. She was doing this once more to me. She was having me make her hair beautiful so she could go off to the spirit world and seduce the one man there who could love me. This would be Thūy's final triumph over me. My hands trembled at this thought and it persisted. I saw this clearly: Thūy arriving in heaven and her hair lying long and soft down her back and her breasts are clearly beautiful even in the white robe of the angels, and the spirit of some great warrior who fought at the side of the Tru'ng sisters[2] comes to her, and though he has waited nineteen centuries for me, he sees Thūy and decides to wait no more. It has been only the work of my hands that he has awaited and he lifts Thūy's hair and kisses it.

I drew back from Thūy and I stared at her face. I saw it in the mirror at the Continental Palace Hotel and it was very beautiful, but this face before me now was rubbery in death, the beauty was hidden, waiting for my hands. Thūy waited for me to make her beautiful. I had always made her more beautiful. Just by being near her. I was tempted once more to turn away. But that would only let her have her condescending smile at me. Someone else would do this job if I did not, and Thūy would fly off to heaven with her beautiful face and I would be alone in my own shame.

I turned to the sheet now, and the body I had never looked upon in its womanly nakedness was hiding there and this was what Lý had given his love for. The hair and the face had invited him, but it was this hidden body, her secret flesh, that he had longed for. I had seen him less than half an hour ago. He was in Mr. Hoa's office when I arrived. He got up and shook my hand with both of his, holding my hand for a long moment as he said how glad he was that I was here. His eyes were full of tears and I felt very sorry for Lê Văn Lý. A warrior should never cry, even for the death of a beautiful woman. He handed me the bag with Thūy's brush and makeup and he said, "You always know what to do."

What did he mean by this? Simply that I knew how to brush Thūy's hair and paint her face? Or was this something he had seen about me in all things, just as he had once seen that I was a very good tennis player? Did it mean he understood that he had never been with a woman like that, a woman who would always know what to do for him as a wife? When he stood before me in Mr. Hoa's office, I felt like a foolish teenage girl again, with that rush of hope. But perhaps it wasn't foolish; Thūy's breasts were no longer there for his eyes to slide away to.

Her breasts. What were these things that had always defined my place in the world of women? They were beneath the sheet and my hand went out and

---

[2] In A.D. 43, the Tru'ng sisters led a revolt against the Chinese masters of the region.

grasped it at the edge, but I stopped. I told myself it was of no matter now. She was dead. I let go of the sheet and turned to her face of rubber and I took out her eye shadow and her lipstick and her mascara and I bent near and painted the life back into this dead thing.

And as I painted, I thought of where she would lie, in the cemetery behind the Catholic church, in a stone tomb above the ground. It was often necessary in New Orleans, the placing of the dead above the ground, because the water table was so high. If we laid Thůy in the earth, one day she would float to the surface and I could see that day clearly, her rising from the earth and awaking and finding her way back to the main street of Versailles in the heat of the day, and I would be talking with Lý, he would be bending near me and listening as I said all the things of my heart, and suddenly his eyes would slide away and there she would be, her face made up and her hair brushed and her breasts would be as beautiful as ever. But the thought of her lying above the ground made me anxious, as well. As if she wasn't quite gone. And she never would be. Lý would sense her out there behind the church, suspended in the air, and he would never forget her and would take all the consolation he needed from his children and grandchildren.

My hand trembled now as I touched her eyes with the brush, and when I held the lipstick, I pressed it hard against her mouth and I cast aside the shame at my anger and I watched this mouth in my mind, the quick smile of it that never changed in all the years, that never sensed any mood in me but loyal, subordinate friendship. Then the paint was all in place and I pulled back and I angled my face once more into the flow of cool air and I tried to just listen to the grinding of the air conditioner and forget all of these feelings, these terrible feelings about the dead woman who had always been my friend, who I had never once challenged in life over any of these things. I thought, What a coward I am.

But instead of hearing this righteous charge against me, I looked at Thůy and I took her hair in my hands and I smoothed it all together and wound it into a bun and I pinned it at the nape of her neck. She was a fifty-year-old woman, after all. She was as much a fifty-year-old woman as I was. Surely she was. And at this I looked to the sheet.

It lay lower across the chest than I thought it might. But her breasts were also fifty years old, and they were spread flat as she lay on her back. She had never let her dear friend see them, these two secrets that had enchanted the man I loved. I could bear to look at them now, vulnerable and weary as they were. I stepped down and I grasped the edge of the sheet at her throat, and with the whisper of the cloth I pulled it back.

And one of her breasts was gone. The right breast was lovely even now, even in death, the nipple large and the color of cinnamon, but the left breast was gone and a large crescent scar began there in its place and curved out of sight under her arm. I could not draw a breath at this, as if the scar was in my own chest where my lungs had been yanked out, and I could see that her scar was old, years old, and I thought of her three years in California and how she had never spoken at all about this, how her smile had hidden all that she must have suffered.

I could not move for a long moment, and then at last my hands acted as if on their own. They pulled the sheet up and gently spread it at her throat. I suppose this should have brought back my shame at the anger I'd had at my friend Thủy, but it did not. That seemed a childish feeling now, much too simple. It was not necessary to explain any of this. I simply leaned forward and kissed Thủy on her brow and I undid the bun at the back of her neck, happy to make her beautiful once more, happy to send her off to a whole body in heaven where she would catch the eye of the finest warrior. And I knew she would understand if I did all I could to make Lê Văn Lý happy.

Prisoner on the Hell Planet

1986

A CASE HISTORY

ART SPIEGELMAN [b. 1948]

This self-contained story is imbedded in the relentlessly unsentimental *Maus: A Survivor's Tale*. That work describes, in comic book format, Spiegelman's parents' suffering under the Nazi persecution of the Jews during World War II. The Jews in *Maus* are represented as mice; the Nazis are cats. The book deals, as well, with the author's attempt (as a child of Holocaust survivors) to understand and relate to parents whose lives have been warped by the unspeakable horrors they witnessed and endured. In 1968, Anja, Spiegelman's mother, committed suicide. Spiegelman published "Prisoner on the Hell Planet: A Case History" in Short Order Comix, no. 1 in 1973—and in 1986 included it in *Maus*—the only segment of the book with human rather than animal characters.

The Hebrew passages on page 770 are the opening lines of the Kaddish—the prayer for the dead: "Extolled and hallowed be the name of God throughout the world which he has created and which he governs according to his righteous will. . . . "

* The Hebrew is a prayer for the dead.

THE NEXT WEEK WE SPENT IN MOURNING... MY FATHER'S FRIENDS ALL OFFERED ME HOSTILITY MIXED IN WITH THEIR CONDOLENCES....

ARTHUR—WE'RE *SO* SORRY...

IT'S HIS FAULT—THE PUNK!

THEY THINK IT'S MY FAULT!!

...BUT, FOR THE MOST PART, I WAS LEFT ALONE WITH MY THOUGHTS...

MENOPAUSAL DEPRESSION

HITLER DID IT!

MOMMY!

BITCH.

...ARTIE...

...*I REMEMBERED THE LAST TIME I SAW HER...*

SHE CAME INTO MY ROOM... IT WAS LATE AT NIGHT....

...ARTIE ... YOU ... STILL ... LOVE ... ME .... DON'T YOU? ....

...I TURNED AWAY, RESENTFUL OF THE WAY SHE TIGHTENED THE UMBILICAL CORD...

SURE, MA!

...SHE WALKED OUT AND CLOSED THE DOOR!

CLIK!

AGH!

WELL, MOM, IF YOU'RE LISTENING...

CONGRATULATIONS!... YOU'VE COMMITTED THE PERFECT CRIME ....

...YOU PUT ME HERE .... SHORTED ALL MY CIRCUITS...CUT MY NERVE ENDINGS ...AND CROSSED MY WIRES!....

...YOU *MURDERED* ME, MOMMY, AND YOU LEFT ME HERE TO TAKE THE RAP!!!

PIPE DOWN, MAC! SOME OF US ARE TRYING TO SLEEP!

© art spiegelman, 1972

THE
PRESENCE
OF DEATH

Knight, Death, and the Devil, 1513 by Albecht Dürer

POETRY

The Ruin

ANONYMOUS

ca. 900

Well-wrought this wall: Wierds° broke it.   Fates
The stronghold burst. . . .[1]

Snapped rooftrees, towers fallen,
the work of the Giants, the stonesmiths,
mouldereth.   5
              Rime scoureth gatetowers
              rime on mortar.

Shattered the showershields, roofs ruined,
age under-ate them.
              And the wielders & wrights?   10
Earthgrip holds them—gone, long gone,
fast in gravesgrasp while fifty fathers
and sons have passed.
              Wall stood,
grey lichen, red stone, kings fell often,   15
stood under storms, high arch crashed—
stands yet the wallstone, hacked by weapons,
by files grim-ground . . .
. . . shone the old skilled work
. . . sank to loam-crust.   20

Mood quickened mind, and a man of wit,
cunning in rings, bound bravely the wallbase
with iron, a wonder.

Bright were the buildings, halls where springs ran,
high, horngabled, much throng-noise;   25
these many meadhalls men filled
with loud cheerfulness: Wierd° changed that.   Fate

---

[1] This poem is a fragment; the ellipses indicate missing words and lines.

773

Came days of pestilence, on all sides men fell dead,
death fetched off the flower of the people;
where they stood to fight, waste places   30
and on the acropolis, ruins.

                     Hosts who would build again
shrank to the earth. Therefore are these courts dreary
and that red arch twisteth tiles,
wryeth from roof-ridge, reacheth groundwards. . . .   35
Broken blocks. . . .

              There once many a man
mood-glad, goldbright, of gleams garnished,
flushed with wine-pride, flashing war-gear,
gazed on wrought gemstones, on gold, on silver,   40
on wealth held and hoarded, on light-filled amber,
on this bright burg of broad dominion.

Stood stone houses; wide streams welled
hot from source, and a wall all caught
in its bright bosom, that the baths were   45
hot at hall's hearth; that was fitting . . .
. . . .

Thence hot streams, loosed, ran over hoar stone
unto the ring-tank. . . .
     . . . It is a kingly thing   50
     . . . city. . . .

Edward

ANONYMOUS

1

"Why does your brand° sae° drap wi' bluid,   *sword/so*
        Edward, Edward,
Why does your brand sae drap wi' bluid,
  And why sae sad gang° ye, O?"   *go*
"O I ha'e killed my hawk sae guid,   5
        Mither, mither,
O I ha'e killed my hawk sae guid,
  And I had nae mair but he, O."

2

"Your hawke's bluid was never sae reid,°   red
      Edward, Edward,   10
Your hawke's bluid was never sae reid,
  My dear son I tell thee, O."
"O I ha'e killed my reid-roan steed,
      Mither, mither,
O I ha'e killed my reid-roan steed,   15
  That erst was sae fair and free, O."

3

"Your steed was auld, and ye ha'e gat mair,
      Edward, Edward,
Your steed was auld, and ye ha'e gat mair,
  Some other dule° ye drie,° O."   grief/suffer 20
"O I ha'e killed my fader dear,
      Mither, mither,
O I ha'e killed my fader dear,
  Alas, and wae° is me, O!"   woe

4

"And whatten penance wul ye drie for that,   25
      Edward, Edward?
And whatten penance wul ye drie for that,
  My dear son, now tell me, O?"
"I'll set my feet in yonder boat,
      Mither, mither,   30
I'll set my feet in yonder boat,
  And I'll fare over the sea, O."

5

"And what wul ye do wi' your towers and your ha',
      Edward, Edward?
And what wul ye do wi' your towers and your ha',   35
  That were sae fair to see, O?"
"I'll let them stand tul they down fa',
      Mither, mither,
I'll let them stand tul they down fa',
  For here never mair maun° I be, O."   must 40

6

"And what wul ye leave to your bairns° and your wife,   children
       Edward, Edward?
And what wul ye leave to your bairns and your wife,
  Whan ye gang over the sea, O?"
"The warlde's° room, let them beg thrae° life,   world's /through 45
       Mither, mither,
The warlde's room, let them beg thrae life,
  For them never mair wul I see, O."

7

"And what wul ye leave to your ain mither dear,
       Edward, Edward?   50
And what wul ye leave to your ain mither dear,
  My dear son, now tell me, O?"
"The curse of hell frae° me sall° ye bear,   from/shall
       Mither, mither,
The curse of hell frae me sall ye bear,   55
  Sic° counsels ye gave to me, O."   such

QUESTIONS

1. Why does the mother reject Edward's answers to her first two questions?
2. Does the poem provide any clues as to the motive of the murder?   **3.** Edward has
murdered his father and then bitterly turns away from his mother, wife, and children.
What basis is there in the poem for nevertheless sympathizing with Edward?

WRITING TOPIC

What effects are achieved through the question-and-answer technique and the repetition of lines?

Sonnet   1609

WILLIAM SHAKESPEARE   [1564–1616]

73

That time of year thou mayst in me behold
When yellow leaves, or none, or few, do hang
Upon those boughs which shake against the cold,
Bare ruined choirs, where late the sweet birds sang.

In me thou see'st the twilight of such day   5
As after sunset fadeth in the west;
Which by and by black night doth take away,
Death's second self, that seals up all in rest.
In me thou see'st the glowing of such fire,
That on the ashes of his youth doth lie,   10
As the deathbed whereon it must expire,
Consumed with that which it was nourished by.
This thou perceiv'st, which makes thy love more strong,
To love that well which thou must leave ere long.

Death, Be Not Proud   1633

JOHN DONNE   [1572–1631]

Death, be not proud, though some have calléd thee
Mighty and dreadful, for thou art not so;
For those whom thou think'st thou dost overthrow
Die not, poor Death, nor yet canst thou kill me.
From rest and sleep, which but thy pictures be,   5
Much pleasure; then from thee much more must flow,
And soonest our best men with thee do go,
Rest of their bones, and soul's delivery.
Thou art slave to fate, chance, kings, and desperate men,
And dost with poison, war, and sickness dwell,   10
And poppy or charms can make us sleep as well
And better than thy stroke; why swell'st thou then?
One short sleep past, we wake eternally
And death shall be no more; Death, thou shalt die.

[handwritten annotation: sleep is a picture of death.]

Lines Inscribed upon a Cup Formed from a Skull   1814

GEORGE GORDON, LORD BYRON   [1788–1824]

Start not—nor deem my spirit fled;
    In me behold the only skull,
From which, unlike a living head,
    Whatever flows is never dull.

I lived, I loved, I quaff'd, like thee: 5
   I died: let earth my bones resign;
Fill up—thou canst not injure me;
   The worm hath fouler lips than thine.

Better to hold the sparkling grape,
   Than nurse the earth-worm's slimy brood;   10
And circle in the goblet's shape
   The drink of gods, than reptile's food.

Where once my wit, perchance, hath shone,
   In aid of others' let me shine;
And when, alas! our brains are gone,   15
   What nobler substitute than wine?

Quaff while thou canst: another race,
   When thou and thine, like me, are sped,
May rescue thee from earth's embrace,
   And rhyme and revel with the dead.   20

Why not? since through life's little day
   Our heads such sad effects produce;
Redeem'd from worms and wasting clay,
   This chance is theirs, to be of use.

The Destruction of Sennacherib[1]

1815

GEORGE GORDON, LORD BYRON   [1788–1824]

The Assyrian came down like the wolf on the fold,
And his cohorts were gleaming in purple and gold;
And the sheen of their spears was like stars on the sea,
When the blue wave rolls nightly on deep Galilee.

Like the leaves of the forest when summer is green,   5
That host with their banners at sunset were seen:

The Destruction of Sennacherib
  [1] Byron retells the account of the Assyrian siege of Jerusalem, found in II Kings 19, which culminates in the death of 185,000 Assyrian troops at the hand of the angel of the Lord.

Like the leaves of the forest when autumn hath blown,
That host on the morrow lay withered and strown.

For the Angel of Death spread his wings on the blast,
And breathed in the face of the foe as he passed;   10
And the eyes of the sleepers waxed deadly and chill,
And their hearts but once heaved—and for ever grew still!

And there lay the steed with his nostril all wide,
But through it there rolled not the breath of his pride;
And the foam of his gasping lay white on the turf,   15
And cold as the spray of the rock-beating surf.

And there lay the rider distorted and pale,
With the dew on his brow, and the rust on his mail;
And the tents were all silent, the banners alone,
The lances unlifted, the trumpet unblown.   20

And the widows of Ashur[2] are loud in their wail,
And the idols are broke in the temple of Baal;[3]
And the might of the Gentile,[4] unsmote by the sword,
Hath melted like snow in the glance of the Lord!

Ozymandias[1]   1818

PERCY BYSSHE SHELLEY   [1792–1822]

I met a traveller from an antique land
Who said: Two vast and trunkless legs of stone
Stand in the desert . . . Near them, on the sand,
Half sunk, a shattered visage lies, whose frown,
And wrinkled lip, and sneer of cold command,   5
Tell that its sculptor well those passions read
Which yet survive, stamped on these lifeless things,
The hand that mocked them, and the heart that fed:

The Destruction of Sennacherib
  [2] Another name for Assyria.
  [3] A Canaanite deity.
  [4] A non-Hebrew, in this case Sennacherib, the King of Assyria.
Ozymandias
  [1] Egyptian monarch of the thirteenth century B.C., said to have erected a huge statue of himself.

And on the pedestal these words appear:
"My name is Ozymandias, king of kings:
Look on my works, ye Mighty, and despair!"
Nothing beside remains. Round the decay
Of that colossal wreck, boundless and bare
The lone and level sands stretch far away.

[handwritten: He's dead, he left a statue in his place, but now the statue is crumbling. So are his works.]

10

Ode on a Grecian Urn   1820

JOHN KEATS   [1795–1821]

[handwritten: urn — pictures painted on it]

I

Thou still unravished bride of quietness, *[handwritten: urn]*
    Thou foster child of silence and slow time,
Sylvan historian, who canst thus express *[handwritten: urn]*
    A flowery tale more sweetly than our rhyme:
What leaf-fringed legend haunts about thy shape   5
        Of deities or mortals, or of both,
            In Tempe or the dales of Arcady?[1]
    What men or gods are these? What maidens loath?
What mad pursuit? What struggle to escape?
        What pipes and timbrels? What wild ecstasy?   10

II   *[handwritten: PICTURE #1]*

Heard melodies are sweet, but those unheard
    Are sweeter; therefore, ye soft pipes, play on; *[handwritten: musician]*
Not to the sensual ear, but, more endeared,
    Pipe to the spirit ditties of no tone:
Fair youth, beneath the trees, thou canst not leave *[handwritten: people kissing]*   15
    Thy song, nor ever can those trees be bare;
        Bold Lover, never, never, canst thou kiss, *[handwritten: anticipation is better than the "kiss."]*
Though winning near the goal—yet, do not grieve;
    She cannot fade, though thou hast not thy bliss,
Forever wilt thou love, and she be fair!   20

III

Ah, happy, happy boughs! that cannot shed
    Your leaves, nor ever bid the Spring adieu;
And, happy melodist, unwearièd,

Ode on a Grecian Urn
    [1] Tempe and Arcady are valleys in Greece famous for their beauty. In ancient times, Tempe was regarded as sacred to Apollo.

Forever piping songs forever new;
More happy love! more happy, happy love!   25
  Forever warm and still to be enjoyed,
    Forever panting, and forever young;
All breathing human passion far above,[2]
  That leaves a heart high-sorrowful and cloyed,
  A burning forehead, and a parching tongue.   30

[handwritten annotations: frozen in time on the urn; ← all that instead; human; paint that comes w/ being in ♥]

IV

Who are these coming to the sacrifice?
  To what green altar, O mysterious priest,
Lead'st thou that heifer lowing at the skies,
  And all her silken flanks with garlands dressed?
What little town by river or sea shore,   35
  Or mountain-built with peaceful citadel,
    Is emptied of this folk, this pious morn?
And, little town, thy streets forevermore
  Will silent be; and not a soul to tell
    Why thou art desolate, can e'er return.   40

[handwritten annotation: priest, town, sacrifice]

V

O Attic[3] shape! Fair attitude! with brede
  Of marble men and maidens overwrought,
With forest branches and the trodden weed;
  Thou, silent form, dost tease us out of thought
As doth eternity: Cold Pastoral!   45
  When old age shall this generation waste,
    Thou shalt remain, in midst of other woe
Than ours, a friend to man, to whom thou say'st,
"Beauty is truth, truth beauty,—that is all
  Ye know on earth, and all ye need to know."   50

[handwritten annotations: passionate/static; talking to urn; not alive/cold. a thing; the urn; Art is eternal]

QUESTIONS

1. Describe the scene the poet sees depicted on the urn. Describe the scene the poet imagines as a consequence of the scene on the urn. **2.** Why are the boughs, the piper, and the lovers happy in stanza 3? **3** Explain the assertion of stanza 2 that "Heard melodies are sweet, but those unheard / Are sweeter." **4.** Does the poem support the assertion of the last two lines? What does that assertion mean?

---

[2] I.e., far above all breathing human passion.
[3] Athenian, thus simple and graceful.

WRITING TOPIC

In what sense might it be argued that this poem is about mortality and immortality? In this connection, consider the meaning of the phrase "Cold Pastoral!" (l. 45).

Growing Old   1867

MATTHEW ARNOLD   [1822–1888]

What is it to grow old?
Is it to lose the glory of the form,
The luster of the eye?
Is it for beauty to forego her wreath?
—Yes, but not this alone.   5

Is it to feel our strength—
Not our bloom only, but our strength—decay?
Is it to feel each limb
Grow stiffer, every function less exact,
Each nerve more loosely strung?   10

Yes, this, and more; but not
Ah, 'tis not what in youth we dreamed 'twould be!
'Tis not to have our life
Mellowed and softened as with sunset glow,
A golden day's decline.   15

'Tis not to see the world
As from a height, with rapt prophetic eyes,
And heart profoundly stirred;
And weep, and feel the fullness of the past,
The years that are no more.   20

It is to spend long days
And not once feel that we were ever young;
It is to add, immured
In the hot prison of the present, month
To month with weary pain.   25

It is to suffer this,
And feel but half, and feebly, what we feel.
Deep in our hidden heart
Festers the dull remembrance of a change,
But no emotion—none.   30

It is—last stage of all—
When we are frozen up within, and quite
The phantom of ourselves,
To hear the world applaud the hollow ghost
Which blamed the living man.   35

After Great Pain, a Formal Feeling Comes (ca. 1862)

EMILY DICKINSON   [1830–1886]

After great pain, a formal feeling comes—
The Nerves sit ceremonious, like Tombs—
The stiff Heart questions was it He, that bore,
And Yesterday, or Centuries before?

The Feet, mechanical, go round—   5
Of Ground, or Air, or Ought—
A Wooden way,
Regardless grown,
A Quartz contentment, like a stone—

This is the Hour of Lead—   10
Remembered, if outlived,
As Freezing persons, recollect the Snow—
First—Chill—then Stupor—then the letting go—

QUESTION
1. Is this poem about physical or psychic pain? Explain.

WRITING TOPIC
What is the meaning of "stiff Heart" (l. 3) and "Quartz contentment" (l. 9)? What part do they play in the larger pattern of images?

I Heard a Fly Buzz— When I Died (ca. 1862)

EMILY DICKINSON [1830–1886]

I heard a Fly buzz—when I died—
The Stillness in the Room
Was like the Stillness in the Air—
Between the Heaves of Storm—

The Eyes around—had wrung them dry—   5
And Breaths were gathering firm
For that last Onset—when the King
Be witnessed—in the Room—

I willed my Keepsakes—Signed away
What portion of me be   10
Assignable—and then it was
There interposed a Fly—

With Blue—uncertain stumbling Buzz—
Between the light—and me—
And then the Windows failed—and then   15
I could not see to see—

Apparently with No Surprise (ca. 1884)

EMILY DICKINSON [1830–1886]

Apparently with no surprise
To any happy Flower,
The Frost beheads it at its play
In accidental power.
The blond Assassin passes on,   5
The Sun proceeds unmoved
To measure off another Day
For an Approving God.

To an Athlete Dying Young   1896

A. E. HOUSMAN   [1859–1936]

The time you won your town the race
We chaired you through the market place;
Man and boy stood cheering by,
And home we brought you shoulder-high.

Today, the road all runners come,   5
Shoulder-high we bring you home,
And set you at your threshold down,
Townsman of a stiller town.

Smart lad, to slip betimes away
From fields where glory does not stay,   10
And early though the laurel grows
It withers quicker than the rose.

Eyes the shady night has shut
Cannot see the record cut,
And silence sounds no worse than cheers   15
After earth has stopped the ears:

Now you will not swell the rout
Of lads that wore their honors out,
Runners whom renown outran
And the name died before the man.   20

So set, before its echoes fade,
The fleet foot on the sill of shade,
And hold to the low lintel up
The still-defended challenge cup.

And round that early-laureled head   25
Will flock to gaze the strengthless dead
And find unwithered on its curls
The garland briefer than a girl's.

Sailing to Byzantium[1]   1927

WILLIAM BUTLER YEATS   [1865–1939]

1

That is no country for old men. The young
In one another's arms, birds in the trees
—Those dying generations—at their song,
The salmon-falls, the mackerel-crowded seas,
Fish, flesh, or fowl, commend all summer long   5
Whatever is begotten, born, and dies.
Caught in that sensual music all neglect
Monuments of unaging intellect.

2

An aged man is but a paltry thing,
A tattered coat upon a stick, unless   10
Soul clap its hands and sing, and louder sing
For every tatter in its mortal dress,
Nor is there singing school but studying
Monuments of its own magnificence;
And therefore I have sailed the seas and come   15
To the holy city of Byzantium.

3

O sages standing in God's holy fire
As in the gold mosiac of a wall,
Come from the holy fire, perne in a gyre,[2]
And be the singing-masters of my soul.   20
Consume my heart away; sick with desire
And fastened to a dying animal
It knows not what it is; and gather me
Into the artifice of eternity.

---

[1] Capital of the ancient Eastern Roman Empire, Byzantium (modern Istanbul) is celebrated for its great art, including mosaics (in ll. 17–18, Yeats addresses the figures in one of these mosaics). In *A Vision*, Yeats cites Byzantium as possibly the only civilization which had achieved what he called "Unity of Being," a state where "religious, aesthetic and practical life were one. . . ."

[2] I.e., whirl in a spiral motion. Yeats associated this motion with the cycles of history and the fate of the individual. Here he entreats the sages represented in the mosaic to take him out of the natural world described in the first stanza and into the eternal world of art.

4

Once out of nature I shall never take   25
My bodily form from any natural thing,
But such a form as Grecian goldsmiths make
Of hammered gold and gold enameling
To keep a drowsy Emperor awake;³
Or set upon a golden bough to sing   30
To lords and ladies of Byzantium
Of what is past, or passing, or to come.

QUESTIONS
1. This poem incorporates a series of contrasts, among them "That" country and Byzantium, the real birds of the first stanza and the artificial bird of the final stanza. What others do you find? **2.** What are the meanings of "generations" (l. 3)? **3.** For what is the poet "sick with desire" (l. 21)? **4.** In what sense is eternity an "artifice" (l. 24)?

WRITING TOPIC
In what ways are the images of bird and song used throughout this poem?

Richard Cory   1897

EDWIN ARLINGTON ROBINSON   [1869–1935]

Whenever Richard Cory went down town,
We people on the pavement looked at him:
He was a gentleman from sole to crown,
Clean favored, and imperially slim.

And he was always quietly arrayed,   5
And he was always human when he talked;
But still he fluttered pulses when he said,
"Good-morning," and he glittered when he walked.

And he was rich—yes, richer than a king—
And admirably schooled in every grace: 10
In fine, we thought that he was everything
To make us wish that we were in his place.

Sailing to Byzantium
³ "I have read somewhere," Yeats wrote, "that in the Emperor's palace at Byzantium was a tree made of gold and silver, and artificial birds that sang." The poet wishes to become an artificial bird (a work of art) in contrast to the real birds of the first stanza.

So on we worked, and waited for the light,
And went without the meat, and cursed the bread;
And Richard Cory, one calm summer night,   15
Went home and put a bullet through his head.

Mr. Flood's Party   1921

EDWIN ARLINGTON ROBINSON   [1869–1935]

Old Eben Flood, climbing alone one night
Over the hill between the town below
And the forsaken upland hermitage
That held as much as he should ever know
On earth again of home, paused warily.   5
The road was his with not a native near;
And Eben, having leisure, said aloud,
For no man else in Tilbury Town to hear:

"Well, Mr. Flood, we have the harvest moon
Again, and we may not have many more;   10
The bird is on the wing, the poet says,
And you and I have said it here before.
Drink to the bird." He raised up to the light
The jug that he had gone so far to fill,
And answered huskily: "Well, Mr. Flood,   15
Since you propose it, I believe I will."

Alone, as if enduring to the end
A valiant armor of scarred hopes outworn,
He stood there in the middle of the road
Like Roland's ghost winding a silent horn.   20
Below him, in the town among the trees,
Where friends of other days had honored him,
A phantom salutation of the dead
Rang thinly till old Eben's eyes were dim.

Then, as a mother lays her sleeping child   25
Down tenderly, fearing it may awake,
He set the jug down slowly at his feet
With trembling care, knowing that most things break;
And only when assured that on firm earth
It stood, as the uncertain lives of men   30
Assuredly did not, he paced away,
And with his hand extended paused again:

"Well, Mr. Flood, we have not met like this
In a long time; and many a change has come
To both of us, I fear, since last it was   35
We had a drop together. Welcome home!"
Convivially returning with himself,
Again he raised the jug up to the light;
And with an acquiescent quaver said:
"Well, Mr. Flood, if you insist, I might.   40

"Only a very little, Mr. Flood—
For auld lang syne. No more, sir; that will do."
So, for the time, apparently it did,
And Eben evidently thought so too;
For soon amid the silver loneliness   45
Of night he lifted up his voice and sang,
Secure, with only two moons listening,
Until the whole harmonious landscape rang—

"For auld lang syne." The weary throat gave out,
The last word wavered, and the song being done,   50
He raised again the jug regretfully
And shook his head, and was again alone.
There was not much that was ahead of him,
And there was nothing in the town below—
Where strangers would have shut the many doors   55
That many friends had opened long ago.

After Apple-Picking   1914

ROBERT FROST   [1874–1963]

My long two-pointed ladder's sticking through a tree
Toward heaven still,
And there's a barrel that I didn't fill
Beside it, and there may be two or three
Apples I didn't pick upon some bough.   5
But I am done with apple-picking now.
Essence of winter sleep is on the night,
The scent of apples: I am drowsing off.
I cannot rub the strangeness from my sight
I got from looking through a pane of glass   10
I skimmed this morning from the drinking trough
And held against the world of hoary grass.
It melted, and I let it fall and break.

But I was well
Upon my way to sleep before it fell,   15
And I could tell
What form my dreaming was about to take.
Magnified apples appear and disappear,
Stem end and blossom end,
And every fleck of russet showing clear.   20
My instep arch not only keeps the ache,
It keeps the pressure of a ladder-round.
I feel the ladder sway as the boughs bend.
And I keep hearing from the cellar bin
The rumbling sound   25
Of load on load of apples coming in.
For I have had too much
Of apple-picking: I am overtired
Of the great harvest I myself desired.
There were ten thousand thousand fruit to touch,   30
Cherish in hand, lift down, and not let fall.
For all
That struck the earth,
No matter if not bruised or spiked with stubble,
Went surely to the cider-apple heap   35
As of no worth.
One can see what will trouble
This sleep of mine, whatever sleep it is.
Were he not gone,
The woodchuck could say whether it's like his   40
Long sleep, as I describe its coming on,
Or just some human sleep.

QUESTIONS
1. What does apple-picking symbolize?   **2.** At the end of the poem, why is the speaker uncertain about what kind of sleep is coming on him?

Nothing Gold Can Stay   1923

ROBERT FROST   [1874–1963]

Nature's first green is gold,
Her hardest hue to hold.
Her early leaf's a flower;
But only so an hour.
Then leaf subsides to leaf.   5

So Eden sank to grief,
So dawn goes down to day.
Nothing gold can stay.

QUESTIONS
1. Does this poem protest or accept the transitoriness of things?   **2.** Why does Frost use the word *subsides* in line 5 rather than a word like *expands* or *grows*?   **3.** How are "Nature's first green" (l. 1), "Eden" (l. 6), and "dawn" (l. 7) linked together?

'Out, Out—'[1]   1916

ROBERT FROST   [1874–1963]

The buzz-saw snarled and rattled in the yard
And made dust and dropped stove-length sticks of wood,
Sweet-scented stuff when the breeze drew across it.
And from there those that lifted eyes could count
Five mountain ranges one behind the other   5
Under the sunset far into Vermont.
And the saw snarled and rattled, snarled and rattled,
As it ran light, or had to bear a load.
And nothing happened: day was all but done.
Call it a day, I wish they might have said   10
To please the boy by giving him the half hour
That a boy counts so much when saved from work.
His sister stood beside them in her apron
To tell them 'Supper.' At the word, the saw,
As if to prove saws knew what supper meant,   15
Leaped out at the boy's hand, or seemed to leap—
He must have given the hand. However it was,
Neither refused the meeting. But the hand!
The boy's first outcry was a rueful laugh,
As he swung toward them holding up the hand   20
Half in appeal, but half as if to keep
The life from spilling. Then the boy saw it all—
Since he was old enough to know, big boy
Doing a man's work, though a child at heart—
He saw all spoiled. 'Don't let him cut my hand off—   25
The doctor, when he comes. Don't let him, sister!'
So. But the hand was gone already.
The doctor put him in the dark of ether.

'Out, Out—'
   [1] The title is taken from the famous speech of Macbeth upon hearing that his wife has died (*Macbeth*, Act V, Scene 5).

He lay and puffed his lips out with his breath.
And then—the watcher at his pulse took fright.   30
No one believed. They listened at his heart.
Little—less—nothing!—and that ended it.
No more to build on there. And they, since they
Were not the one dead, turned to their affairs.

Stopping by Woods
on a Snowy Evening   1923

ROBERT FROST   [1874–1963]

Whose woods these are I think I know.
His house is in the village though;
He will not see me stopping here
To watch his woods fill up with snow.

My little horse must think it queer   5
To stop without a farmhouse near
Between the woods and frozen lake
The darkest evening of the year.

He gives his harness bells a shake
To ask if there is some mistake.   10
The only other sound's the sweep
Of easy wind and downy flake.

The woods are lovely, dark and deep,
But I have promises to keep,
And miles to go before I sleep,   15
And miles to go before I sleep.

QUESTIONS
1. What does the description of the horse tell us about the speaker?   **2.** What function does the repetition in the last two lines of the poem serve?   **3.** Why does the speaker refer to the owner of the woods in the opening stanza?

Design

1936

ROBERT FROST   [1874–1963]

I found a dimpled spider, fat and white,
On a white heal-all, holding up a moth
Like a white piece of rigid satin cloth—
Assorted characters of death and blight
Mixed ready to begin the morning right,   5
Like the ingredients of a witches' broth—
A snow-drop spider, a flower like a froth,
And dead wings carried like a paper kite.

What had that flower to do with being white,
The wayside blue and innocent heal-all?   10
What brought the kindred spider to that height,
Then steered the white moth thither in the night?
What but design of darkness to appall?—
If design governs in a thing so small.

WRITING TOPIC
Compare this poem with Emily Dickinson's "Apparently with No Surprise."

Tract

1917

WILLIAM CARLOS WILLIAMS   [1883–1963]

I will teach you my townspeople
how to perform a funeral—
for you have it over a troop
of artists—
unless one should scour the world—   5
you have the ground sense necessary.
See! the hearse leads.
I begin with a design for a hearse.
For Christ's sake not black—
nor white either—and not polished!   10
Let it be weathered—like a farm wagon—
with gilt wheels (this could be
applied fresh at small expense)
or no wheels at all:
a rough dray to drag over the ground.   15

Knock the glass out!
My God—glass, my townspeople!
For what purpose? Is it for the dead
to look out or for us to see
how well he is housed or to see   20
the flowers or the lack of them—
or what?
To keep the rain and snow from him?
He will have a heavier rain soon:
pebbles and dirt and what not.   25
Let there be no glass—
and no upholstery! phew!
and no little brass rollers
and small easy wheels on the bottom—
my townspeople what are you thinking of!   30

A rough plain hearse then
with gilt wheels and no top at all.
On this the coffin lies
by its own weight.
by its own weight.   35
                    No wreaths please—
especially no hot-house flowers.
Some common memento is better,
something he prized and is known by:
his old clothes—a few books perhaps—   40
God knows what! You realize
how we are about these things,
my townspeople—
something will be found—anything—
even flowers if he had come to that.   45
So much for the hearse.

For heaven's sake though see to the driver!
Take off the silk hat! In fact
that's no place at all for him
up there unceremoniously   50
dragging our friend out of his own dignity!
Bring him down—bring him down!
Low and inconspicuous! I'd not have him ride
on the wagon at all—damn him—
the undertaker's understrapper!   55
Let him hold the reins
and walk at the side
and inconspicuously too!

Then briefly as to yourselves:
Walk behind—as they do in France,   60
seventh class, or if you ride
Hell take curtains! Go with some show
of inconvenience; sit openly—
to the weather as to grief.
Or do you think you can shut grief in?   65
What—from us? We who have perhaps
nothing to lose? Share with us
share with us—it will be money
in your pockets.
in your pockets.   70
                    Go now
I think you are ready.

Dulce et Decorum Est   1920

WILFRED OWEN   [1893–1918]

Bent double, like old beggars under sacks,
Knock-kneed, coughing like hags, we cursed through sludge,
Till on the haunting flares we turned our backs,
And towards our distant rest began to trudge.
Men marched asleep. Many had lost their boots,   5
But limped on, blood-shod. All went lame, all blind;
Drunk with fatigue; deaf even to the hoots
Of gas-shells dropping softly behind.

Gas! GAS! Quick, boys!—An ecstasy of fumbling,
Fitting the clumsy helmets just in time,   10
But someone still was yelling out and stumbling
And flound'ring like a man in fire or lime.—
Dim through the misty panes and thick green light,
As under a green sea, I saw him drowning.
In all my dreams before my helpless sight   15
He plunges at me, guttering, choking, drowning.

If in some smothering dreams, you too could pace
Behind the wagon that we flung him in,
And watch the white eyes writhing in his face,
His hanging face, like a devil's sick of sin,   20
If you could hear, at every jolt, the blood

Come gargling from the froth-corrupted lungs
Bitter as the cud
Of vile, incurable sores on innocent tongues,—
My friend, you would not tell with such high zest   25
To children ardent for some desperate glory,
The old lie: *Dulce et decorum est*
Pro patria mori.[1]

nobody loses all the time   1926

E. E. CUMMINGS   [1894–1962]

nobody loses all the time

i had an uncle named
Sol who was a born failure and
nearly everybody said he should have gone
into vaudeville perhaps because my Uncle Sol could   5
sing McCann He Was A Diver on Xmas Eve like Hell Itself which
may or may not account for the fact that my Uncle

Sol indulged in that possibly most inexcusable
of all to use a highfalootin phrase
luxuries that is or to   10
wit farming and be
it needlessly
added

my Uncle Sol's farm
failed because the chickens   15
ate the vegetables so
my Uncle Sol had a
chicken farm till the
skunks ate the chickens when

my Uncle Sol   20
had a skunk farm but
the skunks caught cold and
died and so
my Uncle Sol imitated the
skunks in a subtle manner   25

Dulce et Decorum Est
[1] A quotation from the Latin poet Horace, "It is sweet and fitting to die for one's country."

or by drowning himself in the watertank
but somebody who'd given my Uncle Sol a Victor
Victrola and records while he lived presented to
him upon the auspicious occasion of his decease a
scrumptious not to mention splendiferous funeral with   30
tall boys in black gloves and flowers and everything and

i remember we all cried like the Missouri
when my Uncle Sol's coffin lurched because
somebody pressed a button
(and down went   35
my Uncle
Sol

and started a worm farm)

QUESTIONS
1. Explain the title.   **2.** What is the speaker's attitude toward Uncle Sol?

Landscape with the Fall of Icarus, ca. 1560 by Pieter Brueghel the Elder

martyr - one who chooses to suffer death
rather than renounce religious principles.
martyrdom - the state of being a martyr

Musée des Beaux Arts   1940

W. H. AUDEN   [1907–1973]

About suffering they were never wrong,
The Old Masters: how well they understood
Its human position; how it takes place
While someone else is eating or opening a window or just walking dully
    along;   5
How, when the aged are reverently, passionately waiting
For the miraculous birth, there always must be
Children who did not specially want it to happen, skating
On a pond at the edge of the wood:
They never forgot   10
That even the dreadful <u>martyrdom</u> must run its course
Anyhow in a corner, some untidy spot
Where the dogs go on with their doggy life and the torturer's horse
Scratches its innocent behind on a tree.

In Brueghel's Icarus,[1] for instance: how everything turns away   15
Quite leisurely from the disaster; the plowman may
Have heard the splash, the forsaken cry,
But for him it was not an important failure; the sun shone
As it had to on the white legs disappearing into the green
Water; and the expensive delicate ship that must have seen   20
Something amazing, a boy falling out of the sky,
Had somewhere to get to and sailed calmly on.

Elegy for Jane   1958

MY STUDENT, THROWN BY A HORSE

THEODORE ROETHKE   [1908–1963]

I remember the neckcurls, limp and damp as tendrils;
And her quick look, a sidelong pickerel smile;
And how, once startled into talk, the light syllables leaped for her,
And she balanced in the delight of her thought,
A wren, happy, tail into the wind,   5
Her song trembling the twigs and small branches.
The shade sang with her;
The leaves, their whispers turned to kissing;
And the mold sang in the bleached valleys under the rose.

Oh, when she was sad, she cast herself down into such a pure depth,   10
Even a father could not find her:
Scraping her cheek against straw;
Stirring the clearest water.

My sparrow, you are not here,
Waiting like a fern, making a spiny shadow.   15
The sides of wet stones cannot console me,
Nor the moss, wound with the last light.

If only I could nudge you from this sleep,
My maimed darling, my skittery pigeon.

Musée des Beaux Arts
   [1] This poem describes and comments on Pieter Brueghel's painting *Landscape with the Fall of Icarus* (See p. 798). According to myth, Daedalus and his son Icarus made wings, whose feathers they attached with wax, to escape Crete. Icarus flew so near the sun that the wax melted and he fell into the sea.

Over this damp grave I speak the words of my love: 20
I, with no rights in this matter,
Neither father nor lover.

Between the World and Me   1935

RICHARD WRIGHT   [1908–1960]

And one morning while in the woods I stumbled suddenly upon the
   thing,
Stumbled upon it in a grassy clearing guarded by scaly oaks and elms.
And the sooty details of the scene rose, thrusting themselves between the
   world and me. . . .
There was a design of white bones slumbering forgottenly upon a cushion
   of ashes.
There was a charred stump of a sapling pointing a blunt finger accusingly at
   the sky.   5
There were torn tree limbs, tiny veins of burnt leaves, and a scorched coil
   of greasy hemp;
A vacant shoe, an empty tie, a ripped shirt, a lonely hat, and a pair of trousers stiff with black blood.
And upon the trampled grass were buttons, dead matches, butt-ends of cigars and cigarettes, peanut shells, a drained gin-flask, and a whore's lipstick;
Scattered traces of tar, restless arrays of feathers, and the lingering smell of
   gasoline.
And through the morning air the sun poured yellow surprise into the eye
   sockets of a stony skull. . . .   10
And while I stood my mind was frozen with a cold pity for the life that was
   gone.
The ground gripped my feet and my heart was circled by icy walls of fear—
The sun died in the sky; a night wind muttered in the grass and fumbled
   the leaves in the trees; the woods poured forth the hungry yelping of
   hounds; the darkness screamed with thirsty voices; and the witnesses rose
   and lived: The dry bones stirred, rattled, lifted, melting themselves into
   my bones.
The grey ashes formed flesh firm and black, entering into my flesh.
The gin-flask passed from mouth to mouth; cigars and cigarettes glowed,
   the whore smeared the lipstick red upon her lips,   15
And a thousand faces swirled around me, clamoring that my life be
   burned. . . .
And then they had me, stripped me, battering my teeth into my throat till
   I swallowed my own blood.

My voice was drowned in the roar of their voices, and my black wet body
   slipped and rolled in their hands as they bound me to the sapling.
And my skin clung to the bubbling hot tar, falling from me in limp
   patches.
And the down and quills of the white feathers sank into my raw flesh, and I
   moaned in my agony.   20
Then my blood was cooled mercifully, cooled by a baptism of gasoline.
And in a blaze of red I leaped to the sky as pain rose like water, boiling my
   limbs.
Panting, begging I clutched childlike, clutched to the hot sides of death.
Now I am dry bones and my face a stony skull staring in my yellow surprise
   at the sun. . . .

Do Not Go Gentle into That Good Night   1952

DYLAN THOMAS [1914–1953]

Do not go gentle into that good night,
Old age should burn and rave at close of day;
Rage, rage against the dying of the light.

Though wise men at their end know dark is right,
Because their words had forked no lightning they
Do not go gentle into that good night.

Good men, the last wave by, crying how bright
Their frail deeds might have danced in a green bay,
Rage, rage against the dying of the light.

Wild men who caught and sang the sun in flight,   10
And learn, too late, they grieved it on its way,
Do not go gentle into that good night.

Grave men, near death, who see with blinding sight
Blind eyes could blaze like meteors and be gay,
Rage, rage against the dying of the light.   15

And you, my father, there on the sad height,
Curse, bless, me now with your fierce tears, I pray.
Do not go gentle into that good night.
Rage, rage against the dying of the light.

QUESTIONS
1. What do wise, good, wild, and grave men have in common? **2.** Why does the poet use the adjective *gentle* rather than the adverb *gently*? **3.** What is the "sad height" (l. 16)?

Aubade[1]   1977

PHILIP LARKIN   [1922–1985]

I work all day, and get half drunk at night.
Waking at four to soundless dark, I stare.
In time the curtain-edges will grow light.
Till then I see what's really always there:
Unresting death, a whole day nearer now;   5
Making all thought impossible but how
And where and when I shall myself die.
Arid interrogation: yet the dread
Of dying, and being dead,
Flashes afresh to hold and horrify.   10

The mind blanks at the glare. Not in remorse
—The good not done, the love not given, time
Torn off unused—nor wretchedly because
An only life can take so long to climb
Clear of its wrong beginnings, and may never;   15
But at the total emptiness for ever,
The sure extinction that we travel to
And shall be lost in always. Not to be here,
Not to be anywhere,
And soon; nothing more terrible, nothing more true.   20

This is a special way of being afraid
No trick dispels. Religion used to try,
That vast moth-eaten musical brocade
Created to pretend we never die,
And specious stuff that says *No rational being*   25
Can fear a thing it will not feel, not seeing
That this is what we fear—no sight, no sound.
No touch or taste to smell, nothing to think with.
Nothing to love or link with,
The anaesthetic from which none come round.   30

Aubade
[1] An aubade is a morning song.

And so it stays just on the edge of vision,
A small unfocused blur, a standing chill
That slows each impulse down to indecision.
Most things may never happen: this one will.
And realisation of it rages out   35
In furnace-fear when we are caught without
People or drink. Courage is no good:
It means not scaring others. Being brave
Lets no one off the grave.
Death is no different whined at than withstood.   40

Slowly light strengthens, and the room takes shape.
It stands plain as a wardrobe, what we know,
Have always known, know that we can't escape,
Yet can't accept. One side will have to go.
Meanwhile telephones crouch, getting ready to ring   45
In locked-up offices, and all the uncaring
Intricate rented world begins to rouse.
The sky is white as clay, with no sun.
Work has to be done.
Postmen like doctors go from house to house.   50

Mid-American Tragedy   1992

DENISE LEVERTOV   [b. 1923]

They want to be their own old vision
of Mom and Dad. They want their dying son
to be eight years old again, not a gay man,
not ill, not dying. They have accepted him,
they would say if asked, unlike some who shut   5
errant sons out of house and heart,
and this makes them preen a little, secretly;
but enough of that, some voice within them
whispers, even more secretly, *he's our kid,*
Mom and Dad are going to give him   10
what all kids long for, a trip to Disney World,
what fun, the best Xmas ever.
And he, his wheelchair strung with bottles and tubes,
glass and metal glittering in winter sun,
shivers and sweats and tries to breathe as *Jingle Bells*   15
pervades the air and his mother, his father,
chatter and still won't talk, won't listen,
will never listen, never give him

the healing silence
in which they could have heard   20
his questions, his answers,
his life at last.

QUESTIONS

1 What do you suppose the son is dying of? **2.** How do his parents apparently feel?
How do they actually feel? **3** What does "his mother, his father, / chatter and still
won't talk, won't listen" (ll. 16–17) mean?

WRITING TOPICS

1. In an essay, describe an incident in which some relative or friend chattered to you
without communicating and heard you without listening. How did you respond?
2. If you were terminally ill, how would you like those close to you to behave?

After a Time   (1961?)

CATHERINE DAVIS   [b. 1924]

After a time, all losses are the same.
One more thing lost is one thing less to lose;
And we go stripped at last the way we came.

Though we shall probe, time and again, our shame,
Who lack the wit to keep or to refuse,   5
After a time, all losses are the same.

No wit, no luck can beat a losing game;
Good fortune is a reassuring ruse:
And we go stripped at last the way we came.

Rage as we will for what we think to claim,   10
Nothing so much as this bare thought subdues:
After a time, all losses are the same.

The sense of treachery—the want, the blame—
Goes in the end, whether or not we choose,
And we go stripped at last the way we came.   15

So we, who would go raging, will go tame
When what we have we can no longer use:
After a time, all losses are the same;
And we go stripped at last the way we came.

QUESTIONS
1. What difference in effect would occur if the refrain "After a time" were changed to "When life is done"?   **2.** What are the various meanings of "stripped" in line 3 and line 19?   **3.** Explain the meaning of "The sense of treachery" (l. 13).   **4.** Does this poem say that life is meaningless? Explain.

WRITING TOPIC
Compare this poem with Dylan Thomas's "Do Not Go Gentle into That Good Night."

Woodchucks

1972

MAXINE KUMIN   [b. 1925]

Gassing the woodchucks didn't turn out right.
The knockout bomb from the Feed and Grain Exchange
was featured as merciful, quick at the bone
and the case we had against them was airtight
both exits shoehorned shut with puddingstone,   5
but they had a sub-sub-basement out of range.

Next morning they turned up again, no worse
for the cyanide than we for our cigarettes
and state-store Scotch, all of us up to scratch.
They brought down the marigolds as a matter of course   10
and then took over the vegetable patch
nipping the broccoli shoots, beheading the carrots.

The food from our mouths, I said, righteously thrilling
to the feel of the .22, the bullets' neat noses.
I, a lapsed pacifist fallen from grace   15
puffed with Darwinian pieties for killing,
now drew a bead on the littlest woodchuck's face.
He died down in the everbearing roses.

Ten minutes later I dropped the mother. She
flipflopped in the air and fell, her needle teeth   20
still hooked in a leaf of early Swiss chard.
Another baby next. O one-two-three
the murderer inside me rose up hard,
the hawkeye killer came on stage forthwith.

There's one chuck left. Old wily fellow, he keeps   25
me cocked and ready day after day after day.

All night I hunt his humped-up form. I dream
I sight along the barrel in my sleep.
If only they'd all consented to die unseen
gassed underground the quiet Nazi way.   30

To Aunt Rose   1961

ALLEN GINSBERG   [b. 1926]

[handwritten annotation: rheumatism – any of several pathological conditions of the muscles, tendons, joints, bones, or nerves characterized by discomfort & disability]

Aunt Rose—now—might I see you
with your thin face and buck tooth smile and pain
          of <u>rheumatism</u>—and a long black heavy shoe
              for your bony left leg
     limping down the long hall in Newark on the running carpet
          past the black grand piano
              in the day room
                   where the parties were
          and I sang Spanish loyalist songs[1]
               in a high squeaky voice   10
                   (hysterical) the committee listening
          while you limped around the room
               collected the money—
Aunt Honey, Uncle Sam, a stranger with a cloth arm
               in his pocket   15
                   and huge young bald head
                        of Abraham Lincoln Brigade

—your long sad face
          your tears of sexual frustration
               (what smothered sobs and bony hips   20
                   under the pillows of Osborne Terrace)
     —the time I stood on the toilet seat naked
          and you powdered my thighs with Calomine
               against the poison ivy—my tender
                   and shamed first black curled hairs   25

To Aunt Rose
   [1] Between 1936 and 1939, a civil war occurred in Spain in which rebel forces under General Francisco Franco defeated the Loyalist forces supporting the politically liberal monarchy. In some ways a foreshadowing of World War II, the Spanish Civil War attracted the attention of the great powers, with Russia supporting the Loyalist forces and Germany and Italy supporting the rebel forces. Many American writers and intellectuals saw the war as a struggle between fascism and democracy and supported the Loyalist cause energetically; the Abraham Lincoln Brigade (line 17) was a volunteer unit of Americans that fought on the Loyalist side.

what were you thinking in secret heart then
        knowing me a man already—
and I an ignorant girl of family silence on the thin pedestal
        of my legs in the bathroom—Museum of Newark.

                    Aunt Rose   30
Hitler is dead, Hitler is in Eternity; Hitler is with
        Tamburlane and Emily Brontë[2]

Though I see you walking still, a ghost on Osborne Terrace
        down the long dark hall to the front door
        limping a little with a pinched smile   35
        in what must have been a silken
           flower dress
welcoming my father, the Poet, on his visit to Newark
        —see you arriving in the living room
           dancing on your crippled leg   40
        and clapping hands his book
        had been accepted by Liveright[3]

Hitler is dead and Liveright's gone out of business
The Attic of the Past and *Everlasting Minute* are out of print
        Uncle Harry sold his last silk stocking   45
        Claire quit interpretive dancing school
        Buba sits a wrinkled monument in Old
           Ladies Home blinking at new babies

last time I saw you was the hospital
        pale skull protruding under ashen skin   50
        blue veined unconscious girl
           in an oxygen tent
        the war in Spain has ended long ago
           Aunt Rose

---

[2] Tamburlane (1336?–1405), Mongol conqueror; Emily Brontë (1818–1848), English novelist.
[3] A publishing firm.

Casual Wear   1984

JAMES MERRILL   [1926–1995]

Your average tourist: Fifty. 2.3
Times married. Dressed, this year, in Ferdi Plinthbower
Originals. Odds 1 to 9^{10}
Against her strolling past the Embassy

Today at noon. Your average terrorist: 5
Twenty-five. Celibate. No use for trends,
At least in clothing. Mark, though, where it ends.
People have come forth made of colored mist

Unsmiling on one hundred million screens
To tell of his prompt phone call to the station,   10
"Claiming responsibility"—devastation
Signed with a flourish, like the dead wife's jeans.

Five Ways to Kill a Man   1963

EDWIN BROCK   [b. 1927]

There are many cumbersome ways to kill a man:
you can make him carry a plank of wood
to the top of a hill and nail him to it. To do this
properly you require a crowd of people
wearing sandals, a cock that crows, a cloak   5
to dissect, a sponge, some vinegar and one
man to hammer the nails home.

Or you can take a length of steel,
shaped and chased° in a traditional way,   ornamented
and attempt to pierce the metal cage he wears.   10
But for this you need white horses,
English trees, men with bows and arrows,
at least two flags, a prince and a
castle to hold your banquet in.

Dispensing with nobility, you may, if the wind   15
allows, blow gas at him. But then you need
a mile of mud sliced through with ditches,

not to mention black boots, bomb craters,
more mud, a plague of rats, a dozen songs
and some round hats made of steel.   20

In an age of aeroplanes, you may fly
miles above your victim and dispose of him by
pressing one small switch. All you then
require is an ocean to separate you, two
systems of government, a nation's scientists,   25
several factories, a psychopath and
land that no one needs for several years.

These are, as I began, cumbersome ways
to kill a man. Simpler, direct, and much more neat
is to see that he is living somewhere in the middle   30
of the twentieth century, and leave him there.

For the Anniversary
of My Death   1967

W. S. MERWIN   [b. 1927]

Every year without knowing it I have passed the day
When the last fires will wave to me
And the silence will set out
Tireless traveller
Like the beam of a lightless star   5

Then I will no longer
Find myself in life as in a strange garment
Surprised at the earth
And the love of a woman
And the shamelessness of men   10
As today writing after three days of rain
Hearing the wren sing and the falling cease
And bowing not knowing to what

People*

(trans. 1962)

YEVGENY YEVTUSHENKO [b. 1933]

No people are uninteresting.
Their fate is like the chronicle of planets.

Nothing in them is not particular,
and planet is dissimilar from planet.

And if a man lived in obscurity   5
making his friends in that obscurity
obscurity is not uninteresting.

To each his world is private,
and in that world one excellent minute.

And in that world one tragic minute.   10
These are private.

In any man who dies there dies with him
his first snow and kiss and fight.
It goes with him.

They are left books and bridges   15
and painted canvas and machinery.

Whose fate is to survive.
But what has gone is also not nothing:

by the rule of the game something has gone.
Not people die but worlds die in them.   20

Whom we knew as faulty, the earth's creatures.
Of whom, essentially, what did we know?

Brother of a brother? Friend of friends?
Lover of lover?

We who knew our fathers   25
in everything, in nothing.

---

* Translated by Robin Milner-Gulland and Peter Levi.

They perish. They cannot be brought back.
The secret worlds are not regenerated.

And every time again and again
I make my lament against destruction.   30

The long death   1980

FOR WENDY TERESA SIMON (SEPTEMBER 25, 1954–AUGUST 7, 1979)

MARGE PIERCY   [b. 1936]

Radiation is like oppression,
the average daily kind of subliminal toothache
you get almost used to, the stench
of chlorine in the water, of smog in the wind.

We comprehend the disasters of the moment,   5
the nursing home fire, the river in flood
pouring over the sandbag levee, the airplane
crash with fragments of burnt bodies
scattered among the hunks of twisted metal,
the grenade in the marketplace, the sinking ship.   10

But how to grasp a thing that does not
kill you today or tomorrow
but slowly from the inside in twenty years.
How to feel that a corporate or governmental
choice means we bear twisted genes and our   15
grandchildren will be stillborn if our
children are very lucky.

Slow death can not be photographed for the six
o'clock news. It's all statistical,
the gross national product or the prime   20
lending rate. Yet if our eyes saw
in the right spectrum, how it would shine,
lurid as magenta neon.

If we could smell radiation like seeping
gas, if we could sense it as heat, if we   25

could hear it as a low ominous roar
of the earth shifting, then we would not sit
and be poisoned while industry spokesmen
talk of acceptable millirems and .02
cancer per population thousand.   30

We acquiesce at murder so long as it is slow,
murder from asbestos dust, from tobacco,
from lead in the water, from sulphur in the air,
and fourteen years later statistics are printed
on the rise in leukemia among children.   35
We never see their faces. They never stand,
those poisoned children together in a courtyard,
and are gunned down by men in three-piece suits.

The shipyard workers who built nuclear
submarines, the soldiers who were marched   40
into the Nevada desert to be tested by the H-
bomb, the people who work in power plants,
they die quietly years after in hospital
wards and not on the evening news.

The soft spring rain floats down and the air   45
is perfumed with pine and earth. Seedlings
drink it in, robins sip it in puddles,
you run in it and feel clean and strong,
the spring rain blowing from the irradiated
cloud over the power plant.   50

Radiation is oppression, the daily average
kind, the kind you're almost used to
and live with as the years abrade you,
high blood pressure, ulcers, cramps, migraine,
a hacking cough: you take it inside   55
and it becomes pain and you say, not
They are killing me, but *I am sick now.*

QUESTIONS

1. What sort of corporate or governmental choices (ll. 14–15) might result in "twisted genes"?   **2.** In what sense is "slow death . . . statistical" (ll. 18–19)?   **3.** Who acquiesces "at murder so long as it is slow" (l. 31)? Why?   **4.** Do you find the last three lines ironic? Explain.   **5.** What "prosaic" qualities do you find in this piece? Do they overbalance its "poetic" qualities? Explain.

WRITING TOPIC
In an argumentative essay, either support or attack the assertion that the benefits derived from some avoidable industrial pollution outweigh the relatively modest damage it causes.

The Ignominy of the Living

1989

KATHLEEN NORRIS   [b. 1947]

The undertaker had placed pink netting
around your face. I removed it
and gave you a small bouquet, encumbering you
into eternity. "Impedimenta," I hear you say,
scornfully, the way you said it at Penn Station   5
when we struggled to put your bag onto a contraption
of cords and wheels. "Laurel and Hardy[1] got paid for this,"
I said the third time it fell off,
narrowly missing my foot.

You would have laughed   10
at the place we brought you to, the hush of carpet,
violins sliding through "The Way We Were."
"Please turn the music off," I said, civilly,
to the undertaker's assistant.
We had an open grave—no artificial turf—   15
and your friends lowered you into the ground.

Once you dreamed your mother sweeping
an earthen floor
in a dark, low-ceilinged room.
I see her now: I, too, want to run.   20
And the "ignominy of the living,"
words you nearly spat out
when one of your beloved dead
was ill-remembered; I thought of that
as I removed the netting.   25

The Ignominy of the Living
    [1] Stan Laurel (1890–1965) and Oliver Hardy (1892–1957) were a celebrated comedy team who made many popular movies during the 1920s, 1930s, and 1940s.

Today I passed St. Mary's
as the Angelus[2] sounded.
You would have liked that, the ancient practice
in the prairie town not a hundred years old,
the world careering disastrously toward the twenty-first century. 30
I stopped and prayed for you.
Then a recording of "My Way" came scratching out
on the electronic carillon.
"Oh, hell," I said,
and prayed for Frank Sinatra, too. 35

QUESTIONS

1. Explain the title.   **2.** Why does the speaker ask the assistant undertaker to turn off the music? In this connection, why does she say, "Oh, hell" at the end when she hears the electronic carillon playing "My Way"?   **3.** Explicate lines 17–19.

WRITING TOPIC

If you have ever attended the funeral of someone you knew well, describe your feelings and reactions to the service. Did it seem appropriate and tasteful? Did it leave you satisfied that the tribute was sincere and honest, that the person being eulogized was the person you knew?

God, A Poem   1984

JAMES FENTON   [b. 1949]

A nasty surprise in a sandwich,
A drawing-pin caught in your sock,
The limpest of shakes from a hand which
You'd thought would be firm as a rock,

A serious mistake in a nightie,   5
A grave disappointment all round
Is all that you'll get from th'Almighty,
Is all that you'll get underground.

Oh he *said*: "If you lay off the crumpet
I'll see you alright in the end.   10

The Ignominy of the Living
    [2] In the Roman Catholic Church, a bell rung as a call to prayer.

Just hang on until the last trumpet.
Have faith in me, chum—I'm your friend."

But if you remind him, he'll tell you:
"I'm sorry, I must have been pissed—
Though your name rings a sort of a bell. You   15
Should have guessed that I do not exist.

"I didn't exist at Creation,
I didn't exist at the Flood,
And I won't be around for Salvation
To sort out the sheep from the cud—   20

"Or whatever the phrase is. The fact is
In soteriological terms
I'm a crude existential malpractice
And you are a diet of worms.

"You're a nasty surprise in a sandwich.   25
You're a drawing-pin caught in my sock.
You're the limpest of shakes from a hand which
I'd have thought would be firm as a rock,

"You're a serious mistake in a nightie,
You're a grave disappointment all round—   30
That's all that you are," says th'Almighty,
"And that's all that you'll be underground."

Fast Break   1985

IN MEMORY OF DENNIS TURNER, 1946–1984

EDWARD HIRSCH   [b. 1950]

A hook shot kisses the rim and
hangs there, helplessly, but doesn't drop,

and for once our gangly starting center
boxes out his man and times his jump

perfectly, gathering the orange leather   5
from the air like a cherished possession

and spinning around to throw a strike
to the outlet who is already shoveling

an underhand pass toward the other guard
scissoring past a flat-footed defender   10

who looks stunned and nailed to the floor
in the wrong direction, trying to catch sight

of a high, gliding dribble and a man
letting the play develop in front of him

in slow motion, almost exactly   15
like a coach's drawing on the blackboard,

both forwards racing down the court
the way that forwards should, fanning out

and filling the lanes in tandem, moving
together as brothers passing the ball   20

between them without a dribble, without
a single bounce hitting the hardwood

until the guard finally lunges out
and commits to the wrong man

while the power-forward explodes past them   25
in a fury, taking the ball into the air

by himself now and laying it gently
against the glass for a lay-up,

but losing his balance in the process,
inexplicably falling, hitting the floor   30

with a wild, headlong motion
for the game he loved like a country

and swiveling back to see an orange blur
floating perfectly through the net.

QUESTIONS
1. What suggests that this poem is about more than a basketball game?   **2.** The last
three stanzas describe an event on the basketball court; what might that event
suggest about the life of Dennis Turner, to whom the poem is dedicated?

WRITING TOPIC

In an essay, use the rules and language of any sport as an extended metaphor for an event in your life.

Funeral Home   1991

MARIANNE BURKE   [b. 1957]

Let us think of you spared, carried gently
in the arms of the ocean that's piped
through speakers, spreading a hush in Parmele's[1]
where we sit, adrift, on the parlor couch
between time, in death's <u>caesura.</u>   *a pause in a line of verse dictated by sense, or natural speech rhythm rather than by metrics*

The funeral director ticks off a list
of questions. He wants the facts, reduces you
to an abstract—mother with a capital "M."
Nowhere will it say how petite you were,
that your wedding ring fits my pinkie finger,   10

or that, tucked into your coffin, you will look
like a doll we will never outgrow.
Downstairs, he shows us his fleet
of caskets, satin-lined, open-lidded—
music boxes whose strains are too fine   15

for us to hear, like your voice,
utterless, our names dead on your tongue.
Even here the ocean's cold hush.

You are lost at sea.
To think we must choose a vessel,   20
one that will not float but sink.
Mahogany is what we set you in—
our mother of pearl, our buried treasure.

QUESTIONS

1. Trace the sea and ship imagery within the poem. Do you find it appropriate? Explain.   **2.** How is the funeral director characterized? How does the speaker respond to his behavior?

---

[1] The name of the funeral home.

THE
PRESENCE
OF DEATH

Tombstones, 1942 by Jacob Lawrence

DRAMA

No Exit

1944

JEAN-PAUL SARTRE [1905–1980]

CHARACTERS

Valet   Estelle
Garcin   Inez

Huis Clos (No Exit) *was presented for the first time at the Théâtre du Vieux-Colombier, Paris, in May 1944.*

SCENE. *A drawing-room in Second Empire style. A massive bronze ornament stands on the mantelpiece.*

Garcin (*enters, accompanied by the room-valet, and glances around him*).   Hm! So here we are?

Valet.   Yes, Mr. Garcin.

Garcin.   And this is what it looks like?

Valet.   Yes.

Garcin.   Second Empire furniture, I observe. . . . Well, well, I dare say one gets used to it in time.

Valet.   Some do. Some don't.

Garcin.   Are all the other rooms like this one?

Valet.   How could they be? We cater for all sorts: Chinamen and Indians, for instance. What use would they have for a Second Empire chair?

Garcin.   And what use do you suppose *I* have for one? Do you know who I was? . . . Oh, well, it's no great matter. And, to tell the truth, I had quite a habit of living among furniture that I didn't relish, and in false positions. I'd even come to like it. A false position in a Louis-Philippe dining-room—you know the style?—well, that had its points, you know. Bogus in bogus, so to speak.

Valet.   And you'll find that living in a Second Empire drawing-room has its points.

Garcin.   Really? . . . Yes, yes, I dare say. . . . (*He takes another look around.*) Still, I certainly didn't expect—this! You know what they tell us down there?

Valet. What about?

Garcin. About (*makes a sweeping gesture*) this—er—residence.

Valet. Really, sir, how could you believe such cock-and-bull stories? Told by people who'd never set foot here. For, of course, if they had—

Garcin. Quite so. (*Both laugh. Abruptly the laugh dies from Garcin's face.*) But, I say, where are the instruments of torture?

Valet. The what?

Garcin. The racks and red-hot pincers and all the other paraphernalia?

Valet. Ah, you must have your little joke, sir!

Garcin. My little joke? Oh, I see. No, I wasn't joking. (*A short silence. He strolls around the room.*) No mirrors, I notice. No windows. Only to be expected. And nothing breakable. (*Bursts out angrily.*) But, damn it all, they might have left me my toothbrush!

Valet. That's good! So you haven't yet got over your—what-do-you-call-it?— sense of human dignity? Excuse me smiling.

Garcin (*thumping ragefully the arm of an armchair*). I'll ask you to be more polite. I quite realize the position I'm in, but I won't tolerate . . .

Valet. Sorry, sir. No offense meant. But all our guests ask me the same questions. Silly questions, if you'll pardon me saying so. Where's the torture-chamber? That's the first thing they ask, all of them. They don't bother their heads about the bathroom requisites, that I can assure you. But after a bit, when they've got their nerve back, they start in about their toothbrushes and what-not. Good heavens, Mr. Garcin, can't you use your brains? What, I ask you, would be the point of brushing your teeth?

Garcin (*more calmly*). Yes, of course you're right. (*He looks around again.*) And why should one want to see oneself in a looking-glass? But that bronze contraption on the mantelpiece, that's another story. I suppose there will be times when I stare my eyes out at it. Stare my eyes out—see what I mean? . . . All right, let's put our cards on the table. I assure you I'm quite conscious of my position. Shall I tell you what it feels like? A man's drowning, choking, sinking by inches, till only his eyes are just above water. And what does he see? A bronze atrocity by—what's the fellow's name?—Barbedienne. A collector's piece. As in a nightmare. That's their idea, isn't it? . . . No, I suppose you're under orders not to answer questions; and I won't insist. But don't forget, my man, I've a good notion of what's coming to me, so don't you boast you've caught me off my guard. I'm facing the situation, facing it. (*He starts pacing the room again.*) So that's that; no toothbrush. And no bed, either. One never sleeps, I take it?

Valet. That's so.

Garcin. Just as I expected. *Why* should one sleep? A sort of drowsiness steals on you, tickles you behind the ears, and you feel your eyes closing—but why sleep? You lie down on the sofa and—in a flash, sleep flies away. Miles and miles away. So you rub your eyes, get up, and it starts all over again.

Valet. Romantic, that's what you are.

Garcin. Will you keep quiet, please! . . . I won't make a scene, I shan't be sorry for myself, I'll face the situation, as I said just now. Face it fairly and squarely. I won't have it springing at me from behind, before I've time to size it up. And you call that being "romantic"! . . . So it comes to this; one doesn't need rest. Why bother about sleep if one isn't sleepy? That stands to reason, doesn't it? Wait a minute, there's a snag somewhere; something disagreeable. Why, now, should it be disagreeable? . . . Ah, I see; it's life without a break.

Valet.   What do you mean by that?

Garcin.   What do I mean? (*Eyes the Valet suspiciously.*) I thought as much. That's why there's something so beastly, so damn bad-mannered, in the way you stare at me. They're paralyzed.

Valet.   What are you talking about?

Garcin.   Your eyelids. We move ours up and down. Blinking, we call it. It's like a small black shutter that clicks down and makes a break. Everything goes black; one's eyes are moistened. You can't imagine how restful, refreshing, it is. Four thousand little rests per hour. Four thousand little respites—just think! . . . So that's the idea. I'm to live without eyelids. Don't act the fool, you know what I mean. No eyelids, no sleep; it follows, doesn't it? I shall never sleep again. But then—how shall I endure my own company? Try to understand. You see, I'm fond of teasing, it's a second nature with me—and I'm used to teasing myself. Plaguing myself, if you prefer; I don't tease nicely. But I can't go on doing that without a break. Down there I had my nights. I slept. I always had good nights. By way of compensation, I suppose. And happy little dreams. There was a green field. Just an ordinary field. I used to stroll in it. . . . Is it daytime now?

Valet.   Can't you see? The lights are on.

Garcin.   Ah yes, I've got it. It's *your* daytime. And outside?

Valet.   Outside?

Garcin.   Damn it, you know what I mean. Beyond that wall.

Valet.   There's a passage.

Garcin.   And at the end of the passage?

Valet.   There's more rooms, more passages, and stairs.

Garcin.   And what lies beyond them?

Valet.   That's all.

Garcin.   But surely you have a day off sometimes. Where do you go?

Valet.   To my uncle's place. He's the head valet here. He has a room on the third floor.

Garcin.   I should have guessed as much. Where's the light-switch?

Valet.   There isn't any.

Garcin.   What? Can't one turn off the light?

Valet.   Oh, the management can cut off the current if they want to. But I can't remember their having done so on this floor. We have all the electricity we want.

Garcin.   So one has to live with one's eyes open all the time?

Valet.   To *live*, did you say?

Garcin.   Don't let's quibble over words. With one's eyes open. Forever. Always broad daylight in my eyes—and in my head. (*Short silence.*) And suppose I took that contraption on the mantelpiece and dropped it on the lamp—wouldn't it go out?

Valet.   You can't move it. It's too heavy.

Garcin (*seizing the bronze ornament and trying to lift it*).   You're right. It's too heavy.

(*A short silence follows.*)

Valet.   Very well, sir, if you don't need me any more, I'll be off.

Garcin.   What? You're going? (*The Valet goes up to the door.*) Wait. (*Valet looks around.*) That's a bell, isn't it? (*Valet nods.*) And if I ring, you're bound to come?

Valet.   Well, yes, that's so—in a way. But you can never be sure about that bell. There's something wrong with the wiring, and it doesn't always work. (*Garcin goes to the bell-push and presses the button. A bell purrs outside.*)

Garcin.   It's working all right.

Valet (*looking surprised*).   So it is. (*He, too, presses the button.*) But I shouldn't count on it too much if I were you. It's—capricious. Well, I really must go now. (*Garcin makes a gesture to detain him.*) Yes, sir?

Garcin.   No, never mind. (*He goes to the mantelpiece and picks up a paper-knife.*) What's this?

Valet.   Can't you see? An ordinary paper-knife.

Garcin.   Are there books here?

Valet.   No.

Garcin.   Then what's the use of this? (*Valet shrugs his shoulders.*) Very well. You can go. (*Valet goes out.*)

(*Garcin is by himself. He goes to the bronze ornament and strokes it reflectively. He sits down; then gets up, goes to the bell-push, and presses the button. The bell remains silent. He tries two or three times, without success. Then he tries to open the door, also without success. He calls the Valet several times, but gets no result. He beats the door with his fists, still calling. Suddenly he grows calm and sits down again. At the same moment the door opens and Inez enters, followed by the Valet.*)

Valet.   Did you call, sir?

Garcin (*on the point of answering "Yes"—but then his eyes fall on Inez*).   No.

Valet (*turning to Inez*).   This is your room, madam. (*Inez says nothing.*) If there's any information you require—? (*Inez still keeps silent, and the Valet looks slightly huffed.*) Most of our guests have quite a lot to ask me. But I won't insist. Anyhow, as regards the toothbrush, and the electric bell, and that thing on the mantelshelf, this gentleman can tell you anything you want to know as well as I could. We've had a little chat, him and me. (*Valet goes out.*) (*Garcin refrains from looking at Inez, who is inspecting the room. Abruptly she turns to Garcin.*)

Inez. Where's Florence? (*Garcin does not reply.*) Didn't you hear? I asked you about Florence. Where is she?

Garcin. I haven't an idea.

Inez. Ah, that's the way it works, is it? Torture by separation. Well, as far as I'm concerned, you won't get anywhere. Florence was a tiresome little fool, and I shan't miss her in the least.

Garcin. I beg your pardon. Who do you suppose I am?

Inez. You? Why, the torturer, of course.

Garcin (*looks startled, then bursts out laughing*). Well, that's a good one! Too comic for words. I the torturer! So you came in, had a look at me, and thought I was—er—one of the staff. Of course, it's that silly fellow's fault; he should have introduced us. A torturer indeed! I'm Joseph Garcin, journalist and man of letters by profession. And as we're both in the same boat, so to speak, might I ask you, Mrs.—?

Inez (*testily*). Not "Mrs." I'm unmarried.

Garcin. Right. That's a start, anyway. Well, now that we've broken the ice, do you *really* think I look like a torturer? And, by the way, how does one recognize torturers when one sees them? Evidently you've ideas on the subject.

Inez. They look frightened.

Garcin. Frightened! But how ridiculous! Of whom should they be frightened? Of their victims?

Inez. Laugh away, but I know what I'm talking about. I've often watched my face in the glass.

Garcin. In the glass? (*He looks around him.*) How beastly of them! They've removed everything in the least resembling a glass. (*Short silence.*) Anyhow, I can assure you I'm not frightened. Not that I take my position lightly; I realize its gravity only too well. But I'm not afraid.

Inez (*shrugging her shoulders*). That's your affair. (*Silence.*) Must you be here all the time, or do you take a stroll outside, now and then?

Garcin. The door's locked.

Inez. Oh! . . . That's too bad.

Garcin. I can quite understand that it bores you having me here. And I, too—well, quite frankly, I'd rather be alone. I want to think things out, you know; to set my life in order, and one does that better by oneself. But I'm sure we'll manage to pull along together somehow. I'm no talker, I don't move much; in fact I'm a peaceful sort of fellow. Only, if I may venture on a suggestion, we should make a point of being extremely courteous to each other. That will ease the situation for us both.

Inez. I'm not polite.

Garcin. Then I must be polite for two.

(*A longish silence. Garcin is sitting on a sofa, while Inez paces up and down the room.*)

Inez (*fixing her eyes on him*).   Your mouth!

Garcin (*as if waking from a dream*).   I beg your pardon.

Inez.   Can't you keep your mouth still? You keep twisting it about all the time. It's grotesque.

Garcin.   So sorry. I wasn't aware of it.

Inez.   That's just what I reproach you with. (*Garcin's mouth twitches.*) There you are! You talk about politeness, and you don't even try to control your face. Remember you're not alone; you've no right to inflict the sight of your fear on me.

Garcin (*getting up and going towards her*).   How about you? Aren't you afraid?

Inez.   What would be the use? There was some point in being afraid *before*; while one still had hope.

Garcin (*in a low voice*).   There's no more hope—but it's still "before." We haven't yet begun to suffer.

Inez.   That's so. (*A short silence.*) Well? What's going to happen?

Garcin.   I don't know. I'm waiting.

(*Silence again. Garcin sits down and Inez resumes her pacing up and down the room. Garcin's mouth twitches; after a glance at Inez he buries his face in his hands. Enter Estelle with the Valet. Estelle looks at Garcin, whose face is still hidden by his hands.*)

Estelle (*to Garcin*).   No! Don't look up. I know what you're hiding with your hands. I know you've no face left. (*Garcin removes his hands.*) What! (*A short pause. Then, in a tone of surprise*) But I don't know you!

Garcin.   I'm not the torturer, madam.

Estelle.   I never thought you were. I—I thought someone was trying to play a rather nasty trick on me. (*To the Valet*) Is anyone else coming?

Valet.   No, madam. No one else is coming.

Estelle.   Oh! Then we're to stay by ourselves, the three of us, this gentleman, this lady, and myself. (*She starts laughing.*)

Garcin (*angrily*).   There's nothing to laugh about.

Estelle (*still laughing*).   It's those sofas. They're so hideous. And just look how they've been arranged. It makes me think of New Year's Day—when I used to visit that boring old aunt of mine, Aunt Mary. Her house is full of horrors like that. . . . I suppose each of us has a sofa of his own. Is that one mine? (*To the Valet*) But you can't expect me to sit on that one. It would be too horrible for words. I'm in pale blue and it's vivid green.

Inez.   Would you prefer mine?

Estelle.   That claret-colored one, you mean? That's very sweet of you, but really—no, I don't think it'd be so much better. What's the good of worrying, anyhow? We've got to take what comes to us, and I'll stick to the green one. (*Pauses.*) The only one which might do, at a pinch, is that gentleman's. (*Another pause.*)

Inez.   Did you hear, Mr. Garcin?

Garcin (*with a slight start*).   Oh—the sofa, you mean. So sorry. (*He rises.*) Please take it, madam.

Estelle.   Thanks. (*She takes off her coat and drops it on the sofa. A short silence.*) Well, as we're to live together, I suppose we'd better introduce ourselves. My name's Rigault. Estelle Rigault. (*Garcin bows and is going to announce his name, but Inez steps in front of him.*)

Inez.   And I'm Inez Serrano. Very pleased to meet you.

Garcin (*bowing again*).   Joseph Garcin.

Valet.   Do you require me any longer?

Estelle.   No, you can go. I'll ring when I want you. (*Exit Valet, with polite bows to everyone.*)

Inez.   You're very pretty. I wish we'd had some flowers to welcome you with.

Estelle.   Flowers? Yes, I loved flowers. Only they'd fade so quickly here, wouldn't they? It's so stuffy. Oh, well, the great thing is to keep as cheerful as we can, don't you agree? Of course, you, too, are—

Inez.   Yes. Last week. What about you?

Estelle.   I'm—quite recent. Yesterday. As a matter of fact, the ceremony's not quite over. (*Her tone is natural enough, but she seems to be seeing what she describes.*) The wind's blowing my sister's veil all over the place. She's trying her best to cry. Come dear! Make another effort. That's better. Two tears, two little tears are twinkling under the black veil. Oh dear! What a sight Olga looks this morning! She's holding my sister's arm, helping her along. She's not crying, and I don't blame her; tears always mess one's face up, don't they? Olga was my bosom friend, you know.

Inez.   Did you suffer much?

Estelle.   No. I was only half conscious, mostly.

Inez.   What was it?

Estelle.   Pneumonia. (*In the same tone as before*) It's over now, they're leaving the cemetery. Good-by. Good-by. Quite a crowd they are. My husband's stayed at home. Prostrated with grief, poor man. (*To Inez*) How about you?

Inez.   The gas stove.

Estelle.   And you, Mr. Garcin?

Garcin.   Twelve bullets through my chest. (*Estelle makes a horrified gesture.*) Sorry! I fear I'm not good company among the dead.

Estelle.   Please, please don't use that word. It's so—so crude. In terribly bad taste, really. It doesn't mean much, anyhow. Somehow I feel we've never been so much alive as now. If we've absolutely got to mention this—this state of things, I suggest we call ourselves—wait!—absentees. Have you been—been absent for long?

Garcin.   About a month.

Estelle.   Where do you come from?

Garcin.   From Rio.

Estelle.   I'm from Paris. Have you anyone left down there?

Garcin.   Yes, my wife. (*In the same tone as Estelle has been using*) She's waiting at the entrance of the barracks. She comes there every day. But they won't let her in. Now she's trying to peep between the bars. She doesn't yet know I'm—absent, but she suspects it. Now she's going away. She's wearing her black dress. So much the better, she won't need to change. She isn't crying, but she never did cry, anyhow. It's a bright sunny day and she's like a black shadow creeping down the empty street. Those big tragic eyes of hers—with that martyred look they always had. Oh, how she got on my nerves!

(*A short silence. Garcin sits on the central sofa and buries his head in his hands.*)

Inez.   Estelle!

Estelle.   Please, Mr. Garcin!

Garcin.   What is it?

Estelle.   You're sitting on my sofa.

Garcin.   I beg your pardon. (*He gets up.*)

Estelle.   You looked so—so far away. Sorry I disturbed you.

Garcin.   I was setting my life in order. (*Inez starts laughing.*) You may laugh, but you'd do better to follow my example.

Inez.   No need. My life's in perfect order. It tidied itself up nicely of its own accord. So I needn't bother about it now.

Garcin.   Really? You imagine it's so simple as that. (*He runs his hand over his forehead.*) Whew! How hot it is here! Do you mind if—? (*He begins taking off his coat.*)

Estelle.   How dare you! (*More gently*) No, please don't. I loathe men in their shirt-sleeves.

Garcin (*putting on his coat again*).   All right. (*A short pause.*) Of course, I used to spend my nights in the newspaper office, and it was a regular Black Hole, so we never kept our coats on. Stiflingly hot it could be. (*Short pause. In the same tone as previously*) Stifling, that it *is*. It's night now.

Estelle.   That's so. Olga's undressing; it must be after midnight. How quickly the time passes, on earth!

Inez.   Yes, after midnight. They've sealed up my room. It's dark, pitch-dark, and empty.

Garcin.   They've slung their coats on the backs of the chairs and rolled up their shirt-sleeves above the elbow. The air stinks of men and cigar-smoke. (*A short silence.*) I used to like living among men in their shirt-sleeves.

Estelle (*aggressively*).   Well, in that case our tastes differ. That's all it proves. (*Turning to Inez*) What about you? Do you like men in their shirt-sleeves?

Inez.   Oh, I don't care much for men any way.

Estelle (*looking at the other two with a puzzled air*).   Really I can't imagine why they put us three together. It doesn't make sense.

Inez (*stifling a laugh*).   What's that you said?

Estelle. I'm looking at you two and thinking that we're going to live together. . . . It's so absurd. I expected to meet old friends, or relatives.

Inez. Yes, a charming old friend—with a hole in the middle of his face.

Estelle. Yes, him too. He danced the tango so divinely. Like a professional. . . . But why, why should we of all people be put together?

Garcin. A pure fluke, I should say. They lodge folks as they can, in the order of their coming. (*To Inez*) Why are you laughing?

Inez. Because you amuse me, with your "flukes." As if they left anything to chance! But I suppose you've got to reassure yourself somehow.

Estelle (*hesitantly*).   I wonder, now. Don't you think we may have met each other at some time in our lives?

Inez. Never. I shouldn't have forgotten you.

Estelle. Or perhaps we have friends in common. I wonder if you know the Dubois-Seymours?

Inez. Not likely.

Estelle. But *everyone* went to their parties.

Inez. What's their job?

Estelle. Oh, they don't do anything. But they have a lovely house in the country, and hosts of people visit them.

Inez. I didn't. I was a post-office clerk.

Estelle (*recoiling a little*).   Ah, yes. . . . Of course, in that case—(*A pause.*) And you, Mr. Garcin?

Garcin. We've never met. I always lived in Rio.

Estelle. Then you must be right. It's mere chance that has brought us together.

Inez. Mere chance? Then it's by chance this room is furnished as we see it. It's an accident that the sofa on the right is a livid green, and that one on the left's wine-red. Mere chance? Well, just try to shift the sofas and you'll see the difference quick enough. And that statue on the mantelpiece, do you think it's there by accident? And what about the heat here? How about that? (*A short silence.*) I tell you they've thought it all out. Down to the last detail. Nothing was left to chance. This room was all set for us.

Estelle. But really! Everything here's so hideous; all in angles, so uncomfortable. I always loathed angles.

Inez (*shrugging her shoulders*).   And do you think I lived in a Second Empire drawing-room?

Estelle. So it was all fixed up beforehand?

Inez. Yes. And they've put us together deliberately.

Estelle. Then it's not mere chance that *you* precisely are sitting opposite *me*? But what can be the idea behind it?

Inez. Ask me another! I only know they're waiting.

Estelle. I never could bear the idea of anyone's expecting something from me. It always made me want to do just the opposite.

Inez. Well, do it. Do it if you can. You don't even know what they expect.

Estelle (*stamping her foot*).   It's outrageous! So something's coming to me from you two? (*She eyes each in turn.*) Something nasty, I suppose. There are some faces that tell me everything at once. Yours don't convey anything.

Garcin (*turning abruptly towards Inez*).   Look here! Why are we together? You've given us quite enough hints, you may as well come out with it.

Inez (*in a surprised tone*).   But I know nothing, absolutely nothing about it. I'm as much in the dark as you are.

Garcin.   We've *got* to know. (*Ponders for a while.*)

Inez.   If only each of us had the guts to tell—

Garcin.   Tell what?

Inez.   Estelle!

Estelle.   Yes?

Inez.   What have you done? I mean, why have they sent you here?

Estelle (*quickly*).   That's just it. I haven't a notion, not the foggiest. In fact, I'm wondering if there hasn't been some ghastly mistake. (*To Inez*) Don't smile. Just think of the number of people who—who become absentees every day. There must be thousands and thousands, and probably they're sorted out by—by understrappers, you know what I mean. Stupid employees who don't know their job. So they're bound to make mistakes sometimes. . . . Do stop smiling. (*To Garcin*) Why don't you speak? If they made a mistake in my case, they may have done the same about you. (*To Inez*) And you, too. Anyhow, isn't it better to think we've got here by mistake?

Inez.   Is that all you have to tell us?

Estelle.   What else should I tell? I've nothing to hide. I lost my parents when I was a kid, and I had my young brother to bring up. We were terribly poor and when an old friend of my people asked me to marry him I said yes. He was very well off, and quite nice. My brother was a very delicate child and needed all sorts of attention, so really that was the right thing for me to do, don't you agree? My husband was old enough to be my father, but for six years we had a happy married life. Then two years ago I met the man I was fated to love. We knew it the moment we set eyes on each other. He asked me to run away with him, and I refused. Then I got pneumonia and it finished me. That's the whole story. No doubt, by certain standards, I did wrong to sacrifice my youth to a man nearly three times my age. (*To Garcin*) Do *you* think that could be called a sin?

Garcin.   Certainly not. (*A short silence.*) And now, tell me, do you think it's a crime to stand by one's principles?

Estelle.   Of course not. Surely no one could blame a man for that!

Garcin.   Wait a bit! I ran a pacifist newspaper. Then war broke out. What was I to do? Everyone was watching me, wondering: "Will he dare?" Well, I dared. I folded my arms and they shot me. Had I done anything wrong?

Estelle (*laying her hand on his arm*).   Wrong? On the contrary. You were—

Inez (*breaks in ironically*).   —a hero! And how about your wife, Mr. Garcin?

Garcin.   That's simple. I'd rescued her from—from the gutter.

Estelle (*to Inez*).   You see! You see!

Inez.   Yes, I see. (*A pause.*) Look here! What's the point of play-acting, trying to throw dust in each other's eyes? We're all tarred with the same brush.

Estelle (*indignantly*).   How dare you!

Inez.   Yes, we are criminals—murderers—all three of us. We're in hell, my pets; they never make mistakes, and people aren't damned for nothing.

Estelle.   Stop! For heaven's sake—

Inez.   In hell! Damned souls—that's us, all three!

Estelle.   Keep quiet! I forbid you to use such disgusting words.

Inez.   A damned soul—that's you, my little plaster saint. And ditto our friend there, the noble pacifist. We've had our hour of pleasure, haven't we? There have been people who burned their lives out for our sakes—and we chuckled over it. So now we have to pay the reckoning.

Garcin (*raising his fist*).   Will you keep your mouth shut, damn it!

Inez (*confronting him fearlessly, but with a look of vast surprise*).   Well, well! (*A pause.*) Ah, I understand now. I know why they've put us three together.

Garcin.   I advise you to—to think twice before you say any more.

Inez.   Wait! You'll see how simple it is. Childishly simple. Obviously there aren't any physical torments—you agree, don't you? And yet we're in hell. And no one else will come here. We'll stay in this room together, the three of us, for ever and ever. ... In short, there's someone absent here, the official torturer.

Garcin (*sotto voce*).   I'd noticed that.

Inez.   It's obvious what they're after—an economy of man-power—or devil-power, if you prefer. The same idea as in the cafeteria, where customers serve themselves.

Estelle.   What ever do you mean?

Inez.   I mean that each of us will act as torturer of the two others.

(*There is a short silence while they digest this information.*)

Garcin (*gently*).   No, I shall never be your torturer. I wish neither of you any harm, and I've no concern with you. None at all. So the solution's easy enough; each of us stays put in his or her corner and takes no notice of the others. You here, you here, and I there. Like soldiers at our posts. Also, we mustn't speak. Not one word. That won't be difficult; each of us has plenty of material for self-communings. I think I could stay ten thousand years with only my thoughts for company.

Estelle.   Have *I* got to keep silent, too?

Garcin.   Yes. And that way we—we'll work out our salvation. Looking into ourselves, never raising our heads. Agreed?

Inez.   Agreed.

Estelle (*after some hesitation*).   I agree.

Garcin.   Then—good-by.

(*He goes to his sofa and buries his head in his hands. There is a long silence; then Inez begins singing to herself.*)

Inez (*singing*).

> What a crowd in Whitefriars Lane!
> They've set trestles in a row,
> With a scaffold and the knife,
> And a pail of bran below.
> Come, good folks, to Whitefriars lane,
> Come to see the merry show!
>
> The headsman rose at crack of dawn,
> He'd a long day's work in hand,
> Chopping heads off generals,
> Priests and peers and admirals,
> All the highest in the land.
> What a crowd in Whitefriars Lane!
>
> See them standing in a line,
> Ladies all dressed up so fine.
> But their heads have got to go,
> Heads and hats roll down below.
> Come, good folks, to Whitefriars Lane,
> Come to see the merry show!

(*Meanwhile Estelle has been plying her powder-puff and lipstick. She looks round for a mirror, fumbles in her bag, then turns towards Garcin.*)

Estelle.   Excuse me, have you a glass? (*Garcin does not answer.*) Any sort of glass, a pocket-mirror will do. (*Garcin remains silent.*) Even if you won't speak to me, you might lend me a glass. (*His head still buried in his hands, Garcin ignores her.*)

Inez (*eagerly*).   Don't worry. I've a glass in my bag. (*She opens her bag. Angrily*) It's gone! They must have taken it from me at the entrance.

Estelle.   How tiresome!

(*A short silence. Estelle shuts her eyes and sways, as if about to faint. Inez runs forward and holds her up.*)

Inez.   What's the matter?

Estelle (*opens her eyes and smiles*).   I feel so queer. (*She pats herself.*) Don't you ever get taken that way? When I can't see myself I begin to wonder if I really and truly exist. I pat myself just to make sure, but it doesn't help much.

Inez.   You're lucky. I'm always conscious of myself—in my mind. Painfully conscious.

Estelle. Ah yes, in your mind. But everything that goes on in one's head is so vague, isn't it? It makes one want to sleep. (*She is silent for a while.*) I've six big mirrors in my bedroom. There they are. I can see them. But they don't see me. They're reflecting the carpet, the settee, the window—but how empty it is, a glass in which I'm absent! When I talked to people I always made sure there was one near by in which I could see myself. I watched myself talking. And somehow it kept me alert, seeing myself as the others saw me. . . . Oh dear! My lipstick! I'm sure I've put it on all crooked. No, I can't do without a looking-glass for ever and ever, I simply can't.

Inez. Suppose I try to be your glass? Come and pay me a visit, dear. Here's a place for you on my sofa.

Estelle. But—(*Points to Garcin.*)

Inez. Oh, he doesn't count.

Estelle. But we're going to—to hurt each other. You said it yourself.

Inez. Do I look as if I wanted to hurt you?

Estelle. One never can tell.

Inez. Much more likely *you'll* hurt *me.* Still, what does it matter? If I've got to suffer, it may as well be at your hands, your pretty hands. Sit down. Come closer. Closer. Look into my eyes. What do you see?

Estelle. Oh, I'm there! But so tiny I can't see myself properly.

Inez. But *I* can. Every inch of you. Now ask me questions. I'll be as candid as any looking-glass.

(*Estelle seems rather embarrassed and turns to Garcin, as if appealing to him for help.*)

Estelle. Please, Mr. Garcin. Sure our chatter isn't boring you?

(*Garcin makes no reply.*)

Inez. Don't worry about him. As I said, he doesn't count. We're by ourselves. . . . Ask away.

Estelle. Are my lips all right?

Inez. Show! No, they're a bit smudgy.

Estelle. I thought as much. Luckily (*throws a quick glance at Garcin*) no one's seen me. I'll try again.

Inez. That's better. No. Follow the line of your lips. Wait! I'll guide your hand. There. That's quite good.

Estelle. As good as when I came in?

Inez. Far better. Crueler. Your mouth looks quite diabolical that way.

Estelle. Good gracious! And you say you like it! How maddening, not being able to see for myself! You're quite sure, Miss Serrano, that it's all right now?

Inez. Won't you call me Inez?

Estelle. Are you sure it looks all right?

Inez.   You're lovely, Estelle.

Estelle.   But how can I rely upon your taste? Is it the same as *my* taste? Oh, how sickening it all is, enough to drive one crazy!

Inez.   I *have* your taste, my dear, because I like you so much. Look at me. No, straight. Now smile. I'm not so ugly, either. Am I not nicer than your glass?

Estelle.   Oh, I don't know. You scare me rather. My reflection in the glass never did that; of course, I knew it so well. Like something I had tamed. . . . I'm going to smile, and my smile will sink down into your pupils, and heaven knows what it will become.

Inez.   And why shouldn't you "tame" *me?* (*The women gaze at each other, Estelle with a sort of fearful fascination.*) Listen! I want you to call me Inez. We must be great friends.

Estelle.   I don't make friends with women very easily.

Inez.   Not with postal clerks, you mean? Hullo, what's that—that nasty red spot at the bottom of your cheek? A pimple?

Estelle.   A pimple? Oh, how simply foul! Where?

Inez.   There. . . . You know the way they catch larks—with a mirror? I'm your lark-mirror, my dear, and you can't escape me. . . . There isn't any pimple, not a trace of one. So what about it? Suppose the mirror started telling lies? Or suppose I covered my eyes—as he is doing—and refused to look at you, all that loveliness of yours would be wasted on the desert air. No, don't be afraid, I can't help looking at you, I shan't turn my eyes away. And I'll be nice to you, ever so nice. Only you must be nice to me, too.

(*A short silence.*)

Estelle.   Are you really—attracted by me?

Inez.   Very much indeed.

(*Another short silence.*)

Estelle (*indicating Garcin by a slight movement of her head*).   But I wish he'd notice me, too.

Inez.   Of course! Because he's a Man! (*To Garcin*) You've won. (*Garcin says nothing.*) But look at her, damn it! (*Still no reply from Garcin.*) Don't pretend. You haven't missed a word of what we've said.

Garcin.   Quite so; not a word. I stuck my fingers in my ears, but your voices thudded in my brain. Silly chatter. Now will you leave me in peace, you two? I'm not interested in you.

Inez.   Not in me, perhaps—but how about this child? Aren't you interested in her? Oh, I saw through your game; you got on your high horse just to impress her.

Garcin.   I asked you to leave me in peace. There's someone talking about me in the newspaper office and I want to listen. And, if it'll make you any happier, let me tell you that I've no use for the "child," as you call her.

Estelle. Thanks.

Garcin. Oh, I didn't mean it rudely.

Estelle. You cad!

(*They confront each other in silence for some moments.*)

Garcin. So that's that. (*Pause.*) You know I begged you not to speak.

Estelle. It's *her* fault; she started. I didn't ask anything of her and she came and offered me her—her glass.

Inez. So you say. But all the time you were making up to him, trying every trick to catch his attention.

Estelle. Well, why shouldn't I?

Garcin. You're crazy, both of you. Don't you see where this is leading us? For pity's sake, keep your mouths shut. (*Pause.*) Now let's all sit down again quite quietly; we'll look at the floor and each must try to forget the others are there.

(*A longish silence. Garcin sits down. The women return hesitantly to their places. Suddenly Inez swings round on him.*)

Inez. To forget about the others? How utterly absurd! I *feel* you there, in every pore. Your silence clamors in my ears. You can nail up your mouth, cut your tongue out—but you can't prevent your *being there.* Can you stop your thoughts? I hear them ticking away like a clock, tick-tock, tick-tock, and I'm certain you hear mine. It's all very well skulking on your sofa, but you're everywhere, and every sound comes to me soiled, because you've intercepted it on its way. Why, you've even stolen my face; you know it and I don't! And what about her, about Estelle? You've stolen her from me, too; if she and I were alone do you suppose she'd treat me as she does? No, take your hands from your face, I won't leave you in peace—that would suit your book too well. You'd go on sitting there, in a sort of trance, like a yogi, and even if I didn't see her I'd feel it in my bones—that she was making every sound, even the rustle of her dress, for your benefit, throwing you smiles you don't see. . . . Well, I won't stand for that, I prefer to choose my hell; I prefer to look you in the eyes and fight it out face to face.

Garcin. Have it your own way. I suppose we were bound to come to this; they knew what they were about, and we're easy game. If they'd put me in a room with men—men can keep their mouths shut. But it's no use wanting the impossible. (*He goes to Estelle and lightly fondles her neck.*) So I attract you, little girl? It seems you were making eyes at me?

Estelle. Don't touch me.

Garcin. Why not? We might, anyhow, be natural. . . . Do you know, I used to be mad about women? And some were fond of me. So we may as well stop posing, we've nothing to lose. Why trouble about politeness, and decorum, and the rest of it? We're between ourselves. And presently we shall be naked as—as new-born babes.

Estelle.   Oh, let me be!

Garcin.   As new-born babes. Well, I'd warned you, anyhow. I asked so little of you, nothing but peace and a little silence. I'd put my fingers in my ears. Gomez was spouting away as usual, standing in the center of the room, with all the pressmen listening. In their shirt-sleeves. I tried to hear, but it wasn't too easy. Things on earth move so quickly, you know. Couldn't you have held your tongues? Now it's over, he's stopped talking, and what he thinks of me has gone back into his head. Well, we've got to see it through somehow. . . . Naked as we were born. So much the better; I want to know whom I have to deal with.

Inez.   You know already. There's nothing more to learn.

Garcin.   You're wrong. So long as each of us hasn't made a clean breast of it—why they've damned him or her—we know nothing. Nothing that counts. You, young lady, you shall begin. Why? Tell us why. If you are frank, if we bring our specters into the open, it may save us from disaster. So—out with it! Why?

Estelle.   I tell you I haven't a notion. They wouldn't tell me why.

Garcin.   That's so. They wouldn't tell me, either. But I've a pretty good idea. . . . Perhaps you're shy of speaking first? Right. I'll lead off. (*A short silence.*) I'm not a very estimable person.

Inez.   No need to tell us that. We know you were a deserter.

Garcin.   Let that be. It's only a side-issue. I'm here because I treated my wife abominably. That's all. For five years. Naturally, she's suffering still. There she is: the moment I mention her, I see her. It's Gomez who interests me, and it's she I see. Where's Gomez got to? For five years. There! They've given her back my things; she's sitting by the window, with my coat on her knees. The coat with the twelve bullet-holes. The blood's like rust; a brown ring round each hole. It's quite a museum-piece, that coat; scarred with history. And I used to wear it, fancy! . . . Now, can't you shed a tear, my love? Surely you'll squeeze one out—at last? No? You can't manage it? . . . Night after night I came home blind drunk, stinking of wine and women. She'd sat up for me, of course. But she never cried, never uttered a word of reproach. Only her eyes spoke. Big, tragic eyes. I don't regret anything. I must pay the price, but I shan't whine. . . . It's snowing in the street. Won't you cry, confound you? That woman was a born martyr, you know; a victim by vocation.

Inez (*almost tenderly*).   Why did you hurt her like that?

Garcin.   It was so easy. A word was enough to make her flinch. Like a sensitive plant. But never, never a reproach. I'm fond of teasing. I watched and waited. But no, not a tear, not a protest. I'd picked her up out of the gutter, you understand. . . . Now she's stroking the coat. Her eyes are shut and she's feeling with her fingers for the bullet-holes. What are you after? What do you expect? I tell you I regret nothing. The truth is, she admired me too much. Does that mean anything to you?

Inez.   No. Nobody admired *me*.

Garcin. So much the better. So much the better for you. I suppose all this strikes you as very vague. Well, here's something you can get your teeth into. I brought a half-caste girl to stay in our house. My wife slept upstairs; she must have heard—everything. She was an early riser and, as I and the girl stayed in bed late, she served us our morning coffee.

Inez. You brute!

Garcin. Yes, a brute, if you like. But a well-beloved brute. (*A far-away look comes to his eyes.*) No, it's nothing. Only Gomez, and he's not talking about *me.* . . . What were you saying? Yes, a brute. Certainly. Else why should I be here? (*To Inez*) Your turn.

Inez. Well, I was what some people down there called "a damned bitch." Damned already. So it's no surprise, being here.

Garcin. Is that all you have to say?

Inez. No. There was that affair with Florence. A dead man's tale. With three corpses to it. He to start with; then she and I. So there's no one left, I've nothing to worry about; it was a clean sweep. Only that room. I see it now and then. Empty, with the doors locked. . . . No, they've just unlocked them. "To Let." It's to let; there's a notice on the door. That's—too ridiculous.

Garcin. Three. Three deaths, you said?

Inez. Three.

Garcin. One man and two women?

Inez. Yes.

Garcin. Well, well. (*A pause.*) Did he kill himself?

Inez. He? No, he hadn't the guts for that. Still, he'd every reason; we led him a dog's life. As a matter of fact, he was run over by a tram. A silly sort of end. . . . I was living with them; he was my cousin.

Garcin. Was Florence fair?

Inez. Fair? (*Glances at Estelle.*) You know, I don't regret a thing; still, I'm not so very keen on telling you the story.

Garcin. That's all right. . . . So you got sick of him?

Inez. Quite gradually. All sorts of little things got on my nerves. For instance, he made a noise when he was drinking—a sort of gurgle. Trifles like that. He was rather pathetic really. Vulnerable. Why are you smiling?

Garcin. Because I, anyhow, am *not* vulnerable.

Inez. Don't be too sure. . . . I crept inside her skin, she saw the world through my eyes. When she left him, I had her on my hands. We shared a bed-sitting-room at the other end of the town.

Garcin. And then?

Inez. Then that tram did its job. I used to remind her every day: "Yes, my pet, we killed him between us." (*A pause.*) I'm rather cruel, really.

Garcin. So am I.

Inez. No, you're not cruel. It's something else.

Garcin. What?

Inez. I'll tell you later. When I say I'm cruel, I mean I can't get on without making people suffer. Like a live coal. A live coal in others' hearts. When I'm alone I flicker out. For six months I flamed away in her heart, till there was nothing but a cinder. One night she got up and turned on the gas while I was asleep. Then she crept back into bed. So now you know.

Garcin.   Well! Well!

Inez.   Yes? What's on your mind?

Garcin.   Nothing. Only that it's not a pretty story.

Inez.   Obviously. But what matter?

Garcin.   As you say, what matter? (*To Estelle*) Your turn. What have you done?

Estelle.   As I told you, I haven't a notion. I rack my brain, but it's no use.

Garcin.   Right. Then we'll give you a hand. That fellow with the smashed face, who was he?

Estelle.   Who—who do you mean?

Inez.   You know quite well. The man you were so scared of seeing when you came in.

Estelle.   Oh, him! A friend of mine.

Garcin.   Why were you afraid of him?

Estelle.   That's my business, Mr. Garcin.

Inez.   Did he shoot himself on your account?

Estelle.   Of course not. How absurd you are!

Garcin.   Then why should you have been so scared? He blew his brains out, didn't he? That's how his face got smashed.

Estelle.   Don't! Please don't go on.

Garcin.   Because of you. Because of you.

Inez.   He shot himself because of you.

Estelle.   Leave me alone! It's—it's not fair, bullying me like that. I want to go! I want to go! (*She runs to the door and shakes it.*)

Garcin.   Go if you can. Personally, I ask for nothing better. Unfortunately, the door's locked.

(*Estelle presses the bell-push, but the bell does not ring. Inez and Garcin laugh. Estelle swings round on them, her back to the door.*)

Estelle (*in a muffled voice*).   You're hateful, both of you.

Inez.   Hateful? Yes, that's the word. Now get on with it. That fellow who killed himself on your account—you were his mistress, eh?

Garcin.   Of course she was. And he wanted to have her to himself alone. That's so, isn't it?

Inez.   He danced the tango like a professional, but he was poor as a church mouse—that's right, isn't it? (*A short silence.*)

Garcin.   Was he poor or not? Give a straight answer.

Estelle.   Yes, he was poor.

Garcin.   And then you had your reputation to keep up. One day he came and implored you to run away with him, and you laughed in his face.

Inez.   That's it. You laughed at him. And so he killed himself.

Estelle.   Did you use to look at Florence in that way?

Inez.   Yes. (*A short pause, then Estelle bursts out laughing.*)

Estelle.   You've got it all wrong, you two. (*She stiffens her shoulders, still leaning against the door, and faces them. Her voice grows shrill, truculent.*) He wanted me to have a baby. So there!

Garcin.   And you didn't want one?

Estelle.   I certainly didn't. But the baby came, worse luck. I went to Switzerland for five months. No one knew anything. It was a girl. Roger was with me when she was born. It pleased him no end, having a daughter. It didn't please *me!*

Garcin.   And then?

Estelle.   There was a balcony overlooking the lake. I brought a big stone. He could see what I was up to and he kept on shouting: "Estelle, for God's sake, don't!" I hated him then. He saw it all. He was leaning over the balcony and he saw the rings spreading on the water—

Garcin.   Yes? And then?

Estelle.   That's all. I came back to Paris—and he did as he wished.

Garcin.   You mean he blew his brains out?

Estelle.   It was absurd of him, really; my husband never suspected anything. (*A pause.*) Oh, how I loathe you! (*She sobs tearlessly.*)

Garcin.   Nothing doing. Tears don't flow in this place.

Estelle.   I'm a coward. A coward! (*Pause.*) If you knew how I hate you!

Inez (*taking her in her arms*).   Poor child! (*To Garcin*) So the hearing's over. But there's no need to look like a hanging judge.

Garcin.   A hanging judge? (*He glances around him.*) I'd give a lot to be able to see myself in a glass. (*Pause.*) How hot it is! (*Unthinkingly he takes off his coat.*) Oh, sorry! (*He starts putting it on again.*)

Estelle.   Don't bother. You can stay in your shirt-sleeves. As things are—

Garcin.   Just so. (*He drops his coat on the sofa.*) You mustn't be angry with me, Estelle.

Estelle.   I'm not angry with you.

Inez.   And what about me? Are you angry with me?

Estelle.   Yes.

(*A short silence.*)

Inez.   Well, Mr. Garcin, now you have us in the nude all right. Do you understand things any better for that?

Garcin.   I wonder. Yes, perhaps a trifle better. (*Timidly*) And now suppose we start trying to help each other.

Inez.   I don't need help.

Garcin.   Inez, they've laid their snare damned cunningly—like a cobweb. If you make any movement, if you raise your hand to fan yourself, Estelle and I feel a little tug. Alone, none of us can save himself or herself; we're linked together inextricably. So you can take your choice. (*A pause.*) Hullo? What's happening?

Inez. They've let it. The windows are wide open, a man is sitting on my bed. *My* bed, if you please! They've let it, let it! Step in, step in, make yourself at home, you brute! Ah, there's a woman, too. She's going up to him, putting her hands on his shoulders. . . . Damn it, why don't they turn the lights on? It's getting dark. Now he's going to kiss her. But that's my room, *my* room! Pitch-dark now. I can't see anything, but I hear them whispering, whispering. Is he going to make love to her on *my* bed? What's that she said? That it's noon and the sun is shining? I must be going blind. (*A pause.*) Blacked out. I can't see or hear a thing. So I'm done with the earth, it seems. No more alibis for me! (*She shudders.*) I feel so empty, desiccated—really dead at last. All of me's here, in this room. (*A pause.*) What were you saying? Something about helping me, wasn't it?

Garcin. Yes.

Inez. Helping me to do what?

Garcin. To defeat their devilish tricks.

Inez. And what do you expect me to do, in return?

Garcin. To help *me.* It only needs a little effort, Inez; just a spark of human feeling.

Inez. Human feeling. That's beyond my range. I'm rotten to the core.

Garcin. And how about me? (*A pause.*) All the same, suppose we try?

Inez. It's no use. I'm all dried up. I can't give and I can't receive. How could I help you? A dead twig, ready for the burning. (*She falls silent, gazing at Estelle, who has buried her head in her hands.*) Florence was fair, a natural blonde.

Garcin. Do you realize that this young woman's fated to be your torturer?

Inez. Perhaps I've guessed it.

Garcin. It's through her they'll get you. I, of course, I'm different—aloof. I take no notice of her. Suppose you had a try—

Inez. Yes?

Garcin. It's a trap. They're watching you, to see if you'll fall into it.

Inez. I know. And you're another trap. Do you think they haven't foreknown every word you say? And of course there's a whole nest of pitfalls that we can't see. Everything here's a booby-trap. But what do I care? I'm a pitfall, too. For her, obviously. And perhaps I'll catch her.

Garcin. You won't catch anything. We're chasing after each other, round and round in a vicious circle, like the horses on a roundabout. That's part of their plan, of course. . . . Drop it, Inez. Open your hands and let go of everything. Or else you'll bring disaster on all three of us.

Inez. Do I look the sort of person who lets go? I know what's coming to me. I'm going to burn, and it's to last forever. Yes, I *know* everything. But do you think I'll let go? I'll catch her, she'll see you through my eyes, as Florence saw that other man. What's the good of trying to enlist my sympathy? I assure you I know everything, and I can't feel sorry even for myself. A trap! Don't I know it, and that I'm in a trap myself, up to the neck, and there's nothing to be done about it? And if it suits their book, so much the better!

Garcin (*gripping her shoulders*).   Well, I, anyhow, can feel sorry for you, too. Look at me, we're naked, naked right through, and I can see into your heart. That's one link between us. Do you think I'd want to hurt you? I don't regret anything, I'm dried up, too. But for you I can still feel pity.

Inez (*who has let him keep his hands on her shoulders until now, shakes herself loose*).   Don't. I hate being pawed about. And keep your pity for yourself. Don't forget, Garcin, that there are traps for you, too, in this room. All nicely set for you. You'd do better to watch your own interests. (*A pause.*) But, if you will leave us in peace, this child and me, I'll see I don't do you any harm.

Garcin (*gazes at her for a moment, then shrugs his shoulders*).   Very well.

Estelle (*raising her head*).   Please, Garcin.

Garcin.   What do you want of me?

Estelle (*rises and goes up to him*).   You can help *me*, anyhow.

Garcin.   If you want help, apply to her.

(*Inez has come up and is standing behind Estelle, but without touching her. During the dialogue that follows she speaks almost in her ear. But Estelle keeps her eyes on Garcin, who observes her without speaking, and she addresses her answers to him, as if it were he who is questioning her.*)

Estelle.   I implore you, Garcin—you gave me your promise, didn't you? Help me quick. I don't want to be left alone. Olga's taken him to a cabaret.

Inez.   Taken whom?

Estelle.   Peter. . . . Oh, now they're dancing together.

Inez.   Who's Peter?

Estelle.   Such a silly boy. He called me his glancing stream—just fancy! He was terribly in love with me. . . . She's persuaded him to come out with her tonight.

Inez.   Do you love him?

Estelle.   They're sitting down now. She's puffing like a grampus. What a fool the girl is to insist on dancing! But I dare say she does it to reduce. . . . No, of course I don't love him; he's only eighteen, and I'm not a baby-snatcher.

Inez.   Then why bother about them? What difference can it make?

Estelle.   He belonged to me.

Inez.   Nothing on earth belongs to you any more.

Estelle.   I tell you he was mine. All mine.

Inez.   Yes, he *was* yours—once. But now—Try to make him hear, try to touch him. Olga can touch him, talk to him as much as she likes. That's so, isn't it? She can squeeze his hands, rub herself against him—

Estelle.   Yes, look! She's pressing her great fat chest against him, puffing and blowing in his face. But, my poor little lamb, can't you see how ridiculous she is? Why don't you laugh at her? Oh, once I'd have only had to glance at them and she'd have slunk away. Is there really nothing, nothing left of me?

Inez.   Nothing whatever. Nothing of you's left on earth—not even a shadow. All you own is here. Would you like that paper-knife? Or that ornament on the mantelpiece? That blue sofa's yours. And I, my dear, am yours forever.

Estelle.   You mine! That's good! Well, which of you two would dare to call me his glancing stream, his crystal girl? You know too much about me, you know I'm rotten through and through. . . . Peter dear, think of me, fix your thoughts on me, and save me. All the time you're thinking "my glancing stream, my crystal girl," I'm only half here, I'm only half wicked, and half of me is down there with you, clean and bright and crystal-clear as running water. . . . Oh, just look at her face, all scarlet, like a tomato! No, it's absurd, we've laughed at her together, you and I, often and often. . . . What's that tune?—I always loved it. Yes, the *St. Louis Blues.* . . . All right, dance away, dance away. Garcin, I wish you could see her, you'd die of laughing. Only— she'll never know I *see* her. Yes, I see you Olga, with your hair all anyhow, and you do look a dope, my dear. Oh, now you're treading on his toes. It's a scream! Hurry up! Quicker! Quicker! He's dragging her along, bundling her round and round—it's too ghastly! He always said I was so light, he loved to dance with me. (*She is dancing as she speaks.*) I tell you, Olga, I can see you. No, she doesn't care, she's dancing through my gaze. What's that? What's that you said? "Our poor dear Estelle"? Oh, don't be such a hum- bug! You didn't even shed a tear at the funeral. . . . And she has the nerve to talk to him about her poor dear friend Estelle! How dare she discuss me with Peter? Now then, keep time. She never could dance and talk at once. Oh, what's that? No, no. Don't tell him. Please, please don't tell him. You can keep him, do what you like with him, but please don't tell him about— that! (*She has stopped dancing.*) All right. You can have him now. Isn't it *foul*, Garcin? She told him everything, about Roger, my trip to Switzerland, the baby. "Poor Estelle wasn't exactly—" No, I wasn't exactly—True enough. He's looking grave, shaking his head, but he doesn't seem so very much surprised, not what one would expect. Keep him, then—I won't haggle with you over his long eyelashes, his pretty girlish face. They're yours for the asking. His glancing stream, his crystal. Well, the crystal's shattered into bits. "Poor Estelle!" Dance, dance, dance. On with it. But do keep time. One, two. One, two. How I'd love to go down to earth for just a moment, and dance with him again. (*She dances again for some moments.*) The music's growing fainter. They've turned down the lights, as they do for a tango. Why are they playing so softly? Louder, please. I can't hear. It's so far away, so far away. I—I can't hear a sound. (*She stops dancing.*) All over. It's the end. The earth has left me. (*To Garcin*) Don't turn from me— please. Take me in your arms.

(*Behind Estelle's back, Inez signs to Garcin to move away.*)

Inez (*commandingly*).   Now then, Garcin!

(*Garcin moves back a step, and, glancing at Estelle, points to Inez.*)

Garcin.   It's to her you should say that.

Estelle (*clinging to him*).   Don't turn away. You're a man, aren't you, and surely I'm not such a fright as all that! Everyone says I've lovely hair and, after all, a man killed himself on my account. You have to look at something, and there's nothing here to see except the sofas and that awful ornament and the table. Surely I'm better to look at than a lot of stupid furniture. Listen! I've dropped out of their hearts like a little sparrow fallen from its nest. So gather me up, dear, fold me to your heart—and you'll see how nice I can be.

Garcin (*freeing himself from her, after a short struggle*).   I tell you it's to that lady you should speak.

Estelle.   To her? But she doesn't count, she's a woman.

Inez.   Oh, I don't count? Is that what you think? But, my poor little fallen nestling, you've been sheltering in my heart for ages, though you didn't realize it. Don't be afraid; I'll keep looking at you for ever and ever, without a flutter of my eyelids, and you'll live in my gaze like a mote in a sunbeam.

Estelle.   A sunbeam indeed! Don't talk such rubbish! You've tried that trick already, and you should know it doesn't work.

Inez.   Estelle! My glancing stream! My crystal!

Estelle.   *Your* crystal? It's grotesque. Do you think you can fool me with that sort of talk? Everyone knows by now what I did to my baby. The crystal's shattered, but I don't care. I'm just a hollow dummy, all that's left of me is the outside—but it's not for you.

Inez.   Come to me, Estelle. You shall be whatever you like: a glancing stream, a muddy stream. And deep down in my eyes you'll see yourself just as you want to be.

Estelle.   Oh, leave me in peace. You haven't any eyes. Oh, damn it, isn't there anything I can do to get rid of you? I've an idea. (*She spits in Inez's face.*) There!

Inez.   Garcin, you shall pay for this.

(*A pause. Garcin shrugs his shoulders and goes to Estelle.*)

Garcin.   So it's a man you need?

Estelle.   Not *any* man. You.

Garcin.   No humbug now. Any man would do your business. As I happen to be here, you want me. Right! (*He grips her shoulders.*) Mind, I'm not your sort at all, really; I'm not a young nincompoop and I don't dance the tango.

Estelle.   I'll take you as you are. And perhaps I shall change you.

Garcin.   I doubt it. I shan't pay much attention; I've other things to think about.

Estelle. What things?

Garcin. They wouldn't interest you.

Estelle. I'll sit on your sofa and wait for you to take some notice of me. I promise not to bother you at all.

Inez (*with a shrill laugh*).   That's right, fawn on him, like the silly bitch you are. Grovel and cringe! And he hasn't even good looks to commend him!

Estelle (*to Garcin*).   Don't listen to her. She has no eyes, no ears. She's— nothing.

Garcin. I'll give you what I can. It doesn't amount to much. I shan't love you; I know you too well.

Estelle. Do you want me, anyhow?

Garcin. Yes.

Estelle. I ask no more.

Garcin. In that case—(*He bends over her.*)

Inez. Estelle! Garcin! You must be going crazy. You're not alone. I'm here too.

Garcin. Of course—but what does it matter?

Inez. Under my eyes? You couldn't—couldn't do it.

Estelle. Why not? I often undressed with my maid looking on.

Inez (*gripping Garcin's arm*).   Let her alone. Don't paw her with your dirty man's hands.

Garcin (*thrusting her away roughly*).   Take care. I'm no gentleman, and I'd have no compunction about striking a woman.

Inez. But you promised me; you promised. I'm only asking you to keep your word.

Garcin. Why should I, considering you were the first to break our agreement?

(*Inez turns her back on him and retreats to the far end of the room.*)

Inez. Very well, have it your own way. I'm the weaker party, one against two. But don't forget I'm here, and watching. I shan't take my eyes off you, Garcin; when you're kissing her, you'll feel them boring into you. Yes, have it your own way, make love and get it over. We're in hell; my turn will come.

(*During the following scene she watches them without speaking.*)

Garcin (*coming back to Estelle and grasping her shoulders*).   Now then. Your lips. Give me your lips. (*A pause. He bends to kiss her, then abruptly straightens up.*)

Estelle (*indignantly*).   Really! (*A pause.*) Didn't I tell you not to pay any attention to her?

Garcin. You've got it wrong. (*Short silence.*) It's Gomez; he's back in the pressroom. They've shut the windows; it must be winter down there. Six months since I—Well, I warned you I'd be absent-minded sometimes, didn't I? They're shivering, they've kept their coats on. Funny they should feel the cold like that, when I'm feeling so hot. Ah, this time he's talking about me.

Estelle.   Is it going to last long? (*Short silence.*) You might at least tell me what he's saying.

Garcin.   Nothing. Nothing worth repeating. He's a swine, that's all. (*He listens attentively.*) A god-damned bloody swine. (*He turns to Estelle.*) Let's come back to—to ourselves. Are you going to love me?

Estelle (*smiling*).   I wonder now!

Garcin.   Will you trust me?

Estelle.   What a quaint thing to ask! Considering you'll be under my eyes all the time, and I don't think I've much to fear from Inez, so far as you're concerned.

Garcin.   Obviously. (*A pause. He takes his hands off Estelle's shoulders.*) I was thinking of another kind of trust. (*Listens.*) Talk away, talk away, you swine. I'm not there to defend myself. (*To Estelle*) Estelle, you *must* give me your trust.

Estelle.   Oh, what a nuisance you are! I'm giving you my mouth, my arms, my whole body—and everything could be so simple. . . . My trust! I haven't any to give, I'm afraid, and you're making me terribly embarrassed. You must have something pretty ghastly on your conscience to make such a fuss about my trusting you.

Garcin.   They shot me.

Estelle.   I know. Because you refused to fight. Well, why shouldn't you?

Garcin.   I—I didn't exactly refuse. (*In a far-away voice*) I must say he talks well, he makes out a good case against me, but he never says what I should have done instead. Should I have gone to the general and said: "General, I decline to fight"? A mug's game; they'd have promptly locked me up. But I wanted to show my colors, my true colors, do you understand? I wasn't going to be silenced. (*To Estelle*) So I—I took the train. . . . They caught me at the frontier.

Estelle.   Where were you trying to go?

Garcin.   To Mexico. I meant to launch a pacifist newspaper down there. (*A short silence.*) Well, why don't you speak?

Estelle.   What could I say? You acted quite rightly, as you didn't want to fight. (*Garcin makes a fretful gesture.*) But, darling, how on earth can I guess what you want me to answer?

Inez.   Can't you guess? Well, *I* can. He wants you to tell him that he bolted like a lion. For "bolt" he did, and that's what's biting him.

Garcin.   "Bolted," "went away"—we won't quarrel over words.

Estelle.   But you *had* to run away. If you'd stayed they'd have sent you to jail, wouldn't they?

Garcin.   Of course. (*A pause.*) Well, Estelle, am I a coward?

Estelle.   How can I say? Don't be so unreasonable, darling. I can't put myself in your skin. You must decide that for yourself.

Garcin (*wearily*).   I can't decide.

Estelle.   Anyhow, you must remember. You must have had reasons for acting as you did.

Garcin.   I had.

Estelle. Well?

Garcin. But were they the real reasons?

Estelle. You've a twisted mind, that's your trouble. Plaguing yourself over such trifles!

Garcin. I'd thought it all out, and I wanted to make a stand. But was that my real motive?

Inez. Exactly. That's the question. Was that your real motive? No doubt you argued it out with yourself, you weighed the pros and cons, you found good reasons for what you did. But fear and hatred and all the dirty little instincts one keeps dark—they're motives too. So carry on, Mr. Garcin, and try to be honest with yourself—for once.

Garcin. Do I need you to tell me that? Day and night I paced my cell, from the window to the door, from the door to the window. I pried into my heart, I sleuthed myself like a detective. By the end of it I felt as if I'd given my whole life to introspection. But always I harked back to the one thing certain—that I had acted as I did, I'd taken that train to the frontier. But why? Why? Finally I thought: My death will settle it. If I face death courageously, I'll prove I am no coward.

Inez. And how did you face death?

Garcin. Miserably. Rottenly. (*Inez laughs.*) Oh, it was only a physical lapse—that might happen to anyone; I'm not ashamed of it. Only everything's been left in suspense, forever. (*To Estelle*) Come here, Estelle. Look at me. I want to feel someone looking at me while they're talking about me on earth. . . . I like green eyes.

Inez. Green eyes! Just hark to him! And you, Estelle, do you like cowards?

Estelle. If you knew how little I care! Coward or hero, it's all one—provided he kisses well.

Garcin. There they are, slumped in their chairs, sucking at their cigars. Bored they look. Half-asleep. They're thinking: "Garcin's a coward." But only vaguely, dreamily. One's got to think of something. "That chap Garcin was a coward." That's what they've decided, those dear friends of mine. In six months' time they'll be saying: "Cowardly as that skunk Garcin." You're lucky, you two; no one on earth is giving you another thought. But I—I'm long in dying.

Inez. What about your wife, Garcin?

Garcin. Oh, didn't I tell you? She's dead.

Inez. Dead?

Garcin. Yes, she died just now. About two months ago.

Inez. Of grief?

Garcin. What else should she die of? So all is for the best, you see; the war's over, my wife's dead, and I've carved out my place in history.

(*He gives a choking sob and passes his hand over his face. Estelle catches his arm.*)

Estelle. My poor darling! Look at me. Please look. Touch me. Touch me. (*She takes his hand and puts it on her neck.*) There! Keep your hand there.

(*Garcin makes a fretful movement.*) No, don't move. Why trouble what those men are thinking? They'll die off one by one. Forget them. There's only me, now.

Garcin.   But *they* won't forget *me*, not they! They'll die, but others will come after them to carry on the legend. I've left my fate in their hands.

Estelle.   You think too much, that's your trouble.

Garcin.   What else is there to do now? I was a man of action once. . . . Oh, if only I could be with them again, for just one day—I'd fling their lie in their teeth. But I'm locked out; they're passing judgment on my life without troubling about me, and they're right, because I'm dead. Dead and done with. (*Laughs.*) A back number.

(*A short pause.*)

Estelle (*gently*).   Garcin.

Garcin.   Still there? Now listen! I want you to do me a service. No, don't shrink away. I know it must seem strange to you, having someone asking you for help; you're not used to that. But if you'll make the effort, if you'll only *will* it hard enough, I dare say we can really love each other. Look at it this way. A thousand of them are proclaiming I'm a coward; but what do numbers matter? If there's someone, just one person, to say quite positively I did not run away, that I'm not the sort who runs away, that I'm brave and decent and the rest of it—well, that one person's faith would save me. Will you have that faith in me? Then I shall love you and cherish you for ever. Estelle—will you?

Estelle (*laughing*).   Oh, you dear silly man, do you think I could love a coward?

Garcin.   But just now you said—

Estelle.   I was only teasing you. I like men, my dear, who're real men, with tough skin and strong hands. You haven't a coward's chin, or a coward's mouth, or a coward's voice, or a coward's hair. And it's for your mouth, your hair, your voice, I love you.

Garcin.   Do you mean this? *Really* mean it?

Estelle.   Shall I swear it?

Garcin.   Then I snap my fingers at them all, those below and those in here. Estelle, we shall climb out of hell. (*Inez gives a shrill laugh. He breaks off and stares at her.*) What's that?

Inez (*still laughing*).   But she doesn't mean a word of what she says. How can you be such a simpleton? "Estelle, am I a coward?" As if she cared a damn either way.

Estelle.   Inez, how dare you? (*To Garcin*) Don't listen to her. If you want me to have faith in you, you must begin by trusting me.

Inez.   That's right! That's right! Trust away! She wants a man—that far you can trust her—she wants a man's arm round her waist, a man's smell, a man's eyes glowing with desire. And that's all she wants. She'd assure you you were God Almighty if she thought it would give you pleasure.

Garcin.   Estelle, is this true? Answer me. Is it true?

Estelle.   What do you expect me to say? Don't you realize how maddening it is to have to answer questions one can't make head or tail of? (*She stamps her foot.*) You do make things difficult. . . . Anyhow, I'd love you just the same, even if you were a coward. Isn't that enough?

(*A short pause.*)

Garcin (*to the two women*).   You disgust me, both of you. (*He goes towards the door.*)

Estelle.   What are you up to?

Garcin.   I'm going.

Inez (*quickly*).   You won't get far. The door is locked.

Garcin.   I'll *make* them open it. (*He presses the bell-push. The bell does not ring.*)

Estelle.   Please! Please!

Inez (*to Estelle*).   Don't worry, my pet. The bell doesn't work.

Garcin.   I tell you they shall open. (*Drums on the door.*) I can't endure it any longer, I'm through with you both. (*Estelle runs to him; he pushes her away.*) Go away. You're even fouler than she. I won't let myself get bogged in your eyes. You're soft and slimy. Ugh! (*Bangs on the door again.*) Like an octopus. Like a quagmire.

Estelle.   I beg you, oh, I beg you not to leave me. I'll promise not to speak again, I won't trouble you in any way—but don't go. I daren't be left alone with Inez, now she's shown her claws.

Garcin.   Look after yourself. I never asked you to come here.

Estelle.   Oh, how mean you are! Yes, it's quite true you're a coward.

Inez (*going up to Estelle*).   Well, my little sparrow fallen from the nest, I hope you're satisfied now. You spat in my face—playing up to him, of course—and we had a tiff on his account. But he's going, and a good riddance it will be. We two women will have the place to ourselves.

Estelle.   You won't gain anything. If that door opens, I'm going, too.

Inez.   Where?

Estelle.   I don't care where. As far from you as I can.

(*Garcin has been drumming on the door while they talk.*)

Garcin.   Open the door! Open, blast you! I'll endure anything, your red-hot tongs and molten lead, your racks and prongs and garrotes—all your fiendish gadgets, everything that burns and flays and tears—I'll put up with any torture you impose. Anything, anything would be better than this agony of mind, this creeping pain that gnaws and fumbles and caresses one and never hurts quite enough. (*He grips the door-knob and rattles it.*) Now will you open? (*The door flies open with a jerk, and he just avoids falling.*) Ah! (*A long silence.*)

Inez.   Well, Garcin? You're free to go.

Garcin (*meditatively*).   Now I wonder why that door opened.

Inez.   What are you waiting for? Hurry up and go.

Garcin.   I shall not go.

Inez.   And you, Estelle? (*Estelle does not move. Inez bursts out laughing.*) So what? Which shall it be? Which of the three of us will leave? The barrier's down, why are we waiting? . . . But what a situation! It's a scream! We're inseparables!

(*Estelle springs at her from behind.*)

Estelle.   Inseparables? Garcin, come and lend a hand. Quickly. We'll push her out and slam the door on her. That'll teach her a lesson.

Inez (*struggling with Estelle*).   Estelle! I beg you, let me stay. I won't go, I won't go! Not into the passage.

Garcin.   Let go of her.

Estelle.   You're crazy. She hates you.

Garcin.   It's because of her I'm staying here.

(*Estelle releases Inez and stares dumbfoundedly at Garcin.*)

Inez.   Because of me? (*Pause.*) All right, shut the door. It's ten times hotter here since it opened. (*Garcin goes to the door and shuts it.*) Because of me, you said?

Garcin.   Yes. *You*, anyhow, know what it means to be a coward.

Inez.   Yes, I know.

Garcin.   And you know what wickedness is, and shame, and fear. There were days when you peered into yourself, into the secret places of your heart, and what you saw there made you faint with horror. And then, next day, you didn't know what to make of it, you couldn't interpret the horror you had glimpsed the day before. Yes, you know what evil *costs*. And when you say I'm a coward, you know from experience what that means. Is that so?

Inez.   Yes.

Garcin.   So it's you whom I have to convince; you are of my kind. Did you suppose I meant to go? No, I couldn't leave you here, gloating over my defeat, with all those thoughts about me running in your head.

Inez.   Do you really wish to convince me?

Garcin.   That's the one and only thing I wish for now. I can't hear them any longer, you know. Probably that means they're through with me. For good and all. The curtain's down, nothing of me is left on earth—not even the name of coward. So, Inez, we're alone. Only you two remain to give a thought to me. She—she doesn't count. It's you who matter; you who hate me. If you'll have faith in me I'm saved.

Inez.   It won't be easy. Have a look at me. I'm a hard-headed woman.

Garcin.   I'll give you all the time that's needed.

Inez.   Yes, we've lots of time in hand. *All* time.

Garcin (*putting his hands on her shoulders*).   Listen! Each man has an aim in life, a leading motive; that's so, isn't it? Well, I didn't give a damn for wealth, or for love. I aimed at being a real man. A tough, as they say. I staked everything on the same horse. . . . Can one possibly be a coward when one's deliberately courted danger at every turn? And can one judge a life by a single action?

Inez.   Why not? For thirty years you dreamt you were a hero, and condoned a thousand petty lapses—because a hero, of course, can do no wrong. An easy method, obviously. Then a day came when you were up against it, the red light of real danger—and you took the train to Mexico.

Garcin.   I "dreamt," you say. It was no dream. When I chose the hardest path, I made my choice deliberately. A man is what he wills himself to be.

Inez.   Prove it. Prove it was no dream. It's what one does, and nothing else, that shows the stuff one's made of.

Garcin.   I died too soon. I wasn't allowed time to—to do my deeds.

Inez.   One always dies too soon—or too late. And yet one's whole life is complete at that moment, with a line drawn neatly under it, ready for the summing up. You are—your life, and nothing else.

Garcin.   What a poisonous woman you are! With an answer for everything.

Inez.   Now then! Don't lose heart. It shouldn't be so hard, convincing me. Pull yourself together, man, rake up some arguments. (*Garcin shrugs his shoulders.*) Ah, wasn't I right when I said you were vulnerable? Now you're going to pay the price, and what a price! You're a coward, Garcin, because I wish it. I wish it—do you hear?—I wish it. And yet, just look at me, see how weak I am, a mere breath on the air, a gaze observing you, a formless thought that thinks you. (*He walks towards her, opening his hands.*) Ah, they're open now, those big hands, those coarse, man's hands! But what do you hope to do? You can't throttle thoughts with hands. So you've no choice, you must convince me, and you're at my mercy.

Estelle.   Garcin!

Garcin.   What?

Estelle.   Revenge yourself.

Garcin.   How?

Estelle.   Kiss me, darling—then you'll hear her squeal.

Garcin.   That's true, Inez. I'm at your mercy, but you're at mine as well.

(*He bends over Estelle. Inez gives a little cry.*)

Inez.   Oh, you coward, you weakling, running to women to console you!

Estelle.   That's right. Inez. Squeal away.

Inez.   What a lovely pair you make! If you could see his big paw splayed out on your back, rucking up your skin and creasing the silk. Be careful, though! He's perspiring, his hand will leave a blue stain on your dress.

Estelle. Squeal away, Inez, squeal away! . . . Hug me tight, darling; tighter still—that'll finish her off, and a good thing too!

Inez. Yes, Garcin, she's right. Carry on with it, press her to you till you feel your bodies melting into each other; a lump of warm, throbbing flesh. . . . Love's a grand solace, isn't it, my friend? Deep and dark as sleep. But I'll see you don't sleep.

(*Garcin makes a slight movement.*)

Estelle. Don't listen to her. Press your lips to my mouth. Oh, I'm yours, yours, yours.

Inez. Well, what are you waiting for? Do as you're told. What a lovely scene: coward Garcin holding baby-killer Estelle in his manly arms! Make your stakes, everyone. Will coward Garcin kiss the lady, or won't he dare? What's the betting? I'm watching you, everybody's watching. I'm a crowd all by myself. Do you hear the crowd? Do you hear them muttering, Garcin? Mumbling and muttering. "Coward! Coward! Coward! Coward!"— that's what they're saying. . . . It's no use trying to escape, I'll never let you go. What do you hope to get from her silly lips? Forgetfulness? But I shan't forget you, not I! "It's I you must convince." So come to me. I'm waiting. Come along, now. . . . Look how obedient he is, like a well-trained dog who comes when his mistress calls. You can't hold him, and you never will.

Garcin. Will night never come?

Inez. Never.

Garcin. You will always see me?

Inez. Always.

(*Garcin moves away from Estelle and takes some steps across the room. He goes to the bronze ornament.*)

Garcin. This bronze. (*Strokes it thoughtfully.*) Yes, now's the moment; I'm looking at this thing on the mantelpiece, and I understand that I'm in hell. I tell you, everything's been thought out beforehand. They knew I'd stand at the fireplace stroking this thing of bronze, with all those eyes intent on me. Devouring me. (*He swings round abruptly.*) What? Only two of you? I thought there were more; many more. (*Laughs.*) So this is hell. I'd never have believed it. You remember all we were told about the torture-chambers, the fire and brimstone, the "burning marl." Old wives' tales! There's no need for red-hot pokers. Hell is—other people!

Estelle. My darling! Please—

Garcin (*thrusting her away*). No, let me be. She is between us. I cannot love you when she's watching.

Estelle. Right! In that case, I'll stop her watching.

(*She picks up the paper-knife from the table, rushes at Inez, and stabs her several times.*)

Inez (*struggling and laughing*).   But, you crazy creature, what do you think you're doing? You know quite well I'm dead.
Estelle.   Dead?

(*She drops the knife. A pause. Inez picks up the knife and jabs herself with it regretfully.*)

Inez.   Dead! Dead! Dead! Knives, poison, ropes—all useless. It has happened *already*, do you understand? Once and for all. So here we are, forever. (*Laughs.*)
Estelle (*with a peal of laughter*).   Forever. My God, how funny! Forever.
Garcin (*looks at the two women, and joins in the laughter*).   For ever, and ever, and ever.

(*They slump onto their respective sofas. A long silence. Their laughter dies away and they gaze at each other.*)

Garcin.   Well, well, let's get on with it. . . .

Curtain

QUESTIONS
1. Characterize Garcin, Inez, and Estelle as they first appear. What sort of person does each *appear* to be?   **2.** Why was Garcin damned? Inez? Estelle?   **3.** Why are there no mirrors in the room?   **4.** Find out what Second Empire furniture and interior decoration are like. Why is such a room made the private hell of these three characters?   **5.** When the door suddenly opens late in the play, why does Estelle want to expel Inez? Why does Garcin refuse? Why do the three of them choose to remain in the room?   **6.** What is the significance of Estelle's knife attack on Inez?   **7.** Which character do you sympathize with most? Least? Explain.

WRITING TOPIC
This play was first performed in Paris in 1944, during World War II, while the city was occupied by the army of Nazi Germany. Consider the play in its historical context, and in an essay, discuss *No Exit* as an attack on Sartre's own countrymen. Your argument might include a discussion of France under the Second Empire, the social and political positions of the three damned characters, the reasons for their damnation, the absence of mirrors, the unwillingness of any of them to leave the room when they have the opportunity, and the knife attack.

Death Knocks

1968

WOODY ALLEN [b. 1935]

The play takes place in the bedroom of Nat Ackerman's two-story house, somewhere in Kew Gardens. The carpeting is wall-to-wall. There is a big double bed and a large vanity. The room is elaborately furnished and curtained, and on the walls there are several paintings and a not really attractive barometer. Soft theme music as the curtain rises. Nat Ackerman, a bald, paunchy fifty-seven-year-old dress manufacturer, is lying on the bed finishing off tomorrow's Daily News. *He wears a bathrobe and slippers, and reads by a bed light clipped to the white headboard of the bed. The time is near midnight. Suddenly we hear a noise, and Nat sits up and looks at the window.*

Nat. What the hell is that?

(Climbing awkwardly through the window is a sombre, caped figure. The intruder wears a black hood and skintight black clothes. The hood covers his head but not his face, which is middle-aged and stark white. He is something like Nat in appearance. He huffs audibly and then trips over the windowsill and falls into the room.)

Death *(for it is no one else).*   Jesus Christ. I nearly broke my neck.
Nat *(watching with bewilderment).*   Who are you?
Death.   Death.
Nat.   Who?
Death.   Death. Listen—can I sit down? I nearly broke my neck. I'm shaking like a leaf.
Nat.   Who *are* you?
Death.   *Death.* You got a glass of water?
Nat.   Death? What do you mean, Death?
Death.   What is wrong with you? You see the black costume and the whitened face?
Nat.   Yeah.
Death.   Is it Halloween?
Nat.   No.
Death.   Then I'm Death. Now can I get a glass of water—or a Fresca?
Nat.   If this is some joke—
Death.   What kind of joke? You're fifty-seven? Nat Ackerman? One eighteen Pacific Street? Unless I blew it—where's that call sheet? *(He fumbles through pocket, finally producing a card with an address on it. It seems to check.)*
Nat.   What do you want with me?
Death.   What do I want? What do you think I want?
Nat.   You must be kidding. I'm in perfect health.

Death (*unimpressed*).   Uh-huh. (*Looking around*) This is a nice place. You do it yourself?

Nat.   We had a decorator, but we worked with her.

Death (*looking at picture on the wall*).   I love those kids with the big eyes.

Nat.   I don't want to go yet.

Death.   *You* don't want to go? Please don't start in. As it is, I'm nauseous from the climb.

Nat.   What climb?

Death.   I climbed up the drainpipe. I was trying to make a dramatic entrance. I see the big windows and you're awake reading. I figure it's worth a shot. I'll climb up and enter with a little—you know . . . (*Snaps fingers*) Meanwhile, I get my heel caught on some vines, the drainpipe breaks, and I'm hanging by a thread. Then my cape begins to tear. Look, let's just go. It's been a rough night.

Nat.   You broke my drainpipe?

Death.   Broke. It didn't break. It's a little bent. Didn't you hear anything? I slammed into the ground.

Nat.   I was reading.

Death.   You must have really been engrossed. (*Lifting newspaper Nat was reading*) "NAB COEDS IN POT ORGY." Can I borrow this?

Nat.   I'm not finished.

Death.   Er—I don't know how to put this to you, pal. . . .

Nat.   Why didn't you just ring downstairs?

Death.   I'm telling you, I could have, but how does it look? This way I get a little drama going. Something. Did you read "Faust"?

Nat.   What?

Death.   And what if you had company? You're sitting there with important people. I'm Death—I should ring the bell and traipse right in the front? Where's your thinking?

Nat.   Listen, Mister, it's very late.

Death.   Yeah. Well, you want to go?

Nat.   Go where?

Death.   Death. It. The Thing. The Happy Hunting Grounds. (*Looking at his own knee*) Y'know, that's a pretty bad cut. My first job, I'm liable to get gangrene yet.

Nat.   Now, wait a minute. I need time. I'm not ready to go.

Death.   I'm sorry. I can't help you. I'd like to, but it's the moment.

Nat.   How can it be the moment? I just merged with Modiste Originals.

Death.   What's the difference, a couple of bucks more or less.

Nat.   Sure, what do you care? You guys probably have all your expenses paid.

Death.   You want to come along now?

Nat (*studying him*).   I'm sorry, but I cannot believe you're Death.

Death.   Why? What'd you expect—Rock Hudson?

Nat.   No, it's not that.

Death.   I'm sorry if I disappointed you.

Nat.   Don't get upset. I don't know, I always thought you'd be . . . uh . . . taller.

Death.   I'm five seven. It's average for my weight.

Nat.   You look a little like me.

Death.   Who should I look like? I'm your death.

Nat.   Give me some time. Another day.

Death.   I can't. What do you want me to say?

Nat.   One more day. Twenty-four hours.

Death.   What do you need it for? The radio said rain tomorrow.

Nat.   Can't we work out something?

Death.   Like what?

Nat.   You play chess?

Death.   No, I don't.

Nat.   I once saw a picture of you playing chess.

Death.   Couldn't be me, because I don't play chess. Gin rummy, maybe.

Nat.   You play gin rummy?

Death.   Do I play gin rummy? Is Paris a city?

Nat.   You're good, huh?

Death.   Very good.

Nat.   I'll tell you what I'll do—

Death.   Don't make any deals with me.

Nat.   I'll play you gin rummy. If you win, I'll go immediately. If I win, give me some more time. A little bit—one more day.

Death.   Who's got time to play gin rummy?

Nat.   Come on. If you're so good.

Death.   Although I feel like a game . . .

Nat.   Come on. Be a sport. We'll shoot for a half hour.

Death.   I really shouldn't.

Nat.   I got the cards right here. Don't make a production.

Death.   All right, come on. We'll play a little. It'll relax me.

Nat (*getting cards, pad, and pencil*).   You won't regret this.

Death.   Don't give me a sales talk. Get the cards and give me a Fresca and put out something. For God's sake, a stranger drops in, you don't have potato chips or pretzels.

Nat.   There's M&M's downstairs in a dish.

Death.   M&M's. What if the President came? He'd get M&M's too?

Nat.   You're not the President.

Death.   Deal.

(*Nat deals, turns up a five.*)

Nat.   You want to play a tenth of a cent a point to make it interesting?

Death.   It's not interesting enough for you?

Nat.   I play better when money's at stake.

Death.   Whatever you say, Newt.

Nat.   Nat, Nat Ackerman. You don't know my name?
Death.   Newt, Nat—I got such a headache.
Nat.   You want that five?
Death.   No.
Nat.   So pick.
Death (*surveying his hand as he picks*).   Jesus, I got nothing here.
Nat.   What's it like?
Death.   What's what like?

(*Throughout the following, they pick and discard.*)

Nat.   Death.
Death.   What should it be like? You lay there.
Nat.   Is there anything after?
Death.   Aha, you're saving twos.
Nat.   I'm asking. Is there anything after?
Death (*absently*).   You'll see.
Nat.   Oh, then I will actually see something?
Death.   Well, maybe I shouldn't have put it that way. Throw.
Nat.   To get an answer from you is a big deal.
Death.   I'm playing cards.
Nat.   All right, play, play.
Death.   Meanwhile, I'm giving you one card after another.
Nat.   Don't look through the discards.
Death.   I'm not looking. I'm straightening them up. What was the knock card?
Nat.   Four. You ready to knock already?
Death.   Who said I'm ready to knock. All I asked was what was the knock card.
Nat.   And all I asked was is there anything for me to look forward to.
Death.   Play.
Nat.   Can't you tell me anything? Where do we go?
Death.   We? To tell you the truth, *you* fall in a crumpled heap on the floor.
Nat.   Oh, I can't wait for that! Is it going to hurt?
Death.   Be over in a second.
Nat.   Terrific. (*Sighs*) I needed this. A man merges with Modiste Originals . . .
Death.   How's four points?
Nat.   You're knocking?
Death.   Four points is good?
Nat.   No, I got two.
Death.   You're kidding.
Nat.   No, you lose.
Death.   Holy Christ, and I thought you were saving sixes.
Nat.   No. Your deal. Twenty points and two boxes. Shoot. (*Death deals.*) I

must fall on the floor, eh? I can't be standing over the sofa when it happens?

Death. No. Play.

Nat. Why not?

Death. Because you fall on the floor! Leave me alone. I'm trying to concentrate.

Nat. Why must it be on the floor? That's all I'm saying! Why can't the whole thing happen and I'll stand next to the sofa?

Death. I'll try my best. Now can we play?

Nat. That's all I'm saying. You remind me of Moe Lefkowitz. He's also stubborn.

Death. I remind you of Moe Lefkowitz. I'm one of the most terrifying figures you could possibly imagine, and him I remind of Moe Lefkowitz. What is he, a furrier?

Nat. You should be such a furrier. He's good for eighty thousand a year. Passementeries. He's got his own factory. Two points.

Death. What?

Nat. Two points. I'm knocking. What have you got?

Death. My hand is like a basketball score.

Nat. And it's spades.

Death. If you didn't talk so much.

(*They redeal and play on.*)

Nat. What'd you mean before when you said this was your first job?

Death. What does it sound like?

Nat. What are you telling me—that nobody ever went before?

Death. Sure they went. But I didn't take them.

Nat. So who did?

Death. Others.

Nat. There's others?

Death. Sure. Each one has his own personal way of going.

Nat. I never knew that.

Death. Why should you know? Who are you?

Nat. What do you mean who am I? Why—I'm nothing?

Death. Not nothing. You're a dress manufacturer. Where do you come to knowledge of the eternal mysteries?

Nat. What are you talking about? I make a beautiful dollar. I sent two kids through college. One is in advertising, the other's married. I got my own home. I drive a Chrysler. My wife has whatever she wants. Maids, mink coat, vacations. Right now she's at the Eden Roc. Fifty dollars a day because she wants to be near her sister. I'm supposed to join her next week, so what do you think I am—some guy off the street?

Death. All right. Don't be so touchy.

Nat. Who's touchy?

Death. How would you like it if I got insulted quickly?

Nat. Did I insult you?

Death. You didn't say you were disappointed in me?

Nat. What do you expect? You want me to throw you a block party?

Death. I'm not talking about that. I mean me personally. I'm too short, I'm this, I'm that.

Nat. I said you looked like me. It's like a reflection.

Death. All right, deal, deal.

(They continue to play as music steals in and the lights dim until all is in total darkness. The lights slowly come up again, and now it is later and their game is over. Nat tallies.)

Nat. Sixty-eight . . . one-fifty . . . Well, you lose.

Death (*dejectedly looking through the deck*).   I knew I shouldn't have thrown that nine. Damn it.

Nat. So I'll see you tomorrow.

Death. What do you mean you'll see me tomorrow?

Nat. I won the extra day. Leave me alone.

Death. You were serious?

Nat. We made a deal.

Death. Yeah, but—

Nat. Don't "but" me. I won twenty-four hours. Come back tomorrow.

Death. I didn't know we were actually playing for time.

Nat. That's too bad about you. You should pay attention.

Death. Where am I going to go for twenty-four hours?

Nat. What's the difference? The main thing is I won an extra day.

Death. What do you want me to do—walk the streets?

Nat. Check into a hotel and go to a movie. Take a *schvitz*.[1] Don't make a federal case.

Death. Add the score again.

Nat. Plus you owe me twenty-eight dollars.

Death. *What?*

Nat. That's right, Buster. Here it is—read it.

Death (*going through pockets*).   I have a few singles—not twenty-eight dollars.

Nat. I'll take a check.

Death. From what account?

Nat. Look who I'm dealing with.

Death. Sue me. Where do I keep my checking account?

Nat. All right, gimme what you got and we'll call it square.

Death. Listen, I need that money.

Nat. Why should you need money?

---

[1] Steam bath.

Death. What are you talking about? You're going to the Beyond.

Nat. So?

Death. So—you know how far that is?

Nat. So?

Death. So where's gas? Where's tolls?

Nat. We're going by car!

Death. You'll find out. (*Agitatedly*) Look—I'll be back tomorrow, and you'll give me a chance to win the money back. Otherwise I'm in definite trouble.

Nat. Anything you want. Double or nothing we'll play. I'm liable to win an extra week or a month. The way you play, maybe years.

Death. Meantime I'm stranded.

Nat. See you tomorrow.

Death (*being edged to the doorway*). Where's a good hotel? What am I talking about hotel, I got no money. I'll go sit in Bickford's[2] (*He picks up the News.*)

Nat. Out. Out. That's my paper. (*He takes it back.*)

Death (*exiting*). I couldn't just take him and go. I had to get involved in rummy.

Nat (*calling after him*). And be careful going downstairs. On one of the steps the rug is loose.

(*And, on cue, we hear a terrific crash. Nat sighs, then crosses to the bedside table and makes a phone call.*)

Nat. Hello, Moe? Me. Listen, I don't know if somebody's playing a joke, or what, but Death was just here. We played a little gin . . . No, *Death*. In person. Or somebody who claims to be Death. But, Moe, he's such a *schlep!*[3]

Curtain

QUESTIONS

1. Upon what allusions does this play depend for its humor?   **2.** Characterize the speech patterns of the characters. How do they contribute to the play's effect?

---

[2] Bickford's was a chain of inexpensive all-night cafeterias in New York City.
[3] Boring jerk.

THE
PRESENCE
OF DEATH

St. George and the Dragon, late fifteenth-century painting

ESSAYS

Meditation XVII, from *Devotions upon Emergent Occasions*   1623

JOHN DONNE   [1572–1631]

> *Nunc lento sonitu dicunt morieris.*
> *Now this bell tolling softly for another says to me, Thou must die.*

Perchance he for whom this bell tolls may be so ill as that he knows not it tolls   1
for him; and perchance I may think myself so much better than I am, as that
they who are about me and see my state may have caused it to toll for me, and
I know not that. The church is catholic, universal, so are all her actions; all that
she does belongs to all. When she baptizes a child, that action concerns me;
for that child is thereby connected to that head which is my head too, and
ingrafted into that body whereof I am a member. And when she buries a man,
that action concerns me: all mankind is of one author and is one volume; when
one man dies, one chapter is not torn out of the book, but translated into a
better language; and every chapter must be so translated. God employs several
translators; some pieces are translated by age, some by sickness, some by war,
some by justice; but God's hand is in every translation, and his hand shall bind
up all our scattered leaves again for that library where every book shall lie open
to one another. As therefore the bell that rings to a sermon calls not upon the
preacher only, but upon the congregation to come, so this bell calls us all; but
how much more me, who am brought so near the door by this sickness. There
was a contention as far as a suit[1] (in which piety and dignity, religion and
estimation, were mingled) which of the religious orders should ring to prayers
first in the morning; and it was determined that they should ring first that rose
earliest. If we understand aright the dignity of this bell that tolls for our
evening prayer, we would be glad to make it ours by rising early, in that

---

[1] An argument settled by a lawsuit.

application, that it might be ours as well as his whose indeed it is. The bell doth toll for him that thinks it doth, and though it intermit again, yet from that minute that that occasion wrought upon him, he is united to God. Who casts not up his eye to the sun when it rises? but who takes off his eye from a comet when that breaks out? Who bends not his ear to any bell which upon any occasion rings? but who can remove it from that bell which is passing a piece of himself out of this world? No man is an island, entire of itself; every man is a piece of the continent, a part of the main. If a clod be washed away by the sea, Europe is the less, as well as if a promontory were, as well as if a manor of thy friend's or of thine own were. Any man's death diminishes me, because I am involved in mankind; and therefore never send to know for whom the bell tolls; it tolls for thee. Neither can we call this a begging of misery or a borrowing of misery, as though we were not miserable enough of ourselves but must fetch in more from the next house, in taking upon us the misery of our neighbors. Truly it were an excusable covetousness if we did; for affliction is a treasure, and scarce any man hath enough of it. No man hath affliction enough that is not matured and ripened by it, and made fit for God by that affliction. If a man carry treasure in bullion, or in a wedge of gold, and have none coined into current moneys, his treasure will not defray him as he travels. Tribulation is treasure in the nature of it, but it is not current money in the use of it, except we get nearer and nearer our home, heaven, by it. Another man may be sick too, and sick to death, and this affliction may lie in his bowels as gold in a mine and be of no use to him; but this bell that tells me of his affliction digs out and applies that gold to me, if by this consideration of another's danger I take mine own into contemplation and so secure myself by making my recourse to my God, who is our only security.

QUESTIONS
1. John Donne is justly admired for his use of figurative language. What extended metaphors does he use to characterize humankind and death?   **2.** What does Donne mean when he asserts that the death bell "tolls for thee"?   **3.** Toward the end of his meditation, Donne states that "tribulation is treasure." What does he mean? What will that treasure purchase?

WRITING TOPIC
In what sense is "No man is an island, entire of itself" an accurate description of the human condition? In what sense is it inaccurate?

Lost in the Snow[1]

MARK TWAIN   [1835–1910]

Plainly the situation was desperate. We were cold and stiff and the horses were   1
tired. We decided to build a sage-brush fire and camp out till morning. This
was wise, because if we were wandering from the right road and the snow-
storm continued until another day our case would be the next thing to hopeless if we kept on.

All agreed that a camp fire was what would come nearest to saving us, now,   2
and so we set about building it. We could find no matches, and so we tried to
make shift with the pistols. Not a man in the party had ever tried to do such
a thing before, but not a man in the party doubted that it *could* be done, and
without any trouble—because every man in the party had read about it in
books many a time and had naturally come to believe it, with trusting simplicity, just as he had long ago accepted and believed *that other* common
book-fraud about Indians and lost hunters making a fire by rubbing two dry
sticks together.

We huddled together on our knees in the deep snow, and the horses put   3
their noses together and bowed their patient heads over us; and while the
feathery flakes eddied down and turned us into a group of white statuary, we
proceeded with the momentous experiment. We broke twigs from a sage
brush and piled them on a little cleared space in the shelter of our bodies. In
the course of ten or fifteen minutes all was ready, and then, while conversation
ceased and our pulses beat low with anxious suspense, Ollendorff applied his
revolver, pulled the trigger and blew the pile clear out of the county! It was the
flattest failure that ever was.

This was distressing, but it paled before a greater horror—the horses were   4
gone! I had been appointed to hold the bridles, but in my absorbing anxiety
over the pistol experiment I had unconsciously dropped them and the released
animals had walked off in the storm. It was useless to try to follow them, for
their footfalls could make no sound, and one could pass within two yards of the
creatures and never see them. We gave them up without an effort at recovering them, and cursed the lying books that said horses would stay by their
masters for protection and companionship in a distressful time like ours.

We were miserable enough, before; we felt still more forlorn, now. Patiently,   5
but with blighted hope, we broke more sticks and piled them, and once more
the Prussian shot them into annihilation. Plainly, to light a fire with a pistol
was an art requiring practice and experience, and the middle of a desert at

---

[1] Mark Twain's *Roughing It* (1872) recounts his experiences in California and Nevada prospecting for silver. In this episode, Twain and his friends are caught in a snowstorm while returning to Carson City, Nevada, from the Humboldt mining district in California.

861

midnight in a snow-storm was not a good place or time for the acquiring of the accomplishment. We gave it up and tried the other. Each man took a couple of sticks and fell to chafing them together. At the end of half an hour we were thoroughly chilled, and so were the sticks. We bitterly execrated the Indians, the hunters and the books that had betrayed us with the silly device, and wondered dismally what was next to be done. At this critical moment Mr. Ballou fished out four matches from the rubbish of an overlooked pocket. To have found four gold bars would have seemed poor and cheap good luck compared to this. One cannot think how good a match looks under such circumstances—or how lovable and precious, and sacredly beautiful to the eye. This time we gathered sticks with high hopes; and when Mr. Ballou prepared to light the first match, there was an amount of interest centered upon him that pages of writing could not describe. The match burned hopefully a moment, and then went out. It could not have carried more regret with it if it had been a human life. The next match simply flashed and died. The wind puffed the third one out just as it was on the imminent verge of success. We gathered together closer than ever, and developed a solicitude that was rapt and painful, as Mr. Ballou scratched our last hope on his leg. It lit, burned blue and sickly, and then budded into a robust flame. Shading it with his hands, the old gentleman bent gradually down and every heart went with him—everybody, too, for that matter—and blood and breath stood still. The flame touched the sticks at last, took gradual hold upon them—hesitated—took a stronger hold— hesitated again—held its breath five heartbreaking seconds, then gave a sort of human gasp and went out.

Nobody said a word for several minutes. It was a solemn sort of silence; even the wind put on a stealthy, sinister quiet and made no more noise than the falling flakes of snow. Finally a sad-voiced conversation began, and it was soon apparent that in each of our hearts lay the conviction that this was our last night with the living. I had so hoped that I was the only one who felt so. When the others calmly acknowledged their conviction, it sounded like the summons itself. Ollendorff said: 6

"Brothers, let us die together. And let us go without one hard feeling towards each other. Let us forget and forgive bygones. I know that you have felt hard towards me for turning over the canoe, and for knowing too much and leading you round and round in the snow—but I meant well; forgive me. I acknowledge freely that I have had hard feelings against Mr. Ballou for abusing me and calling me a logarythm, which is a thing I do not know what, but no doubt a thing considered disgraceful and unbecoming in America, and it has scarcely been out of my mind and has hurt me a great deal—but let it go; I forgive Mr. Ballou with all my heart and—" 7

Poor Ollendorff broke down and the tears came. He was not alone, for I was crying too, and so was Mr. Ballou. Ollendorff got his voice again and forgave me for things I had done and said. Then he got out his bottle of whiskey and said that whether he lived or died he would never touch another drop. He said 8 he had given up all hope of life, and although ill-prepared, was ready to submit humbly to his fate; that he wished he could be spared a little longer, not for any selfish reason, but to make a thorough reform in his character, and by devoting himself to helping the poor, nursing the sick, and pleading with the people to guard themselves against the evils of intemperance, make his life a beneficent example to the young, and lay it down at last with the precious reflection that it had not been lived in vain. He ended by saying that his reform should begin at this moment, even here in the presence of death, since no longer time was to be vouchsafed wherein to prosecute it to men's help and benefit—and with that he threw away the bottle of whiskey.

Mr. Ballou made remarks of similar purport, and began the reform he could   9 not live to continue, by throwing away the ancient pack of cards that had solaced our captivity during the flood[2] and made it bearable. He said he never gambled, but still was satisfied that the meddling with cards in any way was immoral and injurious, and no man could be wholly pure and blemishless without eschewing them. "And therefore," continued he, "in doing this act I already feel more in sympathy with that spiritual saturnalia necessary to entire and obsolete reform." These rolling syllables touched him as no intelligible eloquence could have done, and the old man sobbed with a mournfulness not unmingled with satisfaction.

My own remarks were of the same tenor as those of my comrades, and I   10 know that the feelings that prompted them were heartfelt and sincere. We were all sincere, and all deeply moved and earnest, for we were in the presence of death and without hope. I threw away my pipe, and in doing it felt that at last I was free of a hated vice and one that had ridden me like a tyrant all my days. While I yet talked, the thought of the good I might have done in the world and the still greater good I might *now* do, with these new incentives and higher and better aims to guide me if I could only be spared a few years longer, overcame me and the tears came again. We put our arms about each other's necks and awaited the warning drowsiness that precedes death by freezing.

It came stealing over us presently, and then we bade each other a last   11 farewell. A delicious dreaminess wrought its web about my yielding senses, while the snow-flakes wove a winding sheet about my conquered body. Oblivion came. The battle of life was done.

I do not know how long I was in a state of forgetfulness, but it seemed an   12 age. A vague consciousness grew upon me by degrees, and then came a gathering anguish of pain in my limbs and through all my body. I shuddered. The thought flitted through my brain, "this is death—this is the hereafter."

Then came a white upheaval at my side, and a voice said, with bitterness: 13

---

[2] Earlier in the narrative, Twain and his friends had been trapped in a cabin during a flash flood.

"Will some gentleman be so good as to kick me behind?" 14

It was Ballou—at least it was a towzled snow image in a sitting posture, with 15
Ballou's voice.

I rose up, and there in the gray dawn, not fifteen steps from us, were the 16
frame buildings of a stage station, and under a shed stood our still saddled and
bridled horses!

An arched snow-drift broke up, now, and Ollendorff emerged from it, and 17
the three of us sat and stared at the houses without speaking a word. We really
had nothing to say. We were like the profane man who could not "do the
subject justice," the whole situation was so painfully ridiculous and humiliating that words were tame and we did not know where to commence anyhow.

The joy in our hearts at our deliverance was poisoned; well-nigh dissipated, 18
indeed. We presently began to grow pettish by degrees, and sullen; and then,
angry at each other, angry at ourselves, angry at everything in general, we
moodily dusted the snow from our clothing and in unsociable single file
plowed our way to the horses, unsaddled them, and sought shelter in the
station.

I have scarcely exaggerated a detail of this curious and absurd adventure. It 19
occurred almost exactly as I have stated it. We actually went into camp in a
snowdrift in a desert, at midnight in a storm, forlorn and hopeless, within
fifteen steps of a comfortable inn.

For two hours we sat apart in the station and ruminated in disgust. The 20
mystery was gone, now, and it was plain enough why the horses had deserted
us. Without a doubt they were under that shed a quarter of a minute after they
had left us, and they must have overheard and enjoyed all our confessions and
lamentations.

After breakfast we felt better, and the zest of life soon came back. The world 21
looked bright again, and existence was as dear to us as ever. Presently an
uneasiness came over me—grew upon me—assailed me without ceasing. Alas,
my regeneration was not complete—I wanted to smoke! I resisted with all my
strength, but the flesh was weak. I wandered away alone and wrestled with
myself for an hour. I recalled my promises of reform and preached to myself
persuasively, upbraidingly, exhaustively. But it was all vain, I shortly found
myself sneaking among the snow-drifts hunting for my pipe. I discovered it
after a considerable search, and crept away to hide myself and enjoy it. I
remained behind the barn a good while, asking myself how I would feel if my
braver, stronger, truer comrades should catch me in my degradation. At last I
lit the pipe, and no human being can feel meaner and baser than I did then.
I was ashamed of being in my own pitiful company. Still dreading discovery,
I felt that perhaps the further side of the barn would be somewhat safer, and
so I turned the corner. As I turned the one corner, smoking, Ollendorff turned
the other with his bottle to his lips, and between us sat unconscious Ballou
deep in a game of "solitaire" with the old greasy cards!

Absurdity could go no further. We shook hands and agreed to say no more 22
about "reform" and "examples to the rising generation."

QUESTIONS

1. What is the first indication that Twain's piece is humorous?   **2.** In the end, Twain and his friends are disgusted with themselves for backsliding, the author even going so far as to say, "I was ashamed of being in my own pitiful company." Is this a serious judgment the reader is expected to share? Explain.

WRITING TOPIC

Analyze the ways in which Twain achieves humor by examining both the situations he creates and the language he uses.

The American Way of Death
1963

JESSICA MITFORD [b. 1917]

O Death, where is thy sting? O grave, where is thy victory?[1] Where, indeed. 1
Many a badly stung survivor, faced with the aftermath of some relative's
funeral, has ruefully concluded that the victory has been won hands down by
a funeral establishment—in disastrously unequal battle.

Much has been written of late about the affluent society in which we live, 2
and much fun poked at some of the irrational "status symbols" set out like
golden snares to trap the unwary consumer at every turn. Until recently, little
has been said about the most irrational and wierdest of the lot, lying in
ambush for all of us at the end of the road—the modern American funeral.

If the Dismal Traders (as an eighteenth-century English writer calls them) 3
have traditionally been cast in a comic role in literature, a universally recognized symbol of humor from Shakespeare to Dickens to Evelyn Waugh, they
have successfully turned the tables in recent years to perpetrate a huge, macabre and expensive practical joke on the American public. It is not consciously conceived as a joke, of course; on the contrary, it is hedged with
admirably contrived rationalizations.

Gradually, almost imperceptibly, over the years the funeral men have con- 4
structed their own grotesque cloud-cuckooland where the trappings of Gracious Living are transformed, as in a nightmare, into the trappings of Gracious
Dying. The same familiar Madison Avenue language, with its peculiar adjec-
tival range designed to anesthetize sales resistance to all sorts of products, has
seeped into the funeral industry in a new and bizarre guise. The emphasis is
on the same desirable qualities that we have all been schooled to look for in
our daily search for excellence: comfort, durability, beauty, craftsmanship. The
attuned ear will recognize too the convincing quasi-scientific language, so
reassuring even if unintelligible.

So that this too, too solid flesh might not melt, we are offered "solid 5
copper—a quality casket which offers superb value to the client seeking long-
lasting protection," or "the Colonial Classic Beauty—18 guage lead coated
steel, seamless top, lap-jointed welded body construction." Some are equipped
with foam rubber, some with innerspring mattresses. Elgin offers "the revolutionary 'Perfect-Posture' bed." Not every casket need have a silver lining, for
one may choose between "more than 60 color matched shades, magnificent
and unique masterpieces" by the Cheney casket-lining people. Shrouds no
longer exist. Instead, you may patronize a grave-wear couturière who promises
"handmade original fashions—styles from the best in life for the last memory—dresses, men's suits, negligees, accessories." For the final, perfect groom-

---

[1] See 1 Corinthians 15:55.

ing: "Nature-Glo—the ultimate in cosmetic embalming." And, where have we heard the phrase "peace of mind protection" before? No matter. In funeral advertising, it is applied to the Wilbert Burial Vault, with its ⅜-inch precast asphalt inner liner plus extra-thick, reinforced concrete—all this "guaranteed by Good Housekeeping." Here again the Cadillac, status symbol par excellence, appears in all its gleaming glory, this time transformed into a pastel-colored funeral hearse.

You, the potential customer for all this luxury, are unlikely to read the lyrical descriptions quoted above, for they are culled from *Mortuary Management* and *Casket and Sunnyside*, two of the industry's eleven trade magazines. For you there are ads in your daily newspaper, generally found on the obituary page, stressing dignity, refinement, high-caliber professional service and that intangible quality, *sincerity*. The trade advertisements are, however, instructive, because they furnish an important clue to the frame of mind into which the funeral industry has hypnotized itself.

A new mythology, essential to the twentieth-century American funeral rite, has grown up—or rather has been built up step by step—to justify the peculiar customs surrounding the disposal of our dead. And, just as the witch doctor must be convinced of his own infallibility in order to maintain a hold over his clientele, so the funeral industry has had to "sell itself" on its articles of faith in the course of passing them along to the public.

The first of these is the tenet that today's funeral procedures are founded in "American tradition." The story comes to mind of a sign on the freshly sown lawn of a brand-new Midwest college: "There is a tradition on this campus that students never walk on this strip of grass. This tradition goes into effect next Tuesday." The most cursory look at American funerals of past times will establish this parallel. Simplicity to the point of starkness, the plain pine box, the laying out of the dead by friends and family who also bore the coffin to the grave—these were the hallmarks of the traditional funeral until the end of the nineteenth century.

Secondly, there is a myth that the American public is only being given what it wants—an opportunity to keep up with the Joneses to the end. "In keeping with our high standard of living, there should be an equally high standard of dying," says the past president of the Funeral Directors of San Francisco. "The cost of a funeral varies according to individual taste and the niceties of living the family has been accustomed to." Actually, choice doesn't enter the picture for the average individual, faced, generally for the first time, with the necessity of buying a product of which he is totally ignorant, at a moment when he is least in a position to quibble. In point of fact the cost of a funeral almost always varies, not "according to individual taste" but according to what the traffic will bear.

Thirdly, there is an assortment of myths based on half-digested psychiatric theories. The importance of the "memory picture" is stressed—meaning the last glimpse of the deceased in open casket, done up with the latest in embalming techniques and finished off with a dusting of makeup. A newer one, impressively authentic-sounding, is the need for "grief therapy," which is beginning to go over big in mortuary circles. A historian of American funeral directing hints at the grief-therapist idea when speaking of the new role of the undertaker—"the dramaturgic role, in which the undertaker becomes a stage manager to create an appropriate atmosphere and to move the funeral party through a drama in which social relationships are stressed and an emotional catharsis or release is provided through ceremony."

Lastly, a whole new terminology, as ornately shoddy as the satin rayon casket 11 liner, has been invented by the funeral industry to replace the direct and serviceable vocabulary of former times. Undertaker has been supplanted by "funeral director" or "mortician." (Even the classified section of the telephone directory gives recognition to this; in its pages you will find "Undertakers—see Funeral Directors.") Coffins are "caskets"; hearses are "coaches," or "professional cars"; flowers are "floral tributes"; corpses generally are "loved ones," but mortuary etiquette dictates that a specific corpse be referred to by name only—as, "Mr. Jones"; cremated ashes are "cremains." Euphemisms such as "slumber room," "reposing room," and "calcination—the *kindlier* heat" abound in the funeral business.

If the undertaker is the stage manager of the fabulous production that is the 12 modern American funeral, the stellar role is reserved for the occupant of the open casket. The decor, the stagehands, the supporting cast are all arranged for the most advantageous display of the deceased, without which the rest of the paraphernalia would lose its point—*Hamlet* without the Prince of Denmark. It is to this end that a fantastic array of costly merchandise and services is pyramided to dazzle the mourners and facilitate the plunder of the next of kin.

Grief therapy, anyone? But it's going to come high. According to the funeral 13 industry's own figures, the *average* undertaker's bill in 1961 was $708 for casket and "services," to which must be added the cost of a burial vault, flowers, clothing, clergy and musician's honorarium, and cemetery charges. When these costs are added to the undertaker's bill, the total average cost for an adult's funeral is, as we shall see, close to $1,450.

The question naturally arises, *is* this what most people want for themselves 14 and their families? For several reasons, this has been a hard one to answer until recently. It is a subject seldom discussed. Those who have never had to arrange for a funeral frequently shy away from its implications, preferring to take comfort in the thought that sufficient unto the day is the evil thereof. Those who have acquired personal and painful knowledge of the subject would often rather forget about it. Pioneering "Funeral Societies" or "Memorial Associations," dedicated to the principal of dignified funerals at reasonable cost, have existed in a number of communities throughout the country, but their membership has been limited for the most part to the more sophisticated element in the population—university people, liberal intellectuals—and those who, like doctors and lawyers, come up against problems in arranging funerals for their clients.

Some indication of the pent-up resentment felt by vast numbers of people 15 against the funeral interests was furnished by the astonishing response to an article by Roul Tunley, titled "Can You Afford to Die?" in *The Saturday Evening Post* of June 17, 1961. As though a dike had burst, letters poured in from every part of the country to the *Post*, to the funeral societies, to local newspapers. They came from clergymen, professional people, old-age pensioners, trade unionists. Three months after the article appeared, an estimated six thousand had taken pen in hand to comment on some phase of the high cost of dying. Many recounted their own bitter experiences at the hands of funeral directors; hundreds asked for advice on how to establish a consumer organization in communities where none exists; others sought information about pre-need plans. The membership of funeral societies skyrocketed. The funeral industry, finding itself in the glare of public spotlight, has begun to engage in serious debate about its own future course—as well it might.

Is the funeral inflation bubble ripe for bursting? A few years ago, the United   16
States public suddenly rebelled against the trend in the auto industry towards ever more showy cars, with their ostentatious and nonfunctional fins, and a demand was created for compact cars patterned after European models. The all-powerful auto industry, accustomed to *telling* the customer what sort of car he wanted, was suddenly forced to *listen* for a change. Overnight, the little cars became for millions a new kind of status symbol. Could it be that the same cycle is working itself out in the attitude towards the final return of dust to dust, that the American public is becoming sickened by ever more ornate and costly funerals, and that a status symbol of the future may indeed be the simplest kind of "funeral without fins"?

QUESTIONS
1. What four "articles of faith" does Mitford attribute to the funeral industry?   **2.** In the final three paragraphs, Mitford speculates about what most people want. What assumptions does she put forward? Do you agree with her? Explain.

WRITING TOPIC
What other "costly and ornate" cultural customs would you consider open to ridicule? Imitating Mitford's approach and style, write an essay critical of "The American Way of ___." (Examples might include high school proms, weddings, football halftime shows, etc.)

The Discus Thrower   1977

RICHARD SELZER [b. 1928]

I spy on my patients. Ought not a doctor to observe his patients by any means   1
and from any stance, that he might the more fully assemble evidence? So I
stand in the doorways of hospital rooms and gaze. Oh, it is not all that furtive
an act. Those in bed need only look up to discover me. But they never do.

   From the doorway of Room 542 the man in the bed seems deeply tanned.
Blue eyes and close-cropped white hair give him the appearance of vigor and
good health. But I know that his skin is not brown from the sun. It is rusted,
rather, in the last stage of containing the vile repose within. And the blue eyes
are frosted, looking inward like the windows of a snowbound cottage. This man
is blind. This man is also legless—the right leg missing from midthigh down,
the left from just below the knee. It gives him the look of a bonsai, roots and
branches pruned into the dwarfed facsimile of a great tree.

   Propped on pillows, he cups his right thigh in both hands. Now and then he
shakes his head as though acknowledging the intensity of his suffering. In all
of this he makes no sound. Is he mute as well as blind?

   The room in which he dwells is empty of all possessions—no get-well cards,
small, private caches of food, day-old flowers, slippers, all the usual kickshaws
of the sickroom. There is only the bed, a chair, a nightstand, and a tray on
wheels that can be swung across his lap for meals.

   "What time is it?" he asks.   5
   "Three o'clock."
   "Morning or afternoon?"
   "Afternoon."
   He is silent. There is nothing else he wants to know.
   "How are you?" I say.   10
   "Who is it?" he asks.
   "It's the doctor. How do you feel?"
   He does not answer right away.
   "Feel?" he says.
   "I hope you feel better," I say.   15
   I press the button at the side of the bed.
   "Down you go," I say.
   "Yes, down," he says.

   He falls back upon the bed awkwardly. His stumps, unweighted by legs and
feet, rise in the air, presenting themselves. I unwrap the bandages from the
stumps, and begin to cut away the black scabs and the dead, glazed fat with
scissors and forceps. A shard of white bone comes loose. I pick it away. I wash

the wounds with disinfectant and redress the stumps. All this while, he does not speak. What is he thinking behind those lids that do not blink? Is he remembering a time when he was whole? Does he dream of feet? Of when his body was not a rotting log?

He lies solid and inert. In spite of everything, he remains impressive, as though he were a sailor standing athwart a slanting deck.   20

"Anything more I can do for you?" I ask.

For a long moment he is silent.

"Yes," he says at last and without the least irony. "You can bring me a pair of shoes."

In the corridor, the head nurse is waiting for me.

"We have to do something about him," she says. "Every morning he orders   25
scrambled eggs for breakfast, and, instead of eating them, he picks up the plate and throws it against the wall."

"Throws his plate?"

"Nasty. That's what he is. No wonder his family doesn't come to visit. They probably can't stand him any more than we can."

She is waiting for me to do something.

"Well?"

"We'll see," I say.   30

The next morning I am waiting in the corridor when the kitchen delivers his breakfast. I watch the aide place the tray on the stand and swing it across his lap. She presses the button to raise the head of the bed. Then she leaves.

In time the man reaches to find the rim of the tray, then on to find the dome of the covered dish. He lifts off the corner and places it on the stand. He fingers across the plate until he probes the eggs. He lifts the plate in both hands, sets it on the palm of his right hand, centers it, balances it. He hefts it up and down slightly, getting the feel of it. Abruptly, he draws back his right arm as far as he can.

There is the crack of the plate breaking against the wall at the foot of his bed and the small wet sound of the scrambled eggs dropping to the floor.

And then he laughs. It is a sound you have never heard. It is something new under the sun. It could cure cancer.

Out in the corridor, the eyes of the head nurse narrow.   35

"Laughed, did he?"

She writes something down on her clipboard.

A second aide arrives, brings a second breakfast tray, puts it on the nightstand, out of his reach. She looks over at me shaking her head and making her mouth go. I see that we are to be accomplices.

"I've got to feed you," she says to the man.

"Oh, no you don't," the man says.   40

"Oh, yes I do," the aide says, "after the way you just did. Nurse says so."

"Get me my shoes," the man says.

"Here's oatmeal," the aide says. "Open." And she touches the spoon to his lower lip.

"I ordered scrambled eggs," says the man.

"That's right," the aide says.   45

I step forward.

"Is there anything I can do?" I say.

"Who are you?" the man asks.

In the evening I go once more to that ward to make my rounds. The head nurse reports to me that Room 542 is deceased. She has discovered this quite by accident, she says. No, there had been no sound. Nothing. It's a blessing, she says.

I go into his room, a spy looking for secrets. He is still there in his bed. His   50
face is relaxed, grave, dignified. After a while, I turn to leave. My gaze sweeps the wall at the foot of the bed, and I see the place where it has been repeatedly washed, where the wall looks very clean and very white.

QUESTIONS
1. Why does the patient in Room 542 hurl his scrambled eggs against the wall? **2.** What unstated assumptions govern the nurse's attitude towards the dying man?

WRITING TOPICS
1. Compare the characterization of this dying man with the characterization of Iván Ilých in Tolstoy's story. **2.** Analyze the essay's rhetorical devices with special attention to sentence structure, images, and understatement. How does Selzer's rhetoric contribute to this account of a patient's death?

Two Scenes
from a Hospital

1993

MELVIN I. UROFSKY   [b.1939]

Two things a person does alone, the ancient maxim held, are come into the   1
world and leave it. It is true that for most of human existence, people died by
themselves, the victims of predators, war, disease, or aging. As civilization
tamed humanity, people died at home, in their own beds, surrounded by
loving family who might ease the final pains but could do nothing to delay the
death. Only in the recent past have people gone to hospitals to die, and only
within the last decade or so has medicine developed drugs, procedures, and
technology to hold off death.

These developments raise a host of questions, but in the end they all come   2
down to what does the individual want, and if the individual is incapable of
deciding, what does the family want. But there are others who now demand a
voice in the decision—doctors, nurses, hospital administrators, insurance com-
panies, and, very often, agents of the state. In most instances, the person dies
without interference, since there is still little that medicine can do when age
or disease have taken their ultimate toll. But in other situations, instead of
death coming peacefully and with dignity, there is conflict and suffering, rage
and public controversy.

In these cases, the key issue is who will decide whether or not care should   3
be provided or withheld, whether enormous energy and resources should be
expended to delay death, or whether nothing should be done, so that death
may have its way. Who decides, and what role, if any, should the law play in
this process? These are not easy questions, as can be seen in the following
stories.

Rocco Musolino was a big man, one who enjoyed good food and drink and   4
people, a gregarious man who had run a liquor store in College Park, Maryland,
until his retirement. He also hated hospitals, and never wanted to end his days
in one.[1]

To avoid that possibility, Musolino wrote a living will in 1989 in which he   5
specifically declared that if he were terminally ill, he did not want to be kept
alive by machine. Aware that if he were really sick he might not be able to
make decisions on his own, he also signed a durable power of attorney giving
his wife of fifty years, Edith, the authority to make decisions about his care.

---

[1] Rocco Musolino's story is based on an extensive feature by Susan Okie in the *Washington
Post*, June 16, 1991. [This, and subsequent notes, are Urofsky's.]

Repeatedly he told his family he did not want to be hooked up to any "damn machine" or "kept alive as a vegetable."

Rocco Musolino had drawn up his living will shortly after he had suffered a   6
major heart attack in 1988. While he was in the hospital at that time doctors had performed a catheterization procedure that revealed that he had severe blockages in the coronary arteries and that one-fourth of his heart muscle was already dead. The damage was so extensive that doctors ruled out coronary bypass surgery.

Musolino had no illusions as to the prognosis of the disease, nor the fact   7
that his diabetes seriously compounded the problem. In the two years following his heart attack, his condition deteriorated to the point that he had difficulty moving around his house. "If he made it to the bathroom, that was a big deal," his daughter Edith Scott said. "He couldn't shave. He would get all out of breath."

On October 24, 1990, following a night of chest pains and difficulty breath-   8
ing, he told his wife he couldn't stand the pain anymore. She called an ambulance to take him to Georgetown University Medical Center. There his regular cardiologist, Dr. Richard Rubin, examined Musolino, and then called in a surgeon, Dr. Nevin Katz, who told the family that Rocco's only hope lay in bypass surgery, the same procedure that had been ruled out two years earlier.

"He'll die without an operation," Katz told Edith Musolino. "He's got a   9
50-50 chance with it." The family agreed reluctantly, since it appeared that potential kidney failure would also require dialysis, the type of machine treatment that Musolino had always feared. Musolino stayed in the hospital to undergo tests and build up his strength, and the medical staff scheduled him for bypass surgery on November 12. The night before the operation, Dr. Rubin went in to visit his patient, and later said that Rocco expressed a strong desire to live, even if it meant he might have to go onto dialysis for the rest of his life.

Later that night, Musolino suffered two cardiac arrests but survived, and   10
Rubin and Katz decided to go ahead with the surgery. Rubin called to get Edith Musolino's consent and then wrote in the patient's record: "He is awake and wishes to proceed. He is aware of the risk. I have reviewed the high risk of death (40 percent), high risk of renal failure (long term about 50 percent) with wife and daughter." His daughter later said she could not recall any such discussion.

The operation appeared successful, at least in relieving strain on the heart,   11
but Musolino's kidneys failed, and he required dialysis several times a week. Since he could not breathe without a respirator, his wife reluctantly agreed to a tracheotomy, in which doctors inserted a breathing tube into his neck. In addition to causing constant pain, the breathing tube left Rocco unable to talk.

Musolino remained conscious and aware of what was happening, but his   12
family claims he was never fully alert, and his medical records seem to bear this out. Doctors' notes show that he slept a lot, and often responded to questions

only with a grimace. A neurologist who examined him noted that his fluctuating state of consciousness resulted from severe medical problems; if he overcame them, he would probably regain full mental clarity.

But Rocco Musolino did not improve, and as the weeks went on his family concluded that he would never recover. In late November they asked the doctors to put a "Do Not Resuscitate" order on his chart, so that he would not be treated if he suffered another cardiac arrest. Dr. Katz refused. When the family requested that he stop some of the medication, he angrily told them: "I stay awake at night trying to keep your father alive, and you want me to kill him. What is wrong with you people?" Only after his patient's condition deteriorated further did Katz agree to a "DNR" order.

Edith Musolino watched her husband's condition worsen. "Everything that could be wrong with him was wrong with him. I knew he was dying. I knew his body couldn't take any more." She made up her mind in December to ask the hospital to stop the dialysis sessions and to let her husband die in peace.

On December 21, 1990, the hospital's ethics committee met to consider the request, and recommended a psychiatric examination to determine whether Musolino was mentally competent. Under District of Columbia law, if he were declared incompetent, then the durable power of attorney would become operative, and his wife would have the authority to make the medical decisions.

The hospital named Dr. Steven A. Epstein to do the evaluation, and he visited Musolino twice at times when the patient seemed to rally a bit. Epstein's initial report, dated December 27, was inconclusive, and the family pushed for a second evaluation. This time the doctor reported the patient "lethargic and barely responding to voice. Today he clearly cannot make health care decisions on his own." Musolino, he told the family, was not mentally competent.

On New Year's Day 1991, Edith Musolino filed a note in her husband's medical records withdrawing her consent for dialysis. According to her, doctors, hospital administrators, and the hospital's lawyers agreed that she had the authority; they ordered dialysis stopped and removed the tube used to connect Musolino to the machine. Advised that without the treatment he would probably die within a few days, she and her children went to a funeral home and made the necessary arrangements.

They returned to the hospital to learn that Katz had changed his mind, and wanted to restart dialysis. He wrote on January 2, "I cannot in good conscience carry out their request," and he asked the hospital's lawyers and the chairman of the ethics committee to reopen the case.

The family now tried to find another physician or to have Musolino transferred to another hospital that would honor their requests. Katz agreed to turn over the case if the family could find a heart specialist with intensive-care experience. As Scott Musolino reported: "I called so many doctors. No one was willing to touch my father."

The next day Georgetown Hospital's lawyers wrote to the family's attorney informing them that the hospital would seek "emergency temporary guard-ianship" unless the family agreed to resume dialysis. Edith Musolino felt she had no choice but to agree.

Ten days later, her husband's condition deteriorating, her frustration and 21 anger at the indignities that had been heaped upon him in spite of his express wishes finally erupted in a confrontation with Katz at Rocco's bedside. With her husband's legs and arms twitching, his face grimacing, she demanded of Katz: "What are you trying to prove here? You have made him suffer so much."

Katz asked her what she wanted. She said she wanted another doctor, 22 Taveira Da Silva, the head of the hospital's intensive-care unit, who had earlier agreed to take the case on condition that dialysis be continued. Katz agreed, and the next morning nurses wheeled Rocco to the ICU, where the staff gradually began treating him as a dying patient. While Da Silva described Musolino as "terminal," he nonetheless continued dialysis, even though by this point the patient had become totally disoriented and his arms had to be tied down during the procedure.

His family had reached the end of their patience as well and had agreed that 23 the only way to save Rocco from further indignity was to take him home. At a meeting on January 24, Dr. Da Silva agreed to stop the dialysis if they wanted to do that. A few days later, however, Da Silva finally came to the conclusion the family had reached much earlier—Rocco Musolino had "virtually a fatal, irreversible disease," that no medical care could help, and that the living will, which the hospital and doctors had ignored for three months, should be enforced. He told Edith that he would stop the dialysis and let her husband die in the hospital.

Instead of relief that her husband's long ordeal would soon be over, Edith 24 Musolino felt only anger. "You know, Doctor," she said, "I was beginning not to know who to pray to anymore. Do I pray to you, or do I pray to God?"

On February 2, 1991, Rocco Musolino died, after a stay of 102 days in 25 Georgetown University Medical Center, a place he had never wanted to be and where he and his family had lost all power to decide his fate.

While Rocco Musolino's wife fought to get hospital authorities to stop 26 treating him, halfway across the continent hospital officials were trying to get a patient's family to consent to a cessation of treatment.

On December 14, 1989, Helga Wanglie, an eighty-six-year-old retired 27 schoolteacher, tripped on a scatter rug in her home in Minneapolis and frac-tured her hip. After surgery in a small private hospital, she developed breathing problems and was transferred to Hennepin County Medical Center. There, although on a respirator, she remained fully conscious and alert, writing notes to her husband, since the breathing tube prevented her from talking.

After five months, the hospital weaned her from the respirator in May 1990, 28 and she entered Bethesda Lutheran Hospital across the river in St. Paul, a facility specializing in the care of respiratory ailments. A few days later, her heart stopped suddenly, and by the time doctors and nurses could resuscitate her, she had suffered severe brain damage. An ambulance brought her back to Hennepin Medical in a comatose state, her breathing sustained by a ventilator. When it became clear that doctors could do nothing for Mrs. Wanglie, they spoke with her husband of fifty-three years, Oliver, a retired attorney, about turning off the ventilator.

Although her husband and sons recognized that Helga had no cognition and   29
might never regain consciousness, they would not hear of turning off the machine. His wife had strong religious convictions, Oliver told reporters, and they had talked about the possibility that if anything happened to her, she wanted "everything" done to keep her alive. "She told me, 'Only He who gave me life has the right to take life.' . . . It seems to me [the hospital officials] are trying to play God. Who are they to determine who's to die and who's to live? I take the position that as long as her heart is beating there's life there."

Eight months after readmitting Helga Wanglie and trying to convince her   30
family to stop treatment, Hennepin Medical Center officials announced they would go to court seeking the appointment of a guardian to determine Helga Wanglie's medical treatment. The hospital did not request that the court authorize discontinuing treatment. To the best of my knowledge, no hospital has ever made such a request, nor has there been any case law on it. Rather, the hospital sought the appointment of a "stranger" conservator, that is, one independent of both family and hospital, to make decisions based on the best interests of the patient. The hospital believed that a neutral party would agree with its position.

While in most right-to-die cases it is the patient or the family that wants the   31
hospital to stop treatment, the Wanglie case is the rarely seen other side of the coin. Dr. Michael B. Belzer, the hospital's medical director, said he sympathized with the Wanglie family, but a heartbeat no longer signified life, since machines could artificially do the heart's work. The real question, he believed, was whether the hospital had an obligation to provide "inappropriate medical treatment."

Mrs. Wanglie's medical bills were paid in full by her insurance company, so   32
money was not an issue in the hospital's decision. "This is a pure ethics case," said Dr. Arthur Caplan, director of the Center for Biomedical Ethics at the University of Minnesota. For years, he explained, we've used the "smokescreen of 'Can we afford to do this?' There's been a harder question buried under that layer of blather about money, namely: 'What's the point of medical care?' "

Dr. Belzer noted that Hennepin had the facilities and "the technology to   33
keep fifty Helga Wanglies alive for an indefinite period of time. That would be the easy thing to do. The harder thing is to say just because we can do it, do we have to do it?"

Hennepin Medical Center is a public hospital, one of the best in the upper   34
midwest, and before it could petition a court to appoint a conservator or guardian for Mrs. Wanglie (in order to have consent for turning off the life support), it needed the approval of the county's Board of Commissioners. The

board members gave the hospital permission by a 4–3 vote, with the tiebreaker cast by a member who had known the Wanglie family for more than thirty years. It took him a month to make up his mind.

The commissioner, Randy Jackson, said that he finally voted to let the hospital go to the courts because "I don't think this is a decision to be made by a board of elected commissioners who happen to be trustees of the hospital. These are issues that we're going to be confronted with more and more often as medical machinery becomes more and more able to keep people alive."[2]

Hospital attorneys presented their case to county judge Patricia Belois on May 28, 1991, asking her to appoint a conservator to decide Mrs. Wanglie's fate. They did not question her husband's sincerity, but argued instead that her condition was hopeless, and respirators had never been intended to prolong life in such cases.

On July 1, Judge Belois ruled against the hospital and left power to decide decisions on Helga's medical treatment in her husband's hands. "He is in the best position to investigate and act upon Helga Wanglie's conscientious, religious, and moral beliefs." After the decision Oliver Wanglie said "I think she'd be proud of me. She knew where I stood. I have a high regard for the sanctity of human life."[3]

A little while after this decision, Helga Wanglie died.

The key issue is that of who decides what is best for a terminally ill person and what role the law and the courts have in that process. In an ideal world, perhaps, the interests of patients, families, doctors, hospitals, and courts would all coincide. But aside from the fact that this is an imperfect world, the interests of these groups are not necessarily congruent.

For centuries doctors have sworn to uphold life, and now for the first time they are being asked, openly and at times defiantly, what gives them the right to decide other people's fate? Hospitals, caught in a crunch between escalating expenses and new technology, must weigh costs that never before mattered. Moreover, in a society as litigious as ours, doctors and hospitals walk in constant fear that a "wrong" judgment will lead to a ruinous lawsuit. While elective bodies are responsible for broad policy decisions, it is difficult if not impossible to frame legislation in such a way as to cover all contingencies, and so courts must step in to interpret not only what the laws say and mean, but also what the limits of self-autonomy are under both the common law and constitutional protection.

Two things a person does alone, the ancient maxim held: come into the world and leave it. But at the end of the twentieth century, before one can

---

[2] New York Times, January 10, 1991; Time, January 21, 1991, 67.
[3] In re the Conservatorship of Wanglie, No. PX-91-283, Minnesota Dist. Ct., Probate Div. [July 1991].

leave this world, he or she may find it necessary to traverse a bewildering legal, moral, and medical maze.

QUESTIONS
1. Do you think Rocco Musolino's physician was justified in refusing to put a "Do Not Resuscitate" order on his patient's chart? Defend your view.   **2.** Do you think Helga Wanglie's husband and sons were justified in refusing to give permission to end the treatments that were keeping her alive? Defend your view.

WRITING TOPICS
1. Write an essay in which you examine the relationship between public officials, the courts, doctors, and the family in the case of Helga Wanglie, and define your own position on how such problems should be treated.   **2.** Compare and contrast the writing style of this essay with the style of Richard Selzer's "The Discus Thrower." At the conclusion of your essay, discuss the relationship between style and purpose in these two works.   **3.** In an essay, describe your own experience of the death of someone close to you.

The Rhino

1990

GARY SOTO [b. 1952]

I got up quickly on my knees in the back seat of our Chevy and stared at a   1
charging rhino painted on the side of a tire company. His legs were pleated
with lines, his horn broken, and his eyes yellow and furious. I stared at the
rhino until my father's car pulled around the corner, its sluggish shadows
following closely behind, and we flew onto the freeway.

I looked at Father. His shirt was brilliant white in the late sun. He was   2
working something from his teeth with a matchbook cover, and Mother was
penciling words into a black book. I wanted to ask about the rhino but I knew
that they would shush me.

It scared me to think that tires were being made from rhinoceros hides. So   3
many things were possible. We were eating cows, I knew, and drinking goats
milk in cans. Pigs feet came stuffed into cloudy jars. Cheese came in blocks
from an animal that ate something very orange or very yellow. The Molinas
stirred bony pigeons in pots of boiling water, and a pig's happy grin showed up
on the bacon wrapper. Hop-Along Cassidy was a face that appeared on milk
cartons, his hand on his pistol, and what I noticed was that his horse didn't
have any feet. I imagined that someone had cut off his hooves and the horse
had to lay down for the rest of his life.

I knew some of our clothes were cut from hides. Father's belt had an   4
alligator look, his lathering brush was the whiskers of a docile pony, and his
shoes, whose tips were mirror-bright, were cowhide. My own shoes were also
leather and small as toy trucks. Mother's sweater was wool. Her pillow was a
restrained cloud of chicken feathers. Her key chain was a rabbit's foot with a
claw that drew blood when raked against the skin.

Our neighbor had a bear skin rug spread on his living room floor. Uncle   5
Junior had a shrunken head that swayed from a car mirror. The mouth was
stitched closed with black thread and the left eye was half-open. My aunt
wore a fox with claws clipped together in friendship. The fox's eyes were
smoke-brown marbles, but his teeth, jagged as my aunt's, were real. And my
cousin Isaac, two years older with kindergarten already behind him, showed
me a bloody finger in a gift box. He wiggled the finger and I jumped back,
terrified.

I sat back down. I watched mostly the sky, billboards, and telephone poles.   6
A sonic boom scared Mother and had me back on my knees looking around.
The sky was pink as a scar in the west where the sun struggled to go down.
Birds huddled on a chain link fence, and because I could count to ten I used
all my fingers to tell Mother there were eight. Mother looked up from her
book, turned on her knees, and ran a comb through my hair.

Father pulled off the freeway, and after two sharp turns, he pulled into my   7
nina's yard, scattering chickens and a large black dog. The dog sniffed us as we
got out, and I was so scared that he might bite, Father pulled me into his arms
and put me on a low peach tree while he went inside the house. I thought of
eating one of the peaches but knew that the fuzz would make my face itchy. I
pressed a finger into a brown sap, counted the number of peaches, and peeled
bark from the limb. The dog trotted away and the chickens returned to peck at
the dust.

That evening we watched boxing. Father drank beer and I sat near him with   8
two links of Tinkertoy. The first television was on, and he and my godfather were
watching two boxers hurt each other very badly. They sat on the edge of their
chairs, their fists opening and closing. Father had taken off his shirt. Godfather's
watch lay on an end table, glowing in the semi-dark of the living room. Both
shouted and crushed beer cans when their fighter stumbled into the ropes. I let
the Tinkertoys fight each other and grunt like boxers. I said, "Mine is winning."

Back home I asked Father if our car tires were made from rhinos, and he   9
laughed. Mother laughed and wiped her hands into a chicken-print apron.
Uncle with his panther tattoo, claws tipped with blood, pulled on my cheek
and said I was crazy. He assured me tires didn't come from rhino hides but
from rubber that dripped from trees into buckets. He turned on the porch-
light, a feast of orange light for the moth, and led me down the brick steps to
the Chevy that ticked from a cooling engine. He pounded a front tire with his
fist. I tried to wiggle free, but his grip held me there. He made me pound the
tire and pet it like an animal. Black rhino dust came off, dust and fear that I
washed with a white bar of soap when we returned inside.

I was four and already at night thinking of the past. The cat with a sliver in   10
his eye came and went. The blimp came and went, and the black smudge of
tire. The rose could hold its fiery petals only so long, and the three sick pups
shivered and blinked twilight in their eyes. We wet their noses with water.
We pulled muck from the corners of their eyes. Mother fed them a spoonful
of crushed aspirin, but the next day they rolled over into their leaf-padded
graves.

Now the rhino was dying. We were rolling on his hide and turning corners   11
so sharply that the shadows mingled with the dust. His horn was gone, his
hooves and whale eyes. He was a tire pumped with evil air on a road of
splattered dogs and cats and broken pigeons in the grills of long, long cars.

QUESTIONS

1. Who is the speaker in this essay? What effect does Soto achieve by adopting such
a viewpoint?   **2.** How does watching boxing (paragraph 8) relate to the rest of the
essay? How does the speaker define the boxing match? What is the child's response
to the boxing match?   **3.** Why does the speaker call attention to his uncle's tattoo
(paragraph 9)?   **4.** What is this essay about, and why do you suppose the editors
placed it in the section devoted to death?

WRITING TOPICS
1. Examine the animal images in this piece—you might include descriptive passages about humans, as well. In an essay, analyze the animal images and describe the feelings the animal images generate.   **2.** In an essay, recollect some early childhood misunderstanding of your own, and describe the feelings that the misunderstanding created.

The Presence of Death

QUESTIONS AND WRITING TOPICS

1. Although Housman's "To an Athlete Dying Young" and Roethke's "Elegy for Jane" employ different poetic forms, they both embody a poetic mode called *elegy*. Define *elegy* in terms of the characteristic tone of these poems. Compare the elegiac tone of these poems. **Writing Topic:** Compare the elegiac tone of one of these poems with the tone of Owen's "Dulce et Decorum Est" or Thomas's "Do Not Go Gentle into That Good Night."

2. What figurative language in the prose and poetry of this section is commonly associated with death itself? With dying? Contrast the characteristic imagery of this section with the characteristic imagery of love poetry. **Writing Topic:** Compare the imagery in Shakespeare's sonnet 18 with the imagery in sonnet 73.

3. In Tolstoy's "The Death of Iván Ilých" and Donne's sonnet "Death, Be Not Proud," death and dying are considered from a religious viewpoint. **Writing Topic:** Discuss whether these works develop a similar attitude toward death, or whether the attitudes they develop differ crucially.

4. State the argument against resignation to death made in Thomas's "Do Not Go Gentle into That Good Night." State the argument of Catherine Davis's reply, "After a Time." **Writing Topic:** Using these positions as the basis of your discussion, select for analysis two works that support Thomas's argument and two works that support Davis's.

5. Malamud's "Idiots First" and Fenton's "God, A Poem" both present a grim picture of the human condition, yet they are often funny. What function does humor serve in each work? **Writing Topic:** Which work embodies a more hopeful vision of the human condition? Explain.

6. Contrast the attitudes toward death revealed in Donne's "Meditation XVII" and Selzer's "The Discus Thrower." **Writing Topic:** Analyze the figurative language and other stylistic elements in each essay. How does style account for the contrasting attitudes toward death expressed in these essays?

7. Which works in this section treat death and dying in a way that corresponds most closely with your own attitudes toward mortality? Which contradict your attitudes? **Writing Topic:** Choose two works, each of which affects you differently, and isolate and discuss the elements responsible for your response.

APPENDICES

The Librarian, 1566 by G. Arcimboldo

APPENDICES

Reading Fiction

An author is a god, creator of the world he or she describes. That world has a limited and very special landscape. It is peopled with men and women of a particular complexion, of particular gifts and failings. Its history, almost always, is determined by the interaction of its people within its narrow geography. Everything that occurs in a work of fiction—every figure, every tree, every furnished room and crescent moon and dreary fog—has been *purposely* put there by its creator. When a story pleases, when it moves its reader, he or she has responded to that carefully created world. The pleasure, the emotional commitment, the human response are not results of analysis. The reader has not registered in some mental adding machine the several details that establish character, the particular appropriateness of the weather to the events in the story, the marvelous rightness of the furnishings, the manipulation of the point of view, the plot, the theme, the style. The reader has recognized and accepted the world of the author and has been delighted (or saddened or angered) by what happens in it.

But how does it come about that readers recognize the artificial worlds, often quite different from their own, that authors create? And why is it that readers who recognize some fictional worlds effortlessly are bewildered and lost in other fictional worlds? Is it possible to extend the boundaries of readers' recognition? Can more and more of the landscapes and societies of fiction be made available to that onlooking audience?

The answer to the first of these questions is easy. Readers are comfortable in literary worlds that, however exotic the landscapes and the personalities that people them, incorporate moral imperatives that reflect the value system in the readers' world. Put another way, much fiction ends with its virtuous characters rewarded and its villains punished. This we speak of as poetic justice, and *poetic* seems to suggest that somehow such endings are ideal rather than "real." Not much experience of life is required to recognize that injustice, pain, frustration, and downright villainy often prevail, that the beautiful young heroine and the strong, handsome hero do not always overcome all obstacles, marry, and live happily ever after, that not every man is strong and handsome nor every woman beautiful. But readers, knowing that, respond to tragic fiction as well—where virtue is defeated, where obstacles prove too much for the men and women, where ponderous forces result in defeat, even death. Unhappy outcomes are painful to contemplate, but it is not difficult to recognize the world in which they occur. That world is much like our own. And unhappy outcomes serve to emphasize the very ideals that we have established as the aims and targets of human activity. Consequently, both the "romantic" comedies that gladden with justice and success and the "realistic" stories that end in defeat provide readers with recognizable and available emotional worlds, however exotic the settings and the characters in those stories might be.

If we look at fiction this way, the answer to the question "Why is it that some readers are bewildered and lost in some fictional worlds?" is clearly implied. Some fictional worlds *seem* to incorporate a strange set of moral imperatives. Readers are not altogether certain who are the virtuous characters and who are the villains or even what constitutes virtue and evil. Sometimes tragic oppositions in a fictional world that brooks no compromise puzzle readers who live in a world where compromise has become almost a virtue. Sometimes, particularly in more recent fiction that reflects the ever-widening influence of psychoanalytic theory, the landscape and the behavior of characters is designed to represent deep interiors, the less-than-rational hearts and minds of characters. Those weird interiors are not part of the common awareness of readers; the moral questions raised there are not the same moral questions that occupy most of our waking hours. Such fictional worlds are difficult to map, and bewildered readers may well reject these underworlds for the sunshine of the surfaces they know more immediately.

Fiction and Reality

Why do people read fiction (or watch TV narratives or go to movies)? The question is not so easy to answer as one might suppose. The first response is likely to have something to do with "amusement" or "entertainment." But you have doubtless read stories and novels (or seen movies) that end tragically. Is it accurate to say that they were amusing or entertaining? Is it entertaining to be saddened or to be angered by the defeat of "good" people? Or does the emotional impact of such stories somehow enlarge our own humanity? Fiction teaches its readers by providing them a vast range of experience that they could not acquire otherwise. Especially for the relatively young, conceptions of love, of success in life, of war, of malignant evil and cleansing virtue are learned from fiction, including movies and TV—not from life. And herein lies a great danger, for literary artists are notorious liars, and their lies frequently become the source of people's convictions about human nature and human society.

To illustrate, a huge number of television series based on the exploits of the FBI, or an urban police force, or the dedicated surgeons at the general hospital, or the young lawyers always end with a capture, with a successful (though dangerous) operation, with justice triumphant. But, in the real world, police are able to resolve only about 10 percent of reported crime, disease ravages, and economic and political power often extends into the courtroom. The very existence of such television drama bespeaks a yearning that things should be different; its heroes are heroic in that they regularly overcome those obstacles that we all experience, but that, alas, we do not overcome.

Some writers, beginning about the middle of the nineteenth century, were particularly incensed at the real damage that a lying literature promotes, and they devoted their energies to exposing and counteracting the lies of the novelists, particularly those lies that formed attitudes about what constituted human success and happiness. Yet that popular fiction, loosely called *escapist,* is still most widely read for reasons that would probably fill several studies in social psychology. It needs no advocate. The fiction in this book, on the other hand, has been chosen largely because it does not lie about life—at least it does not lie about life in the ordinary way. And the various authors employ a large variety of literary methods and modes in an effort to illuminate the deepest wells of human experience. Consequently, many of these stories do not retail high adventure (though some do), since an adventurous inner life does not depend on an incident-filled outer life. Some stories, like Toomer's "Theater," might almost be said to be about what does *not* happen rather than what does—not-happening being as much incident, after all, as happening.

All fiction attempts to be interesting, to involve readers in situations, to force some aesthetic response from them—most simply put, in the widest sense of the word, to entertain. Some fiction aspires to nothing more. Other fiction seeks, as well, to establish some truth about the nature of humankind—Hemingway's "A Clean, Well-Lighted Place" and Giles's "Rough Translations" ask readers to perceive the inner life of central figures. Some fiction seeks to explore the relationships among people—Faulkner's "A Rose for Emily," Toomer's "Theater," and Butler's "Preparation" depend for their force on the powerful interaction of one character with another. Still other fiction seeks to explore the connection between people and society—Ellison's " 'Repent, Harlequin!' Said the Ticktockman" acquires its force from the implied struggle between people seeking a free and rich emotional life and the tyrannically ordering society that would sacrifice their humanity to some ideal of social efficiency.

We have been talking about that aspect of fiction that literary theorists identify as *theme.* Theorists also talk about plot, characterization, setting, point of view, and conflict—all terms naming aspects of fiction that generally have to do with the author's technique. Let us here deal with one story—James Joyce's "Araby" (p. 27). Read it. Then compare your private responses to the story with what we hope will be helpful and suggestive remarks about the methods of fiction.

The Methods of Fiction

One can perceive only a few things simultaneously and can hardly respond to everything contained in a well-wrought story all at once. After reading the story, the reader likely thinks back, makes adjustments, and reflects on the significance of things before reaching the emotional and intellectual experiences that we refer to as _response_. Most readers of short stories respond first to what may be called the _tone_ of the opening lines. Now tone is an aspect of literature about which it is particularly difficult to talk, because it is an aura—a shimmering and shifting atmosphere that depends for its substance on rather delicate emotional responses to language and situation. Surely, before readers know anything at all about the plot of "Araby," they have experienced the tone.

> North Richmond Street, being blind, was a quiet street except at the hour when the Christian Brothers' School set the boys free. An uninhabited house of two storeys stood at the blind end, detached from its neighbours in a square ground. The other houses of the street, conscious of decent lives within them, gazed at one another with brown imperturbable faces.

Is the scene cheerful? Vital and active? Is this opening appropriate for a story that goes on to celebrate joyous affirmations about life and living? You will probably answer these questions negatively. Why? Because the dead-end street is described as "blind," because the Christian Brothers' School sounds much like a prison (it "sets the boys free"), because a vacant house fronts the dead end, because the other houses, personified, are "conscious of decent lives within" (a mildly ironic description—_decent_ suggesting ordinary, thin-lipped respectability rather than passion or heroism), because those houses gaze at one another with "brown imperturbable faces"—_brown_ being nondescript, as opposed, say, to scarlet, gold, bright blue, and _imperturbable faces_ reinforcing the priggish decency within.

Short stories, of course, are short, but this fact implies some serious considerations. In some ways, a large class of good short fiction deals with events that may be compared to the tip of the proverbial iceberg. The events animating the story represent only a tiny fraction of the characters' lives and experiences; yet, that fraction is terribly important because it provides the basis for wide understanding both to the characters within the story and to its readers.

In "Araby," the _plot_—the connected sequence of events—may be simply stated. A young boy who lives in a rather drab, respectable neighborhood develops a crush on the sister of one of his playmates. She asks him if he intends to go to a charity fair that she cannot attend. He resolves to go and purchase a gift for her. He is tormented by the late and drunken arrival of his uncle who has promised him the money he needs. When the boy finally arrives at the bazaar, he is disappointed by the difference between his expectation and the actuality of the almost deserted fair. He perceives some minor events, overhears some minor conversation, and finally sees himself "as a creature driven and derided by vanity." Yet this tiny stretch of experience out of the life of the boy introduces him to an awareness about the differences between imagination and reality, between his romantic infatuation and the vulgar reality all about him. We are talking now about what is called the *theme* of the story. Emerging from the mundane events that constitute the story's plot is a general statement about intensely idealized childish "love," the shattering recognition of the false sentimentality that occasions it, and the enveloping vulgarity of adult life. The few pages of the story, by detailing a few events out of a short period of the protagonist's life, illuminate one aspect of the loss of innocence that we all endure and that is always painful. In much of the literature in the section on innocence and experience, the protagonists learn painfully the moral complexities of a world that had once seemed uncomplicated and predictable. That education does not always occur, as in "Araby," at an early age, either in literature or life.

Certainly theme is a centrally important aspect of prose fiction, but "good" themes do not necessarily ensure good stories. One may write a wretched story with the same theme as "Araby." What, then, independent of theme, is the difference between good stories and bad stories? Instinctively you know how to answer this question. Good stories, to begin with, are interesting; they present characters you care about; however fantastic, they are yet somehow plausible; they project a moral world you recognize. One of the obvious differences between short stories and novels is that story writers develop characters rapidly and limit the number of developed characters. Many stories have only one fleshed character; the other characters are frequently two-dimensional projections or even stereotypes. We see their surface only, not their souls. Rarely does a short story have more than three developed characters. Again, unlike novels, short stories usually work themselves out in a restricted geographical setting, in a single place, and within a rather short period of time.

We often speak of character, setting, plot, theme, and style as separate aspects of a story in order to break down a complex narrative into more manageable parts. But it is important to understand that this analytic process of separating various elements is something we have done to the story—the story (if it is a good one) is an integrated whole. The more closely we examine the separate elements, the clearer it becomes that each is integrally related to the others.

It is part of the boy's character that he lives in a brown imperturbable house in North Richmond Street, that he does the things he does (which is, after all, the plot), that he learns what he does (which is the theme), and that all of this characterization emerges from Joyce's rich and suggestive style. Consider this paragraph:

> Her image accompanied me even in places the most hostile to romance. On Saturday evenings when my aunt went marketing I had to go to carry some of the parcels. We walked through the flaring streets, jostled by drunken men and bargaining women, amid the curses of labourers, the shrill litanies of shop-boys

> who stood on guard by the barrels of pigs' cheeks, the nasal chanting of street-singers, who sang a *come-all-you* about O'Donovan Rossa, or a ballad about the troubles in our native land. These noises converged in a single sensation of life for me: I imagined that I bore my chalice safely through a throng of foes. Her name sprang to my lips at moments in strange prayers and praises which I myself did not understand. My eyes were often full of tears (I could not tell why) and at times a flood from my heart seemed to pour itself out into my bosom. I thought little of the future. I did not know whether I would ever speak to her or not or, if I spoke to her, how I could tell her my confused adoration. But my body was like a harp and her words and gestures were like fingers running upon the wires.

This paragraph furthers the plot. But it suggests much more. The boy thinks of his friend's sister even when he carries parcels for his aunt during the shopping trips through a crowded and coarse part of town. In those coarse market streets the shop-boys cry shrill "litanies," the girl's name springs to his lips in strange "prayer and praises," and the boy confesses a confused "adoration." Further, he bears his "chalice safely through a throng of foes." Now the words *litanies, prayers, praises, adoration,* all come from a special vocabulary that is easy to identify. It is the vocabulary of the Roman Catholic Church. The *chalice* and the *throng of foes* come from the vocabulary of chivalric romance, which is alluded to in the first line of the quoted paragraph. Joyce's diction evokes a sort of holy chivalry that characterizes the boy on this otherwise altogether ordinary shopping trip. This paragraph suggests to the careful reader that the boy has cast his awakening sexuality in a mold that mixes the disparate shapes of the heroic knight, winning his lady by force of arms, and the ascetic penitent, adoring the Blessed Virgin, Mother of God.

Playing the word game, of course, can be dangerous. But from the beginning of this story to its end, a certain religious quality shimmers. That now-dead priest of the story's second paragraph had three books (at least). One is a romantic chivalric novel by Sir Walter Scott; one is a sensational account of the adventures of a famous criminal-turned-detective; one is what a priest might be expected to have at hand—an Easter week devotional guide. That priest who read Scott novels might have understood the boy's response—that mixture of religious devotion and romance.

Shortly after the shopping trip, the boy finally speaks to the girl, and it is instructive to see her as he does. He stands at the *railings* and looks up (presumably) at her, she bowing her head towards him. "The light from the lamp opposite our door caught the white curve of her neck, lit up her hair that rested there and, falling, lit up the hand upon the railing. It fell over one side of her dress and caught the white border of a petticoat, just visible as she stood at ease." Skip the petticoat, for a moment. Might the description of Mangan's sister remind the careful reader of quite common sculptured representations of the Virgin Mary? But the petticoat! And the white curve of her neck! This erotic overlay characterizes the boy's response. The sexuality is his own; the chivalry, the religious adoration, come from the culture in which he is immersed—come from Scott, the ballads sung in the market place, the "Arab's Farewell to His Steed" that the boy's uncle threatens to recite, and from his Catholic background. And it is the culture that so romanticizes and elevates the boy's yearning.

He finally gets to Araby—"the syllables of the word . . . were called to [him] through the silence in which [his] soul luxuriated and cast an Eastern enchantment over [him]." His purpose is to serve his lady—to bring her something from that exotic place. What he finds is a weary-looking man guarding a turnstile, the silence that pervades a church after a service, and two men counting money on a salver (that tray is called a *salver* by design). And in this setting he overhears a young woman flirting with two gentlemen:

> "O, I never said such a thing!"
> "O, but you did!"
> "O, but I didn't!"
> "Didn't she say that?"
> "Yes, I heard her."
> "O, there's a . . . fib!"

This is Araby, this is love in a darkened hall where money is counted. Is it any wonder that the boy, in the moment of personal illumination that Joyce calls an epiphany, sees himself as a creature driven and derided by vanity?

"Araby" is a careful, even a delicate story. Nothing much happens—what does occurs largely in the boy's perception and imagination. The story focuses on the boy's confusion of sexual attraction and the lofty sentiments of chivalry and religion. The climax occurs when he confronts the darkened, money-grubbing fair and the banal expression of the sexual attraction between the gentlemen and the young woman. The result is a sudden deflation of the boy's ego, his sense of self, as he recognizes his own delusions about the nature of love and the relationship between men, women, heroism, God, and money.

We would like to conclude with a discussion of one feature of fiction that sometimes proves troublesome to many readers. Often the events of a story, upon which much depends, puzzle or annoy readers. Why does that fool do that? Why doesn't X simply tell Y the way he or she feels and then the tragedy would be averted? In a sense, such responses reflect the intrusion of a reader into the world of the story. The reader, a sensible and sensitive person, understands some things about life after all and is oppressed by the characters' inability to understand at least as much. Characters choose to die when they might proceed safely. They suffer the pain of an unfortunate marriage when with a little trouble they might be free to live joyously. If the "whys" issuing from the reader are too insistent, too sensible, then the story must fail, at least for that reader. But many "whys" are not legitimate. Many are intrusions of the reader's hindsight, the reader's altogether different cultural and emotional fix. Henry James urged that the author must be allowed his or her *donnée*, his or her "given." The author creates the society and the rules by which it operates within his or her own fictional world. Sometimes this creation is so close to the reader's own world that it is hardly possible to object. Many African American readers will recognize the tensions in Walker's "Everyday Use." Those who have grown up in a southern town will recognize the atmosphere of Faulkner's "A Rose for Emily." But few readers of this book know 1895 Dubin and Irish middle-class society, which plays a brooding role in "Araby" (as it does in almost all of Joyce's work). None know the futuristic world of Harlan Ellison's Harlequin. In every case, we must finally imagine those worlds, even where setting is familiar. If we cannot, the events that take place in them will be of no consequence. If those worlds are unimaginable, then the stories must fail. If they too much strain belief or remain too foreign to the reader's heart, they must likewise fail. But all response to fiction depends on the reader's acquiescence to the world of the author and the reader's perceptions of the moral consequences of acts and attitudes in that world. At best, that acquiescence will provide much pleasure as well as emotional insight into his or her own existence.

Reading Poetry

When I Heard the Learn'd Astronomer

1865

WALT WHITMAN [1819–1892]

When I heard the learn'd astronomer,
When the proofs, the figures, were ranged in columns before me,
When I was shown the charts and diagrams, to add, divide, and measure them,
When I sitting heard the astronomer where he lectured with much applause
   in the lecture-room,
How soon unaccountable I became tired and sick,   5
Till rising and gliding out I wander'd off by myself,
In the mystical moist night-air, and from time to time,
Look'd up in perfect silence at the stars.

    The distinction implicit in Walt Whitman's poem between the mind (intellectual knowledge) and the heart (emotion and feelings) is very old, but still a useful one. All of us have no doubt felt at some time that the overexercise of the mind interfered with our capacity to feel. Compelled to analyze, dissect, categorize, and classify, we finally yearn for the simple and "mindless" pleasure of unanalytical enjoyment. But the distinction between the mind and the heart cannot be pushed too far before it breaks down. You may very well enjoy Dylan Thomas's poem "Fern Hill" without recognizing its patterns of imagery or the intricate way Thomas weaves together the past and the present. But understanding these elements will certainly deepen the pleasure the poem can give you.

    We don't mean to suggest by this that every poem needs to be studied long and hard. Some poems are straightforward, requiring little analysis; others, dense and complex, seem to yield little without some study. To test this out, you might want to read right now two short poems (both twelve lines long), Emily Dickinson's "After Great Pain, a Formal Feeling Comes" and Countee Cullen's "Incident." You will probably read straight through the Cullen poem and understand what the poet is saying. If the Dickinson poem doesn't stump you in the first line, it certainly will in the next three lines. Yet you will surely understand (whatever "understand" might mean) the somber, serious tone and the image with which the poem ends.

    Knowing a little about what poetry is and about its history can also enhance your appreciation. If your instructor asked you to define poetry, you would probably say it's the kind of writing that uses rhyme, regular rhythm, unusual word order, and vivid, even unusual language and images. This kind of formal definition describes a good deal of poetry although by no means all, as a glance at any anthology (including this one) will quickly show. Up until about a century ago, poetry was governed by precise and often elaborate rules and conventions. Further, there existed a long tradition of poetic types (epic, elegy, ode, etc.), each with specific rules and characteristics. While these traditions still retain some force, the old notion that these forms are part of the natural scheme of things has been largely abandoned. Under the influence of Walt Whitman (the nineteenth-century poet who virtually invented "free verse") and the explosion of experimentalism beginning in the twentieth century, no one nowadays insists that what we call poetry must exhibit a combination of fixed characteristics (demonstrating once again that theory usually follows practice).

If the old formal criteria are no longer adequate, neither can we say that poetry deals only with certain subjects. Dylan Thomas's "Fern Hill" deals with death and the lost innocence of childhood in an elevated and formal language and an extremely complex stanzaic pattern. These formal characteristics along with the "lofty" subject matter mark it clearly as a poem. Anthony Hecht's "The Dover Bitch" uses a flat, conversational language and lines that have no apparent formal pattern. There is nothing lofty or noble about the woman who is the subject of the poem. But it *looks* like a poem—the lines end at different places on the right-hand side of the page! Carolyn Forché's "The Colonel" doesn't even *look* like a poem. The point is, like the formal characteristics, no hard-and-fast rules can be laid down about the subjects of poetry. The seventeenth-century poet John Milton declared that he had written his great epic *Paradise Lost* "to justify the ways of God to men." Archibald MacLeish tells us in "Ars Poetica" that "A poem should not mean / But be." They are both poems.

However we may define poetry, no culture we know about has been without it. We know that in ancient societies, the arts were not divided by types or differentiated from science. Poetry, dance, sculpture, and painting might all be parts of a tribal ceremony designed to propitiate the gods and so ensure a full harvest or a successful hunt. Poetry, then, was part of an early "science" that defined and helped order the natural world. Nature and the gods who controlled it might be harsh and unpredictable; the function of ritual was to influence and appease these goods (to ensure rain, for example). But ritual also nurtured and strengthened the individual's communal spirit. The work in this anthology closest to this view of the world is Sophocles' tragedy *Antigonê*, a highly ritualized work that combines poetry (it is written in verse), dance (the Chorus moves in a choreographed fashion throughout), and painting and sculpture (the masks worn by the actors).

We in the modern West, of course, live very different lives. We inhabit an enormous industrialized society that over centuries abandoned "primitive" explanations and sought others. That development was marked by a differentiation and specialization of human endeavors, as science broke away from art and both divided into separate if related disciplines. Science became astronomy, biology, physics, and the like, while art branched into various types of aesthetic creation. And it was modern science, not poetry or the other arts, that produced profound and measurable changes in people's lives. Poetry might movingly and memorably remind us of the sorrow of unrequited love or the ravages of growing old, but the technology that science made possible produced undreamed-of material wealth and power.

It would be misleading to suggest that the scientist and the poet exist in separate worlds. But there are important differences. Science seeks the truth of physical reality. Social sciences such as psychology, sociology, and economics have tried to demonstrate that human behavior can be understood in terms of a set of definite and quantifiable mechanisms. Science can explain to us the physical phenomenon of death and explain its role in the ceaseless evolutionary struggle. But to understand the terror or emotional meaning of death, we turn to the poet. To return to the head / heart metaphor, we can say that the poet does speak to our heart while the scientist speaks to our head. But we should remember that the metaphor is not meant to suggest that one is superior to the other. We cannot exist without either the head or the heart. And at a deeper level, we might even say that the realm of science deals as much with beauty and mystery as the realm of poetry.

But poetry does speak more immediately, obviously, and powerfully to us about our inner lives. It helps us to learn who we are and to articulate what we feel. You may wonder what such an assertion means. What we feel, we feel. We don't need a poem to tell us. Not so. Often we don't know what we feel except in a vague way. A powerful poem articulates and thereby clarifies. Although the literary historian might observe that it is an academic exercise in wit, Andrew Marvell's poem "To His Coy Mistress" may well help readers understand their own feelings about the connection between physical love and mortality. The outrageous absurdity of death cutting down a person whose life has barely begun is articulated in Robert Frost's " 'Out, Out—' " and Theodore Roethke's "Elegy for Jane."

Poetry at its highest and most general level is a form of communication, a means of defining, affirming, and deepening our humanity. This is not to say that we should approach poetry solemnly, expecting always to be loftily enlightened. We may, for instance, look upon a poem as a kind of game in which the poet skillfully works within a set of self-imposed rules—patterns of rhymes, rhythms, stanzas—while at the same time playing with language to achieve surprise, wit, and freshness. We delight in the comic effect Lord Byron achieves when he rhymes "intellectual" with "henpecked you all" or "maxim" with "tax 'em." In E. E. Cummings's "if everything happens that can't be done," the telescoping of two syntactic units in the lines "and buds know better / than books / don't grow" ("books" is both the object of the preposition "than" and the subject of "don't grow") is surprising, clever, and thematically appropriate.

Anyone familiar with Plato's theory that everything in our world is an imperfect replica of an ideal heavenly form will appreciate the beauty and condensed brilliance of William Butler Yeats's lines from "Among School Children":

> Plato thought nature but a spume that plays
> Upon a ghostly paradigm of things.

Some will discover, as children often do in nursery rhymes, the pleasure of rhythm, meter, and sound—the musical aspects of poetry. The pleasures of poetry range from the loftiest insights and discoveries to memorable lines and clever rhymes.

What follows are brief discussions about the major techniques and devices of poetry that will give you the tools for discussing and analyzing poems.

The Words of Poetry

It is not unusual to hear an original philosopher, sociologist, or economist referred to as a mediocre writer. Even while judging the writing poor, one may at the same time honor the originality and significance of the writer's ideas. Such a distinction cannot be made in poetry. If a poem is written poorly, it is a poor poem. "In reading prose," Ralph Waldo Emerson said, "I am sensitive as soon as a sentence drags; but in poetry as soon as one word drags." *Where* a poem arrives is inseparable from *how* it arrives. Everything must be right in a poem, every word. "The correction of prose," said William Butler Yeats, "is endless; a poem comes right with a click like a closing box."

Critics often describe poetry as "heightened language," meaning that the poet strives for precision and richness in the words he or she uses. For the poet, "precision" and "richness" are not contradictory. Words have dictionary or denotative meanings as well as associative or connotative meanings; they also have histories and relationships with other words. The English language is rich in synonyms, words whose denotative meanings are roughly the same but whose connotations vary widely (*excite, stimulate, titillate, inflame; poor, impoverished, indigent, destitute*). Many words are identical in sound and often in spelling but different in meaning (*forepaws, four paws; lie [recline], lie [fib]*). The meanings of words have changed over time, and the poet may deliberately select a word whose older meaning adds a dimension to the poem. There are, of course, no hard-and-fast rules for judging a poet's effectiveness and skill in the handling of words (or anything else, for that matter). All we can do is look at particular works for examples of how a good poet uses words.

In a moving and passionate poem on his dying father, "Do Not Go Gentle into That Good Night," Dylan Thomas pleads with his father not to accept death passively but rather to "Rage, rage against the dying of the light." He declares that neither "wise men" nor "good men" nor "wild men" accept death quietly. And neither, Thomas adds, do "grave men," punning on *grave* in its meaning of both "serious" and "burial place." William Blake's poem about the inhumane jobs children were forced into in eighteenth-century England, "The Chimney Sweeper," begins:

> When my mother died I was very young,
> And my Father sold me while yet my tongue
> Could scarcely cry "'weep! 'weep! 'weep! 'weep!"
> So your chimneys I sweep, and in soot I sleep.

"'Weep," a clipped form of "sweep," is what the boy cries as he walks a street looking for work, but *weep* clearly evokes the tears and sorrow of his mother's death and the sadness of the small boy's cruel life. "Cry" is also an effective pun, the precise word to describe how the boy seeks work while simultaneously reinforcing the emotional meaning of *weep*.

Henry Reed's "Naming of Parts" develops a contrast between the instructions a group of soldiers are receiving on how to operate a rifle (in order to cause death) and the lovely world of nature (representing life and beauty). In the fourth stanza, bees are described as "assaulting and fumbling the flowers." "Fumbling," with its meaning of awkwardness and nervous uncertainty, may at first strike us as a puzzling word. Yet anyone who has watched a bee pollinating a flower will find the word denotatively effective. In addition, *fumbling* describes the actions of human beings caught up in sexual passion—a connotation appropriate to the poet's purposes, since pollination is a kind of sexual process. Furthermore, the meanings of *fumbling* contrast powerfully with the cold, mechanical precision of the death-dealing instruments the recruits are learning to use. The next line of the poem exhibits yet another resource of words: "They call it easing the Spring." The line is an exact repetition of a phrase used two lines earlier except *Spring* is now capitalized. While *Spring* retains its first meaning as part of the bolt action of the rifle, the capitalization makes it the season of the year when flowers are pollinated and the world of nature is reborn. With a typographical change, Reed is able to evoke in a single word the contrast (the cold steel of a rifle and the fecund beauty of nature) that gives the poem its structure and meaning.

Figurative Language

Figurative language is the general phrase we use to describe the many devices of language that allow us to speak nonliterally in order to achieve some special effect. When we wish to communicate a subjective state with more precision than the words of English give us, we reach for figurative language. When Robert Burns compares his love to a red rose in his poem "A Red, Red Rose," it's not because he can't find the literal language he needs but because what he wants to say can only be expressed in figurative language. The interior world of emotions, feelings, and attitudes remains shadowy and insubstantial until figurative language gives it form and substance.

Figurative language allows us—and the poet—to transcend the confinement of the literal and the vagueness of the abstract through the use of *imagery*. The world is revealed to us through our senses—sight, sound, taste, touch, and smell. And while some philosophers and psychologists might disagree, it seems pretty clear that much, if not all, of our knowledge is linked to sensory experience. Through imagery, the poet creates a recognizable world by drawing on a fund of common experiences. Bad poetry is often bad because the imagery is stale ("golden sunset," "the smiling sun," "the rolling sea") or so skimpy that the poem dissolves into vague and meaningless abstraction.

A good poet never loses touch with the sensory world. The invisible, the intangible, the abstract, are anchored to the visible, the tangible, the concrete. Andrew Marvell begins his poem "To His Coy Mistress" with an elaborate statement of how he would court his beloved if their lives were measured in centuries rather than in years. He then describes the reality:

> But at my back I always hear
> Time's wingéd chariot hurrying near.
> And yonder all before us lie
> Deserts of vast eternity.
> Thy beauty shall no more be found,
> Nor, in thy marble vault, shall sound
> My echoing song; then worms shall try
> That long-preserved virginity,
> And your quaint honor turn to dust,
> And into ashes all my lust:
> The grave's a fine and private place,
> But none, I think, do there embrace.

Time, eternity, honor, and *lust* are all abstractions, vague and diffuse as abstractions always are. To overcome his mistress's coyness, Marvell needs to impart a sense of passionate urgency, to make her (and the reader) *see* these abstractions by linking them to the concrete. He does this by making time a *chariot,* eternity endless *deserts,* having honor turn to *dust,* and lust dwindle into *ashes.*

The difference between good and bad poetry often turns on the skill with which imagery (or other figurative language) is used. When Robert Frost in his poem "Birches" compares life to a "pathless wood" (line 44), the image strikes us as natural and appropriate (the comparison of life to a path or road is a common one, as is a state of moral bewilderment to a wood or forest).

However, when John Donne in "A Valediction: Forbidding Mourning" describes the relationship between him and his beloved in terms of a drawing compass, the image may seem jarring or even ludicrous. How can such a prosaic object help the poet define the nature of love, especially a love based upon spiritual affinities? In using such a conceit (see "Glossary of Literary Terms"), Donne startles the reader into attention, maybe even hoping to create resistance or doubt that such an image is appropriate for a love poem. But as Donne elaborates the comparison through various stages, concluding it with the brilliantly appropriate image of the completed circle, our resistance and doubt give way to admiration for what Donne has done.

Words and phrases may take on figurative meaning over a period of time. Consider, for example, these familiar old sayings: "The grass is always greener on the other side of the fence"; "A rolling stone gathers no moss"; "A bird in the hand is worth two in the bush"; "The early bird catches the worm." While these sayings make literal sense (the grass you see from a distance *does* look greener than the grass under your feet), their meaning to a native speaker of English is clearly nonliteral. When we use them, we are making general and highly abstract observations about human attitudes and behavior. Yet strangely, these generalizations and abstractions are embodied in concrete and sensuous imagery. Try to explain what any of these expressions mean and you will quickly discover that you are using many more words and much vaguer language than the expression itself. This is precisely what happens when you try to put into your own words (paraphrase) a poem. Like poetry, these sayings rely on the figurative use of language.

Since poetry is an intense and heightened use of language that explores the worlds of feeling, it relies upon more frequent and original use of figurative language than does ordinary speech. One of the most common figurative devices, *metaphor*, where one thing is called something else, occurs frequently in ordinary speech. "School is a rat race," we say, or "He is a tower of strength," and the meaning is perfectly clear—too clear, perhaps, because these metaphors are so common and unoriginal they have lost what vividness they once had. But when John Donne says, "I am a little world made cunningly" or Henry David Thoreau declares, "I am a bundle of vain strivings," we have metaphors that are original and arresting (and provide the vehicle by which both authors define themselves). When W. H. Auden, commenting on the death of William Butler Yeats, says, "Let the Irish vessel lie / Emptied of his poetry," he pays a complex tribute to the great Irish poet.

Simile is closely related to metaphor. But where metaphor says that one thing is another, simile says that one thing is like another, as in Burns's "O My Luve's like a red, red rose" and Frost's "life is too much like a pathless wood." The distinction between simile and metaphor, while easy enough to make technically, is often difficult to distinguish in terms of effect. Frost establishes a comparison between life and a pathless wood and keeps the two even more fully separated by adding the qualifier "too much." Burns's simile maintains the same separation and, in addition, because it occurs in the opening line of the poem, eliminates any possible confusion the reader might experience if the line were, "O My Luve is a red, red rose." You can test the difference in effect by changing a metaphor into a simile or a simile into a metaphor to see if the meaning is in any way altered.

Another important use of figurative language is the *symbol*. In its broadest sense, a symbol is anything that stands for something else. In this sense, most words are symbolic: the word *tree* stands for an object in the real world. When we speak of a symbol in a literary work, however, we usually mean something more precise. In poetry, a symbol is an object or event that suggests more than itself. It is one of the most common and powerful devices available to the poet, for it allows him or her to convey economically and simply a wide range of meanings.

It is useful to distinguish between two kinds of symbols, *public symbols* and *contextual symbols*. Public symbols are those objects or events that history has invested with rich meanings and associations, for example, national flags or religious objects such as the cross. William Butler Yeats uses such a symbol in his poem "Sailing to Byzantium," drawing upon the celebrated and enduring art of the ancient Byzantine Empire as a symbol of timelessness. In "Curiosity," Alastair Reid uses cats and their proverbial curiosity to symbolize the kind of human beings who live the best and truest lives.

In contrast to public symbols, contextual symbols are objects or events that are symbolic by virtue of the poet's handling of them in a particular work—that is, by virtue of the context. Consider, for example, the opening lines of Robert Frost's "After Apple-Picking":

> My long two-pointed ladder's sticking through a tree
> Toward heaven still,
> And there's a barrel that I didn't fill
> Beside it, and there may be two or three
> Apples I didn't pick upon some bough.

The apple is a literal tree, but as one reads through the poem, it becomes clear that the apple tree symbolizes the speaker's life, with a wide range of possible meanings (do the few apples he hasn't picked symbolize the hopes, dreams, aspirations that even the fullest life cannot satisfy?).

Amy Lowell's "Patterns" is rich in symbols. The aristocratic speaker describes herself as walking down garden paths laid out in precise patterns. Her elegant gown is real; the path is a real path. But it quickly becomes apparent that her gown and the paths symbolize the narrowly restricted and oppressive life she is fighting against.

The paths in Amy Lowell's poem are clear and easily recognizable examples of contextual symbols. However, contextual symbols by their very nature tend to present more difficulties than public symbols, because recognizing them depends on a sensitivity to everything else in the poem. In T. S. Eliot's dense and difficult "The Love Song of J. Alfred Prufrock," the speaker twice says, "In the room the women come and go / Talking of Michelangelo," a baffling couplet because it seems to have no connection with what precedes and follows it. But once we see the pattern of Christian religious imagery in the poem and recall that Michelangelo, one of the great Renaissance artists, created some of the greatest religious art of all time, including the *Pietà* of the Vatican and the paintings in the Sistine Chapel, we can at least begin to connect the couplet to the rest of the poem.

The reader who fails to recognize a symbol misses an important part of a poem's meaning. On the other hand, you want to avoid becoming so intent on finding symbolic meanings that you lose sight of the fact that an object must first have a literal meaning before it can function as a symbol. Or, to put it in terms of our earlier definition, an object or event must be itself before it can be something else. Finally, even careful readers may well disagree on whether something should be taken as a symbol. When this occurs, the best criterion for judgment is probably, Does the symbolic interpretation add meanings to the poem that are consistent with other elements in the poem? As you will see in the Glossary of Critical Approaches (p. 919), disagreement on virtually every matter of literary interpretation is a hallmark of modern theories of literature.

Music

The *music* of poetry, by which we mean the poetic use of all the devices of sound and rhythm inherent in language, is at once central to the poetic effect and yet the most difficult to account for. We can discuss the ways in which figurative language works with some clarity because we are using words to explain words. Any listener who has ever tried to explain the effect of a piece of music (or who has read music criticism) will be familiar with the problem of describing a nonverbal medium with words.

The possible musical effects of language are complex. The terms we have to describe various musical devices deal only with the most obvious and easily recognizable patterns. *Alliteration, assonance, consonance, caesura, meter, onomatopoeia, rhythm,* and *rhyme* (all of them defined in the Glossary of Literary Terms) are the key traditional terms for discussing the music of poetry. Along with the other terms already introduced, they are an indispensable part of the vocabulary one needs to discuss poetry. But the relationship between sound and sense is illustrated nicely in a celebrated passage from Alexander Pope's "An Essay on Criticism," in which his definitions of bad verse and then of well-managed verse are ingeniously supported by the music of the lines:

> These[1] equal syllables alone require,
> Though oft the ear the open vowels tire;
> While expletives their feeble aid do join;
> And ten low words oft creep in one dull line;
> While they ring round the same unvaried chimes,
> With sure returns of still expected rhymes;
> Where 'er you find "the cooling western breeze,"
> In the next line, it "whispers through the trees";
> If crystal streams "with pleasing murmurs creep,"
> The reader's threatened (not in vain) with "sleep";
> Then, at the last and only couplet fraught
> With some unmeaning thing they call a thought,
> A needless Alexandrine[2] ends the song
> That, like a wounded snake, drags its slow length along.

---

[1] Bad poets.
[2] Twelve-syllable line.

. . . . .

> True ease in writing comes from art, not chance,
> As those move easiest who have learned to dance.
> 'Tis not enough no harshness gives offense,
> The sound must seem an echo to the sense:
> Soft is the strain when Zephyr gently blows,
> And the smooth stream in smoother numbers flows;
> But when loud surges lash the sounding shore,
> The hoarse, rough verse should like the torrent roar:
> When Ajax[3] strives some rock's vast weight to throw,
> The line too labors, and the words move slow;
> Not so, when swift Camilla[4] scours the plain,
> Flies o'er the unbending corn, and skims along the main.

When Pope speaks of open vowels, the line is loaded with open vowels. When Pope condemns the use of ten monosyllables, the line contains ten monosyllables. When Pope urges that the sound should echo the sense and speaks of the wind, the line is rich in sibilants that hiss, like the wind. When he speaks of Ajax striving, the combination of final consonants and initial sounds slow the line; when he speaks of Camilla's swiftness, the final consonants and initial sounds form liaisons that are swiftly pronounceable.

Or, consider the opening lines of Wilfred Owen's poem "Dulce et Decorum Est," describing a company of battle-weary World War I soldiers trudging toward their camp and rest:

> Bent double, like old beggars under sacks,
> Knock-kneed, coughing like hags, we cursed through sludge.

These lines are dominated by a series of harsh, explosive consonant sounds (*b, d, k, g*) that reinforce the meaning of the lines. More specifically, the first two syllables of each line are heavily stressed, which serves to slow the reading. And, finally, while the poem ultimately develops a prevailing meter, the meter is only faintly suggested in these opening lines, through the irregular rhythms used to describe a weary, stumbling march.

Let us remember, then, that analysis of musical (or for that matter any other) devices can illuminate and enrich our understanding of poetry. But let us also remember that analysis has its limitations. Dylan Thomas once remarked:

> You can tear a poem apart to see what makes it technically tick and say to yourself when the works are laid out before you—the vowels, the consonants, the rhymes, and rhythms—"Yes, this is it. This is why the poem moves me so. It is because of the craftsmanship." But you're back where you began. The best craftsmanship always leaves holes and gaps in the

---

[3] A Greek warrior celebrated for his strength.
[4] A swift-footed queen in Virgil's *Aeneid*.

works of the poem so that something that is not in the poem can creep, crawl, flash, or thunder in.

Another writer, X. J. Kennedy, puts the same idea with less reverence:

ARS POETICA   1985

The goose that laid the golden egg
Died looking up its crotch
To find out how its sphincter worked.
Would you lay well? Don't watch.

Reading Drama

Plays are fundamentally different from other literary forms. Unlike stories and poems, almost all plays are designed to be performed, not to be read. Thus, the reader (with the aid of some meager stage directions) must imagine the aural and the visual aspects of the drama, which should be at least as important as its dialogue. Great effort is invested in such matters as costuming, set design, lighting effects, and stage movement by the director and his or her staff; all of that effort is lost to the reader who must somehow contrive to supply imaginatively some of those dramatic features not contained on the printed page.

As much as possible, the way to read a play is to imagine that you are its director. Hence you will concern yourself with creating the set and the lighting. You will see people dressed so that their clothes give support to their words. You will think about timing—how long between events and speeches—and blocking—how the characters move as they interact on stage. Perhaps the best way to confront the literature of the stage, to respond most fully to what is there, is to attempt to produce some scenes in class or after class. If possible, attend the rehearsals of plays in production on campus. Nothing will provide better insight into the complexities of the theater than attending a rehearsal where the problems are encountered and solved.

As an exercise, read the opening speeches of any of the plays here and make decisions. How should the lines be spoken (quietly, angrily, haltingly)? What should the characters do as they speak (remain stationary, look in some direction, traverse the stage)? How should the stage be lit (partially, brightly, in some color that contributes to the mood of the dialogue and action)? What should the characters who are not speaking do? What possibilities exist for conveying appropriate signals solely through gesture and facial expression—signals not contained in the words you read?

Staging

Since plays are written to be staged, the particular kind of theater available to the dramatist is often crucial to the structure of the play. The Greek theater of Dionysius in Athens, for which Sophocles wrote, was an open-air amphitheater seating about 14,000 people. (See p. 906). The skene, or stage house, from which actors entered, was fixed, though it might have had painted panels to suggest the scene. Consequently, there is no scene shifting in *Antigonê*. All the dialogue and action take place in the same location before the skene building, which represents the Palace of Creon. Important things happen

904

elsewhere, but the audience is informed of these events by messenger. Three deaths occur, but none in sight of the audience, partly as a matter of taste and partly because the conditions of the Greek stage prevented the playwright from moving the action inside the palace or to that terrifying mausoleum where both Antigonê and her betrothed choose death before submission. Later dramatists, writing for a more flexible stage and a more intimate theater, were able to profit from the intensely dramatic nature of murder and suicide, but the Greeks, almost invariably, chose to tell, rather than show, the most gripping physical events in their stories.

Further, an outdoor theater of vast dimensions implies obvious restrictions on acting style. Facial expression can play no important role in such a theater, and, in fact, the actors of Sophoclean tragedy wore masks, larger than life and probably equipped with some sort of megaphone device to aid in voice projection. Those voices were denied the possibility of subtle variety in tone and expression, and the speeches were probably delivered in rather formal declamatory style. The characters wore special built-up footwear that made them larger than life. In addition to these limitations, Sophocles had as well to write within the formal limitations imposed by the Athenian government, which made available only three principal actors, all male, as the cast (exclusive of the chorus) for each play. Consequently, there are never more than three players on stage at once, and the roles are designed so that each actor takes several parts—signified by different masks. Yet, despite the austerity of production values, the unavoidable clumsiness of fortuitous messengers appearing at all the right moments, and the sharply restricted dramatis personae, among the few Greek plays that have survived are some still universally regarded as superlatively fine dramatic representations of tragic humanity.

Until recently we thought we had a clear conception of what Shakespeare's stage looked like. Scholarship has raised some doubts about this conception, but though we no longer accept the accuracy of the reconstruction shown here, we still have a good enough understanding of the shape of the playing area to re-create roughly the staging of a Shakespearean play. (See pp. 906–907.) That staging was altogether different from the Greek. Though both theaters were open air, the enclosure around the Elizabethan stage was much smaller, and the audience capacity limited to something between 2,000 and 3,000. As in classical drama, men played all the roles, but they no longer wore masks, and a stage that protruded into the audience made for great intimacy. Hence the actors' art expanded to matters of facial expression, and the style of speech and movement was certainly closer than was Greek style to what we might loosely call realism. Shakespeare has Hamlet caution the actors: "Suit the action to the word, the word to the action, with this special observance, that you o'erstep not the modesty of nature: for anything so overdone is from the purpose of playing, whose end, both at first and now, was and is, to hold as 't were, the mirror up to nature. . . ." But the characteristic matter of Shakespearean tragedy certainly did not lend itself to a modern realistic style. Those great speeches are written in verse; they frequently are meant to augment the rather meager set design by

The ancient theater at Epidaurus, Greece

The Globe Theatre

Interior of the Swan Theatre, London, 1596

Hypothetical reconstruction of the interior of the Globe Theatre in the days of Shakespeare

A seventeenth-century French box stage

providing verbal pictures to set the stage; they are much denser in texture, image, and import than is ordinary speech. These characteristics all serve to distinguish the Shakespearean stage from the familiar realism of most recent theater.

The Elizabethan stage made possible a tremendous versatility for the dramatist and the acting company. Most of the important action was played out on the uncurtained main platform, jutting into the audience and surrounded on three sides by spectators. The swiftly moving scenes followed each other without interruption, doubtless using different areas of the stage to signify different locations. There was some sort of terrace or balcony one story above the main stage, and there was an area at the back of the main protruding stage that could be curtained off when not in use. Although Shakespeare's plays are usually divided into five separate acts in printed versions, they were played straight through, without intermission, much like a modern motion picture.

Though more versatile and intimate than the Greek stage, the Elizabethan stage had limitations that clearly influenced the playwright. Those critical imperatives of time, place, and action (i.e., the time represented should not exceed one day, the location should be fixed in one place, and the action should be limited to one cohesive story line—one plot), the so-called unities that Aristotle discovered in the drama of Sophocles, may well reflect the physical conditions of the Greek theater. Elizabethan dramatists largely ignored them, and in *Othello* we move from Venice to Cyprus, from the fortifications of the island to the city streets to Desdemona's bedchamber. Certainly some props were used to suggest these locations, but nothing comparable to the furniture of Ibsen's nineteenth-century stage. Instead, the playwright often wove a sort of literary scenery into the speeches of the character. For example, in *Othello*, Roderigo has occasion to say to Iago, "Here is her father's house; I'll call aloud." The second act of *Othello* opens with some gentlemen at "an open place near the Quay." Notice the dialogue:

> **Montano.** What from the cape can you discern at sea?
> **First Gentleman.** Nothing at all: it is a high-wrought flood;
>   I cannot 'twixt the heaven and the main
>   Descry a sail.
> **Montano.** Methinks the wind hath spoke aloud at land;
>   A fuller blast ne'er shook our battlements;
>   If it hath ruffian'd so upon the sea,
>   What ribs of oak, when mountains melt on them,
>   Can hold the mortise?

There is no sea, of course, and Elizabethan technology was not up to a wind machine. The men are, doubtless, looking offstage and creating the stormy setting through language. An open-air theater that played in daylight had few techniques for controlling lighting, and speeches had to be written to supply the effect:

> But look, the morn, in russet mantle clad,
> Walks o'er the dew of yon high eastern hill.

Further, the company had not the resources to place armies on the stage; hence, a speaker in *King Henry* V boldly invites the audience to profit from imagination:

> Piece out our imperfection with your thoughts;
> Into a thousand parts divide one man,
> And make imaginary puissance;
> Think, when we talk of horses, that you see them
> Printing their proud hoofs i' the receiving earth.
> For 'tis your thoughts that now must deck our kings.

The theater in the Petit-Bourbon Palace, built about twenty-five years after Shakespeare's death, was a forerunner of the common "box stage" on which so much recent drama is acted. Essentially, this stage is a box with one wall removed so that the audience can see into the playing area. (See p. 907.) Such a stage lends itself to realistic settings. Since the stage is essentially a room, it can easily be furnished to look like one. If street scenes are required, painted backdrops provide perspective and an accompanying sense of distance. Sets at an angle to the edge of the stage might be constructed. The possibilities for scenic design allowed by such a stage soon produced great set designers, and the structure of such a stage led to the development of increasingly sophisticated stage machinery, which in turn freed the dramatist from the physical limitations imposed by earlier stages. By Ibsen's time the versatility of the box stage enabled him to write elaborately detailed stage settings for the various locations in which the drama unfolds. Further, the furnishing of the stage in Ibsen's plays sometimes functions symbolically to convey visually the choking quality of certain bourgeois life-styles.

None of the historical stages has passed into mere history. The modern theater still uses Greek amphitheaters such as that at Epidaurus, constructs approximations of the Elizabethan stage for Shakespeare festivals, and employs the box stage with ever-increasing inventiveness. Early in the twentieth century, some plays were produced in the "round," the action taking place on a stage in the center of the theater with the audience on all sides. A number of theaters were built that incorporated a permanent in-the-round arrangement. But versatility has become so important to the modern production designer that some feel the very best theater is simply a large empty room (with provisions for technical flexibility in the matter of lighting) that can be rearranged to suit the requirements of specific productions. This ideal of a "theater space" that can be freely manipulated has become increasingly attractive—some have been constructed—since it frees the dramatist and the performance from limitations built into permanent stage design.

Drama and Society

The history of dramatic literature (like the history of literature in general) provides evidence for another kind of history as well—the history of changing attitudes, changing values, and even changing taste. In ancient Greece, in

Elizabethan England when Shakespeare wrote his enduring tragedies, right up to the end of the eighteenth century, certain expectations controlled the nature of tragedy. Those expectations were discussed by Aristotle as early as 335 B.C.; they involved the fall of a noble figure from a high place. Such tragedy reflects important cultural attitudes. It flourished in conjunction with a certain sort of politics and certain notions about human nature. The largest part of an audience of several thousand Athenians in the fifth century B.C. was certainly not itself noble. Neither was Shakespeare's audience at the Globe Theatre in London. That audience, much as a modern audience, was composed of tradespeople, artisans, and petty officials. In Greece, even slaves attended the tragedy festivals. Why then were there no tragedies in which the central figure was a storekeeper, a baker, or a butcher?

There have been many attempts to answer this difficult question, and those answers tend to make assumptions about the way individuals see themselves and their society. If the butcher down the street dies, well, that is sad, but after all rather unimportant to society. If the king falls, however, society itself is touched, and a general grief prevails that makes possible sweeping observations about the chancy conditions of life. A culture always elevates some of its members to the status of heroes—often by virtue of the office they hold. Even now, societies are collectively moved, and moved profoundly, by the death of a president, a prime minister—a Kennedy, a de Gaulle, a Churchill—when they are not nearly so moved by immense disasters such as killing storms or earthquakes or civil wars. But things have changed.

New cultural values and new attitudes about human nature developed in the West during the nineteenth century, especially since the advent of industrialism and the publication of Freud's systemic observations about the way people's minds interact with their bodies. The result has been an increasing humanization of those who used to be heroes and an increasing realization of the capacity for heroism in those who are merely bakers and butchers. Thus Henrik Ibsen, frequently referred to as "the father of modern drama," can compel a serious emotional response from his audience over the tribulations of middle-class families. Such plays succeed in spite of their commonplace heroes because Western society can now accept the experiences of ordinary people as emblems of its own. Perhaps it can because modern political institutions have, at least theoretically, exalted the common person and rejected political aristocracy. Certainly the reasons for the change are complex. But it remains true that neither Sophocles nor Shakespeare could have written any of Ibsen's plays.

Dramatic Irony

Dramatic irony allows the audience to know more than the characters do about their own circumstances. Consequently, that audience *hears more* (the ironic component) than do the characters who speak. Shakespeare's *Othello* provides an excellent illustration of the uses of dramatic irony. At the end of Act II,

Cassio, who has lost his position as Othello's lieutenant, asks Iago for advice on how to regain favor. Iago, who, unknown to Cassio, had engineered Cassio's disgrace, advises him to ask Desdemona, Othello's adored wife, to intervene. Actually this is good advice; ordinarily the tactic would succeed, so much does Othello love his wife and wish to please her. But Iago explains, in a soliloquy to the audience, that he is laying groundwork for the ruin of all the objects of his envy and hatred—Cassio, Desdemona, and Othello:

> . . . for while this honest fool
> Plies Desdemona to repair his fortunes,
> And she for him pleads strongly to the Moor,
> I'll pour this pestilence into his ear
> That she repeals him for her body's lust;
> And, by how much she strives to do him good,
> She shall undo her credit with the Moor.
> So will I turn virtue into pitch,
> And out of her own goodness make the net
> That shall enmesh them all.

Of course Desdemona, Cassio, and Othello are ignorant of Iago's enmity. Worse, all of them consider Iago a loyal friend. But the audience knows Iago's design, and that knowledge provides the chilling dramatic irony of Act III, scene 3.

When Cassio asks for Desdemona's help, she immediately consents, declaring, "I'll intermingle every thing he does / With Cassio's suit." At this, the audience, knowing what it does, grows a little uneasy—that audience, after all, rather likes Desdemona and doesn't want her injured. As Iago and Othello come on stage, Cassio, understandably ill at ease, leaves at the approach of the commander who has stripped him of his rank, thus providing Iago with a magnificent tactical advantage. And as Cassio leaves, Iago utters an exclamation and four simple words that may rank among the most electrifying in all of English drama:

> Ha! I like not that.

They are certainly not very poetic words; they do not conjure up any telling images; they do not mean much either to Othello or Desdemona. But they are for the audience the intensely anticipated first drop of poison. Othello hasn't heard clearly:

> What dost thou say?

Maybe it all will pass, and Iago's clever design will fail. But what a hiss of held breath the audience expels when Iago replies:

> Nothing, my lord: or if—I know not what.

And Othello is hooked:

> Was not that Cassio parted from my wife?

The bait taken, Iago beings to play his line:

> Cassio, my lord? No, sure, I cannot think it,
> That he would steal away, so guilty-like,
> Seeing you coming.

And from this point on in the scene, Iago cleverly and cautiously leads Othello. He assumes the role of Cassio's great friend—reluctant to say anything that might cast suspicion on him. But he is also the "friend" of Othello and cannot keep silent in his suspicions. So honest Iago (he is often called "honest" by the others in the play), apparently full of sympathy and kindness, skillfully brings the trusting Othello to emotional chaos. And every word they exchange is doubly meaningful to the audience, which perceives Othello led on the descent into a horrible jealousy by his "friend." The scene ends with Othello visibly shaken and convinced of Desdemona's faithlessness and Cassio's perfidy:

> Damn her, lewd minx! O, damn her!
> Come, go with me apart; I will withdraw,
> To furnish me with some swift means of death
> For the fair devil. Now art thou my lieutenant.

To which Iago replies:

> I am your own for ever.

Now, all of Iago's speeches in this scene operate on the audience through dramatic irony. The tension, the horror, the urge to cry out, to save Cassio, Desdemona, and Othello from the devilish Iago—all the emotional tautness in the audience results from irony, from knowing what the victims do not know. The play would have much less force if the audience did not know Iago's intentions from the outset and did not anticipate as he bends so many innocent events to his own increasingly evil ends. Note that dramatic irony is not limited to drama; poetry, sometimes (as in William Blake's "The Chimney Sweeper"), and fiction, often (as in Kate Chopin's "The Storm"), make use of this technique. But dramatic irony is the special tool of the dramatist, well suited to produce an electric tension in a live audience that overhears the interaction of people on stage.

Drama and Its Audience

Scholarly ordering that identifies the parts of drama and discusses the perceptive distinctions made by Aristotle among its parts can help you confront a play and understand how your responses were triggered by the playwright, the designers of the play, and the performers. But such an analysis cannot substitute for the emotional experience produced by successful drama. Plays, perhaps more than other art forms, address the complex mélange of belief, attitude, intellect, and awareness that constitutes a human psyche. As in *Antigonê*, sometimes the play torments its audience by imposing on a courageous central character a duty that must be performed and must end in a tragic death. Sometimes, as in David Henry Hwang's *M. Butterfly*, the play mocks widely held cultural values and compels the audience to reexamine some of its fundamental attitudes. If, in our humanity, we did not share the capacity for possessive love as well as jealousy, with all its terror, all its threat to self-esteem, then the tragedy of *Othello* would be incomprehensible.

A lyric poem may simply meditate on the transience of life or express the pain of love unrequited. Plays, however, set characters within demanding social and cultural settings. Those cultural imperatives create dissatisfaction and conflict that may lead to a heightened awareness of or an insight into one's own limitations. What happens when the viewer's (or reader's) assumptions and beliefs conflict with those embodied in the play? If we do not believe that the world is ruled by the gods or a God, can we appreciate *No Exit*? Such questions cannot be answered easily. We can say, however, that one of the functions of art is to force us to reexamine our most cherished abstract beliefs in the revealing light of the artist's work.

Reading Essays

Essays differ from fiction in that they generally do not create imaginary worlds inhabited by fictional characters. We know, for example, through media accounts and the testimony of his friends, that Martin Luther King, Jr., was indeed jailed in Birmingham, Alabama, where he wrote his famous argument for social justice, "Letter From Birmingham Jail." And, although we cannot independently verify that George Orwell actually shot an elephant, or that Richard Selzer is describing a real patient, their works exhibit the formal nonfictional qualities of the essay rather than the imagined world of the short story.

Writers turn to the essay form when they wish to confront their readers directly with an idea, a problem (often with a proposed solution), an illuminating experience, an important definition, some flaw (or virtue) in the social system. Usually, the essay is relatively short, and almost always it embodies the writer's personal viewpoint. And although the essay may share many elements with other literary forms, it generally speaks with the voice of a real person about the real world. The term *essay* derives from the French verb *essayer*, "try," "attempt." That verb, in turn, derives from the Latin verb *exigere*, "weigh out," "examine."

While the French term calls attention to the personal perspective that characterizes the essay, the Latin verb suggests another dimension. The essay not only examines personal experiences but also explores and clarifies ideas, argues for or against a position. Thus, "My First Encounter with Death" is obviously the title of an essay. So is "The American Way of Death." The titles, however, suggest that the first essay will be intensely personal and the second will be less personal and more analytical, perhaps even argumentative.

As you read an essay, you need to ask yourself, "What is the central argument or idea?" Sometimes the answer is obvious. One essay attacks extravagant funerals fostered by the undertaker industry, another justifies feminism by revealing the miserable position of women in Elizabethan society. In either case, these essays, if successful, will change—or, perhaps, reinforce—the reader's attitudes toward death rituals and the status of women.

Some essays address the inner lives of their readers. John Donne's "Meditation XVII," for example, does not attack or justify anything. Rather, it insists that we be aware of our mortality; that awareness might well alter our behavior, our interaction with or perception of the people around us. Such essays often investigate the nature of love, of courage, of what it means to be human.

Types of Essays

In freshman composition, you probably read and were required to write narrative, descriptive, expository, and argumentative essays. Let us recall the characteristics of each of these types, while keeping in mind that in the real world, essays, more interested in effectiveness than in purity of form, frequently combine features of different formal types.

Narrative Essays

Narrative essays recount a sequence of related events and are often autobiographical. But those events are chosen because they suggest or illustrate some truth or insight. In "Shooting an Elephant," for example, George Orwell narrates an episode from his life that led him to an important insight about imperialism. In "Rage," James Baldwin uses an episode from his life to show how a frustrating powerlessness can lead to self-destructive behavior. In these narrative essays, the writers discover in their own experiences the evidence for generalizations about themselves and their societies.

Descriptive Essays

Descriptive essays depict in words sensory observations—they evoke in the reader's imagination the sights and sounds, perhaps even the smells, that transport him or her to such places as Joan Didion's Death Valley or Lars Eighner's Dumpster. Sometimes, the writer is satisfied simply to create a lifelike evocation of some engaging object or landscape; but Didion and Eighner use their descriptions as vehicles for expressing ideas about morality and poverty. The descriptive essay, like the narrative essay, often addresses complex issues that trouble our lives—but it does so by appealing primarily to sensory awareness—sight, sound, touch, taste, smell—rather than to intellect. The power of description is so great that narrative and expository essays often use lengthy descriptive passages to communicate forcefully.

Expository Essays

Expository essays attempt to explain and elucidate, to organize and provide information. Often they embody an extended definition of a complex conception such as love or patriotism. Or expository essays may describe a process—how to do something. This essay, for example, is clearly not narrative, because it doesn't depend for its form on a chronological sequence of meaningful events. It is not descriptive in the pure sense of that type, because it does not depend on conveying sensory impressions of anything. It is, in fact, expository. It acquaints its readers with the techniques and types of essays and provides some tips to help students read essays both analytically and pleasurably. To that end, we have made use of a number of rhetorical strategies that you will remember from your freshman writing course. We *classify* essays by type; we *compare and contrast* them; we use *definition*; we give *examples* to make a point; we imply that there is a *cause and effect* relationship between what readers bring to an essay and the pleasure they derive from it. Similarly, the essayists represented in this book use a variety of such rhetorical strategies to achieve their aims.

Argumentative Essays

Although we described Orwell's "Shooting an Elephant" as a narrative essay, we might reasonably assert that it is also argumentative, because it is designed to convince readers that imperialism is as destructive to the oppressors as to the oppressed. The argumentative essay wishes to persuade its readers. Thus, it usually deals with controversial ideas; it marshals arguments and evidence to support a view; it anticipates and answers opposing arguments. Martin Luther King, Jr., accomplishes all these ends in his "Letter from Birmingham Jail." So does Jonathan Swift in "A Modest Proposal," although his approach is more complicated in that he relies on irony and satire.

Analyzing the Essay

The Thesis

The best way to begin analyzing an essay is to ask "What is the point of this piece of writing; what is the author trying to show, attack, defend, or prove?" If you can answer that question satisfactorily and succinctly, then the analysis of the essay's elements (that is, its rhetorical strategies, its structure, style, tone, and language) becomes easier. Lewis Thomas's "The Iks" is a very short and relatively simple essay, and the author clearly states the thesis when he says, "Nations have themselves become too frightening to think about, but we might learn some things by watching [the Iks]." On the other hand, a much more complex and ambitious essay such as Virginia Woolf's "What if Shakespeare Had Had a Sister?" does not yield up its thesis quite so easily. We might say that Woolf's examination of the historical record leads her to argue that women did not write during the Elizabethan period because literary talent could not flourish in a social system that made women the ill-educated property of men. This defensible formulation of the essay's thesis, as you will see when you read the essay, leaves a good deal out—notably the exhortation to action with which Woolf concludes the piece.

Structure and Detail

Read carefully the first and last paragraphs of a number of essays. Attend to the writers' strategy for engaging you at the outset with an irresistible proposition.

> In Moulmein, in Lower Burma, I was hated by large numbers of people—the only time in my life that I have been important enough for this to happen to me.

> If I speak in tongues of men and of angels, but have not love, I am a noisy gong or a clanging cymbal.

> I spy on my patients.

These randomly chosen opening sentences are startling, and most readers will eagerly read on to find out what it was that made the writer so hated in Burma, why love is so important, why the doctor spies on his patients. You will find that the opening lines of all well-wrought essays instantly capture your attention.

Endings, too, are critical. And if you examine the concluding lines of any of the essays in this collection, you will find forceful assertions that focus the matter that precedes them to sharp intensity. Essayists, unsurprisingly, systematically use gripping beginnings and forceful endings.

Let us turn to what comes between those beginnings and endings.

Essays often deal with abstract issues—the nature of love, the inevitability of death, the evils of imperialism. Though such abstractions do significantly influence our lives, they tend to remain impersonal and distant. Reading about great ideas becomes a sort of academic task—we may record the ideas in notebooks, but we tend to relegate them to some intellectual sphere, separate from the pain and passion of our own humanity. The accomplished essay writer, however, forces us to confront such issues by converting abstract ideas into concrete and illustrative detail.

For example, George Orwell points out early in "Shooting an Elephant" that the "anti-European feeling was very bitter" in British-controlled Burma. But he immediately moves from the abstraction of "anti-European feeling" to "if a European woman went through the bazaars alone somebody would probably spit betel juice over her dress" and "when a nimble Burman tripped me up on the football field and the referee (another Burman) looked the other way, the crowd yelled with hideous laughter." The tiny bits of hateful experience, because they are physical and concrete, powerfully reinforce the abstract assertion about "anti-European feeling" that lies at the center of Orwell's essay, and the narrative account of the speaker's behavior in front of the mob culminates in an illuminating insight—"I perceived in this moment that when the white man turns tyrant it is his own freedom that he destroys." The large generality emerges from deeply felt personal experience.

In another essay, Richard Selzer spies on his terminally ill patient who has become a "discus thrower." How, after all, can a writer, trying to deal with the inevitability of death, convey the intense pain and emotional agony of a dying person? Selzer's patient concretizes that pain and agony in a simple repetitive act:

> In time the man reaches to find the rim of the tray, then on to find the dome of the covered dish. He lifts off the cover and places it on the stand. He fingers across the plate until he probes the eggs. He lifts the plate in both hands, sets it on the palm of his right hand, centers it, balances it. He hefts it up and down slightly, getting the feel of it. Abruptly, he draws back his right arm as far as he can.
>
> There is the crack of the plate breaking against the wall at the foot of his bed and the small wet sound of the scrambled eggs dropping to the floor.
>
> And then he laughs. It is a sound you have never heard.

Can you imagine any objective and clinical description of the anguish and rage of a dying person that would convey the feeling more effectively than the concrete details of this understated anecdote?

Style and Tone

The word *style* refers to all the writing skills that contribute to the effect of any piece of literature. And *tone*—the attitude conveyed by the language a writer chooses—is a particularly significant aspect of writing style. As an illustration of the effect of tone, consider these opening lines of two essays—Margaret Sanger's "The Turbid Ebb and Flow of Misery" and William Saroyan's "Five Ripe Pears."

> During these years in New York trained nurses were in great demand. Few people wanted to enter hospitals; they were afraid they might be "practiced" upon, and consented to go only in desperate emergencies. Sentiment was especially vehement in the matter of having babies. A woman's own bedroom, no matter how inconveniently arranged, was the usual place for her lying-in. I was not sufficiently free from domestic duties to be a general nurse, but I could ordinarily manage obstetrical cases because I was notified far enough ahead to plan my schedule. And after serving my two weeks I could get home again.

> If old man Pollard is still alive I hope he reads this because I want him to know I am not a thief and never have been. Instead of making up a lie, which I could have done, I told the truth and got a licking. I don't care about the licking because I got a lot of them in grammar school. They were part of my education. Some of them I deserved and some I didn't. The licking Mr. Pollard gave me I didn't deserve, and I am going to tell him why. I couldn't tell him that day because I didn't know how to explain what I knew.

Although both are first-person accounts, Sanger's tone is rather formal—in every sentence but the last, she uses some form of the verb *be*, and she often employs the passive voice: "they might be 'practiced' upon," "I was notified." As well, Sanger marshals a host of rather weighty Latinate words: *practiced, consented, desperate, sentiment, vehement, inconveniently, sufficiently, notified.*

Saroyan's tone, in contrast, is personal and informal. He uses slang (*licking*) and contractions. Most of his verbs are active. Although a reminiscing adult describes the event, the writer creates the voice of a child by using simple grammar and a kind of artless repetition, as well as a child's vocabulary. The tonal differences between these two passages reflect the authors' differing aims.

The tone a writer creates contributes substantially to the message he or she conveys. Jonathan Swift might have written a sound, academic essay about the economic diseases of Ireland and how to cure them—but his invention of the speaker of "A Modest Proposal," who ironically and sardonically proposes the establishment of a human-baby meat-exporting industry, jars the readers in ways no scholarly essay could. The outraged tone of Jessica Mitford's "The American Way of Death" comically reinforces her attack on greedy undertakers. The high seriousness of Donne's tone in "Meditation XVII" perfectly suits his contemplation of the relationship among the living, the dying, and the dead.

Style is a more difficult quality to define than tone. Dictionaries will tell you that style is both "a manner of expression in language" and "excellence in expression." Certainly it is easier to distinguish between various *manners* of expression than it is to describe just what constitutes *excellence* in expression. For example, the manners of expression of John Donne in "Meditation XVII," of Richard Selzer in "The Discus Thrower," of Jessica Mitford in "The American Way of Death" clearly differ. The first muses about death in a style characterized by formality and complex extended images. The second achieves informality with a style characterized by short direct sentences and understatement. The essay's figurative language describes the dying patient rather than the nature of death. The third uses the breezy style of a muckraking journalist, replete with contemptuous asides and sardonic exclamations.

Nonetheless, we can describe the excellence of each style. Donne, an Anglican priest, meditates on the community of all living humans and the promise of eternal life in the face of physical death. He creates a remarkable image when he argues that "all mankind is of one author." Not so remarkable, you might argue; God is often called the "author of mankind." But Donne insists on the figurative quality of God as author and the intimate relationship among all people when he adds that all humankind "is one volume." Then he extends this metaphor by arguing that "when one man dies, one chapter is not torn out of the book, but translated into a better language." The daring image is further extended. "God," Donne tells us, "employs several translators; some pieces are translated by age, some by sickness, some by war, some by justice." By alluding to the actual making of a book by the bookbinder, Donne elaborates on the central image and reestablishes the idea of community—"God's hand is in every translation, and his hand shall bind up all our scattered leaves again for that library where every book shall lie open to one another." Surely, this magnificent figurative characterization of death (regardless of your personal beliefs) exhibits stylistic excellence.

Richard Selzer also deals with death.

> From the doorway of Room 542 the man in the bed seems deeply tanned. Blue eyes and close-cropped white hair give him the appearance of vigor and good health. But I know that his skin is not brown from the sun. It is rusted, rather, in the last stage of containing the vile repose within. And the blue eyes are frosted, looking inward like the windows of a snowbound cottage. This man is blind.

Here you see a very different style. Whereas Donne's sentences are long and move with the rolling cadence of oratory, Selzer's are terse and direct. Selzer's metaphors and similes characterize the ugliness of dying. The man's skin is not tanned by the sun; it is "rusted." His sightless eyes are frosted "like the windows of a snowbound cottage." These images, together with the artful simplicity of Selzer's short, halting sentences, powerfully convey the degradation and the impotence of the dying. Here again, style plays a significant role.

Jessica Mitford's attack on the American funeral industry begins:

> O Death, where is thy sting? O grave, where is thy victory? Where, indeed. Many a badly stung survivor, faced with the aftermath of some relative's funeral, has

> ruefully concluded that the victory has been won hands down by a funeral establishment—in disastrously unequal battle.

This essay opens with a quote from Paul's Letter to the Corinthians—certainly a sober and exalted allusion. But immediately, the tone turns sardonic with the question "Where indeed?" And the writer compounds the sarcasm by extending the biblical metaphor that compares death with a painful bee-sting to the equally painful experience of the "stung" survivor who has been conned into enormous expenditure by a funeral establishment. Her breezy style juxtaposes the ancient biblical promise of a spiritual victory over death with the crass modern reality—the only victor, nowadays, is the greedy funeral director. The perception is "rueful," and the victory "has been won hands down" in an encounter characterized as a "disastrously unequal battle." Mitford's language, playing off the high seriousness of the biblical quotation, stylistically advances her purpose by introducing a note of mockery. Certainly her argument gains force from the pervasive sardonic tone that characterizes her style.

Three different writers, all discussing some aspect of death, exhibit three distinctive manners of expression and three distinctive varieties of excellence—in short, three distinctive styles.

Your principal concern, when reading an essay, must always be to discover the essay's central thesis. What does the writer wish you to understand about his or her experience, the world, or yourself? Once you have understood the essay's thesis, you can increase your pleasure by examining the means the author used to convey it and, perhaps, recognize techniques that will enhance the quality of your own writing. To that end, you ought to examine the essay's structure and the rhetorical strategies that shape it. How does it begin and end? What type is it—narrative, descriptive, expository, argumentative? How do rhetorical strategies—definition, cause and effect, classification, exemplification, comparison and contrast—function to serve the author's purposes? Then, discover the sources of reading pleasure by closely analyzing the language of the essay. Watch writers energize abstract ideas with details and moving experience; consider the uses of figurative language—the metaphors and similes that create both physical and emotional landscapes in the prose; respond to the tone of voice and the stylistic choices that create it. When you have done all this successfully, when you have discovered not only *what* the author has said, but also *how* the author moved you to his or her point of view—then you will have understood the essay.

Glossary of Critical Approaches

Introduction

This alphabetically arranged glossary attempts to define, briefly, and in general terms, some major critical approaches to literature. Because literary criticism has to do with the *value* of literature, not with its history, judgments tend to be subjective and disagreements frequent and even acrimonious. The truth of a work of art is, obviously, very different from the truth of a mathematical formula. Certainly one's attitudes toward war, religion, sex, and politics are irrelevant to the truth of a formula but quite relevant to one's judgment of a literary work.

Yet any examination of the broad range of literary criticism reveals that groups of critics (and all readers, ultimately, are critics) share certain assumptions about literature. These shared assumptions govern the way critics approach a work, the elements they tend to look for and emphasize, the details they find significant or insignificant, and, finally, the overall value they place on the work.

We do not suggest that one approach is more valid than another or that the lines dividing the various approaches are always clear and distinct. Readers will, perhaps, discover one approach more congenial to their temperament, more "true" to their sense of the world, than another. More likely, they will find themselves utilizing more than one approach in dealing with a single work. Many of the diverse approaches described here actually overlap, and even those critics who champion a single abstract theory often draw on a variety of useful approaches when they write about a particular work.

Formalist critics assume that a literary text remains independent of the writer who created it. The function of the critic, then, is to discover how the author has deployed language to create (or perhaps failed to create) a formal and aesthetically satisfying structure. The influential American formalists of the 1940s and 1950s (the New Critics) were fond of describing literary texts as "autonomous," meaning that political, historical, biographical, and other considerations were always secondary if not irrelevant to any discussion of the work's merits.

Further, formalist critics argue, the various elements of a "great" work interweave to create a seamless whole that embodies "universal" values. Unsurprisingly, the "universal" values formalist critics praise, upon close analysis, tend to parallel the moral, political, and cultural ideals of the critics' social class.

But the formalist point of view, cherishing the artwork's structure, spawned its own antithesis—a group of theorists called *deconstructionists*. These writers argued that language itself was too shifty to support the expectations of formalist criticism. One reader might read a sentence literally, while another might read it ironically. Hence, their "understanding" of the text would be diametrically opposed.

The deconstructionists believe that intelligent, well-educated readers cannot be expected to ignore those responses that interfere with some "correct" or "desirable" reading of the piece. Given what they see as the notoriously ambiguous and unstable nature of language, deconstructionist critics argue that a literary text can never really be absolutely known. They, unlike the formalists, who search for coherence in texts, almost playfully insist on a (sometimes quite significant) incoherence in texts that, by their very nature, can have no fixed meaning.

While the formalists and deconstructionists wrestle over the philosophy of language and its implications for the nature of literary texts, other critics pursue quite different primary interests. The literary critic Wayne Booth, in his book *The Company We Keep: An Ethics of Fiction* (1988), examines the meaning and relevance of "ethical criticism," which he characterizes as "this most important of all forms of criticism." The term *ethical criticism* describes a variety of approaches, all of which argue that literature, like any other human activity, connects to the real world, and, consequently, influences real people.

Ethical criticism may range from a casual appraisal of a work's moral content to the more rigorous and systematic analysis driven by a coherent set of stated beliefs and assumptions. A *religious* critic (committed to certain moral positions) might attack a work—regardless of its artfulness or brilliance—because it does not condemn adultery. A *feminist* critic might focus on the way literary works devalue women, a *black* critic on the way they stereotype blacks, a *Marxist* critic on the way they support class divisions, a *new historicist* critic on the way a dominant class interprets history to protect its own interests. But all of them agree that literary works invite ethical judgments. Most of them also agree that literary works must be judged as another means by which a society both defines and perpetuates its political institutions and cultural values. The feminist, the black, and the Marxist critics would also agree that the political institutions and cultural values of most Western societies have been carefully designed to serve the interests of a dominant class: male, white, and wealthy.

Other critical approaches analyze literary works from yet other perspectives. *Reader-response* critics assert that a work of art is created as much by its audience as by the artist. For these critics, art has no significant abstract existence—a reader's experience of the work gives birth to it and contributes crucially to its power and value. Further, since each reader embodies a unique set of experiences and values, each reader's response to the work will give birth to a unique, personal artwork. Beauty is in the eye of the beholder. *Psychoanalytic* criticism, similar to reader-response, is nevertheless distinctive in its application of psychoanalytic principles to works of art. Those principles were originally derived from the work of Sigmund Freud (1856–1939), but now often reflect the views of more recent theorists such as Jacques Lacan and others. There is, finally, the recently emergent approach called *new historical* criticism, which brings historical knowledge to bear on the analysis of literary works in new and sophisticated ways. The result is a sometimes dizzying proliferation of analyses that argue for the relationship between literature and life.

The glossary that follows, along with the quotations, reveals the widely diverse and often contradictory views expressed by professional theorists and critics.

There is, first, the literature of knowledge; and, secondly, the literature of power. The function of the first is—to teach; the function of the second is—to move; the first is a rudder; the second an oar or a sail. The first speaks to mere discursive understanding; the second speaks, ultimately, it may happen, to the higher understanding or reason, but always through affections of pleasure and sympathy. . . . It is in relation to [the] great moral capacities of man that the literature of power, as contradistinguished from that of knowledge, lives and has its field of action.

THOMAS DE QUINCEY, "THE LITERATURE OF KNOWLEDGE AND THE LITERATURE OF POWER" [1848]

The Affective Fallacy is a confusion between the poem and its results (what it is and what it does). . . . It begins by trying to derive the standard of criticism from the psychological effect of the poem and ends in impressionism and relativism.

W. K. WIMSATT, JR., "THE AFFECTIVE FALLACY," IN *THE VERBAL ICON* [1954]

There is no such thing as a literary work or tradition which is valuable in itself, regardless of what anyone might have said or come to say about it. "Value" is a transitive term: it means whatever is valued by certain people in specific situations, according to particular criteria and in light of given purposes. . . . There is no such thing as literature which is "really" great or "really" anything, independently of the ways in which that writing is treated within specific forms of social or institutional life.

TERRY EAGLETON, *LITERARY THEORY: AN INTRODUCTION* [1983]

Deconstructionism   This approach grew out of the work of certain twentieth-century European philosophers, notably the Frenchman Jacques Derrida, whose study of language led to the conclusion that since we could only know through the medium of language and language is unstable and ambiguous, it is impossible to talk about truth and knowledge and meaning in any absolute sense. Verbal structures, deconstructionist critics maintained, inevitably contained within themselves oppositions. Derrida asserted that in the Western world, language leads us to think in terms of opposites (soul/body, man/woman, master/slave, etc.) that imply what he called "a violent hierarchy" with one of the terms (the first) always being superior to the other (the second). The aim of deconstruction is to show that this hierarchy of values cannot be permanent and absolute.

Intelligent and well-educated readers therefore cannot be expected to ignore the oppositions and contradictions in a text just because they do not contribute to some "correct" or "desirable" reading of the piece which might uphold a particular political, social, or cultural view.

Formalism assures us that the successful artist is the master of language and that he or she consciously deploys all its resources to achieve a rich and unified work. Sensitive and intelligent readers can aspire to a complete understanding of a work undistorted by their own idiosyncrasies, subjective states, or ideological biases.

Rejecting the formalist assumption about authorial control and conscious design, deconstruction attempts to show that by its very nature, language is constantly "saying" more than the writer can control or even know. Thus, a close study of any text (literary or otherwise) will reveal contradictory and irreconcilable elements.

Deconstructionist critics do not necessarily reject the validity of feminist, Marxist, formalist, and other critical approaches. In fact, they often draw upon the insights furnished by them. But the deconstructionist critic says that any discourse or critical approach that fails to recognize the inherently shifting and unstable nature of language is bound to produce only a partial if not misleading interpretation. For example, in his study *America the Scrivener: Deconstruction and the Subject of Literary Studies* (1990), Gregory S. Jay finds Emily Grierson, the protagonist of William Faulkner's story "A Rose for Emily," a "puzzle" and warns against simplistic interpretations:

> As feminist subject, her story speaks of a revolutionary subversion of patriarchy; as herself, a figure of racial and class power, Emily also enacts the love affair of patriarchy with its own past, despite all the signs of decline and degradation. She is a split subject, crossed by rival discourses. What the text forces us to think about, then, is the complex and ironic alliances between modes of possession and subjection, desire and ownership, identity and position.

Like Marxism and feminism, deconstruction defines itself both as a critical theory of literature and as a philosophy of human values. Hence, it is applicable, not only to literature, but also to an understanding of the power relations among humans and the societies they create. In insisting that we recognize the way language embodies and supports class, gender, and other biases, deconstruction challenges both the ethnocentrism of political structures and the idea of "universal values" in literary works.

> Deconstruction is not synonymous with destruction. . . . It is in fact much closer to the original meaning of the word analysis, which etymologically means "to undo"—a virtual synonym for "to de-construct." The de-construction of a text does not proceed by random doubt or arbitrary subversion, but by the careful teasing out of warring forces of signification within the text itself. If anything is destroyed in reading, it is not the text, but the claim to unequivocal domination of one mode of signifying over another.
>
> BARBARA JOHNSON, THE CRITICAL DIFFERENCE (1980)

> Deconstructive criticism does not present itself as a novel enterprise. There is, perhaps, more of a relentless focus on certain questions, and a new rigor when it comes to the discipline of close reading. Yet to suggest that meaning and language do not coincide, and to draw from that a peculiar strength, is merely to restate what literature has always revealed. There is the difference, for instance, between sound and sense, which both stimulates and defeats writers. Or the difference which remains when we try to reduce metaphorical expressions to the proper terms they have displaced. Or the difference between a text and the commentaries that elucidate it, and which accumulate as a variorum of readings that cannot all be reconciled.
>
> GEOFFREY HARTMAN, DECONSTRUCTION AND CRITICISM (1984)

Feminist Criticism Feminist critics hold that literature is merely one of many expressions of a patriarchal society whose purpose is to keep women subordinate to men. Thus literature, in the way it portrays gender roles, helps to condition women to accept as normal a society that directs them to become nurses rather than doctors, secretaries rather than attorneys or corporate executives, sex symbols rather than thinkers, elementary school teachers rather than university professors. Beyond this general critique of patriarchy, feminists differ in their detailed analyses. Some have reexamined history to show that a literary canon created by males has slighted and ignored female authors. Others, studying canonical works from a feminist perspective, have come up with fresh readings that challenge conventional interpretations, focusing on how women are empowered *in* literary texts or *through writing* literary texts. Some, believing that language itself allows men to impose their power, use literary analyses to expose the gender bias of language. Why, they ask, is the English language so rich in words to describe a quarrelsome, abusive woman ("shrew," "harridan," "termagant") but so lacking in comparable terms for men? Some feminists believe that the male bias of language, far deeper than mere words, is actually structural. The constellation of qualities connoted by "masculine" and "feminine," they say, reveals how deeply the positive (male) and negative (female) values are embedded in the language.

While a psychoanalytic critic might use Freud's Oedipal theories to explain Emily's relationship to Homer Barron in William Faulkner's "A Rose for Emily," the feminist critic Judith Fetterley maintains that the explanation is to be found in the fact that a patriarchal culture instills in us the notion "that men and women are made for each other" and that " 'masculinity' and 'femininity' are the natural reflection of that divinely ordained complement." In a society where there is "a massive differentiation of everything according to sex, one sees that in reality a sexist culture is one in which men and women are not simply incompatible but murderously so. . . . Emily murders Homer Barron because she must at any cost get a man" (*The Resisting Reader: A Feminist Approach to American Fiction*, 1978).

The objection to their voting is the same as is urged in the lobbies of legislatures against clergymen who take an active part in politics;—that if they are good clergymen they are unacquainted with the expediencies of politics, and if they become good politicians they are worse clergymen. So of women, that they cannot enter this arena without being contaminated and unsexed.

RALPH WALDO EMERSON, "WOMAN" (A LECTURE READ BEFORE THE WOMAN'S RIGHTS CONVENTION, BOSTON, SEPTEMBER 20, 1855)

Feminine work has always been ahistorical by the definition of male historians: raising children and keeping house have customarily been viewed as timeless routines capable of only minor variations.

ANN DOUGLAS, THE FEMINIZATION OF AMERICAN CULTURE (1977)

She [Emily Dickinson] was neither a professional poet nor an amateur; she was a private poet who wrote indefatigably as some women cook or knit. Her gift for words and the cultural predicament of her time drove her to poetry instead of antimacassars.

R. P. BLACKMUR, "EMILY DICKINSON" (1937)

> *Literature is political. It is painful to have to insist on this fact, but the necessity of such insistence indicates the dimensions of the problem. John Keats once objected to poetry "that has a palpable design upon us." The major works of American fiction constitute a series of designs on the female reader, all the more potent in their effect because they are "impalpable." One of the main things that keeps the design of our literature unavailable to the consciousness of the woman reader, and hence impalpable, is the very posture of the apolitical, the pretense that literature speaks universal truths through forms from which all the merely personal, the purely subjective, has been burned away or at least transformed through the medium of art into the representa- tive. . . .*

JUDITH FETTERLEY, THE RESISTING READER: A FEMINIST APPROACH TO AMERICAN FICTION (1978)

> *The intellectual trajectory of feminist criticism has taken us from a concentration on women's literary subordination, mistreatment, and exclusion, to the study of wom- en's separate literary traditions, to an analysis of the symbolic construction of gender and sexuality within literary discourse. It is now clear that what we are demanding is a new universal literary history and criticism that combines the literary experi- ences of both women and men, a complete revolution in the understanding of our literary heritage.*

ELAINE SHOWALTER, THE NEW FEMINIST CRITICISM (1985)

Formalist Criticism   Like deconstruction, formalism focuses on the ambiguous and multilayered nature of language but does so in order to achieve the precisely op- posite effect. Formalism assures us that the successful artist is the master of lan- guage and consciously deploys all its resources to achieve a rich and unified work. Sensitive and intelligent readers can aspire to a complete understanding of a work undistorted by their own idiosyncrasies or subjective states or ideological biases. The formalist rejects the central tenet of the reader-response critic, that a work comes into existence, so to speak, through the interaction of the reader with the work. For the formalist, the work exists independent of any particular reader. The work is a structured and formal aesthetic object comprising such elements as symbol, image, and sound patterns. Political, biographical, or historical considerations not embod- ied in the work itself are irrelevant.

The formalist sees literature as a sort of Platonic ideal form—immutable and objective. Works close to that ideal are praised for their aesthetic energy and their "universality" (a characteristic of the greatest literature). Works that do not ex- hibit this prized formal coherence are dispraised, and often dismissed as neither "universal" nor important. Because formalism focuses on the internal structure of literature above all else, it rejects didactic works. During the 1940s and 1950s, when the New Critics (as the formalists were called) dominated academic literary criticism, social protest writing was generally dismissed as subliterary because it lacked the "universality" of great literature. What was important in a work of art was not that it might change people's behavior, but that its parts coalesced into a beautiful whole. Consider the following comment by two formalist critics on Nathaniel Hawthorne's "Young Goodman Brown":

> *The dramatic impact [of "Young Goodman Brown"] would have been stronger if Hawthorne had let the incidents tell their own story: Goodman Brown's behavior to his neighbors and finally to his wife shows us that he is a changed man. Since fiction is*

a kind of shorthand of human behavior and one moment may represent years in a man's life, we would have concluded that the change was to last his entire life. But Hawthorne's weakness for moralizing and his insufficient technical equipment betray him into the anticlimax of the last paragraph.

CAROLINE GORDON AND ALLEN TATE, THE HOUSE OF FICTION (1950)

Black writers and critics, for example, especially complained that the criterion of universality was merely a way of protecting "white," conservative social and political dominance. The New Critics dismissed black literature that sought to deal with racism and the struggle for equality as mere didacticism or agitprop, not to be compared with the great "white" literary productions that achieved "universal" import. In a seminal work of New Criticism published in 1952, the influential critic R. P. Blackmur dismissed *Native Son*, a powerful and now classic novel about white racism, as "one of those books in which everything is undertaken with seriousness except the writing."

All art constantly aspires towards the condition of music.

WALTER PATER, STUDIES IN THE HISTORY OF THE RENAISSANCE (1873)

Poetry is not a turning loose of emotion, but an escape from emotion; it is not the expression of personality, but an escape from personality.

T. S. ELIOT, "TRADITION AND THE INDIVIDUAL TALENT," FROM THE SACRED WOOD (1920)

Modern criticism, through its exacting scrutiny of literary texts, has demonstrated with finality that in art beauty and truth are indivisible and one. The Keatsian overtones of these terms are mitigated and an old dilemma solved if for beauty we substitute form, and for truth, content. We may, without risk of loss, narrow them even more, and speak of technique and subject matter. Modern criticism has shown us that to speak of content as such is not to speak of art at all, but of experience; and that it is only when we speak of the achieved content, the form, the work of art as a work of art, that we speak as critics. The difference between content, or experience, and achieved content, or art, is technique.

MARK SCHORER, "TECHNIQUE AS DISCOVERY" (1948)

A poem should not mean
But be.

ARCHIBALD MACLEISH, FROM "ARS POETICA" (1926)

Marxist Criticism   The Marxist critic sees literature as one activity among many to be studied and judged in terms of a large and all-encompassing ideology derived from the economic, political, and social doctrines of Karl Marx (1818–1883). Marxism offers a comprehensive theory about the nature of humans and the way in which a few of them manage to seize control of the means of production and thereby exploit the masses of working people. But Marxism is about more than analysis. As Karl Marx himself said, "It is not enough to analyze society; we must also change it."

The Marxist critic analyzes literary works to show how, wittingly or unwittingly, they support the dominant social class, or how they, in some way, contribute to the struggle against oppression and exploitation. And since the Marxist critic views literature as just one among the variety of human activities that reflect power relations and class divisions, he or she is likely to be more interested in what a work says than in its formal structure.

The Marxist argues that one cannot properly understand a literary work unless one understands how it reflects the relationship between economic production and social class. Further, this relationship cannot be explored adequately without examining a range of questions that other critical approaches, notably formalism, deem irrelevant. How does the work relate to the profit-driven enterprise of publishing? What does the author's biography reveal about his or her class biases? Does the work accurately portray the class divisions of society? Does the work expose the economic bases of oppression and advance the cause of liberation?

And since Marxist critics see their duty—indeed, the duty of all responsible and humane people—as not merely to describe the world but to change it, they will judge literature by the contribution it makes to bringing about revolution or in some way enlightening its readers about oppression and the necessity for class struggle.

For example, a Marxist critic's analysis of Matthew Arnold's poem "Dover Beach" might see it not as a brilliantly structured pattern of images and sounds but as the predictable end product of a dehumanizing capitalist economy in which a small class of oligarchs is willing, at whatever cost, to protect its wealth and power. The Marxist critic, as a materialist who believes that humans make their own history, would find Arnold's references to "the eternal note of sadness" (line 14) a mystic evasion of the real sources of his alienation and pain: Arnold's misery can be clearly and unmystically explained by his fearful responses to the socioeconomic conditions of his time.

Arnold's refusal to face this fact leads him to the conclusion typical of a bourgeois artist-intellectual who cannot discern the truth. But the cure for Arnold's pain, the Marxist would argue, cannot be found in a love relationship, because relations between people are determined crucially by socioeconomic conditions. The cure for the pain he describes so well will be found in the world of action, in the struggle to create a society that is just and humane. "Dover Beach," the Marxist critic would conclude, is both a brilliant evocation of the alienation and misery caused by a capitalist economy and a testimony to the inability of a bourgeois intellectual to understand what is responsible for his feelings.

The methods of formal analysis are necessary, but insufficient. You may count up the alliterations in popular proverbs, classify metaphors, count up the number of vowels and consonants in a wedding song. It will undoubtedly enrich our knowledge of folk art, in one way or another; but if you don't know the peasant system of sowing, and the life that is based on it, if you don't know the part the scythe plays, and if you have not mastered the meaning of the church calendar to the peasant, or the time when the peasant marries, or when the peasant women give birth, you will have only understood the outer shell of folk art, but the kernel will not have been reached.

LEON TROTSKY, LITERATURE AND REVOLUTION (1925)

When we say that the relationship between literature and reality is important for the Marxist critic, we do not mean that one goes to literature for illustration of knowledge that can be derived just as well from other sources, from the sciences or Marxist theory, for example. On the contrary, one looks to the arts as an independent way of discovering and knowing the truth about man and society; the knowledge that comes from this source is unique and indispensable, not simply a substitute for some other kind of knowledge.

GAYLOR C. LE ROY AND URSULA BEITZ, PRESERVE AND CREATE: ESSAYS ON MARXIST LITERARY CRITICISM (1973)

> *Marxist criticism is part of a larger body of theoretical analysis which aims to understand ideologies—the ideas, values and feelings by which men experience their societies at various times. And certain of those ideas, values, and feelings are available to us only in literature. To understand ideologies is to understand both the past and the present more deeply; and such understanding contributes to our liberation.*
>
> TERRY EAGLETON, MARXISM AND LITERARY CRITICISM (1976)

> *My present judgment is that it [Marxist literary theory] can be made to work and that, together with feminism (a problematic "together"), it is the only body of thought capable of giving theoretical guidance to socialist practice (and this includes guidance in the struggle against the repressive regimes of state capitalism and authoritarian party structures). In particular, it is a compelling alternative to the various forms of liberal humanism which in their indefinite deferral of political positioning have been able to offer no serious resistance to the depredations of a power which is neither liberal nor humane.*
>
> JOHN FROW, MARXISM AND LITERARY HISTORY (1986)

New Historical Criticism   There is nothing "new" about historians drawing upon literary works as significant documents to support and illuminate historical analysis; nor is there anything "new" about literary critics drawing upon history to illuminate literary works. For the historian, Sophocles's *Oedipus Rex* and *Antigonê* tell us much about the conflict between the old-time religion and the new secularism in fifth-century B.C. Athens. The literary critic of *Othello* goes to the historian to understand the way in which Shakespeare and his contemporaries viewed black Africans. But until recently, the provinces of the historian and of the literary critic were pretty much mutually exclusive.

The new historians (influenced by modern theories of language and literature) began to question the very idea of history as it had been practiced. The historians of the past tended, for the most part, to think of history in terms of overarching themes and theses, and attempted to understand it in terms of some perceived "Geist" or "spirit" of the time. This kind of history was often linked to nationalism. Hence (for one example), nineteenth-century Americans created the idea of Manifest Destiny, and then used it to explain and justify the Western movement and its attendant atrocities. When the Nazis came to power in Germany, they developed the idea that "true" Germans were descended from a superior Aryan race, and then used that idea to deprive "inferior races" of civil rights, of property, and, finally, of life.

More abstractly, the purpose of writing history was to articulate and reinforce the values and beliefs that gave a culture unity. By that means, some new historians note, history became the story (and the ideas and beliefs and culture) of the rich, the powerful, the privileged, the victorious. The new historians see history not as the search for some grand, unifying thesis but as the articulation of the various kinds of "discourse" that compete with, contradict, overlap, and modify one another in the constant struggle for dominance. Indeed, the new historians, influenced by deconstructionist views of language, came to question the very idea of historical "truth."

The new historians also reject the traditional division between history and other disciplines, appropriating to historical studies many kinds of texts—including literary texts—that traditional historians left to others. These critics assert that without an understanding of the historical context that produced it, no work of literature could really be understood and, therefore, literature "belongs" as much to the historian as to the literary critic. Such critics aim at what they call a "thick" description of a literary work, one that brings to bear on a text as much information as can be gathered about every aspect of the author, the work, and the times. For example, Thomas McGann in *The Beauty of Inflections* (1985) shows how the literary journal in which Keats published his "Ode on a Grecian Urn" tells us something important about the meaning of the poem.

Finally, it should be noted that new historicism has developed relatively recently and cannot be defined in detail. While its practitioners generally share the fundamental ideas outlined above, they can differ widely in the tools and methodologies they bring to bear on a literary text. That is to say, a new historian may also be a Marxist, feminist, or deconstructionist.

The burden of the past that weighs like a nightmare on the brain of the West is an imperial burden, the anxiety that it might not all be of one piece, that secret histories, forgotten facts, other imaginations operate in all that we do and make, and that our massive ignorance of Othernesses is working to undermine what we do. Like Napoleon moving inexorably toward the capture of Moscow, Great Traditions follow their difficult and equivocal victories of imagination to an ultimate destruction.

JEROME MCGANN, "THE THIRD WORLD OF CRITICISM" (1989)

. . . What is at stake in today's cultural debates is whether or not it is appropriate to raise questions of power, domination, exclusion, and emancipation in conjunction with the study of literature.

BROOK THOMAS, THE NEW HISTORICISM AND OTHER OLD-FASHIONED TOPICS (1991)

Psychoanalytic Criticism   Psychoanalytic criticism always proceeds from a set of principles that describes the inner life of all men and women. Though differing psychological theorists argue for diverse views, all analysts and all psychoanalytic critics assume that the development of the psyche is analogous to the development of the body. Doctors can provide charts indicating physical growth stages; analysts can supply similar charts indicating stages in the growth of the psyche. Sigmund Freud, for all practical purposes, invented psychoanalysis by creating a theoretical model for the human (mostly male) psyche.

The Oedipus complex is a significant element in that model. Freud contends that everyone moves through a childhood stage of erotic attachment to the parent of the opposite sex, and an accompanying hostility and aggression against the parent of the same sex, who is seen as a rival. Such feelings, part of the natural biography of the psyche, pass or are effectively controlled in most cases. But sometimes, the child grown to adulthood is still strongly gripped by the Oedipal mode, which then may result in neurotic or even psychotic behavior.

A famous analysis of Shakespeare's *Hamlet* argues that he is best understood as gripped by Oedipal feelings—Hamlet hates Claudius not as the murderer of his father but as the interloper between Hamlet and his mother. But how could Shakespeare create an Oedipal Hamlet when Freud was not to be born for some two and a half centuries? The answer is that Freud did not invent the Oedipus feelings—he simply described it. It was always there, especially noticeable in the work of great literary artists who, in every era, demonstrate a special insight into the human condition.

Along with Oedipal feelings, the psyche inevitably embodies aggressive feelings—

the urge to attack those who exercise authority, who deny us our primal desires. For the young, the authority figure is frequently a parent. Adults must deal with police, government officials, the boss at the office. As far back as the Hebrew Bible story of the Tower of Babel and the old Greek myths in which the giant Titans, led by Cronus, overthrow their father, Uranus, and Zeus and the Olympians subsequently overthrow Cronus, there appears evidence of the rebellion against the parent-authority figure. Freud views that aggressive hostility as another component of the developing psyche. But, in the interest of civilization, society has developed ways to control that aggressiveness.

Freud saw us as divided selves. An unconscious *id* struggles to gratify aggressive and erotic primal urges, while a *superego* (roughly what society calls "conscience"), by producing guilt feelings, struggles to control the id. The *ego* (the self) is defined by the struggle. Thus the Freudian psychoanalytic critic is constantly aware that authors and their characters suffer and resuffer a primal tension that results from the conflict between psychic aggressions and social obligations.

Freud has been succeeded by a number of psychological theorists who present quite different models of the psyche—and recent literary theory has responded to these post-Freudian views. Among the most important are Carl Gustav Jung (1875–1961), who argued that there exists a collective (as well as a racial and individual) unconscious. Residing there are archetypes—original patterns—that emerge into our consciousness in the form of shadowy images that persistently appear and reappear in literature (for example, the search for the father, death and resurrection, the quest, and the double).

The psychoanalytic critic understands literature in terms of the psychic models that Freud and others defined. Originally, such critics tended to analyze literature in an attempt to identify the author's neuroses. More recently, psychoanalytic critics have argued that the symptoms they discover in works allow us to tap into and, perhaps, resolve our own neuroses.

> . . . *"Cinderella" cannot fail to activate in us those emotions and unconscious ideals which, in our inner experience, are connected with our feelings of sibling rivalry. From his own experience with it, the child might well understand—without "knowing" anything about it—the welter of inner experiences connected with Cinderella. Recalling, if she is a girl, her repressed wishes to get rid of Mother and have Father all to herself, and now feeling guilty about such "dirty" desires, a girl may well "understand" why a mother would send her daughter out of sight to reside among cinders, and prefer her other children. Where is the child who has not wished to be able to banish a parent at some time, and who does not feel that in retaliation, he merits the same fate? And where is the child who has not wanted to wallow to his heart's desire in dirt or mud; and, being made to feel dirty by parental criticism in consequence, become convinced that he deserves nothing better than to be relegated to a dirty corner?*
>
> BRUNO BETTELHEIM, THE USES OF ENCHANTMENT: THE MEANING AND IMPORTANCE OF FAIRY TALES (1977)

> . . . *Modern culture has become increasingly differentiated from traditional societies by the enormous enlargement of fictions through the fiction-producing qualities of the media. Newspapers, popular magazines, movies, and, most of all, television have so flooded modern culture with fictions that many people have difficulty distinguishing between social relations that are real and those that are fantasized. "Fictive culture" more accurately describes contemporary social life than do such phrases as "narcissis-*

tic," "minimalist," or "post-modern" culture; for the profusion of fictions is central to the creativity—and the crisis—of our modern condition.

JAY MARTIN, WHO AM I THIS TIME? UNCOVERING THE FICTIVE PERSONALITY (1988)

Reader-Response Criticism   Reader-response criticism (also called transactional theory) emerged in the 1970s as one of the many challenges to formalist principles. Reader-response critics focus on the interaction between the work and the reader, holding that, in a sense, a work exists only when it is experienced by the reader. If the work exists only in the mind of the reader, the reader becomes an active participant in the creative process rather than a passive receptacle for an "autonomous" work. The creation of a work thus becomes a dynamic enterprise between the reader and the text, each acting on the other. The study of the affective power of a work becomes not a "fallacy," as formalism holds, but the central focus of criticism. The task of the critic is to investigate this dynamic relationship between reader and text in order to discover how it works.

We know that various readers respond differently to the same text. In fact, the same reader might respond to the text quite differently at a different time. The reader-response critic wants to know why. In what ways do such conditions as age, gender, upbringing, and race account for differing responses? Does the reader's mood at the time of reading make a difference? If you accept the principles of reader-response criticism, the inevitable conclusion—*reductio ad absurdum*, its critics would say—is that there is no limit to the possible readings of any text. Consequently, many reader-response critics qualify the intense subjectivity of their approach by admitting that an "informed" or "educated" reader is likely to produce a more "valid" reading than an "uninformed" or "uneducated" one.

"Gaps" or "blanks" in literary texts provide particular opportunities to readers. Every narrative work omits, for example, periods of time that the reader must fill in. In Nathaniel Hawthorne's "Young Goodman Brown" the author omits all the years of Brown's life between his emergence from the forest and his death. The reader is free to imagine that history. In Sophocles' *Antigonê* we never see *Antigonê* and her betrothed, Haimon, together. The reader will supply the energy of that courtship. The filling in of these blanks enables readers to participate in "creating" a text, and reinforces the arguments of reader-response theorists.

Nothing, no power, will keep a book steady and motionless before us, so that we may have time to examine its shape and design. As quickly as we read, it melts and shifts in memory; even at the moment when the last page is turned, a great part of the book, its finer detail, is already vague and doubtful. A little later, after a few days or months, how much is really left? A cluster of impressions, some clear points, emerging from a mist of uncertainty, this is all we can hope to possess, generally speaking, in the name of a book. The experience of reading it has left something behind, and these relics we call by the book's name; but how can they be considered to give us the material for judging and appraising the book?

PERCY LUBBOCK, THE CRAFT OF FICTION (1921)

All readings originate in the reader's personality—all are "subjective" in that sense. Some readings take a close account of the words-on-the-page and some do not, but no matter how much textual, "objective" evidence a reader brings into his own reading, he structures and adapts it according to his own inner needs.

NORMAN N. HOLLAND, 5 READERS READING (1975)

... *The text as an entity independent of interpretation and (ideally) responsible for its career [as formalism maintains] drops out and is replaced by the texts that emerge as a consequence of our interpretive activities. There are still formal patterns, but they do not lie innocently in the world; rather, they are themselves constituted by the interpretive act.*

STANLEY FISH, IS THERE A TEXT IN THE CLASS? THE AUTHORITY OF INTERPRETIVE
COMMUNITIES (1980)

You may well ask, if a range of responses is recognized as probable and acceptable, how can one response be more "valid" than another? How can validity be measured? Within the context of the transactional theory of the literary work, validity of a reading is identified in relation to a consistent set of criteria, implicit or explicit. Adequacy of interpretation can be measured against constraints of the text: to what degree does the individual response include the various features of the text and the nuances of language; to what degree does it include aspects that do not reflect the text; to what degree has the reading evoked a consistent work? Thus, the out-of-context response—a memory or experience triggered by something in the text—takes the reader far afield or the strongly skewed response leads to the neglect of features of the text. These may be valuable responses for the reader but, given the criteria, invalid or less valid transactions with the text.

NICHOLAS J. KAROLIDES, READER RESPONSE IN THE CLASSROOM: EVOKING AND INTERPRETING
MEANING IN LITERATURE (1992)

Writing about Literature*

Writing about literature compels the student to discover and come to terms with his or her response to an author's work. Every element in a literary work has been deliberately incorporated by the author—the description of the setting, the events that constitute the plot, the dialogue, the imagery. A rather mysterious intellectual and emotional event occurs within the reader as a result of the writer's purposeful manipulation of language. An essay about literature inevitably attempts some description of the author's purposes and techniques and some discussion of the reader's response.

As an illustration of the relationship between author's purpose and reader's response, consider these opening lines of a poem by W. H. Auden (the poem appears on p. 543):

> That night when joy began
> Our narrowest veins to flush,
> We waited for the flash
> Of morning's levelled gun.

The stanza tells of a new joy, probably erotic, that the speaker and his companion experience one night. But the reader must see that the speaker is apprehensive about that joy. The writer has created that mood of apprehension by using a violent image—the flash of morning's gun—to characterize the speaker's fears about the consequences of possible discovery. The images in the subsequent stanzas of the poem suggest that the lovers are trespassers and that the leveled gun they fear belongs to the keeper of the forbidden fields they enjoyed. Thus, the reader responds to the poem with an awareness that the lovers have risked danger for the sake of joy.

Though the correspondence between "writer's purpose" and "reader's response" is by no means exact, any attempt to write about literature is, in one way or another, an attempt to discover and describe that correspondence. In other words, whatever the assignment, your fundamental task is to provide the answers to two questions: "How do I respond to this piece? How has the author brought about my response?"

The Journal

Many instructors will require you to keep a journal, a day-by-day account of your reactions to and reflections about what you've been reading. Even if a

---

* See, as well, the appendices "Reading Fiction," "Reading Poetry," "Reading Drama," and "Reading Essays," and the "Glossary of Critical Approaches." Those discussions may well suggest useful approaches to writing assignments.

journal is not required, you might want to keep one for a variety of reasons. From a purely practical perspective, a journal provides valuable mental exercise: forcing yourself to write in a journal regularly is an excellent way to limber up your writing abilities and overcome the fear of facing a blank page. Because journals are like diaries in the sense that they are for yourself alone, you need not worry about whether you are constructing grammatical sentences, whether you are writing cohesive paragraphs and developing your ideas, or even whether you are always making sense. You are free to comment on some aspect of a work or set down a highly personal recollection that something in the work triggered. What is important is that you are recording your reactions, ideas, feelings, questions.

When the time comes to write a formal essay for your class, the journal can provide you with a large range of possible topics. Suppose while you were reading Alastair Reid's poem "Curiosity" you confided to your journal your own curiosity about the reasons the poet selected cats and dogs to carry the theme. You might write an interesting essay on this topic, based on the thesis that, although both are domestic animals, the cat is a far wilder creature than the more docile dog.

You can also use a journal to record unfamiliar words that you encounter in your reading and plan to look up later. In reading Stevie Smith's "To Carry the Child," for example, you might wonder what *carapace* means. You enter the word in your journal, and when you look it up, you find that *carapace* means a bony shell, such as a turtle's. With this knowledge you can return to the poem and appreciate the image, which might suggest a topic for an essay.

Some of your journal entries will probably be confessions of bafflement and confusion. Why does Tolstoy begin "The Death of Iván Ilých" at the end? Why does Crane in "The Bride Comes to Yellow Sky" open Part III with a reference to a character's shirt and the place where it was made as well as the ethnic origin of the people who made it? Working out an answer to either of these questions could lead to an interesting essay.

Anything you want to enter in your journal is relevant, including the most personal feelings and recollections triggered by a work. Dylan Thomas's "Fern Hill" might remind you of feelings you experienced during a particular period of your childhood. Exploring your own childhood feelings and comparing them with those expressed in Thomas's poem could lead in any number of ways to a fascinating essay (for example, how poets give memorable and vivid expression to experiences we've all had). Or you might jot down, after reading Kate Chopin's "The Storm," your moral disapproval of the story's central event—marital infidelity. You might then reread the story to discover whether it seems to disapprove of infidelity or whether you have imposed on it your own personal moral values. Sorting out such feelings could result in an essay on the interaction between the moral values of a reader and those embodied in a particular work.

Finally, remember that (unless your instructor has specific guidelines for your journal keeping) your journal will be the one place where you can write as much or as little as you please, as often or infrequently as you wish, with care and deliberation or careless speed. Its only purpose is to serve your needs. But if you write fairly regularly, you will probably be surprised not only at how much easier the act of writing becomes but also at how many ideas suddenly pop into your head in the act of writing. Henry Adams was surely right when he observed, "The habit of expression leads to the search for something to express."

Essays

Your journal will allow you to struggle privately with your reading. It may produce wonders of understanding; it should, as well, reveal to you lapses in understanding. The journal, while a useful tool for recording thoughts, responses, and impressions, remains, after all, a set of rough notes. Most instructors will demand some organization of those notes—they will ask you to write formal essays that provide evidence of your talent for critical response. Formal essays in introduction-to-literature courses characteristically fall into one of three modes: explication, analysis, and comparison and contrast.

Explication

In explication, you examine a work in as much detail as possible, line by line, stanza by stanza, scene by scene, explaining each part as fully as you can and showing how the author's techniques produce your response. An explication is essentially a demonstration of your thorough understanding of the poem, the story, or the play.

Here is a sample essay that explicates a relatively difficult poem, Dylan Thomas's "Do Not Go Gentle into That Good Night." (The poem appears on p. 801.)

> Dylan Thomas's villanelle "Do Not Go Gentle into That Good Night" is addressed to his aged father. The poem is remarkable in a number of ways, most notably in that contrary to most common poetic treatments of the inevitability of death, which argue for serenity or celebrate the peace that death provides, this poem urges resistance and rage in the face of death. It justifies that unusual attitude by describing the rage and resistance to death of four kinds of men, all of whom can summon up the image of a complete and satisfying life that is denied to them by death.
>
> The first tercet of the intricately rhymed villanelle opens with an arresting line. The adjective gentle appears where we would expect the adverb gently. The strange diction suggests that gentle may describe both the going (i.e., gently dying) and the person (i.e., gentleman) who confronts death. Further, the speaker characterizes "night," here clearly a figure for death, as "good." Yet in the next line, the speaker urges that

the aged should violently resist death, characterized as the "close of day" and "the dying of the light." In effect, the first three lines argue that however good death may be, the aged should refuse to die gently, should passionately rave and rage against death.

In the second tercet, the speaker turns to a description of the way the first of four types of men confronts death (which is figuratively defined throughout the poem as "that good night" and "the dying of the light"). These are the "wise men," the scholars, the philosophers, those who understand the inevitability of death, men who "know dark is right." But they do not acquiesce in death "because their words had forked no lightning," because their published wisdom failed to bring them to that sense of completeness and fulfillment that can accept death. Therefore, wise as they are, they reject the theoretical "rightness" of death and refuse to "go gentle."

The second sort of men—"good men," the moralists, the social reformers, those who attempt to better the world through action as the wise men attempt to better it through "words"—also rage against death. Their deeds are, after all, "frail." With sea imagery, the speaker suggests that these men might have accomplished fine and fertile things—their deeds "might have danced in a green bay." But with the "last wave" gone, they see only the frailty, the impermanence of their acts, and so they, too, rage against the death that deprives them of the opportunity to leave a meaningful legacy.

So, too, the "wild men," the poets who "sang" the loveliness and vitality of nature, learn, as they approach death, that the sensuous joys of human existence wane. As the life-giving sun moves toward dusk, as death approaches, their singing turns to grieving, and they refuse to surrender gently, to leave willingly the warmth and pleasure and beauty that life can give.

And finally, with a pun suggestive of death, the "grave men," those who go through life with such high seriousness as never to experience gaiety and pleasure, see, as death approaches, all the joyous possibilities that they were blind to in life. And they, too, rage against the dying of a light that they had never properly seen before.

The speaker then calls upon his aged father to join these men raging against death. Only in this final stanza do we discover that the entire poem is addressed to the speaker's father and that, despite the generalized statements about old age and the focus upon types of men, the poem is a personal lyric. The edge of death becomes a "sad height," the summit of wisdom and experience old age attains includes the sad knowledge of life's failure to satisfy the vision we all pursue. The depth and complexity of the speaker's sadness is startlingly given in the second line when he calls upon his father to both curse and bless him. These opposites richly suggest several related possibilities. Curse me for not living up to your expectations. Curse me for remaining alive as you die. Bless me with forgiveness for my failings. Bless me for teaching you to rage against death. And the curses and blessings are contained in the "fierce tears"—fierce because you will burn and rave and rage against death. As the poem closes by bringing together the two powerful refrains, we may reasonably feel that the speaker himself, while not facing imminent death, rages because his father's death will cut off a relationship that is too incomplete.

The explication, as you can see, deals with the entire poem by coming to grips with each element in it. This same mode can be used to write about the drama as well, but the length of plays will probably require that you focus on a single segment—a scene, for example—rather than the entire play.

You can learn a great deal about the technique of drama by selecting a short, self-contained scene and writing a careful description of it. This method, a variety of explication, will force you to confront every speech and stage direction and to come to some conclusion regarding its function. Why is the set furnished as it is? Why does a character speak the words he or she does or remain silent? What do we learn of characters from the interchanges among them? Assume that everything that occurs in the play, whether on the printed page or on the stage, is put there for a purpose. Seek to discover the purpose, and you will, at the same time, discover the peculiar nature of dramatic art.

Fiction, too, can be treated effectively in a formal explication. As with drama, it will be necessary to limit the text—you will not be able to explicate a 10-page story in a 1,000-word essay. Choose a key passage—a half page that reflects the form and content of the overall story, if possible. Often the first half page of a story, where the author, like the playwright, must supply information to the reader, will make a fine text for an explication. Although the explication will deal principally with only an excerpt, feel free to range across the story and show how the introductory material foreshadows what is to come. Or, perhaps, you can explicate the climax of the story—the half page that most pointedly establishes the story's theme—and subject it to a close line-by-line reading that illuminates the whole story.

Analysis

Breaking a literary work down into its elements is only the first step in literary analysis. When you are assigned an analysis essay, you are expected to focus on one of the elements that contributes to the complex compound that is the substance of any work of literary merit. This process requires that you extricate the element you plan to explore from the other elements that you can identify, study this element—not only in isolation but also in relation to the other elements and the work as a whole—and, using the insights you have gained from your special perspective, make an informed statement about it.

This process may sound complicated, but if you approach it methodically, each stage follows naturally from the stage that precedes it. If, for example, an instructor assigns an analysis essay on some aspect of characterization in *Othello*, you would begin by thinking about each character in the play. You would then select the character whose development you would like to explore and reread carefully those speeches that help to establish his or her substance. Exploring a character's development in this way involves a good deal of explication: in order to identify the "building blocks" that Shakespeare uses to create a three-dimensional role, you must comb very carefully through that character's speeches and actions. You must also be sensitive to the ways in which other characters respond to these speeches and actions. When you have completed this investigation, you will probably have a good understanding of why you intuitively responded to the character as you did when you first read the play. You will also probably be prepared to make a statement about the character's development: "From a realistic perspective, it is hard to believe that a man of Othello's position could be so gullible; however, Shakespeare develops the role with such craft that we accept the Moor as flesh and blood." At this point, you have moved from the broad *subject* "characterization in *Othello*" to a *thesis*, a statement that you must prove. As you formulate your thesis, think of it as a position that you intend to *argue* for with a reader who is not easy to persuade. This approach is useful in any essay that requires a thesis—in other words, in any essay in which you move beyond simple explication and commit yourself to a stand. Note that "From a realistic perspective, it is hard to believe that a man of Othello's position could be so gullible; however, Shakespeare develops the role with such craft that we accept the Moor as flesh and blood." is *argumentative* on two counts. "Characterization in *Othello*" is not remotely argumentative. Further, you have more than enough material to write a well-documented essay of 1,000 words supporting your proposition; you cannot write a well-documented 1,000-word essay on the general subject of characterization in *Othello* without being superficial.

You may be one among the many students who find it difficult to find a starting point. For example, you have been assigned an analysis essay on a very broad subject, such as "imagery in love poetry." A few poems come to mind, but you don't know where to begin. You read these poems and underline all the images that you can find. You look at these images over and over, finding no relation among them. You read some more poems, again underlining the images, but you still do not have even the germ of a thesis.

The technique of freewriting might help to overcome your block. You have read and reread the works you intend to write about. Now, put the assignment temporarily out of your mind and start writing about one or two of the poems without organizing your ideas, without trying to reach a point. Write down what you like about a poem, what you dislike about it, what sort of person the speaker is, which images seemed striking to you—anything at all about the work. If you do this for perhaps ten minutes, you will probably discover that you are voicing opinions. Pick one that interests you or seems the most promising to explore.

There are a few variations on the basic form of the analysis assignment. Occasionally, an instructor will narrow the subject to a specific assignment: analyze the development of Othello's character in Act I. This sort of assignment saves you the trouble of selecting a character on whom to focus and also limits the amount of text that you will have to study. However, the process from this point on is no different from the process that you would employ addressing a broader subject. Sometimes instructors will supply you with a thesis, and you will have to work backward from the thesis to find supporting material. Again, careful analysis of the text is required. The problem you will have to address when writing an analytical essay remains the same regardless of the literary genre you are asked to discuss. You must find an arguable thesis that deals with the literary sources of your response to the work.

Suppose your instructor has made the following assignment: write an analysis of Harlan Ellison's story, " 'Repent, Harlequin!' Said the Ticktockman," in which you discuss the theme of the story in terms of the characters and the setting. Now consider the following opening (taken from a student paper):

> " 'Repent, Harlequin!' Said the Ticktockman" is a story depicting a society in which time governs one's life. The setting is the United States, the time approximately A.D. 2400 somewhere in the heart of the country. Business deals, work shifts, and school lessons are started and finished with exacting precision. Tardiness is intolerable as this would hinder the system. In a society of order, precision, and punctuality, there is no room for likes, dislikes, scruples, or morals. Thus, personalities in people no longer exist. As these "personless" people know no good or bad, they very happily follow in the course of activities that their society has dictated.

At the outset, can you locate a thesis statement? The only sentences that would seem to qualify are the last three in the paragraph. But notice that, although those sentences are not unreasonable responses to the story, they do not establish a thesis that is *responsive to the assignment*. Because the assignment calls for a discussion of theme in terms of character and setting, there should be a thesis statement about the way in which character and setting embody the theme. Here is another opening paragraph on the same assignment (also taken from a student paper):

> Harlan Ellison's " 'Repent, Harlequin!' Said the Ticktockman" opens with a quotation from Thoreau's essay "Civil Disobedience," which establishes the story's theme. Thoreau's observations about three varieties of men, those who serve the state as machines, those who serve it with their heads, and those who serve it with their consciences, are dramatized in Ellison's story, which takes place about 400 years in the future in a set-

ting characterized by machinelike order. The interaction among the three characters, each of whom represents one of Thoreau's types, results in a telling restatement of his observation that "heroes, patriots, martyrs, reformers in the great sense, and <u>men</u> . . . necessarily resist [the state] and . . . are commonly treated as enemies by it."

Compare the two opening paragraphs sentence by sentence for their responsiveness to the assignment. The first sentence of the first opening does not refer to the theme of the story (or to its setting or characterization). In the second sentence, the discussion of the setting ignores the most important aspect—that the story is set in a machine- and time-dominated future. The last three sentences deal obliquely with character, but they are imprecise and do not establish a thesis. The second opening, on the other hand, immediately states the theme of the story. It goes on to emphasize the relevant aspects of the futuristic setting and then refers to the three characters that animate the story in terms of their reactions to the setting. The last sentence addresses the assignment directly and also serves as a thesis statement for the paper. It states the proposition that will be developed and supported in the rest of the paper. The reader of the second opening will expect the next paragraph of the paper to discuss the setting of the story and subsequent paragraphs to discuss the response to the setting of the three principal characters.

The middles of essays are largely determined by their opening paragraphs. However long the middle of any essay may be, each of its paragraphs ought to be responsive to some explicit statement made at the beginning of the essay. Note that it is practically impossible to predict what the paragraph following the first opening will address. Here is the first half of that next paragraph as the first student wrote it.

> The Harlequin is a man in the society with no sense of time. His having a personality enables him to have a sense of moral values and a mind of his own. The Harlequin thinks that it is obscene and wrong to let time totally govern the lives of people. So, he sets out to disrupt the time schedule with ridiculous antics such as showering people with jelly beans in order to try to break up the military fashion in which they are used to doing things.

The paragraph then goes on to discuss the Ticktockman, the capture and brainwashing of the Harlequin, and the resulting lateness of the Ticktockman.

Note that nothing in the opening of this student's paper prepared readers for the introduction of the Harlequin. In fact, the opening concluded rather inaccurately that the people within the story "happily follow in the course of activities which their society has dictated." Hence, the description of the Harlequin in the second paragraph is wholly unexpected. Further, because the student has not dealt with the theme of the story (remember the assignment explicitly asked for a discussion of *theme* in terms of character and setting), the comments about the Harlequin's antics remain disconnected from any clear purpose. They are essentially devoted to what teachers constantly warn against: a mere plot summary. The student has obviously begun to write before she has analyzed the story sufficiently to understand its theme. With further thought, the student would have perceived that the central thematic issue is resistance to an oppressive state—the issue stated in the epigraph from Thoreau. On the other hand, because the second opening makes that thematic point clearly, we can expect it to be followed by a discussion of the environment (that is, the setting) in which the action occurs. Here is such a paragraph taken from the second student's paper:

> Ellison creates a society that reflects one possible future develop-
> ment of the modern American passion for productivity and efficiency. The
> setting is in perfect keeping with the time-conscious people who inhabit
> the city. It is pictured as a neat, colorless, and mechanized city. No men-
> tion is made of nature: grass, flowers, trees, and birds do not appear. The
> buildings are in a "Mondrian arrangement," stark and geometrical. The
> cold steel slidewalks, slowstrips, and expresstrips move with precision.
> Like a chorus line, people move in unison to board the movers without a
> wasted motion. Doors close silently and lock themselves automatically.
> An ideal efficiency so dominates the social system that any "wasted time"
> is deducted from the life of an inefficient citizen.

Once the setting has been established, as in the paragraph just quoted, writers attentive to the assignment will turn to the characters. But they will insistently link those characters to thematic considerations. It might be well to proceed with a short transitional paragraph that shapes the remainder of the middle of the essay:

> Into this smoothly functioning but coldly mechanized society, Elli-
> son introduces three characters: Pretty Alice, one of Thoreau's machine-
> like creatures; the Ticktockman, one of those who "serve the state chiefly
> with their heads, and, as they rarely make any moral distinctions, they
> are as likely to serve the devil without intending it, as God"; and Everett
> C. Marm, the Harlequin, whose conscience forces him to resist the oppres-
> sive state.

The reader will now expect a paragraph devoted to each of the three characters:

> Pretty Alice is, probably, very pretty. (Everett didn't fall in love
> with her brains.) In the brief section in which we meet her, we find her

hopelessly ordinary in her attitudes. She is upset that Marm finds it necessary to go about "annoying people." She finds him ridiculous and wishes only that he would stay home, as other people do. Clearly, she has no understanding of what Everett is struggling against. Though her anger finally leads her to betray him, Everett himself can't believe that she has done so. His own loyal and understanding nature colors his view of her so thoroughly that he cannot imagine the treachery that must have been so simple and satisfying for Pretty Alice, whose only desire is to be like everybody else.

The Ticktockman is more complex. He sees himself as a servant of the state, and he performs his duties with resolution and competence. He skillfully supports a System he has never questioned. The System exists; it must be good. His conscience is simply not involved in the performance of his duty. He is one of those who follows orders and expects others to follow orders. As a result, the behavior of the Harlequin is more than just an irritant or a rebellion against authority. It is unnerving. The Ticktockman wishes to understand that behavior, and with Everett's time-card in his hand, he muses that he has the name of "what he is . . . not who he is. . . . Before I can exercise proper revocation, I have to know who this what is." And when he confronts Everett, he does not just liquidate him. He insists that Everett repent. He tries to convince Everett that the System is sound, and when he cannot win the argument, he dutifully reconditions Everett, since he is, after all, more interested in justifying the System than in destroying its enemies. It is easy to see this man as a competent servant of the devil who thinks he is serving God.

But only Everett C. Marm truly serves the state, because his conscience requires him to resist. He is certainly not physically heroic. His very name suggests weak conformity. Though he loves his Pretty Alice, he cannot resign from the rebellious campaign on which his conscience insists. So, without violence, and mainly with the weapon of laughter, he attacks the mechanical precision of the System and succeeds in breaking it down simply by making people late. He is himself, as Pretty Alice points out, always late, and the delays that his antics produce seriously threaten the well-being of the smooth but mindless System he hates. He is, of course, captured. He refuses, even then, to submit and has his personality destroyed by the authorities that fear him. The Ticktockman is too strong for him.

An appropriate ending emerges naturally from this student's treatment of the assignment. Having established that the story presents characters who deal in different ways with the oppressive quality of life in a time- and machine-obsessed society, the student concludes with a comment on the author's criticisms of such a society:

> Harlequin is defeated, but Ellison, finally, leaves us with an optimistic note. The idea of rebellion against the System will linger in the minds of others. There will be more Harlequins and more disruption of this System. Many rebels will be defeated, but any System that suppresses individualism will give birth to resistance. And Harlequin's defeat is by no means total. The story ends with the Ticktockman himself arriving for work three minutes late.

Comparison and Contrast   *points of similarities & difference*

An essay in comparison and contrast, showing how two works are similar to and different from one another, almost always starts with a recognition of similarities, most likely similarities of subject matter. While it is possible to compare *any* two works, the best comparison and contrast essays emerge from the analysis of two works similar enough to illuminate each other (most comparison and contrast assignments involve two works of the same genre). Two works about love, or death, or conformity, or innocence, or discovery give you something to begin with. But these are very large categories; two random poems about the same subject may be so dissimilar that a comparison and contrast essay about them would be very difficult. Both Shelley's "Ozymandias" and Wilfred Owen's "Dulce et Decorum Est" are about death, but they deal with the subject so differently that they would probably not yield a very interesting essay. On the other hand, not only are Dickinson's "Apparently with No Surprise" and Frost's "Design" both about death, but they both use remarkably similar events as the occasion for the poem. And starting with these similarities, you would soon find yourself noting the contrasts (in tone, for example, and theme) between nineteenth-century and twentieth-century views of the nature of God.

Before you begin writing your paper, you ought to have clearly in mind the points of comparison and contrast you wish to discuss and the order in which you can most effectively discuss them. You will need to give careful thought to the best way to organize your paper. As a general rule, it is best to avoid dividing the essay into separate discussions of each work. That method tends to produce two separate, loosely joined analysis essays. The successful comparison and contrast essay treats some point of similarity or contrast between the two works, then moves on to succeeding points, and ends with an evaluation of the comparative merits of the works.

Like analysis essays—indeed like any essay that goes beyond simple explication—comparison and contrast essays require theses. However, a comparison and contrast thesis is generally not difficult to formulate: you must identify the works under consideration and summarize briefly your reasons for making the comparison.

Here is a student paper that compares and contrasts a Dylan Thomas poem ("Do Not Go Gentle into That Good Night," explicated earlier in this discussion) with the poetic response it triggered from a poet with different views.

Dylan Thomas's "Do Not Go Gentle into That Good Night" and Catherine Davis's "After a Time" demand comparison: Davis's poem was written in deliberate response to Thomas's. Davis assumes the reader's familiarity with "Do Not Go Gentle," which she uses to articulate her contrasting ideas. "After a Time," although it is a literary work in its own right, might even be thought of as serious parody—perhaps the greatest compliment one writer can pay another.

"Do Not Go Gentle into That Good Night" was written by a young man of thirty-eight who addresses it to his old and ailing father. It's interesting to note that the author himself has very little of his own self-destructive life left as he was composing this piece. Perhaps that is why he seems to have more insight into the subject of death than most people of his age. He advocates raging and fighting against it, not giving in and accepting it.

"After a Time" was written by a woman of about the same age and is addressed to no one in particular. Davis has a different philosophy about death. She "answers" Thomas's poem and presents her differing views using the same poetic form—a villanelle. Evidently, she felt it necessary to present a contrasting point of view eight years after Thomas's death.

While "Do Not Go Gentle" protests and rages against death, Davis's poem suggests a quiet resignation and acquiescence. She seems to feel that raging against death is useless and profitless. She argues that we will eventually become tame, anyway, after the raging is done. At the risk of sounding sexist, I think it interesting that the man rages and the woman submits, as if the traditionally perceived differences between the behavior of men and women are reflected in the poems.

Thomas talks about different types of men and why they rage against death. "Wise men" desire immortality. They rage against death occurring before they've made their mark on history. "Good men" lament the frailty of their deeds. Given more time, they might have accomplished great things. "Wild men" regret their constant hedonistic pursuits. With more time they could prove their worth. "Grave men" are quite the opposite and regret they never took time for the pleasures in life. Now it is too late. They rage against death because they are not ready for it.

His father's death is painful to Thomas because he sees himself lying in that bed; his father's dying reminds him of his own inevitable death. The passion of the last stanza, in which the poet asks his father to bless and curse him, suggests that he has doubts about his relationship with his father. He may feel that he has not been enough of a son. He put off doing things with and for his father because he always felt there would be time later. Now time has run out and he feels cheated. He's raging for his father now. He'll rage for himself later.

Catherine Davis advocates a calm submission, a peaceful acquiescence. She feels raging is useless and says that those of us who rage will finally "go tame / When what we have we can no longer use." When she says "One more thing lost is one thing less to lose," the reader can understand and come to terms with the loss of different aspects of the mind and body, such as strength, eyesight, hearing, and intellect. Once we've lost one of these, it's one thing less to worry about losing. After a time, everything will be lost, and we'll accept that, too, because we'll be ready for it.

In a contest of imagery, Thomas would certainly win the day. His various men not only rage and rave, they burn. Their words "forked no lightning," their deeds might have "danced in a green bay," they "sang the sun in flight," and they see that "blind eyes could blaze like meteors." Davis's images are quiet—generally abstract and without much sensory suggestiveness. She gives us "things lost," a "reassuring ruse," and "all losses are the same." Her most powerful image—"And we go stripped at last the way we came"—makes its point with none of the excitement of Thomas's rage. And yet, I prefer the quiet intelligence of Davis to the high energy of Thomas.

"And we go stripped at last the way we came" can give strange comfort and solace to those of us who always envied those in high places. Death is a great leveler. People are not all created equal at birth, not by a long shot. But we will bloody well all be equal when we make our final exit. Kings, popes, and heads of state will go just as "stripped" as the rest of us. They won't get to take anything with them. All wealth, power, and trappings will be left behind. We will all finally and ultimately be equal. So why rage? It won't do us any good.

Exploring Fiction, Poetry, Drama, and Essays

Here are some questions you might ask yourself when you are faced with the task of writing about literature. Your answers to these questions can help you overcome the awful whiteness of the empty page.

Fiction

1. From what point of view is the story told? Can you speculate on the appropriateness of that point of view? If a story is told from the point of

view of a first-person narrator who participates in the action, what significant changes would occur if it were told from the point of view of an omniscient author? And, of course, *vice versa*. Note that first-person narrators do not know what other characters think. On the other hand, omniscient narrators know everything about the lives of the characters. How would the story you are writing about be changed if the viewpoint were changed?

2. Who are the principal characters in the story? (There will rarely be more than three in a short story—the other characters will often be portrayed sketchily; sometimes they are even stereotypes.) What functions do the minor characters serve? Do any of the characters change during the course of the story? How, and why?

3. What is the plot of the story? Do the events that constitute the plot emerge logically from the nature of the characters and circumstances, or are the plot elements coincidental and arbitrary?

4. What is the setting of the story? Does the setting play an important role in the story, or is it simply the place where things happen? You might ask yourself what the consequences of some other setting might be for the effectiveness of the story.

5. What is the tone of the story? The first several paragraphs of the story establish that tone. Does the tone change with events, or remain fixed? How does the tone contribute to the effect of the story?

6. Do you find ambiguities in the story? That is, can you interpret some element of the story in more than one way? Does that ambiguity result in confusion, or does it add to the complexity of the story?

7. Does the story seem to support or attack your own political and moral positions?

8. Bring your knowledge of history and contemporary events to bear on your reading of the story. Does the story clarify, enhance, or contradict your understanding of history?

9. What is the theme of the story? This, finally, is the most significant question to answer. All the elements of fiction—point of view, tone, character, plot, setting—have been marshaled to project a theme—the moral proposition the author wishes to advance. When you write about fiction, or any literary form, you must resist the tendency to do the easiest thing—retell the plot, incident by incident. You must, indeed, come to understand the devices the author uses to convey his or her theme, and, in your paper, reveal that understanding.

Poetry

1. Who is the speaker? What does the poem reveal about the speaker's character? In some poems the speaker may be nothing more than a voice

meditating on a theme, while in others the speaker takes on a specific personality. For example, the speaker in Shelley's "Ozymandias" is a voice meditating on the transitoriness of all things; except for the views expressed in the poem, we know nothing about the speaker's character. The same might be said of the speaker in Hopkins's "Spring and Fall" but with this important exception: we know that he is older than Margaret and therefore has a wisdom she does not.

2. Is the speaker addressing a particular person? If so, who is that person, and why is the speaker interested in him or her? Many poems, like "Ozymandias," are addressed to no one in particular and therefore to anyone, any reader. Others, such as Donne's "A Valediction: Forbidding Mourning," while addressed to a specific person, reveal nothing about that person because the focus of the poem is on the speaker's feelings and attitudes. In a dramatic monologue (see "Glossary of Literary Terms"), the speaker usually addresses a silent auditor. The identity of the auditor will be important to the poem.

3. Does the poem have a setting? Is the poem occasioned by a particular event? The answer to these questions will often be "no" for lyric poems, such as Frost's "Fire and Ice." It will always be "yes" if the poem is a dramatic monologue or a poem that tells or implies a story, such as Tennyson's "Ulysses" and Lowell's "Patterns."

4. Is the theme of the poem stated directly or indirectly? Some poems, such as Frost's "Provide, Provide" and Owen's "Dulce et Decorum Est," use language in a fairly straightforward and literal way and state the theme, often in the final lines. Others may conclude with a statement of the theme that is more difficult to apprehend because it is made with figurative language and symbols. This difference will be readily apparent if you compare the final lines of the Frost and Owen poems mentioned above with, say, the final stanzas of Stevens's "Sunday Morning."

5. If the speaker is describing specific events, from what perspective (roughly similar to point of view in fiction) is he or she doing so? Is the speaker recounting events of the past or events that are occurring in the present? If past events are being recalled, what present meaning do they have for the speaker? These questions are particularly appropriate to the works in the section "Innocence and Experience," many of which contrast an early innocence with adult experience.

6. Does a close examination of the figurative language (see "Glossary of Literary Terms") of the poem reveal any patterns? Yeats's "Sailing to Byzantium" may begin to open up to you once you recognize the pattern of bird imagery. Likewise, Thomas's attitude toward his childhood in "Fern Hill" will be clearer if you detect the pattern of biblical imagery that associates childhood with Adam and Eve before the Fall.

7. What is the structure of the poem? Since narrative poems, those that tell stories, reveal a high degree of selectivity, it is useful to ask why the poet has focused on particular details and left out others. Analyzing the structure of a nonnarrative or lyric poem can be more difficult because it does not contain an obvious series of chronologically related events. The structure of Thomas's "Fern Hill," for example, is based in part on a description of perhaps a day and a half in the speaker's life as a child. But more significant in terms of its structure is the speaker's realization that the immortality he felt as a child was merely a stage in the inexorable movement of life toward death. The structure of the poem, therefore, will be revealed through an analysis of patterns of images (biblical, color, day and night, dark and light) that embody the theme. To take another example, Marvell's "To His Coy Mistress" is divided into three verse paragraphs, the opening words of each ("Had we . . . ," "But . . . ," "Now therefore . . . ,") suggesting a logically constructed argument.

8. What do sound and meter (see "Glossary of Literary Terms") contribute to the poem? Alexander Pope said that in good poetry "the sound must seem an echo to the sense," a statement that is sometimes easier to agree with than to demonstrate. For sample analyses of the music of poetry, see the section on music in the appendix "Reading Poetry" (p. 903).

9. What was your response to the poem on first reading? Did your response change after study of the poem or class discussions about it?

Drama

1. How does the play begin? Is the exposition presented dramatically through the interaction among characters, or novelistically through long, unrealistic, and unwieldy speeches that convey a lot of information, or through some device such as the reading of long letters or lengthy reports delivered by a messenger?

2. How does the information conveyed in exposition (which may occur at various moments throughout the play) establish the basis for dramatic irony—that is, the ironic response generated in an audience when it knows more than do the characters? For example, because we know that Iago is a villain in Shakespeare's *Othello*, we hear an ironic dimension in his speeches that the characters do not hear, and that irony is the source of much tension in the audience. An assessment of dramatic irony in a play makes an interesting and instructive writing assignment.

3. Who are the principal characters, and how are the distinctive qualities of each dramatically conveyed? Inevitably, there will be minor characters in a play. What function do they serve? A paper that thoughtfully assesses the role of minor characters can often succeed better than the attempt to

analyze the major figures who may embody too much complexity to deal with in 1,000 words.

4. Where is the play set? Does it matter that it is set there? Why? Does the setting play some significant role in the drama, or is it merely a place, any place?

5. What is the central conflict in the play? How is it resolved? Do you need to know something of the historical circumstances out of which the play emerged, or something of the life of the author in order to appreciate the play fully? If so, how does the information enhance your understanding?

6. Since plays are usually written to be performed rather than read, what visual and auditory elements of the play are significant to your response? Obviously, if you are writing from a reading text, you will have to place yourself in the position of the director and the actors in order to respond to this aspect of drama.

7. What is the play's theme? How does the dramatic action embody that theme?

Note that any one of these questions might provoke an effective paper—one could do a thousand words on the settings of *Othello*, or the minor characters of *A Doll's House*, or the methods of exposition in *Antigonê*. But each of those papers, to be successful, needs to relate the issues it deals with to the thematic force of the play. Plot summaries (except as a variety of note taking) are unsatisfactory.

Essays

1. What is the author's thesis (or unifying idea)? What evidence or arguments does the author advance to support the thesis? Is the thesis convincing? If not, why not? Does the author rely on any basic but unstated assumptions?

2. What is the author's tone? Select for analysis a passage you consider illustrative of the author's tone. Does the author maintain that tone consistently throughout the essay?

3. How would you characterize the author's style? For example, are the syntax, length of sentences, and diction elevated and formal or familiar and informal?

4. What rhetorical strategies does the author use? For example, can you identify the effective use of classification, comparison and contrast, analogy, cause and effect, or definition? Note that one of these rhetorical strategies may constitute the unifying idea of the essay and the means of structuring it. Jessica Mitford's "The American Way of Death" is an essay in definition that effectively uses comparison and contrast and analogy.

5. What are the major divisions in the essay, and how are they set off? Are the transitions between the divisions effective and easy to follow?

6. Analyze the author's opening paragraph. Is it effective in gaining the reader's attention? Does it clearly state the essay's thesis? If it does not, at what point does the author's thesis and purpose become clear?

Suggested Topics for Writing

Here are some specific suggestions for essay topics based on pieces collected in this book.

Fiction

1. Explicate the opening paragraph or page of a story in order to demonstrate how it sets the tone and anticipates what is to follow.

2. Select a story that uses a central symbol or symbolic event and analyze its function. Some suggestions:

   A. Iván's fall from the ladder in Tolstoy's "The Death of Iván Ilých."

   B. The pink ribbon in Hawthorne's "Young Goodman Brown."

   C. Hair in Butler's "Preparation."

   D. The quilt in Walker's "Everyday Use."

   E. The ANC pin in Gordimer's "Something for the Time Being."

3. Select a story in which the narrative does not unfold chronologically and explain why.

4. Here are some suggestions for essays in comparison and contrast:

   A. Compare and contrast the nature and function of the dream sequences in Hawthorne's "Young Goodman Brown" and Giles's "Rough Translations."

   B. Compare and contrast the nature of jealousy in Borges's "The Intruder" and Moravia's "The Chase."

   C. Compare and contrast the idea of "the hero" in Crane's "The Bride Comes to Yellow Sky" and Thurber's "The Greatest Man in the World."

   D. Compare and contrast the attitude toward sexuality in Chopin's "The Storm" and Shaw's "The Girls in Their Summer Dresses."

   E. Compare and contrast the marriages in Shaw's "The Girls in Their
      Summer Dresses" and Carver's "What We Talk about When We Talk
      about Love."

5. Write an essay on an interesting story title.

6. Did the ending of any story you read violate your expectations? What led
   you to those expectations? Do you find the author's ending more satisfactory than the one you had anticipated?

7. Select a story you feel is weak, and explain why you feel so. You might
   consider the credibility of the plot or of a character's behavior.

Poetry

1. Select a short lyric poem you found difficult, and explicate it line by line.
   Conclude with a paragraph or two describing how the process of explication helped you to clarify the meaning of the poem.

2. Here is a list of poems about poets and poetry. Select two and compare
   and contrast their treatment of the subject.
       Housman, "Terence, This Is Stupid Stuff"
       MacLeish, "Ars Poetica"
       Kennedy, "Ars Poetica"
       Giovanni, "For Saundra"
       Cruz, "Today Is a Day of Great Joy"

3. The poems listed below tell or imply a story. Select one, and write out the
   story in your own words. Use your imagination to fill in details.
       Anonymous, "Bonny Barbara Allen"
       Anonymous, "Edward"
       Tennyson, "Ulysses"
       Browning, "My Last Duchess"
       Hardy, "The Ruined Maid"
       Lowell, "Patterns"
       Eliot, "The Love Song of J. Alfred Prufrock"
       Owen, "Dulce et Decorum Est"
       Wright, "Between the World and Me"
       Peacock, "Say You Love Me"
       Kearney, "Father Answers His Adversaries"

4. Analyze a poem in which the author uses a particular kind of diction.
   Identify the pattern, and explain how it functions in the poem. Some
   suggestions:

   A. The language of bureaucracy in Auden's "The Unknown Citizen" or
      Baker's "Formal Application."

   B. Contrasting patterns of diction in Reed's "Naming of Parts."

C. Colloquial and formal diction in Hughes's "Same in Blues."

D. Prosaic diction in Forché's "The Colonel" or Mezey's "My Mother."

E. Colloquial diction in Kizer's "Bitch."

5. As an exercise to illuminate the importance of connotation, select a poem that you like, identify some of its key words, and then consult a dictionary or thesaurus for synonyms of those key words. Reread the poem, substituting the synonyms for the words the poet used (for purposes of this exercise, ignore that fact that the synonyms may have more or fewer syllables and thus alter the rhythm). Write an essay analyzing the effects of your substitutions. Provide a sample of the rewritten poem.

6. Select one of the following titles for an essay in comparison and contrast.

A. The Cost of Conformity: Dickinson's "What Soft—Cherubic Creatures" and Cummings's "the Cambridge ladies who live in furnished souls."

B. The Psychology of Hate: Blake's "A Poison Tree" and Allen's "A Moment Please."

C. The Meaning of Love: Marvell's "To His Coy Mistress" and Donne's "A Valediction: Forbidding Mourning."

D. The Logic of Love: Campion's "I Care Not for These Ladies" and Marvell's "To His Coy Mistress."

E. The Images of Love: Shakespeare's Sonnet 18 and Sonnet 130.

F. The Death of Love: Sexton's "The Farmer's Wife" and Schnackenberg's "Complaint."

G. Remembering Childhood: Frost's "Birches" and Thomas's "Fern Hill."

H. What the Young Can Never Understand: Housman's "When I Was One-and-Twenty" and Hopkins's "Spring and Fall."

I. The Woman's Role: Rich's "Living in Sin" and Sexton's "The Farmer's Wife."

J. The Meaning of Nature: Dickinson's "Apparently with No Surprise" and Frost's "Design."

K. The Meaning of Old Age: Arnold's "Growing Old" and Yeats's "Sailing to Byzantium."

L. Untimely Death: Frost's " 'Out, Out—' " and Housman's "To an Athlete Dying Young" or Roethke's "Elegy for Jane" and Hirsch's "Fast Break."

M. Confronting Death: Stevens's "Sunday Morning" and Thomas's "Do Not Go Gentle into That Good Night."

7. Analyze the allusions in a poem. Include in your discussion an explanation of the allusion and what it contributes to the poem. Some suggestions:
Eliot's "The Love Song of J. Alfred Prufrock"
Auden's "The Unknown Citizen"
Frost's "Provide, Provide"
Reid's "Curiosity"
Wordsworth's "The World Is Too Much With Us"
Cummings's "the Cambridge ladies who live in furnished souls"
Arnold's "Dover Beach"
Plath's "Daddy"
Yeats's "Sailing to Byzantium"
Frost's " 'Out, Out—' "
Baker's "Formal Application"

8. Analyze the use of irony in a poem. Some suggestions:
Blake's "The Chimney Sweeper"
Browning's "My Last Duchess"
Arnold's "Growing Old"
Hardy's "The Ruined Maid"
Robinson's "Richard Cory"
Frost's " 'Out, Out—' "
Bishop's "One Art"

9. Analyze the use of one form of figurative language in a poem. Some suggestions:

A. Hyperbole in Burns's "A Red, Red Rose" or Marvell's "To His Coy Mistress."

B. Simile and metaphor in Donne's "A Valediction: Forbidding Mourning," Marvell's "To His Coy Mistress," Burns's "A Red, Red Rose," Keats's "On First Looking into Chapman's Homer," Shakespeare's sonnets 18 and 130, or MacLeish's "Ars Poetica."

C. Symbols in Waller's "Go, Lovely Rose!" Blake's "The Tyger," Frost's "Fire and Ice," Lowell's "Patterns," Reid's "Curiosity," or Meinke's "Advice to My Son."

D. Paradox in Meinke's "Advice to My Son," Yeats's "Easter 1916," Blake's "The Tyger," Stevens's "Sunday Morning," or Donne's "Death, Be Not Proud."

10. Look carefully at the reproduction of Brueghel's painting *The Fall of Icarus* (p. 798), and jot down your impressions of it. Include a sentence or two on the "statement" you think Brueghel is making. Now read Auden's poem "Musée des Beaux Arts." In an essay, compare your impressions of the painting with those of the poet. If the poem taught you something about the painting, include that in your essay.

Drama

1. Explicate the opening scene of a play in order to demonstrate how the dramatist lays the groundwork for what is to follow. Some questions you might consider: What information necessary to understand the action are we given? What do we learn about the characters and their relationships? Do settings and costumes contribute to the exposition?

2. Analyze a play in order to show how nonverbal elements, such as costumes and stage sets, contribute to the theme.

3. Select a minor character in a play, and analyze that character's function. Some possibilities: Roderigo in *Othello*; Marc in *M. Butterfly*; the Valet in *No Exit*.

4. Analyze the language of a play for patterns of imagery that contribute to the development of character, mood, or theme. Some suggestions: images of bestial sexuality in Shakespeare's *Othello*; animals in Ibsen's *A Doll's House*; furniture in Sartre's *No Exit*.

5. Assume you are the director of one of the plays in this anthology. For one of the major characters, write a set of director's notes intended for the actor playing the role, in which you describe your conception of how the role should be played.

6. In an essay, describe the playwright's method for achieving dramatic irony in one of the plays you have read.

7. When you attend a performance of a play, you are usually given a program indicating, among other things, the number of acts, the elapsed time between acts, the time and place of the action. It will not include the stage directions of the printed version of the play. Examine the stage directions of a play, and suggest how a director might convey in a performance what the dramatist describes in the stage directions.

Essays

1. Carefully analyze the first paragraph or two of an essay in order to demonstrate how it sets the tone and attracts the reader's attention. Look for unusual language, imagery, prose rhythm, and notable sentence structure as evidence to support your assertions.

2. Select an essay that uses a central symbol or symbolic event and analyze its function. Some suggestions:

   A. Shooting the elephant in Orwell's essay.

   B. The Iks in Thomas's essay.

   C. The tolling bell in Donne's "Meditation XVII."

D. The rhino in Soto's "The Rhino."

E. The plate in Selzer's "The Discus Thrower."

3. Here are some suggestions for studies in comparison and contrast:

A. Compare and contrast the attitude toward political power in Orwell's "Shooting an Elephant" and King's "Letter from Birmingham Jail."

B. Compare and contrast the experience of minorities as revealed in Baldwin's "Rage" and King's "Letter from Birmingham Jail."

C. Compare and contrast the satirical methods of Swift in "A Modest Proposal" and Thomas in "The Iks."

D. Compare and contrast the prose style of Didion's "On Morality" and Woolf's "What if Shakespeare Had Had a Sister?"

4. Select an essay you particularly like and create a set of notes in which you systematically convert the original to brief study aids. After a few days, try to recreate the essay, or a portion of it, from your notes. Compare your effort with the original and write an analysis of the differences.

5. Discover, describe, and analyze the unspoken assumptions on which an author depends. Some suggestions:

A. The sacredness of life in Swift's "A Modest Proposal."

B. The solemnity of death in Didion's "On Morality."

C. The survival of the soul in Donne's "Meditation XVII."

D. The nature of power in Orwell's "Shooting an Elephant."

E. The right to equal justice in King's "Letter from Birmingham Jail."

F. Deathbed promises in Twain's "Lost in the Snow."

G. Tension between the sexes in Tweedie's "The Experience."

H. The proper response to death in Mitford's "The American Way of Death."

And one final general question: One of the commonly accepted notions of art is that it helps us to clarify our own feelings, to give us in vivid and memorable form what we had perhaps felt or thought only vaguely. Select a work (one that you found especially relevant to your own life), and describe how it clarified your own feelings.

Some Matters of Form

Titles

The first word and all main words of titles are capitalized. Ordinarily (unless they are the first or last word), articles (*a, an,* and *the*), prepositions (*in, on, of with, about*, etc.), and conjunctions (*and, but, or*, etc.) are not capitalized.

The titles of parts of larger collections, short stories, poems, articles, essays, and songs are enclosed in quotation marks.

The titles of plays, books, movies, periodicals, operas, paintings, and newspapers are italicized. In typed and handwritten manuscripts, italics are represented by underlining.

The title you give your own essay is neither placed in quotation marks nor underlined. However, a quotation used as a part of your title would be enclosed in quotation marks (see the following section on quotations). Similarly, the title of a literary work used as a part of your title would be either placed in quotation marks or underlined depending on the type of work it is.

Quotations

Quotation marks indicate you are transcribing someone else's words; those words must, therefore, be *exactly* as they appear in your source.

As a general rule, quotations of not more than four lines of prose or two lines of poetry are placed between quotation marks and incorporated in your own text:

> Near the end of "Young Goodman Brown," the narrator asks, "Had Goodman Brown fallen asleep in the forest and only dreamed a wild dream of a witch-meeting?"

If you are quoting two lines of verse in your text, indicate the division between lines with a slash. Leave a space before and after the slash:

> Prufock hears the dilettantish talk in a room where "the women come and go / Talking of Michelangelo."

Longer quotations are indented ten spaces and are double-spaced. They are not enclosed in quotation marks, since the indentation signals a quotation.

As noted above, anything quoted, whether enclosed in quotation marks or indented, must be reproduced exactly. If you insert anything—even a word—the inserted material must be placed within brackets. If you wish to omit some material from a passage in quotation marks, the omission (ellipsis) must be indicated by three spaced periods: . . . (an ellipsis mark). When an ellipsis occurs between complete sentences or at the end of a sentence, a fourth period, indicating the end of the sentence, should be inserted. No space precedes the first period.

Full quotation from original:

> As one critic puts it, "Richard Wright, like Dostoevsky before him, sends his hero underground to discover the truth about the upper world, a world that has forced him to confess to a crime he has not committed."

With insertion and omissions:

> As one critic puts it, "Richard Wright . . . sends his hero [Fred Daniels] underground to discover the truth about the upper world. . . ."

Use a full line of spaced periods to indicate the omission of a line or more of poetry (or of a whole paragraph or more of prose):

> For I have known them all already, known them all—
> Have known the evenings, mornings, afternoons,
> I have measured out my life with coffee spoons;
> . . . .
> And I have known the eyes already, known them all—
> The eyes that fix you in a formulated phrase.

Periods and commas are placed *inside* quotation marks:

> In "The Lesson," the narrator describes Miss Moore as someone "who always looked like she was going to church, though she never did."

Other punctuation marks go outside the quotation marks unless they are part of the material being quoted.

For poetry quotations, provide the line number or numbers in parentheses immediately following the quotation:

> With ironic detachment, Prufrock declares that he is "no prophet" (1. 83).

Documentation

You must acknowledge the source of ideas you paraphrase and material you quote. Such acknowledgments are extremely important, for even an unintentional failure to give formal credit to others for their words or ideas can leave you open to an accusation of plagiarism—that is, the presentation of someone else's ideas as your own.

If you use published works as you prepare your paper, you should list those sources as the last page of your essay. Then, in the body of your essay, you will use parenthetical citations that refer to the works you quote or paraphrase. Here is a sample list of works cited that illustrates the mechanical form for different kinds of sources. These samples will probably satisfy your needs, but if you use kinds of sources not listed here, you should consult Joseph Gibaldi, *MLA Handbook for Writers of Research Papers*, 4th ed. (New York: Modern Language Association, 1995). That handbook provides sample entries for every imaginable source.

Works Cited

Abcarian, Richard, and Marvin Klotz, eds. Literature: The Human Experience, Shorter 6th ed. with Essays. New York: St Martin's. 1996.

Cooper, Wendy. Hair, Sex, Society, Symbolism. New York: Stein, 1971.

Fiedler, Leslie. "Come Back to the Raft Ag'in, Huck Honey." Partisan Review 15 (1948): 664–71.

Joyce, James. "Araby." Literature: The Human Experience. Shorter 6th ed. with Essays. Ed. Richard Abcarian and Marvin Klotz. New York: St. Martin's, 1996. 27–31.

———. Dubliners. Ed. Robert Scholes and A. Walton Litz. New York: Peguin, 1976.

The first of these citations is this book. You would use it if you used materials from the editors' introduction or critical appendices. The entry illustrates the form for citing a book with two editors. Note that the first editor's name is presented surname first, but the second is presented with the surname last.

The second entry illustrates the form for citing a book with one author. The third gives the form for an article published in a periodical (note that the title of the article is in quotes and the title of the journal is underlined). The fourth entry shows how to cite a work included in an anthology. The fifth citation, because it is by the same author as the fourth, begins with three hyphens in place of the author's name.

The following paragraph demonstrates the use of parenthetical citations.

> Leslie Fiedler's controversial view of the relationship between Jim and Huck (669–70) uses a method often discussed by other critics (Abcarian and Klotz 1278–79). Cooper's 1971 study (180) raises similar issues, but such methods are not useful when one deals with such a line as "North Richmond Street, being blind, was a quiet street except at the hour when the Christian Brothers' School set the boys free" (Joyce, "Araby" 27). But when Joyce refers to the weather (Dubliners 224), the issue becomes clouded.

This rather whimsical paragraph illustrates the form your parenthetical citations should take. The first citation gives only the page reference, which is all that is necessary because the author's name is given in the text and only one work by that author appears in the list of works cited.

The second citation gives the editors' names and thus identifies the work being cited. It then indicates the appropriate pages.

The third citation, because the author's name is mentioned in the text, gives only a page reference.

The fourth citation must provide the author's name *and* the work cited, because two works by the same author appear in the list of works cited.

The last citation, because it refers to an author with two works in the list of works cited, gives the name of the work and the page where the reference can be found.

In short, your parenthetical acknowledgment should contain (1) the *minimum* information required to lead the reader to the appropriate work in the list of works cited and (2) the location within the work to which you refer.

Rather than parenthetical references, some instructors may prefer footnotes (or endnotes). Here is the paragraph documented with footnotes.

> Leslie Fiedler's controversial view of the relationship between Jim and Huck[1] uses a method often discussed by other critics.[2] Cooper's 1971 study[3] raises similar issues, but such methods are not useful when one deals with such a line as "North Richmond Street, being blind, was a quiet street except at the hour when the Christian Brothers' School set the boys free."[4] But when Joyce refers to the weather,[5] the issue becomes clouded.

> [1] "Come Back to the Raft Ag'in, Huck Honey," Partisan Review 15 (1948): 664–71.
> [2] Richard Abcarian and Marvin Klotz, eds., Literature: The Human Experience, Shorter 6th ed. with Essays (New York: St. Martin's, 1996) 930–32.
> [3] Hair, Sex, Society, Symbolism (New York: Stein, 1971) 180.
> [4] James Joyce, "Araby," Literature: The Human Experience, Shorter 6th ed. with Essays, ed. Richard Abcarian and Marvin Klotz (New York: St. Martin's, 1996) 27.
> [5] Dubliners, ed. Robert Scholes and A. Walton Litz (New York: Penguin, 1976) 224.

Note that when the author's name is given in the text, you do not have to repeat it in the footnote. Subsequent references to a work generally require only the surname of the author (or authors, editor, or editors) and the page number; thus:

> [6] Cooper 175.

If you need to find a model for a different kind of source, don't despair. Simply refer to the *MLA Handbook* (1995).

The main thing to remember about footnoting, and about citations in general, is that the object is to give credit to others whenever it is due and to enable your reader to go directly to your sources, if he or she wishes to do so, as quickly and easily as possible.

A Checklist for Your Final Draft

Here are some questions to ask yourself before turning in your essay.

1. Is my essay clearly responsive to the assignment?

2. Does my essay put forward a clearly defined thesis at the outset?

3. Does each paragraph have an identifiable topic sentence?

4. Have I marshaled my paragraphs in logical order and provided appropriate transitions?

5. Do I support my assertions with evidence?

6. Have I used direct quotations appropriately, and have I transcribed them accurately?

7. Do I document the sources of other people's ideas and the direct quotations I use? Is the documentation in appropriate form?

8. Have I written syntactically correct sentences (no run-ons, and no fragments except by design)?

9. Have I eliminated as many passive constructions and forms of the verb *to be* as possible?

10. Have I avoided long sequences (say three or more) of prepositional phrases?

11. Can I feel good about this essay? Does it embody serious thinking in attractive form (free of typos and other errors)? Can I put my name on the paper with pride?

Biographical Notes on the Authors

Samuel Allen (b. 1917)   Born in Columbus, Ohio, the son of a member of the clergy, Allen attended Fisk University and graduated from Harvard Law School in 1941. He spent a year as deputy assistant district attorney in New York City, had his own private law practice, and held an assortment of posts including assistant deputy counsel for the U.S. Information Agency (1961–1964). Previously a professor of law (Texas Southern University) and humanities (Tuskegee Institute), Allen joined the English department of Boston University in 1971, the same year he won the National Endowment for the Arts award for poetry. He published *Every Round and Other Poems* in 1987. Allen's translations, essays, and poems have appeared in scores of anthologies and journals, including *Presence Africaine* and *Journal of Afro-American Studies*, often under the pen name Paul Vesey.

Woody Allen (b. 1935)   After being dismissed from both City College of New York and New York University, this precocious and prototypical New Yorker became a television comedy writer at the age of eighteen. He wrote two successful Broadway plays; his first screenplay, *What's New Pussycat?*, appeared in 1965. A dozen years in show business gave him the confidence to set out on his own, and he began performing as a standup comic. Soon after, he embarked on the filmmaking career—writing, performing, directing, and producing—for which he is famous. His talents, and those of the actors and technical group he has bought together as a kind of filmmaking repertory company, account for his reputation as an innovative contributor to cinema history. (His 1977 film, *Annie Hall*, won four Academy Awards.) In his spare time, he plays the clarinet in a Dixieland jazz group at a New York nightspot, and continues to write occasional pieces like *Death Knocks*.

Catherine Anderson (b. 1954)   Born in Detroit, Michigan, Anderson is the author of *In the Mother Tongue* (1983), a book of poems published by Alice-jamesbooks of Cambridge, Mass. She was the Cornelia Ward Fellow for Poetry at Syracuse University in 1976, where she received an M.A. in English and creative writing in 1979. She works as a community journalist and organizer in Boston's immigrant communities and has published in many journals, including *The American Voice*, *The Antioch Review*, and *The Harvard Review*.

Matthew Arnold (1822–1888)   Born in Middlesex, England, Arnold attended Rugby School (where his father was headmaster) and studied classics at Oxford. Following his graduation in 1844, he became a fellow at Oxford and a master at Rugby School. In 1851, he was appointed inspector of schools in England and was sent by the government to observe educational systems in Europe. He remained in that post for some thirty-five years. As a poet, Arnold took inspiration from Greek tragedies, Keats, and Wordsworth. His collections include *Empedocles on Etna and Other Poems* (1852). An eminent social and literary critic in his later years, Arnold lectured in America in 1883 and 1886. His essay "The Function of Criticism" sheds light on his transition from poet to critic. Much of his work is collected in *Complete Prose Works* (11 volumes, 1960–1977).

W. H. Auden (1907–1973)   A poet, playwright, translator, librettist, critic, and editor, Wystan Hugh Auden was born in York, son of a medical officer and a nurse. He attended Oxford from 1925 to 1928, then taught, traveled, and moved from faculty to faculty of several universities in the United States (where he became a naturalized citizen in 1946). He won the Pulitzer Prize in 1948 for his collection *The Age of Anxiety,* an expression he coined to describe the 1930s. While his early writing exhibited Marxist sympathies and reflected the excitement of new Freudian psychoanalytic thought, he later embraced Christianity and produced sharply honed verse in the rhyme and meter of traditional forms.

Donald W. Baker (b. 1923)   Born in Boston, son of a cabdriver, Baker earned a Ph.D. in 1955 from Brown University, where he taught English from 1948 to 1953. He joined the faculty of Wabash College in Crawfordsville, Indiana, in 1953, served six years as the director of drama, and was named poet-in-residence in 1964. Married in 1945 and the father of two, Baker has enjoyed giving readings and workshops. However, he is no stranger to writer's block and wryly admits: "I'm not prolific and have a lot of trouble producing anything at all."

James Baldwin (1924–1987)   Born in New York City, the son of a Harlem minister, Baldwin began preaching as a young teenager. Some years later, he experienced a religious crisis, left the church, and moved to New York City's bohemian Greenwich Village, where he began his career as a writer, supporting himself with menial jobs and publishing occasional articles in journals such as the *Nation* and *Commentary.* By the end of the 1940s, Baldwin's anger over the treatment of African Americans led him into exile in France. There, Baldwin completed his acclaimed first novel, *Go Tell It on the Mountain* (1953), a work in which he drew heavily on his own childhood to depict the lives of members of a Harlem church, focusing on a minister's son. His next work, *Notes of a Native Son* (1955), a collection of personal, literary, and social essays, secured Baldwin's reputation as a major American writer. Two later collections of essays, *Nobody Knows My Name* (1961) and *The Fire Next Time* (1963), established Baldwin as one of the most powerful voices of the turbulent civil rights movement of the 1960s. But as riots, bombings, and other violence grew more frequent, Baldwin grew increasingly pessimistic over the prospect that white America could ever overcome its racism. That pessimism was deepened by two traumatic events: the 1964 bombing of the Sixteenth Avenue Baptist Church in Birmingham, Alabama, that killed four young girls attending a Sunday school class and the assassination of the Reverend Martin Luther King, Jr., in 1968. Baldwin began making periodic trips to France, settling there permanently in 1974.

Toni Cade Bambara (b. 1939)   Born in New York City, Bambara was educated there and in Italy and Paris. Early in her career she worked as an investigator for the New York State Department of Social Welfare but has devoted herself for many years to teaching and writing. One of the best representatives of a group of African American writers who emerged in the 1960s, Bambara has been a consistent civil rights activist, both politically and culturally involved in African American life. Much of her writing focuses on African American women, particularly as they confront experiences that force them to new awareness. She is the author of three collections of short stories, *Gorilla, My Love* (1972), *Tales and Stories for Black Folks* (1971), and *The Sea Birds Are Still Alive: Collected Stories* (1977), and two novels, *The Salt Eaters* (1980) and *If Blessing Comes* (1987). She is also editor of *The Black Woman: An Anthology* (1970).

Elizabeth Bishop (1911–1979)   Bishop was born in Worcester, Massachusetts. Her father died before she was a year old; four years later, when her mother suffered a mental breakdown, Bishop was taken to live with her grandmother in Nova Scotia. Although her mother lived until 1934, Bishop saw her for the last time in 1916, a visit recalled in one of her rare autobiographical stories, "In the Village." Bishop planned to enter Cornell Medical School after graduating from Vassar, but was persuaded by Marianne Moore to become a writer. For the next fifteen years, she was a virtual nomad, traveling in Canada, Europe, and North and South America. In 1951, she finally settled in Rio de Janeiro, where she lived for almost twenty years. During the final decade of her life, Bishop continued to travel, but she resumed living in the United States and taught frequently at Harvard. She was an austere writer, publishing only four slim volumes of poetry: *North and South* (1946); *A Cold Spring* (1955), which won the Pulitzer Prize; *Questions of Travel* (1965); and *Geography III* (1976), which won the National Book Critics' Circle Award. *The Complete Poems (1927–1979)* was published after her death, as was a collection of her prose. Despite her modest output, she has earned an enduring place of respect among twentieth-century poets.

William Blake (1757–1827)   Born in London to an obscure family, Blake was educated at home until he was ten, then enrolled in a drawing school, advancing ultimately to a formal apprenticeship as an engraver. At an early age, Blake exhibited talent as both an artist and a poet, and throughout his life read widely among modern philosophers and poets. Throughout his life, he experienced mystical visions that provided him with the inspiration for many of his poems. Blake devised a process he called illuminated printing, which involved the preparation of drawings and decorative frames to complement his poems. He published *Songs of Innocence* (1789) and *Songs of Experience* (1794) in this fashion. These books, as well as the many subsequent works he wrote and illustrated, earned him a reputation as one of the most important artists of his day. Many of Blake's works assert his conviction that the established church and state hinder rather than nurture human freedom and the sense of divine love.

Jorge Luis Borges (1899–1986)   Borges was born in Buenos Aires, Argentina, to a middle-class family that spoke both Spanish and English at home. His love of literature began early, encouraged by a father who had himself aspired to a writing career. As a young man, he traveled and studied in Europe, where he published reviews, essays, and poetry. When he returned to Buenos Aires in 1921, he became a well-known exponent of experimental writing. However, he remained relatively unknown outside Argentina until he received an important international literary prize in 1961, the Prix Formentor. The fame that came with the prize led to the simultaneous publication in six countries of a collection of short stories, *Fictions* (1945), and to the first of his many lecture tours in the United States. Borges created much of his best-known fiction during his later years, when failing eyesight (eventually resulting in blindness) and poor health made him a semi-invalid. By the time of his death, his prolific and innovative writing had earned him a reputation and influence that extended far beyond his native Argentina.

Elizabeth Brewster (b. 1922)   Born in Chipman, New Brunswick, Canada, Elizabeth Brewster earned a B.A. (1946) from the University of New Brunswick, and an A.M. (1947) from Radcliffe College. She completed a degree in library science in 1953 at the University of Toronto, and worked as a library cataloger at Carleton University, Ottawa, for several years thereafter. She moved to the University of Indiana library in 1957, and completed her Ph.D. there in 1962. Her first book of poems, *East Coast*, was published in 1951, and she has produced, over the years, a half-dozen volumes of poetry as well as a novel (*The Sisters* [1974]). She has been twice recognized by the Canada Council with Senior Artist Awards (1971, 1976). Her professional career shifted from the library to the classroom in 1971, when she became a professor at the University of Saskatchewan.

Edwin Brock (b. 1927)   Born in London, Brock served two years in the Royal Navy. He was a police officer when he completed his first poetry collection, *An Attempt at Exorcism* (1959). Influenced by American confessional poets, Brock writes about family relationships, childhood memories, and sometimes shifts into the linguistic mode of an advertising copywriter (which he became in 1959). Suggesting that all poetry is to some extent autobiographical, Brock argues "that most activity is an attempt to define oneself in one way or another: for me poetry, and only poetry, has provided this self-defining act." His works include over a dozen poetry collections; a novel, *The Little White God* (1962); and an autobiography, *Here. Now. Always.* (1977).

Gwendolyn Brooks (b. 1917)   Brooks was born in Topeka, Kansas, attended public schools in Chicago, and graduated from Wilson Junior College in 1936. Her poetic talent was recognized when she attended a poetry workshop at Chicago's Southside Community Art Center. Shortly after, she published her first book of poems, *A Street in Bronzeville* (1945). She soon established her reputation as a major poet and won many honors, including the Pulitzer Prize for poetry in 1950. No African American woman before her had ever achieved such critical acclaim as a poet. While her poetry has always focused on the hardships and joys of being poor and black in America, she steadily moved away from the apolitical integrationist views of her early years until, by the 1960s, she had become a passionate advocate of African American consciousness and activism. Besides reworking traditional forms such as the ballad and sonnet, Brooks achieves great power in many of her poems by juxtaposing formal speech with black vernacular. Among her other works are *Annie Allen* (1949), *The Bean Eaters* (1960), *In the Mecca* (1968), and *To Disembark* (1981).

Robert Browning (1812–1889)   Born in London, Browning attended a private school and was later tutored at home. After one year as a student of Greek at the University of London, he moved with his family to Hatcham, where he studied, wrote poetry, and practiced writing for the theater. In 1845, he began exchanging poems and letters with the already famous poet Elizabeth Barrett; they eloped in 1846. They moved to Italy, where Browning completed most of his work. When Elizabeth died in 1861, he returned to England and began to establish his own reputation. He is noted especially for his fine dramatic monologues in which a wide range of characters reveal the complexity of human belief and passion. His many volumes of poetry include *Dramatis Personae* (1864), and *The Ring and the Book* (1868–1869).

Marianne Burke (b. 1957)   Born in Poughkeepsie, New York, Marianne Burke started writing poetry in her sophomore year at Vassar. She went on to Stanford University, where she earned an M.A. She won writing fellowships to both

Yaddo (1991) and McDowell (1992), and has published her poems in various magazines, including the *Southern Poetry Review,* the *Threepenny Review,* and the *New Yorker.* Until recently she worked in the *New Yorker*'s editorial department. She lives in New York City. When asked to comment about her work she pointed out that "one of my earliest teachers, the poet William Heyen, used to say that it was possible to write too much. I'm just beginning to understand what he means. For instance, my poem 'Funeral Home' took two years to write. I needed that much time to write both feelingly and impersonally about my mother's death. Having lost both my parents at too early an age, death is one of my favorite subjects. I don't write poems to merely record my losses or to open old wounds, but to recover some of life's sweetness and mystery."

Robert Burns (1759–1796) Born in Scotland to a family of poor tenant farmers, Burns was working in the fields with his father by age twelve. During these early years, the family moved often in fruitless attempts to improve its lot. Although Burns received formal education only intermittently, he read widely on his own. After the death of his father, Burns and his brother worked vainly to make their farm pay, an effort Burns was able to abandon when his first volume of poetry, *Poems, Chiefly in the Scottish Dialect* (1786) brought him overnight fame. One result of this fame was his appointment as an excise officer, a position that gave him some financial security while he continued to write poetry. Burns's humble origins instilled in him a lifelong sympathy for the poor and downtrodden, the rebels and iconoclasts, as well as a disdain for religion, particularly Calvinism and what he considered the hypocrisy of its "devout" ministers.

Robert Olen Butler, Jr. (b. 1945) Born in Granite City, Illinois, Butler attended Northwestern University as a theater major (B.S., 1967) and then switched to playwriting at the University of Iowa (M.A., 1969). He rose to the rank of sergeant in the Army Military Intelligence while serving in Vietnam (1969–1972). There he became a fluent speaker of the language and came to understand and honor Vietnamese culture. In 1972 he married the poet Marilyn Geller—they have one child. After the usual collection of odd jobs, including steel mill labor, taxi driving, and substitute teaching in high schools, Butler joined Fairfield Publications and worked on such trade publications as *Electronic News.* He became editor-in-chief of *Energy User News* in 1975. Although his first published novel, *The Alleys of Eden* (1981), was rejected twenty-one times before it was finally published, it was well received and even nominated for a number of literary prizes. *Sun Dogs* (1982), as did his first novel, makes use of Butler's Vietnam experiences, and his collection of short stories, *A Good Scent from a Strange Mountain* (1992), reveals his remarkable ability to identify with the Vietnamese refugees trying to remake their lives in the United States. In a review of Butler's first novel, the writer praised Butler's "ability to catch tiny shifts of feeling, momentary estrangements, sudden dislocations of mood—a tool as valuable to the novelist as a scalpel to the surgeon." A *Good Scent from a Strange Mountain* was awarded the 1993 Pulitzer Prize for fiction.

George Gordon, Lord Byron (1788–1824)   Born in London of an aristocratic family, Byron was educated at the best grammar schools and at Cambridge. He early became a public figure, as much for the notoriety of his personal life as for the popularity of his irreverent, satiric poetry. Among his scandalous affairs, the one he was rumored to have had with his half-sister forced him into European exile in 1816. His political life was equally flamboyant: he began his career in the House of Lords with a speech defending the working classes and he met his death in Greece as the result of a fever he contracted while fighting for Greek independence. Byron published a volume of poetry while at Cambridge, but fame and popularity came with later volumes of poems, notably *Childe Harold's Pilgrimage* (1812–1818) and *Don Juan* (1819–1824). Despite Byron's acknowledged literary greatness and popularity, he was deemed morally unfit for burial in Westminster Abbey.

Thomas Campion (1567–1620)   Campion spent his early childhood in London, studied at Cambridge, then returned to London in 1586 to study law. It appears that Campion served, for a short time, as a soldier in France. In 1595, he published a collection of Latin poems, *Poemata*. After the publication of this volume, he apparently went abroad to study medicine and, later, music (though it is not known when or where). His first volume of English poems, *A Book of Ayres*, appeared in 1601; the other three volumes appeared between 1601 and 1617. Campion also wrote masques for presentation at court, often composing the music for his own lyrics. Toward the end of his life, he wrote a treatise on music that became a standard text.

Raymond Carver (1938–1989)   Carver was born in Clatskanie, Oregon, the son of a sawmill worker and a mother who did odd jobs. He graduated from high school at eighteen and was married and the father of two children before he was twenty. The following years were difficult as he struggled to develop a writing career while supporting a family. While at Chico State College (now California State University, Chico), Carver took a creative writing course that profoundly affected him. He went on to earn a B.A. degree (1963) from Humboldt State College in Eureka; he spent the following year studying writing at the University of Iowa. As he became known, he began to lecture on English and creative writing at various universities, including the University of Iowa Writer's Workshop. He taught at Goddard College in Vermont and was from 1980 to 1983 professor of English at Syracuse University. In 1983, he received the Mildred and Harold Straus living award, which allowed him for the next five years to devote himself full-time to writing. His first collection of short stories, *Will You Please Be Quiet, Please* (1976), was nominated for the National Book Award. Other short story collections include *What We Talk about When We Talk about Love* (1981) and *Cathedral* (1984). He also published five volumes of poems, among them *Near Klamath* (1968), *Ultramarine* (1986), and *A New Path to the Waterfall* (1989), his last book. During the last years of his life, Carver lived with the poet and short story writer Tess Gallagher, whom he married shortly before his death.

Kate Chopin (1851–1904)   Born Kate O'Flaherty in St. Louis, Missouri, Chopin was raised by her mother, grandmother, and great-grandmother, all widows, after her father's death when she was four. In 1870, following her graduation from Sacred Heart Convent, she married Oscar Chopin and moved to New Orleans, where she became a housewife and mother (she had six children). Upon her husband's death in 1882, she returned to her mother's home in St. Louis and began her career as a writer. Her first novel, *At Fault* (1890), and her stories, collected in *Bayou Folk* (1894) and *A Night in Acadie* (1897), gained her a reputation as a vivid chronicler of the lives of Creoles and Acadians ("Cajuns") in Louisiana. Many of these stories explore a female protagonist's attempts to achieve self-fulfillment. Her novel *The Awakening* (1899) is probably her most ambitious exploration of this theme. It is the story of a woman whose awakening to her passion and inner self leads her to adultery and suicide. The storm of controversy with which this work was met virtually ended Chopin's literary career.

Lucille Clifton (b. 1936)   Born in Depew, New York, Clifton attended Howard University (1953–1955) and Fredonia State Teachers College. She worked as a claims clerk in the New York State Division of Employment, Buffalo (1958–1960), and as literature assistant in the Office of Education in Washington, D.C. (1960–1971). In 1969, she received the YM-YWHA Poetry Center Discovery Award, and her first collection, *Good Times*, was selected as one of the ten best books of 1969 by the *New York Times*. From 1971 to 1974 she was poet-in-residence at Coppin State College in Baltimore, and in 1979 she was named poet laureate of the state of Maryland. She has written many collections for children and a free-verse chronicle of five generations of her family, *Generations: A Memoir* (1976). Her most recent volume of poetry is *Quilting: Poems 1987–1990* (1991). Noted for celebrating ordinary people and everyday things, Clifton has said "I am a black woman poet, and I sound like one."

Stephen Crane (1871–1900)   Born in Newark, New Jersey, the fourteenth and youngest child of a Methodist minister who died when Stephen was nine years old, Crane was raised by his strong-minded mother. His brief college career, first at Lafayette College and then at Syracuse University, was dominated by his interest in baseball; he left college after two semesters, and moved on to a bohemian life in New York City. There he wandered through the slums, observing and developing a strong sympathy for the underclass of boozers and prostitutes that inhabited the Bowery. His first novel, *Maggie: A Girl of the Streets* (1893), described the inevitable consequences of grinding poverty—but no publisher would take a chance on Crane's bleak and biting vision. He published it at his own expense, but it found no audience. Without any military experience, and at the age of twenty-four, Crane produced *The Red Badge of Courage* (1895), a novel that made him famous and became an American classic. For the remainder of his life, he traveled about the world as a writer and war correspondent. He died of a tubercular infection in Badenweiler, Germany. Despite the brevity of his writing career, Crane left behind a substantial volume of work that includes a number of brilliant short stories and innovative poems.

Victor Hernández Cruz (b. 1949)   Cruz was born in Aguas Buenas, Puerto Rico, and came with his family to New York City in 1954. He recalls, "My family life was full of music, guitars and conga drums, maracas and songs. . . . Even when it was five below zero in New York [my mother] sang warm tropical ballads." By 1966, he had already completed a collection of verse, *Papo Got His Gun*, and in 1969 published *Snaps*. He has edited *Umbra* magazine in New York, lectured at the University of California, Berkeley, and taught at San Francisco State University. Cruz says he writes in three languages: Spanish, English, and Bilingual. "From the mixture a totally new language emerges, an intense collision, not just of words, but of attitudes." His other works include *Mainland* (1973), *Topicalizations* (1976), and *Rhythm, Content, and Flavor: New Selected Poems* (1989).

Countee Cullen (1903–1946)   Born Countee L. Porter in New York City, Cullen was adopted by the Reverend and Mrs. Cullen in 1918 and raised in Harlem. He was extraordinarily precocious, and by 1920 his poems had been published in *Poetry*, the *Nation*, and *Harper's*. He published his famous poem "Heritage" in 1925, the year he graduated from New York University. After earning an M.A. in English from Harvard in 1926, he taught French in a junior high school and was assistant editor of the National Urban League's *Opportunity: Journal of Negro Life*. Cullen, along with Langston Hughes and Jean Toomer, was a central figure in the Harlem Renaissance of the 1920s. He received a Guggenheim Fellowship in 1929. In addition to five volumes of poetry, he published a novel, *One Way to Heaven* (1932), which deals with the interaction between upper- and lower-class African Americans in Harlem in the 1920s.

E. E. Cummings (1894–1962)   Born in Cambridge, Massachusetts, Edward Estlin Cummings attended Harvard (B.A., 1915; M.A. 1916), served as a volunteer ambulance driver in France during World War I, was imprisoned for three months in a French detention camp, served in the United States Army (1918–1919), then studied art and painting in Paris (1920–1924). His prose narrative, *The Enormous Room* (1922), a recollection of his imprisonment, brought instant acclaim. Several volumes of poetry followed. His experiments with punctuation, line division, and capitalization make his work immediately recognizable. In a letter to young poets published in a high school newspaper, Cummings said, "[N]othing is quite so easy as using words like somebody else. We all of us do exactly this nearly all the time—and whenever we do it, we're not poets."

Kate Daniels (b. 1953)   Born in Richmond, Virginia, Daniels was educated at the University of Virginia (B.A., 1975) and Columbia University (M.A., 1977). She has taught at the University of Virginia, the University of Massachusetts, and Louisiana State University. Since 1979, she has been coeditor of *Poetry East*. Her first collection of poems, *The White Wave* (1984), won the Agnes Lynch Starrett Poetry Prize of the University of Pittsburgh in 1983. In 1985 she was awarded a fellowship from the Mary Ingraham Bunting Institute of Harvard University for her literary biography of the poet Muriel Rukeyser (1984). Her works have been published by many journals, among them the *Virginia Quarterly Review*, the *Massachusetts Review*, and the *New England Review*.

Emily Dickinson (1830–1886)   Dickinson, one of three children, was born in Amherst, Massachusetts. Her father was a prominent lawyer. Except for one year away at a nearby college and a trip with her sister to Washington, D.C., to visit her father when he was serving in Congress, she lived out her life, unmarried, in her parents' home. During her trip to Washington, she met the Reverend Charles Wadsworth, a married man, whom she came to characterize as her "dearest earthly friend." Little is known of this relationship except that Dickinson's feelings for Wadsworth were strong. In 1862 Wadsworth moved to San Francisco, an event that coincided with a period of Dickinson's intense poetic creativity. Also in that year, she initiated a literary correspondence with the critic T. W. Higginson, to whom she sent some of her poems for his reactions. Higginson, although he recognized her talent, was puzzled by her startling originality, and urged her to write more conventionally. Unable to do so, she concluded, we may surmise, that she would never see her poems through the press. In fact, only seven of her poems were published while she was alive, none of them with her consent. After her death, the extraordinary richness of her imaginative life came to light with the discovery of her more than one thousand lyrics.

Joan Didion (b. 1934)   A fifth-generation Californian, Didion was born in Sacramento and raised in the great central plain of California, an area she often describes nostalgically in her work. As an undergraduate English major at the University of California, Berkeley, she won an essay prize sponsored by *Vogue* magazine. As a result, *Vogue* hired her, and for eight years, she lived in New York City, while she rose to associate features editor. She published her first novel, *Run River*, in 1963 and in the same year, married the writer John Gregory Dunne. In 1964 the couple returned to California, where they remained for twenty-five years. Although Didion wrote three more novels, her reputation rests on her essays collected as *Slouching toward Bethlehem* (1968) and *The White Album* (1979). In addition to her work as a columnist, essayist, and fiction writer, she has collaborated with her husband on a number of screenplays. She has focused her trenchant powers of observation in two documentary, book-length studies: *Salvador* (1983) and *Miami* (1987). Her reputation as a prose stylist is reflected in a comment by one critic who asserts that "nobody writes better English prose than Joan Didion. Try to rearrange one of her sentences, and you've realized that the sentence was inevitable, a hologram." Didion characterizes herself as uneasy with abstractions: "I would try to think about the Great Dialectic and I would find myself thinking instead about how the light was falling through the window in an apartment I had on the North Side. How it was hitting the floor."

John Donne (1572–1631)   Born in London into a prosperous Roman Catholic family of tradespeople, at a time when England was staunchly anti-Catholic, Donne was forced to leave Oxford without a degree because of his religion. He studied law and, at the same time, read widely in theology in an attempt to decide whether the Roman or the Anglican church was the true Catholic church, a decision he was not able to make for many years. In the meantime, he became known as a witty man of the world and the author of original, often dense, erotic poems. Donne left his law studies, participated in two naval expeditions, and then became secretary to a powerful noble, a job he lost when he was briefly sent to prison for secretly marrying his patron's niece. In 1615, at the age of forty-two, Donne accepted ordination in the Anglican church. He quickly earned a reputation as one of the greatest preachers of his time. He was Dean of St. Paul's from 1621 until his death. In his later years, Donne rejected the poetry of his youth.

Paul Laurence Dunbar (1872–1906)   The son of former slaves, Dunbar was born in Dayton, Ohio, where he graduated from Dayton High School (1891) and worked for two years as an elevator operator. In 1894, he worked in Chicago at the World's Columbian Exhibition. His first verse collection, *Oak and Ivy*, was published in 1893. William Dean Howells, an eminent editor, author, and critic, encouraged him to write and had him join a Lecture Bureau in 1896. Dunbar read his own works in the United States and traveled to Europe in 1897. While Dunbar maintained that African American poetry was not much different from white (and wrote many poems in standard English), he often wrote poems in black dialect that seemed to cater to the racial stereotypes of his white audience. He died of tuberculosis in 1906. His complete works appear in *The Dunbar Reader* (1975).

Lars Eighner (b. 1948)   Born in Corpus Christi, Texas, Eighner was two when his parents divorced and he and his mother, a teacher of the deaf, moved to Houston. He became a student at the University of Texas in 1966 but dropped out after three years and took a job as a counselor in a drug-crisis center in Austin. In 1979, he was hired as an attendant at Austin State Hospital but lost his job after quarreling with his supervisor. Unable to support himself by writing stories, he was finally evicted from his Austin home and became a homeless itinerant. By 1990 Eighner, who has described himself as "a homosexual pornographer," had many stories published in obscure gay publications. In 1991, he became more widely known when the *Threepenny Review* published two of his essays on homelessness. The publication in 1993 of *Travels with Lizbeth,* an account of his three years of homelessness, was widely and enthusiastically reviewed. He is the author of two collections of stories, *Bayou Boy* and *B.M.O.C.* (both 1993). Eighner now lives with Lizbeth, his dog, in an apartment in Austin, Texas.

T. S. Eliot (1888–1965)   Thomas Stearns Eliot was born in St. Louis, Missouri. His father was president of the Hydraulic Press Brick Company, his mother a teacher, social worker, and writer. Educated in private academies, Eliot earned two philosophy degrees at Harvard (B.A., 1909; M.S., 1910). After graduate study in Paris and England, he worked for eight years as a clerk in Lloyd's Bank in London, and became a naturalized British citizen in 1927. He was editor, then director of Faber & Gwyer Publishers (later Faber & Faber) from 1925 to 1965, and spent time in the United States as a visiting lecturer and scholar. Admirers and detractors agree that Eliot was the most imposing and influential poet writing between the world wars. His poems "The Love Song of J. Alfred Prufrock" (1917) and *The Waste Land* (1922) are among his earliest and most famous. Acknowledging his dependence on a preexisting cultural tradition, Eliot explained: "The existing order is complete before the new work arrives; for order to persist after the supervention of novelty, the whole existing order must be altered." Eliot also wrote plays, including *Murder in the Cathedral* (1935) and *The Cocktail Party* (1950). The long-running Broadway musical *Cats* is based on his 1939 verse collection, *Old Possum's Book of Practical Cats.* He won the Nobel Prize for literature in 1948.

Harlan Ellison (b. 1934)   Born in Cleveland, Ohio, Ellison published his first story when he was thirteen. He left Ohio State University after two years and worked at a variety of odd jobs while establishing himself as a writer. In a career spanning over thirty-seven years, he has written or edited fifty-eight books, more than twelve hundred stories, essays, reviews, articles, motion picture scripts, and teleplays. He has won the Hugo award eight and a half times, the Nebula three times, the Edgar Allan Poe award of the Mystery Writers of America twice, the Bram Stoker award of Horror Writers of America twice, the World Fantasy Award, the British Fantasy Award, and the Silver Pen award for journalism from P.E.N. He is the only scenarist in Hollywood ever to have won the Writers Guild of America award for Most Outstanding Teleplay four times for solo work. His latest books are *The Harlan Ellison Hornbook*, a thirty-five-year retrospective of his work; *The Essential Ellison;* and *The City on the Edge of Forever*, the first book publication of his *Star Trek* script in its original (not aired) version. He lives with his wife, Susan, in the Lost Aztec Temple of Mars somewhere in the Los Angeles area.

Louise Erdrich (b. 1954)   Born in Little Falls, Minnesota, Erdrich grew up in Wahepton, North Dakota, a member of the Turtle Mountain Band of Chippewa. Her grandfather was for many years tribal chair of the reservation where her parents taught in the Bureau of Indian Affairs School. She attended Dartmouth College, earning a degree in anthropology (1976) as well as prizes for fiction and poetry, including the American Academy of Poets Prize. She returned to North Dakota for a brief period of teaching before going on to study creative writing at Johns Hopkins University (M.A., 1979). The following year, she returned to Dartmouth as a writer-in-residence. Her works have appeared in the *New England Review* and *Redbook* as well as such anthologies of Native American writing as *Earth Power Coming* and *That's What She Said: Contemporary Poetry and Fiction by Native American Women*. She has published two collections of poems, *Jacklight* (1984) and *Baptism of Desire* (1989). Her novel *Love Medicine* (1984) won the National Book Critics' Circle Award. *Beet Queen* (1986) and *Tracks* (1988) extend the histories of families dealt with in *Love Medicine*. In 1991, Erdrich and her husband, Michael Dorris, a professor of Native American Studies at Dartmouth, published *The Crown of Columbus*, a collaborative novel about Christopher Columbus's discovery of America. They have pledged to donate a part of their royalties to American Indian charities.

William Faulkner (1897–1962)   Faulkner was born in New Albany, Mississippi, and lived most of his life in Oxford, the seat of the University of Mississippi. Although he did not graduate from high school, he did attend the university as a special student from 1919 to 1921. During this period, he also worked as a janitor, a bank clerk, and a postmaster. His southern forebears had held slaves, served during the Civil War, endured the indignities of Reconstruction, fought duels, even wrote the occasional romance of the old South. Faulkner mined these generous layers of history in his work. He created the mythical Yoknapatawpha County in northern Mississippi, and traced the destinies of its inhabitants from the colonial era to the middle of the twentieth century in such novels as *The Sound and the Fury* (1929), *Light in August*

(1932), and *Absalom, Absalom!* (1936). Further, Faulkner described the decline of the pre–Civil War aristocratic families and the rise of mean-spirited money grubbers in a trilogy: *The Hamlet* (1940), *The Town* (1957), *The Mansion* (1959). Recognition came late, and Faulkner fought a constant battle to keep afloat financially. During the 1940s, he wrote screenplays in Hollywood. But, finally, his achievement brought him the Nobel Prize in 1950.

James Fenton (b. 1949)   Born in Lincoln, England, Fenton earned a B.A. (1970) from Magdalen College, Oxford University. His earliest volumes of verse appeared during his undergraduate years: *Our Western Furniture* (1968) and *Put Thou Thy Tears into My Bottle* (1969). He wrote for the *New Statesman* and *Nation* and continued to publish relatively few but always finely crafted poems. Almost half of his collection *Children in Exile: Poems 1968– 1984* is light verse, but often those poems move from whimsey to horror. He won the 1984 Geoffrey Faber Memorial Prize for his poetry. He translated the lyrics of Verdi's opera *Rigoletto*, controversially setting the action in the 1950s New York Mafia world. He accompanied Redmond O'Hanlon on a remarkable trip to Borneo that served as the source for O'Hanlon's comic travel book *Into the Heart of Borneo* (1984). *Children in Exile's* appearance in the United States (1985) generated an enthusiastic response to the relatively unknown British poet. More recently, Fenton has published a collection of essays, *The Snap Revolution* (1986) and a travel book with political overtones, *All the Wrong Places: Adrift in the Politics of the Pacific Rim* (1988).

Lawrence Ferlinghetti (b. 1919)   Born Lawrence Ferling, this irreverent writer restored his original family name in 1954. He earned a B.A. in journalism from the University of North Carolina in 1941, became lieutenant commander in the U.S. Naval Reserve during World War II, then received graduate degrees from Columbia and the Sorbonne. He worked as a translator of French before rising to prominence in the "beat" poetry movement of the 1950s, which sought to rejuvenate and popularize poetry. His controversial work drew raves from many critics, even though one critic called it "real jivy, real groovy, all that—but ultimately kind of stupid." Known chiefly for his poetry, he has written a novel, *Her* (1960), and some unsympathetically reviewed plays. As a successful publisher (he cofounded the San Francisco bookstore, City Lights, and the two publishing enterprises, City Lights Books and the Pocket Poets Series), Ferlinghetti appreciates the irony of his ascendance in a system he has repudiated. His early work, *A Coney Island of the Mind* (1958), remains a best-selling poetry collection.

Carolyn Forché (b. 1950)   Born in Detroit, Forché earned a B.A. in international relations and creative writing at Michigan State University in 1972. After graduate study at Bowling Green State University in 1975, she taught at the University of Virginia, the University of Arkansas, New York University, Vassar, and Columbia. She won the Yale Series of Younger Poets Award in 1976 for her first collection, *Gathering the Tribes*. Other honors include a Guggenheim Fellowship and the Lamont Award (1981). Forché was a journalist for Amnesty International in El Salvador in 1983 and Beirut correspondent for the National Public Radio program "All Things Considered." Her collection *The Country between Us* (1981) embodies an unusual combination of political passion and technical proficiency.

Robert Frost (1874–1963)   Frost was born in San Francisco but from the age of ten lived in New England. He attended Dartmouth College briefly, then became a teacher, but soon decided to resume his formal training and enrolled at Harvard. He left Harvard after two years without a degree, and for several years supported himself and his growing family by tending a farm his grandfather bought for him. When he was not farming, he read and wrote intensively, though he received little recognition. Discouraged by his lack of success, he sold the farm and moved his family to England, where he published his first volumes of poetry, *A Boy's Will* (1913) and *North of Boston* (1914). After three years in England, Frost returned to America a recognized poet. Later volumes, notably *Mountain Interval* (1916), *New Hampshire* (1923), *West-Running Brook* (1928), and *A Further Range* (1936), won Frost numerous awards, including two Pulitzer Prizes, and a wide popularity. By the time he delivered his poem, "The Gift Outright," at the inauguration of President John F. Kennedy in 1962, Frost had achieved the status of unofficial poet laureate of America, widely revered and beloved for his folksy manner and seemingly artless, accessible poems.

Tess Gallagher (b. 1943)   Born in Port Angeles, Washington, to a mother and father who were both loggers, Gallagher was educated at the University of Washington, where she earned a B.A. (1963) and an M.A. (1970). She received an M.F.A. (1974) from the University of Iowa. She has taught creative writing at various universities, including the University of Montana, Missoula; the University of Arizona, Tucson; and Syracuse University in New York. Her 1976 volume of poetry, *Instructions to the Double*, won the Elliston Award for the "best book of poetry published by a small press" in 1977. Among other honors, she received the *American Poetry Review* award for best poem of 1980. Gallagher has been a prolific writer in all genres. Beginning with *Outside* (1974), she has published some half dozen volumes of poems, the most recent being *Amplitude: New and Selected Poems* (1987) and *Moon Crossing Bride* (1992). *A Concert of Tenses* (1986) is a collection of her essays on poetry. She has written a teleplay, *The Wheel* (1970), and a screenplay, *The Night Belongs to the Police* (1982). She has also been a columnist for the *American Poetry Review* and a contributor of stories, poems, and essays to many periodicals.

Gallagher lived with the writer Raymond Carver during the last decade of his life and married him shortly before his death.

Willard Gaylin (b. 1925) Gaylin was educated at Harvard University (A.B., 1947), Western Reserve (now Case Western Reserve) University (M.D., 1951), and Columbia University, where, after earning a certificate in psychoanalytic medicine, he served as a faculty member (1956). A practicing psychiatrist and psychoanalyst, he is also cofounder and president of the Hastings Center, which researches ethical issues in the life sciences. Among his publications are *In the Service of Their Country: War Resisters in Prison* (1970), *Feelings: Our Vital Signs* (1979), *The Killing of Bonnie Garland: A Question of Justice* (1982), *The Rage Within: Anger in Modern Life* (1984), and *Adam and Eve and Pinocchio: On Being and Becoming Human* (1990).

Molly Giles (b. 1942) Giles was born and educated in California. She married in 1961, divorced in 1974, and is the mother of two children. She attended the University of California, Berkeley, and San Francisco State University, where she received a B.A. (1978) and an M.A. (1980). From 1980 to 1986, she taught creative writing at San Francisco State University. Her works have been published in the *North American Review*, the *New England Review*, *Redbook*, and *Playgirl*. *Rough Translations* (1985) is a collection of her short stories told mostly from a woman's point of view.

Allen Ginsberg (b. 1926) Ginsberg was born in Newark, New Jersey, earned an A.B. from Columbia in 1948, and became one of the most influential writers of the 1950s as the preeminent "beat" poet. His long poem *Howl* (1956), formally influenced by Walt Whitman's work, cried out against a brutal, stifling society. Because of graphic, sexual language in *Howl*, San Francisco police declared it obscene and arrested its publisher, Lawrence Ferlinghetti. In a well-publicized trial, Judge Clayton W. Horn ruled the work not obscene. A lifelong consciousness-raiser, Ginsberg helped create the "flower power" movement of the 1960s, cultivated meditation and mantra-chanting, and converted to Buddhism in 1972. While Ginsberg was largely ignored or attacked by the mainstream literary establishment in the 1950s and 1960s, in 1974 he won a National Book Award for *The Fall of America: Poems of These States 1965–1971* (1972). For all his literary ground breaking, Ginsberg considers himself a follower of Thoreau, Emerson, and Whitman, carrying "old-time American transcendentalist individualism ... into the 20th century."

Dana Gioia (b. 1950) Born in Los Angeles, Gioia (pronounced *Joy-uh*) grew up in a working-class family, his father a cab driver and his mother a telephone operator. He received a B.A. with high honors and an M.B.A. from Stanford University (1973; 1977) and an M.A. from Harvard University (1975). He went to work for General Foods Corporation in 1977, first as manager of new business development and, since 1988, as marketing manager. In addition to contributing poems and reviews to many magazines, he has served since 1985 on the board of directors of Wesleyan University Writers Conference. His publications include three volumes of poetry, *Summer* (1983), *Daily Horoscope* (1986), and *The Gods of Winter* (1991).

Nikki Giovanni (b. 1943)   Born Yolande Cornelia Giovanni, Jr., in Knoxville, Tennessee, daughter of a probation officer and a social worker, Giovanni graduated with honors from Fisk University in 1967. She attended the University of Pennsylvania School of Social Work and Columbia School of the Arts, was assistant professor of black studies at Queens College (1968), associate professor of English at Rutgers University (1968–1970), and founded a publishing firm, Niktom, in 1970. Giovanni's early work reflected her social activism as an African American college student in the 1960s. Later, she fell outside the mainstream of African American poetry, concentrating on the individual struggle for fulfillment rather than the collective struggle for black empowerment. Her books include *Black Feeling, Black Talk* (1970), *My House* (1972), and *The Women and the Men* (1975). A collection of essays, *Sacred Cows . . . and Other Edibles*, appeared in 1988.

Emma Goldman (1869–1940)   Socialist, anarchist, and feminist, Goldman was born in Russia and emigrated in 1885 to New York City, where she worked in clothing factories and began writing and lecturing on behalf of reform movements, including feminism and birth control. In 1893, she was arrested for inciting a riot after urging a group of unemployed workers to take food by force. In 1919, after serving time in prison for agitating against military conscription and U.S. involvement in World War I, she was deported to Russia, whose revolution in 1917 she had hailed as the dawn of a just society. After two years, she left Russia to travel in a number of countries, including Germany, England, and Canada. In two books, *My Disillusionment with Russia* (1923) and *My Further Disillusionment with Russia* (1924), Goldman announced her break with the Russian regime. She spent her final years in Canada, anxiously awaiting word on her request to end her exile. The request was denied. She died in Canada and is buried in Chicago. Other works include *Anarchism and Other Essays* (1911) and the autobiography *Living My Life* (1931).

Nadine Gordimer (b. 1923)   Gordimer was born and spent her childhood in the gold-mining town of Springs, Transvaal, South Africa. Her father, a Jew who had emigrated to Africa at thirteen, was a jeweler; her mother was born in England. Educated privately at the University of Witwatersrand, Johannesburg, Gordimer was a rebellious child, both as student and daughter. She disliked the convent school her parents sent her to and refused to follow the conventional path—school, low-level job, marriage—expected of white, middle-class women. She was an early reader and writer, winning her first writing prize at fourteen. By this time, she had begun to take a keen interest in politics and the oppression of black South Africans. She ultimately came to reject the system of apartheid, and despite her frequent travels, has continued to make Johannesburg her home. She has made writing her career (she is a wife and mother as well) and has lectured at many American universities, including Harvard, Princeton, Northwestern, Columbia, and Tulane. She has received many prizes and honors, among them honorary degrees from Harvard and Yale (both 1987) and the New School for Social Research (1988). In 1991, she was awarded the Nobel Prize for literature. Among her many novels are *The Lying Days* (1953), *A World of Strangers* (1958), *Burger's Daughter* (1979), and *A Sport of Nature* (1987). Her collections of short stories include *Face to Face* (1949), *The Soft Voice of the Serpent* (1952), *Not for Publication* (1965), *Selected Stories* (1975), and *Something Out There* (1984). Her nonfiction works include *South African Writing Today* (1967; coeditor), *The Black Interpreters: Notes on African Writing* (1973), *Lifetimes under Apartheid* (1986), and *The Essential Gesture: Politics and Places* (1988). Her most recent publications are *My Son's Story* (1990), about apartheid and politics in South Africa; and *Jump: And Other Stories* (1991).

Thomas Hardy (1840–1928)   Hardy was born near Dorchester, in southeastern England (on which he based the "Wessex" of many of his novels and poems). Hardy worked for the ecclesiastical architect John Hicks from 1856 to 1861. He then moved to London to practice architecture, and took evening classes at King's College for six years. In 1867, he gave up architecture to become a full-time writer, and after writing short stories and poems found success as a novelist. *The Mayor of Casterbridge* (1886) and *Tess of the d'Urbervilles* (1891) reveal Hardy's concern for victims of circumstance and his appeal to humanitarian sympathy in readers. After his novel *Jude the Obscure* (1896) was strongly criticized, Hardy set aside prose fiction and returned to poetry—a genre in which he was most prolific and successful after he reached the age of seventy.

Nathaniel Hawthorne (1804–1864)   The son of a merchant sea captain who died in a distant port when Nathaniel was four, Hawthorne grew up in genteel poverty in Massachusetts and Maine. His earliest American ancestor, the magistrate William Hathorne, ordered the whipping of a Quaker woman in Salem. William's son John was one of the three judges at the Salem witch trials of 1692. Aware of his family's role in colonial America, Hawthorne returned to Salem after graduating from Bowdoin College (where future president Franklin Pierce was a friend and classmate), determined to be a writer. He recalled and destroyed copies of his first novel, the mediocre *Fanshawe* (1828). His short stories, often set in Puritan America, revealed a moral complexity that had not troubled his righteous ancestors William and John. His success as an author allowed him to marry Sophia Peabody in 1842 (after a four-year engagement). Though his stories were critically praised, they did not earn much money, and, in 1846, he used his political connections with the Democratic party to obtain a job at the Salem custom house. His dismissal in 1849 (when the Democrats lost) produced both anger and resolve. The result was a great American novel, *The Scarlet Letter* (1850), which made him famous and improved his fortune. Although he was friendly with Emerson and his circle of optimistic transcendentalists (some of whom established the utopian social community at Brook Farm), Hawthorne's vision of the human condition was considerably darker. Herman Melville dedicated *Moby Dick* to Hawthorne, and characterized him as a man who could say "No" in thunder.

Robert Hayden (1913–1980)   Born in Detroit, Hayden studied at Wayne State University and the University of Michigan (M.A., 1944). In 1946, he joined the faculty of Fisk University. He left Fisk in 1968 for a professorship at the University of Michigan, where he remained until his death. He produced some ten volumes of poetry but did not receive the acclaim many thought he deserved until late in life, with the publication of *Words in the Mourning Time: Poems* (1971). In the 1960s, he aroused some hostility from African Americans who wanted him to express more militancy. But Hayden did not want to be part of what he called a "kind of literary ghetto." He considered his own work "a form of prayer—a prayer for illumination, perfection."

Bessie Head (1937–1986)   Bessie Head was born in Pietermaritzburg, South Africa, the daughter of a racially mixed marriage. She was taken from her white mother and raised by foster parents until she was thirteen, and then placed in an orphanage; she overcame this difficult childhood and trained to be a primary-school teacher. After four years as a teacher, two years as a journalist, and a failed marriage in South Africa, she emigrated to Botswana where she lived for many years in deep poverty. She spent fifteen years in a refugee community at the Bamangwato Development Farm before winning Botswanian citizenship. At the development farm, she continued her distinguished career as a writer, though she had to plead for small advances from her publisher in order to buy paper to write on. Her writing brought her recognition and prominence, and she represented Botswana at international writers' conferences in the United States, Canada, Europe, and Australia. She died of hepatitis at age forty-nine. Along with several collections of short stories, she published three novels and two historical chronicles of African life. In an interview, Head acknowledged "that the regularity of her life in the refugee community brought her the peace of mind she sought: 'In South Africa, all my life I lived in shattered little bits. All those shattered bits began to grow together here. . . . I have a peace against which all the turmoil is worked out!' "

Anthony Hecht (b. 1923)   Born in New York City, Hecht attended Bard College (B.A., 1944). After three years in the U.S. Army, serving in Europe and Japan, he continued his education at Columbia University (M.A., 1950). Hecht has taught at several universities, including the University of Rochester, where he was professor of poetry and rhetoric in 1967. He is presently a professor in the graduate school of Georgetown University. His awards include a 1951 Prix de Rome, and Guggenheim, Rockefeller, and Ford Foundation Fellowships, as well as the Bollingen Prize in Poetry. His first book of poetry, A *Summer of Stones* (1954), was followed by *Hard Hours* (1968), which won a Pulitzer Prize for poetry, *Millions of Strange Shadows* (1977), and *Venetian Vespers* (1979). His most recent collection of poems is *The Transparent Man* (1990). Hecht is also the author of a collection of critical essays, *Obbligati* (1986). Acclaimed for his technical expertise, Hecht was first devoted to traditional poetic forms, and his work was sometimes described as "baroque" and "courtly." More recently, his work has become less decorative.

Ernest Hemingway (1899–1961)   Born in Oak Park, Illinois, Hemingway became a cub reporter after high school. He was seriously wounded while serving as an ambulance driver in World War I. After the war, he lived in Paris, a member of a lively and productive expatriate community characterized by Gertrude Stein as "a lost generation." He lived an active life, not only as a writer, but as a war correspondent, big-game hunter, and fisherman. In such novels as *The Sun Also Rises* (1926), *A Farewell to Arms* (1929), and *For Whom the Bell Tolls* (1940), his fictional characters exhibit a passion for courage and integrity, for grace under pressure. Hemingway's spare, unembellished style reinforced his central theme that one must confront danger and live honorably. He won the Nobel Prize in 1954. In 1961, unable to write because treatment for mental instability affected his memory, he killed himself with the shotgun he had so often used as a hunter.

William Heyen (b. 1940)   William Heyen's father immigrated from Germany in 1928 and made a living as a bartender and carpenter. Heyen was born in Brooklyn but grew up on suburban Long Island. He attended the State University of New York at Brockport (B.S.Ed., 1961), where, at six feet, four inches, he played basketball and twice earned All-American recognition in soccer. He received a Ph.D. from Ohio University in 1967 and joined the faculty of his alma mater at Brockport the same year. He won a Fulbright grant to Germany (1971–1972). Heyen married in 1962 and has two children. His father's two brothers remained in Germany, fought on the Nazi side, and were killed during World War II. His family history clearly marked Heyen powerfully—three of the dozen books of poems he has produced (*The Swastika Poems* [1977], *Erika: Poems of the Holocaust* [1984], and, with Daniel Brodsky, *Falling from Heaven: Holocaust Poems of a Jew and a Gentile* [1991]) deal with Nazi Germany and the Holocaust. As well, Heyen's passion for nature is manifested in *Pterodactyl Rose: Poems of Ecology* (1991). The work of this prolific poet has been repeatedly honored with prizes: among others, he won the Borestone Mountain poetry award in 1966, the annual *Ontario Review* poetry prize in 1978, and a Guggenheim Fellowship in 1977–1978. In addition to his poetry, which has appeared in over one hundred periodicals, Heyen has edited three anthologies of American poets and produced a novel, *Vic Holyfield and the Class of 1957* (1986).

Edward Hirsch (b. 1950)   Hirsch was born in Chicago and earned a B.A. from Grinnell College in Iowa (1972). With a Ph.D. from the University of Pennsylvania (1979), he joined the English department at Wayne State University in Detroit. He has won prizes for poetry from several bodies including the Academy of American Poets and the Ingram Merrill Foundation. He is a Fellow of the American Council of Learned Societies. In addition to poems, Hirsch has published articles and stories in such journals as the *New Yorker*, the *North American Review*, the *Partisan Review*, the *Nation*, and the *New Republic*. His first book of poetry, *For the Sleepwalkers*, appeared in 1981. Later books include *Wild Gratitude* (1986) and *The Night Parade* (1989). Asked about his work, Hirsch replied: "My goal is to write a few poems that are unforgettable. I love enchanted stories, magical realism, secret signs, and the great modern artists of childhood—Archille Gorky and Paul Klee. Jean Cocteau once said that the goal of every artist should be his own extremity. I want to write poems that are imaginative, astonishing, playful, mysterious, and extreme."

Linda Hogan (b. 1947)   Hogan was born in Denver, Colorado, and educated at the University of Colorado, where she received her M.A. in 1978. For a time, she supported herself with odd jobs and freelance writing. By 1980, her success as a writer led to her appointment as writer-in-residence for the states of Colorado and Oklahoma. In 1982 she became an assistant professor in the TRIBES program at Colorado College, Colorado Springs. She is now associate professor of American Indian studies at the University of Minnesota. In 1980, her play, *A Piece of Moon*, won the Five Civilized Tribes Playwriting Award. In 1983, she received the *Stand* magazine fiction award. Her writings include five volumes of poetry, *Calling Myself Home* (1979), *Daughters, I Love You* (1981), *Eclipse* (1983), *Seeing through the Sun* (1985), and *Savings* (1991), and two collections of stories, *That Horse* (1985) and *The Big Woman* (1987).

Gerard Manley Hopkins (1844–1889)   Raised in London, Hopkins won a scholarship to Balliol College, Oxford, where he studied classical literature. He converted to Roman Catholicism in 1866 and two years later entered the Jesuit Novitiate. In 1877, he was ordained as a Jesuit priest and served in missions in London, Liverpool, Oxford, and Glasgow until 1882. From 1884 to his death in 1889, he was professor of Greek at University College, Dublin. A technically innovative poet, Hopkins saw only three of his poems published during his lifetime, but gained posthumous recognition in 1918 when a friend (the Poet Laureate Robert Bridges) published his complete works. His early poems celebrate the beauty of God's world, but later works reflect his poor health and depression.

A. E. Housman (1859–1936)   Born in Fockbury, England, and an outstanding student, Alfred Edward Housman nonetheless failed his final examinations at Oxford in 1881 (possibly as a result of emotional chaos caused by his love for a male classmate). Working as a clerk in the Patent Office in London, he pursued classical studies on his own, earned an M.A., and was appointed to the Chair of Latin at University College, London. In 1910, he became professor of Latin at Cambridge, where he remained until his death in 1936. As a poet, Housman was concerned primarily with the fleetingness of love and the decay of youth. After his first collection, *A Shropshire Lad*, was rejected by several publishers, Housman published it at his own expense in 1896. It gained popularity during World War I, and his 1922 collection, *Last Poems*, was well received. In his lecture "The Name and Nature of Poetry" (1933), Housman argued that poetry should appeal to emotions rather than intellect. *More Poems* (1936) was published posthumously.

Pam Houston (b. 1962)   Houston grew up in New Jersey, the only child of an actress and an unsuccessful businessman. After graduating in English from Denison University in Ohio, she rode across Canada on a bicycle and then down to Colorado, where she worked at various odd jobs, among them bartender and flagwoman on a highway crew. Eventually, she entered a doctoral program at the University of Utah but is presently taking time off from her studies to teach creative writing at her alma mater in Ohio. Her first collection of short stories, *Cowboys Are My Weakness*, was published in 1992. Her stories have also appeared in *Crazyhorse*, *Cimarron*, *Puerto del Sol*, the *Apalachee Quarterly*, and *Mademoiselle* and her nonfiction has appeared in *Mirabella*. She and her husband, a safari guide from South Africa, live in Utah, where she occasionally works as a licensed river guide. In explaining her pursuit of outdoor and often dangerous activities during her early twenties, she says: "You think I spent three summers leading hunters through Alaska because I like watching guys like David Duke shoot sheep? No. It was because if I didn't go with my boyfriend, somebody else would. I wanted to win."

Langston Hughes (1902–1967)   Hughes was born in Joplin, Missouri. His father was a businessperson and lawyer, his mother a teacher. Hughes attended Columbia, graduated from Lincoln University in 1929, traveled throughout the world, and held many odd jobs as a young man. While Hughes had a long and prolific career as a writer in all genres, he is still remembered as the central figure of the Harlem Renaissance of the 1920s, a movement which committed itself to the examination and celebration of black life in America and its African heritage. He was the Madrid correspondent for the Baltimore *Afro-American* (1937) and a columnist for the *Chicago Defender* (1943–1967) and the New York *Post* (1962–1967). His poems of racial affirmation and protest are often infused with the rhythms of blues and jazz music. He wrote over two dozen plays (many musicalized) and founded the Suitcase Theater (Harlem, 1938), the New Negro Theater (Los Angeles, 1939), and the Skyloft Players (Chicago, 1941). His works include *The Weary Blues* (1926), *Montage of a Dream Deferred* (1951), and *The Panther and the Lash: Poems of Our Times* (1969).

Ted Hughes (b. 1930)   Born in Yorkshire, Hughes served two years in the Royal Air Force and attended Pembroke College, Cambridge (B.A. in archeology and anthropology, 1954; M.A., 1959). His first wife was poet Sylvia Plath, who committed suicide in 1963. A full-time writer of plays, essays, and children's verse, and an editor of many anthologies, Hughes created a poetry of animals, full of primitive passion and violence. The most famous of these is the title character of his 1970 volume, *Crow*. One critic calls Hughes a "20th-century Aesop whose fables lack an explicit moral." Many have found in his animal subjects a telling portrayal of the human condition.

David Henry Hwang (b. 1957)   Born in Los Angeles to immigrants, his father a banker and his mother a professor of piano, Hwang graduated from Stanford University in 1979. But by 1978 he had already written his first play, *FOB* [Fresh Off the Boat], which won the 1981 Obie Award as the best new play of the season when Joseph Papp brought it to Off-Broadway in New York. Hwang attended the famous Yale School of Drama during 1980 and 1981. Two more promising plays, *The Dance and the Railroad* and *Family Devotions*, based on the problems of immigrants—trying sometimes to assimilate and sometimes to avoid assimilation in a new culture—appeared in 1981. His 1985 marriage to Ophelia Y. M. Chong, an artist, ended in divorce. Hwang continued to write and direct during the 1980s, moving from the relatively narrow early material to "wider concerns of race, gender, and culture." His 1988 Broadway hit, *M. Butterfly*, won the Tony Award for best play, and established him as a major modern American playwright. A critic writing in *Time* argued that "the final scene of *M. Butterfly*, when the agony of one soul finally takes precedence over broad-ranging commentary, is among the most forceful in the history of the American theater. . . . If Hwang can again fuse politics and humanity, he has the potential to become the first important dramatist of American public life since Arthur Miller, and maybe the best of them all."

Henrik Ibsen (1828–1906)   Ibsen was born in Skien, Norway (a seaport about a hundred miles south of Oslo), the son of a wealthy merchant. When Ibsen was eight, his father's business failed, and at fifteen he was apprenticed to an apothecary in the tiny town of Grimstad. He hated this profession. To solace himself, he read poetry and theology and began to write. When he was twenty-two, he became a student in Christiania and published his first play. In 1851, his diligent, though unremarkable, writing earned him an appointment as "theater-poet" to a new theater in Bergen, where he remained until 1857, learning both the business and the art of drama. He wrote several plays based on Scandinavian folklore, held positions at two theaters in Christiania, and married. When he was thirty-six, he applied to the government for a poet's pension—a stipend that would have permitted him to devote himself to writing. The stipend was refused. Enraged, he left Norway, and, though he was granted the stipend two years later, spent the next twenty-seven years in Italy and Germany, where he wrote the realistic social dramas that established his reputation as the founder of modern theater. Such plays as *Ghosts* (1881), *An Enemy of the People* (1882), and *A Doll's House* (1878) inevitably generated controversy as Ibsen explored venereal disease, the stupidity and greed of the "compact majority," and the position of women in society. In 1891, he returned to live in Christiania, where he was recognized and honored as one of Norway's (and Europe's) finest writers.

June Jordan (b. 1936)   Jordan was born in Harlem, New York, and educated at Barnard College (1953–1955) and the University of Chicago (1955–1956). A poet, novelist, and writer of children's books, she has taught widely at university campuses, including the City College of the City University of New York (1966–1968) and Connecticut College (1969–1974), where she both taught English and served as director of Search for Education, Elevation and Knowledge (SEEK). She is currently professor of English at the State University of New York, Stony Brook. In addition to many appointments as visiting professor, she has served as Chancellor's Distinguished Lecturer, University of California, Berkeley (1986). Her numerous honors include the Prix de Rome in Environmental Design (1970–1971) and the Nancy Bloch Award (1971) for her reader *The Voice of the Children*, and the achievement award from the National Association of Black Journalists (1984). Her many books include *His Own Where* (1971), *Dry Victories* (1972), and *Kimako's Story* (1981), all for juvenile and young adult readers. Her collections of poetry include *Things That I Do in the Dark* (1977), *Living Room: New Poems, 1980–1984* (1985), *Naming Our Destiny: New and Selected Poems* (1989), and *Poetic Justice* (1991). Jordan is also the author of *On Call: New Political Essays, 1981–1985* (1985).

James Joyce (1882–1941)   Though educated in Jesuit schools, Joyce came to reject Catholicism; though an expatriate living in Paris, Trieste, and Zurich for most of his adult life, he wrote almost exclusively about his native Dublin. Joyce's rebelliousness, which surfaced during his university career, generated a revolution in modern literature. His novels *Ulysses* (1922) and *Finnegans Wake* (1939) introduced radically new narrative techniques. "Araby," from his first collection of short stories, *Dubliners* (1914), is one of a series of sharply realized vignettes based on Joyce's experience in Ireland, the homeland he later characterized as "a sow that eats its own farrow." Joyce lived precariously on earnings as a language teacher and modest contributions from wealthy patrons. That support Joyce justified—he is certainly one of the most influential novelists of the twentieth century. Because *Ulysses* dealt frankly with sexuality and used coarse language, the U.S. Post Office charged that the novel was obscene, and forbade its importation. A celebrated 1933 court decision lifted the ban in the United States.

John Keats (1795–1821)   Keats was born in London, the eldest son of a stablekeeper who died in an accident in 1804. His mother died of tuberculosis shortly after remarrying, and the grandmother who raised Keats and his siblings died in 1814. At eighteen Keats wrote his first poem, "Imitation of Spenser," inspired by Edmund Spenser's long narrative poem *The Faerie Queene*. The thirty-three poems he wrote while training to be a surgeon were published in 1817, and Keats then gave up medicine for writing. After more traumatic losses in 1818, including the departure of one brother for America and the death of his older brother of tuberculosis, Keats wrote his second collection, *Lamia, Isabella, The Eve of St. Agnes, and Other Poems* (1820). Ill with tuberculosis himself, Keats was sent to Rome to recover. He died at twenty-six, but despite his short career, he is a major figure of the Romantic period.

X. J. Kennedy (b. 1929)   Born Joseph Charles Kennedy in Dover, New Jersey, Kennedy published his own science fiction magazine, *Terrifying Test-Tube Tales*, at age twelve. He honed his writing skills at Seton Hall University and earned an M.A. degree from Columbia in 1951. From 1951 to 1955, he served in the U.S. Navy, at one time publishing a daily newssheet for the entertainment-starved crew of a destroyer at sea. Kennedy notes: "Nothing I have ever written since has been received so avidly." After further study, at the Sorbonne in Paris and the University of Michigan, Kennedy taught English at the University of North Carolina and moved to Tufts University in Massachusetts in 1963. His first poetry collection, *Nude Descending a Staircase* (1961), won the Lamont Award for that year. A freelance writer since 1979, Kennedy prefers writing within the constraints of rhyme and metrical patterns. His most recent volume, with Dorothy M. Kennedy, is *Talking Like the Rain: A First Book of Poems* (1992).

Martin Luther King, Jr. (1929–1968)   King was born in Atlanta, Georgia, where his father was pastor of the Ebenezer Baptist Church. He attended public schools (skipping the ninth and twelfth grades) and entered Morehouse College in Atlanta. He was ordained as a Baptist minister just before his graduation in 1948. He then enrolled in Crozer Theological Seminary in Pennsylvania and after earning a divinity degree there, attended graduate school at Boston University, where he earned a Ph.D. in theology in 1955. At Boston University, he met Coretta Scott; they were married in 1953. King's rise to national and international prominence began in Montgomery, Alabama, in 1955. In that year, Rosa Parks, an African American woman, was arrested for refusing to obey a city ordinance that required African Americans to sit or stand at the back of municipal buses. The African American citizens of the city (one of the most thoroughly segregated in the South) organized a bus boycott in protest and asked King to serve as their leader. Thousands boycotted the buses for more than a year, and despite segregationist violence against them, King grounded their protests on his deeply held belief in nonviolence. In 1956, the U.S. Supreme Court ordered Montgomery to provide integrated seating on public buses. In the following year, King and other African American ministers founded the Southern Christian Leadership Conference (SCLC) to carry forward the nonviolent struggle against segregation and legal discrimination. As protests grew, so did the unhappiness of King and his associates with the unwillingness of the president and Congress to support civil rights. The SCLC, therefore, organized massive demonstrations in Montgomery (King wrote "Letter from Birmingham Jail" during these demonstrations). With the civil rights movement now in the headlines almost every day, President Kennedy proposed to Congress a far-reaching civil rights bill. On August 28, 1963, over 200,000 blacks and whites gathered at the Lincoln Memorial in Washington, D.C., where King delivered his now famous speech, "I Have a Dream." In the following year, Congress passed the Civil Rights Act of 1964, prohibiting racial discrimination in public places and calling for equal opportunity in education and employment. In that year, King received the Nobel Peace Prize. In 1965, King and others organized a march to protest the blatant denial of African Americans' voting rights in Selma, Alabama, where the march began. Before the protesters were able to reach Birmingham, the state capital, they were attacked by police with tear gas and clubs. This outrage, viewed live on national television, led President Johnson to ask Congress for a bill that would eliminate all barriers to voting rights. Congress responded by passing the landmark Voting Rights Act of 1965. King remained committed to nonviolence, but his conviction that economic inequality—not just race—was one of the root causes of injustice led him to begin organizing a Poor People's Campaign that would unite all poor people in the struggle for justice. These views also led him to criticize the role played by the United States in the Vietnam War. The Poor People's Campaign took King to Memphis, Tennessee, to support a strike of African American sanitation workers, where on April 4, 1968, he was shot and killed while standing on the balcony of his hotel room. Riots immediately erupted in scores of cities across the nation. A few months later, Congress enacted the Civil Rights Act of 1968, banning discrimination in the sale and rental of housing. King is the author of *Stride toward Freedom* (1958), dealing with the Montgomery bus boycott; *Strength to Love* (1953), a collection of sermons; and *Why We Can't Wait* (1964), a discussion of his general views on civil rights.

Carolyn Kizer (b. 1925)   Kizer was born in Spokane, Washington. Her father was a lawyer, her mother a biologist and professor. After graduating from Sarah Lawrence College in 1945, Kizer pursued graduate study at Columbia and the University of Washington. From 1959 to 1965, she was editor of *Poetry Northwest* (which she founded in 1959 in Seattle), and spent 1964 and 1965 as a State Department specialist in Pakistan, where she taught at a women's college and translated poems from Urdu into English. She chose to leave government service after the U.S. decision to bomb North Vietnam in 1965. Later, she joined archeological tours in Afghanistan and Iran. She has worked as director of literary programs for the National Endowment for the Arts in Washington, D.C., has taught at several universities, and was poet-in-residence at the University of North Carolina and Ohio University. Her works include *Poems* (1959) and *Mermaids in the Basement: Poems for Women* (1984).

Etheridge Knight (1933–1991)   Knight was born in Corinth, Mississippi, attended two years of public high school in Kentucky, and served in the U.S. Army from 1948 to 1951. Convicted on a robbery charge and sentenced in 1960 to twenty years in Indiana State Prison, he discovered poetry; his first collection is entitled *Poems from Prison* (1968). Knight was paroled after eight years. From 1968 to 1971 he was poet-in-residence at several universities. An important African American voice in the 1960s and 1970s, Knight rejected the American and European esthetic tradition, arguing that "the red of this esthetic rose got its color from the blood of black slaves, exterminated Indians, napalmed Vietnamese children." His collection *Belly Song and Other Poems* was nominated for the National Book Award and the Pulitzer Prize in 1973. His awards include National Endowment for the Arts and Guggenheim grants, and the 1987 American Book Award for *The Essential Etheridge Knight* (1986).

Maxine Kumin (b. 1925)   Born Maxine Winokur, Kumin attended Radcliffe College (B.A., 1946; M.A., 1948), and has lectured at many universities, including Princeton, Tufts, and Brandeis. She is the author of several collections of poetry, including *Up Country* (1972), for which she won a Pulitzer Prize, and, most recently, *Nurture* (1989) and *Looking for Luck: Poems* (1992). She has also published several novels, a collection of short stories, and more than twenty children's books, three of them in collaboration with the poet Anne Sexton.

Philip Larkin (1922–1985)   Born in Coventry, Larkin attended St. John's College, Oxford (B.A., 1943; M.A., 1947). He was appointed librarian at the University of Hull in 1955, wrote jazz feature articles for the London *Daily*

Telegraph from 1961 to 1971, and won numerous poetry awards, including the Queen's Gold Medal (1965) and the Benson Medal (1975). His first collection, *The North Ship* (1945), was not well received, but he gained recognition after publication of *The Less Deceived* (1960). Larkin once said "Form holds little interest for me. Content is everything."

Ursula K. Le Guin (b. 1929)   The daughter of distinguished University of California, Berkeley, anthropologists, Le Guin graduated from Radcliffe and earned an M.A. from Columbia. She enjoyed early success writing for science fiction and fantasy magazines (a genre often stigmatized as subliterary popular fiction). But she quickly established a reputation that places her alongside such modern writers as Kurt Vonnegut, Jr., and in the tradition of older writers who used fantastic circumstances to shape their understanding of the human condition, such as Jonathan Swift, Edgar Allan Poe, and H. G. Wells. In addition to speculative fiction, she has written poetry and children's books.

John Lennon (1940–1980) **and Paul McCartney** (b. 1942)   Lennon and McCartney met at a church fete in 1957 where they were both performing. Later that year, they formed a duo called The Nurk Twins. By 1962, after various incarnations and personnel changes, Lennon, McCartney, George Harrison, and Ringo Starr emerged as the Beatles and were launched on their successful career by their new manager, Brian Epstein. Lennon and McCartney wrote most of The Beatles' songs. "Love Me Do," their first recording with EMI, sold 100,000 copies in 1962. Exhausted by obsessed fans at sold-out concerts around the world, the foursome became a studio band in 1966. Epstein's death in 1967 and Lennon's marriage to Yoko Ono in 1969 contributed to the group's demise. Ego problems plagued their 1971 movie *Let It Be*, and the group officially disbanded a month after its release. Lennon and McCartney continued their songwriting careers separately. Lennon was murdered by an obsessed fan on December 8, 1980.

Denise Levertov (b. 1923)   Born in Ilford, England, Levertov was raised in a literary household (her father was an Anglican priest) and educated privately. She was a nurse at a British hospital in Paris during World War II; after the war, she worked in an antique store and bookstore in London. Married to an American writer, she came to the United States in 1948, became a naturalized citizen in 1956, and taught at several universities, including M.I.T. and Tufts. Levertov began as what she called a "British romantic with almost Victorian background" and has become more politically active and feminist with time. She protested U.S. involvement in the Vietnam War and has also been involved in the antinuclear movement. Regarding angst-filled confessional poetry, Levertov once said, "I do not believe that a violent imitation of the horrors of our times is the concern of poetry. . . . I long for poems of an inner harmony in utter contrast to the chaos in which they exist." Her works include *The Double Image* (1946), *Relearning the Alphabet* (1970), and *A Door in the Hive* (1989).

C. Day Lewis (1904–1972) Born in Ireland, son of a minister, Cecil Day Lewis began writing poetry at age six. He attended Oxford, taught for seven years, served as editor for the Ministry of Information (1941–1946), was professor of poetry at Oxford (1951–1956), and visiting professor at Harvard (1964–1965). His early works *From Feathers to Iron* (1931) and *The Magnetic Mountain* (1933) reflect a politically radical ideology, but Lewis mellowed enough to be named poet laureate in 1968. From 1935 to 1964 he wrote nearly two dozen detective novels under the pseudonym Nicholas Blake. He commented, "In my young days, words were my antennae, my touch-stones, my causeway over a quaking bog of mistrust."

Barry Holstun Lopez (b. 1945) Born in Port Chester, ·New York, Lopez graduated from the University of Notre Dame in 1966, married, and earned an M.A.T. there in 1968. He went on to further graduate study at the University of Oregon (1969–1970). He envisioned his earliest fiction, *Desert Notes: Reflections in the Eye of a Raven* (1976), as the first of a trilogy which, ultimately, would include *River Notes: The Dance of Herons* (1979) and *Animal Notes.* Keenly interested in the traditions of the Northwest Indians, as well as natural history, he published a collection of Indian legends, *Giving Birth to Thunder, Sleeping with His Daughter* (1977). The nonfiction study *Of Wolves and Men* followed in 1978. A collection of short stories, *Winter Count* (1981), reveals how deeply Lopez feels about the American Indian experience, and in 1990 he published a children's book based on Indian traditions, *Crow and Weasel.* *Arctic Dreams: Imagination and Desire in a Northern Landscape* appeared in 1986. Lopez's skill as a photographer is evident in the illustrations included in several of his works. A collection of essays, *The Rediscovery of North America*, appeared in 1991.

Audre Lorde (1934–1992) Born to middle-class, West Indian immigrant parents in New York City, Lorde grew up in Harlem and attended the National University of Mexico (1954), Hunter College (B.A., 1959) and Columbia (M.L.S., 1961). She married in 1962, had two children, and divorced in 1970. During these early years, she worked as a librarian, but in 1968 her growing reputation as a writer led to her appointment as lecturer in creative writing at City College in New York and, in the following year, lecturer in the education department at Herbert H. Lehman College. In 1970, she joined the English department at John Jay College of Criminal Justice and in 1980 returned to Hunter College as professor of English. Besides teaching, Lorde combined raising a son and a daughter in an interracial lesbian relationship with political organizing of other black feminists and lesbians, and in the early 1980s, helping to start Kitchen Table: Women of Color Press. In 1991, she was named New York State Poet. Lorde is probably best known for her prose writings, among them two collections of essays, *Sister Outsider* (1984) and *Burst of Light* (1988), and the autobiographical *Zami: A New Spelling of My Name* (1982) and *The Cancer Journals* (1980), a chronicle of her struggle with the breast cancer that ultimately claimed her life. Her poetry publications include *The First Cities* (1968), *The Black Unicorn* (1978), and *Undersong: Chosen Poems Old and New* (1993). Near the end of her life, Lorde made her home on St. Croix, U.S. Virgin Islands, and adopted the African name Gamba Adisa ("Warrior—She Who Makes Her Meaning Known").

Amy Lowell (1874–1925)   Born to a prominent family in Brookline, Massachusetts, Lowell was privately educated. After the death of her parents, she inherited the family's ten-acre estate, including a staff of servants and a well-stocked library. Lowell wrote a great deal of undistinguished poetry that, unfortunately, prejudiced critics and readers against her better work. While traveling abroad, she became associated with the Imagists, a group of English and American poets in London who felt that sharply realized images gave poetry its power, and she gained recognition promoting their work in America after 1913. Her first collection of poems, *A Dome of Many-Coloured Glass*, appeared in 1912. Though her poetry never reached a wide audience, her criticism helped shape American poetic tastes of the time.

Bernard Malamud (1914–1986)   Born in Brooklyn, New York, and educated at the City College of New York and Columbia, Malamud is one of a number of post–World War II writers whose works drew heavily on their urban New York, Jewish backgrounds. Malamud's works often dramatize the tension arising out of the clash between Jewish conscience and American energy and materialism or the difficulty of keeping alive the Jewish sense of community and humanism in American society. *A New Life* (1961), *The Fixer* (1966; winner of both a National Book Award and a Pulitzer Prize), and *Pictures of Fidelman* (1969) all have protagonists who struggle with these problems. Some of his other novels are *The Natural* (1952), *The Assistant* (1957), *The Tenants* (1971), and *God's Grace* (1982). His short stories are collected in *The Magic Barrel* (1958; winner of the National Book Award in 1959), *Idiots First* (1963), and *Rembrandt's Hat* (1973).

Christopher Marlowe (1564–1593)   Born in Canterbury, Marlowe was educated at Cambridge, where he embarked on a career of writing and political activity, eventually giving up his original intention of entering the priesthood. He was arrested in 1593 on a charge of atheism, but before he could be brought to trial he was murdered in a brawl apparently involving a wealthy family that had reason to want him silenced. Marlowe's literary reputation rests primarily on his plays, powerful in their own right and the most significant precursors of Shakespeare's poetic dramas. The most important are *Tamburlaine, Parts I and II* (ca. 1587–1588; published 1590), *The Jew of Malta* (1589; published 1633), and *The Tragical History of the Life and Death of Dr. Faustus* (1592; published 1604).

Andrew Marvell (1621–1678)   Born in Yorkshire and educated at Cambridge, Marvell received an inheritance upon his father's death that allowed him to spend four years traveling the Continent. Though not a Puritan himself, Marvell supported the Puritans' cause during the civil war and held a number of posts during the Puritan regime, including that of assistant to the blind John Milton, Cromwell's Latin Secretary. In 1659, a year before the Restoration, Marvell was elected to Parliament, where he served until his death. Soon after the Restoration, Marvell expressed strong disagreements with the government in a series of outspoken satires. It was for these satires, rather than for his many love poems, that he was primarily known in his own day.

Katherine McAlpine (b. 1948)   Katherine McAlpine grew up in western New Jersey. She studied voice with Leon Kurzer of the Vienna Opera and worked for a number of years as a singer and voice teacher. She now lives in Downeast, Maine, where she works as a freelance writer. Her poetry has appeared in a wide variety of magazines and in several anthologies. She was a 1992 winner of the *Nation*'s Discovery Award and the Judith's Room Award for emerging women poets.

Claude McKay (1890–1948)   Born in Sunny Ville, Jamaica, McKay had already completed two volumes of poetry before coming to the United States in 1912 at the age of twenty-three (the two volumes earned him awards, which paid his way). The racism he encountered as a black immigrant brought a militant tone to his writing. His popular poem "If We Must Die" (1919) helped to initiate the Harlem Renaissance of the 1920s. Between 1922 and 1934 he lived in Great Britain, Russia, Germany, France, Spain, and Morocco. His writings include four volumes of poems, many essays, an autobiography (*A Long Way from Home* [1937]), a novel (*Home to Harlem* [1928]), and a sociological study of Harlem. His conversion to Roman Catholicism in the 1940s struck his audience as an ideological retreat. McKay wrote in a letter to a friend: "[T]o have a religion is very much like falling in love with a woman. You love her for her . . . beauty, which cannot be defined."

Bill McKibben (b. 1960)   Born in Palo Alto, California, McKibben graduated from Harvard University (B.A., 1982), and immediately was hired as an editor at the *New Yorker* magazine. At age twenty-six, dissatisfied with the frantic pace of urban life and work, he quit his job at the *New Yorker* and moved with his wife, writer Sue Halperin, to an isolated house (the nearest town is twelve miles away) in the Adirondack Mountains, in New York State. There, his concern over the growing threat to the earth's ecosystem posed by chemical pollution led him to the research and reflections described in his book *The End of Nature* (1989). Besides writing, McKibben spends much of his time hiking in the woods. He has said that he overcame a crisis in religious belief "to a greater or lesser degree by locating God in nature."

Peter Meinke (b. 1932)   Born in Brooklyn, New York, son of a salesman, Meinke served in the U.S. Army from 1955 to 1957, attended Hamilton College (B.A., 1955), the University of Michigan (M.A., 1961), and earned his Ph.D. at the University of Minnesota (1965). He taught English at a New Jersey high school, Hamline University, and Presbyterian College (now Eckerd College) in Florida, where he began directing the writing workshop in 1972. His reviews, poems, and stories have appeared in periodicals such as the *Atlantic*, the *New Yorker*, and the *New Republic*. The latest of his three books in the Pitt Poetry Series is *Nightwatch on the Chesapeake* (1987). His collection of stories, *The Piano Tuner*, won the 1986 Flannery O'Connor Award. Also, he has been the recipient of an NEA Fellowship in Poetry.

Herman Melville (1819–1891)   The death of his merchant father when Melville was twelve shattered the economic security of his family. The financial panic of 1837 reduced the Melvilles to the edge of poverty, and, at age nineteen, Melville went to sea. Economic conditions upon his return were still grim, and after a frustrating stint as a country school teacher, he again went to sea—this time on a four-year whaling voyage. He deserted the whaler in the South Pacific, lived some time with cannibals, made his way to Tahiti and Hawaii, and finally joined the navy for a return voyage. He mined his experiences for two successful South Sea adventure books, *Typee* (1846) and *Omoo* (1847). On the strength of these successes he married, but his next novel, *Mardi* (1849), was too heavy-handed an allegory to succeed. Driven by the obligation to support his growing family, Melville returned to sea adventure stories, with moderate success. But neither his masterpiece, *Moby Dick* (1851), nor his subsequent short stories and novels found much of an audience, and, in 1886, he accepted an appointment as customs inspector in Manhattan, a job he held until retirement. He continued to write, mostly poetry, and lived to see himself forgotten as an author. *Billy Budd*, found among his papers after his death and published in 1924, led to a revival of interest in Melville, now recognized as one of America's greatest writers.

James Merrill (1926–1995)   Born into a wealthy New York family (his father cofounded the Merrill Lynch stockbrokerage firm), Merrill was privately educated at home and then at Amherst College, where he received a B.A. degree in 1947. His first volume of poems, *First Poems* (1951), established his reputation as a writer of technical virtuosity, urbane eloquence, and wit. With the more personal and passionate poems of *Nights and Days* (1966) and *Mirabell: Books of Number* (1979), both recipients of the National Book Award, Merrill gained a wider and more enthusiastic audience. Merrill is probably most widely known as "the Ouija poet" for his narrative poems that record the Ouija board sessions he and a friend conducted with "spirits from another world." Merrill has also written plays (*The Immortal Husband* [1956] and *The Bait* [1960]) and novels (*The Seraglio* [1957] and *The (Diblos) Notebook* [1957]). In 1990, Merrill won the Bobbitt Prize from the Library of Congress.

W. S. Merwin (b. 1927)   Born in New York City and raised in New Jersey and Pennsylvania, Merwin graduated from Princeton in 1947. His first poetry collection, *A Mask for Janus* (1952), completed while he tutored in Europe, won the Yale Series of Younger Poets Award. Associated with contemporary oracular poets, Merwin has offered a unique vision of solitude and nothingness. His collection *A Carrier of Ladders* (1970) won the Pulitzer Prize in 1971. He has published several other collections, four plays, and a number of translations. His latest work, *The Lost Upland* (1992), is a collection of stories set in France.

Robert Mezey (b. 1935)   Born in Philadelphia, Mezey attended Kenyon College and served a troubled hitch in the U.S. Army before earning his B.A. from the University of Iowa in 1959. He worked as a probation officer, advertising copywriter, and social worker, did graduate study at Stanford, and began teaching English at Case Western Reserve University in 1963. After a year as poet-in-residence at Franklin and Marshall College, he joined the English department of California State University, Fresno, spent three years at the University of Utah, and settled in 1976 at Pomona College in Claremont, California. Winner in 1960 of the Lamont Award for *The Lovemaker*, he has published many poetry collections, coedited *Naked Poetry* (1969), and was one of several translators for *Poems from the Hebrew* (1973). *Evening Wind*, a book of poems, appeared in 1987.

John Milton (1608–1674)   Born in London to an affluent and artistic family, Milton was educated privately as a child and later attended Cambridge, where he wrote both Latin and English poems. After leaving Cambridge, he was supported for five years by his family while he read the classics, wrote, and traveled. When civil war broke out in 1642, Milton actively supported the Puritans against the Crown. The Puritan victory in 1649 led to his appointment as Latin Secretary to Oliver Cromwell, his main duty being to translate foreign diplomatic correspondence. He voluntarily wrote many pamphlets defending the new regime, including a justification of the execution of Charles I in 1649. Doctors warned him that continued writing would damage his eyesight, but Milton ignored their advice and at age forty-three he became totally blind. Thereafter, Andrew Marvell assisted him in his secretarial duties. With the Restoration of Charles II in 1660, Milton went into retirement and was able to devote himself to composing the epic work he had long contemplated. This project reached fruition in 1667 with the publication of *Paradise Lost*, a blank verse epic in which Milton announced that he would "justify the ways of God to men." One of Milton's last works, often seen as autobiographical, is *Samson Agonistes* (1671), a poetic drama about the blind Samson triumphing over the treachery of those around him.

Jessica Mitford (b. 1917)   One of six sisters, Mitford was born in Gloucestershire, England, into an aristocratic and rather eccentric family. She was educated at home and early adopted political views that contrasted violently with those of her sister Diana, who married Sir Oswald Mosley, the pre–World War II leader of the British Fascist movement. Jessica, on the other hand, traveled to Loyalist Spain during its civil war, where she met her first husband. He was killed in action during World War II, and she later married a labor lawyer. They moved to California and joined the Communist party. They left the party in 1958, and Jessica embarked on a successful career as a muckraking journalist and writer. Her first work, *Lifeitselfmanship*, was privately published in 1956, but her attack on undertakers in *The American Way of Death* (1963) established her reputation as an incisive and witty enemy of social and economic pretentiousness. Her many books include *Kind and Usual Punishment: The Prison Business* (1973), the autobiographical *A Fine Old Conflict* (1979), and a collection of articles, *Poison Penmanship: The Gentle Art of Muckracking* (1979).

Felix Mnthali (b. 1933)   Mnthali was born and grew up in Malawi in south central Africa. He was educated in Malawi University and Cambridge University in England. He returned to Africa, and as a visiting academic at the University of Ibadan in Nigeria, he wrote and privately published *Echoes from Ibadan* (1961). Back in his homeland he became the head of the department of English at Malawi University. He recently left Malawi to reside in Botswana.

Alberto Moravia (1907–1990)   Born in Rome, Moravia contracted tuberculosis as a child and was educated privately at home. Following the publication of his first novel, *A Time of Indifference* (1929), he traveled widely in Europe and America, supporting himself by writing articles for Italian newspapers. Moravia's writings brought him into conflict with the Fascist regime, and he was forced to flee Italy when the Germans occupied Rome. Moravia's international fame was established in the postwar period with the publication of such novels as *The Woman of Rome* (1947), *Conjugal Love* (1949), and *The Conformist* (1951). Many of his short stories appear in *Roman Tales* (translated in 1956) and *More Roman Tales* (translated in 1963).

Bharati Mukherjee (b. 1940)   Mukherjee was born in Calcutta, India. Her father was a chemist. She attended the University of Calcutta (B.A., 1959), the University of Baroda (M.A., 1961), and the University of Iowa, where she took an M.F.A. in 1963 and a Ph.D. in 1969. In 1963 she married Clark Blaise, a Canadian writer and professor, and joined the faculty at McGill University in Montreal. In 1973, Mukherjee and her husband visited India together and kept separate diaries of the trip, published as *Days and Nights in Calcutta* (1977). The diaries reveal marked differences in their responses: Mukherjee found her home environs, especially the status of women, worse than she remembered, while Blaise, after an initial revulsion at the squalor and poverty, found India a fascinating and attractive culture compared to the West. Mukherjee "left Canada after fifteen years due to the persistent effects of racial prejudice against people of my national origin," and joined the faculty at Skidmore College, Saratoga Springs, New York. Later she moved to Queens College of the City University of New York. Her fiction frequently explores the tensions inevitable in intercultural relationships. Her first novel, *The Tiger's Daughter* (1972), deals with the disappointment of an expatriate's return to India. In her second novel, *Wife* (1975), a psychologically abused woman finally kills her husband. *The Middleman and Other Stories* appeared in 1988.

Kathleen Norris (b. 1947)   Norris was born in Washington, D.C., and educated at Bennington College in Vermont (B.A., 1969). From 1969 to 1973, she worked for the Academy of American Poets in New York and was later affiliated with Leaves of Grass, Inc., in Lemmon, South Dakota, where she lives. Her awards include a Provincetown Fine Arts Center Fellowship (1972) and a Creative Artists Public Service Grant from the state of New York (1972–1973). Her works have appeared in many periodicals, including *Dragonfly*, *Lillabulero*, and the *New Yorker*. She is the author of two collections of poems, *Falling Off* (1971) and *The Middle of the World* (1981).

Edna O'Brien (b. 1936)   O'Brien was born in a rural, Catholic village of about two hundred people in the west of Ireland and grew up on a farm. Educated at local schools and in a convent, she escaped rural life by briefly attending Pharmaceutical College in Dublin. Shortly after her marriage in 1952, she and her husband (Czech-Irish author Ernest Gebler) moved to London; they divorced after twelve years. O'Brien remained in London, where she raised her two sons alone. She has, since 1986, taught creative writing at City College of the City University of New York. Among her honors are the Kingsley Amis Award (1962) and the *Los Angeles Times* Book Prize (1990).

O'Brien's prolific output includes *Johnny I Hardly Knew You* (1977), *The High Road* (1988), *The Country Girls Trilogy and Epilogue* (1989), and *Time and Tide* (1990). Among her half-dozen collections of stories are *A Scandalous Woman* (1974), *A Fanatic Heart* (1984), and *Lantern Slides* (1990). She has also written stories for juveniles, stage plays, television plays, screenplays, and been a contributor to magazines such as the *New Yorker*, the *Ladies' Home Journal*, and *Cosmopolitan*. Of the connection between her writing and her life, O'Brien says, "It is as if the life lived has not been lived until it is set down in this unconscious sequence of words."

Flannery O'Connor (1925–1964)   Afflicted with lupus erythematosus, O'Connor spent most of her tragically short life in Milledgeville, Georgia. She began writing while a student at Georgia State College for Women in her hometown and in 1947 earned an M.F.A. degree from the University of Iowa. Back in Milledgeville, she lived on a farm with her mother, raised peacocks, and endured the indignity of constant treatment for her progressive and in- curable disease. She traveled and lectured when she could. She wrote two novels, *Wise Blood* (1952) and *The Violent Bear It Away* (1960), and two collections of stories, *A Good Man Is Hard to Find* (1955) and *Everything That Rises Must Converge* (1965). She was deeply religious, and wrote numerous book reviews for Catholic newspapers. Her southern gothic tales often force readers to confront physical deformity, spiritual depravity, and the violence they often engender.

Sharon Olds (b. 1942)   Born in San Francisco, Olds attended Stanford (B.A., 1964) and Columbia (Ph.D., 1972). She joined the faculty of Theodor Herzl Institute in 1976 and has given readings at many colleges. She won the Made- line Sadin Award from the *New York Quarterly* in 1978 for "The Death of Marilyn Monroe." Often compared to confessional poets Sylvia Plath and Anne Sexton, Olds published her first collection, *Satan Says*, in 1980, and won both the National Book Critics' Circle Award and the Lamont Award for *The Dead and the Living* in 1983. *The Gold Cell* was published in 1987, and her most recent book of poems, *The Father*, appeared in 1992.

Mary Oliver (b. 1935)   Mary Oliver was born in Cleveland, Ohio. She spent one year at Ohio State University and a second year at Vassar. Her distinctive poetic talent led to an appointment as the chair of the writing department of the Fine Arts Workshop in Provincetown, Massachusetts (1972–1973). Though she never graduated from college, she was awarded the Mather Vis- iting Professorship at Case Western Reserve University for 1980 and 1982, and, among her many awards and honors, she received a National Endowment of the Arts Fellowship (1972–1973) and a Guggenheim Fellowship (1980– 1981). The first of her several volumes of poems, *No Voyage and Other Poems*, appeared in 1963. *New and Selected Poems* appeared in 1992. One critic, commenting on her work, asserts that "her vision of nature is celebratory and religious in the deepest sense."

George Orwell (1903–1950)   Born Eric Blair in India, the son of a minor British colonial officer, Orwell was raised in England. His education at good grammar schools, culminating with a stay at Eton, introduced him to what he later called the snobbish world of England's middle and upper classes. Denied a university scholarship, he joined the Indian Imperial Police in 1922 and served in Burma until he resigned in 1927, disgusted with the injustice of British imperialism in India and Burma. He was determined to be a writer and living at the edge of poverty, deliberately mingled with social outcasts and impoverished laborers. These experiences produced *Down and Out in Paris and London* (1933). Although he was a socialist, his experiences while fighting alongside the leftists during the Spanish Civil War disillusioned him, and he embodied his distaste for any totalitarian system in *Animal Farm* (1945), a satirical attack on the leadership of the Soviet Union. In his pessimistic novel *1984* (1949), he imagined a social order shaped by a propagandistic perversion of language, in which the government, an extension of "Big Brother," uses two-way television to control the citizenry. Orwell succumbed to tuberculosis at the age of forty-seven, but not before he produced six novels, three documentary works, over seven hundred newspaper articles and reviews, and a volume of essays.

Wilfred Owen (1893–1918)   Born in the Shropshire countryside of England, Owen had begun writing verse before he matriculated at London University, where he was known as a quiet and contemplative student. After some years of teaching English in France, Owen returned to England and joined the army. He was wounded in 1917 and killed in action leading an attack a few days before the armistice was declared in 1918. Owen's poems, published only after his death, along with his letters from the front to his mother, are perhaps the most powerful and vivid accounts of the horror of war to emerge from the First World War.

Paul (d. ca. A.D. 64)   Paul was born in Tarsus of Cilicia (located near the Mediterranean Sea in central Turkey, near Syria). As an adult, he was an important Jerusalem Pharisee (his name then was Saul), and, according to accounts in the Acts of the Apostles, he vigorously attacked (both intellectually and physically) those who proclaimed the deity of Jesus. The same source (Chapter 9) provides an account of Paul's conversion, though Paul himself never mentions it. Traveling to Damascus to arrest followers of Jesus, he experienced an intense light that blinded him, and heard a voice that declared, "I am Jesus, whom you are persecuting." In Tarsus, his blindness was cured by

Ananius, a follower of Jesus, and Paul became, arguably, the most important disciple of Jesus in the early Church—his letters (and those attributed to him) comprise a quarter of the New Testament. His attempts to preach the new Way in the synagogues of the region were rebuffed, sometimes violently, and Paul was frequently jailed. He became the apostle to the Gentiles, traveling throughout the Mediterranean region to establish churches. His epistles were addressed to those young and fragile congregations to help formulate the political, legal, and spiritual institutions of the early Church. His final arrest brought him to Rome to answer charges where, after two years of imprisonment, he died about A.D. 64.

Molly Peacock (b. 1947)   Born in Buffalo, New York, Peacock was educated at the State University of New York at Binghamton (now Binghamton University) and at Johns Hopkins University, where she received an M.A. with honors in 1977. From 1970 to 1973, she was the director of academic advising at her alma mater in Binghamton. She was appointed honorary fellow at Johns Hopkins in 1977 and, in the following year, poet-in-residence at the Delaware State Arts Council in Wilmington. Since 1979, she has directed the Wilmington Writing Workshops. She has published in many magazines, including the *Southern Review*, the *Ohio Review*, and the *Massachusetts Review*. She has published three books of poems, *And Live Apart* (1980), *Raw Heaven* (1984), and *Take Heart* (1989), the latter dealing with her father's alcoholism and the mental and physical abuse she endured while growing up.

Marge Piercy (b. 1936)   Born in Detroit, Marge Piercy was the first of her family to attend college. In 1957, she graduated from the University of Michigan (where she won prizes for poetry and fiction) and earned an M.A. from Northwestern University (1958). She was active in social and political causes and fought for equal treatment of women and minorities while opposing the Vietnam War. She supported herself with odd jobs in Chicago as she pursued a writing career, but her first novel was not published until after her 1969 move to Wellfleet, Massachusetts (where she still lives). She remains an extraordinarily prolific writer—eleven novels, a dozen volumes of poetry, plays, several nonfiction volumes, and recordings. Her list of prizes and honors covers seventeen lines in *Contemporary Authors*, and her work has appeared in over one hundred anthologies. In the introduction to a volume of selected poems, *Circles on the Water* (1982), Piercy asserted that she wanted her poems to be "useful." "What I mean by useful is simply that readers will find poems that speak to and for them, will take those poems into their lives and say them to each other and put them up on the bathroom wall and remember bits and pieces of them in stressful or quiet moments. . . . To find ourselves spoken for in art gives dignity to our pain, our anger, our lust, our losses."

Sylvia Plath (1932–1963)   Plath was born in Boston, Massachusetts, where her parents taught at Boston University. She graduated summa cum laude in

English from Smith College (1955), earned an M.A. as a Fulbright scholar at Newnham College, Cambridge (1955–1957), and married British poet Ted Hughes (1956). Plath's poetry reveals the anger and anxiety that would eventually lead to her suicide. Her view that all relationships were in some way destructive and predatory surely darkened her life. Yet in 1963, during the month between the publication of her only novel, *The Bell Jar* (about a suicidal college student), and her death, Plath was extraordinarily productive; she produced finished poems every day. One critic suggests that for her, suicide was a positive act, a "refusal to collaborate" in a world she could not accept. Her *Collected Poems* was published in 1981.

Alexander Pope (1688–1744)   Born in London to a prosperous merchant family, Pope was educated mostly by tutors because schools and universities were closed to Roman Catholics. Despite this situation and an illness that left him hunchbacked and stunted, his brilliance as a wit and poet early gained him entry into the most sophisticated circles of London society. By age thirty, he was acknowledged as the premier poet of England. He came to typify an age known for its sense of order, balance, and decorum, as well as its concern for the relation of the individual to society. Pope's poetry reflects these concerns in the polished and balanced heroic couplets he uses to write about the social, religious, and philosophical issues of his age. His *Essay on Criticism* (1711) and *Essay on Man* (1733–1734) are heavily didactic, while his satires, such as *The Rape of the Lock* (1712–1714), *The Dunciad* (1728), and *Epistle to Dr. Arbuthnot* (1735) try to instill reasonableness and proportion by ridiculing the follies and absurdities of humankind.

Sir Walter Ralegh (1554–1618)   Born in Devonshire, England, into the landed gentry, Ralegh attended Oxford but dropped out after a year in order to fight for the Huguenot cause in France. He returned to England, began the study of law, but again was drawn to a life of adventure and exploration. Through the influence of friends he came to the attention of Queen Elizabeth, and thenceforth his career flourished: he was knighted, given a number of lucrative commercial monopolies, made a member of Parliament and, in 1587, named captain of the Yeoman of the Guard. During these years, he invested in various colonies in North America, but all his settlements failed. He was briefly imprisoned in the Tower of London for offending the Queen but was soon back in favor and in command of an unsuccessful expedition to Guiana (now Venezuela) in 1595. In 1603, he was again imprisoned in the Tower, this time on a probably trumped-up charge of treason, where he remained until 1616, spending part of his time writing *A History of the World* (1614). After his release, he undertook still another expedition to Guiana but again returned empty-handed. As a consequence of more political intrigue, James I ordered him executed. Although Ralegh epitomized the great merchant adventurers of Elizabethan England, he was also a gifted poet.

Dudley Randall (b. 1914)   Born in Washington, D.C., Randall worked during the Depression in the foundry of the Ford Motor Company in Dearborn, Michigan, and then as a carrier and clerk for the U.S. Post Office in Detroit. He served in the U.S. Army Signal Corps (1942–1946), and graduated from Wayne State University (B.A., 1949) and the University of Michigan (M.A.L.S., 1951). He was a librarian at several universities, and founded the Broadside Press in 1965 "so black people could speak to and for their people." Randall told *Negro Digest*, "Precision and accuracy are necessary for both white and black writers. . . . 'A black aesthetic' should not be an excuse for sloppy writing." He urges African American writers to reject what was false in "white" poetry but not to forsake universal concerns in favor of a racial agenda. His works include *On Getting a Natural* (1969) and *A Litany of Friends: New and Selected Poems* (1981).

Henry Reed (b. 1914)   Reed was born in Birmingham, England, earned a B.A. from the University of Birmingham (1937), worked as a teacher and freelance writer (1937–1941), and served in the British Army (1941–1942). His early poetry dealt with political events before and during World War II. "Naming of Parts" and "Judging Distances" were based on his frustrating experience in cadet training. His only collection of poetry, *A Map of Verona* (1946), revealed a formal, reverent, but also humorous and ironic voice. Reed began writing radio plays in 1947 and has generated as many as four scripts a year. His best-known satirical work is the "Hilda Tablet" series, a 1960s BBC-Radio production that parodied British society of the 1930s.

Alastair Reid (b. 1926)   Born in Scotland, son of a minister, Reid graduated with honors from St. Andrews University after serving in the Royal Navy. He taught at Sarah Lawrence College (1951–1955) and, after his appointment as staff writer at the *New Yorker* in 1959, occasionally enjoyed visiting professorships across the United States and in England, teaching Latin American studies and literature. Acclaimed for his light, engaging style, Reid has been enthusiastically received as a poet, translator, essayist, and author of children's books, moving between genres as easily as he has moved between countries. Reid has lived in Spain, Latin America, Greece, and Morocco (to name a few places) and rejects the label "Scottish" writer. His deliberate rootlessness shows in his poetry, which is characterized by, in one critic's words, "natural irregularity."

Adrienne Rich (b. 1929)   Born to a middle-class family, Rich was educated by her parents until she entered public school in the fourth grade. She graduated Phi Beta Kappa from Radcliffe College in 1951, the same year her first book of poems, *A Change of World*, appeared. That volume, chosen by W. H. Auden for the Yale Series of Younger Poets Award, and her next, *The Diamond*

Cutters and Other Poems (1955), earned her a reputation as an elegant, controlled stylist. In the 1960s, however, Rich began a dramatic shift away from her earlier mode as she took up political and feminist themes and stylistic experimentation in such works as *Snapshots of a Daughter-in-Law* (1963), *The Necessities of Life* (1966), *Leaflets* (1969), and *The Will to Change* (1971). In *Diving into the Wreck* (1973) and *The Dream of a Common Language* (1978), she continued to experiment with form and to deal with the experiences and aspirations of women from a feminist perspective. In addition to her poetry, Rich has published many essays on poetry, feminism, motherhood, and lesbianism. Her most recent collection of poems, *An Atlas of the Difficult World*, appeared in 1991.

Alberto Ríos (b. 1952)   Born in Nogales, Arizona, to a Mexican father and an English mother, Ríos was educated at the University of Arizona, where he received a B.A. in English and creative writing (1974) and an M.F.A. (1975). He began teaching at Arizona State University in 1983 and is presently professor of English there. Ríos has served on various state and national boards and commissions devoted to the arts. His awards include a first place in the Academy of American Arts poetry contest (1977) and the Chicanos Por La Causa Community Appreciation Award (1988). Ríos's publications include three poetry chapbooks, *Elk Heads on the Wall* (1979), *Sleeping on Fists* (1981), and *Whispering to Fool the Wind* (1982), as well as a collection of stories, *The Iguana Killer: Twelve Stories of the Heart* (1984). His most recent volume of poetry is *Teodoro Luna's Two Kisses* (1990). Ríos's poetry has been set to music in a cantata called "Tito's Story" on an EMI release, "Away from Home." He is also featured in the documentary *Birthwrite: Growing Up Hispanic.*

Edwin Arlington Robinson (1869–1935)   Robinson grew up in Gardiner, Maine, attended Harvard, returned to Gardiner as a freelance writer, then settled in New York City in 1896. His various odd jobs included a one-year stint as subway-construction inspector. President Theodore Roosevelt, a fan of his poetry, had him appointed to the United States Customs House in New York, where he worked from 1905 to 1909. Robinson wrote about people, rather than nature, particularly New England characters remembered from his early years. Describing his first volume of poems, *The Torrent and the Night Before* (1896), he told a friend there was not "a single red-breasted robin in the whole collection." Popular throughout his career, Robinson won three Pulitzer Prizes (1921, 1924, 1927).

Theodore Roethke (1908–1963)   Born in Saginaw, Michigan, Roethke was the son of a greenhouse owner; greenhouses figure prominently in the imagery of his poems. He graduated magna cum laude from the University of Michigan in 1929, where he also earned an M.A. in 1936 after graduate study at Harvard. He taught at several universities, coached two varsity tennis teams, and settled at the University of Washington in 1947. Intensely introspective and demanding of himself, Roethke was renowned as a great teacher, though sometimes incapacitated by an ongoing manic-depressive condition. His collection *The Waking: Poems 1933–1953*, won the Pulitzer Prize in 1954. Other awards include Guggenheim Fellowships in 1945 and 1950, and a National Book Award and the Bollingen Prize in 1959 for *Words for the Wind* (1958).

Muriel Rukeyser (1913–1980)   Born in New York City, Rukeyser attended Vassar and Columbia, then spent a short time at Roosevelt Aviation School, which no doubt helped shape her first published volume of poetry, *Theory of Flight* (1935). In the early 1930s, she joined Elizabeth Bishop, Mary McCarthy, and Eleanor Clark in founding a literary magazine that challenged the policies of the *Vassar Review*. (The two magazines later merged.) A social activist, Rukeyser witnessed the Scottsboro trials (where she was one of the reporters arrested by authorities) in 1933. She visited suffering tunnel workers in West Virginia (1936) and went to Hanoi to protest U.S. involvement in the Vietnam War. She gave poetry readings across the United States and received several awards, including a Guggenheim Fellowship and the Copernicus Award. *Waterlily Fire: Poems 1935–1962* appeared in 1962, and later work was collected in *29 Poems* (1970). *The Collected Poems of Muriel Rukeyser* appeared in 1978. Her only novel, *The Orgy*, appeared in 1965.

Margaret Sanger (1883–1966)   The sixth of eleven children, Margaret Higgins Sanger was born in Corning, New York. She chose nursing as a career, and the tragic events that determined the course of her life occurred while she worked as an obstetrical nurse in the impoverished Lower East Side of Manhattan. Her experiences with the poor and desperate women she nursed compelled her to action; she decided to educate women about birth control (an expression she invented) and help them avoid pregnancy. She founded the National Birth Control League in 1914 under the slogan "No gods; no masters!," and began publishing a magazine, *Woman Rebel*. In 1915, she was indicted for sending birth-control information through the mail, and in 1916, she was arrested and jailed for operating a birth-control clinic in Brooklyn, New York. While in prison, she founded and edited *Birth Control Review*. Her personal integrity and her prodigious energy finally triumphed, and legislative changes allowed doctors to provide sex education and prescribe contraceptives. Her work culminated in 1952, in Bombay, India, when the International Planned Parenthood Federation was established and made her its first president.

Sappho (ca. 610–ca. 580 B.C.)   Almost nothing certain is known of the finest woman lyric poet of the ancient world. She was born to an aristocratic family, had three brothers, one of whom was a court cupbearer (a position limited to the sons of good families). She is associated with the island of Lesbos in the Aegean Sea. She married and had a daughter. Until recently, her reputation depended on fragments of her work quoted by other ancient authors. However, in the late nineteenth century a cache of papyrus and vellum codices (dating from the second to the sixth centuries A.D.) containing authentic transcriptions of a few of her lyrical poems was discovered in Egypt. Unlike other ancient Greek poets, she wrote in ordinary Greek rather than an exalted literary dialect; her lyrics, despite their simple language, conveyed women's concerns with intense emotion.

William Saroyan (1908–1981)   Born and raised in Fresno, California, to Armenian immigrant parents, Saroyan's first success as a writer came with the publication in 1934 of his story "The Daring Young Man on the Flying Trapeze." He went on to a prolific career as a writer of fiction and plays, notable for their optimism and romantic celebrations of ordinary people pursuing the American dream. Among his best-known novels are *My Name is Aram* (1940) and *The Human Comedy* (1943), both dealing with children growing up in the San Joaquin Valley in California. His many plays include *My Heart's in the Highlands* and *The Time of Your Life* (both 1939). Saroyan refused the Pulitzer Prize for the latter play on the grounds that wealthy business people were incapable of judging art. His autobiographical works include *The Bicycle Rider in Beverly Hills* (1952), *Places Where I've Done Time* (1972), and *Obituaries* (1979). Five days before he died, he said to the Associated Press, "Everybody has got to die, but I have always believed an exception would be made in my case. Now what?"

May Sarton (b. 1912)   Born in Belgium, Sarton was brought to the United States in 1916 and became a naturalized citizen in 1924. She was educated at various private schools, including the Cambridge High and Latin School. In 1929, the year her first poems were published, she turned down a scholarship to Vassar College to become an apprentice with Eva Le Gallienne's Civic Repertory Theatre in New York. In 1936, when the Associated Actors Theatre, which she directed, disbanded, Sarton began to devote herself to writing. Her prolific output of poetry, fiction, and nonfiction has brought her many honors, including appointment as a Guggenheim Fellow in poetry (1954–1955) and awards from the Poetry Society of America (1952), the Johns Hopkins University Poetry Festival (1961), the Before Columbus Foundation (1985), and the Women's Building/West Hollywood Conexxus Women's Crisis Center (1987). She has taught widely in American colleges and universities and is the recipient of numerous honorary doctorate degrees. She is the author of eighteen novels, among them *The Single Hound* (1938), *Mrs. Stevens Hears the Mermaids Singing* (1965), and *The Education of Harriet Hatfield* (1989). Her volumes of poetry include *Encounter in April* (1937), *Collected Poems: 1930–*

1973 (1974), and *The Silence Now: New and Uncollected Earlier Poems* (1988). In 1986, Sarton suffered a stroke. In describing her difficult recuperation, she remarked to an interviewer that since her illness, her poems explore "where I am now, as a woman . . . who has really faced growing old for the first time."

Jean-Paul Sartre (1905–1980)   Sartre was born in Paris, the son of a naval officer who died when Sartre was a child. He graduated from the prestigious École Normale Supérieure (1930), and spent his early career as a philosophy professor. During World War II, he was imprisoned in Germany for nine months, and, when released, joined the French Resistance (1941–1944). At the conclusion of the war, Sartre devoted himself to his extraordinary writing career. His philosophical writings, dating from as early as 1936, gave shape to existentialism. His first novel, *Nausea* (1938), won the first of many prizes awarded for his work. Some of these, including the Nobel Prize for Literature (1964), Sartre refused. In addition to his copious output as a technical philosopher and fiction writer, Sartre became a distinguished playwright, a discerning literary critic, and a prolific apologist for leftist political theory. Although they never married, Sartre maintained a durable relationship with Simone de Beauvoir, the eminent French writer and feminist. In 1956, the *New Statesman and Nation* wrote: "The Vatican has placed his works on the Index; yet Gabriel Marcel, himself a militant Catholic, regarded him as the greatest of French thinkers. The State Department found his novels subversive; but *Les Mains Sales* [Dirty Hands] was the most effective counter-revolutionary play of the entire cold war. Sartre has been vilified by the Communists in Paris and feted by them in Vienna. No great philosopher ever had fewer disciples, but no other could claim the intellectual conquest of an entire generation."

Gjertrud Schnackenberg (b. 1953)   Born in Tacoma, Washington, Schnackenberg graduated from Mount Holyoke College in 1975 and was honored by her alma mater with an honorary doctorate in 1985. She has published three volumes of poetry: *Portraits and Elegies* (1982), *The Lamplit Answer* (1985), and *A Gilded Lapse of Time* (1992). She has received numerous awards, including the Rome Prize in literature from the American Academy and Institute of Arts and Letters, which provided a year at the American Academy in Rome (1983), and fellowships from the National Endowment for the Arts and the Guggenheim Foundation.

Richard Selzer (b. 1928)   The son of a family doctor, Selzer was born in Troy, New York. He attended Union College in Schenectady, New York, and earned an M.D. at Albany Medical College in 1953. He wrote *Rituals of Surgery* (1974), a collection of short stories, and he subsequently published numerous essays and stories in such magazines as *Redbook, Esquire,* and *Harper's.* These he collected in two volumes of essays, *Mortal Lessons* (1977) and *Confessions of a Knife* (1979), and a volume of essays and fiction, *Letters to a Young Doctor* (1982). In his writing, he draws upon his experience as a surgeon, and as one critic points out, he "forces physicians to think about the morality of medicine."

Anne Sexton (1928–1974) Born in Newton, Massachusetts, Sexton attended Garland Junior College and Boston University, where she studied under Robert Lowell. She worked for a year as a fashion model in Boston and later wrote her first poetry collection, *To Bedlam and Part Way Back* (1960), while recovering from a nervous breakdown. Writing a poem almost every day was successful therapy for her. From 1961 to 1963, Sexton was a scholar at the Radcliffe Institute for Independent Study. A confessional poet, Sexton acknowledged her debt to W.D. Snodgrass, whose collection of poetry, *Heart's Needle* (1959), influenced her profoundly. Her second collection, *All My Pretty Ones* (1962), includes a quote from a letter by Franz Kafka that expresses her own literary philosophy: "A book should serve as the axe for the frozen sea within us." *Live or Die* (1967), her third collection of poems, won a Pulitzer Prize. She committed suicide in 1974.

William Shakespeare (1564–1616) Shakespeare was born at Stratford-on-Avon in April 1564. His father became an important public figure, rising to the position of high bailiff (equivalent to mayor) of Stratford. Although we know practically nothing of his personal life, we may assume that Shakespeare received a decent grammar school education in literature, logic, and Latin (though not in mathematics or natural science). When he was eighteen, he married Anne Hathaway, eight years his senior; six months later their son was born. Two years later, Anne bore twins. We do not know how the young Shakespeare supported his family, and we do not hear of him again until 1592, when a rival London playwright sarcastically refers to him as an "upstart crow." Shakespeare seems to have prospered in the London theater world. He probably began as an actor, and earned enough as author and part owner of his company's theaters to acquire property. His sonnets, which were written during the 1590s, reveal rich and varied interests. Some are addressed to an attractive young man (whom the poet urges to marry); others to the mysterious dark lady; still others suggest a love triangle of two men and a woman. His dramas include historical plays based on English dynastic struggles; comedies, both festive and dark; romances such as *Pericles* (1608) and *Cymbeline* (1611) that cover decades in the lives of their characters; and the great tragedies: *Hamlet* (1602), *Othello* (1604), *King Lear* (1605), and *Macbeth* (1606). About 1611 (at age forty-seven), he retired to the second largest house in Stratford. He died in 1616, leaving behind a body of work that still stands as a pinnacle in world literature.

Irwin Shaw (1913–1984)   Born and educated in New York City, where he received a B.A. from Brooklyn College in 1934, Shaw began his career as a scriptwriter for popular radio programs of the 1930s, then went to Hollywood to write for the movies. Disillusioned with the film industry, Shaw returned to New York. His first piece of serious writing, an antiwar play entitled *Bury the Dead*, was produced on Broadway in 1936. About this time, Shaw began contributing short stories to such magazines as the *New Yorker* and *Esquire*. His first collection of stories, *Sailor off the Bremen and Other Stories* (1939), earned him an immediate and lasting reputation as a writer of fiction. While continuing to write plays and stories, Shaw turned to the novel and published in 1948 *The Young Lions*, which won high critical praise as one of the most important novels to come out of World War II. The commercial success of the book and the movie adaptation brought Shaw financial independence and allowed him to devote the rest of his career to writing novels, among them *The Troubled Air* (1951), *Lucy Crown* (1956), *Rich Man, Poor Man* (1970), and *Acceptable Losses* (1982). Shaw's stories are collected in *Short Stories: Five Decades* (1978).

Percy Bysshe Shelley (1792–1822)   Born near Horsham, England, Shelley was the son of a wealthy landowner who sat in Parliament. At University College, Oxford, he befriended Thomas Jefferson Hogg. Both became interested in radical philosophy and quickly became inseparable. After one year at Oxford they were expelled together for writing and circulating a pamphlet entitled "The Necessity of Atheism." Shelley married Harriet Westbrook soon after leaving Oxford. Though they had two children, the marriage was unsuccessful, and in 1814, Shelley left Harriet for Mary Wollstonecraft Godwin (author of *Frankenstein* [1818]). After Harriet's death (an apparent suicide), Shelley and Godwin were married. Escaping legal problems in England, he settled in Pisa, Italy, in 1820, and died in a sailing accident before his thirtieth birthday. A playwright and essayist as well as a romantic poet, Shelley is admired for his dramatic poem "Prometheus Unbound" (1820).

Stevie Smith (1902–1971)   Born Florence Margaret Smith in Hull, England, Stevie Smith was a secretary at Newnes Publishing Company in London from 1923 to 1953, and occasionally worked as a writer and broadcaster for the BBC. Though she began publishing verse, which she often illustrated herself, in the 1930s, Smith did not reach a wide audience until 1962—with the publication of *Selected Poems* and her appearance in the Penguin Modern Poets Series. She is noted for her eccentricity and mischievous humor, often involving an acerbic twist on nursery rhymes, common songs, or hymns. Force-fed with what she considered lifeless language in the New English Bible, she often aimed satirical barbs at religion. Smith won the Queen's Gold Medal for poetry in 1969, two years before her death. She published three novels in addition to her eight volumes of poetry.

Robert C. Solomon (b. 1942)   Solomon was born in Detroit. His father was a lawyer, his mother, an artist. After earning a B.A. (1963) at the University of Pennsylvania, he moved to the University of Michigan for an M.A. (1965) and Ph.D. (1967). He has held several teaching positions at such schools as Princeton University, the University of California, Los Angeles, and the University of Pittsburgh. In 1972, he moved to the University of Texas at Austin where he is now a professor of philosophy. His more than fifteen books include *The Passions* (1976), *Love: Emotion, Myth, and Metaphor* (1981), *Above the Bottom Line: An Introduction to Business Ethics* (with Kristine R. Hansen) (1983), and the source of the essay reprinted in this text, *About Love: Reinventing Romance for Our Times* (1988). He is also a published songwriter. Responding to the standard questionnaire that asked him his religion, he wrote: "Peter Pantheist." As his avocations he listed "Travel, food, love, animals, life."

Sophocles (496?–406 B.C.)   Born into a wealthy family at Colonus, a village just outside Athens, Sophocles distinguished himself early in life as a performer, musician, and athlete. Our knowledge of him is based on a very few ancient laudatory notices, but he certainly had a brilliant career as one of the three great Greek classical tragedians (the other two are Aeschylus, an older contemporary, and Euripides, a younger contemporary). He won the drama competition associated with the Dionysian festival (entries consisted of a tragic trilogy and a farce) at least twenty times (far more often than his two principal rivals). However, *Oedipus Rex*, his most famous tragedy, and the three other plays it was grouped with, took second place (ca. 429 B.C.). He lived during the golden age of Athens, when architecture, philosophy, and the arts flourished under Pericles. In 440 B.C., Sophocles was elected as one of the ten *strategoi* (military commanders), an indication of his stature in Athens. But his long life ended in sadder times—when the Peloponnesian War (431–404 B.C.), between the Athenian empire and an alliance led by Sparta, darkened the region. Though Sophocles wrote some 123 plays, only 7 have survived; nonetheless, these few works establish him as the greatest of the ancient Western tragedians.

Helen Sorrells (b. 1908)   Born in Stafford, Kansas, the daughter of farmers, Sorrells earned a B.S. from Kansas State University in 1931. She married a technical writer, had two children, and was approaching her seventh decade when she won the Borestone Award for her poem "Cry Summer." In 1968, she won the *Arizona Quarterly Award* for poetry and in 1973 received a creative writing grant from the National Endowment for the Arts, as well as the Poetry Society of America's Cecil Hemley Award for the poem "Tunnels." She has contributed to *Esquire* and *Reporter*, among others, and published a collection of poems, *Seeds as They Fall* (1971).

Gary Soto (b. 1952)   Gary Soto was born in Fresno, California, to working-class Mexican American parents. He grew up in the San Joaquin Valley, and worked as a migrant laborer in California's rich agricultural region. Uncertain of his abilities, he began his academic career at Fresno City College, moving on to California State University, Fresno, and the University of California, Irvine, where he earned an M.F.A. degree (1976). In 1975, he married Carolyn Oda, a woman of Japanese ancestry. Although his work earned him recognition as early as 1975 (an Academy of American Poets Prize), his first book of poems, *The Elements of San Joaquin*, grim pictures of Mexican American life in California's central valley, appeared in 1977. In 1985, he joined the faculty at the University of California, Berkeley, where he teaches in both the English and Chicano Studies departments. His prolific output of poetry, memoirs, essays, and fiction continues unabated and has earned him numerous prizes, including an American Book Award from the Before Columbus Foundation for *Living up the Street* (1985). One critic points out that Soto has transcended the social commentary of his early work and shifted to "a more personal, less politically motivated poetry." Another argues that "Gary Soto has become not an important Chicano poet but an important American poet."

Art Spiegelman (b. 1948)   Spiegelman's parents, Anja and Vladek, were Polish Jews who survived imprisonment in the Nazi concentration camp at Auschwitz. Spiegelman was born in Stockholm, Sweden, and his family immigrated to the United States. He attended Harpur College (now Binghamton University) from 1965 to 1968. His mother, Anja, committed suicide in 1968. In 1977, he married Francoise Mouly, a publisher. As a student, Spiegelman developed his talent for drawing and writing and became a creative consultant, designer, and writer for Topps Chewing Gum, Inc., where he produced novelty packaging and bubble gum cards. But he was fascinated by the provocative underground comics of the sixties, and began to create original and powerful comic book work addressed to an adult audience. *The Complete Mr. Infinity* appeared in 1970, succeeded by numerous other productions that culminated in *Maus: A Survivor's Tale* (1986). *Maus*, based on his father's experience as a Nazi concentration camp survivor, was nominated for a National Book Critics' Circle Award, and won the Joel M. Cavior Award for Jewish Writing. In his "comic book," Spiegelman portrays the Nazis as cats and the Jews as their victim mice. He published the second volume of *Maus—And Here My Troubles Began* (*From Mauschwitz to the Catskills and Beyond*) in 1991. Spiegelman is currently art director at the *New Yorker*.

Wallace Stevens (1879–1955)   Born in Reading, Pennsylvania, Stevens graduated from Harvard in 1900, worked for a year as a reporter for the New York *Herald Tribune*, graduated from New York University Law School in 1903, and practiced law in New York for twelve years. From 1916 to 1955, Stevens worked for the Hartford Accident and Indemnity Company, where he was appointed vice-president in 1934. He was in his forties when he published his first book of poetry, *Harmonium, Ideas of Order* (1923). Stevens argued that poetry is a "supreme fiction" that shapes chaos and provides order to both nature and human relationships. He illuminates his philosophy in *Ideas of Order* (1935) and *Notes toward a Supreme Fiction* (1942). His *Collected Poems* (1954) won the Pulitzer Prize and established him as a major American poet.

Jonathan Swift (1667–1745)   Born in Dublin, Ireland, of English parents, Swift moved to England following his graduation from Trinity College, Dublin. In 1695, he was ordained minister of the Anglican church of Ireland and five years later became a parish priest in Laracor, Ireland. The conduct of church business took Swift to England frequently, where his wit and skill in defense of Tory politics made him many influential friends. He was rewarded for his efforts in 1713, when Queen Anne appointed him dean of St. Patrick's Cathedral in Dublin. The accession of George I to the throne in the following year, followed by the Tory's loss of the government to Whig control, ended the political power of Swift and his friends. He spent the rest of his life as dean of St. Patrick's, writing during this period his most celebrated satirical narrative, *Gulliver's Travels* (1726), and his most savage essay, "A Modest Proposal" (1729). Among his many other works are *A Tale of a Tub* and *The Battle of the Books* (both 1704), and many poems.

Dylan Thomas (1914–1953)   Born in Swansea, Wales, Thomas decided to pursue a writing career directly after grammar school. At age twenty, he published his first collection, *Eighteen Poems* (1934), but his lack of a university degree deprived him of most opportunities to earn a living as a writer in England. Consequently, his early life (as well as the lives of his wife and children) was darkened by a poverty compounded by his free spending and heavy drinking. A self-proclaimed romanticist, Thomas called his poetry a "record of [his] struggle from darkness towards some measure of light." *The Map of Love* appeared in 1939 and *Deaths and Entrances* in 1946. Later, as a radio playwright and screenwriter, Thomas delighted in the sounds of words, sometimes at the expense of sense. *Under Milk Wood* (produced in 1953) is filled with his private, onomatopoetic language. He suffered from alcoholism and lung ailments, and died in a New York hospital in 1953. Earlier that year, he noted in his *Collected Poems:* "These poems, with all their crudities, doubts and confusions are written for the love of man and in Praise of God, and I'd be a damn fool if they weren't."

Lewis Thomas (1913–1993)   Thomas was born in Flushing, New York. The son of a surgeon, he graduated from Princeton University and in 1937 earned an M.D. from Harvard. In his distinguished medical career, he combined an active practice with teaching and administration. He served as dean of the medical schools of Yale and New York universities and was chief executive officer of the Sloan-Kettering Institute in New York City at the time of his death. His many scientific papers earned him membership in the National Academy of Sciences. But even as a medical student, Thomas displayed literary ambition and published a number of poems. In 1971, he began contributing a regular column, "Notes of a Biology Watcher," to the prestigious *New England Journal of Medicine*. Some of these essays he collected and published in 1974 as *The Lives of a Cell: Notes of a Biology Watcher*. These graceful essays found a sizable audience and won the National Book Award. Subsequent essay collections include *The Medusa and the Snail* (1979) and *Late Night Thoughts on Listening to Mahler's Ninth Symphony* (1983). *The Youngest Science: Notes of a Medicine Watcher* (1983) describes the making of a doctor.

James Thurber (1894–1961)   Born in Columbus, Ohio, Thurber went through the local public schools and graduated from Ohio State University. He began his writing career as a reporter, first for an Ohio newspaper, and later in Paris and New York City, before he became a staff member of the *New Yorker*. There he wrote the humorous satirical essays and fables (often illustrated with his whimsical drawings of people and animals) upon which his reputation rests—the most famous being "The Secret Life of Walter Mitty." In 1929, he and another *New Yorker* staffer, E. B. White, wrote *Is Sex Necessary? or, Why You Feel the Way You Do*, a spoof of the increasingly popular new psychological theories. In 1933, he published his humorous autobiography, *My Life and Hard Times*. With Elliott Nugent, he wrote *The Male Animal* (1940), a comic play that pleads for academic freedom, and, in 1959, he memorialized his associates at the *New Yorker* in *The Years with Ross*.

Leo Tolstoy (1828–1910)   Born in Russia into a family of aristocratic landowners, Tolstoy cut short his university education and joined the army, serving among the primitive Cossacks, who became the subject of his first novel, *The Cossacks* (1863). Tolstoy left the army and traveled abroad but was disappointed by Western materialism and returned home. After a brief period in St. Petersburg, he became bored with the life of literary celebrity and returned to his family estate. There he wrote his two greatest novels, *War and Peace* (1869) and *Anna Karenina* (1877). Around 1876, Tolstoy experienced a kind of spiritual crisis that ultimately led him to reject his former beliefs, way of life, and literary works. Henceforth, he adopted the simple life of the Russian peasants, rejecting orthodoxy in favor of a rational Christianity that disavowed private property, class divisions, secular and institutional religious authority, as well as all art (including his own) that failed to teach the simple principles he espoused.

Jean Toomer (1894–1967)   Descended from Pinckney Benton Stewart Pinchback, a Reconstruction governor of Louisiana whose mother had been a slave, Jean Toomer became one of the leaders in the literary world of the Harlem Renaissance and produced one of that movement's most distinguished works, *Cane* (1923). He also worked in the mainstream white New York literary scene.

Although his best work illuminates the African American experience of the Georgia sugar cane fields, he once wrote "I would consider it libelous for anyone to refer to me as a colored man, for I have not lived as one." Born in Washington, D.C., he graduated from public school and, aiming for a law degree, enrolled briefly at the University of Wisconsin and the City College of New York. But college life proved ungratifying, and he wandered, living among a variety of social and racial groups. He married twice—first a novelist, who died in childbirth, then the daughter of a wealthy New York broker. Both his wives were white. He said of himself: "I am of no particular race, I am of the human race, a man at large in the human world, preparing a new race."

Mark Twain (1835–1910)   Born Samuel L. Clemens in Florida, Missouri, Twain grew up in Hannibal, Missouri, on the banks of the Mississippi River (*mark twain*, a phrase meaning "two fathoms deep," was used by Mississippi riverboat pilots in making soundings). Sometime after his father's death in 1847, Twain left school to become a printer's apprentice, worked as a journeyman printer and newspaper reporter in the East and Middle West, and became a steamboat pilot on the Mississippi River until the outbreak of the Civil War. In 1861, he departed for Nevada with his brother, spent a year prospecting for silver, then returned to newspaper work as a reporter. In 1867, a San Francisco newspaper sent him as correspondent on a cruise ship to Europe and the Holy Land. He used the dispatches he wrote about this voyage as the basis for his first, highly successful book, *The Innocents Abroad* (1869). His second book, *Roughing It* (1872), described his western years and added to his already considerable reputation as an irreverent humorist. No longer explicitly autobiographical but still drawing on his own life, Twain published his masterpieces, the novels *The Adventures of Tom Sawyer* (1876) and *The Adventures of Huckleberry Finn* (1884). Twain remained a prolific and important writer and by the time of his death had become something of a national institution, although he never again quite matched the achievements of these early works. Financial problems and personal tragedies contributed to his increasingly bleak view of the human condition, expressed most powerfully in such works as *A Connecticut Yankee in King Arthur's Court* (1889), *Pudd'nhead Wilson* (1894), *The Man That Corrupted Hadleyburg* (1900), and the posthumously published *The Mysterious Stranger* (1916).

Jill Tweedie (1936–1993)   A reviewer of Jill Tweedie's autobiography, *Eating Children: Young Dreams and Early Nightmares* (1993), reveals that she was born into an economically comfortable family of "impeccable rectitude," presided over by her father, "a Scottish patriarch pathologically incapable of affection." Tweedie was encouraged to become "feminine" and marriageable; she was given ballet lessons and sent to a Swiss finishing school, while her brother, and only sibling, was given an academic education. Her inevitable rebellion when she was eighteen years old precipitated a disastrous marriage (the first of three) to a jealous and abusive Hungarian count. After an acrimonious separation, she took her two children to a hippie commune in Wales where she discovered that, even there, women were burdened with "women's work" while the men, generally, did no work at all. She moved to London and lived in poverty while she struggled to support her household by writing—the only skill she commanded. Ultimately, she became the *Guardian*'s regular columnist on feminist issues. She has written several volumes on feminist themes, among them, *Letters from a Faint-hearted Feminist* (1982). Shortly before her death, when asked about the changes feminism had generated, she replied: "Assumptions about women are what has changed most radically. And a woman's whole psychic energy isn't wrapped up in men or nurturing the male ego. Young women don't appreciate that vast liberation."

Melvin I. Urofsky (b. 1939)   Melvin Urofsky was born and grew up in New York City, where he earned an A.B. (1961), M.A. (1962), and Ph.D. (1968) from Columbia University. He taught at Ohio State University, State University of New York at Albany, and is chair of the history department at Virginia Commonwealth University. In 1984, he earned a law degree from the University of Virginia. He has written and edited more than fifteen books, including a four-volume edition of the letters of Supreme Court Justice Louis D. Brandeis (with David W. Levy, 1971–1978). Urofsky has written and edited several books on the American Jewish experience, and was chair of the Zionist Academic Council (1976–1979). In *Letting Go: Death, Dying, and the Law* (1993), he examines the vexing relationships among dying patients, their physicians, their families, medical ethics, and the law.

Alice Walker (b. 1944)   Born in Eatonton, Georgia, the eighth child of sharecroppers, Walker was educated at Spelman College and Sarah Lawrence College. She has been deeply involved in the civil rights movement, working to register voters in Georgia and on behalf of welfare rights and Head Start in Mississippi. She also worked for the New York City Department of Welfare. She has taught at Wellesley and Yale and been an editor of *Ms.* Her nonfiction works include a biography for children, *Langston Hughes: American Poet* (1973); numerous contributions to anthologies about African American writers; and a collection of essays, *In Search of Our Mothers' Gardens: Womanist Prose* (1983). She has published several novels dealing with the African American experience: *The Third Life of Grange Copeland* (1973), *Meridian* (1976), *The Color Purple* (1982), which won the Pulitzer Prize and established her as a major writer, and *The Temple of My Familiar* (1989). Her short stories are collected in two volumes, *In Love and Trouble: Stories of Black Women* (1973) and *You Can't Keep a Good Woman Down* (1981). Among her collections of poetry are *Good Night, Willie Lee, I'll See You in the Morning* (1979) and *Horses Make a Landscape Look More Beautiful* (1984). Her most recent novel, *Possessing the Secrets of Joy*, appeared in 1992.

Edmund Waller (1606–1687)   Born in Hertfordshire, England, Waller was privately instructed as a young child, then sent to Eton and Cambridge. He served for several years as a member of Parliament, first as an opponent of the Crown and later, as a Royalist. His advocacy of the Royalist cause and his attempts to moderate between the Crown and the Puritans in an increasingly revolutionary period led to his imprisonment and exile. He made his peace with Cromwell and returned to England in 1651. When the monarchy was restored in 1660, Waller regained his seat in Parliament. Waller was one of the earliest poets to use the heroic couplet, a form that was to dominate English poetry for over a century.

Walt Whitman (1819–1892)   One of nine children, Whitman was born in Huntington, Long Island, in New York, and grew up in Brooklyn, where his father worked as a carpenter. At age eleven, after five years of public school, Whitman took a job as a printer's assistant. He learned the printing trade and, before his twentieth birthday, became editor of the *Long Islander*, a Huntington newspaper. He edited several newspapers in the New York area and one in New Orleans before leaving the newspaper business in 1848. He then lived with his parents, worked as a part-time carpenter, and began writing *Leaves of Grass*, which he first published at his own expense in 1855. After the Civil War (during which he was a devoted volunteer, ministering to the wounded), Whitman was fired from his job in the Department of the Interior by Secretary James Harlan, who considered *Leaves of Grass* obscene. Soon, however, he was rehired in the attorney general's office, where he remained until 1874. In 1881, after many editions, *Leaves of Grass* finally found a publisher willing to print it uncensored. Translations were enthusiastically received in Europe, but Whitman remained relatively unappreciated in America, where it was only after his death that a large audience would come to admire his original and innovative expression of American individualism.

Kathleen Wiegner (b. 1938)   Wiegner was born in Milwaukee, Wisconsin, to parents who were both educators. She earned three degrees including a Ph.D. (1967) from the University of Wisconsin–Madison. Thereafter, she joined the faculty at the University of Wisconsin at Milwaukee, where she remained until 1973. She has a daughter, but her 1960 marriage ended in divorce in 1970. In 1974 she moved to California and became an associate editor at the West Coast Bureau of *Forbes* magazine. She received the poetry prize from the Wisconsin Writers Council for *Country Western Breakdown* (1974) and has published several volumes of verse. She once remarked that "My secret ambition would be to live in a world where poems were performed in Las Vegas, where the poet sat on a piano like Ruth Etting and 'sang' poems to an audience that clapped and wept."

Richard Wilbur (b. 1921)   Son of a portrait artist, Wilbur was born in New York City, graduated from Amherst College in 1942, became staff sergeant in the U.S. Army during World War II, then earned an M.A. from Harvard in 1947. He taught English at Harvard, Wellesley, and Wesleyan University, and was named writer-in-residence at Smith College in 1977. Winner of the Pulitzer Prize, National Book Award, and the Bollingen Prize, Wilbur has distinguished himself, in his several volumes of poetry, by using established poetic forms and meters, mining new insights from common, tangible images. A translator of French plays by Molière and Racine, Wilbur was colyricist (with Lillian Hellman) of *Candide*, the 1957 Broadway musical based on Voltaire's satirical novel. *New and Collected Poems* appeared in 1988 and *More Opposites* in 1991.

William Carlos Williams (1883–1963)   Born in Rutherford, New Jersey, Williams graduated from the University of Pennsylvania, (M.D., 1906), interned at hospitals in New York City for two years, studied pediatrics in Leipzig, then returned to practice medicine in his hometown. As a general practitioner, Williams found ample poetic inspiration in his patients, and scribbled down lines between appointments and on the way to house calls. His early collections include *The Tempers* (1913), *Kora in Hell: Improvisations* (1920), and *Sour Grapes* (1921). A stroke in the mid-1950s forced him to retire from his medical practice, but gave him more time to write. His many honors include the National Book Award (1950) and the Pulitzer Prize (1963). *The Williams Reader* was published in 1966.

Virginia Woolf (1882–1941)   Born in London, where she spent most of her life, Woolf, because of her frail health and her father's Victorian attitudes about the proper role of women, received little formal education (none at the university level). Nevertheless, the advantages of an upper-class family (her father, Sir Leslie Stephen, was a distinguished scholar and man of letters who hired tutors for her) and an extraordinarily powerful and inquiring mind allowed Woolf to educate herself. She began keeping a regular diary in her early teens. After moderate success with her first novels, the publication of *To the Lighthouse* (1927) and *Orlando* (1929) established her as a major novelist. While Woolf's reputation rests primarily on her novels, which helped revolutionize fictional technique, she was also a distinguished literary and social critic. A strong supporter of women's rights, she expressed her views on the subject in a series of lectures published as *A Room of One's Own* (1929) and in a collection of essays, *Three Guineas* (1938). Her reputation grew with the publication of her letters and diaries following her suicide by drowning.

William Wordsworth (1770–1850)   Born in Cockermouth, in the Lake District of England, Wordsworth was educated at Cambridge. During a summer tour in France in 1790, Wordsworth had an affair with Annette Vallon that resulted in the birth of a daughter. The tour also made of Wordsworth an ardent defender of the French Revolution of 1789 and kindled his sympathies for the plight of the common person. Wordsworth's acquaintance with Samuel Taylor Coleridge in 1795 began a close friendship that led to the collaborative publication of *Lyrical Ballads* in 1798. Wordsworth supplied a celebrated preface to the second edition in 1800, in which he announced himself a nature poet of pantheistic leanings, committed to democratic equality and the language of common people. He finished *The Prelude* in 1805, but it was not published until after his death. As he grew older, Wordsworth grew increasingly conservative and, while he continued to write prolifically, little that he wrote during the last decade of his life attained the heights of his earlier work. In 1843, he was appointed poet laureate.

Richard Wright (1908–1960)   Wright grew up in Memphis, Tennessee, where his sharecropper father moved the family after he was forced off the farm near Natchez, Mississippi, where Wright was born. When Wright was six, his father abandoned the family, leaving his mother to support Wright and his younger brother with whatever jobs she could find. While their mother worked, the boys shifted for themselves. When he was eight, Wright's mother enrolled him in grammar school, but she fell ill and was unable to work. Consequently, Wright and his brother were placed in an orphanage; reunited, the family lived with relatives, and Wright was able to resume his education, graduating from high school as valedictorian in 1925. Wright left the South for Chicago in 1927, hoping, as he said, that "gradually and slowly I might learn who I was, what I might be." After working at odd jobs, his efforts at writing paid off when he received a job as publicity agent for the Federal Negro Theater. Wright joined the Communist party in 1932 and was a member of the Federal Writers' Project from 1935 to 1937. He published his first collection, *Uncle Tom's Children*, in 1938. About the same time, he began a novel about a poor and angry ghetto youth who accidentally murders the daughter of his white, millionaire employer. The novel, *Native Son* (1940), was published to much critical and popular acclaim and remains his best-known work. Unable to accept party discipline, Wright quit the Communist party in 1944, and in the following year published *Black Boy*, an autobiography of his early years. Discouraged with the racism of America, Wright soon moved his family to France, where he spent the remainder of his life writing and supporting the cause of African independence. His later works include the novels *The Outsider* (1953) and *The Long Dream* (1958), the nonfiction works *Black Power* (1954) and *White Man, Listen!* (1957).

William Butler Yeats (1865–1939)   Yeats was born in Ireland and educated in both Ireland and London. Much of his poetry and many of his plays reflect his fascination with the history of Ireland, particularly the myths and legends of its ancient, pagan past, as well as his interest in the occult. As Yeats matured, he turned increasingly to contemporary subjects, expressing his nationalism in poems about the Irish struggle for independence from England. In 1891, he became one of the founders of an Irish literary society in London (the Rhymers' Club) and of another in Dublin the following year. Already a recognized poet, Yeats helped to establish the Irish National Theater in 1899; its first production was his play *The Countess Catheen* (written in 1892). His contribution to Irish cultural and political nationalism led to his appointment as a senator when the Irish Free State was formed in 1922. Yeats's preeminence as a poet was recognized in 1923, when he received the Nobel Prize for Literature. Among his works are *The Wanderings of Oisin and Other Poems* (1889), *The Wind among the Reeds* (1899), *The Green Helmet and Other Poems* (1910), *Responsibilities: Poems and a Play* (1914), *The Tower* (1928), and *Last Poems and Two Plays* (1939).

Yevgeny Yevtushenko (b. 1933)   Son of two geologists, Yevtushenko was born in Siberia. He attended Gorky Literary Institute from 1951 to 1954, and worked on a geological expedition, at the same time establishing himself as an influential Soviet poet. During the 1950s, his books were published regularly and he was allowed to travel abroad. In 1960, he gave readings in Europe and the United States, but was criticized by Russians for linking them with anti-Semitism in his poem "Babi Yar," the name of a ravine near Kiev where 96,000 Jews were killed by Nazis during World War II. Although considering himself a "loyal revolutionary Soviet citizen," he elicited official disapproval by opposing the 1968 occupation of Czechoslovakia (a performance of his play *Bratsk Power Station* [1967] was cancelled as a result) and for sending a telegram to then-Premier Brezhnev expressing concern for Aleksandr Solzhenitsyn after his arrest in 1974. His works include *A Precocious Autobiography* (1963) and *From Desire to Desire* (1976). His analysis of recent Russian history, *Fatal Half Measures: The Culture of Democracy in the Soviet Union*, appeared in 1991.

Glossary of Literary Terms

Abstract Language   Language that describes ideas, concepts, or qualities, rather than particular or specific persons, places, or things. *Beauty, courage, love* are abstract terms, as opposed to such concrete terms as *man, stone, woman*. George Washington, the Rosetta Stone, and Helen of Troy are particular concrete terms. Characteristically, literature uses *concrete* language to animate *abstract* ideas and principles. When Robert Frost, in "Provide, Provide" (p. 99), describes the pain of impoverished and lonely old age, he doesn't speak of an old, no longer beautiful female. He writes:

> The witch that came (the withered hag)
> To wash the steps with pail and rag,
> Was once the beauty Abishag.

Alexandrine   In poetry, a line containing six iambic feet (iambic hexameter). Alexander Pope, in "An Essay on Criticism" (p. 901), reveals his distaste for the form in a couplet: "A needless Alexandrine ends the song, / That like a wounded snake, drags its slow length along." *See* Meter.

Allegory   A narrative in verse or prose, in which abstract qualities (*death, pride, greed*, for example) are personified as characters. In Bernard Malamud's story "Idiots First" (p. 738), Ginzburg is the personification of death.

Alliteration   The repetition of the same initial consonant (or any initial vowel) sounds in close proximity. The "w" sounds in these lines from Robert Frost's "Provide, Provide" (p. 99) alliterate: "The witch that came (the withered hag) / To wash the steps with pail and rag, / Was once the beauty Abishag."

Allusion   A reference in a literary work to something outside the work. The reference is usually to some famous person, event, or other literary work.

Ambiguity   A phrase, statement, or situation that may be understood in two or more ways. In literature, ambiguity is used to enrich meaning or achieve irony by forcing readers to consider alternative possibilities. When the duke in Robert Browning's "My Last Duchess" (p. 88) says that he "gave commands; / Then all smiles stopped together. There she stands / As if alive," the reader cannot know exactly what those commands were or whether the last words refer to the commands (as a result of which she is no longer alive) or merely refer to the skill of the painter (the painting is extraordinarily lifelike).

Anapest   A three-syllable metrical foot consisting of two unaccented syllables followed by an accented syllable. *See* Meter.

Antagonist   A character in a story, play, or narrative poem who stands in opposition to the hero (*see* Protagonist). The conflict between antagonist and protagonist often generates the action or plot of the story.

Antistrophe   *See* Strophe.

Apostrophe   A direct address to a person who is absent, or to an abstract or inanimate entity. In one of his Holy Sonnets (p. 777), John Donne admonishes: "Death, be not proud." And Wordsworth speaks to a river in Wales: "How oft, in spirit, have I turned to thee, / O sylvan Wye! thou wanderer through the woods."

Archaism   The literary use of obsolete language. When Keats, in "Ode on a Grecian Urn" (p. 780), writes: "with brede / Of marble men and maidens overwrought," he uses an archaic word for *braid* and intends an obsolete definition, "worked all over" (that is, "ornamented"), for *overwrought*.

Archetype   Themes, images, and narrative patterns that are universal and thus embody some enduring aspects of human experience. Some of these themes are the death and rebirth of the hero, the underground journey, and the search for the father.

Assonance   The repetition of vowel sounds in a line, stanza, or sentence. For example, Gwendolyn Brooks, in "The Children of the Poor" (p. 305), describes a character whose "lesions are legion." By using assonance that occurs at the end of words—*my, pie*—or a combination of assonance and consonance (that is, the repetition of final consonant sounds)—*fish, wish*—poets create rhyme. But some poets, particularly modern poets, often use assonantial and consonantial off rhymes (*see* Near Rhyme). W. H. Auden, in "Five Songs" (p. 543) writes:

> That night when joy began
> Our narrowest veins to flush,
> We waited for the flash
> Of morning's levelled gun.

Flush and *gun* are assonantial, *flush* and *flash* are consonantial (and, of course, alliterative.)

Atmosphere   *See* Tone.

Aubade   A love song or lyric to be performed at sunrise. Richard Wilbur's comic "A Late Aubade" (p. 547) is a modern example. Philip Larkin's "Aubade" (p. 802) uses the form ironically in a somber contemplation of mortality.

Ballad   A narrative poem, originally of folk origin, usually focusing upon a climactic episode and told without comment. The most common ballad form consists of quatrains of alternating four- and three-stress iambic lines, with the second and fourth lines rhyming. Often, the ballad will employ a *refrain*—that is, the last line of each stanza will be identical or similar. "Edward" (p. 774) and "Bonny Barbara Allan" (p. 521) are traditional ballads. Dudley Randall's "Ballad of Birmingham" (p. 302) is a twentieth-century example of the ballad tradition.

Blank Verse   Lines of unrhymed iambic pentameter. Shakespeare's dramatic poetry and Milton's *Paradise Lost* (p. 281) are written principally in blank verse. *See* Meter.

Cacophony   Language that sounds harsh and discordant, sometimes used to reinforce the sense of the words. Consider the plosive *b, p,* and *t* sounds in the following lines from Shakespeare's Sonnet 129 (p. 525): "and till action, lust / Is perjured, murderous, bloody, full of blame, / Savage, extreme, rude, cruel, not to trust." *Compare* Euphony.

Caesura   A strong pause within a line of poetry. Note the caesuras in these lines from Robert Browning's "My Last Duchess" (p. 88):

> That's my last Duchess painted on the wall,
> Looking as if she were alive. ‖ I call
> That piece a wonder, now: ‖ Frà Pandolf's hands
> Worked busily a day, ‖ and there she stands.

Carpe Diem   Latin, meaning "seize the day." A work, usually a lyric poem, in which the speaker calls the attention of the auditor (often a young woman) to the short-ness of youth, and life, and then urges the auditor to enjoy life while there is time. Andrew Marvell's "To His Coy Mistress" (p. 529) is among the best of the carpe diem tradition in English. The opening stanza of a famous Robert Herrick poem nicely illustrates carpe diem principles.

> Gather ye rosebuds while ye may,
> Old Time is still a-flying
> And this same flower that smiles today,
> Tomorrow will be dying.

Catharsis   A key concept in the *Poetics* of Aristotle that attempts to explain why representations of suffering and death in drama paradoxically leave the audience feeling relieved rather than depressed. According to Aristotle, the fall of a tragic hero arouses in the viewer feelings of "pity" and "terror"—pity because the hero is an individual of great moral worth, and terror because the viewer identifies with and, consequently, feels vulnerable to the hero's tragic fate. Ideally, the circumstances within the drama allow viewers to experience a catharsis that purges those feelings of pity and terror and leaves them emotionally purified.

Central Intelligence   *See* Point of View.

Chorus   Originally, a group of masked dancers who chanted lyric hymns at religious festivals in ancient Greece. In the plays of Sophocles, the chorus, while circling around the altar to Dionysius, chants the odes that separate the episodes. These odes, in some respects, represented an audience's reaction to, and comment on, the action in the episodes. In Elizabethan drama, and even, on occasion, in modern drama, the chorus appears, usually as a single person who comments on the action.

Comedy   In drama, the representation of situations that are designed to delight and amuse, and which end happily. Comedy often deals with ordinary people in their human condition, while tragedy deals with the ideal and heroic and, until recently, embodied only the high born as tragic heroes. *Compare* Tragedy.

Conceit   A figure of speech that establishes an elaborate parallel between unlike things. The *Petrarchan conceit* (named for the fourteenth-century Italian writer of love lyrics) was often imitated by Elizabethan sonneteers until the device became so hackneyed that Shakespeare mocked the tendency in Sonnet 130 (p. 526):

> My mistress' eyes are nothing like the sun;
> Coral is far more red than her lips' red;
> If snow be white, why then her breasts are dun;
> If hairs be wires, black wires grow on her head.

The *metaphysical conceit*, as used by John Donne for example, employs strange, even bizarre, comparisons to heighten the wit of the poem. Perhaps the most famous metaphysical conceit is Donne's elaborate and extended parallel of a drawing com-pass to the souls of the couple in "A Valediction: Forbidding Mourning" (p. 527).

Concrete Language   *See* Abstract Language.

Conflict   The struggle of a protagonist, or main character, with forces that threaten to destroy him or her. The struggle creates suspense and is usually resolved at the end of the narrative. The force opposing the main character may be either another person—the antagonist—(as in Flannery O'Connor's "Good Country People," p. 36), or society (as in Harlan Ellison's "'Repent, Harlequin!' Said the Ticktockman," p. 528), or natural forces (as in Bernard Malamud's "Idiots First," p. 738). A fourth type of conflict reflects the struggle of opposing tendencies within an individual (as in Tolstoy's "The Death of Iván Ilých," p. 695).

Connotation   The associative and suggestive meanings of a word, in contrast to its literal or *denotative* meaning. One might speak of an *elected official*, a relatively neutral term without connotative implications. Others might call the same person a *politician*, a more negative term; still others might call him or her a *statesman*, a more laudatory term. *Compare* Denotation.

Consonance   Repetition of the final consonant sounds in stressed syllables. In the following verse from W. H. Auden's "Five Songs" (p. 543), lines one and four illustrate consonance, as do lines two and three.

> That night when joy began
> Our narrowest veins to flush,
> We waited for the flash
> Of morning's levelled gun.

Couplet   A pair of rhymed lines—for example, these from A. E. Housman's "Terence, This is Stupid Stuff" (p. 93).

> Why, if 'tis dancing you would be,
> There's brisker pipes than poetry.

Dactyl   A three-syllable metrical foot consisting of an accented syllable followed by two unaccented syllables. *See* Meter.

Denotation   The literal dictionary definition of a word, without associative and suggestive meanings. *See* Connotation.

Denouement   The final revelations that occur after the main conflict is resolved; literally, the "untying" of the plot following the climax.

Deus ex Machina   Latin for "god from a machine." Difficulties were sometimes resolved in ancient Greek and Roman plays by a god, who was lowered to the stage by means of machinery. The term is now used to indicate the use of unconvincing or improbable coincidences to advance or resolve a plot.

Diction   The choice of words in a work of literature, and hence, an element of style crucial to the work's effectiveness. The diction of a story told from the point of view of an inner-city child (as in Toni Cade Bambara's "The Lesson," p. 51) will differ markedly from a similar story told from the point of view of a cosmopolitan lawyer (as in Herman Melville's "Bartleby the Scrivener," p. 211).

Didactic   A term applied to works with the primary and avowed purpose of persuading the reader that some philosophical, religious, or moral doctrine is true. Hence, although some didactic works are nonetheless successful works of art, the emphasis on moral purposes usually occurs at the expense of aesthetic considerations and produces preachy narratives.

Dimeter   A line of poetry consisting of two metrical feet. *See* Meter.

Distance   The property that separates an author or a narrator from the actions of the characters he or she creates, thus allowing a disinterested, or aloof, narration of events. Similarly, distance allows the reader or audience to view the characters and events in a narrative dispassionately.

Dramatic Irony   *See* Irony.

Dramatic Monologue   A type of poem in which the speaker addresses another person (or persons) whose presence is known only from the speaker's words. During the course of the monologue, the speaker (often unintentionally) reveals his or her own character. Such poems are dramatic because the speaker interacts with another character at a specific time and place; they are monologues because the entire poem is uttered by the speaker. Robert Browning's "My Last Duchess" (p. 88), Matthew Arnold's "Dover Beach" (p. 535), and T. S. Eliot's "The Love Song of J. Alfred Prufrock" (p. 537) are dramatic monologues.

Elegy   Usually, a poem lamenting the death of a particular person, but often used to describe meditative poems on the subject of human mortality. A. E. Housman's "To an Athlete Dying Young" (p. 785) and Theodore Roethke's "Elegy for Jane" (p. 799) are elegies.

End-Rhyme   *See* Rhyme.

End-Stopped Line   A line of verse that embodies a complete logical and grammatical unit. A line of verse that does not constitute a complete syntactic unit is called *run-on*. For example, in the opening lines of Robert Browning's "My Last Duchess" (p. 88): "That's my last Duchess painted on the wall, / Looking as if she were alive. I call / That piece a wonder, now: . . . ." The opening line is end-stopped, while the second line is run-on because the direct object of *call* runs on to the third line.

English Sonnet   Also called *Shakespearean sonnet. See* Sonnet.

Enjambment   The use of run-on lines. *See* End-Stopped Line.

Epigraph   In literature, a short quotation or observation related to the theme and placed at the head of the work. T. S. Eliot's "The Love Song of J. Alfred Prufrock" (p. 537) has an epigraph, as does Donald W. Baker's "Formal Application" (p. 307).

Epiphany   In literature, a showing forth, or sudden manisfestation. James Joyce used the term to indicate a sudden illumination that enables a character (and, presumably, the reader) to understand his situation. The narrator of Joyce's "Araby" (p. 27) experiences an epiphany toward the end of the story, as does Iván Ilých in Tolstoy's "The Death of Iván Ilých" (p. 695).

Epode   *See* Strophe.

Euphony   Language embodying sounds pleasing to the ear. *Compare* Cacophony.

Exposition   Information supplied to readers and audiences that enables them to understand narrative action. Often, exposition establishes what has occurred before the narrative begins or informs the audience about relationships among principal characters. The absence of exposition from some modern literature, particularly modern drama, contributes to the unsettling feelings sometimes experienced by the audience.

Farce   A type of comedy, usually satiric, that relies on exaggerated character types, ridiculous situations, and, often, horseplay.

Feminine Rhyme   A two-syllable rhyme in which the second syllable is unstressed, as in the second and fourth lines of these verses from Edward Arlington Robinson's "Miniver Cheevy" (p. 289)

> Miniver Cheevy, child of scorn,
> Grew lean while he assailed the seasons;
> He wept that he was ever born,
> And he had reasons.

Figurative Language   A general term covering the many ways in which language is used nonliterally. *See* Hyperbole, Irony, Metaphor, Metonymy, Paradox, Simile, Symbol, Synecdoche, Understatement.

First-Person Narrator   *See* Point of View.

Foot   *See* Meter.

Free Verse Poetry, usually unrhymed, that does not adhere to the metrical regularity of traditional verse. Although free verse is not metrically regular, it is nonetheless clearly more rhythmic than prose and makes use of other aspects of poetic discourse—such as alliteration, assonance, parallelism, etc.—to achieve its effects.

Heroic Couplet Iambic pentameter lines that rhyme *aa, bb, cc,* and so on. Usually, heroic couplets are *closed*—that is, the couplet's end coincides with a major syntactic unit so that the line is end-stopped. These lines from Alexander Pope's "Essay on Man" illustrate the form: "And, spite of pride, in erring reason's spite, / One truth is clear; Whatever IS, is RIGHT."

Hexameter A line of verse consisting of six metrical feet. *See* Meter.

Hubris In Greek tragedy, arrogance resulting from excessive pride.

Hyperbole Figurative language that embodies overstatement or exaggeration. The boast of the speaker in Robert Burns's "A Red, Red Rose" (p. 531) is hyperbolic: "And I will luve thee still, my dear, / Till a' the seas gang dry."

Iamb A metrical foot consisting of an unstressed syllable followed by a stressed syllable. *See* Meter.

Imagery Language that embodies an appeal to a physical sense, usually sight, although the words may invoke sound, smell, taste, and touch as well. The term is often applied to all figurative language.

Internal Rhyme *See* Rhyme.

Irony Figurative language in which the intended meaning differs from the literal meaning. *Verbal irony* includes overstatement (hyperbole), understatement, and opposite statement. The following lines from Robert Burns's "A Red, Red Rose" (p. 531) embody overstatement:

> As fair as thou, my bonnie lass,
> So deep in luve am I;
> And I will luve thee still, my dear,
> Till a' the seas gang dry.

These lines from Andrew Marvell's "To His Coy Mistress" (p. 529) understate: "The grave's a fine and private place, / but none, I think, do there embrace." W. H. Auden's ironic conclusion to "The Unknown Citizen" (p. 300) reveals opposite statement: "Was he free? Was he happy? The question is absurd: / Had anything been wrong, we should certainly have heard." *Dramatic irony* occurs when a reader or audience knows things a character does not and, consequently, hears things differently. For example, in Shakespeare's *Othello* (p. 571), the audience knows that Iago is Othello's enemy, but Othello doesn't. Hence, the audience's understanding of Iago's speeches to Othello differs markedly from Othello's.

Italian Sonnet Also called *Petrarchan sonnet. See* Sonnet.

Lyric Originally, a song accompanied by lyre music. Now, a relatively short poem expressing the thought or feeling of a single speaker. Almost all the nondramatic poetry in this anthology is lyric poetry.

Metaphor A figurative expression consisting of two elements in which one element is provided with special attributes by being equated with a second, unlike element. In Theodore Roethke's "Elegy for Jane" (p. 799), for example, the speaker addresses his dead student: "If only I could nudge you from this sleep, / My maimed darling, my skittery pigeon." Here, Jane is characterized metaphorically as a "skittery pigeon," and all the reader's experience of a nervous pigeon's movement becomes attached to Jane. *See* Simile.

Meter   Refers to recurrent patterns of accented and unaccented syllables in verse. A metrical unit is called a *foot*, and there are four basic accented patterns. An *iamb*, or *iambic foot*, consists of an unaccented syllable followed by an accented syllable (bĕfóre, tŏdáy). A *trochee*, or *trochaic foot*, consists of an accented syllable followed by an unaccented syllable (fúnñy, phántŏm). An *anapest*, or *anapestic foot*, consists of two unaccented syllables followed by an accented syllable (in the line "Ĭf ĕv́ ‖ erv̆thĭng háp ‖ peňs thăt cán't ‖ bĕ dóne," the second and third metrical feet are anapests). A *dactyl*, or *dactylic foot*, consists of a stressed syllable followed by two unstressed syllables (sýllăblĕ, métrĭcăl). One common variant, consisting of two stressed syllables, is called a *spondee*, or *spondaic foot* (dáybŕeak, moónshíne).

Lines are classified according to the number of metrical feet they contain.

one foot	monometer
two feet	dimeter
three feet	trimeter
four feet	tetrameter
five feet	pentameter
six feet	hexameter (An iambic hexameter line is an *Alexandrine*.)

Here are some examples of various metrical patterns:

Tŏ eách ‖ hĭs súff ‖ erĭngs: áll ‖ aŕe mén,	*iambic tetrameter*
Cŏndemńed ‖ ăliké ‖ tŏ groán;	*iambic trimeter*
Ońce ŭp ‖ oń ă ‖ mídnĭght ‖ dréarў, ‖ whíle Ĭ ‖ póndeŕed ‖ wéak ănd ‖ wéarў	*trochaic octameter*
Thĕ Ässýr ‖ iăn caḿe dowń ‖ likĕ ă wólf ‖ oň ŧhe fóld	*anapestic tetrameter*
Ĭš thís ‖ thĕ rég ‖ iŏn, thís ‖ thĕ soíl, ‖ thĕ clíme,	*iambic pentameter*
Fóllŏw ĭt ‖ úttĕrlў,	*dactylic dimeter*
Hópe bĕ ‖ yońd hópe:	*dimeter line—trochee and spondee*

Metonymy   A figure of speech in which a word stands for a closely related idea. In the expression "The pen is mightier than the sword," *pen* and *sword* are metonyms for written ideas and physical force.

Muses   Nine goddesses, the daughters of Zeus and Mnemosyne (memory), who preside over various humanities. Although there are some variations, generally they may be assigned as follows: Calliope, epic poetry; Clio, history; Erato, lyric poetry; Euterpe, music; Melpomene, tragedy; Polyhymnia, sacred poetry; Terpsichore, dance; Thalia, comedy; and Urania, astronomy.

Near Rhyme   Also called *off rhyme*, *slant rhyme*, or *oblique rhyme*. Usually the occurrence of consonance where rhyme is expected, as in *pearl*, *alcohol* or *heaven*, *given*. *See* Rhyme.

Octave   An eight-line stanza. More often, the opening eight-line section of an Italian sonnet, rhymed *abbaabba*, followed by the sestet that concludes the poem. *See* Sonnet.

Ode   Usually, a long, serious poem on exalted subjects, often in the form of an address. Keats's "Ode on a Grecian Urn" (p. 780) is representative. In Greek dramatic poetry, odes consisting of three parts, the *strophe*, the *antistrophe*, and the *epode*, were sung by the chorus between the episodes of the play. *See* Strophe.

Off Rhyme   *See* Near Rhyme.

Omniscient Point of View   *See* Point of View.

Onomatopoeia   Language that sounds like what it means. Words like *buzz, bark,* and *hiss* are onomatopoetic. Also, sound patterns that reinforce the meaning may be designated onomatopoetic. Alexander Pope illustrates such onomatopoeia in a passage from "An Essay on Criticism" (p. 901):

> 'Tis not enough no harshness gives offense,
> The sound must seem an echo to the sense:
> Soft is the strain when Zephyr gently blows,
> And the smooth stream in smoother numbers flows;
> But when loud surges lash the sounding shore,
> The hoarse, rough verse should like the torrent roar:
> When Ajax strives some rock's vast weight to throw,
> The line too labors, and the words move slow;
> Not so, when swift Camilla scours the plain,
> Flies o'er th'unbending corn, and skims along the main.

Opposite Statement   *See* Irony.

Ottava Rima   An eight-line, iambic pentameter stanza rhymed *abababcc*. Originating with the Italian poet Boccaccio, the form was made popular in English poetry by Milton, Keats, and Byron, among others.

Oxymoron   Literary, "acutely silly." A figure of speech in which contradictory ideas are combined to create a condensed paradox: *thunderous silence, sweet sorrow, wise fool.*

Paean   In classical Greek drama, a hymn of praise, usually honoring Apollo. Now, any lyric that joyously celebrates its subject.

Paradox   A statement that seems self-contradictory or absurd but is, somehow, valid. The conclusion of Donne's "Death, Be Not Proud" (p. 777) illustrates: "One short sleep past, we wake eternally / And death shall be no more; Death, thou shalt die." In Holy Sonnet 14, Donne, speaking of his relationship with God, writes: "Take me to You, imprison me, for I, / Except You enthrall me, never shall be free, / Nor ever chaste, except You ravish me."

Pastoral   *Pastor* is Latin for "shepherd," and the pastoral is a poetic form invented by ancient Roman writers that deals with the complexities of the human condition as if they exist in a world peopled by idealized rustic shepherds. Pastoral poetry suggests that country life is superior to urban life. In the hands of such English poets as Marlowe and Milton, the pastoral embodies highly conventionalized and artificial language and situations. Christopher Marlowe's "The Passionate Shepherd to His Love" (p. 522) is a famous example, as is Sir Walter Ralegh's mocking response, "The Nymph's Reply to the Shepherd" (p. 523).

Pentameter   A line containing five metrical feet. *See* Meter.

Persona   Literally, "actor's mask." The term is applied to a first-person narrator in fiction or poetry. The persona's views may differ from the author's.

Personification   The attribution of human qualities to nonhuman things, such as animals, aspects of nature, or even ideas and processes. When Donne exclaims in "Death, Be Not Proud" (p. 777), "Death, thou shalt die," he uses personification, as does Edmund Waller when the speaker of "Go, Lovely Rose!" (p. 528) says:

> Go, lovely rose!
> Tell her that wastes her time and me

> That now she knows,
> When I resemble her to thee,
> How sweet and fair she seems to be.

Petrarchan Sonnet Also called *Italian sonnet. See* Sonnet.

Plot A series of actions in a story or drama that bear a significant relationship to each other. E. M. Forster illuminates the definition: " 'The King died, and then the Queen died,' is a story. 'The King died, and then the Queen died of grief,' is a plot."

Poetic License Variation from standard word order to satisfy the demands of rhyme and meter.

Point of View The person or intelligence a writer of fiction creates to tell the story to the reader. The major techniques are:

First person, where the story is told by someone, often, though not necessarily, the principal character, who identifies himself or herself as "I" (as in James Joyce's "Araby") (p. 27).

Third person, where the story is told by someone (not identified as "I") who is not a participant in the action and who refers to the characters by name or as "he," "she," and "they" (as in Harlan Ellison's " 'Repent, Harlequin!' Said the Ticktockman") (p. 258).

Omniscient, a variation on the third person, where the narrator knows everything about the characters and events, can move about in time and place as well as from character to character at will, and can, whenever he or she wishes, enter the mind of any character (as in Tolstoy's "The Death of Iván Ilých") (p. 695).

Central intelligence, another variation on the third person, where narrative elements are limited to what a single character sees, thinks, and hears.

Prosody The study of the elements of versification, such as *rhyme, meter, stanzaic patterns,* and so on.

Protagonist Originally, the first actor in a Greek drama. In Greek, *agon* means "contest." Hence, the protagonist is the hero, the main character in a narrative, in conflict either with his or her situation or with another character. *See* Antagonist.

Quatrain A four-line stanza.

Refrain The repetition within a poem of a group of words, often at the end of ballad stanzas.

Rhyme The repetition of the final stressed vowel sound and any sounds following (*cat, rat; debate, relate; pelican, belly can*) produces perfect rhyme. When the last stressed syllable rhymes, the rhyme is called masculine (*cat, rat*). Two-syllable rhymes with unstressed last syllables are called feminine (*ending, bending*). When rhyming words appear at the end of lines, the poem is *end-rhymed.* When rhyming words appear within one line, the line contains *internal rhyme.* When the correspondence in sounds is imperfect (*heaven, given; began, gun*) *off rhyme, slant rhyme,* or *near rhyme* is produced.

Rhythm The quality created by the relationship between stressed and unstressed syllables. A regular pattern of alternation between stressed and unstressed syllables produces *meter.* Irregular alternation of stressed and unstressed syllables produces *free verse.* Compare the rhythm of the following verses from Robert Frost's "Stopping by Woods on a Snowy Evening" (p. 792) and Walt Whitman's "Out of the Cradle Endlessly Rocking":

Whose woods these are I think I know.
His house is in the village though;
He will not see me stopping here
To watch his woods fill up with snow.

Out of the cradle endlessly rocking,
Out of the mocking-bird's throat, the musical shuttle,
Out of the Ninth-month midnight,
Over the sterile sands and the fields beyond, where the child leaving his bed
    wander'd alone, bareheaded, barefoot,
Down from the shower'd halo,

Run-On Line   *See* End-Stopped Line.

Satire   Writing in a comic mode that holds a subject up to scorn and ridicule, often with the purpose of correcting human vice and folly. Harlan Ellison's " 'Repent, Harlequin!' Said the Ticktockman" (p. 258) satirizes a society obsessed with time and order.

Scansion   The analysis of patterns of stressed and unstressed syllables in order to establish the metrical or rhythmical pattern of a poem.

Sestet   The six-line resolution of a Petrarchan sonnet. *See* Sonnet.

Setting   The place where a story occurs. Often the setting contributes significantly to the story; for example, the dreary academic setting of Barry Holstun Lopez's "Winter Count 1973" (p. 274) serves as a foil to Native American history.

Shakespearean Sonnet   Also called *English sonnet*. *See* Sonnet.

Simile   Similar to metaphor, the simile is a comparison of unlike things introduced by the words *like* or *as*. Robert Burns, in "A Red, Red Rose" (p. 531), for example, exclaims, "O My Luve's like a red, red rose," and Shakespeare mocks extravagant similes when he admits in Sonnet 130, "My mistress' eyes are nothing like the sun" (p. 526).

Slant Rhyme   *See* Rhyme.

Soliloquy   A dramatic convention in which an actor, alone on the stage, speaks his or her thoughts aloud. Iago's speech that closes Act I of Shapespeare's *Othello* (p. 571) is a soliloquy, as is Othello's speech in Act III, Scene 3, lines 258–78.

Sonnet   A lyric poem of fourteen lines, usually of iambic pentameter. The two major types are the Petrarchan (or Italian) and Shakespearean (or English). The Petrarchan sonnet is divided into an octave (the first eight lines, rhymed *abbaabba*) and sestet (the final six lines, usually rhymed *cdecde* or *cdcdcd*). The Shakespearean sonnet consists of three quatrains and a concluding couplet, rhymed *abab cdcd efef gg*. In general, the sonnet establishes some issue in the octave or three quatrains and then resolves it in the sestet or final couplet. Robert Frost's "Design" (p. 793) is an Italian sonnet; several Shakespearean sonnets appear in the text.

Spondee   A metrical foot consisting of two stressed syllables, usually a variation within a metrical line. *See* Meter.

Stanza   The grouping of a fixed number of verse lines in a recurring metrical and rhyme pattern. Keats's "Ode on a Grecian Urn" (p. 780), for example, employs ten-line stanzas rhymed *ababcdecde*.

Stream-of-Consciousness   The narrative technique that attempts to reproduce the full and uninterrupted flow of a character's mental process, in which ideas, memories, and sense impressions may intermingle without logical transitions. Writers using this technique sometimes abandon conventional rules of syntax and punctuation.

Strophe   In Greek tragedy, the unit of verse the chorus chanted as it moved to the left in a dance rhythm. The chorus sang the *antistrophe* as it moved to the right and the *epode* while standing still.

Style   The way an author expresses his or her matter. Style embodies, and depends upon, all the choices an author makes—the diction, syntax, figurative language, and sound patterns of the piece.

Subplot   A second plot, usually involving minor characters. The subplot is subordinate to the principal plot, but often is resolved by events that figure in the main plot. For example, Iago's manipulation of Roderigo in Shakespeare's *Othello* (p. 571) is a subplot that enters the main plot and figures prominently in the play's climax.

Symbol   An object, an action, or a person that represents more than itself. In Stephen Crane's "The Bride Comes to Yellow Sky" (p. 18), Scratchy represents the old mythic West made obsolete by the encroachment of Eastern values. The urn in Keats's "Ode on a Grecian Urn" (p. 780) symbolizes the cold immortality of art. In both of these, the symbolism arises from the *context*. *Public* symbols, in contrast to these *contextual symbols*, are objects, actions, or persons that history, myth, or legend has invested with meaning—the cross, Helen of Troy, a national flag.

Synecdoche   A figure of speech in which a part is used to signify the whole. In "Elegy Written in a Country Churchyard," Gray writes of "Some heart once pregnant with celestial fire; / Hands that the rod of empire might have swayed." That heart, and those hands, of course, refer to whole persons who are figuratively represented by significant parts.

Synesthesia   An image that uses a second sensory impression to modify the primary sense impression. When one speaks of a "cool green," for example, the primary *visual* evocation of green is combined with the *tactile* sensation of coolness. Keats, in "Ode to a Nightingale," asks for a drink of wine "Tasting of Flora and the country green, / Dance, and Provençal song, and sunburnt mirth!" Here, the *taste* of wine is synesthetically extended to the sight of flowers and meadows, the movement of dance, the sound of song, and the heat of the sun.

Tetrameter   A verse line containing four metrical feet. *See* Meter.

Theme   The abstract moral proposition that a literary work advances through the concrete elements of character, action, and setting. The theme of Harlan Ellison's " 'Repent, Harlequin!' Said the Ticktockman" (p. 258), in which an ordinary person defies an oppressive system, might be that to struggle against dehumanizing authority is obligatory.

Third-Person Narrator   A voice telling a story that refers to characters by name or as "he," "she," or "they." *See* Point of View.

Tone   The attitude embodied in the language a writer chooses. The tone of a work might be sad, joyful, ironic, solemn, playful. Compare, for example, the somber tone of Matthew Arnold's "Dover Beach" (p. 535) with the comic tone of Anthony Hecht's "The Dover Bitch" (p. 548).

Tragedy   The dramatic representation of serious and important actions that culminate in catastrophe for the protagonist, or chief actor, in the play. Aristotle saw tragedy as the fall of a noble figure from a high position and happiness to defeat and misery as a result of *hamartia*, some misjudgment or frailty of character. *Compare* Comedy.

Trimeter   A verse line consisting of three metrical feet. *See* Meter.

Triplet   A sequence of three verse lines that rhyme.

Trochee   A metrical foot consisting of a stressed syllable followed by an unstressed syllable. *See* Meter.

Understatement   A figure of speech that represents something as less important than it really is, hence, a form of irony. When in Robert Browning's "My Last Duchess" (p. 88) the duke asserts ". . . This grew; I gave commands; / Then all smiles stopped together . . .," the words ironically understate what was likely an order for his wife's execution.

Villanelle   A French verse form of nineteen lines (of any length) divided into six stanzas—five tercets and a final quatrain—employing two rhymes and two refrains. The refrains consist of lines one (repeated as lines six, twelve, and eighteen) and three (repeated as lines nine, fifteen, and nineteen). Dylan Thomas's "Do Not Go Gentle into That Good Night" (p. 801) and Catherine Davis's response "After a Time" (p. 804) are villanelles.

1031

T. S. Eliot, "The Love Song of J. Alfred Prufrock." From *Collected Poems 1909–1962* by T. S. Eliot. Reprinted by permission of the publisher, Harcourt Brace Company, and by permission of Faber & Faber Ltd.

Harlan Ellison, " 'Repent, Harlequin!' Said theTicktockman." Copyright © 1965 by Harlan Ellison. Renewed copyright © 1993 by Harlan Ellison. Reprinted by arrangement with, and permission of, the Author and the Author's agent, Richard Curtis Associates, Inc., New York. All rights reserved.

Louise Erdrich, "The Red Convertible." From *Love Medicine* by Louise Erdrich. Copyright © 1984, 1993 by Louise Erdrich. Reprinted by permission of Henry Holt and Co., Inc.

William Faulkner, "A Rose for Emily." From *Collected Stories of William Faulkner.* Copyright 1930 and renewed 1958 by William Faulkner. Reprinted by permission of Random House, Inc.

James Fenton, "God, A Poem." From *Children in Exile* by James Fenton. Copyright 1993 by James Fenton. Reprinted by permission of Sterling Lord Literistic, Inc.

Lawrence Ferlinghetti, "Constantly Risking Absurdity" and "In Goya's Greatest Scenes." From *A Coney Island of the Mind.* Copyright © 1958 by Lawrence Ferlinghetti. Reprinted by permission of New Directions Publishing Corporation.

Carolyn Forché, "The Colonel." From *The Country between Us* by Carolyn Forché. Copyright © 1980 by Carolyn Forché. Reprinted by permission of HarperCollins Publishers Inc.

Robert Frost, "After Apple-Picking," "Birches," "Design," "Fire and Ice," "Nothing Gold Can Stay," "Out, Out—" "Provide, Provide," "Stopping by Woods on a Snowy Evening." From *The Poetry of Robert Frost* edited by Edward Connery Lathem. Copyright 1916, 1923, 1930, 1939, © 1969 by Holt, Rinehart and Winston. Copyright 1936, 1942, 1944, 1951, © 1958 by Robert Frost. Copyright © 1964, © 1967, © 1970 by Lesley Frost Ballantine. Reprinted by permission of Henry Holt and Co., Inc.

Tess Gallagher, "Conversation with a Fireman from Brooklyn." Copyright 1984 by Tess Gallagher. Reprinted from *Willingly* with permission of Graywolf Press, Saint Paul, Minnesota.

Willard Gaylin, "What's So Special about Being Human?" From *Adam and Eve and Pinocchio* by Willard Gaylin. Copyright © 1990 by Willard Gaylin. Used by permission of Viking Penguin, a division of Penguin Books USA Inc.

Molly Giles, "Rough Translations." From *Rough Translations* by Molly Giles. Copyright © by Molly Giles. Reprinted by permission of The University of Georgia Press.

Allen Ginsberg, "To Aunt Rose." From *Collected Poems 1947–1980* by Allen Ginsberg. Copyright © 1958 by Allen Ginsberg. Reprinted by permission of HarperCollins Publishers Inc.

Dana Gioia, "Sunday News." From *Daily Horoscope* by Dana Gioia. Reprinted by permission of Graywolf Press, Saint Paul, Minnesota.

Nikki Giovanni, "Dreams." From *The Women and the Men* by Nikki Giovanni. Copyright © 1970, 1974, 1975, by Nikki Giovanni. Reprinted by permission of William Morrow & Company, Inc.

Nikki Giovanni, "For Saundra." From *Black Feeling, Black Talk, Black Judgment* by Nikki Giovanni. Copyright © 1968, 1970 by Nikki Giovanni. Reprinted by permission of William Morrow & Company, Inc.

Nadine Gordimer, "Something for the Time Being." Copyright © 1960, renewed © 1988 by Nadine Gordimer, from *Selected Stories* by Nadine Gordimer. Used by permission of Viking Penguin, a division of Penguin Books USA Inc.

Robert Hayden, "Those Winter Sundays." Reprinted from *Angle of Ascent, New and Selected Poems,* by Robert Hayden, by permission of Liveright Publishing Corporation. Copyright © 1975, 1972, 1970, 1966 by Robert Hayden.

Bessie Head, "Looking for a Rain God." Copyright © The Estate of Bessie Head. From *The Collector of Treasures,* Heinemann Educational Books, African Writers Series, 1977. Permission granted by John Johnson Ltd., London.

Anthony Hecht, "More Light! More Light!" and "The Dover Bitch." From *Collected Earlier Poems* by Anthony Hecht. Copyright © 1990 by Anthony E. Hecht. Reprinted by permission of Alfred A. Knopf, Inc.

Ernest Hemingway, "A Clean, Well-Lighted Place." Reprinted with permission of Charles Scribner's Sons, an imprint of Macmillan Publishing Company, from *Winner Take Nothing* by Ernest Hemingway. Copyright 1933 by Charles Scribner's Sons; renewal copyright © 1961 by Mary Hemingway.

William Heyen, "The Trains." From *Falling from Heaven: Holocaust Poems of a Jew and a*

permission granted by The Executor of Henry Reed's Estate 1991. Reprinted by permission of Oxford University Press.

Alastair Reid, "Curiosity." From *Weathering* (Dutton) © 1959 Alastair Reid. Originally published in *The New Yorker*. Reprinted by permission of *The New Yorker*.

Otto Reinert, Notes on Shakespeare's *Othello*. Copyright 1964. Reprinted by permission of the author.

Adrienne Rich, "Living in Sin." From *The Fact of a Doorframe* by Adrienne Rich. Reprinted by permission of W. W. Norton & Company, Inc. Copyright © 1984 by Adrienne Rich. Copyright © 1975, 1978 by W. W. Norton & Company Inc. Copyright © 1981 by Adrienne Rich.

Alberto Ríos, "Teodoro Luna's Two Kisses." From *Teodoro Luna's Two Kisses* by Alberto Ríos. Reprinted by permission of W. W. Norton & Company, Inc. Copyright © 1990 by Alberto Ríos.

Theodore Roethke, "My Papa's Waltz," "Elegy for Jane." From *The Collected Poems of Theodore Roethke* by Theodore Roethke. "My Papa's Waltz," copyright 1942 by Hearst Magazines, Inc. "Elegy for Jane," copyright 1950 by Theodore Roethke. Used by permission of Doubleday, a division of Bantam Doubleday Dell Publishing Group, Inc.

Muriel Rukeyser, "Myth." From *Out of Silence*, copyright, William L. Rukeyser, 1992, Triquarterly Books, Evanston, IL. Reprinted by permission of William L. Rukeyser.

Margaret Sanger, "The Turbid Ebb and Flow of Misery." Reprinted by permission of Grant Sanger.

Sappho, "With His Venom." *Sappho: A New Translation* by Mary Barnard. Copyright © 1958 The Regents of the University of California; © renewed 1984 Mary Barnard. Reprinted by permission of the University of California Press.

William Saroyan, "Five Ripe Pears." From *The Saroyan Special*. Books for Libraries Press. Permission granted by Ayer Co. Publishers.

May Sarton, "AIDS." Reprinted from *The Silence Now; New and Uncollected Earlier Poems* by May Sarton. By permission of W. W. Norton & Company, Inc. Copyright © 1988 by May Sarton.

Jean-Paul Sartre, "No Exit." From *No Exit and The Flies* by Jean-Paul Sartre, trans. S. Gilbert. Copyright 1946 by Stuart Gilbert. Copyright renewed 1974, 1975 by Maris Agnes Mathilde Gilbert. Reprinted by permission of Alfred A. Knopf, Inc. Canadian rights: "In Camera" from *Huis Clos* by Jean-Paul Sartre. Translated by Stuart Gilbert (Hamish Hamilton, 1946). Translation copyright © Stuart Gilbert, 1946. Reprinted by permission of Hamish Hamilton Ltd.

Gjertrud Schnackenberg, "Complaint." From *The Lamplit Answer* by Gjertrud Schnackenberg. Copyright © 1982, 1985 by Gjertrud Schnackenberg. Reprinted by permission of Farrar, Straus & Giroux, Inc.

Richard Selzer, "The Discus Thrower." From *Confessions of a Knife*. Copyright © 1979 by David Goldman and Janet Selzer, Trustees. Reprinted by permission of William Morrow & Company, Inc.

Anne Sexton, "The Farmer's Wife." From *To Bedlam and Part Way Back* by Anne Sexton. Copyright © 1960 by Anne Sexton. Reprinted by permission of Houghton Mifflin Company. All rights reserved.

Irwin Shaw, "The Girls in Their Summer Dresses." Reprinted by permission of the Irwin Shaw Literary Estate.

Stevie Smith, "Not Waving but Drowning" and "To Carry the Child." From *The Collected Poems of Stevie Smith* by Stevie Smith. Copyright © 1972 by Stevie Smith. Reprinted by permission of New Directions Publishing Company.

Robert C. Solomon, "Love Stories." From *About Love* by Robert C. Solomon. Copyright © 1988 by Robert C. Solomon. Reprinted by permission of Melanie Jackson Agency.

Sophocles, *Antigonê*. From *Sophocles, The Oedipus Cycle: An English Version* by Dudley Fitts and Robert Fitzgerald. Copyright 1939 by Harcourt Brace & Company and renewed 1967 by Dudley Fitts and Robert Fitzgerald. Reprinted by permission of the publisher.

CAUTION: All rights, including professional, amateur, motion picture, recitation, lecturing, performance, public reading, radio broadcasting, and television are strictly reserved. Inquiries on all rights should be addressed to Harcourt Brace & Company, Permissions Department, Orlando, FL 32887.

Helen Sorrells, "From a Correct Address in a Suburb of a Major City." From *Seeds as They Fall* by Helen Sorrells. Published by Vanderbilt University Press, 1971. Reprinted by permission of Vanderbilt University Press.

Gary Soto, "The Rhino." From *A Summer Life.* Copyright © 1990 by University Press of New England. By permission of University Press of New England.

Art Spiegelman, "Prisoner on the Hell Planet." From *Maus: A Survivor's Tale* by Art Spiegelman. Copyright © 1973, 1980, 1981, 1982, 1983, 1984, 1985, 1986 by Art Spiegelman. Reprinted by permission of Pantheon Books, a division of Random House, Inc.

Wallace Stevens, "Sunday Morning." From *Collected Poems* by Wallace Stevens. Copyright 1923 and renewed 1951 by Wallace Stevens. Reprinted by permission of Alfred A. Knopf, Inc.

Dylan Thomas, "Do Not Go Gentle into That Good Night," "Fern Hill." From *The Poems of Dylan Thomas,* copyright 1945 by the Trustees for the Copyrights of Dylan Thomas, 1952 by Dylan Thomas. Reprinted by permission of New Directions Publishing Corporation and David Hingham Associates.

Lewis Thomas, "The Iks." Copyright © 1973 by The Massachusetts Medical Society, from *The Lives of a Cell* by Lewis Thomas. Used by permission of Viking Penguin, a division of Penguin Books USA Inc.

James Thurber, "The Greatest Man in the World." Copyright 1935 James Thurber. Copyright 1963 Helen W. Thurber and Rosemary A. Thurber. From *The Middle-Aged Man on the Flying Trapeze,* published by Harper & Row.

Jean Toomer, "Theater." Reprinted from *Cane* by Jean Toomer, by permission of Liveright Publishing Corporation. Copyright © 1923 by Boni & Liveright. Copyright renewed 1951 by Jean Toomer.

Jill Tweedie, "The Experience." Reprinted by permission of Curtis Brown, Ltd. Copyright © 1979 by Jill Tweedie.

Melvin I. Urofsky, "Two Scenes from a Hospital." Reprinted with the permission of Charles Scribner's Sons, an imprint of Macmillan Publishing, from *Letting Go* by Melvin I. Urofsky. Copyright 1993 Melvin I. Urofsky.

Alice Walker, "Everyday Use." From *In Love & Trouble: Stories of Black Women* copyright © 1973 by Alice Walker. Reprinted by permission of Harcourt Brace & Company.

Kathleen K. Wiegner, "At Times." From *Country Western Breakdown* by Kathleen K. Wiegner. Published by Crossing Press 1974 under the title "Hard Mornings (1)." Copyright 1974 by Kathleen Wiegner.

Richard Wilbur, "A Late Aubade." From *Walking to Sleep: New Poems and Translations,* by Richard Wilbur. Copyright © 1968 by Richard Wilbur. Reprinted by permission of Harcourt Brace & Company. Originally appeared in *The New Yorker.*

William Carlos Williams, "Tract." From *The Collected Poems of William Carlos Williams, 1909–1939, vol. I.* Copyright 1938 by New Directions Publishing Corporation. Reprinted by permission of New Directions Publishing Corporation.

Virginia Woolf, "What If Shakespeare Had Had a Sister?" From *A Room of One's Own* by Virginia Woolf. Copyright 1929 by Harcourt Brace & Company and renewed 1957 by Leonard Woolf. Reprinted by permission of the publisher.

Richard Wright, "Between the World and Me" by Richard Wright. Reprinted by permission of Ellen Wright. Copyright Ellen Wright.

Yevgeny Yevtushenko, "I Would Like." From *Selected Poems* by Yevgeny Yevtushenko edited by Albert C. Todd. Copyright © 1991 by Henry Holt and Co., Inc. Reprinted by permission of Henry Holt and Co., Inc.

Yevgeny Yevtushenko, "People." From *Selected Poems* by Yevgeny Yevtushenko. Translated by Robin Milner-Gulland and Peter Levi, (Penguin Books, 1962). Copyright © Robin Milner-Gulland and Peter Levi, 1962. Reprinted by permission of Penguin Books Ltd.

PICTURE CREDITS

Innocence and Experience

Part Opener, pp. 2–3: *The Garden of Peaceful Arts* (Allegory of the Court of Isabelle d'Este), ca. 1530 by Lorenzo Costa. The Louvre, Paris. Photograph, Bridgeman/Art Resource.

Fiction, p. 6: *Woman and Child on a Beach,* ca. 1901 by Pablo Picasso. Private collection. Photograph, Bridgeman/Art Resource. © 1989 ARS NY / SPADEM

Poetry, p. 78: *Il castello di carte* (The House of Cards) by Zinaida Serebriakova. Scala/Art Resource, NY.

Drama, p. 122: *Belisarius and the Boy*, 1802 by Benjamin West. Oil on canvas, 67 × 48 cm. © The Detroit Institute of Arts, Gift of A. Leonard Nicholson.

Essays, p. 180: *Child in a Straw Hat*, 1886 by Mary Cassatt. National Gallery of Art, Washington; Collection of Mr. and Mrs. Paul Mellon.

Conformity and Rebellion

Part Opener, pp. 206–7: *Le Ventre Legislatif*, 1834 by Honore Daumier. Lithograph. Art Resource, NY.

Fiction, p. 210: *The Trial*, 1950 by Keith Vaughan. Worthing Museum and Art Gallery, England.

Poetry, p. 280: *Adam and Eve*, Sistine Chapel (photograph of restored figures). © Nippon Television Network Corporation, Tokyo, 1991.

Drama, p. 322: *Self Portrait*, ca. 1900–1905 by Gwen John. National Portrait Gallery, London.

Essays, p. 414: *The Accused*, 1886 by Odilon Redon. Charcoal, sheet: 21 × 14⅝″. Collection, The Museum of Modern Art, New York. Acquired through the Lillie P. Bliss Bequest.

Love and Hate

Part Opener, pp. 466–67: *Mr. and Mrs. Clark and Percy*, 1970–1971 by David Hockney. The Tate Gallery, London/Art Resource, NY.

Fiction, p. 470: *A Husband Parting From His Wife and Child*, 1799 by William Blake. Pen and watercolor on paper, 11⅞ × 8⅞″. '64-110-3, Philadelphia Museum of Art: Given by Mrs. William T. Tonner.

Poetry, p. 520: *La fontana della giovinezza, Eroe e Eroina*, (partial), 15th century by Giacomo Jaquerio. Scala/Art Resource, NY.

Drama, p. 570: *Judith and Her Maidservant with the Head of Holofernes*, ca. 1625 by Artemisia Gentileschi. Oil on canvas, 72½ × 55¾″ (185.2 × 141.6 cm). © The Detroit Institute of the Arts, gift of Mr. Leslie H. Green.

Essays, p. 666: *Grosse Heidelberger Liederhandschrift "Codex Manesse" fol 249v*. Universitatsbibliothek, Heidelberg.

The Presence of Death

Part Opener, pp. 690–91: *Dream of a Sunday Afternoon in the Alameda*, (detail), 1947–1948 by Diego Rivera. Schalkwijk/AMI/Art Resource, NY.

Fiction, p. 694: *The Dead Mother* by Edvard Munch. Marburg/Art Resource, NY.

Poetry, p. 772: *Knight, Death, and the Devil*, 1513 by Albrecht Durer. Engraving. Art Resource, NY.

P. 798: *Landscape with the Fall of Icarus*. ca. 1560 by Pieter Brueghel the Elder. Museum of Fine Arts, Brussels. Photograph, Art Resource, New York.

Drama, p. 818: *Tombstones*, 1942 by Jacob Lawrence. Gouache, 29 × 20¾″. Collection of Whitney Museum of American Art.

Essays, p. 858: *St. George and the Dragon*, late fifteenth-century painting. Photograph, courtesy of the Bettmann Archive.

Appendices

Opening, p. 884: *The Librarian*, 1566 by G. Arcimboldo. Skoklosters Slott, Stockholm.

Pp. 906–7: *The Globe Theatre; Interior of the Globe Theatre in the days of Shakespeare; and a French theater during Moliere's management*: Courtesy of the Bettmann Archive, Inc. *Interior of the Swan Theatre*, London: Courtesy of Culver Pictures. *The Greek theater at Epidaurus*: Courtesy of the Greek National Tourist Office.

Index of Authors and Titles